June 9–13, 2018
Hong Kong

Association for
Computing Machinery

Advancing Computing as a Science & Profession

DIS 2018

Proceedings of the 2018 Conference on Designing Interactive Systems

Sponsored by:
ACM SIGCHI

General Chairs: **Ilpo Koskinen (University of Twente) & Youn-kyung Lim (KAIST)**

Program Chairs: **Teresa Cerratto-Pargman (Stockholm University)**
Kenny Chow (The Hong Kong Polytechnic University)
William Odom (Simon Fraser University)

Pictorial Chairs: **Laura Devendorf (University of Colorado in Boulder),**
Jung-Joo Lee (National University of Singapore) & Tom Jenkins (Georgia Tech)

Association for
Computing Machinery

Advancing Computing as a Science & Profession

The Association for Computing Machinery
2 Penn Plaza, Suite 701
New York, New York 10121-0701

ISBN: 978-1-4503-5198-0 (Digital)

ISBN: 978-1-4503-6146-0 (Print)

Additional copies may be ordered prepaid from:

ACM Order Department
PO Box 30777
New York, NY 10087-0777, USA

Phone: 1-800-342-6626 (USA and Canada)
+1-212-626-0500 (Global)
Fax: +1-212-944-1318
E-mail: acmhelp@acm.org
Hours of Operation: 8:30 am – 4:30 pm ET

Design and Diversity: Welcome to DIS2018 in Hong Kong

We are pleased to welcome Designing Interactive Systems DIS 2018 to Hong Kong. DIS 2018 is the first of its kind in two ways. It is in Asia for the first time. It is also in an art and design school for the first time.

The theme of the conference is Design and Diversity. The theme reflects a classic design theme - and also a foundational distinction in philosophy - of universals and particulars. Should we, as designers, follow Silicon Valley in its quest for products that engage everyone on the planet, or the architect Glenn Murcutt's conviction that he can only build in places he knows so well that his designs can be outstanding? The underlying logic of this question divides designers and design disciplines and emerges in every design process.

This theme operated as a guiding tool for selecting our four keynotes, professors Jodi Forlizzi, Kun-pyo Lee, Phoebe Sengers and Erik Stolterman. During their years in design, they have lived through its diversities. We were happy that they accepted the challenge to share their experiences and thoughts about diversity to the benefit of our community. The theme was also our tool for directing the DIS community into the future. A few years from now, we hope, we will start to see answers to the challenges our keynotes are posing to us.

The nucleus of the conference organization were two chairs and three technical chairs. This small group invited sixteen Subcommittee Chairs, three Pictorials chairs, and two chairs each for Workshops, Provocations and Work-in-Progress, Doctoral Consortium, and Demos. These chairs recruited 100 Associate Chairs, who recruited 1818 reviewers. Our review and decision schedule was brutal, but the organization worked through it efficiently, always with humor, and with collegial respect.

DIS 2018 received 645 submissions: 405 for full papers and notes submissions; 71 for pictorials; 23 for workshops submissions; 107 for Provocations and Work-in-Progress (out of these, 19 were Provocations); 20 for Doctoral Consortium Submissions; and 19 for Demos. Acceptance rates were: 23% for papers and notes, 24% Pictorials, 55% for Workshops, 73% for Demos, 53% for PWiPs, and 50% for Doctoral Consortium.

All this work led into a highly competitive conference between 9-13 June. June 9-10 were reserved for Workshops and Doctoral Consortium, and June 11-13 for 28 paper sessions. Pictorials are not in separate sessions; they are treated the same way as Full Papers. The 11th of June became an Experience Night of Demos, PWiPs, and a small design exhibition, which illuminated interaction design in Hong Kong and the Pearl River Delta. As extra, we organized a post-conference trip to a few technology companies in Shenzhen, China.

The program reflects the highly diverse nature of our discipline. We could not see any particular trends in papers, but a few observations may be possible. Two thirds of submissions focused on the following two human-oriented subcommittees: Experience and Methods and Processes. In comparison, the two technically oriented committees were smaller, but the quality of papers was particularly impressive in the Technical Innovation subcommittee. We expected to see more papers in design fiction, but with few exceptionally creative exceptions, fictional papers did not fare well in the review process. We also expected more papers on diversity, sustainability, global and civic issues, but did not. Looking at our own PhD students, however, we believe this work is maturing over the next few years. We saw several papers that try to bridge the gap between interaction design and more traditional fields of design like crafts. Machine learning is becoming a research topic, as is everyday life, with all its richness including themes like interaction with pets, microbes, and food.

Finally, our sincere thanks to sponsors. The Chairs also want to thank the chairs of DIS 2016 and DIS 2017. In particular, Ilpo Koskinen wants to thank Oli Mival and Marcus Foth; their help was crucial in creating the architecture of the conference. From Subcommittee Chairs to reviewers, the community came together beautifully. It was their volunteer work that keeps this community going; our sincere thanks goes for all of them. At the back end, we want to thank ACM and the Hong Kong Polytechnic University for their support. Our thanks also goes to Lisa Tolles for preparing the publication on tight schedule. Our local committee, especially the treasurer Christine Tsin, deserves a big thanks; this conference would not have happened without her. Our final thanks of course goes to the participants, who took a week off from their busy lives to travel to Hong Kong to present their work for their peers and to mingle with the community.

We welcome you to enjoy DIS 2018 in Hong Kong, one of the world's iconic, albeit less well known cities!

General Chair	**Co-Chair**	**Technical Chairs**
Ilpo Koskinen	*Youn-kyung Lim*	*Teresa Cerratto-Pargman*
		Kenny Chow
		William Odom

Table of Contents

Session 3: Personal Health & Wellness

Session 4: Making Diversity

Session 5: Augmenting Reality

Session 6: Therapeutic Design

Session 7: Expanding Domestic Design

Session 8: Supporting Designers

Session 9: Aging and Changing

Session 10: Things of Inquiry & Knowledge Creation

Session 11: Places of Interaction

Session 12: Designing with Machine Learning

Session 13: Fingers, Gestures & Bodies

Session 14: Co-performing with Machines

Session 15: Reflection, Remembrance & Connection

Session 16: Design Research Methods

Session 17: Immersive Experiences, Scenarios & Technologies

Session 18: Interacting with Conversational Agents

Session 19: Animals & Wilderness

Session 20: Design Issues in the Wild

Session 21: Sports and Training

Session 22: Exploring Interaction Design

Session 23: Crafting Fabrication

Session 24: Design for Collective Action

Session 25: Micro-Sites of Interaction

Session 26: Creativity and Design

Session 27: Measurements and Guidelines

Session 28: Values & Ethics

DIS 2018 Organization

General Chairs:	Ilpo Koskinen *(University of Twente)* Youn-kyung Lim *(KAIST)*
Program Chairs:	Teresa Cerratto-Pargman *(Stockholm University)* Kenny Chow *(The Hong Kong Polytechnic University)* William Odom *(Simon Fraser University)*
Pictorial Chairs:	Laura Devendorf *(University of Colorado in Boulder)* Jung-Joo Lee *(National University of Singapore)* Tom Jenkins *(Georgia Tech)*
Provocations and Work-in-progress Chairs:	Karthikeya Acharya *(Aarhus University)* Daniel Saakes *(KAIST)*
Workshop Chairs:	Peter Benz *(Hong Kong Baptist University* Marco Rozendaal *(Delft University of Technology)*
Demo Chairs:	Erik Grönvall (ITU Copenhagen) Peter Hasdell *(The Hong Kong Polytechnic University)*
Doctoral Consortium Chairs:	Ron Wakkary *(Simon Fraser University)* John Vines *(Northumbria University)*
Industry Engagement Chairs:	Jorn Buhring *(The Hong Kong Polytechnic University)* David Williams *(Asian Digital MOJO)*
Publicity and Social Chairs:	Rico Chan *(The Hong Kong Polytechnic University)* Pierre Tam *(The Hong Kong Polytechnic University)*
Visual Design and Web:	Clive Ng *(The Hong Kong Polytechnic University)* Christine Tsin *(The Hong Kong Polytechnic University)*
Student Volunteer Chair:	Leon Buker *(The Hong Kong Polytechnic University)*
Treasurer & Registration Chair:	Christine Tsin *(The Hong Kong Polytechnic University)*
Steering Committee Chair:	Steve Harrison *(Virginia Tech)*
Steering Committee:	Wendy Ju *(Stanford University)* Kim Halskov *(Aarhus University)* Marcus Foth *(Queensland University of Technology Brisbane)* Jack Carroll *(Penn State University)* Ron Wakkary *(Simon Fraser University)* Peter Wright *(Newcastle University)*

Subcommittee Chairs: Madeline Balaam *(Royal Institute of Technology in Stockholm)*
Jeffrey Bardzell *(Indiana University)*
Eric Baumer *(Lehigh University)*
Mark Blythe *(Northumbria University)*
Tone Bratteteig *(University of Oslo)*
Melanie D. Feinberg *(University of North Carolina)*
Joep Frens *(Technical University of Eindhoven)*
Jonas Fritsch *(ITU Copenhagen)*
Marianne Graves Petersen *(Aarhus University)*
Marc Hassenzahl *(University of Siegen)*
Uta Hinrichs *(University of St. Andrews)*
Lars-Erik Holmquist *(Northumbria University)*
Eva Hornecker *(Weimar University)*
Netta Iivari *(University of Oulu)*
Andres Lucero *(Aalto University)*
Eric Paulos *(University of California Berkeley)*

Associate Chairs:

Syed Ishtiaque Ahmed
Tanja Aitamurto
Jason Alexander
Dzmitry Aliakseyeu
Swamy Ananthanarayan
Mariam Asad
Louise Barkhuus
Tom Bartindale
Bo Begole
Andrea Bianchi
Simon Bowen
Jed Brubaker
Miguel Bruns Alonso
Daniel Buzzo
John Carroll
Adrian Clear
Sara Colombo
Rob Comber
Aykut Coskun
Paul Coulton
Lynne Coventry
Peter Dalsgaard
Sebastian Deterding
Tawanna Dillahunt
Lynn Dombrowski
Niklas Elmqvist
Chris Elsden
Sarah Fox
Mike Fraser
Christopher Frauenberger
Verena Fuchsberger
Mathias Funk
Colin Gray
Jonna Hakkila
Marcus Hanratty
Lone Hansen
Karin Hansson
Chris Harrison
Bart Hengeveld
Trevor Hogan
Christian Holz
Jonathan Hook
Kristina Höök
Gary Hsieh
Jörn Hurtienne
Minna Isomursu
Cecilia Katzeff
Aisling Kelliher
Ahmed Kharrufa
Rohit Ashok Khot
Vera Khovanskaya
Marianne Kinnula

Associate Chairs (continued):

David Kirk
Ben Kirman
Jesper Kjeldskov
Clemens Klokmose
Per Ola Kristensson
Sari Kujala
Neha Kumar
Stacey Kuznetsov
Matthias Laschke
Effie Law
Shaun Lawson
Stephen Lindsay
Daria Loi
Geke Ludden
Thomas Ludwig
Lindsay MacDonald Vermeulen
Wendy Moncur
Kellie Morrissey
Tek-Jin Nam
Nuno Nunes
Lora Oehlberg
Thomas Olsson
Deger Ozkaramanli
Minna Pakanen
Nadia Pantidi
Young-Woo Park
Majken Kirkegaard Rasmussen
Janet Read
Stuart Reeves
Francesca Rizzo
Jennifer Rode
Daniela Rosner
Corina Sas
Petr Slovak
Gunnar Stevens
Norman Su
Ozge Subasi
Anthony Tang
Nick Taylor
Daniel Tetteroo
Anja Thieme
Oscar Tomico
Austin Toombs
Vasiliki Tsaknaki
Victor Dibia
Jo Vermeulen
Lining Yao
John Zimmerman

DIS 2018 Sponsors & Supporters

DIS 2018 would like to thank the following Sponsors & Supporters

Supporters:

To Study Interaction and Interfaces: An Approach and Some Findings

Erik Stolterman
Indiana University
Bloomington, Indiana, USA
estolter@indiana.edu

ABSTRACT

It is hard to deny that our artifacts and environments are becoming more and more complex, more and more "alive," and as a consequence more and more demanding. We have to interact more. There seems to be no retreat or escape from interactivity. Some well-informed critics worry that the proliferation of interactions and interactive things has already gone too far. Their concerns raise many questions. Does interactivity in fact increase? How can we know? What does it really mean to claim that it does? And if indeed it is increasing, what does it mean? And why is this happening? And should something be done? Despite this development there seems to be no precise idea of what interaction is and what being interactive means, beyond a vague notion that it is some kind of interplay, usually optimistically understood as good-natured cooperation.

In this talk I will present the work I have done for many years, together with my colleague Lars-Erik Janlert. As our approach, maybe best described as analytical and philosophical, we have examined properties and qualities of designed artifacts and systems; primarily those properties that are open for manipulation to designers, that is, properties that designers can and do intentionally affect by their design decisions (and thus in principle are possible to control). Rather than taking users and their subjective experiences of the artifacts and systems as the primary target for examination, unfashionable as it may be, we have chosen to be objective in the sense of focusing on the artifacts and systems. Apart from discussing our approach, I will briefly introduce some of our main results consisting of some developed definitions of existing (and some new) concepts, such as, interactivity, interactability, interactiveness. I will end with some comments on what this kind of investigation can tell us about the future by introducing the notions of faceless interaction, interactivity clutter, and interactivity fields.

ACM Classification Keywords

H.5.2. User Interfaces

ACM ISBN 978-1-4503-5198-0/18/06.
DOI: https://doi.org/10.1145/3196709.3196796

Author Keywords

Interaction, interactivity, interface

BIOGRAPHY

Erik Stolterman is Professor in Informatics and the Senior Executive Associate Dean of the School of Informatics, Computing, and Engineering at Indiana University, Bloomington. He is also professor at the Institute of Design at Umeå University, Sweden. Stolterman is co-Editor for the *Design Thinking/Design Theory* book series by MIT Press, and on several editorial boards for international journals. Stolterman's main work is within the areas of HCI, interfaces, interactivity, interaction design, design practice, philosophy and theory of design. Stolterman has published a large number of articles and five books, including "Thoughtful Interaction Design" (MIT Press) and "The Design Way" (MIT Press) and the recently published "Things That Keep Us Busy--The Elements of Interaction" (MIT Press, 2017).

Data and Design for Action

Jodi Forlizzi
Carnegie Mellon University
Pittsburgh, PA, USA
forlizzi@cs.cmu.edu

ABSTRACT

This is an interesting era for design in terms of the diverse ways that designers need to work. The advent of cloud computing and the sensors in the mobile phones we carry means that there is a vast amount of data collected about what people do. There is a vast opportunity for designers to leverage this data to create products, services and systems that are tailored to individual needs. At the same time, designers at Google are designing products and services that millions of people use every day. This sets up an interesting dichotomy for today's designers, who need to take into account both personal and adaptive and global and scaled in how they think, design, and take action.

ACM Classification Keywords
H.5.2. User Interfaces

DIS 2018, June 9–13, 2018, Hong Kong.

ACM ISBN 978-1-4503-5198-0/18/06.
DOI: https://doi.org/10.1145/3196709.3196797

Author Keywords
Interaction design, service design, AI, machine learning

BIOGRAPHY

Jodi Forlizzi is a the Geschke Director and a Professor of Human-Computer Interaction in the School of Computer Science at Carnegie Mellon University and a Co-founder of Pratter.us, a healthcare startup. Her current research interests include designing educational games that are engaging and effective, designing robots, AVs, and other technology services that adapt to people's needs, and designing for healthcare. Jodi is a member of the ACM CHI Academy and has been honored by the Walter Reed Army Medical Center for excellence in HRI design research. Jodi has consulted with Disney and General Motors to create innovative product-service systems.

Design Research, for What? Different Perspectives on Design Research

Kun-Pyo LEE
KAIST
Daejon, South Korea
kplee@kaist.ac.kr

ABSTRACT

The notion of research in the field of design has a relatively short history compared to other well established academic disciplines, and therefore the relationship between design academia and design practice is not very closely intertwined. Particularly this disconnecting phenomenon becomes more serious as the rapid introduction of new technologies such as AI is challenging the validity of the existing body of knowledge, methods, and processes.

Faced with this new big changes the healthy cycle of coexistence of academia and practice is required more than ever. In addition, in order to establish a single academic discipline, mutual synergetic collaboration between academia and practice is inevitable. Practical designers regard research as something done in the pre-stage of the design concept development, whereas academia perceives research as an instrument for knowledge generation. Design research in practice and academia significantly differ in respect to goal, deliverables, applicability, methods, scope, venue, and other things.

What are the diversifying factors of design research in academia and practice, and how can they be interconnected while maintaining the advantages of being diverse?

The issue of diversity in design research will be addressed by some comparative research with interview with design researchers in industry and review of papers presented in design research conferences.

ACM Classification Keywords

H.5.m. Information interfaces and presentation

Author Keywords

Design Research; Practice, Education, Collaboration, Methods, Process

DIS 2018, June 9–13, 2018, Hong Kong.

ACM ISBN 978-1-4503-5198-0/18/06.
DOI: https://doi.org/10.1145/3196709.3196822

BIOGRAPHY

Kun-pyo LEE is professor at the Department of Industrial Design, KAIST, South Korea and the director of the Human-Centered Interaction Design Lab for more than 30 years. He is co-founder and president emeritus of IASDR (International Association of Societies of Design Research). He also served as Chief Design Officer (Executive Vice President) of Corporate Design Center, LG Electronics.

He is well known in Asia as an early pioneer in the field of design research, UX design and user-centered design, for which he was recognized as Honorary Fellow of the Design Research Society, and Local Hero at CHI 2015.

After returning back to KAIST from LG with unique experiences in industry and academia he has been focusing on establishing a new design education paradigm under the name of Design 3.0 – Big, Deep and Open.

Diversifying Design Imaginations

Phoebe Sengers
Cornell University
Ithaca, NY USA
sengers@cs.cornell.edu

ABSTRACT
The act of designing technologies does not simply create functionality; it also offers possibilities for action, ways of looking at the world, and modes through which we can relate to one another. How we design technologies reflects what we value; who we think is important, and in what ways; which places, people and possibilities are in our imaginations, and which are not.

Current ways of designing technologies frequently narrow these possibilities, in two ways. The first is that technology design is dominated by a narrow demographic: predominantly white and Asian, white collar, highly educated, urban. These designers' ways of imagining new technological worlds are shaped by the worlds they themselves know and value, which are only a small slice of global ways of being. The second is that even as technology design is being increasingly engaged in around the world by and for people outside this demographic, local adaptations are frequently judged and limited by what makes sense from the perspective of Silicon Valley and other urban high-tech centers.

Supporting the rich diversity of human experience requires explicitly identifying and appreciating values and experiences outside of mainstream technology design logics.

ACM Classification Keywords
K.4.2. Social Issues; H.5.2. User Interfaces

Author Keywords
Interaction design; speculative futures; values in design; diversity; postcolonial computing; ethnography

BIOGRAPHY
Phoebe Sengers is an Associate Professor at Cornell in Information Science and Science & Technology Studies, where she leads the Culturally Embedded Computing group. Her work integrates ethnographic and historical analysis of the social implications of technology with design methods to suggest alternative future possibilities. Her group explores rural, working-class and global South experiences of technologies, traces the emerging entanglements between people and data, and uses design to speculate about alternative pasts and futures.

Sengers led the Cornell campus of the Intel Science & Technology Center for Social Computing, has been a Fulbright Fellow, a Fellow in the Cornell Society for the Humanities, and a Public Voices Fellow, and received an NSF CAREER award. She holds an interdisciplinary PhD in Artificial Intelligence and Cultural Theory from Carnegie Mellon University.

ACKNOWLEDGEMENTS
This work was supported by the US National Science Foundation under grants 1217685 and 1526155, by the Intel Science & Technology Center for Social Computing, by the Cornell Institute for Social Sciences, and by Memorial University of Newfoundland & Labrador.

DIS 2018, June 9–13, 2018, Hong Kong.

ACM ISBN 978-1-4503-5198-0/18/06.
DOI: https://doi.org/10.1145/3196709.3196823

Exploring Trust in Digital Civics

Eric Corbett **Christopher A. Le Dantec**
Georgia Institute of Technology
Atlanta, GA. USA
{ecorbett, ledantec}@gatech.edu

ABSTRACT
Digital civics research seeks to understand how technology can create new forms of relationships and services between public officials and citizens in governance. To accomplish this, design in digital civics emphasizes the importance of relationships based on dialogue, empowerment, and participation; all of which are contingent upon the existence of trust. Currently, however, these relationships are most often characterized by entrenched distrust which problematizes opportunities for dialogue and participation. In this paper, we explore how design might support trust in the relational aims of digital civics. To do so, we led 13 public officials in a large US city through a design-based inquiry centered around the role of trust in their various efforts to engage communities. In our findings, we discuss four strategies for supporting trust in digital civics.

Author Keywords
Digital Civics; Trust; Community Engagement

ACM Classification Keywords
H.5.m. Information interfaces and presentation (e.g., HCI): Miscellaneous;

INTRODUCTION
Digital civics is a research agenda interested in how to bring about "new configurations of government and citizenry that is relational rather than transactional" [40]. The emphasis on relational civic encounters "enables us to begin to view governments (local or national) as composed through relations with constituents" [1]. Thus, rather than focusing on how design might make government efficient (e-government), or make existing modes of democratic participation more accessible (digital democracy), design in digital civics focuses on how to create relationships in participatory experiences between public officials and citizens based on mutual learning, empowerment, and co-creation [1,34].

DIS '18, June 9–13, 2018, Hong Kong

ACM ISBN 978-1-4503-5198-0/18/06...$15.00
https://doi.org/10.1145/3196709.3196715

The turn to relational encounters presented by digital civics is timely given the widespread distrust that currently characterizes interactions between public officials and citizens throughout many modern democracies [10,45,47]. In fact, this distrust now is so pervasive that "it is a given and perhaps even a framework that conditions all possible [civic] relationships" [31]. Moreover, despite the importance that trust plays in civic institutions, and its role in the digital systems we build to support and access those institutions, trust is often bracketed out as either an externality to the design space or assumed to be a built-in attribute of technology itself [19]. It is only more recently that trust has become a first-order concern of research and design for HCI in this space [12,28].

To further explore trust as a design value in digital civics, we conducted a workshop with municipal officials from a large US city. The goal of the workshop was to develop design insights for digital civics drawn from how these officials view the role of trust and technology in the work of community engagement. We focus exclusively on municipal officials in this study to better understand the role of trust within the organizational and institutional arrangements of governing and providing public services. Our study helps expand recent work in HCI that tends to approach digital civics exclusively as citizen-to-public official; an unnecessarily narrow view given the importance of buy-in and support of public officials as a key factor in the long term success of digital civic systems [43,44].

Our findings provide four strategies for supporting trust in digital civics: historicizing engagement, focusing on experience, mediating expectations and preserving institutional relationships. Taken together, these strategies provide insight into how technology should be designed to support trust in the work of community engagement. Through our analysis of the workshop material, we reveal several tensions that need to be confronted to advance digital civics. These include: supporting the needs and challenges public officials face in their efforts to engage communities; and on the other, achieving the transformative, democratic goals the research ascribes to. We end by discussing how focusing on the affordances derived from the four strategies we developed could address these tensions.

BACKGROUND
There are two elements that setup the areas of focus for this paper: the first is the turn to digital civics as a way to reimagine civic systems to support relational interactions; the second is taking on trust as an under-studied attribute of

systems that is needed in order to support action in the face of imperfect knowledge, unequal power relations, and political conflict.

Digital Civics

In a move beyond the privileged and professionalized versions of democratic participation, digital civics seeks to understand and design technologies for a wider range of civic interactions and experiences. There are two key elements to digital civics. The first is a turn to participatory systems described by McCarthy and Wright as enabling "an open, empathic, and critical questioning relationship... [that] construct[s] new imaginaries through mutual learning" [34]. By engaging in conflicts and counter narratives, digital civics enables a kind of shared learning and shared ownership about issues and their resolution [15,22]. Importantly, there is an inclination to examine civic transformation—institutional or community centered—as incremental rather than immediate.

The incremental impact of participatory systems leads to the second element of digital civics: a focus on relational interaction [8,40,46]. By attending to the relations that underpin our civic lives, we open the design space to include modes of identity- and place-making [16,22], as well as sites of advocacy and activism [2,14,15]. The focus on relational interactions reframes civic encounters such that government services are created in the doing that happens *between* officials and citizens and not simply delivered *to* citizens. By focusing on the co-created outcomes of civic life, we can begin to view governments (local or national) as composed through myriad relations with constituents, and it is precisely these relations that matter most in day-to-day civic life [4,8].

By looking beyond the narrow scope of rational deliberative decision making, digital civics confronts governance—and technology's role in governance—not as a means to more perfect knowledge—via sensors, databases, and algorithms—but as interactions based in power dynamics, social and political capital, and local histories. Across the different kinds of interactions of place making [15], identity building [22], and fostering civic engagement, the conditions of trust (or its absence) plays a crucial role [1,14]. Yet trust, as a first-order concern for design, has remained under examined, particularly as it relates to institutional processes and historic experiences with government in HCI.

Trust and Governance

While trust is a vital component to enabling cooperative action in situations of risk [5], the role of trust in community engagement is less clear: some scholars suggest distrust from citizens provides a healthy and necessary check against the power of public officials and serves as the primary motivator for engagement [25]; while others argue that trust is essential to enabling and facilitating engagement [41]. This debate stems from how cooperative work in political relationships are inherently problematic for trust as "the mere fact that a social relationship has become political throws into question the very conditions for trust" [54:1]. Those conditions are predicated on a need to overcome uncertainty and risk.

Trust, as we use it throughout this research, is a mechanism for dealing with uncertainty. Without uncertainty, there would be no risk; no risk would obviate the need for trust [37]. For this reason, trust comes into play only when the risk presented by a situation cannot be reduced entirely. The process of trust is best described as how one comes to form expectations that allow the "leap" over uncertainty [38]. The mechanisms that enable that process derive from "distinct cognitive, emotional, and behavioral dimensions which are merged into a unitary social experience" [32]; this then allows for the "reduction of complexity, [and] discloses possibilities for action which would have remained improbable and unattractive without trust" [33].

In this regard, the question of how to trust is the essence of political relationships where compromises and actions can only ever be made with partial knowledge and varying degrees of risk. Further, it is within the larger debate of whether engagement is motivated by trust or by distrust that design in digital civics finds itself.

Clearly, digital civics' focus on participatory and relational interactions between public officials and citizens is preconditioned by the current environment of distrust [41,42,45]. How will (or should) design in digital civics contend with this condition? In prior work within the same municipal setting, we established a conceptual framework that describes how trust develops as a process with distinct stages: initiating trust, building trust, and finally retaining trust [12]. The degree of trust increases in each stage, creating evermore possibilities for cooperative actions between public officials and citizens. Moving across the stages is done through a collection of practices we called "trust work." This work is performed by public officials in order to overcome barriers to trust in both interpersonal and institutional relationships with their constituencies.

In completing our initial research into trust and community engagement, we recognized that the trust work performed by public officials is at best poorly supported in the current landscape of digital technology and at worst completely incompatible. To begin to address this gap between the tools municipal official have to do the work of community engagement, and the need to directly respond to different stages of trust, we designed a workshop to specifically explore how trust might be operationalized to support the work of community engagement in digital civics. In doing so, we are adding to the larger understanding of how to build systems to bring government and citizens together (e.g., ([6,28,29]).

WORKSHOP STRUCTURE

In order to explore trust as a design value in digital civics, we organized a workshop with public officials. We recruited 13 public officials representing 12 departments/organizations from our home municipality—a large US city with a populous urban core and a much larger metro region (Table

Department/Organization	
Public Health NGO	P1, P2
Parks and Recreation	P3
City Planning	P4
Watershed Management	P5
Public Works	P6
Immigrant Affairs	P7
Economic Development	P8
Public Safety	P9
Beltline Partnership	P10
Parks Advocacy	P11
Public Health UNIVERSITY	P12
Regional Planning	P13

Table 1. List of departments/organizations and participant code.

1). We were intentionally broad in recruiting participants looking for a wide representation from the breadth of municipal entities that exist across the city. The workshop ran concurrently in three sessions over the course of two weeks. Each session was approximately two hours and took place on our campus. One researcher recorded ethnographic field and photo documentation while the lead author ran the workshops. We also audio recorded the workshops which we then partially transcribed to provide additional fidelity to key exchanges identified in our ethnographic notes.

The workshop was designed around the conceptual elements of trust in community engagement we developed in previous work [12]. The first of these concepts were the 'trust circles' —canvases we designed to represent the three stages of how trust is developed in the work of community engagement (Figure 1). The workshop activity required participants–working individually—to think through each stage of the trust process—initiating, building, and retaining—by matching together three forms of prompts: barriers, actions, and technologies (Table 2). We designed the trust circles to force participants to decompose the process of trust into the stages represented on the canvas; building on our prior work we understood that each stage required different responses to the provided prompts. Each participant had their own trust circle, individual sets of the prompts, and blank cards they could use to introduce new prompts as they saw fit.

At the center of each trust circle was a goal the participant identified as part of their current work (Figure 1). The goals pursued during the workshop ranged from specific project outcomes to more general organizational imperatives. P1, P2 and P13 pursued goals that aimed to improve different communities they work within: P1 and P2 each had goals tied to specific health interventions; P13 sought to improve communities across the city by facilitating access to the technical planning resources his organization provides. P3, P6, P7 and P9 pursued goals aimed at expanding institutional relationships with different segments of the community: P3 sought to connect the department with new constituents; P6 with millennials to improve the city's recycling initiatives; P9 with minority and underserved communities; P7 with immigrant communities. P4 and P11 pursued goals aimed at increasing community input into decision making processes: P4 through coordinating the city's neighborhood planning units which provide a mechanism for communities to provide input on zoning, land use and city ordinances; P11 by facilitating community led master planning processes for city parks. P5 and P8 pursued goals to improve their department's communication with communities: P5 wanted to make sure customers understood how to interact with the department for billing and service requests; P8 wanted to provide a better public understanding of what her agency is and its purpose. P10 and P12 pursued goals to create community ownership of department initiatives: P10 wanted to better involve communities in customizing how his agency's infrastructure project would impact neighborhoods; P12 pursued this goal generally as it is vital to the sustainability of initiatives across all his agency's work.

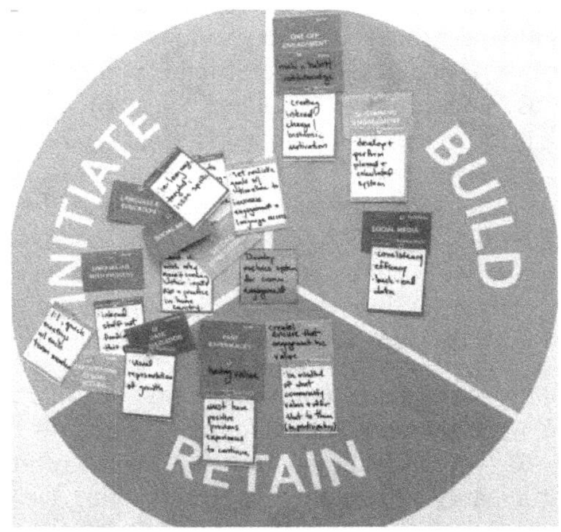

Figure 1. Completed trust circle. The circle is broken down into the three stages of the trust process: Initiate, Build and Retain. Each participant had their own trust circle with their goal placed in the center on the pink post-it

These goals grounded the activity so that participants could link specific challenges they were facing with the different stages of trust, the barriers to moving forward, and the actions they were or could be taking to advance toward their goal. Once the goals were established, participants pinned the different prompts to their trust circles, adding descriptive detail that further explained why they selected the prompt. At the end of each stage we brought the participants together to share their selection of barriers, actions, and technologies to the group.

The *barrier* prompts (Table 2) included 14 barriers to trust that represented the most salient forms of risk in community engagement identified from our previous work [12,13].

Participants would select the barriers they felt were important to address in in order to develop trust to the next stage—from initiating to building, and from building to retaining. The barriers general issues such as *misinformation, fear of change, language and education* while others were more specific to trust in the context of community engagement and municipal government such as *speed of progress*, *one-off engagement* and *cycles of leadership*. We provided general descriptions of the barriers but encouraged participants to interpret them openly in the context of their work.

Similar to the barriers, we developed 10 *action* prompts (Table 2) also identified through previous work [12]. These actions included practices public officials would commonly describe as important to building trust in community engagement (described as "trust work" in [12]). Participants would select actions they felt could address the barriers pinned to the trust circle. Like the barriers, each of the actions were briefly described while allowing an open, flexible interpretation. For instance, the action *educating community* could be carried out in many ways: formal training or workshops, informal conversations, or website information.

Finally, there were 18 *technology* prompts (Table 2). We selected a wide range of technologies in order to provide flexibility for various municipal work domains represented by our participants. In selecting the technologies, we wanted a mixture between those that were conventional and familiar (*website, survey, text messaging*), to existing but new (*virtual meeting, crowd sourcing),* to the more future orientated, distant technologies (*holograms, drones, smart cities*). Participants selected technology prompts based on how the technology could augment their trust processes by either improving how an action was performed or helping to address a barrier.

As an example of the whole workshop activity, a participant might choose the barrier *misinformation* to describe the skepticism citizens might feel toward official communication channels. In response to that barrier, the participant could choose some form of action, for instance *educating community* as a remedy. Pushing that remedy into technology, they might choose *virtual meeting* to mediate the action *educating community* in order to address the barrier *misinformation.* Throughout the workshops we encouraged participants to approach technology selections that were a mixture between those that were familiar and unfamiliar. In this way, we hoped to elicit selections that were both pragmatic as well as those that were explorative and future orientated.

In short, during the workshop each participant worked individually on reaching their goal by thinking through each stage of the trust process represented by the trust circle (Figure 1) matching the barriers they felt were relevant—to actions that would address those barriers—and finally technologies they have access to (or envision having access to) that would aid their process (Table 2). This allowed us to get a wide view of how public officials across a range of municipal roles address barriers for trust in their goals of community engagement.

Barriers	*Actions*	*Technologies*
Speed of Progress; Misinformation; Cycles of Leadership; Perception of Equity; Input Doesn't Matter; Language and Education; Availability for Engagement; Past Experiences; Accessibility; Sense of Voicelessness; Unfamiliar with Process; One-off Engagement; Out of the Loop; Fear of Change	Being Present; Setting Expectations; Sharing Decision Making; Sustaining Engagement; Listening; Educating Community; Participating in Goal Setting; Managing Expectations; Meeting people where they are; Raising Awareness	Mobile App; Website; Survey; Virtual Meeting; Drone; Data Visualization; Broadcast Media; Group Messaging; Crowd Sourcing; Hologram; Open Data Portal; Smart City; Blog; Virtual Reality; Social Media; Electronic Polling; Text Messaging; Data Visualization

Table 2. List of design prompts: 14 Barriers; 10 Actions; 18 Technologies

Analysis

The data collected from the workshop, comprising the selections of barriers, actions, technologies, goals, field notes, photos and audio, were subject to inductive analysis [36] in order to connect the nascent strategies for addressing trust that developed across the different workshop instances. We decided to organize our analysis around the barrier prompt selections as these were the central material of the workshop activity. We started by first identifying the most frequent barrier prompts selected in the workshop. These were (in descending order of frequency): *speed of progress*, *past experiences*, *unfamiliar with process*, *misinformation*, *one-off engagement* and *cycles of leadership*. We then looked for strategies in how these barriers were addressed—interrogating the data by asking and comparing: What actions were selected and why? How did the technologies factor in? How were selections differentiated by participant domain as well as goals? The common strategies that emerged form the foundation for how we can move systems design forward when considering the need to account for and develop trust between institutional actors—here city officials and departments—and individuals outside those institutions—i.e. city residents.

DESIGN STRATEGIES

We present four strategies developed by analyzing the themes in how barriers, actions and technologies (Table 2) were aligned to develop trust during the workshop: *historicizing engagement, focusing on experience, mediating expectations* and *preserving institutional relationships*. These strategies are meant to provide design advice drawn from how public official view the role of trust and technology in the work of community engagement. Each of the strategies focus on a particular barrier: historicizing engagement addresses the barrier of past experiences; focusing on experience confronts the barrier of one-off engagement; mediating expectations is a way to address the barrier of speed of progress; preserving institutional relationships helps bridge the barrier of cycles of leadership.

Each of the strategies also falls into a particular stage of the trust process. First, historicizing engagement is important to the initiating stage as it addresses past experiences that need to be acknowledged and then adjusted to. Next, focusing on experience falls in between the initiating and building stages as it addresses how to provide an experience of engagement that will lead to ongoing interactions that further build trust. Then, mediating expectations falls in-between building and retaining stages as it addressed how to maintain momentum to sustain trust over time. Finally, preserving institutional relationships is most relevant to the retaining stage as it addresses how relationships established over the course of the trust process can be preserved for future work.

Historicizing Engagement

Historicizing engagement is a strategy for addressing instances of the barrier *past experiences* which impact the ability to develop trust in the present. While trust as process is future orientated, it is forged upon past experiences which serve as material in the process of forming expectations [37]. Thus, a key part of trust as a process is overcoming fear and doubt that may stem from negative past experiences. In this way, past experience is the primary, fundamental barrier for trust. For this reason, we began with this strategy as it initiates the trust process and thus sets the stage for the remaining three strategies to unfold during the building and retain stages.

The barrier of past experiences manifested in a variety of contexts and forms in the workshop. P5 in watershed management had to contend with the past experiences of poor responsiveness to issues with service. Responsiveness was also the challenge with P9 in public safety which he described: "*many people have past experiences where crimes have been committed against them or family and friends that they feel were not taken seriously.*" For P10 in infrastructure development, past experience was the history of broken promises of neighborhood revitalization in minority communities. For P12 in community health, it was the history of negligence that underserved communities felt towards outsiders who alleged to work benevolently but in the end used engagement to further their own agendas.

There were two key concerns that underlie historicizing engagement: *engaging the past* and *altering engagement* in a manner that is historically aware and appropriate. First, there is the work of engaging the past which was primarily about developing empathy with it: both P9 and P10 selected the actions 'meeting people where they are' and 'listening' to achieve this. P9 described this work as the need to build understanding: "*Take time to get a handle at how the community lives. Understand what's normal and what's not.*" P10 felt these actions would build relationships by establishing a presence with (and within) the community: "[making] *yourself present, available and engrained in the community.*" For the technology prompts, both P9 and P10 selected 'social media' and 'surveys' to help learn, listen and connect. In this way, the technology selections augment the actions: social media provides a way of meeting people where they are (online) and surveys provide a structured way to listen.

The second key concern of this strategy, altering engagement, was described by P12 as the need to be flexible in engagement: "*being prepared to go slower and/or move away from the agenda*" when necessary. In this case, P12 is aware that flexibility engenders trust—allowing agency to express concerns with the speed or direction of a process. This is especially important given the history of experiences in the community he is working in. He selected the technology 'electronic polling' as way to feel when and where flexibility might be needed by gauging feelings periodically throughout an engagement process. He thought electronic polling provided a safe, comfortable way for people to express feelings that they otherwise might not be willing to in one-on-one or larger group meetings. For P5, altering engagement was a matter of increasing responsiveness by following up and sustaining communication patterns. She selected the technology 'open data portal' to compliment responsiveness by increasing visibility and openness of her department's processes. For P10, altering engagement was expressed as a sensitivity towards decisions about technology use in engagement. He selected the action 'sharing decision making' which he felt was important to address the barrier 'perception of equity'. This action and barrier were important for his department's goal of involving communities—some which are very uneasy due to the history of inequity in development work in the city—in customizing how development would impact neighborhoods. P10 initially selected the technology 'crowdsourcing' to augment his action; however, upon reflection he later altered this selection by adding in paper-based surveys because, "*everything we do has to be mirrored in a non-technology way too.*" In this case, P10 is sensitive to the history of this community being left out of conversations in development. As a result, he is careful not to exacerbate this history by introducing technology that may be inappropriate to the level of access, familiarity, and comfort. So, while crowdsourcing might be well suited as medium to achieve shared decision-making care must be taken that it does not present a new barrier while doing so.

The key affordance of this strategy is history—how to attend to the memories, emotions and experiences of the past that can create barriers for trust in the present. Due to the idiosyncrasies of history, the strategy of historicizing engagement is complex and requires nuanced response; nonetheless, there are some key takeaways for digital civics that arise in the ways in which past experiences are addressed. First, the technologies used highlight the importance of increasing the flow of communication from resident-to-public official. While altering engagement suggest systems that are flexible and adaptable to the needs of past experiences rather that rigid or primarily concerned with making engagement more efficient. On the point of efficiency, there is the tension between on one hand how public officials doing the work of engagement are typically overworked and under staffed therefore increasing the efficiency of engagement work is rightly desirable. On the other hand, historicizing engagement may require work to slow down and agendas to be altered thus reducing efficiency.

Focusing on Experience

While the previous strategy focuses on conditions of the past that form barriers for initiating trust, focusing on experience addresses conditions of the present that must be addressed in order build trust further. The primary barrier this strategy addresses is *one-off engagement*. This barrier arises from inconsistency in community engagement which is problematic for trust—as ongoing, continuous and frequent interactions are its building blocks [38]. The most prevalent cause of one-off engagement were issues with the experience of engagement that can prevent citizens from engaging in an ongoing manner. For instance, P11, whose goal was increasing public input by facilitating community-led master planning processes for city parks, believes the experience of engagement is typically too narrow as citizens are given limited agency in the larger picture of how decision-making process play out. He believes this leads citizens to devalue engagement—resulting in one-off engagements that ultimately reduce input because citizens often participate once but never return. In this case, P11 chose the action 'educating community' by creating citizen academies which would be trained (and eventually train others) with an expanded view of participation in the planning process. He selected 'blogs' as technology that could amplify the reach of these academies by offering citizen presentations on those blogs.

P4 also pursues the goal of increasing input through his department's work of coordinating the city's neighborhood planning units (NPUs) that provide a mechanism for communities to provide input on zoning, land use and city ordinances. P4 deals with the inconsistency of citizens experiences in participating in the NPU system as the nature of these units vary significantly based on current leadership and active members. P4 selected the action 'sustaining engagement' which he described as continuing to develop an understanding of the different pain points for citizen experiences in NPUs. He selected the technology 'electronic polling' as way to gather data and inform improvement work in an efficient and convenient manner.

P13 wanted to address the experience of engagement feeling transactional: "*agencies can get a bad rap for only engaging communities when they must put together a periodic plan for funders, etc. Agencies can been seen as disingenuous or inauthentic if they only engage communities in these 3 or 4 year intervals.*" Transactional experiences stem from when engagement occurs only to satisfy institutional needs rather than the needs for ongoing relationships with the communities that they serve. P13 selected the action 'educating community' as way to provide a more regular, direct linking with residents to understand their needs and concerns. He selected the technology prompt 'virtual meeting' as a way to mitigate the resources strain that his action selection would introduce.

The key affordance of this strategy is the experience of engagement; however, as Asad et al noted "community engagement is to cities what user experience is to computing: it signifies a large and multi-faceted category that simultaneously speaks to general qualities of interaction and to specific ways of doing that interaction" [1]. Thus, given the inherent variability of experiences—this strategy resists prescriptive implications for design of trust in digital civics. Rather, than prescriptions, the value of this strategy is simply in how it calls focus to the quality of experience in engagement which can be overlooked in comparison to other aspects such as empowerment, access, and social justice. While these are important nonetheless (as both outcomes and conditions of engagement), this strategy suggests a holistic view of the conditions that affect the quality of the "user experience" overall.

Mediating Expectations

Having addressed issues of the past and present in the previous two strategies, we move to the strategy mediating expectations which focuses on issues with future expectations. Conceptually, this strategy falls into the building stage of trust. The primary barrier this strategy addresses is *speed of progress* which refers to the speed in which the results of the work of community engagement come to fruition. Speed of progress can either be too slow, or too fast; both of which are problematic for trust. For P9 in public safety, his goal of expanding relationships with minority and underserved communities is problematized by the speed of progress being too slow in issues like systemic neighborhood crime or ongoing police accountability. For planners like P3 and P10, speed of progress can be too fast when it comes to introducing change to the built environment causing fear of change. In both cases, deferential expectations of speed (what one considers a reasonable timeframe) is the issue.

Expectation is what enables trust—trust is the process of how one comes to form positive expectations in the face of uncertainty [38]. In this way, expectation and time are the primary elements of trust. These elements are interlocked as the strength of trust (or distrust) at any given point is dependent upon sustaining expectations. In the work of community engagement this means that trust will fluctuate over the course of an engagement process—as the momentum of expectations meets the friction of the passage of time. This was evident for P13 in regional planning where projects run for many years with multiple moving parts and contingencies that results in oscillating momentum. This was also the case for P10 whose work in infrastructure development operates on a timescale of decades whilst the economic, social and cultural ramifications of the work do not (and may not ever) align with the physical manifestations of the work. This makes expectations difficult to sustain as P10 describes, "[i]t *can be a frustration that change isn't coming fast enough...*"

We developed the strategy mediating expectations based upon the two key concerns in how speed of progress was addressed: *shaping expectations* and *maintaining momentum*. The first concern of this strategy shaping expectations starts with providing a basic understanding of the factors that impact speed of progress so that expectations can be formulated. An example of this was in how P5 in watershed management selected the action 'educating community' which meant making sure residents had at least a basic awareness of the processes of her department: "*it is important the public know that we do have a process for services offered.. sometimes they just don't know... they may just reach out to their council member on Twitter rather than call our hotline.*" After expectations are in place, the second concern comes into play—as it then becomes important to engage regularly as a way to maintain momentum. Illustrating this second concern, P13 in regional planning selected the action 'sustaining engagement' which is important, "*because it helps citizens track with the progress of projects that cannot be seen at a glance. It also helps them better understand the process of funding and implementation.*" Here, sustaining engagement not only does the work of maintaining momentum but also helps to expand understanding of the process as it develops over time.

The technology prompts selected in this strategy fell into two categories: *visualizing processes* and *facilitating ongoing conversation*. Both P3 and P9 selected technologies that would mediate expectations through visual representation. P3 selected onsite 'holograms' to show final plans or where a plan is at in order to help with the action 'setting expectations.' He selected 'data visualization' to help 'sustain engagement' which was using data visuals to update and educate in a way that would be easy to understand and remember. Likewise, P9 selected 'data visualization' to help momentum by, "*being able to visualize what the progress is... getting the community hope... something to look forward to.*"

P5, P6, P10 and P13 all selected technologies to facilitate ongoing interactions. For P5 and P6, (both in service providing departments) this took the form of custom 'mobile apps' for their departments that would mediate expectations through providing a communication channel that is real-time and customizable. P6 described the benefits of this as, "*Mobile app may allow ratepayers the ability to interact with department in real-time see status of issues, more effectively pay bill (this helps with speed of progress).*" P10 selected 'text messaging' to facilitate ongoing interactions because it is, "*digital divide friendly... even if you don't have smart phone to use our app.*" Whereas P13 selected 'blogs', "*because it allows anyone to read about the progress of projects at any time. It also allows comments and Q&A features so learning can take place.*"

The key affordance of this strategy is expectation which is mediated by altering perception, experience and interaction. Expectation is vital for trust—as trust is future orientated—providing the suspension of doubt that enables one to pursue actions toward a desired future [33]. The challenge for trust in community engagement is in how to sustain ongoing work necessary to reach some desired future in the face of uncertainty and setbacks.

Preserving Institutional Relationships

The last strategy, preserving institutional relationships, falls into the retaining stage of the trust process as is it is concerned with the ways in which trust can be retained in relationships over time. The primary barrier this strategy addresses is *cycles of leadership*. Cycles of leadership refers to the cyclical nature of civic relationships: how contact points on both sides of the relationship are constantly shifting making trust difficult to hold in place over time. On the government side, this barrier reverberates through the political cycles of elected officials moving in and out of power, who then appoint new department leaders who in turn hire new employees.

We developed the strategy preserving institutional relationships based upon the concern of *preservation* that was central to how cycles of leadership were addressed. Preservation was pursued by extending the focal point of institutional contact beyond top leadership in such a way that preserves relationships through cycles. The action 'sustaining engagement' is a key component of this strategy as P8 describes, "*have*[ing] *consistent outlets for the community to engage us regardless of changes in leadership.*" Here, "us" refers to internal staff rather external contacts such as mayor or city council. Both P8 and P13 selected technologies that would facilitate more frequent and regular contact from within their respective entities: P8 thought staff use of 'text messaging' would be a good way to have casual conversations while P13 chose 'blogs' and 'social media' to remain in contact with communities over the duration of planning processes.

P11's focus was on how to preserve visions throughout cycles of political regimes that unfold during the timeframe of master plans, "*plans like these happen on a scale of time that ends up being in between regimes (not something that happens on an annual basis) — even the best plans etched in stone have the challenge of becoming someone's else vision... how do you work through that?*" P11 selected the action 'managing expectations' which he described as making it clear to citizens that even after a planning process produces a vision—this vision is not self-fulling. Rather, ongoing work is needed to keep the vision alive through cycles of leadership. His choice of technology was 'website' but he wondered how to avoid the tendency for websites to become static repositories rather than an ongoing source of engagement capable of sustaining visions, "[websites] *become artifacts of the past rather than a living breathing thing...like the plan itself.*"

The key affordance for this strategy is preservation; but rather than preservation in the sense of documenting the past statically—preservation is future orientated and dynamic. For P8 and P13, preservation was a matter of facilitating ongoing casual conversation and social interactions by increasing contact from internal leadership. Whereas for P11, preservation was aimed at sustaining engagement necessary to carry on the visions embodied in plans. Preserving institutional relationships addresses the barrier cycles of leadership by extending the focal point of institutional contact thus drawing away from over-dependence on singular, transitory relationships by distributing where, how, and with whom does institutional contact occur. This has implications for trust in community engagement where interpersonal and institutional trust have complimentary yet distinct roles. Generally public officials tend to emphasize interpersonal trust. This was reflected during the workshop (and our previous work [12]) in an instance where P8 expressed difficulty in thinking about how technology could be used in the retaining stage remarking, "*this is hard because trust is people to people.*" P11 added, "*people don't trust institutions they trust people...*" In the end, design will need to take care in how trust is mediated in community engagement; balancing support of trust in both its institutional and interpersonal forms [12].

DISCUSSION

This paper posed the question: how might design support trust in the relational aims of digital civics? Through our design based inquiry with public officials, we developed four strategies towards answering this question: historicizing engagement, focusing on experience, mediating expectations and preserving institutional relationships. These strategies are grounded in the work of community engagement from the point of view of public officials. This purview presents an opportunity and challenge for digital civics. The opportunity is in how we understand the perspective and needs of public officials within the context of digital civics. The challenge is that designing for present needs and practices does not align with the goals of digital civics that aim to transform civic interactions and confront established modes of neoliberal governance. Reconciling the challenge of designing for what is, instead of what might be, prompts us to ask a more fundamental question of digital civics: should digital civics provide tools and support for the work of community engagement as is—responding to user need, such as it were? Or, do we design tools that reflect what we expect of public officials and residents alike in the work of governance?

In the end, we are left with the situation that on one hand, the perspective from public officials tends to leave participation, democracy, and power relations in place; while on the other, buy-in and adoption of new technologies by public officials is key to the success and longevity of digital civics [9,43,44]. One possible bridge between these conflicting goals is by focusing on the common denominator—the need for trust. Trust underlies the relational aims of digital civics and is also vital to the work of community engagement [26,41]. However, as we have argued, trust's importance is implicit in digital civics but also under-theorized in terms of design guidelines. Moreover, the use of digital tools in the work of community engagement to support trust is limited [12,26]. For this reason, orientating digital civics around trust serves to align digital civics with the work of community engagement performed by public officials. Doing so means developing a better understanding of the affordances within the strategies developed in our workshops.

History

While design is inherently future orientated—supporting relationships in digital civics will need to actively engage history to be successful. To engage history, we mean the ways in which past experiences can be brought to bear on current systems and processes. In the civic space, this can be difficult as history is often linked to inequity, injustice, broken promises, and ultimately distrust.

Digital civics has provided several examples we can draw from history to productively build relations between different constituencies. For instance, Crivellaro et al [16] explored how history of place was fundamental to the design of technologies to solicit oral history and build relations between past and future residents of public housing. The briefcase they designed was fitted with various audio recording and playback mechanisms and was passed from resident to resident, accumulating stories of place that set the stage for future engagement around the identity of the community. The key to success in Crivellaro's design intervention was by allowing residents agency in engaging history on their own terms, rather than accepting narratives developed from others.

In another example, Le Dantec and Fox's community historians project [22], local history was engaged through participatory design encounters to empower an underserved community through the creation of shared identity. In this case, sensing technology was used as a medium to explore how the community might further goals, communicate values, and utilize social capital. In these examples, agency and empowerment—both of which are vital to trust—were enabled through focusing on history in the design and use of digital media. These two examples point to ways in which history can be productive tethered by technology to establish a pathway to, and basis for trust. The challenge for design is moving these kinds of design interventions out of the community settings where they were developed, and into institutional settings where instrumental performance takes precedent over community building and affective experience. The concerns that P10 and P12 expressed during the workshop about technology's role in addressing historical breakdowns means that we need to find new ways of capturing, codifying, and sharing historical experience—not just knowledge and data. One potential avenue is by focusing on agency and empowerment, both within the municipal workplace, and in relation to the municipal official and the community they serve.

Experience

Experience in the public sector is most often framed around customer service. One of the traits of neoliberal governance is by directly adopting the private sector perspective of business and technology to improve experience by running government like a business and treating citizens as customers. Of course, improving the experience of government along these lines is important—there are elements of local government that are best modeled as service providers with customer—but the larger point is to not conflate the experience of receiving service from the government with the experience of participating in the decision-making processes of government. Recognizing the difference between private and public sector needs is especially important given that the methods applied to improving experience in the former can be fundamentally incompatible to the values of experience in the latter [1,24].

In contrast, experience in digital civics is framed as "participative experiences [34]" that "emphasizes dialogue, reflexivity and mutual learning" [40]. A key quality of participative experiences is reconfiguring social relations in terms of the roles actors play and how these change through participation. Trust is developed gradually over these experiences by developing empathy and understanding—"making visible what is invisible to the other" [34]. Overall, McCarthy and Wright suggest trust is both the means and ends of participative experience—with design enabling participation and then responding to the dialogue created within [34].

Participatory experience thus construed seems well suited to addressing the challenges with experience that arose during the workshop. However, there is a dissonance between how experience is viewed by public officials and how it is framed within the research agenda of digital civics. In digital civics, experience is both the means and ends in bringing about fundamental changes to services, processes, relationships, and ultimately power. In comparison, the perspective of experience of our participants was much more incremental and pragmatic—the assumption is one of working within the status quo, rather than creating something entirely new. The unwillingness to break from the familiar was clear in how the technology selections of workshop participants were fitted into existing processes and tuned to amplifying reach or collecting data. Unfortunately, focusing on experience in this manner would be insufficient to address the primary barrier of one-off engagement that worried our participants (and which contributed to troubled histories of interaction).

Ultimately, civic design needs a middle ground. A potential example can be found in Johnson et al's community conversational platform [27]. Community conversational gamifies the experience of local consultation processes to encourage and structure conversations. The platform also featured an interface for searching and filtering data to support analysis by officials. In this way, the platform creates a participatory experience that can be used directly to support the work of community engagement. The second example is Sens-Us, which focused on the experience of citizen participation with surveys [23]. In order to spur more engagement with surveys (which are typically unappealing and tedious experience) Golsteijn et al explored how materiality and space could create a more enticing and enjoyable interaction. Promising in both of these examples is how creative, playful, and explorative experiences are wedded with the practical needs for gathering data and informing decision making that characterizes the work of community engagement performed by public officials.

In the end, research in digital civics is foregrounded by a commitment to experience, and to that end, provides several exemplar interventions [15,16,23,30]. However, the key question we raise here is how can these experiences achieve the other commitment of digital civics, "to support citizens becoming agents of democracy through technology and dialogue *with public institutions that actualize public will*" [46].

Expectation

At the most basic level, trust is a process of forming expectations. Thus, enabling trust is essentially about supporting how expectations are formed and maintained [38]. The challenge of supporting expectations arises from uncertainty and time; both of which are especially problematic in the work of community engagement. This was exemplified in the challenges with the barrier of 'speed of progress' that participants raised in the workshop—engagement must continue and manage differing expectations about how quickly or how long something should, or does take.

Supporting expectations through design is perhaps the most straightforward of the four affordances. The most common form this affordance comes through interfaces like data dashboards and other associated visualizations of public data. Such systems are designed to share information and provide a common understanding and set of expectations of a process or service. While common, supporting expectations with open data and visualizations is not without its problems and limitations. For instance, McMillan et al discussed the problems public officials face when opening up data—the "messy realities of what it means to collect, curate, control, and disseminate data relating to the lives and practices of citizens" [35]. Creating and managing open data is a resource intense process that requires constant work of curating and translating across boundaries of accountability and influence [18]. Additionally, there is always the potential threat public officials face that the data they share could be used to subvert city functioning. Moreover, in addition to the problems McMillan identified, O'Hara's study of open data and transparency initiatives in the UK examines the interaction between open data and trust, pushing back against the simplistic determinism in much of the popular discourse surrounding the ability for open data to enable trust [39]. A key concern for O'Hara was that top down approaches—where public institutions decide alone what to release and what not to—fail to be meaningful for citizens and thus fail to engender trust.

Using data dashboards and open data to manage expectations is also more bound to questions of accountability than to efforts to build trust in relationships. In fact, accountability is often a product and response to distrust, therefore necessitating the need for increased oversight. In this way, open data as means to engender trust is paradoxical—as society becomes increasingly more complex and interdependent, the ability to monitor, predict, and calculate is reduced, which explains the allure of efforts around smart cities where instrumentation and machine learning are deployed to manage these growing complexities. However, by applying complex systems to manage complex systems, we only increase uncertainty. Thus, ultimately the proliferation of data can,s in fact increase complexity and therefore risk which problematizes the process of forming positive expectations. In reality, people do not have the cognitive resources to perceive the multitude of vulnerabilities, so instead they trust (or rely) on institutions, others and systems [47].

A more appropriate approach to supporting expectations to sustain trust in digital civics can be drawn from Davis's work exploring participatory design in ambient persuasive technology [19]. Davis tries to solve the possibility of manipulation inherent in persuasive technology by introducing participatory design "by involving potential users in design helps to avoid some potential ethical issues with persuasive technology. Without participatory design, the designer stands outside of the community and intends to change the behavior of community members. With participatory design, the persuasive intent comes in part from community members who want to change the community's behavior from within." The possibility of manipulation Davis raises is also very relevant in supporting expectations generally and even more so if open-data is the method. In fact, both McMillan and O'Hara allude to the dangers of manipulation with open data—in terms of selecting, withholding data, scrubbing data and outright falsification. In comparison, participatory design as a method of supporting expectations would work by bringing people into the process of forming expectations—much the same as how Davis sought to create persuasive intent from within users. So rather than expectations being supported 'from afar' with open data and data visualizations which we have argued is just a way of increasing visibility of work being done by public officials—participatory design offers an alternative to support expectations 'from within' by working with public officials in formation of expectations. Thus, participatory methods of developing and opening up data present a promising approach to the affordance of expectations in digital civics. To this end, existing work around participatory data visualizations [11,17,20,21]—provide good examples of how this might pursued.

Preservation

On the whole, trust as a process is time consuming and arduous. Thus, preservation of relationships—which are the end products of the trust process—will always be important. On this point, digital civics and the needs of public officials are most aligned when it comes to preservation. For digital civics, preservation is implicit in creating participatory experiences in how these should focus on the durational quality of relationships to establish trust [34]. This necessitates extended ongoing encounters and a commitment to making lasting changes to relationships. Many of these elements McCarthy points out were also present in how preservation was approached in the workshop—supporting ongoing encounters, improving durational quality, and the commitment to lasting relationships revealed by P8, P11 and P13.

That being said, one important aspect of how preservation was pursed in the workshop was the distributive nature in the ways in which preservation was carried out—distributing where, how and with whom does institutional contact occur. This distributive aspect is both promising and problematic for trust. Bosman has recently detailed how the impact of technology on trust in society is tangled by how digital technology's fundamental impact on trust is distributive: trust becomes proliferated across systems, platforms and infrastructures [7]. A good example of distributive trust in digital civics is the CrowdMemo platform by Balestrini et al[3]. The platform was a socio-technical system for generating and circulating microdocumentaries in order to help preserve local heritage in a rural town. A key factor in the success of CrowdMemo was in how it distributed interactions across several different classes of relationships throughout the community. In this regard, the CrowdMemo project was an exemplar display of preservation in HCI.

On the other hand, distributive trust as means of achieving preservation is not without its problems. While in the past trust was centralized in institutions—through leaders or key officials (as was discussed in the workshop)—Bosman argues that distributive trust weakens institutional trust. This in turn reverberates to how trust operates interpersonally; trust is ultimately the product of interpersonal relationships as well as institutional which are intertwined in such a manner that, "trust cannot be fully understood and studied exclusively on either the psychological level or on the institutional level, because it so thoroughly permeates both" [32]. Ultimately, the take-away here is designing for preservation should be careful to consider the interrelated nature of both forms of trust.

CONCLUSION

In order to support trust in digital civics, we developed four strategies: historicizing engagement, focusing on experience, mediating expectations and preserving institutional relationships. These strategies are derived from the relationships between public officials and the citizens they work to engage. While digital civics has used as a point of departure the community perspective and experience, here we add balance by working from the institutional side. Thus, this work expands the design space by addressing a facet of digital civics that has gone under-studied: how design could approach creation of tools to support the work of community engagement performed by public officials. To this end, the four affordances we discussed provide a useful starting point to orientate future design interventions.

ACKNOWLEDGMENTS

We are grateful to our partners with the City of Atlanta. This project was supported in part by the NSF under grant IIS-1524380.

REFERENCES

1. Mariam Asad, Christopher A. Le Dantec, Becky Nielsen, and Kate Diedrick. 2017. Creating a Sociotechnical API. In *Proceedings of the 2017 CHI Conference on Human Factors in Computing Systems - CHI '17*, 2295–2306. https://doi.org/10.1145/3025453.3025963
2. Mariam Asad and Christopher A Le Dantec. 2015. Illegitimate Civic Participation: Supporting Community Activists on the Ground. In *CSCW '15: Proceedings of the 18th ACM Conference on Computer Supported Cooperative Work & Social Computing*, 1694–1703.
3. Mara Balestrini, Jon Bird, Paul Marshall, Alberto Zaro, and Yvonne Rogers. 2014. Understanding Sustained Community Engagement: A Case Study in Heritage Preservation in Rural Argentina. *Proceedings of the SIGCHI Conference on Human Factors in Computing Systems*: 2675–2684. https://doi.org/10.1145/2556288.2557323
4. Shakuntala Banaji and David Buckingham. 2013. *The Civic Web*. MIT Press.
5. Bernard Barber and Diego Gambetta. 1992. Trust: Making and Breaking Cooperative Relations. *Contemporary Sociology 21*, 401. https://doi.org/10.2307/2076328
6. a. Borning, B. Friedman, Janet L. Davis, and P. Lin. 2005. Informing Public Deliberation : Value Sensitive Design of Indicators for a Large-Scale Urban Simulation. *Proceedings of the ECSCW 2005 European Conference on Computer-Supported Cooperative Work*, September: 449–468. https://doi.org/10.1007/1-4020-4023-7
7. Rachel Botsman. 2017. *Who can you trust? : how technology brought us together : and why it could drive us apart*. Penguin UK: Kindle Edition.
8. Harry C Boyte. 2010. *Everyday Politics*. University of Pennsylvania Press.
9. Aurélien Buffat. 2015. Street-Level Bureaucracy and E-Government. *Public Management Review* 17, 1: 149–161. https://doi.org/10.1080/14719037.2013.771699
10. Pew Research Center. 2015. *Beyond Distrust: How Americans View Their Government*. https://doi.org/10.1017/CBO9781107415324.004
11. Rachel Clarke, Peter Wright, Madeline Balaam, and John Mccarthy. 2013. Digital portraits: Photo-sharing after domestic violence. *Proc. CHI '13*: 2517–2526. https://doi.org/10.1145/2470654.2481348
12. Eric Corbett and Christopher A Le Dantec. 2018. Going the Distance : Trust Work for Citizen Participation. In *Proceedings of the 2018 CHI Conference on Human Factors in Computing Systems - CHI '18*.
13. Eric Corbett and Christopher Le Dantec. The Problem of Community Engagement : Disentangling the Practices of Municipal Government. In *Proceedings of the 2018 CHI Conference on Human Factors in Computing Systems - CHI '18*.
14. Clara Crivellaro, Rob Comber, J Bowers, Peter C Wright, and Patrick Olivier. 2014. A Pool of Dreams: Facebook, Politics and the Emergence of a Social Movement. In *CHI '14: Proceedings of the 32nd annual ACM conference on Human factors in computing systems*, 3573–3582.
15. Clara Crivellaro, Rob Comber, Martyn Dade-Robertson, Simon J. Bowen, Peter Wright, and Patrick Olivier. 2015. Contesting the city: enacting the pollitical through digitally supported urban walks. *CHI '15: Proceedings of the 33rd Annual ACM Conference on Human Factors in Computing Systems*: 2853–2862. https://doi.org/10.1145/2702123.2702176
16. Clara Crivellaro, Alex Taylor, Vasillis Vlachokyriakos, Rob Comber, Bettina Nissen, and Peter Wright. 2016. Re-Making Places: HCI,'Community Building'and Change. In *Proceedings of the 2016 CHI Conference on Human Factors in Computing Systems*, 2958–2969.
17. Catherine D'Ignazio and Lauren F Klein. 2016. Feminist data visualization. In *Workshop on Visualization for the Digital Humanities (VIS4DH), Baltimore. IEEE.*
18. Christopher a Le Dantec and W Keith Edwards. 2010. Across Boundaries of Influence and Accountability: The Multiple Scales of Public Sector Information Systems. *Proceedings of the SIGCHI Conference on Human Factors in Computing Systems*: 113–122. https://doi.org/10.1145/1753326.1753345
19. Janet Davis. 2009. Early experiences with participatory design of ambient persuasive technology. In *CHI'09: Workshop on defining the role of HCI in the challenges of sustainability*, 119–128.

20. Carl DiSalvo, Jeff Maki, and Nathan Martin. 2007. Mapmover: a case study of design-oriented research into collective expression and constructed publics. *Proc. CHI 2007*: 1249–1252. https://doi.org/10.1145/1240624.1240813

21. Carl DiSalvo, Illah Nourbakhsh, David Holstius, Ayça Akin, and Marti Louw. 2008. The Neighborhood Networks project: a case study of critical engagement and creative expression through participatory design. In *Proceedings of the Tenth Anniversary Conference on Participatory Design 2008*, 41–50.

22. Sarah Fox and Christopher A Le Dantec. 2014. Community Historians : Scaffolding Community Engagement through Culture and Heritage.

23. Connie Golsteijn, Sarah Gallacher, Licia Capra, and Yvonne Rogers. 2016. Sens-Us. *Proceedings of the 2016 ACM Conference on Designing Interactive Systems - DIS '16*: 39–49. https://doi.org/10.1145/2901790.2901877

24. Eric Gordon and Stephen Walter. 2016. Meaningful Inefficiencies: Resisting the Logic of Technological Efficiency in the Design of Civic Systems. *Civic Media: Technology, Design, Practice*: 243.

25. Russell Hardin. 1999. Do we want trust in government? *Democracy and trust*: 22–41.

26. Mike Harding, Bran Knowles, Nigel Davies, and Mark Rouncefield. 2015. HCI, Civic Engagement & Trust. *Proceedings of the 33rd Annual ACM Conference on Human Factors in Computing Systems - CHI '15*: 2833–2842. https://doi.org/10.1145/2702123.2702255

27. Ian G Johnson, Alistair Mcdonald, Jo Briggs, Jennifer Manuel, Karen Salt, Emma Flynn, and John Vines. 2017. Community Conversational : Supporting and Capturing Deliberative Talk in Local Consultation Processes.

28. Jonghyuk Jung, Eun-young Ko Songyi, Han Chang, Won Lee, Juho Kim, and Jihee Kim. 2016. BudgetMap : Engaging Taxpayers in the Issue-Driven Classification of a Government Budget. 1028–1039.

29. Juho Kim, Eun-young Ko, Jonghyuk Jung, Chang Won Lee, Nam Wook Kim, and Jihee Kim. 2015. Factful: Engaging Taxpayers in the Public Discussion of a Government Budget. *Proceedings of the ACM CHI'15 Conference on Human Factors in Computing Systems* 1: 2843–2852. https://doi.org/10.1145/2702123.2702352

30. Matthias Korn and Jon Back. 2012. Talking it further: from feelings and memories to civic discussions in and about places. *Proceedings of the 7th Nordic Conference on Human-Computer Interaction: Making Sense Through Design*: 189–198. https://doi.org/10.1145/2399016.2399046

31. Charles H Levine. 2015. Citizenship and Service Delivery. *The age of direct citizen participation* 44: 78.

32. J David Lewis and Andrew Weigert. 1985. Trust as a Social Reality. *Source: Social Forces* 63, 4: 967–985. https://doi.org/10.1093/sf/63.4.967

33. Niklas Luhmann. 1979. Trust and Power. *Cooperation without Trust* 8: 208.

34. John McCarthy and P Wright. 2015. *Taking [A]part*. MIT Press.

35. Donald McMillan, Arvid Engström, Airi Lampinen, and Barry Brown. 2016. Data and the City. *Proceedings of the 2016 CHI Conference on Human Factors in Computing Systems - CHI '16*: 2933–2944. https://doi.org/10.1145/2858036.2858434

36. Matthew B Miles, A Michael Huberman, and J Saldana. 1984. Qualitative data analysis: A sourcebook. *Beverly Hills*.

37. Guido Mollering. 2001. The Nature of Trust: From Georg Simmel to a Theroy fo Expectation, Interpertation ad Suspension. *Sociology* 35, 2: 403–420.

38. Guido Möllering. 2006. *Trust: Reason, routine, reflexivity*. Emerald Group Publishing.

39. Kieron O'Hara. 2012. Transparency, open data and trust in government. *Proceedings of the 3rd Annual ACM Web Science Conference on - WebSci '12*: 223–232. https://doi.org/10.1145/2380718.2380747

40. Patrick Olivier and P Wright. 2015. Digital civics: Taking a local turn. *Interactions* 22, 4: 61–63. https://doi.org/10.1145/2776885

41. Simon Parker, Phil Spires, Faizal Farook, and Melissa Mean. 2008. State of Trust. How to Build better Relationships between Councils and the Public. *Demos, London*.

42. Pew Research Center. 2015. *Beyond Distrust: How Americans View Their Government*. https://doi.org/10.1017/CBO9781107415324.004

43. Julie Simon, Theo Bass, Victoria Boelman, and Geoff Mulgan. 2017. *NESTA Digital Democracy: the tools transforming political engagement*.

44. Jon Sotsky and Jonathan Kartt. 2018. *Scaling Civic Tech: Paths to a Sustainable Future*.

45. Eran Vigoda-Gadot and Shlomo Mizrahi. 2014. *Managing democracies in turbulent times: Trust, performance, and governance in modern states*. https://doi.org/10.1007/978-3-642-54072-1

46. Vasillis Vlachokyriakos, Clara Crivellaro, Christopher A Le Dantec, Eric Gordon, Pete Wright, and Patrick Olivier. 2016. Digital Civics. In *Proceedings of the 2016 CHI Conference Extended Abstracts on Human Factors in Computing Systems - CHI EA '16* (CHI EA '16), 1096–1099. https://doi.org/10.1145/2851581.2886436

47. Mark E Warren. 1999. *Democracy and trust*. Cambridge University Press.

Beyond the Prototype: Maintenance, Collective Responsibility, and Public IoT

Sarah E. Fox, Rafael M. L. Silva, and Daniela K. Rosner
University of Washington
Seattle, WA USA
{sefox, rafaelsi, dkrosner}@uw.edu

ABSTRACT

This paper describes the reparative Internet of Things (Riot), a project investigating the role of IoT devices in maintaining public resource accessibility. Drawing on a mix of interviews, technology development, and ethnographic engagements, we explore the distribution and stratification of menstrual hygiene resources in Seattle, WA. We redesigned menstrual product dispensers placed in public settings by outfitting them with networked sensor inserts to make them easier to stock by custodial staff and easier to access by members of the public. We use this case to show how such newly connected devices structure experiences of hygiene access and help expose important consequences of integrating those devices into the socioeconomic logics and infrastructure of public life. Our interventions further examine the role of public IoT devices once they pass the proof-of-concept stage, revealing their capacity to cultivate and maintain collective responsibility.

Author Keywords

Internet of Things; menstruation; maintenance; public life.

ACM Classification Keywords

K.4.0 Computers in Society: general.

INTRODUCTION

Over the last decade, design researchers have increasingly helped articulate and imagine the possibility of a civic internet of things (IoT) — connected devices distributed throughout a city that contribute to public engagement, governance, and coordinated action. From pollution sensing [19] to foraging [12], scholars have used IoT devices to instrument urban landscapes, giving new momentum to the phrase "smart cities." Less visible in this body of research, however, is a thorough accounting for design's role in what repair studies scholar Lara Houston has called the "timeliness" of such infrastructures [25], the ways computational remainders, fragments, and breakdowns may not be contained in the tidier stories of technology prototyping that we circulate as design researchers. This paper investigates this work to maintain public IoT around the important but under-examined (and often stigmatized) topic of menstrual hygiene resource accessibility.

DIS '18, June 9–13, 2018, Hong Kong

ACM ISBN 978-1-4503-5198-0/18/06...$15.00
https://doi.org/10.1145/3196709.3196710

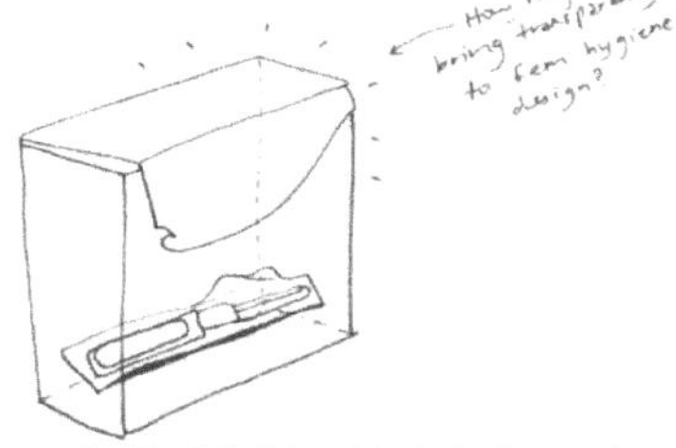

Figure 1: Rethinking Public IoT with Riot, networked sensor inserts that make menstrual product dispensers easier to stock and access.

Over the past few years, shifting government policies have sparked a flurry of interest in topic of menstruation — from local, state and federal policy initiatives calling for free and ready access to hygiene products to the formation of over a dozen startups with tens of millions in venture capital backing [46]. Alongside these efforts exist longer running programs that install and maintain dispensers in public restrooms and the efforts of activists who collect and re-distribute menstrual resources to people unable to afford them [7].

Responding to and building on recent activism, including a growing body of design work on menstruation [15,34,41] and reproductive health [1,1,3,11], this paper describes a process of outfitting restroom menstrual product dispensers with networked sensors, a project we call Riot—or, the reparative Internet of Things. The sensors collect data on product levels in the dispensers and publically share that information on an online map so that the machines might be more easily stocked by maintenance and custodial staff and accessed by members of the public. Further, we discuss how the advocacy organization we worked with to design Riot used data from the dispensers to support particular legislation aimed at promoting "menstrual equity" statewide. To inform this design process, we drew on interviews and field visits with facilities organizations across Seattle, WA, a process that unfolded over three years, from 2015-2018.

With this case, we not only contribute a rich case study of IoT development around the stigmatized topic of menstrual health, but also begin to explore what it takes to move an activist IoT project beyond the prototyping stage — as well as what is learned as a result. Reflecting our design work beyond this specific case, our paper makes three key contributions to research literatures on IoT, maintenance, and design activism. First, we use Riot to highlight the forms of maintenance both expected and made possible through IoT deployments. Our deployment, for example, revealed political stakes of the municipal electric power grid as well as subtle class hierarchies around maintenance that we didn't see through interviews. Second, we surface collective responsibility as a core concern of IoT development, shaping both our ways of *doing* design research (in groups rather than as individual investigators and stakeholders) as well as our ways of *conceptualizing* it (framing the maintenance of menstrual resources as a collective rather than individual burden). Lastly, we explore how IoT may work not only as a proof-of-concept (a solution to the defined problem of public resource distribution); it may also create spaces and opportunities to reframe the very problem of access such interventions are meant to address.

LITERATURE REVIEW

The ideas and literature that inform our project sit at the nexus of three central bodies of work. First is the constellation of design scholarship that examines the incorporation of IoT devices and infrastructures into the fabric of public life. A range of recent work explores the public nature of IoT designed for civic engagement [2,5,13]. Carl DiSalvo and Tom Jenkins, for example, adopt feminist scholars J.K. Gibson-Graham's notion of "communing" to challenge the narrow positioning of IoT and other sensing devices within diverse economies such as foraging [12]. Instead of reject sensing devices around communing, they write, "what is needed is careful attention to how they configure experience and agency, and perhaps, imagine ways they might in fact contribute to an even richer understanding of nonhumans in diverse economies" [ibid:55].

In a second body of work, researchers have highlighted activism for the here and now of technology development. For instance, Susan Leigh Star famously highlighted the concept of *invisible work* after doing what she terms "feminist activist work," unpaid housework that puts laborers, often women, into the role of an "unseeable" domestic servant [42]. For HCI, this concept draws attention to expropriations and power discrepancies that design researchers may help expose [28], resonating with early participatory design orientations focusing on re-centering devalued forms of labor practice in the face of authority and power differentials [14]. Embodying this commitment, designers and artists like Sputniko! (also known as Hiromi Ozaki) have begun examining the technological domain around menstruation. In the Menstruation Machine, Sputniko! equipped a wearable device with a blood dispensing mechanism and lower-abdomen stimulating electrodes to simulate select physical symptoms of menstruation for those with a desire to experience them [34]. Within the HCI community, Epstein et al. offered an analysis of the motivations and methods behind the use of period tracking applications and put forth several key design considerations, from improving the app's accuracy to avoiding gender stereotypes within interface design [15]. Søndergaard and Hansen moved this conversation back to the realm of the speculative with PeriodShare, a connected menstrual cup that quantifies and shares menstrual data automatically, reflecting on the contemporary and near future politics of intimate forms of self-tracking [41]. Altogether these works have offered a glimpse into the range of considerations that design research on menstruation might take up—from those oriented toward the whimsical, to the sociocultural, to the practical.

Alongside these activist encounters, we look to the growing interdisciplinary field of maintenance and repair studies, an area of research and design practice given recent definition by several edited collections [9,27]. Early studies of digital maintenance include Julian Orr's [33] rich accounts of Xerox technicians and the social nature of the expertise, lessons broadened in other work by Graham and Thrift [22] and later Houston [26], Jackson [29], and Rosner and colleagues [36,37,40]. Underlying this focus on maintenance is a commitment to thinking of design as only one (widely valorized) moment within the long-term lifecycle of computational goods. As feminist scholar and former Xerox ethnographer Lucy Suchman explains, "the basic change implied by rethinking the technological object is from a view of design as the creation of discrete devices, or even networks of devices, to a view of systems development as entry into the networks of working relations – including both contests and alliances – that make technical systems possible" [43:2]. Important for our work, Jérôme Denis and David Pontille recently enumerate the regimes of practice that make up repair, including mending, repairing, fixing, restoring, preserving, cleaning, recycling, and up-keeping. Turning to the regime of things, they write, "maintenance enacts what we might think of as two-sided objects, fragile in the eyes and hands of maintainers, reliable in the eyes of users" [10]. It is this particular argument that we take up in the work that follows to consider the maintenance of IoT infrastructure.

OUR PROJECT

Riot began as a part of a wider investigation of public IoT, the sorts of connected digital systems and modes of interaction that might support public engagement. Our early work included design investigations of people's movement through public space and modes of lighting along such paths [17,38,39]. As our work continued, we quickly turned our attention to restrooms—spaces integral to participation in public life, yet often overlooked in popular depictions of the internet of things, public or otherwise.

Methodology

To investigate the role of public IoT in menstrual resource accessibility we deploy feminist approaches to situated inquiry [23,31] and modes of interventionist research tied to traditions of participatory [6,30] and speculative design [32,35]. The first acknowledges the ways in which investigators' political and social conditions shape their ways of knowing. Following this line of inquiry, we take up approaches of ethnographic observation and interviewing to investigate existing forms of menstrual access across the city. The second uses engagements of collaborative design in order to build encounters both speculative and real at the same time. In this case, we grasp for a vision of feminist internet of things, while offering repairs to the systems already in place.

Our project uses the above investigative tools to draw out the social conditions that define access to public resources, while also contending with those circumstances through design encounters. In particular, we adopt elements of participatory inquiry to explore two core questions: (1) *What does access to menstrual resources mean to those maintaining public restrooms?* (2) *What forms of menstrual accessibility could IoT encourage or engender?*

Design Process

Our design process included two main phases: (1) ethnographic fieldwork within sites of menstrual resource distribution, and (2) design and ethnographic engagements around our Riot intervention.

To understand ongoing activity in Seattle public restrooms, for example, we conducted ethnographic field visits during the first phase across:

1. *Seattle public parks & recreational facilities' restrooms,* spaces meant for public use and open without a fee or an implicit expectation of consumer exchange. Seattle Parks and Recreation is responsible for the repair and maintenance of basic services at the city's parks and community centers. This work involves the day-to-day upkeep of the park facilities and grounds maintenance, including cleaning restrooms, removing litter, clearing trails, landscaping, painting over graffiti, and making building repairs. The organization is responsible for a 6,414-acre park system, including 485 parks and 120 miles of trails (occupying 12% of the city's land area). Those involved in this work include people in managerial positions such as district supervisors and lead crew workers, as well as grounds crew and administrative staff.
2. *Our home institution's facilities organization,* a group made up of 10 departments (e.g. building services, maintenance and construction, and transportation), each serving the university community by performing repairs, maintenance, and cleaning for campus buildings and grounds. The work of the staff involves care for over 1,300 restrooms and maintenance of "643 acres of grounds, 22 miles of roads and pathways, and services including power, HVAC, cleaning, waste, maintenance and construction for more than 15 million square feet" [49]. Among those on staff are supervisors who oversee the various departments, building managers who supervise the care of either high traffic centers or several smaller buildings, custodians who manage the day-to-day cleaning and maintenance of buildings within a certain area, and office personnel who administer service requests and address internal human resource needs.
3. *The Womxn's Action Commission (WAC)* an organization that has worked since the 1960s to promote gender equity on the university campus and amongst the broader Seattle community by hosting events and advocating for institutional and regional policy shifts. In its current form, the WAC takes an intersectional approach to justice, seeking to "[recognize] and [affirm] the multiple and intersecting identities held by woman-identified and/or female-identified-at-birth constituents" [50]. Contemporary programs of the WAC include a yearly production of the ___ monologues (a challenge to the cisgender focus of the widely known The Vagina Monologues), workshops and panel discussions on Gender in STEM, Queer Narratives, Disability Justice, health programs such as a Check Your Boobies Party, and a Queer and Trans Artists of Color series. In addition to these events, each year the group selects a political issue or cause to pursue with the support of their staff and interns. During the 2016-17 school year, they elected to support menstrual equity through both student government proposals and state legislation.

By engaging these sites, we began to deepen our understanding of menstrual resource accessibility across the Seattle community writ large (from maintenance to advocacy), while also forming partnerships across various concerns, contingencies, and ideological commitments.

Data Collection

Our design research methods draw on ethnographic fieldwork and collaborations spanning a three-year period (from the winter of 2015 to the winter of 2018), including a wide range of interviews and observations with custodial professionals (at parks, community centers, and homeless shelters) and members of activist and advocacy organizations such as the Womxn's Action Commission (WAC). Data included:

- *Ethnographic fieldnotes* based on first-hand accounts produced by Sarah Fox while she worked as a custodian and a front desk volunteer at two hygiene centers (one specifically for women and children, and the other all gender)—spaces offering free access to restrooms, showers, and laundry—for a total of 6 months. There we began to learn about the limitations of access throughout the city. For instance, though day centers offered menstrual products to visitors, they were closed in the evenings and on weekends. This meant clients needed to stockpile products or go without for times when centers were inaccessible. We also learned about individual preferences when it came to particular products, noting that many gravitated toward pads and high absorbency tampons in order to avoid regular changing when without easy access to restrooms.

We also collected fieldnotes from observations with staff of the Seattle public parks and recreational facilities, as well as our home institution's facilities organization, including visiting 46 restrooms. At each restroom site we documented the sorts of objects, resources, and infrastructure we found inside. Often these spaces included paper towel dispensers, hand dryers, sinks, mirrors, toilets, toilet paper rolls, condom dispensers, and trashcans, but rarely did we find operational menstrual product dispensers. We charted this initial fieldwork on a city map, beginning to note the spatial relationships to access (the online map of Riot later borrowed from this form).

- *Interview data* collected across each of our field sites. Specifically, building on our public restroom facilities observations, we conducted 15 interviews with members of the municipal maintenance staff, learning about the processes and political structures that guide their labor and define public hygiene accessibility. We also interviewed 13 organizers of local activist and nonprofit organizations that collect and distribute pads, tampons, and other menstrual resources. Additionally, we interviewed representatives of the largest manufacturer of menstrual product dispensers in the country, Congress members and staff of state and US governments, and social entrepreneurs focusing on promoting change to the treatment of menstrual resource accessibility through enterprise-based initiatives.

Data analysis

We thematically analyzed our data drawing on inductive techniques of contextualized grounded theory [8] to highlight the forms of menstrual accessibility enabled within public spaces and the role IoT might play in them. During weekly meetings, we reviewed reflective memos that we developed based on our field notes and other empirical materials. Across later rounds of analysis, we iteratively revisited and refined our interpretations to build emergent themes such as collective responsibility, as outlined in the sections below.

Riot

The Riot insert is a lightweight, networked sensor outfitted for commonplace menstrual hygiene dispensers. The device counts the number of menstrual products (e.g. tampons and pads) inside the dispensers and stores and shares this information for both maintenance staff and public viewing. The insert comprises two distance sensors—a low-cost microcontroller with Wi-Fi capability and a simple, portable power bank—all housed in a custom cardboard box fitted to the dimensions of prominent dispenser models.

PHASE I: SETTING THE GROUNDWORK FOR RIOT

To help set the stage for our discussion of Riot, we begin by introducing the alliances we built with members of WAC and other key organizations developed to collectively direct the project's outcomes. We recognize that in concentrating on our organizational partnerships, we lose out on providing detail on 'users' of the restrooms (a focus we take up in other accounts [16]), yet we believe this focus is worthwhile for two key reasons. The first has to do with the nature of our collaborative process, which involved not only enrolling individual stakeholders (as is common in other prevailing design methods [18]), but also understanding what is required for producing and maintaining those connections. We sought to examine the integral role that policy, media, and organizational structures play in the development and, crucially, the sustainability of our collective work. The second reason for emphasizing our partnerships has to do with the recognition that despite developing novel IoT infrastructure, like many other digital designs, the broader initiative was not wholly new. Indeed, we built on many existing menstrual advocacy efforts, as outlined below. Our project thus required charting the WAC's evolution and the emergence of central advocacy concerns over the years leading up to our interventions.

Public Restrooms Maintenance

We began our project with site visits to public parks and community centers where we later conducted interviews and observations with members of the municipal maintenance staff, learning about the processes and political structures that guide their labor and define public hygiene accessibility. In one interview with custodial staff, an administrator to a district head named Debra described how the city introduced soap to restrooms in municipal parks, a relatively new addition from the 1990s. It was one "very adamant" resident, she told us, who "gathered the forces, communicated to all layers of government," and convinced those at the head of the parks department to revise their policy on this form of hygiene infrastructure. Prior to this advocacy, Debra told us, soap was considered a "courtesy" and was thus left for individual area supervisors to decide if it was worth the cost and additional labor to upkeep. From a maintenance lead named Linda, we later learned that it was not just any adamant resident, it was the spouse of a city councilmember. Linda claimed he also took up the cause, advocating to his colleagues in city government who, in turn, put pressure "back down" on the department. Those who tended get their voices heard and their needs met, Linda told us, were the ones who had "time on their hands" or "know the system"—likely those already in positions of prominence, as the case of the soap illustrates.

Those unlikely to have a seat at the table were members of the city's homeless population who spent time in the parks, and who many of the maintenance staff described as perpetrators of "vandalism," the name they gave to perceived malicious destruction or defacement of the restroom infrastructure that they were left to fix. Lead maintenance crew member Robert told us that his district had to deal with the remains of bathrooms burned to the ground in what he described as "arson." As we continued chatting, he told us that he had an idea for why this arson was happening with such frequency. He had spent time sleeping outside while deployed in the military, he said, and, "used do a lot of things to keep warm." "If this is the only paper [referring to toilet paper] you had, then this is what you burn to stay warm," he continued.

In this recollection, we saw experiences of the maintenance staff such as Robert and others resembling the circumstances of people they accused of vandalism and arson. But rather than form a sense of connection with these residents, crew members instantiated programs to limit homeless people's access to the sites—locking the restrooms in the early evening and calling the police or service workers when maintenance staff spotted people they believed to be "campers." Across the areas and districts we observed, maintenance crews took up similar approaches to deter the homeless population from spending time in public parks, with an express preference for the "good people" (middle class families or those with regular access to housing). We noticed that maintenance staff like Deborah, Linda, and Robert could sympathize with people using restrooms but ultimately couldn't see past their own assumptions about the types of inhabitances they saw as fit for these sites. Some kind of connection between the homeless lived experience and restroom maintenance seemed missing.

Seeds of an intervention

Early in our fieldwork we noticed that when discussions with city maintenance staff turned to menstrual hygiene infrastructure, maintenance staff often expressed ignorance or apathy. Most staff didn't know where someone might go to find menstrual resources, much less determine who was responsible for them. One maintenance crew member suggested that dispensers were only available at community centers, while community center staff told us they were not required to install them and thus many did not have them. Much like we observed with the councilmember-led soap dispenser campaign, the lack of institutionalized policies created uneven access across districts.

With this new understanding of the city's public restroom landscape, we gained new sensitivities to what access meant in these sites. This sensitivity involved better understanding the maintenance labor involved in sustaining the present infrastructure and the political will that would likely be needed to shift or expand it. We proceeded puzzling the question: how might we design an intervention to probe at this space, while recognizing the crucial work of those already there?

University Facilities Organization Staff

To answer this question, we turned back to our own institutional context to see what existing initiatives we might contribute to or partner with locally. Following city-wide efforts, we organized a drive out of our university lab, collecting items such as pads, tampons, and menstrual cups (often under-donated to shelters and day centers [21]), as well as other products like lotion, toothpaste, and denture cream to be donated to youth and emergency shelters in the area. As we circulated an email announcement for the drive, we were met with messages expressing support and questions on how best to contribute. In one of these emails, we were connected with a representative from our university union (representing both graduate student workers and staff) who inquired about our research and suggested we get in touch with fellow members from our home institution's facilities organization. With this introduction, we met an institution plumber who contributed to initiatives such as the implementation of lactation stations and all-gender restrooms. The plumber eventually connected us with the members of the broader university facilities organization.

Echoing our prior fieldwork with municipal facilities staff, the university custodians described a tedious process of maintaining existing menstrual infrastructure, alongside their other duties. A group of facilities managers told us about struggling to keep track of the single, unique key for each dispenser and a constant need to troubleshoot broken devices. Machines often featured signs of struggle attributed to what the managers called "vandalism," where a visitor might have tried to break in after a failed attempt at buying a tampon or pad or to take the handful of coins inside.

Reparability here was difficult to establish. The machines held small, indispensable parts and staff had few options for their repair other than replacing coin mechanisms or installing entirely new units, which a facilities manager told us ran upwards of $300 for even older models. To deal with the labor and financial costs associated with keeping up the dispensers, the organization opted to divvy up access. Rather than installing the machines in every restroom, they selected a subset of buildings that would feature them (determined by "building use, traffic, and accessibility"). The staff then put in their absence a piece of paper listing the sites where dispensers were placed (not a map that might show how to navigate to them, but a text-based list). We later learned that this practice had first come under scrutiny by the WAC about two decades earlier.

Local Histories and the Womxn's Action Commission

Looking across these first two sites—the Seattle public restrooms and the university facilities organization—we found tensions played out over decades, sometimes in productive ways and other times recursively. In the early 1980s, the university facilities organization made the decisive move to remove all menstrual product dispensers "due to vandalism and maintenance costs," the then director told the campus newspaper [44]. For almost a decade, the university community did without the dispensers. Yet, due to student pressure throughout the 1990s, maintenance crews incrementally reintroduced them, with an initial installation of 55 devices across campus.

By 1998, the Womxn's Action Commission (WAC), the main student organization concerned with women's issues, had secured more than 1,000 signatures on a petition lobbying for an additional 19 dispensers. Successful with this push, they moved on campus menstrual infrastructure once again in 2010, scrutinizing what they took to be the uneven upkeep of machines and a lack of revisions to the list meant to guide visitors to available dispensers (which purportedly had not been updated for the decade following the WAC's last effort). The then director of WAC pleaded to the university newspaper, "If you're going to have those machines, you need to fill them" [47]. Following this attention, the university facilities organization formed a committee to review the dispensers, repairing broken and jammed machines and adding a half dozen more.

Upon learning of this history, we knew that familiarizing ourselves with the WAC should be our next step. As we interviewed those currently working for the university facilities organization we found similar maintenance issues emerging again (about 6 years on from WAC's last push). For instance, a plumber detailed the ways in which the placement of machines and the rapidness of repair was unevenly distributed amongst the units of the same institution. She described services being relayed more quickly to larger, more resource-rich departments. These departments already had dedicated maintenance staff (rather than employees covering multiple buildings, as with most) and could afford preventative infrastructural care such as checking for leaks.

It was at this point that our own building manager emailed us with the WAC's appeal for support in their latest campaign to seek permanent menstrual infrastructure through the institutional and state legislature. She suggested that we connect with the group directly, seeing productive overlaps between our design research and their aims of policy revision.

In the coming weeks we learned that the WAC planned for a suite of three legislative proposals that would guarantee residents of the area the same resources. The first proposal, introduced to the student government in the fall of 2016, codified the installation of dispensers in newly built all gender restrooms. This bill gained quick, sweeping approval in the student senate and acknowledged the need for private spaces of menstrual management for the community's transgender and gender non-conforming members. The second piece of legislation, a measure also introduced to the student government in late fall of 2016, proposed enforcing access to menstrual products in the campus' 15 busiest buildings. The third and final measure, planned for introduction to the Washington state government during the 2018 legislative session, would propose policy requiring all public schools (from elementary to university) to stock these items. In control of their own budgets, the student government was seen by members of the WAC as providing a uniquely rapid path to institutional change (with a board of some 65 people to convince, rather than with city- or state-wide bills that would likely require bipartisan negotiation). Together, these initiatives became a part of a longer legislative trajectory that began with the hyperlocal (just a few restrooms) and moved incrementally toward broader access for more and more (expanding with each level of government).

In our first meeting with both the university facilities organization and the WAC, their political astuteness became clear as members discussed shared goals for improving menstrual accessibility and how each group might aid the other toward this end. For instance, a member of the WAC touted the press coverage fellow institutions received after the launch of similar programs, such as initiatives at Brown University and University of Wisconsin, Madison. Meanwhile, the university facilities organization lent legitimacy to this effort by giving their support, stating they would explore options for funding the program themselves if the legislation did not pass. Here, a conversation at the intersection of maintenance, policy, and design set in motion a partnership that would later scaffold menstrual access.

PHASE II: DESIGNING AND DEPLOYING RIOT

Throughout our engagements with these key sites—the public restrooms, the university facilities organization, and the WAC—our design team sketched and imagined ideas for menstrual hygiene access. Initial concepts focused on developing a sensing technique capable of integrating within pre-existing dispenser models already in place in the public bathrooms we surveyed. We settled on the idea of counting product levels after exploring various sensing options (described in more detail in the Appendix) and abandoned ideas that might compromise the privacy and security of those visiting the restroom.

Proof-of-Concept Prototypes

Our first prototypes mobilized the gap inside the typical dispenser's cache, which becomes wider as tampons and pads are discharged. A set of two distance sensors (one for pads and the other for tampons) monitors this gap, prompting the system to calculate the number of remaining items (see Appendix for more detail on our sensor selection process). During this proof-of-concept phase, our team created an off-the-shelf Arduino-based structure to collect the field data as well as a web-platform for registering new restrooms and providing public-facing records of product counts from across the city. We used an Arduino Uno as the baseboard, ultrasonic sensors, a power management circuit integrated with a LiPo battery, and a Wi-Fi shield. The setup allowed us to explore this approach, with it capturing and sending data during a limited period of time (a few hours to several days). Yet, as we attempted to extend our

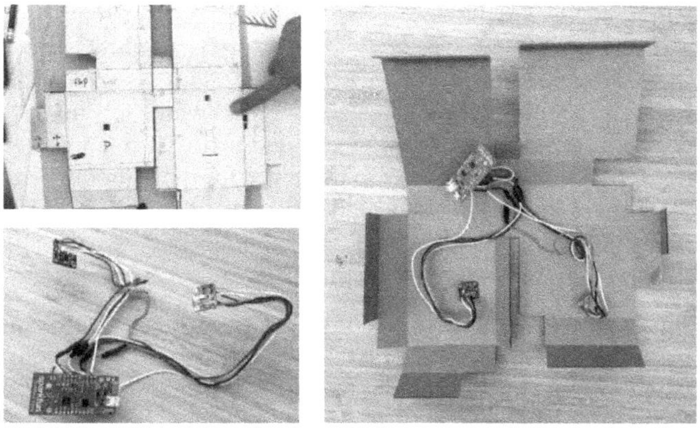

Figure 2: The Riot design is comprised of two distance sensors, a low-cost microcontroller with Wi-Fi capability, and a simple, portable power bank—all housed in a custom cardboard box.

trial beyond our design lab or a couple of targeted sites, we faced challenges around scalability and maintainability.

Designing for Reproducibility and Sustainable Maintenance

As we learned more about maintenance labor and the potential for a broad, public deployment within our field sites, we focused our next iteration on emerging issues of adaptability. Specifically, we worked on longer power operation, more consistent internet connectivity, better precision in product count, and lowering the cost of the unit. Each of these factors reflected concerns for how the device would be taken up in our sites—from staying powered on for long periods in spaces constructed of cinderblock (power and connectivity) to ensuring the output was useful and reliable to those who look to the data (product count). Toward this end, we replaced the Arduino Uno, Wi-Fi shield, and power boost board with a newly released DIY toolkit called the ESP8266. This reduced the overall cost (by $50, from about $95 to $45) and lessened power consumption and the physical dimensions of the insert. We also replaced the sonic sensors with laser-based ranging sensors, allowing more accurate distance measurements. To address concerns for electrical power, we used a disassembled portable charger, connecting the microcontroller directly to its internal 18650 battery cells (a practice growing within the DIY community to produce projects such as domestic power walls for "off the grid" houses).

Mixed (Initial) Reactions

When we introduced the concept of Riot to members of our key field sites we received mixed reactions, from curiosity to ambivalence to annoyance. Two crew members of a Seattle Parks maintenance crew told us that the device would likely end up being just one more thing to be vandalized and in need of repair. They advocated instead for "minimalism," or fewer rather than more restroom artifacts, thinking it would reduce maintenance demands. Yet, the device occupied the imagination of members of our home institution's facilities organization, who viewed it as a connective link to the student body and as a means of contributing to research on campus. As the design work continued, they also saw links to the state of the art of bathroom design—later, entertaining a pitch from the multi-national "personal hygiene" corporation Kimberly-Clark on smart restrooms during the week of our first deployment.

Members of the WAC saw utility for the Riot dispenser design beyond our own understanding of it as a maintenance tool. When holding discussions with building managers, for instance, they heard a concern first and foremost for funding the proposed shift to free products: how much would it cost? With many comparable programs across the country still in their infancy, they could not point to an agreed upon average amount. Instead, they needed to estimate through current usage patterns and viewed the dispenser inserts as a source of data to gauge the potential cost of the proposed legislation, with plans to also use it as a means of tracking the program's uptake if the law were to pass. In doing so, they invited us to view Riot as a form of data advocacy, or as data gathering object to be used in support of their cause. This effort became particularly potent as one of the earliest campus campaigns from Columbia University came to a quick halt after administrators suggested there was a lack of interest on the part of students [24]. Even when passed, these initiatives were vulnerable to swift rollbacks.

Deployment

We conducted two deployments of the sensor system over several months, from September to December 2017. In both cases, we deployed the sensor system at our home institution with members of the facilities organization who assisted in identifying the restrooms to use for testing and advised us on how to hang the sensor system within the dispensers. With each, we affixed the device to the top interior portion of the dispenser with the support of a removable adhesive Velcro strip. This allowed for the sensor insert to be both secured in place and also easily detached for regular maintenance by members of the facilities team, for the replacement of batteries by the research team, and for the eventual removal of the insert at the end of the deployment term. The use of the Velcro also ensured that we made no lasting alteration to the dispenser (for instance, avoiding drilling holes or using stronger glue that might have left a mark), for this would impact the maintenance of the machine in the longer term.

In both deployments, the sensor platforms operated for about a month at a time without interruption, sending data to a web server hosted by our home institution. In each case, the device housing successfully protected the components and secured them to the dispenser. The boxes remained in the dispensers in the precise location where they were initially attached, as did the sensors themselves. Furthermore, the platform continued to operate when we monitored it in the field (and it is still in operation during the writing of this paper). Based on our continued development of power handling over the course of the deployment period, we estimated that our design could support between 7 to 8 weeks of monitoring.

Installing Riot, uncovering existing entanglements

The installation invited additional opportunities to understand the way access developed across the university restrooms. Consider, for example, an episode during our field engagements when the first author, Sarah Fox, met building manager Felicia to implement a long-term deployment in the restroom of a heavily trafficked campus building.

Though Felicia had volunteered to be a part of the research, and although she was at first curious about the device, when we met her at the campus building she appeared to oscillate between excitement and skepticism over the course of the installation. As Fox told her how the system worked, for example, Felicia said under her breath, "just bring [the tampon] from home," referring to students in need of menstrual products. She seemed disappointed, pointing to individual accountability as the answer to the problem of too few public menstrual resources. After a moment of reflection, however, she shifted tone; "although, I guess it comes in handy sometimes," she said. Her view of responsibility seemed to change over the course of our conversation—from institutional to individual and back again.

This tension between individual and collective responsibility remerged as we turned to the machine itself. When Felicia opened the door of a dispenser we noticed there was nothing inside. Fox asked if she had any menstrual products to fill the machine, and she responded, "Oh, you need those?" To her, the device was the solution to the problem—the technological standalone that would ease the burden of upkeep and make certain visitors had the menstrual resources they needed. It seemed tales of design solutionism had preceded us. Yet, Riot was no such thing. Instead, the IoT device relied on a web of connections between maintenance, advocacy, and design intervention—interdependent, much like the relationships that gave rise to it.

Without products already in place, we were unable to calibrate the device. Without calibration, the device was unable to count the products. And without the count, we were left facing an empty, under-considered machine once again. This revelation exposed something about our design we had not yet considered: the machines had to be filled for the system to work. It highlighted an assumption we were making about the types of enrollment we assumed from our collaborators—namely, we expected them to know where to locate the products. But this insight also represented an immediate intervention into the way maintenance practice worked. The machines had to be filled, right then and there.

After calling a crew member to locate the products, Felicia found pads in a nearby supply closet, but the tampons were "all the way at the tower," a building easily a half-mile away or more from where we stood. As she went to retrieve them, Fox waited by the open machine, with visitors to the restroom commenting, "thank you" and "Finally!" Continuing to stand there, Fox found a tiny, ripped post-it note stuck to the door next to the lever for the tampons with a handwritten message. It read, "Empty July 2017 :(". The dispenser had been unfilled for months, but not without notice from the menstruating public.

As our fieldwork continued we noticed that custodians passed by the dispenser as well, peaking into the restrooms when they saw Fox standing there. "Are we going to do that again?" one woman asked as she passed by on her way through the hall, referring to stocking the machine. "We just had to do it a long time ago. Are we starting again this year?" she continued. When Fox described the Riot project and its installation the woman nodded and continued walking. Minutes later, from another custodial professional, "Are we supposed to do that?"

Marked by our presence, the dispenser gained new attention and prompted questions of responsibility. Whose duty was it to maintain these machines? For the visitors who moved through the space during the installation, there seemed to be a quiet desire that dispensers be kept by university staff, but when that job was left undone there was only small evidence of resistance (in the form of a post-it note). Custodial staff, on the other hand, expressed curiosity, asking if it was something that might be under their authority to do.

When Felicia returned from her mile-long journey, she had two large trash bags full of individually wrapped tampons and pads. She began filling the dispenser and asked how the system works. Walking through the different IoT components, Fox described what each part did and how it communicated with the online system. In response, Felicia's face relaxed a bit. She said that she hoped this platform would help facilities see how difficult it is for building managers to keep the machines up. Custodians aren't allowed to fill the dispensers, she told Fox. Instead, building managers or their superiors have to travel between the areas under their supervision, empty the coins, and fill the machines with more products. This work currently sits outside of their regular tasks of managing schedules and it involves overseeing the facilities of many buildings at once, which means the work often goes undone, she admitted. Those closest to and with arguably greater knowledge of individual restrooms and their care, the custodians who maintain them, were not entrusted with the replenishment of the machines because of the money handling involved. Felicia laughed at the thought of this and offered to count the money inside of the machine in front of me. Pulling out a separate, and even smaller key she opened a small metal box in the interior of the dispenser and counted the coins there, "$2.25." She counted again just to be sure, "Yeah, $2.25," and laughing again.

Through this encounter with Felicia we gained a deeper appreciation of the forms of labor enacted (and made invisible) in public sites such as university restrooms. Our presence during the installation prompted reflection on the varied responsibilities expected of and entrusted to those maintaining the restrooms. It also surfaced larger questions of individual accountability and collective responsibility in regards to public resources. What is and isn't considered vital to sustaining a healthy public? Who is expected to supply the material to support it? In some ways these questions were made more fascinating by the fact that we only discovered them at what might be considered the end of a traditional design encounter: the deployment.

Reflecting back, we find it interesting to contemplate what our project might have looked like had we learned about these conditions and questions sooner. Would the project have shifted to reflect these power differentials—focusing further on class or labor relations? Or, could it have confronted more directly the fact that the responsibility of resource distribution is unevenly assigned? Without the slow-collaborative design process and installation, it seems unlikely that we would have uncovered these complexities at all.

DISCUSSION

With Riot we began to reveal the kinds managerial and service labor hidden away and deeply intertwined with IoT deployments. Our project exposed the value of frequent and repeated engagements with key community allies, but also the way we built those alliances across multiple sites in parallel, and not in isolation. Where typical community-based design projects partner with local groups to develop design solutions, Riot required understanding the numerous histories of advocacy and maintenance our deployments operated within. This understanding developed as part of iteratively refining the Riot platform and, in particular, re-defining what it meant to build a robust technology. The project necessitated that we conceptualize the robustness of our IoT devices from "two sides," as Denis and Pontille [10] might say. We examined their fragility from the perspective of the custodians who maintain them and their reliability from the perspective of the people who look to them for access and support.

Adopting this dual attention to repair, we illustrated a design approach that in some ways contrasts with typical IoT development. For the IoT dispenser to live in public, it had to enroll a variety of actors, each with numerous influences, concerns, and interdependencies. From limited power supplies to uneven authority, we found that defining discrete stakeholders and identifying their needs or desires could not capture or do justice to the web of relationships our design inhabited. Even from our small glimpse at these arrangements, we began to see how the Riot platform demanded multiple scales of engagement. At the device-level, Riot opened possibilities for extending menstrual resource accessibility. At the infrastructural-level, it showed us how prototyping was insufficient for understanding the range of dependencies and interests at play. At the policy level, it occupied the imagination of grassroots organizers and facilities staff, offering opportunities for advocacy. Rather than ground its design in the interests and desires of individual actors, each with the perceived ability to take up the device toward their own ends, our project began to show what it might look like for designers to take seriously the broader political, economic, and historical forces shaping IoT design as well as the collective concerns of those implicated in accessibility (here, custodial staff, advocacy organizations, and menstruating peoples, for example).

Although the design of an IoT for public hygiene resource distribution—a timely and important topic for the DIS community—has been ostensible focus of this paper, this work was not simply about the creation of a novel digital tool to serve a stigmatized need. Instead, drawing on traditions of design inquiry [4,20,48], we focused on what our tool exposed about those public sites: showing how that which is novel or digital cannot work in a vacuum if it must survive beyond proof-of-concept deployment. Our design interventions always interact with a complex constellation of organizational actors with their own histories of design and policy work, each opening some paths for design while closing others. Below we discuss three of these broader lessons for maintenance around IoT design.

Designing Lasting IoT Installations through Adaptability

A crucial concern for our research around Riot was how our installation would last over time, a relatively important but under-explored concern within design research projects around IoT. For our initial design, we focused on proving that an IoT deployment could be achieved—emphasizing the selection of the right sensors. However, as we continued with different phases of the design process, we began to stress reparability and sustained use instead, trying to make the device cheaper and more easily maintainable. In partnership with the WAC and the university facilities organization, we saw the need for IoT to live in the world and not just be a prototype. It was critical that we were not the only ones interested or able to maintain it.

Moving forward, this insight has useful implications for design research on smart cities and public sensing. Interactive systems development within IoT projects typically serves populations for short periods of a research cycle. By ending a deployment early, or according to academic timelines, design researchers may unwittingly cut short the advantages their tools offer the groups or the communities they engage. Our work suggests that the responsibility for design interventions in the long term—the care and attention required for sustained engagement—needs further examination in the now. For us this meant understanding how community partners may take up and continue to use, service, mend, and rework IoT infrastructure, work that may be as important or challenging as devising the initial design concept.

As we saw throughout our fieldwork, some of the steadiest figures of the menstrual movement have been community activists running product drives and sewing circles—filling gaps of access using the tactics of grassroots organizing. Although the WAC's recent push for institutional legislation helped advance the codification of menstrual policy, their ongoing advocacy for wide product availability and transparency—over 25 years of work—has produced a proposed bill that has yet to appear in the state congress. This slow and unpredictable process offers lessons on flexibility, posing collective adaptability as a key concern for the development of any community resource or product design effort. With this concern in mind, we ask: what might a flexible IoT look like, one that is adaptable and community supported? To start with, designing for such IoT may not only mean attending to the particulars of component selection or environmental surroundings (in our case, building menstrual resources), but also the regimes of maintenance (in our case, WAC advocacy efforts) that envelope and define it.

Harnessing Collective Responsibility

Connected to concerns for maintenance, our investigation into menstrual resource distribution also holds lessons for the shared authorship and responsibility of public IoT. When the WAC was not able to get their second proposal for broad ranging menstrual equity through the appropriate channels of the student government, the directors of the university facilities organization took up the proposal anyhow. They installed our sensors in university restrooms and piloted a program that made free products available in select restrooms across campus. Thus, our partners reconceptualized the maintenance of menstrual resources as a collective rather than an individual burden.

This case suggests that the design of public IoT takes not only work, but certain kinds of work that meaningfully extend IoT design methods through collective responsibility. Our intervention reveals for design researchers the types of obligations held by different organizational actors, and the classed nature of those commitments. In our case, custodial staff were not interested in the $2.25 worth of coins sitting in each dispenser, yet the organization shifted the responsibility for emptying the coins away from such staff — ultimately making the majority of machines unusable. Here, the rules and policies guiding the practices of those attending to the restrooms reflected deeply entrenched power differentials and forestalled forms of collective responsibility that could exist, highlighting again the importance of attending to the conditions of one's deployment site.

Alongside finding a power outlet or securing the device, the historical and political matter of IoT may just as critically inform how an intervention works. Rather than merely focus on particular utilitarian gains, our project exposes how IoT can also work as what Sherry Turkel might call an "evocative object" [45] contributing to wider debates on access, resource distribution, and public health. It is this ability to inspire and imagine, and to do so collectively, that point to key implications for public IoT beyond the individual.

Sustained Prototyping: Making IoT "work"

When we began this project, something like a networked counting device made sense for a deployment since it supported the interests of both the facilities organization and the WAC. It was a tool that addressed a defined need: accounting for and supporting the necessary expansion of menstrual resource distribution across our community. In this sense, our initial proof-of-concept was simultaneously a real and speculative campaign. Yet, as the parallel efforts of advocacy and design unfolded, the utility of that particular IoT object turned out to only hold so much weight. It was not able to fully solve the problem of access on its own, as perhaps Felicia had imagined, nor did it capture the imagination of all who encountered it (as was the case with the Seattle Parks crew members). Instead, our Riot platform affected change in other ways. For example, it served as an object for gathering around, for forming partnerships that had long elided the facilities organization and the WAC. It also shed light on issues of menstrual accessibility more broadly, amongst those at our home institution, the wider city community, and our academic circles, while showing signs of design solidarity with those advocating across the country. Even as the technology itself became less central, it produced something larger, a connection that might live on beyond the tenure of the device.

CONCLUSION

With Riot we have sought to extend HCI's concerns for IoT to consider its place in the distribution of public resources. We began by outfitting dispensers with networked sensor inserts to make them easier to stock by custodial staff and easier to access by members of the public. However, our goal was not to suggest our device as the core solution to problems of menstrual resource accessibility. Nor did we seek to produce a generalizable technical intervention that might move to other contexts unchanged. Rather, we brought a sensitivity to the political and social dimensions of public resource maintenance, and explored the textures and dependencies of the partnerships that emerged through the design and deployment of Riot. In doing so, we focus new attention on role of public IoT devices once they move on from the proof-of-concept stage, revealing their capacity to cultivate and maintain forms of collective responsibility.

AKNOWLEDGEMENTS

We deeply appreciate the generosity of our community partners. We also thank Ankur Agrawal, Allie Deford, Kiley Sobel, Carl DiSalvo, James Pierce, Tom Jenkins, and our anonymous reviewers. This work was made possible by NSF grants 1453329, 1423074, and 1523579.

REFERENCES

1. Teresa Almeida, Rob Comber, Gavin Wood, Dean Saraf, and Madeline Balaam. 2016. On Looking at the Vagina Through Labella. In *Proceedings of the 2016 CHI Conference on Human Factors in Computing*

Systems (CHI '16), 1810–1821. https://doi.org/10.1145/2858036.2858119
2. Mariam Asad and Christopher A. Le Dantec. 2015. Illegitimate Civic Participation: Supporting Community Activists on the Ground. In *Proceedings of the 18th ACM Conference on Computer Supported Cooperative Work & Social Computing* (CSCW '15), 1694–1703. https://doi.org/10.1145/2675133.2675156
3. Madeline Balaam, Rob Comber, Ed Jenkins, Selina Sutton, and Andrew Garbett. 2015. FeedFinder: A Location-Mapping Mobile Application for Breastfeeding Women. In *Proceedings of the 33rd Annual ACM Conference on Human Factors in Computing Systems* (CHI '15), 1709–1718. https://doi.org/10.1145/2702123.2702328
4. Jeffrey Bardzell, Shaowen Bardzell, and Lone Koefoed Hansen. 2015. Immodest Proposals: Research Through Design and Knowledge. In *Proceedings of the 33rd Annual ACM Conference on Human Factors in Computing Systems* (CHI '15), 2093–2102. https://doi.org/10.1145/2702123.2702400
5. Thomas Binder, Giorgio De Michelis, Pelle Ehn, Giulio Jacucci, Per Linde, and Ina Wagner. 2011. *Design Things*. The MIT Press, Cambridge, Mass.
6. Erling Bjögvinsson, Pelle Ehn, and Per-Anders Hillgren. 2012. Design Things and Design Thinking: Contemporary Participatory Design Challenges. *Design Issues* 28, 3: 101–116. https://doi.org/10.1162/DESI_a_00165
7. Chris Bobel. 2010. *New Blood: Third-wave Feminism and the Politics of Menstruation*. Rutgers University Press.
8. Kathy Charmaz. 2014. *Constructing Grounded Theory*. SAGE.
9. Jérôme Denis, Alessandro Mongili, and David Pontille. 2016. Maintenance & Repair in Science and Technology Studies. *TECNOSCIENZA: Italian Journal of Science & Technology Studies* 6, 2: 5–16.
10. Jérôme Denis and David Pontille. 2017. Beyond breakdown: Exploring Regimes of Maintenance. *continent.* 6, 1: 13–17.
11. Catherine D'Ignazio, Alexis Hope, Becky Michelson, Robyn Churchill, and Ethan Zuckerman. 2016. A Feminist HCI Approach to Designing Postpartum Technologies: "When I First Saw a Breast Pump I Was Wondering if It Was a Joke." In *Proceedings of the 2016 CHI Conference on Human Factors in Computing Systems* (CHI '16), 2612–2622. https://doi.org/10.1145/2858036.2858460
12. Carl DiSalvo and Tom Jenkins. 2017. Fruit Are Heavy: A Prototype Public IoT System to Support Urban Foraging. In *Proceedings of the 2017 Conference on Designing Interactive Systems* (DIS '17), 541–553. https://doi.org/10.1145/3064663.3064748
13. Carl DiSalvo, Jonathan Lukens, Thomas Lodato, Tom Jenkins, and Tanyoung Kim. 2014. Making Public Things: How HCI Design Can Express Matters of Concern. In *Proceedings of the 32Nd Annual ACM Conference on Human Factors in Computing Systems* (CHI '14), 2397–2406. https://doi.org/10.1145/2556288.2557359
14. Pelle Ehn. 1990. *Work-Oriented Design of Computer Artifacts*. L. Erlbaum Associates Inc., Hillsdale, NJ, USA.
15. Daniel A. Epstein, Nicole B. Lee, Jennifer H. Kang, Elena Agapie, Jessica Schroeder, Laura R. Pina, James Fogarty, Julie A. Kientz, and Sean Munson. 2017. Examining Menstrual Tracking to Inform the Design of Personal Informatics Tools. In *Proceedings of the 2017 CHI Conference on Human Factors in Computing Systems* (CHI '17), 6876–6888. https://doi.org/10.1145/3025453.3025635
16. Sarah E. Fox. 2016. Casting a Feminist Eye on Public Infrastructure. Retrieved January 9, 2018 from http://www.4sonline.org/meeting/16
17. Sarah Fox, Daniela K. Rosner, Margaret E. Morris, and Kathi R. Kitner. 2015. Inviting Participation through IoT: Experiments and Performances in Public Spaces. *Aarhus Series on Human Centered Computing* 1, 1: 3. https://doi.org/10.7146/aahcc.v1i1.21395
18. Friedman Batya, Kahn Peter H., and Borning Alan. 2009. Value Sensitive Design and Information Systems. *The Handbook of Information and Computer Ethics*. https://doi.org/10.1002/9780470281819.ch4
19. Jennifer Gabrys. 2014. Programming Environments: Environmentality and Citizen Sensing in the Smart City. *Environment and Planning D: Society and Space* 32, 1: 30–48. https://doi.org/10.1068/d16812
20. William Gaver. 2012. What Should We Expect from Research Through Design? In *Proceedings of the SIGCHI Conference on Human Factors in Computing Systems* (CHI '12), 937–946. https://doi.org/10.1145/2207676.2208538
21. Eleanor Goldberg. 2015. For Homeless Women, Getting Their Period Is One Of The Most Difficult Challenges. *Huffington Post*. Retrieved March 29, 2018 from https://www.huffingtonpost.com/2015/01/14/homeless-women-tampons_n_6465230.html
22. Stephen Graham and Nigel Thrift. 2007. Out of Order: Understanding Repair and Maintenance. *Theory, Culture and Society* 24. https://doi.org/10.1177/0263276407075954
23. Donna Haraway. 1988. Situated Knowledges: The Science Question in Feminism and the Privilege of Partial Perspective. *Feminist Studies* 14, 3: 575–599. https://doi.org/10.2307/3178066
24. Larson Holt. 2016. Columbia Health stops providing free tampons, pads to students. *Columbia Daily Spectator*. Retrieved January 9, 2018 from columbiaspectator.com/news/2016/09/12/columbia-health-stops-providing-free-tampons-pads-students/
25. Lara Houston. 2017. The Timeliness of Repair. *continent.* 6, 1: 51–55.

26. Lara Houston, Steven J. Jackson, Daniela K. Rosner, Syed Ishtiaque Ahmed, Meg Young, and Laewoo Kang. 2016. Values in Repair. In *Proceedings of the 2016 CHI Conference on Human Factors in Computing Systems* (CHI '16), 1403–1414. https://doi.org/10.1145/2858036.2858470
27. Lara Houston, Daniela K. Rosner, Steven J. Jackson, and Jamie Allen. 2017. Letter from the Editors. *continent.* 6, 1: 1–3.
28. Lilly C. Irani and M. Six Silberman. 2013. Turkopticon: Interrupting Worker Invisibility in Amazon Mechanical Turk. In *Proceedings of the SIGCHI Conference on Human Factors in Computing Systems* (CHI '13), 611–620. https://doi.org/10.1145/2470654.2470742
29. Steven J. Jackson. 2013. Rethinking Repair. In *Media Meets Technology*, Pablo Boczkowski, Kirsten Foot and Tarleton Gillespie (eds.). MIT Press.
30. Christopher A. Le Dantec. 2016. *Designing Publics.* MIT Press.
31. Celia Lury and Nina Wakeford (eds.). 2013. *Inventive Methods: The Happening of the Social.* Routledge, London.
32. Luiza Prado de O. Martins and Pedro J. S. Vieira de Oliveira. 2016. Breaking the Cycle of Macondo: Design and Decolonial Futures. *XRDS* 22, 4: 28–32. https://doi.org/10.1145/2930880
33. Julian E. Orr. 1996. *Talking about Machines: An Ethnography of a Modern Job.* ILR Press, Ithaca, N.Y.
34. Hiromi Ozaki. 2010. Menstruation Machine. *Design Interactions.* Retrieved January 9, 2018 from http://www.di10.rca.ac.uk/hiromiozaki/menstruation-machine.html
35. search results and search results. 2014. *Speculative Everything: Design, Fiction, and Social Dreaming.* MIT Press, Cambridge, Massachusetts ; London.
36. Daniela K. Rosner. 2014. Making Citizens, Reassembling Devices: On Gender and the Development of Contemporary Public Sites of Repair in Northern California. *Public Culture* 26, 1 (72): 51–77. https://doi.org/10.1215/08992363-2346250
37. Daniela K. Rosner and Morgan Ames. 2014. Designing for Repair?: Infrastructures and Materialities of Breakdown. In *Proceedings of the 17th ACM Conference on Computer Supported Cooperative Work & Social Computing* (CSCW '14), 319–331. https://doi.org/10.1145/2531602.2531692
38. Daniela K. Rosner, Margaret E. Morris, Ariel Duncan, Sarah E. Fox, Kathi R. Kitner, Ankur Agrawal, and Mei J. Chen. 2016. Designing for Movement in Public Life with Itinerant Probes. In *Proceedings of the 2016 ACM Conference on Designing Interactive Systems* (DIS '16), 1072–1082. https://doi.org/10.1145/2901790.2901913
39. Daniela K. Rosner, Hidekazu Saegusa, Jeremy Friedland, and Allison Chambliss. 2015. Walking by Drawing. In *Proceedings of the 33rd Annual ACM Conference on Human Factors in Computing Systems* (CHI '15), 397–406. https://doi.org/10.1145/2702123.2702467
40. Daniela K. Rosner and Fred Turner. 2015. Theaters of Alternative Industry: Hobbyist Repair Collectives and the Legacy of the 1960s American Counterculture. In *Design Thinking Research.* Springer, Cham, 59–69. https://doi.org/10.1007/978-3-319-06823-7_5
41. Marie Louise Juul Søndergaard and Lone Koefoed Hansen. 2016. PeriodShare: A Bloody Design Fiction. In *Proceedings of the 9th Nordic Conference on Human-Computer Interaction* (NordiCHI '16), 113:1–113:6. https://doi.org/10.1145/2971485.2996748
42. Susan Leigh Star and Anselm Strauss. 1999. Layers of Silence, Arenas of Voice: The Ecology of Visible and Invisible Work. *Computer Supported Cooperative Work (CSCW)* 8, 1–2: 9–30. https://doi.org/10.1023/A:1008651105359
43. Lucy Suchman. 2007. *Human-Machine Reconfigurations: Plans and Situated Actions.* Cambridge University Press.
44. Lael Telles. 2010. The dispensing dilemma. *The Daily of the University of Washington.* Retrieved January 9, 2018 from http://www.dailyuw.com/news/article_3c73f744-0907-5fad-bfcf-7835ad37d2d5.html
45. Sherry Turkle. 2011. *Evocative Objects: Things We Think With.* MIT Press.
46. Jennifer Weiss-Wolf. 2017. *Periods Gone Public: Taking a Stand for Menstrual Equity.* Skyhorse Publishing Inc.
47. Joon Yi. 2011. Waiting for Tampons. *The Daily of the University of Washington.* Retrieved January 9, 2018 from http://www.dailyuw.com/news/article_c5a7a517-9122-5dec-ad48-7441599a973d.html
48. John Zimmerman, Jodi Forlizzi, and Shelley Evenson. 2007. Research Through Design As a Method for Interaction Design Research in HCI. In *Proceedings of the SIGCHI Conference on Human Factors in Computing Systems* (CHI '07), 493–502. https://doi.org/10.1145/1240624.1240704
49. Who We Are. *Facilities Services.* Retrieved January 9, 2018 from https://facilities.uw.edu/about
50. About the Womxn's Action Commission. *Womxn's Action Commission.* Retrieved January 9, 2018 from http://women.asuw.org/about/

Designing Future Employment Applications for Underserved Job Seekers: A Speed Dating Study

Tawanna R. Dillahunt[1], **Jason Lam**[1,2], **Alex Lu**[1,2], **Earnest Wheeler**[1]
University of Michigan, School of Information[1], School of Social Work[2]
Ann Arbor, MI 48109
{tdillahu,lamcj,alexjlu,earnestw}@umich.edu

ABSTRACT
Modern Information and Communication Technologies (ICTs) support job searches, resume creation, career development, and professional self-presentation. However, these technology tools are often tailored to high-income, highly educated users and white-collar professionals. It is unclear what interventions address the needs of job seekers who have limited resources or education, or who may be underserved in other ways. We gathered insights from the literature and generated ten tangible design concepts to address the needs of underserved job seekers. We then conducted a needs validation and speed dating study to understand which concepts were most viable among our population. We found that the three most preferred concepts immediately addressed job seekers' *social* and *personal* needs, where addressing social needs meant mediating job seekers' connections to others and supporting job seekers' limited access to strong ties.

Author Keywords
Needs validation; speed dating; design; employment, underserved job seekers

ACM Classification Keywords
H.5.m. Information Interfaces and Presentation: Misc.

INTRODUCTION
Many technologies facilitate the needs of relatively affluent populations, and there is generally less consideration for the needs of underserved populations [15, 18, 28]. As a result, offline social injustices [20] are often transferred to online job applications. For example, LinkedIn caters to high-income and highly educated users and to white-collar professionals [31, 39]. Further, while employment researchers have established that companies seek higher-skilled employees from sites such as LinkedIn, now even government services and companies seeking employees *without* a 4-year degree are moving their employment and recruiting process online [13, 35]. This leaves fewer opportunities to encounter recruiters face-to-face and to connect to social and other job resources.

DIS'18, June 9-13, 2018, , Hong Kong.

ACM ISBN 978-1-4503-5198-0/18/06...$15.00
https://doi.org/10.1145/3196709.3196770

Figure 1. Storyboard of Review-Me, one of ten concepts used in the needs validation session.

According to a 2015 Pew Research report, Americans who could benefit the most from using socio-technical systems to support their employment endeavors (e.g., underserved job seekers) are the ones who find these tools most challenging to use [38]. Despite this, information and communication technologies (ICTs) have done little to support individuals who do not have the knowledge, skills, or experience to participate in these online venues. More and more individuals living in the United States have broadband access and availability; however, they often lack the skill set needed to make the most of Internet availability [46].

To provide insights into the features and requirements needed to build digital employment tools for this population, we conducted a literature review to investigate the needs and challenges of job seekers from underserved populations. A review of HCI research in this space identified job seeker barriers such as financial hardships, low wages, limited resources, lack of transportation, and homelessness [14, 15, 16, 17, 19, 26, 27, 43, 45]. Underserved job-seeking populations also include those on the autism spectrum [25]. From this review, we categorized the challenges as personal, social, and societal. Our literature review highlights barriers such as the lack of (*personal*) feedback from potential employers, limited *social* networks, and *societal* issues such as workers' limited support for wage theft and employee rights and limited reliable transportation. However, few interventions exist to overcome these barriers and it is unclear whether interventions that address these challenges are viable solutions among these job seekers. Drawing from past studies (e.g., [12, 34, 48]), we created short storyboards to convey ten employment concepts, which we assessed using Ajzen's Theory of Planned Behavior (TPB) [2], a major theoretical perspective that has been used to frame the effects of employment interventions [10, 41, 47]. We then conducted a needs validation and speed dating study (see Figure 1) to understand which concepts are most viable among our target population. Findings from past research suggest that the most desirable tools for job seekers are those that either provide connections to others, or adhere to the *social* needs of job seekers. However, we found that the three most preferred concepts are those that immediately addressed job seekers' *social and personal* needs, where addressing social needs means supporting job seekers' limited access to strong social ties. These concepts provide job seekers with resume feedback [15], assist job seekers in articulating their skills based on their past jobs, and suggest a concrete path to achieve their goals. These concepts address the most practical needs of our participants and could increase their self-efficacy.

Our work builds on this past research to contribute:

- A literature review of HCI research investigations of underserved job seekers, the barriers they face, and the key design insights from these investigations. We contribute three job seeker need categories for future interventions: *social, personal, and societal*;
- A set of ten tangible design concepts for future employment tools that build on these design insights to address the needs of our targeted job seekers and their rank order;
- An analysis of our participants' feedback regarding the three most and three least popular concepts to expose the issues our job seekers faced and wished to address.

LITERATURE REVIEW

We frame our related work on two distinct categories based on the literature: (1) underserved job seekers' needs and challenges; (2) design insights from those applications that targeted underserved job seekers.

Job Seeker Needs and Challenges

We categorize job seeker needs, challenges, and design insights based on the literature as *social*, which refers to the need for social networks, social resources, social support, feedback, mentorship, assistance and emotional support; *personal*, or those needs requiring effort from one's self such as reflection on the job process and the ability to articulate one's skills; and *societal* [27], which refers to challenges that require community and/or government implementation, such as support for transportation, childcare access, combating discrimination, and access to job opportunities that are suitable to the skills of the current job seekers. Below, we discuss each of these categories of job seeker needs in detail.

Social

Social needs are those that are met by our social ties or social connections. Research shows that bridging ties—the ties that connect people across lines of race, class, ethnicity, and age—are valuable [37], particularly for job searching [32]. Granovetter argues that these ties are better sources of information [23]. However, some underserved job seekers are disadvantaged by social isolation and have limited access to ties of social worth [40]. These barriers suggest opportunities for technologies to aid in fostering social capital. Facilitating access to social connections that can provide mentorship and information about employment opportunities is also a recommended course of action for supporting job seekers, per a literature review on job search [24] and other recent reports [14, 43].

Researchers have investigated the viability of sharing economy applications such as Lyft, Uber, TaskRabbit, NeighborGoods and Airbnb as tools that could address these barriers among low-income, unemployed, and underemployed populations [17]. This research uncovered the need for trust, social support, and feedback. The need for feedback was also articulated by low-resourced job seekers in [43]. In an employment study of homeless youth, Hendry et al. found that assistance and emotional support were vital for successful employment and that external social resources were often needed to meet basic needs [26, 27].

Personal

We identify personal needs as those needs requiring effort from oneself, such as reflection on one's current life situation and how that could impact the job process. Personal needs also relate to an individual's ability to understand and articulate her current skillset and where she fits into the work environment. A common suggestion between Dillahunt et al. and Wheeler and Dillahunt's investigations was to support job seekers in articulating their current skills [15, 43]. Wheeler and Dillahunt also proposed that digital systems should encourage job seekers to reflect on the job process and educate them about the advantages their social networks could provide in the job search [43].

Hendry et al. identified two challenges in investigating work among homeless youth: *identity*, which is a problem these youth face when they must represent themselves for employment, and *availability* of job opportunities [26, 27]. They found that work is linked to life circumstances, which are deeply personal.

Societal

Societal-related needs require support from the community or government and sometimes also require regulations that would be difficult to implement by a single individual or tool. Dillahunt acknowledged that systemic issues such as income and social inequality exist beyond our control and that it might be difficult for technological interventions to address these issues [14]. For example, job seekers face types of discrimination such as age, gender, race, disability, and other factors [11]. Very little empirical research investigates interventions that aim to tackle employment discrimination—perhaps because technology is unable to address these issues.

Separate studies of underserved and low-resource job seekers identified barriers related to reliable access to transportation [16] needed to get to interviews. In addition, parents with limited transportation who need to take care of their children during an interview are also left behind because they might have limited access to childcare or lack the funds to pay for it [8].

Although there is some consistency among the research findings regarding challenges job seekers face, there have been few attempts to conceptualize and make any design insights concrete. Next we discuss what we know of these attempts from the literature.

Design Insights from Applications Targeting Underserved Job Seekers

The studies that exist to our knowledge have evaluated current tools; conceptualized new tools; or designed, implemented, and evaluated new tools. The tools to address the needs outlined previously are somewhat limited. For example, one study has conceptualized a tool that addresses societal needs for homeless young adults. Researchers in two other studies have designed, implemented, and evaluated feedback tools—one resume feedback tool and one interview feedback tool—for low-resource job seekers and young autistic job seekers respectively.

Evaluations of Existing Tools

Perhaps one of the earliest assessments in the HCI space of employment tools that target underserved job seekers was done by Jen et al. [28]. In this work-in-progress, authors conducted a competitive analysis to assess seven existing employment tools against three user profiles with characteristics reflecting those of underserved job seekers. Other work has extended this research by using these profiles among job seekers facing similar challenges to assess the potential value of various web services and sharing economy applications for this population [14, 17]. Hendry et al. conducted a similar investigation of six work-related systems to determine whether the systems could be altered to address the needs of homeless young adults [27]. These authors discussed three key findings: (1) these applications fell short in providing homeless young adults with suitable jobs and job sponsors that conformed to regulations; (2) these applications did not support life skills development or lead to self-efficacy and confidence among the youth; and (3) the applications were not sensitive to the effects of being homeless (flexible job schedules). The authors took the results of their study to provide a storyboard that envisioned a socio-technical concept, the *U-District Job Co-op*, as a solution [27].

Concepts for New Tools

Hendry et al.'s [27] concept represents a service that matches jobs that community members post to homeless job seekers who can perform the work. The co-op pays and provides emotional support and mentorship to the job seeker, which leads to confidence, a stronger resume, and individuals who can serve as references, which aligns with Dillahunt's findings regarding economically distressed job seekers [14]. The overall concept was viewed positively among all stakeholders involved; however, issues of trust arose, and these trust issues were similar to issues raised in [14], where community members had reservations about hiring individuals with felony records. The socio-technical solution, as discussed in Hendry et al., requires the implementation of varying levels of trust [26]. While the past investigations have included evaluations of existing tools and the envisioning of new ones, none of these implemented or piloted the tools that were suggested.

New Tool Implementation

Dillahunt et al. followed a user-centered design process to design, develop and pilot a resume review tool for disadvantaged job seekers [15]. The researchers built this tool as an extension of their prior work [14, 17]. One of the researchers' goals was to understand who continued to be left behind after implementing a tool designed for disadvantaged job seekers. The evaluation results revealed the limitations for disadvantaged job seekers with limited digital literacy skills and with criminal records, as well as unexpected issues with digital access and document storage [15].

Hayes et al. investigated video modeling and video prompting as potential solutions for teaching interview skills among youth with autism spectrum disorder (ASD) [25]. They designed, implemented, and evaluated VidCoach, an iOS software prototype that demonstrated video modeling and prompting techniques in seven interview videos. The authors randomized 15 students with ASD into either a control or VidCoach condition. All students received a mock employment interview at the beginning and end of a 1-month period: students in the control group did not use VidCoach whereas those in the intervention group used VidCoach as frequently as they wished during the 1-month period (on average they used the tool twice per day, which increased to four times per day 3 days before conducting the second set of mock interviews). The results suggest that those in the VidCoach group made a statistically significant improvement in terms of their evaluation performance as rated by employers. The students also showed improvement in presenting succinct and logical ideas, in their health care and hygiene, and with reduced fidgeting, and the students rated the tool highly.

In summary, past employment concepts and interventions have worked to eliminate barriers that would prevent underserved job seekers from being able to use employment tools, connected job seekers to social resources and helped to improve self-efficacy, and provided tools to access expert feedback.

Key Social Factors

Given the focus of past employment concepts and interventions, we applied Ajzen's Theory of Planned Behavior (TPB) [2] as a theoretical model for assessing the design concepts we developed in this work (see Table 1). The TPB is a major theoretical perspective that has been widely used to model the effectiveness of job search interventions on employment [10, 32, 41, 47].

In the TPB, intention is the central determinant of behavior [2] and is determined by *attitude*, *subjective norms*, and *perceived behavioral control*. Intention describes an individual's willingness to try to perform a behavior—in this case, how worthwhile it is to put effort into the job search. Attitude toward the job search is the individual's personal evaluation of how worthwhile it is to put effort into the job search. For example, job seekers with a positive job search attitude would believe that applying more effort to their resume or practicing for interviews would be very beneficial for their eventual success, while those with a negative job search attitude might believe that even preparing a resume would be useless. Subjective norms are the degree to which a person perceives social pressure to perform or not to perform. This includes a person's motivation to meet external expectations [3, 33, 36]. Finally, Ajzen defines perceived behavioral control as the "perceived ease or difficulty of performing the behavior" [3, p.665]. This has been consistently operationalized in the job-seeking literature as job search self-efficacy, which is an individual's internal belief about their ability to perform job-search-related actions effectively [5, 32]. This also relates to whether individuals believe that they have the opportunities and skills required to succeed at tasks in the job search process [32].

These three factors (job search attitudes, subjective norms/social support, and perceived behavioral control/self-efficacy) contribute to the job search intentions that inform actions and have been shown to positively predict job attainment. Therefore, employment interventions that aim to address these factors have the potential to improve employment outcomes. These constructs can also be considered in relation to the three levels of barriers and needs (personal, social, and societal) that we described in the previous section. In general, interventions that address personal needs are expected to increase job seekers' self-efficacy because they augment job seekers' abilities. Interventions that address social barriers do so in a variety of ways: some help job seekers leverage existing social capital, while others help create opportunities to build social capital or provide social resources through alternative means. We expect those interventions that help a job seeker build capital or provide increased access would increase self-efficacy, while those that help job seekers leverage existing social resources would increase subjective norms. We would expect interventions aimed at societal barriers to increase self-efficacy and improve job search attitude. In the next section, we introduce each of our ten concepts and their expected value in the context of our three types of identified needs (social, personal, and societal) and the Theory of Planned Behavior.

DESIGN CONCEPTS

This section describes each of the ten design concepts—all inspired by the literature. For the sake of brevity, we refrain from providing technical implementation details, or extensive detail about concepts that were less popular among our participants. Our goal was to validate the theoretical needs underlying each concept and to evaluate each concept's perceived usefulness from the perspective of potential users. Table 1 provides an overview of the categories of needs and aspects of behavioral intention that each concept aims to address. The majority of our concepts (N=8) would promote users' confidence in their job search practices, and two would increase subjective norms. We argue that all ten concepts are likely to improve users' job search attitude and note three cases in which specific forms of feedback *could* lead to negative outcomes (see * in Table 1).

	Categories of Needs			Aspects of Behavioral Intention		
Tool	Social	Personal	Societal Related	Self-Efficacy	Subjective norms	Job-search attitudes
Vouch for Me	✓				✓	✓
Review-Me	✓	✓		✓		*
Interview4	✓	✓		✓		*
WeCandoIt	✓	✓		✓	✓	*
ForgetAboutIt	✓		✓	✓		✓
Anon-Inerviews			✓			✓
Skills Identifier		✓		✓		✓
DreamGigs		✓		✓		✓
Job Score		✓	✓	✓		✓
MediaTutorial		✓		✓		✓

Table 1. Categories of Needs and Aspects of Behavioral Intention met by Concept Applications. Note that an * indicates that the interventions could lead to positive or negative job search attitudes.

Based on past literature from sociology and HCI, [14, 15, 23, 26, 27, 44], we predicted that concepts that aimed to address social needs and increase job seekers' access to important resources would be ranked highest among the concepts. We thought that concepts that additionally aim to address the personal needs of job seekers—such as Review-Me, Interview4, and WeCanDoIt—could increase self-efficacy and lead to positive job-search attitudes, and would be among the highest ranked. WeCanDoIt could also lead to increased social norms and we thought the concept would be successful among our participants.

Vouch for Me

Vouch for me allows freelancers or any job seeker to gather testimonials from their past clients and customers; it is somewhat similar to LinkedIn Recommendations, which allows people to provide informal recommendations about another person's work. Hendry et al. [27] and participants providing feedback about sharing economy applications [17] described benefits of having access to references, or someone who could vouch for him or her. Vouch for Me was derived for individuals who may have difficulties finding references and provides a platform for some individuals to collect testimonials as an alternative to traditional references.

Vouch for Me addresses social needs by enabling job seekers to use idle social resources, in the form of testimonials, to improve their application materials. We also hypothesized that this would increase subjective norms because users would feel greater pressure to exert effort in the job search process from the contacts who provide testimonials.

Review-Me

Review-Me extends the pilot application evaluated in [15]. Review-Me sources volunteers to provide resume feedback to job seekers. The concept addressed the timing barriers identified in [15]. In the needs validation study, we implied that the feedback was immediate.

Review-Me addresses both social and personal job seeker needs. First, the concept provides expert resume feedback, which is traditionally drawn from mentors and other social connections. Second, the feedback requires some reflection from the job seeker in order to update his or her resume. This system would increase users' self-efficacy in the job search by increasing their confidence in their application materials and their understanding of what a "good" resume is. This system could improve users' attitude toward the job search, though it is also possible for job seekers to be discouraged by the feedback they receive.

Interview4

Interview4 [1] is an existing tool designed for employers, service providers, and job candidates to support the interviewing process. Interview4 is a free online video tool that allows candidates to practice and record interviews. While the current tool relies on self-reflection like VidCoach [25], our concept sourced feedback from professionals and is similar to Review-Me, except that Interview4 supports reviews of interviews rather than resumes. We expect that Interview4 would provide the same types of support for job seekers as Review-Me.

WeCanDoIt

WeCanDoIt is an online support group where people can support one another in the job search process and share practical tips on how they go about job searches and interviews. Such a support group could also provide positive affirmation to help everyone stay motivated. For example, a job seeker may hear that hiring is slow right now for larger companies but people have had success with local organizations. This information might lead a job seeker to change his or her strategy and spend more time networking and applying for jobs at local businesses.

WeCanDoIt addresses the social needs of job seekers (e.g., social and emotional support, feedback, information). These conversations also enable users to reflect on their process [43] and get useful feedback [15, 43], addressing job seekers' personal needs. We argue that WeCanDoIt could increase self-efficacy and subjective norms in users, by providing valuable information and emotional support to increase job seekers' confidence in their ability to perform during the job search, and also create a community where they feel expected to do their best in the job search. However, WeCanDoIt could have a positive or negative effect on job search attitudes, depending on the content of discussion or information provided.

ForgetAboutIt

ForgetAboutIt is the only service concept. The service helps to arrange transportation and babysitting services for job seekers who must manage childcare. For a small (unspecified) fee, job seekers are able to arrange a babysitter to come to their house so that they can leave on time for interviews without issues.

ForgetAboutIt aims to alleviate structural barriers in the job search process, such as child-care [6] or transportation [30], that would otherwise be addressed through the use of social or societal resources. We argue that ForgetAboutIt would improve self-efficacy and attitude in the job search because job seekers would feel more confident that they could overcome barriers that they encounter during their efforts to secure a job.

[1] https://www.interview4.com/.

Anon-Interviews

Anon-Interviews masks identifying information that could lead to discrimination such as name, age, and gender. This concept addresses issues of discrimination, such as those identified in [14, 19, 43]. These are societal issues that can possibly be mitigated via technology but must be regulated externally. This concept would have a positive effect on users' job search attitude because it would increase the belief that the job search process is fair and that effort exerted by the users directly relates to the outcomes of their search.

Skills Identifier

Skills Identifier helps job seekers identify and communicate their current skill set. Imagine a job seeker, Andy, who wants to work in a customer-service job but is unsure how his previous experiences are related to customer service. Using Skills Identifier, Andy would enter his previous job as a construction worker and Skills Identifier would determine that customer service jobs and construction jobs both require problem-solving skills and teamwork skills. Andy would then update his resume and cover letter to highlight his skills in problem-solving and team work.

This concept addresses an important personal need in the job search process, enabling job seekers to understand and articulate the skills they already possess and focus on how to improve their resumes accordingly. This tool should lead to increased self-efficacy because it improves users' ability to articulate their skills. Based on work with low-resourced populations [15], we also hypothesized that this system would improve job-search attitudes by increasing job seekers' awareness of their skills.

DreamGigs

DreamGigs helps job seekers understand what career-related skills they need to reach their ideal, or "dream" gig or job. Dream Gigs is an extension of SkillsIdentifier and allows job seekers to specify the positions that they have held in the past. However, the tool also specifies: (1) the skills the job seeker would need to develop to achieve his or her ideal job and (2) available positions that job seekers could pursue to acquire these skills.

Like SkillsIdentifier, DreamGigs aims to address some of the personal needs important in the job search process, by helping job seekers articulate their skills and identify a path towards a long-term employment goal. The concept requires the job seeker to reflect on the skills he or she has already and what path he or she should take to obtain those needed skills, thus boosting one's self-efficacy. In related work [18, 44], job seekers have explicitly stated their desire for a path to achieve their career aspirations, so we argue that this system would improve users' job search attitudes.

Job Score

Job Score provides detailed job information for a specified geographic area or location and allows job seekers to evaluate how accessible jobs are (e.g., on bus routes, walkable, bikeable) and evaluate whether or not he or she should try to move to other areas or train for new skills.

Job Score addresses some of the personal and societal concerns raised by Hendry et al. about the lack of potential jobs available for individuals based on their skill set [26]. Users of this system would be afforded the ability to understand the types of jobs available in their area, and the opportunity to consider new job search strategies. We argue that users of this system would experience higher levels of self-efficacy because they would have more information to inform their job seeking practices, and more positive job search attitudes because this system would expose barriers and biases that previously made the job search seem unfair.

MediaTutorial

MediaTutorial helps job seekers develop a professional online brand. The concept helps job seekers who may rely on contract work and wish to advertise their skills. For example, take Samantha, who is a freelance designer looking for a way to get her name out there. She could use MediaTutorial to identify free platforms to help her display her work and advertise her work. MediaTutorial would also scan her Facebook and LinkedIn sites to determine what content to change and remove. MediaTutorial helps job seekers with their presentation and with managing their personal identity.

MediaTutorial addresses the fragile issue of *identity* as uncovered in Hendry et al. [26, 27] and builds on job seekers' motivation to find ways to leverage their networks to advertise their skills [14, 17]. The tool primarily supports personal job seeker needs because it helps to improve how a job seeker would convey his or her personal identity. MediaTutorial could help to increase self-efficacy of users by educating them about valuable ways of finding employment and thereby improve job search attitudes.

METHODOLOGY

We drew from studies on need validation and speed dating (e.g., [12, 34, 48]) and created a set of short storyboards [42] to convey our concepts[2]. We conducted pilot sessions of our storyboards with five participants to clarify and refine our concepts before our formal study. The results of these pilot sessions were not included in our final results.

Our goal was to understand which concepts are most viable among our target population. The needs validation and speed dating study allowed us to rapidly iterate through our concepts for feedback. The next subsections describe our recruitment process and research setting and the details of the need validation and speed dating study.

Recruitment and Research Setting

We conducted our study in December 2017 in southeastern Michigan, USA. We recruited from non-profit organizations that focused on economic mobility and finding employment for underserved job seekers, as well as job seekers from a pool of past study participants, and we asked participants to refer others to our study via snowball sampling. We also posted advertisements to Craigslists' "Gigs" section. To be eligible for our study, job seekers also needed to (1) be at least 18 years of age, (2) have less than a four-year college degree, and (3) have been searching for jobs in the past 6 months.

Needs Validation and Speed Dating

We conducted needs validation and speed dating studies one-on-one with each job seeker at local institutions such as cafes, libraries, and community centers. Participants completed surveys upon completion of the study. We presented participants with ten storyboards illustrating common issues job seekers face, and the concept for a tool to address this issue. We randomized the order we presented the storyboards for each participant. We asked participants to read each storyboard and to describe their initial thoughts after reading each one. We probed for details and asked clarification questions as needed. After participants read all ten storyboards, we held a general debriefing session and asked participants about their overall thoughts, specific concepts that stood out, and unaddressed needs.

Next, we asked participants to rank each concept from most to least preferred, specifying that they should base their rankings on their own challenges in the job search, not someone else's challenges. After participants ranked each concept, we asked participants to discuss their reasons for their ranking. We assigned participants' most preferred tool a value of 10 and their least preferred tool a value of 1. To provide a final ranking for all concepts, we summed rankings for all the tools from all the participants and the highest value was considered the most preferred.

At the end of the study, participants completed a survey consisting of 13 questions. The survey included questions about demographics, job status, and familiarity with technology. Demographic questions included gender, date of birth, ZIP code, race, education level, marital status, and number of individuals in the household. Job status questions included job seeking status and type of job desired. Familiarity with technology questions, included those about devices owned, type of device used to access the Internet, and familiarity with and use of web and job-related web services.

RESULTS

We recruited a total of 11 participants from local community organizations. We recruited the most participants (N=4) from an organization that provided housing for families and individuals who were homeless or at-risk for homelessness. The organization used the U.S. Department of Housing and Urban Development's definition of homelessness: "a person sleeping in a place not meant for human habitation or living in a homeless emergency shelter" [3].The remaining participants (N=7) saw our Craigslist advertisement, were past study participants, or were participants who were referred to our study.

[2]Please refer to https://doi.org/10.7302/Z2BV7DSF for the full set of storyboards.

[3]https://www.hud.gov/

Name	ID	Age	Race	Sex	Employment Status	Top 3 Tool Preferences	Bottom 3 Tool Preferences
Geoff	P1	42	African American	M	Looking for full time position	1. DreamGigs; 2. Interview4 3. Review-Me	1. MediaTutorial; 2.Vouch for Me 3.ForgetAboutIt
Angel	P2	42	African American	F	Looking for full time position	1. Review-Me; 2. DreamGigs 3. SkillsIdentifier	1. WeCanDoIt; 2. ForgetAboutIt 3. Vouch for Me
Ignacio	P3	28	African American	M	Looking for short-term part-time position	1. Interview4; 2. Review-Me 3. SkillsIdentifier	1. DreamGigs; 2.WeCanDoIt 3. ForgetAboutIt
Tamara	P4	38	African American	F	Looking for long-term part-time position	1. Review-Me; 2. DreamGigs 3. SkillsIdentifier	1. ForgetAboutIt; 2. Vouch for Me 3. MediaTutorial
Chelsea	P5	40	Caucasian	F	Looking for long-term part-time position	1. DreamGigs; 2. SkillsIdentifier 3. Anon-Interviews	1.ForgetAboutIt 2. MediaTutorial; 3. Vouch for Me
Elizabeth	P6	55	Caucasian	F	Looking for long-term part-time position	1. Review-Me; 2. Interview4 3. Anon-Interviews	1. DreamGigs 2. Vouch for Me; 3. MediaTutorial
Aaron	P7	55	Caucasian	M	Looking for long-term part-time position	1. DreamGigs; 2. Review-Me 3. Vouch for Me	1. Anon-Interview; 2. ForgetAboutIt 3. MediaTutorial
Erica	P8	31	African American	F	Looking for full time position	1. We Can Do It; 2. DreamGigs 3. SkillsIdentifier	1. Interview4; 2. MediaTutorial 3. Job Score
Allynna	P9	31	African American	F	Looking for full time position	1. Job Score; 2. ForgetAboutIt 3. WeCanDoIt	1. Anon-Interview; 2. Interview4 3. Vouch for Me
Jill	P10	29	African American	F	Not currently looking for any additional employment	1. Review-Me; 2. Interview4 3. MediaTutorial	1. DreamGigs; 2. Anon-Interview 3. SkillsIdentifier
Chrissy	P11	38	African American	F	Looking for long-term part-time position	1. SkillsIdentifier 2. Vouch for Me; 3. ForgetAboutIt	1. Job Score; 2. DreamGigs 3. Anon-Interview

Table 2. Participant Details and Participants' Top and Bottom 3 Tool Preferences

Sessions lasted 1 hour: participants spent approximately 20 minutes looking over the ten storyboards and the remaining time (40 minutes) discussing the concepts. All participants (N=11) completed the demographic survey. Out of the 11 participants, eight were female and three were male. Participants were 28 to 55 years old (M=39, STD=9.39), single/separated/divorced, and living in households of one or two people. Education levels varied with most participants having completed high school.

All participants had access to the Internet and access to at least one digital device such as a smartphone, desktop computer, or personal laptop. The majority of our participants used a smart phone as the main tool to access the Internet (N=7). Two participants (N=2) did not have a personal smartphone and accessed the Internet using public computers at the library and public housing. Participants seemed proficient in the use of digital tools as demonstrated by taking the online survey. All participants used Google's search engine, and most participants expressed familiarity with Facebook (N=9) but did not use it every day. The main job search tools used by our participants were Indeed.com (N=5) and Google (N=4). See Table 2 for additional participant details. In the next subsections, we discuss the three most and least validated concepts. Table 3 provides a summary of the rankings from most to least preferred.

Design Concepts

We anticipated that concepts aiming to provide social support, or address the *social* needs of job seekers, would be highly ranked. We specifically thought Review-Me, Interview4, and WeCanDoIt would be the top three highest ranked tools because they also addressed the personal needs of job seekers. While Review-Me was the highest ranked concept of our participants, Skills Identifier and DreamGigs, which address a personal need among job seekers, were ranked second and third (see Table 3). The lowest ranked concepts were ForgetAboutIt (*social and societal*), Vouch for Me (*social*), and the MediaTutorial (*personal*). We discuss the details of these rankings next.

Review-Me

Overall, Review-Me was ranked as the most preferred concept tool by the participants. Specifically, 7 of the 11 interviewees listed it as a top-three choice, and all the participants expressed that the problem of developing appealing resumes was personally relatable. During the needs validation and speed dating sessions, most participants recognized the importance of resumes in getting a job. Many job seekers expressed they had limited resume-building skills and believed that Review-Me was a viable solution.

Participants struggled to include their related experiences on the resume and tailor it to different industries and valued Review-Me for this capability. For example, Tamara (P4) indicated that she struggled in terms of finding the right experience to list on her CV. Erica (P8), who had a criminal background, mentioned that she needed to make a resume because of her poor job history from the past. It is also worth mentioning that four (N=4) participants sought help from external resources such as job centers and libraries. Angel (P2) mentioned that she used to go to the local job center to receive similar services as Review-Me from a job coach. She viewed Review-Me as a service to provide to those with no means to reach the center and for those unable to pay for paid services.

Given the capability for spelling and grammar checking in standard word-processing tools, a finding that stood out was that most participants felt that Review-Me could be used to ensure that their grammatical errors were addressed. Participants often discussed challenges with online job-seeking and the need for help getting past the initial screening process. Participants also noted seeking help from others. Elizabeth (P6) emphasized this in her discussion of Review-Me:

> My son helps me because he grew up with computers. He lives with me but it's taken me a long time to learn

> the computer and how to maximize my phone even... So, if I didn't have him, I'd be in trouble.

When asked about what issues job seekers were currently facing, Geoff (P1) described his challenge with online applications:

> This ain't like it was maybe back in like 2000. They want to see that you can do your resume online. You know most of the time you gave them a paper resume. They don't take that no more. Sometimes you have to put it online. I have a computer but sometimes my computer is messing up I can't really do that way I have to go to Lowe's to get a paper resume printed out.

Skills Identifier

Skills Identifier was the second highest rated concept, with 6 out of 11 participants ranking Skills Identifier in their top three choices. Participants expressed career transitions as a common experience and Skills Identifier as a viable solution to aid in these transitions. Seven of our participants (N=7) believed that Skills Identifier could help them identify related skills and transfer the related experiences during the process of career transition. Angel (P2) described her previous experience of switching industries:

> I went from bookkeeper/office manager to working with food, [and I am now] looking to go back into an office-type position. I was a supervisor and it was like I went from one field to the next, from one extreme to the next.

Participants considered the most beneficial application of Skills Identifier was as a tool for building more competitive resumes. Job seekers also indicated that Skills Identifier would enable them to align resumes with the different requirements across industries. Similarly, job seekers who were discouraged during the job seeking process indicated that Skills Identifier could help them examine what opportunities were available and could do so immediately. Erica (P8) stated:

> Because a lot of us really don't see what other people see. The skill identifier would break it down to a point where you could see how one job actually relates to another. I like that. Like you might have good customer service skills. That doesn't mean that that can't work maybe in a law office...I think it motivates you to actually see yourself doing other things...

DreamGigs

DreamGigs was the third highest ranked concept, and 6 of the 11 participants ranked it in their top three tools. As mentioned above, job seekers sought a path to reach their desired careers [18, 43], and this was echoed in participants' responses. Most participants liked the transparency of DreamGigs because it provides job seekers with clear steps to build their skillsets.

Erica (P8) saw the similarities between DreamGigs and Skills Identifier and expressed that DreamGigs also enables you to identify the skills you have. Most participants considered skill-building to be essential for individuals looking for high-level positions or those searching for higher-paying jobs. Allynna (P9) stated that DreamGigs could help those who:

Participant	ID	Review-Me	Skills Identifier	DreamGigs	Interview4	We Can Do It	Anon-Interview	Job Score	Forget About It	Vouch For Me	Media Tutorial
Geoff	P1	8	4	10	9	5	7	6	1	2	3
Angel	P2	10	8	9	4	3	6	7	2	1	5
Ignacio	P3	9	8	3	10	1	7	5	2	6	4
Tamara	P4	10	8	9	6	5	7	4	3	2	1
Chelsea	P5	5	9	10	6	7	8	4	3	1	2
Elizabeth	P6	10	6	3	9	7	8	4	5	2	1
Aaron	P7	9	7	10	4	6	3	5	2	8	1
Erica	P8	6	8	9	3	10	4	1	7	5	2
Allyana	P9	5	6	4	2	8	3	10	9	1	7
Jill	P10	10	1	3	9	7	2	4	6	5	8
Chrissy	P11	5	10	2	6	7	1	3	8	9	4
Totals		**87**	**75**	**72**	**68**	**66**	**56**	**53**	**48**	**42**	**38**

Table 3. Final Ratings. Note that in this table, higher numbers are assigned to top preferences.

> Don't want to settle for low-wage [jobs], and the tool could help these people to go volunteer somewhere and get that job shadowing, and be able to hone the skills.

Job seekers were also looking for ways to get additional support on how to achieve their job-related goals. Tamara (P4) responded to DreamGigs with the following:

> Like, you know there are some sites out there that will give you information on what you should include in your resume that sort of thing. But if you don't have those skills, no one tells you how to get those skills. It just tells you what skills you need to have, but doesn't follow up on how to get them.

On the other hand, it is notable that 5 of the 11 participants listed DreamGigs in their bottom four choices. Most of these participants gave DreamGigs a relatively low ranking because they already received similar training services from different organizations, including their past employers and public job centers.

Next, we discuss the three lowest ranking concepts among our participants.

ForgetAboutIt

ForgetAboutIt was our third-lowest-rated concept, with 6 of the 11 participants listing it as one of their bottom three choices. Participants considered ForgetAboutIt as a useful tool for people who have children and transportation needs, but most of our participants did not feel personally connected to the concept. Ignacio (P3) stated:

> I would say that's definitely realistic as far as the concept of [ForgetAboutIt]. I believe it's a good concept. If I had children, I would use it [...].

However, three of our participants (N=3) who had difficulties with child care and transportation gave ForgetAboutIt a relatively high ranking. Two of these three participants were single mothers. Chrissy (P11) described how ForgetAboutIt could have addressed her childcare needs and benefited her job search:

> I have a child with special needs, and she was having problems with school. That was my main reason for not job searching for at least a year or two to last before now. And a service like [ForgetAboutIt] would be wonderful, [so I can] leave [the] house without any issues and being stressed out, worries, and go job searching.

Vouch for Me

Vouch for Me was the second lowest rated concept, and 6 of the 11 participants rated it as one of the bottom three tools. The key issue regarding this concept was its credibility. Six of our participants (N=6) did not believe Vouch for Me could contribute reliable references for job searching. For example, Jill (P10) stated that testimonials should be made by people who have deep connections with job seekers:

> If a person that you know speaks about you, they're gonna be more passionate and they're gonna talk with care. Versus somebody that's actually somebody you have no idea, and they just read your profile off a piece of paper. It's just based off of what they see, it's not based off what they actually know of you.

Along the same lines, participants expressed the need for access to social resources; some received this from their external networks and local job organizations, while others did not have access to either. Not having access to networks put our participants at a disadvantage, and caused participants to rank certain concepts lower than others. For example, while we anticipated Vouch for Me to raise job seekers' self-efficacy, some participants thought that this tool could be discouraging if they had limited connections. Erica (P8) mentioned that she had a hard time building a solid and reliable friend circle to get support. Allynna (P9) described similar experiences:

> [...] they always say it's not what you know, it's who you know, and if a person don't know nobody, how can they get out there and network with people, and get a job.

> [Vouch for Me] depends on how you network with people out here, because with *my* experience, it's like I done been around a lot of stuff where you're dealing with the human trafficking, where they will work you for free, and they would get in your mind, and brainwash. And [Vouch for Me] would probably go good for people that got good friends and [a] good network.

MediaTutorial

MediaTutorial was the least preferred concept among participants. While eight of our participants (N=8) believed that building a professional online image was a common need for general job seekers, most of our participants did not feel personally connected to the scenario and only saw the need for this tool among those who were looking for "decent" and professional jobs, and those who owned small businesses. Given that this did not represent our population, MediaTutorial was the lowest ranked concept for our participants, with 7 of the 11 participants ranking MediaTutorial among their bottom three choices. Most participants believed that MediaTutorial could be more beneficial for people and groups who needed online marketing or were looking for professional jobs. They believed that traditional job seekers would not benefit from this type of tool. For example, Erica (P8) stated:

> [MediaTutorial] is useful for people in a professional field, but [not useful] for getting a dishwasher job and stuff like that. I have never had no one look at my Facebook to my knowledge. But I would think in the medical field and social work and lawyers and different things like that, it would be useful.

In addition, the limited accessibility to information technology and the relatively low level of computer literacy reduced job seekers desire to develop an online brand. Two participants (N=2) expressed never having used social media platforms. Chrissy (P11) raised general concerns about the limited digital literacy among job seekers:

> [MediaTutorial is not helpful for] people who are not computer literate. I believe [MediaTutorial] will be eventually needed by a lot of people, [because] everything is gonna be [online]. I think more computer training is needed in society, because a lot of people are not [computer literate] and that puts a lot of fear when you're job searching.

MediaTutorial's evaluation demonstrated that many of our participants did not perceive a need to curate their online identity.

DISCUSSION

We would like to first acknowledge that the aim of this work was not to contribute a ranking of employment tools among our job seekers, but a discussion about *why* our participants liked or disliked some of the concepts, and how this fits into the the broader employment literature. To maintain this goal, we discuss three key findings of this work. First, the most salient result was the overwhelming preference for employment tools that immediately address job seekers' *personal* and *social* needs—resume feedback, support for articulating job skills, and help determining concrete paths to achieve career goals. Second, we discuss our findings around the importance and challenges of social networks and maintaining an online brand for employment. Finally, those tools addressing *societal* needs were not ranked highly among our concepts.

Our top-rated concepts supported job seekers' self-efficacy and addressed their immediate and practical needs: resume feedback (Review-Me), and support for articulating job skills (SkillsIdentifier) and providing concrete paths to achieve career goals (DreamGigs). These concepts supported job seekers' *social* and *personal* needs and confirmed past findings that job tools should provide transparency and feedback during the job search process [43] as well as self-efficacy [32]. Further data solidify the need for immediacy. For example, ForgetAboutIt's results were somewhat polarized because the tool was ranked highly among those participants who had children and ranked lowest by those who did not. Although issues of discrimination were not salient in our main findings, some of our oldest participants ranked Anon-Interviews higher than others, reflecting the pervasiveness of age discrimination in employment [7].

The top-rated concept, Review-Me, provides access to a *social* resource; however, the tool mediates this interaction and removes the onus from job seekers to find a person who can provide this level of service. We discuss why this mediation of social resources might have been important to our job seekers next. Findings from our literature review support social capital theory and, particularly, the strength of weak ties [23]—social ties and connections are critical in the job search process. In fact, as quoted in [29], according to Matt Youngquist, the president of a career coaching outplacement firm, between 70-80% of jobs are not published and are filled via trusted friends and acquaintances. Such statistics are the impetus for professional networking sites such as LinkedIn.

LinkedIn assumes that individuals have professional networks that could benefit them in the job-seeking process. While professional networking sites are beneficial for job seekers, most of our job seekers were discouraged by the Vouch for Me concept, which was rated second to last overall among our job seekers. Our participants had limited education and did not experience networking among college friends, professors, or career counselors, who are often called upon when individuals look beyond their own personal connections for job leads [9]. Further, long periods of unemployment remove an individual from social environments and from social networks populated with people who have higher social and human capital [9, 21]. Therefore, our job seekers might actually be disadvantaged by a concept like Vouch for Me.

Interestingly, Erica (P8) and Allynna (P9), who discussed the overall importance of having strong social networks, were supporters of Vouch for Me, which addresses a social need, yet ranked WeCanDoIt among their lowest concepts. WeCanDoIt, however, was ranked much higher than Vouch for Me among our job seekers overall. WeCanDoIt, contrary to Vouch for Me, provides a supportive network and addresses a social *and* a personal need to job seekers without a strong social network. Could a tool like WeCanDoIt provide the forms of support needed by those who lack access to strong social ties? Future research should investigate this question.

Another salient finding among new job-seeking literature is the rise of social media for branding and social identity, particularly among white-collar workers [22]. According to CareerBuilder's annual social media recruitment survey, 70% of employers use social media to screen candidates, 58% of employers are less likely to interview a candidate they can't find online, and 54% had decided not to hire a candidate based on their social media profiles [1]. Yet, the MediaTutorial, a concept aimed to support job seekers in developing a professional online brand, was ranked the lowest among participants. There were concerns of limited digital literacy [14, 15, 16, 38] around the ability to manage their social media in this way. However, our participants were perceptive in their realization that this tool was not useful for the types of jobs that they were seeking. In fact, Gershon found that identity branding is not as effective as some white collar workers believe, and less effective than social ties who can vouch for one's ability to be an effective employee [22]. This work supports our participants' belief that there is little value for them in social branding.

Finally, tools addressing societal needs (ForgetAboutIt, Anon-Interviews, and JobScore) were not ranked highly among our concepts. Our current results show that these concepts were preferred by some job seekers and not others. ForgetAboutIt, the only service concept, did not address the immediate needs of childless job seekers; Anon-Interviews was preferred among older adults. Although these results are reflective of the limitation of our small corpus, our findings suggest opportunities for employment tools to be more inclusive of the various barriers job seekers face (e.g., limited access to daycare, transportation, digital literacy, social networks).

Future research should investigate interventions that support other stakeholders in the job search, such as employment agencies and workforce development centers, whose existing efforts to support specific job-seeker needs could be amplified by technology. Future research should also investigate commonalities among these findings and those found in information and communication technologies for development (ICTD) literature. Despite the differences in geographic and work context (i.e. formal versus informal labor economies), the individual focuses on the discontinuity in employment, the importance of informal networks, and the existing structural barriers to seeking jobs are similar (e.g., [4]).

CONCLUSION AND FUTURE WORK

To conclude, we contributed a literature review of HCI research investigations of underserved job seekers and a set of ten tangible design concepts for future employment tools. We conducted a needs validation and speed dating study with underserved job seekers and found that the three most preferred concepts immediately address job seekers' most practical needs. These concepts provide job seekers with resume feedback, assist job seekers in articulating their skills based on their past jobs, and provide job seekers with a concrete path to achieve their goals.

There are opportunities for future researchers to validate the findings of our study across a larger and broader set of job seekers, and understand the potential for these tools to support external stakeholders such as career counselors, employers, and employment agencies. These questions could be addressed via a large-scale survey.

ACKNOWLEDGMENTS

We thank our participants and FII.org for supporting this project. We also thank Julie Hui, Ilana Gershon, and our reviewers for their thoughtful reviews and discussion, and members of the Social Innovations Group who provided us with early feedback. This work was supported by the NSF award IIS-1717186.

REFERENCES

1. Number of employers using social media to screen candidates at all-time high, finds latest careerbuilder study. *CareerBuilder* press release. june 2017. http://press.careerbuilder.com/2017-06-15-number-of-employers-using-social-media-to-screen-candidates-at-all-time-high-finds-latest-careerbuilder-study.

2. Ajzen, I. The theory of planned behavior. *Organizational behavior and human decision processes 50*, 2 (1991), 179–211.

3. Ajzen, I. Perceived behavioral control, self-efficacy, locus of control, and the theory of planned behavior.

Journal of applied social psychology 32, 4 (2002), 665–683.

4. Bajpai, K., Larson, J. B., and Mehta, K. Like a hustler: Aligning intervention design with informal labor practices. In *Proceedings of the Sixth International Conference on Information and Communication Technologies and Development: Full Papers - Volume 1*, ICTD '13, ACM (New York, NY, USA, 2013), 177–184.
5. Bandura, A. *Self-efficacy: The exercise of control.* Macmillan, 1997.
6. Baum, C. L. A dynamic analysis of the effect of child care costs on the work decisions of low-income mothers with infants. *Demography 39*, 1 (2002), 139–164.
7. Bayl-Smith, P. H., and Griffin, B. Age discrimination in the workplace: identifying as a late-career worker and its relationship with engagement and intended retirement age. *Journal of Applied Social Psychology 44*, 9 (2014), 588–599.
8. Bouchard, M. Transportation emerges as crucial to escaping poverty. The New York Times (May 2015).
9. Calvo-Armengol, A., and Jackson, M. O. The effects of social networks on employment and inequality. *American economic review 94*, 3 (2004), 426–454.
10. Caska, B. A. The search for employment: Motivation to engage in a coping behavior. *Journal of Applied Social Psychology 28*, 3 (1998), 206–224.
11. Darity, W. A., and Mason, P. L. Evidence on discrimination in employment: Codes of color, codes of gender. *Journal of Economic Perspectives 12*, 2 (1998), 63–90.
12. Davidoff, S., Lee, M. K., Dey, A. K., and Zimmerman, J. Rapidly exploring application design through speed dating. In *Proceedings of the 9th International Conference on Ubiquitous Computing*, UbiComp '07, Springer-Verlag (Berlin, Heidelberg, 2007), 429–446.
13. Davidson, M. M. The computerization of career services: Critical issues to consider. *Journal of Career Development 27*, 3 (2001), 217–228.
14. Dillahunt, T. R. Fostering social capital in economically distressed communities. In *Proceedings of the SIGCHI Conference on Human Factors in Computing Systems*, CHI '14, ACM (New York, NY, USA, 2014), 531–540.
15. Dillahunt, T. R., Bose, N., Diwan, S., and Chen-Phang, A. Designing for disadvantaged job seekers: Insights from early investigations. In *Proceedings of the 2016 ACM Conference on Designing Interactive Systems*, DIS '16, ACM (New York, NY, USA, 2016), 905–910.
16. Dillahunt, T. R., Kameswaran, V., Li, L., and Rosenblat, T. Uncovering the values and constraints of real-time ridesharing for low-resource populations. In *Proceedings of the 2017 CHI Conference on Human Factors in Computing Systems*, ACM (2017), 2757–2769.
17. Dillahunt, T. R., and Malone, A. R. The promise of the sharing economy among disadvantaged communities. In *Proceedings of the 33rd Annual ACM Conference on Human Factors in Computing Systems*, CHI '15, ACM (New York, NY, USA, 2015), 2285–2294.
18. Dillahunt, T. R., Ng, S., Fiesta, M., and Wang, Z. Do massive open online course platforms support employability? In *Proceedings of the 19th ACM Conference on Computer-Supported Cooperative Work & Social Computing*, CSCW '16, ACM (New York, NY, USA, 2016), 233–244.
19. Dombrowski, L., Alvarado Garcia, A., and Despard, J. Low-wage precarious workers' sociotechnical practices working towards addressing wage theft. In *Proceedings of the 2017 CHI Conference on Human Factors in Computing Systems*, CHI '17, ACM (New York, NY, USA, 2017), 4585–4598.
20. Dombrowski, L., Harmon, E., and Fox, S. Social justice-oriented interaction design: Outlining key design strategies and commitments. In *Proceedings of the 2016 ACM Conference on Designing Interactive Systems*, DIS '16, ACM (New York, NY, USA, 2016), 656–671.
21. Gayen, K., McQuaid, R., and Raeside, R. Social networks, age cohorts and employment. *International Journal of Sociology and Social Policy 30*, 5/6 (2010), 219–238.
22. Gershon, I. *Down and out in the new economy: How people find (or dont find) work today*. University of Chicago Press, 2017.
23. Granovetter, M. S. The strength of weak ties. *American journal of sociology 78*, 6 (1973), 1360–1380.
24. Green, A. E., Hoyos, M. d., and Li, Y. Job search study: literature review and analysis of the labour force survey. Department for Work and Pensions, London, England (March 2011).
25. Hayes, G. R., Custodio, V. E., Haimson, O. L., Nguyen, K., Ringland, K. E., Ulgado, R. R., Waterhouse, A., and Weiner, R. Mobile video modeling for employment interviews for individuals with autism. *Journal of Vocational Rehabilitation 43*, 3 (2015), 275–287.
26. Hendry, D. G., Abokhodair, N., Kinsley, R. P., and Woelfer, J. P. Homeless young people, jobs, and a future vision: Community members' perceptions of the job co-op. In *Proceedings of the 8th International Conference on Communities and Technologies*, C&T '17, ACM (New York, NY, USA, 2017), 22–31.
27. Hendry, D. G., Woelfer, J. P., and Duong, T. U-district job co-op: constructing a future vision for homeless young people and employment. *Information Technology & People 30* (2017), 602–628.
28. Jen, B., Kaur, J., De Heus, J., and Dillahunt, T. R. Analyzing employment technologies for economically distressed individuals. In *CHI '14 Extended Abstracts on Human Factors in Computing Systems*, CHI EA '14, ACM (New York, NY, USA, 2014), 1945–1950.

29. Kaufman, W. A successful job search: It's all about networking. *National Public Radio.*, Feb 2011.

30. Lichtenwalter, S., Koeske, G., and Sales, E. Examining transportation and employment outcomes: Evidence for moving beyond the bus pass. *Journal of Poverty 10*, 1 (2006), 93–115.

31. LinkedIn. Quarterly numbers of linkedin members. Statista (2015).

32. Liu, S., Huang, J. L., and Wang, M. Effectiveness of job search interventions: A meta-analytic review. *Psychological bulletin 140*, 4 (2014), 1009.

33. Maio, G., and Haddock, G. *The psychology of attitudes and attitude change*. Sage, 2014.

34. Park, S. Y., and Zimmerman, J. Investigating the opportunity for a smart activity bag. In *Proceedings of the SIGCHI Conference on Human Factors in Computing Systems*, CHI '10, ACM (New York, NY, USA, 2010), 2543–2552.

35. Powell, A., Bryne, A., and Dailey, D. The essential internet: Digital exclusion in low-income american communities. *Policy & Internet 2*, 2 (2010), 161–192.

36. Prochaska, J. O., DiClemente, C. C., and Norcross, J. C. In search of how people change: Applications to addictive behaviors. *American psychologist 47*, 9 (1992), 1102.

37. Putnam, R. D. Bowling alone: America's declining social capital. *Journal of democracy 6*, 1 (1995), 65–78.

38. Smith, A. Searching for work in the digital era. In *Pew Research Center: Internet, Science & Tech* (Nov 2015).

39. Smith, C. Linkedin may not be the coolest social network, but it's only becoming more valuable to businesses. Business Insider (Jul 2014).

40. Smith, S. S. *Lone pursuit: Distrust and defensive individualism among the black poor*. Russell Sage Foundation, 2007.

41. Song, Z., Wanberg, C., Niu, X., and Xie, Y. Action–state orientation and the theory of planned behavior: A study of job search in China. *Journal of Vocational Behavior 68*, 3 (2006), 490–503.

42. Truong, K. N., Hayes, G. R., and Abowd, G. D. Storyboarding: an empirical determination of best practices and effective guidelines. In *Proceedings of the 6th conference on Designing Interactive systems*, ACM (2006), 12–21.

43. Wheeler, E., and Dillahunt, T. R. Navigating the job search as a low-resourced job seeker. In *Proceedings of the 36th Annual ACM Conference on Human Factors in Computing Systems*, CHI '18, ACM (New York, NY, USA, 2018).

44. Wheeler, E., Dillahunt, T. R., and Rieh, S. Y. Opportunities to address information poverty with social search. In *Proceedings of the 2017 CHI Conference Extended Abstracts on Human Factors in Computing Systems*, CHI EA '17, ACM (New York, NY, USA, 2017), 2224–2231.

45. Woelfer, J. P., and Hendry, D. G. Homeless young people's experiences with information systems: Life and work in a community technology center. In *Proceedings of the SIGCHI Conference on Human Factors in Computing Systems*, CHI '10, ACM (New York, NY, USA, 2010), 1291–1300.

46. Zickuhr, K., and Smith, A. Digital differences. Pew Research Center: Internet, Science & Tech (Apr 2012).

47. Zikic, J., and Saks, A. M. Job search and social cognitive theory: The role of career-relevant activities. *Journal of Vocational Behavior 74*, 1 (2009), 117–127.

48. Zimmerman, J., Forlizzi, J., Finkenaur, J., Amick, S., Ahn, J. Y., Era, N., and Tong, O. Teens, parents, and financial literacy. In *Proceedings of the 2016 ACM Conference on Designing Interactive Systems*, DIS '16, ACM (New York, NY, USA, 2016), 312–322.

Designing for Intersections

Marisol Wong-Villacres[†‡] **Arkadeep Kumar**[†] **Aditya Vishwanath**[†]
Naveena Karusala[Φ] **Betsy DiSalvo**[†] **Neha Kumar**[†]

[†] Georgia Institute of Technology
{lvillacr, arkadeepkumar, adityavishwanath, bdisalvo, neha.kumar}@gatech.edu

[‡] Escuela Superior Politecnica del Litoral
lvillacr @espol.edu

[Φ] University of Washington
naveenak @cs.uw.edu

ABSTRACT

In response to the recent call for a more intersectionally-aware field of human-computer interaction (HCI), we aim to operationalize intersectionality for technology design in HCI. We develop our lens of intersectionality by drawing on the work of Rita Kaur Dhamoon, and use it to analyze data collected from a multi-sited ethnographic study of seven low-resource learning environments in the Indian states of Maharashtra, Tamil Nadu, and West Bengal. Our research contributions are threefold. First, we extend conversations in Intersectional HCI by expanding its scope from understanding users to recognizing social processes. Second, we emphasize the importance of factoring in both penalties and privileges when conducting research in underserved contexts. Finally, we engage situated comparisons as a methodology to identify pathways for designing interactive systems across intersectionally diverse environments.

Author Keywords

Intersectionality; HCI4D; Education; India

ACM Classification Keywords

H.5.m. Information Interfaces and Presentation (e.g. HCI): Miscellaneous

INTRODUCTION

The growing presence, power, and versatility of information and communication technologies (ICTs) in the Global South suggest tremendous potential for supporting diverse domains for development, such as health and education [20, 49, 50]. To harness this potential, researchers and practitioners in the field of ICTs and Development (ICTD) have proposed various innovative technology-enhanced interventions with some success [22, 56, 59, 72, 76]. However, technology design for diversely disadvantaged groups in the Global South tends to fall short of targeted impact [65, 72, 80]. One underlying reason is that most initiatives operate with partial understanding, at best, of the complexities of these groups' experiences [16, 50, 73]. Dwelling on constraints and deficits, they disregard potential that might be harnessed for realizing technosocial opportunities towards greater equity [43]. The question is still pending: *how might we study these diversely disadvantaged groups to imagine ways of integrating ICTs into the broader social and cultural fabric of their everyday contexts?*

We address the question above by focusing specifically on imagining context-appropriate roles for technology within *diversely* low-resource learning environments (LRLEs) located across India. To work towards a more holistic understanding that factors in the realities of learners' homes, schools, and communities [50], we engage deeply with the lens of intersectionality. Thus we focus on how *"the complex, irreducible, varied, and variable effects which ensue when multiple axes of differentiation—economic, political, cultural, psychic, subjective, and experiential—intersect in historically specific contexts"* [11].

Leveraging findings from our multi-sited ethnography across seven culturally and infrastructurally distinct LRLEs in the Indian states of Maharashtra, Tamil Nadu, and West Bengal, we unpack monolithic assumptions of what *"low-resource"* might entail. We analyze this data using Dhamoon's lens on *mainstreaming intersectionality* [28] for an enriched understanding of the realities of LRLEs. Dhamoon's proposal for intersectional-type analyses allows us to go beyond identifying power dynamics due to intersecting axes of differentiation such as gender, race, and education [26] to understanding the interacting cultural and historical processes and systems underlying these differences. It is in this interaction of processes, Dhamoon argues, that we can identify the *penalties* that individuals and communities endure, as well as the *privileges* they mobilize to resist modes of differentiation. Using Dhamoon's method of *situated comparisons*, we identify pathways for design based on how experiences from one LRLE might inform technology design for others.

Our research makes an important contribution to the ICTD community that routinely grapples with complex sociotechnical environments and multiple *isms* or systems of domination, engages with constraints and values assets-based approaches [53], and targets technology interventions (but could do so more holistically). We also contribute to feminist scholarship in HCI by extending recently introduced conversations on intersectionality in HCI that have thus far emphasized reshaping the collection and reporting of user data [71]. Specifically, we demonstrate how investigating and comparing sites of interaction between penalties and privileges can unearth novel pathways for technology design.

DIS 2018, June 9–13, 2018, Hong Kong.

ACM ISBN 978-1-4503-5198-0/18/06 ...$15.00.
http://dx.doi.org/10.1145/3196709.3196794

RELATED WORK

We now situate our research in the education literature of ICTD, highlighting the need for design to better leverage the potential of LRLEs. We then describe how intersectionality assists to this end. To do this, we cover its origins and position our work within ongoing theoretical debates in feminist scholarship. We draw upon Yuval-Davis' practicable approach for devising intersectional policy initiatives [86] to structure and justify a methodology for using Dhamoon's intersectional-type analysis towards holistic design decisions for LRLEs and beyond [28].

Education and ICTD

Current education research in ICTD has largely focused on identifying or overcoming constraints in the learning environment, such as the lack of social infrastructure (in the form of teachers and parents), physical infrastructure, and financial resources for accessing and maintaining technology [83]. For example, several studies from 2004 onwards have engaged with the constraints of rural schools in India by deploying video-based instruction, mobile-phone based language learning [42, 41], and various technologies such as polling systems [23] and flash drive learning platforms [18]. Extensive work has been done on unsupervised and group learning techniques, modifying ICTs to overcome the cost of technology [48, 4, 38, 39, 62]. Education research in ICTD has also scaled up to overcome constraints. Breazeal et al. presented a novel platform hosted on mobile devices with a cloud backend to deliver educational content to marginalized children in different countries, with a focus on improving low literacy levels [12]. Cutrell et al. explored a blended learning initiative for an underserved context, combining online and in-person instruction as an alternative to a purely online classroom [25]. In 2016, Kazakos et al. presented the development of an interactive voice response system that enables real-time interaction and functions as a community radio [46].

While much prior research has been careful to introduce technology that is low-cost and usable in underserved communities, the focus on identifying constraints in learning environments presents challenges. This approach can require leapfrogging on the part of students and teachers and is not always sustainable [16, 24, 81]. Additionally, presenting more perceived constraints, such as users being slow to adopt or learn interventions due to lack of expertise or training, reinforce the idea that users are an obstacle to adoption [24]. Compounding this perspective, multiple studies have also emphasized that a lack of social infrastructure cannot simply be overcome by the addition of technological infrastructure to ensure learning [5, 33, 60, 83, 84]. These studies certainly caution against using ICTs as a short-term solution, but also leave us with only a partial perspective of what LRLEs might afford the agency to accomplish. Focusing on constraints also prompts the question of what action designers can actually take based on knowledge of such constraints. We sought to learn how using ethnographic data that captures the everyday constraints people face and how they resist them might be a step towards a more holistic approach to integrating ICTs into the broader sociocultural fabric of LRLEs [50].

Intersectionality: from 1989 to 2018

Crenshaw introduced the term *intersectionality* to feminist theory in 1989 as a label for the pressing notion that critical theory and feminism should not be siloed from conversations about racism [85, 86]. Through the decades, intersectionality has been taken up widely by feminist scholars across the world and in work ranging from social movements and sociology to electoral behavior research [26, 35]. However, there are ongoing debates in feminist studies about the conceptualization of the theory itself [26]. We now carefully consider the intense debates on what intersectionality is and position our ideas about how intersectionality might be operationalized to inform design in HCI.

From its original conception, two strands of intersectionality have developed, each with different vocabularies and mechanisms. The first strand, used by feminist race scholars and focused on women of color, has been associated with the *systemic* approach [67], the *additive* approach [86], and the use of categories to classify identities [55]. This strand has been most popularized in the United States (and the field of HCI so far). This approach views systems of domination as having unilateral power over how people are socially divided and how they experience identities, leading to a sole focus on how identities bear oppression in the context being studied [67]. It necessitates the naming (black, Muslim, woman) and categorization (race, religion, gender) of identities to *divide and then add* their experiences to create an intersection.

The second strand of intersectionality used more generally by postmodern feminists has been associated with the *constructionist* approach [67], the *constitutive* approach [66, 86], and critiques of categories and classification processes [10, 55, 67, 77]. This strand problematizes the notion of static categories and the systems of power that get to create them; it focuses on the *construction* of identity and one's ever-changing relationship to power structures [51, 67]. In this approach, falling into a certain category does not determine one's experiences or the usefulness of intersectionality; people *construct* their identity through conveyance of their own unique experiences, which can include privilege, oppression, and resistance [67]. Prins suggests that, as a result, *"the scripts of gender, race, ethnicity and class play a constitutive role, but never in the same way, never as mere determining factors"* [67]. This strand of intersectionality aligns with Feminist HCI and Postcolonial Computing theories, which critique the way HCI and ICTD research tends to view culture as unchanging and generalizable across individual experience and time [6, 40]. In relating this perspective to design, the rejection of such categorization might make operationalization more difficult because there is no predefined starting point (such as categories) for studying people's unique experiences of identity [51]. However, we argue that this strand of intersectionality is apt for taking into account complexity and agency in operationalization—we align with Suchman's suggestion that we can still problematize the dominant system that creates and deploys categories [77] and the idea that we can more purposefully recognize an individual's cultural capital and ability to use it in different ways over time [85].

As this theoretical debate continues, there has been a growing body of work in HCI, including at recent workshops [31, 32, 74], that point to a burgeoning need for the operationalization of intersectionality for design. These works have looked at problems such as the design of gendered or racialized virtual agents [78], racial bias in technology use and creation [37], understanding technology and media consumption among diverse children and families [3], or how different identities access health information online [58]. Most recently, Blackwell et al.'s work on classifying online abuse point out how important it is for technology to take into account complexity of experience [9]. There has been work that takes this understanding of intersectionality's importance further [13, 71]. Notably, Schlesinger et al.'s call for Intersectional HCI in 2017 highlighted how we might better understand and represent the *"user"* in terms of the static identity categories they fall into, something which they show the HCI community has not been addressing properly [71]. Their work contributes to the practical application of intersectionality by engaging with step one of Yuval-Davis' proposed four-step methodology: collecting diverse and desegregated data about users [86]. In the next section, we detail how we aim to complete the remaining three steps (which we have adapted for HCI): contextually *analyze* complex experiences of identity, *review* systems to understand their role in users' experiences, and *implement* opportunities for design based on this data [86].

Designing for Intersections

To operationalize Yuval-Davis' blueprint for engaging the lens of intersectionality towards technology design [86], we considered the scholarship of Hancock, Prins, Ludvig, and Dhamoon [36, 67, 28]. In particular, we sought a constitutive approach that would allow us to engage with rich, multi-sited ethnographic data at the individual, community, and institutional levels of analysis. Dhamoon was a good fit [28]; Hancock focused on a quantitative approach that placed constraints on the kind of data we could analyze [36], and Prins [67] and Ludvig [51] focused only on the individual.

Dhamoon formulates an intersectional-type analysis that focuses on *processes of differentiation* (such as racialization and sexualization) and *systems of domination* (such as racism and patriarchy) [28]. She sees these processes as being interrelated; for example, imperialism cannot exist without sexism or class exploitation [28]. She also discusses how these interrelated processes take place at different levels (of the individual, community, and institution), manifesting differently at each [28]. Dhamoon emphasizes that these processes affect individuals variously—those seen as marginalized might still exercise *privilege*, and those seen as beneficiaries of systems of domination may also incur *penalties* [28]. This conceptualization serves us well because it *"denaturalizes what is taken as a given,"* allowing us to go beyond studying oppression to focus on the processes and systems *"in which meanings of privilege and penalty are produced, reproduced, and resisted in contingent and relational ways"* [28].

Due to the various complexities in these processes, researchers and practitioners must deconstruct assumptions around what differentiation looks like and the impact it might have. To this end, Dhamoon recommends conducting *situated comparisons* [28]. This could mean contrasting how different combinations of processes interrelate, how processes unfold at distinct societal levels, or how differentiation serves to uphold power structures [28]. Dhamoon's approach allows us to operationalize the last three steps of Yuval-Davis' blueprint by enabling us to *(1) analyze* ethnographic data that deconstructs the penalties and privileges in the sites we studied, *(2) review* the existing situation of the sites by comparing them, and *(3) implement* change through ideas for technology design that account for *"the different kinds of difference"* across sites [86].

RESEARCH APPROACH

Our research objective was to identify pathways for technology design that might stem from an enriched understanding of the *"different kinds of difference"* [86] present across the LRLEs we studied. To attain this enriched understanding, we chose the lens of intersectionality. We were particularly informed by the practicability of Yuval-Davis' approach towards devising implementable intersectional policy initiatives [86]. As such, our methodology consisted of the following: *(1)* collection of desegregated data through multi-sited ethnography, *(2)* contextual analysis of the data using Dhamoon's intersectional-type framework [28], and *(3)* situated comparisons across sites for imagining points of intervention. Below we describe our execution of these steps.

Data Collection

We studied seven disparate, geographically separated LRLEs in the Indian states of Maharashtra, Tamil Nadu, and West Bengal from June 2015 to July 2017 (see Table 1). To collect data from these settings, we chose Marcus' multi-sited ethnographic approach [52], which assisted us in examining how beliefs, experiences, and discourses around LRLEs varied (or not) across India. We selected our LRLEs because of the diverse struggles they face in supporting students' learning. They represent historically, culturally, and organizationally distinct contexts—from North to South India, public to NGO-run, rural to urban, and formal to after-school educational environments. Our choice was not shaped, however, by the processes of differentiation interacting with the LRLEs' work; these were uncovered only later, during data collection.

Our fieldwork included extensive participant observation and targeted interviews with teachers, parents, children, and other stakeholders present. In June 2015, we visited the villages of Uthiramerur, Vadanallur, and Kulathakarai in the district of Kancheepuram (Tamil Nadu). There we conducted participant observations for six weeks, held semi-structured interviews with five instructors and five staff members, and directly interacted with all 60 students (evenly distributed from third grade to sixth grade). From December 2015 to July 2017, we continued our fieldwork across sites in the states of Maharashtra and West Bengal. In Powai, we conducted 120 hours of participant observations and 58 semi-structured interviews (six staff, 12 teachers, six volunteers, 29 students, five parents). At Nehru Nagar, we observed and participated in four classroom sessions over two weeks. We later interviewed two teachers whose classrooms we had previously visited. In West Bengal, we studied two after-school centers near Kolkata: one in the suburb of Kamarhati and another in the suburb of Baruipur (that catered to nearby villages). In Kamarhati, we interviewed six teachers and engaged with students. In Baruipur, we conducted 25 hours of participant observation and semi-structured interviews with three teachers, three staff members, ten mothers, and ten twelfth grade students. In addition, we conducted multiple group interviews with 40 other students. The data we collected was in the form of field notes, photographs, and audio recordings of interviews (that we transcribed).

Data Analysis

Following Yuval-Davis [86], we sought an intersectional approach for engaging in contextual analysis of our data. Relying on an inductive thematic analysis alone had the risk of flattening out the multiple dimensions of our data. A categorical approach to intersectionality—one that identifies how the intersection of categories of difference and identity (such as race, gender, and class) is engendering and reinforcing systems of domination and marginalization [55]—was not suitable for our purposes. A focus on foregrounding intersecting categories can certainly highlight inequities and limitations of current approaches to relevant issues pertaining to the user (*e.g,* unearthing how HCI research has acknowledged the user's identity [71] and making recommendations for improvement). Also, the creation of a system of categories can be the outcome of participatory design processes that acknowledge individual experiences and systems of social oppression [9]. However, when intending to achieve a holistic understanding of individuals and groups, such an approach tends to mostly emphasize the marginalized aspects of individuals and communities [36, 67, 27], diminishing the visibility of people's modes of resistance against penalties. Further, the static nature of categories can create issues for uncovering the dynamic, culturally- and historically-shaped everyday experiences of people and their contexts; categories can tell us the current status, but cannot explain the reasons underlying that status [36]. After extensive literature review, we found Dhamoon's ideas for mainstreaming intersectionality [28] more apt for our research goals, as explained earlier.

Drawing on Dhamoon's approach, we proceeded to unpack the degrees and forms of penalties and privileges already present in each LRLE [28], which in turn illuminated constraints for technology integration as well as assets we could mobilize for the same. We interpret penalties as the different disadvantages that individuals, communities, or organizations must grapple with on an everyday basis (*e.g.,* not being able to attend school due to having to work), and privileges as circumstances that individuals (could) harness to attain their goals (*e.g.,* having parents who care about one's well-being). The presence of privileges does not imply a lesser degree of penalties, and vice-versa (*e.g.,* a child may have parents who care about their well-being but who deemed that sending them to work instead of to school was in their best interest). To deconstruct penalties and privileges, we followed a two-step approach. First, we conducted an inductive thematic analysis of all data to identify common trends. Examples of themes that emerged were *"gender equity initiatives at school," "gendering of education,"* and *"technology use in the classroom"*. After iteratively distilling our themes, we arrived at four large themes that were transversal to our data: *"Issues of Gender", "Parental Engagement", "Everyday use of Technology",* and *"Technology Adoption in the Classroom"*. From there, for each theme, we crafted narratives of the LRLEs we visited and then conducted narrative analysis [51, 67]. Our purpose was to deductively identify interacting processes of differentiation and systems of domination, and uncover how individuals (teachers, parents, children), communities (LRLEs), and organizations (non-governmental and governmental organizations) interacted with those, to uphold or to resist them. It was in those interactions that we were able to see the dynamically-shifting nature of penalties and privileges. This, in turn, highlighted both challenges to technology adoption and supporting structures for new technology designs.

State	School (Locale, Structure)
Maharashtra	Nehru Nagar (Urban, Formal) Powai (Suburban, After-School)
West Bengal	Baruipur (Rural, After-School) Kamarhati (Suburban, After-School)
Tamil Nadu	Kancheepuram (Rural, Formal)

Table 1. Field Sites

To identify processes and systems, we used Matsuda's recommendation to *"ask the other question"*: *"When I see something that looks racist, I ask, 'Where is the patriarchy in this?' When I see something that looks sexist, I ask, 'Where is the heterosexism in this?' When I see something that looks homophobic, I ask, 'Where are the class interests in this?"' [54].* This method highlighted the processes that were salient in our data, such as those relating to gender, caste, geography, and levels of education.

In our final step of analysis, we subjected our narratives from across sites to Dhamoon's method of situated comparisons [28]. This allowed us to better glean how the promises and pending challenges for teachers, students, parents, and LRLEs at one site might suggest points of intervention at others.

Self-Disclosure

Following Schlesinger et al.'s [71] recommendation that authors disclose aspects of their identity that influence their research, we clarify that Marisol (first author), Naveena, and Neha (advising author) are women of color from Ecuador, the United States, and India, with a shared commitment to feminist perspectives in HCI. Arkadeep and Aditya were responsible for all fieldwork and data collection, in the languages spoken at each site—also their native languages. Betsy originates from the United States (U.S.) and has extensive experience with researching LRLEs in the U.S. All authors worked together to ensure that our assumptions were double-checked.

AN INTERSECTIONAL-TYPE ANALYSIS

We now execute on the steps proposed by Yuval-Davis [86]. We present our *intersectional-type analysis* (as Dhamoon calls it [28]), and focus on foregrounding the *penalties* and *privileges* present in the LRLEs we studied. Our primary goal is to explore how these penalties and privileges might highlight constraints to account for and assets we might leverage to imagine points of intervention. Our analysis is organized into four themes that were transversal to our empirical data. For each theme, we present narratives from the LRLEs we visited. In particular, we describe how individuals, communities, and institutions mobilize privileges to enact forms of resistance against penalties. We present four (out of several potential) *situated comparisons* that consider both challenges and forms of resistance across narratives. Finally, we propose pathways for technology design that account for both penalties and privileges.

The Importance of Addressing Girls' and Boys' Needs

The gendering of education was a salient process of differentiation across our sites, taking various forms and resulting in different penalties for girls and boys. Each of the LRLEs we visited chose to mobilize its privileges in different ways to help students resist the effects of gendering. Below we present and contrast the gender equity initiatives organized by two NGO-run after-school centers—Baruipur and Kamarhati—in rural and suburban West Bengal, respectively. Our analysis shows that, although boys are also impacted by gendering processes, LRLEs tend to focus their gender equity initiatives on girls alone. We conclude that conducting initiatives for granting boys opportunities for resistance as well is a pending challenge for NGO-run LRLEs. We envision ways in which technology might play a role in addressing such a challenge.

Baruipur is a girls-only LRLE that caters to villages near Kolkata. These villages have been historically affected by the sex trafficking industry [70], with many implications for girls' education. When abducted by sex traffickers, girls certainly end up missing educational opportunities. However, as one of the mothers we spoke to explained, parents' response to the danger of sex trafficking might also limit girls' educational opportunities: *"We have to raise the girls and then we run the risk of losing them to traffickers. It is better for us to marry them off as soon as possible."*. Cognizant of the penalties inflicted upon girls, Baruipur mobilizes its privileges as an NGO-run organization (such as provision of education, infrastructure, and volunteers) to grant its students various opportunities for resistance. It ensures that girls continue their education, learn to protect themselves, and imagine alternate futures for their lives. For example, the center sends its volunteers to nearby villages to provide girls with educational support; this helps the girls perform better academically and keeps parents motivated to send their daughters to school. Baruipur also offers the girls regular orientation on women's issues (*e.g.*, adolescent health, child marriage, teen pregnancy, and domestic violence) to help them gain self-reliance. Moreover, the center provides girls with vocational, computer, and English training to improve their chances of securing jobs after they have completed their schooling.

Baruipur's initiatives of resistance are forms of power that, when interacting with sexist discourses such as child marriage, shape girls' perspectives on their identities. Some girls we interviewed perceived marriage as restrictive and burdensome, sharing that they had discussed the topic of marriage with their parents and even changed their parents' convictions. These girls told us they now felt more confident about their abilities to attain day jobs and financially support their families and themselves. Some also expressed a desire to get a college education they could finance themselves. Baruipur's case demonstrates how gender equity initiatives need to acknowledge the different processes that inflict penalties on students (*e.g.*, gender violence, sexist discourses) and interact with them to help students realize that they are able to change their present and future.

Kamarhati, an after-school center run by an NGO in peri-urban Kolkata, struggles with boys' low attendance rates. Interacting processes and systems—such as the industrialization of the area, families' economic struggles due to casteism and capitalism, and the gendering of factory work as a male activity—have resulted in the burgeoning of early labor occupations for boys. This is a penalty that hinders boys' opportunities for an education. Teachers recognize this problem and make individual efforts to help students resist this oppressive power. Rakesh, a teacher at Kamarhati, recounted how he had made sure that his students continued to attend school by regularly talking to their parents to convince them about the advantages of attaining an education. However, Kamarhati as an institution limits its gender equity initiatives that aid boys specifically in imagining future selves through educational attainment. Rather, the LRLE aims to harness its educational and infrastructural privileges to counteract yet another form of power: the historic violence against women in the area. The center takes initiatives to instill gender norms in students that can protect girls in the long run. For example, at Kamarhati, boys are encouraged to challenge gender stereotypes by having them participate in traditionally feminine activities such as cooking.

Our data shows that some NGO-funded after-school centers in India have educational, financial, and infrastructural assets, and social capital. They can potentially mobilize these privileges to conduct gender equity initiatives that empower students to construct new, alternative futures. Baruipur is an example of how an after-school center can address the many fronts that penalize girls' lives by providing the opportunity to grow through education. However, as our narratives show, systematically working towards granting opportunities for resistance to boys is still a challenge for LRLEs. Kamarhati's focus on helping girls resist gender violence takes away from devising other kinds of initiatives for boys that could systematically address the effects of child labor. After-school centers such as Kamarhati thus need support to *(1)* further explore the processes that engender penalties for both boys and girls, and *(2)* broaden boys' and girls' notions of future opportunities.

We now offer examples to illustrate how a situated comparison of the narratives above can illuminate pathways for technology design that are not only sensitive to the unique penalties boys and girls confront when imagining positive futures but also still support sensitivity to the opposite gender. First, constructionist technologies that foster students' self-expression [63] can assist teachers at LRLEs to further understand the processes underlying gender-related penalties for boys and girls. From this understanding, these teachers could devise mechanisms for mobilizing privileges. Considering that not all children attend school, one approach might involve opening co-located interaction spaces where boys and girls can engage in activities that challenge normalized perspectives on gender, perhaps through makerspaces [7]. This could also enable boys and girls to be more aware of gender equity issues. Second, technology could help LRLEs broaden boys' and girls' knowledge of alternative occupational options. For example, technology could play a role in connecting learners with professionals and students from other places (including urban areas in India, for example) who may have undergone similar challenges to pursue education. Learning from others' aspirations and discussing their process of constructing new identities can help learners envision greater possibilities for their futures.

Parental Engagement and the Alignment of Values

Across sites, we found that one of the main issues LRLEs face is in finding ways to engage parents in their children's education. Casteism interacts with gendering processes and lack of education to prevent parents from actively participating in children's academic activities. This can lead to several problems, from hindering learning at home to withdrawing children from school so they can be put to work or married early. We analyze how the after-school centers of Powai (suburban Maharashtra) and Baruipur (rural West Bengal) interact with the casteism that shapes parents' attitudes toward school. Our analysis highlights the relevance for LRLEs to understand parents beyond traditional assumptions around lower-caste groups and explore how to use parents' cultural values, beliefs, and aspirations as assets to improve children's educational opportunities. We also demonstrate, however, that such exploration can be difficult for LRLEs. Parents' values can entail both potential penalties and privileges for children's futures and it is up to the LRLE to decide how to interact with those values in ways that can help the children. Our analysis concludes that LRLEs need support in negotiating with parents a shared understanding of the benefits of supporting children's academic endeavors. Technology can have a key role in supporting that process.

Powai, a mixed-gender after-school center near Mumbai, is exemplary of the issues that arise when LRLEs clash with the values that casteism can engender. Most of Powai's parents are daily-wage laborers with limited capacity—and thus, willingness—to devote to children's education. The following account from Ishita, a mother, demonstrates this: *"I dont have time to focus on what my son does in school. I expect the school will do what it is supposed to do; why am I expected to intervene and supervise how my child is progressing? It's not the parent's job! Isn't that the teacher's job?"* However, casteism interacts with capitalism in an urban setting—where there is exposure to stories of academic success—to drive these parents to value education as a vehicle for upward mobility. One of the fathers explained his expectations: *"I want my son to have a different future, to do better than me. I did not have the opportunity to learn but I'm giving that opportunity to my child, I want my child to take advantage of it."* The expectation of moving away from their castes, thus, represents an important motivation to send their children to an after-school center. However, this support is weakened by the clash of values that occurs between parents and the teachers and administrators at Powai.

As an NGO-funded institution, Powai attracts instructors who hold progressive values around issues such as gender equity. These teachers' experiences with systems such as casteism and sexism motivate them to instill change in society. For example, many of them promote learning experiences where boys and girls can interact freely and be welcoming towards each other. Such progressive initiatives, however, go against parents' traditional values around gender, which frames the free interaction of single men and women as a social taboo [1]. A teacher explained: *"Parents don't always like this. So many parents go around with the opinion—I'm not going to send my daughter to Powai—the coordinator there gives children too much freedom or the coordinator lets boys and girls talk with each other..."* The case of Powai shows that by not exploring how parents interact with casteism on a daily basis, the center is unable to harness the privileges this system of oppression might produce. The center thus misses the opportunity to fully harness parents' willingness to support education to attain a better future for their children. Further, it shows the relevance of acknowledging traditional values, for though they stem from systems of domination such as patriarchy, can override pragmatic values such as support for children's education. This, in turn, represents a penalty for children when they miss out on educational opportunities.

Instead of assuming the values of low-caste parents as constraints, Baruipur tries to deconstruct the values that casteism engenders, to identify how parents' values can be leveraged as assets to support girls' educational attainment. There are two values that Baruipur uncovers as assets: parents' care for their children and collectivist values that drive them to seek the support of their children later in life. We now describe how Baruipur unpacks these values towards furthering its educational initiative. At first sight, one might conclude that parents at Baruipur do not care for the future of their daughters. On one hand—and in contrast to the urban parents at Powai—parents at Baruipur often disregard the education of girls as a sign of upward mobility. This is due to several interacting processes. For one, being of lower caste in rural settings gives these parents less exposure to stories of academic success. Further, patriarchal norms drive parents to assume marriage to be the only plausible future for their daughters. One of the mothers further explained: *"When [my daughter] started failing at school, we decided it'd be better for her to help us at home. It is safer for her and in that way she can be more prepared for when she gets married."*. A deeper engagement with the interactive processes underlying parents' actions allows us to see that, for parents at Baruipur, marriage is a form of protection. As we highlighted previously, the risk of sexual exploitation prevalent in the area [70] drives parents to marry their daughters earlier than laws allow. Despite the negative connotations around child marriage, in the case of Baruipur, it is itself a form of resistance drawing from parents' care for their children. Baruipur sees this care as a privilege parents mobilize, and, as we will show, uses it to motivate parents to support their children's education.

Baruipur also harnesses the collectivist values predominant in rural India. Via collectivism, parents expect to find support in their children later on in life [82]. Collectivism interacts with patriarchy, however, to determine that it is men and not women who will have the ability to take care of their parents when they age [17]. Baruipur mobilizes its infrastructure and volunteers along with parents' care and collectivist values to shape parents' minds about girls' abilities. The center offers girls vocational training for landing urban jobs to convince parents that girls can attain safe, prosperous futures and support their families. Further, it sends volunteers to visit parents at home and explain the benefits of supporting girls. One of the teachers shared: *"If your girl finishes school she can become a teacher in a tutor center, she can then earn money and support herself and you in your old age."* Kamini, a mother, explained how this changed her perspective: *"I have supported my child to become educated and now she is studying in a college to become a nurse. I hope she will take care of me in old age."* Baruipur's strategy demonstrates the relevance of further exploring the implications of being a low-caste parent. By identifying privileges within the values that casteism engenders, Baruipur is able to devise an educational initiative that is sustainable because it aligns with parents' values.

Research on parent-school relationships advises schools to foster a two-way connection between the home and learning environment so that parents feel welcome to engage in their child's education [15, 57]. Our narratives highlight, however, that LRLEs in India need a different approach. These schools need to show how students receiving an education can align with parents' values and aspirations. Baruipur's mobilization of care and collectivism as assets demonstrates that aligning with parents' values requires LRLEs to have a good understanding of parents' contexts and practices. Parents' rejection of Powai's gender sensitization initiative shows that LRLEs need to be able to negotiate a shared understanding with parents of how a change of practices can align with their values.

Pathways for technology design emerge in this regard. Easy-to-share videos with stories of students' and parents' alternative (positive and negative) futures can be one way to support parental engagement in these scenarios. Another way could be through simple visualizations showing parents information that they find valuable, such as the financial payoff of sending their children to school compared to how much they will make if their children go to work immediately instead. Technology could also help schools connect with parents whose children have pursued higher education so as to coordinate talks and personalized advising for those who are still supporting their children. These one-on-one interactions can help LRLEs better understand how interacting processes and systems of oppression shape parents' actions. Learning from others while building a community can help parents engage in ways they find valuable and feasible.

Improving Meaningful Connectivity

Previous work on digital inequities has suggested that meaningful digital connectivity—that is, the ability to engage technology and mobilize information resources to address everyday goals and concerns [45]—is a crucial component for addressing social marginalization [44, 64]. We sought to analyze the penalties and privileges students experience in terms of attaining meaningful connectivity. Our purpose was to imagine how those penalties and privileges could be translated into constraints and assets for technology-enhanced interventions. Our analysis of urban Mumbai (Maharashtra), where we visited two LRLEs, and the rural areas around Baruipur (West Bengal), where we visited several villages catered by one LRLE, confirm the rural/urban divide in access and meaningful connectivity. In particular, the interaction between two processes—the limited exposure to people and technology in rural sites and practices of sexualization—engender privacy-related penalties for young girls. These, in turn, hinder girls' ability to devise new uses for technology. From our analysis on these interacting processes, we identified, however, the following four assets for technology design to improve meaningful connectivity: *(1)* students' pollination of ideas, *(2)* parents' willingness to learn from teachers, *(3)* parents' interest in gaming apps, and *(4)* the transfer of knowledge between girls with limited internet access and individuals with easy access to mobile technologies.

As mentioned before, the parents we studied in Mumbai were seen as low-caste, daily-wage laborers. However, life in urban settings affords both parents and children a series of technology-related privileges that the children mobilize for resisting monolithic notions of being from lower caste. These forms of resistance entail different opportunities for meaningful connectivity. For example, we might consider that the forces of capitalist consumerism have made smartphones cheaper, engendering a privilege for low-caste families: they have now the possibility of accessing these devices and sharing them with children. Living in Mumbai also gives students exposure to diverse ways of using technologies, often leading to new technology-enhanced learning practices. Prabhu, a student from Nehru Nagar, one of the LRLEs we visited, explained: *"Outside the school I have friends who are going to other schools. They talked to me about a YouTube channel for solving math problems, and when I had the chance, I used it on my Dad's phone."* As students grow older and gain access to their own phones, the exposure that their urban contexts afford shape their technology practices further. For example, Rohan, an eleventh grader in Powai, told us he had purchased a second-hand phone so he could join his classmates' WhatsApp group and chat with them. As a result of mobilizing these privileges, students in Mumbai were able to connect in meaningful ways. A teacher from Nehru Nagar shared how this connectivity took place in Mumbai: *"If they are told there is this project and you can use internet, they do use it. Nowadays a lot of them first try to use Wikipedia. They know that is a medium they can access (for information or general knowledge)."*

Regarding the use of other educational apps, we observed that—despite their urban exposure—parents were not aware of existing options. They preferred to use cellphones mostly for playing games (*e.g.*, Fruit Ninja and Subway Surfers) and accessing social media (*e.g.*, Facebook) instead. However, parents' relationship with teachers usually engenders a privilege, for teachers often make recommendations to parents and children about novel uses of technology. Naresh, a parent, described further how he harnessed this privilege to learn new things: *"My son's teacher suggested I install an app for helping [my son] learn to pronounce English. I tried it out and now I use it regularly, it's pretty good!"* Teachers' knowledge about technologies for learning as well as parents' willingness to learn from teachers signal a key asset that technology-based interventions could leverage.

In the villages near Baruipur, the processes of sex trafficking, and gendering of technology access and use, interact with the technological isolation of rural sites to heavily constrain girls' engagement with technology. To resist sex trafficking and protect girls, parents and schools discourage them from using phones. Nipun, a teacher at Baruipur explained the rationale behind this practice:

> *"You get some missed call from an unknown person, then you ring back, and you talk, develop a relationship with that boy. Then that person calls you somewhere and you go there, and fall in trouble [alluding to sexual assault]. Moreover, we have got so many girls who have got trafficked due to mobiles!"*

Roughly a third of the girls we interviewed had mobile devices; among them, around 15% had smartphones. Internet costs and constrained access to cellphones limited technology use even further. Despite such issues of access, girls' interactions with teachers from NGOs from urban sites, who regularly visited the villages, gave them opportunities to learn about Facebook and WhatsApp. In this case, teachers mobilized their privileged access and education to support girls in resisting existing differentiations.

Despite the digital divide between rural and urban settings, our narratives highlight privileges for both kinds of locations that can be harnessed to foster meaningful connectivity. Further, juxtaposing Mumbai's forms of use with Baruipur's case illustrates how to grant rural children safer exposure to different technology practices. Our analysis suggests (at least) four pathways technology designers might take to support meaningful connectivity. First, drawing on students' knowledge-sharing practices, we suggest exploring how social computing can support the pollination of ideas between rural and urban students. Second, families' willingness to learn from teachers can be harnessed to develop applications through which teachers can send parents periodic suggestions about new educational apps. Third, parents' preference for gaming apps could also be leveraged to tailor popular mobile games for progressively leading parents and students to other kinds of technology uses. Fourth, girls' intermediated access to technology in Baruipur signals the need to consider women's safety when designing for intermediated internet access [69].

Towards Meaningful Technology Integration

The use of technology for teaching and learning is steadily increasing worldwide [8, 34]. However, achieving meaningful technology integration in learning environments—that is, using technology in the classroom so that young people achieve empowered forms of learning [79]—remains a challenge [29, 34, 75]. To better understand where technology deployment initiatives in schools fail or succeed, we analyzed the LRLEs in Kancheepuram (rural public schools), Powai, and Baruipur. These LRLEs represent a range of organizational structures, contexts (rural, peri-urban, urban), and levels of technological engagement. Our analysis shows that the paternalism of the government and NGOs as a system of domination was present across failed infrastructural deployments at the schools. Paternalism interacting with other processes, such as the rural versus urban gap, takes away from the motivation to enact change and flexibility to appropriate initiatives. However, our analysis unearths privileges that teachers in rural and urban settings harness to counteract the effects of paternalism. We conclude that bottom-up approaches where integrations are informed by the knowledge and needs of teachers and students—rather than imposed by schools or other organizations—can engender meaningful integrations for the learning environment and beyond.

Kancheepuram's case foregrounds the challenge with top-down technology integration initiatives. Further, it helps inform the changes needed in how technology is integrated so as to properly take into account teachers' support. In Kancheepuram, several key processes interact and often conflict with each other to shape teachers' attitudes towards their job. On the one hand, the government's paternalism and restricted exposure to diversity in rural settings impacts teachers' motivation for conducting and supporting important changes in the classroom. For example, teachers are required to fulfill goals imposed by the government (*e.g.*, a state-mandated curriculum) while their salary and access to educational resources (*e.g.*, labs, libraries) are always constrained by the government's budget. On the other hand, the closeness of teachers to students and their families engenders an interest for children's well-being, and thus, a willingness to go the extra mile for them. For example, their care for children motivates them to go around the village 30 minutes before school starts to remind parents to send their children to class, and even offer to drop children home after school ends. Teachers also expressed their care by identifying priorities for the school to offer a better education, such as a library and science lab.

In our visit to Kancheepuram, we learned that such care for children, however, was not sufficient to engage teachers in an NGO-run technology-integration initiative. In trying to understand why that was the case, we identified key aspects to consider for harnessing teachers' care towards children as an asset for future technology-integration initiatives. Again, several interacting factors led to the failure of the technology-integration initiative. Amongst them was a paternalistic approach towards technology introduction. The initiative entailed the provision of technological infrastructure (tablets with educational materials and a WiFi router for internet access) and training for teachers to learn how to apply educational technologies in the classroom. However, the initiative did not stem from teachers' but from the NGO's assessment of educational needs in rural contexts. The teachers thus felt that their perspectives and preferences in terms of what the school needed were being disregarded. Moreover, the initiative disrupted teachers' everyday lives by demanding that they arrive 30 minutes early to charge their devices. Given that public school teachers already operate under low motivation, they decided to reject the initiative entirely. Teachers' participation (or lack thereof) in this process of technology integration suggests two factors as key for harnessing teachers' care for children as assets in such initiatives: *(1)* the initiative needs to match teachers' assessments of what is valuable in the learning environments where they work, and *(2)* the new practices the initiative demands must align with teachers' operational, everyday practices.

As mentioned before, being in an urban environment is a privilege that the students in Mumbai mobilized to counteract the effects of casteism interacting with classism. As an NGO-run after-school center, Powai (near Mumbai) also holds privileges (*e.g.,* progressive teachers, flexibility to design a new curriculum, and the ability to secure technology resources with more ease than a public institution). Motivated to help students further resist fixed notions about their future, the center fosters technology use in ways that students and teachers value. Dr. Usha, the Powai coordinator, explained the school's vision of technology integration:

> *"My students should take the initiative to pursue their interests. I give them the freedom to use the WiFi, and explore the internet whenever they want. Yes, we maintain some discipline with regards to what they browse, but we still give them that opportunity to explore."*

Powai leveraged its privileges to equip one lab with five desktop computers, one printer, five tablets, and a WiFi network. It had two classrooms, each with a wall-mounted television and a desktop whose screen could be projected onto the TV. Support from the school allowed teachers to pursue bottom-up approaches of technology deployment in the classroom. For example, one teacher would use the TV or tablet to stream YouTube videos related to the topic she was teaching at least twice a week, to supplement her lessons. She paused each lecture at least once to Google images (*e.g.,* Mount Everest) related to the lesson (*e.g.,* geography) so that students could use the tablets to connect better with what they were taught. This bottom-up integration also changed students' self-perception as technology users: now they had the ability to decide which projects to engage in. For example, we observed that some students started scanning YouTube for Do It Yourself (DIY) tutorials on topics such as movie animation and graphics, cooking recipes, and making toys.

Baruipur sought a different bottom-up approach to technology integration. As mentioned before, the after-school center mobilizes its privileges to help rural girls resist the interaction of sexism, gendering, and patriarchy. Towards that pursuit, the center has helped girls develop different aspirations for their future, including using technology for furthering their careers and lives. Motivated by girls' requests to receive computer training, Baruipur decided to conduct an exploratory initiative for 40 girls to receive computer and spoken English classes for one day a week through six months. The training entailed learning basic computer skills such as typing and using Microsoft Office. Due to lack of resources in rural settings, the Baruipur LRLE does not have computers for students, nor teachers for computer training. However, the center was able to harness its funding to rent time and space in a nearby local computer learning center and hire the training services of another center in Kolkata. Girls had to travel from different villages to Baruipur to receive this training.

This initiative's bottom-up nature—for it was motivated by the students' interests—allowed the girls and the center to construct their own values around a technology-supported education. It also drove them to reflect on ways in which it could be improved. After the training, a few of the girls had secured jobs as store attendants in retail outlets in the nearby city of Kolkata. We interviewed a few who had started working. These girls were not satisfied with their jobs and felt strongly that *a different kind of* computer training could have helped further:

> *"They taught us very basic computers, not enough for most of the work which is based on computers. If we had been given more of computer training as opposed to retail training it would have been better. They are giving us jobs at very good places but we are lagging because of our insufficient computer training."*

Baruipur's example highlights that bottom-up approaches can help resist complex interacting process and systems, including the lack of exposure to technology in rural settings It also reveals how it is possible for modes of resistance to shape the self-perceptions of students and their sense of empowerment.

Juxtaposing Baruipur's and Powai's bottom-up forms of resistance for students against the lack of motivation of Kancheepuram's teachers towards paternalistic initiatives suggests the need for a new perspective on technology integration. In LRLEs, integration might not necessarily entail large deployments of technology, which usually require major changes in practices and hard-to-obtain/maintain resources [30, 68]. Instead, integration could stem from teachers, students, and LRLEs, who need support in broadening their ideas about how to harness privileges such as care, assessment of students' needs, and personal technology use. One integration initiative could be to expand self-organized learning [56] to structured environments such as public schools. Another idea we find valuable—due to its special focus on teachers—could be to provide progressive, scaffolded support to teachers to develop their own strategies of how to introduce technology in the classroom (such as by regularly communicating suggestions to teachers' phones about what might be possible in the classroom, given existing resources, technology-based or not).

DESIGNING FOR INTERSECTIONS

Our paper develops conversations in Intersectional HCI that were begun by Schlesinger et al. at CHI 2017 [71]. We propose a focus on processes rather than users when imagining points of intervention. We also inform research on underserved contexts by proposing an approach that holistically engages both penalties and privileges. Finally, our intersectional-type analysis makes a methodological contribution to facilitate working across multiple intersections to identify pathways for technology design.

Intersectional HCI: From Users to Processes

We extend conversations in Intersectional HCI by contributing an approach that shifts focus from users' categories of identity (such as race or gender) to interacting processes. Examining these processes allows us to *(1)* challenge conceptions of the user as a static individual without agency, *(2)* look beyond the user at other levels of interaction such as the social and the organizational, and *(3)* recognize the influence of users' cultural/historical backgrounds on their actions.

The focus on dynamic processes of subject formation allows us to identify when individuals mobilize their agency to deploy different aspects of their identity. A focus on intersecting traits of the user's identity—as prior work on intersectionality in HCI has adopted [13, 58, 71]—runs the risk of representing users and their contexts as static entities with little agency [61, 67], needing to be "helped". In contrast, our approach's focus on processes lets us view users as possible creators of their own stories. Also, by recognizing how users respond to interacting processes of differentiation and systems of domination, new pathways for design that support resistance may emerge. This possibility aligns with the feminist quality of *advocacy* that Bardzell proposed for shaping interaction design [6]. In our work, exploring processes instead of users' identities allowed us to see the girls of Baruipur as agents of change, and further explore ways in which technology might support them in their resistance.

Looking at processes allowed us to go beyond identifying challenges individuals face to analyzing how—by interacting with *other* individuals or organizations—they resist or enact forms of power. When we focus only on individual traits, we may only see experiences of marginalization [19, 14, 67, 86], disregarding what people's everyday interactions with others can tell us about the feasibility of change. By contrast, our focus on processes allows us to identify what social relationships, values, and infrastructures are key for imagining points of intervention. This view can enable, in turn, the design of technologies that are *"ecologically appropriate"*—as Bardzell discusses them in her presentation of Feminist HCI [6]; that is, technology designed to consider the widest range of stakeholders, and the possible effects design artifacts can have in their broadest contexts. For example, by looking at the interaction between gendering practices and patriarchy affecting girls in Baruipur, we can see the importance of the NGO's relationship with the girls and consider ways for new technologies to harness that relationship.

Finally, by focusing on the dynamic nature of processes that take place in what Irani et al. call a *"generative"* view of culture [40], we can recognize the influence of users' cultural/historical backgrounds on their actions. We can also reflect on what interventions may be feasible for certain communities. For example, looking at parents' reactions to the interaction of practices of sexism and a traditional patriarchal system in Baruipur, we are forced to think deeper about parents' motives to marry their girls early, and then see that it is their care for the girls and the reliance on collectivist values that drives them to such decisions; these values must be taken into account when designing technology for this context.

A Holistic View Entails Both Privileges and Penalties

In response to feminist and critical perspectives that call for a holistic understanding of the everyday contexts of marginalized populations [21, 27, 85], we explored privileges and penalties prevalent in LRLEs across India [50]. Investigating privileges allows us to acknowledge the dignity of individuals and communities [2, 53]. Prior research has also critiqued the idea of needs-based problem-solving, arguing that labeling a community as riddled with problems that need fixing perpetuates the idea that problems cannot be solved from within [47, 53]. A lens that examines the ways in which individuals address the limitations they face on an everyday basis can reveal key supporting structures for new designs [3].

Our intersectional-type analysis highlighted the importance of recognizing both penalties and privileges for devising meaningful, sustainable interventions. For example, recognizing that girls in Baruipur face restrictions in accessing technology for safety reasons is key to identifying a possible problem space. However, this constraint by itself does not indicate how an environment might mobilize itself to tackle the problem. By identifying the interactions girls have with urban instructors as privileges, we can uncover more stakeholders to be taken into account for design, and redefine the problem space from *"girls need access"* to *"how might we make intermediated access safer for girls?"*. A holistic understanding through deconstruction of privileges and penalties may also benefit other fields that address concerns of vulnerable groups, such as health informatics and/or civic design.

Situated Comparisons Reveal Pathways for Design

By emphasizing similarities and differences across contexts, our situated comparisons—as recommended by Dhamoon [28]—allowed us to identify which processes were more salient where, and what pending challenges could be addressed, also highlighting how one group's acts of resistance could help identify design opportunities for another. For example, our comparison of gendering practices across LRLEs recommended supporting collaboration in open spaces (*e.g.*, makerspaces) as an opportunity for NGOs to explore specific gender-related needs. Makerspaces can foster mixed-gender interactions that challenge normalized perspectives of gender. Also, by juxtaposing the Mumbai children's sharing of ideas with Baruipur's lack of exposure to diversity, we were able to devise new roles for social computing to enable students in rural areas to participate in activities for pollinating ideas. Situated comparisons thus helped us uncover penalties and privileges to unearth pathways for contextually relevant technology design across intersectionally diverse contexts, enabling contributions to the ICTD, HCI, and DIS communities.

REFERENCES

1. 2015. Engineering lesson 1: Boys shouldn't speak to girls. `http://timesofindia.indiatimes.com/india/Engineering-lesson-1-Boys-shouldnt-speak-to-girls/articleshow/21010464.cms`. (2015).
2. Antwi A Akom, Julio Cammarota, and Shawn Ginwright. 2008. Youthtopias: Towards a new paradigm of critical youth studies. *Youth Media Reporter* 2, 4 (2008), 1–30.

3. Meryl Alper, Vikki S Katz, and Lynn Schofield Clark. 2016. Researching children, intersectionality, and diversity in the digital age. *Journal of Children and Media* 10, 1 (2016), 107–114.

4. Saleema Amershi, Meredith Ringel Morris, Neema Moraveji, Ravin Balakrishnan, and Kentaro Toyama. 2010. Multiple mouse text entry for single-display groupware. In *Proceedings of the 2010 ACM conference on Computer supported cooperative work*. ACM, 169–178.

5. Payal Arora. 2010. Hope-in-the-Wall? A digital promise for free learning. *British Journal of Educational Technology* 41, 5 (2010), 689–702.

6. Shaowen Bardzell. 2010. Feminist HCI: taking stock and outlining an agenda for design. In *Proceedings of the SIGCHI conference on human factors in computing systems*. ACM, 1301–1310.

7. Angela Calabrese Barton, Edna Tan, and Day Greenberg. 2016. The makerspace movement: Sites of possibilities for equitable opportunities to engage underrepresented youth in STEM. *Teachers College Record* (2016).

8. Bryan Berrett, Jennifer Murphy, and Jamie Sullivan. 2012. Administrator insights and reflections: Technology integration in schools. *The Qualitative Report* 17, 1 (2012), 200.

9. Lindsay Blackwell, Jill Dimond, Sarita Schoenebeck, and Cliff Lampe. 2017. Classification and Its Consequences for Online Harassment: Design Insights from HeartMob. *Proc. ACM Hum.-Comput. Interact.* 1, CSCW, Article 24 (Dec. 2017), 19 pages. DOI: http://dx.doi.org/10.1145/3134659

10. Geoffrey C Bowker and Susan Leigh Star. 2000. *Sorting things out: Classification and its consequences*. MIT press.

11. Avtar Brah and Ann Phoenix. 2004. Ain't IA woman? Revisiting intersectionality. *Journal of international women's studies* 5, 3 (2004), 75–86.

12. Cynthia Breazeal, Robin Morris, Stephanie Gottwald, Tinsley Galyean, and Maryanne Wolf. 2016. Mobile Devices for Early Literacy Intervention and Research with Global Reach. In *Proceedings of the Third (2016) ACM Conference on Learning@ Scale*. ACM, 11–20.

13. Samantha Breslin and Bimlesh Wadhwa. 2014. EnGendering Design: Implementing Interdisciplinarity. (2014).

14. Wendy Brown. 2008. The impossibility of women's studies. *Women's Studies on the Edge* (2008), 17–38.

15. Gustavo Pérez Carreón, Corey Drake, and Angela Calabrese Barton. 2005. The importance of presence: Immigrant parents' school engagement experiences. *American Educational Research Journal* 42, 3 (2005), 465–498.

16. Ruy Cervantes, Mark Warschauer, Bonnie Nardi, and Nithya Sambasivan. 2011. Infrastructures for low-cost laptop use in Mexican schools. In *Proceedings of the SIGCHI Conference on Human Factors in Computing Systems*. ACM, 945–954.

17. Rakesh K Chadda and Koushik Sinha Deb. 2013. Indian family systems, collectivistic society and psychotherapy. *Indian Journal of Psychiatry* 55, Suppl 2 (2013), S299.

18. Malolan Chetlur, Ashay Tamhane, Vinay Kumar Reddy, Bikram Sengupta, Mohit Jain, Pongsakorn Sukjunnimit, and Ramrao Wagh. 2014. Edupal: Enabling blended learning in resource constrained environments. In *Proceedings of the Fifth ACM Symposium on Computing for Development*. ACM, 73–82.

19. Patricia Hill Collins. 2002. *Black feminist thought: Knowledge, consciousness, and the politics of empowerment*. Routledge.

20. Regin Joy Conejar, Haeng-Kon Kim, and Roger Y Lee. 2016. Opportunities Ahead the Future Mobile Learning. In *Software Engineering, Artificial Intelligence, Networking and Parallel/Distributed Computing*. Springer, 85–96.

21. Kimberle Crenshaw. 1989. Demarginalizing the intersection of race and sex: A black feminist critique of antidiscrimination doctrine, feminist theory and antiracist politics. *U. Chi. Legal F.* (1989), 139.

22. Julian Cristia, Pablo Ibarrarán, Santiago Cueto, Ana Santiago, and Eugenio Severín. 2017. Technology and child development: Evidence from the one laptop per child program. *American Economic Journal: Applied Economics* 9, 3 (2017), 295–320.

23. Andrew Cross, Edward Cutrell, and William Thies. 2012. Low-cost audience polling using computer vision. In *Proceedings of the 25th annual ACM symposium on User interface software and technology*. ACM, 45–54.

24. Larry Cuban and Petar Jandrić. 2015. The dubious promise of educational technologies: Historical patterns and future challenges. *E-Learning and Digital Media* 12, 3-4 (2015), 425–439.

25. Edward Cutrell, Jacki O'Neill, Srinath Bala, B Nitish, Andrew Cross, Nakull Gupta, Viraj Kumar, and William Thies. 2015. Blended learning in Indian colleges with massively empowered classroom. In *Proceedings of the Second (2015) ACM Conference on Learning@ Scale*. ACM, 47–56.

26. Kathy Davis. 2008. Intersectionality as buzzword: A sociology of science perspective on what makes a feminist theory successful. *Feminist theory* 9, 1 (2008), 67–85.

27. Rita Dhamoon. 2015. A feminist approach to decolonizing anti-racism: Rethinking transnationalism, intersectionality, and settler colonialism. *Feral Feminisms* 4 (2015), 20–37.

28. Rita Kaur Dhamoon. 2011. Considerations on mainstreaming intersectionality. *Political Research Quarterly* 64, 1 (2011), 230–243.
29. Amandeep Dhir, Nahla M Gahwaji, and Göte Nyman. 2013. The role of the iPad in the hands of the learner. *J. UCS* 19, 5 (2013), 706–727.
30. Conrado I Dotong, Evelyn L De Castro, and Joselito A Dolot. 2016. Barriers for Educational Technology Integration in Contemporary Classroom Environment. *Asia Pacific Journal of Education, Arts and Sciences* 3, 2 (2016).
31. Sarah Fox, Mariam Asad, Katherine Lo, Jill P Dimond, Lynn S Dombrowski, and Shaowen Bardzell. 2016. Exploring Social Justice, Design, and HCI. In *Proceedings of the 2016 CHI Conference Extended Abstracts on Human Factors in Computing Systems*. ACM, 3293–3300.
32. Sarah Fox, Amanda Menking, Stephanie Steinhardt, Anna Lauren Hoffmann, and Shaowen Bardzell. 2017. Imagining Intersectional Futures: Feminist approaches in CSCW. In *Companion of the 2017 ACM Conference on Computer Supported Cooperative Work and Social Computing*. ACM, 387–393.
33. Joseph B Giacquinta, Jo Anne Bauer, and Jane E Levin. 1993. *Beyond technology's promise: An examination of children's educational computing at home*. Cambridge University Press.
34. Javier Gil-Flores, Javier Rodríguez-Santero, and Juan-Jesús Torres-Gordillo. 2017. Factors that explain the use of ICT in secondary-education classrooms: The role of teacher characteristics and school infrastructure. *Computers in Human Behavior* 68 (2017), 441–449.
35. Ange-Marie Hancock. 2007. When multiplication doesn't equal quick addition: Examining intersectionality as a research paradigm. *Perspectives on politics* 5, 1 (2007), 63–79.
36. Ange-Marie Hancock. 2013. Empirical intersectionality: a tale of two approaches. *UC Irvine L. Rev.* 3 (2013), 259.
37. David Hankerson, Andrea R Marshall, Jennifer Booker, Houda El Mimouni, Imani Walker, and Jennifer A Rode. 2016. Does Technology Have Race?. In *Proceedings of the 2016 CHI Conference Extended Abstracts on Human Factors in Computing Systems*. ACM, 473–486.
38. Kurtis Heimerl, Janani Vasudev, Kelly G Buchanan, Tapan Parikh, and Eric Brewer. 2010a. A case study on designing interfaces for multiple users in developing regions. In *Proceedings of the First ACM Symposium on Computing for Development*. ACM, 9.
39. Kurtis Heimerl, Janani Vasudev, Kelly G Buchanan, Tapan Parikh, and Eric Brewer. 2010b. Metamouse: Improving multi-user sharing of existing educational applications. In *Proceedings of the 4th ACM/IEEE International Conference on Information and Communication Technologies and Development*. ACM, 19.
40. Lilly Irani, Janet Vertesi, Paul Dourish, Kavita Philip, and Rebecca E Grinter. 2010. Postcolonial computing: a lens on design and development. In *Proceedings of the SIGCHI conference on human factors in computing systems*. ACM, 1311–1320.
41. Matthew Kam, Anuj Kumar, Shirley Jain, Akhil Mathur, and John Canny. 2009a. Improving literacy in rural India: Cellphone games in an after-school program. In *Information and Communication Technologies and Development (ICTD), 2009 International Conference on*. IEEE, 139–149.
42. Matthew Kam, Akhil Mathur, Anuj Kumar, and John Canny. 2009b. Designing digital games for rural children: a study of traditional village games in India. In *Proceedings of the SIGCHI conference on Human factors in computing systems*. ACM, 31–40.
43. Naveena Karusala, Aditya Vishwanath, Arkadeep Kumar, Aman Mangal, and Neha Kumar. 2017. Care as a Resource in Underserved Learning Environments. In *Proceedings of the ACM on Computer-Supported Collaborative Work*, Vol. 1. 1–22.
44. Vikki S Katz and Carmen Gonzalez. 2016a. Community variations in low-income Latino families' technology adoption and integration. *American Behavioral Scientist* 60, 1 (2016), 59–80.
45. Vikki S Katz and Carmen Gonzalez. 2016b. Toward meaningful connectivity: using multilevel communication research to reframe digital inequality. *Journal of Communication* 66, 2 (2016), 236–249.
46. Konstantinos Kazakos, Siddhartha Asthana, Madeline Balaam, Mona Duggal, Amey Holden, Limalemla Jamir, Nanda Kishore Kannuri, Saurabh Kumar, Amarendar Reddy Manindla, Subhashini Arcot Manikam, and others. 2016. A Real-Time IVR Platform for Community Radio. In *Proceedings of the 2016 CHI Conference on Human Factors in Computing Systems*. ACM, 343–354.
47. John Kretzmann and John P McKnight. 1996. Assets-based community development. *National Civic Review* 85, 4 (1996), 23–29.
48. Anuj Kumar, Anuj Tewari, Geeta Shroff, Deepti Chittamuru, Matthew Kam, and John Canny. 2010. An exploratory study of unsupervised mobile learning in rural India. In *Proceedings of the SIGCHI Conference on Human Factors in Computing Systems*. ACM, 743–752.
49. Neha Kumar, Trevor Perrier, Michelle Desmond, Kiersten Israel-Ballard, Vikrant Kumar, Sudip Mahapatra, Anil Mishra, Shreya Agarwal, Rikin Gandhi, Pallavi Lal, and others. 2015. Projecting health: Community-led video education for maternal health. In *Proceedings of the Seventh International Conference on Information and Communication Technologies and Development*. ACM, 17.

50. Sonia Livingstone and Monica E Bulger. 2013. A global agenda for children's rights in the digital age. (2013).
51. Alice Ludvig. 2006. Differences between women? Intersecting voices in a female narrative. *European Journal of Women's Studies* 13, 3 (2006), 245–258.
52. George E Marcus. 1995. Ethnography in/of the world system: The emergence of multi-sited ethnography. *Annual review of anthropology* 24, 1 (1995), 95–117.
53. Alison Mathie and Gord Cunningham. 2005. Who is driving development? Reflections on the transformative potential of asset-based community development. *Canadian Journal of Development Studies/Revue canadienne d'études du développement* 26, 1 (2005), 175–186.
54. Mari J Matsuda. 1991. Beside my sister, facing the enemy: Legal theory out of coalition. *Stanford Law Review* (1991), 1183–1192.
55. Leslie McCall. 2005. The complexity of intersectionality. *Signs: Journal of women in culture and society* 30, 3 (2005), 1771–1800.
56. Sugata Mitra. 2015. Minimally Invasive Education: Pedagogy for Development in a Connected World. In *International Perspectives on Home Education.* Springer, 254–277.
57. Luis C Moll, Cathy Amanti, Deborah Neff, and Norma Gonzalez. 1992. Funds of knowledge for teaching: Using a qualitative approach to connect homes and classrooms. *Theory into practice* 31, 2 (1992), 132–141.
58. Allison J Morgan, Yuvay Meyers Ferguson, and Eileen M Trauth. 2015. Consumer Demographics and Internet Based Health Information Search in the United States: The Intersectionality of Gender, Race, and Class. *International Journal of E-Health and Medical Communications (IJEHMC)* 6, 1 (2015), 58–72.
59. Preeti Mudliar and Joyojeet Pal. 2013. ICTD in the popular press: media discourse around Aakash, the'world's cheapest tablet'. In *Proceedings of the Sixth International Conference on Information and Communication Technologies and Development: Full Papers-Volume 1.* ACM, 43–54.
60. Bonnie A. Nardi and Vicki L. O'Day. 1999. *Information Ecologies: Using Technology with Heart.* MIT Press, Cambridge, MA, USA.
61. Jennifer C Nash. 2008. Re-thinking intersectionality. *Feminist review* 89, 1 (2008), 1–15.
62. Joyojeet Pal, Udai Singh Pawar, Eric A Brewer, and Kentaro Toyama. 2006. The case for multi-user design for computer aided learning in developing regions. In *Proceedings of the 15th international conference on World Wide Web.* ACM, 781–789.
63. Seymour Papert and Idit Harel. 1991. Situating constructionism. *Constructionism* 36, 2 (1991), 1–11.
64. Katy E Pearce and Ronald E Rice. 2013. Digital divides from access to activities: Comparing mobile and personal computer Internet users. *Journal of Communication* 63, 4 (2013), 721–744.
65. Jahnavi Phalkey and Sumandro Chattapadhyay. 2015. The Aakash tablet and technological imaginaries of mass education in contemporary India. *History and Technology* 31, 4 (2015), 452–481.
66. Ann Phoenix and Pamela Pattynama. 2006. Intersectionality. (2006).
67. Baukje Prins. 2006. Narrative accounts of origins: a blind spot in the intersectional approach? *European Journal of Women's Studies* 13, 3 (2006), 277–290.
68. Jayson W Richardson. 2011. Challenges of adopting the use of technology in less developed countries: The case of Cambodia. *Comparative Education Review* 55, 1 (2011), 008–029.
69. Nithya Sambasivan, Ed Cutrell, Kentaro Toyama, and Bonnie Nardi. 2010. Intermediated technology use in developing communities. In *Proceedings of the SIGCHI Conference on Human Factors in Computing Systems.* ACM, 2583–2592.
70. Kamalesh Sarkar, Baishali Bal, Rita Mukherjee, Sekhar Chakraborty, Suman Saha, Arundhuti Ghosh, and Scott Parsons. 2008. Sex-trafficking, violence, negotiating skill, and HIV infection in brothel-based sex workers of eastern India, adjoining Nepal, Bhutan, and Bangladesh. *Journal of health, population, and nutrition* 26, 2 (2008), 223.
71. Ari Schlesinger, W Keith Edwards, and Rebecca E Grinter. 2017. Intersectional HCI: Engaging Identity through Gender, Race, and Class. In *Proceedings of the 2017 CHI Conference on Human Factors in Computing Systems.* ACM, 5412–5427.
72. Ariel Schwartz, Eva Kaplan, Evviva Weinraub Lajoie, Trey Terrell, and Esther Ajambo. 2015. Using a principal agent model to explain user-centered design challenges for mother tongue reading in Kenya. In *Proceedings of the Seventh International Conference on Information and Communication Technologies and Development.* ACM, 3.
73. Carly Shuler, Niall Winters, and Mark West. 2013. The future of mobile learning: Implications for policy makers and planners. *United Nations Educational, Scientific and Cultural Organization (UNESCO)* (2013), 7–35.
74. Kiley Sobel, Julie A Kientz, Tamara L Clegg, Carmen Gonzalez, and Jason C Yip. 2017. Equity & Inclusivity at IDC. In *Proceedings of the 2017 Conference on Interaction Design and Children.* ACM, 761–767.
75. J Michael Spector. 2001. An overview of progress and problems in educational technology. *Interactive educational multimedia: IEM* 3 (2001), 27–37.

76. Roy Steiner and Duncan Hanks. 2016. Digital Green: enabling a collective process of learning in rural development. In *Harnessing the Power of Collective Learning*. Routledge, 42–56.

77. Lucy Suchman. 1994. Speech acts and voices: Response to Winogradet al. *Computer supported cooperative work (CSCW)* 3, 1 (1994), 85–95.

78. M Sweeney. 2016. The intersectional interface. *The intersectional internet: Race, sex, class and culture online* (2016), 215–228.

79. Jo Tondeur, Johan van Braak, PA Ertmer, and Anne Ottenbreit-Leftwich. 2016. Understanding the relationship between teachers' pedagogical beliefs and technology use in education: A systematic review of qualitative evidence. *Educational Technology Research and Development* (2016).

80. Kentaro Toyama. 2011. Technology as amplifier in international development. In *Proceedings of the 2011 iConference*. ACM, 75–82.

81. Jan van Akker and Nienke Nieveen. 2017. The Role of Teachers in Design Research in Education. In *Making Change Happen*. Springer, 75–86.

82. Jyoti Verma and Harry C Triandis. 1999. The measurement of collectivism in India.. In *International Congress of the International Association for Cross-Cultural Psychology., 14th, Aug, 1998, Western Washington U, Bellingham, WA, US*. Swets & Zeitlinger Publishers.

83. Mark Warschauer. 2004. *Technology and social inclusion: Rethinking the digital divide*. MIT press.

84. Mark Warschauer. 2006. *Laptops and literacy: Learning in the wireless classroom*. Teachers College Press.

85. Tara J Yosso*. 2005. Whose culture has capital? A critical race theory discussion of community cultural wealth. *Race ethnicity and education* 8, 1 (2005), 69–91.

86. Nira Yuval-Davis. 2006. Intersectionality and feminist politics. *European Journal of Women's Studies* 13, 3 (2006), 193–209.

VMotion: Designing a Seamless Walking Experience in VR

Misha Sra
MIT Media Lab
Cambridge, MA USA
sra@media.mit.edu

Xuhai Xu
Tsinghua University
Beijing, China
xxh14@mails.tsinghua.edu.cn

Aske Mottelson
University of Copenhagen
Copenhagen, Denmark
amot@di.ku.dk

Pattie Maes
MIT Media Lab
Cambridge, MA USA
pattie@media.mit.edu

ABSTRACT
Physically walking in virtual reality can provide a satisfying sense of presence. However, natural locomotion in virtual worlds larger than the tracked space remains a practical challenge. Numerous redirected walking techniques have been proposed to overcome space limitations but they often require rapid head rotation, sometimes induced by distractors, to keep the scene rotation imperceptible. We propose a design methodology of seamlessly integrating redirection into the virtual experience that takes advantage of the perceptual phenomenon of *inattentional blindness*. Additionally, we present four novel visibility control techniques that work with our design methodology to minimize disruption to the user experience commonly found in existing redirection techniques. A user study ($N = 16$) shows that our techniques are imperceptible and users report significantly less dizziness when using our methods. The illusion of unconstrained walking in a large area ($16 \times 8m$) is maintained even though users are limited to a smaller ($3.5 \times 3.5m$) physical space.

ACM Classification Keywords
H.5.1. Information Interfaces and Presentation (e.g. HCI): Artificial, augmented, and virtual realities

Author Keywords
Virtual Reality; Reorientation; Seamless Experience; Context-Sensitive Design; Visibility Control; Locomotion;

INTRODUCTION
The ability to move is a fundamental requirement for exploration in both real and virtual worlds (VWs). Natural exploration is desirable for many practical virtual reality (VR) applications in areas of education, tourism, rehabilitation, and entertainment. Mapping physical space to a virtual space of the same size can support walking for navigation and interaction and provide a compelling experience [27, 34]. However, a major limitation is that physical dimensions of the tracked space constrain the size of the VWs that can be explored on foot. While navigation techniques, both design and device based like teleportation [1], magic carpets [15], miniaturization [35], or 360° treadmills [26] allow for experiencing VWs that are much larger than the tracked physical space, the sensation of walking is still not satisfactorily addressed. If the user cannot naturally move and engage with the virtual environment as if it were real, presence or the sense of 'being there' may break [24]. Research suggests that users navigate best with locomotion techniques that provide vestibular and proprioceptive feedback such as real walking [21]. Additionally, locomotion techniques that stimulate the vestibular and proprioceptive systems are less likely to cause VR sickness than locomotion interfaces that do not stimulate them [2, 21].

DIS '18, June 9–13, 2018, , Hong Kong

ISBN 978-1-4503-5198-0/18/06...$15.00
DOI: https://doi.org/10.1145/3196709.3196792

Redirected walking, a technique for continuous manipulation of mapping between physical and virtual rotations to steer the user away from the tracked space boundaries [20], has been shown to be effective for allowing natural and unconstrained walking in VWs. Other real walking locomotion interfaces include scaled translation gain [6, 39] or motion compression [14]. Both these interfaces either rotate the VW or scale the user's motion. While numerous redirection studies have demonstrated promising results, redirection techniques are still somewhat limited in their practical applicability for the typical consumer [33]. The techniques typically require a large physical space [18, 28], have difficulty changing a user's direction when the user gets close to tracked space boundaries [31], need frequent and rapid head rotations to keep the VW rotation imperceptible [20], and can cause virtual reality sickness [10].

Resetting, also known as reorientation, is a class of techniques used to steer the user away from physical boundaries. While redirection techniques are applied continuously as the user walks around, resetting techniques stop and reorient the user only at the boundary of the tracked physical space. Reorientation techniques rotate the VW around the user's current position. The user must also reorient their body by physically turning to be able to follow their desired path in the rotated VW. Williams et al. [40] proposed a reset technique that directs the user to walk backwards or to physically turn around while the VW remains frozen. A notable disadvantage of resetting is that it interrupts the experience and can thereby decrease presence and immersion. To address the need for rapid head rotation for redirection, Peck et al. [17] introduce a fast moving object called a distractor, which encourages users to rapidly turn their head back and forth for tracking its movements. However, the usefulness of the distractor is weakened as it can disrupt the user's experience and it requires users to be trained to follow it whenever it appears [3, 18]. General purpose distractors that effectively serve their purpose but intrude upon the scenario context, interrupt the flow of the narrative and can break the user's sense of presence.

In this paper, we present a design methodology and four visibility control techniques that work together to overcome previous limitations by integrating distractors into the narrative and making them part of the user's main activity in the VW. In our design, the distractors are what make the experience interactive and engaging and hence, in the rest of this work we refer to them as attractors. We leverage human perception, specifically, *inattentional blindness* [11] and some aspects of how the human visual system [37] functions to design interaction which allows us the opportunity to imperceptibly rotate the VW when needed. Unlike previous distractor-based methods that manipulate a user's physical trajectory by combining reorientation with redirection techniques [17], our methods do not use redirection (continuous VW rotation). We hypothesize that our embedded or context-sensitive design methodology along with visibility control techniques can help minimize breaks in presence from disruptions to the user's main activity, preclude the need for frequent and rapid user head rotation, reduce physical space requirements, successfully steer users away from boundaries, lessen virtual reality sickness, and maintain high presence in the virtual experience.

Our methodology of embedded or context-sensitive reorientation is based on the perceptual phenomenon of *inattentional blindness*, which suggests that a user does not perceive items that are in plain view [11] when they are intently focused on a different task. The methodology entails creating experiences that embed scene-relevant and task-relevant attractors into the narrative and the user's main activity in VR. The attractors spawn in appropriate spatio-temporal positions and fully engage users, allowing for organically integrating reorientation into the experience of, and interaction with the VW.

For designing interactions with the embedded attractors, we introduce the idea of using elements of visual and motion perception [37]. Specifically, we propose four general visibility control techniques: *reduced field of view*, *limited viewing distance*, *tilted viewing angle* and *shallow depth of field*. To demonstrate how the visibility control techniques and the embedded attractors work together, we present a fully working VR experience. Our study results show that VW rotation using our techniques is less noticeable than VW rotation without these techniques and has minimal impact on the experience even when users do notice the associated scene rotation. Reported dizziness using our techniques is significantly lower due to using real-walking for locomotion and imperceptibility of VR rotation, leading to a more comfortable and seamless VR experience. Because users are simply performing their intended activities, and the attractors are not disruptors, the users' sense of immersion and presence is maintained.

The key contributions of our work are:

- Design of visibility control techniques based on elements of visual perception to make reorientation imperceptible.
- A design methodology to seamlessly integrate reorientation into the user's main activity through *attractors*.
- Four design strategies based on the perceptual phenomenon of inattentional blindness for VR designers who want to create seamless real-walking experiences in VR.

RELATED WORK

This paper presents a design methodology and visibility control techniques that together enable walking through an immersive VW that is considerably larger than the available tracked space. We summarize below a few of the most directly related works.

Real Walking in Virtual Reality

The benefits of supporting natural body movement in VWs have been extensively studied. Real walking has been shown to provide a greater sense of presence than walking-in-place or flying [35], better performance on search tasks [21], and benefits for memory and cognition [41]. Redirected walking or redirection has been shown to successfully support real walking in VR [20]. Two common approaches to redirection are: introducing a VW rotational gain in order to imperceptibly rotate the scene such that the user stays away from the boundaries of the tracked space [20], and (2) scaling linear movement to enable travel over larger distances in the VW [6]. Other techniques for supporting walking in virtual environments like estimating walkable areas automatically from a 3D scan of the physical space [27] or by using simultaneous localization and mapping (SLAM) [13] have also been explored. A study on redirected walking shows that users can be physically turned approximately 49% more or 20% less than the perceived virtual rotation without visibly noticing [28]. A walking arc with a radius of at least 22m is necessary for scene rotation or curvature gains to be imperceptible to the user though most users do not have this much tracked space [28]. As both redirection approaches introduce a visual-vestibular conflict, they can cause dizziness or virtual reality sickness [4]. In contrast to redirection techniques, our method does not continuously manipulate the mapping between physical and virtual motions. Instead, we rotate the scene only when the user is engaged in interacting with the VW, thereby making any rotation largely imperceptible.

Reorientation

While redirection techniques are applied continuously as the user walks around, reorientation or resetting techniques stop and reorient the user only at the boundary of the tracked physical space [40]. A notable disadvantage of resetting is that it interrupts the user and depending on the frequency of interruption, it can negatively impact the immersive experience. To mitigate potential breaks in presence, Peck et al. [17] combined distractors with redirection. The distractors were preferred over visual or audio reset instructions. However, the out of place distractors and the user training required to look at the distractors impeded the flow of narrative by distracting from the user's main goal in the virtual experience. Our method integrates the reorientation techniques into the user's primary activity. We use interactions with attractors in the VW to advance the narrative and manipulate a user's physical path. We rotate the scene, only when the user is engaged in a task, towards the direction that can lead them away from the boundary.

Perception

Magicians have been exploiting the limits of perception and attention for centuries. Redirection and reorientation techniques work because visual perception dominates proprioception in VR if the magnitude of the conflict is within tolerable limits [20, 28]. In Infinite Walking [30], the VR scenario instructs users to explore the environment while stopping at specific points to take panoramic photos in the virtual world. To take a panoramic photo, the user needs to turn 360° and while they are turning, the virtual world is rotated such that when they stop, they are correctly aligned to walk forward in both the virtual and physical spaces [30]. Visual motion perception serves many roles, including perception of depth, the separation of objects, and the estimation of the motion of objects in the world [38]. Everyday visual experience shows that humans can see things move and can judge how fast and in what direction they move, with some accuracy. Research indicates that three dimensional perception of position and orientation is largely affected by reference objects in the field of view [37, 38]. Hence, the fewer reference elements in the scene, the less a user will be aware of the self body scale information [37], and thus, be less sensitive to any changes of the background. In order to make movement unnoticeable, we exploit the underlying process of motion perception in our visibility control techniques.

Change blindness [23], a perceptual phenomenon when a person fails to detect an obvious change to an object or scene, has been successfully used as a redirection technique [32]. Another type of phenomenon is inattentional blindness, where a user does not perceive items that are plainly in view [11]. The famous Invisible Gorilla Test shows that when humans keep their attention on the main task, they fail to notice other unexpected changes [22]. The difference between change blindness and inattentional blindness lies in the fact that the former is the failure to notice an obvious change in the scene from before while the latter is the failure to notice something incongruent in plain view [7]. The design of our visibility control techniques is based on the perceptual phenomenon of inattentional blindness.

DESIGN METHODOLOGY

Embedded Context-Sensitive Distractors

An attractor is presented when the user approaches the boundary of the safe area. We define the term embedded context-sensitive attractor to encompass the general notion of attractors

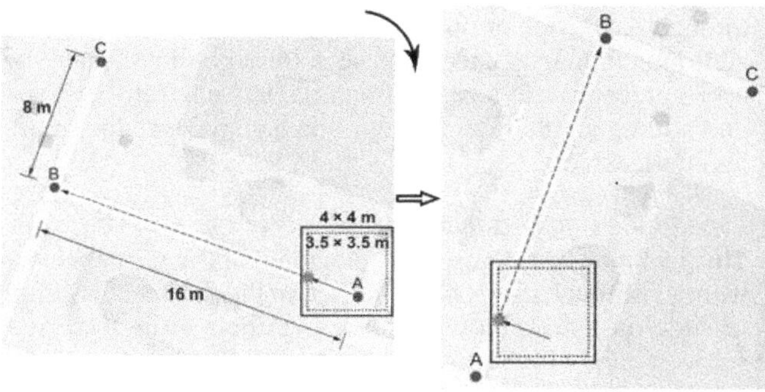

Figure 1: Virtual world rotation. Black square is the tracked space. Left: At the boundary of the safe area (red dot), one of our reorientation techniques is triggered randomly to engage the user in an interactive activity relevant to their goal. During the interaction, the VW is rotated by 90 ° to lead the user away from the safe area boundary. Right: The user (red dot) position shows newly available walking space inside the tracked area after virtual world rotation.

that are coherent with the narrative, related user interactions, and the virtual environment. For example, in games modeled after real world places, attractors like a bird in a park or an enemy in a battle scene would not feel out of place and any interaction with them could be seamlessly integrated into the user's activity and goals in that VR experience. Blending reorientation events into the narrative, such that interaction with them feels natural and organic, requires designing the experience with reorientation in mind instead of layering the techniques *post-factum*. Seamless integration allows the scene to be rotated while the user interacts with the attractor (see Figure 1) thereby reorienting their physical trajectory while maintaining the virtual one. The result is reduced interruption of primary activity and enhanced presence that comes from natural, non-disrupted real-walking based movement, and the VR experience.

Visibility Control Techniques

We propose a new type of reorientation method with four visibility control techniques: *reduced field of view*, *limited viewing distance*, *tilted viewing angle* and *shallow depth of field*, designed to manipulate elements of human visual and motion perception. According to Gibson [5], everyday living depends on direct perception that guides action intuitively and automatically. Our visibility control techniques work with embedded attractors to engage the user in scene and activity relevant tasks. This provides us the "opportunity" to furtively rotate the virtual scene when the user is performing a task as part of their VR experience.

Reduced Field of View

This technique requires users to look through devices or small openings that are appropriate for the task they need to perform. Doing so effectively limits a user's field of view (FoV) which in turn can make it difficult for them to notice VW rotation. Examples of devices include looking through a pair of binoculars, a telescope or microscope, a camera viewfinder or any other type of reticle. Examples of openings include holes, cracks, slits, or other similar apertures. The narrative needs to provide a reason (embedded attractor) for the user to look through the device or opening. Binoculars or microscopes can additionally magnify the view seen through them, changing a user's perception of size and motion relative to self-body scale, and adding another component that can make scene rotation less noticeable.

Limited Viewing Distance
This technique involves using elements of the virtual environment to limit the user's ability to see in the distance. Examples include dust, fog, blowing leaves, garden sprinklers, heavy snow or rain which reduce the distance that users can see to a few meters. Reducing distance visibility removes visual reference points from the viewable scene which can make VW rotation imperceptible. Mixed with nearby attractors to allow the user to focus on or interact with something instead of feeling lost, this technique can provide another opportunity to rotate the VW.

Tilted Viewing Angle
This technique requires users to look towards the clear sky or any background that has a limited number of objects which can act as visual reference points for indicating motion. The user can be made to look up or down by using an attractor. The attractor needs to be designed such that it fills the user's field of view, when held or looked at against a partially empty background. Doing so provides an opportunity to subtly rotate the VW. Examples include reading a book up close or inspecting an insect or other object closely against a plain background.

Shallow Depth of Field
Depth of field (DoF) is the distance between the nearest and farthest objects in a scene where objects appear acceptably sharp in an image. In cinema, manipulating DoF is used as a method to guide the viewer's attention by selectively bringing objects into focus while blurring others. For example, changing the center of attention in a scene by having a foreground object in focus, with the background out of focus. VR hardware uses fixed-focus displays, making it difficult to attain a natural depth of field as the user's eyes shift focus from objects in background to those in the foreground. Like the storytelling mechanic from cinema, this technique simulates DoF by blurring the background and keeping the foreground in focus thereby indirectly guiding the user's attention. The foreground object is the distractor while the blurred background and inattentional blindness allow for imperceptibly rotating the VW.

In both *Limited Viewing Distance* and *Shallow Depth of Field*, visibility of background reference points is masked to reduce noticeability of scene rotation. The difference lies in the design of the interaction. The former involves passively tracking moving objects in the scene while the latter involves active interaction through dialog or other means with one or more characters in the scene.

Implementation Criteria
The two main implementation criteria in our design are, 1) having tasks or attractors along a path that are coherent with the scene or experience, and 2) having elements in the scene that can affect the user's visibility temporarily such as reducing their field of view or limiting the viewing distance. Both design elements serve to create opportunities for interaction and visibility control which in turn allow us to imperceptibly rotate the virtual world, leading to a seamless walking experience. While several linear narrative based experiences could take advantage of our design, what constitutes the *attractors* and which scene objects can aid the design of visibility control may not be readily obvious for all scenarios. Sandbox experiences that support open-ended exploration over task completion for making progress through the experience, may also be able to use our design if suitable attractors and other objects exist in the scene.

Below are three exemplary scenarios that meet our implementation criteria that show that within the stated scope, there are a variety of VR experiences where our design is suitable.

Treasure hunt
Users follow a map to the treasure which would require them to stay on a predetermined path. The attractors would be objects that provide clues to the location of the treasure like small puzzles or tasks. Scene elements affecting visibility would be things such as a pirate's spyglass or a large wind blown pirate flag or the ship's sail. Looking through the spyglass would *reduce field of view* while a flag or sail billowing in the wind would temporarily *limit viewing distance*.

Job Simulator extension
Job Simulator is one of the most popular VR games currently available *. In our version of the game, that allows users to walk around naturally, the chef would walk to and from the kitchen along a specified path that goes between the restaurant tables. Cooking and cleaning interactions, talking with customers, and dropped objects would serve as attractors. Visibility would be affected by things like waiters walking by with platters of food (*limited viewing distance*) or the user peering into the fridge for food (*reduced field of view*).

Pokemon like game
Here the main task would be to walk along a fixed path through the forest collecting things or monsters, interacting with them, and battling them. Trees or insect swarms would serve to affect visibility by blocking the user's *field of view* or *reducing viewing distance*.

We believe the designed visibility control techniques can significantly impact a user's visual and motion perception in VR. When used with appropriate embedded attractors, they can make users less aware of VW rotation.

IMPLEMENTATION
To investigate the capabilities of the embedded design methodology and the visibility control techniques, we created a virtual experience set in park (see Figure 1). In the game, we ask the user to walk from point A to B and then to C where the points are located on three corners of a $16 \times 8m$ rectangle. The rectangle defines the paved walking paths in the virtual park.

*https://owlchemylabs.com/job-simulator-sales-milestone/

Figure 2: View of the park looking at the starting point A in the foreground and the first destination point B marked by a yellow star at the end of the 16*m* long straight path.

Background Story

In order to seamlessly integrate reorientation into the experience, we designed tasks that a user needs to accomplish as part of the game experience. Our user is a young naturalist, who goes to an small park for collecting data on exotic birds and bugs. The naturalist begins their quest near the fountain in the center of the park (point A). They are told that successfully arriving at point B in the distance will give them new tools to help analyze their gathered data (see Figures 1 and 2). After arriving at point B, they are asked to walk to the next checkpoint C, which holds information about secret locations teeming with even more exotic flora and fauna. As the naturalist walks towards points B and C, they are presented with opportunities to collect data. Gathering data involves careful observation of birds or insects, whether it is viewing through binoculars or through unveiling treasures hidden in amber. On occasion, the naturalist interacts with other people in the park, who are fellow naturalists or park visitors, looking for help or information.

Reorientation Techniques

The physical tracking area is a $4 \times 4m$ square and the "safe area" is set to a $3.5 \times 3.5m$ inner square. Whenever the user is about to walk out of the safe area, a reorientation event is triggered, i.e., a task-relevant attractor is spawned causing the user to stop and interact. The reorientation rotates the VW by 90°, which reorients the user away from the boundary that they originally approached. Our $3.5 \times 3.5m$ space is about half the size of the tracking space used by Peck et al. [17] for moving in a comparably sized virtual space. While still larger than the tracking space that most consumers may have at home, we believe in our future work we can design a system that can support a seamless walking experience for most home VR users.

The current design can support branching paths (though not tested in the user study) by presenting appropriate attractors as incentives for decision making. For example, showing participants an attractor some distance away from a T-junction or a crossroads to encourage them to take one of the many path options. The current setup can also support slightly curved paths in the virtual world while allowing the user to walk on curved paths in the tracked space. However, given the small tracking space, the experience is not very different from users walking on a straight path. Prior work shows that truly walking on a curved path while thinking you are walking in a straight line in the virtual world requires a path of radius 22m [28].

Before we describe each technique's implementation in the game in detail, we first introduce *directionally constant* need-based rotation in contrast to directionally variable continuous rotation [17], as our scene rotation method. When the user approaches the boundary, the desired direction of the scene after reorientation has already been determined based on the user's position, approach angle, and future direction. For instance, in Figure 1 when the user starting at point A reaches the red dot at the inner square's boundary, we know that we need to rotate the scene clockwise by 90°. If the user approaches a boundary by walking straight at it, then either a clockwise or a counterclockwise rotation works. We define *directionally constant* rotation as – a method to insert desired rotation that does not change direction once the scene starts rotating. This is different from directionally variable and continuous rotation where the VW rotation direction is based on the user's head rotation direction [17] and changes continuously.

We set the *directionally constant* rotation gain rate to 0.5 but this rate can be adjusted as needed depending on the size of the physical space. When the user turns in the desired direction while interacting with the environment, the VW rotates half as fast. However when the user turns in the opposite direction, instead of rotating the scene 1.5 times faster, we temporarily set the world's rotation speed to be the same as the user's turning speed. This is because prior research shows that users are more sensitive to scene motion if the scene moves against head rotation than if the scene moves with head rotation [8, 28]. Compared to the distractors in Peck's work that always move in one direction [16], the *directionally constant* rotation method introduces asymmetric rotations that allow both the user and the attractors to move in any direction, hence enlarging the design space of attractors.

$$\begin{aligned} Gain &= \frac{rotation_{virtual}}{rotation_{user}} \\ &= \begin{cases} 0.5 & \text{user rotates in the desired direction} \\ 1.0 & \text{user rotates in the opposite direction} \end{cases} \end{aligned}$$

Note that our methods do not continuously manipulate the mapping between the physical and virtual motions, thereby avoiding a visual-vestibular conflict and accompanied dizziness. We only rotate the scene when the user is interacting with the attractors. Since our physical space is much smaller than spaces used previously to demonstrate redirection techniques [17, 33], the effectiveness of slow, continuous redirection is limited. Our pilot study found that continuous rotation in a small space is very noticeable and can cause nausea. An added benefit of rotating the scene only when the user is busily engaged is the level of control it allows designers. For example, if the path in the virtual world is long and straight, then the physical path will consist of a number of short relatively straight line segments. Compared to a set of unpredictable curves that arise due to continuous rotation, the straight line segments can be more easily controlled and designed.

Because we only use reorientation events and not continuous redirection, we can easily calculate the minimum number of reorientation events needed for a space of known size. For instance, if the safe area is a square (as is the case in our space) with width d and the user needs to walk a straight path with length l, then the ideal number of reorientation events c can be calculated as:

$$c = \max\{\frac{l}{d} - 1, 0\}$$

This number can be used as a reference by designers and developers for planning and creating the requisite number of attractors and visibility control methods.

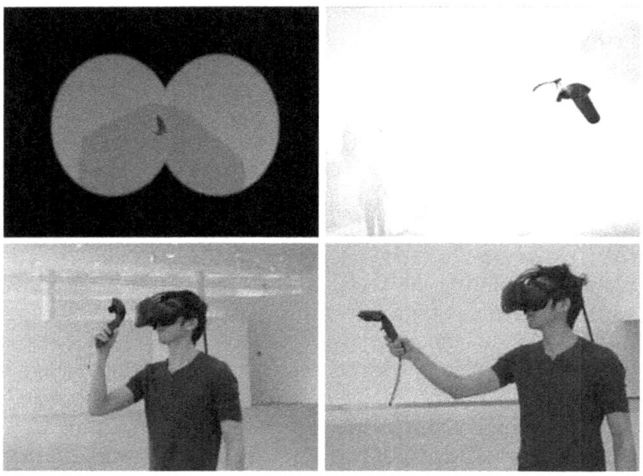

(a) Viewing through Device (b) Change in Environment

Figure 3: (a): The bird is 3m above the ground, 5m horizontally away from the user. It flies in a 180° arc with the user as the center of the circle (radius 5m). The user holds the 'binoculars' close to their eyes to look at the bird through them. (b): The insects are 1.5m above the ground, 1m horizontally away from the user. They fly in a circle of radius 1m with the user as the center. The user can reach out with their hand to 'touch' the dragonflies.

Viewing through Device

This technique uses the *Reduced Field of View* visibility control method. It is implemented as an exotic bird that appears in the distance as our naturalist walks down the path towards points B or C. When the bird appears, the user receives a notification (both text and audio) asking them to pick up binoculars from the ground to observe the bird (see Figure 3a). The bird, acting as an attractor, flies around the user in a pre-determined path in the sky. To keep the bird inside the binoculars' reduced FoV, the user needs to turn their head and body. As the user follows the movement of the bird through the binoculars, the *directionally constant* rotation gain is injected into the VW. If the user stops looking through the binoculars, the rotation is halted. The bird leaves once the VW is rotated 90°. A notification informs the user that enough data on the bird has been collected and they can put down the binoculars. The user adjusts their body orientation (if any) to allow them to continue walking along the path.

Change in Environment

We implement this technique using the *Limited Viewing Distance* method. Generating fog around the user obscures the background. Several insects swarm when the fog rises and fly around the user a circle with random directions and speeds (see Figure 3b). The radius of the circle is set small enough for the user to see the attractors (insects) but not much else beyond the fog is visible. A notification asks the user to observe the insects and to keep at least one of them in focus, which causes the user to turn their head and rotate as the insect leads them. When the fog is thick enough to cover the background, the VW is rotated. Similar to the first technique, once the world rotates 90°, the insects leave and the fog gradually dissipates. Another notification pops up indicating the end of data collection and asking the user to continue walking to their destination.

Interaction with Object

This technique is based on the *Tilted Viewing Angle* visibility control method. It is triggered when the naturalist walks by a tree. An opaque piece of amber drops close to them and a notification directs their attention to the fallen amber. They are asked to pick it and hold it up high against the sky. While doing so, they are also directed to spin their body until they find the correct light and viewing angle to see the insect trapped inside. *Tilt angle* or viewing angle is defined as the head pitch angle, positive for looking up and negative for looking down. When the *tilt angle* reaches a threshold (empirically set at 45° in our example), the user needs to rotate their body to find the right light and viewing angle conditions for the amber to become transparent (see Figure 4a). They need to spin 180° (either clockwise or counter-clockwise, depending on the desired direction of the scene after reorientation) in the physical world to accomplish this task. The amber becomes clearer as the user spins until becoming completely transparent when the user is fully turned to reveal the insect inside. The *directionally constant* rotation gain is added to the VW when the user is spinning while looking up. A message saying "collecting data" shows up for three seconds after the user's body is fully turned to allow time for rotating the VW. The user is then asked to put the amber back on the ground and continue walking to their destination.

Interaction with Character

This technique is instantiated by a human character approaching our naturalist to ask about other locations for collecting data or to ask if the naturalist happened to come across a set of lost keys. It is based on the *Shallow Depth of Field* method. As the user turns to locate the source of the sound (the character), the background is blurred to mimic shallow DoF but the character in the foreground stays in focus (see Figure 4b). The character paces back and forth in a predetermined circle around the user, which induces the user to turn back and forth as they listen to and engage with the character. A conversation is made possible by the user responding to questions asked by the character. The VW is rotated when the character

(a) Interaction with Object (b) Interaction with Character

Figure 4: (a): The green slider indicates the head tilt, with 45° as the maximum. The blue slider indicates how much the user has rotated the body, with 180° as the maximum. The user holds a piece of amber up high against the sky. (b): The virtual character is 1.5m away from the user and depth of field is set as 2m. The character walks back and forth in a 180° arc with the user as the center (radius 1.5m). The user waves to the character.

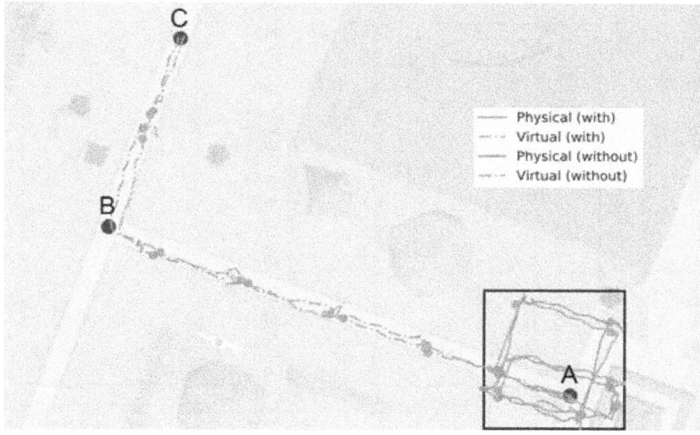

Figure 5: Physical and virtual paths of one participant in the park as seen from a top-down view. Dots represent the points where reorientation was triggered.

paces. Even though the world rotation ends fairly quickly, the character continues talking for a few more seconds to end the conversation in a natural manner.

EVALUATION

Participants and Apparatus

We invited 16 participants (6 females) to evaluate our techniques, with an average age of 21.9 ($SD = 5.1$). We used an HTC Vive headset during the study, as it gave us a room-scale tracked space without requiring any third party position tracking systems. Our tracked area was set as $4 \times 4m$, and the user was required to walk along the edge of a $16 \times 8m$ rectangle in the virtual scene.

Design

We investigated the effect of our visibility control techniques on the participants' sense of presence, level of dizziness, and reported discernibility of virtual world rotation in a within-subjects study. Each participant experienced two sessions, one with our visibility techniques, hereon referred to as *with* session and the other without the techniques, hereon referred to as *without* session. Half of the participants began with the *with* condition and the other half experienced the *without* condition first.

In the *with* session, when reorientation was triggered, i.e., the participant got near the boundary of the inner square, the system automatically and randomly selected one of the four methods described above and displayed relevant instructions to the participant for accomplishing the task. In contrast, during the *without* session, the four visibility manipulation techniques were removed but the attractors appeared and the scene was rotated like the originally proposed redirection technique [20]. For the reduced *Reduced Field of View* technique, binoculars were removed but the bird attractor still appeared. Instructions were modified to remove any reference to binoculars and participants were asked to simply look at the bird. In the case of *Limited Viewing Distance*, no fog was generated and the user was asked to look at the nearby flying insects. In the *Tilted Viewing Angle*, the *tilt angle* threshold was removed and participants could spin their body without needing to hold the amber up against the sky for viewing. Finally, in the *Shallow Depth of Field* technique, the background was not blurred during the interaction with the virtual character. All other factors (e.g., tasks, attractors, environment) remained unchanged in the *without* session.

After each session, the participant completed a questionnaire, hereon referred to as Q1, which consisted of the following parts:

1. Demographic questions and a previous VR experience question (1-7 point Likert Scale, Never before – A great deal)

2. Four questions from the Slater-Usoh-Steed (SUS) presence questionnaire [36] (7-point Likert Scale, Not at all - A lot)

3. One experience of dizziness question from the Kennedy Simulator Sickness questionnaire [9] modified from a 4-point scale to a 7-point Likert scale (Not at all – A lot)

4. An open ended question about anything the participant found unusual during the experience.

In order to eliminate the carry-over effect between questions about presence, the demographic questions were interspersed with the other questions, as suggested by [25]. Since participants needed to fill the questionnaire after each session, they ended up answering the demographic questions twice. After a participant finished both sessions, we asked them to fill another questionnaire, hereon referred to as Q2, which was composed of five questions. Four questions asked participants to compare noticeability of VW rotation between *with* and *without* conditions for each visibility technique. The fifth question asked them to compare overall noticeability of scene rotation in both conditions.

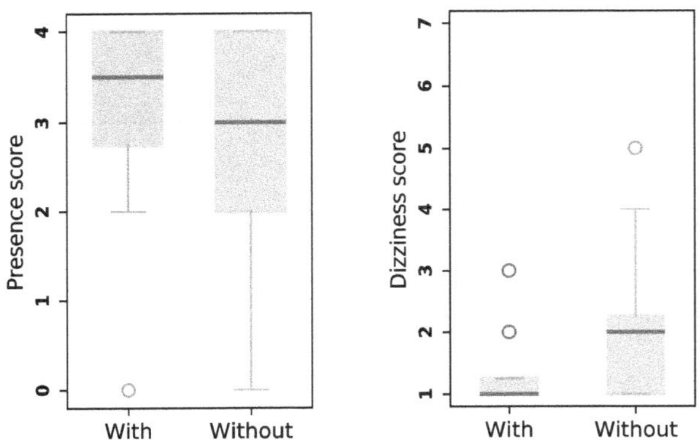

(a) Presence Score (b) Dizziness Score

Figure 6: Presence and dizziness scores in the *with* session and *without* sessions. Overall, participants reported high presence and low dizziness in both conditions.

Procedure

Before starting the first session, participants were asked to sign a consent form and read the background story. They were provided with a list of tasks to accomplish in the park. They were also shown how to use the Vive hand controller for picking up objects. We helped them put on the HMD and headphones before getting started with the first session. Each session took about 7-8 minutes, following which the participants answered Q1. A researcher held the Vive cables to prevent the participant from accidentally tripping. After completing both sessions, we told the participants that they had walked in a virtual park which was 8 times larger than the physical area they were in. We explained how scene rotation worked when they interacted with birds, insects and virtual characters in the park. When the participants indicated understanding the reorientation concept, we asked them to complete Q2 for comparing how obvious was the VW rotation in either session.

RESULTS

Participants walked to the final destination with an average of 6.8 reorientation events ($SD = 1.0$). A paired t-test did not show any significant difference between the two sessions on the number of reorientation events (6.7 ± 1.3 for *with* vs 6.9 ± 0.8 for *without*, $p = 0.41$) or on the average duration (18.2 ± 5.5 for *with* vs 16.9 ± 3.0 for *without*, $p = 0.14$) of reorientation. Figure 5 shows four walking paths of one participant, two for each session (virtual and physical). Note the similarity between the sessions, both in the paths and in the positions where the reorientation events happened. This indicates that users behaved very similarly in both sessions and removes the effect of behavior difference on the results of our questionnaires.

Presence and Dizziness

In Q1, four questions are related to presence. The presence score is the count of questions answered with 5 or higher [12, 17], and can range from 0 to 4. Figure 6a shows the scores of the *with* (3.8 ± 1.1) and the *without* (3.3 ± 1.3) sessions. Treating the presence score as binomially distributed for logistic regression on session, as intended by the SUS approach [25], there is no significant difference between the two sessions ($\chi^2_1 = 0.5, p = 0.49$). Participants in both sessions were able to maintain high presence during the study.

The results for the question about the experience of dizziness are shown in Figure 6b, which indicate that overall participants experienced low dizziness in both sessions (1.4 ± 0.7 for *with* and 2.1 ± 1.2 for *without*). However, there still exists a difference between the two conditions: 75% of the participants rated the lowest score in the *with* session while only 37.5% rated 1 in the *without* session. According to whether a player rated dizziness 1 or not, the chi-square test shows a significant difference in dizziness between the two conditions ($\chi^2_1 = 4.6, p = 0.03$). Players in the *without* condition experienced higher dizziness than those in the *with* condition.

Reorientation Noticeability

We discovered interesting results from the last question in Q1, which asked participants if they noticed anything unusual during the experience. Note that when the user answered this question after each session, they had not yet been informed about the rotation of the virtual world. In *with* session, 14 out of 16 users did not notice the reorientation at all. While in *without* session, seven reported feeling the virtual world rotation. Chi-square test shows significant difference between the two sessions ($\chi^2_1 = 3.9, p = 0.05$). This means our techniques decreased the obviousness of rotation effectively.

Among the 10 users who rated their previous VR experience below four, four users explicitly mentioned noticing rotation of the world in the *without* session. *"I was able to realize that the scene shifted directions when I was performing a task."* (P1). *"When rotating my head the direction of the path changed while looking away. Sometimes rotating and walking felt like they were happening more quickly than if I was doing those actions in real life."* (P2). However, none of the 10 participants mentioned the rotation of the world in the *with* session. Among the remaining six participants who reported being familiar with VR, three of them noticed the rotation of the scene in the *without* session. Two of these three participants also noticed the rotation in the *with* session. One user explicitly expressed their preference for the techniques in the *with* session. *"I liked the obscure mist and vignette binoculars. It helped reduce nausea."* (P15). Splitting participants into two groups based on VR experience (answer above 4 or not), chi-square test was applied on two sessions respectively. The results (*with* session: $\chi^2_{1,with} = 3.8, p_{with} = 0.05$, *without* session: $\chi^2_{1,without} = 1.6, p_{without} = 0.21$) indicate that unexperienced VR users were less aware of the reorientation, especially in *with* session.

We arrive at a similar conclusion from the results of Q2. Fifteen participants responded to Q2. 11 of them agreed that the rotation with our methods was less obvious (see Figure 7). Among the four techniques, *Limited Viewing Distance* had the best performance, with 12 out of 16 users saying rotation with

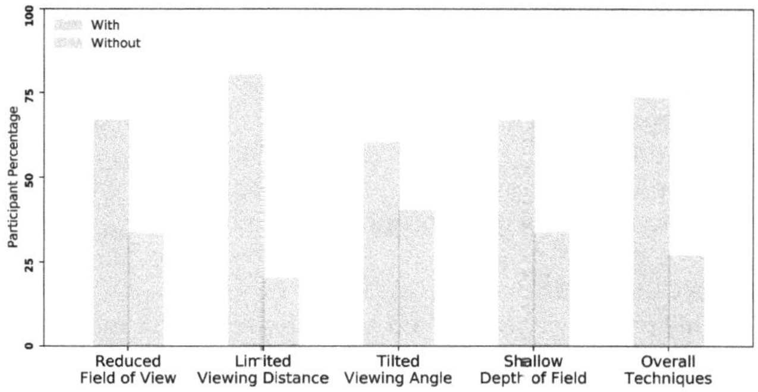

Figure 7: Number of participants who found VW rotation imperceptible for each visibility control technique when asked to compare between the *with* and *without* conditions.

fog is less obvious. *Tilted Viewing Angle* comparatively performed the worst, with only 9 users supporting that technique.

Discussion

According to the context-sensitive design method, attractors were embedded into the narrative in both sessions of the user study, and the only difference was the presence or absence of visibility control methods. User interaction with the attractors (bird, amber, character and insects) was part of the participants' main activity of data collection as a naturalist. Embedding attractors into the main activity reduced disruptions and did not require experimenter intervention to keep users within the tracked space bounds, likely leading to a high presence score.

The results from our user study are very promising. Presence was high in both conditions (Median$_{with}$ = 3.5, Median$_{without}$ = 3, with 4 as the maximum) likely because the participants could walk to navigate the VW and there was visuo-motor synchrony in their hand-head movements [24, 35]. The visibility control methods decreased reported dizziness significantly. Moreover, a majority of the participants reported that the rotation in the *with* session was less obvious than in the *without* session. Both these results support the effectiveness of our techniques and can be explained by the workings of the human motion perception system [38].

Ratings on the noticeability questions indicated that inattentional blindness is quite effective in virtual environments. Only two participants out of 16 (both experienced 3D gamers) noticed the world rotate in the *with* condition when asked to identify any unusual events in the qualitative questionnaire. All other participants stated they did not notice anything unusual about rotation of the VW.

Given the difference in dizziness for each condition, we believe our reorientation techniques proved quite effective and thus desirable for inclusion in VR design. Inattentional blindness when paired with an appropriate attractor can successfully create a natural walking experience in a small space.

Another interesting finding from the study is that participants with experience playing video games reported higher sensitivity to the reorientation. We speculate that because playing video games improves spatial skills [29], participants were able to discern changes in the virtual environment, though specific reasons for this difference are not evident in our data.

STRATEGIES FOR EMBEDDING ATTRACTORS

The main goal is for designers to think about and plan for reorientation through interaction with *attractors* as part of the narrative design process. By attracting a user's attention away from the horizon to objects up close or up above, designers can remove or mask reference objects in the scene, that can otherwise make scene rotation obvious. Designers should think about *attractors* as the moving elements in the scene while static objects or objects used to interact with the *attractors* form the essence of visibility control. For e.g., the bird in the presented implementation is the *attractor* while the binoculars represent one type of visibility control technique, namely *Reduced Field of View*.

Design of Attractors

For the design of attractors, Peck et al. [17] answered the question of *when* should the attractors appear and disappear. We answer the question of *what* should appear during the reorientation. Our design focuses on mechanisms for integrating attractors into the narrative and the user's main activity, which can reduce disruption of the immersive experience caused by non-integrated attractors [16]. In our work, we embed the attractors into the biological data collection task that the naturalist needs to accomplish. Not only are attractors seamlessly embedded into the experience serving to forward the narrative, they are also the primary interactive elements in the VW. Designers and developers need to identify potential attractors in their scenarios and distinguish the moving and interactive attractors that can be incorporated into a task the user may need to do for progressing through the experience.

Designing Visibility Controls

The design of visibility control methods serves to reduce the noticeability of the reorientation while the user is engaged in interaction with the distractor. Developers can use any visibility manipulation method that is appropriate for their scenario, for e.g., a microscope in a virtual classroom or an ash filled volcanic eruption. The design of visibility control approaches should stay separated from the design of attractors for lending more flexibility and variety in the creation of interaction mechanics.

Attractors and Space Size

Traditional redirection methods that involve continuous scene rotation can become annoying if the tracking space is very small, which is the case for a large number of consumer room-scale setups [19]. The small space causes reorientation events to be triggered frequently in order to keep users in the tracked area and continuous and fast scene rotation can cause dizziness and nausea. Our pilot study showed that on average users got bored after the same reorientation technique was repeated more than 5 times (e.g., a mocking bird frequently appearing and disappearing) thereby reducing their sense of presence. However, our methodology allows for the design of diverse attractor and visual control technique combinations given that most VR experiences have moving objects and interactivity, the two main constituents of an attractor. For added variety, in our virtual data collection task, we implemented more than 20 types of birds and insects. Using 3D models with high detail and adding stats for discovered items can make each reorientation event seem novel, even though the interaction or reorientation mechanic is repeated. This is related to item collection games like the incredibly popular Pokémon[†], where the Pokémon capturing mechanism is repeated but individual Pokémon look different and have different stats and fighting capabilities. The combination of attractors and visibility control techniques can thus generate a large number of possible reorientation mechanics that can be used frequently, based on space size, without immediately and negatively impacting the user's experience.

Rotation as Gameplay

Our reorientation methods embed rotation of the virtual world into the users' interactive experience. Previous research suggests that a 0.5 rotation gain rate is very noticeable by 80% when used by itself [4, 28]. However, in our study, less than 40% of the participants perceived the rotation in the *without* session. The percentage was even lower (less than 20%) in the *with* session. This indicates that our embedded techniques may have a positive effect on reducing the obviousness of world rotation which can lead to improved satisfaction with the VR experience and reduced VR sickness.

When attractors are part of the experience, users may be less aware of the secondary function of the attractors, which is to allow us to rotate the VW imperceptibly. Together, functional and interactive attractors with visibility manipulation techniques can more easily elicit *inattentional blindness*, leading users to overlook the rotation of the virtual world. This gives designers and developers an interesting arsenal of tools at their disposal to integrate real walking in their VR applications.

LIMITATIONS AND FUTURE WORK

There are some limitations of our work. First, there is the cost of integrating reorientation into the VR experience. Designing integrated techniques, compared to using hard reset methods [40], out of context distractors [17] or adding non-walking navigation mechanisms like teleportation, takes time and effort. Second, there is a possibility that users may disregard the attractor, either unconsciously or consciously, and exit the tracked area. This can be partially resolved by providing a warning system like the chaperone on the HTC Vive (a blue grid that appears at the boundary of the tracked area when the user gets close). Adding a warning system may prevent the user from leaving the tracked space but it can disrupt presence. Lastly, users may walk too fast in a space that is too small, and not fully interact with the presented distractors, leading them to quickly step outside the safe and tracked areas. A possible solution to this may be implement a mechanism that asks users to step back into the safe area by marking its position in the virtual world and modifying the experience accordingly.

The current design focuses on scenarios where a user needs to move along a specified path. In the future, we plan on expanding our design methodology and implemented techniques to allow for walking on curved paths or walking freely in open spaces as well as exploring movement in indoor places. An interesting possibility may be to combine real-walking with artificial navigation techniques that fit the narrative like walking around the entirety of Star Trek's USS Enterprise and using teleportation to travel to different planets and then walking again to interact with life forms on the planets.

[†]http://www.pokemon.com/us/

CONCLUSION

In this paper, we introduced a design methodology that integrates reorientation into the user's primary activity in the VR environment. We showed how our embedded context-sensitive reorientation can improve the VR experience, resulting in a high sense of presence, significantly reduced dizziness and reduced noticeability of virtual scene rotation. We showed an example implementation of four novel visibility manipulation techniques, which work with attractors and are integrated in the narrative, tasks, and the virtual environment to further reduce users' sensitivity towards rotational changes of the virtual world. We believe that our methodology is an important step towards making natural walking a more effective and practical navigation mechanism for consumer virtual reality and can successfully provide a seamless experience with high presence.

REFERENCES

1. Doug A Bowman, David Koller, and Larry F Hodges. 1997. Travel in immersive virtual environments: An evaluation of viewpoint motion control techniques. In *Virtual Reality Annual International Symposium, 1997., IEEE 1997*. IEEE, 45–52.
2. Sarah S Chance, Florence Gaunet, Andrew C Beall, and Jack M Loomis. 1998. Locomotion mode affects the updating of objects encountered during travel: The contribution of vestibular and proprioceptive inputs to path integration. *Presence: Teleoperators and Virtual Environments* 7, 2 (1998), 168–178.
3. Haiwei Chen and Henry Fuchs. 2017. Towards Imperceptible Redirected Walking: Integrating a Distractor into the Immersive Experience. In *Proceedings of the 21st ACM SIGGRAPH Symposium on Interactive 3D Graphics and Games (I3D '17)*. ACM, New York, NY, USA, Article 22, 2 pages. DOI: http://dx.doi.org/10.1145/3023368.3036844
4. David Engel, Cristóbal Curio, Lili Tcheang, Betty Mohler, and Heinrich H. Bülthoff. 2008. A Psychophysically Calibrated Controller for Navigating Through Large Environments in a Limited Free-walking Space. In *Proceedings of the 2008 ACM Symposium on Virtual Reality Software and Technology (VRST '08)*. ACM, New York, NY, USA, 157–164. DOI: http://dx.doi.org/10.1145/1450579.1450612
5. James J Gibson. 1978. The ecological approach to the visual perception of pictures. *Leonardo* 11, 3 (1978), 227–235.
6. Victoria Interrante, Brian Ries, and Lee Anderson. 2007. Seven league boots: A new metaphor for augmented

locomotion through moderately large scale immersive virtual environments. In *3D User Interfaces, 2007. 3DUI'07. IEEE Symposium on*. IEEE.

7. Melinda S Jensen, Richard Yao, Whitney N Street, and Daniel J Simons. 2011. Change blindness and inattentional blindness. *Wiley Interdisciplinary Reviews: Cognitive Science* 2, 5 (2011), 529–546.
8. Jason Jerald, Tabitha Peck, Frank Steinicke, and Mary Whitton. 2008. Sensitivity to scene motion for phases of head yaws. In *Proceedings of the 5th symposium on Applied perception in graphics and visualization*. ACM, 155–162.
9. Robert S Kennedy, Norman E Lane, Kevin S Berbaum, and Michael G Lilienthal. 1993. Simulator sickness questionnaire: An enhanced method for quantifying simulator sickness. *The international journal of aviation psychology* 3, 3 (1993), 203–220.
10. Joseph J LaViola Jr. 2000. A discussion of cybersickness in virtual environments. *ACM SIGCHI Bulletin* 32, 1 (2000), 47–56.
11. Arien Mack and Irvin Rock. 1998. *Inattentional blindness*. Vol. 33. MIT press Cambridge, MA.
12. Michael Meehan. 2001. *Physiological reaction as an objective measure of presence in virtual environments*. Ph.D. Dissertation. University of North Carolina at Chapel Hill.
13. Thomas Nescher, Markus Zank, and Andreas Kunz. 2016. Simultaneous Mapping and Redirected Walking for ad hoc Free Walking in Virtual Environments. In *IEEE Virtual Reality Conference 2016*. IEEE, 239–240.
14. Norbert Nitzsche, Uwe D Hanebeck, and Günther Schmidt. 2004. Motion compression for telepresent walking in large target environments. *Presence: Teleoperators and Virtual Environments* 13, 1 (2004), 44–60.
15. Joseph Paradiso, Craig Abler, Kai-yuh Hsiao, and Matthew Reynolds. 1997. The Magic Carpet: Physical Sensing for Immersive Environments. In *CHI '97 Extended Abstracts on Human Factors in Computing Systems (CHI EA '97)*. ACM, New York, NY, USA, 277–278. DOI: http://dx.doi.org/10.1145/1120212.1120391
16. Tabitha C Peck, Henry Fuchs, and Mary C Whitton. 2009. Evaluation of reorientation techniques and distractors for walking in large virtual environments. *IEEE Transactions on Visualization and Computer Graphics* 15, 3 (2009), 383–394.
17. Tabitha C Peck, Henry Fuchs, and Mary C Whitton. 2010. Improved redirection with distractors: A large-scale-real-walking locomotion interface and its effect on navigation in virtual environments. In *Virtual Reality Conference (VR), 2010 IEEE*. IEEE, 35–38.
18. Tabitha C Peck, Henry Fuchs, and Mary C Whitton. 2011. An evaluation of navigational ability comparing Redirected Free Exploration with Distractors to Walking-in-Place and joystick locomotio interfaces. In *Virtual Reality Conference (VR), 2011 IEEE*. IEEE, 55–62.
19. PersonGuy. SteamVR Play Area Size Stats. http://steamcommunity.com/app/358720/discussions/0/350532536103514259/. (????). 2017 (Accessed September 9, 2017).
20. Sharif Razzaque, Zachariah Kohn, and Mary C Whitton. 2001. Redirected walking. In *Proceedings of EUROGRAPHICS*, Vol. 9. Citeseer, 105–106.
21. Roy A Ruddle and Simon Lessels. 2009. The benefits of using a walking interface to navigate virtual environments. *ACM Transactions on Computer-Human Interaction (TOCHI)* 16, 1 (2009), 5.
22. Daniel J Simons and Christopher F Chabris. 1999. Gorillas in our midst: Sustained inattentional blindness for dynamic events. *Perception* 28, 9 (1999), 1059–1074.
23. Daniel J Simons and Daniel T Levin. 1997. Change blindness. *Trends in cognitive sciences* 1, 7 (1997), 261–267.
24. Mel Slater. 2009. Place illusion and plausibility can lead to realistic behaviour in immersive virtual environments. *Philosophical Transactions of the Royal Society B: Biological Sciences* 364, 1535 (2009), 3549–3557.
25. Mel Slater, Martin Usoh, and Anthony Steed. 1994. Depth of presence in virtual environments. *Presence: Teleoperators & Virtual Environments* 3, 2 (1994), 130–144.
26. Mel Slater, Martin Usoh, and Anthony Steed. 1995. Taking Steps: The Influence of a Walking Technique on Presence in Virtual Reality. *ACM Trans. Comput.-Hum. Interact.* 2, 3 (Sept. 1995), 201–219. DOI: http://dx.doi.org/10.1145/210079.210084
27. Misha Sra, Sergio Garrido-Jurado, Chris Schmandt, and Pattie Maes. 2016. Procedurally Generated Virtual Reality from 3D Reconstructed Physical Space. In *Proceedings of the 22Nd ACM Conference on Virtual Reality Software and Technology (VRST '16)*. ACM, New York, NY, USA, 191–200. DOI: http://dx.doi.org/10.1145/2993369.2993372
28. Frank Steinicke, Gerd Bruder, Jason Jerald, Harald Frenz, and Markus Lappe. 2010. Estimation of detection thresholds for redirected walking techniques. *IEEE Transactions on Visualization and Computer Graphics* 16, 1 (2010), 17–27.
29. Kaveri Subrahmanyam and Patricia M Greenfield. 1994. Effect of video game practice on spatial skills in girls and boys. *Journal of applied developmental psychology* 15, 1 (1994), 13–32.
30. Evan A Suma, Mahdi Azmandian, Timofey Grechkin, Thai Phan, and Mark Bolas. 2015. Making small spaces feel large: Infinite walking in virtual reality. In *ACM SIGGRAPH 2015 Emerging Technologies*. ACM, 16.

31. Evan A Suma, Gerd Bruder, Frank Steinicke, David M Krum, and Mark Bolas. 2012. A taxonomy for deploying redirection techniques in immersive virtual environments. In *Virtual Reality Short Papers and Posters (VRW), 2012 IEEE*. IEEE, 43–46.

32. Evan A Suma, Seth Clark, David Krum, Samantha Finkelstein, Mark Bolas, and Zachary Warte. 2011. Leveraging change blindness for redirection in virtual environments. In *2011 IEEE Virtual Reality Conference*. IEEE, 159–166.

33. Evan A Suma, Zachary Lipps, Samantha Finkelstein, David M Krum, and Mark Bolas. 2012. Impossible spaces: Maximizing natural walking in virtual environments with self-overlapping architecture. *IEEE Transactions on Visualization and Computer Graphics* 18, 4 (2012), 555–564.

34. Qi Sun, Li-Yi Wei, and Arie Kaufman. 2016. Mapping virtual and physical reality. *ACM Transactions on Graphics (TOG)* 35, 4 (2016), 64.

35. Martin Usoh, Kevin Arthur, Mary C Whitton, Rui Bastos, Anthony Steed, Mel Slater, and Frederick P Brooks Jr. 1999. Walking> walking-in-place> flying, in virtual environments. In *Proceedings of the 26th annual conference on Computer graphics and interactive techniques*. ACM Press/Addison-Wesley Publishing Co., 359–364.

36. Martin Usoh, Ernest Catena, Sima Arman, and Mel Slater. 2000. Using presence questionnaires in reality. *Presence: Teleoperators & Virtual Environments* 9, 5 (2000), 497–503.

37. John Wann and Mark Mon-Williams. 1996. What does virtual reality NEED?: human factors issues in the design of three-dimensional computer environments. *International Journal of Human-Computer Studies* 44, 6 (1996), 829–847.

38. Andrew B Watson and Albert J Ahumada. 1985. Model of human visual-motion sensing. *JOSA A* 2, 2 (1985), 322–342.

39. Betsy Williams, Gayathri Narasimham, Tim P McNamara, Thomas H Carr, John J Rieser, and Bobby Bodenheimer. 2006. Updating orientation in large virtual environments using scaled translational gain. In *Proceedings of the 3rd Symposium on Applied Perception in Graphics and Visualization*. ACM, 21–28.

40. Betsy Williams, Gayathri Narasimham, Bjoern Rump, Timothy P McNamara, Thomas H Carr, John Rieser, and Bobby Bodenheimer. 2007. Exploring large virtual environments with an HMD when physical space is limited. In *Proceedings of the 4th symposium on Applied perception in graphics and visualization*. ACM, 41–48.

41. Catherine A Zanbaka, Benjamin C Lok, Sabarish V Babu, Amy Catherine Ulinski, and Larry F Hodges. 2005. Comparison of path visualizations and cognitive measures relative to travel technique in a virtual environment. *IEEE Transactions on Visualization and Computer Graphics* 11, 6 (2005), 694–705.

Attending to Breath: Exploring how the cues in a virtual environment guide the attention to breath and shape the quality of experience to support mindfulness

Mirjana Prpa
School of Interactive Arts+Technology, SFU
Surrey, Canada
mprpa@sfu.ca

Kıvanç Tatar
School of Interactive Arts+Technology, SFU
Surrey, Canada
ktatar@sfu.ca

Jules Françoise
LIMSI, CNRS, Univ. Paris-Sud,Univ. Paris-Saclay,
Orsay, France
jules.francoise@limsi.fr

Bernhard Riecke
School of Interactive Arts+Technology, SFU
Surrey, Canada
ber1@sfu.ca

Thecla Schiphorst
School of Interactive Arts+Technology, SFU
Surrey, Canada
thecla@sfu.ca

Philippe Pasquier
School of Interactive Arts+Technology, SFU
Surrey, Canada
pasquier@sfu.ca

ABSTRACT

Busy daily lives and ongoing distractions often make people feel disconnected from their bodies and experiences. Guided attention to self can alleviate this disconnect as in focused-attention meditation, in which breathing often constitutes the primary object on which to focus attention. In this context, sustained breath awareness plays a crucial role in the emergence of the meditation experience. We designed an immersive virtual environment (iVE) with a generative soundtrack that supports sustained attention on breathing by employing the users' breathing in interaction. Both sounds and visuals are directly mapped to the user's breathing patterns, thus bringing the awareness researched. We conducted micro-phenomenology interviews to unfold the process in which breath awareness can be induced and sustained in this environment. The findings revealed the mechanisms by which audio and visual cues in VR can elicit and foster breath-awareness, and unfolded the nuances of this process through subjective experiences of the study participants. Finally, the results emphasize the important role that a sense of agency and control have in shaping the overall quality of the experience. This can in turn inform the design specifications of future mindfulness-based designs focused on breath awareness.

ACM Classification Keywords

H.5.1. Information Interfaces and Presentation (e.g. HCI): Multimedia Information Systems – Artificial, augmented, and virtual realities

DIS'18, June 9–13, 2018, Hong Kong

ISBN 123-4567-24-567/08/06... $15.00

DOI: https://doi.org/10.1145/3196709.3196765

Author Keywords

Mindfulness; Breath Awareness; Virtual Reality; Immersion; Well-Being; Embodiment.

INTRODUCTION

An increasing amount of our daily interactions in the world are mediated by digital technologies. With the rise of ubiquitous computing, an increasing number of our actions are measured, stored and quantified. Smart-phones and wearable technologies track our location, social interactions, and physical activity. The rise of these technologies for the 'quantified self' [77] often focuses on increasing our productivity by tightly monitoring our actions in the world. However, the more we focus on these outward uses of technology, the less we experience an embodied self [70]. Yet, there are opportunities beyond quantification. By designing technologies "as experiences" [40] and by minimizing distractions and bringing focus on the self, we can move toward improving the quality of our interactions and quality of life [5].

In this context, a growing thread of HCI research investigates how embodied approaches to interaction design can support an increased attention to the self [60, 22]. From this body of work, we have focused on designs built upon the concept of *mindfulness*, defined as "the awareness that emerges through paying attention on purpose, in the present moment, and non-judgmentally to the unfolding of experience moment by moment" [26]. Our work builds upon *mindfulness-based design* evolving around the practice of *focused-attention meditation* (FAM) [33]. FAM is a practice of sustaining focused attention on one, "primary", object of attention (internal, such as breathing, or external, such as a candle light). Focused attention on breathing is a widely accepted practice that aims at cultivating a sense of being present with a demonstrated impact on well-being. Engaging in breathing exercises influence cognition, memory, and emotional processing [24, 79, 51], and decreases anxiety and stress [24], even in a young population [30].

A large number of mindfulness-based designs are built upon nuances of FAM with a focus on breathing. Mindfulness-based design can be used to guide a user's attention to breath, for example through Virtual Environments (VEs) that employ breathing cues [64, 52]. Despite a significant number of mindfulness-based designs that guide the attention to breath, our understanding of how breath awareness is elicited and how the design of VEs can sustain the user's attention on breath are still limited. This is what motivates the research effort presented here.

In this paper, we investigate how a continuous interaction between breathing patterns and a virtual environment can induce and support the breath awareness of users. Our inquiry is motivated by the preliminary findings in [54] that showed the potential of the VE and interaction design to elicit and sustain the user's awareness of their breathing. Hence, our goal in this study is to better understand (1) how the users of the *Pulse Breath Water* system become aware of their breathing in a VE without verbal guidance during the interaction, (2) how the cues in the VE can support sustained attention on breathing, and (3) gain a deeper understanding of the actual experience of becoming aware and sustained awareness of one's breath. To answer these research questions we (1) built the *Pulse Breath Water* system, and (2) propose an empirical qualitative study employing micro-phenomenology interviews [50].

BACKGROUND

Mindfulness-Based Design

The third wave in HCI [4] brought the embodied approach to interaction [11] to the forefront by acknowledging the importance of the embodied experience in sense-making of the experience. A number of design approaches position the body at the center of a user's experience. For instance, *Somaesthetics* designs cultivate an aesthetic appreciation of bodily experience [62, 59]. *Somaesthetic Appreciation design* gives rise to the experience through guided attention inwards, to the self; excluding external distractions and making space for somatic awareness to arise [23]. Yet another concept, *Somatic Connoisseurship*, demonstrates how "body-based awareness skills" can be utilized in experience design and designing for the experience of the self, by building upon somatic phenomenology and first-person practices for self-awareness [61].

The designs we focus on are built upon mindfulness principles and encourage a shift of attention inwards, towards bodily sensations, in order to support well-being and self-regulation processes [3]. Mindfulness has been defined as a state of being non-judgmental and present in the moment-to-moment unfolding of the experience [26]. Mindfulness-based designs aim to bring one to the state of mindfulness through various approaches. For example, Zhu et al. [80] recognized four approaches to designing for mindfulness: *Digitalized mindfulness* that is a digital equivalent to guided meditation; *Personalized mindfulness* that addresses personal preferences regarding mindful meditation; *Quantified mindfulness* that is built upon applications that offer real-time sensing and feedback; and *Presence-in and Presence-with* approach that goes beyond tools and offers a way of mindful being rather than doing.

The most common mindfulness-based designs take the form of a mobile application [8] that tackle mindfulness from different angles: mobile applications that guide a user to distance itself from troubling thoughts [78, 47], foster mindful walking through ambient sound generated from walking and breathing patterns [7], applications that serve as mindfulness meditation timers [48], applications for didactic guided meditation sessions [69], or applications that integrate mindfulness principles within a broader framework such as *acceptance and commitment therapy* [1]. Beside mobile and computer applications, mindfulness-based designs have taken on the form of audio installations - *Sonic Cradle* [73, 74], virtual environments [41] - *The Meditation Chamber* [64], *RelaWorld* [32], *Sanctuarium* [12], *PsychicVR* [2] and more recently, mixed reality environments - *Inner Garden* [58].

Focused-Attention Meditation

Mindfulness practices encompass various approaches to bringing the user's awareness to the present moment. A growing number of mindfulness-based designs revolve around the practice of focused-attention meditation (FAM) [37, 38]. In FAM a practitioner shifts their attention from external stressors to internal sensations such as breathing [55], and is considered the most widely accessible practice among novice meditators [38]. Practicing sustained focused attention on breath has been shown to reduce stress and improve well-being [31]. Most importantly, FAM fosters interoceptive awareness, an ability to receive and attend to the signals originating in our bodies [14, 21], which is shown to not only improve attention task performance but as well contribute to emotion regulation [10, 44].

Designs for Breath Awareness

How can we support the meditation community with technology [9] is an open-end question that is explored within the HCI community from many different angles. We focus on designs that "facilitate mindful moments" of being present and self-aware by directing the user's attention to their breathing [55]. We review systems using multi-sensory feedback to support mindful reflection, by "bringing unconscious aspects of experience to conscious awareness" [63]: p.50. Many designs for breath awareness have been proposed in HCI [66]. *Sonic Cradle* [73] was designed for cultivating mindfulness through a soundscape in which sounds are triggered by breathing. *BrightBeat* [18] was designed for cultivating calmness and focus through utilizing screen brightness with breathing patterns and audio feedback to guide a user towards intended breathing. *SomaMat and Breathing Light* demonstrated a different approach to mindfulness through breathing by emphasizing breath-related somaesthetic qualities through light and heat feedback [67].

Specifically, we focus on Virtual Reality (VR) as an "embodied technology" that can support the user's attention to bodily sensations using the sense of immersion and presence [56]. By employing audio-visual cues to breath as another representation cue, VR can provide a sensory-augmentation dimension that supports the user in focusing attention on breath. Because immersion in VEs minimizes external distractions, VR is a promising medium to support mindfulness practice and elicit breath awareness [65, 55].

Different approaches to designing for breath awareness and FAM in virtual reality have been proposed. In *Solar* [52], breathing and electroencephalography (EEG) data are mapped to the elements in the virtual environment that provides audio and visual cues and is presented on a desktop screen. *Guided Meditation VR* [42] and *JunoVR* [75] immerse the user in a VEs that resemble nature and uses audio instructions to guide the user's attention to breathing. Similarly, abstracted natural environments are used as a design element in: *Lumen* [43] that employs guided meditation and gaze interaction for navigation through an enchanted forest; *Life Tree* in which the growth and liveness of the tree are controlled by the user's breathing rhythm [49], and in *Deep* which depicts an underwater fantasy world which the user navigates by deepening their breathing and adjusting to a slow pace [71]. Other applications employ continuous – and potentially ambiguous – feedback to guide the users' attention. The *Meditation Chamber* [64], provides biofeedback in a VE using multimodal data – breathing, electrodermal activity (EDA), and blood volume pressure – along with guided instructions, and presented on HMD. Similarly, in *Strata*, breathing, heart rate, EDA, and brain activity determine the visuals and the audio of the virtual environment depicting five different worlds unified into a single experience [13].

However, while some of these applications are built upon the gamification paradigm [25], and often include guided meditation as an invite to the experience, our interest is in the experiences that can guide user's attention to breathing through the cues in the environment. Therefore, our approach does not involve any guided meditation instructions, nor have we intended for our VE design to be a game. Our focus is on VR applications presented on immersive HMD and without verbal guidance into the practice. Hence, we designed *Pulse Breath Water* as a generative environment in which the events are determined by breathing pattens and the system's decision (by AI agent), where the user's breathing is employed as one and only modality for the cues in the iVE.

Despite a significant number of mindfulness-based VEs that support breath awareness, there is still a lack of a deeper understanding of how specifically breath awareness is elicited through different cues and interactions in VR. In this work, we aim to get a detailed understanding of user experiences of a particular design using micro-phenomenology interviews. Our design employs breathing data in a continuous audio and visual feedback in the virtual environment. The complexity of the visual elements is kept minimal to minimize dispersion of attention. The immersiveness of the medium contributes to decreased external distractions and an ability to elicit body sensations and direct attention towards one's breath, supported by generative audio that responds in real time to the changes in breathing patterns.

Micro-Phenomenology: A Methodology for the Study of Experience

To understand the subjective experiences of the participants, we chose *micro-phenomenology*, an inquiry method developed by Petitmengin [50, 45] upon Vermersch's *Explicitation interviews* technique [72]. The objective of micro-phenomenology is to obtain explicit descriptions of *singular experiences* as they unfold in a larger, chronological structure of the experience, bypassing generalized typical post-hoc descriptions.

For the descriptions of the experience to emerge in the interview, the interviewer and the interviewee use a precise communication-protocol as a tool for mediating the first-person point of view of the interviewee through the second-person position of the interviewer. The interviewee accesses the experience retrospectively following the guidance of the interviewer who takes a role of a mediator. The interviewer's role is to guide and stabilize the interviewee's attention, guide them through the process of evoking the experience, and then direct their attention to a particular dimension of the experience. Once the interviewee's attention is stabilized and they are in an *evocative state* – a state of re-living the experience – the interviewer guides the interviewee in deepening the description to the required level of precision.

Micro-phenomenology and *Explicitation interview* have been explored in HCI context in the past. Light [34] discussed the explicitation interview in the context of gathering experiences of using websites [34] and receiving mobile phone calls [35, 36]. Hogan [20] used the method to gather the users' experiences of data representation. Françoise et al. [15] utilized the method to evaluate the system they built for kinesthetic awareness while the same method was used by Candau et al. [6] to explore how interaction informed by somatic practices and embodied cognition contributes to cultivating kinesthetic awareness. To our knowledge, while the interest in micro-phenomenology to understand user experiences is growing, no published research has used the methodology in VR.

A VIRTUAL ENVIRONMENT DESIGNED TO SUPPORT BREATH AWARENESS

Pulse Breath Water system was initially created as an artwork [53] that evolved and doubled into a research instrument over time. We undertake a research-through-design [16] approach, and design iterations are informed by the exploratory studies we conduct.

Interaction Scenario

The main design premise is that the events in the virtual environment are determined by the breathing patterns. Deep slow breathing triggers slower, more sustained movement on the up/down-axis, allowing users to observe, reflect, and position in a particular part of the environment. Sustained breaths allow for staying in a place, while fast, strong breaths cause erratic movement. Metaphoric mapping [39] of movement allows for interaction that is easy to understand: on the participant's inhale, the position of the participant rises in the environment, and on the exhale they sink, just like when submerged in water. In our VE, the respiration data guides the audio generation in the affective space. The eventfulness of the audio is mapped to the appearance of the waves in the ocean. More eventful breathing generates more eventful audio that then generates a more disturbed ocean surface and increased waves. The element that depicts the passage of time is the sky that changes color from light gray to pitch black within a span of 6 minutes.

System design

Our design brings together three components: (1) A respiration sensor and respiration analysis module that drives (2) an immersive virtual environment (displayed on Oculus Rift SDK2), and (3) a generative sound environment. The novelty of the system, compared to other VR systems presented above, is in the generative audio and the AI agent that determines the events in the environment based on eventfulness of breathing that, to our best knowledge, have not been utilized so far in iVE.

The overall system outline is represented in Figure 1. One respiration sensor (Thought Technology) [76] attached to the user's abdominal area streams respiration data to M+M middleware [46] to MAX MSP [1] patch. The audio is generated by an autonomous agent that selects samples from the audio corpus according to the frequency of the user's breathing. All audio samples are tagged with different eventfulness properties using a state of the art music emotion recognition algorithm [68]. The overall eventfulness values of the audio environment is sent to the 3D game engine Unity 3D [2] along with respiration data via OSC messages. This data generates visual changes in the VE presented to the user via HMD. The user listens to the audio environment with circumaural noise-canceling headphones. A second respiration sensor was placed around the chest, and was used for data collection and as a reference, however chest data was not employed in the design.

Musical Agent: listening and responding through sound

Musical agents are artificial agents that automatize musical tasks. The hybrid musical agent generates the audio environment using the patterns of the user's breathing: slower subtle breathing triggers the agent to play less eventful sounds, and vice versa, faster deeper breaths result in the agent playing sounds that will be perceived as more eventful. The audio corpus contains piano recordings of musical chords that do not create musical tension and resolution. These recordings are further processed so that the origin of the recordings are not clear to the listeners. The recordings are all labeled with vectors with two dimensions: average pleasantness and average eventfulness based on Music Emotion Recognition algorithm [68]. Using Music Emotion Recognition, the agent maps the breathing to the eventfulness of audio samples to create an interactive sonic environment.

We apply signal processing to the respiration data using a wavelet transform. The wavelet transform outputs 24 frequency bands and these bands are mapped to the audio corpus' eventfulness range. The pleasantness range of the audio samples are substantially smaller than the range of eventfulness. The agent applies a random walk on the pleasantness dimension to create variations on the sample selection. The agent uses the generated eventfulness and pleasantness values to choose samples from the audio corpus. The selected sample is played by one of four playback engines of the agent.

In addition to piano sounds, a wave-table synthesizer [57] is used to generate a heartbeat-like sound controlled by the speed of user's breathing: the pulsation sound in the audio environment slows down as the user's breathing slows down. The interaction between the user and the audio environment is further enhanced by introducing a low-pass filter. As the user breaths in and out, the timbre of the audio environment oscillates between a muddy, low-frequency prominent audio environment and a full-spectrum audio environment. This also enhances the submersion feeling associated with being under the virtual water surface in the virtual environment (see section below *Virtual Environment: ART and Ambiguity of relationship as an invitation to the experience*).

Lastly, the agent applies Music Emotion Recognition algorithm to estimate the eventfulness and pleasantness of the generated sonic environment. The estimation algorithm is the online version of the estimation algorithm that is used to label the audio in the agent's memory. The output of online affect estimation is a vector with two dimensions: eventfulness and pleasantness. These values are further used to control the parameters of the virtual reality environment.

Virtual Environment: ART and Ambiguity of relationship as an invitation to the experience

Immersive environments can positively affect the user's attention, which was explained by Kaplan in *Attention Restoration Theory (ART)*[29]. ART focuses on the correlation between type of stimuli and restorative potential of nature environments [28]. The environments with stimuli that modestly capture attention are preferred over the stimuli that elicits mental fatigue and cognitive overload, and the design of our system relies on this principle. We used Unity 3D to generate the environment and 3D elements of a body of water - an ocean. The aesthetics of the scene is intentionally minimal, displaying the ocean and the sky in a range of gray-scale shades. The use of color is minimal. Design of elements in the VE is informed by the concept of *beholder's share* [27] in which the user's previous experiences guide the process of meaning-making of ambiguous stimuli. The ambiguity of visual stimulus encourages an interpretative relationship between a user and the environment [17]. In particular, *ambiguity of relationship* [17] between the user and the visual stimulus evokes users to project their values and experiences in reflection and meaning-making. For example, the ambiguous environment can be perceived as frightening and anxiety-inducing by one person or calm that elicits relaxation and peaceful feelings in other, building upon each person's previous real life experiences with real-life environments. Finally, continuous breathing patterns allow users to control the environment and curate their own experience.

Respiration data from an abdominal sensor controls the user's position in the environment. After initial testing, we decided to include movement on a vertical axis because the movement on a horizontal axis (along the ocean surface) was inducing motion-sickness. The mapping was informed by metaphoric mapping [39] built upon cognitive schema of "more is up, less is down (for example)". The more the participant breathes in, the higher in the VE they will go. We limited the height to which participants can move to prevent falling down from a high distance as that was reported as anxiety inducting by pilot participants. The eventfulness level is mapped to waves on the ocean surface: more eventful audio will cause more excited waves, and vice versa.

[1]https://cycling74.com

[2]Unity 3D: https://unity3d.com/

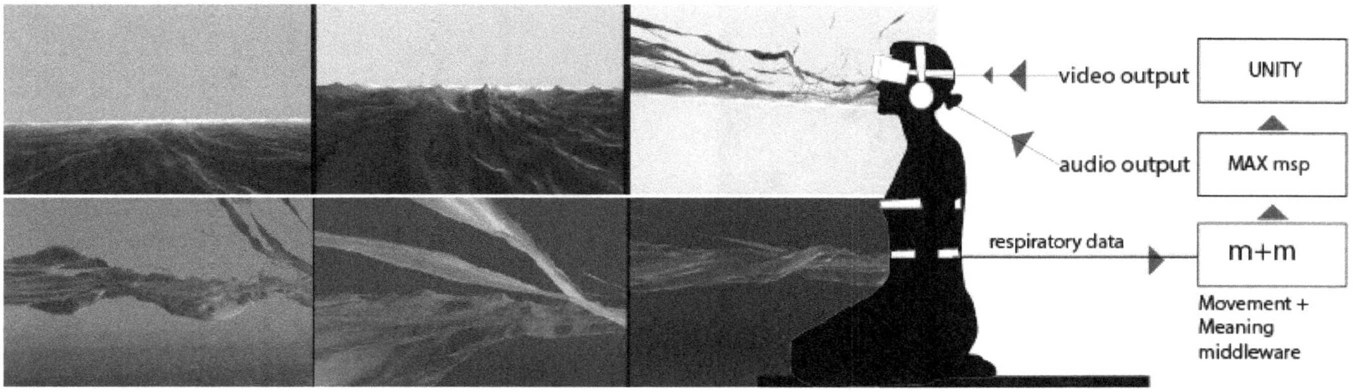

Figure 1. The system design

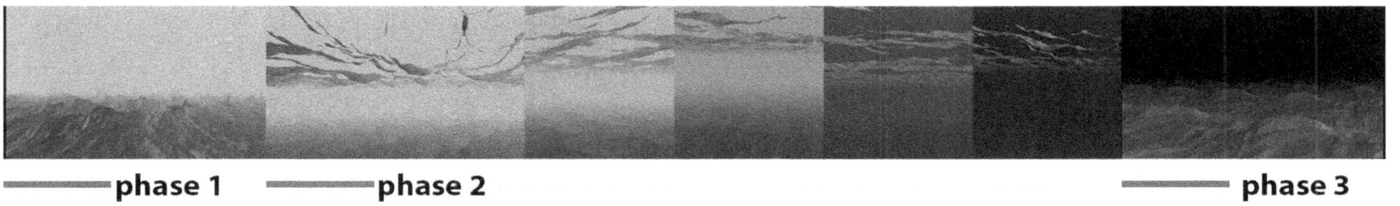

Figure 2. Duration: phase 1 (1 min) starts off with light gray sky and a stationary user's position above the ocean surface level; Phase 2 (4 min) is when the breath to movement mapping in the VE is activated and the user is moving along the vertical axis according to their breathing; the sky colour progresses from gray to black; Phase 3 (1 min)- the user is stationary again, and the only difference between this and phase 1 is in the colour of the sky

USER STUDY: UNDERSTANDING PERSONAL EXPERIENCES THROUGH MICRO-PHENOMENOLOGY

We conducted an exploratory study investigating how audio and visual cues mapped to breathing in the VE give rise and support to sustained breath awareness. The study aims to understand the experience of becoming aware of breath, and the nuances of the system that either support or distract a user in attending to self and becoming breath-aware. The participants were introduced to the VE following a four-part protocol described in more detail in Section *Protocol* (below). The insights are induced using micro-phenomenology interviews [50] after each completed session.

Artwork as a research instrument The initial design of our system was built upon the idea of a real-time generated piece, without narrative, end or beginning. To allow for gradual transition to and out of the environment that would enable us to inquire about the process of eliciting breath awareness, we iterated the system previously created as an artwork *Pulse Breath Water* [53] and added three phases. In the first and the last phase (phases 1 and 3) (see Figure 2), the user has a stationary position above the ocean and is presented with the cues of their agency through an audio environment. In the second phase, the user's agency is reflected not just through the audio (as in phase 1, and 3) but also their breathing controls the vertical position in the environment, moving the user above the ocean's surface with breath in and below the surface with breath out. The third phase is the same as the first phase, and the user is back to the starting position above the water while exposed to the cues of their breathing through the audio.

Designing 3 phases allowed for a variety of cues of the user's agency in the VE that could have influenced different mechanisms for eliciting breath awareness that we aimed to reveal in the interviews. The main points of interest were the switches between the phases in which the user's breath started impacting the environment (first reflected through audio cues in phase 1, then increasing the agency in phase 2 by adding movement cues, and then decreasing agency in phase 3 by presenting the audio cues only).

The length of the phases was determined in a pilot study conducted with 6 participants. The criteria was to find the balance between the time that seemed to keep the user's interest and flow state, and the point when the familiarity and lack of events in the environment becomes dull. Taking these pilot sessions into account, we reduced the length of the phases without agency as the users reported them as dull. Finally, the first phase is 60 seconds long, the second phase is 240 seconds long, and finally, the third phase is 60 seconds adding to the VE's duration to 6 minutes total (see Figure 2).

Participants

We recruited 11 participants (7 female) through the university mailing list and social media channels. Participants' ages ranged from 24 to 44 (mean: 27.1, SD: 5.87). Two participants had never tried VR before, eight participants had been exposed to it less than ten times overall, and one is an expert VR user. Regarding mindfulness practice, three participants meditate regularly, one has never meditated, and the rest meditate irregularly. All participants reported good health condition and normal vision.

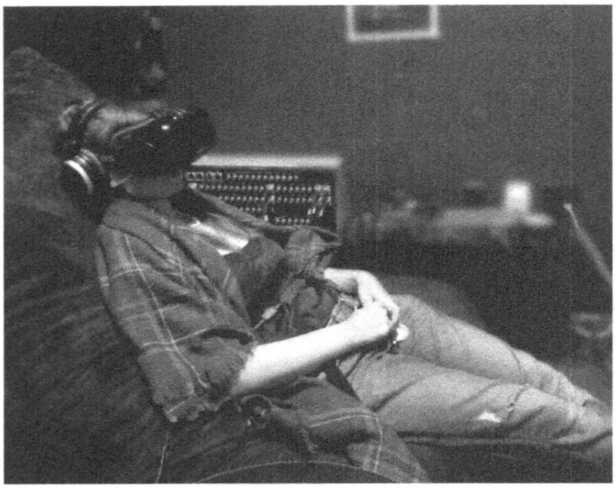

Figure 3. The participant interacting with the VE, wearing breathing sensors, headphones, and Oculus Rift while seated on the cushion

Apparatus and Data collection

The participants were seated comfortably on a large bean bag pillow (see Figure 3), one at the time, in a dark room, at the computer station. The VE was presented on Oculus SDK2 at the rate of 90 FPS. The audio component of the VE was played on noise-canceling headphones. Participants wore respiration sensors (Thought technology [76]) positioned on the abdomen and chest and that data was captured. Also, interviews were audio and video recorded.

Protocol

Upon arrival, the participants read a description of the study. After agreeing to participate by signing the consent form, participants were equipped with two breathing sensors: abdominal and chest, and Oculus Rift, and the noise-canceling headphones. Prior to the sessions, we informed all participants that: "the virtual environment is reacting to your breathing" and we invited the participants to explore the experience without disclosing mapping details. The session was divided into four parts (see Figure 4):

1. *Session 1: Exploration*: The participants interacted with the virtual environment using their breathing for a duration of 6 minutes.

2. *Did the participant understand control and mapping details?*: After Session 1, we started interviews with all participants. Very early in these interviews we were able to determine whether participants made sense of the interaction and if they understood the correlation between the breath and the movement and sonic events in the environment (i.e., if they understood the mapping).

3. *Interview*: If they did, we would proceed to a full-length micro-phenomenology interview (this was the case with 3 participants [3]). If they did not make this connection (8 participants), they were instead invited to proceeded with Session 2 followed by the full-length interview.

[3]we will elaborate on this further in the Discussion section

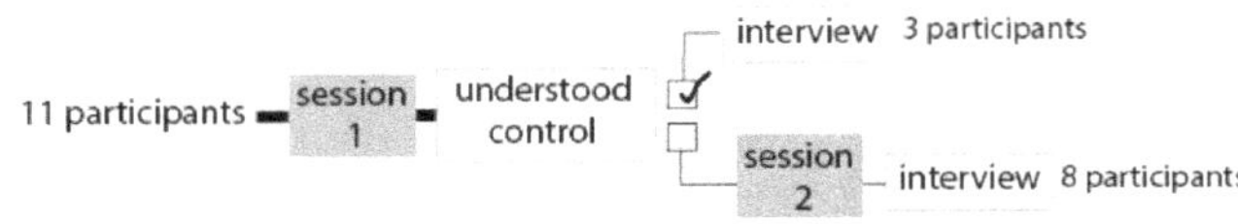

Figure 4. the illustration of the protocol

4. *Session 2: disclosed mapping details*: The 8 participants who did not make a sense of the control they had over the cues in the environment via their breathing, were explained the mapping details, that is how their breathing influences the virtual visual and sonic environment. Finally, they were asked to explore the environment again for another 6 minutes going through the 3 phases already described.

5. *Interview*: After the second session we conducted micro-phenomenology interviews, each 30 minutes in length.

Analysis

All interviews were transcribed and coded using the nVivo software for qualitative analysis. All interview data was structured in chronological order, and the descriptions of singular experiences were identified. The coding was done in two stages: first, interviews were coded line-by-line. Our coding system in this stage included the codes: control, attention, breath, body sensations, imagery, sound, feeling, inner voice, and were informed by six pilot interviews that we conducted prior to the study. In the second stage of coding, we identified common themes from the codes identified in the first stage of coding. Two researchers (the authors number 1 and 5), both trained in conducting micro-phenomenology interview, discussed and agreed on the themes.

FINDINGS

Unfolding the process of eliciting breath awareness

Attention shifts in becoming aware of breath

The complexity of the environment and the novelty of the experience can potentially be overwhelming to the participants. However, the three phases of the experience offered the possibility for a gradual transition of the focus from the environment to the bodily sensations related to the movement, and finally to the breath. Once aware of their control of the elements in the environment, a majority of the participants would direct attention first to the waves, the vertical movement patterns, and then to changes in the sonic environment, thus gradually discovering the nuances of the control they had over the environment, before starting to focus their awareness on their breathing. However, participants with meditation experience tended to immediately focus on the breath before shifting their attention to the environment, and finally to their bodily sensations:

> *At the very beginning I was focusing on my breath, just trying to listen and understand what was happening. And then the second part because I got the connection instead of listening to my own breath I changed my breath playing with the images and then I went to first state of listening to my body but I wasn't anxious anymore about motion sickness and the storms in the ocean and... I was focusing on really listening.* (P17)

Focused attention

Once familiarized with the environment, participants directed their attention to preferred parts in the experience by practicing controls they experientially learned during the session:

> *Initially I was repeating it, long breath in out in out but I didn't hold my breath even inside. After some time when it went on for some cycles then I started different things different rhythm of my breath as if I am controlling it. I was just trying to control that up and down... after that I realized [that] inside I'm feeling good, then I started staying inside.*(P14)

> *My focus is just I guess on the tranquility and lack of sharp noises and you know... how much air do I need to stay... like when should I take my next breath, and you know if I take my next breath is it going to be really deep breath.* (P9)

Finally when transitioning to phase 3 and losing the movement on a vertical axis, their attention shifted back to their body and "letting go":

> *OK, now I'm controlling my breath, and then with the white peaceful situation I attuned to my body and that was it, I wasn't controlling. I let that go...* (P17)

Cues in the VE for eliciting breath awareness

One of the most common difficulties for beginners in mindfulness breath FAM is attending to breathing without being distracted. In our design, this process was supported by the visual representation of breathing as a movement in the environment. As a matter of fact, participants were expected to first direct their attention outwards to the environment in order to be able to redirect it to the self. Their vertical position being controlled by how full their chest was simply allowed them to literally visualize their breathing, thus expliciting it.

> *I was more conscious of it [of breath] because of what I was seeing at the same time. [How did that make you conscious of breath?] I wasn't really concentrating only on my breath but also on what I saw... so I knew that I was breathing in but also by seeing where I was... or... at what point I was by seeing where I was.* (P10)

Figure 5 depicts the moment in which participant 17 became aware of the relationship between breath and the changes in the environment. The plot shows a change in their breathing pattern after the realization of their agency and control of the environment. The participant described this change as:

> *After a couple [breaths] I was like "no that's me, if I'm holding my breath I see down, every time I'm exhaling I'm down there, and every time I'm inhaling I'm up there" and then I tried to hold my breath both in the inhalation and exhalation and I was like* ***"Hey, yay, I got it"***. (P17)

Regarding the audio cues, the majority of participants made a connection between the sound and the breath through the visual cues of their position in the environment:

> *When I'm staying level there [on the surface]... the sound gets a little bit violent I guess. It was just like, there was some sort of something like chords going on with some dissonance pattern maybe bit when I was level there I felt like there something transcendental creature got real angry about what I was doing and like the sound got violent and even although I enjoyed being level there for a while I felt "for this sound to change I have to move" and I went back to breathe in breathe out pattern again.*(P15)

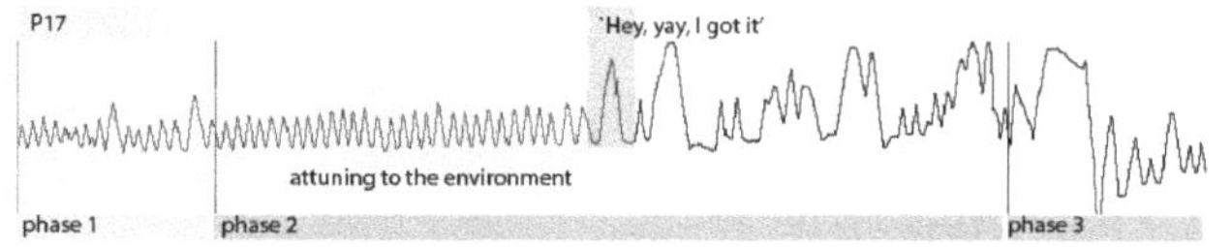

Figure 5. Change in breathing pattern following realization of how the participant's breathing influences the system

Finally, some participants related the perceived motion cues to perceived bodily sensations of the breath. After the initial "a-ha" moment of breath awareness, the motion cues caused participants to be more aware of the range, rhythm, depth, and other subtleties of their breathing and the other bodily sensations that accompany inhalation and exhalation.

> *I paid attention to correlation and inhaling... feeling my body move, and also like the airflow through my nose, and my mouth... I feel like when my body became still I inhaled completely, and there is moment of no movement then that's when the motion stopped.* (P11)

Breathing patterns and perceived sense of agency

The comparison of breathing data of Session 1 (participants unaware of agency) and Session 2 (participants aware of the agency and interacting with the environment) revealed different breathing patterns and the qualities of the experience associated with the interaction. This is depicted in Figures 6 and 7. The upper images of both Figure 6 and Figure 7 reveal that when these two participants were not aware of their agency in the environment (were not aware of the changes their breathing was causing to the environment), the breathing patterns remained somewhat consistent within all three phases. However, the bottom images demonstrate that the changes in the phases are followed by the changes in the breathing patterns, indicating that the perceived agency in the environment in this case, influenced how the user interacted with the environment (leading them to take on more active role) and their experience of it.

> *The first one I feel like because I didn't know that I had any control over what was happening I think it was lot more chaotic in my mind. And the second one was lot more calming because I felt I had that control.* (P10)

An interesting finding is that the sense of agency in some participants defined the perceptive position of the participant. In the first trials, those who were not aware of the direct control they had of the system were more likely inclined to take a passive role in the environment similar to the "observer's perspective" or that the system was pushing them up and down.

> *In the first one I was thinking that something is pushing me up and down like bouncing... this time I was thinking*

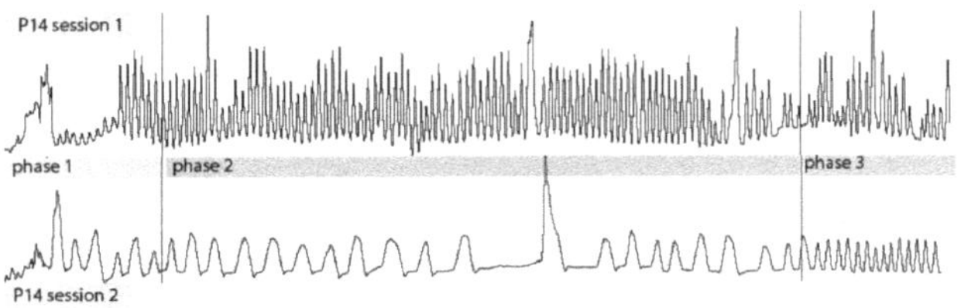

Figure 6. breathing data during Session 1: no perceived sense of agency vs breathing data in the Session 2: perceived agency (bottom image).

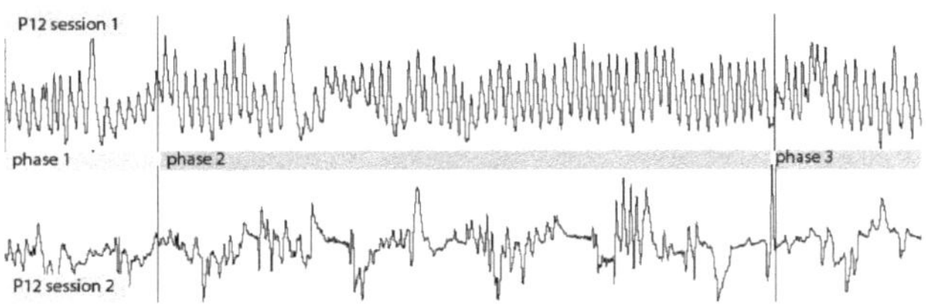

Figure 7. (upper image) breathing data in the Session 1 vs breathing data in the Session 2 (bottom image)

> *I am controlling this and I can calm this ocean... so I was feeling this was inside my body, it's not the system, it's inside of me.* (P12) (see Figure 7)

Creating the experience from "within"

Once the participants became aware of their breath, of the agency that their breath has in the environment and how they can control the experience, they started exploring the environment. After participants got familiar with the elements of the environment and identified the most pleasurable parts they started directing the experience from "within", through their breathing. Curating the experience through agency and perceived control over the environment helped the users to leverage the initial personal differences in initial reaction to the environment, while gradually familiarizing with the control they had in the environment.

Personal differences in experiencing ambiguous VE

Previous, real-life experiences influenced participants' experience of the environment; participants who fear water made negative associations with our environment and vice versa, participants who relate positive experiences to being in the water found the environment more pleasurable.

> *I didn't like the feeling of going underneath... probably not because of this experience but probably related to other experiences with water and because it looks a lot like water... [how does this make you feel] it's like a little bit of anxiety... or like fear in a way but not really fear because I know I can breathe.* (P10)

Following the evocation of previous experiences, the immersiveness of the medium triggered strong bodily sensations related to the overall quality of the experience.

> *I did experience that feeling of euphoria as I was coming up and and traveling upwards I did get that sensation of actually moving up and when I looked down I just really felt compelled this was overwhelming feeling for me to wanna go deeper... and I just wanted so hard to get rid of all of my breath so I could go deeper.* (P13)

> *It was kind of like swimming and holding a breath underneath the water... and then like I could feel that physical aspect to it.* (P7)

Perception of control alters the experience

A few participants initially experienced VE as anxiogenic or fear-inducing. However, they alleviated these initial negative associations once they realized that they were in control.

> *I was like "oh I'm in control actually" and that's very comfortable, because that anxiety went away straight away... it's very comfortable that anxiety was out of it... I can stay under the water as long as I want. That's totally fine – I told myself... and then I also see the patterns below and then I felt this urge to explore it.* (P15)

Curating the experience from a conscious control of a breath

In the second phase, once the participants were aware of their breath and control that they had over the environment, they would purposefully manipulate their breathing patterns to either stay in a preferred location in the environment or avoid potentially unpleasant stimuli.

> *I kind of found myself holding my breath when I breathe out because I liked the blue better the description of the VE... so I found myself kind of breathing out lot more than what I was inhaling that's what I was observing when I was really focused on my breathing.* (P16)

Some of the participants were able to identify moments when their breathing changed as a response to the environment, which induced a reaction. The reactions to irregular breath varied from focusing on breath closely to trying to change the position in the environment to a preferred one.

> *In that first phase I'd say I think I was just attuning to the environment. [how?] I listened to my breath and I realized because I'm not doing well, I suffer of sea sickness, so I was "I don't know if this is going work" and I realize that my breath was going faster than what would normally happen, but then I just tried to listen to my breath and that was pretty much what I did.* (P17)

Associating irregularity of breath with a particular part of the environment that helped participants know how to regulate breath when it becomes irregular:

> *Then I was asking myself: ok now I'm breathing quite heavily so... uhm... can I also maybe just try to get back to the white plane again?* (P8)

Subtle and unaware of influence of the environment on breathing patterns

In Session 1, only three participants were immediately aware of their agency. The data plots of the remaining eight participants indicate that there is an influence of the system on their breathing patterns. This influence is particularly clear in the moments of phase changes, revealing two trends:

1. Transient perturbation of breath by changes in the mapping
Figure 8 depicts the respiration sensor data for participant 16 in

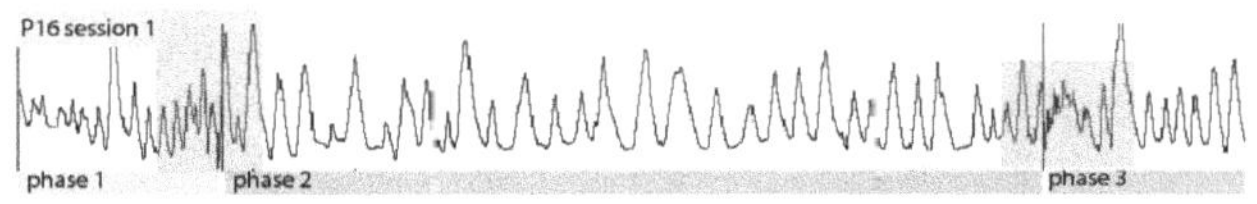

Figure 8. Respiration sensor data for participant 16 in the first session. Although P16 was not aware that their breath controlled the visual feedback, we observe shifts in breathing patterns following the changes between the three phases.

the first session. Although P16 was not aware that their breath controlled the feedback, we observe that transitions from phase 1 to phase 2 and from phase 2 to phase 3 were followed by changes in breathing patterns. Even though participants were not aware of the fact that they influenced the system, the data suggests that changes in the mapping of breath to the visual feedback induced perturbations of the participants' breathing patterns.

2. Sustained Influence of the mapping on the breathing patterns
Finally, the comparison of breathing patterns across phases showed that participants' breathing patterns changed on a longer time scale throughout the session. For example, the breathing period of P16 significantly changed between phase 1 and phase 2, as highlighted in Figure 8. In phase 2 participants tended to breathe at a slower rate, extending inhalation and exhalation over longer periods of time compared to phase 1.

DISCUSSION

In this section, we discuss the findings in the context of designing for breath awareness. This discussion is informed by participants' accounts about the process of becoming aware of their breath, and by our design decisions.

The role of sense of agency and control in overall experience

Understanding the control and engaging in the interaction impacts the quality of the experience and thus influences the experience-driven designs [12]. In our study protocol, we allowed participants to explore our system in Session 1 without giving away the details about how the system reacts to their breathing. Eight participants did not make an explicit connection between their breathing and changes in the environment in Session 1. We speculate that this happened due to an overall novelty with virtual reality applications, the lack of knowledge regarding the respiratory sensor, and that once immersed in the environment the participants were engaged in sense making of the scene rather than raising focus and awareness to the interaction. That could possibly explain why some of the participants reported that "something" [P12] was pushing them up and down, without realizing that that "something" was their breathing. Feeling of being dependent on the system while immersed in the VE caused unpleasant feelings that were alleviated once the participants became aware of their agency on the system. We find this to be a challenge to be addressed in future work. How we can design systems that make users aware of their agency in a subtle, less instructed way is yet to be addressed.

Interestingly, three participants did make an immediate connection between their breath and the environment. After the interview, when asked whether they meditate, and how often, those three participants reported that they regularly meditate. While we are careful not to draw strong conclusions from this observation, it has been shown that meditators have more accurate visual attention compared to non-meditators [19, 37] and this might explain why those three participants made an immediate connection.

In conclusion, while the system did not change, perceived sense of agency and control over the system determined the qualities of the experience: if the sense of agency was not perceived, the experience was more likely to be unpleasant. Understanding how the system could be controlled was crucial in a further unfolding of the experience. Participants exercised control especially in the parts of the environment that were more likely to induce fear and anxiety. At signs of discomfort caused either by the movement or audio-visual feedback, participants consciously changed their breathing to influence changes in the environment towards creating a more pleasant experience.

Complexity of the VE mediated through gradual introduction of the elements through phases

During the design process we were faced with the decision of how much feedback is optimal for eliciting breath awareness while preventing possible distractions. Through an iterative design process we decided to gradually increase the threshold for the stimulus, introducing sound as the first cue, and then movement as the second cue to breathing. This allowed participants to familiarize themselves with the environment before introducing more stimulating, and more obvious cues such as the movement along the vertical axis.

The majority of the participants described the up-down movement as the most dominating cue to one's breathing in our environment. One explanation might be that of the immersiveness of VR as a medium that can elicit bodily sensations related to locomotion. Moving on the vertical axis up and down was described as being on the roller coaster or a swing. In the second phase, the majority of participants' reports about breathing were related to the movement rather than sound. Sound as a cue was discussed within the first and third phase, when the movement cues were absent. The absence of the movement allowed the participants to listen and "attune" to their breath:

> *[in the end the third phase] I was just watching and I heard a sound but my attention and my focus was inside and just listening what was happening... in the second [the second phase] I was still doing that but because I knew I could control what I was watching instead of attuning to my breath I was using my breath to change what I was observing.* (P17)

Despite our attempts to understand an optimal amount of cues to guide the user's attention through the pilot study from which we drew insights for the final design presented here, some of the participants' accounts imply that a few things distracted them from fully attending to breathing. The main distractions are related to the interaction design: the velocity of the movement on the vertical axis was reported as too fast. Since the mapping of the movement was not elaborate in this iteration of the system, we see the potential of fine-tuning the mapping of the movement and better controlling for the velocity. We speculate that fine-tuning of the movement parameters will provide more opportunities for variety in how users interact with the system and how breath awareness can be raised in more subtle movements in the environment, and this will be explored in our future work.

Attuning to the environment

While we expected to see the changes in breathing patterns within different phases in Session 2 when the participants were aware of their agency and how they control the changes in the environment, unexpected findings emerged from Session 1. Even though the participants were not aware of the differences between the three phases, nor were they aware of how they influence changes in the environment, breathing data revealed that breathing patterns changed in participants (9 out of 11 participants) following shifts between phase 1 to phase 2 to phase 3. This suggests that our virtual environment influenced the breathing patterns through implicit mechanisms, and we are curious to explore this further.

Meditation tool

As a part of inquiry after the micro-phenomenology interview, we asked the participants: "If we tell you that this VE is a tool, what would you use this tool for?". The majority of the participants responded that they would use it to: overcome a fear of water, reflect, isolate themselves from distractions, or meditate. One of the participants even compared the breath-driven control to breathing exercises often done as an intro to mindfulness meditation practice:

> *it felt... it's kind of when you are meditating and you do breath work before. And so I felt kind of the same in terms I wasn't using breathing technique but to say "ok now I'm controlling my breath" and then with the white peaceful situation I attuned to my body and that was it, I wasn't controlling I let that go.* (P17)

Presence of visual cues helped the participants focus on their breath which is commonly reported as an obstacle in novice meditators:

> *You can pay more attention to the visual or what's in front of you in environment to make that difference in your body instead of having to pay attention to your breathing to a affect your breathing, you pay attention to the environment to affect your breathing.* (P10)

Traditional mindfulness meditation requires mediators to maintain some kind of *meta-awareness* so they can notice once their mind wanders off and they lose focus on their breathing and gently guide their attention back to their intended point of focus. This need to maintain a meta-awareness constitutes one of the main meditation challenges and obstacles especially for novice meditators. Similar to the playful interaction paradigm in the auditory environment of *Sonic Cradle* [73, 74], the audio-visual virtual environment in the current study was designed to subtly and unobtrusively help users to re-focus their attention to their breathing once they lost it – as if the system would simulate the meta-awareness that the users might not have developed yet. Instead of requiring users to maintain meta-awareness, our system was designed to help users re-orient their focus in a more playful manner, which we hope will eventually help them to more easily re-direct focus in their everyday life.

Commentary on the methodology: Can we trust the participant's descriptions?

In this study, the interviewer has been trained in the method, but none of our participants have been subject to a micro-phenomenology interview prior to participating in our study. While no method to our knowledge can provide us with conclusive evidence that participant's actual experience matches their description of it, we found some signs of such matchings. When we compared participants' interviews with their breathing data, it showed that the descriptions explained the breathing data such as changes in breathing rhythm patterns when participants reported that they changed their breathing, or holding the breath to stay in a particular part of the environment, or sudden deep inhales/exhales showed in plots. Despite the difficulties that some of the participants experienced with an evocation of the experience, we are confident in the validity of the descriptions because their descriptions can explain the breathing data and the breathing data corroborates their descriptions. However, we are yet to explore what is the level of detail in the descriptions that we can obtain from participants and how fine-grained descriptions correlate with the breathing data.

CONCLUSION

Our motivation was to gain a deeper understanding of how the experience of becoming aware of breath in VE unfolds. Previous mindfulness-based designs that employ breath demonstrated the important role that breathing and breath awareness hold in mindfulness practices. However, the understanding of the process of how people become aware of breath through embodied interaction was largely missing and the goal of this study was to take us a step closer to that knowledge. Our contribution is threefold: First, we presented the design of a system that employs breathing as embodied interaction in VE for eliciting breath awareness; Second, we conducted a micro-phenomenology inquiry and unveiled the mechanisms of becoming aware of breath; Third, we presented the findings that revealed the process of becoming aware of breathing in VE and demonstrated the importance of a sense of agency, understanding of control and possible subtle impact of the environment on breathing patterns without users being aware of it. In addition, some of the initial unpleasant experiences and personal differences in the quality of how participants experienced VE can be alleviated if users are enabled to curate their experiences. Finally, we contribute to the research on micro-phenomenology and HCI by revealing that participants' descriptions of their experience can describe their breathing data. This indicates the potential of micro-phenomenology and motivates us to continue to explore this methodology paired with physiological data in future work.

ACKNOWLEDGMENTS

The authors would like to thank all the volunteers for participating in the study, Ash Tanasiychuk for tireless proofreading, and the reviewers for their valuable feedback.We would like to acknowledge that this research would not be otherwise possible without the grant support from The Social Sciences and Humanities Research Council of Canada (SSHRC), and equipment support from Natural Sciences and Engineering Research Council (NSERC).

REFERENCES

1. Aino Ahtinen, Elina Mattila, Pasi Välkkynen, Kirsikka Kaipainen, Toni Vanhala, Miikka Ermes, Essi Sairanen, Tero Myllymäki, and Raimo Lappalainen. 2013. Mobile mental wellness training for stress management: feasibility and design implications based on a one-month field study. *JMIR mHealth and uHealth* 1, 2 (2013).
2. Judith Amores, Xavier Benavides, and Pattie Maes. 2016. Psychicvr: Increasing mindfulness by using virtual reality and brain computer interfaces. In *Proceedings of the 2016 CHI Conference Extended Abstracts on Human Factors in Computing Systems*. ACM, 2–2.
3. Kirk Warren Brown and Richard M Ryan. 2003. The benefits of being present: mindfulness and its role in psychological well-being. *Journal of personality and social psychology* 84, 4 (2003), 822.
4. Susanne BÃ¸dker. 2006. When Second Wave HCI Meets Third Wave Challenges. In *Proceedings of the 4th Nordic Conference on Human-computer Interaction: Changing Roles (NordiCHI '06)*. ACM, New York, NY, USA, 1–8. DOI:http://dx.doi.org/10.1145/1182475.1182476
5. Rafael A Calvo and Dorian Peters. 2014. *Positive computing: technology for wellbeing and human potential*. MIT Press.
6. Yves Candau, Jules Françoise, Sarah Fdili Alaoui, and Thecla Schiphorst. 2017. Cultivating kinaesthetic awareness through interaction: Perspectives from somatic practices and embodied cognition. In *Proceedings of the 4th International Conference on Movement Computing*. ACM, 21.
7. Sixian Chen, John Bowers, and Abigail Durrant. 2015. 'Ambient Walk': A Mobile Application for Mindful Walking with Sonification of Biophysical Data. In *Proceedings of the 2015 British HCI Conference (British HCI '15)*. ACM, New York, NY, USA, 315–315. DOI: http://dx.doi.org/10.1145/2783446.2783630
8. Luca Chittaro and Andrea Vianello. 2014. Computer-supported Mindfulness: Evaluation of a Mobile Thought Distancing Application on Naive Meditators *Int. J. Hum.-Comput. Stud.* 72, 3 (March 2014), 337–348. DOI: http://dx.doi.org/10.1016/j.ijhcs.2013.11.001
9. Katie Derthick. 2014. Understanding Meditation and Technology Use. In *CHI '14 Extended Abstracts on Human Factors in Computing Systems (CHI EA '14)*. ACM, New York, NY, USA, 2275–2280. DOI: http://dx.doi.org/10.1145/2559206.2581368
10. Anselm Doll, Britta K Hölzel, Satja Mulej Bratec, Christine C Boucard, Xiyao Xie, Afra M Wohlschläger, and Christian Sorg. 2016. Mindful attention to breath regulates emotions via increased amygdala–prefrontal cortex connectivity. *NeuroImage* 134 (2016), 305–313.
11. Paul Dourish. 2004. *Where the action is: the foundations of embodied interaction*. MIT press.
12. Laura L Downey. 2015. *Well-being technologies: Meditation using virtual worlds*. Ph.D. Dissertation. Nova Southeastern University.
13. Isabelle Du Plessis. 2017. Strata: a biometric VR experience. In *ACM SIGGRAPH 2017 VR Village*. ACM, 14.
14. Norman Farb, Jennifer Daubenmier, Cynthia J Price, Tim Gard, Catherine Kerr, Barnaby D Dunn, Anne Carolyn Klein, Martin P Paulus, and Wolf E Mehling. 2015. Interoception, contemplative practice, and health. *Frontiers in psychology* 6 (2015), 763.
15. Jules Françoise, Yves Candau, Sarah Fdili Alaoui, and Thecla Schiphorst. 2017. Designing for Kinesthetic Awareness: Revealing User Experiences through Second-Person Inquiry. In *Proceedings of the 2017 CHI Conference on Human Factors in Computing Systems*. ACM, 5171–5183.
16. William Gaver. 2012. What Should We Expect from Research Through Design?. In *Proceedings of the SIGCHI Conference on Human Factors in Computing Systems (CHI '12)*. ACM, New York, NY, USA, 937–946. DOI:http://dx.doi.org/10.1145/2207676.2208538
17. William W. Gaver, Jacob Beaver, and Steve Benford. 2003. Ambiguity As a Resource for Design. In *Proceedings of the SIGCHI Conference on Human Factors in Computing Systems (CHI '03)*. ACM, New York, NY, USA, 233–240. DOI: http://dx.doi.org/10.1145/642611.642653
18. Asma Ghandeharioun and Rosalind Picard. 2017. BrightBeat: Effortlessly Influencing Breathing for Cultivating Calmness and Focus. In *Proceedings of the 2017 CHI Conference Extended Abstracts on Human Factors in Computing Systems*. ACM, 1624–1631.
19. Holley S Hodgins and Kathryn C Adair. 2010. Attentional processes and meditation. *Consciousness and cognition* 19, 4 (2010), 872–878.
20. Trevor Hogan. 2015. Tangible Data, a Phenomenology of Human-Data Relations. In *Proceedings of the Ninth International Conference on Tangible, Embedded, and Embodied Interaction (TEI '14)*. ACM Press, Stanford, CA, USA, 425–428. DOI: http://dx.doi.org/10.1145/2677199.2691601
21. Britta K Hölzel, Sara W Lazar, Tim Gard, Zev Schuman-Olivier, David R Vago, and Ulrich Ott. 2011. How does mindfulness meditation work? Proposing mechanisms of action from a conceptual and neural perspective. *Perspectives on psychological science* 6, 6 (2011), 537–559.

22. Kristina Höök, Martin P Jonsson, Anna Ståhl, and Johanna Mercurio. 2016. Somaesthetic Appreciation Design. In *Proceedings of the 2016 CHI Conference on Human Factors in Computing Systems (CHI '16)*. ACM, San Jose, CA, USA, 3131–3142. DOI: http://dx.doi.org/10.1145/2858036.2858583

23. Kristina Höök, Martin P. Jonsson, Anna Ståhl, and Johanna Mercurio. 2016. Somaesthetic Appreciation Design. In *Proceedings of the 2016 CHI Conference on Human Factors in Computing Systems (CHI '16)*. ACM, New York, NY, USA, 3131–3142. DOI: http://dx.doi.org/10.1145/2858036.2858583

24. Ravinder Jerath, Molly W Crawford, Vernon A Barnes, and Kyler Harden. 2015. Self-regulation of breathing as a primary treatment for anxiety. *Applied psychophysiology and biofeedback* 40, 2 (2015), 107–115.

25. Daniel Johnson, Sebastian Deterding, Kerri-Ann Kuhn, Aleksandra Staneva, Stoyan Stoyanov, and Leanne Hides. 2016. Gamification for health and wellbeing: A systematic review of the literature. *Internet Interventions* 6 (2016), 89–106.

26. Jon Kabat-Zinn. 2003. Mindfulness-Based Interventions in Context: Past, Present, and Future. *Clinical Psychology: Science and Practice* 10, 2 (2003), 144–156. DOI: http://dx.doi.org/10.1093/clipsy.bpg016

27. Eric Kandel. 2016. *Reductionism in Art and Brain Science: Bridging the Two Cultures*. Columbia University Press.

28. Stephen Kaplan. 1995. The restorative benefits of nature: Toward an integrative framework. *Journal of environmental psychology* 15, 3 (1995), 169–182.

29. Stephen Kaplan. 2001. Meditation, Restoration, and the Management of Mental Fatigue. *Environment and Behavior* 33, 4 (July 2001), 480–506. DOI: http://dx.doi.org/10.1177/00139160121973106

30. Kiat Hui Khng. 2016. A better state-of-mind: deep breathing reduces state anxiety and enhances test performance through regulating test cognitions in children. *Cognition and Emotion* (2016), 1–9.

31. Bassam Khoury, Tania Lecomte, Guillaume Fortin, Marjolaine Masse, Phillip Therien, Vanessa Bouchard, Marie-Andrée Chapleau, Karine Paquin, and Stefan G Hofmann. 2013. Mindfulness-based therapy: a comprehensive meta-analysis. *Clinical psychology review* 33, 6 (2013), 763–771.

32. Ilkka Kosunen, Mikko Salminen, Simo Järvelä, Antti Ruonala, Niklas Ravaja, and Giulio Jacucci. 2016. RelaWorld: neuroadaptive and immersive virtual reality meditation system. In *Proceedings of the 21st International Conference on Intelligent User Interfaces*. ACM, 208–217.

33. Tatia MC Lee, Mei-Kei Leung, Wai-Kai Hou, Joey CY Tang, Jing Yin, Kwok-Fai So, Chack-Fan Lee, and Chetwyn CH Chan. 2012. Distinct neural activity associated with focused-attention meditation and loving-kindness meditation. *PLoS One* 7, 8 (2012), e40054.

34. Ann Light. 2006. Adding method to meaning: A technique for exploring peoples' experience with technology. *Behaviour & Information Technology* 25, 2 (2006), 175–187. DOI: http://dx.doi.org/10.1080/01449290500331172

35. Ann Light. 2008. Transports of delight? What the experience of receiving (mobile) phone calls can tell us about design. *Personal and Ubiquitous Computing* 12, 5 (2008), 391–400.

36. Ann Light. 2009. Negotiations in space: The impact of receiving phone calls on the move. *The reconstruction of space and time: Mobile communication practices* (2009), 191–213.

37. Dominique P Lippelt, Bernhard Hommel, and Lorenza S Colzato. 2014. Focused attention, open monitoring and loving kindness meditation: effects on attention, conflict monitoring, and creativity–A review. *Frontiers in psychology* 5 (2014).

38. Antoine Lutz, Heleen A Slagter, John D Dunne, and Richard J Davidson. 2008. Attention regulation and monitoring in meditation. *Trends in cognitive sciences* 12, 4 (2008), 163–169.

39. Anna Macaranas, Alissa N Antle, and Bernhard E Riecke. 2015. What is intuitive interaction? balancing users' performance and satisfaction with natural user interfaces. *Interacting with Computers* 27, 3 (2015), 357–370.

40. John McCarthy and Peter Wright. 2004. Technology As Experience. *interactions* 11, 5 (Sept. 2004), 42–43. DOI: http://dx.doi.org/10.1145/1015530.1015549

41. A Relaxing Virtual Reality Application / Guided Meditation. 2017. (2017). http://guidedmeditationvr.com/about-2/

42. Cubicle Ninjas.Virtual Reality Meditation. 2016. (2016). http://guidedmeditationvr.com/about-2/

43. Lumen VR meditation. 2016. (2016). https://www.viveport.com/apps/c666dd8d-e42b-403c-91d3-58693f268220

44. W-E Mehling. 2001. The experience of breath as a therapeutic intervention–psychosomatic forms of breath therapy. A descriptive study about the actual situation of breath therapy in Germany, its relation to medicine, and its application in patients with back pain. *Complementary Medicine Research* 8, 6 (2001), 359–367.

45. Claire Petitmengin : Micro-phenomenology. 2017. (2017). https://www.microphenomenology.com/

46. Movement and Meaning | Canarie Middleware. 2017. (2017). http://www.mplusm.ca/

47. Just Let Go on the App Store. 2011. (2011). https://itunes.apple.com/us/app/just-let-go/id439683407?mt=8

48. Lotus Bud Mindfulness Bell on the App Store. 2012. (2012). https://itunes.apple.com/us/app/lotus-bud-mindfulness-bell/id502329366?mt=8

49. Rakesh Patibanda, Florian'Floyd' Mueller, Matevz Leskovsek, and Jonathan Duckworth. 2017. Life Tree: Understanding the Design of Breathing Exercise Games. In *Proceedings of the Annual Symposium on Computer-Human Interaction in Play*. ACM, 19–31.

50. Claire Petitmengin. 2006. Describing one's subjective experience in the second person: An interview method for the science of consciousness. *Phenomenology and the Cognitive Sciences* 5, 3-4 (2006), 229–269. DOI: http://dx.doi.org/10.1007/s11097-006-9022-2

51. Pierre Philippot, Gaëtane Chapelle, and Sylvie Blairy. 2002. Respiratory feedback in the generation of emotion. *Cognition & Emotion* 16, 5 (2002), 605–627.

52. Mirjana Prpa, Karen Cochrane, and Bernhard E. Riecke. 2015. Hacking Alternatives in 21st Century: Designing a Bio-Responsive Virtual Environment for Stress Reduction. In *Pervasive Computing Paradigms for Mental Health*, Silvia Serino, Aleksandar Matic, Dimitris Giakoumis, Guillaume Lopez, and Pietro Cipresso (Eds.). Number 604 in Communications in Computer and Information Science. Springer International Publishing, 34–39. http://link.springer.com/chapter/10.1007/978-3-319-32270-4_4 DOI: 10.1007/978-3-319-32270-4_4.

53. Mirjana Prpa, Kivanc Tatar, Philippe Pasquier, and Bernhard Riecke. 2016. Pulse Breath Water. http://madzie.com/portfolio/pulse-breath_-water/. (2016). [Online; accessed March 2018].

54. Mirjana Prpa, Kıvanç Tatar, Bernhard E Riecke, and Philippe Pasquier. 2017. The Pulse Breath Water System: Exploring Breathing as an Embodied Interaction for Enhancing the Affective Potential of Virtual Reality. In *International Conference on Virtual, Augmented and Mixed Reality*. Springer, 153–172.

55. Cassandra L Reese. 2017. *Breath in Motion: Breath Awareness Design Research Study*. Ph.D. Dissertation. Kent State University.

56. Giuseppe Riva, Rosa M Baños, Cristina Botella, Fabrizia Mantovani, and Andrea Gaggioli. 2016. Transforming experience: the potential of augmented reality and virtual reality for enhancing personal and clinical change. *Frontiers in Psychiatry* 7 (2016).

57. Curtis Roads. 1996. *The Computer Music Tutorial*. The MIT Press, Cambridge, Mass.

58. Joan Sol Roo, Renaud Gervais, and Martin Hachet. 2016. Inner garden: An augmented sandbox designed for self-reflection. In *Proceedings of the TEI'16: Tenth International Conference on Tangible, Embedded, and Embodied Interaction*. ACM, 570–576.

59. Thecla Schiphorst. 2009a. soft(n). In *Proceedings of the 27th international conference extended abstracts on Human factors in computing systems (CHI EA '09)*. ACM, Boston, MA, USA, 2427. DOI: http://dx.doi.org/10.1145/1520340.1520345

60. Thecla Schiphorst. 2009b. *The Varieties of User Experience: Bridging Embodied Methodologies from Somatics and Performance to Human Computer Interaction, Ph.D. dissertation*. Ph.D. dissertation. Simon Fraser University. http://www.sfu.ca/~tschipho/PhD/PhD_thesis.html

61. Thecla Schiphorst. 2011. Self-evidence: applying somatic connoisseurship to experience design. In *CHI'11 extended abstracts on human factors in computing systems*. ACM, 145–160.

62. Richard Schusterman. 2012. Somaesthetics definition. In *ncyclopedia of Human-Computer Interaction. Interaction Design Foundation*.

63. Phoebe Sengers, Kirsten Boehner, Shay David, and Joseph 'Jofish' Kaye. 2005. Reflective Design. In *Proceedings of the 4th Decennial Conference on Critical Computing: Between Sense and Sensibility (CC '05)*. ACM, New York, NY, USA, 49–58. DOI: http://dx.doi.org/10.1145/1094562.1094569

64. C. Shaw, D. Gromala, and A. Fleming Seay. 2007. The meditation chamber: Enacting autonomic senses. *Proc. of ENACTIVE* 7 (2007), 405–408. http://www.sfu.ca/~shaw/papers/Enactive07MedChamber.pdf

65. Jacek Sliwinski, Mary Katsikitis, and Christian Martyn Jones. 2015. Mindful gaming: how digital games can improve mindfulness. In *Human-Computer Interaction*. Springer, 167–184.

66. Jacek Sliwinski, Mary Katsikitis, and Christian Martyn Jones. 2017. A Review of Interactive Technologies as Support Tools for the Cultivation of Mindfulness. *Mindfulness* (2017), 1–10.

67. Anna Ståhl, Martin Jonsson, Johanna Mercurio, Anna Karlsson, Kristina Höök, and Eva-Carin Banka Johnson. 2016. The Soma Mat and Breathing Light. In *Proceedings of the 2016 CHI Conference Extended Abstracts on Human Factors in Computing Systems*. ACM, 305–308.

68. Kıvanç Tatar and Philippe Pasquier. 2017. MASOM: A Musical Agent Architecture based on Self Organizing Maps, Affective Computing, and Variable Markov Models. In *Proceedings of the 5th International Workshop on Musical Metacreation (MUME 2017)*. Atlanta, Georgia, USA.

69. The Mindfulness App: Guided & Silent Meditations to Relax on the App Store. 2012. (2012). https://itunes.apple.com/us/app/mindfulness-app-guided-silent/id417071430?mt=8

70. Sherry Turkle. 2011. Alone together. (2011).

71. Marieke Van Rooij, Adam Lobel, Owen Harris, Niki Smit, and Isabela Granic. 2016. DEEP: A biofeedback virtual reality game for children at-risk for anxiety. In *Proceedings of the 2016 CHI Conference Extended Abstracts on Human Factors in Computing Systems*. ACM, 1989–1997.

72. Pierre Vermersch. 2009. Describing the Practice of Introspection. *Journal of Consciousness Studies* 16, 10-12 (2009), 10–12.

73. Jay Vidyarthi and Bernhard E. Riecke. 2013. Mediated Meditation: Cultivating Mindfulness with Sonic Cradle. In *CHI '13 Extended Abstracts on Human Factors in Computing Systems*. ACM, New York, NY, USA, 2305–2314. DOI: http://dx.doi.org/10.1145/2468356.2468753

74. Jay Vidyarthi, Bernhard E Riecke, and Diane Gromala. 2012. Sonic Cradle: designing for an immersive experience of meditation by connecting respiration to music. In *Proceedings of the designing interactive systems conference*. ACM, 408–417.

75. Juno VR. 2017. (2017). http://junovr.com/blog/2017/2/11/a-breathing-sensor-for-virtual-reality

76. Thought Technology Ltd. ProComp2 2 Channel Biofeedback & Neurofeedback System w/ BioGraph Infiniti Software Thought Technology Ltd. 2017. (2017). http://thoughttechnology.com

77. Gary Wolf. 2010. The data-driven life. *The New York Times* 28 (2010), 2010.

78. Throw your worry away! 2011. (2011). http://cdn.appshopper.com/icons/437/253188_larger.png

79. Christina Zelano, Heidi Jiang, Guangyu Zhou, Nikita Arora, Stephan Schuele, Joshua Rosenow, and Jay A Gottfried. 2016. Nasal respiration entrains human limbic oscillations and modulates cognitive function. *Journal of Neuroscience* 36, 49 (2016), 12448–12467.

80. Bin Zhu, Anders Hedman, and Haibo Li. 2017. Designing Digital Mindfulness: Presence-In and Presence-With Versus Presence-Through. In *Proceedings of the 2017 CHI Conference on Human Factors in Computing Systems (CHI '17)*. ACM, New York, NY, USA, 2685–2695. DOI: http://dx.doi.org/10.1145/3025453.3025590

Your Place and Mine: Designing a Shared VR Experience for Remotely Located Users

Misha Sra
MIT Media Lab
Cambridge, MA USA
sra@media.mit.edu

Aske Mottelson
University of Copenhagen
Copenhagen, Denmark
amot@di.ku.dk

Pattie Maes
MIT Media Lab
Cambridge, MA USA
pattie@media.mit.edu

ABSTRACT
Virtual reality can help realize mediated social experiences where distance disappears and we interact as richly with those around the world as we do with those in the same room. The design of social virtual experiences presents a challenge for remotely located users with room-scale setups like those afforded by recent commodity virtual reality devices. Since users inhabit different physical spaces that may not be the same size, a mapping to a shared virtual space is needed for creating experiences that allow everyone to use real walking for locomotion. We designed three mapping techniques that enable users from diverse room-scale setups to interact together in virtual reality. Results from our user study ($N = 26$) show that our mapping techniques positively influence the perceived degree of togetherness and copresence while the size of each user's tracked space influences individual presence.

ACM Classification Keywords
H.5.1. Information Interfaces and Presentation (e.g. HCI): Artificial, augmented, and virtual realities

Author Keywords
Virtual Reality; Embodiment; Room-scale VR; Social; Dancing

Figure 1: Participant 1 (top, male) in their physical and virtual space respectively, waving at participant 2 (bottom, female) in a different physical space, who waves back. To support shared virtual spaces for geographically distributed participants in room-scale setups of different sizes, we created three physical-to-virtual space mapping techniques.

INTRODUCTION
Twentieth century philosopher Merleau-Ponty said humans are fundamentally related to space and based on their capacity to perceive through their body, they make meaning of space [28]. Of all digital technologies, nowhere are the notions of 'being' and 'space' of more consequence than in virtual reality (VR) as characterized by the fundamental concepts of *embodiment* and *presence*. Both 'being' and 'space' contribute to a user's sense of presence defined as "...the strong illusion of being in a place in spite of the sure knowledge that you are not there" [36].

A user is immersed in VR in two ways: first, through the representation of computer generated surroundings displayed from a first person point of view, and second, through a match between proprioceptive signals about the movements of their body with those of a corresponding virtual body [39]. In practice, a virtual body is often replaced by disembodied hands, which creates a conflict between proprioceptive data which tells the user their body is there, and sensory data in VR where the body does not exist. Embodiment is an attempt to reduce the conflict by providing a body representation where virtual body movements correspond with real body movements [36]. Studies have shown that reported presence is higher if the match between proprioception and sensory data is high [38, 40]. Because of this match, natural walking is a desired feature in VR applications [50], and has repeatedly been shown to be superior to other navigation methods such as flying or using game controllers [41, 50].

Embodied social VR can help realize the utopian environment where distance disappears and we interact as richly with friends, family, and colleagues around the world as we do with those around us. This could also allow us to have natural interactions with those who cannot travel to meet physically. In order to create such rich experiences, there are certain challenges we need to overcome. Room-scale VR systems allow users to freely walk around in a designated tracking area with their body positions translated into VR in realtime, thereby supporting natural movement in VR. Taking advantage of

DIS '18, June 9--13, 2018, , Hong Kong

ISBN 978-1-4503-5198-0/18/06. . . $15.00
DOI: https://doi.org/10.1145/3196709.3196788

natural movement afforded by room-scale VR, co-located room-scale VR experiences can allow all users physically located in the same tracking space to move around naturally in a shared virtual space. However, when users are remotely located, each user inhabits a different physical space. All the different spaces need to be mapped to a shared virtual space to can allow remote users to interact in close proximity.

In this paper, we present three approaches for mapping users' physical spaces to a shared virtual space for remote users to interact in virtual proximity. Our goal is to create experiences where users interact as richly over distance as they do with those in the same room. Our approach is novel in that prior work supporting multiuser interactions in VR does not take into account the size and shape of each individual user's tracking space. By mapping the different room-scale spaces into a single shared virtual space, our system allows each user to move in the shared virtual environment by walking in their physical space.Since walking has been shown to be the most natural form of virtual locomotion and consistently elicits higher presence than other navigation techniques [50], supporting natural walking was one of our design goals. In our study setup, two remotely located users with full body tracked avatars (see Figure 5) get a dance lesson together in VR. The lesson takes place in a park environment where a group of virtual onlookers also copy some of the instructors' dance moves (see Figure 3) presented during the lesson. We chose a dance lesson as our social scenario because dancing together affords natural exploration of space and body-based interaction, as opposed to tasks like modeling a car or city planning [49] that center around hand-based interactions. Prior research in virtual dance lessons has mostly focused on the analysis of a single user's whole body motion through different motion capture techniques [8, 18].

Our user study reports on the implications of three different strategies for mapping two physical tracked spaces to a single shared virtual space, namely *Scale*, *Kernel*, and *Overlap*. The different space mappings afford different activities and movement patterns. Our results show that partially or completely overlapping two spaces of different sizes allows for experiences with high levels of copresence. Adding a translation gain to the movements of a user in the smaller space allows them to access a shared virtual area as big as the larger space in the Scale mapping technique. However, this mapping technique showed to be the least preferred.

To the best of our knowledge, this paper is the first of its kind to report on the effects of spatial mapping strategies that support embodied multiplayer interactions for remotely located participants in room-scale VR.

The key contributions of our work for remotely located multiuser room-scale VR systems are the following:

1. Three novel physical space to shared virtual space mappings, and their associated trade-offs.
2. Insights from a user study ($N = 26$) exploring the impact of physical to virtual space mappings on presence, copresence, social interaction, and togetherness.
3. Four design guidelines for creating shared virtual spaces for remotely located users. These are derived from our experience and analysis of the user study results.

RELATED WORK

The work presented in this paper explores the influence of space mapping techniques on social interaction in a VR scenario where users are geographically distributed and have avatars that they can fully control through their own body movements. We summarize below a few most directly related works in areas of proxemics, the relationship between proprioception from real walking and corresponding visual feedback in VR, and multiuser or social VR experiences.

Proxemics

In an influential paper, Hall categorized interpersonal space into four zones of intimate, personal, social, and public distances that people maintain towards each other in the real world [19]. People adhere to similar norms in VR, keeping greater distances from humanoid avatars than cylinders [1]. Participants moved out of the way when approached by virtual avatars and also kept greater distances when there was mutual gaze [2]. Other studies have also shown that real world proxemics behaviors work similarly in VR [17, 52]. Skin conductance response was shown to vary with the distance of one or many virtual characters as expected on the basis of proxemics theory [26]. While face-to-face interaction generates the most vivid sense of copresence [14], the feeling of being in the same place with others is enhanced by embodiment [54]. The experience of ''togetherness'' in our dance lesson experience is facilitated by close interpersonal interactions made possible by physical to virtual space mapping, real walking for locomotion, and full body tracking.

Proprioception

Walking is a basic form of interaction with the real world and similarly fundamental and desirable in VR [22]. Studies have found that real walking is significantly better than both walking-in-place and flying in terms of simplicity, straightforwardness, and naturalness of locomotion in VR [41, 50]. Research shows that a proprioceptive match between real and virtual body movements can enhance presence [39, 42]. These findings have led to research that supports walking through the development of tracking systems so users can move about in the physical space [51] and the building of mechanical walking devices such as treadmills, roller skates, and foot plates [7, 9, 22, 23]. Recently, walking in VR has been made possible for consumers through room-scale tracking included with the HTC Vive and mechanical devices like the Virtuix Omni[1]. Presence in VR is impacted by perception through the visual, auditory, and kinesthetic senses. Subjective presence is significantly correlated with the degree of association with a virtual body which suggests that substantial presence gains can be had from tracking all limbs and customizing avatar appearance [50]. Natural body movements in VR also provide improved task performance [32], and benefits for memory and cognition [53]. Our system is designed to support two

[1] http://www.virtuix.com/

users with different tracked space sizes. The mapping techniques allow virtual movement through physical walking, and embodiment affords natural interactions in the shared virtual space.

Multiuser VR

The first established work where more than one person could simultaneously inhabit the same virtual world was called 'Reality Built for Two', proposed in 1990 [6]. Following this, several other systems were created for two or more users [13, 15] and today, support for online multiplayer systems is fast becoming commonplace. Outside the home, VR entertainment centers (The VOID or VRcade) provide playful experiences in warehouse-size spaces to multiple users simultaneously while allowing natural walking for locomotion. Another type of multiuser system is device-based asymmetrical VR where a VR user interacts with one or more non-VR users who may be in the same physical space or remotely connected through a PC or tablet [16, 44]. SnowballVR creates a space-based asymmetrical VR experience where the size of the tracked area is used to assign appropriate roles to each user [44]. Social VR applications like *Facebook Spaces* and *AltspaceVR* allow people from around the world to participate from seated or room-scale setups respectively. Neither of these social VR systems support full body tracking such as presented in Metaspace [45] for co-located users. Our system supports full body tracking for remotely located participants using off the shelf trackers. It does not require expensive motion capture suits or tracking systems which are the norm for full body tracking. We show that physical interaction supported by full body tracking and embodiment enables realistic behaviors in VR.

Collaborative Virtual Environments

Collaborative Virtual Environments (CVEs) involve the use of networked virtual reality systems to support group work [4, 49]. The key concept behind CVEs is that of shared virtual worlds whose occupants are represented to one another in graphical form and who interact with each other and with the virtual environment [10]. Oliviera et al. presented an early example of asymmetric collaboration where a VR user received guidance and instruction from a PC user [30]. CVEs do not necessarily need to reflect or embody the characteristics of conventional environments to enable them to support particular forms of activity or interaction [11, 40]. It has previously been shown that presence in VR is related to what the users can do and less so with the visual fidelity of the environment [37]. Our system uses a collaborative dancing lesson to facilitate social interaction.

SYSTEM DESCRIPTION

This paper investigates social interaction for a geographically distributed set of two users. The designed experience requires proximity afforded through a mapping of each user's physical space to a shared virtual space. To examine distinct physical to virtual space mappings, we implement the task of taking a VR dance lesson. This section starts by defining some terminology. We present four design goals and describe three space mapping approaches that we implemented. We follow with a description of the dance lesson application.

Terminology

- **Virtual environment or world** is the virtual space that is much larger than each user's tracked space.
- **Room-scale** is a type of VR setup that allows users to freely walk around a tracked area, with their real-life motion reflected in the VR environment.
- **Physical space or tracked space** is the real world area in which a user's body position and movements are tracked by sensors and relayed to the VR system.
- **Shared virtual space** is an area in the virtual world where remotely located users can 'come together' to interact with one another in close proximity. The shared area can be as big as the largest tracked space depending on the space mapping technique used. Each user can walk to and in the shared area by walking in their own tracked space.
- **Presence** is defined as the sense of ''being there.'' It is the ''...the strong illusion of being in a place in spite of the sure knowledge that you are not there'' [36].
- **Copresence**, also called ''social presence'' is used to refer to the sense of being in a computer generated environment with others [5, 35, 12, 34].
- **Togetherness** is a form of human co-location in which individuals become ''accessible, available, and subject to one another'' [14]. We use togetherness to refer to the experience of doing something together in the shared virtual environment.

While it is easy for multiple participants to be copresent in the same virtual world, supporting proximity and shared tasks that can elicit a sense of togetherness is much harder.

Design Goals

We outline a series of goals for our system inspired by [15] to enable remote social VR systems that allow for more natural experiences than currently available. Specific design goals of our system include:

Spatial Connection: supporting natural and realtime interaction between participants from different locations, and direct perception of others through their positions and orientations.

Space Heterogeneity: allowing users with different room-scale setups to interact within a shared virtual space.

Identity: using humanoid avatars with visuo-motor synchrony between the real and virtual bodies to support realtime interactions and natural behaviors similar to the real world.

Activity Diversity: supporting different activities that involve movement in space with occasional physical proximity (e.g., training, learning, creating).

Space Mapping

We designed and implemented three approaches for mapping two physical spaces of different sizes (L: $4m \times 4m$, larger space; S: $2m \times 2m$, smaller space) to a shared virtual space. These sizes were informed by 1) the most common quadratic play area as reported by the popular consumer VR platform [46], and 2) by the largest allowed play area for the

HTC Vive. The size of the shared space differs in each configuration but it does not prevent each user from using the entirety of their own tracked space for non-shared activities.

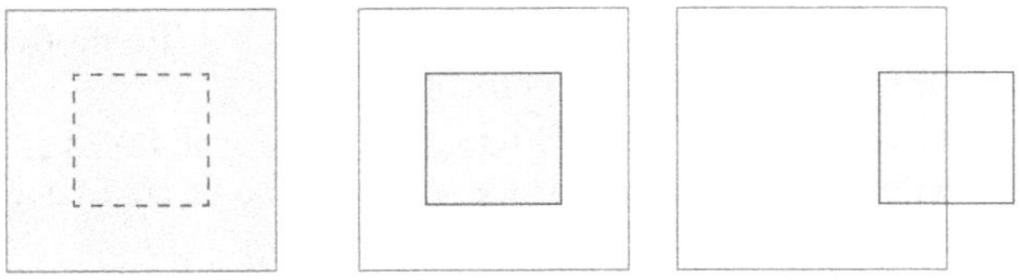

(a) (b) (c)

Figure 2: The three physical space to shared virtual space mapping techniques we designed: (a) Scale, (b) Kernel, and (c) Overlap. The red outline shows the larger physical space (L) and the blue outline shows the smaller physical space (S). Shared virtual space is shown in gray.

Scale stretches the smaller space to match the size of the larger space (see Figure 2a). This requires scaling the user's movements in the smaller space by a factor of L/S. A user in space **L** will thus find the user in space **S** moving twice as fast as normal while the user in **S** will find the user in **L** moving at a normal speed. The shared space coincides with the entirety of each user's tracked space. The area of the shared space equals that of the larger space for the two spaces R_1 and R_2; $max(R_1.size, R_2.size)$.

Kernel places the smaller tracked space in the center of the larger tracked space (see Figure 2b), making the shared virtual space coincide with the entirety of the smaller physical space. The user in **L** can walk around freely in their space but close interactions with the other user are limited to the shared space. The area of the shared space equals $min(R_1.size, R_2.size)$.

Overlap places the two tracked spaces next to each other with half of the smaller space overlapped with the larger space (see Figure 2c). This results in a shared space that coincides with half of the smaller tracked space. This is the smallest shared space of the three with an area of $.5 \times min(R_1.size, R_2.size)$.

Table 1 shows the virtual space as created by the different space mapping techniques and specific employed room sizes in our user study.

	Union space	Shared virtual space
Scale	16 m^2	16 m^2
Kernel	16 m^2	4 m^2
Overlap	18 m^2	2 m^2

Table 1: Union is the area of the combined physical space in each mapping configuration. The shared virtual space size varies with mapping technique resulting in the largest for Scale and smallest for Overlap.

Environment and Activity

Our goal was to find a collaborative activity that would address our design goals, namely a multiuser activity where spatial factors between people would determine the social dimension of the activity. We also wanted an environment where users could freely choose to engage with each other socially such that there would be no wrong way to use the system.

We created a virtual city park (see Figure 3) with a small creek, trees and picnic benches. Users were placed in the center of an open area in the park. A few virtual characters were placed in a circle around the users. Each user could see the boundary of their tracked space but could not see the other person's space boundary nor the shared space outline. This prevented any confusion about where the user should stay or move to and allowed for more natural interactions.

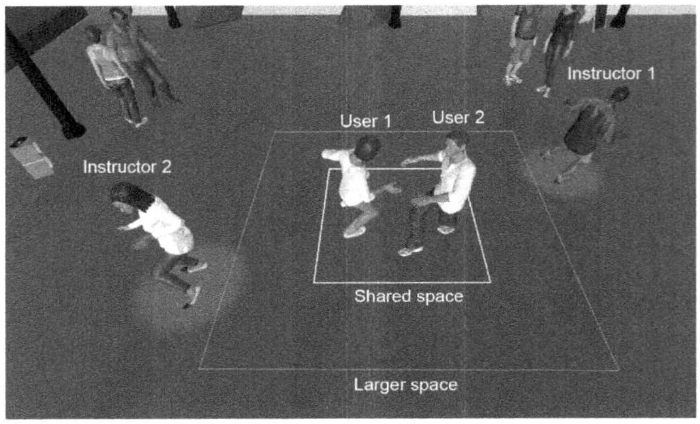

Figure 3: The dance lesson park setting as seen from a 3rd person point of view. The figure shows two users dancing together in the Kernel mapping technique, each with their own instructor in the spotlight who is facing away from them. The brightness of lights in the park has been turned up for the image though in the actual experience the lights are dimmed down which makes the spotlight stand out (see Figure 4).

We implemented a dance lesson experience. Each user had a personal dance instructor visible only to them and placed behind their dance partner (Figure 3). The instructor had its back facing the user to make it easy to follow dance moves (see Figures 3 and 4). Instructors were identifiable by a spotlight on them, their facing direction and their location in the scene which were different from all other characters. Users could choose to follow their instructor or improvise with each other.

Figure 4: Users copying their instructors' dance move. Top: Male user in tracked space (left), and his corresponding VR view (right). His dance instructor is shown in the spotlight behind the female participant. Bottom: Female user in tracked space (right), and her corresponding view (left). Her instructor is visible in the spotlight, behind the male user.

The lesson consisted of two *routines*; each routine comprised of four *dance moves*, done for around 10-15 seconds each, with a small break in between. The dance moves required users to move their arms or move their body and were designed to make the users come closer on occasion without requiring them to touch one another. The four dance moves were:

1. *Wave*: moving the body like a wave, from right to left.
2. *Push-the-roof*: both arms in the air moving up and down.
3. *Forward and backward*: moving two steps forward, and two steps backward.
4. *Sidestep*: taking two steps sideways to the left, and two to the right.

Body Tracking

Each user's body was tracked using a combination of three Vive Trackers[2] placed one on each foot and one on the lower back, two hand controllers and the HMD, along with an inverse kinematics system to create a realtime motion capture setup. The tracked points and the inverse kinematics system together create a system that provides real-time visuo-motor synchrony, between the real and the virtual body, which is considered one of the primary reasons for presence in VR [33, 48]. Users were represented as size and gender matched humanoid avatars with visuo-motor synchrony between the real and virtual bodies (see Figure 5).

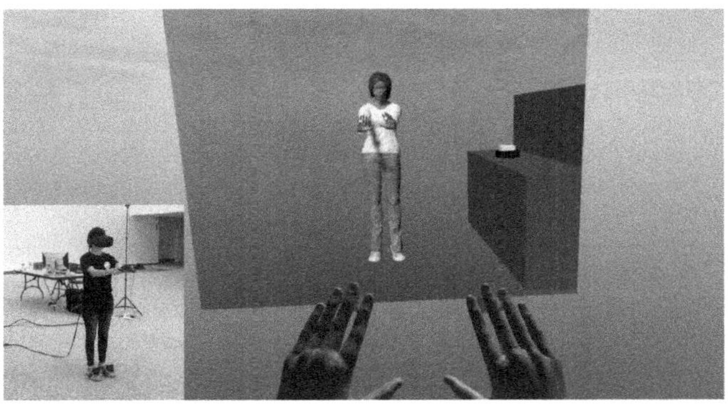

Figure 5: Before entering the park, participants go through an embodiment phase. Inset shows a participant in the physical space with Vive trackers on their feet and body; rest of the figure shows the participant's perspective. A mirror provides a full body view.

The hand controllers provided haptic feedback upon collisions with the other user's virtual body for an additional sense of awareness of the other person's location in the virtual space. This was especially useful in the *Scale* mapping because of high possibility of collisions due to user movement scaling. Research also shows that users consistently underestimate the spatial dimensions in VR [20]. Anecdotally, a few subjects mentioned that despite the avatar matching their height and arm span, it seemed bigger and the tracked space felt smaller in VR than in real life.

EXPERIMENT

We ran a user study to compare the three space mappings and to understand the fundamentals of embodied social VR from the users' perspectives.

[2] https://www.vive.com/us/vive-tracker/

Participants

We recruited 28 participants who were mainly local students. We paired participants in groups of two (14 groups) based on the time slots they requested; three groups consisted of participants who were familiar with each other. Nine participants were female; the average age was 20 years. Most participants had little to no previous experience with VR ($M = 2.0$, on a scale of 1-to-7; 1 being no experience, 7 being very experienced). One group (two participants) was discarded due to bad body tracking distorting the embodiment; the resulting analysis is done on 26 participants (13 groups). We reimbursed participants the equivalent of $10 USD, for one hour of participation.

Apparatus

We had two identical HTC Vive setups consisting of two base stations, an HMD, two hand controllers and three trackers, connected to a desktop PC (Windows 10; 16GB RAM; GEFORCE GTX 1080Ti). To increase mobility of participants we extended all cables by $3m$. To reduce network latency, the PCs were setup on a LAN connected with ethernet cables. We created the VR system in Unity with FinalIK for inverse kinematics. The 3D models were downloaded from the Unity Asset store and animations from Mixamo.

Task

We wanted to study social aspects in VR using a task that allowed us to compare participants' movements across different space sizes and mappings. We sought a multiuser task with a fixed progression to allow for assessment of both individual and collaborative performance. Unlike many collaborative tasks, choreographed dancing provides a proposed trajectory that allows for an objective assessment of both individual and collective effort. Dancing has previously been used in HCI to reason about embodied aspects of interaction design [25].

We intentionally chose not to employ common collaborative tasks such as a puzzle, or model building, since these seldom use room-scale movements or require body movements. Tasks like attending a lecture or viewing data visualizations together have been explored in prior work as collaborative VR tasks where multiple users are present in the same virtual space looking at the same thing together [29]. Our task is similarly collaborative as both users are in the same virtual space dancing together. Some dance moves are performed together, i.e., participants approach one another while facing each other, while other dance movements are performed independently but in proximity.

The choreography consisted of four different moves (wave, push-the-roof, stepping forward and backward, and sidestepping). While participants were encouraged to dance together, each participant had their own dance instructor, located behind the other participant, showing how to perform each move. Music accompanied the choreography. Each trial required participants to perform the choreography twice, matching the length of the music. Each trial lasted about 4 minutes, the length of the song (1 trial = 2 rounds $\times$ 4 dance moves $\times$ 15 seconds, excluding breaks). The total duration of the study was one hour per group, with three trials and questionnaires filled out after each trial.

Data Collection

We collected different types of data (see full list in Table 2):

Tracking. We recorded all raw position data for all sensors.

Interaction. We recorded collisions between avatars.

Self-report. Participants answered questionnaires about presence, togetherness, and social presence, three times each; once after each trial.

Design

The study was a mixed-design experiment with two independent variables: room size, administered between-subjects, and space mapping technique, administered within-subjects. All groups did three trials, one for each space mapping. The order of the trials was counter-balanced using a latin-square assignment. Dependent variables came from movement patterns and self-reports (see all dependent variables in Table 2).

Room Size

We manipulated the physical tracked room size as an independent variable to observe differences across space mappings attributable to the size of the room. We employed two different room size configurations: $2m \times 2m$ and $4m \times 4m$. One participant from each group was placed in the smaller space and the other one in the larger space.

We disabled the chaperone system (the blue 3D safety grid that warns users as they approach the tracked area boundary) but made each user's tracked space visible in VR with a green outline on the ground. The virtual park environment was identical for each user in both room sizes.

Space Mapping

All groups did a trial with each of the different space mappings (Scale, Kernel, and Overlap), in counter-balanced order.

Procedure

Participants were recruited using an internal email list and signed up for our experiment online in groups of two. After signing a consent form, participants were asked to read a short background story that fit the environment and task. Following that we attached the Vive trackers and helped the participants put on the HMD.

The experience was divided into two scenes. The participants went through an embodiment phase in the first scene where they stepped into the body of an avatar and spent a few minutes getting comfortable with the idea that moving their own hands or legs resulted in corresponding body part movements in their embodied avatar. Once satisfied, they pushed down on a big yellow button in the scene which took them to the park. At that point the two VR systems were connected and participants could see each other's avatars in addition to everything else in the park. Audio instructions were provided upon entering the park scene, and also during the experiment to tell the participant when to switch dance moves. An evaluator carried the cable behind each participant from a safe distance, making sure that it did not interfere with the participant's movements.

Participants spawned in the center of the shared space, one after the other. A yellow cross showed both participants where to walk to, before the dancing started. The crosses were placed close to the outer bounds of the shared space in a way that made the participants face each other, one meter apart.

Participants were asked to dance with abandon as an experimenter managed the cables to prevent tripping. We conducted the study in an open space with no physical obstacles so there was no fear of running into objects either. Most all participants danced freely, with observable playfulness in friend pairs who tried different movements in addition to following their dance instructors.

RESULTS

In this section we report on the insights from our study. We organize the results by dimensions from Table 2. We employed 5 dependent variables, with a total of 13 statistical tests.

Presence

Presence is defined as the sense of *being there* [42]. Presence was determined using the questions from the SUS-inventory [40] presented in a random order after each trial. The scores reflect how many questions (out of four) were answered with a score of 5 or higher (on a scale of 1-to-7) [27]. A score of 2 thus means that a participant reported a high score (≥ 5) on two of the four protocols in the questionnaire.

Room Size

We treat the SUS count as binomially distributed for a logistic regression on group (as in [27]). We found a significant difference for presence on room size ($\chi^2 = 3.97$ on 1 df, $p < .05$); the larger physical space created a higher sense of presence (see Figure 6).

Dimension	Source	Data			Measures
Presence	SUS [40]			S	Presence measures.
Togetherness	Basdogan et al. [3]			S	Sense of being together measures.
Copresence	GEQ (Social Presence Module) [21]; Jakobsen & Hornbæk [24]			S	Social presence measures.
Movement and use of space	Jakobsen & Hornbæk [24]		T	S	Movement patterns, VR sickness.
Interference and conflicts	Jakobsen & Hornbæk [24]	I	T		Collisions and conflicting actions.

Table 2: The investigated dimensions and their associated measures and analysis methods: Tracking data, Interaction data, Self-report.

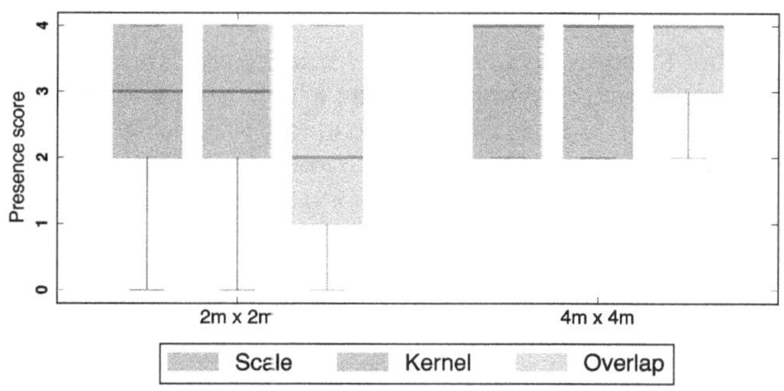

Figure 6: Presence scores divided between room size and space mapping. Room size significantly alters presence in VR, while the space mappings provide consistent levels of presence. Thick horizontal lines show medians, and the boxes represent interquartile ranges.

Space Mapping

We found no significant difference between space mapping techniques on presence; $\chi^2 = 0.35$ on 1 df, $p = .84$.

Summary

The results show that larger tracked areas lead to higher perceived sense of presence, even if the virtual spaces are otherwise identical. We also show that participants perceive comparable sense of presence regardless of the employed multi-room space mapping technique.

Togetherness

Five questions on the sense of being together (from [3]) were placed in random order in the questionnaire administered after each trial; each question was rated on a 1-to-7 scale. Table 3 shows the mean score for each question, and a togetherness score (1-to-5), computed as the number of questions (of five), which had a 'high' response (≥ 5). A Cronbach's alpha shows the internal consistency of the inventory.

	Scale	Kernel	Overlap
Sense of being with another person	4.5	5.3	5.2
You were not the only one involved	4.0	4.2	4.3
You and your dance partner danced together	3.3	4.0	4.5 *
A real experience of doing something together	4.3	4.5	4.9
Another human being interacted with you	4.2	5.2	4.9
Togetherness ($\alpha = .85$)	**2.3**	**2.9**	**3.0**

Table 3: Mean scores for items in the togetherness inventory. Scale scores consistently lower than the other space mappings. The scores that showed significantly different from Scale with a Wilcoxon rank-sum test on .05 are shown with *.

Room Size

Room size did not impact the degree to which participants had the sense of being together; togetherness for $2m \times 2m$ was $M = 2.5$ ($SD = 1.6$), and for $4m \times 4m$ it was $M = 2.9$ ($SD = 1.8$). A logistic regression for togetherness on room size showed as not significant, $\chi^2 = 0.65$ on 1 df, $p = .42$.

Space Mapping

Kernel and *Overlap* showed very similar degrees of togetherness (see Table 3), no significant differences were shown for any items between *Kernel* and *Overlap*. *Scale* consistently scored lower on all items compared to *Kernel* and *Overlap*. While only two of these were significantly different (and only for Overlap vs Scale), we believe that the scores together show that *Scale* is less optimal for experiences requiring high degrees of togetherness, and that *Kernel* and *Overlap* offer comparable degrees of togetherness.

Summary

We did not find a correlation with the size of a person's tracked space and the perceived degree of being together with another person in VR.

On the contrary, the employed space mapping technique seems to have an influence on the degree with which participants feel together. Scaling scores lower on all items in the togetherness inventory, one which showed significantly different on 0.05. *Kernel* and *Overlap* appear comparable in terms of togetherness, even if Kernel had twice the shared virtual space, and Overlap had a larger union virtual space.

Social Presence

Five questions on social presence (from [21, 24]) were presented in a random order in the questionnaire administered after each trial; each question was rated on a 1-to-7 scale. Table 4 shows the mean score for each question, and a copresence score (1-to-5), computed as the number of questions (of five), which had a 'high' response (≥ 5). A Cronbach's alpha shows the internal consistency of the inventory.

	Scale	Kernel	Overlap
I knew what my dance partner was doing	4.3	5.3 *	5.4 *
My dance partner knew what I was doing.	4.2	4.8	5.1
I felt connected with my dance partner.	3.5	4.6 *	4.5 *
What my dance partner did affected what I did.	3.7	4.2	4.3
What I did affected what my partner did.	3.5	4.0	3.9
Copresence ($\alpha = .93$)	**2.0**	**2.9**	**2.8**

Table 4: Mean scores for items in the social presence inventory. Scale scores consistently lower than the other space mappings. The scores that showed significantly different from Scale with a Wilcoxon rank-sum test on .05 are shown with *.

Room Size

Room size showed to have no significant effect on social presence experienced by the participants; copresence for 2×2 was $M = 2.3$ ($SD = 2.1$), and for 4×4 it was $M = 2.8$

($SD = 1.9$). A logistic regression for copresence showed no significant effect on room-size, $\chi^2 = .76$ on 1 df, $p = .38$.

Space Mapping

We found no significant differences between Kernel and Overlap on social presence. Scale, however, showed lower average scores on all items in the social presence inventory compared to the two other methods (see Table 4). For two of the questions, these differences were significantly different on .05 between Scale and the other methods, shown with a Wilcoxon rank-sum test.

Summary

We found no differences on social presence attributable to room size, while we found differences attributable to the space mapping technique.

Interestingly, this finding is the inverse of (single-person) presence; our findings suggest that the degree of being present in VR alone is mostly altered by the available walking space, while the social dimension of being in VR with another person is to a larger degree controlled by how the virtual shared space is mapped and what it affords.

Movement and Use of Space

We looked at the raw tracking data to assess how factors relating to the use of space changed across experimental conditions. We merged the data from the two VR stations, such that the potential data loss due to networking would not affect the logs.

Distance Traversed

We looked at which space mapping caused the greatest traversed distance in the virtual world. Figure 7 shows that, except for Scale, people in larger spaces move around more ($F(1,75) = 11.3, p = .001$); it also shows that Scale caused less overall movement. We speculate that scaling movements makes locomotion less desirable, and thus affects users' movement patterns. Walked distances in the real world can be upscaled by 26 percent, when they are mapped to virtual motions [47]. In the Scale mapping technique, user movements were upscaled by 100 percent, much higher than the formerly established imperceptibility threshold. Movements in VR that do not correspond to equivalent real world movements can cause a visuo-vestibular conflict which is believed to cause motion or VR sickness [31].

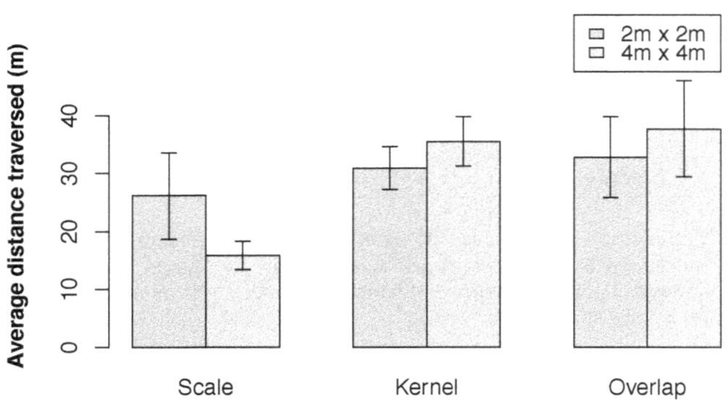

Figure 7: The mean distance traversed split into space mapping and room size. Error bars show standard deviation.

Raw Movements

Figure 8 shows the aggregated virtual movements visualized for each space mapping technique which reveals some notable trends. As evident in Figure 8a, contrary to expectations, Scale participants in the $4m \times 4m$ space moved much less than those in the $2m \times 2m$ space. Compared to the other two techniques also, participants in the larger space moved much less than participants in the smaller space in the Scale mapping. This is likely to avoid collisions because of unpredictable movements of the person in the smaller space, resulting from a translation gain of 1.5. This is possibly also the reason why we see low copresence scores for *Scale*.

Kernel (Figure 8b) shows the shared space to be inhabited primarily by the user in the small space, even if the person in the larger space is unaware of the boundary of the shared space; roughly half of the positions of the person in the larger space are observed in the shared space.

Overlap (Figure 8c) shows surprisingly little proximity between users; the small space user almost exclusively inhabits the shared space. It also seems to condense movements to a more fixed space (along the x-axis), compared to the other space mappings. Additionally it can be seen that the person in the smaller space overstepped the actual boundary (which was possible due to the lack of physical walls); this could have shifted all activity towards that direction.

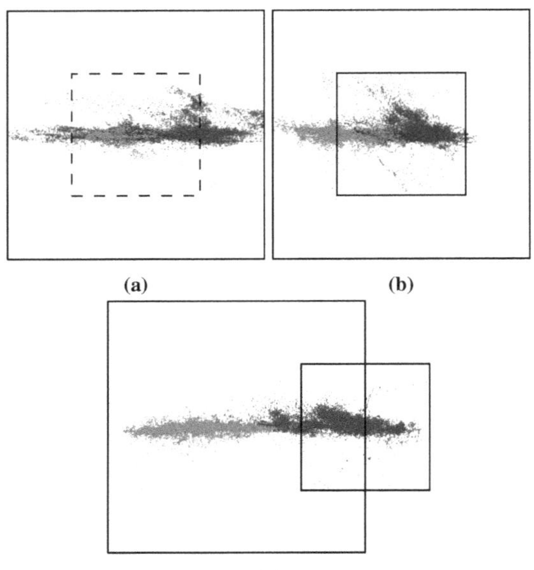

Figure 8: Raw virtual positions for all participants. Black borders show the large and small tracked spaces for both users. Blue observations show positions of participants in the smaller room; red observations are from participants in the larger room. Figures show how movement differed across the space mappings: (a) Scale, (b) Kernel, and (c) Overlap.

Distance Between Participants

We computed the average distance between the two virtual avatars throughout the entire study: Scale $1.01m$ ($SD = 0.36$), Kernel $1.09m$ ($SD = 0.31$), Overlap $1.92m$ ($SD = 0.29$).

Overlap caused significantly more distance between users; $F(1,76) = 68.2, p < .001$; due to the smaller shared space and the larger combined space. Scale and Kernel showed similar proximity between users' avatars; $F(1,50) = .4, ns$.

Table 5 shows how much time participants spent in different proxemic zones, as defined by Hall [19]; intimate (0-46cm), personal (46-120cm), and social (120-240cm). We note that Scale affords the most intimate interaction; Kernel mostly personal; and Overlap mostly interaction in the social zone.

Because we disabled the chaperone system and conducted our study in an open space without walls to prevent any accidental collisions with obstacles, users were able to walk outside of their virtual spaces. This however only happened to a small extent, and almost exclusively for Overlap (see Figure 8).

	Intimate	Personal	Social
Scale	24%	35%	41%
Kernel	9%	51%	40%
Overlap	2%	11%	87%

Table 5: Time participants spent in different proxemic zones.

VR Sickness

Participants in our study experienced very low VR sickness; on a scale of 1-to-7 on the question *How dizzy, sick or nauseous did you feel resulting from the experience, if at all?*, $M = 1.46$. Using an ANOVA we found no significant difference on room size; $F(1,75) = .59, p = .45$. We also found no significant difference on space mapping; $F(1,75) = .02, p = .88$.

Summary

We observed several differences in movement patterns due to both room size and space mapping technique; larger rooms cause more movement; Scaling causes little movement (especially by users immersed in the larger space); With Scale, users have the most intimate interaction; using the Overlap mapping causes larger distance between users. The participants overstepped the boundary to a very limited degree.

Interference and Conflicts

We provided participants with vibrotactile feedback through the hand controllers upon collisions between the avatars. That way participants were informed about bumping into each other even if it was not visually clear to them. Here we report movement conflicts defined as the average number of collisions between avatars lasting longer than 1 second. Our records show that, as expected, Scaling causes more conflicts than the other space mappings; Overlap causes the fewest: Scale $M = 5.0$ ($SD = 6.7$); Kernel $M = 1.0$ ($SD = 1.8$); Overlap $M = 0.1$ ($SD = 0.4$). These results reflect Hall's zones of interaction [19] and confirm previous findings about users exhibiting real world proxemics behaviors in VR.

DISCUSSION

Here we summarize our main findings, with a discussion of design implications for remotely located social VR experiences. Additionally, we provide some unanswered questions that can pave the way for future research directions.

The goal of our study was to examine the impact of space mapping techniques on copresence, social interaction, and the sense of being together for remotely located participants in room-scale VR setups. Even if no significant differences were found for copresence based on each user's tracked space size, we found differences in copresence between the three mapping techniques. Scale showed significantly worse than the other two techniques. We believe this may have been due to unpredictable and unnatural movement of the person in the smaller space (moving at 2x speed) as visible to the person in the larger space. Some participants remarked upon how the shared virtual space in Kernel (2x2m) felt crowded with two people while they felt comfortable sharing a similarly sized space with another person in the real world. The avatars were scaled to match each participant, so this difference in spatial perception and its resulting impact on proxemics may be due to factors unrelated to proprioception and warrants further exploration.

Similar to copresence, the sense of being together was not influenced by the size of the tracked area but the mapping techniques did influence the perceived sense of togetherness. In contrast, individual presence was dependent on each user's tracked space size and did not change between the mapping techniques. Even though Scale was found to be an undesirable mapping strategy for natural social interactions, we believe it still has potential if used with lower translation gain. We envision Scale being used for creating interesting gameplay involving super human capabilities. For example, if we were to replace the humanoid avatar with a flying wisp character, we think the fast unpredictable movements of the user in the smaller space, will become readily acceptable in the newer context, as they will be more in line with user expectations.

In summary, we found that two of the three mapping techniques provided a high sense of copresence and togetherness. Surprisingly, we found that the space mapping with the smallest shared space (Overlap) resulted in the least amount of proximity as it ended up being occupied mostly by the small space user. The different types of interactions afforded by the different mapping techniques suggest that experiences need to be specifically designed and matched with a mapping technique. They also suggest the audience for the designed experiences. For example, we may only want to create experiences for family members or friends when we know that the resulting personal space will be low. We summarize the findings relating to the design of mapping techniques in Table 6.

DESIGN GUIDELINES

We derived four guidelines from our experience of building and evaluating our system. We consider these guidelines useful for designing shared virtual experiences for remotely located participants, especially where each user has a different room-scale setup and is allowed to physically walk in VR. The guidelines focus on the structural elements of a shared virtual experience created by mapping different room-scale setups. Collaborative tasks, defined broadly, can be partly, completely, or not-at-all overlapping, and we have shown different mappings that support all these.

	Scale	Kernel	Overlap
shared space size	large	fair	small
personal space	high	fair	low
presence	high	high	high
social presence	low	high	high
togetherness	low	high	high
collisions	many	few	few
use of space	little	little	good
activity examples	travel games creativity	collaboration training education	sports healthcare tabletop

Table 6: Design implications for the three space mappings summarized.

Support Shared Space: To make the most of a room-scale setup, design experiences should allow participants to come together in the shared space when needed and explore individually at other times. This will support the most flexible use of each person's physical space while still supporting real-walking for locomotion and natural interaction in the shared virtual space. Depending on the type of experience (see Table 6) to be designed, the appropriate space mapping can be selected. For example, if the shared activity requires a lot of movement for each user, then Kernel is the best mapping technique. For example, remote collaboration for designing a large 3D object together where both need to freely move around the static objects or in education scenarios like viewing the structure of an enlarged molecule and viewing and manipulating it together.

Leverage Asymmetry: Instead of trying to fit all types of tasks into one type of shared virtual space, designers should leverage the inherent advantages of the different sizes of tracked spaces and the resulting mappings to design relevant tasks. For example, the Overlap technique is best suited for tasks where each user needs to maximize their movement space but the shared space can be small. Such a setup affords sports activities like ping-pong or tennis, or collaborative tasks where each user is placed on either end of a table, a room, or a hallway (meeting, tabletop games, or doctor/patient interactions in clinical psychology).

Design for Interaction: While all users are located in different physical spaces, they perceive the same virtual world. All users can hear and see each other doing things in VR, even if they are not directly involved with one another which can be distracting or engaging. Design tasks that require teamwork through shared manipulation of objects for creating challenging, productive and fun experiences.

Natural Embodiment: Our empirical work confirms that participants highly valued having an avatar that gave them the ability to ''physically'' and naturally engage with each other. Similarly physically walking in VR provided a satisfying sense of presence. We encourage creators of collaborate VREs to design shared spaces and interactions using natural locomotion, and only use teleportation or related transportation methods as a fallback technique if the space limit requires it.

Limitations and Future Work

This paper shows a first of its kind exploration of mapping techniques for remotely located multiuser VR systems. We decided on the three techniques because of their difference to cover a wide spectrum of applicative possibilities, given the physical space configurations supported by the HTC Vive. To entirely cover the gradient of social engagement, tasks and space mappings need to be modeled and studied as pairs. Our findings are based on two remotely located people taking a dance lesson together in a shared virtual environment.

In the future, we plan to extend our system to incorporate more simultaneous users to understand the limits of natural locomotion techniques and to explore combination navigation mechanisms. This will allow us to further investigate the novel design space of embodied remotely located VR experiences with natural locomotion and the impact of mapping techniques on social dynamics. Expanding the shared activity to include dances that require touching (e.g., waltz, tango) would benefit from exploration into haptics beyond vibrotactile feedback as included in the presented work. In such a scenario, the visual representation of solidity would be of special concern, such that when users interact, it should not appear as though their hands go through the other person's hands or body. It would be worthwhile to study mapping techniques for irregular space layouts as afforded by systems that use inside-out tracking similar to spaces created by [43].

We presented the design and user experience of three novel space mapping techniques together with their associated trade-offs in terms of phenomena like togetherness and use of space. Naturally, many more ways to blend physical spaces into multi-user virtual space are possible; we encourage further exploration in the area, that encompasses both algorithmic and user centric design challenges. Also, we encourage research in dynamic space mappings that may impact how space is mapped during immersion, based on, for example, users' activity and location.

CONCLUSION

In this paper we described the design, implementation, and evaluation of a VR system that allows geographically distributed embodied users to engage in a social dancing activity. We explored three ways of mapping two differently sized physical spaces to shared virtual spaces, and we report on how the mapping techniques influenced presence, social presence, togetherness, and movement. We found that the two mapping techniques, Kernel and Overlap, offered a high sense of copresence and togetherness, but caused different movement patterns, specifically when users were in close proximity. The mapping techniques support the design of different social activities based on movement and proximity requirements. A third mapping technique, Scale, showed reduced social presence and togetherness, but we foresee its usefulness in playful VR applications. We concluded with a set of design guidelines for creating social VR experiences for non co-located users.

ACKNOWLEDGEMENTS

We would like to thank Orson Xu for helping out with the user studies.

REFERENCES

1. Jeremy N. Bailenson, Jim Blascovich, Andrew C. Beall, and Jack M. Loomis. 2001. Equilibrium Theory Revisited: Mutual Gaze and Personal Space in Virtual Environments. *Presence: Teleoper. Virtual Environ.* 10, 6 (Dec. 2001), 583--598. DOI: http://dx.doi.org/10.1162/105474601753272844
2. Jeremy N. Bailenson, Jim Blascovich, Andrew C. Beall, and Jack M. Loomis. 2003. Interpersonal distance in immersive virtual environments. *Personality and Social Psychology Bulletin* 29, 7 (2003), 819--833. DOI: http://dx.doi.org/10.1177/0146167203029007002
3. Cagatay Basdogan, Chih-Hao Ho, Mandayam A. Srinivasan, and Mel Slater. 2000. An Experimental Study on the Role of Touch in Shared Virtual Environments. *ACM Trans. Comput.-Hum. Interact.* 7, 4 (Dec. 2000), 443--460. DOI:http://dx.doi.org/10.1145/365058.365082
4. Steve Benford, John Bowers, Lennart E. Fahlén, Chris Greenhalgh, and Dave Snowdon. 1995. User Embodiment in Collaborative Virtual Environments. In *Proceedings of the SIGCHI Conference on Human Factors in Computing Systems (CHI '95)*. ACM Press/Addison-Wesley Publishing Co., New York, NY, USA, 242--249. DOI: http://dx.doi.org/10.1145/223904.223935
5. Frank Biocca and Chad Harms. 2002. Defining and Measuring Social Presence: Contribution to the Networked Minds Theory and Measure. *Proceedings of PRESENCE* 2002 (2002), 7--36.
6. Chuck Blanchard, Scott Burgess, Young Harvill, Jaron Lanier, Ann Lasko, Mark Oberman, and Mike Teitel. 1990. Reality Built for Two: A Virtual Reality Tool. *SIGGRAPH Comput. Graph.* 24, 2 (Feb. 1990), 35--36. DOI:http://dx.doi.org/10.1145/91394.91409
7. Frederick P. Brooks, Jr. 1987. Walkthrough&Mdash;a Dynamic Graphics System for Simulating Virtual Buildings. In *Proceedings of the 1986 Workshop on Interactive 3D Graphics (I3D '86)*. ACM, New York, NY, USA, 9--21. DOI: http://dx.doi.org/10.1145/319120.319122
8. Jacky C. P. Chan, Howard Leung, Jeff K. T. Tang, and Taku Komura. 2011. A Virtual Reality Dance Training System Using Motion Capture Technology. *IEEE Trans. Learn. Technol.* 4, 2 (April 2011), 187--195. DOI: http://dx.doi.org/10.1109/TLT.2010.27
9. Robert R. Christensen, John M. Hollerbach, Yangming Xu, and Sanford G. Meek. 2000. Inertial-Force Feedback for the Treadport Locomotion Interface. *Presence: Teleoperators and Virtual Environments* 9, 1 (2000), 1--14. DOI:http://dx.doi.org/10.1162/105474600566574
10. E. F. Churchill and D. Snowdon. 1998. Collaborative Virtual Environments: An Introductory Review of Issues and Systems. *Virtual Real.* 3, 1 (March 1998), 3--15. DOI:http://dx.doi.org/10.1007/BF01409793
11. Paul Dourish, Annette Adler, Victoria Bellotti, and Austin Henderson. 1996. Your Place or Mine? Learning from Long-term Use of Audio-video Communication. *Comput. Supported Coop. Work* 5, 1 (Sept. 1996), 33--62. DOI:http://dx.doi.org/10.1007/BF00141935
12. Nat Durlach and Mel Slater. 2000. Presence in Shared Virtual Environments and Virtual Togetherness. *Presence: Teleoper. Virtual Environ.* 9, 2 (April 2000), 214--217. DOI: http://dx.doi.org/10.1162/105474600566736
13. Emmanuel Frécon and Mårten Stenius. 1998. DIVE: A Scaleable Network Architecture for Distributed Virtual Environments. *Distributed Systems Engineering* 5, 3 (1998), 91. DOI: http://dx.doi.org/10.1088/0967-1846/5/3/002
14. Erving Goffman. 2008. *Behavior in Public Places*. Free Press.
15. Chris Greenhalgh and Steven Benford. 1995. MASSIVE: A Collaborative Virtual Environment for Teleconferencing. *ACM Trans. Comput.-Hum. Interact.* 2, 3 (Sept. 1995), 239--261. DOI: http://dx.doi.org/10.1145/210079.210088
16. Jan Gugenheimer, Evgeny Stemasov, Julian Frommel, and Enrico Rukzio. 2017. ShareVR: Enabling Co-Located Experiences for Virtual Reality Between HMD and Non-HMD Users. In *Proceedings of the 2017 CHI Conference on Human Factors in Computing Systems (CHI '17)*. ACM, New York, NY, USA, 4021--4033. DOI: http://dx.doi.org/10.1145/3025453.3025683
17. A. Guye-Vuillème, T. K. Capin, S. Pandzic, N. Magnenat Thalmann, and D. Thalmann. 1999. Nonverbal Communication Interface for Collaborative Virtual Environments. *Virtual Reality* 4, 1 (01 Mar 1999), 49--59. DOI:http://dx.doi.org/10.1007/BF01434994
18. Koaburo Hachimura, Hiromu Kato, and Hideyuki Tamura. 2004. A Prototype Dance Training Support System with Motion Capture and Mixed Reality Technologies. In *13th IEEE International Workshop on Robot and Human Interactive Communication*. IEEE, 217--222. DOI: http://dx.doi.org/10.1109/ROMAN.2004.1374759
19. Edward Twitchell Hall. 1966. The Hidden Dimension. (1966).
20. D. Henry and T. Furness. 1993. Spatial Perception in Virtual Environments: Evaluating an Architectural Application. In *Proceedings of the 1993 IEEE Virtual Reality Annual International Symposium (VRAIS '93)*. IEEE Computer Society, Washington, DC, USA, 33--40. DOI:http://dx.doi.org/10.1109/VRAIS.1993.380801
21. W. A. Ijsselsteijn, Y. A. W. de Kort, and K. Poels. 2013. The Game Experience Questionnaire. (2013).

22. Hiroo Iwata. 1999. Walking About Virtual Environments on an Infinite Floor. In *Proceedings of the IEEE Virtual Reality (VR '99)*. IEEE Computer Society, Washington, DC, USA, 286--. http://dl.acm.org/citation.cfm?id=554230.835685

23. Hiroo Iwata, Hiroaki Yano, and Fumitaka Nakaizumi. 2001. Gait Master: A Versatile Locomotion Interface for Uneven Virtual Terrain. In *Proceedings of the Virtual Reality 2001 Conference (VR'01) (VR '01)*. IEEE Computer Society, Washington, DC, USA, 131--. http://dl.acm.org/citation.cfm?id=580521.835815

24. Mikkel R. Jakobsen and Kasper Hornbæk. 2016. Negotiating for Space?: Collaborative Work Using a Wall Display with Mouse and Touch Input. In *Proceedings of the 2016 CHI Conference on Human Factors in Computing Systems (CHI '16)*. ACM, New York, NY, USA, 2050--2061. DOI: http://dx.doi.org/10.1145/2858036.2858158

25. David Kirsh. 2013. Embodied Cognition and the Magical Future of Interaction Design. *ACM Trans. Comput.-Hum. Interact.* 20, 1, Article 3 (April 2013), 30 pages. DOI: http://dx.doi.org/10.1145/2442106.2442109

26. Joan Llobera, Bernhard Spanlang, Giulio Ruffini, and Mel Slater. 2010. Proxemics with Multiple Dynamic Characters in an Immersive Virtual Environment. *ACM Trans. Appl. Percept.* 8, 1, Article 3 (Nov. 2010), 12 pages. DOI:http://dx.doi.org/10.1145/1857893.1857896

27. Michael Meehan. 2001. *Physiological Reaction as an Objective Measure of Presence in Virtual Environments*. Ph.D. Dissertation. University of North Carolina.

28. Maurice Merleau-Ponty. 1996. *Phenomenology of Perception*. Motilal Banarsidass Publishe.

29. Teresa Monahan, Gavin McArdle, and Michela Bertolotto. 2008. Virtual reality for collaborative e-learning. *Computers & Education* 50, 4 (2008), 1339--1353.

30. Jauvane C. Oliveira, Xiaojun Shen, and Nicolas D Georganas. 2000. Collaborative virtual environment for industrial training and e-commerce. *IEEE VRTS* 288 (2000).

31. Clare Regan. 1995. An Investigation into Nausea and Other Side-effects of Head-coupled Immersive Virtual Reality. *Virtual Reality* 1, 1 (01 Jun 1995), 17--31. DOI: http://dx.doi.org/10.1007/BF02009710

32. Roy A. Ruddle and Simon Lessels. 2009. The Benefits of Using a Walking Interface to Navigate Virtual Environments. *ACM Trans. Comput.-Hum. Interact.* 16, 1, Article 5 (April 2009), 18 pages. DOI: http://dx.doi.org/10.1145/1502800.1502805

33. Maria V Sanchez-Vives and Mel Slater. 2005. From presence to consciousness through virtual reality. *Nature Reviews Neuroscience* 6, 4 (2005), 332--339.

34. Ralph Schroeder. 2002. Copresence and Interaction in Virtual Environments: An Overview of the Range of Issues. In *Presence 2002: Fifth international workshop*. 274--295.

35. J. Short, E. Williams, and B. Christie. 1976. *The Social Psychology of Telecommunications*. Wiley.

36. Mel Slater. 2009. Place Illusion and Plausibility can Lead to Realistic Behaviour in Immersive Virtual Environments. *Philosophical Transactions of the Royal Society of London B: Biological Sciences* 364, 1535 (2009), 3549--3557. DOI: http://dx.doi.org/10.1098/rstb.2009.0138

37. Mel Slater and Maria V. Sanchez-Vives. 2016. Enhancing Our Lives with Immersive Virtual Reality. *Frontiers in Robotics and AI* 3 (2016), 74. DOI: http://dx.doi.org/10.3389/frobt.2016.00074

38. Mel Slater and Martin Usoh. 1993. Representations Systems, Perceptual Position, and Presence in Immersive Virtual Environments. *Presence: Teleoperators and Virtual Environments* 2, 3 (1993), 221--233. DOI: http://dx.doi.org/10.1162/pres.1993.2.3.221

39. Mel Slater and Martin Usoh. 1994. Body Centred Interaction in Immersive Virtual environments. *Artificial life and virtual reality* 1, 1994 (1994), 125--148.

40. Mel Slater, Martin Usoh, and Anthony Steed. 1994. Depth of Presence in Virtual Environments. *Presence: Teleoper. Virtual Environ.* 3, 2 (Jan. 1994), 130--144. DOI:http://dx.doi.org/10.1162/pres.1994.3.2.130

41. Mel Slater, Martin Usoh, and Anthony Steed. 1995. Taking Steps: The Influence of a Walking Technique on Presence in Virtual Reality. *ACM Trans. Comput.-Hum. Interact.* 2, 3 (Sept. 1995), 201--219. DOI: http://dx.doi.org/10.1145/210079.210084

42. Mel Slater and Sylvia Wilbur. 1997. A Framework for Immersive Virtual Environments Five: Speculations on the Role of Presence in Virtual Environments. 6, 6 (Dec. 1997), 603--616. DOI: http://dx.doi.org/10.1162/pres.1997.6.6.603

43. Misha Sra, Sergio Garrido-Jurado, Chris Schmandt, and Pattie Maes. 2016a. Procedurally Generated Virtual Reality from 3D Reconstructed Physical Space. In *Proceedings of the 22Nd ACM Conference on Virtual Reality Software and Technology (VRST '16)*. ACM, New York, NY, USA, 191--200. DOI: http://dx.doi.org/10.1145/2993369.2993372

44. Misha Sra, Dhruv Jain, Arthur Pitzer Caetano, Andres Calvo, Erwin Hilton, and Chris Schmandt. 2016b. Resolving Spatial Variation And Allowing Spectator Participation In Multiplayer VR. In *Proceedings of the 29th Annual Symposium on User Interface Software and Technology (UIST '16 Adjunct)*. ACM, New York, NY, USA, 221--222. DOI: http://dx.doi.org/10.1145/2984751.2984779

45. Misha Sra and Chris Schmandt. 2015. MetaSpace: Full-body Tracking for Immersive Multiperson Virtual Reality. In *Adjunct Proceedings of the 28th Annual ACM Symposium on User Interface Software & Technology (UIST '15 Adjunct)*. ACM, New York, NY, USA, 47--48. DOI:http://dx.doi.org/10.1145/2815585.2817802

46. STEAM. 2017. Steam Hardware & Software Survey: July 2017. http://store.steampowered.com/hwsurvey. (2017). [Accessed 01-August-2017].

47. Frank Steinicke, Gerd Bruder, Jason Jerald, Harald Frenz, and Markus Lappe. 2010. Estimation of detection thresholds for redirected walking techniques. *IEEE transactions on visualization and computer graphics* 16, 1 (2010), 17--27.

48. Jonathan Steuer. 1992. Defining virtual reality: Dimensions determining telepresence. *Journal of communication* 42, 4 (1992), 73--93.

49. Haruo Takemura and Fumio Kishino. 1992. Cooperative Work Environment Using Virtual Workspace. In *Proceedings of the 1992 ACM Conference on Computer-supported Cooperative Work (CSCW '92)*. ACM, New York, NY, USA, 226--232. DOI: http://dx.doi.org/10.1145/143457.269747

50. Martin Usoh, Kevin Arthur, Mary C. Whitton, Rui Bastos, Anthony Steed, Mel Slater, and Frederick P. Brooks, Jr. 1999. Walking > Walking-in-place > Flying, in Virtual Environments. In *Proceedings of the 26th Annual Conference on Computer Graphics and Interactive Techniques (SIGGRAPH '99)*. ACM Press/Addison-Wesley Publishing Co., New York, NY, USA, 359--364. DOI: http://dx.doi.org/10.1145/311535.311589

51. Mark Ward, Ronald Azuma, Robert Bennett, Stefan Gottschalk, and Henry Fuchs. 1992. A Demonstrated Optical Tracker with Scalable Work Area for Head-mounted Display Systems. In *Proceedings of the 1992 Symposium on Interactive 3D Graphics (I3D '92)*. ACM, New York, NY, USA, 43--52. DOI: http://dx.doi.org/10.1145/147156.147162

52. Laurie M. Wilcox, Robert S. Allison, Samuel Elfassy, and Cynthia Grelik. 2006. Personal Space in Virtual Reality. *ACM Trans. Appl. Percept.* 3, 4 (Oct. 2006), 412--428. DOI: http://dx.doi.org/10.1145/1190036.1190041

53. Catherine A. Zanbaka, Benjamin C. Lok, Sabarish V. Babu, Amy C. Ulinski, and Larry F. Hodges. 2005. Comparison of Path Visualizations and Cognitive Measures Relative to Travel Technique in a Virtual Environment. *IEEE Transactions on Visualization and Computer Graphics* 11, 6 (Nov. 2005), 694--705. DOI: http://dx.doi.org/10.1109/TVCG.2005.92

54. Shanyang Zhao. 2003. Toward a Taxonomy of Copresence. *Presence: Teleoper. Virtual Environ.* 12, 5 (Oct. 2003), 445--455. DOI: http://dx.doi.org/10.1162/105474603322761261

VRSpinning: Exploring the Design Space of a 1D Rotation Platform to Increase the Perception of Self-Motion in VR

Michael Rietzler Teresa Hirzle Jan Gugenheimer
Julian Frommel Thomas Dreja Enrico Rukzio
Institute of Mediainformatics
Ulm University, Ulm
firstname.lastname@uni-ulm.de

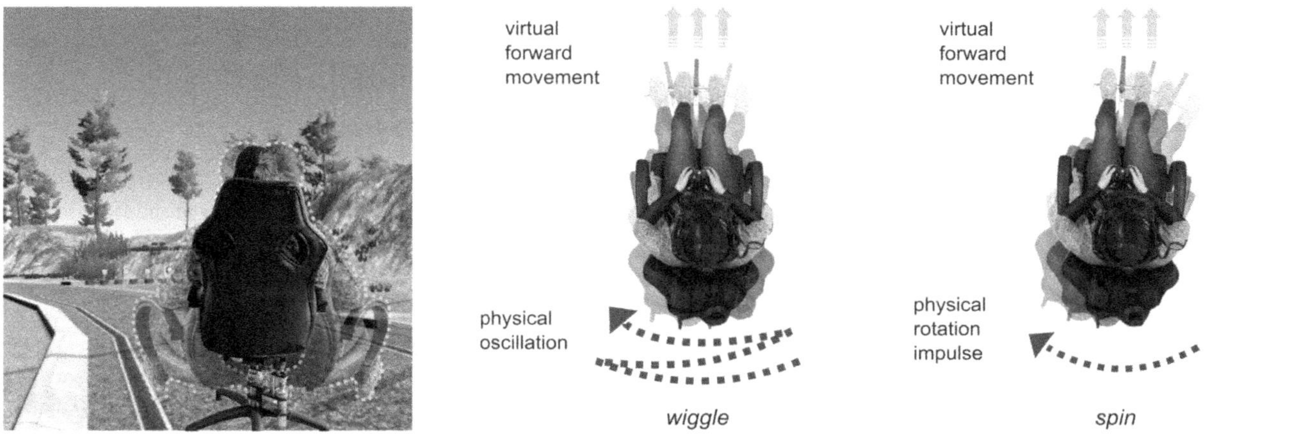

Figure 1. Forward motion approaches of *VRSpinning* to increase vection and reduce simulator sickness: *wiggle* movement to simulate steps or environmental events in VR (left middle), *spin* movement to simulate forward acceleration in VR by applying a short rotational impulse.

ABSTRACT

Current approaches for locomotion in virtual reality are either creating a visual-vestibular conflict, which is assumed to cause simulator sickness, or use metaphors such as teleportation to travel longer distances, lacking the perception of self motion. We propose *VRSpinning*, a seated locomotion approach based around stimulating the user's vestibular system using a rotational impulse to induce the perception of linear self-motion. In a first study we explored the approach of oscillating the chair in different frequencies during visual forward motion and collected user preferences on applying these feedback types. In a second user study we used short bursts of rotational acceleration to match the visual forward acceleration. We found that this rotational stimulus significantly reduced simulator sickness and increased the perception of self-motion in comparison to no physical motion.

DIS '18, June 9–13, 2018, Hong Kong

ISBN 978-1-4503-5198-0/18/06... $15.00
DOI: https://doi.org/10.1145/3196709.3196755

ACM Classification Keywords

H.5.1 Multimedia Information Systems: virtual realities; H.5.2 User Interfaces: Prototyping

Author Keywords

virtual reality; simulator sickness; vection; seated navigation.

INTRODUCTION

The majority of current locomotion techniques for virtual reality (VR) are focused around standing and short term walking experiences (e.g. HTC Vive or Oculus Rift) using teleportation as a metaphor for traveling longer distances. However, this excludes applications such as driving or flight simulators, where self-motion cannot be solved by teleportation. Additionally, virtual reality requires to be designed to immerse the user for a longer duration than most current short demonstrations (e.g. Fallout 4 VR, Skyrim VR, Doom VR, Gran Tourismo VR) to become a relevant medium for entertainment. All of these recent AAA titles and most likely the upcoming games depend on some kind of locomotion suitable for a longer exposure.

The two currently most dominant forms of locomotion are either physical movement through a tracked space (e.g. HTC Vive) or virtual metaphors such as teleportation (e.g. Fallout 4 VR, Doom VR) and virtual movement (e.g. Resident Evil VR). Since a tracked space is often smaller than the virtual world the user explores, physical movement is often combined with a form of virtual metaphors, when a user reaches the physical limits. Physical movement over time results in high levels of fatigue and will become uncomfortable for longer experiences. Virtual metaphors on the other hand can be used over a longer duration (also while seated) but lack the perception of vection (e.g. teleportation) and can result in higher levels of simulator sickness (e.g. virtual movement) [5]. Therefore, VR requires a (physical) locomotion feedback that creates the feeling of self-motion without causing simulator sickness.

We propose to use physical feedback generated through a motion platform on an actuated swivel chair, which we call *VRSpinning*. We implemented different actuation patterns (*wiggle*, *spin*) and introduce the concept of presenting a visual stimulus (forward acceleration) synchronously with a short and non-matching vestibular stimulus (rotational acceleration), tricking human perception into interpreting the rotational acceleration cue as a forward acceleration (see Figure 1). We found that this approach significantly reduces simulator sickness and increases the perception of self-motion.

To fine tune the stimuli we developed *VRSpinning* using a user centered design approach. We explored two different rotational stimuli to enhance the feeling of forward motion and ran two studies. In the first study we used oscillation for simulating three different movement approaches for forward motion (walking, driving, flying). We ran an exploratory study, exposing the user with the technique and having a think aloud feedback session, collecting calibration values and preferences. We found that users quickly mapped the oscillation to virtual steps but disliked the continuous stimulus when virtually driving or flying. Based on this feedback we redesigned the stimulus to be a short physical rotational acceleration only at the start of a visual forward motion. We countered the physical rotation inside of VR so that users are physically rotated but still keep looking in the same virtual direction. In the second study we measured vection, simulator sickness and presence compared to no physical rotation. We found that the rotational impulse of *VRSpinning* reduced simulator sickness and significantly increased vection as well as the feeling of acceleration compared to no physical motion.

The main contributions of our work are:

- The concept of presenting a visual stimulus (forward acceleration) synchronously with a short and non-matching vestibular stimulus (rotational acceleration), tricking human perception into interpreting the rotational acceleration cue as a forward acceleration.
- Findings from an exploratory user study on an oscillating stimulus for a walking metaphor and resulting user preferences.
- Findings from a second comparative study showing the decrease of simulator sickness and increase of vection using the *VRSpinning* concept for forward motion in virtual reality.

RELATED WORK

Vection

According to [1] and [19] vection can be defined as a *conscious subjective experience of self-motion*, which includes both perceptions and feelings of self-motion. Vection is thereby induced by optokinetic stimulation, but is also influenced by other sensory systems including the vestibular one.

It has been shown that during circular vection, i.e. illusory self-rotation, the perceived direction is opposite to the actual moving direction. This effect is caused by three semi-circular canals of the inner ear that act similar to leaky integrators. Therefore, a constant signal of velocity will decay after less than a minute, which causes that humans are not able to detect rotational movement without visual stimuli [7]. A similar effect can be observed in terms of forward motion. As the vestibular system only detects changes of velocity (accelerations), it will not respond to a constant velocity and also not detect any conflict (since the null signal is expected). This effect is referred to as onset latency, which can vary from a few seconds to half a minute [23]. We leverage this effect by applying a rotational acceleration in order to simulate forward movement in virtual reality. We assume that the direction of a short term acceleration cannot be recognized. However, it should be enough to support the feeling of self-motion induced by the visual stimulus.

Simulator Sickness

The phenomenon of simulator sickness is a well known problem of VR applications. It is commonly considered as a subset of motion sickness, therefore symptoms are related and include eye strain, headache, sweating, vertigo and nausea [15]. The cause of simulator sickness is of polygenic nature [12], however, scientific consent points towards vection as a possible cause of simulator sickness [10]. The two perceptual systems that are mainly involved in perception of self-motion are the vestibular and the visual sensory system. The vestibulo-ocular reflex, which ensures that the eyes are kept in place while the head is moving, elucidates the important relationship between these two senses [15]. Three main theories (sensory conflict theory [21], postural instability theory [22] and poison theory [27]) give an explanation for the phenomenon. The sensory conflict theory is the oldest and most accepted one [15]. It states that the body is not able to handle dissimilar information from different sensory systems. In VR a person usually perceives motion visually, while the vestibular system signals stasis. We counter this by giving a vestibular stimulus (rotational acceleration) synchronously with a visual stimulus. Though conflicting concerning the direction of acceleration, we assume that the short application of physical stimulation is long enough to be perceived as vestibular stimulus, but short enough to prevent the perception of the actual direction. Combined with the fact that the visual stimulus is considered more dominant lead to our assumption that using a rotational impulse combined with visual motion could increase vection and reduce simulator sickness.

Vection During Sensory Conflicts

The human central nervous system integrates visual and vestibular information to get a compelling perception of motion. According to the sensory conflict theory, conflicts arise when merging sensory information does not lead to a coherent and robust perception. One way to constitute a solution is the dominance of one sense over the others.

Although the visual sense is able to dominate the perception of motion, it is not clear how vestibular information integrates with visual information. Wright [28] tested horizontal and vertical visual motions on seated participants during forward motion. For both horizontal and vertical motion, participants' reported perception of self-motion coincided with the visual phase (not the inertial one). Even when the actual forward inertial motion was orthogonal to the visual one. Additionally, the perceived feeling of self-motion increased correspondingly to the amplitude of the inertial feedback. Berthoz et al. [3] tested the perception of forward self-motion induced by peripheral vision and also found that vision dominated in conflicting situations in which visual cues contradicted vestibular ones. According to these findings the feeling of vection increases with the amplitude of vestibular feedback, but does not primarily depend on its direction. We build up on these findings by using a physical, rotational acceleration to increase the feeling of self-motion during a visual forward motion scenario.

Motion Feedback

To solve conflicts arising from visual and vestibular perceptual information in terms of using real motion various approaches were made. One of them is to stimulate human sensory systems by inducing false sensory input, which, combined with visual information, is interpreted as realistic information by the brain. Galvanic vestibular stimulation (GVS) stimulates the vestibular system by sending electrical signals to the inner ear. Maeda et al. [17] indicate that a visually induced feeling of self-motion can be increased by combining visual stimuli with GVS. Further, Gálvez-García et al. [6] point out that galvanic cutaneous stimulation (GCS) mitigates simulator sickness symptoms. However, technical limitations and medical concerns are currently too immense for GVS and GCS to be used in consumer grade hardware.

Walking setups are another approach to bridge the gap between vestibular and visual information. Room scale tracking allows the user to freely roam around in the real world, free of any sensory conflict as real and virtual motion match. However, in most settings only limited space is available. Therefore, redirected walking [20] aims at redirecting the users steps in the real world to walk curved paths while walking straight in the virtual world. Another way to provide natural and immersive virtual locomotion is the walking-in-place (WIP) approach. VR-STEP [26] offers intuitive real-time pedometry to implement virtual locomotion. Users stand and provide continuous stepping input while walking through the virtual wold. In combination with head-tilt WIP can even be used for multidirectional navigation in the direction of the user's gaze [25]. However, redirected walking and WIP approaches may not be used for longer periods of time due to physical exhaustion.

Another way to create motion in the real world when moving in the virtual one are motion platforms that create real related motions to match virtual ones. While in the past motion platforms with six degrees of freedom were used to create motion [16, 11], it has been shown that smaller setups suffice to create a sense of realistic motion. The advantage of these smaller platforms and feedback devices is that they can be used in domestic settings. *HapSeat* [4] uses three actuators for both arms and head to simulate motion through applying force feedbacks on the user's seated body. Ouarti et al. [18] use a haptic force feedback in the hands of the user to enhance the sensation of self-motion. When coherent with the virtual camera motion, the force feedback stimulation creates a higher sensation of self-motion in contrast to visual feedback alone in moving a virtual environment. However, these systems only create a sensation of motion by simulating motion through an applied force feedback. But humans perceive motion by interpreting information from their visual, auditory, vestibular and kinesthetic sensory systems [2, 9]. Therefore, *VRSpinning* is based on a swivel chair [8] that creates real motion instead of simulating it.

ON THE DESIGN OF MOTION USING ROTATION

Our aim was to represent both, forward and rotational motion in VR based on a swivel chair as motion platform. Since the vestibular system measures acceleration, but does not detect constant motion, we concentrated on representing rotational and forward accelerations in VR. While rotation is rather easy to represent, forward motion is more problematic as it cannot be displayed as a one to one match by the chair. As indicated by related work, the vestibular system is not very accurate and human perception can be tricked into interpreting an acceleration stimulus as orthogonal or opposite to its actual direction. We take advantage of the inaccuracy of human perception and present visual stimuli synchronously with non-matching vestibular stimuli (rotational acceleration) that are interpreted as forward acceleration.

Besides the limits of human perception, usability should be considered. Motion platforms may increase the feeling of self-motion by adding physical motion to the virtual one. However, accelerations are known to cause simulator sickness. More aspects that have to be considered are peoples' preferences on what kind of motions should be enriched with motion feedback (e.g. walking, driving, flying). Therefore, we used an user-centered design approach to get further insights on how to design a motion approach on the basis of an actuated swivel chair as motion platform.

FIRST PROTOTYPE

We implemented a first prototype based on the SwiVRChair platform [8] (see Figure 2). The prototype consists of a motorized swivel chair with a VR ready laptop on its back.

In terms of feedback we used a one to one mapping of virtual to physical rotations (e.g. when the user rotated left inside the virtual world the chair would rotate left). Additionally, we added an oscillation of the chair when a forward motion was performed inside of the virtual environment (*wiggle*). The main idea of that oscillation was to stimulate the users' vestibular system and trick him into perceiving a forward motion. The concept is illustrated in Figure 3.

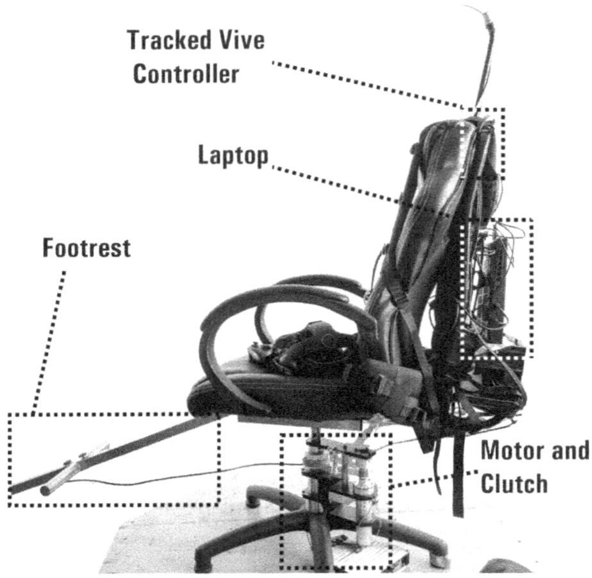

Figure 2. Technical setup of our prototype. A footrest is attached to the chair to have a more comfortable position and to not perceive rotational direction. A VR ready laptop is attached to the back of the chair, as well as an HTC Vive controller, the rotation values of which are used to remove the chair's physical rotation from the virtual view (participant keeps looking in the same direction although the chair is rotating).

While the driving and flying conditions included an avatar in form of a car or a cockpit, the player was represented only by a marker on the ground in the walking condition.

Setup

We equipped a swivel chair with a gearbox, a clutch and an electric motor to enable automatic rotation of the chair. To alleviate some performance issues, several design modification were made. The wireless connection was replaced with an USB connection to reduce latency and increase reliability, which are both crucial for the feedback mechanism we evaluated. Additionally, the motor driver board was replaced with an additional 20 V power supply to enable a gentler motion of the chair, while enhancing the grip of the clutch, which could then be powered with the full 24 V. Furthermore, the Samsung Gear VR headset used in the SwiVRChair project was replaced with the HTC Vive, which drastically increased processing power and overall performance. The chair's physics integration into the virtual world was one of the most challenging parts of the setup, as it's virtual representation had to match the real world object. Therefore, we attached a Vive controller to the back of the chair. We only regarded the Euler angle's Y component to describe the chair's rotation in 3D space, since the other parts are most of all results of tilting the chair. Finally, we added a footrest to the setup (see Figure 2) to avoid participants perceiving the direction of the rotation by having their feet drag over the floor.

Design

We chose a study method which is a mix between a quantitative and qualitative approach aimed towards better understanding user preferences and the overall experience of a 1D motion platform. The study was conducted using a within-subject design with the type of motion (*walking, driving, flying*) as independent variable. Additionally three options of motion feedback were applied (*chair rotation, chair oscillation, chair rotation & oscillation*). Participants were free to turn the options on/off according to their preferences using an Xbox 360 controller. The three scenarios were presented to the participants using a Latin square for counterbalancing. Users were encouraged to talk out loud and the whole session was video recorded, transcribed and analyzed. The motion feedback options worked as follows:

Chair rotation Using this option the chair was rotated synchronously with the virtual rotation at a fixed rotation speed. This feature could either be turned on or off.
Chair oscillation This option was applied during forward motion. Besides turning the feature on and off, participants could adjust frequency and motor strength during the oscillation.
Oscillation during rotation While either moving forward or rotating, either the rotation or the oscillation was presented. Rotating while being in motion is though a combination of both. We therefore decided to include another option that allowed participants to combine the chair rotation with the oscillation. This feature could either be turned on or off.

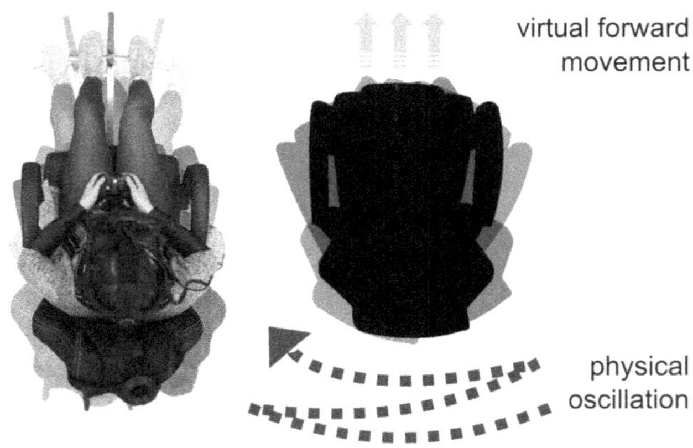

Figure 3. The *wiggle* concept is realized by letting the chair oscillate within a given rate during visual forward or backward motions. The movement is mapped e.g. steps during walking.

We designed three applications including the most common motion types: walking, driving and flying (see Figure 4).

Procedure

The study was conducted in an university lab. Participants were introduced to the topic of the study, stated their consent, and completed a demographics questionnaire. They also self-assessed their susceptibility to motion and cybersickness. After introducing the setup (chair, HMD, Xbox controller), participants were given some time to freely explore and get familiar with the setup. Then each of the three scenarios was presented in a counterbalanced order. Participants were asked to freely move in the virtual environment and test the different options for force feedback. Participants were encouraged to constantly talk about their decisions and explain why they

Figure 4. The different motion types used in the first study: a) walking scenario; b) car driving scenario; c) flying through asteroids.

did what. This was audio recorded and later transcribed and coded to deeper understand the needs for such a rotational locomotion platform.

Participants

The study was conducted with 24 participants (5 female) with an average age of 24.7 ($SD = 3.03$) years. All participants were university students or employees and participated voluntarily. Although participants showed great interest in VR technologies (mdn 6 on a 7-point Likert-scale), their experience levels varied greatly. However, the effect of this potential bias on the results could be neglected, as the target demographic of this study are all potential VR users. Participants reported low susceptibility towards motion sickness (mdn 2 on a 7-point Likert-scale), values for cybersickness were slightly higher (mdn 3 on a 7-point Likert-scale).

Measures

The study aimed to include users early in the design process of evaluating forward motion approaches for a rotational locomotion platform. We mainly wanted to find out what type of feedback can be used and how people react to the *wiggling* we designed for forward motion. We further aimed to elicit user preferences and leverage ideas about designing a locomotion platform solely on a rotational impulse. Additionally, we collected participants' preferences on oscillation and rotation values (frequency and motor strength).

Quantitative Results

The following results are based on the preferences we logged during the study and the user feedback we recorded.

Chair Rotation was a desired feature, which most participants turned on (see Fig. 5). Most of the participants that turned the rotation off reasoned their decision by the circumstance that the behavior of the character becomes too unrealistic when following the physical boundaries of acceleration. Other participants talked about an increase of the perception of actually turning and the reduction of simulator sickness.

Chair Oscillation was seen as controversial. While some participants turned it on in all conditions, others turned it off for each condition. The majority of participants desired to map chair oscillation to a virtual event (e.g. driving off-road or clashing with an asteroid), instead of using it for actual motion. As long as there was no mapping they stated to prefer some

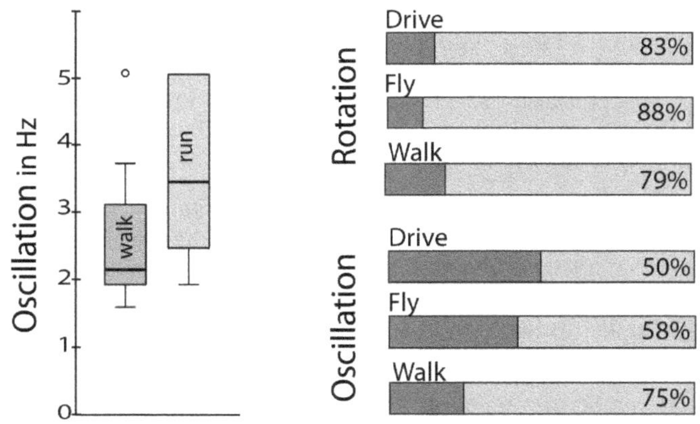

Figure 5. Participants set the oscillation to very low frequencies. As the results of the think aloud suggest, the oscillation was mapped to steps, with having a higher frequency for running (green) then for slow walking (blue). Most participants liked to be rotated with the virtual avatar, while the oscillation was only appreciated in the walking condition.

kind of vibration instead of oscillation, which they would map to the motor. In the case of walking however, 75% of the participants turned oscillation on as they mapped it on steps. Here, they chose a low frequency (2.2 Hz) for slow walking and a slightly higher frequency (3.4 Hz) for running. Participants who did not use the oscillation feature, argued again with the too intense feeling of motion, which would disturb them during longer experience.

Discussion and Calibration Results

The following results are based on the thematic analysis of the transcript of each participant and the verbal feedback we collected about the rational behind each decision.

Wiggling as a good metaphor for walking: Participants mainly adapted the frequency of the *wiggle* to match a walking motion (slow for walking fast for running). Since we already are familiar with a slight nudge while walking this metaphor was positively perceived. Participants reported this could potentially increase the sense of presence but did not work perfectly with the rotation. When rotating on the spot the inertia of the chair lead to the perception one is sitting inside a robot. Overall, participants reported that it is a nice feedback mechanism but it could become annoying and cumbersome to use over a longer duration.

Stabilization of the head compensated the wiggle: During the study we observed an interesting effect when using the wiggling mechanism. When being inside the virtual scene and focusing on a certain point participants always managed to keep their head stable and thereby compensated the *wiggle*. Similar to the stabilization of the head of a chicken humans also tend to stabilize certain motion when focused on a target. Therefore, we could not use this *wiggle* motion to induce any form of signal to the vestibular system.

Wiggling as a force feedback of the environment: Participants reported that most types of feedback should rather come from the environment and would fit better to simulate the surrounding virtual world than a motion. When hit by some virtual object the chair could imitate the impact. When driving over a rough road the wiggling could mimic the underground. When flying through an asteroid field the wiggling could simulate the impact the asteroids do on the spaceship. We deducted that the wiggling motion is mainly usable to simulate environmental impact rather than using it as a metaphor for acceleration.

No big differences between the motion metaphors: Besides the incidental metaphor of walking and wiggling, participants reported no big differences between the three motion approaches (walking, flying, driving). Since the main preference was to map the feedback on the environment the actual simulation of the motion should be similar across all the modalities.

Based on the quantitative and qualitative findings we learned that our wiggling approach works best to simulate environmental properties or that it can be used as metaphor for steps during walking. Furthermore, we used the feedback to design an new motion approach. Since people reported that a constant *wiggle* is cumbersome we decided to only use one short impulse burst when a virtual acceleration occurs. To also avoid the stabilization of the head we decided to not have a one to one mapping between virtual and physical rotation of the chair but compensate for every physical rotation so the virtual direction is always fixed. This allowed us to have physical rotation while visually being stable and having a forward acceleration. This should potentially stimulate the vestibular system with an impulse and also trick the user in perceiving a forward motion. Since participants asked for the same form of motion along all three motion approaches we decided not to distinguish between them anymore and design one motion approach suitable for the general concept of forward acceleration.

SECOND PROTOTYPE

For the second prototype we implemented a general motion approach for virtual reality aiming to represent forward motion. To give vestibular cues during forward acceleration we stimulated the vestibular system with a short rotational impulse presented synchronously with visual acceleration. To make sure the rotational acceleration impulse would be mapped to forward movement we subtracted the chair's physical rotation from the visual one (see Video). By iterative testing, we adjusted the physical rotation to be short (50 ms of acceleration), but relatively strong (up to~$20^{\circ}/m$). The idea was to create a vestibular stimulus that is strong enough to be recognized, but too short to be mapped to the actual direction. The concept is illustrated in Figure 6.

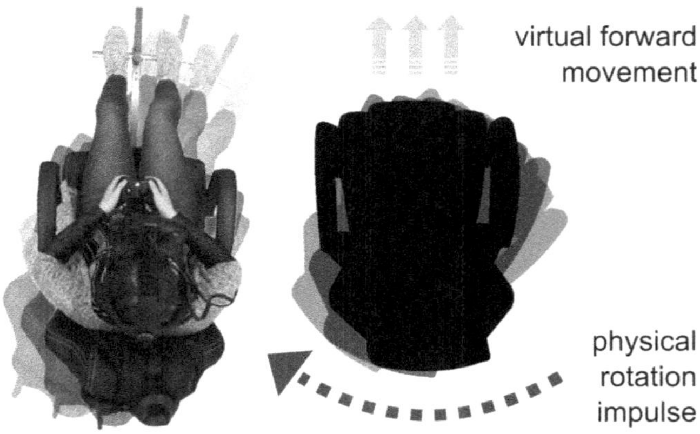

Figure 6. The *spin* concept is realized by a short rotational acceleration impulse synchronous to the visual forward or backward acceleration.

Setup

We used the same motorized swivel chair and HMD as in the first iteration. As physical and virtual rotation should be separated for this second study we used the HTC Vive controller attached to the back of the swivel chair. We added the controller's inverse rotation value to the virtual camera's one in order to remove the chair's rotation from the view. This way, the virtual camera remains in the same orientation even when the chair is rotating.

Design

The study was conducted in a within-subjects design with the form of rotational stimulus as independent variable. The participants experienced a strong but short ($20\ ^{\circ}/s^2$ over 0.3s) rotation to the right at the start of an acceleration and the inverse when braking (or accelerating backwards). The two tested conditions were (1) visual stimulus only (*visual*) and (2) visual and physical stimuli (*physical*). The order was counterbalanced using a Latin square.

Procedure

The study took place in an university lab. Participants were introduced to the topic of the study, stated their consent, and completed a demographic questionnaire. Then they were placed in a virtual environment using an HTC Vive while sitting on the motorized swivel chair. The virtual environment contained a virtual road (see Figure 7) and participants took part in an experience similar to car driving on the road. The experience comprised of several phases of acceleration and braking (as well as accelerating backwards). We designed the application in a way that acceleration, braking and constant motion alternated within small time frames. The longest phase of moving with a constant velocity was three seconds long. Overall the participants were exposed around one minute to virtual motion. For both conditions participants were passive observers of the virtual scene and did not have an active task.

After they finished all conditions, participants were compensated with 10€. The respective experiment lasted for around 30 minutes.

Figure 7. In the second experiment the participants drove through a virtual canyon.

Participants

We recruited 20 participants (8 female) with an average age of 24.3 (*SD* = 2.7) years. They were mostly university students with a technological background. Their previous experience in virtual reality was comparably low. Seven participants stated that they had never experienced VR before, while two stated they consumed more than 50 hours of VR (mdn: 1-10 hours). 11 participants reported that they get motion sick, e.g. when reading in a moving car.

Measures

In this experiment we were interested in the participants' levels of simulator sickness, presence, and experience of vection. Simulator sickness was measured in two ways. The sickness during the experience was assesed by using the question "On a scale from 1 to 10, 1 being how you felt before the test, 10 is that you wanted to stop, how did you feel during your time in the virtual world?". To measure the symptoms after the experience we used the SSQ [13]. The participants' presence was assessed using Slater, Usoh, and Steed's (SUS) presence questionnaire [24]. To measure vection, we employed a question asking the participants to rate their feeling of self-motion similar to [10]. They propose to present an explanation of the illusion of self-motion and to rate to which degree they experienced such on a 4-point Likert scale from "no feelings of self-motion" to "very strong feelings of self-motion".

Since vection is based on the feeling of self-motion, which can also occur during longer phases of forward movement, we also asked for the more critical aspects of self-motion: acceleration and braking. These situations are also the ones considered to cause simulator sickness, which made them to be of special interest. This is also the reason why we did not include longer phases of forward motion, but included multiple, alternating accelerations and braking time frames. In addition to the prior named questions, the participants should state how much they agree to the following statements: "I felt a physical acceleration" and "I felt a physical braking". In addition, we asked the participants to state how realistic the perception of acceleration and braking was ("The feeling of physical acceleration(/braking) felt realistic". The used scale was from 1: "not at all" to 7: "absolutely".

Results

Vection: We count the vection item, as well as the own items concerning acceleration and breaking to be contributing to vection. We compared each item separately using the Wilcoxon signed rank test. Differences are considered to be significant on the 5% level, while being highly significant when being below the 1% level. Boxplots of the results are shown in Figure 8. We found a highly significant increase of vection in the *physical* condition ($p < .01$, $Z = -2.24$, $r = .50$). The feeling of acceleration ($p < .01$, $Z = -2.06$, $r = .46$) and braking ($p < .01$, $Z = -2.37$, $r = .53$) was also highly significantly increased. The perceived realism of acceleration ($p < .01$, $Z = -2.19$, $r = .49$) and braking ($p < .01$, $Z = -2.01$, $r = .45$) was also increased highly significantly.

Simulator Sickness: We asked the participants to rate the intensity of symptoms of simulator sickness during the experience on a scale from 1 to 10. Additionally, we included the SSQ questionnaire to measure the symptoms after the VR experience. Boxplots of the results are shown in Figure 8. Sickness symptoms during the experience (measured using the single question) were significantly stronger in the *visual* condition ($p < .05$, $Z = -1.57$, $r = -.35$) than in the *physical* one. Sickness symptoms after the experiences (measured with the SSQ) were rather low (visual: 19.2 (mdn), physical: 9.6 (mdn)) and did not vary significantly between both conditions ($p = .11$, $Z = -1.12$, $r = -.25$).

Presence: The SUS presence score was increased highly significant by introducing the short vestibular stimulus ($p < .01$, $Z = -1.83$, $r = .41$) and is illustrated in Figure 8.

DISCUSSION

Vection: We found that the short rotational acceleration we applied strongly increased vection compared to presenting visual stimuli only. Similar to Wright [28] we found an increased feeling of self-motion in the condition with vestibular stimulus compared to using only visual cues, though the vestibular stimulus was applied in another direction. We assume that the short duration of the vestibular stimulus was enough to increase the feeling of self-motion, while being too short to perceive its direction.

Simulator Sickness: Concerning the question how participants felt during their time in the virtual world, a significant decrease of simulator sickness in the physical condition compared to the visual one could be found. For the symptoms that occurred after the VR exposure no significant difference could be found, as for both conditions SSQ values were relatively low (visual: 19.2 (mdn), physical: 9.6 (mdn)). Although we did not find a significant difference, we observed an interesting trend towards decreased SSQ scores in the physical condition compared to the visual one. These findings were quite surprising as we applied various stimuli that are known to increase simulator sickness (multiple accelerations/brakes and short amounts of time driving with constant velocity).

Presence: Applying rotational stimuli did significantly increase the feeling of being present in the virtual world. Therefore, we assume our forward motion approach to be a natural way of simulating forward motion in virtual reality.

Countering the Conflict: Our results indicate that the approach of simulating forward (or backward) accelerations in virtual reality increases the feeling of self-motion while decreasing simulator sickness at the same time during the VR experience.

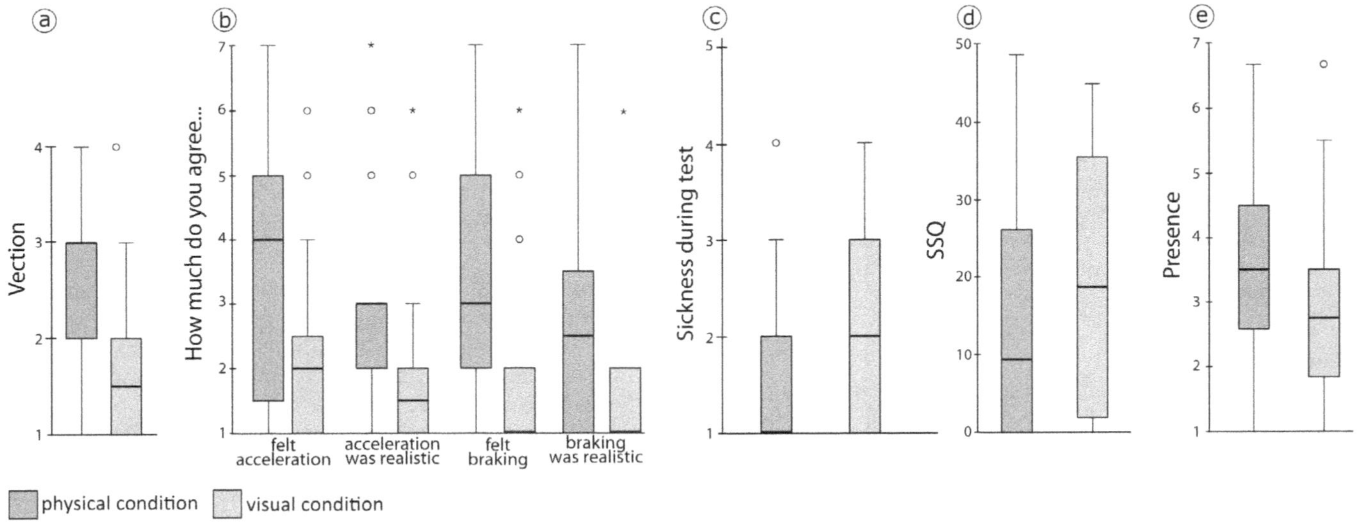

Figure 8. The results of the second study: (a) vection was significantly increased when a physical rotation was applied. (b) participants stated a higher feeling of acceleration and braking in the *physical* condition. In both conditions acceleration and braking were not considered as *realistic*, however, ratings for both were slightly increased by the physical rotation. (c) simulator sickness symptoms during the test were significantly reduced by the physical rotation. (d) there was no significant difference regarding simulator sickness symptoms after the test. (e) the SUS presence score was significantly higher during the *physical* condition.

Interestingly, these findings are in contrast to the results proposed by related work, where it is stated that an increased feeling of vection also leads to an increase of simulator sickness [10, 14]. Although we applied a rather short rotational stimulus it seems to suffice in duration and force to positively influence the experience of simulator sickness. We explain the results by avoiding a sensory conflict, which is assumed to cause simulator sickness [21], as we present visual stimuli synchronously with short vestibular stimuli and trick human perception into interpreting a rotational acceleration cue as forward acceleration.

Inducing Acceleration: Due to the short time of physical accelerating the chair, it also came to rest after a short time. We therefore used the same physical rotation stimulus for both kinds of acceleration, although they differed in terms of direction. Thus, braking was not simulated by actually reducing the velocity of rotation, but by increasing it in the inverse direction. Although participants gave lower values for the feeling of braking than for accelerating, they still had a stronger feeling of slowing down compared to the *visual only* condition. Participants also gave comparable values for realism of accelerating and braking when a physical rotation stimulus was applied. While vection can occur during longer phases of constant velocity, the feeling of acceleration is different. It is harder to induce by visual cues only, since acceleration is – in contrast to constant velocity – also measured by the vestibular system. Our results show that even acceleration can be perceived using our approach.

Less is More: While fine tuning our impulse, we were surprised how little movement actually was physically needed to simulate the acceleration that happens visually (see video). We only had to rotate for approx. $8^\circ/s^2$ with a short burst to mimic this form of visual forward acceleration. When we used a longer impulse we found several side effect that were considered unpleasant (e.g. when spinning for too long and too fast moving the head resulted in the perception of the gyroscopic effect). However, applying our short bursts resulted in a more realistic experience. We argue that this is even an advantage since it implies that to simulate this form of locomotion a 360 degree rotational platform is not necessary. To counter simulator sickness it could be enough to have 180 degree or even less.

CONCLUSION

In this work we presented *VRSpinning*, a seated locomotion approach based around stimulating the user's vestibular system using rotational impulses to amplify the perception of forward or backward self motion. We designed the feedback in a user centered design approach, involving participants early in the process and iterating the feedback mechanism. We found that participants preferred the *wiggle* mechanism as a form of feedback of the environmental impact. We further found that using a short burst of rotation with a corresponding visual forward acceleration leads to a significantly increased perception of self motion and reduces simulator sickness. Our work shows that to tackle the problem of simulator sickness and vection in virtual reality we can leverage the inaccuracy of the human vestibular system. We showed that a rotational acceleration during a visual forward acceleration can induce a perception of self motion. Based on our results we argue that different forms of "non-matching" stimuli should be tested synchronously to visual linear motion to generate the perception of self motion and fight simulator sickness.

We plan to test our approach in a self-controlled racing game to measure long term effects on simulator sickness and the effect on presence and enjoyment.

ACKNOWLEDGEMENTS

This work was supported by the Emmy Noether research group "Mobile Interaction with Pervasive User Interfaces" funded by DFG.

REFERENCES

1. April Ash, Stephen Palmisano, Deborah Apthorp, and Robert S Allison. 2013. Vection in depth during treadmill walking. *Perception* 42, 5 (2013), 562–576.
2. Alain Berthoz. 2000. *The brain's sense of movement.* Vol. 10. Harvard University Press.
3. A Berthoz, B Pavard, and LR Young. 1975. Perception of linear horizontal self-motion induced by peripheral vision (linearvection) basic characteristics and visual-vestibular interactions. *Experimental brain research* 23, 5 (1975), 471–489.
4. Fabien Danieau, Julien Fleureau, Philippe Guillotel, Nicolas Mollet, Anatole Lécuyer, and Marc Christie. 2012. HapSeat: producing motion sensation with multiple force-feedback devices embedded in a seat. In *Proceedings of the 18th ACM symposium on Virtual reality software and technology*. ACM, 69–76.
5. Julian Frommel, Sven Sonntag, and Michael Weber. 2017. Effects of Controller-based Locomotion on Player Experience in a Virtual Reality Exploration Game. In *Proceedings of the 12th International Conference on the Foundations of Digital Games (FDG '17)*. ACM, New York, NY, USA, Article 30, 6 pages. DOI: http://dx.doi.org/10.1145/3102071.3102082
6. Germán Gálvez-García, Marion Hay, and Catherine Gabaude. 2015. Alleviating simulator sickness with galvanic cutaneous stimulation. *Human factors* 57, 4 (2015), 649–657.
7. Fred E Guedry Jr. 1974. Psychophysics of vestibular sensation. In *Vestibular System Part 2: Psychophysics, Applied Aspects and General Interpretations*. Springer, 3–154.
8. Jan Gugenheimer, Dennis Wolf, Gabriel Haas, Sebastian Krebs, and Enrico Rukzio. 2016. Swivrchair: A motorized swivel chair to nudge users' orientation for 360 degree storytelling in virtual reality. In *Proceedings of the 2016 CHI Conference on Human Factors in Computing Systems*. ACM, 1996–2000.
9. Laurence R Harris, MR Jenkin, D Zikovitz, Fara Redlick, P Jaekl, UT Jasiobedzka, HL Jenkin, and Robert S Allison. 2002. Simulating self-motion I: Cues for the perception of motion. *Virtual Reality* 6, 2 (2002), 75–85.
10. Lawrence J Hettinger, Kevin S Berbaum, Robert S Kennedy, William P Dunlap, and Margaret D Nolan. 1990. Vection and simulator sickness. *Military Psychology* 2, 3 (1990), 171.
11. Saurabh Hindlekar, Victor B Zordan, Emerson E Smith, John C Welter, and William Garrett Mckay. 2016. MechVR: interactive VR motion simulation of Mech biped robot. In *ACM SIGGRAPH 2016 VR Village*. ACM, 14.
12. Robert S Kennedy and Jennifer E Fowlkes. 1992. Simulator sickness is polygenic and polysymptomatic: Implications for research. *The International Journal of Aviation Psychology* 2, 1 (1992), 23–38.
13. Robert S Kennedy, Norman E Lane, Kevin S Berbaum, and Michael G Lilienthal. 1993. Simulator sickness questionnaire: An enhanced method for quantifying simulator sickness. *The international journal of aviation psychology* 3, 3 (1993), 203–220.
14. Behrang Keshavarz, Bernhard E Riecke, Lawrence J Hettinger, and Jennifer L Campos. 2015. Vection and visually induced motion sickness: how are they related? *Frontiers in psychology* 6 (2015).
15. Joseph J LaViola Jr. 2000. A discussion of cybersickness in virtual environments. *ACM SIGCHI Bulletin* 32, 1 (2000), 47–56.
16. Woon-Sung Lee, Jung-Ha Kim, and Jun-Hee Cho. 1998. A driving simulator as a virtual reality tool. In *Robotics and Automation, 1998. Proceedings. 1998 IEEE International Conference on*, Vol. 1. IEEE, 71–76.
17. Taro Maeda, Hideyuki Ando, and Maki Sugimoto. 2005. Virtual acceleration with galvanic vestibular stimulation in a virtual reality environment. In *Virtual Reality, 2005. Proceedings. VR 2005. IEEE*. IEEE, 289–290.
18. Nizar Ouarti, Anatole Lécuyer, and Alain Berthoz. 2014. Haptic motion: Improving sensation of self-motion in virtual worlds with force feedback. In *Haptics Symposium (HAPTICS), 2014 IEEE*. IEEE, 167–174.
19. Allison R. S. Schira M. M. Barry R. J. Palmisano, S. 2015. Future challenges for vection research: definitions, functional significance, measures, and neural bases. *Frontiers In Psychology* 6 (2015).
20. Sharif Razzaque, Zachariah Kohn, and Mary C Whitton. 2001. Redirected walking. In *Proceedings of EUROGRAPHICS*, Vol. 9. Manchester, UK, 105–106.
21. James T Reason and Joseph John Brand. 1975. *Motion sickness.* Academic press.
22. Gary E Riccio and Thomas A Stoffregen. 1991. An ecological theory of motion sickness and postural instability. *Ecological psychology* 3, 3 (1991), 195–240.
23. Bernhard E Riecke and Daniel Feuereissen. 2012. To move or not to move: can active control and user-driven motion cueing enhance self-motion perception (vection) in virtual reality?. In *Proceedings of the ACM Symposium on Applied Perception*. ACM, 17–24.
24. Mel Slater, Martin Usoh, and Anthony Steed. 1994. Depth of presence in virtual environments. *Presence: Teleoperators & Virtual Environments* 3, 2 (1994), 130–144.

25. Sam Tregillus, Majed Al Zayer, and Eelke Folmer. 2017. Handsfree Omnidirectional VR Navigation using Head Tilt. In *Proceedings of the 2017 CHI Conference on Human Factors in Computing Systems*. ACM, 4063–4068.

26. Sam Tregillus and Eelke Folmer. 2016. Vr-step: Walking-in-place using inertial sensing for hands free navigation in mobile vr environments. In *Proceedings of the 2016 CHI Conference on Human Factors in Computing Systems*. ACM, 1250–1255.

27. Michel Treisman. 1977. Motion sickness: an evolutionary hypothesis. *Science* 197, 4302 (1977), 493–495.

28. W Geoffrey Wright. 2009. Linear vection in virtual environments can be strengthened by discordant inertial input. In *Engineering in Medicine and Biology Society, 2009. EMBC 2009. Annual International Conference of the IEEE*. IEEE, 1157–1160.

A Situated Exploration of Designing for Personal Health Ecosystems through Data-enabled Design

Sander Bogers[2,1], Janne van Kollenburg[1,2], Eva Deckers[1], Joep Frens[2], Caroline Hummels[2]

[1] Philips Design,
Eindhoven, the Netherlands
janne.van.kollenburg@philips.com

[2] Eindhoven University of Technology,
Eindhoven, the Netherlands
s.j.a.bogers@tue.nl

ABSTRACT
This paper presents a design case study from industry that explores designing for personal health ecosystems. Following on from previous work on ecologies that gives a predominantly theoretical perspective, we present a more applied and design-oriented perspective. To do so, we build on our previously-developed data-enabled design approach, which utilizes contextual, behavioral and experiential data from situated design experiments as creative material. This approach comprises two steps, of which this paper presents the first (contextual) step. We introduced a small adaptable ecosystem of multiple artifacts, in four family homes over a period of eight weeks, through which we explored and further expanded on valuable ecosystem relationships. The insights gained were translated into three design opportunities that inform a future second step. We highlight and discuss practical examples from our situated explorations, and discuss how our data-enabled design approach served in designing for the complexity and versatility inherent to these ecosystems.

Author Keywords
Data-enabled Design; Ecosystems; Personal Health.

ACM Classification Keywords
H.5.2. User Interfaces.

INTRODUCTION
The recent proliferation of (internet-) connected interactive products [28], which are often data-intensive, has created exciting new opportunities for design, but also posed new challenges. Everyday artifacts equipped with ubiquitous sensing [51] capabilities and data analytics (often driven by artificial intelligence), are better able to understand their context and usage, allowing for more dynamic and personalized interactions for their users. But their connected nature also introduces new levels of complexity as they break with the more traditional 'one person - one product' dictum [15, 44]. Interactions with one product may have consequences for other products (e.g. multiple devices can control a Philips Hue [44]). As a result, experiences and responses of product interactions become very unpredictable, as people's experiences in the system are no longer simple accumulations of the single human-product interaction experiences [25, 17].

DIS '18, June 9–13, 2018, Hong Kong

ACM ISBN 978-1-4503-5198-0/18/06...$15.00
https://doi.org/10.1145/3196709.3196769

From our daily practice at Philips Design, we see multiple design challenges surfacing throughout the company. Philips is transforming from a hardware-oriented company to a digital and product-platform oriented one, with a presence in many areas of the health and wellbeing domain [41]. Where the company used to focus on designing traditional hardware products (e.g. electric shavers, baby bottles, electric toothbrushes), as illustrated by figure 1.a, it has gradually evolved towards more one-to-one, connected solutions (fig 1.b) (e.g. the connected shaver that offers style advice, the smart baby bottle sleeve that gives feeding advice [43] or the connected toothbrush that helps optimize your brushing routine [42]). Beyond Philips there is also a proliferation of devices in this category (e.g. Fitbit activity tracker [13], the Vessyl smart cup [50] or the Lumo Lift posture sensor [32]).

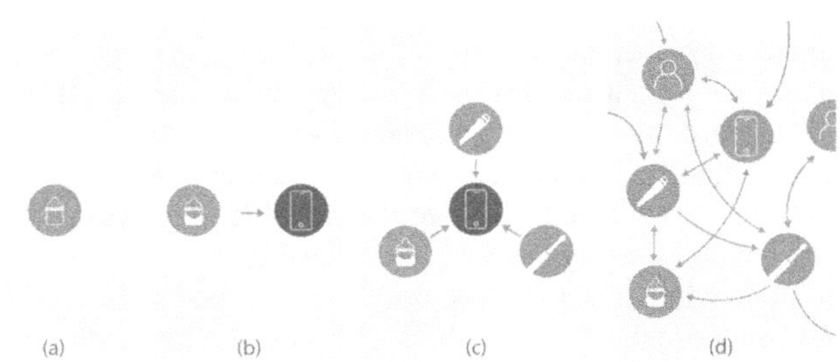

Figure 1. (a) non-connected (b) one-to-one connected (c) multiple-to-one connected (d) ecosystem

As a next step, companies aim to go beyond one-to-one connected devices and instead develop systems of connected devices. Philips, for example, built the uGrow digital parenting platform [40]. Data from different connected devices (e.g. smart baby bottle, thermometer, baby monitor) come together in one app insight into to give greater insight (i.e. personal informatics) [30]. Another example is Nokia

Withings [39], which connects activity monitors, weight scales and blood pressure meters. Such systems (figure 1.c.) generally have one-directional connections. Devices collect data through these ubiquitous sensing capabilities, and an app presents it. The multiple, single-connected devices usually do not interrelate with each other. One exception to this is the Xiaomi Miband activity tracker, which updates its step goal based on the Xiaomi weight scale [52]. But, in general, products in such systems do not make good on the promise of artifact/information/product ecology design theory [3, 35, 23, 14], as there is little interrelation and interdependence between products.

Outside the domain of personal health systems, for example in home automation, we do see examples that relate more closely to available theory on ecologies and ecosystems. Multiple products connect to each other, with multiple users, through bidirectional connections (figure 1.d). For example, If This Then That (IFTTT) can turn the light on when the TV turns off [21]. Google Home [20] or Amazon Alexa [1] can control devices and provide multi-user interactions. However, these connections mostly take place on a functional level (i.e. action A triggers action B).

As part of the Philips Design innovation group, we set out to explore the value of a personal health ecosystem of connected products (fig 1.d) by emphasizing the inter-relational and interdependent nature of these systems. For example, the baby bottle, toothbrush and shaver each have their own individual functionality (fig 1.a), and their digital (connected) layer has proven to be valuable in a one-to-one (fig 1.b) and sometimes multiple-to-one (fig 1.c) setup. We explored how they can leverage each other as they become part of the same ecosystem (fig 1.d). Our aim was to extend the ecosystem to cover different domains in personal health, unlike most commonly-known ecosystems, which usually have a clear focus (e.g. losing weight, healthy activity).

This paper starts by giving a detailed overview on how prior work in HCI has addressed this system design challenge. Based on Nardi and O'Day's [37] definition of *information ecologies* we outline different ecology characteristics that we use to introduce related work on those characteristics. Based on this mainly theoretical work, we argue for a more practical and design-oriented perspective to this discussion, and explore how to *design* for these ecosystems. As a starting point, we introduce our previously-developed *data-enabled design* approach [6, 26], which consists of a contextual step followed by an informed step. As this has proven to be valuable in the design of a single-connected device (fig 1.b), we set out to further develop it to cope with the challenges of designing for ecosystems. We then introduce the case study about designing a personal health ecosystem. We present results from the first contextual step – an eight- week exploration with four families (16 participants) – as well as three design opportunities which resulted from our contextualized understanding of personal health ecosystems. Finally, we discuss how this case study has given us insights into design challenges acquainted with designing for ecosystems, and illustrate how we utilized and modified our data-enabled design approach to address these new challenges.

The contribution of this paper is therefore twofold. Firstly, it presents a practical design case study (from industry), that sets out to identify ecological relationships between artifacts and presents three design opportunities for a personal health ecosystem. In doing so it provides an alternative perspective on the until-now more theoretical discussion on ecologies. Secondly, we utilize and further develop our data-enabled design approach. We discuss how it served in designing for ecosystems, and describe changes that have been made in response to the more complex design challenges.

RELATED WORK

There is an extensive body of design theory available in HCI that addresses designing for systems [14, 3, 34, 35, 10, 23, 4, 5, 29, 15]. This originates from various perspectives (e.g. sociology [14], biology [8], psychology [3], philosophy [34]). Nardi and O'Day [37] introduce the notion of *ecology* to describe complex systems of people, practices, values and technologies in a particular local environment. Their concept of information ecologies puts the spotlight on human activities that are served by technology, instead of on the technology itself.

Building on characteristics of biological ecology, they introduce five characteristics to describe information ecologies: *system, diversity, coevolution, keystone species* and *locality.* We briefly introduce these below, together with related work in the domain of designing for artifact, product and information ecologies [14, 4, 23], as this provides a valuable framework in which to position other work in this domain.

The *system* describes the strong interrelationships and dependencies between different elements in the ecology. When one element is changed, changes can be felt throughout. There are various perspectives on these relationships. Forlizzi et al [14] introduce their product ecology framework, which emphasizes extending pure functionality towards social and emotional relationships between different elements. Bodker et al. [4] focus on the human-artifact relationship in their artifact ecologies. Jung et al. [23, 33] introduce the concept of ecological factors and ecological layers to describe different artifact-artifact relationships in systems. Ecological factors describe more direct relationships between artifacts, as for example connections through functions or connections through information flow. Ecological layers provide a more holistic perspective that describes relationships of artifacts in similar contexts or values.

Diversity is used to emphasize the variety of roles and functions in the ecology, for humans as well as artifacts. The complexity of the ecology ensures there are always new niches that can be further explored. Diversity is necessary to accommodate the continuously changing nature of the system. Cila et al. [9] offer a pluralistic approach to meaningful interactions between all ecosystem elements involved in a context [12, 18, 22, 24, 36]. This work strongly builds on principles from Actor Network Theory (ANT) [29], which emphasizes how connections between both human and non-human entities can lead to "the creation of new entities that do not necessarily practice the sum of characteristics of constituent entities." [11]

A healthy ecology is not static, as it continually *coevolves*. Elements migrate to fill niches (see *Diversity*), which affects other elements (see *System*). With constant change, even in apparent equilibrium, coevolution is always present. Especially for the technological systems we discuss here, the pace at which new artifacts are introduced into the system is unparalleled. Frens and Overbeeke present a vision on growing systems [15, 16]. They take a strong artifact-oriented perspective and focus on the (rich and embodied) interactions between different artifacts in the system, and how these can evolve together with the system. From a more analytical perspective, building on their human-artifact model, Bodker et al. [5] describe the dynamics in artifact ecologies. Based on their ethnographic analysis of new iPhone users, they present different states to illustrate how experiences in the ecosystem evolve over time. To study this changing nature they argue for more longitudinal studies around artifact ecologies.

Every ecology has *keystone species* which are essential to the existence of the system. These can be artifacts or humans. A developed world hospital ecology can, for example, almost never function properly without imaging equipment nor the specialists controlling it. Bodker et al. [4] discuss that it is often not clear what the artifact in the artifact ecology is, let alone the keystone species. The artifact can be seen as the smartphone, but also as the individual apps that are continuously installed and removed. Identifying keystone species is challenging, as the complexity of the ecology often makes it hard to grasp what the effect of certain changes is (i.e. whether it is essential or instrumental to the ecology).

Locality is a particularly important attribute of ecology. It defines how people perceive (parts of) these ecologies. A dentist's drill plays a completely different role in an ecology for a dentist than for the patient undergoing treatment. This characteristic has received significant attention in HCI. Schütz's work [45] for example discusses intersubjectivity, arguing that our own subjective worlds influence the way we perceive things. This work builds on Merleau-Ponty's [33] work on phenomenology, that describes how the perceptive skills of our bodies enable meaning to emerge in the interaction between artifact and person, in context. Through *situated action*, Suchman [48] argues that human action is constantly reconstructed through dynamic interactions with the world. Here, too, meaning emerges in situated action. This work provides a valuable perspective on locality, although not necessarily specific to *designing* ecosystems.

Conclusions

The systemic nature of these ecologies emphasizes the close interrelations and dependencies of both human-artifact and artifact-artifact relationships. Through this, we see that the challenges for design have moved from designing the individual elements (in a product design era) [25] to designing the relationships between these elements. However, this will have clear consequences for the individual products too. Although our work gives a mainly theoretical perspective on describing and evaluating ecosystems, it does provide valuable pointers on how to design for these ecosystem challenges. We recognize that an ecosystem is always part of other ecosystems. It is never isolated and its relationships to others ecosystems are as important as the ones within. The focus is not only on introducing new elements to the ecosystem, but also on designing elements so that new relationships can be formed between them. This way we allow for meaning in interaction to arise. Besides, it is evident that ecosystems are never static. Elements can be introduced or removed, or evolve over time, as can their relationships to other elements. The elements should be designed to facilitate this ever-changing nature. Lastly, the presented work shows that people create their own definitions and relationships to derive meaning from these systems. To embrace the idiosyncratic values of individuals in our personal health ecosystems, we see a clear need for affording a variety of use cases and values so people can discover and create personally-relevant ecosystems.

APPROACH

We concluded that designing for ecosystems means designing for the relationships between elements and for how the individual elements can support these. We also confirmed the need to embrace the complexity, richness and versatility acquainted with the design challenge and context the ecosystems are situated in.

In our previous work we developed a data-enabled design approach to designing data-driven products. Through the case study of a connected baby bottle [6] and a case study that explored how parent-tracked baby data could be relevant in interactions with different healthcare professionals [26], we described a two-step approach in which real-life data from situated design explorations are used as creative material for design. Through a combination of contextual data (e.g. feeding environment), behavioral data (e.g. moments of feeding during the day and how long these feedings take) and experiential data (e.g. "this was a very stressful feeding") we were able to get a detailed and nuanced understanding of the design space. Based on these continuously and remotely collected insights, we were able to continuously make changes to our design prototypes (remotely). Hence, our field study was no longer a static means of inquiry, as in field trials or home-placement tests, but an active situated exploration for design. This makes data-enabled design significantly different from a more well-known data-driven design approach [31], which uses data as evidence upon which to base or evaluate design decisions.

The starting point for this case study is that various qualities of data-enabled design overlapping with the system design challenges identified earlier. Through its situated approach, data-enabled design could embrace the complexity of these (networked) ecosystems in their context of use. This clearly follows Latour [29] and Forlizzi's [14] suggestion that ecologies can best be explored through empirical fieldwork. From the start of the design process we set out to place artifacts that enriched sensing capabilities in an everyday life context. We treat artifacts as open and malleable means to facilitate exploration of context and design ideas. By making our ecosystem experiential we allow the emergence of new values through personal meaning (i.e. locality).

The first – contextual – step of data-enabled design sets out to gain contextualized understanding of the design space by utilizing a combination of quantitative sensor data and qualitative user insights from everyday life explorations. The sensor data allows us, together with participants, to gain highly detailed insights in behavioral patterns, while the qualitative insights provide a more experiential perspective. This step is an open exploration, resulting in a collection of anecdotes, details, nuances and design opportunities that give a better understanding of the design space. These further inform and inspire the scope of the second step.

The second – informed – step sets out to iteratively design while the prototype(s) remain in the field. The informed step introduces an open and dynamic set of collection tools that facilitate our (remote) exploration (e.g. physical prototypes, researcher dashboards, app interfaces). We called this the data-enabled design canvas. The contextual step is instrumental in shaping this canvas so it allows for a variety of on-the-fly design explorations in this step. The canvas needs to grow together with our solution to enable continuity of the design explorations [47]. This growing nature of the data canvas in the informed step closely matched the dynamic nature of the ecosystems described by Nardi [37], Frens [16] and Bodker [4].

CASE STUDY

In this case study we explored what the value of a systemic approach to personal health could be (figure 1.d) in a collection of one-to-one connected solutions (figure 1.c). Following our data-enabled design approach we set out to introduce a collection of connected artifacts in context that allowed us to explore and generate insights into a variety of aspects. As we still had little idea what elements a personal health ecosystem could be comprised of, let aside what the keystone species are, we decided to start with a minimalistic set of artifacts. For this, we involved different types of data trackers as part of our data-enabled canvas to explore which artifacts, and more importantly, which relationships between these artifacts, could be relevant. Throughout the situated explorations we extended the ecosystem based on contextualized insights. Only in the informed step did we start designing for these relationships and build towards an ecosystem (figure 1.d).

For this exploration we invited four families from the Netherlands, with four family members each (i.e. father, mother, two children). We deliberately sought diversity in relationships, behaviors and experiences. The children, for example, ranged from toddlers to teenagers and the parents had different backgrounds and interests. The number of families was kept relatively small so we could provide highly personalized attention. We needed to keep the system up and running, analyze all the family data and build and introduce new devices on-the-fly. To facilitate this, and to allow for a more longitudinal and rich data-collection, we involved these families for eight weeks. As we knew from experience [6, 7, 26] that most technical challenges would surface in the first weeks, we use a phased approach. Families would start in consecutive weeks as this would allow us to respond to issues quickly. Therefore, the study would run for 12 weeks in total.

We chose the bathroom environment as starting point for this exploration. In addition to being one of the key locations in the personal health domain, it is probably one of the most personal and intimate spaces. We deliberately chose this for the data-enabled exploration to touch upon ethics and privacy topics from the start, as these will be key in designing for a personal health ecosystem [35].

Family members needed to be familiar with electric toothbrushes, and at least one male family member needed to use an electric shaver. We also appreciated if they showed some interest in using new (connected) products and if they were familiar with contemporary technology (smartphones, apps, connected devices). Table 1 shows a brief overview of the selected families. This study setup was positively evaluated by a Philips internal ethical committee board.

Family	Father	Mother	Oldest child	Youngest child
Family 1	41	41	10 (female)	6 (female)
Family 2	51	52	18 (female)	16 (male)
Family 3	43	43	16 (male)	13 (female)
Family 4	35	34	3 (female)	1 (female)

Table 1. Participants of the study

A data-enabled canvas

The data-enabled design canvas contains all elements that facilitated our situated explorations. This comprises both the series of artifacts placed in the families' homes (1) (see figure 2) as well as the design research tools that allowed for the dynamic nature of our explorations (2).

(1) The Family System of Artifacts

By sensor-equipping a series of artifacts that are used for personal health in the bathroom, we aimed to gain a better understanding of how these artifacts could play a role in a personal health ecosystem. As we were still exploring what artifacts could provide valuable connections we selected a mix of different data collectors. Firstly, we used device-specific data collectors, which could give us more detailed insights into how people use these devices, also in relation to each other. Some of these devices have sensor-equipped versions on the market (e.g. the Philips Sonicare toothbrush). For others we had to create custom prototypes ourselves (e.g. the Philips Shaver 7000 and the Philips Visapure Advanced cleansing brush). Table 2 shows an overview of what devices were initially set up together with their functionality.

Secondly, we used generic data collectors (figure 3) [26]. Participants could decide for themselves what they wanted these data collectors to keep track of. In this category we had one 'automated' data collector (a Wi-Fi connected accelerometer module), and a 'manual' data collector (a Wi-Fi connected rotary knob). The accelerometer would operate when it was moved, and saved a continuous stream of data describing how it moved. The rotary knob could be used to capture more subjective data. Participants could label what the knob represented (using the tablet), after which it could be used to save a value between very low to very high (a continuous scale from 0 to 100). For example, the knob could be labelled 'how well I slept' with a minimum value of 'very poorly' and a maximum of 'awesome'. The goal of these generic data collectors was to allow participants to actively explore what data could play a valuable role in their personal health ecosystem.

Finally, there was a dedicated iPad installed in the bathroom (with its camera blocked), running a custom-built application. The app had various purposes.

(a) It was used to display all of the connected devices and show their status so the participants could see if everything was still working.

(b) A check-in/check-out button on the screen for each family member meant we could receive extra data about who was in the bathroom for how long. (figure 4).

(c) Design researchers could ask questions in, or at least close to, the moment. (e.g. showing simple visualizations that required further explanation by the participant). This explanation, which generates data of a more subjective nature, could give greater insight into experiences and stories.

(d) Facilitating the (technical) connection to all Bluetooth devices. In this way it functioned as a hub or gateway to the researchers.

(2) Design Researcher Playground

The design researcher playground comprises two major components; the data dashboard and the system composer.

The data dashboard displays data from all data collectors, from all families, and allows the design researchers to explore this data (together with participants). This can be done on multiple levels. There is a timeline view that for example gives insight into routines during the day and changing patterns over time (see figure 5). Next to this, there is a raw data view that allows for more detailed analysis of different data points. It can, for example, be used to compare how one participant brushes his/her teeth in the morning and the evening on a highly detailed level (see figure 6). This web-based dashboard was set up so new data visualizations could easily be built to further explore specific activities and experiences. Besides being able to look at incoming data, the data dashboard allowed the design researchers to send out messages or questions to the participants' iPads.

The system composer was instrumental in facilitating the pace required for our explorative approach. This custom-built toolset can be used to quickly set up new families, connect specific devices to families or family members, and monitor their status. Devices could be prototypes (e.g. accelerometer modules, modified shavers) or off-the-shelf third-party devices. After a drag-and-drop configuration, all data management and organization is handled by the composer's backend, regardless of the type of device.

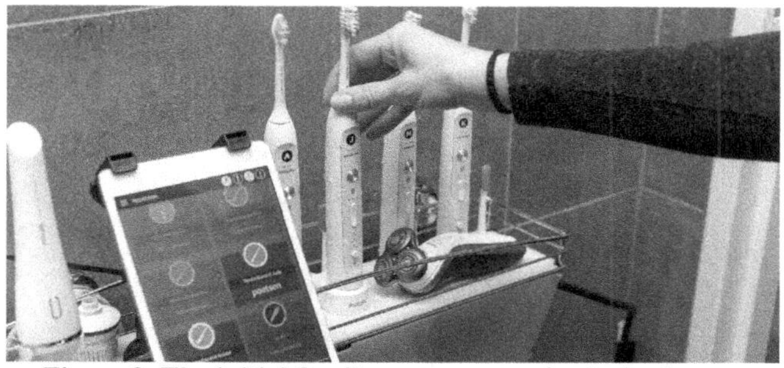

Figure 2. The initial family system setup in the bathroom

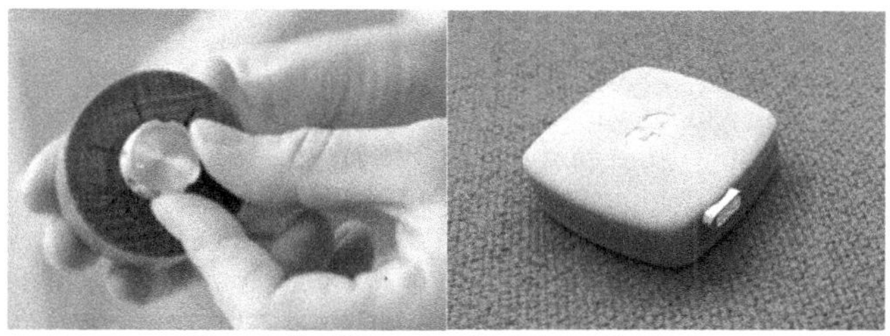

Figure 3. The generic data collectors

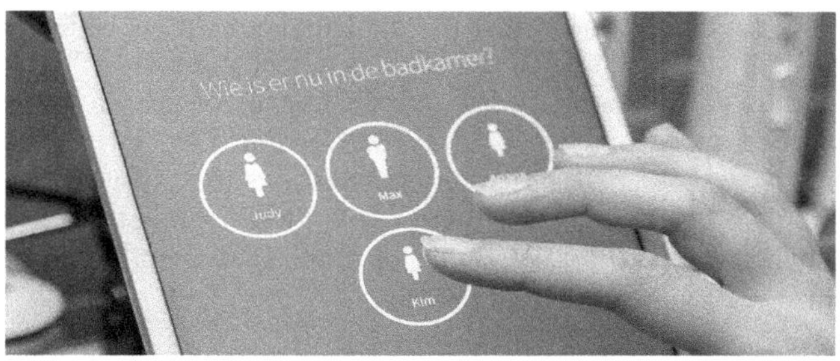

Figure 4. The check-in screen, which is also the screensaver

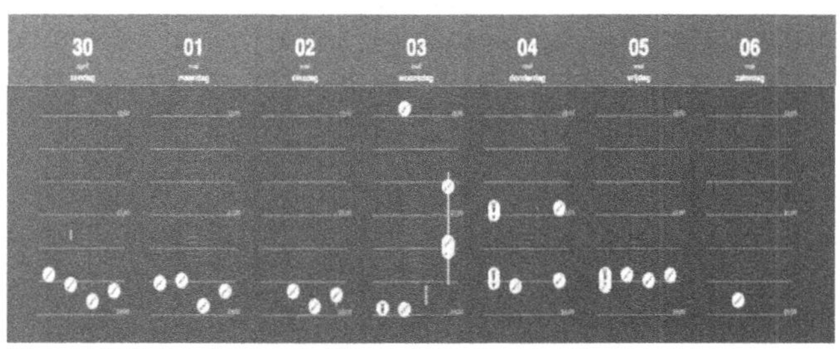

Figure 5. Timeline of daily and weekly routines

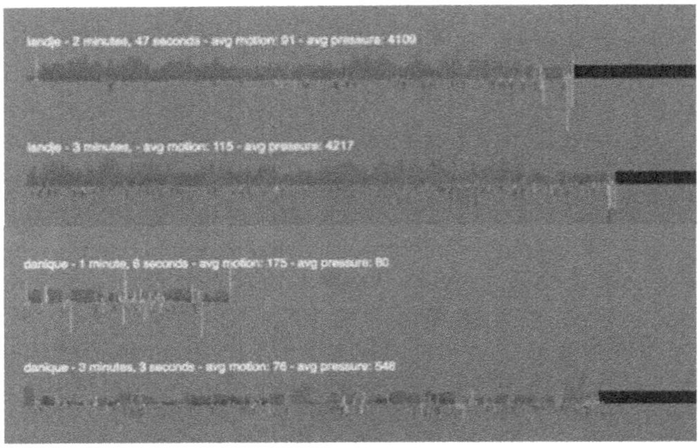

Figure 6. The raw data of three teeth-cleaning sessions involving a father and daughter

Figure 7. System setup in the context of one of the families

Procedure

In the introductory meeting, at each family's home (figure 7), we introduced the purpose of the study, set up the family system and demonstrated its functionality. We emphasized that this was an explorative study, not a validation of a new concept, and encouraged them to be actively involved. In an adjacent interview, we explored bathroom routines and general health issues for different family members, and explained how our devices or data could help in giving some insight. This would also serve as a benchmark to better anticipate what kind of data could come in. We also told the participants that we would expect to return for interviews every week or two, based on the questions that would arise from both sides. The topics of these semi-structured interviews were not defined prior to the study, but would be inspired by insights from the study.

All results and insights from interviews and data dashboard reviews were discussed in a weekly design meeting,. Topics could range from participant quotes to technical difficulties or bug fixes. Based on these insights the team would collectively brainstorm and decide which actions had the highest priority (e.g. new data dashboard visualizations, building new connected devices or fixing bugs).

SITUATED EXPLORATIONS

In this section we present three design opportunities for a personal health ecosystem, and highlight the use cases and insights of the situated explorations which were most influential in formulating these opportunities.

The situated explorations, with 16 participants over a period of eight weeks, resulted in about 900 days' worth of data. In total we collected entries from 48 data collectors, of which the toothbrush was by far the most frequently-used. Based on insights from the data and from interviews, we extended the families' ecosystems with 15 additional data collectors (including five entirely new ones, see table 2). On average we visited families for six interviews, and discussed topics such as daily routines, health issues in the past, present and future, connected devices and family dynamics.

Initially, participants struggled to find purpose for the generic data collectors, as it was both unclear what to use them for and how that data could be valuable. Later, the purpose was found in diverse ways. For example, keeping track of showering durations of different family members by placing it on the shower door; tracking candy consumption by attaching it to the door of the cupboard where the candy was stored, or tracking diaper changing frequency through diaper drawer usage.

As design researchers, we (together with the participants) struggled to find value for our personal health ecosystem in the routine data (gathered by the generic trackers). The timeline in the data dashboard gave an overview of when artifacts of the ecosystem were used, and for how long. For example, it showed family routines (e.g. a mother always waking up first, then other family members in the same order). By exploring data using different visualizations, we also found clear differences between family members and families. For example, figure 6 shows how different teeth-cleaning sessions were in one family. But when all sessions of all participants were displayed in one visualization, we saw that families are more alike than we expected.

Although the data from the data collectors provided insight into (a limited scope of) everyday (bathroom) routines, it gave little insight into the underlying experiences and context. Fortunately, our open study setup and data canvas allowed us to quickly change our approach. The following two examples clearly illustrate how a better contextual and experiential understanding of the behavioral data, gained throughout the interviews, provided a completely different perspective to the individual data collectors.

(1) As Family 3 was interested in being more active throughout the day, we provided them with Fitbit activity trackers [13]. In our data dashboard we could see when they were active and how active they were. In one of the weekly interviews the 13-year-old daughter explained:

'I'm interested in keeping track of my step count throughout the day because, at school, I have to carry a heavy backpack with books around all day. I can use this [Fitbit data] to show my teachers that my complaining is justified.' – Family 3, daughter

To her, the Fitbit data has a more specific purpose. Daily step counts are not (directly) of interest. How many steps she takes with her backpack, and how this affects her back, is what she is curious about. It was through the specific context of this participant that we learned about the personal value of this artefact.

(2) In the data dashboard we could see that the Visapure cleansing brush was frequently used by Family 1 and Family 2. In addition, we gained insights into how it was used (e.g. for how long, how the brush was moving and which brush head was used). In the dataset of Family 1, two Visapure sessions often appeared per day, with a time interval of about 15 minutes. During the interviews the family elaborated that not only the mother used it on a daily basis, but also the 10-year old daughter was actively using the same brush. Together they built a cleaning routine for the child's first blackheads (figure 8). In Family 2's data we recognized surprisingly extensive Visapure usage; besides using it as a cleansing device, the mother found a different purpose:

'I frequently suffer from migraine. I found that the Visapure with massage head [originally intended to enhance blood circulation for a healthy-looking glow] provides great relief when applied on the pressure points in my neck and head'. – Family 2, mother

Without this understanding, the Visapure data would have only told us that the device was used frequently, in a number of different ways.

The data from the data collectors (together with participants' explanations) provided insight into (a limited scope of) everyday routines, but, gave little insight into how devices could be of value to each other. From a health perspective, the interviews were instrumental in unravelling issues and concerns, allowing us to think beyond routines. As a result, we were able to introduce new (relevant) data collectors, based on personal interests. We describe these insights in more detail through three design opportunities, which emerged after the situated explorations.

Levels of Care

This explorative study started with a focus on bathroom routines. For the first couple of weeks, with the first two families, we struggled to find a way in which a personal health ecosystem could be valuable within these routines, as there were little to no health-related issues or concerns. But, based on our introductory interview with Family 3, we came to a widely different perspective.

Our personal health focus had mainly revolved around relatively 'small' personal health topics (e.g. optimized morning routines). However, Family 3 was and had been coping with much more serious problems. In the past, the son was diagnosed with cancer and the family had been travelling to the hospital several times a week. Fortunately, the boy recovered, but the situation caused depression in the mother. When our study started, the father had just lost his job and was going through a difficult period. These are only

Figure 8. Daughter (10) using the Visapure Advanced

some of the issues that we came across in the introductory interview. We felt that there was a stark contrast between the devices in our ecosystem (and our routine thinking at the time) and the lives of these people. As we set out to expand and develop the family ecosystems, based on what we would discover during these situated explorations, we challenged ourselves to see how the artifacts in our personal health ecosystem would develop within this new context. As a result, we introduced different 'levels of caring', as we argued that the ability of the system to understand the context of these issues was crucial if we wanted it to be valuable beyond simple routine advice.

We therefore introduced three levels of care: (1) I'm fine, (2) I'm worried, (3) I receive or need (professional) help. Depending on the level of care, the system could react differently. For instance, on the *I'm fine* level of teeth cleaning, the toothbrush could keep an eye on whether you brush regularly. In case you deviate too much it could occasionally nudge you (e.g. once a week or month). On the *I'm worried* level the user could have issues with gum health, and could therefore be more receptive to feedback. This would allow the system to be more present and give advice on how to best brush. On the *I receive or need (professional) help* level, issues have a more medical nature. Here, a dentist could, for example, provide a more intensive flossing schedule for a tooth implant.

For this exploration, identifying which issues were positioned on which levels of care was done manually and was based on the data dashboards, interviews and empathic understanding of the design researchers. We found a diverse set of care topics; for example, *snoring* (Family 1), *migraine during menstruation* (Family 2), *night lenses* (Family 3), *vitamin intake for kids* (Family 4) on the 'I'm fine' level; *hyperventilation* (Family 1), *light sleeping* (Family 2), *back pain* (Family 3) and *stress* (Family 4) on the 'I'm worried' level; and *burn-out* (Family 3) and *separation anxiety* (Family 4) on the 'I receive or need professional help' level.

Caring, When it Matters

In the 'Levels of Care' section we introduced the system's ability to position issues on different levels of care, and to respect the distinct nature of such issues. However, we found that these issues often change rapidly, and realized that a personal health ecosystem should embrace this dynamic nature. Topics that are relevant today may no longer relevant next week, as also reflected by Nardi's coevolution characteristic. Together with participants we concluded that a health ecosystem that cares about you should be there for you when it matters most. Although we didn't focus on translating our data in rule-sets for automation, we see clear starting points as described below.

When the system is (actively) used for a longer period of time, the data from the data collectors starts to show clear patterns. We referred to these earlier as daily- and session-specific routines. We noticed that sudden changes within these patterns often relate to special events or issues. Sudden changes in teeth cleaning routines (e.g. exhaustive brushing) can for example indicate an upcoming dentist visit or new brush head.

Although these examples presented insights that remain within the same category (i.e., an insight based on toothbrush data gives teeth cleaning advice), we also saw clear examples that managed to extend beyond their own category. For example, as already mentioned the father of Family 3 lost his job during the experiment. The interviews confirmed that this was a difficult time for him. A shaver, that was initially introduced to get more insight into shaving behavior, started showing less frequent use and thereby possibly diminished interest in personal care. The teeth cleaning routine, which was quite predictable before, now started deviating. It was more often at midday and midnight instead of morning and evening. Without having sleep-tracking devices, the toothbrush data indicated there might have been a sleeping routine shift.

Reflecting on our design challenge, which was to explore the value of an ecosystem compared to a collection of one-to-one connected devices, this is a clear example. For the next step we strongly argue for a common place where different devices can share their knowledge beyond their own domain.

As a note to this, we realize that a system can never embrace full contextual complexity, and thus will be incapable of interpreting reasons for behavioral change without stigmatizing. Neither will it be able to accurately predict users' preferred follow up. Hence, we propose that personal health ecosystems should analyze data, highlight changes, and only *guide towards* the preferred behavioral change. In this guidance there should always be room for personal and subjective input (as advocated by the locality argument of Nardi).

Designing an ecosystem that, together with users, aims to unravel relevant health topics and subsequently gives guidance throws up many questions related to privacy and trust. In this study these topics were barely raised by participants. Probably because their rights, the study purpose and the security of the system were discussed in detail and confirmed by signing informed consents. Likewise, the system forwarded neither conclusions nor guidance. However, these topics are essential when considering a commercial system .

Personalized Growth

We started this exploration with the intention of finding a collection of devices that could together play a role in our health ecosystem. As it proved challenging to define our 'keystone species' from the drawing board, we decided to start with a limited set of devices, that we would extend with other devices based on insights gathered during the experiment.

Table 2 gives an overview of how the different family systems all grew in a different direction. For example, for Family 1 we introduced Beddit sleep trackers [2] based on (family) sleep-related questions. For Family 3 we introduced Fitbit activity trackers [13] based on interests in a more healthy and active lifestyle. And for Family 4 we introduced Netatmo weather stations [38] to address the issue of ventilation during sleeping. Other devices we introduced were a connected vacuum cleaner (prototype) and a connected power socket [49].

device	functionality	Fam 1	Fam 2	Fam 3	Fam 4
Philips Sonicare Toothbrush	XYZ–orientation, duration of use, time of use, pressure, brushing modes, brushing Intensity.	1-8	1-8	1-8	1-8
Philips Shaver	XYZ-orientation, duration of use, time of use	1-8	1-8	1-8	1-8
Philips Visapure	XYZ-orientation, duration of use, time of use, head identification	1-8	1-8	1-8	1-8
iPad	Check in, check out, (duration & who is in the bathroom)	1-8	1-8	1-8	1-8
Accelerometer	XYZ-orientation, duration of use, time of use	1-8	1-8	1-8	1-8
Rotary Knob	(manual input) between 0 and 10, time of use	1-8	1-8	1-8	1-8
Beddit Sleep Tracker	sleep stages, environmental factors (temperature, humidity), heart rate, breathing rate	4-8			
Fitbit Activity tracker	Activity levels, sleep stages, heart rate		3-6	4-8	7,8
Netatmo Weather station	Room temperature, humidity, CO_2 levels, noise levels	6-8			5-8
Philips Vacuum Cleaner	XYZ-orientation, duration of use, time of use, noise levels, light, pressure, dust.		6		
Ubiquity Power Socket	Power consumption, duration of use, time of use.	5-8			3-8

Table 2. Overview of devices, functionality and in which week the devices were introduced

When reflecting on our insights from the previous two concepts, this growth is easily connected to the personal health topics that were at hand. Since our exploration produced such a variety in ecosystems – despite the fact that only four families were involved and all started with the same set of devices – we propose a model that allows for personalized growth. This is especially true if we think about how these artifact ecosystems will evolve. We see it as highly unlikely that people will buy all connected products at once, but instead will buy new devices when the need or (personal) interest is there. An informed step should further explore how an automated ecosystem could facilitate personalized growth, from a similar minimalistic starting point.

DISCUSSION

In this paper we presented a data-enabled design case study as a more practical angle to the thus-far dominantly theoretical discussion on ecosystems. Throughout the situated explorations we encountered multiple examples of unexpected use cases emerging, and discovered relations to other personal health elements of everyday life. In this section we discuss how this case study has given us insight into design challenges acquainted with designing for ecosystems, and illustrate how we utilized and modified our data-enabled design approach to address these new challenges.

An experiential-behavior approach to exploring system relationships

Prior work on ecologies [3, 4, 9, 15] and the Internet of Things [8, 27, 46] emphasized functional relationships between artifacts or artifacts and humans. This was clearly reflected in our initial thinking. At the start of the study, we expected to discover design opportunities or values for our *systemic* approach by focusing on the direct connections and relationships between devices (e.g. how data from the toothbrush could be relevant in interactions with a shaver). The only relationships we, together with participants, found (through the behavioral data) was how devices were connected through time (i.e. routine timelines) and how different users had distinct usage patterns (i.e. session timelines). Although devices were located and used in the same environment, they seemed to share little functional relations (apart from as reminders if a part of the routine was forgotten). If the value of the systemic approach should only come from these routine-like relationships, we strongly questioned the value of this systemic approach for a personal health ecosystem. Only after we visited Family 3 for the introductory interview – the family with the more serious health-related issues – did we find relationships between artifacts on a different layer. As the health issues provided a clear context for the artifacts, we could explore how the different artifacts could leverage or contribute to this contextual perspective.

Where ideas resulting from our initial perspective could be effortlessly mapped on Jung's [23] *ecological factors*: *functional* (e.g. exchangeable chargers), *informational* (e.g. routine data of toothbrush being relevant to your shaver), *interactional* (e.g. one interaction language for all Philips devices) and *physical* (e.g. a connected bathroom station), the latter relationships are more similar to their *ecological layers*. It allowed us to describe relationships based on similar context (e.g. teeth cleaning and sleep data were both instrumental in understanding everyday routines when going through a burn-out.), or similar values (e.g. the Visapure and topicals both relate to beautiful skin).

Previous data-enabled case studies started from a behavioral data point of view and used this as a starting point to involve more experiential data. However, this ecosystem study threw up broader, more open-ended and complex design challenges. These clearly benefited from a more experiential starting point. The behavioral data initially gave little insight into context and experiences, and it was therefore difficult to unravel how it could be meaningfully related to other artifacts. The experiential data (collected through the interviews) gave context to the explorations by understanding health issues and worries. Once these became clearer, the behavioral data could again be used to generate insights into more detailed and nuanced aspects of these topics (as explained in the reflection on ecological functions and layers).

An open and continuous approach to ever-changing ecosystems

In the related work section, we introduced the *coevolution* characteristic of ecologies and Frens' work on growing systems [16], both of which stressed the ever-changing nature of ecosystems. As it was challenging to initially determine the focus for our ecosystem, we used this growing quality to extend (i.e. grow) our ecosystem based on empirical behavioral and experiential insights. The flexibility and pace of device introductions, enabled by our data-enabled canvas, was instrumental in this. It allowed us to quickly act based on insights gathered in the field, and follow up on interesting aspects by introducing actors in the system (i.e. find new niches). The diversity of the final ecosystems demonstrates how this supported the idiosyncratic values and diversity of these families.

As already mentioned, data-enabled design strongly builds on the ability to continuously gain insights and execute new design interventions, in response to these insights. Where earlier case studies emphasized this continuity mostly in the second informed step, we see its value in the contextual step. It was unclear what data from which artifacts could play a role in this exploration. Neither did we know what *keystone species* would be because of the openness of the challenge. This study therefore benefited heavily from a flexible data-enabled canvas in the contextual step, which allowed for exploration in multiple directions. In addition, insights on an experiential level from the interviews triggered new questions on a behavioral level. This meant not only introducing new devices but also a renewed focus on existing data (e.g. sleep patterns in the toothbrush data). This continuous approach helped address the challenges associated with the dynamic nature of ecosystems.

It is relevant to point out that our current approach relies heavily on the empathic skills of the designer in understanding experiences and relations between elements of the ecosystem. This level of personal attention is what facilitated the extremely personalized growth at this point. The next – informed – step has to challenge us to translate the values associated with this personal understanding in an automated and scalable system. Although the challenge is of a different magnitude, the previous data-enabled design cases have shown similar developments towards more automated and personalized systems in the next step.

A situated and experiential approach to locality

The situated and experiential qualities, strongly advocated by the data-enabled design approach, were valuable in tackling the challenges posed by the design for ecosystems. They were instrumental in exploring emerging *diversity* relationships and strongly emphasized Nardi's *locality* characteristics through our personalized approach. The value of the ecosystem differed per family, as illustrated through different use cases. For example, the value of the cleansing brush was different for a participating mother suffering from migraine that was for a young girl spotting her first blackhead.

Taking these ecosystems out of their context would significantly reduce the complexity involved in this design challenge, but would also reduce the relevance of its findings. To us, this complexity, richness and versatility is inherently part of these system challenges. We see them as a fundamental quality of a personal health ecosystem, rather than something that should be reduced to be able to design for it. Our situated and open approach allowed for a rich collection of use cases, relations, topics, issues and values to emerge, which inspired new explorations and the design opportunities we presented.

Compared to the previous data-enabled design case studies, this contextual exploration ran for a longer period of time (i.e. eight weeks instead of four). As the challenge was less clearly defined, we decided to find direction throughout our situated explorations. The additional time was needed to facilitate new artifact introductions and to understand how relationships developed over time.

A critical note

In all data-enabled design case studies so far we involved a limited number of participants, as we valued extensive personal attention and tailored design interventions over large scale experiments that could be more conclusive but would give less insight into inspirational details. Although we were able to collect a rich and diverse set of insights that we were able to base our three design directions on, it is good to note that our participants have significantly affected our outcomes. Arguably, even without Family 3, the outcomes could have been widely different. On the other hand, with a larger-scale approach these issues would probably not have surfaced, as it would not have been possible to achieve the same level of personal detail.

As we were designing for personalized ecosystems, it is instructive to note that – although we set out to involve a heterogeneous group of participants – the families that involved in the study were all middle-income Dutch families. Although relatively diverse in the health issues they brought to the table, this selection offers a limited perspective of the user base we envision (e.g. culturally, socially, demographically). This arguably made it easier to come up with scalable personalized ecosystem concepts, as these people have more in common with each other than a random selection of the envisioned population. It is important to understand that the design directions were inspired by the insights, not a direct implementation of them. There is always a design step involved that abstracts these insights into opportunities for a larger target group. Moving further along in this process, to the next informed steps, these opportunities are further explored and evaluated along the way.

CONCLUSION

From a data-enabled perspective, the design for ecosystems was a significantly broader challenge than the previous ones that focused on designing (single) connected products. This required a shift from designing individual elements to designing for the relationships between these elements. Prior work on ecologies addressing this new challenge has been predominantly theoretical, and used to describe and evaluate ecosystems. In this paper we have presented a design exploration of a personal health ecosystem, to explore how data-enabled design could be used for these ecosystem challenges. We introduced a dynamic contextual step that started with a minimalistic, open and malleable ecosystem that was expanded based on situated insights. Where we previously relied mostly on sensor data, quickly turning this into behavioral data, this ecosystem challenge showed how a stronger initial focus on experiential data could be used to further inform the relevance of behavioral data. Being able to quickly switch between both types allowed us to gain insight on more holistic health levels as well as very detailed and personal use cases. Our data-enabled design approach is useful in addressing the systemic challenges posed by the complexity of designing for ecosystems, because it embraces relational, growing and locality characteristics through our experiential and situated approach. Although the highly personalized approach helped in emphasizing individual uniqueness, challenges remain on how diversity can be addressed in such small-scale studies. A next, informed, step can further explore the presented design opportunities and challenge their relevance.

ACKNOWLEDGEMENTS

Jos-Marien Janssen, Pepijn Verburg, Joep Elderman, Iris Roijakkers, Emmanuel Yeboah and other Philips Design colleagues, thank you for your help and commitment in running this project! This research was supported by the IMPULS perinatology framework.

REFERENCES

1. Amazon Digital Services LLC. 2017. Echo & Alexa. Retrieved December 11, 2017 from https://www.amazon.com/echo
2. Beddit. 2017. Better Sleep starts with not thinking about it. Retrieved December 11, 2017 from Beddit.com
3. Eli Blevis, Susanne Bodker, John Flach, Jodi Forlizzi, Heekyoung Jung, Victor Kaptelinin, Bonnie Nardi and Antonio Rizzo. 2015. Ecological Perspectives in HCI, Promise, Problems, and Potential. In *proceedings the Conference Extended Abstracts on Human Factors in Computing Systems (CHI EA'15)*, 2401-2404.
4. Susanne Bodker and Clemens Nylandstad Klokmose. 2011.The Human-artifact model an activity theoretical approach to artifact ecologies. *Human-Computer Interaction* 26(40), 315-371
5. Susanne Bodker and Clemens Nylandsted Klokmose. 2012. Dynamics in Artifact Ecologies. In *proceedings of Nordic conference on Human-computer interaction NordiCHI'12*, 448-457.
6. Sander Bogers, Joep Frens, Janne van Kollenburg, Eva Deckers, Caroline Hummels. 2016. Connected Baby Bottle: A design case study towards a framework for data-enabled design. In *proceedings of the Conference on Designing Interactive Systems (DIS'16)*, 301-311.
7. Sander Bogers, Janne van Kollenburg, Joep Frens and Tom Djajadiningrat. 2016. Data-Enabled-Design, a Situated Exploration of Rich Interactions. In *proceedings of the Conference Companion Publication on Designing Interactive Systems (DIS'16)*, 45-48.
8. Gerard Briscoe, Suzanne Sadedin and Philippe De Wilde. 2011. *Digital Ecosystems: Ecosystem-Oriented Architectures*. Natural Computing 10(3), 1143-1194
9. Nazli Cila, Iskander Smit, Elisa Giaccardi and Bend Krose. 2017. Products as Agents: Metaphors for Designing the Products of the IoT Age. *In proceedings of the Conference on Computer Human Interaction (CHI'17)*, 422-459.
10. Torkil Clemmensen, Victor Kaptelinin and Bonnie Nardi. 2016. Making HCI theory work: an analysis of the use of activity theory in HCI research. *Behaviour & Information Technology*, 35(8), 608-627
11. Ritske Dankert. 2011. Using Actor-Network Theory (ANT) doing research. Retrieved December 11, 2017 from https://ritskedankert.nl/using-actor-network-theory-ant-doing-research/
12. Carl Di Salvo and Jonathan Lukens. 2011. Nonanthropocentrism and the non-human in design: Possibilities for designing new forms of engagement with and through technology. In *From social butterfly to engaged citizen*. MIT Press, 421-437
13. Fitbit. Find your fit. 2017. Retrieved December 11, 2017 from www.fitbit.com/
14. Jodi Forlizzi. 2007. The Product Ecology: Understanding Social Product Use and Supporting Design Culture. *International Journal of Design* 2(1), 11-20.
15. Joep Frens, and Kees Overbeeke. 2009. Setting the stage for the design of highly interactive systems. In *proceedings of International Association of Societies of Design Research (IASDR'09)*, 1-10.
16. Joep Frens. 2017. Designing for Embodied and Rich Interaction in Home IoT. In *proceedings of the Conference on Design and Semantics of Form and Movement DeSForM'17*
17. Paul Gardien, Eva Deckers and Geert Christiaansen. 2014. Innovating Innovation: Deliver Meaningful Experiences in Ecosystems. In *proceedings of the Academic Design Management Conference (DMI'14).*
18. Elisa Giaccardi, Chris Speed, Nazli Cila, Melissa L. Caldwell. 2016. Things as co-ethnographers: Implications of a thing perspective for design and anthropology. In *Design Anthropological Futures, Rachel C. Smith, Kasper T. Vaskilde, Mette G. Kjaersgaard, Ton Otto, Joachim Halse, Thomas Binder (eds.)*. Bloomsbury Academic, 235-248
19. James J. Gibson. 1977. The theory of affordances. In *Perceiving, Acting and Knowing, R. Shaw and J. Bransford (eds.)*, Erlbaum
20. Google LLC. 2017. Google Home. Retrieved December 11, 2017 from https://store.google.com/category/home_entertainment
21. IFTTT Inc. 2017. IFTTT helps your apps and devices work together in new ways. Retrieved December 11, 2017 from https://ifttt.com/
22. Tom Jenkins, Christopher A. Le Dantex, Carl DiSalvo, Thomas Ladato and Mariam Asad. 2016. Object-Oriented Publics. In *proceedings of Conference on Human Factors in Computing Systems (CHI '16)*, 827-839
23. Heekyoung Jung, Erik Stolterman, Will Ryan, Tonya Thompson and Marty Siegel. 2008. Toward a Framework for Ecologies of Artifacts: How are Digital Artifacts Interconnected within a Personal Life? In *proceedings of Nordic conference on Human-computer interaction NordiCHI'08*, 201-210.
24. Jorn Georg Sannes Knutsen. 2014. Uprooting products of the networked city. *International Journal of Design* 8(1), 127-142.
25. Janne van Kollenburg, Eva Deckers, Paul Gardien and Caroline Hummels. 2015. People Research for Ecosystem propositions: a theoretical framework towards the future of interaction design. In *proceedings*

of the Conference on Design and Semantics of Form and Movement (DeSForM'17), 102-110.

26. Janne van Kollenburg, Sander Bogers, Heleen Rutjes, Eva Deckers, Joep Frens, Caroline Hummels 2018. Exploring the Value of Parent-Tracked Baby Data in Interactions with Healthcare Professionals: A Data-Enabled Design Exploration. In *proceedings of the Conference on Computer Human Interaction (CHI'18).*
27. Treffyn Lynch Koreshoff, Toni Robertson and Tuck Wah Leong. 2013. Internet of Things: a review of literature and products. In *proceedings of Australian Computer-Human Interaction Conference (OzCHI'13)*, 335-344.
28. Mike Kuniavsky. 2010. *Smart Things: Ubiquitous Computing User Experience Design*. Elsevier
29. Bruno Latour. 2011. Networks, societies, spheres: Reflections of an actor-network theorist. *International Journal of Communication* 5(15), 786-810.
30. Ian Li, Anind Dey and Jodi Forlizzi. 2010. A Stage-based Model of Personal Informatics Systems. In *proceedings of the Conference on Human Factors in Computing Systems (CHI'10)*, 557-566.
31. Rochelle King, Elizabeth Churchill, Caitlin Tan. 2017. *Designing with Data.* O'Reilly Media.
32. Lumo Bodytech Inc. 2017. Lumo Lift. Retrieved December 11, 2017 from https://www.lumobodytech.com/lumo-lift/
33. Maurice Merleau-Ponty. 1962. *Phenomenology of Perception, Translation: Collin Smith*. New York: Humanities Press.
34. Carl Mitcham 1994. *Thinking through Technology: The Path between Engineering and Philosophy*. The University of Chicago Press.
35. Richard Mortier, Hamed Haddadi, Tristan Henderson, Derek McAuley, and Jon Crowcroft. 2014. Human-data interaction: the human face of the data-driven society. arXiv:1412.6159 [cs.CY]
36. Bjorn Nansen, Luke van Ryn, Frank Vetere, Toni Robertson, Margot Brereton and Paul Dourish. 2014. An internet of social things. In *proceedings of Australian Computer-Human Interaction Conference on Designing Futures (OzCHI '14)*, 87-96
37. Bonnie Nardi, Vicky O'Day. 1999. *Information Technologies, Using Technology with heart.* MIT Press, Cambridge.
38. Netatmo. 2017. Personal Weather Station: Master your own climate measurements on your smartphone. Retrieved December 11, 2017 from https://www.netatmo.com/product/weather/weatherstation
39. Nokia. 2017. An ideal weight loss companion. Retrieved December 11, 2017 from https://health.nokia.com/us/en/body-plus
40. Philips AVENT. 2017. uGrow- the world's first medical baby app with connected devices giving you personal advice that matters. Retrieved December 11, 2017 from http://www.philips.co.uk/c-m-mo/ugrow-healthy-baby-development-app
41. Philips Design. 2017. 90 years of years of design. Retrieved December 11, 2017 from www.philips.com/design
42. Philips Healthtech B.V. 2017. FlexCare Platinum Connected. Retreived December 11, 2017 from www.usa.philips.com/c-m-pe/electric-toothbrushes/flexcare-platinum/connected
43. Philips Healthtech B.V. 2017. Factsheet for CES – Philips Avent uGrow digital parenting platform. Retreived December 11, 2017 from https://www.philips.com/c-dam/corporate/newscenter/global/standard/resources/healthcare/2017/ces2017/CES-2017-Philips-Avent-uGrow-FactSheet.pdf
44. Philips Lighting B.V. 2017. Meet Hue, Personal Wireless Lighting. Retrieved December 11, 2018, from http://www.meethue.com/
45. Alfred Schütz. 1967. *The Phenomenology of the Social World.* Northwestern University Press.
46. Henrik Sorensen, Dimitrios Raptis, Jesper Kjeldskov and Mikael B. Skov. 2014. The 4C Framework: Principles of Interaction in Digital Ecosystems. In *proceedings of International Joint Conference on Pervasive and Ubiquitous Computing (UbiComp'14)*, 87-97
47. Jelle Stienstra, Sander Bogers and Joep Frens. 2015. Designerly Handles: Dynamic and Contextualized Enablers for Interaction Designers. In *proceedings of the Conference on Design and Semantics of Form and Movement (DeSForM'15)*, 86-94.
48. Lucy A. Suchman.1987. *Plans and Situated Actions: The problem of human-machine communication.* Cambridge UK: Cambridge University Press.
49. Ubiquiti Networks, Inc. 2017. mFi® Controllable Power Outlets. Retrieved December 11, 2017 from https://www.ubnt.com/mfi/mpower/
50. Vessyl. Inc. 2017.Vessyl automatically knows and tracks everything you drink. Retrieved December 11, 2017 from https://www.myvessyl.com/
51. Mark Weiser. 1991. The Computer for the 21st Century. *Scientific American* 265(3), 94-104
52. Xiaomi. 2017. Xiaomi Mi band 2 Black. Retrieved December 11, 2017 from https://xiaomi-mi.com/mi-band/xiaomi-mi-band-2-black/

Social Support Mosaic: Understanding Mental Health Management Practice on College Campus

Sun Young Park
Stamps School of Art and Design, School of Information
University of Michigan
Ann Arbor, MI, USA
sunypark@umich.edu

ABSTRACT
Mental health wellness concerns are a significant issue among emerging adults due to the compounded stressors of life changes, new responsibilities, and career-related burdens. Due to a lack of support and the stigma associated with seeking help, they often do not receive adequate professional care. In this paper, we show how emerging adults seek help managing their mental wellness through social support. We conducted 19 interviews with students at a large university in the U.S. Midwest. Our study identifies that students maintain different social support groups, selectively sharing their concerns based on each group's role, benefits, and limitations. We call this support network the Mosaic of Social Support. We discuss opportunities for technology design that enhances the Mosaic of Social Support, allowing it to be more accessible, safe, and sustainable, thus providing tailored help to serve the students' unmet needs.

Author Keywords
Social support; emerging adults; mental health; mental wellness.

ACM Classification Keywords
H.5.m. Information interfaces and presentation (e.g., HCI): Miscellaneous.

INTRODUCTION
Mental health issues, growing both in severity and prevalence, are becoming a serious concern among emerging adults who are experiencing increased independence and exploring various life possibilities [6]. Emerging adults have particular difficulties maintaining their mental health wellness because of the burden of managing both personal and career-related life transitions. According to a recent U.S. national survey [2], 49.8% of students reported feeling hopeless, and 85.1% felt overwhelmed with their given tasks. Nearly 10% had seriously considered committing suicide in the last year. 75% of mental disorders have first onset by age 24 [37] and account for nearly 50% of the disease burden for young adults in the U.S. [80].

DIS '18, June 9–13, 2018, Hong Kong

ACM ISBN 978-1-4503-5198-0/18/06...$15.00
https://doi.org/10.1145/3196709.3196787

Research has provided a variety of evidence for the importance of social support to mental health wellness [1,62,67,70]. Effective social support is tailored according to the needs of the receiver, whether building resilience to stress [62], increasing self-esteem [11,34,35], or providing coping skills for the adaptation to stressful life circumstances [25,34,58,73]. Family support is crucial to decreasing depression for emerging adults [67], while peers' social support provides students with a sense of belonging [33], validation in their struggles [53], and help with developing empathy for others [69]. Despite these benefits, seeking and receiving social support is frequently hindered by various barriers. Stigma, secrecy, and negative cultural attitudes towards mental illness suppress help-seeking behavior [14,23,45]. Stigma not only affects the person with the mental illness, but also others (e.g., friends, family, physicians), resulting in a culture of "don't ask, don't tell." Consequently, individuals do not receive timely, proactive help [20]; and those who need the most help are often those left with the largest lack of support resources.

Technology has played a role in facilitating mental health, and the HCI community has investigated a variety of ways to support young adults and adolescents with mental health wellness. Starting with self-tracking or passively monitoring users' statuses [40,50,75], researchers have explored providing therapy modules [66], developing games as a way to provide treatment or social support [15], and using social media to understand their conditions [17,18,24,57]. Using such technologies provides more promising opportunities to address mental health's stigma and increase access to therapeutic tools. However, more work is required to examine how technologies can provide tailored social support – that is, support properly targeted and of the quality that the literature has presented as helpful and effective. HCI researchers and designers are well-positioned to create tools that enhance collaborative and tailored social support to address this unmet need in mental health.

To better provide social support for emerging adults' mental health wellness, we needed to understand emerging adults' current use of social support and the role, benefits, and challenges of seeking and receiving social support. To do so, we conducted 19 interviews with undergraduate and graduate students at a large public university. We found that students utilized and managed different social groups of people, selectively sharing distinct concerns with each group depending on the groups' availability, the tailored support each social group could provide, and the limitations each group had. We call this social support practice *mosaic of social support*. In this paper, we discuss how *mosaics* – tailored, flexible, yet intertwined social support practices – can shed light on the potential role of technology-mediated social support for emerging adults. We then present opportunities for designing technologies to enhance social support mosaics, unique to individuals' needs and situations, to be more accessible, safe, and sustainable.

BACKGROUND

Emerging adulthood is a well-known term for the new life stage between adolescence and young adulthood, roughly lasting through one's twenties. Five distinct characteristics of emerging adulthood are: identity exploration, instability, self-focus, feelings of being in-between adolescence and adulthood, and having a sense of broad possibilities for the future [6]. Emerging adults often face a number of stressors that affect mental health due to the transition from adolescence to college life [49] and changes in lifestyle, including increased personal responsibility and independence [4,6,43]. Students must manage the pressure of academics [29,32,41] and at the same time build relationships with friends, as well as develop a sense of belonging [3,28,68,72]. Although there have been some efforts to provide resources and aids to address student mental health issues, such as college campus counseling services, educational materials, workshops, and online help [39], they remain under-utilized for preventative visits and are utilized primarily for emergency services [12,56]. Social stigma also prohibits help-seeking behavior [23], and negative cultural attitudes towards professional help [14,45] reduce the likelihood of students seeking help when they need it.

Social support is defined as "support accessible to an individual through social ties to other individuals, groups, and the larger community" [47], and as "support available in times of need to give psychological, physical, and financial help" [81]. High levels of social support can protect against the impacts of mental illness on students' lives [62] by providing encouragement and help with social adjustment and college transition [16,52], as well as reducing depressive symptoms and risk of suicide [30,31].

Social support that is tailored to targeted populations and specific mental illnesses is essential to providing a more effective solution. For instance, in the treatment of sexual assault survivors with PTSD, using social support to build resilience and self-esteem to reduce self-blame and promote avoidance coping has been found crucial [77]. For those suffering from severe social anxiety, close friends who provide high peer group acceptance is effective [42].

Technology has been utilized significantly as an effective mental health solution for the young adult population by enhancing social support. Phone calls and texts are the most useful technologies to get social support from family, friends, and peers [26]. Online support communities and social networks are beneficial for managing mental illness and a multitude of studies have shown their effectiveness in improving mental illness outcomes [24,36,46,61]. For instance, an online peer support system helped match peers through similarities beyond diagnosis [61]. Moderated online social therapy has also shown success in developing a sense of belonging, security, positivity, and protection [44]. These tools have not only actively or passively augmented physical presence in remote settings, but also helped in actually providing mental support among users. At the heart of these successes lies anonymity and accessibility; Balani and De Choudhury found being anonymous in online support groups allowed individuals' honest and candid expressions of thoughts, experiences, and beliefs [9]. However, it is worth noting that excessive social media use, particularly among adolescent populations, has been correlated with depression symptoms [63] and linked to cyberbullying [64], potentially leading to Internet addiction [13], and causing lower self-esteem [78].

HCI researchers and designers have developed technologies to enhance support exchanges among existing social networks. Digital family portraits [38,59,60,71] have augmented connections between extended family members and elderly adults. CoupleVIBE [10] and MissU [48] explored the power of implicit communication between distant partners; Eichhorn et al. simulated the effects of physical intimacy through a physical stroking device for long-distance couples [22].

As such, HCI work has investigated augmenting a variety of social support sources: online support groups and social media for mental health, and tangible media for significant others and family members. Even though some of this prior work shows the outcomes, benefits, and challenges of using technologies for people with mental health issues, more work can shed light on stigma-related challenges in seeking help around mental health for the emerging adult population who are transitioning from being dependent to being partially independent. Furthermore, more work is required to gain a more qualitative, descriptive understanding of the existing social support practices of this population, in addition to using quantitative approaches through surveying their experiences and opinions and examining online posts, which have been the dominant methods used in prior studies in this field.

Our goals in this paper are to: (1) broaden the understanding of how emerging adults currently seek and receive social support in their daily lives, (2) understand how other factors, such as stigma, affect these practices, and (3) highlight opportunities for future technology that can support and augment such practice.

METHODS

Participants

The literature has described attending college as one of the critical contributors to the challenges that emerging adults experience because of lifestyle changes including increased personal responsibility, independence, and stress from school and work [6,29]. Emerging adults are those aged between 18-29, or roughly, in their 20s. Thus, we recruited both undergraduate and graduate students at a large university in the U.S. Midwest. We recruited 19 participants between the ages of 20-28, consisting of 13 females and six males. They were six undergraduate and 13 graduate students; there were seven international students among them. The 19 participants consisted of diverse ethnic backgrounds: six non-Hispanic White, six East Asians, five Indians, and two African-Americans. Two had been clinically diagnosed with a mental disorder, and 13 had past experience with professional counseling services. We recruited participants through school-wide departmental e-mailing lists and word-of-mouth.

Data Collection and Analysis

We conducted a qualitative study using interviews to understand how students managed their mental health and what social support resources they used. We chose individual participant interviews as our study method since this allowed us to gain a deeper understanding of students' experience, challenges, opinions, and perceptions of seeking and receiving social support than surveys or focus groups could. The participants shared their stressors, their experiences of seeking and receiving social support, and the tools they used in the process. Building upon prior literature on the overall climate of students on college campus (e.g., how many students struggle with anxiety, stress, and depression and using resources), we wanted to explore the kinds of stressors students deal with, the coping strategies they develop, the kinds of social support they have, seek, and want, and the challenges they face. Our exploratory study, using in-depth qualitative interviews, helped us gain a deeper understanding of students' current experiences with and perspectives of social support.

All interviews were audio recorded and transcribed for analysis. Three researchers conducted the data analysis, using the open coding method [27] using the Atlas.Ti 7 qualitative coding software program. Once we identified the core themes, we conducted axial coding to systematically explore the properties and dimensions of each theme. As a group, we compared, discussed and revised the themes through a series of iterations until agreement was reached. We used affinity diagramming on a shared Google Sheet to collaboratively generate and examine these themes. The Institutional Review Boards of the authors' universities approved the study. Below, we describe how our participants exchanged social support to manage their mental health, and then follow with the suggested role of technology-mediated social support for students on college campuses.

STUDENTS' SOCIAL SUPPORT SEEKING PRACTICES

In this study, we found that during times of distress, our participants actively made efforts to cope with their struggles by seeking support from the various social groups in their lives. All of our participants maintained more than one social group. These social groups ranged from close friends and parents to acquaintances and anonymous individuals. Each of these groups had a unique role and had different benefits and limitations when fulfilling the needs of the participants, significantly affecting how students selected groups with which to share more private concerns. The ways in which participants shared their concerns with each group were largely dependent upon the kinds of needs the participant had, the types of help they expected, as well as any potential conflicts or limitations present in their relationship with members of each group. Our study showed that various levels of stigma associated with sharing one's concerns generated the most significant limitation in using these social groups as support. In this section, we present each social group, their roles in supporting participants' mental health and their limitations.

Close Friends: Active Listening, Proactive Support, and Sociocultural Sensitivity

The most salient social group our participants interacted with to share their concerns was their close friends, a dedicated and intimate group. Participants found that close friends provided intimacy, trust, and comfort by offering active listening, which was one of the most important factors they looked for in support. Because of the comfort and intimacy they shared with close friends, the participants were mostly able to share concerns spontaneously and informally through casual conversations.

Active listening was a "*rare*" quality that their close friends provided: *"I have a lot of friends but not all of them are very good listeners ... people generally like to talk and then listen."* (P14) Participants found that many people gave superficial comfort by listening and then stating *"Oh you're doing good. You're doing well. Don't worry."* (P17) However, close friends listened to the participants' problems and provided sincere feedback and encouragement: *"I just talk to them about all of the stress that I have right now. They will share with me their stress, too. They will talk to me, 'Okay, I'm at the same page with you, but we can do this.'"* (P16)

In addition, close friends were commonly able to provide proactive help for each other. Close friends were sensitive and responsive enough to each other to sense one another's moods on daily basis; thus, support was sometimes given without the participants actively seeking it or expressing their concerns upfront. In our interviews, many participants reported that their close friends sensed when they were not feeling well and would routinely intervene and proactively offer support: *"I have several very close friend. Every time*

I feel depressed, I think they can tell. Because I just stop showing up in classes. They will say, "Where are you?" I'll say, "I'm at home. I don't feel really good. I probably feel a little bit stressed." They will probably ask me why, what's the trigger? I'll say, "Because of the paper. Because of what. Because of this. Because of that." If they are at the same class with me, we'll just talk about the paper, talk about their ideas, and share ideas, start working on it. That will be really helpful. They will talk to me, "Okay, I'm at the same page with you, but we can do this. They will just cheer me up, and we just go out and eat, and do some dessert. They know dessert's really helpful." (P16) Thus, participants felt that their closest friends would be there to provide support for them whenever they needed it, without necessarily expecting anything in return.

Our participants also expected deeper understanding and more empathy from their close friends since, in many cases, close friends have similar ethnic, religious, educational, and socioeconomic backgrounds. In our interviews, the students described how it was critical that members of their close friends groups had similar education levels or ethnicities.

"They have to [already] have undergrad degree because I feel like if the education background are so different, they probably don't understand my stress. I want them to have the ability or the background to understand my concerns. That would be, I think education is one of my concern." (P16)

"I have a very good friend who study in Netherland. She's just graduated. She encounters pretty much the same stress as I have here. I'm finding an internship, she is finding a full-time job. We were struggling going back to Taiwan or stay or not. A lot of same issues... We have very similar situations." (P10)

In the case of P10, even though her Taiwanese friend was studying in the Netherlands, they still shared the similar struggle of being Taiwanese, studying abroad, and looking for a job in a foreign country. Thus, they were easily able to understand each other's concerns and situation. Having same ethnicities was especially critical to international students in particular. Other international students in our study also described feeling more closely connected to people of the same ethnic group as they were able to help each other with issues related to acculturation and assimilation while they lived in a foreign country.

Due to the benefits of culturally relevant and culturally sensitive support, the participants often turned to their close friends instead of other social groups when they struggled with issues that especially needed empathy. They expected that their close friends would be able to best understand and empathize with their situations and issues. For instance, one student was able to share her "sexual deviance" with her friends and found them to be the best help while she faced difficulties sharing the complexities of her identity with a health professional who was unable to comprehend her bisexuality in the context of her conservative Catholic upbringing. Another student explained his distinctive expectation for the kinds of support he would gain from close friends, compared to other social groups: *"Friends [are] good sources to vent, rather than asking for solutions because they don't have the knowledge to solve my issue, but they have a similar issue and concern at the same time."* (P1)

Limitations

Since close friends were critical to the participants' daily lives, many of the participants also felt pressure to maintain these relationships by trying to meet certain expectations the friends might have for them. For example, P2 feared that revealing too much of himself would change the relationship he had with his friends, stating that even close friends had expectations for each other, such as maintaining a positive and fun attitude when hanging out. This was a significant stressor shared by many participants and placed limits on how much help the participants would seek from their close friends. As P2 explained, *"It's very difficult and I feel uncertain if I were to reveal a little bit my personal self, would they still be the same towards you know, friendship or not. I think that was something really halting me from seeking help when very stressful things happened."* (P2)

Similarly, another student expressed her fear that sharing her struggles might burden her friends and end up ruining her friendships: *"I think everybody likes to hang out with somebody that lifts them up, that makes them happy. Not a lot of people want to hang out with somebody who's just constantly complaining about their life or they're feeling sad all the time. A lot of those types of people end up not having a lot of friends, because not a lot of people want to hear just sadness all the time. I think it's good to vent to your friends, but you can't be a person that's just constantly sad and leaning on your friends, because that's a lot of burden for them to carry too."* (P7)

Our study shows that the close friends group offered support through active listening, proactive help, and sociocultural understanding. This enabled students to expect a high level of intimacy, empathy, and comfort from their close friends. At the same time, worries about being a good friend and maintaining their friendships often hindered the participants from asking for help. These benefits, perceived limitations and participant expectations affected how participants decided to share their issues with their close friends.

Parents: Unconditional Love, Guidance, and Versatile Help

Parents were another important social group for the students we spoke with, but a complex one, encompassing the extreme ends of the support qualities. A majority of our participants felt that their parents had the potential to provide unconditional love, guidance and versatile help, but also felt that poor relations and past conflicts led to certain obstacles to a complete source of social support.

Participants' parents often provided unconditional love and a strong belief in their children; this level of support helped the participants turn to their parents as their last resort in extreme situations. For instance, a couple of participants recalled that they thought of their parents during dangerous moments like when they had suicidal thoughts. However, such a reliable connection required openness and comfort: *"I'm very open. My parents are sort of very modern thinkers. They've never said that anything is off the table to discuss. We've always been very open about sex or drinking or whatnot."* (P5)

Another quality parents provided as a crucial support group was reassurance with unconditional support, a different type of support than the other social groups. An interviewee described how her mom gave her reassurance with love and encouragement: "She's not *just baby[ing] me about it. You're not being productive right now... You need to get it together. You can do it, I know you can do it, make sure you're using the strategies that I know you have in your toolkit from your therapist."* (P13).

Parents also provided significant guidance and gave advice based on their own seasoned, lived experience, including help making career decisions (P9, P5), strategies for managing school work (P5, P13), and how to deal with medical issues (P5, P13). Because many parents had experience dealing with similar issues in the past, some participants relied on them for advice when faced with certain situations, wanting *"somebody else's opinion who's been around the block a few times..."* (P5).

We also found that many participants considered their parents, particularly their mother, their crucial supporter when making a rational decision or in need of practical help with their mental health. While close friends could provide intimacy and comfort by offering active listening, understanding, and similarity, parents could help them become more aware of a problematic situation and take action to improve it. One participant mentioned how her mother helped her realize that she had a problem and suggested she get professional help immediately: *"I was sitting in my room thinking about how to kill myself. So, my thought was not to really talk to anyone about it. I mean, I talked to a friend. But the reason why I ended up going [to the mental health therapy] in the end was because my mom suggested it. I think what ended up happening was I got a C- in school, which is not something that I ever did. And I started hyperventilating with her over the phone. And she was like, "This is not normal." So, she asked around, and someone had a friend. And so, my mom really set me up with this person to go see her."* (P19)

Limitations

While most parents provided unconditional love and belief in their child, we found that some participants could not share intimate problems because they lacked trust with their parents due to past conflicts, or conflicting values and expectations. Painful or unpleasant experiences in the past, such as child abuse (P3), memories of frequent arguments with the parents (P1), and drug problems in the family (P2) were obvious causes of our participants not being open with their parents. More subtle forms of conflicts included the inability to meet family expectations (P1), judgment over mental health issues (P4), and disagreements with cultural values (P19). P10 stated that she felt that her parents had "invested" in her education and she had a duty to "repay" them; thus, sharing her stressors in school was not an option.

Additionally, not all parents could provide useful guidance and advice for their children. Some mentioned that their parents could not help with their stress with school curriculums and career building because their parents lacked similar experiences or their experiences did not match up (P12, 19). Similarly, when there was too much of a gap between their parents' lifestyle and their own current lifestyle, participants neither wanted to share with their parents nor had the expectation of receiving help since their parents could not relate to their issues or situations. These participants often chose not to discuss personal issues with their parents, forcing them to reach out to others, such as close friends or other trusted elders. With their parents, these students chose to only talk about significant life updates or have general conversations about daily life. For instance, P12 and P19 felt that they could not discuss their issues with their parents because their parents could not understand or relate to the stress of student life. P12 explains, *"...sometimes it is difficult to explain the situation to my family because they are not in the university setting, so when I am stressed I can't really explain it to my mom because she needs more context, and that in itself is a bit of more pain..."* (P12)

Lastly, some participants showed concerns about adding an extra burden to their parents or causing their parents to become overprotective or overreact by sharing their problems. These students would rather face their problems themselves or confide in their friends. In her interview, P16 demonstrated her worry that her mom might have noticed her stress: "*My family? Not really. I don't want to make my parents feel stressful. Most of the time, I just tell them good news, not the bad news. If I'm really stressful, I'd probably ... How do I say? Normally, my mom will call me three times a week, but if I feel really depressed or very stressful, I'll just text my mom. I don't tell her the reason, I just tell her I'm busy, but because I'm not in a good mood, I'm not in a good condition I don't want her to see me because she can tell. Every time we video chat, she says, "Oh you look really happy recently, right?" I then say, "Yeah." When I feel really depressed, I don't want to her see it.*" (P16)

In sum, our findings show that getting reassurance, encouragement, practical guidance, and solutions to their problems allowed the students to seek more versatile support from the parents group, compared to other social groups. Nonetheless, limitations, including conflicted family relationships, different lifestyles, and worry about burdening their parents, often impeded the students' sharing of their problems and seeking help from their parents.

Acquaintances and Anonymous Individuals: Maneuvering Stigma and Secrecy, Forming New Relationships

The next two groups – acquaintances and anonymous individuals – provided participants with groups to fall back on when problems arose with their closer social network groups, such as friends and parents, either due to stigma or unavailability. Although our participants generally preferred sharing their concerns with their close social groups, they sometimes wanted to detach themselves when the subject was too personal or there was a potential stigma or unwanted consequences. In these cases, by confiding in people outside of their close networks, participants hoped to create a degree of separation between their issues and their personal lives. For example, P14 stated, *"I'd rather have somebody I don't know learn about what I was going through rather than have someone I know remember this for my entire lifetime... I didn't want my friends to remember me to be somebody who is very sad or is stressed out. I didn't want them to judge me that way."* (P14)

Acquaintances

Acquaintances include individuals that participants met in person outside their close networks of friends and family, such as contacts from classes, school, or part-time work. Unlike those in the close networks, who may have personal stakes in the issues that the participant was facing, acquaintances could provide objective and outside perspectives, addressing issues that had stigma with social distance. At the same time, our participants also mentioned that they only turned to acquaintances who had the qualities of genuine concern, compassion, and a desire to have discussions.

Participants felt that having a common background, to some degree, was still crucial for the acquaintances group. If they had no common background with an acquaintance, students felt it was useless to share their concerns because that person would not understand their issues appropriately. Similar backgrounds also helped to provide an opportunity to create and develop a new relationship. The students felt it was important that they had the potential to mold positive images of themselves in the space of these newly formed relationships, allowing them to separate their troubled pasts from the relationships that they would form going forward. One student mentioned how she occasionally shared her issues with people she just met at a dance club and her excitement about developing a fresh relationship with them without the burden of her past issues: *"... the people I do know here aren't people I've known in the past. Even they're only getting to know me now. I didn't want them to remember me that way."* (P14)

We also found that a few students in our study had some expectation that health professionals would be the acquaintances group outside their close network when they looked for a professional help, rather than looking for a specific treatment. The students in the study who had prior experience with professional therapists described not finding the treatment effective since the suggested treatment did not align with their personal interests (e.g., being told to write a letter or breathing strategy). Instead, they found being able to talk to a person who had the interest of hearing them out, yet who was outsider, a lot more valuable.

Anonymous Individuals

In addition to the in-person acquaintances group, several participants used the Internet to connect with anonymous users when seeking help or advice. Anonymous platforms allowed the students to find and connect with others who had similar struggles and needed resources, without the risk of dealing with stigma or worrying about others knowing their identity. With issues that were uncommon or difficult to find others who could understand among their existing social groups, participants tended to go online to talk to people, instead of sharing with their friends or family members. For example, one participant used online forums to connect with other people also struggling with autoimmune diseases and received anonymous help from a support group.

One salient benefit to sharing with an anonymous group was to be able to reduce the fear of stigma even more so than sharing with acquaintances because their identity was completely concealed, including their appearance. Thus, students often utilized Reddit or other online forums to anonymously interact with others through posts and messages, rather than merely using their social media accounts. Our participants used anonymous on-line groups to find others who were struggling with similar issues, read others' stories to reflect on their own problems, gain indirect comfort/support from replies and messages, and learn useful coping skills.

With anonymous groups, students also considered feeling safe and comfortable the foremost quality since they were able to be vulnerable by putting themselves out there and asking for support. One student explained that feeling safe needed to be guaranteed in order for people to open up, which was the main draw of being anonymous:

"People who go to [online forum name] want to be themselves. Even though they don't know who they are, but they want to be themselves. Meaning that they want to sacrifice that...(inaudible). Safety is definitely one of the biggest sacrifices and that turns everything to the bad side. You want to be safe there. That is the bottom line. You are not going to talk anything if you feel it is not safe. For instance, if I feel I will be judged when I say it, like socially, I am not going to go [online]." (P1)

Limitations

In terms of utilizing the acquaintances and anonymous group as social support, developing trust was somewhat challenging and/or intimidating. Thus, participants found that there was an initial hurdle involved in seeking help from groups and sharing private information: *"I felt like talking to a stranger was a little bit, like, awkward because I didn't really know her that well I wasn't really sure like how much initial like trust we had."* (P4); *"I'm not too sure I could talk to random people who are not professionals ... You have a different mental state when you're a therapist compared to talking to just anonymous people."* (P14)

In addition, despite the benefit of being able to keep their identity disclosed and being able to connect with others who were in similar situations, the students found that anonymous individuals could not provide help that was as useful as in-person sources of support. Since the anonymous individuals, unlike professionals, neither had the training nor expertise to properly handle someone's concerns, nor knew their personal history or personality, participants did not really expect the help of the anonymous group to be that practical or personal. As one student explained,

"You have a different mental state when you're a therapist compared to talking to just anonymous people... Most of us [in the anonymous group] would just give them responses like just don't worry about it and things like that whereas a therapist would have a better way... They [professionals] might have suggestions of how to go about things and they're always much more understanding than regular people." (P14)

Similarly, another student expressed his doubt about the quality of help from the anonymous group, compared to the direct advice given from the other social groups who had real connections to his life and understood his past life history and personality. Thus, it was generally believed that anonymous supporters were only capable of providing generic support and advice that may or may not be relevant to the participant seeking help.

Lastly, a few students who utilized online communities to discuss their problems mentioned that there were potential risks in doing so, such as cyber bullying and harassment. The risks that the students perceived were varied, based on individual attitudes about and past experiences with online communities. As reported previously [61], these perceived risks potentially led to participants limiting use, avoiding, and even abandoning technology for social support, with the consequence of furthering isolation.

DISCUSSION

This study examines emerging adults' practices of seeking and receiving social support for mental wellness. Our study uncovers their needs when building various social support groups, the types of tailored support each group provides, and the limitations participants experience with each group.

Below, we discuss the *mosaic of social support* observed from the social support seeking practices of the participants, in which they actively developed and used social groups to share their concerns and seek help. We then discuss design opportunities for future tools to incorporate the needs of these emerging adults and enhance the development and utility of their tailored social support.

Mosaic of Social Support

All of our study participants developed and maintained a variety of social groups that were uniquely supportive of their mental health needs and constraints. These social groups were somewhat structured, but also adaptable, meeting the different needs of each individual at different times. This flexible but tightly intertwined form of social support was crucial in maintaining the students' mental wellness.

To describe this support structure, we use the concept of the *mosaic*. The Merriam-Webster dictionary defines *mosaic* as: "a surface decoration made by inlaying small pieces of variously colored material to form pictures or patterns; *also*: the process of making it" [82]. Here, the "small pieces" refer to the "different social groups," and the "formed pictures or patterns" are the "uniquely tailored social support structure" each individual has to manage. Our findings present how our participants create their own *mosaic of social support* as they try to address their immediate needs and work around the limitations of the social groups around them. As part of the pieces of the mosaic, the close friends group offers active listening, proactive support, and a sense of belonging; the parents group provides practical advice as experienced individuals and unconditional love and belief in them; and finally, the acquaintance / anonymous groups provide support in de-stigmatization and opportunities for new relationships. At the same time, different participants differently construe the roles and constraints of each group when seeking social support givers.

Since the mosaics the students develop and maintain consist of various social groups that provide different types of help, the mosaics are not static, but flexible and adaptable; students make decisions about whom to turn to, what to share, and how to share based on the types of support needed at a given time, as well as the limitations each group has at that moment. For instance, P1 chose to vent private concerns to close friends rather than seek solutions or strategies. P1 did so because her friends did not have sufficient knowledge to solve her issues, but they had had similar experiences and they could listen and understand what P1 was going through. On the other hand, P19 preferred not to disclose private information to her close friends because some of the information she wanted to share could affect her current status as "fun" to her close friends group. Accordingly, P19 turned to a distant friend living in a different country.

When seeking more concrete solutions, P1 sought help from a more experienced, seasoned individual, such as her advisor, rather than her friends who lacked the appropriate knowledge. Although her parents could have provided advice, P1 felt she had a strained relationship with them, where her parents overemphasized the parts of her life that she didn't care as much about. On the other hand, other participants (e.g., P5, P9, P13) saw their parents as people to share life experiences with, and to seek help from when making career decisions, managing school work, and dealing with medical issues.

As such, the social groups in a mosaic are pieced together to compensate for other groups' limitations according to each individual's needs, constraints, and expectations. The students flexibly adapted and used their various social groups together in tailored ways that best supported their mental wellness, resembling a mosaic. As students encounter various stressors during their emerging adulthood, they develop a mosaic that continues to adapt and evolve in a manner that best supports them and their evolving mental health needs. Over time, mosaics may evolve by changing in terms of the size, quality, benefits, and limitations of each group (e.g., college friends become the close friends group, replacing the high school friends; finding different acquaintances).

Mosaic of Social Support as an Exemplar Case of Emerging Adulthood

The literature showed how social and cultural stigma, negative attitudes, and lack of support for mental illnesses affect the quality and timing of emerging adults' receiving professional help, making them passive in the process [8, 14, 34]. University students with Asian ethnic backgrounds, in particular, were known to have a high level of stigma towards mental health issues, leading to increased emergency situations [7,51]. Adding to this stigma, discrimination and prejudice among minorities (e.g., ethnicity, gender identity) can generate serious mental health problems [55]. These stigmatized, hidden mental diseases among young adults, if untreated, lead to substance abuse, violence, and poor reproductive and sexual health [65].

Nonetheless, all of our participants actively sought help with their struggles using their multiple social groups. Having engagement with different social groups, such as close friends, parents, and acquaintances, and selectively socializing with anonymous individuals enabled them to create an optimal support environment to address their mental health-related needs. The value of receiving social support from different social groups has been acknowledged in prior literature from the field of psychology [30,54,79]. For instance, Milevsky [8] described the compensatory patterns of social support and how individuals compensate for a lack of support by drawing from different sources (e.g., using friends to compensate for a lack of family support). Arnett et al. [5] presented the need of emerging adults to form healthy, varied social relationships to develop "personal mastery." The more variety in the social relationships they build, the more their developmental challenges (e.g., sexual identity) can be ameliorated. Developmental psychology work by Subrahmanyam et al. [74] discussed how emerging adults used online social networks to strengthen the weaker aspects of their offline connections. This psychology literature provides a theoretical foundation for the importance of spontaneous, multifaceted social support during emerging adulthood and addressing the need to compensate for missing support from various social groups. The support systems our participants created — their mosaics of social support — resemble what the literature discussed as compensatory patterns and help seeking practices that lead to constructive, personal mastery. Building upon this prior theoretical foundation in psychology, our study on the mosaic of social support makes a novel contribution by extending it to focus on the underlying mechanism of the social support practices engaged in by emerging adults and providing useful, concrete insights for future technology design in the healthcare domain.

We acknowledge that the students in our study were those who were able to come forward voluntarily and disclose their interests and needs around mental health. Accordingly, our data might be biased towards those who have resources or the situational ability to seek help when they needed it. Still, we find the students express experiences similar to those in the literature described as hiding and suffering with their problems. What we find in the study, however, sheds light on the ways in which our participants actively attempt to cope with their struggles, share, and improve their stressful situations utilizing various social groups. Thus, our findings provide an exemplary social support seeking mechanism that emerging adults as university students can practice to cope; this is the mosaic of social support. While being mindful of each individual's differing capacity and ability to construct this mosaic, our findings indicate valuable insights for future mental health support system design for emerging adults.

Learning from Mosaic of Social Support: Opportunities for Technology-Mediated Social Support

Our study provides an important foundation for understanding current social support practices in university students and the role of social support in managing mental wellness. Barriers to accessing mental health care leave the majority of students with mental illnesses without professional care. Social support has been shown to address gaps in care; and with technology it could be advanced by helping reduce the students' burden in reaching out to others, enhance their relationships with support groups, and scale to wider support audiences. Since the existing technology design for mental health social support mainly focuses on providing online peer support groups [24], we sought to better understand and augment the current experiences with and perspectives of emerging adulthood social support, uncovering the need for and mechanisms of a mosaic of social support.

Based on our empirical findings, we propose the following technology design opportunities for fostering the social support mosaic for mental health. We hope the key opportunities outlined here can inform designers and researchers in developing social support technologies for mental health for young adults, beyond online support groups and social media.

Ensuring the mosaic accessible and workable

All of the participants in our study had more than one social group and managed multiple groups to better address their needs. However, the groups were not always readily available when the participants needed to ask for help. Additionally, sometimes for a particular problem, a social group did not exist. For such cases, we suggest that technology help match alternative supporters who can fill the void to make the mosaic of social support more accessible and workable. We will describe this design suggestion through two scenarios based on our findings.

First, students have moments when all their close friends are too busy with their own job searches or exams to have time to listen or share; sometimes, close friends become too remote to stay frequently connected after graduation or getting jobs. To help the mosaic become more accessible and available, technology can provide in-the-moment-based support by finding and matching alternative supporters within the mosaic. Initially, a user can predefine his/her social support mosaic in a mobile-based system by categorizing contacts into each different social group, and update it as needed. This mobile application can then learn the user's relationships with each group – the ways in which the social support mosaic works for this user – based on the communication frequency and interaction patterns over time. Upon the user's request regarding the absence of the supporters available, the application can suggest that the user express his or her concerns in an implicit way, such as using photographs, scribbles, music, or doodles, similar to Twitter or Tumblr. With this, users can express their concerns or needs in a subtle and abstract form, which will be shared among contacts within the groups they have selected. Then, people from the selected social groups who are available and have relevant knowledge and experience can jump in to fill that need. Or, using a semantic scan of an image, the application can interpret a user's mood to help the user feel better on his or her own and choose the right group(s). This will enable students to be connected with appropriate alternative supporters based on in-the-moment availability and accessibility, and also broaden the benefits as well as their knowledge of possible social groups that can provide similar intimacy or sympathy as the original, intended social group.

Second, some users may find their mosaic deficient and incomplete, where social groups do not have sufficient capacity or the right qualities to fulfill their needs. For example, their parents did not have any experience of attending college or living in a big city to be able to give useful advice and guidance, or their parents had already passed away. To cope with this lacking or deficient mosaic, a system can help through providing potential surrogates for that missing group. Once it recognizes the lack of a certain group in the user's social support mosaic, the mobile application can make more informative suggestions for potential surrogates, based on the representative role and benefit of that certain missing group, by virtually pairing the students with mentorship organizations such as Mental Health America or compensating them with delegated social group, such as sibling support. Such cases would be particularly useful when social stigma could be involved – such as for those who did not want to be honest with parents due to degraded relationships. Although the qualities of these surrogate groups might not be able to match exactly the same quality of the original social groups (e.g., unconditional love of parents), studies report relationships, such as siblings' support over unsatisfying school friendships [21] or spousal support to overcome job strains [76], to be as effective in improving socioemotional outcomes.

Suggesting an alternative group to fall back on

Acquaintances and anonymous social groups helped to make our participants feel their concerns were de-stigmatized and their privacy was somewhat protected. Acquaintances and anonymous social groups can be included in the technology as an alternative group that the users can fall back on if the desired support is not available in the users' existing support mosaic. Their quality of help might seem inferior compared to that of the other social groups, and some users may perceive them negatively due to a lack of trust. However, our study revealed that the role and quality of acquaintances and anonymous groups is crucial to coping with breakdowns in the mosaic, such as social stigma. By providing something to *fall back on* when others are either not available or there are barriers preventing access to their support, this group can help to amend the problems, albeit temporarily.

Therefore, our work suggests that designing a system to educate students and enhancing their help-seeking skills is an important step to making it safe and beneficial to access acquaintances and anonymous groups for mental health support. Based on the subject of concern, the system can make recommendations for potential acquaintances, experts on a subject matter, or relevant online groups. Beyond making recommendations, to ensure safety and an ethical environment, the system could also monitor and detect harmful behavior and language among anonymous interactions or provide features, such as reporting, flagging and blocking, utilizing machine-learning techniques, which is similar to automated interventions for online communities using language processing tools in prior works [19,61]. In this way, we can enable students to recognize the need for proper acquaintances and anonymous support and for creating and experiencing other potential social groups based on their needs.

Maintaining sustainability of social groups

Our study indicates that most students take the time and make a good effort to keep and maintain the status quo of "good relationships and expectations" with their social groups through selective sharing. Many participants expressed concerns about ruining their friendships by overusing their friends to vent, while making an effort to stay connected as a good friend. Similarly, participants also struggled with the tension between sharing problems with parents and not wanting to cause their parents to have an extra burden or worry about them. Such tensions can be a critical stressor if they hinder the support mosaic from completing its role.

Thus, we suggest that technology can offer a way to ameliorate these tensions and provide sustainable ways to help maintain the sustainability of each social group, while understanding the evolving needs of the user. For instance, by tracking a user's engagement level, and the quality and frequency of interactions with social groups (e.g., the numbers of messages/calls sent/received, hours a user is active physically or virtually, etc.), the system can foster the needed interactions by generating reminders or prompts as triggers (e.g., shared memory, newsletter, interests) among users and groups. This way, the system can help not only ease the burden on users to maintain their relationships with each group in terms of frequency and quality, but also help users gradually develop relationships and sustain the benefits and qualities found to be important in maintaining a healthy mosaic of social support.

Lastly, our students experience major life changes, such as changing schools, leaving home, or moving to a foreign country for their career, especially as they move on to different stages of life over time. Along with the life changes of emerging adults, their social support mosaic should be regenerated accordingly. Thus, we suggest that technology can help facilitate this process of updating their mosaic by introducing and connecting them to new resources (e.g., sports activities at a new school to find new friends with common interests). This way, one's current network can not only be maintained, but also "repaired." The benefits and qualities identified in our study should not be considered final, since the social support mosaic evolves as each group runs into limitations, generating new ways and qualities to cope with the issues.

CONCLUSION

Our study examines the practices of emerging adults' seeking and receiving social support in a university setting. We introduce the concept of the mosaic of social support, the assemblage of various social groups that are flexible, adaptable, but closely intertwined, which in turn provides insights into how technologies can facilitate the social support practice, while helping students navigate stigma around mental health. The contribution of this work is an understanding of the roles, benefits, and limitations of social groups for students in managing their mental health. Our work further contributes to identifying technology design opportunities to support relatively understudied populations who suffer from a lack of proper support by opening up conversations to quality-driven technology design that can fit into students' daily lives in managing mental health.

REFERENCES

1. Francesca Agostini, Erica Neri, Paola Salvatori, Sara Dellabartola, Laura Bozicevic, and Fiorella Monti. 2015. Antenatal depressive symptoms associated with specific life events and sources of social support among Italian women. *Maternal and child health journal* 19, 5: 1131–1141.
2. American College Health Association. 2017. *American College Health Association-National College Health Assessment II: Reference Group Executive Summary Fall 2016*. Hanover, MD: American College Health Association.
3. William S. Aquilino. 2006. Family Relationships and Support Systems in Emerging Adulthood. In *Emerging adults in America: Coming of age in the 21st century.*, Jeffrey Jensen Arnett and Jennifer Lynn Tanner (eds.). American Psychological Association, Washington, 193–217.
4. Jeffrey Jensen Arnett. 2007. Emerging Adulthood: What Is It, and What Is It Good For? *Child development perspectives* 1, 2: 68–73.
5. Jeffrey J. Arnett, Rita Žukauskienė, and Kazumi Sugimura. 2014. The new life stage of emerging adulthood at ages 18-29 years: implications for mental health. *The lancet. Psychiatry* 1, 7: 569–576.
6. J. J. Arnett. 2000. Emerging adulthood. A theory of development from the late teens through the twenties. *The American psychologist* 55, 5: 469–480.
7. Donald R. Atkinson and Ruth H. Gim. 1989. Asian-American cultural identity and attitudes toward mental health services. *Journal of counseling psychology* 36, 2: 209–212.
8. Avidan Milevsky. 2005. Compensatory patterns of sibling support in emerging adulthood: Variations in loneliness, self-esteem, depression and life satisfaction. *Journal of social and personal relationships* 22, 6: 743–755.
9. Sairam Balani and Munmun De Choudhury. 2015. Detecting and Characterizing Mental Health Related Self-Disclosure in Social Media. In *Proceedings of the 33rd Annual ACM Conference Extended Abstracts on Human Factors in Computing Systems* (CHI EA '15), 1373–1378.
10. Elizabeth Bales, Kevin A. Li, and William Griwsold. 2011. CoupleVIBE: Mobile Implicit Communication to Improve Awareness for (Long-distance) Couples. In *Proceedings of the ACM 2011 Conference on Computer Supported Cooperative Work* (CSCW '11), 65–74.
11. G. W. Brown, B. Andrews, T. Harris, Z. Adler, and L. Bridge. 1986. Social support, self-esteem and depression. *Psychological medicine* 16, 4: 813–831.
12. Yves J. A. Chaput and Marie-Josée Lebel. 2007. Demographic and clinical profiles of patients who make multiple visits to psychiatric emergency services. *Psychiatric services* 58, 3: 335–341.
13. Dimitri A. Christakis and Megan A. Moreno. 2009.

Trapped in the net: will internet addiction become a 21st-century epidemic? *Archives of pediatrics & adolescent medicine* 163, 10: 959–960.
14. Kyaien O. Conner, Gary Koeske, and Charlotte Brown. 2009. Racial differences in attitudes toward professional mental health treatment: the mediating effect of stigma. *Journal of gerontological social work* 52, 7: 695–712.
15. David Coyle, Gavin Doherty, Mark Matthews, and John Sharry. 2007. Computers in talk-based mental health interventions. *Interacting with computers* 19, 4: 545–562.
16. M. Scott DeBerard, Glen Spielmans, and Deana Julka. 2004. Predictors of academic achievement and retention among college freshmen: A longitudinal study. *College student journal* 38, 1: 66–80.
17. Munmun De Choudhury, Scott Counts, and Eric Horvitz. 2013. Social Media As a Measurement Tool of Depression in Populations. In *Proceedings of the 5th Annual ACM Web Science Conference* (WebSci '13), 47–56.
18. Munmun De Choudhury, Michael Gamon, Scott Counts, and Eric Horvitz. 2013. Predicting Depression via Social Media. *ICWSM* 13: 1–10.
19. Munmun De Choudhury, Emre Kiciman, Mark Dredze, Glen Coppersmith, and Mrinal Kumar. 2016. Discovering Shifts to Suicidal Ideation from Mental Health Content in Social Media. In *Proceedings of the 2016 CHI Conference on Human Factors in Computing Systems* (CHI '16), 2098–2110.
20. J. P. Docherty. 1997. Barriers to the diagnosis of depression in primary care. *The Journal of clinical psychiatry* 58 Suppl 1: 5–10.
21. Patricia L. East and Karen S. Rook. 1992. Compensatory Patterns of Support Among Children's Peer Relationships: A Test Using School Friends, Nonschool Friends, and Siblings. *Developmental psychology* 28, 1: 163–172.
22. Elisabeth Eichhorn, Reto Wettach, and Eva Hornecker. 2008. A Stroking Device for Spatially Separated Couples. In *Proceedings of the 10th International Conference on Human Computer Interaction with Mobile Devices and Services* (MobileHCI '08), 303–306.
23. Daniel Eisenberg, Marilyn F. Downs, Ezra Golberstein, and Kara Zivin. 2009. Stigma and help seeking for mental health among college students. *Medical care research and review: MCRR* 66, 5: 522–541.
24. Gunther Eysenbach, John Powell, Marina Englesakis, Carlos Rizo, and Anita Stern. 2004. Health related virtual communities and electronic support groups: systematic review of the effects of online peer to peer interactions. *BMJ* 328, 7449: 1166.
25. A. F. Fontana, R. D. Kerns, R. L. Rosenberg, and K. L. Colonese. 1989. Support, stress, and recovery from coronary heart disease: a longitudinal causal model. *Health psychology: official journal of the Division of Health Psychology, American Psychological Association* 8, 2: 175–193.
26. Katrina Gay, John Torous, Adam Joseph, Anand Pandya, and Ken Duckworth. 2016. Digital Technology Use Among Individuals with Schizophrenia: Results of an Online Survey. *JMIR mental health* 3, 2: e15.
27. B. Glasser and A. Strauss. 1967. The discovery grounded theory: strategies for qualitative inquiry. *Aldin, Chicago.*
28. B. M. Hagerty and R. A. Williams. 1999. The effects of sense of belonging, social support, conflict, and loneliness on depression. *Nursing research* 48, 4: 215–219.
29. Stephen F. Hamilton and Mary Agnes Hamilton. 2006. School, Work, and Emerging Adulthood. In *Emerging adults in America: Coming of age in the 21st century.*, Jeffrey Jensen Arnett and Jennifer Lynn Tanner (eds.). American Psychological Association, Washington, 257–277.
30. Jennifer Hefner and Daniel Eisenberg. 2009. Social support and mental health among college students. *The American journal of orthopsychiatry* 79, 4: 491–499.
31. Charles W. Hennig, Craig R. Crabtree, and David Baum. 1998. Mental health CPR: Peer contracting as a response to potential suicide in adolescents. *Archives of suicide research: official journal of the International Academy for Suicide Research* 4, 2: 169–187.
32. Jameson K. Hirsch and Jon B. Ellis. 1996. Differences in life stress and reasons for living among college suicide ideators and non-ideators. *College student journal.* Retrieved from http://psycnet.apa.org/psycinfo/1997-07633-008
33. Marybeth Hoffman, Jayne Richmond, Jennifer Morrow, and Kandice Salomone. 2002. Investigating "Sense of Belonging" in First-Year College Students. *Journal of college student retention: research, theory & practice* 4, 3: 227–256.
34. Scott M. Hyman, Steven N. Gold, and Melissa A. Cott. 2003. Forms of Social Support That Moderate PTSD in Childhood Sexual Abuse Survivors. *Journal of family violence* 18, 5: 295–300.
35. F. Ebru Ikiz and Firdevs Savi Cakar. 2010. Perceived social support and self-esteem in adolescence. *Procedia - Social and Behavioral Sciences* 5, Supplement C: 2338–2342.
36. Sue Jamison-Powell, Conor Linehan, Laura Daley, Andrew Garbett, and Shaun Lawson. 2012. I can't get no sleep: discussing# insomnia on twitter. In *Proceedings of the SIGCHI Conference on Human Factors in Computing Systems*, 1501–1510.
37. Ronald C. Kessler, Patricia Berglund, Olga Demler, Robert Jin, Kathleen R. Merikangas, and Ellen E. Walters. 2005. Lifetime prevalence and age-of-onset distributions of DSM-IV disorders in the National

Comorbidity Survey Replication. *Archives of general psychiatry* 62, 6: 593–602.
38. Julie A. Kientz, Shwetak N. Patel, Brian Jones, Ed Price, Elizabeth D. Mynatt, and Gregory D. Abowd. 2008. The Georgia Tech Aware Home. In *CHI '08 Extended Abstracts on Human Factors in Computing Systems* (CHI EA '08), 3675–3680.
39. Martha Anne Kitzrow. 2003. The Mental Health Needs of Today's College Students: Challenges and Recommendations. *NASPA Journal* 41, 1: 167–181.
40. Predrag Klasnja and Wanda Pratt. 2012. Healthcare in the pocket: mapping the space of mobile-phone health interventions. *Journal of biomedical informatics* 45, 1: 184–198.
41. James P. Kohn and Gregory H. Frazer. 1986. An Academic Stress Scale: Identification and Rated Importance of Academic Stressors. *Psychological reports* 59, 2: 415–426.
42. A. M. La Greca and N. Lopez. 1998. Social anxiety among adolescents: linkages with peer relations and friendships. *Journal of abnormal child psychology* 26, 2: 83–94.
43. Larry J. Nelson and Carolyn McNamara Barry. 2005. Distinguishing Features of Emerging Adulthood: The Role of Self-Classification as an Adult. *Journal of adolescent research* 20, 2: 242–262.
44. Reeva Lederman, Greg Wadley, John Gleeson, Sarah Bendall, and Mario Álvarez-Jiménez. 2014. Moderated Online Social Therapy: Designing and Evaluating Technology for Mental Health. *ACM Trans. Comput. - Hum. Interact.* 21, 1: 5:1–5:26.
45. Sunmin Lee, Hee-Soon Juon, Genevieve Martinez, Chiehwen E. Hsu, E. Stephanie Robinson, Julie Bawa, and Grace X. Ma. 2009. Model minority at risk: expressed needs of mental health by Asian American young adults. *Journal of community health* 34, 2: 144–152.
46. Morton A. Lieberman, Mitch Golant, Janine Giese-Davis, Andy Winzlenberg, Harold Benjamin, Keith Humphreys, Carol Kronenwetter, Stefani Russo, and David Spiegel. 2003. Electronic support groups for breast carcinoma. *Cancer* 97, 4: 920–925.
47. N. Lin, R. S. Simeone, W. M. Ensel, and W. Kuo. 1979. Social support, stressful life events, and illness: a model and an empirical test. *Journal of health and social behavior* 20, 2: 108–119.
48. Danielle Lottridge, Nicolas Masson, and Wendy Mackay. 2009. Sharing Empty Moments: Design for Remote Couples. In *Proceedings of the SIGCHI Conference on Human Factors in Computing Systems* (CHI '09), 2329–2338.
49. L. Lu. 1994. University transition: major and minor life stressors, personality characteristics and mental health. *Psychological medicine* 24, 1: 81–87.
50. Deborah Lupton. 2014. Self-tracking Cultures: Towards a Sociology of Personal Informatics. In *Proceedings of the 26th Australian Computer-Human Interaction Conference on Designing Futures: The Future of Design* (OzCHI '14), 77–86.
51. Akihiko Masuda and Matthew S. Boone. 2011. Mental Health Stigma, Self-Concealment, and Help-Seeking Attitudes among Asian American and European American College Students with No Help-Seeking Experience. *International Journal for the Advancement of Counselling* 33, 4: 266–279.
52. Jonathan F. Mattanah, Jean F. Ayers, Bethany L. Brand, Leonie J. Brooks, Julie L. Quimby, and Scot W. McNary. 2010. A Social Support Intervention to Ease the College Transition: Exploring Main Effects and Moderators. *Journal of college student development* 51, 1: 93–108.
53. Shery Mead and Cheryl MacNeil. 2006. Peer support: What makes it unique. *International Journal of Psychosocial Rehabilitation* 10, 2: 29–37.
54. S. Melinda Spencer and Julie Hicks Patrick. 2009. Social Support and Personal Mastery as Protective Resources During Emerging Adulthood. *Journal of adult development* 16, 4: 191–198.
55. Ilan H. Meyer. 2003. Prejudice, social stress, and mental health in lesbian, gay, and bisexual populations: conceptual issues and research evidence. *Psychological bulletin* 129, 5: 674–697.
56. Sharon L. Mitchell, Mahrin Kader, Melinda Z. Haggerty, Yogesh D. Bakhai, and Calvert G. Warren. 2013. College Student Utilization of a Comprehensive Psychiatric Emergency Program. *Journal of College Counseling* 16, 1: 49–63.
57. S. Anne Moorhead, Diane E. Hazlett, Laura Harrison, Jennifer K. Carroll, Anthea Irwin, and Ciska Hoving. 2013. A new dimension of health care: systematic review of the uses, benefits, and limitations of social media for health communication. *Journal of medical Internet research* 15, 4: e85.
58. Rudolf H. Moos and Jeanne A. Schaefer. 1993. Coping resources and processes: Current concepts and measures. *Handbook of stress: Theoretical and clinical aspects*: 234–257.
59. Elizabeth D. Mynatt, Irfan Essa, and Wendy Rogers. 2000. Increasing the Opportunities for Aging in Place. In *Proceedings on the 2000 Conference on Universal Usability* (CUU '00), 65–71.
60. Elizabeth D. Mynatt, Jim Rowan, Sarah Craighill, and Annie Jacobs. 2001. Digital Family Portraits: Supporting Peace of Mind for Extended Family Members. In *Proceedings of the SIGCHI Conference on Human Factors in Computing Systems* (CHI '01), 333–340.
61. Kathleen O'Leary, Arpita Bhattacharya, Sean A. Munson, Jacob O. Wobbrock, and Wanda Pratt. 2017. Design Opportunities for Mental Health Peer Support Technologies. In *Proceedings of the 2017 ACM Conference on Computer Supported Cooperative Work and Social Computing*, 1470–1484.
62. Fatih Ozbay, Douglas C. Johnson, Eleni Dimoulas, C.

A. Morgan, Dennis Charney, and Steven Southwick. 2007. Social support and resilience to stress: from neurobiology to clinical practice. *Psychiatry* 4, 5: 35–40.

63. Igor Pantic, Aleksandar Damjanovic, Jovana Todorovic, Dubravka Topalovic, Dragana Bojovic-Jovic, Sinisa Ristic, and Senka Pantic. 2012. Association between online social networking and depression in high school students: behavioral physiology viewpoint. *Psychiatria Danubina* 24, 1: 90–93.
64. Justin W. Patchin and Sameer Hinduja. 2006. Bullies move beyond the schoolyard: A preliminary look at cyberbullying. *Youth violence and juvenile justice* 4, 2: 148–169.
65. Vikram Patel, Alan J. Flisher, Sarah Hetrick, and Patrick McGorry. 2007. Mental health of young people: a global public-health challenge. *The Lancet* 369, 9569: 1302–1313.
66. Yael Perry, Aliza Werner-Seidler, Alison L. Calear, and Helen Christensen. 2016. Web-Based and Mobile Suicide Prevention Interventions for Young People: A Systematic Review. *Journal of the Canadian Academy of Child and Adolescent Psychiatry = Journal de l'Academie canadienne de psychiatrie de l'enfant et de l'adolescent* 25, 2: 73–79.
67. Jeremy W. Pettit, Robert E. Roberts, Peter M. Lewinsohn, John R. Seeley, and Ilya Yaroslavsky. 2011. Developmental relations between perceived social support and depressive symptoms through emerging adulthood: blood is thicker than water. *Journal of family psychology: JFP: journal of the Division of Family Psychology of the American Psychological Association* 25, 1: 127–136.
68. Jeremy W. Pettit, Robert E. Roberts, Peter M. Lewinsohn, John R. Seeley, and Ilya Yaroslavsky. 2011. Developmental relations between perceived social support and depressive symptoms through emerging adulthood: blood is thicker than water. *Journal of family psychology: JFP: journal of the Division of Family Psychology of the American Psychological Association* 25, 1: 127–136.
69. Julie Repper and Tim Carter. 2011. A review of the literature on peer support in mental health services. *Journal of mental health* 20, 4: 392–411.
70. Jan Risser, Alice Cates, Hafeez Rehman, and William Risser. 2010. Gender differences in social support and depression among injection drug users in Houston, Texas. *The American journal of drug and alcohol abuse* 36, 1: 18–24.
71. Jim Rowan and Elizabeth D. Mynatt. 2005. Digital Family Portrait Field Trial: Support for Aging in Place. In *Proceedings of the SIGCHI Conference on Human Factors in Computing Systems* (CHI '05), 521–530.
72. Inge Seiffge-Krenke. 2006. Coping With Relationship Stressors: The Impact of Different Working Models of Attachment and Links to Adaptation. *Journal of youth and adolescence* 35, 1: 24.
73. C. A. Shively, T. B. Clarkson, and J. R. Kaplan. 1989. Social deprivation and coronary artery atherosclerosis in female cynomolgus monkeys. *Atherosclerosis* 77, 1: 69–76.
74. Kaveri Subrahmanyam, Stephanie M. Reich, Natalia Waechter, and Guadalupe Espinoza. 2008. Online and offline social networks: Use of social networking sites by emerging adults. *Journal of applied developmental psychology* 29, 6: 420–433.
75. Melanie Swan. 2009. Emerging patient-driven health care models: an examination of health social networks, consumer personalized medicine and quantified self-tracking. *International journal of environmental research and public health* 6, 2: 492–525.
76. J. Syrotuik and C. D'Arcy. 1984. Social support and mental health: direct, protective and compensatory effects. *Social science & medicine* 18, 3: 229–236.
77. Sarah E. Ullman, Stephanie M. Townsend, Henrietta H. Filipas, and Laura L. Starzynski. 2007. Structural Models of the Relations of Assault Severity, Social Support, Avoidance Coping, Self-Blame, and PTSD Among Sexual Assault Survivors. *Psychology of women quarterly* 31, 1: 23–37.
78. Patti M. Valkenburg, Jochen Peter, and Alexander P. Schouten. 2006. Friend networking sites and their relationship to adolescents' well-being and social self-esteem. *Cyberpsychology & behavior: the impact of the Internet, multimedia and virtual reality on behavior and society* 9, 5: 584–590.
79. Heather R. Walen and Margie E. Lachman. 2000. Social support and strain from partner, family, and friends: Costs and benefits for men and women in adulthood. *Journal of social and personal relationships* 17, 1: 5–30.
80. 2014. WHO | The global burden of disease: 2004 update. Retrieved July 16, 2017 from http://www.who.int/healthinfo/global_burden_disease/2004_report_update/en/
81. NCI Dictionary of Cancer Terms. *National Cancer Institute*. Retrieved September 18, 2017 from https://www.cancer.gov/publications/dictionaries/cancer-terms?cdrid=440116
82. Definition of MOSAIC. Retrieved January 8, 2018 from https://www.merriam-webster.com/dictionary/mosaic

Examining Self-Tracking by People with Migraine: Goals, Needs, and Opportunities in a Chronic Health Condition

Jessica Schroeder[1], Chia-Fang Chung[2], Daniel A. Epstein[1], Ravi Karkar[1], Adele Parsons[2], Natalia Murinova[3], James Fogarty[1], and Sean A. Munson[2]
[1]Computer Science & Engineering | [2]Human Centered Design & Engineering | [3]Headache Clinic
DUB Group, University of Washington
{jesscs, cfchung, depstein, rkarkar, adelepa, nataliam, jaf1978, smunson}@uw.edu

ABSTRACT

Self-tracked health data can help people and their health providers understand and manage chronic conditions. This paper examines personal informatics practices and challenges in migraine, a condition characterized by unpredictable, intermittent, and poorly-understood symptoms. To investigate how people with migraine track and use data related to their condition, we surveyed 279 people with migraine and conducted semi-structured interviews with 13 survey respondents and 6 health providers. We find four distinct goals people bring to tracking and data: 1) answering questions about migraines, 2) predicting and preventing migraines, 3) monitoring and managing migraines over time, and 4) enabling motivation and social recognition. Each goal suggests different needs for the design of tools to support migraine tracking. We also find needs resulting from an individual's goals evolving over time, their varied personal experiences, and their communication and collaboration with providers. We discuss these goals and needs in terms of opportunities for personal informatics tools to facilitate learning to: 1) avoid common pitfalls; 2) support customization and flexibility; 3) account for burden, negativity, and lapsing; and 4) support management with uncertainty.

ACM Classification Keywords

H.5.m. Information Interfaces and Presentation (e.g., HCI).

Author Keywords

Personal Informatics; Health; Chronic Condition; Migraine.

INTRODUCTION

As part of diagnosing and managing health conditions, people and their health providers often utilize data about a person's environment, behaviors, and symptoms. Such data can be especially helpful in the management of chronic conditions. Prior research has examined opportunities for technology to support personal informatics practices in managing a range of chronic conditions (e.g., asthma [35] , diabetes [16,29,53], hypertension [10,31,32], irritable bowel syndrome [38,39,62]). However, people with migraine present additional goals and needs that can be particularly difficult to support, due in part to the unpredictable, intermittent, and poorly-understood nature of migraine symptoms [57]. An estimated 14% of the population experiences migraine, the third most prevalent disease in the world [65]. Symptoms can be debilitating, often including pain, sensitivity to light, and impaired cognition. Migraine is a leading cause of loss of workplace productivity [64] and is the seventh-highest cause of years lost due to disability [65]. People often turn to personal data to better understand and manage their migraines, but struggle to control symptoms [4], motivating additional research in the design of personal informatics tools for people with migraine.

DIS '18, June 9–13, 2018, Hong Kong

ISBN 978-1-4503-5198-0/18/06... $15.00
DOI: https://doi.org/10.1145/3196709.3196738

Building upon Park and Chen's identification of migraine as an important condition largely unstudied by the human-computer interaction and design research community [57], this paper examines how people navigate their goals for using self-tracked data to understand and manage migraine, as well as the challenges and pitfalls they encounter. Our focus on self-tracked data builds upon and contributes to research in personal informatics that examines how people attempt to gather and interpret personal data (e.g., [12,27,38,46]). Because people with migraine often turn to providers for help in managing migraine, we additionally build upon and contribute to research in patient-provider collaboration that examines how patient data can inform consultations and how current tools can better support associated needs (e.g., [15,62,69]). This paper therefore bridges an important gap between the challenges people with migraine face in managing their condition and the additional design challenges and opportunities for supporting people with migraine and their providers in their use of self-tracked data.

To characterize how people with migraine track and use data about their condition, we surveyed 279 people with migraine and then conducted semi-structured interviews with 13 survey respondents and 6 health providers. Our contributions include:

- Identifying four distinct goals that people bring to migraine-related tracking and data, each suggesting different needs for the design of tools to support migraine tracking: 1) answering questions about migraines, 2) predicting and preventing migraines, 3) monitoring and managing migraines over time, and 4) enabling motivation and social recognition.
- Characterizing additional design needs and challenges that result from an individual's goals evolving over time, from the variety of personal migraine experiences, and from a desire to communicate and collaborate with providers.
- Describing design opportunities in migraine self-tracking, including in facilitating learning to avoid common pitfalls; in customization and flexibility of tracking; in accounting for burden, negativity, and lapsing in tracking; and in tracking to support management with uncertainty.

BACKGROUND AND RELATED WORK

This section presents background in the domain of migraine and introduces additional challenges that migraine presents relative to other chronic conditions. We then review related research in personal informatics for health and in patient-provider collaboration with patient-generated health data.

Study Context: Migraine

Migraine is a prevalent and debilitating condition that can severely affect quality of life and productivity [64]. To help reduce the frequency and severity of symptoms, people often attempt to identify "triggers", or factors that cause or worsen their personal symptoms [52]. Because triggers vary across individuals [2,43], health providers often encourage self-tracking as part of attempts to identify personal triggers [63]. Both patients and providers believe self-tracked migraine data can help in communication and collaboration [8].

However, prior research examining a variety of conditions has found that people self-tracking to identify symptom triggers encounter multiple pitfalls: tracking too many factors, failing to track factors needed to answer their questions, and accepting dubious conclusions due to insufficient rigor [12]. Such pitfalls motivate examining how technology can support self-tracking to identify symptom triggers (e.g., helping people with irritable bowel syndrome identify foods that trigger their symptoms [38, 39, 62]). In contrast to previously-studied conditions, self-tracking in migraine can be especially difficult. A greater range of factors are relevant, including diet (e.g., alcohol, caffeine), environment (e.g., glare, noise, weather), menstruation, sleep patterns, and stress and mood. In addition, multiple factors often must accumulate before precipitating migraine symptoms [43,68]. This wide variety of factors, and interactions between them, further complicates and confounds identification of an individual's symptom triggers and increases the likelihood of inaccurate conclusions.

In their examination of challenges that people encounter in managing migraine [57], Park and Chen interviewed 12 people with migraine and 2 providers to characterize needs. These needs include: 1) determining whether a person's symptoms result from migraine, 2) determining what might trigger a person's symptoms, 3) developing strategies to manage symptoms, and 4) coordinating social recognition and assistance. We build upon and advance this work with a focused and in-depth examination of how people gather and use self-tracking data (e.g., in identifying triggers, in monitoring symptoms, in social recognition). To better understand the range of self-tracking needs and practices, we employed a mixture of methods that allowed examining a greater number of participants. To better understand provider perspectives on patient data as well as tensions between patient and provider expectations, we also recruited a larger and more diverse set of health provider participants, including both primary care physicians and headache clinic specialists. Our discussion further highlights additional design needs and challenges revealed in our focus on self-tracking data in migraine.

Personal Informatics for Health

Prior research has examined personal informatics practices and tools (e.g., [12,27,38,46]), including in the management of chronic conditions such as asthma (e.g., [35]), diabetes (e.g., [16, 29, 53]), and hypertension (e.g., [10, 31, 32]). Compared to migraine, these conditions have relatively well-understood relationships between symptoms and contributing factors, and technology generally focuses on teaching people about those relationships or helping them learn how to manage them in the context of their lives.

Other research investigates chronic conditions with more acute, episodic symptoms. For example, symptoms of irritable bowel syndrome are often triggered by foods. Personal informatics tools can help determine what foods impact an individual's symptoms, such as through visualizations of self-tracked food and symptom data [62] or through a guided self-experimentation process [38, 39]. Research has also examined how to support people in maintaining control of their lives despite intermittent symptoms, as with intermittent fatigue in multiple sclerosis (e.g., [6,71]). Our focus is on personal informatics in migraine, a condition characterized by unpredictable symptoms with individual and poorly-understood relationships to triggers. Successful management often requires learning about an individual's symptoms and collaborating with providers to identify appropriate combinations of behavior change, medication, and other treatments that fit the needs of that individual. Personal informatics challenges presented by migraine are therefore likely to draw upon and extend those in previously-studied conditions (e.g., conditions with well-understood symptoms, conditions better suited to self-experimentation).

Prior research in other contexts has studied many factors that can impact migraine (e.g., diet [9,19,38,53], menstruation [26], physical activity [18, 48], sleep [40, 60], stress [54]). However, current tools generally isolate data in domain-specific siloes [27,28]. Despite prior research emphasizing that intensive self-tracking is generally unsustainable (e.g., [12, 20, 25]), current tools also generally fail to support challenges presented by lapsing, resumption, or abandonment [17,25,27]. Migraine requires a more holistic and longer-term approach to facilitate understanding and addressing how multiple factors impact an individual's symptoms [43,68], suggesting new needs and opportunities for personal informatics research and tools.

Clinical Use of Patient-Generated Health Data

Many people turn to health providers for help making sense of collected data [12, 14, 15, 23, 30, 72], both because interpretation is often difficult [12,46] and because tracking is sometimes initiated at the suggestion of providers [14,30]. Reviewing patient-generated health data can help providers understand and contextualize patient health [67], which can lead to improved diagnoses, treatments, and health outcomes [14,55,66]. Sharing self-tracked data with providers can also foster motivation and accountability [14, 44, 46] and can ground and provide objectivity during consultations (e.g., [15,26,62]). Reviewing patient-generated data can also foster a sense of collaboration, with providers contributing their medical expertise while patients contribute detailed knowledge of their data and behaviors [7,62].

Despite potential benefits of patient-generated health data, providers face barriers attempting to use such data. Providers often lack time to review data or feel unequipped to interpret it, especially because data is often incomplete, disorganized, and unreliable [14,69]. Current tools are generally not designed to support data sharing or collaboration in a manner compatible with provider workflows [14,30]. When existing tools fail to allow patients to collect the data providers want, providers sometimes recommend paper-based tracking [14,15]. Paper provides flexibility, but interpretation then generally requires manually sifting through pages attempting to identify patterns. No validated method exists for providers to interpret journal data, so the process is generally difficult and error-prone [34,36]. Due in part to these challenges, many patients who share their data with health providers report disappointment in provider engagement with that data [30]. Patient-provider collaboration around self-tracking data can also break down when patients and providers have different goals or expectations [15]. In addition, some patients find self-tracking a negative experience that emphasizes health difficulties [1]. People with migraine face similar challenges when seeking help from providers, such that they often decide to discontinue clinical consultations [50,51]. Our research aims to help address these barriers by engaging both patients and providers in characterizing needs and opportunities for self-tracking data and improved tools for understanding and managing migraine.

DATA COLLECTION AND ANALYSIS

To examine how people and providers work to manage migraine, with a focus on the role of patient-generated data, we conducted a survey examining experiences with migraine and then conducted follow-up interviews with a subset of survey participants. We also interviewed 6 providers for their perspective on working with patients with migraine. Summary information for all participants is in Table 1. Participants skew female, which matches migraine prevalence in the United States: women are three times as likely to experience migraines than men [59]. We refer to survey participants as SX, interview participants as IX, and provider participants as PX.

Survey of 279 People with Migraine

We surveyed 279 people about how they understand, track, and manage their migraines. The survey asked primarily open-ended questions about experiences with migraine, tracking related to migraine, and consulting with health providers about migraine. We focused on understanding what people found particularly helpful and unhelpful about tracking, health consultations, and sharing their data. Participants were recruited through university mailing lists, Facebook posts, and posts to two Reddit subreddits: one dedicated to migraine and another to surveys. Participants were entered into drawings for a single $100 and three $25 Amazon gift cards.

Three researchers conducted an affinity diagram analysis of open-ended survey responses. The first author then created a preliminary code book based on emergent themes. We coded three different categories of participant experiences: 1) using apps to understand, track, and manage migraines; 2) consulting with health providers about migraines; and 3) sharing data with providers during consultations. The three researchers discussed and iterated on codes to develop the final code book, which consisted of 40 codes. The first author then coded 100% of the data, while the other two

	Survey Participants (279 People)
Gender	222 female, 51 male, 2 FtM transgender, 1 genderqueer, 1 genderqueer man, 2 no answer
Age	18–96, $\bar{x}$ = 33.8 (7 no answer)
Years with Migraine	1–65, $\bar{x}$ = 17
Apps Tried (106 people)	Migraine Buddy (71); 40 apps with <10 people each (14 could not remember)
Apps Used (56 People)	Migraine Buddy (30); 23 apps with <10 people each
Other Resources Tried (196 People)	paper journals (83), online articles about migraine (70), online forums such as reddit (44), custom spreadsheets (30), calendars (24), books about migraine (14); 17 methods with <10 people each

	Migraine Interview Participants (13 People)
Gender	11 female, 1 male, 1 genderqueer man
Age	20–61, $\bar{x}$ = 32.15
Years with Migraine	1–30, $\bar{x}$ = 15.8
Apps Tried (8 people)	Migraine Buddy (5), Migraine Coach (2), Fitbit (1), Clue (1), Pacifica (1), Curelator (1), iHeadache (1), PTracker (1), Grid Diary (1) (1 could not remember)
Apps Used (3 People)	Migraine Buddy (1), Migraine Coach (1), Clue (1), Pacifica (1)
Other Resources Tried (13 People)	paper journals (7), custom spreadsheets (5), online articles about migraine (4), online forums such as Reddit (4), calendars (3), books about migraine (1), tracking help from family (1), discussions with other people with migraine (1)

Provider Interview Participants (6 People)

Participant	Area of Practice	Provider Type
P1	Family Medicine	Medical Doctor, Master of Public Health
P2	Family Medicine	Medical Doctor
P3	Headache Clinic	Nurse Practitioner
P4	Primary Care	Nurse Practitioner
P5	Headache Clinic	Nurse Practitioner
P6	Primary Care	Medical Doctor

Table 1: Summary information for all survey and interview participants.

researchers each coded 10% of the data. We then calculated inter-rater reliability, defining "agreement" as use of the same code within a given question response. As preliminary code agreement varied ($\kappa = 0.16 - 1$, $\bar{x} = 0.67$ for the 28 codes used more than 10 times, with 0.8 or higher for 11 codes), the researchers discussed and resolved any disagreements. Most disagreements resulted from misunderstandings about the code book and in infrequently-occurring codes. The first author then took a second pass through the data based on the discussion.

Interviews of 13 People with Migraine

After analyzing survey data, we identified themes to explore in more detail. We wanted to learn more about people who commented on successes or failures in tracking. For example, we reached out to individuals who said data had helped their health consultations, as well as those who had struggled to interpret and act upon data. We were particularly interested in people who had struggled with apps and turned to alternative methods. We emailed 23 people who had agreed to be contacted about follow-up interviews, and 13 responded to our request.

Semi-structured interviews were conducted by Skype or phone. Interviews covered: 1) the participant's general experience with migraine, 2) how the participant collected data, 3) what they liked and disliked about their method, and 4) how and with whom they shared data (e.g., family, friends, coworkers, providers). Questions encouraged participants to discuss their experiences, thoughts, and behaviors. Interviews were approximately 30 minutes, compensated with a $20 Amazon gift card.

A third-party service transcribed the audio recordings. Two researchers then open coded 2 transcripts. The first author open coded the remaining 11 transcripts, then affinity diagrammed the resulting codes and created a code book of 70 codes from emergent themes. Finally, two researchers coded the data using the code book. Inter-rater reliability is not often calculated on semi-structured interview data because different people can apply the same code to different parts of a conversation [3]. We therefore did not calculate reliability between researchers.

Interviews of 6 Health Providers

Finally, after learning about the expectations and experiences that people with migraine have when bringing their data to providers, we interviewed 6 health providers from a range of specialties about their experiences with patients with migraine (see Table 1). Interviews were semi-structured, 5 conducted in person and 1 by phone. Each interview covered: 1) general experiences working with patients with migraine; 2) experiences with patients who tracked information about their migraine, focusing on whether and how the provider interacted with patient data; and 3) provider reactions to specific examples of migraine tracking methods, collected from our interviews of people with migraine. Providers were recruited via email introductions from our medical collaborators and compensated with a $30 Amazon gift card. A third-party service transcribed audio recordings. Resulting transcripts were analyzed via a similar process of open-coding, affinity diagramming of codes to create a code book, and coding using the resulting code book.

Limitations

Many of the people with migraine we surveyed and interviewed were associated with professional and social networks of the researchers. Participants skew more highly-educated than the general population: 38% of survey participants have an advanced degree, and an additional 32% a bachelor's degree. Recruitment, particularly via a subreddit for migraine, may have biased our sample to people who seek an online community for migraine resources. Prior work suggests people who get migraines less frequently or less severely are less likely to dedicate as much time to tracking and management [57], so they may also not engage in such a community. Finally, 84% of survey participants were from the United States, as were all 6 provider participants. Tracking habits and care strategies may differ in other cultures or countries, so care must be taken when generalizing our findings.

RESULTS

Of 279 survey participants, 106 had used an app to try to understand, track, or manage their migraines, and 56 still used an app. Participants primarily reported using apps for tracking migraines (n=80), determining triggers (n=59), and tracking medication use (n=13). The majority of participants had used resources or tools other than apps to try to understand, track, or manage their migraines (n=196), instead of or in addition to such apps. The most common use of other technological and paper resources was tracking, but participants also described online research and community support (see Table 1).

Many found technology useful for migraine-related tracking. Those who had used apps often felt their app was easy to use (53/106) and helped them identify trends and triggers (42/106). However, many found the tools they used failed to fully support their goals. This section discusses four challenges we found current technologies fail to fully support: 1) variety in personal tracking goals, 2) tracking goals that evolve over time, 3) variety in personal experiences with migraine, and 4) support for data sharing and collaboration with health providers.

Although we report counts of participants who expressed perspectives, the open-ended nature of survey and interview questions means not every participant was explicitly prompted about each perspective. As a result, additional participants beyond those in each count may have agreed with a perspective.

Tracking for a Variety of Goals

Informed by and building upon prior research on self-tracking goals (e.g., [12, 26, 42, 46, 46, 61]), we find four primary goals people bring to migraine-related self-tracking: 1) answering questions about migraines, 2) predicting and preventing migraines, 3) monitoring and managing migraines over time, and 4) enabling motivation and social recognition. Participants often had simultaneous and overlapping goals, but explicitly distinguishing them better facilitates consideration of the design implications of each goal for self-tracking data.

Goal 1: Answering Questions About Migraines

Many people who track information about their migraines do so with a goal of *diagnostic self-tracking*, or self-tracking to answer a specific question about a person's health [61]. Common questions include what behaviors or other factors contribute to an individual's symptoms and whether a new treatment or preventative medication seems to improve symptoms.

For example, of 106 survey participants who had tried an app, 65 had used it to attempt to identify factors that contributed to their migraines. Some apps provide graphs or analyses to help identify factors that correlate with symptoms, and 16 survey participants mentioned feeling that apps helped them interpret their data. However, another 16 survey participants explicitly discussed finding data hard to interpret. When asked in interviews, 10 of 13 participants described similar challenges (*I1, I4, I5, I6, I8, I9, I10, I11, I12, I13*). Because individual apps generally do not support tracking the wide range of factors potentially relevant to an individual's migraine, participants often track data across multiple apps. To identify trends, participants then needed to integrate data across apps themselves. *I10* explained she *"found it stressful ... there's no place in any of those apps for a whole health picture of, like, OK, I was nauseated today. I had a migraine today"*. *S66* lamented that no single app helped him track and understand his data: *"I wish a program like a general health app (e.g, Lose-It) would track everything and do correlations."* *S258* summarized that apps made it *"[t]oo difficult to put all the pieces together"*. When people collect data in separate apps, the data typically remains siloed, creating additional barriers and burdens in interpretation.

Participants often used data to compare symptoms before and after a change. If people feel symptoms improve after a change, they may be more likely to commit to that change, especially if it requires behavior change or incurs side effects. If they do not feel symptoms improve, they may return to the prior behavior or ask their provider for another solution. Such "before and after" comparisons are therefore useful to get a sense for whether a treatment is helpful. 7 of 13 interview participants mentioned that tracking had helped them identify treatment-related trends (*I1, I2, I6, I9, I10, I11, I12*), with *I11* explaining *"you basically turn your life into a control of a experiment and try to change one thing at a time and see what works"*. All 6 providers also wanted their patients to track as part of enabling comparisons to determine effectiveness and whether to continue a treatment.

Despite considering data useful for answering such questions, however, providers were wary of patients focusing too much on a single potential trigger. 4 of 6 providers (*P1, P3, P4, P5*) expressed concern people might see false patterns, leading them to make changes that could be unnecessary or inappropriate. When discussing participants who track foods to attempt to identify specific dietary triggers, *P1* explained that the practice was not only often futile, but also potentially dangerous:

> There can be a lot of overlap between dysfunctional eating and tracking, and so sometimes [tracking foods] reinforces dysfunctional eating like, "Oh, I got a headache after I ate bread, so now eliminate gluten from my diet", when it's just a way to kind of normalize dysfunctional eating.

Goal 2: Predicting and Preventing Migraines

Distinct from tracking to determine what factors increase an individual's likelihood of symptoms (i.e., Goal 1), many people track with a goal of predicting and preventing migraines. Of 106 survey participants who had tried an app, 15 had used it to try to predict their migraines. Because migraines often occur due to an accumulation of multiple factors [43, 68], people may not need to entirely eliminate factors that can contribute to a migraine. Other factors that may contribute are outside of a person's control. People therefore must not only identify their potential migraine contributors, but also be cognizant of exposure to factors that impact their likelihood of symptoms. 4 interview participants (*I1, I3, I6, I7*) described trying to predict likely migraines by paying attention to what they are exposed to, so they can take other actions to attempt to prevent a migraine. For example, *I6* described using the MigraineX app to get alerts whenever the barometric pressure was going to drop. When she gets those alerts, she explained:

> I do what I can to make sure that I'm really well hydrated ... that I get my best sleep ... that everything else in my body is as healthy as possible so that hopefully I can ride through that weather front without any other triggers.

Even when a migraine could not be prevented, participants benefited when a prediction provided an opportunity to prepare. For example, a person's menstrual cycle can be an important trigger of migraine symptoms, and *S257* described tracking to predict symptoms: *"The app can be validating: when I feel a migraine coming on I can see that it might be roughly the usual time in my [menstrual] cycle to get one. Instead of fighting it, I can just try to adjust my schedule and get through it."*

I7 additionally explained how predicting a migraine allowed her to prepare: *"Even if it's just throwing extra rescue meds in my purse. It's an incredibly helpful thing instead of sitting there and floundering while you're on the train ride on the way home like 'oh my God, I wish had something to take right now'"*.

Tracking for prediction and prevention is often complicated by people struggling to identify factors that impact their symptoms, especially because some important factors are surprising to many people with migraine. For example, 4 of 6 providers described overuse of acute medications as the top mistake among patients. Many people with migraine take acute medications (e.g., 224 of 279 survey respondents reported trying over-the-counter medication to stop a migraine, 201 of 279 reported trying a prescription acute medication). However, medication overuse can actually cause more frequent migraines, creating a cycle in which a person gets more migraines, which prompts them to take more medication, which leads to still more migraines [49]. Providers emphasized a need for education about trigger accumulation and medication overuse, as tracking other factors is likely futile absent this foundation. Many participants also wanted technology to be more prescriptive, including 5 interview participants (*I3, I4, I6, I11, I13*) saying they wanted apps to provide recommendations and make suggestions about what they might track or changes they might try.

Goal 3: Monitoring and Managing Migraines Over Time

Although many participants tracked to learn about their migraines (i.e., Goal 1) or predict migraines (i.e., Goal 2), others tracked to monitor and manage their condition. Tracking migraine symptoms was the most common reason survey participants reported using an app, with 80 of 106 people who had used an app reporting symptom tracking as among their goals. In contrast to prior goals, monitoring and managing migraines over time often focuses on symptom-related data, and therefore cannot help identify correlations with factors that might be related to symptoms. However, 10 interview participants discussed how such symptom tracking helped them remember and monitor their experiences (*I2, I3, I4, I5, I6, I7, I9, I10, I11, I13*). For example, *I2* talked about how tracking helped her monitor her symptoms, ensure she was not getting worse, and notice any need for changes:

> [my provider] saw the January and February and she's like, "Oh, that's a reasonable number of headaches", and then she saw March and April and was like, "That's too many headaches" ... And she was like, "Okay if you're still getting six or seven headaches a month in a couple months, we're gonna talk about doing something else".

Many providers encourage patients to track, and providers often use the resulting data to support diagnoses and treatment decisions. All 6 providers recommended patients track migraine symptoms under some circumstances. Of the 47 survey participants who had shared data with a provider, 10 felt that having the data directly influenced their diagnosis or treatment, and all 6 providers said the same. To support such migraine monitoring and management, patients and providers need data about migraine frequency and severity, as well as information about what treatments a person has been pursuing.

Goal 4: Enabling Motivation and Social Recognition

Although providers often recommend patients track to gain information, they also believe tracking can help motivate people to make changes to improve their symptoms. *P3* and *P5* work at a headache clinic, where they recommend behavior changes that can help reduce migraine frequency and severity (e.g., increasing exercise, modifying diet, relieving stress). Patient-tracked symptom data helps providers show patients that behavior changes actually impact their migraines. *P3* explained:

> [a patient] might think, "I'm doing so horrible, I'm doing so horrible", and then you look at it, and you're like "you actually cut back your severity by 50%" ... you kind of shift your perspective as you go on, and the new horrible becomes just the same horrible, even though it's improved. So, it's helpful to show that improvement more than anything.

The "before and after" comparison *P3* describes has similarities to interpreting what factors impact symptoms (i.e., Goal 1) and to monitoring migraines (i.e., Goal 3), but also differs in its purpose. For example, a person may make multiple small behavior changes, and then need to examine a larger, cumulative comparison to motivate themselves that all of these changes together are justified because they result in an overall improvement. Although data collection may be similar, a person seeking motivation to continue the overall process can therefore need different representations of data than when investigating a specific trigger or monitoring symptoms.

In addition to using data as motivation by demonstrating improvement, *P5* described using it to inspire accountability:

> We want to know whether they are really following the plan, the recommendations, because sometimes some patients say, "Oh, I'm not getting better, I'm doing everything." Well, what is everything? ... besides giving me information for diagnosis, treatment, and plan management, I think when they keep a diary, it also gives them accountability.

Outside of the patient-provider context, people also want to share data with others. Of 106 survey participants who had used apps, 23 mentioned that apps lacked support for social sharing. Similarly, 9 of 13 interview participants expressed a desire to be able to share data with friends or family (*I1, I3, I5, I6, I7, I9, I11, I12, I13*) and 5 of 13 with a boss (*I1, I2, I7, I11, I12*). Some already shared their data, despite the lack of explicit design support. For example, *I9* tracked her migraines on a Google calendar that she shared with her husband "*so he could see when I did have them and how I was feeling*".

Sharing was motivated in part by a hope that people would better acknowledge their symptoms (e.g., family, friends, coworkers, providers). 3 participants shared data to prove their symptoms really existed and were as bad as they thought (*I1, I5, I12*). *I1* started getting migraines when she was a teenager, and felt that "*nobody believed me. They thought I was just being a melodramatic teenager with headaches who didn't want to go to class or something*". She therefore started tracking to "*[be] able to say, 'No, look, here's documentation of the last six months of my life that have been horrible. Please help me'*". Similarly, 3 interview participants mentioned they shared in order to prove to people that they were actually

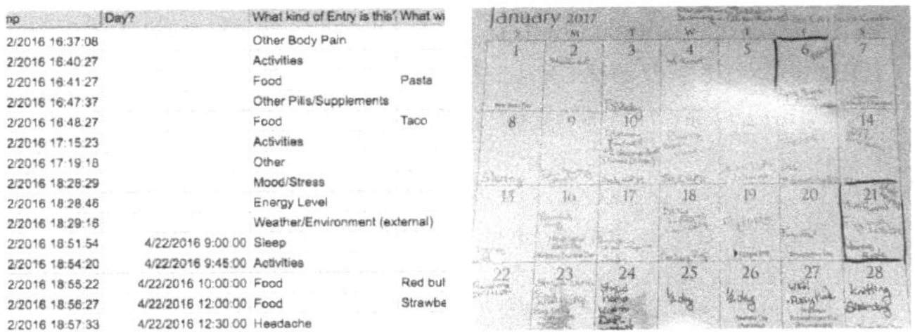

Figure 1: *I02* initially used a Google Sheet to track migraine symptoms and potential triggers. She chose this method because it provided flexibility to track exactly what and how she wanted. Now that she understands her triggers, she just tracks bad migraine days on a calendar.

taking action to try to manage symptoms (*I1, I11, I12*). For example, *I12* shared his data with his boss, "*just to show them, 'Hey, I've been struggling with this ... and this is the work that we've been doing with my neurologist, we're working towards it. We're actively working on stuff'*". Overall, these goals illustrate myriad motivations and needs for sharing migraine data, each requiring different design considerations.

Tracking for Goals that Evolve Over Time

Whether, what, when, and how people want to track often depends on their current understanding of their migraine and whether they consider their situation stable. 10 of 13 migraine interview participants discussed how their tracking changed over time (*I1, I2, I3, I6, I7, I9, I10, I11, I12, I13*). We examine goal evolution in migraine to identify resulting design needs.

Participants often initially tracked intensively with a goal of better understanding migraines (i.e., Goal 1), then transitioned to more minimal tracking with goals focused on management (i.e., Goal 2, Goal 3). For example, *I2* originally had a goal of determining her symptom contributors. She therefore spent three months using a custom spreadsheet to track everything she thought might be relevant (e.g., activities, environmental factors, foods, mood, sleep). After identifying some high-likelihood contributors, she felt she had answered her questions. Her goal then evolved to management over time (see Figure 1). She now only tracks days on which her symptoms are severe enough that she takes her prescription medication, in a paper calendar she also uses for general everyday coordination.

Though the progression from intensive to minimal tracking was common, some found it insufficient. People often must return to goals they previously considered fulfilled, as *I7* explained:

> [I used to track] daily, but that was right back when I started on new meds, so I wanted to make sure that I was keeping track of absolutely anything in the worst case scenario sort of thing. Now I just keep track when something major changes. Like most recently I was supposed to up my dose to a 30 milligram day of my preventative, and that just wasn't working out. I feel like if I hadn't kept track of each day-by-day, I might have doubted myself, and been like, "no, no, no just keep doing what your doctor told you [to do]".

With each adjustment of her treatment, *I7* therefore returns to asking questions about her symptoms (i.e., Goal 1). Without this change in her tracking goal, she may not have realized her treatment modification had been detrimental.

As goals change, transitions in tracking strategies are often motivated by tracking burdens. To be prepared to answer questions that may arise, some initially wanted to track as much as possible about symptoms, treatments, and potential contributors. However, such intensive tracking is generally unsustainable, and 7 of 13 interview participants found their tracking experiences negative (*I1*, *I2*, *I5*, *I6*, *I11*, *I12*, *I13*), with all 6 providers additionally mentioning negative patient tracking experiences.

In addition to direct burdens, participants described frustration with negative emotions in tracking. *I11* explained, "*You're supposed to enter [information] everyday, which I totally get the validity of and rationalization behind, but it's just one more thing about the day that's dedicated to my disease and it isn't what I want to be doing with my time*". *P4*, *S107*, and *S140* further described a concern that tracking can worsen a person's overall experience with their condition, as with *S140*:

> when I track my pain closely, I pay more attention to it, and I'm less happy. I stopped my migraine diary after a couple of years and I honestly think ceasing to consciously observe my pain level every minute of the day made me feel better.

Some participants feared that migraine tracking could itself be a contributing factor. *I7* commented: "*The more I was focusing, tracking, journaling, the more migraines I was getting*". When participants suspected tracking was making their migraines worse, they often wanted to abandon tracking, despite potential benefits.

Given this combination of burden and negative experience, all 6 providers felt patients should track according to their goals, rather than indefinitely. *P3* explained "*we recommend they do ongoing tracking, as long as they're working with us. But once you're in a stable point, it's probably less important to keep tracking unless it's helpful for the patient, because it can become a burden*". *I6* similarly motivated a need to support lapsing, resumption, and abandonment in migraine tracking:

> Having it so you don't feel like when you have a gap in your data, you have just start from zero [is helpful]. Whatever [app designers] can do to kind of make it easy to fill in those gaps makes it less intimidating to get back in there.

Finally, despite concerns for minimizing tracking and its burdens, participants also described appropriate tracking as an important part of maintaining motivation (i.e., Goal 4). 4 interview participants (*I1*, *I2*, *I6*, *I7*) described tracking as empowering, especially over the long term, as *I1* explained:

> Just being able to look back at that however many years of journals and calendars stacked up and see that I'm not in the pain that I used to be and that I can live my life and understand the choices that I've made without being scared that I'm gonna be incapacitated the next day. That's a reward and I hope more people can get to that point.

From a provider perspective, *P3* also described modifying a patient's tracking according to motivational needs. She explained that if a patient was not seeing the benefit, she would have them "*flip their tracking, and have them track good moments*". Although such approaches do not remove concerns for burden, encouraging people to see positive aspects can help them in achieving tracking that supports their goals.

Tracking for Varying Personal Experience

Within and across tracking goals, varying personal differences require an ability customize tracking. 6 of 13 interview participants (*I1*, *I2*, *I3*, *I4*, *I10*, *I11*) and 5 of 6 providers (*P2*, *P3*, *P4*, *P5*, *P6*) mentioned the variety of experiences with migraine. 72 of 106 survey participants who had used apps and 11 of 13 interview participants expressed a desire for apps to better support customization (*I1*, *I2*, *I3*, *I4*, *I5*, *I6*, *I7*, *I9*, *I10*, *I11*, *I12*).

A key dimension of customization is *what* a person tracks. For example, *I1* explained she did not like using apps to record her migraines because she "*[doesn't] get all the symptoms that other people do*". *I11* explained a similar frustration with journaling data that she knew was not relevant for her:

> I have been doing this for 20 years now. There are some things I can just cross off my list ... say, whether I ate onions or something? ... I know this isn't a trigger. It's not a problem for me, can I just stop answering questions about onions?

Although customization can allow adding or removing factors to track, defaults and explicit support for particular factors will affect what people consider potentially relevant. *I3* explained how defaults influenced what she believed could be important:

> It makes sense that they would have a limited option of things to choose from, and then allow you to add more things. But it would be nice if that list was a little bit longer, because sometimes you're not sure if something you're feeling or something you did is relevant to the migraine. Or it may not occur to you, if you don't see it in a list, that it would be relevant.

A second key dimension is *when* a person tracks, specifically whether they prefer tracking *during* or *after* migraine symptoms. Of 13 interview participants, 7 reported tracking either during or after a migraine (*I1*, *I2*, *I4*, *I6*, *I7*, *I9*, *I19*), 4 reported only tracking after a migraine (*I3*, *I8*, *I11*, *I13*), and 2 reported only tracking during a migraine (*I5*, *I12*). Some people cannot track during a migraine: 36 survey participants mentioned having trouble using apps because interacting with a screen during a migraine was painful. *I4* described how her migraines impacted her cognitive ability to the point that data tracked during a migraine was often useless: "*The cloudy head makes it very difficult to put words into focus, I guess, and if I [tracked] during a migraine I'd look back and say, 'What the hell was I talking about?'*". In contrast, *I5* always wanted to record that she was taking medication during a migraine, before actually taking it. She explained that tracking during a migraine was necessary because it helped her remember to record the data:

> Usually ... when I'm starting to feel better, there are things [I had been unable to do] that I would want to do. It's often that I'd forget to write [the fact that I took the medication] down ... Record keeping wise, it was more accurate for me to write it down before I took the medication.

Because *I5* needs to track during migraines to ensure reliable data, she was wary of tracking with an app, as she feared doing so would worsen her migraines. She therefore needs to be able to record data without interacting with a screen, thus highlighting a third key dimension of flexibility in *how* people track.

Data in Communication and Collaboration with Providers

As mentioned above, people with migraine often wanted to share tracked data with their health providers. Of 47 survey participants who reported bringing data to a health consultation, 22 mentioned that concrete data was helpful. Similarly, 12 of 13 interview participants (all except *I8*) said tracking helped their consultations. 10 of 13 interview participants mentioned tracking, and the resulting data, helped them remember their experiences (*I2, I4, I6, I7, I8, I9, I10, I11, I12*), and 6 felt it helped them more effectively communicate experiences to a provider (*I1, I2, I6, I7, I9, I10*). *I6* explained:

> Really what I needed was a tool to talk to my doctor about, because it's really hard to just go in there and be like, "I have them a lot." When you speak in vague terms, you get vague treatment. That's essentially what I needed, was an empowerment tool to go in and say, "This is frequency. I need to know what treatment's doing. I need to know what's working, what's not".

I7 similarly explained benefits of her tracking and data, even when data was not directly shared with her provider:

> I'll bring out the report that I printed out in with me, and even if [my health provider] doesn't ask to see it, I feel like it's good for me to have it there in case I forget anything. Mostly it's just helping me check on myself so that I don't forget something important, or exaggerate something wildly, when I'm like, actually it wasn't that bad. Yeah, it's just like having a set of checks and balances for me, by me.

Providers also appreciated their patients self-tracking. All 6 providers we interviewed reported they had recommended a patient track their migraines. 4 of the 6 providers said self-tracked data can help communication and collaboration (*P1, P3, P5, P6*). All 6 providers said they wanted to be able to see a patient's data in some circumstances. *P3* explained:

> It's a way to avoid misunderstanding, because a lot of time people will be talking about their headaches. Let's say they're talking about their migraines, but really they're just talking about their most severe migraines, and you're making this assumption that the five days a month are the only headaches they're having. When really they're having daily headache, it's just these five migraines that are really bothering them ... I feel like [having the data] takes those assumptions out of the way.

However, when patients and providers collaborate around data in a clinic appointment, they often struggle to interpret it. Of 47 survey participants that reported sharing data with their provider, 6 noted the volume of data made it difficult. *S136* explained: "*Because it was so dense and not in an easily digestible form like a chart, I don't think it was very helpful in our appointment*". All 6 providers reported they had struggled to interpret data in a clinic appointment, and 4 additionally said they did not want to see patient-generated data in some circumstances (*P1, P2, P5, P6*). These circumstances included patients bringing an overwhelming volume of data, as well as patients bringing data the provider is unprepared to or uncomfortable with interpreting (e.g., food-related data).

Although consistent with prior findings that patient-provider collaboration to interpret data can be difficult (e.g., [15, 62]), migraine data magnifies these difficulties due to: 1) the many factors that are potentially relevant to an individual's symptoms, and 2) the fact that those factors are generally siloed in their own app or other tracking method. *S198* explained that compensating for siloes is time-consuming and burdensome: "*I usually write things out ahead of time because the reports I want aren't quickly accessible or I have to wade through info and pick out what I need*". 6 of 13 interview participants similarly described integrating their data (*I1, I6, I7, I9, I10, I11*), with *I11* saying, "*Having to coordinate all the apps together and then when I'm at my headache appointment, I feel like I have to take 20 minutes before I go and ... copy all of the data out long-hand so that I have it all pieced together*". Some participants attempted to address integration challenges by using calendars or custom spreadsheets so they could track exactly what they wanted. However, 5 of 6 providers (*P1, P2, P3, P4, P5*) expressed that such custom spreadsheets were particularly difficult to interpret during a clinical consultation. Migraine tracking must account for the many factors that are potentially relevant to an individual's symptoms, but current approaches and tools for capturing and integrating the wide range of potentially-relevant factors can create challenges in effectively communicating and collaborating with providers around that data.

Of 47 survey participants who had shared data with their provider, 13 felt their provider did not engage as much as they hoped. A common breakdown is for patients to expect providers to directly review data. In part because of the challenges discussed in this section, providers often preferred patients interpret data themselves, on their own time. *P2* described trying to avoid misunderstanding by telling her patients, "*this is for you. This is you trying to do the detective work of figuring out what's going on here. You're going to be the best person to figure this out. I'm not going to be the best person to figure this out*".

In addition to aligning migraine tracking goals, successful collaboration around migraine requires agreeing about overall management goals. *I2* described a misalignment with her provider wherein both sought to use data for understanding (i.e., Goal 1), but within different overall management goals:

> [My doctor's] approach was much more like, "Let me figure out what drugs I can give you to have you stop having these headaches", rather than figuring out why I'm having them. I'm much more like, "I want to know why this is happening to me".

The complexity of migraine data and the variety of goals people bring to that data therefore present additional needs in self-tracking and patient-provider collaboration.

DISCUSSION

Our findings illustrate how people navigate their goals for using self-tracked data to understand and manage migraine, building upon prior research in migraine [57], personal informatics (e.g., [12, 27, 38, 46]), and patient-provider collaboration with patient-generated data (e.g., [15, 62, 69]). With our focus on the role of self-tracked data in migraine management, some of our results provide additional insights and detail within themes identified by Park and Chen. For example, Park and Chen characterize trigger identification as an important challenge, within which we provide greater insight into specific barriers and design opportunities (e.g., emphasizing an accumulation of contributing factors rather than any single trigger, data integration challenges presented by using multiple apps to track different migraine-related data). We also surface data-centric insights that are distinct from the themes identified by Park and Chen (e.g., the importance of many different "before and after" questions in migraine management, roles for data in motivation and accountability in patient-provider collaborations, design challenges resulting from a person's migraine-related goals evolving over time).

Informed by our findings, this section discusses additional design requirements and opportunities for personal informatics tools to support people with migraine, organized into themes of: 1) facilitating learning to avoid common pitfalls; 2) supporting customization and flexibility; 3) accounting for burden, negativity, and lapsing; and 4) supporting management with uncertainty. Our findings, design requirements, and design opportunities also warrant exploration in other conditions with unpredictable, intermittent, and poorly-understood symptoms.

Facilitating Learning to Avoid Common Pitfalls

People often track to develop personalized understanding (i.e., Goal 1), but lack necessary background information to identify potentially relevant factors. Absent guidance on how to systematically answer questions, many people reach conclusions that are dubious, that lead them to needlessly avoid things they enjoy, or that are otherwise problematic (e.g., *P1*'s concern for dysfunctional eating facilitated by a spurious association resulting from an individual relating gluten to their symptoms after a single episode). Park and Chen emphasized a need for education regarding potential triggers of migraine symptoms, and integrating learning into health self-tracking tools is an important theme of prior research (e.g., in making healthy decisions throughout pregnancy [58], in making healthy interpretations and decisions around sleep tracking [60], in maintaining a healthy diet while identifying and avoiding foods that trigger symptoms in irritable bowel syndrome [62]). Our research extends these ideas by emphasizing key priorities for migraine learning in the context of self-tracking and resulting data.

Prior to using self-tracking data to robustly answer questions about their migraine, individuals must address two prerequisites: 1) controlling acute medication usage (i.e., over-the-counter and prescription pain relievers), and 2) understanding that migraine symptoms generally result from an accumulation of factors, rather than a single trigger. We have noted the first is important because overuse of acute medication often causes symptoms, leading to a cycle in which a person takes more medication, leading to still more migraines [49]. Tools should prioritize support for learning about medication overuse, and could support tracking an acute medication "budget", but should ensure this support does not create unnecessary burdens for people who already understand and have addressed this aspect of their migraine management. Designs should similarly emphasize accumulation of multiple factors, rather than overly emphasizing efforts to identify a single "trigger". An emphasis on accumulation also enables learning about health behavior change (e.g., healthier eating, increased physical activity, better sleep), which our providers described encouraging as a means to improve an individual's overall resilience to factors that contribute to their symptoms.

Failing to address these prerequisites can easily lead to data being misinterpreted (e.g., attributing migraines that result from medication overuse to other spurious correlations, identification of spurious factors that happen to occur at a time when other factors accumulate). Growing interest in techniques for individualized understanding (e.g., [21, 22, 38, 39, 45]) fosters a desire to extend approaches from specific domains into general-purpose tools. Our results balance this desire by highlighting a need to ensure tools account for condition-specific challenges and pitfalls. A general-purpose tool that does not account for medication overuse, or which emphasizes individual factors instead of accounting for their accumulation, could easily confound or mislead in the context of migraine.

Supporting Customization and Flexibility

Within and across tracking goals, tools need to support customization and flexibility in what, when, and how people track. In deciding what to track, appropriate default options are important, in part because they influence what people consider potentially relevant. But the wide variety of relevant factors and personal experiences mean many people will not want to track all default options and may have other data they do want to track. Additional challenges are presented by data that is siloed in different tools or must be abandoned when a person changes tools due to a change in tracking goals. Similarly, people with migraine need flexibility in when they track, so tracking can be adapted to their needs and symptoms. Tracking designs often emphasize tracking "in the moment", but such a requirement is inappropriate for many people with migraine.

People with migraine often turn to paper-based tracking rather than tracking via an app. In addition to allowing greater flexibility, paper-based tracking does not require interacting with a screen during a migraine, which participants described as important. Unfortunately, resulting data is difficult to integrate, analyze, and interpret. Opportunities exist to explore hybrid solutions, such as tracking on paper and later digitizing data. Paper forms could be customized and printed according to an individual's current needs. Research in low-resource environments has examined using phones in digitization of paper forms (e.g., [11,24,56]), and technology-centric research has explored augmented paper (e.g., [5,33,47,70]), but potential needs and opportunities for hybrid paper-digital tracking are largely unexplored in personal informatics research.

Support for customization must also consider provider needs, including provider goals, limited time, expectations that patients lead the interpretation process, and the difficulty of interpreting data in formats that vary across individual patients. One possibility may be to define common or important questions (e.g., the various "before and after" questions in each of the tracking goals), then develop tools for quickly curating a person's data into a more standard format for answering these questions. Such tools might be used by a person prior to a clinic appointment, either because they intend to share the resulting data and visualizations with their provider or because they want to review the data themselves prior to the appointment.

Accounting for Burden, Negativity, and Lapsing

Tools also need to account for burden and negativity. Tracking can impose many burdens [20, 25], and participants described additional negativity (e.g., that tracking was a constant reminder of difficulties of their health condition, that stress associated with tracking could contribute to symptoms). Even when a person's information goals suggest "more data is better", tools must support people in balancing this desire for data against their lived experience with tracking [27, 61]. Current tools instead often assume continuous tracking and provide little or no explicit support for lapsing [17, 25, 27]. Research in other domains has noted tools often fail to support people as their goals evolve (e.g., healthy eating [13], financial tracking [42], menstrual tracking [26]), and we see a similar need to support lapsing and evolving goals in migraine. For example, a person with a stable understanding of their migraine may stop tracking, later resume symptom-only tracking as part of monitoring (i.e., Goal 3), and much later resume tracking behavioral data as part of asking a new question (i.e., Goal 1). Designs should support people in determining whether and what to track and should minimize any burdens or negative experiences in resumption. Designs will also need to account for such lapses in analyses and visualizations (e.g., in designing how to support "before and after" comparisons in data that includes lapsing and intermittent tracking, in historical visualizations that include many gaps and variation in what data is tracked over time). As tools explore how to support sharing migraine-related data with family, friends, and coworkers, any negative consequences of sharing will also need to be examined and addressed (e.g., embarrassment of the person with migraine, discomfort of the people with whom they share).

Supporting Management with Uncertainty

Diagnostic self-tracking often presents pitfalls to scientific rigor [12], a challenge that has motivated prior research in other domains to support self-experimentation and techniques for individualized understanding (e.g., [21,22,38,39,45]). The "before and after" comparisons found in migraine generally do not constitute rigorous experiments (e.g., they do not account for confounds), but more rigorous methods can often be impractical or unacceptable. First, designing an experiment to robustly test a single factor can be difficult, because of 1) the wide variety of potentially relevant factors, 2) a person's inability to control some factors (e.g., weather), and 3) symptoms generally resulting from an accumulation of factors rather than any single factor. Second, the debilitating nature of symptoms (i.e., being unable to do the things a person wants or needs to do) can mean a person is unwilling to risk inducing symptoms for the sake of a more rigorous experiment. Similarly, if a person makes a change (e.g., a new medication), and that change seems to improve symptoms, they may be unwilling to discontinue the change. When symptoms seem to be improved by changes with other benefits (e.g., increased physical activity), discontinuing for the sake of an experiment seems even more unreasonable. People with migraine will therefore generally have some inherent uncertainty regarding factors relevant to their personal migraine symptoms.

Personal informatics tools may be able to help people navigate this uncertainty by better differentiating the goals people bring to migraine tracking. For example, when tracking is intended to answer questions about a person's migraine (i.e., Goal 1), tools can maximize transparency in analyses, communicate underlying uncertainty, and explain potential confounds. Such tools might adopt existing representations of uncertainty for non-experts (e.g., [41]). Understanding that uncertainty, people may still want to implement a change if it has the potential to improve symptoms (e.g., a person may decide to entirely remove coffee from their diet, while understanding that correlational data behind the decision is limited). Similarly, representations of uncertainty could help people make better decisions in migraine prediction (i.e., Goal 2), analogous to results in other domains [37]. For example, tools could support a person in deciding about their accumulation of risk and what factors they can control (e.g., whether to have a coffee today). Similar to how *I6* used an app to monitor the weather and then acted upon other factors that she could control, tools might use a combination of self-report, modeling, and sensing across multiple factors (e.g., level of physical activity, menstrual patterns, sleep sensing, weather). Such tools would need to communicate their own uncertainty, but might reduce burdens and allow people to more effectively manage their symptoms. Data could also later be integrated across goals (e.g., data collected as part of symptom prevention could also later be used as part of answering questions about a person's migraine). Finally, in some cases, uncertainty may be best addressed by seeking additional expert support. Tools should therefore provide support for patient-provider collaboration throughout a person's tracking, including in determining goals, in interpreting the resulting data, and in deciding on next steps.

CONCLUSION

This paper bridges a gap between the challenges people with migraine face in managing their condition, underlying self-tracking challenges in personal informatics, and patient-provider collaboration with patient-generated data. We surveyed 279 people with migraine and then conducted semi-structured interviews with 13 survey respondents and 6 health providers. We find four distinct goals that people bring to tracking and data: 1) answering questions about migraines, 2) predicting and preventing migraines, 3) monitoring and managing migraines over time, and 4) enabling motivation and social recognition. We also find needs resulting from an individual's goals evolving over time, their varied personal experiences, and their communication and collaboration with providers. We further discuss these goals and needs in terms of opportunities for personal informatics tools to facilitate learning to avoid common pitfalls, to support customization and flexibility, to account for burden, negativity, and lapsing, and to support management with uncertainty. Our research motivates design and development of new personal informatics tools for people with migraine, as well as additional research examining how these results extend to other conditions with unpredictable, intermittent, and poorly-understood symptoms.

ACKNOWLEDGMENTS

We thank our reviewers for their feedback. This research was supported in part by a University of Washington Innovation Research Award and the National Science Foundation under awards SCH-1344613, DGE-1256082, and IIS-1553167.

REFERENCES

1. Jessica S Ancker, Holly O Witteman, Baria Hafeez, Thierry Provencher, Mary Van De Graaf, and Esther Wei. 2015. "You Get Reminded You're a Sick Person": Personal Data Tracking and Patients with Multiple Chronic Conditions. *Journal of Medical Internet Research* 17, 8 (2015). https://doi.org/10.2196/jmir.4209
2. Diane Andress-Rothrock, Wesley King, and John Rothrock. 2010. An Analysis of Migraine Triggers in a Clinic-Based Population. *Headache: The Journal of Head and Face Pain* 50, 8 (2010), 1366–1370. https://doi.org/10.1111/j.1526-4610.2010.01753.x
3. David Armstrong, Ann Gosling, John Weinman, and Theresa Marteau. 1997. The Place of Inter-Rater Reliability in Qualitative Research: An Empirical Study. *Sociology* 31, 3 (1997), 597–606. http://doi.org/10.1177/0038038597031003015
4. Glen Aukerman, Doug Knutson, and William F Miser. 2002. Management of the Acute Migraine Headache. *American Family Physician* 66, 11 (2002), 2123–2130. https://www.ncbi.nlm.nih.gov/pubmed/12484694
5. Daniel Avrahami, Scott E Hudson, Thomas P Moran, and Brian D Williams. 2001. Guided Gesture Support in the Paper PDA. In *Proceedings of the ACM Symposium on User Interface Software and Technology*. ACM, 197–198. https://doi.org/10.1145/502348.502385
6. Amid Ayobi, Paul Marshall, Anna L Cox, and Yunan Chen. 2017. Quantifying The Body and Caring for The Mind: Self-Tracking in Multiple Sclerosis. In *Proceedings of the ACM Conference on Human Factors in Computing Systems*. ACM, 6889–6901. https://doi.org/10.1145/3025453.3025869
7. Stinne Aaløkke Ballegaard, Thomas Riisgaard Hansen, and Morten Kyng. 2008. Healthcare in Everyday Life: Designing Healthcare Services for Daily Life. In *Proceedings of the ACM Conference on Human Factors in Computing Systems*. ACM, 1807–1816. http://doi.acm.org/10.1145/1357054.1357336
8. V Baos, F Ester, A Castellanos, G Nocea, MT Caloto, and WC Gerth. 2005. Use of a Structured Migraine Diary Improves Patient and Physician Communication About Migraine Disability and Treatment Outcomes. *International Journal of Clinical Practice* 59, 3 (2005), 281–286. https://doi.org/10.1111/j.1742-1241.2005.00469.x
9. Eric PS Baumer, Sherri Jean Katz, Jill E Freeman, Phil Adams, Amy L Gonzales, John Pollak, Daniela Retelny, Jeff Niederdeppe, Christine M Olson, and Geri K Gay. 2012. Prescriptive Persuasion and Open-Ended Social Awareness: Expanding The Design Space of Mobile Health. In *Proceedings of the ACM 2012 Conference on Computer Supported Cooperative Work*. ACM, 475–484. https://doi.org/10.1145/2145204.2145279
10. JE Carnahan and Nugent CA. 1975. The Effects of Self-Monitoring By Patients on The Control of Hypertension. *The American Journal of the Medical Sciences* 269, 1 (1975), 69–73. https://www.ncbi.nlm.nih.gov/pubmed/1130437
11. Kuang Chen, Akshay Kannan, Yoriyasu Yano, Joseph M Hellerstein, and Tapan S Parikh. 2012. Shreddr: Pipelined Paper Digitization for Low-Resource Organizations. In *Proceedings of the ACM Symposium on Computing for Development*. ACM. https://doi.org/10.1145/2160601.2160605
12. Eun Kyoung Choe, Nicole B Lee, Bongshin Lee, Wanda Pratt, and Julie A Kientz. 2014. Understanding Quantified-Selfers' Practices in Collecting and Exploring Personal Data. In *Proceedings of the ACM Conference on Human Factors in Computing Systems*. ACM, 1143–1152. http://doi.acm.org/10.1145/2556288.2557372
13. Chia-Fang Chung, Elena Agapie, Jessica Schroeder, Sonali Mishra, James Fogarty, and Sean A Munson. 2017. When Personal Tracking Becomes Social: Examining the Use of Instagram for Healthy Eating. In *Proceedings of the 2017 CHI Conference on Human Factors in Computing Systems*. ACM, 1674–1687. https://doi.org/10.1145/3025453.3025747
14. Chia-Fang Chung, Jonathan Cook, Elizabeth Bales, Jasmine Zia, and Sean A Munson. 2015. More Than Telemonitoring: Health Provider Use and Nonuse of Life-Log Data in Irritable Bowel Syndrome and Weight Management. *Journal of Medical Internet Research* 17, 8 (2015), E203. http://doi.org/10.2196/jmir.4364
15. Chia-Fang Chung, Kristin Dew, Allison Cole, Jasmine K Zia, James Fogarty, Julie A Kientz, and Sean A Munson. 2016. Boundary Negotiating Artifacts in Personal Informatics: Patient-Provider Collaboration with Patient-Generated Data. In *Proceedings of the ACM Conference on Computer-Supported Cooperative Work and Social Computing*. http://doi.acm.org/10.1145/2818048.2819926
16. C Clar, Katharine D Barnard, Ewen Cummins, Pamela Royle, and Norman Waugh. 2010. Self-Monitoring of Blood Glucose in Type 2 Diabetes: Systematic Review. *Health Technology Assessment* 14, 12 (2010), 1–140. http://www.doi.org/10.3310/hta14120
17. James Clawson, Jessica Pater, Andrew D. Miller, Elizabeth D. Mynatt, and Lena Mamykina. 2015. No Longer Wearing: Investigating The Abandonment of Personal Health-Tracking Technologies on Craigslist. In *Proceedings of the ACM Conference on Ubiquitous Computing*. ACM. https://doi.org/10.1145/2750858.2807554

18. Sunny Consolvo, David W McDonald, Tammy Toscos, Mike Y Chen, Jon Froehlich, Beverly Harrison, Predrag Klasnja, Anthony Lamarca, Louis Legrand, Ryan Libby, Ian Smith, and James A Landay. 2008. Activity Sensing in the Wild: A Field Trial of UbiFit Garden. In *Proceedings of the ACM Conference on Human Factors in Computing Systems*. ACM, 1797–1806. https://doi.org/10.1145/1357054.1357335

19. Felicia Cordeiro, Elizabeth Bales, Erin Cherry, and James Fogarty. 2015a. Rethinking The Mobile Food Journal: Exploring Opportunities for Lightweight Photo-Based Capture. In *Proceedings of the ACM Conference on Human Factors in Computing Systems*. ACM, 3207–3216. https://doi.org/10.1145/2702123.2702154

20. Felicia Cordeiro, Daniel A Epstein, Edison Thomaz, Elizabeth Bales, Arvind K Jagannathan, Gregory D Abowd, and James Fogarty. 2015b. Barriers and Negative Nudges: Exploring Challenges in Food Journaling. In *Proceedings of the ACM Conference on Human Factors in Computing Systems*. ACM, 1159–1162. http://doi.org/10.1145/2702123.2702155

21. Nediyana Daskalova, Karthik Desingh, Jin Young Kim, Lixiang Zhang, Alexandra Papoutsaki, and Jeff Huang. 2017. Lessons Learned from Two Cohorts of Personal Informatics Self-Experiments. In *Proceedings of the ACM Conference on Ubiquitous Computing*, Vol. 1. ACM, 46. https://doi.org/10.1145/3130911

22. Nediyana Daskalova, Danaë Metaxa-Kakavouli, Adrienne Tran, Nicole Nugent, Julie Boergers, John McGeary, and Jeff Huang. 2016. SleepCoacher: A Personalized Automated Self-Experimentation System for Sleep Recommendations. In *Proceedings of the Symposium on User Interface Software and Technology*. ACM, 347–358. http://doi.org/bwt4

23. Mary Jo Deering, Erin Siminerio, and Scott Weinstein. 2013. Issue Brief: Patient-Generated Health Data and Health IT. *Office of the National Coordinator for Health Information Technology* (2013).

24. Nicola Dell, Jessica Crawford, Nathan Breit, Timóteo Chaluco, Aida Coelho, Joseph McCord, and Gaetano Borriello. 2013. Integrating ODK Scan into The Community Health Worker Supply Chain in Mozambique. In *Proceedings of the International Conference on Information and Communication Technologies and Development*. ACM, 228–237. https://doi.org/10.1145/2516604.2516611

25. Daniel A Epstein, Monica Caraway, Chuck Johnston, An Ping, James Fogarty, and Sean A Munson. 2016. Beyond Abandonment To Next Steps: Understanding and Designing for Life After Personal Informatics Tool Use. In *Proceedings of the ACM Conference on Human Factors in Computing Systems*. ACM, 1109–1113. https://doi.org/10.1145/2858036.2858045

26. Daniel A Epstein, Nicole B Lee, Jennifer H Kang, Elena Agapie, Jessica Schroeder, Laura R Pina, James Fogarty, Julie A Kientz, and Sean Munson. 2017. Examining Menstrual Tracking To Inform The Design of Personal Informatics Tools. In *Proceedings of the ACM Conference on Human Factors in Computing Systems*. ACM, 6876–6888. https://doi.org/10.1145/3025453.3025635

27. Daniel A Epstein, An Ping, James Fogarty, and Sean A Munson. 2015. A Lived Informatics Model of Personal Informatics. In *Proceedings of the ACM international Joint Conference on Pervasive and Ubiquitous Computing*. ACM, 731–742. https://doi.org/10.1145/2750858.2804250

28. Deborah Estrin and Ida Sim. 2010. Open mHealth Architecture: An Engine for Health Care Innovation. *Science* 330, 6005 (2010), 759–760. http://doi.org/10.1126/science.1196187

29. Aojg Farmer, Oj Gibson, L Tarassenko, and A Neil. 2005. A Systematic Review of Telemedicine Interventions To Support Blood Glucose Self-Monitoring in Diabetes. *Diabetic Medicine* 22, 10 (2005), 1372–1378. DOI: http://dx.doi.org/10.1111/j.1464-5491.2005.01627.x

30. The Robert Wood Johnson Foundation. 2014. Personal Data for The Public Good: New Opportunities To Enrich Understanding of Individual and Population Health. *Health Data Exploration Project* (2014). http://www.rwjf.org/en/library/research/2014/03/personal-Data-For-The-Public-Good.html

31. RH Friedman, LE Kazis, A Jette, MB Smith, J Stollerman, J Torgerson, and Carey K. 1996. A Telecommunications System for Monitoring and Counseling Patients with Hypertension: Impact on Medication Adherence and Blood Pressure Control. *American Journal of Hypertension* 9, 4 (1996), 285–92. https://www.ncbi.nlm.nih.gov/pubmed/8722429

32. Erik Grönvall and Nervo Verdezoto. 2013. Understanding Challenges and Opportunities of Preventive Blood Pressure Self-Monitoring At Home. In *Proceedings of the European Conference on Cognitive Ergonomics*. ACM, 31. https://doi.org/10.1145/2501907.2501962

33. François Guimbretière. 2003. Paper Augmented Digital Documents. In *Proceedings of the ACM Symposium on User Interface Software and Technology*. ACM, 51–60. https://doi.org/10.1145/964696.964702

34. Reetta Heinonen, Riitta Luoto, Pirjo Lindfors, and Clas-Håkan Nygård. 2012. Usability and Feasibility of Mobile Phone Diaries in an Experimental Physical Exercise Study. *Telemedicine and E-Health* 18, 2 (2012), 115–119. http://www.doi.org/10.1089/tmj.2011.0087

35. Susan L Janson, Kelly Wong McGrath, Jack K Covington, Su-Chun Cheng, and Homer A Boushey. 2009. Individualized Asthma Self-Management Improves Medication Adherence and Markers of Asthma Control. *Journal of Allergy and Clinical Immunology* 123, 4 (2009), 840–846. https://doi.org/10.1016/j.jaci.2009.01.053

36. Mehul Jhaveri and Elizabeth Lee. 2007. Performance of Electronic Diaries in Diabetes Clinical Trials Measured Through Overall Satisfaction of Site Coordinators. *Journal of Diabetes Science and Technology* 1, 4 (2007), 522–530. http://www.doi.org/10.1177/193229680700100410

37. Susan L Joslyn and Jared E LeClerc. 2012. Uncertainty Forecasts Improve Weather-Related Decisions and Attenuate the Effects of Forecast Error. *Journal of Experimental Psychology: Applied* 18, 1 (2012), 126. http://doi.org/10.1037/a0025185

38. Ravi Karkar, Jessica Schroeder, Daniel A Epstein, Laura R Pina, Jeffrey Scofield, James Fogarty, Julie A Kientz, Sean A Munson, Roger Vilardaga, and Jasmine Zia. 2017. Tummytrials: A Feasibility Study of Using Self-Experimentation To Detect Individualized Food Triggers. In *Proceedings of the ACM Conference on Human Factors in Computing Systems*. ACM, 6850–6863. https://doi.org/10.1145/3025453.3025480

39. Ravi Karkar, Jasmine Zia, Roger Vilardaga, Sonali R Mishra, James Fogarty, Sean A Munson, and Julie A Kientz. 2015. A Framework for Self-Experimentation in Personalized Health. *Journal of the American Medical Informatics Association* (2015). http://doi.org/10.1093/jamia/ocv150

40. Matthew Kay, Eun Kyoung Choe, Jesse Shepherd, Benjamin Greenstein, Nathaniel Watson, Sunny Consolvo, and Julie A Kientz. 2012. Lullaby: A Capture & Access System for Understanding The Sleep Environment. In *Proceedings of the ACM Conference on Ubiquitous Computing*. ACM, 226–234. https://doi.org/10.1145/2370216.2370253

41. Matthew Kay, Tara Kola, Jessica R Hullman, and Sean A Munson. 2016. When (ish) Is My Bus?: User-Centered Visualizations of Uncertainty in Everyday, Mobile Predictive Systems. In *Proceedings of the ACM Conference on Human Factors in Computing Systems*. ACM, 5092–5103. https://doi.org/10.1145/2858036.2858558

42. Joseph (Jofish) Kaye, Mary Mccuistion, Rebecca Gulotta, and David A Shamma. 2014. Money Talks: Tracking Personal Finances. In *Proceedings of the ACM Conference on Human Factors in Computing Systems*. ACM, 521–530 https://doi.org/10.1145/2556288.2556975

43. L Kelman. 2007. The Triggers or Precipitants of the Acute Migraine Attack. *Cephalalgia* 27, 5 (2007), 394–402. https://doi.org/10.1111/j.1468-2982.2007.01303.x

44. Yoojung Kim, Eunyoung Heo, Hyunjeong Lee, Sookyoung Ji, Jueun Choi, Jeong-Whun Kim, Joongseek Lee, and Sooyoung Yoo. 2017. Prescribing 10,000 Steps Like Aspirin: Designing a Novel Interface for Data-Driven Medical Consultations. In *Proceedings of the 2017 CHI Conference on Human Factors in Computing Systems*. ACM, 5787–5799. https://doi.org/10.1145/3025453.3025570

45. Jisoo Lee, Erin Walker, Winslow Burleson, Matthew Kay, Matthew Buman, and Eric B Hekler. 2017. Self-Experimentation for Behavior Change: Design and Formative Evaluation of Two Approaches. In *Proceedings of the ACM Conference on Human Factors in Computing Systems*. ACM, 6837–6849. https://doi.org/10.1145/3025453.3026038

46. Ian Li, Anind Dey, and Jodi Forlizzi. 2010. A Stage-Based Model of Personal Informatics Systems. In *Proceedings of the ACM Conference on Human Factors in Computing Systems*. ACM, 557–566. http://doi.acm.org/10.1145/1753326.1753409

47. Chunyuan Liao, François Guimbretière, Ken Hinckley, and Jim Hollan. 2008. Papiercraft: A Gesture-Based Command System for Interactive Paper. *ACM Transactions on Computer-Human Interaction (tochi)* 14, 4 (2008), 18. https://doi.org/10.1145/1314683.1314686

48. James J Lin, Lena Mamykina, Silvia Lindtner, Gregory Delajoux, and Henry B Strub. 2006. Fish'n'Steps: Encouraging Physical Activity with an Interactive Computer Game. In *Proceedings of the ACM Conference on Ubiquitous Computing*. ACM, 261–278. https://doi.org/10.1007/11853565_16

49. Richard B Lipton. 2015. Risk Factors for and Management of Medication-Overuse Headache. *Continuum: Lifelong Learning in Neurology* 21, 4, Headache (2015), 1118–1131. http://doi.org/10.1212/CON.0000000000000216

50. Richard B Lipton, Joan C Amatniek, Michel D Ferrari, and Michael Gross. 1994. Migraine. Identifying and Removing Barriers To Care. *Neurology* 44, 6 Suppl 4 (1994), S63–8. https://www.ncbi.nlm.nih.gov/pubmed/8008228

51. Richard B Lipton, Walter F Stewart, and David Simon. 1998. Medical Consultation for Migraine: Results From The American Migraine Study. *Headache: The Journal of Head and Face Pain* 38, 2 (1998), 87–96. https://www.ncbi.nlm.nih.gov/pubmed/9529763

52. Morris Maizels. 1998. The Clinician's Approach To The Management of Headache. *Western Journal of Medicine* 168, 3 (1998), 203. https://www.ncbi.nlm.nih.gov/pmc/articles/PMC1304871/

53. Lena Mamykina, Elizabeth Mynatt, Patricia Davidson, and Daniel Greenblatt. 2008. MAHI: Investigation of Social Scaffolding for Reflective Thinking in Diabetes Management. In *Proceedings of the ACM Conference on Human Factors in Computing Systems*. ACM, 477–486. http://doi.acm.org/10.1145/1357054.1357131

54. Margaret Morris and Farzin Guilak. 2009. Mobile Heart Health: Project Highlight. *IEEE Pervasive Computing* 8, 2 (2009). https://doi.org/10.1109/MPRV.2009.31

55. Lucille ML Ong, Johanna CJM De Haes, Alaysia M Hoos, and Frits B Lammes. 1995. Doctor-Patient Communication: A Review of the Literature. *Social Science & Medicine* 40, 7 (1995), 903–918. https://www.ncbi.nlm.nih.gov/pubmed/7792630

56. Tapan S Parikh, Paul Javid, Sasikumar K, Kaushik Ghosh, and Kentaro Toyama. 2006. Mobile Phones and Paper Documents: Evaluating a New Approach for Capturing Microfinance Data in Rural India. In *Proceedings of the ACM Conference on Human Factors in Computing Systems*. ACM, 551–560. https://doi.org/10.1145/1124772.1124857

57. Sun Young Park and Yunan Chen. 2015. Individual and Social Recognition: Challenges and Opportunities in Migraine Management. In *Proceedings of the ACM Conference on Computer Supported Cooperative Work & Social Computing*. ACM, 1540–1551. https://doi.org/10.1145/2675133.2675248

58. Tamara Peyton, Erika Poole, Madhu Reddy, Jennifer Kraschnewski, and Cynthia Chuang. 2014. Every Pregnancy Is Different: Designing mHealth for The Pregnancy Ecology. In *Proceedings of the Conference on Designing Interactive Systems*. ACM, 577–586. https://doi.org/10.1145/2598510.2598572

59. Birthe Krogh Rasmussen, Rigmor Jensen, Marianne Schroll, and Jes Olesen. 1991. Epidemiology of Headache in a General Population—A Prevalence Study. *Journal of Clinical Epidemiology* 44, 11 (1991), 1147–1157. https://www.ncbi.nlm.nih.gov/pubmed/1941010

60. Ruth Ravichandran, Sang-Wha Sien, Shwetak N Patel, Julie A Kientz, and Laura R Pina. 2017. Making Sense of Sleep Sensors: How Sleep Sensing Technologies Support and Undermine Sleep Health. In *Proceedings of the ACM Conference on Human Factors in Computing Systems*. ACM, 6864–6875. https://doi.org/10.1145/3025453.3025557

61. John Rooksby, Mattias Rost, Alistair Morrison, and Matthew Chalmers Chalmers. 2014. Personal Tracking As Lived Informatics. In *Proceedings of the ACM Conference on Human Factors in Computing Systems*. ACM, 1163–1172. https://doi.org/10.1145/2556288.2557039

62. Jessica Schroeder, Jane Hoffswell, Chia-Fang Chung, James Fogarty, Sean Munson, and Jasmine Zia. 2017. Supporting Patient-Provider Collaboration To Identify Individual Triggers Using Food and Symptom Journals. In *Proceedings of the ACM Conference on Computer-Supported Cooperative Work & Social Computing*. ACM, 1726–1739. https://doi.org/10.1145/2998181.2998276

63. Stephen D Silberstein and The US Headache Consortium. 2000. Practice Parameter: Evidence-Based Guidelines for Migraine Headache (An Evidence-Based Review) Report of the Quality Standards Subcommittee of the American Academy of Neurology. *Neurology* 55, 6 (2000), 754–762. http://doi.org/10.1212/WNL.55.6.754

64. GD Solomon and KL Price. 1997. Burden of Migraine. *Pharmacoeconomics* 11, 1 (1997), 1–10. https://doi.org/10.2165/00019053-199700111-00003

65. Timothy J Steiner, Lars Jacob Stovner, and Gretchen L Birbeck. 2013. Migraine: The Seventh Disabler. *Headache: The Journal of Head and Face Pain* 53, 2 (2013), 227–229. http://doi.org/10.1186/1129-2377-14-1

66. Moira A Stewart. 1995. Effective Physician-Patient Communication and Health Outcomes: A Review. *CMAJ: Canadian Medical Association Journal* 152, 9 (1995), 1423. https://www.ncbi.nlm.nih.gov/pubmed/7728691

67. Cristiano Storni. 2011. Complexity in an Uncertain and Cosmopolitan World. Rethinking Personal Health Technology in Diabetes with The Tag-It-Yourself. *Psychnology Journal* 9, 2 (2011), 165–185.

68. Thomas N Ward. 2012. Migraine Diagnosis and Pathophysiology. *Continuum: Lifelong Learning in Neurology* 18, 4, Headache (2012), 753–763. http://doi.org/10.1212/01.CON.0000418640.07405.31

69. Peter West, Richard Giordano, Max Van Kleek, and Nigel Shadbolt. 2016. The Quantified Patient in the Doctor's office: Challenges & Opportunities. In *Proceedings of the ACM Conference on Human Factors in Computing Systems*. ACM, 3066–3078. http://doi.acm.org/10.1145/2858036.2858445

70. Ron Yeh, Chunyuan Liao, Scott Klemmer, François Guimbretière, Brian Lee, Boyko Kakaradov, Jeannie Stamberger, and Andreas Paepcke. 2006. ButterflyNet: A Mobile Capture and Access System for Field Biology Research. In *Proceedings of the ACM Conference on Human Factors in Computing Systems*. ACM, 571–580. https://doi.org/10.1145/1124772.1124859

71. Kathryn Yorkston, Kurt Johnson, Estelle Klasner, Dagmar Amtmann, Carrie Kuehn, and Brian Dudgeon. 2003. Getting the Work Done: A Qualitative Study of Individuals with Multiple Sclerosis. *Disability and Rehabilitation* 25, 8 (2003), 369–379. http://www.doi.org/10.1080/0963828031000090506

72. Haining Zhu, Joanna Colgan, Madhu Reddy, and Eun Kyoung Choe. 2016. Sharing Patient-Generated Data in Clinical Practice: An Interview Study. *Proceedings of the American Medical Informatics Association* (2016), 1303–1312. https://www.ncbi.nlm.nih.gov/pubmed/28269928

Exploring Self-Defining Memories in Old Age and their Digital Cues

Corina Sas
Lancaster University
Lancaster, UK
c.sas@lancaster.ac.uk

ABSTRACT

Self-defining memories represent significant emotional events capturing the most important concerns in our lives. While much HCI work on memory technologies has focused on autobiographic memories and lifelogging technologies for capturing them, there has been little exploration of self-defining memories and how they may be supported by appropriate cues. This is important as such memories are key in the development and maintenance of the sense of self, particularly in old age. We report on interviews with 8 older adults in their homes. Findings advance the understanding of self-defining memories and their possible cues with new insights into their relationship with self-identities and cues' specific qualities supporting richer emotional recall. Our findings led to several design implications such as novel technologies for curating self-defining memories and their cues, for embedding layered meaning in such cues across the lifespan, for crafting them, and sensitive design for their physical handling.

Author Keywords

Self-defining memories; memory cues; self; older adults.

ACM Classification Keywords

H.5.m. Information interfaces and presentation (e.g., HCI): Miscellaneous.

INTRODUCTION

Sense of self is crucial for our perception of continuity through time, and invaluable for wellbeing [33]. It captures perceptions and attitudes about oneself, often as a set of identities such as personal, relational or collective self [17,42,45]. Sense of self is actively supported by personal memories [57] and in particular by self-defining ones. The latter represent a specific type of autobiographical memories capturing lasting concerns or unresolved conflicts [4,20,28] around significant events, which help people explain how they have become who they are [8].

DIS '18, June 9–13, 2018, Hong Kong

ACM ISBN 978-1-4503-5198-0/18/06...$15.00
https://doi.org/10.1145/3196709.3196767

Fig. 1. Crafted objects as cues for self-defining memory: handmade doll cloth (P1) (left) and embroidery of a regimental badge (P7) (right).

When memory weakens because of cognitive decline of healthy aging or dementia, the sense of self also weakens, with findings showing the painful impact of the disintegrating self on people living with dementia and their families [5]. Much HCI research on memory technologies has focused on the value of lifelogging systems for capturing and archiving large amount of digital memories to support total recall [44]. Such emphasis on capture technologies however does not account for the significance that people attach to their memories and their specific cues. In addition, despite the importance of supporting self-defining memories, and of their much exploration in memory research [4,20,45], we know little about if and how such memories may be cued in healthy ageing and dementia. Relevant HCI work on cueing has focused mostly on autobiographical memories in general [10,14,24,37,38,43,58] albeit with less focused on those representing self-defining memories.

We argue that if the aim is to strengthen the sense of self in old age, then we must move beyond the main emphasis on capture technologies. This paper aims to investigate self-defining memories in older people, and in particular the possible cues that they identify for recalling them. The idea that people can identify memory cues, before they cue, has been previously argued based on meta-memory judgments [56], and on emerging findings on self-chosen cues supporting recall of self-defining memories of people living with dementia [20]. An understanding of what can cue self-defining memories, the content, and format of such cues, where they are stored, and how they are retrieved should support the design of technologies to capture, store, and retrieve digital memory across the lifespan, and to strengthen the sense of self in old age. We report on interviews with 8 older adults in their homes about such memories and how they can be cued. Because of the exploratory nature of our study and the novelty of research topic, we selected participants without signs of dementia; it is arguably easier to explore self-defining memories and their potential cues in healthy older people before the onset of dementia. Our study addresses the following questions:

- What *types* of self-defining memories do people identify? What are their affect, content, and reflected self-identities?
- What *types* of possible cues do people associate with self-defining memories, *where* do they store them, and what *challenges* do they face in identifying such cues?
- What *qualities* do self-defining memory cues have?

RELATED WORK

The study outlined in this paper draws from previous HCI research on memory cues, and memory technologies for aging, and of the growing body of work in psychology of memory and in particular self-defining memories.

Memory Cues in HCI

Most HCI research has focused on technologies for capturing and supporting recall of episodic memories [43,58]. There are two main types of cues supporting this recall namely internal ones consisting of sensorial experiences and feelings, and external cues present in physical environment [56]. The latter may include objects, people, activities and places, and their capture through photos, physical and tangible objects has been particularly explored in interaction design [56].

Much work has looked into the impact on recall of different modalities of memory cues, mostly visual [43] and audio cues [14], although the investigation of other cues such as location-based [24], or crafted cues [37,39] has also started to emerge. Beyond the exploration of cue modalities in isolation, other scholars have looked at combining them. One such example is HP *memory box* [18] which integrates sound-based narrative with stored memorabilia to support episodic recall. A few studies have explored the enduring impact of cue types on retrieval, such as photos, sounds, videos, odors, or physical objects on one-month old autobiographical memories [55]. Findings indicate that no cues condition led to more memory-details. However, with the exception of physical objects crafted by participants, the rest of the cues were generated by researchers, and hence may not have been typical or unique; characteristics considered key for successful cueing. Other HCI work has explored physical or digital possessions and their value for remembering [30,31], building on the link between possessions and sense of identity, and in particular Belk's [2] theory that possessions are components and determinants of sense of self consisting of: collections, money, pets, other people, and body parts. Later work has identified alternative categorizations of possessions in objects of power, self-continuity, and relationships [11], or, for their role in recall, in mementos (reminders of special events), souvenirs (reminders of special places) or heirlooms (family or inherited objects) [12]. Souvenirs relate mostly to holiday memories, are on display in house's public rooms and used for reminiscing [54], while mementos were categorized in artwork, photos or symbols of achievements often on display in public spaces [34]. Memorabilia (serving specific function and occasionally used), and idiosyncratic deeply personal objects tend to be privately stored [34]. A few studies have focused on how older adults' memory and identity are challenged by moving in later life to residential care or downsized homes. Findings suggest that to address limited space and fewer cherished possessions they can be bring with, people document and engage in tagging or telling stories of lost objects [27]. An emerging body of work has looked into how possessions may be questioned when cueing strong negative emotional events, no longer relevant for the current self [40,41].

To summarize, much work has focused on cueing autobiographical memories to support recall [10,14,24,37,43,58] or explore forgetting [40,41]. Most cues are printed photos or physical objects [56] created by researchers or belonging to participants' possessions. Although few prior studies have touched upon the relationship between possessions and self [27,34,40], there has been however limited explicit exploration of self-defining memories and how they may be cued.

Memory Technologies for Aging in HCI

A particular strand of memory research in HCI has focused on older adults to support their memory impairment due to aging or dementia [21,43,59]. *Memento* [60] creates hybrid physical-digital scrapbooks allowing older adults to reminisce. A much used technology is SenseCam, a wearable device which automatically capture photos in daily life. Consistent findings have shown its value in supporting the recall of episodic memories [21], particularly those of personal relevance to people experiencing memory impairment [25]. Other work integrated SenseCam photos with ambient displays for showing both past and recent photos, which has supported the sense of self of people living with Alzheimer's disease [10]. These authors also describe *multimedia biographies* co-designed as collages of personal photos, videos, and narratives on life stages and themes by people with memory impairment. Findings suggest that this practice supports the reminiscence of positive events, but its value for strengthening the sense of self has been less investigated.

To conclude, most HCI work on memory technologies has focused on curating and capturing life events to support older people's recall and share of their episodic memories. The emphasis here is on digital caption of past or very recent life events, but with a few exceptions [10], their value for sense of self and in particular for remembering self-defining memories has been less explored.

Memory Research on Self-Defining Memories

Autobiographical memories contain crucial information about the self [9,35,36] in the form of personal semantics comprising general knowledge and facts about oneself [28], and episodic memories of personal events located in a specific time and space and re-experienced through mental travel of the self [51]. Self-defining memories share characteristics with both episodic memories such as rich phenomenological details and specific spatio-temporal context, and with personal semantics in the form of more generic memories of personal events clustering in patterns over time [45]. What sets self-defining memories apart is one's enduring concerns reflected in events focused on self-discovery, self-understanding and identity [4,20].

Findings have also shown that self-defining memories related to negative emotional events are more challenging to process albeit crucial for one's wellbeing [33]. With respect to content, prior work identified different types of self-defining events such as narratives of threat, disrupted relationships, conflict-free relationships, achievement, failure, exploration, or guilt/shame [4]. Additional studies have also shown that the content of self-defining memories is structured around concerns, unresolved conflicts, and current goals [3].

In terms of healthy aging's impact on self-defining memories, previous findings showed that when compared to college students, older people recall less detailed and more summarized and positive self-defining memories encoded across the lifespan and focusing on meaningful themes such as achievements (32%), relationships (27.5%), life-threatening events (21%), recreation (8%), or guilt (5.5%) [45]. De Vries and colleagues [13] also showed that in life review, older people focus more on career and illness than younger people, suggesting that the former have more self-defining memories around life-threatening events. In terms of the endurance of sense of self in old age, following interviews with people living with dementia in nursing home, Cohen-Mansfield and colleagues [5,6] have shown that all roles deteriorate (professional, family, leisure and personal), while the family role is best maintained.

There is also a wealth of research on self-defining memories in dementia, with consistent findings showing their decline due to the required high level of specificity [28]. Such decline is made responsible for the loss of sense of identity in people living with dementia [4,20]. Unfortunately there is a paucity of studies exploring the retrieval of self-defining memories in dementia. A noticeable exception is Haj and colleagues' work [20]. They showed that exposure to music supports better retrieval of self-defining memories than autobiographical memories, when the music was self-chosen by participants instead of selected by researcher. This important finding can be explained by active involvement in the selection of favorite music of people living with dementia.

To summarize, self-defining memories are key in maintaining the sense of self, but prone to aggressive deterioration in old age and dementia. With a few exceptions there is a lack of studies exploring the possible cues for retrieval of self-defining memories in old age.

METHOD

For our exploratory study, we recruited a convenience sample of 8 older adults (age range 65- 82), 7 female and 1 male (P4). Participants were recruited with help from the local branch of the UK University of the Third Age (U3A), a volunteer charitable organization focusing on learning. The rationale for this choice is threefold: older adults have more self-defining memories to report, arguably larger collections of possessions which may be used to cue recall, and are more inclined to contemplate and reflect on their lives in order to develop coherent narratives [15]. Participants are from the UK so the empirical data is drawn from a similar Western context as most of reviewed work.

We employed contextual interviews in participants' homes [23] to observe people interacting with the identified cues and where they are usually stored. Prior to the interviews, they were asked to think of three self-defining memories described according to Singer and Salovey [46] as remembered clearly, important to them, leading to strong feelings, and helping understand who they are and how they come to be the person they currently are. We sensitively focused only on positive self-defining memories in order to limit the risks of revisiting previous trauma which may be associated with negative self-defining memories [47]. Participants were also asked to give a house tour to identify among their possessions those cueing self-defining memories, leaving it open to them to select physical or digital artifacts.

Interviews took about an hour, were audio recorded and fully transcribed. Data analysis involved a hybrid approach with existing concepts informing the deductive coding, while new ones, grounded in the empirical data, contributed to the inductive coding [16]. The deductive coding included concepts from autobiographical and self-defining memory research [28,45,51], with codes capturing the content and types of such memories and their cues [14,24,37,43], and different self-identities [6,17,45]. Participants' memories were identified as self-defined if they contained specific spatio-temporal and phenomenological details such as thoughts and feelings, as well as integrative meaning as lessons extracted beyond the recalled event [4] contributing to their identity construction, enduring concerns or unresolved conflicts [28]. The coding list was iteratively refined as new codes emerged such as redemption memories, crafted cues, and cues' qualities.

FINDINGS

This section describes the identified self-defining memories in terms affect and content, and how they reflect different self -identities. Then we focus on the possible cues for these memories, and the challenges of identifying them.

Self-defining Memories: Retrieval Process

Only two participants (P2 and P8) reported directly their top three self-defining memories. The others started their free recall with life story narratives identifying self-defining memories throughout life periods. Because of this approach, participants were able recollect the sequence of events leading up to their self-defining memories, demonstrating also how those continued to affect them long after the initial event.

While previous work also indicated that older people's self-defining memories are spread across the lifespan [45], our findings provided new insights into the life periods when such memories were encoded and their weight: childhood (25%), adolescence (15%), young adulthood (15%), adulthood (41%), and old age (4%). Such emphasis on the early life, providing over half of self-defining memories, extends similar findings on episodic memories [28] and reminiscence bump theory [35]. Our findings also contrast those on the life periods from where mementos emerge, i.e., less from formative years and more from recent past and adulthood [34]. This underscores critical distinctions between self-defining memories' cues and mementos, as the former may be shaped by earlier life periods when self-identities are emerging.

Self-Defining Memories: Affect and Content

Participants reported 28 self-defining memories; slightly more than 3 per person. Over three quarters of self-defining memories elicited positive emotions related to events such as achievements and loving relationships, or to negative ones transformed into redemption narratives (Table 1, column 2,3). The latter could be either relationship-focused: taking responsibility for less fortunate others; or self-focused: overcoming personal challenges through self-mastery. These outcomes confirm those on positive self-defining memories of older people [45] underpinned by successful relationships and personal achievements [3,5,6,45]. The content of negative self-defining memories relates to loss or transgression, confirming previous findings on unresolved conflicts [3,28] and disrupted relationships [4] albeit not mortality and guilt [3,4,45,48].

Self-Defining Memories: Identities

Sedikides and Marilynn [42] conceptualized self-identity across three levels: personal self (aspects of the self that differentiate the self from all others), relational self (derived from intimate relationships), and collective self (derived from membership in large social groups).

Our findings show the predominance of self-defining memories focused on relational self, followed by those focused on personal self , and to less extent on collective self (Table 1 column 1), confirming outcomes on older adults' emphasis on relational self, followed by personal, and collective self [1]. We now describe the identified self-defined memories integrating self-identities, with their content and affect.

Self (#)	Content (#) (Participant)	Affect	Identified Cues (#)
Personal (8)	Achievements (8) (P1,P2,P3,P4,P5)	Positive	Ready-made objects (6) Crafted-objects (2)
Relational (18)	Loving relations (15) (P1,P5,P6,P7,P8)	Positive	Ready-made objects (10) Crafted objects (5)
	Redemption narratives (3) (P1,P2,P4,P6)	Positive	Crafted objects (2) Body-based cues (1)
	Challenging relationships(0) (P3,P4,P6)	Negative	None
Collective (2)	Large scale events (2) (P6,P7)	Negative	Place-based cues (2)

Table 1: Relationship between self-identities, content and affect of self-defining memories and their possible cue and their counts

Relational Self: Loving Relationships

All participants recalled self-defining memories capturing key relationships with loved ones. These include memorable events of meeting the spouse-to-be, the first pregnancy, or family leisure time. P8 reports the memory of acquiring a handmade toy (Fig. 2a) in a country fair, signifying the romance with her husband: *"My husband and I went out for a Sunday drive and they were having a country fair, which was unusual for Australia. So we stopped and looked around, and there was a stall where this girl had stuffed toys she handmade, and I fell in love with it. It was twenty dollars, I'll never forget because I thought it was so cheap, [but] it's still going strong, it's a lovely thing. I can't remember if I knew I was pregnant or not, but it was a lovely day, not too hot, and there was this great big field full of stores. That was a happy day. That opens up memories of when my son was born, and of course one of the best memories of my life was when I saw him. This elephant was bigger than him to start with. [And] when we came over to the UK ... my husband came over a few months later holding the elephant with him, and he walked through customs holding onto it"* [P8].

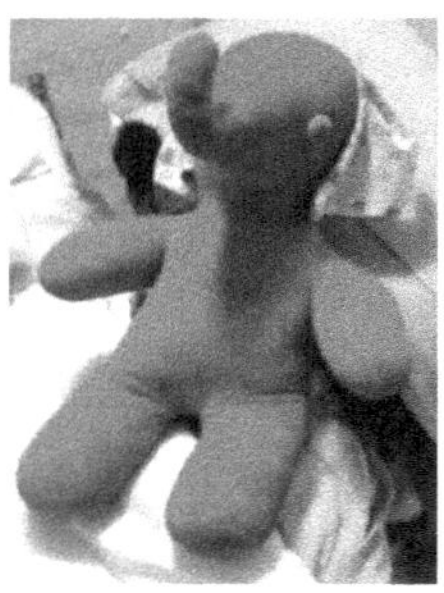

Fig. 2a. *"The elephant represents memories of when the children were born"* [P8]

Fig. 2b. Crafted wooden banister: apprenticeship and meeting of wife-to-be (P4)

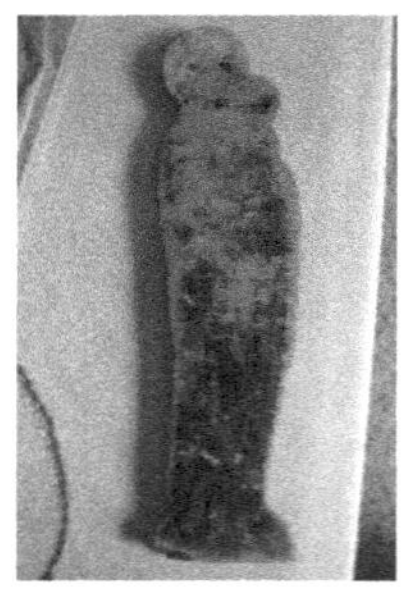

Fig. 2c *"I entered the competition, and I won! I was so pleased"* [P5]

This quote illustrates that the relational identity wraps around multiple roles, both of wife and mother, and the toy's ability to connect in a nexus, key self-defining events about both roles, signifying romance as well as pregnancy, unknown at the time, followed by the birth of her son.

Another positive self-defining memory capturing the relational self is described as the moment of meeting one's future wife: "*I was 20 and still serving my apprenticeship as a joiner [...] and that was the biggest event of my life: meeting her. I was in the society where they would help people in need, so we used to have dances for the youths in the area. And, I hadn't been out with girls at that particular stage, so I used to do the doors and refreshments. And she came to one of the dances and that was it! [Laughs] I couldn't dance and I asked her to dance, [quiet mumbling], that has been the essence of my life*" [P4]. While this memory is about relational self, it also touches upon the personal self because its spatio-temporal context intersects that of apprenticeship stage with its value for personal self.

Relational Self: Challenging Relationships-Transgression & Loss

Three participants mentioned self-defining negative memories in relation to significant hard to reconcile losses, such as the loss of a child through accident or stillbirth, or transgressions such as physical abuse: "*My stepfather was such a bully: sometimes when he was whacking me, the only way I could make him stop was to fall on the floor and pretend to be unconscious. So, I became very afraid of confrontation, disagreement and for lots and lots of years was very much a doormat, and wouldn't hold my ground for anything really*" [P3]. This quote indicates the enduring impact of such experiences on the current self. The fewer episodic details of such memories confirm prior findings on repression [3] as a defensive mechanism intrinsic to self-memory system [7]. Such self-defining memories share the same negative emotions as the original even, but unlike redemption-based memories, they remained unprocessed into a coherent positive resolution [33,59]. HCI work has also started to explore social loss such as the one due to death or separation [41] and its challenging digital traces consisting of poignant evocative and ubiquitous reminders that people feel compelled to delete [40].

Personal Self: Personal Achievements

Five participants mentioned self-defining memories reflecting achievements such as academic success or professional recognition, which shaped their personal self. One such example is from P5 who attended a convent school where she won a handwriting prize (Fig. 2c): "*I always wanted a little statue of our Lady, which I couldn't have, but the prize was this little wooden statue [...] I'd only be young, about 8 or 9. I entered the competition, and I won!*" [P5]. This memory illustrates her faith, education, and values she learned during school. Other participant mentioned an early self-defining memory as a precocious child and her trait as a fast learner: "*I was three years old when I could read and write in two languages, and I knew my Math.*" [P1]. Although not celebrated with a specific award, the achievement and the drive behind it have shaped her identity as determined and ambitious: "*If I didn't enjoy something, I wouldn't waste my time doing it, but if I did, I would practice until I could be the best that I could*" [P1].

Personal Self: Redemption Narratives

Four participants mentioned redemption in their self-defining memories of overcoming hardship, poverty, accidents or disability, confirming previous findings on the importance of coherent, positive resolution [59,33]. An eloquent example is provided by P2 in relation to her perceived inadequacy and physical disability: "*I was failing my 11 year exams and remember sitting on the headmaster's knee being told I'd failed. I knew from that moment I would go to a worse school than everybody else; it made me feel thick and stupid and inferior, and thinking that people who were cast aside because they "weren't good enough" actually had lots of positive strong characteristics and that, kind of followed on from when I had my leg differences. That was definitely a defining memory*" [P2]. The quote illustrates how these limitations have underpinned the development of her personal self, driven by values of equality and diversity. The predominance of positive affect around personal self's defining memories confirms the positive core characteristics of personal self that people are motivated to protect, maintain, or elevate while resisting negative feedback [42]. In this light, redemption narratives represent specific types of personal achievements.

Collective Self: Negative Impactful Events

Collective self focuses on people's identity as members of a valued social group and two participants mentioned large scale events with significant social impact: childhood memories of the World War II or adult memories of youth's riots in 2011 in the UK cities: "*I love Manchester and when all that happened it really affected me [and] I thought for every one of them nasty kids, there are ten good kids out there.*" [P6]. This quote indicates the collective identity of Mancunians and their attempts to reclaim agency, despite the disempowering impact of such events.

To summarize, an important outcome is our integration of self-defining memories with self-identities which prior work has limitedly addressed. More specifically, findings indicate that personal self is reflected in memories of achievements and redemption; relational self captures the significance of both loving and challenging relationships, while collective self reflects predominantly negative events with large social impact.

Possible Cues for Self-Defining Memories

The findings from the home tour data show that the majority of cues for self-defining memories are physical objects (Table 1 column 4). Most of these are ready-made objects followed by crafted objects. The other two types of cues are place-based and body-based cues. The emphasis on physical objects, be them ready-made or crafted, extends findings on the prevalence of physical and tangible objects as external cues for autobiographical memories [56] to self-defining memories. An important finding is the absence of digital artifacts as cues for such memories. Even though non digital printed photos are mentioned, participants have limited preference using them as possible cues. This is surprising as photos figure prominently among digital cherished possessions and mementos [31,40,55]. To explore the preference for different types of cues, we looked at their link with self-identities, content and affect (Table 1).

Personal Self: Achievement Objects as Possible Cues
Five participants mentioned achievement-related objects usually in paper or object format, including for example old school notebooks with high marks (P1,P2), certificates of academic or professional exams subsequently framed (P2), prizes from school competitions (P5) (Fig. 2c), and objects of professional recognition (P4) (Fig. 3).

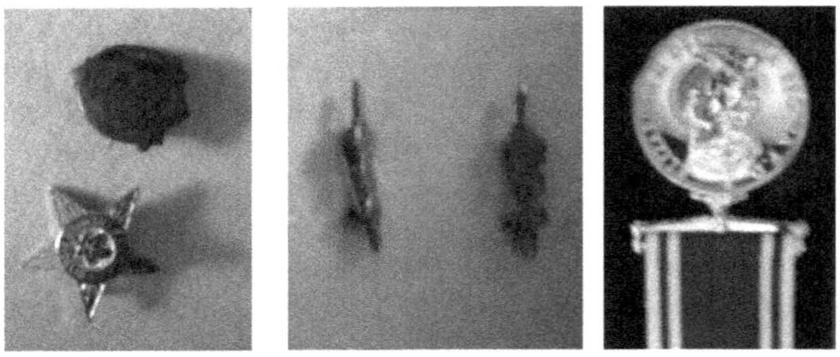

Fig. 3. Awards for professional recognition: emblems (left), oak leaves cufflinks (center), medal (right) (P4)

Such objects are deeply valued for their ability to represent positive emotions related to self-mastery, as key aspect of personal self [17] and content of self-defining memories [3,48,49]. For example, P5's recall of being awarded a handwriting prize in a school competition became richer when the Mary statue was fetched and handled (Fig. 2c). Indeed, P5 expressed more intense emotions illustrating the value of such artifact in recall: "*I was so pleased to get that [smiles intently as she thinks]. It could stand up, you see, and I could put little tiny jars of flowers and things [giggles] I loved every minute of school*" [P5]. She also expressed much care while handling the statue because of its material fragility: "*it is so faded, it's been in a tin*" [P5].

Relational Self: Possessions and Crafted Objects as Cues
An important finding is that one third of positive self-defining memories of loving relationships have been linked to handmade crafted objects. Their ability to facilitate rich emotional recall suggests their value as possible cues. Three participants mentioned such possible cues as crafted objects made by themselves through embroidery (P1) or woodcraft (P4), or by others through sewing or weaving (P2). P2's appreciation for her elephant toy has been earlier described and two other such cues are further detailed. One is the wooden banister (Fig. 2b) mentioned by P4 with respect to the self-defining memory of meeting his wife. He crafted the banister for a church and kept because it represented not only the formative time of his joiner apprenticeship, but more importantly the event at which he met his wife organized by the same church: "*I can go back even now to the churches that I've worked at, and it gives a great deal of satisfaction to see it*" [P4]. Another such cue is a doll cloth handmade by P1 for her daughter to celebrate their bond and for passing on the sewing skills (Fig. 1 left).

Collective Self: Places as Possible Cues
Given the limited number of identified self-defining memories related to collective self, it is not surprising that we have found only a few such cues. However, given the predominantly negative affect characterizing such memories, it is surprising that such possible cues were even suggested. Two participants identified place-based cues as large scale spaces with socially shared meaning. For example, P6 described the music shop destroyed during the UK riots earlier described: "*What really upset me was the music shop. Because my memories took me back to me in town with my grandson*" [P6]. This quote indicates the perceived transgression of participant's favorite music shop and its precious musical instruments where she has spent many moments with her grandson.

The second place-based cue is described by P7, as the place in Normandy where her husband has been wounded during the War World II: "*We went to Normandy on the 6th of June, for services in memory and respect, but it brought my husband a lot of memories of the war [...] we carried on to the place where he was wounded. He was fascinated*" [P6]. Interestingly, this place in Normandy has not been photographed, although the family took pictures during this commemoration trip. Even more striking is the crafting of a cue through embroidery (Fig. 1 right): "*My husband made that stitching of the unit he was with in Normandy to help his fingers after he was wounded*" [P6]. Although the choice of craft was pragmatic, it allows not just the capture but also the processing of negative emotions. This may open up the design space of exploring craft for cueing self-defining memories related to personal self. This finding also indicates that significant others are in position to identify possible cues which may scaffold the recall of loved ones' self-defining memories.

Personal Self: Body-Based Cues for Redemption Narratives
Another interesting cue type is provided by P2 in relation to her physical disability (Fig. 4): "*My leg is really central to how I defined who I was; not a great, strong perfect person but somebody inferior [...] I felt I was never perfect [...] But actually, within that, I gathered a real strength that made me feel very strong and different [...] my legs were key to me growing up [and] they will always be central values to me about differences: different ways of measuring people, and different ways of being, and I think we have to celebrate difference and diversity*" [P2]. Less surprising is finding limited cues for negative self-defining memories of challenging or ended relationships. This may be not because such cues are not necessarily there [40,41], but because people are not much motivated to cue the recall of painful memories. The limited reference to cues for negative self-defining memories focused on relational self may also be the reason for finding fewer cues for relational as opposed to personal self. Together, these findings suggest that people have a strong bias towards identifying possible cues for positive rather than negative self-defining memories.

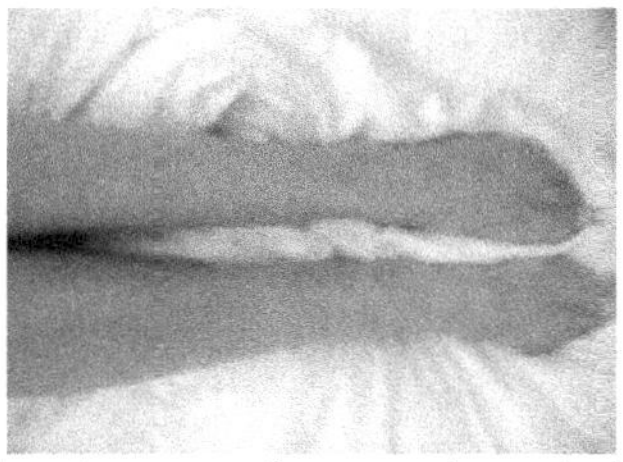

Fig. 4. "*My leg is part of me and my being, and probably defines me really, really strongly*" [P2]

Possible Cues for Self-Defining Memory: Challenges

We now discuss the challenges of identifying possible cues for self-defining memories. They should be identifiable: cues that people can think of, with or without the ability to reach them physically; retrievable, i.e., easy to be physically found; and accessible, i.e., physically seen or touched.

Difficult to Identify

An important finding is that for almost one third of self-defining memories, participants experienced difficulties in identifying specific cues. Most of these memories relate to negative events, either as redemption-based memories, or as memories of unresolved issues pertaining to challenging relationships. While people may lack incentives for cueing the recall of memories of unresolved issues, such cues may be valuable in developing coherent life story once successfully processed [33]. It is surprising however, that some redemption-based memories also lack cues. Apart from their negative affect, it is possible that this lack of cues reflects people's challenges of identifying them among their cherished possessions. We do not argue that such cues cannot be found or created, just that during the interviews, participants did not succeed identifying them. Although most participants have collections of cherished possessions, their link with specific self-defining memories is missing: *"there are loads of things around my house I collect [which] I don't keep consciously to remind me about who I am. I have collected them because they have reminded me about different periods of my life"* [P2]. This is an important finding which may be due either to the fact that people do not usually reflect on how specific artefacts may cue their self-defining memories, or because such artefacts need to meet specific qualities which are not commonly embodied by cherished possessions.

Hidden among Cherished Possessions

Another challenge is that even when participants succeed identifying possible cues, they sometimes could not physically retrieve them. This can occur because such self-defining memory cues have been unwillingly disposed of: *"I did have [school] reports but my mother got rid of them all, which was always about me not being very good but if I'd had those records I would have collected them, but I haven't anymore"* [P2]. This quote suggests that such cues may not be recognized as important by others because of their mundane, unassuming appearance obscuring their meaning revealed only to their owners [53]. Another reason for inaccessible self-defining memory cues is that cherished possessions become scattered in the old age by being passed down to adult children: *"I found a great box which I kept for safe keeping, and my daughter went through and got most of it, more of it than me!"* [P1].

Lost Due to Moving in Later Life

HCI work on ageing and memories has shown that older adults' sense of self is challenged by moving to residential care or downsized homes, which forces them to part with cherished possessions [27]. Our outcomes provide support for this argument by highlighting the negative impact of losing during downsizing or moving house (P1,P3) not only cherished possessions but also possible cues for self-defining memories hidden among them.

Although participants were able to fetch and show some of self-defining memory cues, they were often able to recall other object-based cues which they were no longer able to physically locate. For example, in relation to her self-defining memory of a fast learner, P1 mentioned a second memory box with cherished possessions such as books, newspaper clippings, or recipes from her mother, as well as a special schoolbook that she has kept since she was four years old. It had pages of sums written in different color crayons, and most memorable: the sums were all marked correctly which relates to her self-defining memory of fast learner. However, after moving house, she was no longer able to remember where she has put it. Memory boxes were mentioned by other three participants (P2,P3,P5) who indicated the importance of safeguarding their content. It is in such private places where most possible cues for self-defining memories tend to be stored, with less than one quarter being on display.

To conclude, identifying possible cues for self-defining memories is not trivial, particularly for those with negative emotional content. Possible cues consisting of ready-available objects are often unassuming objects, hidden among cherished possessions, for which people may lack the sensitivity to recognize their recall value. Moreover, collections of cherished possessions are difficult to maintain in old age, becoming lost, scattered or downsized.

THEORETICAL IMPLICATIONS

We now discuss the findings and how they address the research questions outlined in the introduction. The outcomes advance the understanding of self-defining memories and their cues with new insights into their relationship with self-identities. We also discuss the types of such cues and particularly detail their specific qualities supporting richer emotional recall. Suh qualities are important as they can open up novel design opportunities for memory technologies in old age. We also acknowledge the limitation of the sample consisting mainly of female participants and its possible impact on cues generated through the gendered practice of craft. Despite the relationship between gender and emotional aspects of autobiographical memories [19], previous findings indicated limited gender impact on self-defining memories [4]. Future work however is needed for exploring the role of self-defining memories and their cues for older males, and for experimentally assessing the impact of identified cues on the richer recall of people living with dementia.

New Insights on Self-Defining Memories and Identities

Our approach to link identities with self-defining memories is innovative, offering additional insights into their relationship between self-identities. For example, P8's memory of meeting his future wife, P3 and P6's experience of transgression in relational and social self indicate how personal self is also affected. Our findings also show an emerging relationship between self-identities on the one hand, and the affect and content of their self-defining memories on the other hand. Personal self is reflected predominantly in positive memories of achievement or mastery in front of adversities; relational self on positive loving relationships and less on negative challenging ones, while collective self on negative large scale events. Our outcomes on positive affect, characterizing in decreasing order personal, relational, and collective self, echo those showing that people protect and invest significantly more efforts in personal self [42].

Types of Possible Cues for Self-Defining Memories

Possible cues for self-defining memories include mostly objects tailored to the self-identities they aim to support. Cues as ready-made achievement and crafted objects extend the function of mementos from supporting recall of autobiographical memories [34] to self-defining memories. However, our findings suggest that unlike mementos, cues for self-defining memories consist less of artwork, photos, or memorabilia [34]. This may be because such cues are self-relevant:on display when symbolizing achievements, and seldom interacted with, unlike memorabilia.

We now reflect on the distinction between ready-made and crafted objects as possible cues. For the ready-made cues, the encoding of the memory and the identification of its cue tend to take place simultaneously. Often such objects become part of collections of cherished possessions. The value of crafted objects as possible cues emerges when ready-made ones are neither available nor recognized as important. Crafted objects can be identified as powerful cues either during (Fig. 2a and 2b), or after the memory has been encoded (Fig. 1 right). Due to the personal involvement in the generation of these cues, they are arguably more effective in supporting recall. As consistent findings have also shown the impact on retrieval of self-generated encoding cues [26], we argue for the importance of directly involving the self in the making of cues for self-defining memories. The craft practice for making such objects is gendered, with women favoring female-oriented crafting such as embroidery, knitting or sewing, and male engaging in woodcraft. These findings extend Csikszentmihalyi's [11] categories of household objects relevant for the self with the dimension of gendered craft.

We also argue for the novelty of body-based cues which received limited attention in cueing episodic memories. Despite that only one participant identified such a cue, our argument for their value is supported by Belk's [2] theory on components of self including body parts as a distinct category. In addition, as our findings indicate, body-based cues have particular value for self-defining memories of redemption narratives related to personal self. The identified place-based cues also build on previous work on location-based cues [24], extending them with insights emphasizing less the tracking of the place but the construction of its meaning. Moreover, for cueing negative memories with large social impact such as battlefields or riots, photos may be too evocative [37].

We also argue that place-based cues have distinct characteristics from object- or body-based cues pertaining to positive emotions of personal and relational self and their defining memories. Instead, the place-based cues tend to be of a larger scale: cities or battle fields versus handheld objects, and public rather than private thus able to safely contain the recall of and sharing with others negative and collective self-defining memories.

Qualities of Self-Defining Memories' Cues

Although, many identified cues are physical artefacts, we argue for the importance of digital cues. The rationale for this argument is threefold. First, our participants between 65 and 82 years old did not live digitally rich lives, but millennials do [32,40], and in their old age much of their identities will be reflected in digital artefacts. Second, the tangibility of many physical cues is particularly important for recall, and interactive tangible cues could better support it. Third, some physical cues are difficult to identify or locate unlike their potential digital counterparts. We also argue that because of their content and qualities, the identified cues for self-defining memories have the potential of supporting richer recall. Their qualities include tangibility, layered meaning, challenging to identify and access, privately stored and fragile.

Tangibility

Despite the exploratory nature of our study, findings indicate that when physical cues are handled, the mere act of holding and often gently caressing them opens up participants' access to richer emotional content in their recall of associated self-defining memories. This is an important finding, given the considerable decline of self-defining memories in dementia [28]. The richer emotional content triggered by such cues can facilitate access to more specific details required by successful recall of self-defining memories, which in turn can help people with dementia strengthen their sense of identity [4,20]. Arguably, tangible embodied interaction through its ability to support multisensorial recall could open up new design opportunities. Another quality strengthening their value is the ability of such cues to embody layered meaning.

Layered Meanings

An interesting characteristic which makes for strong self-defining memory cues is *layered meanings,* which we define as relating to more than one personal goal or theme embodied in a self-defining memory, to a cluster of self-defining memories occurring close in time, or multiple self-identities involved in the event. For example, the elephant mentioned by P8 (Fig. 2a) cues a powerful memory capturing two crucial themes around love and motherhood and the object imparts its powerful meaning with three family members. Such cue has been acquired at a life transition when the participant was pregnant, in a spatio-temporal context symbolizing romance, abundance and fecundity. Another example is the wooden banister (Fig. 2b), described by P4 capturing both self-mastery as a young apprentice, and the romance of meeting his future wife. This characteristic is also supported by findings showing that some mementos are also rooted in more than one reason [34]. Lifelogging technologies already capture digital traces of self-identities across the lifespan, and tailoring them to identify the self-defining clusters of events or goals can open up valuable design opportunities.

Challenging to Identify or Access

Cues for positive self-defining memories tend to focus on achievements or relationships, and take mostly the form of ready-made or crafted objects. Cues for negative self-defining memories which focus on significant personal or social losses, rather than mortality and guilt as previously suggested [3,48,49], tend to be less available. Interestingly, when available, they are not directly accessible taking the form of place-based cues such as outdoor places seldom visited. Findings also indicate that once identified, self-defining memory cues are valuable in supporting rich recall. However, such object-based cues can become inaccessible at times, as described by almost one third of participants. This can be due to the cues being disposed of by others, misplaced or lost during downsizing or moving house, or being parted with for the benefit of the adult children. Again, lifelogging technologies tailored to identify the self-defining memories across the lifespan could offer easier access to their digital cues. Another surprising finding is the lack of crafted objects for cueing negative self-defining memories, despite the value of craft for processing negative emotions [50]. Here, the value of digital craft can open up new design opportunities.

Privately Stored and Fragile

An important finding is that the majority of accessible self-defining memory cues are stored in private spaces, with fewer being on display. Most of the objects in the public spaces of the house are achievement-related, i.e., framed certificates. In contrast, other achievement-related objects, usually smaller and linked to early school years, or relationship-related objects tend to be kept in private rooms. Such outcomes support previous ones showing that private spaces store mementos as idiosyncratic objects related to intense emotions, and in particular negative ones which are never on display in public spaces [34]. We found that this insight is even more relevant to objects cuing self-defining memories, as there is a clear distinction between those kept on display, and those kept privately. This is reflected in participants' emotions whilst recalling such memories. While the objects on display were talked about and showed with enthusiasm, those stored privately such as the school prize of Mary statue (Fig. 2c) were more emotionally handled; both however facilitated emotionally richer recall.

An important quality of such cues is their unique material *fragility* which strongly limits people's interaction with them. For example, participants P5 expressed concerns of even taking out from her memory box the small booklet where she was practicing her handwriting prior to wining the school prize. Such findings confirm those showing that people tend to have boxes of memories with strong reminiscing power, and that fragility of some mementos requires careful storage [34]. In contrast, their digital counterparts, if sensitively designed could allow for more interaction while still engendering a sense of preciousness.

IMPLICATIONS FOR DESIGN

Study findings offer several implications for the design of memory technology to support self-defining memories. They address the challenge of curating self-defining memories and their cues, the value of embedded layered meaning in such cues, and of crafting them when people cannot identify existing cues for self-defining memories.

Curating Self-Defining Memories and their Cues

Findings indicate that people experience difficulties in identifying their self-defining memories. It may be that from the richness of autobiographical memories, they are not used to discriminate those which are self-defining from other episodic memories or personal semantics.

We suggest novel memory technologies which may scaffold people's effort to identify their self-defining memories. For example, such technologies may integrate life review with a variant of card sorting method to iteratively sort such memories, relate them to major goals within life periods, and in particular to themes of achievements, relationships, redemption, and negative unresolved issues as suggested by our findings.

People also have many self-defining memories without identifiable cues. This is surprising given the vast collections of physical and digital possessions that people acquire throughout life. Such challenge can be addressed through novel tools supporting reflective reminiscing on self-defining memories in order to explicitly identify their cues among personal collections. For example, these may support engagement with cherished possessions, stored both digitally and in private memory boxes, with the aim of creating links between such artefacts and specific self-defining memories. Metadata of digital collections can be used for selecting such cues from digital trails captured through lifelogging or social media.

Embedding Cues with Layered Meaning across Lifespan

Our findings show that richer recall is particularly supported by cues able to prompt retrieval of multiple themes associated with a self-defining memory, multiple such memories or self-identities related to them. We can think of novel memory technologies to support not just the identification of self-defining memories' cues but also the evolving construction of the meaning embedded in them. This may exploit cues acquired or crafted at life transitions when multiple identities intersect, offsetting the risk of not recognizing their associated memories as self-defining at the time. The emerging HCI interest in life transitions offers a useful lens to support the identification of cues for such self-defining memories even before they are encoded [40]. The lifespan approach to identifying and developing these cues is also valuable in addressing the challenge of them being disposed of, lost during downsizing, or unwillingly parted with.

Augmenting cherished objects with digital memories has been previously suggested [34], particularly for tracking such cues during the moving in later life in residential or care home [27]. Arguably, such curatorial acts can be even more valuable when performed across the entire lifespan. Stories attached to self-defining memory cues could mitigate the risk of having them disposed by others, as such stories uncover the deep personal meaning hidden within otherwise unassuming objects. They can also help communicate to adult children the value of such objects for supporting the personal self of their old parents, and mitigate the risk of older people unwillingly parting with them. In addition, digital stories could mitigate the risk of misplacing or losing these cues across the lifespan.

Crafting Self-Defining Memories' Cues

An important finding is that almost one third of self-defining memories have unidentifiable cues. This may be because identifying possible cues for self-defining memories is challenging particularly for those with negative emotional content. Such challenge opens up design opportunities shifting the focus away from personal possessions and possible cues buried in them, to novel technologies for crafting new cues [39]. Moreover, crafting is particularly valuable in facilitating self-involvement whose role in recall has been consistently shown [20,26]. Our study methodology asked participants to actively identify and select their cues, an additional factor which may be responsible for their success. This is supported by findings showing that self-chosen music can cue self-defining memories of people living with dementia [20].

Building on this argument, we could consider extending people's involvement from cue selection to cue generation, since consistent findings have also shown the impact of self-generated encoding cues on recall of autobiographical memories [26]. We argue that precisely this involvement is provided by crafted objects, which may explain their emphasis in our findings. We can imagine novel interactive systems integrating tangible interfaces with elements of art therapy to support not just capturing the event, but also reflecting on and processing of negative self-defining memories and their progression into redemption narratives.

Sensitive Design for Physical Handling of Fragile Cues

An interesting outcome is the value of physical handling of cues for self-defining memories. The mere gentle touch of their surfaces allows for accessing richer emotional content. Such cues tend to be fragile as they stood the test of time accompanying people through their life trajectories. We can imagine new memory technologies consisting of hybrid objects. The physical part could be crafted objects that people will value such jewelry. Such artifacts have the potential to embody both preciousness and fragility. The digital part of these hybrid objects could capture, store, and play short digital stories of its meaning, or even multisensorial digital stories further emphasizing touch. To support their fragility, sensitive design can explore ways in which such hybrid objects could embody the signs of wear of both its physical and digital parts. For example, the physical object could get patina [29], while the digital part through subsequent use may show signs of faded images or crackle sound similar to those of old vinyl records.

CONCLUSION

This study investigates older adults' identification of self-defining memories and their possible cues. We advance the understanding of such memories and cues with new insights into their relationship with self-identities. Personal self is reflected in memories of achievements and redemption; relational self captures loving or challenging relationships, while collective self reflects negative events with large social impact. These tend to be cued by achievement objects, body-based cues, crafted objects, and place-based objects, respectively. The key qualities of such cues include being ordinarily unassuming, difficult to identify and access as they are hidden among cherished possessions, often fragile and privately stored, and rich in layered meanings which allow for strong emotional recall. Our findings suggest novel memory technologies with potential to better support self-defining memories and their cueing than lifelogging technologies. The shift of focus from capture technologies towards those emphasizing the curation of self-defining memories and their cues, the embedding of layered meaning in such cues across lifespan, and of crafting these cues could better support such memories and the fragile sense of self in old age.

ACKNOWLEDGEMENTS

We are indebted to the study participants, and to Megan Rouncefield for completing the fieldwork and preliminary data analysis. This work has been partly supported by AffecTech: Personal Technologies for Affective Health, Innovative Training Network funded by the H2020 Marie Skłodowska-Curie, No 722022, and PACTMAN: Trust, Privacy and Consent in Future Pervasive Environments project funded by the UK EPSRC, No: EP/N028228.

REFERENCES

1. Rose Addis, Donna, and Lynette Tippett.2004. Memory of myself: Autobiographical memory and identity in Alzheimer's disease. *Memory* 12, 1: 56-74.
2. Russel Belk. 1988. *Possessions and self.* John Wiley & Sons, Ltd.
3. Dorthe Berntsen. 2009. *Involuntary autobiographical memories: An introduction to the unbidden past*. New York: Cambridge University Press.
4. Pavel Blagov & Jefferson A. Singer. 2004. Four Dimensions of Self-Defining Memories Specificity, Meaning, Content, and Affect) and Their Relationships to Self-Restraint, Distress, and Repressive Defensiveness. *Journal of personality* 72, 3: 481-511.
5. Jiska Cohen-Mansfield, Hava Golander and Giyorah Arnheim. 2000. Self-identity in older persons suffering from dementia: preliminary results. *Social science & medicine* 51, 3: 381-394.
6. Jiska Cohen-Mansfield, Aleksandra Parpura-Gill, and Hava Golander. 2006. Utilization of self-identity roles for designing interventions for persons with dementia. *The Journals of Gerontology Series B: Psychological Sciences and Social Sciences*, *61,* 4: 202-212.
7. Martin Conway & Christopher Pleydell-Pearce. 2000. The construction of autobiographical memories in the self-memory system. *Psychological Review* 107, 2: 261-288.
8. Martin Conway, Jefferson A. Singer, and Angela Tagini. 2004. The self and autobiographical memory: Correspondence and coherence. *Social Cognition* 22, 5: 491-529.
9. Martin Conway. 2005. Memory and the self. *Journal of Memory and Language, 53, 4:* 594-628.
10. Masashi Crete-Nishihata, Ronald Baecker, Michael Massimi, Deborah Ptak, Rachelle Campigotto, Liam D. Kaufman, Adam M. Brickman, Gary R. Turner, Joshua R. Steinerman & Sandra E. Black. 2012. Reconstructing the past: personal memory technologies are not just personal and not just for memory. *Human–Computer Interaction* 27, 1-2: 92-123.
11. Mihaly Csikszentmihalyi. 1993. Why we need things. In S. Lubar & W. Kingery (Eds). *History from things: Essays on material culture*, Smithsonian Institution Press, 20-29.
12. Mihaly Csikszentmihalyi & Eugene Rochberg-Halton. 1981. *The meaning of things: Domestic symbols and the self.* Cambridge, UK: Cambridge University Press.
13. Brian De Vries, John A. Blando, and Lawrence J. Walker. 1995. An exploratory analysis of the content and structure of the life review. In Haight, Barbara K. (Ed); Webster, Jeffrey Dean (Ed). (1995). The art and science of reminiscing: Theory, research, methods, and applications (pp. 123-137). Philadelphia, PA, US: Taylor & Francis.
14. Lina Dib, Daniela Petrelli, and Steve Whittaker. 2010. Sonic souvenirs: exploring the paradoxes of recorded sound for family remembering. In *Proc. Conf Computer supported cooperative work*, 391-400.
15. Erik Erikson. 1980. *Identity and the life cycle*. New York: Norton. (Original work published 1959).
16. Jennifer Fereday & Eimear Muir-Cochrane. 2006. Demonstrating rigor using thematic analysis: A hybrid approach of inductive and deductive coding and theme development. *International journal of qualitative methods*, *5*, 1: 80-92.
17. William Fitts. 1965. Manual for the Tennessee self-concept scale. *Nashville, TN: Counselor Recordings and Tests*.
18. David Frohlich & Rachel Murphy. 2000. The Memory Box. *Personal Ubiquitous Comput.* 4, 4:238-240.
19. Azriel Grysman, Robyn Fivush, Natalie A. Merrill, and Matthew Graci. 2016. The influence of gender and gender typicality on autobiographical memory across event types and age groups. *Memory & cognition* 44, 6: 856-868.
20. El Haj, Mohamad, Pascal Antoine, Jean Louis Nandrino, Marie-Christine Gély-Nargeot, and Stéphane Raffard. 2015. Self-defining memories during exposure to music in Alzheimer's disease. *International Psychogeriatrics* 27, 10: 1719-1730.
21. Richard Harper, Dave Randall, N. Smythe, C. Evans, L. Heledd, and R. Moore. 2007. Thanks for the memory." In *Proceedings of the 21st British HCI Conference* Volume *2*, 39-42.
22. Steve Hodges, Emma Berry & Ken Wood. 2001. SenseCam: A wearable camera that stimulates and rehabilitates autobiographical memory. *Memory*, *19,* 7: 685-696.
23. Karen Holtzblatt and Sandra Jones. 1995. Conducting and analyzing a contextual interview. In *Readings in Human–Computer Interaction,* R.M. Baecker et al. (Eds). Morgan Kaufman. San Francisco. pp. 241-253.
24. Vaiva Kalnikaite, Abigail Sellen, Steve Whittaker & David Kirk. 2010. Now let me see where I was: understanding how lifelogs mediate memory. In *Proc. CHI* 2010, ACM Press, 2045-2054.
25. Matthew L. Lee and Anind K. Dey. 2007. Providing good memory cues for people with episodic memory impairment. In *Proc. Conference on computers and accessibility*. ACM, New York, NY, USA, 131-138.
26. Meike Kroneisen, Edgar Erdfelder and Axel Buchner. 2013. The proximate memory mechanism underlying the survival-processing effect: Richness of encoding or interactive imagery? *Memory*, *21*(4), pp.494-502.

27. Siân Lindley & Jayne Wallace. 2015. Placing in age: Transitioning to a new home in later life. *ACM Transactions on Computer-Human Interaction (TOCHI)* 22, 4: 20.
28. Pénélope Martinelli, Adèle Anssens, Marco Sperduti, and Pascale Piolino. 2013. The influence of normal aging and Alzheimer's disease in autobiographical memory highly related to the self. *Neuropsychology* 27, 1: 69-79.
29. William Odom, Richard Harper, Abigail Sellen, David Kirk, and Richard Banks. 2010. Passing on & putting to rest: understanding bereavement in the context of interactive technologies. In *Proc. Conference on Human Factors in Computing Systems*, 1831-1840.
30. William Odom, Abigail Sellen, Richard Harper & Eno Thereska. 2012. Lost in translation: Understanding the possession of digital things in the cloud. In *Proc. Conf. on Human Factors in Computing Systems*, 781–790.
31. William Odom, Abigail Sellen, David. Kirk, Richard. Banks, Tim Regan, Mark Selby, Juddi Forlizzi, and John Zimmerman. 2014. Designing for slowness, anticipation and re-visitation: A long term field study of the photobox. In *Proc. CHI'2014*, 1961–1970.
32. William Odom, John Zimmerman, and Jodi Forlizzi. 2011. Teenagers and their virtual possessions: design opportunities and issues. In *Proc. Conference on Human Factors in Computing Systems*, 1491-1500.
33. Jennifer Pals. 2006. Narrative identity processing of difficult life experiences: Pathways of personality development and positive self-transformation in adulthood. *Journal of personality* 74, 4: 1079-1110.
34. Daniela Petrelli, Steve Whittaker, and Jens Brockmeier. 2008. AutoTopography: what can physical mementos tell us about digital memories? In *Proc. Human Factors in Computing Systems*, ACM, 53-62.
35. Clare Rathbone, Chris Moulin, J. and Martin Conway. 2008. Self-centred memories: The reminiscence bump and the self. *Memory and Cognition, 36, 8:*1403-1414.
36. Clare Rathbone, Chris Moulin, J. and Martin Conway, A. 2009. Autobiographical memory and amnesia: Using conceptual knowledge to ground the self. *Neurocase, 15,* 5: 405-418.
37. Corina Sas, Scott Challioner, Christopher Clarke, Ross Wilson, Alina Coman, Sarah Clinch, Mike Harding, and Nigel Davies. 2015. Self-defining memory cues: creative expression and emotional meaning. In *Extended Abstracts on Human Factors in Computing Systems*, 2013-2018.
38. Corina Sas, Shuang Ren, Alina Coman, Sarah Clinch, and Nigel Davies. 2016. Life Review in End of Life Care: A Practitioner's Perspective. In *Extended Abstracts on Human Factors in Computing Systems* 2947-2953
39. Corina Sas, Karen Wisbach, and Alina Coman. 2017. Craft-based Exploration of Sense of Self. In *Extended Abstracts on Human Factors in Computing Systems*, 2891-2899.
40. Corina Sas & Steve Whittaker. 2013. Design for forgetting: disposing of digital possessions after a breakup. In *Proc. Conf. on Human Factors in Computing Systems*, 1823-1832.
41. Corina Sas, Steve Whittaker, and John Zimmerman. 2016. Design for Rituals of Letting Go: An Embodiment Perspective on Disposal Practices Informed by Grief Therapy. *ACM Trans. Comput.-Hum. Interact.* 23, 4: 1-37.
42. Constantine Sedikides &Marilynn Brewer. 2015. *Individual self, relational self, collective self.* Psychology Press.
43. Abigail J. Sellen, Andrew Fogg, Mike Aitken, Steve Hodges, Carsten Rother, and Ken Wood. 2007. Do life-logging technologies support memory for the past? In *Proc. CHI '07*, ACM Press, 81-90.
44. Abigail J. Sellen, and Steve Whittaker. 2010. Beyond total capture: a constructive critique of lifelogging. *Communications of the ACM* 53, 5, 70-77.
45. Jefferson Singer, Blerim Rexhaj, and Jenna Baddeley. 2007. Older, wiser, and happier? Comparing older adults' and college students' self-defining memories. *Memory* 15, 8: 886-898.
46. Jefferson Singer & Peter Salovey. 1993. The remembered self. New York: Free Press.
47. Kylie Sutherland & Richard A. Bryant. 2005. Self-defining memories in post-traumatic stress disorder. *British Journal of Clinical Psychology* 44, 4: 591-598.
48. Avril Thorne & Kate McLean. 2001. Manual for coding events in self-defining memories. Unpublished manuscript, University of California, Santa Cruz.
49. Avril Thorne, Kate C. McLean, and Amy M. Lawrence. 2004. When Remembering Is Not Enough: Reflecting on Self-Defining Memories in Late Adolescence. *Journal of personality* 72, 3: 513-542.
50. Carol Tubbs & Margaret Drake. *Crafts and creative media in therapy*. Slack Incorporated, 2007.
51. Endel Tulving and Thomson Donald. 1973. Encoding specificity and retrieval processes in episodic memory. *Psychological Review*, 80, 5: 352-373.
52. Doménique van Gennip, Elise van den Hoven, and Panos Markopoulos. 2015. Things That Make Us Reminisce: Everyday Memory Cues as Opportunities for Interaction Design. In *Proc. Conf. Human Factors in Computing Systems*, 3443-3452.
53. Elise van den Hoven. 2004. *Graspable Cues for Everyday Recollecting.* PhD thesis, Technische Universiteit Eindhoven, The Netherlands.

54. Elise van den Hoven & Berry Eggen. 2005. Personal souvenirs as ambient intelligent objects. In Proceedings of the 2005 joint conference on Smart objects and ambient intelligence: innovative context-aware services: usages and technologies, 123-128. ACM.

55. Elise van den Hoven and Berry Eggen. 2009. The effect of cue media on recollections. *Human Technology: An Interdisciplinary Journal on Humans in ICT Environments* 5, 1:47-67.

56. Elise van den Hoven and Berry Eggen. 2015. The cue is key. *Zeitschrift für Psychologie* 222, 2: 110-117

57. Elise van den Hoven, Corina Sas, and Steve Whittaker. 2012. Introduction to this special issue on designing for personal memories: past, present, and future. *Human–Computer Interaction* 27, 1-2: 1-12.

58. Huy Viet Le, Sarah Clinch, Corina Sas, Tilman Dingler, Niels Henze, and Nigel Andrew Justin Davies. 2016. Impact of video summary viewing on episodic memory recall: design guidelines for video summarizations, In *Proc. Human Factors in Computing Systems*, 4793-4805.

59. Jayne Wallace, Anja Thieme, Gavin Wood, Guy Schofield, and Patrick Olivier. 2012. Enabling self, intimacy and a sense of home in dementia: an enquiry into design in a hospital setting. In *Proc. Human Factors in Computing Systems*, 2629-2638. ACM.

60. David West, Aaron Quigley, Judy Kay. 2007. Memento: A digital-physical scrapbook for memory sharing. *Personal and Ubiquitous Computing* 11, 4: 313-328.

Making Grooves With Needles: Using e-textiles to encourage gender diversity in embedded audio systems design

Rebecca Stewart
School of Electronic Engineering and Computer Science
Queen Mary University of London
London, UK
rebecca.stewart@qmul.ac.uk

Sophie Skach
School of Electronic Engineering and Computer Science
Queen Mary University of London
London, UK
s.skach@qmul.ac.uk

Astrid Bin
Adam Lab & Center for Music Technology
Georgia Institute of Technology
Atlanta, Georgia, USA
a.bin@gatech.edu

ABSTRACT
Historically, women have been excluded from engineering and computer science disciplines, and interactive audio is no exception. Relatively few women are involved with the designing and building of embedded audio systems with traditional tools such as microprocessors, but when embedded audio systems are built using e-textiles, much larger proportions of women become engaged with technology. In this paper we review theories for this gender disparity and the barriers women face in working with audio technology, and then present a comparison of survey data between an e-textile audio workshop and an audio platform user group. Extrapolating from the case study and the surveyed literature, we propose that flexibility in learning, communal dissemination of knowledge, and gendering of tools are prominent reasons why women engage with technology via e-textiles.

ACM Classification Keywords
H.5.5 Sound and Music Computing: Systems; J.5 Arts and Humanities: Performing Arts; K.4 Computers and Society; K.7 The Computing Profession

Author Keywords
Embedded audio; e-textiles; gender

INTRODUCTION
Significantly fewer women than men participate in the designing and building of embedded interactive audio systems [31, 14, 11, 16, 4, 3, 15]. Contrastingly, electronic textiles (e-textiles) such as the sensor in Figure 1 have historically attracted the engagement of proportionally more women and girls than men and boys, particularly within hand-crafting contexts [6, 7].

Figure 1. E-textile stretch sensor.

Despite a lack of women involved in building audio applications, e-textiles — a practice that includes far more women — have a long history of being used for building audio applications. Noting this disparity, we are examining e-textile practices in order to increase the participation of women in building interactive audio applications.

This paper is in four parts. First, we explore the barriers to participation faced by women in audio technology, in order to understand why this gender disparity exists, and how e-textile practice has the potential to effectively address it. Second, we survey e-textile practice, and consider the nature and history of e-textile practice through a gendered lens. Third, we present a case study of an e-textile audio workshop, and consider the outcomes reported through participant surveys. Finally, we discuss why women may choose to participate in audio technology through e-textiles due to its knowledge formation,

DIS'18, June 9–13, 2018, Hong Kong

ISBN 978-1-4503-5198-0/18/06... $15.00
DOI: http://dx.doi.org/10.1145/3196709.3196716

community, and tools, and how this can inform strategies to encourage wider diversity of participation.

BARRIERS TO WOMEN IN AUDIO TECHNOLOGY

Audio technology refers to the intersection of computer science and electrical engineering with sound generation, analysis, and transmission. This term is also more generally used to describe all sounds, while *music technology* usually refers to only musical sounds (excluding sounds like speech or sound effects). However, both terms are often used interchangeably to refer to the same tools and communities, and both denote interdisciplinary fields drawing on music and engineering. Examples include human-computer interfaces for digital musical instruments, the design of algorithms that create sound, and using software and hardware to control sound. Within academia, university degrees and research labs addressing the same topics could be found in either music or electrical engineering and computer science departments [3].

Women and girls are underrepresented in every aspect of audio technology including academic communities [14, 11], professional music production [16, 31], students enrolled in music technology degrees [4, 3, 31], composers utilising music technology [15] and semi-professional or professional developers of audio technology outside academia [1].

Audio technology is not immune from the social context shaping the broader fields of engineering and computer science, and there is a large body of science and technology studies (STS) documenting ways in which young girls through to grown women are discouraged from being the designers and builders of technology. For example, the way programming is taught can discourage women if they don't conform to certain cultural norms [38]. These do not have to be intentional actions; even the placement of objects in a shared space can discourage women if those objects are associated with a culture that women do not identify with or belong to [10]. This effect remains in place even if there are only women in that shared space.

As audio technology has matured as a field in its own right, STS has focused directly on the gender imbalance that pervades every aspect of it. Born et al. [4] present a thorough analysis of music technology within higher education, and lay out a number of explanations for why girls choose not to even apply to universities to study music technology (such as the explicit and implicit messages that girls are less technically-adept than boys and technology is a masculine pursuit).

Within audio technology culture, there are still gendered cues that indicate women don't belong there, from the language used to describe technical concepts ("punch in", "kill a track") to the violent and sexualized content of advertisements for audio equipment [17]. Far more overt forms of sexism still exist, as well such as sexual harassment and assault [16].

ENGAGEMENT WITH ELECTRONICS AND COMPUTING THROUGH E-TEXTILES

We will first introduce core e-textile technologies along with the community of e-textile practitioners. We will then look at the field's relationship to audio technology.

Introduction to E-Textiles

E-textiles are electrical circuitry made of conductive threads and/or fabrics. The most commonly used threads are metallized by nano-plating or wrapping non-conductive core threads, but yarns can also be constructed by spinning staple fibers with metal fibers similar to how wool yarns are produced. Conductive polymers electro-spun into fibers or used to coat non-conductive textiles are another method commonly employed [28]. There are a number of resources that more thoroughly document the state-of-the-art of e-textiles than is possible here, including [37, 12, 30].

Conductive textile structures can be formed from these yarns by undergoing traditional textile processes such as weaving or knitting. These more complex structures can exhibit particular electrical properties that mean they can be used as sensors, such as a change in resistance when a knit is stretched [36].

Capacitive sensing to detect touch or proximity is another popular sensing technique as it can be constructed using a variety of textile processes. It is particularly effective when combined with digital embroidery where a computer-controlled sewing machine can precisely place conductive threads on non-conductive fabric (see [27, 21]).

E-textiles are more commonly found as sensors or the interconnections between components in a circuit, but they can also perform as actuators. Two such examples are fabrics dyed with thermochromic dyes that change color when electrical current heats the underlying conductive yarn [2] and conductive threads or fabrics acting as voice coils within loudspeakers [25].

Currently, non-textile components are included in e-textile circuitry. Components such as batteries and microcontrollers are not yet available in textile form factors (though there is ongoing work to adapt electronic packages to better integrate directly into yarns [29]). As a result, a number of applications have emerged to make the integration of hard components and soft circuity easier, such as the Arduino Lilypad, a microcontroller that can be sewn into textile applications and runs on a small 3V battery.

The Lilypad Arduino by Buechley introduced sewable pads on PCBs (Printable Circuit Boards) for connections to components like microcontrollers [6]. Its adaptation of traditional PCB manufacturing to accommodate sewn conductive thread allowed it to be produced at scale and be commercially available to professional and hobbyist embedded electronics engineers, opening up e-textile development to those outside academic research labs [7]. The core features of the sewable pads of the Lilypad have been integrated into other e-textiles products such as the Flora by Adafruit, seen in Figure 2.

E-Textile Practitioners

Women have been active researchers in e-textiles since its founding, with the research by Orth and her colleagues recognized as the first publications in the field. They developed novel applications for textile interfaces embroidered with conductive threads and adapted existing fabrics that happened to have conductive properties into circuit substrates [26, 27].

Figure 2. Adafruit Flora microcontroller in an e-textile circuit with conductive fabrics and thread. The Flora iterates on the open source design of the Lilypad using the same sewable connections on the PCB.

Buechley's pioneering contributions through the design and sale of the Lilypad greatly expanded the demographics of who was working with embedded electronics. The Lilypad was created with diversity, and gender diversity in particular, in mind [6]. It built on the Arduino platform, an open source and low cost microcontroller platform designed to be accessible for those with little or no formal education in electrical engineering. The Lilypad made it simpler for users to connect e-textile sensors to a microcontroller allowing those who already worked with textiles such as fashion designers or artists to integrate electronics into their projects with greater ease than ever before.

The Lilypad was immediately successful at engaging women in building and designing their own electronics. Within a few years of the commercial release, Buechley and her research team investigated who was buying and using Lilypads. They found significantly more women were working with Lilypad than the standard Arduino board [7]. When looking at Arduino projects documented online, they found that women were the creators behind 65% of the projects using the LilyPad and only 2% of the projects using an Arduino board other than the LilyPad. When looking at sales figures from the primary retailer of the Lilypad, they found that female customers were more likely to purchase a Lilypad, when buying an Arduino microcontroller board.

On the back of the mainstream success of the Lilypad, e-textiles were quickly becoming a pedagogical tool within schools for teaching engineering and computer science coupled with art and design. The topic was found to attract more girls in after-school clubs such as the one described in [6]. The 10 participants that volunteered to take part consisted of 9 girls and 1 boy, with the boy having more previous computing experience than the girls. This proportion of female to male participants and their respective prior experiences with technology were repeatedly found in other workshops, whether with students in formal educational environments or adults outside of universities [40, 9, 8].

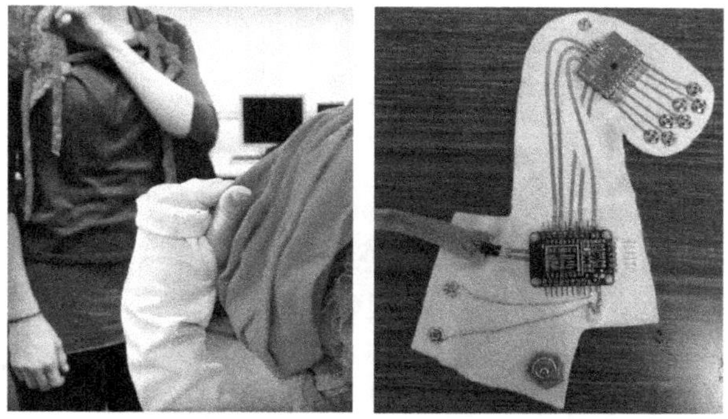

Figure 3. (Left) Touch-detecting wearable audio interfaces integrated into dancers costumes and (right) a portion of the embedded e-textile circuitry from the same interface.

As the Maker Movement grew with technologies like the Arduino platform and domestic 3D printers, hobbyist and semi-professional engineers, designers, and artists were sharing their expertise and experimentation with e-textiles online. Artistic duo Kobakant [1] became significant organizers and contributors to the e-textile community. Their website "How to Get What You Want" and their series of eTextile Summer Camps are resources and networks that are central to the community [32].

E-Textiles and Audio

E-textiles have long been used to sense, control, and generate audio. Much of Orth's groundbreaking work creating e-textile interfaces centered around musical controllers, most notably her MIDI jacket which used capacitive sensing to detect when digitally embroidered motifs were touched [27]. Later work by researchers at Virginia Tech combined weaving with audio signal processing to build large lengths of cloth that could determine the location of passing objects like cars [23].

E-textiles are well-suited for wearable applications as they can be directly integrated into clothing more comfortably than PCBs. This makes them ideal for embodied audio performances as the electronics can form part of the costumes that the performers wear. One such example can be seen in Figure 3 where e-textile capacitive touch sensors are worn by dancers to trigger audio samples [34].

Alongside wearable applications, e-textiles have been a popular technology for creating malleable objects where the ability to stretch or squeeze the object controls the generated audio. Examples include a touch-sensitive embroidered map that plays sounds from that places the embroidery illustrates [21], a pressure and proximity sensitive fabric keyboard [41]; and a multi-touch cloth as a control surface for audio synthesis [13].

WORKSHOP CASE STUDY

Now that we have explored the barriers to participation faced by women in audio technology and the history of e-textile practice through a gendered lens, we present a case study of an e-textile audio workshop, and consider the findings from a series of surveys. In order to more closely examine the barriers for women wishing to develop audio interfaces, we

[1] http://www.kobakant.at

Figure 4. Bela on a fabric breakout circuit board as used in the e-textile workshop.

Figure 5. Group of workshop participants working together on their collaborative project.

examine the responses gathered via two different surveyed groups. Both sets of surveys look at using Bela[2] in embedded audio projects [19]. Bela is a computing platform designed for real-time embedded audio applications. Beginning as a university research project, Bela has evolved into a commercial product with a community of approximately 700 developers [22].

We will refer to as the first surveyed group as the *Bela community*. In June 2017 the Bela team conducted an online user survey to gather data on who was using the platform and how they were interacting with it. This survey was advertised online through the Bela user forum, mailing list and social media accounts and gathered 251 responses.

The second surveyed group will be referred to as the *e-textile workshop participants*. In November 2017 a one-day workshop was held during an electronic music and art festival in the UK [3]. The workshop was advertised as an e-textiles workshop for creating wearable audio interfaces using Bela and handmade fabric sensors. The workshop had 15 attendees in total; 11 of those attendees completed an online pre-workshop survey and 5 completed an online post-workshop survey. The pre- and post-workshop surveys were structured identically to the *Bela community* survey, with additional questions to account for working with textiles.

Workshop Activities

During the workshop the participants were introduced to some of the materials commonly used in e-textiles and taught how to build textile switches, stretch and pressure sensors. Conductive fabrics and yarns (e.g. silver coated fabrics or stainless steel fibers), as well as resistive materials were used to make textile circuits and sensors.

The participants were then shown how to use the data generated by the sensors to control sounds through editing the code running on the Bela, using the browser-based integrated development environment (IDE). Bela was connected to a fabric breakout circuit board so that conductive textile cables prepared for the workshop could be easily snapped into place to allow for rapid prototyping. (Figure 4 shows the Bela on a fabric breakout circuit board; a more detailed technical description of the system can be found in [35]. During the second half of the workshop, participants designed and prototyped projects using the provided kit and materials. They were encouraged to collaborate and to share different skill sets, helping each other with either textile-making techniques or programming skills.

As there were 5 Bela kits for the 15 participants to share, group sizes varied from 2 to 4 participants. Figure 5 shows one of the groups of four. Each group had the same equipment available, which consisted of fabric snap connectors to link the sensors to the Bela breakout board, as well as sewing needles and a variety of conductive yarns and fabrics. There was also a sewing machine and iron available for use. Participants were asked to bring their own laptops to work on the programming sketches that allowed testing of the sensors (these sketches were prepared in advance and shared with attendees by the workshop organizers).

Community Demographics

Though the *workshop participants* are a smaller sample set than the survey of the *Bela community*, we are able to compare their demographic and previous experiences to the larger audio technology community and to previously documented e-textile workshops. The age demographics of both the broader *Bela community* and the *workshop participants* were quite similar. Both ranged from 18 to over 55 years old, with representation from every grouping of five years. Both groups had slightly more representation from respondents in their 30s than the other age bands.

While there were similarities with age distribution, there were significant differences between the two surveys when comparing gender. The respondents to the *Bela community* user survey were overwhelmingly male with 92% (232) identifying as male, 4% (9) as female, and 4% (9) who preferred to not say. The survey did not ask if their gender matched the one they were assigned at birth. This roughly aligns with other measures of gendered participation in the audio technology community such as 3% of the board members and 6% of the

[2] `https://bela.io`

[3] `http://algomech.com/2017/`

authors of a prominent conference being women [11], though is lower than other reported figures of 15% women when considering audio technology within the entertainment industry [16].

Of the 11 respondents to the pre-workshop survey of the *e-textile workshop participants*, 82% (9) identified as female and 18% (2) as male with all but one respondent confirming their current gender is the one assigned them at birth. One respondent preferred to not say whether their gender was the same as the one assigned at birth. (Anecdotally, this is representative of the e-textile workshops that the first author has led and is similar to other workshops described in the literature [6].)

Prior Experience

From the pre-workshop *e-textile workshop participants* survey (N=11), no attendees indicated any experience working with the Bela platform before attending the workshop, but they did have experience with other electronics and coding platforms: 91% (10) had worked with Arduino and 27% (3) with the Raspberry Pi. 27% (3) had experience with audio-specific software, such as Max/MSP or PureData. One workshop attendee said they had no prior experience with coding or electronics, while 45% (5) had completed degrees or were currently university students in computer science or digital arts courses. The rest had limited experience with coding and electronics, largely through "tinkering" at home.

Generally, the *Bela community* had more experience with a variety of embedded computing platforms than the *e-textile workshop participants*, but a similar proportion had exposure to maker platforms: 80% (201) of the *Bela community* and 67% (10) of the *workshop participants* had used Arduino.

There were differences between the groups in self-reported expertise: 9% of the *Bela community* who had experience with Arduino considered themselves to be experts, whereas no *workshop participants* with Arduino experience considered themselves experts. Further, where one *workshop participant* considered themselves expert in Max/MSP (out of 10 suggested languages), 54% (137) of the *Bela community* considered themselves expert in at least one out of the same set of languages.

However, the *e-textile workshop participants* identified their expertise in e-textiles, with 64% (7) of survey respondents citing at least some experience. The skill sets that related to textiles focused on hand craft, such as hand embroidery, knitting, or crochet.

Even though 55% (6) of the *workshop participants* had formal educational qualifications in textiles at the undergraduate or graduate level, and an additional 27% (3) participants had years of experience in pattern making, weaving, printing, knitting or crocheting, only one person identified themselves expert in a textile-related discipline. Though this group had fewer formal qualifications in textiles than in computing, this was not reflected in their survey responses as their self-reported expertise tended to focus on textiles and not technology.

Additionally, 3 of the 7 *e-textile workshop participants* that confirmed they had previous experience with e-textiles had also taught e-textiles skills in other workshops.

Motivation

Both groups were asked to identify themselves from a list of descriptors, including musician, programmer, maker, instrument builder, researcher, visual artist, educator, hardware developers and visual artists. Respondents could select more than one descriptor.

The *Bela community* identified themselves as musicians (79%, 198), programmers (63%, 158), makers (55%, 139), instrument builders (54%, 136), researchers (43%, 109), educators (32%, 80), hardware developers (25%, 62), and visual artists (18%, 46).

Of the *e-textile workshop participants*, 33% (8) identified as makers, 21% (5) as researchers, 13% (3) as visual artists, 8% (2) as programmers, as well as 1 musician and 1 instrument builder. None identified as hardware developer. When asked why the attendees chose to attend the workshop, 90% (10) cited gaining skills (textile, technical or general) as their motivation for participating.

Workshop Outputs

The workshop's primary activity was to design sensors for an embodied sound performance. Most participants worked on accessories like a headband or glove instead of a larger garment. Two groups achieved their goal of creating a wearable sensor network that could be worn on the body, including the Bela attached via snaps or sewn pockets[4].

The sensors that were built on the day were mostly made in the first half of the workshop, when basic e-textile techniques were taught. To accomplish these basic skills and techniques (making switches and pressure sensors, as well as connecting sensors to Bela), *e-textile workshop participants* reported to having needed only little or no guidance. More guidance was needed when integrating the self made sensors in garments or accessories and working with Bela code to process the measured sensor data.

Discussion of Survey Results

There were significant differences in the survey responses of the two groups, but also notable similarities. Each group had a similar age distribution, and though the *Bela community* had more experience with different technology platforms, the *e-textile workshop participants* were experienced with two of those platforms most commonly used in maker communities.

The most obvious difference was gender, as the *Bela community* was predominantly male, and the *e-textile workshop participants* predominantly female. This imbalance suggests that though the outcomes of interactive, sensor-based audio applications are common to both groups, the Bela platform does not attract female users in the same way as a craft-based workshop.

[4]Different items of clothing for both upper and lower body were provided by the organizers.

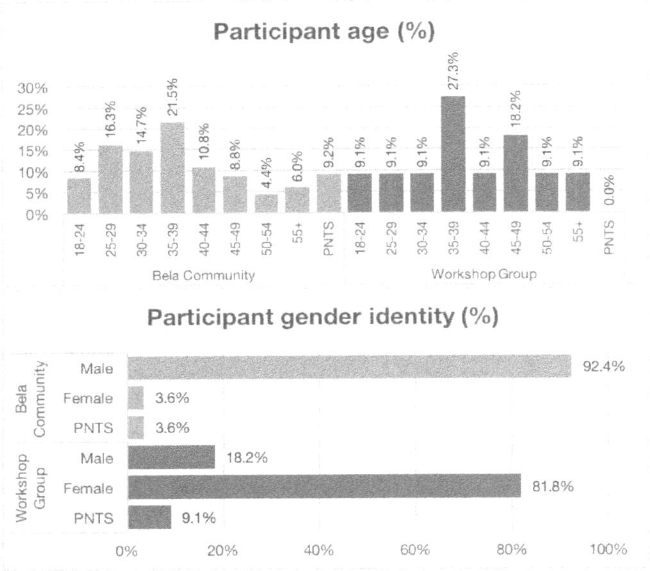

Figure 6. Visualisation of participant data, Bela community survey vs e-textile workshop participants. Top: Ages of participants. Bottom: Gender identity of participants. (PNTS = Prefer Not To Say)

The members of both groups also identified their motivations differently. Though a similar proportion of both groups chose the descriptor maker, the *Bela community* also predominantly identified as musicians and programmers. As well as makers, the *e-textile workshop participants* also identified as researchers and visual artists.

Though no detailed conclusions can be extrapolated from this data given the small sample size, it does suggest that the female-dominated *e-textile workshop participants* are motivated by exploration, while the male-dominated *Bela community* is motivated by task. This is not to suggest that music creation is not exploratory or creative, but rather that the Bela system is viewed more as a tool that can be used, rather than a starting point for open-ended exploration.

Overall the *e-textile workshop participants* did not express confidence in their expertise in any of the technical platforms listed in the survey (with the exception of one attendee who is a professional software developer), while showing more confidence in their textile skills. This did not correlate with the professional qualifications of the group as there were more individuals with university-level computing experience than textile. This could be indicative of women feeling less confident in expressing technical expertise, though this is again stated cautiously as this is a small sample size.

An interesting observation of the *e-textile workshop participants* is that though learning and skill development was listed as a motivator, we observed that participants tended to stay within the fields of practice in which they were already confident (knitters, for example, concentrated on making textile sensors rather than trying out new software to process sensor data), and few tried out techniques they hadn't used before. When experimentation did take place, it appeared that participants with more technical experience were willing to experiment with textile and craft related skills and techniques they had not yet mastered. However, those with craft experience and technical knowledge did not tend to extend their knowledge of software or programming.

Expecting to provide the participants with a sufficient grounding in an audio programming language unfamiliar to most of them is an overly ambitious goal for a single-day workshop, though this trend is still notable. It may be because those with craft skills consider technical skills to be intimidating or that they simply don't know where to start, and those with technical skills might consider crafting something that is low-risk and experimental and are therefore more willing to try. This is a particularly salient finding that requires more study, as understanding the perceptions of technical and craft skills by non-experts in both domains may provide important insights into how technical tools might incorporate styles of learning and using that support a user base with a more diverse range of experiences and abilities. This is examined further in the following section.

MOVING BEYOND 'WOMEN JUST LIKE TO SEW'

It has been demonstrated both in the workshop presented here and the many others that came before it documented in the literature [6, 9, 8, 40] that women and girls want to learn how to work with electronics and code to build audio interfaces of their own design. However, they are not easily found within the various academic, hobbyist and professional established audio technology communities. The introduction of e-textiles to audio technology drastically and consistently changes the gender representation with women outnumbering men.

In this section we explore why this occurs, and move beyond overly simplistic tropes such as "girls like to sew" or "women like knitting". Further, we examine the opportunities that textile practice presents and the barriers they may remove for underrepresented groups within audio technology. We identify three themes that have emerged: flexibility in learning; communal dissemination of knowledge; and gendering of tools.

Flexibility in Learning

Turkle proposes that one of the contributing factors to the lack of women in computer science is the stringent requirements in how skills like programming are learned [38, 39]. There is little accommodation for anyone who does not relate to computers in a way that aligns with the existing technical culture, and common pedagogical approaches. We propose that one of the attractions to e-textiles for women is that field is still relatively young; there isn't a 'right' or 'wrong' way, as long as the desired output is achieved.

Turkle and Papert argue for *epistemological pluralism* where different methods of thinking and learning are valued [39]. This fights against what is called in technology start-ups as "culture fit", where arriving at the correct answer is not sufficient if the steps taken to arrive at that answer did not follow the accepted model. They propose broadening computer science education by encouraging a *bricolage* approach to building knowledge by arranging and rearranging well-known concepts. They emphasize "playing around" and treating code elements as physical materials, sometimes literally by using code to alter the physical world through robotics. This pluralistic approach has directly impacted e-textile development, as Buechley et al. [6] reference the modular style of the robotics kit designed by Papert as a design consideration for the Lilypad, which brought bricolage to e-textiles and microcontrollers.

Epistemological pluralism addresses how an individual learns, but McCartney [18] discusses what feminist epistemologist Code calls "second personhood" within the context of electroacoustic audio. Code proposes that second persons inform how knowledge is created through empathetic knowledge and ecological thinking as opposed to "spectator epistemologies" — colloquially, "bouncing ideas off each other" as a method for the formation of knowledge. Hand crafting textiles are rooted in social interactions between women, and, as will be discussed in the next section, second personhood is a foundation of e-textile culture.

As women are less likely to pursue formal educations in computer science or electrical engineering fields, they need to use alternative educational routes to learn programming or circuit design. Resources like Kobakant's "How to Get What You Want" are one option, but peer-led community workshops are another. We saw this in our workshop attendees with the 3 of the 7 attendees with previous experience in e-textiles having already taught e-textiles skills in other workshop settings.

We suggest that women will engage with technology when it is taught in workshops set within social contexts where attendees are encouraged to interact with and learn from each other. Workshops should include activities that allow for creative exploration and which encourage combining presented concepts in new ways in order to facilitate a deeper understanding.

Communal Knowledge Dissemination

The communal nature of textile crafting is one that has directly influenced e-textiles. Kobakant have grown the e-textile community through virtual and physical activities. Their website "How to Get What You Want" and the eTextile Summer Camps described above have provided a set of central resources for both technical and social cohesion [32].

Workshops are an essential means of transmitting craft knowledge while reinforcing relationships, and can be used as a means to conduct research [33]. They have been used to evaluate e-textiles tools and pedagogy since the development of the Lilypad and continue to be a core research tool [6, 8, 32, 9]. Workshops also serve as a primary means to disseminate information on best practices. In our workshop, connecting with community was declared an important component and sharing knowledge, networking and acquiring skills were named by participants as a motivation for attending the workshop.

In discussing the growth of the Bela platform, Morreale et al. use the term *pluggable communities* to describe how the Bela community has grown by connecting multiple disparate communities already working with audio technology to Bela [22], and cite social experts as key to transferring knowledge between disparate communities. We have found this holds true in this work, and that holding workshops such as ours, where audio, technical, and textile/crafts experts are brought together, allows not only for social experts to meet but also for connections to form and knowledge to be exchanged between their associated communities, which might otherwise have very little interaction.

Tools

Pluggable communities, as discussed in the previous section, center around common tools and toolchains. When those communities are strongly gendered, the associated tools are as well. Electrical engineers have a wide variety of tools designed for precise, specialized tasks. Complex spatial transformations and in-depth understanding of materials are required to realize a physical circuit from its abstract circuit diagram. This is true whether working with fiberglass boards coated with copper or stainless steel threads embroidered onto fabric. However, the tools used with each of those materials are associated with gendered communities. One set of tools and materials are deemed more "serious" and "scientific" than the other. Even though e-textiles have only recently given a reason for a sewing needle or crochet hook to be placed in an electronics lab, handcrafting textiles have long been qualified as a frivolous activity because of its association with women [24].

The gendering of tools is easily seen within mixed gender e-textiles workshops. Buchholz et al. [5] found that during their after-school workshop that boys and girls worked with their historically gendered tools: The girls handled the textile crafting tools like needles and scissors 80% of the time, while the boys handled the electronics tools like the multimeter 75% of the time. We also observed this within two of the groups in our workshop where there was mixed gender collaborations. The men in both groups performed all programming activities while the women hand stitched or crocheted. For gender parity to take place, the gendered nature of tools needs to be challenged, and space needs to be provided for women to assert control over electronics and technical tools, as well as for men to feel comfortable with tools of sewing and crafting.

The tools available to complete a task have the ability to assist or hinder that task, and embedded audio for e-textiles has been limited by the available tools. The Lilypad microcontroller (along with its later iterations such as Adafruit's Flora) has limited processing power that is not designed for audio signal processing. It is only capable of simple tones and beeps unless peripheral hardware is used that can process mp3 files, for example, or the application is connected to a a computer where more complicated processing can take place. This lack of powerful e-textile platforms greatly limits the embedded audio technology systems that can be developed using textile practices.

We addressed this by creating a fabric breakout circuit board for Bela that was used in our workshop (see Figure 4). This breakout provided an easy way to embed a powerful system in a craft application. In this way, we are providing tools that encourage a wider diversity of techniques to be used in creating novel interactive audio systems, by providing a method of interfacing with a powerful system capable of much richer sound possibilities than those that are currently used.

CONCLUSION

Women have historically been excluded from engineering and computer science disciplines, including those involving audio. Relatively few women in proportion to men are involved with the designing and building of embedded audio systems, whether looking at students within school or university education, professionals, or hobbyists. However, the field of e-textiles regularly attracts women and girls in disproportionate numbers to other technical disciplines. When embedded audio systems are built using e-textiles, we see larger proportions of women becoming engaged compared to traditional code-based methods of creation. This implies that women are motivated to work with audio technologies, and we suggest that this is because the methods of working that e-textiles encourage remove, or let women overcome, the barriers that would otherwise prevent them from working with audio technology.

We began by reviewing explanations for this gender disparity and the barriers women face in working with audio technology. The culture surrounding engineering and computing both subtly implies and overtly states that they are inappropriate topics for girls. This influences what they choose to study and how to spend their free time. Outside of education, the environments where technology is designed and built are frequently unwelcoming — and sometimes hostile — for women. This is in contrast to textile-based communities of practice that generally are centered around women's work, even when technology is introduced via e-textiles.

We used an e-textile workshop as a case study to examine the demographics, previous experience, and motivations of the attendees. They learned how to design and build their own embedded audio systems with e-textiles, completing surveys before and after the workshop. We compared these responses to user survey responses from the Bela user community. Bela is the same embedded audio platform used in the e-textile workshop).

We found that the both groups had a similar age distribution, but that the *workshop participants* were overwhelmingly female with the *Bela community* almost entirely male. There were also differences in the way the two groups judged their expertise: the *Bela community* was more willing to consider themselves experts, while the *workshop participants*, despite significant formal education in electronics and computer science, only one participant identified as expert in any of the suggested programming languages or platforms. Further, the *Bela community* was far more confident in their technical abilities with more expertise in a variety of platforms, while the *workshop participants* felt their expertise was limited to textiles.

We identified three key themes from the observed workshop and the surveyed literature to aid in understanding what attracts women to engaging with audio technology within the context of e-textiles. E-textiles allows for multiple and more flexible methods of knowledge formation, brings technology to an already existing community, and utilizes gendered tools that provide space and confidence for women to exert expertise over men.

Both Buechley [7] and Turkle [39] discuss creating new communities around building technology that are designed for women, as opposed to asking women to fit into already established environments that work to exclude them. Focusing on materiality is one way to form these new technological communities. Paint, paper craft and woodworking can all be used to build circuitry, and these crafts each have their own communities and demographics. For example, painting and quilting workshops involving microcontrollers have drawn in an older demographic while for paper circuitry attracts women in similar proportions to e-textiles [20].

Though this study has produced intriguing findings related to gender, it only examines a narrow demographic. We have not discussed a multitude of additional factors that shape an individual's lived experience such ethnicity, immigration status, accessibility requirements, and a myriad of other influences. Future work should explore how the lessons learned from e-textile communities might be applied to encourage participation from other groups marginalised from technology, in order to increase the diversity of technical practice.

ACKNOWLEDGEMENTS

This research was supported by the Centre for Public Engagement at Queen Mary University of London and by the EPSRC and AHRC Centre for Doctoral Training in Media and Arts Technology (EP/L01632X/1).

The authors would like to thank the anonymous reviewers for their valuable comments, and the Bela development team for their support.

REFERENCES

1. Freida Abtan. 2016. Where Is She? Finding the Women in Electronic Music Culture. *Contemporary Music Review* 35, 1 (2016), 53–60. DOI: http://dx.doi.org/10.1080/07494467.2016.1176764
2. Joanna Berzowska and Marguerite Bromley. 2007. Soft Computation Through Conductive Textiles. *Program* 3 (2007), 1–12.
3. Georgina Born and Kyle Devine. 2015. Music technology, gender, and class: Digitization, educational and social change in Britain. *Twentieth-Century Music* 12, 2 (2015), 135–172. DOI: http://dx.doi.org/10.1017/S1478572215000018
4. Georgina Born and Kyle Devine. 2016. Gender, Creativity and Education in Digital Musics and Sound Art. *Contemporary Music Review* 35, 1 (2016), 1–20. DOI:http://dx.doi.org/10.1080/07494467.2016.1177255
5. Beth Buchholz, Kate Shively, Kylie Peppler, and Karen Wohlwend. 2014. Hands on, hands off: Gendered access in crafting and electronics practices. *Mind, Culture, and Activity* 21, 4 (2014), 278–297. DOI: http://dx.doi.org/10.1080/10749039.2014.939762
6. Leah Buechley, Mike Eisenberg, Jaime Catchen, and Ali Crockett. 2008. The LilyPad Arduino : Using Computational Textiles to Investigate Engagement , Aesthetics , and Diversity in Computer Science Education.

In *Proceeding of the 2008 CHI Conference on Human Factors in Computing Systems - CHI '08*. 423–432. DOI: http://dx.doi.org/10.1145/1357054.1357123

7. Leah Buechley and Benjamin Mako Hill. 2010. LilyPad in the wild: : how hardwareÊijs long tail is supporting new engineering and design communities. In *Proceedings of the 8th ACM Conference on Designing Interactive Systems - DIS '10*. 199–207. DOI: http://dx.doi.org/10.1145/1858171.1858206
8. Leah Buechley, Kylie Peppler, Michael Eisenberg, and Kafai Yasmin (Eds.). 2013. *Textile Messages: Dispatches from the World of E-Textiles and Education. New Literacies and Digital Epistemologies*. Peter Lang Publishing Group.
9. Leah Buechley and Hannah Perner-Wilson. 2012. Crafting technology: Reimagining the Processes, Materials, and Cultures of Electronics. *ACM Transactions on Computer-Human Interaction* 19, 3 (2012), 1–21. DOI:http://dx.doi.org/10.1145/2362364.2362369
10. Sapna Cheryan, Victoria C. Plaut, Paul G. Davies, and Claude M. Steele. 2009. Ambient Belonging: How Stereotypical Cues Impact Gender Participation in Computer Science. *Journal of Personality and Social Psychology* 97, 6 (2009), 1045–1060. DOI: http://dx.doi.org/10.1037/a0016239
11. Charlotte Desvages and Alex Wilson. 2017. *Gender Balance at DAFx (or lack thereof)*. Technical Report.
12. Tilak Dias (Ed.). 2015. *Electronic Textiles: Smart Fabrics and Wearable Technology*. Woodhead Publishing, Oxford.
13. Maurin Donneaud, Cedric Honnet, and Paul Strohmeier. 2017. Designing a Multi-Touch eTextile for Music Performances. In *Proceedings of the International Conference on New Interfaces for Musical Expression*. 7–12.
14. Emma Frid. 2017. Sonification of Women in Sound and Music Computing - The Sound of Female Authorship in ICMC , SMC and NIME .... In *Proceedings of the International Computer Music Conference*. Shanghai.
15. Elizabeth Hinkle-Turner. 2003. Women and music technology: Pioneers, precedents and issues in the United States. *Organised Sound* 8, 1 (2003), 31–47. DOI: http://dx.doi.org/10.1017/S1355771803001043
16. Marlene; Mathew, Jennifer; Grossman, and Areti Andreopoulou. 2016. Women in Audio: contributions and challenges in music technology and production. In *Proceeedings of the 141st Audio Engineering Society Convention*. 1–10.
17. Andra McCartney. 1995. Inventing Images: Constructing and Contesting Gender in Thinking about Electroacoustic. *Leonardo Music Journal* 5 (1995), 57–66.
18. Andra McCartney. 2006. Gender, Genre and Electroacoustic Soundmaking Practices. *Intersections: Canadian Journal of Music* 26, 2 (2006), 20–48. DOI: http://dx.doi.org/10.7202/1013224ar
19. Andrew McPherson. 2017. Bela: An embedded platform for low-latency feedback control of sound. *The Journal of the Acoustical Society of America* 141, 5 (2017), 3618.
20. David A Mellis, Sam Jacoby, Leah Buechley, Hannah Perner-wilson, and Jie Qi. 2013. Microcontrollers as material: crafting circuits with paper, conductive ink, electronic components, and an untoolkit. In *Proceedings of the 7th International Conference on Tangible, Embedded and Embodied Interaction*. 83–90. DOI: http://dx.doi.org/10.1145/2460625.2460638
21. Alessia Milo and Joshua D. Reiss. 2017. Aural Fabric : an interactive textile sonic map. In *Proceedings of the 12th International Audio Mostly Conference on Augmented and Participatory Sound and Music Experiences*. London, 37:1–37:5. DOI: http://dx.doi.org/10.1145/3123514.3123565
22. Fabio Morreale, Giulio Moro, Alan Chamberlain, Steve Benford, and Andrew P. McPherson. 2017. Building a Maker Community Around an Open Hardware Platform. In *Proceedings of the 2017 CHI Conference on Human Factors in Computing Systems - CHI '17*. 6948–6959. DOI:http://dx.doi.org/10.1145/3025453.3026056
23. Zahi Nakad, Mark Jones, Thomas Martin, and Ravi Shenoy. 2007. Using electronic textiles to implement an acoustic beamforming array: A case study. *Pervasive and Mobile Computing* 3, 5 (2007), 581–606. DOI: http://dx.doi.org/10.1016/j.pmcj.2007.02.003
24. Rozsika Parker. 2010. *The subversive stitch: Embroidery and the making of the feminine*. IB Tauris.
25. Hannah Perner-Wilson and Mika Satomi. 2012. The Crying Dress. (2012). http://www.kobakant.at/?p=222
26. E.R. Post and M. Orth. 1997. Smart fabric, or washable computing. *Digest of Papers. First International Symposium on Wearable Computers* (1997), 167–168. DOI:http://dx.doi.org/10.1109/ISWC.1997.629937
27. E. R. Post, M. Orth, P. R. Russo, and N. Gershenfeld. 2000. E-broidery: Design and fabrication of textile-based computing. *IBM Systems Journal* 39, 3.4 (2000), 840–860. DOI:http://dx.doi.org/10.1147/sj.393.0840
28. H. Qu and M. Skorobogatiy. 2015. Conductive polymer yarns for electronic textiles. In *Electronic Textiles*, Tilak Dias (Ed.). Elsevier Ltd., Chapter 2, 21–53. DOI: http://dx.doi.org/10.1016/B978-0-08-100201-8.00003-5
29. Anura Rathnayake and Tilak Dias. 2015. Yarns with embedded electronics. In *Proceedings of the 2015 ACM International Joint Conference on Pervasive and Ubiquitous Computing and Proceedings of the 2015 ACM International Symposium on Wearable Computers - UbiComp '15*. ACM Press, New York, New York, USA, 385–388. DOI: http://dx.doi.org/10.1145/2800835.2800919
30. Susan Elizabth Ryan. 2014. *Garments of Paradise: Wearable Discourse in the Digital Age*. MIT Press.

31. Natalie Sappleton, Sunrita Dhar-Bhattacharjee, Haifa Takruri-Rizk, and Rae Baezer. 2006. *WAVE-ing Goodbye to the Women? Explaining Gender Segregation in the Audio Video Industries*. Technical Report. 1–32 pages. http://aberdeen.ac.uk/wes2007/FullPapers/StreamJ/117.NatalieSappletonFP.doc

32. Mika Satomi and Hannah Perner-Wilson. 2011. Future master craftsmanship: where we want electronic textile crafts to go. In *The 17th International Symposium on Electronic Art ISEA 2011*. Istanb, 1–8.

33. Emma Shercliff and Amy Twigger Holroyd. 2016. Making with others: working with textile craft groups as a means of research. *Studies in Material Thinking* 14 (2016).

34. Kate Sicchio, Camille Baker, Tara Baoth Mooney, and Rebecca Stewart. 2016. Hacking the Body 2 . 0 : Flutter / Stutter. *Proceedings of the International Conference on Live Interfaces (ICLI '16)* (2016), 37–42.

35. Sophie Skach, Anna Xambó, Luca Turchet, Ariane Stolfi, Rebecca Stewart, and Mathieu Barthet. 2018. Embodied Interactions with E-Textiles and the Internet of Sounds for Performing Arts. In *In Proceedings of the 12th ACM Conference on Tangible, Embedded, and Embodied Interaction (TEI-18)*. Stockholm.

36. Rebecca Stewart and Sophie Skach. 2017. Initial Investigations into Characterizing DIY E-Textile Stretch Sensors. In *Proceedings of the 4th International Conference on Movement Computing (MOCO '17)*. ACM, New York, NY, USA, 1:1–1:4. DOI: http://dx.doi.org/10.1145/3077981.3078043

37. Matteo Stoppa and Alessandro Chiolerio. 2014. Wearable electronics and smart textiles: A critical review. *Sensors (Switzerland)* 14, 7 (2014), 11957–11992. DOI: http://dx.doi.org/10.3390/s140711957

38. Sherry Turkle. 1986. Computational Retitcience: Why Woman Fear The Intimate Machine. In *Technology and Woman's Voices*. Pegamon Press, New York, NY, USA, 41–61.

39. Sherry Turkle and Seymour Papert. 1991. Epistemological Pluralism and the Revaluation of the Concrete. In *Constructionism*. Chapter 0, 161–191. DOI: http://dx.doi.org/citeulike-article-id:513444

40. Anne Weibert, Andrea Marshall, Konstantin Aal, Kai Schubert, and Jennifer Rode. 2014. Sewing Interest in E-Textiles: Analyzing Making from a Gendered Perspective. In *Proceedings of the 2014 conference on Designing interactive systems - DIS '14*. 15–24. DOI: http://dx.doi.org/10.1145/2598510.2600886

41. Irmandy Wicaksono and Joseph A. Paradiso. 2017. FabricKeyboard : Multimodal Textile Sensate Media as an Expressive and Deformable Musical Interface. In *NIME*. 348–353. http://homes.create.aau.dk/dano/nime17/papers/0066/paper0066.pdf

Open Design, Inclusivity and the Intersections of Making

David Green
University of the West of England
Bristol, UK
david10.green@uwe.ac.uk

David Kirk
Northumbria University
Newcastle, UK
david.kirk@northumbria.ac.uk

ABSTRACT
This paper presents insights from an ethnographic study with a diverse population of *makers* in the city of Newcastle upon Tyne, UK. By engaging individuals, groups and communities who 'make' in different contexts, we reveal under-explored perspectives on 'making' and highlight points of intersection between different *kinds* of making across the city. We reflect on the dynamics of these intersections and connect our observations to emerging discourses around '*open design'*. In doing so, we argue for a renewed focus on 'inclusivity' and highlight a need for new infrastructure to support iterative, collaborative making within – and across – interconnected networks of makers.

Author Keywords
Making; Makers; Open Design; Diversity; Inclusivity; Ethnography; Documentary; Participatory Action Research;

ACM Classification Keywords
H.5.m. Information interfaces and presentation (e.g., HCI): Miscellaneous.

INTRODUCTION
The popular 'maker movement' is often considered to be an exemplar of progressive design values such as openness and collaboration [2, 10, 11, 16]. *Diversity* and *inclusivity* are recurrent themes in the related discourses [1, 17, 23, 38, 43, 60] and '*makerspaces*' (a.k.a. 'hacker-spaces', 'fab-labs', etc.) often extol these kinds of virtues in their formal manifestos/codes of practice [34]. Indeed, studies of makerspaces have tended to reveal supportive communities of co-operative, like-minded people [61, 63, 64, 65]. Yet to characterize 'making' as a unified movement in this way is to oversimplify a complex, multifaceted socio-technical phenomenon [39]. It is to risk overlooking critical nuances in the interactions and intersections between different *kinds* of makers, which might otherwise enrich interaction design work in this area.

There remains a shortage of perspectives from 'places of making' beyond the usual makerspaces, hacker spaces and fab-labs. Some notable exceptions include [45] and [61], but we are still missing insights from places such as home studios, industrial parks and educational facilities, where making takes many forms and reveals (often complex) making practices that complement 'maker culture' in interesting ways. Pioneering work by Lindtner et al [44], which has sought to overcome this challenge, concludes, "*we have to take seriously these* (alternative) *maker practices*", and there are calls for HCI to be visionary about building links with *"other sites of tech innovation*" [45]. In other words – we need to cast our nets wider.

DIS '18, June 9–13, 2018, Hong Kong

ACM ISBN 978-1-4503-5198-0/18/06.
https://doi.org/10.1145/3196709.3196718

A good example of why this is important is the *Fab City* movement [21], which envisions cities with distributed, responsive networks of *fab-labs.* This project reflects an intrinsic value of connecting maker networks; the potential for cross-pollinating ideas and sharing resources. However, there is a risk of tension if the project fails to reflect the diversity of existing maker networks. Perspectives from alternative, atypical and peripheral places of making are not always readily apparent, nor are their internal logics, their community interactions or the shape of their interactions with public-facing 'makerspaces'. In short, our current understanding of the nuanced inter-relationships and complex interactions between different *kinds of makers* in and across online and offline spaces is limited.

This research aims to contribute to an emerging body of work that acknowledges - and is taking steps to overcome - these gaps in our knowledge. In this paper, we present findings from an 8-month study that engaged diverse individuals, groups and communities from the city of Newcastle upon Tyne to explore liminal perspectives on making and points of intersection between different *kinds* of makers. We describe how this was achieved through mixed ethnographic methods (observations, interviews and workshops) and a co-creative, reflexive documentary project, drawing upon participatory action research methods to engage deeply with a diverse cross-section of makers from across the city.

Our contribution is twofold. Firstly, by presenting insights from the peripheries of the maker movement and exploring connections between makers, we are exposing under-researched concerns relating to interactions between different kinds of co-located makers. Secondly, by articulating connections between these concerns and the concept of 'open design', we are strengthening links to a highly relevant discourse that relates to both user-centered design and emerging strategies for digital fabrication. We conclude by advocating 'open design' as an agenda for inclusive making within – and across – networks of makers.

BACKGROUND

Interest in making (as a socio-technical phenomenon), and makers (as both users and creators of digital systems) has been growing steadily in HCI for several years [6]. A key point of focus for interaction design research has been self-identifying 'makers' (e.g. those in 'maker spaces') and the wider movements they align to (e.g. the global 'maker movement'). Another focal point has been the ways particular groups of users engage with particular 'maker technologies' (e.g. *Arduino*). Recent examples include studies with *skateboarders* [28] and *schoolchildren* [48], but such studies have engaged a diverse array of users. The research value of these studies is not in question. However, we are missing some important perspectives. These include people who 'make', but resist the 'maker' label; businesses who 'make', but not with/in makerspaces due to concerns about intellectual property (Hall's "*2-edged sword*" [33]); private or other non-public groups of 'makers' and/or institutions under pressure to be 'more open', (e.g. Universities, who balance public engagement with dedicated support for teaching/research) [11]. We have often considered 'makers' and 'non-makers', but we have tended to overlook *liminal* makers – those on the peripheries of maker culture. These kinds of makers are a sometimes-invisible part of 'maker culture' in-practice.

Different Kinds of *Makers*

The principles of *human-centered* and *user-centered design* remind us that, to design for human users of digital systems (thinking here about 'makers'), we must seek to understand them. This presents an immediate challenge because the terms we use to refer to 'makers' are both varied and flexible. For example, 'making' – like 'hacking' – can be applied to both digital and non-digital activities. These terms can also be ascribed to people with many different skills, abilities and needs, in many different contexts. Professional 'makers', for example, (e.g. industrial designers / mechanical engineers) might be concerned with career-development, profit margins, reputation and the logistics of supply chains and consumer demand in the context of their making practices. Hobbyist 'makers' on the other hand (e.g. garden-shed tinkerers / DIY enthusiasts) may be more concerned with the desire to balance personal enjoyment, disposable household income, shed-space, etc. Embracing this ambiguity, we adopt the term 'maker', both in our framing of this study and in our engagements with participants. We have done so *because* it is an ambiguous term, and inclusive of other labels (e.g. hacker, tinkerer, craftsperson, fabricator, inventor, engineer, designer, artist, artisan, etc), as well as people who do not self-identify in this way. As a principle of inclusivity, we contend that *anyone* can be a maker ([2] also notes, in a similar vein, "*we are all designers now*" (:53)). For the purposes of this study 'makers' are people involved in 'making' (the multifaceted socio-technological phenomenon), not just 'digital making'. In this study, makers include makerspace regulars, university technicians, industrial designers, support workers, administrators, professional engineers, and academic researchers. Our rationale for adopting this approach is that it is *inclusive*; we are interested in exploring interactions between the *different kinds of people involved in making* – not just 'makerspace' makers.

Different Kinds of *Making*

Empirical studies have been revealing of making practices within communities-of-practice, but they have been less revealing about the kinds of interactions *between* communities-of-practice. For example, by studying the interactions of skateboarders and digital fabrication technologies (or, indeed, between schoolchildren and digital fabrication technologies) we gain insights into making that may apply equally to other user-groups as well. However, we do not learn about how a set of shared resources might be used *across* these groups – for example.

A recent shift towards critically re-examining making is taking steps to overcome this by resisting the naïve and utopian thinking that can lead us to idealize makerspace cultures (indeed, [43, 58] explicitly urge caution against "*techno-solutionism*" [49]). An alternative idea within emerging critical discourses – that is now also gaining traction on-the-ground – is to tackle specific challenges with reference to pluralistic values (e.g. care within maker spaces [63]; makers interactions with non-maker communities [62]). This is a pragmatic approach that resonates with similar calls for 'designing our way out' of the limitations of neoliberalism [46]. By focusing less on distant ideals – and more on pragmatically *designing our way out* of unsatisfactory realities, *in the direction of* our ideals (e.g. inclusivity) – we have a better chance of contributing to systems of support that will provide a more sustainable route to achieving those ideals.

Our motivation is therefore to hone in on an explicit practical agenda for diverse and inclusive making. This is a particularly urgent challenge. Recent research [44] suggests the "*promises*" of maker culture have the potential to clash with other cultures of making (e.g. Chinese manufacturing) in unproductive ways. We find cautionary tales in similar ideologically-motivated and digitally-enabled domains [50, 42]. The 'sharing economy' started as a technological-utopian idea, but has since developed in problematic ways; 'tragic neighbours' in *AirBnB*s [22] and tensions between established taxi drivers and users of ridesharing apps. If we want to protect the ideals of the maker movement, which is still characterized by so much goodwill and "*good faith*" [55], we should take steps to pre-emptively address problematic elements in the 'sharing economies' of existing ecologies of making.

We are at a point in time where many in HCI (and beyond) are probing the boundaries of what we think of as 'making'. A recent workshop at CHI'17 [31], built on substantial existing critical mass [25, 26] to explore "*the intersection of maker culture and industrial manufacturing*". At CHI'16, a papers session, *(Re)understanding Making,* proposed a "*critical broadening of maker cultures*". Industrial perspectives also validate this critical direction. [37] is a retrospective that celebrates the maker movement's achievements but acknowledges its potential "*is greater than its current trajectory*" (p30). [20] calls for "*a more holistic approach*" and a "*deeper maker community*" (p31).

Recent work by Taylor et al exploring the wider role of makerspaces in public life [61] reflects on how self-identifying makerspaces act as a "*third place*" (a place away from home and work that plays a key role in public life). Taylor et al's "*Community inventor days*" (matchmaking 'makers' with members of the wider community) also explored the interactions between makers and wider publics [62]. Now that we know such connections yield value, can existing connections between communities be leveraged in similar ways? What connections exist between maker communities? What can we learn from them and what can we do to help develop them further? A conceptual "*maker ecosystem*" in [16] (originally in [32]) characterizes relationships between 'zeros' (those "*at a loss*" with fabrication tools), 'makers' and 'markets'. The unidirectional arrow suggests that (beyond 'gaining new skills' and 'taking an idea to market') the nuances of interactions between makers of different creeds and competencies are proving difficult to articulate (even once we acknowledge, via terms such as "ecosystem", that there *are* nuances in their interactions). A recent study [63] examined a hacker mailing list and identified a variety of subtle social nuances within a single online network of distributed makers. We need to extend this approach to offline and hybrid online/offline contexts as well. We are gradually gaining insights into the varied social roles assumed by makers (e.g. the 'expert amateur' [40]), but there are still many gaps in our understanding.

An open dataset of UK makerspaces [65] focused on self-identifying, public maker spaces. Two are listed in Newcastle but, as our study will show, there are more than twenty (what we call) 'places of making' in the city. Self-identifying, public makerspaces are the tip of the iceberg in Newcastle, as well as other cities such as London [11].

Drawing on our analysis, we have identified a need to explore interactions between individuals, groups and communities of makers and ask: *Who are the liminal, atypical, alternative and peripheral (groups of) makers and what are their points of connection / tension to one another and other makers? What kinds of interactions exist between different kinds of makers?*

STUDY DESIGN

We designed a research study that set out to explore *liminal* perspectives on making and the interactions between different makers in Newcastle upon Tyne (pop. ~ 300,000).

Making in the City

We decided to frame this enquiry within the geographical context of a city for several reasons. First and foremost, the city represents an intermediate position between the *macrocosm* of the global maker movement and the *microcosm* of the individual maker space. It is also a perspective that stands to be especially revealing as global maker movements start to align themselves through concepts such as the *Fab City*. The city also provides a logical focus for a study that is seeking-out complexity since cities are characterized in this way [7]. Perhaps for this reason, studies of making at this scale are rare. Notable exceptions include studies of making from cities in East Asia [e.g. 44] and Northern Europe [e.g. 61]. We felt our small city presented a challenging – yet manageable – scale and, like the previous studies mentioned above, our aim was not to provide a comprehensive account of the entire city. To do so would be resource-intensive and likely obsolesce quickly, as patterns of making change. Rather, our aim was to extend the lines of inquiry beyond the boundaries of one specific group or a single technological intervention.

A key reason for situating the study in Newcastle specifically was its proximity to the researchers. Another key reason was that the lead author is a cross-disciplinary researcher-practitioner with ten years' experience as a 'maker' in this city. The unique perspective this brought to the project informed our research aims by, for example, facilitating the formation of trust relationships with makers across the city. The role assumed by the lead author in this respect is defined in literature on qualitative research methods as an "insider-outsider" [18]. The subjectivity this introduces to the research setting is mitigated by our methodology and accounted for in our analysis; overall, we consider it to be a key strength of the research.

The formal study took place over 8 months and began with a scoping exercise with eight makers in the city with whom we were already acquainted. This took the form of unstructured / semi-structured interviews about general making practices; the kinds of things they as individuals make and how they make them; the other people they interact with in their making practices; the places where they make; the resources they use, etc. This process affirmed the suitability of our methodological approach.

Methodology

Our methodology combines overlapping elements of three qualitative research techniques: (i) documentary, (ii) ethnography and (iii) participatory action research (fig 1). Three 'hybrid' methods formed at the intersections of these techniques; each fulfilling a role, either in service to one (or more) of the techniques and/or as a source of additional data. We outline each of the methods / intersections below.

(i) ***Documentary*** is a method of generating rich media data within qualitative research [57]. It can also have a further value as a stimulus for dialogue [29]. We used it as a conversation-starter, but we also used the framework of a documentary project to give a logical 'resolution' to our engagements with makers, at a fixed time in the future. This enabled highly reflective dialogue with participants, both on- and off-camera as well as constructive conversations about what to film, when and how. Media making activities were concentrated at the end of the project and implemented by the lead researcher. Our approach was not to make a linear documentary; rather, from our participant community, we invited a cross-section of makers to participate in 'vignettes' (short films about their social making practices). These 'vignettes' all conform to a 3-minute template, so that they can be presented as a (synchronized) 'video wall', assembled in an interactive (web-based) documentary. The artistic premise is to highlight similarities between seemingly different makers.

(ii) ***Ethnography***, in this context, refers to our decision to conduct our research 'in the wild' using fieldwork methods - observations, conversations and 'hanging around' at sites of interest. Our approach was to some extent 'auto-ethnographic' [19] (by default) since our 'insider-outsider' configuration overcame the *'initial strangeness'* with participants we were already acquainted with (this applied less as we began to encounter other makers). Our approach was informed by previous HCI work [e.g. 30, 53] that has used similar ethnographic techniques to gain insights into the socio-technical organization of complex communities. We struck a balance between ethnography and documentary by a simple self-imposed rule: visit twice before bringing a camera. To assist in the reflection and cross-referencing of key issues, the lead author kept detailed notes in a notebook/diary over the course of the project.

(iii) ***Participatory Action Research*** (PAR) has proven to be an effective technique in numerous HCI contexts [35, 30] as a way of nurturing ethical relationships with research participants, building sustainable collaborations and giving something of-value back to participant communities. In this project, our intention was not to build sustainable collaborations *per se* (although in some cases, this was a by-product). However, we did want to give back something of-value. To achieve this, we actually produced two short films with each participant; one documentary 'vignette' (*about* them) and a secondary digital video (edited from the same materials) produced *for-and-with* the participants.

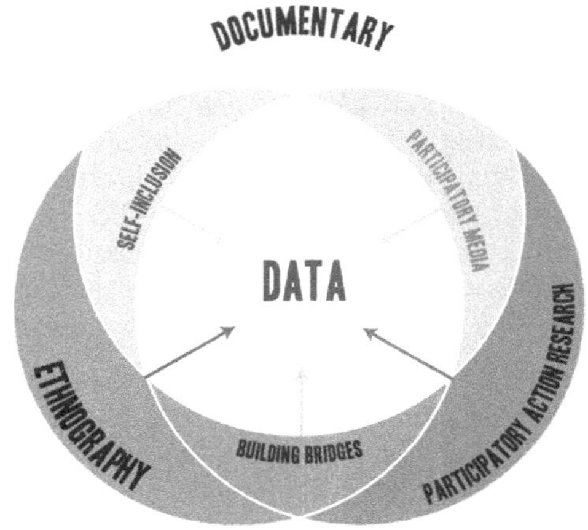

Fig 1 – A visualization of the research methodology. The three points of intersection between PAR, Ethnography and Documentary each generate data.

Intersection 1 - Participatory Media

The short films we made *for-and-with* participants were framed around the participant's own requirements (e.g. a promotional video for a project, a show-reel, etc.). The short films we made *about* the participant (which we refer to as documentary 'vignettes') combined these materials with edited versions of their structured interviews.

Intersection 2 – Building Bridges

We used the opportunity of interacting with lots of different makers in the city to proactively (yet informally) build-bridges between individuals, groups and communities; connecting participants with like-minded makers and sharing opportunities that might be of-value or interest.

Intersection 3 – Self Inclusion

The lead researcher produced a self-reflective documentary about the making of their films – edited to the same template as the others. This was designed to build an empathic rapport with participants and to demonstrate peer-status as a member of the same community (the 'insider' half of our insider-outsider role).

Recruitment

To facilitate our aim of engaging makers from alternative, atypical and peripheral places of making, we 'cast our net' as widely as possible. To achieve this, we used 8 different recruitment vectors (fig 2). Some of these relied on our acquaintances spreading the word. Others made contact with makers directly - or indirectly - via email, at informal meet-ups/open-days or via events (e.g. *Maker Faire*). Once contact was established, we would arrange to visit their 'place of making' and adopt our ethnographic methodology.

The study coincided with a national *Maker Faire* being held in the city. We used this opportunity to experiment with a 'maker mapping' activity that invited makers to create custom 3D avatars, place them on a map and use physical threads to create symbolic connections between them (fig 3). The national scale of this activity extends the scope of this paper, but it was an important aspect of our approach that gave us an opportunity to interact with hundreds of

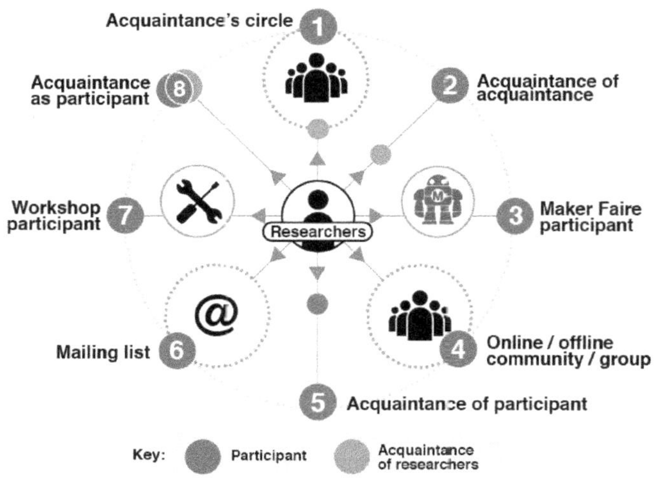

Fig 2 – Participant Recruitment Vectors

makers and engage potential new participants on a face-to-face basis. (We plan to report specifically on the outcomes of this activity in a future publication).

Data Collection & Analysis

We focus our descriptions and analysis on the findings from our ethnographic study. This includes the process of *making* the documentary, but not the final 'vignettes' / documentary (We will report on these in another future publication).

In our scoping exercise, we collected 4 hours of audio recordings with 9 participants (5m/4f 23-68), 20-40 minutes each. Thereafter, we engaged a wide variety of makers from across the city. We collected audio recordings, a diary, notes, and engaged with several participants via email, social media and SMS. In all cases, participants were made aware that we were conducting a research project *and* a documentary project, and where we have collected identifiable data (i.e. quotes and correspondence), participants have given written, informed consent for the data to be collected. We have anonymized all of the data collected during our ethnographic study and used pseudonyms for our final group of 11 participants (fig 4).

We used a two-pass thematic analysis to analyse our data. Our first pass was a *deductive* thematic analysis, framed around our aim of identifying liminal perspectives and articulating the interactions between different kinds of makers. Our second pass was an *inductive* thematic analysis that sought to reveal broader issues. The second-pass analysis resulted in themes that we discuss below. As well as monitoring and reflecting upon our data regularly throughout the study, we performed two validity checks at the end of the study. The first was member checking (with a participant from the scoping study, two from the ethnographic study and a documentary participant). Secondly, after our thematic analysis, we scrutinized our data for discrepant evidence and negative cases [47].

Fig 3 – Interactive 'maker mapping' activity at Maker Faire.

FINDINGS

We present our findings in two sections. Section 1, composed of two sub-sections (1a and 1b) derives from the first (*deductive*) pass of our thematic analysis. In (1a) we present descriptions of five selected makers who represent atypical, alternative and peripheral places of making (i.e. those who make outside from the well-known places of making in the city). In (1b) we present the kinds of interactions we observed, highlighting the 'intra-community' nature of most of these interactions. Section 2 derives from our second (inductive) pass and contains four themes that suggest wider findings / avenues for further research.

Section (1a) – Makers' Perspectives

We interacted with over 200 makers, of which a cross-section of eleven (fig 4) participated in the documentary as well. Here we describe five documentary participants in detail (fig 4: highlighted), as examples of *liminal* perspectives on making.

Aaron is a senior technician at a large university. As part of a small team, he manages a rapid prototyping suite that is accessible to over 10,000 staff and students. He facilitates and oversees the safe use of various CNC machines, including 3D printers, laser-cutters and milling machines. Aaron notes a shift in his focus since taking up the role,

> *"I love making things – that's how I ended up doing this – now I see myself more as a facilitator. I help people. I don't really have time to sit and make. I put my time and enthusiasm into helping other people achieve what they want to achieve."[Aaron]*

Aaron acknowledges steep learning curves and adopts a constructionist - "*make mistakes and improve*" - philosophy within his role. His 'holistic' perspective on making is also revealing; as an everyday user and regular purchaser / researcher of CNC machines, Aaron reminds his students that they are tools like any other (not prototyping 'panacea'). He asserts that the best results come from

Aaron	Senior technician, [Anon] University	4
Barney	Founder, Newcastle Makerspace	1
Callum	Academic researcher / designer	8
Daniel	Retired seafarer and amateur carpenter	6
Easter	PhD student	8
Fatima	Self-employed dressmaker	2
Gary	Electronics Engineer / Homebrewer	3
Hanna	Digital artist, [Anon] Projects	7
Ian	Professional Lithographer, [Anon] Editions;	8
Janet	Support manager, [Anon]	5
Karl	Designer / Bicycle mechanic	8

Fig 4 – Participants n=11 (7m/4f)
Numbers correspond to recruitment vector (fig 2)

knowing how to use them alongside traditional tools,

> *"People think you can just 3D print something and it's done, but it doesn't necessarily work like that [...] you use the other [e.g. manual] tools to finish. I think it's really important to be able to use both sets of tools and not just rely on one or the other." [Aaron]*

Aaron's point is reflected in both the support-infrastructure and the physical layout of the university workshops; Aaron's team of fellow technicians work in adjacent, inter-connected workshops, and take responsibility for different facilities; hand tools, soldering stations, band saws, etc.

Daniel is a retired seafarer whose ambition to learn woodworking after his retirement (in 2014) was realized at *Craftworks* after two local carpenters declined his offer of work in exchange for experience. *Craftworks* is part of a charity that provides experiences, knowledge and skills for adults with disabilities and learning difficulties. When Daniel, who is not disabled, encountered the service "*by accident*", it had just opened and was not at full capacity so Daniel was given access on an informal, short-term basis. Soon *Craftworks* will reach full capacity and Daniel, who has been using the facility for 2 years, must give up his place. However, during his tenure, having been mentored by Craftworks' manager, he has gained the skills he wanted. Daniel was fortunate to be in 'the right place at the right time', but the benefits were also reciprocal; the charity benefitted from Daniel's informal technical and peer-support to other service-users, which he provided in-kind throughout his tenure.

Fatima is a self-employed dressmaker, who openly prefers to 'make' alone and on her own terms.

> *"It's not that I don't work well with other people, because I do, but I have my own ideas about everything and I love working by myself. I prefer working by myself." [Fatima]*

However, she builds close relationships with her customers – whom she describes as "*collaborators*" – and her practice is co-creative – particularly during the development phases. She also acknowledges a need to draw on others' expertise,

> "... *I might have to go to somebody else because I need some equipment that I haven't got* ... [but] ... *in terms of collaborating with other makers, they're mostly kept at a distance. I have a knowledge of who they are, so I can go to them if they can help me in some way, or to work together on small projects." [Fatima]*

Having previously been based in a small city-centre studio (alongside other makers), Fatima now works from home, which benefits her personal circumstances and independent spirit; she also teaches embroidery at a local college, which she describes as,

> *"... almost like I'm moulding my own little community now because I'm teaching them <u>my ways</u>." [Fatima]*

Hanna is the creative director of '*AP*', a participatory arts organization based at 'BH', a city-centre studio that is also home to various other professional artists and creative businesses. AP is *"a platform for collaborations... we put a team together and we do a project*"; projects that tend to combine participatory activities, (e.g. "*workshops with communities*") with Hanna's own creative inventions,

> *"I like combining digital things with physical ones. That implies objects, but also physical spaces like public open spaces, rooms, museums, those kinds of things... [Urban space is] a material; the architecture – the interactions between people – this is a material ... the little details, the way things have been damaged over time" [Hanna]*

Hanna is a member of the city Makerspace, but tends to 'make' either publicly, in a community setting, or in her own studio (a place littered with breadboards, teapots, wires, IT peripherals, sewing kits, and other esoterica). Her studio is a reflection of her culturally diverse experiences and widely varied interests,

> *"I used to work in Providence, RI and there was a place called the Steelyard where you could learn to weld (but) it's difficult in Newcastle to do things with metal." [Hanna]*

Ian is a 'Tamarind master printer', "*trained in the art of collaborative printmaking*". Ian is fiercely independent; "*You try and use what they* [The Tamarind Institute] *teach you ... but I want to see for myself why things don't work.*" Ian has a well-equipped studio in a creative quarter of the city, where he regularly collaborates with national and international artists on printmaking projects, drawing on informal local connections to hone his craft in innovative ways (e.g. laser-cutting lithographic stones).

> *"I like using new technology to do something in the hope that at some point it will be useful. I'll try different things when I've got some time and I'll add it to my arsenal of skills and tools for mark-making to offer to artists - or perhaps myself." [Ian]*

Ian is a busy professional and describes a need to be careful with his time. "*I would love to have the time to learn to do lots of things myself – I'm quite hands on – but there's not enough time in the world.*" However, he acknowledges the importance of an active online presence. To balance his desire to connect online with other printmakers and his time limitations, he avoids online printmaking forums except for a "*secret Facebook group*", where he shares professional advice with other Tamarind master printers.

Section (1b) – Interactions between Makers

We encountered >25 'places of making' in Newcastle, including the city *Makerspace* (MS), private studios, workshops, 'men's sheds', universities, community centers, charities, industrial estates and home studios. There were a surprisingly large number of CNC facilities, but making and making-related activities (e.g. meet-ups) also took place in various other places; public spaces, pubs and cafes and private dwellings, as well as online, via social media, etc. We identified numerous overlapping connections between makers with various combinations of '*who, what, when, where, why* and *how*'. '*Where*', for example: Many makers would meet up to 'make' together with like-minded makers – not just at MS but at formal and informal 'places of making' across the city. Indeed, most of these connections *between* makers took place *within* discreet communities. These typically aligned to a particular *place*, but shared other characteristics such as a social and/or cultural identity (e.g. students, model railway makers, etc).

So, making in Newcastle tends to happen in close-knit communities; however - these communities themselves are fragmented. We now present five examples of such communities and, in each case, outline how they are characterized chiefly by *internal* interactions (rather than interactions with *other* communities). We begin with the city makerspace, and work outwards (fig 5).

Community 1 - Makerspace

Makerspace (MS) is a members-only group, founded and led by Barney. From its launch in 2011 until 2016, MS was based at a street-level shop-front unit in a central, creative district of the city. In 2016, it moved into Studio A, a seven-storey artists studio on the same block. Recently it moved again into the basement of the same building. Several 'keyholders' (regulars with keys to the premises) open-up for members on an ad-hoc basis and communication is primarily via an active (public) Googlegroup. They are a sociable, active group who engage with local maker events (e.g. Maker Faire) and collaborate on interactive projects (e.g. kinetic window displays). Nonetheless, its weekly 'open evenings' are not usually well attended by non-members. Some participants expressed ambivalent attitudes to MS; "*they've got their thing going on and I'm… looking for something different.*". A common observation was that MS members are mostly male and "*quite a specific age-range*". It is also perceived to align to a particular stereotype of 'making' ("*all microcontrollers and soldering irons*"). MS is an archetypal makerspace; a community-of-practice with a shared interest in microelectronics, digital fabrication, ubiquitous computing, Internet-of-Things technologies (e.g. *Arduino*,

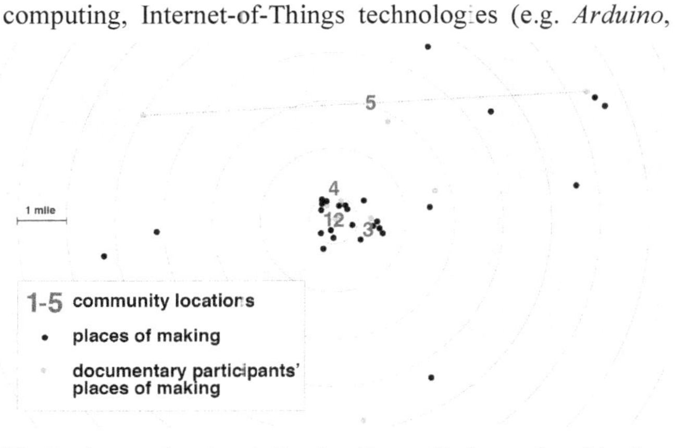

Fig 5 – Approximate relative locations of 'places of making' we visited + corresponding communities.

Raspberry Pi, etc) and digital experimentation. It is nonetheless a welcoming, friendly community, who make a regular weekly effort to embrace new members ("*Welcome Wednesdays*").

Community 2 - Downtown Studios

As well as being home to MS, Studio A is also home to a transient community of (~50) professional creatives (e.g. illustrators, performing artists, musicians, etc.) in individually leased studios. Two floors are managed by *Ampersand*, whose aim is "*to create and manage a multi-functional space that provides a creative and supportive environment for experimental and participatory events, charities and artists.*" BC is a 9-storey studio on the opposite corner of the same block, similarly dedicated to "*the promotion of cross-fertilisation within the arts"*. BC and Studio A are both commercial enterprises and "*friendly rivals*". Despite participating in public 'open days' (e.g. *The Late Shows*), and proactively engaging with other artists in the city (e.g. via the universities), the places of making here (and, by extension, the communities) are not typically 'open', nor are they explicitly 'inclusive'. Two of our participants, Callum and Hanna, have monthly-leased studios at BC. Callum describes the arrangement as follows,

"There is a community of people who have a freelance practice who engage each other as and when they need for the projects that they have, both in terms of work that's happening locally, but also when people come through Newcastle, when there's a commission here and they're seeking local people to produce their work … there's a community of people that then support that." [Callum]

Many in this community rely on public funding, which is increasingly competitive in the UK. The future of this community is therefore uncertain with tenants renting two entire floors of Studio A recently moving out. In the coming months, the ways *Makerspace* will adapt-to (or indeed influence) the community is uncertain. Overall, this is a densely packed network of collaborative artists and makers. Basic, rented 'places of making' are affordable and private, yet public and accessible *enough* to sustain and maintain an active – albeit transient - population.

Community 3 - Creative Quarter

CQ is an established hub. It is a sprawling, ex-industrial area that, over the last 15 years, has evolved into a picturesque home to several large independent studios, 3D design practices (e.g. *RSK*), merchants (e.g. *Q-Timber*), charities, a city farm, stables, independent pubs and cafes. It is now a relatively affluent area but it maintains a laid back atmosphere. LStudios (LS) is a suite of 33 studios, primarily occupied by visual artists (including Ian) with traditional making equipment (e.g. Ian's lithographic press) as well as digital fabrication facilities. Making here tends to be skilled and highly specialized. LS are private studios, but other places (*Q-Timber* and *RSK*) open at street level (the latter, "*a multidisciplinary design and fabrication practice*", offer "*3D solutions*", and their fabrication machines are visible to pedestrians). Ian describes CQ's culture as neighborly and business-like,

> *"I use local services, who are generally makers themselves. If I need things, I know there are people around I can ask and there's people to help ... There are people around who will give you a hand lifting something, or help you install a new press, or help you move buildings. Some people will be like "we can make that for you" and if my skills transfer, then I'll do that too ... I'm a big fan of the barter system." [Ian]*

CQ is a relatively stable cluster of independent makers, who share a strong cultural identity. Interactions are typically social or transactional rather than collaborative. Tenancies are typically long-term and there are strong national and international links to other makers and places of making.

Community 4 - The Universities

The city's two universities have a total of over 60,000 students and staff and their geographical footprint covers most of the city's Northern quarter. Both universities have engineering, art / design, and computer science departments that across the two sites house at least ten different CNC / fabrication facilities. Some are well known and in regular use; others are well-kept secrets (even internally). Some are open access; others are restricted to a few users. Aaron's facility is one of the largest and most widely (internally) accessible of the spaces. The facility used by both Easter and Callum (two laser-cutters and two 3D printers), is relatively exclusive; accessible to a research group with about 100 members, but used regularly by fewer than ten. Both universities use their facilities for teaching and research, as well as to support "third-strand" activities (e.g. consultancy to industry). Many university-affiliated makers (staff and students) have the freedom to use well-equipped fabrication facilities – some even have 24-hour access. As with most universities [8], these facilities are not open to the public, but formal and informal interactions do occur. A formal method is research projects, although these tend to be controlled by and ultimately for the benefit of the university-affiliates who initiate them. An informal method is via social connections to university affiliates. This can lead to informal (or even formal) access, but this unofficial economy remains exclusory to the socially unconnected and it is also open to exploitation. Overall, the two universities are an intersecting pair of stable (yet exclusive) networks, comprising of academics, researchers, students, technicians and engineers. Dedicated access to state-of-the-art fabrication facilities is provided to the affiliated but inaccessible to the majority of the other makers in the city.

Community 5 - The Charity

PCH is an Newcastle-based charity that provides, "*a wide range of high quality, specialist and personalised care and education support to disabled people and their families*" (a.k.a. 'service-users'). *PCH* is based on a social enterprise model that integrates commercial services and professional care provision. Facilities are distributed widely across the city (fig 5) and include *Craftworks* (Daniel's woodworking studio) and *N-Able*, where Janet works as a support manager. Janet is responsible for managing support services across *N-Able's* three co-located facilities; a print studio, a professional kitchen and media-making studios – as well as two remote sites (*Craftworks* and one other). *N-Able* is based at a business park on a large industrial park about 4 miles east of the city centre. The print studio is supervised by Layne, a professional carer with 35 years of experience in the professional printing industry. Layne's primary role is as a carer, but under his supervision, service-users use a variety of (digital and physical) tools to produce flyers for clients in the industrial park and beyond. In a similar arrangement, meals are provided by the kitchen team (service-users, supervised by a chef-turned-professional-carer) and arts events are planned and organized, with promotional media developed in the in-house media studios. As well as being successful commercial enterprises, PCH gives service-users practical experiences of 'making' in a variety of contexts.

> *"We're in a really fortunate position that we're part of an organisation that has been providing care and support for 65 years. There's a really rich and vibrant culture that comes with that and the people we support really contribute to that." [Janet]*

Section 2 – General Findings

2i - Intersecting 'Places of Making' within Communities

In our study, we found clear delineations between community members and non-members in the forms of affiliations and memberships. However, in some cases (*The Universities*, *Downtown Studios* and *Creative Quarter*) multiple unaffiliated co-located 'places of making' shared similar practices, cultures and identities and thus were essentially clustered communities-of-practice. In the case of *The Universities*, despite institutional differences, there were many similarities in the 'making' practices across the two sites; both had similar facilities and networks of professional connections enabled regular interactions between makers across-sites. The main barrier was not individual institutional affiliation, but *any* institutional affiliation. The *Creative Quarter* and *Downtown Studios*, though operating in very similar ways, were comparatively discreet communities; geographically separated by only 2 miles yet with substantively different cultures of making. *Downtown Studios* nurture a *public, collaborative* culture whereas *Creative Quarter* nurtures a more *private, transactional* culture. There are many exceptions, but these cultural differences were widely acknowledged in the wider public as a key distinction between these otherwise similar communities.

2ii - Intersecting Practices within Communities

Each community has its own culture and traditions of making. In each case, this culture co-evolved with practices that are *not making*: trade; education; research; care; artistic co-creation. In most cases, this resulted in potential co-creativity being hindered by cultural incompatibilities elsewhere. For example, we found several examples of tensions between businesses whose commitments to IPR (intellectual property rights) were ideologically opposed to the openness of (e.g.) the makerspace. Yet, in many cases, a shared interest or goal (e.g. Ian's interactions with RSK relating to laser-etching lithographic stones) would transcend these differences, but only in situations where there were mechanisms in place to assuage cultural incompatibilities (e.g. a bartering economy). There were also imbalances in this regard. It was clear how universities would benefit from interactions with local makers (e.g. student placements) but *quid pro quo* access to high-tech equipment was not always possible. Daniel's experience at *Craftworks* highlights how it can be mutually rewarding to connect makers and service-users (even in a sensitive context), provided the terms are explicit and understood.

2iii - Interrogating 'the' Makerspace

MS's central location and self-identification as a makerspace led many to use it as a point of reference. A consequence of this is that it is often used as a basis for comparison; positive aspects of other places were expressed in terms of provisions or qualities that MS lacks. This was initially flagged in our data as criticism of MS, but we also found many examples of praise and apologetic reasons for not attending, so the error was identified. MS is widely respected, but makers have diverse needs that MS cannot always meet; "*sometimes I want to make things out of metal*" [Ian]; "*I need a big space*" [Karl]; "*...it's just not for me*" [Easter]. Despite a relatively small number of our participants being active members of MS, many had visited; others knew members; some were even members (e.g. Hanna and Karl), but only Barney (its founder) was a regular attendee. A final unforeseen side effect of being the dominant makerspace in the city's imagination relates to university researchers ... "*At Makerspace we get at least one request a month ... most of them thought they would be the first academic making contact.*" [Barney].

2iv - Intersecting Vectors

Earlier, we described several vectors that we used to engage potential participants (fig 2). These represented pathways to makers in communities beyond those we were already affiliated to / associated with. These vectors also the same as those that makers might use to connect with makers beyond their own communities, yet a surprisingly small number of our participants identified with multiple communities. For many, the reason was to do with resources. As one university-affiliated participant said,

> *"My motivations for joining [a makerspace] would be about the equipment and the space and at the moment, I have both of those things through the university."*

There were other reasons as well. For Janet and the PCH community, they are geographically distant from the city centre, but also geographically fragmented *themselves*. Their community is defined by affiliation, professional objectives and a strong cultural identity rather than co-location. In the case of *N-Able*, they are surrounded by hundreds of 'makers' on an industrial park. Their neighbours make industrial plastics, undersea robots, etc, and have little in common with the kind of making at *N-Able*. Apart from being friendly acquaintances who "*pop to the same shops*" [Janet], that might be the extent of the connection. Yet Janet has pursued this informal vector to pioneer placement opportunities for service-users at several manufacturers from the industrial park. In doing so, she has transcended the community barrier and formalized an informal connection via an opportunistic vector. *Craftworks* is similar - its facilities are adjacent to a bed factory, where service-users gain work experience; making beds and mattresses, using the skills gained at *Craftworks*. The social enterprise model is another vector of a different kind; *what other vectors did we miss?*

DISCUSSION

Our findings confirmed our hypothesis that - even in a small city like Newcastle - there are 'liminal' makers whose perspectives and practices are varied and insightful. We also found evidence of tensions between different *kinds* of makers that result from the fact that 'making' is just one facet of a community's identity. Connecting making can bring other 'facets' (e.g. business models) into conflict, but also potentially into alignment. We found many interesting interactions between makers: Aaron's holistic mentoring, Daniel's opportunistic apprenticeships, Fatima's co-creation with customers, Hanna's creative interactions with people in urban spaces, and Ian's informal bartering with local service providers. These unique interactions highlight the diversity of 'liminal' makers – and the various vectors that can lead them to interact with one another – as well as 'makerspace' makers.

Enabling Co-Creative Making in Cities

Newcastle is a melting pot of co-creativity, both potential and realised. *PCH* are pioneering inclusive, co-creative making. This is partly achieved by being open to informal requests (e.g. to Daniel - and to this research project!) and partly by seizing upon opportunistic encounters with other liminal makers (e.g. in the industrial park). In academic and creative communities, others are transcending community boundaries by similar determination, but usually with limited resources. Co-creative making (therefore) often tends to piggy-back on other (often commercial) ventures, thereby limiting what is possible to the confines of those projects. Bespoke socio-technical support for making *in public* (cf Hanna's public approach to making) might enable more cross-fertilisation among makers and more inter-community making in cities like Newcastle. Makerspaces fulfil a vital role, but they are not a catch-all for active makers in cities.

As we have demonstrated, there can be communities of makers in cities who are unconnected to each other. Projects like *Fab City* risk alienating local makers if they fail to connect existing 'places of making'. Two strategies might help avoid this. 1- help connect them to each other directly. 2- connect them via a central node. If we connect them through a central node (e.g. a website), the intervention might *influence* the community. This could be a *positive* influence (like Daniel's positive influence at *Craftworks*) or it could be a *negative* influence (e.g. like the Universities, who collectively imposed on the makerspace – or, worse, like a nightmare scenario from the 'sharing economy'; it could result in conflict with existing systems and services). More research is needed, but facilitating multiple direct connections between places of making might be a more sensitive, less risky, and more sustainable approach than a 'one-size-fits-all' approach.

Our study suggests the importance of bridging not just makerspaces, but also other 'places of making' in cities. We have also highlighted the challenge of bridging clusters of communities. The vectors we used in this project were primarily interpersonal, but other vectors such as social enterprises could inform future research. Indeed, further exploration is certainly needed. The current understanding of existing city networks of making is limited and the intersections between networks of maker communities is under-researched. Other researchers might wish to further explore the tensions and connections at the intersections of making – particularly in other city contexts; especially in the global south, where our knowledge is most limited.

'Open Design' as an Agenda for Inclusive Making

In our study, we encountered diverse making practices and makers with diverse needs, including communities of makers who rarely interact with each other. Even collaborative making tends to be with like-minded makers, behind closed doors, or characterized by transactional, goal-oriented interactions that clash with the progressive ambitions for future making. Making in Newcastle is incredibly diverse, yet it remains characterized by subtle forms of *exclusivity*. Of the progressive ideals the maker movement aspires to, diversity rules. This is a paradox: the aim of being both *inclusive* and *diverse* is thwarted by the latter. The majority of the (diverse) making practices we encountered were *exclusive* forms of making (i.e. explicitly *not inclusive*).

The maker movement is defined in-part by its diversity. *Inclusive making* therefore calls for a different strategy; one explicitly aligned to wholly open co-creativity. It must actively resist exclusive elements like ownership, IPR, affiliation - and even notions such as "community", where one can be 'in' or 'out'.

To develop the digital systems and infrastructure necessary to enable this is a substantial challenge, but it aligns to an existing paradigm of radical inclusivity: "*open design*". Open design thereby provides an agenda for explicitly *inclusive* making. In a basic sense, open design is a physical analogy of open source software [51]. Yet it extends the basic concept of 'open source hardware' by incorporating two key elements: *iteration* and *inclusion* [13]. It has been defined as the, "*collaborative creation of artefacts by a dispersed group of otherwise unrelated individuals*" [11].

Aligning 'inclusive making' to the identity of 'open design' could be productive in a number of ways. Firstly, it separates the explicitly progressive notion of *inclusion* from (intentionally or unintentionally) *exclusive* areas of the maker movement. Secondly, it will help the mainstream 'maker movement' avoid the problems of 'sharing economies' (although to 'open design', they remain a key challenge). Thirdly, it provides makers who align to the values of openness and inclusivity a shared identity – thereby providing an impetus, and enriching the maker movement by diversifying it still further. Finally, it opens up an exciting new space for co-design 'mashup'. As well as constructive, 'designerly' input, knowledge-sharing and other traditional forms of contribution, 'open design' or 'inclusive making' might explicitly seek to nurture iterative public making, perhaps by embracing parody, pastiche - even 'trolling' - as legitimate forms of co-creation.

In light of this proposal, an agenda for interaction design is to focus on new ways to facilitate *as many different kinds of maker as possible* to co-create. New forms of support might draw upon those elements we have described; e.g. holistic philosophy, co-creative arts practices, social enterprises, etc. In any case, 'open design' is already happening - at the peripheries of the maker movement. If we want to support 'inclusive' making, we can look there for inspiration.

CONCLUSION

Enabling co-creativity, particularly at scale, remains a complex socio-technical challenge. Indeed, our study has acknowledged new facets of this challenge through a rich account of a diverse population of makers. Through this, we have exposed a critical tension between 'inclusivity' and 'diversity' - so much of the culture and practices of making are (gently) exclusive. By aligning with 'open design', a practical solution space is revealed for digital systems that - via iterative, reflective and distributed co-creation - could enable more *inclusive* cultures of 'making' that complement and diversify existing cultures still further.

ACKNOWLEDGEMENTS

This work was funded by the EPSRC 'Design Your Own Future: Supporting Networked Design Expertise' Project EP/N005848/1.

REFERENCES

1. Morgan G. Ames, Jeffrey Bardzell, Shaowen Bardzell, Silvia Lindtner, David A. Mellis, and Daniela K. Rosner. 2014. Making Cultures: Empowerment, Participation, and Democracy - or Not?. In Proc. CHI EA '14. ACM, 1087–1092. DOI: http://dx.doi.org/10.1145/2559206.2579405
2. Chris Anderson. 2013. *Makers: The New Industrial Revolution.* Random House

3. P. Atkinson. 2006. *Do It Yourself: Democracy and Design*. Journal of Design History, 19(1), 1-10.
4. P. Atkinson. 2010. 'Boundaries? What Boundaries? The Crisis of Design in a Post-Professional Era', Design Journal, 13(2), 137-155.
5. Jeffrey Bardzell, Shaowen Bardzell, and Austin Toombs. 2014. "Now That's Definitely a Proper Hack": Self-made Tools in Hackerspaces. In Proc. CHI '14. ACM, 473–476. DOI: http://dx.doi.org/10.1145/2556288.2557221
6. Jeffrey Bardzell, Shaowen Bardzell, Cindy Lin, Silvia Lindtner and Austin Toombs (2017), "HCI's Making Agendas", Foundations and Trends® in Human–Computer Interaction: Vol. 11: No. 3, pp 126-200. http://dx.doi.org/10.1561/1100000066
7. Shaowen Bardzell. 2015. Utopian Design. In Reconceptualizing Critical Utopia panel at Aarhus 2015, the Decennial Conference on Critical Alternatives. Aarhus, Denmark.
8. T. W., Barrett, et al. 2015. A Review of University Maker Spaces, 2015 ASEE Annual Conference & Exposition, Seattle, Washington. 10.18260/p.23442
9. Michael Batty. 2007. Cities and Complexity: Understanding Cities with Cellular Automata, Agent-Based Models, and Fractals. The MIT Press.
10. Edward P. Clapp, Jessica Ross, Jennifer O. Ryan, Shari Tishman. 2016. *Maker-Centered Learning: Empowering Young People to Shape Their Worlds*, John Wiley & Sons, New York, USA, Dec 2016
11. *Co-Making: Research into London's Open access Makerspaces and Shared Workshops*. 2015. Workshop East with Engel Hadley Kirk & Rhianon Morgan-Hatch, Retrieved August 30, 2017 from: https://www.london.gov.uk/sites/default/files/makerspaces-jan2015.pdf
12. Leon Cruickshank and Paul Atkinson. 2013. *Closing in on Open Design. Comparing Casual and Critical Design Challenges*. In: Proceedings of the 10th European Academy of Design Conference, Gothenburg. [Gothenburg], University of Gothenburg/European Academy of Design.
13. Leon Cruickshank. 2014. *Open Design and Innovation*. Gower.
14. Charlotte A. Davis. 2008. *Reflexive Ethnography: A Guide to Researching Selves and Others*. London & New York: Routledge (second edition).
15. Monica Divitini, Michail N. Giannakos, Simone Mora, Sofia Papavlasopoulou, and Ole Sejer Iversen. 2017. Make2Learn with IoT: Engaging Children into Joyful Design and Making of Interactive Connected Objects. In Proceedings of the 2017 Conference on Interaction Design and Children (IDC '17). ACM, New York, NY, USA, 757-760. DOI: https://doi.org/10.1145/3078072.3081312
16. *The Cultural Role of Makerspaces*. 2016. From-Now-On, Retrieved August 30, 2017 from: https://issuu.com/deehalligan/docs/fno_report
17. Dale Dougherty (2016), *Free to Make*, North Atlantic Books, Berkeley California.
18. Sonya Corbin Dwyer, and Jennifer L. Buckle. 2009. *The Space Between: On Being an Insider-Outsider in Qualitative Research*. International Journal of Qualitative Methods 8.1 (2009): 54-63.
19. Carolyn Ellis, Tony E. Adams, and Arthur P. Bochner. "Autoethnography: an overview." Historical Social Research/Historische Sozialforschung (2011): 273-290.
20. *Envisioning the Future of the Maker Movement: Summit Report*. 2016. American Society for Engineering Education June 2016. Retrieved August 30, 2017 from https://www.asee.org/documents/papers-and-publications/papers/maker-summit-report.pdf
21. *Fab City - Locally Productive Globally Connected Cities,* Retrieved August 30, 2017 from http://fab.city
22. Apostolos Filippas and John Joseph Horton. 2017. The Tragedy of your Upstairs Neighbors: Is the Negative Externality of Airbnb Internalized?. In Proceedings of the 2017 ACM Conference on Economics and Computation (EC '17). ACM, New York, NY, USA, 537-538. DOI: https://doi.org/10.1145/3033274.3085097
23. Sarah Fox. 2015. Feminist Hackerspaces as Sites for Feminist Design. In Proceedings of the 2015 ACM SIGCHI Conference on Creativity and Cognition (C&C '15). ACM, New York, NY, USA, 341-342. DOI= http://dx.doi.org/10.1145/2757226.2764771
24. Verena Fuchsberger, Martin Murer, Manfred Tscheligi, Silvia Lindtner, Shaowen Bardzell, Jeffrey Bardzell, Andreas Reiter, and Pernille Bjorn. 2016. Fabrication & HCI: Hobbyist Making, Industrial Production, and Beyond. In Proceedings of the 2016 CHI Conference Extended Abstracts on Human Factors in Computing Systems (CHI EA '16). ACM, New York, NY, USA, 3550-3557. DOI: http://dx.doi.org/10.1145/2851581.2856491
25. Verena Fuchsberger, Silvia Lindtner, Martin Murer, and Manfred Tscheligi. 2015. Rethinking Technology Innovation: Factories, Fabrication & Design Research. (2015). http://hci.sbg.ac.at/ffdr
26. Verena Fuchsberger, Martin Murer, Manfred Tscheligi, Silvia Lindtner, Andreas Reiter, Shaowen Bardzell, Jeffrey Bardzell, and Pernille Björn. 2015. The Future of Making: Where Industrial and Personal Fabrication Meet. In Critical Alternatives '15. Aarhus Univ. Press.
27. *The Future of Manufacturing: A New Era of Opportunity and Challenge for the UK* - project report.

2013. Foresight / Government Office for Science and Department for Business, Innovation & Skills. BIS/13/809, Retrieved August 30, 2017 from https://www.gov.uk/government/publications/future-of-manufacturing/future-of-manufacturing-a-new-era-of-opportunity-and-challenge-for-the-uk-summary-report

28. Oskar Galewicz and Alma Leora Culén. 2017. Co-creating Interactive Obstacles and DIY Skateboarding Spaces. In Proceedings of the 12th Biannual Conference on Italian SIGCHI Chapter (CHItaly '17). ACM, New `York, NY, USA, Article 27, 10 pages. DOI: https://doi.org/10.1145/3125571.3125595

29. David Philip Green, Simon J. Bowen, Christopher Newell, Guy Schofield, Tom Bartindale, Clara Crivellaro, Alia Sheikh, Peter Wright, and Patrick Olivier. 2015. Beyond Participatory Production: Digitally Supporting Grassroots Documentary. In Proceedings of the 33rd Annual ACM Conference on Human Factors in Computing Systems (CHI '15). ACM, New York, NY, USA, 3157-3166. DOI: https://doi.org/10.1145/2702123.2702203

30. David Philip Green, Guy Schofield, Gary Pritchard, Patrick Olivier, and Peter Wright. 2017. Cinehacking Cape Town - Embracing Informality in Pursuit of High Quality Media. In Proceedings of the 2017 CHI Conference on Human Factors in Computing Systems (CHI '17). ACM, New York, NY, USA, 4753-4764. DOI: https://doi.org/10.1145/3025453.3025481

31. David Philip Green, Verena Fuchsberger, David Kirk, Nick Taylor, David Chatting, Janis Lena Meissner, Martin Murer, Manfred Tscheligi, Silvia Lindtner, Pernille Bjorn, and Andreas Reiter. 2017. Open Design at the Intersection of Making and Manufacturing. In Proceedings of the 2017 CHI Conference Extended Abstracts on Human Factors in Computing Systems (CHI EA '17). ACM, New York, NY, USA, 542-549. DOI: https://doi.org/10.1145/3027063.3027087

32. John Hagel, John Seely Brown, Duleesha Kulasooriya (2014), A Movement in the Making, accessed online, 18th Sept 2017, https://dupress.deloitte.com/dup-us-en/topics/emerging-technologies/a-movement-in-the-making.html

33. Bronwyn H. Hall. 2010. *Open Innovation & Intellectual Property Rights: The Two-edged Sword.* Economy, Culture and History Japan Spotlight Bimonthly 29.1 (2010): 18.

34. Mark Hatch. 2013. *The Maker Movement Manifesto: Rules for Innovation in the New World of Crafters, Hackers, and Tinkerers*. McGraw-Hill

35. Gillian R. Hayes. 2011. The relationship of action research to human-computer interaction. ACM Trans. Comput.-Hum. Interact. 18, 3, Article 15 (August 2011), 20 pages. DOI: https://doi.org/10.1145/1993060.1993065

36. Tapio Ikkala and Airi Lampinen. 2015. Monetizing Network Hospitality: Hospitality and Sociability in the Context of Airbnb. In Proceedings of the 18th ACM Conference on Computer Supported Cooperative Work & Social Computing (CSCW '15). ACM, New York, NY, USA, 1033-1044. DOI: http://dx.doi.org/10.1145/2675133.2675274

37. *Impact of the Maker Movement*. 2014. Deloitte / Makermedia, Retrieved August 30, 2017 from: http://bit.ly/1VZGh2f

38. *Inclusive Making in the Neighborhood*. 2015. Anne Weibert, Konstantin Aal, Andrea Marshall, Thomas von Rekowski, and Volker Wulf. Retrieved August 30, 2017 from: https://hci.sbg.ac.at/wpcontent/uploads/2015/11/Inclusive_Making.pdf

39. Tim Ingold. *Making: Anthropology, Archaeology, Art and Architecture*. Routledge, 2013.

40. Stacey Kuznetsov and Eric Paulos. 2010. Rise of the expert amateur: DIY projects, communities, and cultures. In Proceedings of the 6th Nordic Conference on Human-Computer Interaction: Extending Boundaries (NordiCHI '10). ACM, New York, NY, USA, 295-304. DOI= http://dx.doi.org/10.1145/1868914.1868950

41. C. Leadbeater. 2008. *We-Think: Mass Innovation, not Mass Production: The Power of Mass Creativity.* Profile Books.

42. Mathias Lecuyer, Max Tucker, and Augustin Chaintreau. 2017. Improving the Transparency of the Sharing Economy. In Proceedings of the 26th International Conference on World Wide Web Companion (WWW '17 Companion). International World Wide Web Conferences Steering Committee, Republic and Canton of Geneva, Switzerland, 1043-1051. DOI: https://doi.org/10.1145/3041021.3055136

43. Silvia Lindtner, Shaowen Bardzell, and Jeffrey Bardzell. 2016. Reconstituting the Utopian Vision of Making: HCI After Technosolutionism. In *Proceedings of the 2016 CHI Conference on Human Factors in Computing Systems* (CHI '16). ACM, New York, NY, USA, 1390-1402. DOI: https://doi.org/10.1145/2858036.2858506

44. Silvia Lindtner. 2015. Hacking with Chinese Characteristics The Promises of the Maker Movement against China's Manufacturing Culture. Science, Technology & Human Values (2015).

45. Silvia Lindtner, Garnet D. Hertz, and Paul Dourish. 2014. Emerging Sites of HCI Innovation: Hackerspaces, Hardware Startups & Incubators. In

Proc.CHI '14. ACM, 439–448. DOI: http://dx.doi.org/10.1145/2556288.2557132

46. Paul Mason (2016). *Postcapitalism: A Guide to Our Future.* Macmillan.
47. J. A. Maxwell, & B. A. Miller, 2008. *Categorizing and Connecting Strategies in Qualitative Data Analysis.* in P. Leavy & S. Hesse-Biber (Eds.), Handbook of Emergent Methods (pp. 461–477). New York: Guilford Press.
48. Brenna McNally, Leyla Norooz, Alazandra Shorter, and Evan Golub. 2017. Toward Understanding Children's Perspectives on Using 3D Printing Technologies in their Everyday Lives. In Proceedings of the 2017 Conference on Interaction Design and Children (IDC '17). ACM, New York, NY, USA, 298-303. DOI: https://doi.org/10.1145/3078072.3079735
49. Evgeny Morozov. 2011. *The Net Delusion: The Dark Side of Internet Freedom.* Perseus Books, Cambridge, MA, USA.
50. Sunjoo Oh and Jae Yun Moon. 2016. Calling for a shared understanding of the "sharing economy". In *Proceedings of the 18th Annual International Conference on Electronic Commerce: e-Commerce in Smart connected World* (ICEC '16). ACM, New York, NY, USA, Article 35, 5 pages. DOI: https://doi.org/10.1145/2971603.2971638
51. *Open Design Manifesto.* Ronen Kadushin, 2010, Retrieved August 30, 2017 from: https://www.ronen-kadushin.com/open-design-manifesto/
52. *Power, Access, Status: The Discourse of Race, Gender, and Class in the Maker Movement,* by Lauren Britton. 2015, Retrieved August 30, 2017 from http://tascha.uw.edu/2015/03/power-access-status-the-discourse-of-race-gender-and-class-in-the-maker-movement/
53. Gary Pritchard, John Vines, and Patrick Olivier. 2015. Your Money's No Good Here: The Elimination of Cash Payment on London Buses. In *Proceedings of the 33rd Annual ACM Conference on Human Factors in Computing Systems* (CHI '15). ACM, New York, NY, USA, 907-916. DOI: https://doi.org/10.1145/2702123.2702137
54. Dave Randall, Richard Harper, and Mark Rouncefield. *Ethnography and How To Do It.* in Fieldwork for Design: Theory and Practice (2007): 169-197.
55. Joseph M. Reagle, 2010, *Good Faith Collaboration - The Culture of Wikipedia*, MIT Press, Cambridge, MA.
56. David Roedl, Shaowen Bardzell, and Jeffrey Bardzell. 2015. Sustainable Making? Balancing Optimism and Criticism in HCI Discourse. ACM Trans. Comput.-Hum. Interact. 22, 3, Article 15 (June 2015), 27 pages. DOI: http://dx.doi.org/10.1145/2699742
57. Greg M Scott and Roberta M Garner. 2012. *Doing Qualitative Research: Designs, Methods, and Techniques*, Pearson
58. S. Currie Sivek. 2011. "We Need a Showing of All Hands": Technological Utopianism in MAKE magazine. Journal of Communication Inquiry, 35: 187. Austin L. Toombs, Shaowen Bardzell, and Jeffrey Bardzell. 2015. The Proper Care and Feeding of Hackerspaces: Care Ethics and Cultures of Making. In Proc. CHI '15. ACM, 629–638. DOI: http://dx.doi.org/10.1145/2702123.2702522
59. Oliver Stickel, Dominik Hornung, Konstantin Aal, Markus Rohde and Volker Wulf (2015), 3D Printing with Marginalized Children—An Exploration in a Palestinian Refugee Camp, ECSCW 2015: Proceedings of the 14th European Conference on Computer Supported Cooperative Work, 19-23 September 2015, Oslo, Norway pp 83-102
60. Craig Talmage & Richard C. Knopf. 2017. *Rethinking Diversity, Inclusion, and Inclusiveness: The Quest to Better Understand Indicators of Community Enrichment and Well-Being.* In New Dimensions in Community Well-Being 7-27. 10.1007/978-3-319-55408-2_2.
61. Nick Taylor, Ursula Hurley, and Philip Connolly. 2016. Making Community: The Wider Role of Makerspaces in Public Life. In Proceedings of the 2016 CHI Conference on Human Factors in Computing Systems (CHI '16). ACM, New York, NY, USA, 1415-1425. DOI: http://dx.doi.org/10.1145/2858036.2858073
62. Nick Taylor, Loraine Clarke, and Katerina Gorkovenko. 2017. Community Inventor Days: Scaffolding Grassroots Innovation with Maker Events. In Proceedings of the 2017 Conference on Designing Interactive Systems (DIS '17). ACM, New York, NY, USA, 1201-1212. DOI: https://doi.org/10.1145/3064663.3064723
63. Austin L. Toombs. 2017. Hackerspace Tropes, Identities, and Community Values. In Proceedings of the 2017 Conference on Designing Interactive Systems (DIS '17). ACM, New York, NY, USA, 1079-1091. DOI: https://doi.org/10.1145/3064663.3064760
64. Austin L. Toombs, Shaowen Bardzell, and Jeffrey Bardzell. 2015. The Proper Care and Feeding of Hackerspaces: Care Ethics and Cultures of Making. In Proceedings of the 33rd Annual ACM Conference on Human Factors in Computing Systems (CHI '15). ACM, New York, NY, USA, 629-638. DOI: https://doi.org/10.1145/2702123.2702522
65. *UK Makerspaces – The Data*, Published by Nesta, Retrieved August 30, 2017 from: http://www.nesta.org.uk/uk-makerspaces-data

66. *Who are Makers? You Are* – Make Magazine, Retrieved August 30, 2017 from: http://makezine.com/2016/04/01/what-is-a-maker-you-are/

67. Bas van Abel, Lucas Evers, Roel Klaassen, and Peter Troxler (eds.). 2011. Open Design Now: Why Design Cannot Remain Exclusive. BIS Publishers, Amsterdam.

68. E. von Hippel, (2006). Democratizing Innovation. Cambridge, Mass: MIT Press.

Statement Making: A Maker Fashion Show Foregrounding Feminism, Gender, and Transdisciplinarity

Johanna Okerlund, Madison Dunaway, Celine Latulipe, David Wilson
UNC Charlotte
Charlotte, NC, USA
{jokerlun, mdunawa2, clatulip, davils}@uncc.edu

Eric Paulos
Electrical Engineering & Computer Sciences
University of California, Berkeley
paulos@berkeley.edu

ABSTRACT
Maker culture has been increasingly pervasive in a variety of communities and contexts, in particular devoted spaces such as Makerspaces, Hackerspaces and Fab Labs. Several people, however, have pointed out that while one of the values of these spaces is radical inclusion, the general Maker culture can be exclusive to some based on gender, race, and socioeconomic status. With the goal of disrupting existing Maker culture by developing, diversifying, and empowering our own university Maker community, we created a semi-structured making experience that we call *Statement Making*. Statement Making is a Maker Fashion show that we invited anyone from the community to participate in by "making a statement" for them or a friend to wear in a runway show. We report outcomes and experiences of those who participated. We then discuss the key aspects of the event, especially surrounding its performative aspect, using design principles of Feminist HCI to argue that events with similar aspects might also be successful at disrupting existing culture.

Author Keywords
Maker culture; Fabrication; Education; Feminism; Wearables; Fashion; Performance

ACM Classification Keywords
H.5.m. Information interfaces and presentation (e.g., HCI): Miscellaneous

INTRODUCTION
The term "maker" has become popular recently in various spaces, establishments, and contexts to describe a re-emphasis or refocusing on humankind's need and desire to create things. Surrounding this phenomenon is what has been described as the Maker Movement [14], educational initiatives [24], online platforms [29], communities, and an emerging Maker culture. Much of the increase in prevalence of Making is due in part to spaces that provide access to machines for making and support communities centered around common interests. Makerspaces exist in many public spaces such as elementary schools, universities, libraries, cities, general communities etc. They provide value to their members in terms of access to equipment and the ability to innovate, but also in terms of a social community. The result is not only a stream of innovation, but also a culture. The spaces value democratization, access, low barriers, individualism, open-endedness, and creativity [45, 24, 19, 14, 25]. Makerspace expert Laura Fleming notes that "A visit to a Makerspace should leave you with the impression that the possibilities are endless" [18]. These spaces often develop bottom-up, through grassroots efforts, as opposed to through centralized forces.

Researchers have begun to study the emerging Maker culture, to understand who is part of it and why [43]. Researchers have also pointed to problems in the culture, showing how it is not as equitable as it claims in terms of gender, race, and socioeconomic status [8]. Researchers have targeted these problems and discussed activities or design principles to help mitigate or disrupt these trends [9].

There is a tension, however, between the grassroots nature of the Maker movement and the desire for equity. If the culture is all about open-endedness, grassroots efforts, and letting people generate their own experiences, then this might mean nothing deliberate is being done to ensure equity. As Britton points out, if we leave things without intervention to run their course, then we are naïve to think that this will result in a culture that is equitable rather than one that reinforces existing sources of oppression [8]. Some experiences designed around making are great at disrupting sources of oppression, such as e-textiles [9]. However, even though these experiences have a culture that surrounds the activity itself, and it remains a challenge for that sub-culture to permeate the larger Maker culture. Also, when these experiences are used prescriptively, taken as a solution to a problem, they can introduce other issues. One of the hallmarks of Makerspaces is the complete freedom to do absolutely anything and prescriptive activities take away some of that freedom. As Maker culture grows, we need to figure out ways to create events that are generative rather than prescriptive – they should allow individuals to

DIS '18, June 9–13, 2018, Hong Kong

ACM ISBN 978-1-4503-5198-0/18/06...$15.00
https://doi.org/10.1145/3196709.3196754

generate their own experience and identity in keeping with the hallmarks of Maker culture. At the same time, it is essential to build upon affirming sub-cultures such as e-textiles, and continue to disrupt, rather than reinforce, problematic norms at the cultural level that surround the word Maker.

With these issues in mind, we created a semi-structured making event around fashion that culminated in a public performance. What we mean by semi-structured is that we gave a loose prompt for participation, but did not specify what, how, or why participants were to make. Essentially what we provided was a context and a deadline. This event was designed to develop, diversify, and empower the maker community on our campus by providing a venue that was both generative of multiple possible experiences and disrupted existing norms. The event was a making and digital fabrication fashion show called "Statement Making," where university students and community members were invited to create a wearable piece that was then presented during a runway show. The only prompt for participation was to "Make a Statement" and anything was allowed in the show. What is most novel about the design of the fashion show as a Maker experience is the performance-based aspect. Our results show that it was successful at being an intervention to develop, diversify, and empower the campus Maker community of students, faculty, and staff in that it successfully generated a range of experiences, showcased a range of voices, and was perceived in a positive light.

In this paper, we describe the design of the event and the experiences of the people who participated. We analyze the event through a feminist HCI lens [3] and discuss considerations for the design of future making events with wearables. The contributions of this paper are: 1) A detailed description of a making and digital fabrication fashion show aimed at developing, diversifying, and empowering a campus maker community, 2) A description of the outcomes and experiences from the fashion show event, garnered from personal observations of the creators and from survey data collected from participants, and 3) A set of design considerations to aid communities planning semi-structured making events aimed at developing, empowering and diversifying the maker community, specifically with a performance as the culminating event.

RELATED WORK

Maker, Hacker, and Fab Lab Movement

The Maker, Hacker, and Fab Lab movements are separate but related emerging trends in recent years. The terms are sometimes used interchangeably and the movements are related and overlapping. We discuss the key differences between the trends and the values inherent to each.

The Maker Movement has been characterized by the emergence of community-driven spaces centered around different kinds of making. While these spaces are all different, they generally share the desire to democratize making and build community [25]. Each Makerspace, however, can be radically different in terms of how they are run, who makes the decisions, what the focus is, and what kinds of making the space supports [43]. Some exist in university settings and are run by faculty with the help of students and strive to maximize learning experiences [37, 44]. Others have emerged in a more bottom-up fashion based on the needs or interests of members in a community [46]. A number of libraries have also joined the Maker movement because they believe it fits with their mission of providing access to tools that allow people to both read and write information and provide access to equipment like 3D printers and laser cutters [7, 19, 51, 46].

The Hacker movement, while similar to the Maker movement in its value in communities centered around certain types of making, has different central values. Hackerspaces tend to focus on repurposing, finding new uses for old things, and being clever [4, 47, 20]. They also tend to be more individualistic and anti-authoritarian [47].

The Fab Lab (short for Fabrication Lab) movement was started out of MIT by Neil Gershenfeld and now includes a network of over 1,000 Fab Labs all over the world. Fab Labs have a standardized set of equipment, focusing on digital fabrication tools such as CNC mills, laser cutters, and 3D printers. The commonality of tools allows for a global network of sharing designs, resources, solutions, and ideas [22]. Many Fab Labs serve local needs, allow communities to build the infrastructure around them, and focus on humanitarian needs. In addition to challenges faced by all machine-based spaces such as safety, management, and exclusivity, challenges for Fab Labs include access and literacy [22, 23].

While the movements themselves have different alignments and values, individual spaces are not necessarily directly aligned with any one movement and might be characterized by any or all of a Makerspace, Hackerspace, or Fab Lab. In the rest of the paper, we will primarily use the term Makerspace and making. Some work has been done to look at individual spaces to understand what has emerged from the bottom-up. Sheridan et al. did a case study of several Makerspaces and looked at how they set their goals and interact with the people who use them and conclude how different the spaces are [43]. Several others have looked at the practices to understand the ideas, goals, and perspectives of individual users in terms of their motivations, entry points, practices, challenges they face, and identities [28, 38, 42, 25, 34]. There is still much to learn as practices differ greatly between individuals, regions, contexts, and demographics and we further this research by studying students at a US university participating in a semi-structured making event centered around a fashion show.

Critiques of Making

Even though democratization is one of the values central to Makerspaces, they tend to not be truly equitable with respect to gender, race, or socioeconomic status [8]. Some may think that because Makerspaces and digital fabrication are so new, they are a blank slate where everyone starts off as having equal access, but Adam points out that this is naïve since this ignores systems of oppression that might be embedded in the traditions from which these new spaces emerge [2]. The United States especially suffers from gender, race, and socioeconomic status based oppression in technical and computing-related spaces stemming from socially constructed stereotypes, prior access to certain types of learning experiences, and the privilege of control over how one spends their time [11, 12, 16, 26]. Ensmenger discusses the emergence of the common computing stereotype of a male computer scientist who is antisocial, anti-authoritarian, and highly individualistic [15]. It is reasonable to expect that Makerspaces will suffer from these same stereotypes and cultural biases not only due to the strong technological component in many Makerspaces, but also due to things like the atmosphere, the vulnerability required to tinker in public, and personality traits such as a propensity to dive into things [35, 12, 33, 8].

Feminism and Making

Several researchers have investigated ways to disrupt the emerging inequitable culture surrounding making and studied alternate making identities. One strategy is to ensure that the space offers a solution to problems faced specifically by one particular group, such as daycare, since it is still expected that women in many cultures take care of the children [1]. Another approach is to expand the culture to incorporate forms of making that are not typically included, but that are familiar to certain marginalized groups. For example, Buechley focuses on e-textiles, which combine electronics with sewing and fabrics using conductive thread and sewable electronic components [9]. E-textiles offer an experience of doing technology that incorporates skills, perspectives, and interests that are traditionally part of the feminine realm. Wiebert et al. show that in groups age 8-12, e-textiles are not only successful at sparking the interest of both boys and girls, but also disrupt traditional making stereotypes and allow students to explore making identities outside of the gender binary [50].

Holbert points out that even though activities like e-textiles expand the culture to include people with wider interests, they run the risk of reinforcing stereotypes if they are articulated as a strategy to include women [27]. Similarly, a maker fashion show might be seen as feminist in that it incorporates a traditionally feminized craft into the realm of making, but it could also be seen as anti-feminist because fashion traditionally is about the subjection of women's bodies. Holbert focuses on the principles employed and associated with making. He shows that when making is framed as "a set of practices, skills, and technologies to give back to and support members of one's community" [27], young girls showed interest.

Nagbot discusses the history of feminism and making/hacking, pointing out how things like craft and care have been adopted into technological spaces as part of feminist intervention [39, 48]. Fox and Rosner investigate self-identified feminist hackers to see how they define what they do and how it is part of their identities [20]. For many, it is about hacking, or repurposing something that is oppressive. For example, since fear of failing might be a barrier to participating in making [6], a "Failure Club" changes that into a good thing [20]. Fox, however, is looking into people who identify in a certain way. The likelihood of someone to enter a space that has a certain identity is not necessarily based on that person's gender, but rather based on whether or not they have that identity, even if that identity is based on their gender. Roxane Gay points out how things she does make her feel like a "bad feminist" because they are not part of what is typically construed as a feminist identity [21]. The point is that there is not only one way to be a feminist and not only one way to adopt or not adopt a set of activities as part of a feminist identity. We thus seek to develop a culture where people can form their own identities as this is in line with the open-endedness of Maker culture, but that is not so open-ended that the culture is dominated by the rugged masculinity that seems to perpetuate in technology [15]. We seek to do this in a way such that identities similar to what Fox and Buechley discuss [20, 9] are present and prominent, but in a way that leaves room for the adoption of multiple different identities.

Feminist HCI is an emerging set of methodologies, interaction design principles, and theories to guide HCI in practice and research that are grounded in feminist theory [3]. While feminism has many different connotations, academic accounts of feminist theory are largely concerned with delving into the social and cultural construction of power structures that oppress people due to gender as well as other factors such as race, socioeconomic status, and sexual orientation. Likewise, Feminist HCI is not so much about gender equality or advocating for women in particular, but rather about considering the ways in which technology reinforces or subverts socially constructed oppressive power structures. While as of yet there are no prescriptive steps to take to practice feminist HCI, guiding characteristics and principles that are present in feminist HCI have been identified. We use Bardzell's feminist interaction design principles as a lens through which to discuss the design of the fashion show [3].

Fashion and HCI

Several researchers have explored fashion as it relates to HCI and the way we design interactive systems. Fashion and clothing are part of human culture, history, identity, and daily life. Vaughan points out that there is an intimate relationship between a person and the clothes they wear, discussing what it means to "inhabit design" [49]. Various researchers have taken aspects of our relationship to fashion and clothing and apply them to HCI, for example outfit-centric design [31], asking how questions of intimacy might help design for privacy [30], or using fashion as a lens to understand aesthetics of mobile phones [32]. Pan and Blevis explore the relationship between fashion and sustainable interaction design, deriving design principles from fashion concepts such as its relationship to communities, its adaptation to different environments and lifestyles, and its inherent personalization [40]. Pan and Stolterman discuss explicitly what it would be like if HCI became driven by fashion both in terms of how external concepts of fashion can affect what goes on in the field as well as concepts that go in and out of fashion within the field [41]. We build on this work but focus more on the culture around designing wearable technology to design an experience around making.

STATEMENT MAKING

Statement Making was a campus-wide digital fabrication fashion show designed to develop, diversify and empower the maker community. It was run at the University of North Carolina at Charlotte, a comprehensive research university in the southeast US and was open to students and community members of all disciplines. The organizers of the event were each part of different making and fabrication facilities on the campus. We discuss specifics of the context and the design of the event.

Context

UNC Charlotte has approximately 29,000 undergraduate students and 6,000 graduate students. There are several Makerspaces and Fab Labs at the university in different departments: the College of Arts and Architecture, the College of Computing and Informatics, the Library, and the College of Engineering. Each is relatively new and has different policies and staffing models. For example, the Computer Science Makerspace and the Fine Arts Fab Lab are both open to students of all departments, whereas one has to be a student in a particular class to obtain access to the Engineering makerspace facilities. While all of these spaces and organizations are run by different people and have different purposes, they all share some of the same over-arching goals: to provide access to as many students as possible. Part of that goal is about becoming a cohesive network of resources and people. While the goals of university administration and the departments who fund the spaces include creating a network of spaces, they typically do not have the bandwidth or the time to create those pathways. It was thus leaders and community members of the spaces who took it upon themselves and created this event to forge new pathways.

The Statement Making event was conceived of and run by representatives of the Computer Science Makerspace and the Fine Arts Fab Lab who also help manage the spaces. One was a current PhD student in Computer Science, the other a recent graduate with a BA in Fine Arts who became employed as the lab's team manager after graduating. The event was organized with the help of representatives from the Library, the Engineering department, and several student-run making-related organizations. While the event had the support of administrative entities, it was a grassroots effort led by dedicated community members. Several professors incorporated Statement Making into their curriculum, having their students create pieces in the classes to be worn during the show. In addition to the goal for a more connected campus Maker community, Statement Making was also born out of the informal personal observations of some of the event creators (specifically the supervisors of the Computer Science Makerspace and the Fine Arts Fab Lab, who are both authors on this paper). For example, we noticed that there were few collaborations between students in the spaces and few students had ever ventured to any of the other spaces. This resulted in each space having its own persona of student, its own use cases, and its own unique culture. We also noticed that some students who had shown interest in making had a hard time making the initial jump into a project or making the transition from downloading and printing to developing new skills. The spaces were also all set up as collections of tools. While we talked about the importance of community that precedes the tools, there was nothing we had done specifically as leaders of the spaces to implement that idea. And as Adam says, if you leave a collection of tools in a space for a culture to emerge around, it is unlikely it will be equitable [2]. From these observations, we decided there needed to be something to develop, diversify, and empower the campus-wide Maker community.

The theme for the fashion show was "Statement Making". This means creating physical things that have a purpose, but also plays off how making a statement can mean a verbal statement or something intangible. The logo is a series of colored triangles coming together to make different shapes (Figure 1). The hard angles represent the more technological side and the bright colors are to appeal to a more artistic person. The different colors and angles all come together, similar to how the different departments come together for the event. The mixed typography also speaks to the complementary differences of different disciplines. The hard angles and bright colors were meant to appeal to a range of people.

Figure 1. The Statement Making logo.

The prompt for participation was "make a statement". A statement piece could be anything that is worn — a whole outfit, a hat, an accessory, etc. We encouraged the use of digital fabrication, but also allowed pieces that had been made with traditional sewing machines or needle and thread. The reason for this was so that the overall show would combine traditional craft with new technology.

We also made sure to communicate that while pieces with a strong message were welcomed and encouraged, this was not meant to exclude those who did not know what they wanted their piece to say. We drew attention to the fact that all actions and artifacts in the world make some sort of statement and represent a point of view, even if that was not the explicit intention of their creator. The act of choosing to participate is a statement in itself, as is choosing not to participate. The framing as Statement Making was not a requirement for participation, but rather a prompt to encourage people to reflect on why they make and how the artifacts they make might be perceived by others.

Before the Show

Statement Making was advertised starting about two months before the show would take place. At this time, both the call for participation and the date of the show were announced. We sent out emails to active students, faculty, and staff who participate in the various spaces on campus, emails to the entire school of Arts and Architecture and Computing and Informatics, and posters on the walls of all academic and recreational buildings. Leading up to the show, we held a series of events to provide social, technical, and creative support.

Speed dating – Our first event was an information session with speed dating. After a session on the philosophy of Statement Making and an overview of the available resources on campus, we had students shuffle around and meet each other. We considered helping people match up for collaborations using a spreadsheet based on interest, but speed dating was a more human-focused approach that was not only open for more spontaneous collaborations but also communicated that this was not a traditional academic event. We also liked how the initial stages of a collaboration might make one feel a vulnerability that is similar to what one experiences on a date.

Workshops – Each space held a series of workshops centered around relevant techniques and tools with the hopes of adding to students' toolkit of skills, encouraging exploration, and sparking inspiration.

Model Training – We held a specific workshop for all the models who would be walking on the runway on how to walk with confidence and how to move in a way that draws the most attention to the garment they are wearing.

During the Show

The main part of the show was the runway where the designers or other community members walked down the stage wearing the fabricated pieces. Participants had to register for the event with a short description about what they made and why. Music played as the participants walked and two emcees narrated each piece, using information provided by the creators. There were also tables set up for other maker community members to show things they had been working on and tables for all the maker-related spaces and clubs on campus.

OUTCOMES

We describe the event itself and the pieces featured in it as well as the results of a post-event survey. Data about the event was collected in the form of video and photographs by the event organizers and community members. The survey was administered online via Google forms.

The Event

A total of 50 garments were part of the show. These were created by 29 individuals and 9 collaborative groups. Three individuals and one group made multiple pieces. 43 of the participants were students, 3 were faculty or staff, and 1 was from the outside community. We did not collect data on demographics of all participants in the show.

The show was divided into 5 sections: Intro, Costume, Statement, Collaborative, and LEDs. These sections were decided the day before the event based on descriptions provided in the registration cards associated with each piece. The organizers aimed to make the groups of equal size and to keep the audience engaged. The Intro section had pieces representing a wide range of work, to communicate the scope of the show. The first piece in the show was created and worn by the Dean of the College of Arts and Architecture, who was very excited by the collaboration and made a piece to represent this (Figure 2a). He also wore a bowtie and pocket square that had been 3D modeled and printed by some students.

Some of the pieces from the Costume section were cultural. One piece was a Puerto Rican Vejigante festival mask (Figure 2b). It was made collaboratively using 3D modeling and laser cutting. It also had human-actuated moving parts—the mouth and tongue could move. Other pieces from the cultural section represented or celebrated different cultures such as a Hmong headdress, a paper-cut Aztec design, a laser-cut acrylic ancient Egyptian collar. Other pieces from the costume section featured accessories such as a tail and claws (Figure 2c), a 3D printed spine (Figure 2d), and wings (Figure 2e).

Pieces in the Statement section ranged in focus. Pieces that spoke to oppression surrounding women and women's bodies were popular (Figure 2f). Other issues featured included gendered bathroom laws, Islamophobia, Black Lives Matter, pollution, and the declining bee population.

The collaborative section had pieces that were the result of collaborations between students of the same and different departments. One piece was a collaboration between an electrical engineering student, an art student, and a dancer. Their idea was to make the piece light up based on the dancer's movements. They had to consider the dance, aesthetics, technology, and the overall effect (Figure 2h).

The last section, LEDs, had all of the pieces that lit up and had the most technology directly incorporated into the garments. This was also the section where most of the computer science students' work was featured. Notable pieces included a dress that lit up whenever lightning strikes in the state (Figure 2i), a chameleon dress that uses a color sensor to change to the color of the surroundings, and an LED-lit hijab.

(a) (b) (c) (d) (e)

(f) (g) (h) (i)

Figure 2. (a) The Dean of the College of Arts and Architecture wears a piece he made and 3D printed accessories made by a student; (b) Puerto Rican Vejigante festival mask; (c) Laser cut light up tail and claws modeled by an Arts professor; (d) 3D printed spine; (e) Laser cut wings; (f) Consent Statement; (g) A student explores the materials themselves in the creation of a new textile; (h) The result of a collaboration between an Electrical Engineering student, a dance student, and an art student. The dress lights up based on dance movements; (i) Dress and umbrella light up whenever lightning strikes in the state.

Post-event survey

We administered a survey to all participants 8 months after the event to hear their reflections and gauge the lasting effect of their participation in the show. As the goals of the show were to develop, diversify, and empower the campus Maker community, we designed the survey questions to capture insights around these themes. Since many of the pieces had a political alignment, it seemed that the event was empowering for participants, so we asked questions about the perceived purpose of the show overall. As far as diversifying and developing the community, we wanted to see the extent to which the event was successful at generating a multitude of experiences rather than one singular experience. We also wanted to know to what extent participating pushed people out of their comfort zone, prompted them to grow, and provided them with opportunities to meet new and different people.

Specific survey questions include:

1. Why did you participate in last year's show?

2. What did you make and why?
3. How did your participation in the show push you out of your comfort zone (if at all)?
4. Did you attend the event and watch (at least the majority of) the runway show? If so, how would you describe the event to someone who didn't go?
5. Did you make any connections as a result of your participation? Please describe.
6. Where is your garment now and why?
7. Are you going to participate again this year? Why?

Results were aggregated and coded within each of the questions asked based on emergent themes, which were determined by the authors following a thematic analysis approach [13]. We later discuss the results in terms of Feminist HCI interaction design principles.

Participants

A total of 8 fashion show participants responded to the survey (8/29). All respondents were either current students or recently graduated at the time of participation in the event. Three reported their field of study as Art (P3, P4, P6), two were Graphic Design (P1, P7), one of whom also studies Digital Media (P7). One student was from Architecture (P5), one was a Computer Science student (P2), and one reported their field of study as Electrical Engineering, Business, and Software (P8)

Two of the respondents were in the same collaborative team (P6 and P8). Three of the other respondents were also part of collaborative teams.

Five respondents were men (P1, P2, P4, P7, P8), three were women (P3, P5, P6), and none were non-binary.

Purpose of Participating

We asked participants why they participated in the fashion show. Three reported that they participated in the event due to an existing connection either to one of the maker labs or to the university community (P1, P2, P4). P1 said that he wanted "to support the digital fabrication community on campus". P2 said "It was a great opportunity for [sic] take part in a makerspace event".

Two people participated because of an existing interest in fashion (P3, P6). Two people were drawn to the event simply as something new, exciting, or different (P4, P7). One participant noted his desire "To collaborate with students from different departments" (P8). One participant did not respond to this question (P5).

Purpose of Artifact

In addition to the reasons for participation, we also asked participants why they made what they made. Responses fell into 5 categories, described in more detail below:

- To experiment with a technique or process or do something in a new way (P2, P7)
- To make a statement (P3)
- To bridge fashion and technology (P6, P8)
- To have some sort of functionality (P2, P5)
- To achieve a certain aesthetic (P1, P4)

All participants responded with different reasons for their garments than the reasons they provided for their participation in the show, except for P8. P8, the Electrical Engineer/Business/Software student, was part of a collaborative team with an Art student who reported that his reason for participation was collaboration, also reported that the purpose of the piece his team created was "to show a beautiful amalgamation of fashion and tech community" (P8). P6, who worked with P8, used similar language to describe their piece, saying "The garment was made to bridge the gap between fashion and technology to function as a wearable", though her initial reason for participating in the fashion show was not the collaboration itself, but rather because of her existing experience with fashion.

P2 (Computer Science) and P7 (Graphic Design and Digital Media), both reported the purpose of their pieces as exploratory. P2 was exploring how to take weather data from the web and "display them creatively" using lights. P7 made a laser cut wooden textile because he "wanted to experiment with combining digital and analog processes".

P3 (Art) says she "made three garments that made a statement regarding three different feminist topics. I made these because the show was called "Statement Making" and these were topics I feel very strongly about." P3 was the only one of our survey respondents who made a piece with a political message and was the only who commented on the theme of "Statement Making" as being an integral part of her inspiration.

P2 (Computer Science) and P5 (Architecture) aimed for functionality. P2, in addition to exploring creative ways of visualizing weather data, aimed to make a functional piece that was successful in getting the data and translating it into light. P5 made a transformational dress that "solves the problem of not knowing what to wear".

P1 (Art) and P4 (Art) both discussed the purpose of their piece as being to achieve a certain aesthetic that was of personal interest to them. P1, who made a 3D printed gauntlet "wanted to make something fantasy oriented" and said that the "piece is literally a product of my imagination from when I was a little kid". P4 says that he "love[s] concept art and film design and I wanted to make something of that ilk" and thus made "a sci-fi-esque costume/couture".

Descriptions of Event

When asked how participants would describe the event to someone who had not been there, most mentioned the aesthetic, artistic or fashion-related nature of the pieces and overall feel (P1, P2, P4, P5, P6, P7), saying things like "fun casual fashion show" (P6), and "you could clearly see the passion for fashion" (P4). P2, a computer science student, said it was "an art show where the art is stuck on people".

Two participants described the show as a collaborative or interdisciplinary event (P3, P6). P3 (Art) was the only one who mentioned technology in their description, saying it involved students from different disciplines who "incorporated making statements and different technological aspects".

Two participants commented on the political aspect of the show (P3, P5). And four participants commented in just a general positive way (P4, P6, P7, P8), saying things like "energetic and fun" (P4) and "bold and wonderful" (P8).

Connections and Bridges

When asked if they made any connections, almost all respondents reported some sort of social aspect to their participation (P1 made no connections and P5 did not answer). Four respondents explicitly said they met someone from a different discipline or from the other side of campus (P2, P3, P6, P8). Two respondents mentioned that they met or reconnected with people, but did not say whether they were from the same or a different discipline (P4, P7).

We also asked participants where their garment currently was to see if it had a life beyond the show. One respondent said their garment no longer existed because they had disassembled the garment so others could use the electronic components (P8). For one participant, the piece he made for the show went on to be displayed in another art show (P7). No other participants discussed a definitive way in which their work for the fashion show was a bridge to something else. However, two participants said they were keeping their pieces with some sort of future in mind (P4, P6).

Others stored their garments not for a purpose, but just because they did not know what else to do with it (P1, P2, P3, P5). P1 noted that he is storing the piece he made, but sees no future use for it because it was "for a specific, one-time event". Some participants discussed the impracticality of what they had made for actual wearing (P2, P3, P5).

Learning and Growth

When asked if and how participating in the show pushed respondents out of their comfort zone, only P1 said it did not push him at all. Other respondents said it pushed them to learn a new skill related to sewing (P2, P5, P8), two had never done fashion before (P2, P7), and one mentioned it pushed them to collaborate with someone new (P6).

Two mentioned that having an audience was new for them (P3, P4). For P4, this pushed him in terms of scope to take on something larger than usual. P3 said her "participation as a designer helped to push my creativity of what statement I wanted to make and how. And my participation as a model walking in the show pushed me out of comfort zone [sic] by being on stage and performing in front of a large group of people". P3's work also spoke most directly to the theme of the show, taking the notion of "statement making" to heart. She discussed stepping out of her comfort zone in terms of being in front of people and in terms of considering a new creative medium and plans to push herself further next year. As an art student, the event is likely a valuable experience for her and others to develop their voices through fabrication and fashion.

For some, the benefit was to take an existing skill of theirs and use it either in collaboration with others (P8) or for their own idea (P2). This provided them the opportunity to deepen their learning of the skill and work through any complications of working in a different context. P5, an architecture student, took a very architectural and pragmatic approach to her design, which was a garment that could change shape and "solves the problem of not knowing what to wear". As in architecture, she worked to combine both form and function, thinking not only of the aesthetics, but also of the human interfaces with clothing and how that relationship could be improved.

All participants said they were interested in participating again in next year's show except for P1 who thought since he graduated he would not be able to. P3 was the only participant who expressed the way she would continue to push herself next year, wanting to "collaborate more with other students and incorporate more technology".

DISCUSSION

We discuss takeaways at the level of the individual and at the level of how the individuals relate to the event as an interdisciplinary collaboration. We then discuss the key aspects of our event for consideration during the future design of a performance-centered wearable-based making event. Throughout our discussion, we refer to Bardzell's Feminist HCI interaction design principles (plurality, participation, self-disclosure, advocacy, and ecology) [3].

Development, Diversification, and Empowerment

As the goals of our event were to develop, diversify, and empower the campus community, we discuss our results in terms of these themes. We saw clear evidence of development at both an individual level and at a community level. Examples of the types of individual growth included the opportunity to develop voice (P3), appropriate a skill to a new domain (P2, P5, P8), acting as a catalyst to collaborate (P6, P8), and experimentation (P2, P7). An increase in collaborations and people meeting new people means that the community is developing to be more connected across campus as well as more diverse and less siloed based on lab. The number of political statements shows that the event was an empowering platform for some to voice their opinions. The fact that participants tried new skills shows also that they were empowered to explore in the realm of digital fabrication. Our data also shows evidence of diversification in the form of multiple experiences. There was not just one way or reason for participating or view of the event as a whole. This means that this was successful at generating multiple experiences as opposed to prescribing what the experience should be. Overall, this event builds on the sub-culture of the e-textiles movement in disrupting norms surrounding Maker culture in a way that is in the spirit of the open-endedness of the Maker community.

Key Aspects

Our analysis provides insight and considerations for the design of future semi-structured making events centered around a fashion show or other wearable-based performance. Based on the outcomes of the event we ran, we identified these aspects of our event as key to the experiences and outcomes. We also discuss how these aspects and our results speak to Bardzell's feminist HCI interaction design principles (plurality, participation, self-disclosure, advocacy, and ecology) [3]. Ultimately, by using these principles as a lens through which to look at these generalized aspects of the event we ran, we argue that there is something about these aspects that is Feminist.

The performance

Working towards being in front of people is inherently different than doing or making just for oneself or working alone. Several of our participants pointed out how the performative aspect pushed them to do more or to be bold.

Performance is also inherently different from giving a demonstration, even though both are done in front of people. A demo implies showing and demonstrating an external artifact, whereas performance implies acting and becoming. The performance thus inherently invites consideration of the self, identity, and expression as the artifact is inseparable from the human who is wearing it. Judith Butler talks about gender as a performance, not in the sense that it is like a costume we can choose to put on or take of, but rather in the sense that it is something that is learned, practiced repetitively, and displayed publicly [10]. Thus, the way we perform and our identity are inextricably tied. Creating an event that involved performance provided an opportunity for participants to reflect on identity.

The stage

A performance takes place on a stage, but we define and build the stage well before the performance. It exists in peoples' minds before they even start considering what to make. Some stages are to make people laugh, some are to tell a story. Our stage is a runway, which exists as a place for people to show their fashion designs being worn by models who walk and pose. It is also a place where traditionally women's bodies are put on display and can have connotations of being anti-feminist and oppressive, but we used the "Statement Making" prompt to subvert the historically constructed view of fashion by making the focus on voices, rather than on bodies.

Although a runaway can be gender oppressive, it is at least a place where gender is not invisible. Because fashion is largely gendered (men wear different clothing than women), a piece that is worn by a man will be perceived differently than when that same piece is worn by a woman. Bardzell talks about the feminist design principle of embodiment and calls upon designers to consider differences in socially constructed gendered bodies. Using a runway as a stage provides room for this because the pieces were not shown in isolation, but through an embodied performance. The designers had to consider the body of the human who would be wearing the piece for the show.

The invitation

People were invited to participate in the event. The nature of the invitation was key. Our only prompt for participation was to "Make a Statement". We consider this a generative invitation rather than a prescriptive invitation, in that it allows individuals to generate their own experience rather than us prescribing exactly what their experience will be. This resonates with Feminist HCI design principles of plurality and participation [3]. These two principles are in opposition to the general HCI concept of universal usability. They instead advocate for designs that are sensitive to the complexity and diversity of what constitutes the human experience and the experiences of the marginalized [3]. Digital fabrication is an area of computing that is open to an almost limitless potential of applications, purposes, and perspectives. However, it is often the case that experiences designed around digital fabrication are designed around one particular application, or identity, as Holbert points out with the e-textiles [27] and as Roxane Gay notes in her self-labeling as a "bad feminist" [21]. A particular activity or action might be part of one's identity as a person or as a maker, but there is more than one way for it to be part of them. The fashion show, while culminating in one common event, allowed for a plurality of experiences and pathways to participation that covered a range of what digital fabrication has to offer. The non-competitive nature of the invitation was also key as it encouraged internal and intrinsic reflection rather than external comparison.

The invitation is also where the Feminist HCI design principle of self-disclosure has the most potential to be incorporated [3]. When we invited people to participate, we included who we were and that our goal was to make a fun collaborative event. We did not, however, discuss the event in terms of the Feminist HCI principles such as advocacy or pluralism or the event as a whole as feminist.

The frame and the voice

With any event, there is a purpose that lies within a particular discipline or multiple disciplines. For example, it might be an artistic goal, an educational goal, a creative goal, etc., or the combination of several. Statement Making was in every way interdisciplinary: the coordinators of the event were representatives from Fine Arts and Computer Science, we encouraged collaborations between departments, and the stage brought together fashion and technology. We invited people to participate as individuals or collaborate with someone from a different department, being careful to maintain that while there were different ways of participating, no one discipline was more important than another. However, our results show that the fashion show did not have equal representation or experiences from students of different disciplines. We introduce the notion of the *frame* of the event and the *voice* of an individual to discuss these different experiences.

Lying at the intersection between fashion and technology, Statement Making might be described as doing something creative in fashion through technology (we call this Art-frame) or doing something creative with technology through fashion (we call this Technologist-frame). Given these two framings, we can consider what the voice of either an artist or technologist might say given their perspective as such:

Technologist-voice, Technologist-frame: The future of computing is not screen-based. It is physical, gestural, embedded in the world around us, and ultimately worn on our bodies. For the Statement Making fashion show, let's push the bounds of technology's relationship to the body.

Art-voice, Technologist-frame: The computer scientists are working to push technology to be more wearable. Let's share our skills with them to ensure the aesthetics are intentional and speak to our humanity.

Art-voice, Art-frame: Fashion is about pushing the bounds, being creative, making a statement, doing new things. We use technology to push the field of fashion forward.

Technologist-voice, Art-frame: Artists are always working to push the bounds of creativity. Let's share our skills with them towards that vision.

Interestingly, both students from the art/design side as well as students from the CS/technology side described the event with the Art-frame, articulating the overall purpose as being fashion-related. Even the all-CS team described not only an Art-frame, but also an Art-voice (P2) by viewing the event as "an art show where the art is stuck on people" and seeing their own contribution as a creative exploration rather than a technological innovation.

We discuss the frame and voice here in terms of Bardzell's principle of advocacy. While having a bias towards a certain frame and a certain voice might limit who opts in to participate, it might also engage new participants who would not otherwise be part of the community. It is also likely beneficial for students in one discipline to practice adopting the voice of another discipline. This allows them to deepen their understanding and develop a voice they might not have known that they have.

The community

As with any stage-based event, an entire community gets involved with everything from costumes to scenery to programs. The Fashion Show was the same way, with projects like designing fabricated giveaways and creating foldable popcorn holders. The fact that there were multiple points of entry gave opportunities for more community members to be involved and excited. Also, the spaces of the individuals who hosted the events, the departments involved, and the professors who participated showed that there were existing community infrastructures that contributed to the social dynamics of the event and everything surrounding it. This again resonates with Bardzell's principles of pluralism and participation.

The After-party

Bardzell calls upon designers to consider the ecology of a system in interaction design in terms of how the design fits into a larger system of designs and to consider the way demographics factor into that ecosystem [3]. The fashion show we ran is part of a complex ecology including the spaces involved, the academic departments, the university, the broader maker community, and the broader fashion design community. To consider the ecology, we must consider the most broad and far-reaching impact. Because the fashion show was a one-time event, there is the opportunity and the need to allow the artifacts from the event to permeate other spaces and have a life beyond the event. Responses from our participants support this as they said that they have energy and interest for some sort of continued engagement with what they made and with the community involved in the event.

CONCLUSION

We presented the design and outcomes from running an interdisciplinary maker fashion show at a university campus that had the goal of developing, diversifying, and empowering the campus Maker community. We extracted key aspects from the event and discussed these in terms of Feminist HCI design principles to inform the design of future semi-structured making events culminating in a performance. By using these principles as a lens through which to look at these generalized aspects of the event we ran, we argue that there is something about these aspects that is feminist. Applying these aspects in the design of future making events will help to develop an array of experiences that disrupt the norms of Maker culture and continue to develop, diversify, and empower the Maker community.

ACKNOWLEDGEMENTS

The photographs from the event were taken by Jonathan Helms, Brianna Robinson, and Caleb Roenigk. The logo was designed by Caleb Roenigk. We also acknowledge the hard work of all the designers who participated in the show and all the students, faculty, staff, and community members who helped. Thank you to the UNCC College of Arts and Architecture, College of Computing and Informatics, and Chancellor's Diversity fund for their monetary support of the event. Thank you to the anonymous reviewers for their thoughtful and helpful insights.

REFERENCES

1. Mothership hackermoms. http://mothership.hackermoms.org/. Accessed: 2016-08-22.

2. A. E. Adam, "Hacking into hacking: Gender and the hacker phenomenon," *ACM SIGCAS Computers and Society*, vol. 33, no. 4, p. 3, 2003.
3. Shaowen Bardzell. 2010. Feminist HCI: taking stock and outlining an agenda for design. In *Proceedings of the SIGCHI Conference on Human Factors in Computing Systems* (CHI '10). ACM, New York, NY, USA, 1301-1310. DOI: https://doi.org/10.1145/1753326.1753521
4. Jeffrey Bardzell, Shaowen Bardzell, and Austin Toombs. 2014. "Now that's definitely a proper hack": self-made tools in hackerspaces. In *Proceedings of the SIGCHI Conference on Human Factors in Computing Systems* (CHI '14). ACM, New York, NY, USA, 473-476. DOI: https://doi.org/10.1145/2556288.2557221
5. Shaowen Bardzell, Jeffrey Bardzell, and Sarah Ng. 2017. Supporting Cultures of Making: Technology, Policy, Visions, and Myths. In *Proceedings of the 2017 CHI Conference on Human Factors in Computing Systems* (CHI '17). ACM, New York, NY, USA, 6523-6535. DOI: https://doi.org/10.1145/3025453.3025975
6. Robert Charles Birney, Harvey Burdick, and Richard Collier Teevan. *Fear of failure*. Van Nostrand-Reinhold Co., 1969.
7. Leanne Bowler. Creativity through" maker" experiences and design thinking in the education of librarians. *Knowledge Quest*, 42(5):58, 2014.
8. Laura Britton. Power, access, status: The discourse of race, gender, and class in the maker movement. *University of Washington Technology and Social Change Group*, 2015
9. Buechley, Leah, et al. "The LilyPad Arduino: using computational textiles to investigate engagement, aesthetics, and diversity in computer science education." *Proceedings of the SIGCHI conference on Human factors in computing systems*. ACM, 2008.
10. Butler, Judith. Gender trouble: Feminism and the subversion of identity. routledge, 2011.
11. Debbie Chachra. Why I am not a maker. *The Atlantic*, 23, 2015.
12. Sapna Cheryan, Victoria C Plaut, Paul G Davies, and Claude M Steele. Ambient belonging: how stereotypical cues impact gender participation in computer science. *Journal of personality and social psychology*, 97(6):1045, 2009.
13. Clarke, Victoria, and Virginia Braun. "Thematic analysis." *Encyclopedia of critical psychology*. Springer New York, 2014. 1947-1952.
14. Dougherty, Dale. "The maker movement." *Innovations: Technology, Governance, Globalization* 7.3 (2012): 11-14.
15. Ensmenger, Nathan. "“Beards, Sandals, and Other Signs of Rugged Individualism”: Masculine Culture within the Computing Professions." Osiris 30.1 (2015): 38-65.
16. K. Evans, "Barriers to participation of women in technological education and the role of distance education," *Commonwealth of Learning, Vancouver*, 1995.
17. Laura Fleming. *Worlds of making: best practices for establishing a makerspace for your school.* Corwin Press, 2015.
18. Laura Fleming. A maker culture. *PRINCIPAL*, 95(4):16–19, March April 2016.
19. I. Fourie and A. Meyer, "What to make of makerspaces: Tools and diy only or is there an interconnected information resources space?" *Library Hi Tech*, vol. 33, no. 4, pp. 519–525, 2015.
20. Sarah Fox, Rachel Rose Ulgado, and Daniela Rosner. Hacking culture, not devices: Access and recognition in feminist hackerspaces. In *Proceedings of the 18th ACM conference on Computer supported cooperative work & social computing*, pages 56–68. ACM, 2015.
21. Roxanne Gay. 2014. *Bad feminist*. Hachette UK, 2014.
22. Neil Gershenfeld. 2008. *Fab: the coming revolution on your desktop--from personal computers to personal fabrication.* Basic Books, 2008.
23. Neil Gershenfeld, Alan Gershenfeld, Joel Cutcher-Gershenfeld. 2017 *Designing Reality*. Basic Books, 2017.
24. Halverson, Erica Rosenfeld, and Kimberly Sheridan. "The maker movement in education." *Harvard Educational Review*84.4 (2014): 495-504.
25. Mark Hatch (2013). *The Maker Movement Manifesto*. McGraw-Hill Education.
26. S. Henn, "When women stopped coding," *NPR Planet Money*, vol. 21, 2014.
27. Nathan Holbert. 2016. Bots for tots : building inclusive makerspaces by leveraging "ways of knowing ." In *Proceedings of the ACM Conference on Interaction Design and Children* (IDC 2016), 79–88. http://doi.org/10.1145/2930674.2930718
28. Nathaniel Hudson, Celena Alcock, and Parmit K. Chilana. 2016. Understanding Newcomers to 3D Printing: Motivations, Workflows, and Barriers of

Casual Makers. In *Proceedings of the 2016 CHI Conference on Human Factors in Computing Systems* (CHI '16). ACM, New York, NY, USA, 384-396. DOI: https://doi.org/10.1145/2858036.2858266

29. Instructables. http://www.instructables.com/. Accessed: 2018-28-03
30. Cindy Jacob and Bruno Dumas. 2014. Designing for intimacy: how fashion design can address privacy issues in wearable computing. In Proceedings of the 2014 ACM International Symposium on Wearable Computers: Adjunct Program (ISWC '14 Adjunct). ACM, New York, NY, USA, 185-192. DOI=http://dx.doi.org/10.1145/2641248.2641353
31. Oskar Juhlin, Yanqing Zhang, Cristine Sundbom, and Ylva Fernaeus. 2013. Fashionable shape switching: explorations in outfit-centric design. In Proceedings of the SIGCHI Conference on Human Factors in Computing Systems (CHI '13). ACM, New York, NY, USA, 1353-1362. DOI: https://doi.org/10.1145/2470654.2466178
32. Oskar Juhlin and Yanqing Zhang. 2011. Unpacking social interaction that make us adore: on the aesthetics of mobile phones as fashion items. In Proceedings of the 13th International Conference on Human Computer Interaction with Mobile Devices and Services (MobileHCI '11). ACM, New York, NY, USA, 241-250. DOI: https://doi.org/10.1145/2037373.2037410
33. J. C. Kraft, "Who is a maker?" *Bright*, 2015.
34. Kuznetsov, Stacey, and Eric Paulos. "Rise of the Expert Amateur: Diy Projects, Communities, and Cultures." Proceedings of the 6th Nordic Conference on Human-Computer Interaction: Extending Boundaries ACM, 2010. 295-304.
35. J. Lewis, "Barriers to women's involvement in hackspaces and makerspaces," 2015.
36. Silvia Lindtner, Garnet D. Hertz, and Paul Dourish. 2014. Emerging sites of HCI innovation: hackerspaces, hardware startups & incubators. In Proceedings of the SIGCHI Conference on Human Factors in Computing Systems (CHI '14). ACM, New York, NY, USA, 439-448. DOI: http://dx.doi.org/ 10.1145/2556288.2557132
37. Lee Martin. The promise of the maker movement for education. *Journal of Pre-College Engineering Education Research (J-PEER)*, 5(1):4, 2015.
38. Milne, Andrew. *What Makes a Maker: Common Attitudes, Habits and Skills from the Do-It-Yourself (DIY) Community*. Diss. Communication, Art & Technology: School of Interactive Arts and Technology, 2014.
39. SSL Nagbot. 2016. "Feminist hacking/making: Exploring new gender horizons of possibility." *Journal of Peer Production* 8 (2016): 1-10.
40. Yue Pan and Eli Blevis. 2014. Fashion thinking: lessons from fashion and sustainable interaction design, concepts and issues. In Proceedings of the 2014 conference on Designing interactive systems (DIS '14). ACM, New York, NY, USA, 1005-1014. DOI: https://doi.org/10.1145/2598510.2598586
41. Yue Pan and Erik Stolterman. 2015. What if HCI Becomes a Fashion Driven Discipline?. In Proceedings of the 33rd Annual ACM Conference on Human Factors in Computing Systems (CHI '15). ACM, New York, NY, USA, 2565-2568. DOI: https://doi.org/10.1145/2702123.2702544
42. Rosner, D., and Bean, J. (2009). Learning From IKEA Hacking: I'm Not One to Decoupage a Tabletop and Call It a Day. In *Proc. of CHI2009*. ACM Press.
43. Kimberly Sheridan, et al. (2014). "Learning in the Making: A Comparative Case Study of Three Makerspaces." Harvard Educational Review. 84(4):505-531.
44. Andrew Richard Schrock. Education in disguise: Culture of a hacker and maker space. *InterActions: UCLA Journal of Education and Information Studies*, 10(1), 2014.
45. Schön, Sandra, Martin Ebner, and Swapna Kumar. "The Maker Movement. Implications of new digital gadgets, fabrication tools and spaces for creative learning and teaching." *eLearning Papers* 39 (2014): 14-25.
46. N. Taylor, U. Hurley, and P. Connolly, "Making community: the wider role of makerspaces in public life," in *Proceedings of the 2016 CHI Conference on Human Factors in Computing Systems*. ACM, 2016, pp. 1415–1425.
47. Austin L. Toombs. 2017. Hackerspace Tropes, Identities, and Community Values. In *Proceedings of the 2017 Conference on Designing Interactive Systems* (DIS '17). ACM, New York, NY, USA, 1079-1091. DOI: https://doi.org/10.1145/3064663.3064760
48. Austin L. Toombs, Shaowen Bardzell, and Jeffrey Bardzell. 2015. The Proper Care and Feeding of Hackerspaces: Care Ethics and Cultures of Making. In Proceedings of the 33rd Annual ACM Conference on Human Factors in Computing Systems (CHI '15). ACM, New York, NY, USA, 629-638. DOI: https://doi.org/10.1145/2702123.2702522

49. Laurene Vaughan. 2006. Embodying design: the lived relationship between artefact, user and the lived experience of design. In Proceedings of the ninth conference on Participatory design: Expanding boundaries in design - Volume 1 (PDC '06), Vol. 1 ACM, New York, NY, USA, 41-46. DOI=http://dx.doi.org/10.1145/1147261.1147268

50. Anne Weibert, Andrea Marshall, Konstantin Aal, Kai Schubert, and Jennifer Rode. 2014. Sewing interest in E-textiles: analyzing making from a gendered perspective. In *Proceedings of the 2014 conference on Designing interactive systems* (DIS '14). ACM, New York, NY, USA, 15-24. DOI: https://doi.org/10.1145/2598510.2600886

51. Rebekah Willett (2017): Learning through making in public libraries: theories, practices, and tensions, Learning, Media and Technology, DOI: 10.1080/17439884.2017.1369107

Exploring Aesthetic Enhancement of Wearable Technologies for Deaf Women

Danielle Wilde
SDU Design, University of Southern Denmark, Kolding
d@daniellewilde.com

Patrizia Marti
University of Siena
Siena, Italy
patrizia.marti@unisi.it

ABSTRACT
The Quietude project uses making, participation and co-design to collectively imagine a more sustainable, aesthetically enriched future for deaf women, by developing wearables that respond to the women's needs and desires: those that are well known, and those that may be only dimly glimpsed. We present our motivation and process, and describe our first workshop that brought together deaf women, ethicists, makers, designers and technology experts. The workshop led to the design and development of an ecology of jewellery products: fashionable accessories that enhance the experience of deaf women by translating sounds into vibration, light patterns and shape change. We reflect on the opportunities and challenges of developing aesthetically rich wearables for deaf women, using experimental participatory design methods, and the value of considering disability as an opportunity for wearables design, rather than as an issue that needs to be addressed or solved.

Author Keywords
Disability aesthetics; co-design; research through design; material cultures; wearables.

ACM Classification Keywords
H.5.m. Information interfaces and presentation (e.g., HCI): Miscellaneous.

INTRODUCTION
A common, if problematic, view of disability is as a lack or insufficiency to overcome [82]. As a result, many well-meaning technology experts seek to "solve" the "problem of disability" through tech fixes by (re)making disabled bodies [9]. The resulting technologies may conform well to medical needs, but they often neglect complex aesthetic needs of the individual. Quietude [69] takes a different approach. Rather than seeing disability as a problem, the Quietude project values disability as a form of human variation. We recognise that disability is in part medically constructed, in part socially constructed, and that the economy between social representations and the body is not unidirectional or non-existent, but reciprocal and thus complexly embodied [63]. We agree with feminist philosophers that knowledge is socially situated and adheres in embodiment, that identities are socially constructed (and thus embodied), and that some bodies—in particular disabled bodies—are excluded by dominant social ideologies [33, 34, 63]. We also recognise that, as a result, people in marginal social positions, such as deaf persons in hearing-oriented contexts, "enjoy an epistemological privilege that allows them to theorise society differently from those in dominant social locations" [33, 34, 63]. We therefore consider disability as a source of valuable perspectives from which to design—not only for disabled persons, but for everyone. Grounding our work thus, in theories of complex embodiment, demands mindful attention to the complex embodied expertise of the people we are designing for. It requires we find effective ways of surfacing divergent, perspectives, while being attentive to how radically these perspectives may differ from our own.

Our team includes deaf people—mostly women—from a range of professional backgrounds and with varying levels of deafness, as well as ethicists, designers, makers and technology experts. Our process draws from technology, fashion, material cultures and crafting, and uses a curated form of thinking-through-making, supported by a participatory, applied action-reflection approach to Research through Design [42] to surface the deaf collaborators' needs and desires. We adapt these generative research methods [60] to foreground ethics, and embodied and material approaches to aesthetics, in the specific context of working with deaf people. Our aim is to surface individual perspectives, and collectively imagine more sustainable, aesthetically enriched futures for deaf women, in a world which is strongly oriented towards sound. As we will discuss, this process is affording deep reflection, and diverse responses to our deaf collaborators' needs and desires: those that are well known, and those that may be only dimly glimpsed.

In this article, we discuss our first workshop, and the ways that we use participatory Research through Design and thinking-through-making to bring the diverse team members together. We present our workshop findings, system design and first prototypes, and reflect on the opportunities and challenges of developing aesthetically rich wearables with and for deaf women. We then highlight challenges and

DIS '18, June 9–13, 2018, Hong Kong

ACM ISBN 978-1-4503-5198-0/18/06…$15.00
https://doi.org/10.1145/3196709.3196777.

opportunities of designing for aesthetic enrichment in the context of deaf women. In doing so, we reflect on how working in specific, demanding contexts of use can enrich wearables research for any context. Our contribution, thus, goes beyond the context of wearables development for deaf women, to the development of wearables more broadly.

FASHIONING COMPLEX EMBODIMENT

Culture vs. engineering:

Wearable elements—clothing, modules and devices—can support development of novel, technologically augmented clothing and accessories. Clothing and accessories perform important physical, social and psychological functions [6], among them providing protection and concealment, supporting communication and individualistic expression, and signifying status or affiliation [2]. Fashion designers consciously engage with these functions to produce fashionable and philosophical meanings in tangible form that wearers navigate and adapt to their personal skills, preferences and changing circumstances [7].

While wearables have the potential to significantly enhance such functions, and also define new ones [58, 64], developers of wearables seem to struggle with what may seem competing demands from culture and engineering and typically pay scant attention to idiosyncratic needs of potential wearers—for well-justified economic and technological reasons. As a result, on one hand, we find a wealth of projects that explore the cultural, aesthetic and poetic potential of wearables that typically remain outside the market: in museums, galleries, and design spaces, operating as tantalising thought provocations, unable to be worn, to be adapted to personal contexts, or to impact everyday lives through use. On the other hand, we find increasingly sophisticated technical offerings for use in health, medicine, sports, fitness and safety. These wearables often address a specific need and are brought to market with minimal consideration of cultural meaning, social impact or design aesthetics. The results—particularly in medical and safety contexts—can be out of sync with public opinion and the cultural currency of fashion and dress.

Merging cultural understandings of how and why people engage with dress, and technology-oriented understandings of what might be important to focus on when developing wearables, can bring benefit. Doing so remains a challenge, a challenge that fashion theory can help us to think about.

Fashioning relevance:

Fashion theory foregrounds social and cultural aspects of dress, recognising it as a crucial aspect of embodiment, that shapes the self physically and psychologically [20, 66]. As Entwistle argues [19], the body is a socially constructed phenomenon—at once a physical body, consisting of its biological materials, and a part of culture, influenced by gender, society *and* circumstance. There is thus no single 'body' that is everywhere and always the same that we can design for [2]. This perspective echoes complex theories of embodiment and disability theory [62, 63, 82]. Additionally, the ways that any person wears clothes shifts and adapts in response to both material and cultural concerns [2]. Such needs vary both between and inside cultures, depending on social expectations encountered in daily life, and personal choices that can shift from person to person as well as from moment to moment. Wearables do not typically afford such 'shifting'—between persons, bodies, contexts, circumstances, cultures, or moods.

Dress relates people to each other [8]. The act of dressing is an embodied activity that links society, culture, social interactions and daily lives. It is an intimate expression of the experience and presentation of the self [56] that cannot be isolated from the moving body it adorns [19]. The personal and social entanglement of dressing is a largely overlooked design opportunity for wearables. Our process holds attention to the associated entanglement and shifting.

Embodying felt experience:

A major challenge for design that sits close to the body is to work with relationships between bodies, materials and contexts [68]. As discussed in [86]: "Embodied Design" responds to this challenge. It enlivens design and research potential by leveraging all of a person's senses in an emergent design space. Embodied Design draws on phenomenology [35, 36, 51] and related theoretical frameworks such as pragmatist aesthetics [14, 65], embodied cognition [75] and embodied, embedded and enacted minds [10, 11, 25, 26, 27, 46]. It covers a diversity of methods, approaches, ontological registers, and changing definitions and—like phenomenology—can be considered a "style of thinking" rather than a doctrine or method; a "re-learning to look at the world" that favours reflective attentiveness to "lived experience" [51]. Unlike Embodied Interaction [16], embodied design brings a phenomenologically informed focus to the full cycle of design research and development: ideation, speculation, engagement and analysis, as well as interaction. It thus moves beyond Dourish's proposition for embodied interaction [16, 17] to include methods designed to ensure the perspective of the mobile body [48, 50, 73, 83], to address the mundane and the intimate, to inspire new forms of interactions and new forms of design—for the actual corporeal, pulsating, live, felt body (c.f.[39]). When applied to wearables, Embodied Design connects intimately to theories of fashion and dress, and complex theories of embodiment. It can thus be leveraged to understand how to socially embed wearables in ways that support different wearers' highly personal, and shifting, needs and desires.

WEARABLE TECHNOLOGIES FOR DEAF PEOPLE

In this section, we focus on related research in the area of interactive jewellery, and accessories and wearables for deaf persons—the focus of the Quietude project.

Interactive jewellery

Contemporary jewellery and accessories are diverse in their expression (c.f. [12]), yet this potential remains relatively underexplored within interaction design. Strong foundational research has been undertaken by Sarah Kettley [45] and Jayne Wallace [78], who both argued a decade ago for the potential of interactive capabilities to enhance the capacity of jewellery as "particular, intimate form[s] of object" that play "a strong role within our developing sense of self and within meaningful and personal human relationships" [78]. We now see increasing work in this area, for example, Tsaknaki and Fernaeus who, like Kettley and Wallace, foreground craft in their research [21, 70, 71, 72].

Outside of academic research contexts, Melbourne-based jewellery designer Leah Heiss [37] therapeutically augments medical jewellery using nanotechnologies and micro-electronics. Her work is powerfully oriented towards aesthetics when designing wearable health products. Examples include jewellery for pain-free delivery of diabetes medication, a wearable cardiac monitor, and "emergency jewellery" to identify the wearer, and their allergies in a medical crisis [37]. In March 2018, after "many years" including collaboration with 25 hearing-aid users, deep collaboration between design, engineering, signal processing, manufacturing and audiology, and 130 3D-printed prototypes, Barney Saunders Hears launched Facett, a hearing-aid developed by Heiss [5, 38]. The time and effort required to develop this product reflects how challenging it can be to develop precious, bespoke items for use close to the skin. As Heiss writes: Facett is an emotional technology that is precious rather than medical in its aesthetic. It thus helps shift hearing-aids from *dis*ability to *desir*ability [38]. See also Tsaknaki et al. for discussions of preciousness and the challenge of 'hybrid crafting' in Interaction Design.

Accessories and wearables for deaf persons

If we look beyond hearing assistive devices to other kinds of wearables designed for deaf persons, we find a number of projects that map sound to vibration. Neosensory's Versatile Extra-Sensory Transducer (VEST) [18, 53], for example, maps sound onto the torso to leverage human pattern recognition abilities. While functionally effective, VEST's aesthetic is quite particular and, we suggest, limited in terms of its appeal and thus the contexts in which it might be worn. A more sophisticated embodiment is Cute Circuit's Sound-Shirt [13], which transmits orchestral sound to the body in real time, mapping instrument groups to body locations to afford a fully immersive experience. VEST and Sound-Suit use lights to signal functioning, rendering their use highly performative. As we discuss later, such performativity may or may not be interesting for a deaf person.

Other vibrating accessories for deaf people include Vibrohear [77], a bracelet that signals the presence and volume of sound; Music for Deaf People [55], a concept collar from the German designer Frederik Podzuweit that converts sound into vibration; and Vibering Sensor [76], a concept watch, coupled with two rings, that vibrate according to the distance and position of a sound. Of these examples, only Music for Deaf People makes a tentative move beyond a conservative embodiment of jewellery; and only Vibrohear has attempted the move from prototype to product.

In the realm of products, Patti + Ricky is a website that brings together a range of 'stylish and functional designer products for individuals with 'disAbilities' [54]. The products they carry include hearing aid jewellery, casts and slings, fashionable clothing made to fit wheelchair users, and more. The site proclaims the need for 'stylish empowerment' for people with disabilities, and provides a wide range of products for men, women and children. At present, no products they sell afford technologically supported, *smart* interactions.

Wearable gadgets

An emerging trend of smart jewellery and accessories is to transition existing gadgets into fashionable body-wear. Intel's MICA, for example, like many such gadgets, supports interaction through a touch screen with predefined visual or tactile feedback [52]. Juhlin and Wang argue the need for fashionable perspectives to make such gadgets more appealing [43, 79].

An exception to the screen-based orientation of wearable gadgets is Hsin-Liu Kao et al.'s on-body robot Kino—a kinetic accessory system that "alters the appearance of clothing for aesthetic presentation" [44]. It does this through on garment displacement of small brooch-like robotic modules. Kino affords function-driven applications such as shape-shifting close to the neck of the wearer in the event of an incoming telephone call, or unfolding or refolding a hood in response temperature changes.

This landscape of products demonstrates both lack and opportunity. Bringing attention to the aesthetic needs of individuals is important for wearables. Drawing from fashion theory to support this engagement is coherent. Doing so with an orientation towards body diversity is critical.

QUIETUDE: ENRICHING THE QUALITY OF SILENCE IN A HEARING-ORIENTED WORLD

Quietude has at its core the desire to imagine a more sustainable, aesthetically enriched future for deaf women by developing wearables that respond to the women's needs and desires: those that are well known, and those that may be dimly glimpsed. In this section, we present our motivation and process, our first workshop, which had as its aim to connect the diverse collaborators and illicit inspiration for the system design and prototypes. From this basis, we reflect on opportunities and challenges of developing aesthetically rich wearables, taking into account body diversity.

Motivation

Quietude is funded within the H2020 EU Research Programme, WEAR Sustain [81], which aims to stimulate awareness of ethical issues that can arise when wearable technologies collect users' personal (physiological) data. In line with the purpose of the program, *Quietude* envisions a more sustainable role of users to (1) better understand and articulate their rights to access, own, explore, and use their body data; and (2) play an active role in interpreting this data; both of which are, presently, extremely challenging.

Our team includes deaf women from a range of professional backgrounds and with varying levels of deafness, ethicists, makers, designers and technology experts. The group has been assembled specifically to develop aesthetically sophisticated objects of desire—iconic pieces that draw inspiration from deaf women's personal experiences, the innate sensuality of the body, and the power of accessories to embody desires; acknowledging that personal expression, visibility and discretion can be complexly intertwined and deeply meaningful—and bring these products to market. Crucially, *Quietude* leverages the expertise of deaf experts alongside that of the other team members—as equal contributors driving the final outcome.

The project takes inspiration from the seminal research of Frank Geldard [30] who studied the expressivity and communication capabilities of the body's surface.

The skin is a good break-in sense: cutaneous sensations, especially if aroused in unusual patterns, are highly attention-demanding. [30].

Geldard envisioned the possibility to define a new tactile language *Vibratese*, using tactile stimulation to present complex information to humans. His vision connects to the work of Paul Bach-y-Rita, who developed vibro-tactile displays to enable blind people, for example, to remap their brains and 'see', or people with damaged vestibular systems to 'rewire' their brains and thus develop a 'replacement vestibular' system so they could balance again [1, 15]. Bach-y-Rita focused on the pragmatic possibilities of vibro-tactile language, whereas Geldard's vision incorporates the sensual and poetic aspects. Inspired by their work, we explore the potential of kinetic and tactile stimulation on the body surface to design aesthetically enriched, fashionable accessories for awareness, safety and social sustainability of deaf women in everyday life contexts.

Methodology

In *Quietude,* we adapt thinking-through-making, participatory Research through Design and Co-design to the specific context of working with deaf women.

Thinking-through-making emerged out of Gaver et al's work in *Cultural Probes* [29]. Cultural Probes were developed to give designers access to the thinking and desires of a specific set of users in order to inspire design processes. Probes typically consist of activity prompts sent out to participants, who interpret the activities however they wish and send their responses back to the designers. Our reinterpretation of this process uses *thinking-through-making, moving* and *doing* as the basis for enabling real-time situated exchange between designers and others. Like critical making: "materially productive, hands-on work [is] intended to uncover and explore conceptual uncertainties, parse the world in ways that language cannot, and disseminate the results of these explorations through embodied, material forms" [57].

Thinking-through-making also draws on performative approaches, such as the tightly structured instruction sets commonly used in the Fluxus movement [24], reflecting—or reaching towards—the inherent performativity of wearables [83]. These instruction sets enable a designer-facilitator to prompt participants to engage in an embodied thinking process that results in exploratory objects and ideas that serve as props and prompts in physically engaged activities. The whole process assists participants to move from abstract (personal, knowledge-based) embodied exploration into a specific articulated design space in which they can explore idiosyncratic desires in relation to possible futures. *Thinking-through-making* is enacted within the context of— as a form of—participatory Research through Design.

Research through Design (RtD) is a hybrid approach that employs methods and processes from art and design as legitimate modes of inquiry [23]. RtD is commonly used in technology design research to understand the influence of a new technology on how people think, value, feel, and relate [86]. It makes use of designerly activities as a way of approaching messy situations with unclear or even conflicting agendas [28].

By engaging users in creative play with research ideas and techniques, *participatory RtD* shifts the research focus toward the future, instead of the present or the past. It provides opportunities for community engagement in a discourse and allows consideration of the broader ethics of what is proposed, developed or designed. Further, by leveraging embodied thinking-through-making, the first author's approach to RtD generates personal knowledge, as well as knowledge that can contribute to societally relevant design of future outcomes. Foregrounding the participatory in RtD thus enables researchers to co-investigate design possibilities through an embodied engagement with material and form, and prototype emergent material artefacts that generate reflections and responses around emergent ideas. In this applied action-reflection approach, it is not the outcomes that are the focus. Rather, the making serves as a form of negotiation of emergent ideas. This approach is ideal in a team of collaborators who bring divergent perspectives. It assists people to bring into language things that they may not previously have reflected on in explicit ways or tried to articulate to others.

Finally, *Co-design* enables us to support team members who are not deaf or hearing impaired, in understanding the cultural, societal and usage scenarios encountered by deaf women. Co-design affords collective creativity across the span of a design process. It affords the creativity of designers and people not trained in design to work together in the design development process, bringing differing perspectives to bear on creative decision-making [59]. As one of our deaf experts—a psychologist—stressed, hearing people will never understand the desires of deaf people, because they begin from the assumption that hearing is a desired state. Yet, this assumption is often erroneous. Co-design enables us to

Figure 1: 'Feeling Voice' workshop, Day 1: (*l-r*) *not hearing / being heard* discussions → mind-map →body map (Task 2–3)

navigate the tensions of such insurmountable difference, and articulate more precisely and realistically what might be meaningful for deaf people, and which benefits to aim for.

The careful interweaving of these research processes enables us to bring into being previously unarticulated thoughts and desires, as we consider and discuss concrete and tangible actions to afford different experiential outcomes. Following, we describe the first workshop, which brought the team together for the first time and served to promote empathy among participants, to generate inspirational material, and to elicit values, desires, and unmet needs of deaf participants. Co-design activities were planned in the last two days, to consolidate and materialize what emerged in the first sessions.

Workshop 1: 'Feeling Voice'

Our team—in broad strokes—consists of a fablab group, a design group, an app development team, a group of deaf experts, and a group of ethicists and social sustainability experts who support and work alongside deaf people. These groups are not all discrete. Nonetheless, describing them thus can be helpful to both manage and describe our unfolding process. The social sustainability experts also provide translation services—from deaf-sign to English, the working language of the project.

Our first full project meeting, the 'Feeling Voice' workshop, needed to: (1) establish modes of communication and develop the necessary trust for creative risk-taking among team members, both within and across the different groups; (2) introduce the participatory, RtD and Co-design methods; (3) introduce some technological possibilities we might explore, in particular to collaborators with little or no prior technology experience; and (4) generate inspirational material that the Fab Lab group, design group and app developers might use to make a first, rapid pass at system design and prototyping. The workshop was scheduled to run for 6 Days, as follows:

Day 1 and 2 involved everyone. Day 1 focused on *Feelings*, Day 2, on *Forms*. Days 3–6 involved the Fab Lab and design groups only, including one deaf expert. The app developers worked in tandem. The majority of deaf experts did not participate days 3–6, though they were originally expected to be present on Day 3.

This planning acknowledged the different development requirements of the different groups, including time needed to reflect and respond to emerging ideas. We provide a more detailed breakdown:

DAY 1 ~ FEELINGS

1. *Introduction*: all team members introduced themselves. Of the four deaf experts, one was a psychologist, one an architect one an educator, and one a communication design undergraduate student who had been working in the fab lab. The communication design student was the only deaf expert who had prior experience with rapid prototyping of novel material forms with interactive capabilities.

2. *Feeling-mapping*: *not hearing / being heard*: working in pairs or groups of three, all team members (deaf and hearing) identify feelings they have about *not hearing* or *being heard*. Each feeling is given a name, the name is written on a post-it note, and the note placed on the wall (Figure 1). As a **mind-map** emerges, participants are encouraged to actively group notes and ideas, and identify **keywords**. One particularly potent example was the phrase: "feeling under water."

3. *Body-feeling* pairings: in new pairs or groups, team members (1) make a crude (self-drawn, A3-sized) body-map; (2) choose feelings from the mind-map created in task 2; (3) write these 'feelings' onto new post-its and place them on their **personal body-map**. Choices do not need to follow a particular logic or be coherent with anything done previously. Participants are instructed to follow their instincts no matter how fanciful. Once 'completed', body maps are placed on the wall (Figure 1) and are updated as needed.

4. *Materials introduction*: a wide selection of **materials**, with different characteristics—visual, tactile and behavioural—are arranged on the table. Participants are asked to experiment with how different materials feel and behave, and to try to find the right **material feeling** for the **body/feeling pairings** identified in the previous task.

5. *Technology introduction—vibration:* **a wide selection of technologies**, with different characteristics and interactive

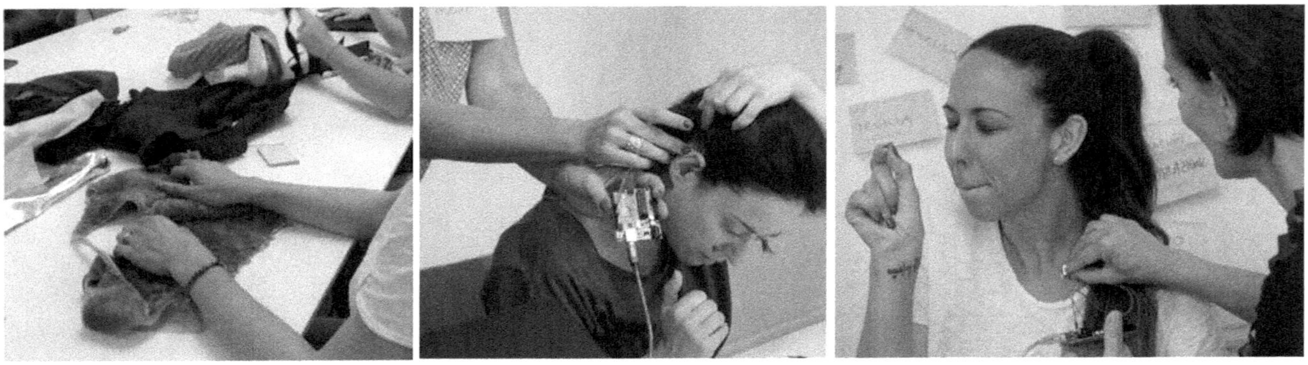

Figure 2: 'Feeling Voice' workshop, Day 1: (*l-r*) Materials, Technologies and Vibration (Tasks 4–6)

attributes, are arranged on the table. Many of them vibrate. The director of the fablab explains different elements. The workshop facilitator dismantles off-the-shelf elements and discusses form-factor and customisation. Participants are encouraged to explore.

6. *Vibration:* Taking inspiration from Vallgårda et al., [74] participants begin experimenting with sexual vibrators as a crude **off-the-shelf technology** that can give direct access to vibration. The incongruity of the sexual vibrator in this context breaks much of the tension around the idea that some at the table hold knowledge or expertise that others lack. We then experiment with **simple vibration circuits** that included a transducer or vibration motor (Figure 2). This process enables us to explore personal sensitivities to vibration, responses and preferences, and discover which parts of the body are best suited to receive or sense vibration input. A range of materials are also used to dampen or attenuate the vibration. This is a first step towards **material customization**, and provides useful information around preferences and impacts in different use-case scenarios. As vibration sensitivities were experimented with and compared, people updated personal body maps as needed. We thus could continually compare the emerging findings.

DAY 2 ~ FORMS

1. *Personal inspiration:* Team members were asked to bring in inspirational images, to share materials, styles and personal desires around the project. Not one team member prepared this task. We thus moved straight to task 2:

2. *Accessorising the Body:* We began with a short presentation to expand how we might be **thinking about accessorising the body**. Images came from fashion, as well as art and performance. The aim was to extend current conceptions of what shapes, forms and materials might be exciting as accessory, and relevant to everyday contexts.

3. *Thinking-through-making*: This task was designed to learn what the deaf women dream of or aspire to—irrespective of whether or not these dreams or aspirations are realistic—by experimenting through form. Following a tightly structured series of tasks, the intention (following [84]) was to bring these desires, including **yet-to-be-imagined desires**, into being.

Following a small mutiny from our deaf collaborators, who were impatient to see outcomes, rather than perform the above task, we engaged in **a lively discussion** of what is important for them: why they are participating in the project, and what they hope we might achieve together. Shortly after starting on day 2, we had discovered that four of the five deaf experts could not be present Day 3, so the benefit of working instinctively—without clearly articulated goals, expressed in advance—seemed frustrating to team members who had little prior experience with generative design processes.

In lieu of task 3, we followed our discussion with an **embodied exploration through materiality**—holding materials and technologies to the body, simulating movement and vibration, testing very rough approximations of what people were trying to express, in order to come to shared understandings of those expressions. This approach, done in a quick and rudimentary way, echoes Tomico's Material Props in Context Method (described in [68]).

At the end of the day, the first author, workshop facilitator, gave a public presentation about her research, during which she showed outcomes from previous *thinking-through-making* workshops. A number of deaf experts subsequently expressed disappointment that we had not undertaken activity 3. We will elaborate our insights in the discussion.

DAY 3 ~ CONCEPT DESIGN

The fablab and design groups formed two mixed groups. Only one deaf expert was present. She collaborated with both groups, so that each group could encompass the full range of expertise of the *Quietude* team. In these groups, we **brainstormed material possibilities** for different use-case scenarios, using materials and technologies at hand, and generated ideas using interim outcomes from Day 1 and 2.

DAY 4–5 ~ PROTOTYPING:

To develop a suite of prototypes, we revisited the different tech options we experimented with on Day 1, and expanded or shifted our ideas in response to the findings from Day 2. Further, we conducted a **lo-fi prototyping session** (Figure 3), using paper, cardboard and simple fabrics, to enable us to explore possibilities without being constrained by technical limitations. The emergent expertise enabled us to map out the accessory space.

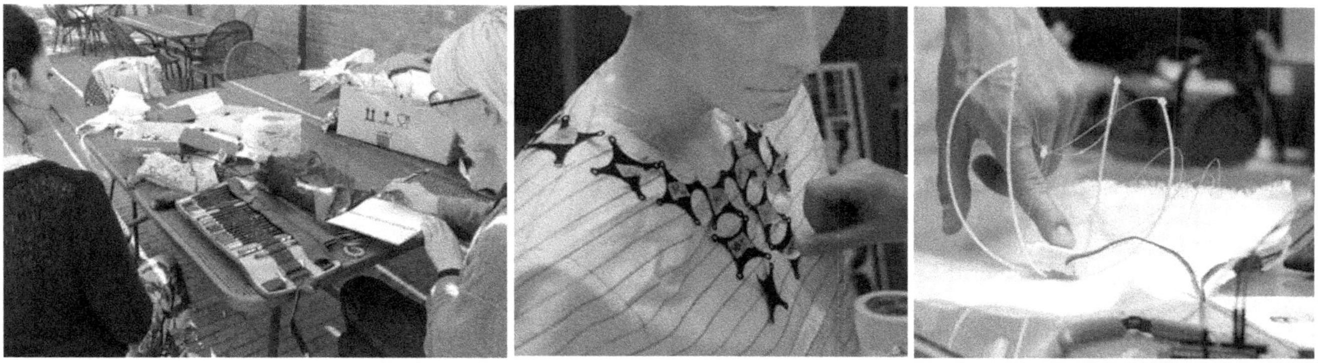

Figure 3: 'Feeling Voice' workshop: (*l-r*) Day 3: Concept brainstorming; Day 4–5: Lo-fi prototyping

We also drew directly from the Day 1 **body maps,** making new maps that complemented, and could be compared to, the previous findings. The aim was to consider the different aesthetics that might come into play, without being constrained by material or technical realities. This approach has proven its value in prior research [85].

DAY 6 ~ TESTING, CONSOLIDATING, REFLECTING: To complete the workshop, we tested and discussed the emerging prototypes—a suite of accessories inspired equally by feelings of being underwater and the needs of our deaf collaborators that emerged during Day 1 and 2, and during reflections.

Throughout the workshop, our design research structures were intentionally fluid, to support a reflective conversation with materials and resources in an ongoing and iterative process [61]. This process involved all of the collaborators and enabled us to support highly aesthetic outcomes.

FROM WORKSHOP TO ACCESSORIES

In this section, we discuss how our workshop findings guided the design of a first suite of accessories.

On Day 1, visibility and invisibility appeared as key words on post-it notes and were placed on the body maps close to the head, face and chest. One deaf expert explained that when people talk to each other they typically focus on the eyes and face of the other person. When focused thus it can be difficult, if not impossible, to realise that the other person is deaf.

Our deaf experts highlighted this invisibility of deafness as both a social and a safety issue, suggesting a counter-trend design compared to that of modern hearing aids. Non-surgically implanted hearing devices sit behind the ear or in the ear. They vary in size, power and circuitry, as well as positioning. Those that hang behind the ear are connected to the outer ear bowl—the concha—by a tube or wire; in-ear devices sit inside the concha (and are typically custom fitted). All hearing aids are designed to be as discreet as possible, with some sitting deep inside the ear canal, virtually invisible.

We learned that this effective invisibility of deafness can lead to challenges in interactions. In social situations, hearing people can forget to attend to deaf people's needs and inadvertently exclude them; in busy public places such as transit centres, the invisibility of deafness can be lead to misunderstandings and missed connections. Our deaf collaborators expressed a desire for an elegant and dignified—even beautiful—response to this issue.

Also on Day 1, our deaf experts showed a wide range of sensitivity to vibration. Some identified the neck area as the most sensitive to vibration, others the shoulder or scapula. Still others considered the wrist and forearm to be ideal parts of the body to enact vibrations and micro-movements. It became clear that being able to choose where and how a vibration plays out on the body through an accessory is crucial. As is being able to turn a vibrating accessory on or off. As our deaf architect noted after experimenting with vibrations on the body:

This day made me reflect on the importance of the link between vibration and information. For example: in any given context, it is important to understand the direction relative to the information the vibration is providing me with, also the quality of the vibration, its frequency or the point of contact with specific parts of the body. Above all it is essential to be able to exercise control over such vibration because getting continuous vibration produces disorientation and annoyance. So, it is necessary to be able to decide to turn it off or not use at all. That means I need my freedom.

On Day 2, one of the designers proposed a necklace that expressively enacts sounds, translating them into vibrations and physical expression. This idea was responded to enthusiastically by the deaf experts. We therefore conducted targeted *Material Props on the Body*-style experiments to clarify some design elements, to inform our thinking around the style of such an element.

On Day 3 the team reflected further on the issue of safety, which came up on Day 1. Sounds from the side or behind that require a quick response can go unnoticed by a deaf

Figure 4: *Quietude,* TRL3 prototype accessories: (*l-r*) Hairpin, Arm Band, Brooch-set, Necklace and App.

person, and the impact, whether the person is alone or with others, can be devastating. From this reflection, a concept was developed for fashion accessories that are both beautiful and functional, that warn the wearer of alarms or other meaningful sounds. Our deaf collaborators highlighted the importance of a range of meaningful sounds including both personal sounds (e.g. their pet, doorbell, name, etc..) and public notifications, such as alarms, airport announcements, police whistles, and more.

We discussed the possibility of "translating" such sounds into vibrations or subtle movements as a form of alert. Our deaf collaborators found this possibility intriguing. They suggested that, in addition to signalling meaningful sounds, the accessories might also reflect ambient qualities of an environment. Further, they discussed use cases where a deaf person is unaware of noises they produce themselves, such as in a library, walking on a wooden floor with heels. Vibrating and shape change accessories were identified as a helpful support in such situations, as they could signal inadvertent noises in a fun, fashionable and elegant way.

On Day 4 and 5 a mixed group of deaf and hearing collaborators built a fascinator of leather twigs attached to a hair clip (Figure 4, left) to signal deafness to others and also critical sound events to the wearer. The pin includes an Arduino and a microphone. The twigs move in response to ambient sounds. Their movement is clearly visible and can be felt through the cranium. The prototype was considered a witty, elegant and functional accessory when tested.

A Suite of Accessories

The team thus designed and developed a modular suite of accessories that can be assembled to create different pieces of jewellery, such as hairpins, armbands, and necklaces (Figure 4). Being modular, the accessories can be configured in a variety of forms related to external (visual) aesthetic and perceptive functionality. This modularity satisfies the need for personalisation that came up repeatedly during the workshop: the need to express an individual sense of style and identity, and to acknowledge personal preferences and sensitivities to vibration.

The design approach was conducted using an adapted fashion design methodology (c.f. [4]) which included development of a mood board [32] (Figure 5) to give visual form to the different sensitivities and styles that emerged during the *thinking-through-making* act on Day 2. The accessories thus have a strong visual and material aesthetic. The modules resemble sea anemones, algae and bubbles; the palette of colours reflects images of sand, deep ocean and coral. The colour palette and forms are inspired by the Day 1 keyword: *feeling under water*, which was proposed by a hearing collaborator, and enthusiastically approved by the deaf collaborators. The notion was used to describe a hushed feeling of the perception of sound. The different elements are made using leather, which adapts well to the body, being soft, comfortable and pleasant to wear, and well adapted to expressive kinetic properties. The modules contain functional and decorative elements that move, vibrate or emit light. The necklace leverages three-dimensional shape-change and will become increasingly sophisticated in this regard in coming iterations (following [49]). These kinetic features are used to signal deafness to others, as well as critical sound events to the wearer. They thus stimulate responsible and responsive behaviour: dual functionality our deaf experts repeatedly requested.

While these artefacts remain first pass prototypes, the accessories are stylish and expressive, and have been well received by our deaf experts and others in public events like the 2017 Florence Biennale of Contemporary Art, where a more advanced jewellery collection was exhibited [22].

System development

The jewellery system is composed of a suite of electronic boards embedded in the accessories. The boards are equipped with microphones, processing units and actuators. The electronics are connected to a smartphone through a Bluetooth personal wireless network, to enable users to manage and personalize sound recording and haptic feedback. The embedded electronics translate different sonic qualities (basically low, medium and high frequencies) of the

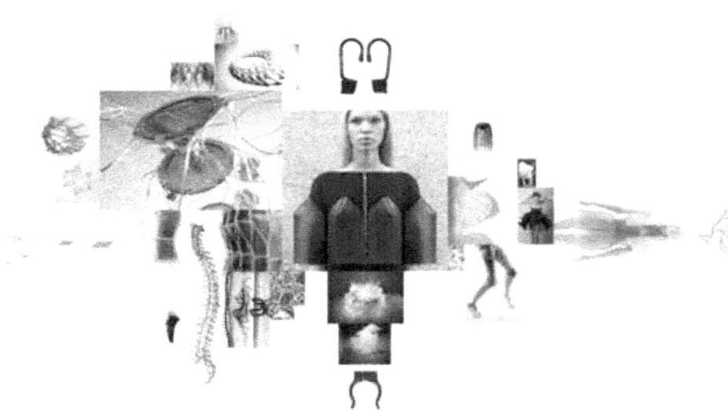

Figure 5. Quietude mood board. Courtesy Michele Tittarelli, Glitch Factory s.r.l.

ambient environment to the wearer. Our deaf experts explained that hearing impaired people may detect some sound frequencies and be totally deaf to others. The accessories reflect a need to perceive sound quality by mapping movement, vibration and light to detected sound frequencies. The embedded servos expressively enact live or recorded sounds, translating them into movement and physical expression. These kinetic properties are tuned to dynamically represent sonic qualities of environmental sounds. The behaviour of these and other actuators (such as the vibrators, for example) can be fine-tuned to achieve a comfortable, expressive, informative and refined, material choreography, adjusted to personal mood or circumstance.

A smart phone app works with the accessories, allowing personalisation of both input and output, and the construction of a personal library of sounds that can be monitored for, and replayed on demand through the accessories. As our experts explained during the workshop, deaf people commonly use apps to assist them in everyday life. Such apps range from video messaging apps (c.f. [31]), apps that stream live music lyrics (c.f. [67]), instant video-relay apps designed, for example, for British Sign Language users (c.f. [41]), and navigation apps (c.f. [80]). As app use is popular in the deaf community, the idea of using an app to control the accessories was readily embraced by our deaf experts.

To construct a personal library of sounds, the app allows recording and naming of sounds (my dog, the doorbell, my name etc.). These sounds are "translated" into vibrations, light patterns or subtle movements of the accessories to advise the wearer when they occur. Preferences related to kinetics and the quality of vibrations can be set and fine-tuned through the app for different contexts, moods and bodily sensitivities. In this way, the real-time feedback provided on the body, through the app, supports the freedom our deaf architect expressed as so crucial.

The app includes a control panel for managing sensor precision and the quality of the haptic feedback. Parameters such as vibration strength, on-off, as well as aspects of sound recording can be set up through a minimal interface, and immediately fed back onto the body through the accessories. The wearer can thus experiment with the quality of vibration, light and movement of the accessories in real time, and adjust them—personalise them—to suit their embodied preferences. Furthermore, sound recording and tagging functionality enables users to record, tag and store preferred sounds in the library, which is held locally on the phone. This is a key feature of the system since stored sounds are used to map an incoming sound (acquired from microphones embedded in the accessories), and to trigger the accessories' actuators.

OPPORTUNITIES AND CHALLENGES

In this section, we reflect on the opportunities and challenges of developing aesthetically rich, socially sustaining wearables for deaf women.

First and foremost, communication between our deaf and hearing collaborators was necessarily mediated by sign-language interpreters. Some of our deaf experts were able to speak in English, Italian or Spanish. Some could lip-read, or through the use of their hearing aids, hear. Nonetheless, communication at its most fundamental level was challenging, and needed to be navigated across a number of factors: basic socio-cultural and linguistic differences; differing values, objectives and practices across design, making and engineering; and the fundamentally different cultures of deaf and hearing. So, while our hearing collaborators were all trying to bring their diverse expertise to a deaf context, negotiating the relevance of the expertise to that context required constant attentiveness.

The fact that the first workshop took place in spaces associated with the fablab, further impacted our ability to contribute equally. Curiously, the frustrations that came about by suddenly losing a day's scheduled collaboration may have been one of the greatest gifts in this situation. While our scheduled events did not play out on Day 2, the improvised conversation allowed us to break through some of the barriers that are inevitable in mediated communication, including the power structures that surfaced—despite the best intentions—when a small group of people with different abilities, came into a technology research space with a range of acknowledged experts who are comfortable in this space and with the technologies and techniques at play. In such a situation, the expertise of the individual can easily be overlooked. In *Quietude*, our deaf team members are experts at being deaf, experts at being deaf women, as well as experts at various professional activities that are more or less related to the research. Yet, to design for their experience in a hearing-oriented world, our first step was to force them to collaborate on our terms, in a hearing-oriented collaborative set-up.

Our experiences prompt the question: How can Co-design be extended to upstream participation from all stakeholders in meaningful ways within the innovation process, yet enable team members to fully leverage textile and technical expertise? While we do not have the answers to this question, our next steps are clear.

Future Steps

Moving forward, we will enter into the deaf women's world to further our collaboration with a, hopefully more balanced (or more equitably unbalanced) hierarchy. After the workshop, two additional suites of prototypes were developed and fully integrated with electronics. These will be used to experiment the qualities of movement, vibration and light.

Participatory RtD will take several forms, moving forward. In addition to the 'Feeling Voice' workshop described here, other participatory and co-design sessions and testing sessions have been organised to allow deaf women to wear the accessories. These sessions enable us to test functionality on many levels, assessing how they feel and perform for the wearer, as well as how their performance is perceived (or not) by the viewer or interlocutor. The emerging prototypes are thus being exposed to the scrutiny of their intended consumer base, and the broader communities that may be impacted by their use.

We will investigate additional ways that *thinking-through-making* might be introduced to the deaf community. When our deaf experts expressed disappointment that they had been unable to experiment with this technique, they were responding to two aspects in particular: (1) the outcomes, like many forms of intermediary knowledge [40], and like responses to cultural probes [29], can be wild and inspirational, but they are often sitting in the adjacent possible—barely out of reach; sufficiently close that they support the bringing into being of potential and viable futures; and (2) *thinking-through-making* operates in an extra-discursive space—for the most part beyond language. Issues of language thus recede into the background as participants explore yet-to-be-articulated thoughts through embodied engagement with material and form. Both aspects show promise when trying to bring into being new forms of accessories, in a team that has no clear foundation from which to communicate as equals. We hope this technique will help us make our way forward to new ways of enacting participatory Research through Design in a Co-design process such as that which we set up in *Quietude.*

CONCLUSION

This paper presents an ongoing research on wearables designed for deaf women. We discussed specific needs that emerged in a participatory RtD workshop, as well as early, experience-able prototypes of smart accessories, and challenges and opportunities that arose from our working process.

Designing wearables for individuals who are considered by more body-typical people as having impairments, should not be limited to functional services that reflect the assumptions of those who are body typical (in our case hearing). Rather, we suggest engaging experts in the articulation and development of products that reflect their idiosyncratic, personal, aesthetic needs. We are certainly not the first to make such a suggestion [47], but hope our case adds a powerful voice to the discussion.

To a large extent, disability is socially constructed [81], and to a certain extent contextual. A deaf person may not hear a crucial event without support; at the same time, a hearing person may find it extremely difficult to focus when bombarded by background noise. One cannot assume that being able to hear is always preferable. Indeed, one of our deaf experts said that she often chooses to turn her hearing aid off, as she often prefers being deaf to hearing, even if hearing may be more practical in many situations.

In our approach to designing for and with deaf women, we lean on complex embodiment theory [63] and fashion theory. We recognise that *the body* is a socially constructed phenomenon—at once a physical body, consisting of its biological materials, and a part of culture, influenced by gender, society *and* circumstance; that there is no one body that can be designed for, but that each and every body is different. We also recognise that the economy between social representations and the body is not unidirectional or non-existent, but is reciprocal and thus complexly embodied, and its shifting nature needs to be taken into account.

As feminist theory tells us, knowledge is socially situated and adheres in embodiment, identities are socially constructed (and thus embodied), and some bodies—in particular disabled bodies—are excluded by dominant social ideologies [33, 34, 63]. As a result of this exclusion, people in marginal social positions, such as deaf persons in hearing-oriented contexts, "enjoy an epistemological privilege that allows them to theorise society differently from those in dominant social locations" [33, 34, 63]. By working from this viewpoint, we can approach disability as a source of valuable perspectives from which to design—not only for disabled persons, but for everyone.

Designing fashionable accessories with and for deaf women is allowing us to bring mindful attention to the nuanced skills and preferences that diverse individuals bring to dressing, and the meaning that accessorising brings to individual needs and personal style/s. Dress relates people to each other [8]. The act of dressing is an embodied activity that links society, culture, social interactions and daily lives. It is an intimate expression of the experience and presentation of the self [56] that cannot be isolated from the body it adorns [19]. By focusing on the particularities—the challenges and opportunities—of designing with and for deaf women, our contribution is able to go beyond the context of wearables development for deaf women, to the development of wearables more broadly.

ACKNOWLEDGEMENTS

Quietude has been developed by a consortium coordinated by the University of Siena in partnership with Glitch Factory and T4All. Consultancy has been provided by the University of Southern Denmark and Siena Art Institute. Funding comes from the H2020 project, WEARSustain, grant agreement No. 732098

REFERENCES

1. Paul Bach-y-Rita, Carter C. Collins, Frank A. Saunders, Benjamin White and Lawrence Scadden. 1969. Vision substitution by tactile image projection. *Nature* 221.5184: 963-964.
2. Malcolm Barnard. 2002. *Fashion as Communication.* Routledge.
3. Roland Barthes. 1967. *The Fashion System.* University of California Press.
4. Mascha Beuthel, Danielle Wilde. Wear.x: developing wearables that embody felt experience. In *Proc. DIS2017, ACM Conference on Designing Interactive Systems.* ACM (2017): 915-927.

5. Blamey Saunders Hears. Facett. Retreived 26 March, 2018 from: https://www.facett.com.au/
6. Andrew Bolton. 2002. *The Supermodern Wardrobe.* V&A Publications.
7. Christopher Breward. 2003. *Fashion (Oxford History of Art).* Oxford University Press.
8. Dani Cavallaro and Alexandra Warwick. 1998. *Fashioning the frame: Boundaries, dress and body.* Oxford: Berg.
9. James L. Cherney. 1999. Deaf culture and the cochlear implant debate: Cyborg politics and the identity of people with disabilities. *Argumentation and Advocacy*, 36: 22–34.
10. Andy Clark. 1998. *Being There: Putting Brain, Body and World Together Again.* MIT Press.
11. Andy Clark. 2010 *Supersizing the Mind Embodiment, Action, and Cognitive Extension.* (Philosophy of Mind). Oxford University Press.
12. Susan Cohn. 2012 *Unexpected Pleasures: The Art and Design of Contemporary Jewelry* (Design Museum, London - Exhibition Catalogues). New York, NY: Skira Rizzoli.
13. Cute Circuit. The Soundshirt. Retrieved September 17, 2017 from: cutecircuit.com/soundshirt/
14. John Dewey. 2005 (1934). *Art as Experience.* New York, N.Y.: Perigee (Penguin, Berkley)
15. Norman Doidge. The brain that changes itself: Stories of personal triumph from the frontiers of brain science. Penguin, 2007.
16. Paul Dourish. 2004. *Where the action is: the foundations of embodied interaction.* MIT press, 2004.
17. Paul Dourish. 2013. Epilogue: Where the action was, wasn't, should have been, and might yet be. *ACM Trans. Comput.-Hum. Interact.* 20, 1, Article 2 (April 2013), 4 pages. DOI: https://doi.org/10.1145/2442106.2442108
18. David Eagleman and Scott Novich. Versatile Extra-Sensory Transducer (VEST). Retrieved September 17, 2017 from: https://www.kickstarter.com/projects/324375300/vest-a-sensory-substitution-neuroscience-project
19. Joanne Entwistle. 2015. *The Fashioned body: Fashion, dress and social theory.* John Wiley & Sons
20. Joanne Entwistle, and Elizabeth B. Wilson, eds. 2001. *Body dressing.* Berg Publishers.
21. Fernaeus, Y., Murer, M., Tsaknaki, V., & Belenguer, J. S. (2014, February). Handcrafting electronic accessories using 'raw' materials. In *Proceedings of the 8th International Conference on Tangible, Embedded and Embodied Interaction* (pp. 369-372). ACM.
22. Florence International Biennial of Contemporary Art, XI edition, eARTh, Creativity and Sustainability, Arte Studio S.r.l., 6-15 October 2017. ISBN 9788868741778.
23. Christopher Frayling, Research in Art and Design. *Royal College of Art Research Papers* series 1.1 (1993): 1-5.
24. Ken Friedman, Owen Smith and Lauren Sawchyn, (ed.s). the Fluxus Performance Workbook: a Performance Research e-publication. 2002.
25. Shaun Gallagher. 2012. *Phenomenology.* Palgrave Macmillan.
26. Shaun Gallagher. 2016. *How the body shapes the mind.* Oxford University Press, (2006)
27. Shaun Gallagher and Dan Zahavi. 2012. *The phenomenological mind.* Routledge; 2nd edition.
28. William Gaver. 2012. What should we expect from research through design? In Proceedings of the SIGCHI conference on human factors in computing systems. (CHI '12), 937-946. DOI: http://dx.doi.org/10.1145/2207676.2208538
29. William Gaver, Anthony Dunne and Elena Pacenti. Cultural Probes. *Interactions*, 6, 1 (1999), 21–29
30. Frank A. Geldard. 1960. Some neglected possibilities of communication. *Science*, 131, 1583–1588
31. Glide. Retrieved January 7, 2018 from: http://www.glide.me/
32. Godlewsky Tanja. 2008 Mood Board. In: Erlhoff M., Marshall T. (eds) Design Dictionary. Board of International Research in Design. Birkhäuser Basel.
33. Donna Haraway. 1991. *Simians, Cyborgs and Women.* Ithica, NY: Cornell University Press
34. Sandra Harding. 1986. *The Science Question in Feminism.* Ithica, NY: Cornell University Press
35. Martin Heidegger. 1977. *The Question Concerning Technology.* trans., W. Lovitt. NY: Harper and Row
36. Martin Heidegger. 1996 *Being and Time.* trans., Joan Stambaugh. State University of New York Press
37. Leah Heiss. Retrieved January 7, 2018 from: http://www.leahheiss.com
38. Leah Heiss. *Modular Hearing Aid.* Retrieved January 7, 2018 from: http://www.leahheiss.com/#/modular-hearing-aid/
39. Kristina Höök. 2018. (forthcoming book). Cambridge, MA: MIT Press.
40. Kristina Höök, Jeffrey Bardzell, Simon Bowen, Peter Dalsgaard, Stuart Reeves, and Annika Waern. 2015. Framing IxD knowledge. *Interactions* 22, 6, 32-36. DOI: https://doi.org/10.1145/2824892
41. Interpreter Now. Retrieved January 7, 2018 from: http://interpreternow.co.uk/
42. Wolfgang Jonas. 2007. Design Research and its Meaning to the Methodological Development of the Discipline. In Ralf Michel (Ed.), *Design Research Now.* Birkhäuser, pp.187-206
43. Juhlin, O., Zhang, Y., Wang, J., & Andersson, A. (2016, October). Fashionable Services for

Wearables: Inventing and Investigating a New Design Path for Smart Watches. In Proceedings of the 9th Nordic Conference on Human-Computer Interaction (p. 49). ACM.

44. Hsin-Liu (Cindy) Kao, Deborah Ajilo, Oksana Anilionyte, Artem Dementyev, Inrak Choi, Sean Follmer, and Chris Schmandt. 2017. Exploring Interactions and Perceptions of Kinetic Wearables. In Proceedings of the 2017 Conference on Designing Interactive Systems (DIS '17), pp 391-396.
45. Sarah Kettley, *Crafting The Wearable Computer Design Process And User Experience.* PhD Diss. Napier University, 2007.
46. Julian Kiverstein and Andy Clark. Introduction: Mind embodied, embedded, enacted: One church or many? *Topoi* 28.1 (2009): 1-7.
47. Richard, E. Ladner. 2015. Design for user empowerment. *Interactions* 22.2 (2015): 24-29.
48. Catriona Macaulay, Giulio Jacucci, Shaleph O'Neill and Tomi Kankaineen (eds.) Special issue on The Emerging Roles of Performance within HCI and Interaction Design. *Interacting with Computers* 18, 5, 869-1164 (September 2006)
49. Majken K. Rasmussen, Giovanni M. Troiano, Marianne G. Petersen, Jakob G. Simonsen, and Kasper Hornbæk. 2016. Sketching Shape-changing Interfaces: Exploring Vocabulary, Metaphors Use, and Affordances. In Proceedings of the 2016 CHI Conference on Human Factors in Computing Systems (CHI '16). ACM, New York, NY, USA, 2740-2751. DOI: https://doi.org/10.1145/2858036.2858183
50. Paul Marshall, Alissa Antle, Elise Van Den Hoven, and Yvonne Rogers (eds.). Special Issue on the Theory and Practice of Embodied Interaction in HCI and Interaction Design ACM *Transactions on Computer-Human Interaction*, 20(1) 2013
51. Maurice Merleau-Ponty. 1996. *Phenomenology of Perception*. trans. Colin Smith. Motilal Banarsidas
52. MICA, My Intelligent Communications Assistant. Retrieved September 17, 2017 from: https://iq.intel. com/mica-intelligent-luxury-fashion-bracelet-stays-alert-with-style/.
53. Neosensory. Versatile Extra-Sensory Transducer (VEST). Retrieved September 17, 2017 from: https://neosensory.com
54. Patti + Ricky. Retrieved September 17, 2017 from: Pattiandricky.com
55. Frederik Podzuweit, Music for Deaf People. Retrieved September 17, 2017 from: https://www.magneticmag.com/2011/11/frederik-podzuweit-music-for-deaf-people/
56. Ted Polhemus, and Lynn Proctor. 1978. *Fashion and Anti-Fashion*. London: Thames and Hudson.
57. Matt Ratto. 2011. Critical Making: Conceptual and Material Studies in Technology and Social Life. *Information Society* 27:4. 252–260. DOI: 10.1080/01972243.2011.583819
58. Susan Elizabeth Ryan. 2014. *Garments of paradise: wearable discourse in the digital age.* MIT Press.
59. Elizabeth B.-N. Sanders and Pieter Jan Stappers. 2008. Co-creation and the new landscapes of design, *CoDesign,* 4:1, 5-18, DOI: 10.1080/15710880701875068
60. Elizabeth B.-N. Sanders and Pieter Jan Stappers. 2012. *Convivial design toolbox: Generative research for the front end of design.* BIS, 2012.
61. Donald Schön. 1983. *The reflective Practitioner*. Basic Books.
62. Tobin Siebers. *Disability Aesthetics*. Ann Arbor, MI: University of Michigan Press, 2010.
63. Tobin Siebers. *Disability Theory.* Ann Arbor, MI: University of Michigan Press, 2008.
64. Sabine Seymour. 2008. *Fashionable Technology.* Springer-Verlag.
65. Richard Shusterman. 2000. *Pragmatist Aesthetics: Living Beauty, Rethinking Art.* 2nd Edition. Rowman and Littlefield
66. Kate Soper. 2001. Dress Needs: Reflections on the Clothed Body, Selfhood and Consumption. In Joanne Entwistle, Elizabeth Wilson, (eds.) *Body Dressing.* Berg.
67. SoundHound Retrieved January 7, 2018 from: https://www.soundhound.com/soundhound
68. Oscar Tomico and Danielle Wilde. Soft, Embodied, Situated & Connected: enriching interactions with soft wearables. *Journal of Mobile User Experience*. Springer. (2016) 5: 3. https://doi.org/10.1186/s13678-016-0006-z.
69. Quietude. Retreived 27 March, 2018 from : http://www.quietude.it/
70. Tsaknaki, V., Fernaeus, Y., & Jonsson, M. (2015). Precious Materials of Interaction: Exploring Interactive Accessories as Jewellery Items. In Nordes (No. 6). Nordes–Nordic Design Research.
71. Tsaknaki, V., Fernaeus, Y., Rapp, E., & Solsona Belenguer, J. (2017, June). Articulating Challenges of Hybrid Crafting for the Case of Interactive Silversmith Practice. In Proceedings of the 2017 Conference on Designing Interactive Systems (pp. 1187-1200). ACM.
72. Tsaknaki, Vasili. (2017) Making Preciousness: Interaction Design through Studio Crafts. *PhD. Diss.* KTH Royal Institute of Technology, Sweden.
73. Astrid Tweneboa Larssen, Toni Robertson, Lian Loke, Jenny Edwards (eds.) Special issue on movement-based interaction. *Personal & Ubiquitous Computing.* 11(8), Springer, 2007
74. Anna Vallgårda, Morten Winther, Nina Mørch, & Edit Emese Vizer. 2015. Temporal Form in Interaction Design. *International Journal of Design.* 9, 3. 1-15

75. Francisco J. Varela, Evan Thompson and Eleanor Rosch. The Embodied Mind: Cognitive Science and Human Experience. MIT Press (1993)
76. Vibering Sensor. Retrieved September 17, 2017 from: http://www.tuvie.com/vibering-sensor-to-help-detect-noises-for-hearing-impaired/
77. Vibrohear. Retrieved September 17, 2017 from: http://www tested.com/tech/535041-10-inventions-restore-lost-senses/item/vibrohear/
78. Jayne Wallace, *Emotionally charged: A practice-centred enquiry of digital jewellery and personal emotional significance.* PhD Diss. Sheffield Hallam University, 2007.
79. Jinyi Wang, Oskar Juhlin, Erika Blomgren, Linnea Bågander, Evelin Kägo, Florian Meier, Mariko Takahashi, and Clemens Thornquist. "Design space of the new materials for fashionable wearables." In Proceedings of the 18th International Conference on Human-Computer Interaction with Mobile Devices and Services Adjunct, pp. 1159-1162. ACM, 2016.
80. Waze Retrieved January 7, 2018 from: https://waze.en.uptodown.com/android
81. WEAR (Wearable technologists Engage with Artists for Responsible innovation) Sustain. Retrieved September 17, 2017 from: wearsustain.eu/about
82. Susan Wendell. 1996. The Social Construction of Disability. In *The Rejected Body*. Susan Wendell. Routledge Taylor & Francis Group. pp57–68
83. Danielle Wilde. A New Performativity : wearables and body devices. Proceedings of Re:live Media Art History Conference 2009 MAH Archive, 184-190. Retrieved January 5, 2018 from: http://www.mat.ucsb.edu/Publications/burbano_MAH2009.pdf
84. Danielle Wilde. Embodying Material Ideation. Proceedings PINC2015. *Participatory Innovation Conference*. Rianne Valkenburg, Coen Dekkers and Jannek Sluijs. ed.s The Hague University of Applied Sciences. Retrieved 9 January 2018 from: https://lirias.kuleuven.be/bitstream/123456789/483524/5/Pin-C+2015+Proceedings.pdf
85. Danielle Wilde and Jenny Underwood. Designing towards the Unknown: Engaging with Material and Aesthetic Uncertainty. *Informatics* 2018, 5(1), 1; doi:10.3390/informatics5010001
86. Danielle Wilde, Anna Vallgårda, and Oscar Tomico. 2017. Embodied Design Ideation Methods: Analysing the Power of Estrangement. Proceedings of the 2017 CHI Conference on *Human Factors in Computing Systems*. ACM 2017.
87. John Zimmerman, Erik Stolterman, and Jodi Forlizzi. An Analysis and Critique of Research through Design: towards a formalization of a research approach. In Proc. *Designing Interactive Systems.* ACM Press, New York, 2010

Interweaving Visual and Audio-Haptic Augmented Reality for Urban Exploration

Yi-Ta Hsieh[1], Valeria Orso[2], Salvatore Andolina[3], Manuela Canaveras[2], Diogo Cabral[4], Anna Spagnolli[2], Luciano Gamberini[2], Giulio Jacucci[1,3]
[1]Helsinki Institute for Information Technology HIIT, Dept. Computer Science, Univ. Helsinki, Finland
first.last@helsinki.fi
[2]Human Inspired Technology Research Centre HIT, Dept. General Psychology, Univ. Padova, Italy
first.last@unipd.it
[3]Helsinki Institute for Information Technology HIIT, Aalto University, Finland
first.last@aalto.fi
[4]Madeira-ITI, University of Madeira, Portugal
first.last@m-iti.org

ABSTRACT
While ordinary touchscreen-based interfaces on urban explorer applications draw much of a user's attention onto the screen, visual and audio-haptic augmented reality interfaces have emerged as the two main streams for enabling direct focus on the surroundings. However, neither interface alone satisfies users in the highly dynamic urban environment. This research investigates how the two complementary augmentation can coexist on one system and how people adapt to the situation by selecting the more suitable interface. A prototype was deployed in a field experiment in which participants explored points of interest in an urban environment with both interfaces. The engagement with the surroundings was compared with a touchscreen-based application. Most participants spontaneously switched between the two interfaces, which manifests the value of the availability of both interfaces on one system. The results point at the situated advantages of either interface and reveal the users' preferences when both interfaces are available.

ACM Classification Keywords
H.5.2. Information Interfaces and Presentation (e.g. HCI): User Interfaces

Author Keywords
Augmented Reality; Multimodal Interaction; Urban Exploration; Audio-Haptic Interface.

DIS 2018, June 9–13, 2018, Hong Kong.

ACM ISBN 978-1-4503-5198-0/18/06 ...$15.00.
http://dx.doi.org/10.1145/3196709.3196733

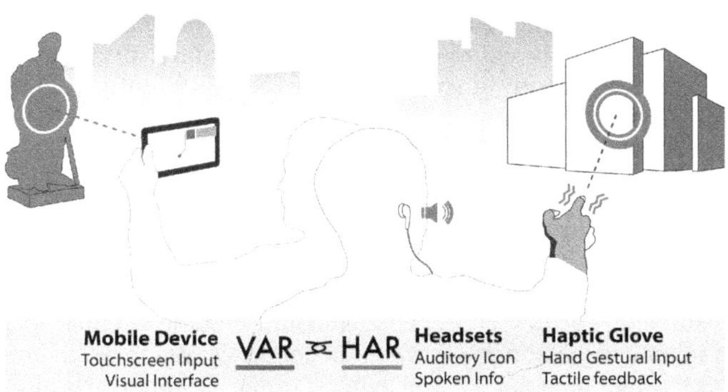

Figure 1. The availability of both VAR and HAR interfaces on one urban heritage explorer enables users to freely choose which interface to use to easily adapt to the highly dynamic environment while maintaining focus on the environment.

INTRODUCTION
This paper investigates how visual augmented reality (VAR) and audio-haptic augmented reality (HAR) interfaces in urban exploration can support users in focusing on the real content—the situated surroundings—rather than on the interface itself, as well as how these two interfaces can coexist on one system to support adaptation to the dynamic environment. It is very common that mobile users tend to focus on interacting with the touchscreen-equipped device, and such head-down interaction results in not only ignoring the surroundings but also increasing unsafe behaviors [11, 27, 15]. This could severely hamper the experience in which the surroundings are the actual content to interact with and the environment is highly dynamic.

Two main streams of augmented reality (AR) solutions have emerged from the interaction design point of view: sensor-based VAR and non-visual HAR approaches. Both proposals adopt the general idea of aligning users' pointing direction, the device, and real-world objects to enable direct focus on the environment. The principle of VAR approach is to utilize on-device sensors to understand users' viewing orientation so that geo-referenced digital content can be overlaid onto the camera preview of the real scene. For example, Wikitude[1] enables users to point the device in a particular direction to look for information associated with objects in the situated surroundings. Similarly, HAR solutions have mainly deployed handheld devices as a "magic wand" to point directly at specific landmarks for fetching associated information [8]. This approach overcomes the requirement of concentrating users' visual attention on the interface, allowing their visual resources to be fully allocated to the surroundings.

Although both VAR and HAR interfaces can enable direct focus on the surroundings, each has specific strengths and weaknesses in different contexts of urban exploration. For instance, when a user's priority is to search for a specific piece of information (e.g., searching the stories about a statue by its name), a VAR interface allows him/her to quickly skim through the contents. On the other hand, when users need to keep their eyes on the environment (e.g., in rush hour by a road), HAR interfaces might serve users better. Urban exploration tools should meet users' dynamic and evolving needs even by supporting the switch between different modalities [37]. This motivates us to investigate how the two complementary interfaces can coexist on one system.

Our aim is to gain insights into designing an urban exploration system equipped with both VAR and HAR interfaces. Since grounding knowledge to design such an integrated system is still unknown, we identified two fundamental aspects to be studied. The first aspect entails identifying the circumstances in which each interface would benefit users the most, in order to further improve the design in each area. Secondly, we aim at understanding how a smooth transition can be designed when switching from one interface to the other. If the effort in the interface switching is too high, users would rather continue using the less suitable interface than switching to the other.

Our research method is to build an urban explorer prototype interwoven with both VAR and HAR interfaces as a research tool and deploy it in a field experiment in which participants explore and locate urban points of interest (POIs). While the pointing techniques in sensor-based VAR interfaces have been well established with various applications available on the market, the interaction techniques in a HAR interface vary from one form factor of the sensing device to another. Since handheld devices occupy the hand, many wearable sensing devices have been developed for eliminating constraints on the freedom of the hand, such as a belt [34], a wristband [12], or a ring [16]. Considering the benefits of leveraging our already-familiar hand gestures to directly interact with landmarks, we adopted a spatial sensing haptic glove (SSH Glove) for the HAR interface. The glove features hand orientation and gestural sensing, as well as providing tactile feedback. As a result, the prototype system incorporates a mobile device, a glove, and a headset (See Fig. 1). The research prototype may seem bulky, but it serves well at this exploratory stage.

[1]http://www.wikitude.com/

We report an experiment in which 18 participants used our prototype to explore the central area of a historic city in the context of public, real-world use. In the three-phase experiment, the participants were allowed to first use VAR and HAR interfaces separately, and then to freely choose and switch between VAR and HAR during the last phase of exploration. We observed spontaneous switching of interfaces from most participants during the exploration, which manifests the value of the availability of both interfaces on one system. Moreover, to reveal the benefits of an urban explorer with both VAR and HAR interfaces, a control group of 18 participants used the Google Maps application to explore the same area. Results indicate that it is possible to predict the way people would use those modes in different situations. Knowledge gained from this research fosters an ultimate visual-audio-haptic AR interface for urban exploration, and could direct further studies that are carried out in the field with realistic tasks but a controlled design.

BACKGROUND

Mobile scenarios have been the favorite research setting to explore new interfaces that extend and augment human capabilities [3] with visual, haptic, and aural augmentations. Such multimodal interaction methods aim at improving human-computer communications by utilizing all available modalities of human input and output in a natural manner [36].

Exploring Surroundings with Visual AR

Based on the "smart lens" technique, VAR interfaces allow users to "see through" a device via the camera preview, hence allowing direct focus on the environment [8]. VAR applications also benefit users by providing information relevant to the current location, enabling access to timely and updated multimedia content and supporting interactive annotations [41, 23]. These multimedia augmentations can provide an immersed experience in the immediate environment. In addition, VAR exploration can increase the chances of finding relevant information, as noted by Schmalstieg and Höllerer [32].

VAR applications have been developed for increasing users' awareness of their surroundings [4, 6] but with certain practical constraints when in use. For example, its outdoor usage presents additional interaction challenges. Schmalstieg and Höllerer [32] state that most of the displays are not bright enough to achieve sufficient contrast in outdoor situations and mobile devices have a bigger risk of creating fatigue, particularly when one has to hold them at eye level. In addition to these issues, there is also the difficulty of touching on a display while holding it at the same time [28] and the difficulty of reading text on small size displays [7, 18]. Such interaction issues could potentially be avoided when audio and haptic modalities are incorporated in the interaction.

Exploring Surroundings with Audio-Haptic AR

Audio and haptic modalities can be incorporated into the interface design so that users' visual resource can be focused even more on the surroundings. McGookin et al. [26] presented Audio Bubbles that associate audio with real-world landmarks to support serendipitous discovery in tourist activities. By overlaying virtual audio in the soundscape of the environment, their approach can increase the awareness of nearby interesting things. Similarly, auditory icons and music icons in the field can support serendipitous discovery, emotional engagement, and implicit navigation [1, 21, 39]. Audio can be further complemented with haptic modality. Combining the two for displaying touristic information results in a higher recognition rate than utilizing each modality alone [29].

Moreover, using the handheld device as a "magic wand" to point directly at real-world objects imposes an even more explicit connection with the surroundings [8]. For example, Magnusson et al. [25] presented an audio-tactile tourist guide on a mobile device through which users can scan for the direction of POIs and receive audio-recorded information. This point-and-select type of interaction is perceived as easy to use and natural [25, 31]. However, it comes at a cost of carrying a device that limits the freedom of users' hands. Moreover, attention is soon drawn back to the device after the selection, rather than remaining on the surroundings [8].

The constraint on the freedom of the hand can be easily confronted by deploying hand-worn form factors on the device while still enjoying the inherited benefits from the "magic wand" technique. Moreover, we wanted to leverage familiar gestures (e.g., finger pointing or grabbing gesture) to construct a stronger augmented experience and connection with the surroundings. As compared to other hand-worn form factors, such as wristbands [12] or rings [16], the glove form factor affords sufficient space for distributing sensors on various locations of the hand for enabling more truthful hand gestural recognition; hence, a more complete gestural language set is possible. For example, Mycpoint, a sensor-equipped wristband, uses a rather counterintuitive gesture—opening one's palm—for selection, possibly due to limited capability in detecting finer finger gestures [12]. There are other wearable form factor options, such as a belt for wayfinding [34, 30]. However, they do not support magic wand-type pointing interaction. Hence, a glove was more suitable than belts or vests. Another benefit of using the glove form factor is to provide tactile feedback on an action-performing body. In sum, using the glove can leverage our existing skills in using the hand to interact with everyday objects, resulting in a more intimate connection with the surroundings through the interaction.

However, delivering information over audio-haptic interfaces could be less efficient than through visual interfaces. At least, the duration of the spoken content is the minimal time needed from users to receive the complete information. Although fast forward is possible on audio interfaces, it is still not as efficient as skimming text on a visual interface. This fact further ascertains how VAR and HAR interfaces could complement each other.

Other Approaches

Vaittinen and McGookin [37] point out that most of current tourism applications are based on maps and lists (e.g., Google Maps[2] and Tripadvisor[3]), and that do not work for all needs, particularly for touristic/urban exploration. The applications would benefit from interfaces that could register the information spatially to the objects, removing the need to divert the focus to the device. Baldauf et al. [2] have compared different (but traditional) visualization techniques of geo-referenced information for supporting mobile urban exploration. They have compared 2D and 3D maps, list and category views, and tag clouds. In their study, the users preferred 2D maps and category view to tag view and 3D maps. However, they missed an opportunity to study VAR and audio-haptic interfaces.

Equipped with see-through displays, smart glasses allow users to view both digital content and a real scene simultaneously, which potentially can be an ideal solution for enabling direct focus on the environment and increasing situational awareness. However, previous studies did not show a major advantage of head-mounted devices when compared with handheld devices [40, 5]. Moreover, the current bulkiness of head-mounted devices [32] and both voice control and eye-level hand gestures raise much concern of social acceptability [35, 14]. Therefore, we do not consider smart glasses in this research.

Both VAR and HAR solutions increase the awareness and the connection with surroundings while exploring an urban environment. Nonetheless, both present advantages and constraints. In our study, we aim to answer how these two complementary interfaces can coexist on one system, overcoming the limitations of each.

SYSTEM DESIGN

In this section, we describe the design of the research prototype, comprising VAR and HAR interfaces for urban exploration and a basic mechanism for switching between the two interfaces. We adopted matured technologies at this explorative stage rather than pursuing technical novelty.

VAR Interface

In addition to the common features on most VAR applications (e.g., mapping virtual content to a real scene through camera preview), our VAR interface presents two additional features: 1) precise positioning of the billboards and 2) an aim-and-shoot technique for one-hand operation. Relying on the device location, orientation, and GPS coordinates of the POIs, ordinary VAR applications derive only the relative angles of the surrounding POIs to the current location. It is very common to see a billboard indicating a POI that is invisible from a current location due to long distance or occlusion. To overcome this issue, we incorporated 3D models for checking the visibility of POIs and placing the billboards on relevant locations, such as elevating the billboard of a clock tower (See Fig. 2).

The second feature is an aim-and-shoot technique for enabling one-hand operation, which is preferred by most users in mobile interaction [20]. Ordinary VAR interface design would require one hand for holding the device and the other for clicking the billboards near the center of the display. Our aim-and-shoot interface includes a crosshair icon in the center and a shooting button on the edge of the screen (See Fig. 2). To select a billboard, users align the crosshair with the target billboard and click on the shooting button that is conveniently reachable by the thumb of the device-holding hand.

[2]https://maps.google.com/

[3]https://www.tripadvisor.com/

Figure 2. Left: Exact POI locations on the VAR interface are indicated by colored circles which are attached to square billboards featuring POI category icons. The billboards are floating on the screen to avoid obscuring the POIs. The interface features a "TARGET" button on the top-left corner for one-hand selection, and a crosshair icon in the center for aiming at billboards. Right: The SSH Glove. The electronic components were covered with an extra layer of fabric during the experiment.

State	*Activation (ms)*	*ISI (ms)*
Browsing	100	900
Matching	100	400
Multi-Matching	100	100

Table 1. The activation and interstimulus intervals for each tactile cue designed for three states in the interaction.

HAR Interface

The HAR interface has three main components: a hand-worn tracking device for enabling mid-air gestures, a headset for delivering audio information, and a mobile device for location and system logic, etc. The same mobile device also supports the VAR interface. Users do not need to interact with the mobile device when using the HAR interface.

We deployed the SSH Glove (See Fig. 2) for hand tracking. The glove features hand orientation and finger pose sensing, and it gives vibrotactile feedback on three fingers. A 9-axis inertial measurement unit (IMU, InvenSense MPU-9150) is mounted on the back of the hand for sensing pointing orientation. Three flex sensors (Spectra Symbol flex sensor) on three fingers (thumb, index, and middle finger) detect the finger pose. Three vibrotactile actuators (Precision Microdrives 10 mm shaftless vibration motor) provide vibration amplitude at 2.4 g and 250 Hz frequency, which falls in the optimal sensitive range of our tactile perception [17]. The Arduino Pro Mini-based glove is wirelessly connected with the mobile device through Bluetooth.

On the HAR interface, information is encoded and delivered through auditory and tactile features. Auditory features include spoken title and description, as well as auditory icons for indicating the POI category. For example, religious POIs were associated with the sound of a church bell and Gregorian chanting. As for the tactile features, burst rate was the primary source for coding. We implemented three tactile cues for different states of the interaction. The cues have the same activation interval with varied interstimulus intervals (ISIs) (See Table 1). The cue design is in line with previous research [17, 10].

The interaction between the system and the user does not start until a pointing gesture (index finger straightened, middle finger bent, and the hand is horizontal regardless of the arm pose) is performed. When pointing, the user can feel the browsing tactile cue presented on the index finger, indicating the activation of the "browsing" state. If the pointing orientation matches the direction of a POI, a faster matching cue is presented to indicate a "matching" state. Meanwhile, the auditory icon and the spoken title of the matched POI is delivered over the headsets. While in "matching" state, the user can make a selecting gesture (bending index finger when in pointing gesture) for receiving the spoken description. When listening to the description, the user can freely move the hand. Nevertheless, a rejection gesture (only thumb bent) can skip the playback of the spoken content. We followed the recommendation for mid-air pointing gesture design [38]: bending index finger (while pointing) as primary gesture for selection and bending thumb for secondary tasks.

One challenge in designing non-visual HAR interfaces for target acquisition tasks is to identify and indicate overlapping targets, which can be very common in an urban environment. When there are more than two POIs falling into the glove "viewing angle," the multi-matching cue is triggered on the index finger, which suggests the user to approach in the pointing direction to discover the POI hot zone. Meanwhile, the title and auditory icon of the best-matching POI (i.e. with the smallest angular difference in pointing) is delivered, as suggested in [24].

Interaction Design for Switching Interfaces

We implemented a simple switching mechanism requiring minimum actions as a probe to investigate the adjustments and efforts required from the users during interface switching. By detecting the device orientation and screen cover status, we can interpret users' intentions on which interface to use. The design was inspired by the switching between 2D map (screen facing up) and VAR view (back camera facing front) on Nokia's City Lens[4] application.

When the mobile device is in landscape orientation and the screen is not covered, VAR is activated, and HAR is disabled to avoid false positives. To switch from VAR to HAR, the user simply covers the device screen (e.g., by storing the device in a pocket). To return to VAR interface, the user can simply uncover the tablet. This mechanism was reliably done with on-device accelerometers and proximity sensors that are commonly available on modern mobile devices.

A smooth transition was implemented for the interface switching as well. When a POI is activated after selection on HAR, switching to VAR would not interrupt the on-going spoken description while visual media of the POI is available on the screen. This allows users to continue listening to the audio content while examining visual media.

Occlusion Geometry

A 3D model can enable visibility checks on surrounding POIs to avoid the confusion resulting from occlusion. Receiving content regarding a POI while pointing at an irrelevant building that occludes the designated POI can be confusing in both VAR

[4]https://help.here.com/wp8/citylens/

and HAR use scenarios. Furthermore, information regarding distance and elevation of a POI can be displayed on VAR (e.g., the billboard of a clock tower far from the current location can be smaller than nearby POIs and elevated above ground floor).

The 3D model runs in the background on our system and is not meant to be accessible for the users. While the point-and-select technique on both VAR and HAR enables direct interaction with the environment, ordinary touchscreen-based interaction for 3D models remains focused on the screen, thus is excluded from this research.

EVALUATION

Goals

One goal of the study was to check whether aligning geo-located information with users' pointing and viewing direction would result in a better visiting experience than that on an ordinary 2D map interface. Common 2D geo-localized digital maps require users to shift the focus between the surroundings and a touchscreen-based interface, which typically results in a head-down interaction. Thus our sample was split into an experimental group using our research prototype and a control group using the popular Google Maps application. The following hypothesis was formulated:

- (H1) The VAR/HAR interface leads to better visiting experience than the 2D map interface.

A second goal was to examine the efficiency and the perceived advantages of each modality, as well as users' preference for any of them under different tasks. Three different conditions were experienced by the experimental group: using VAR alone, using HAR alone, and using both VAR and HAR. Connected to this goal, we wanted to consider whether the different modalities suited different task types differently. We used location tasks where participants locate a pre-assigned POI that they do not know beforehand, and information tasks where the participants fetch information about a POI that interests them. The former task reproduced a situation in which the participant needs to find a specific POI s/he heard of, while the latter simulates a situation in which the participant wants to know more about an object that captured his/her interest. We then expected that:

- (H2) VAR is more efficient than HAR in location tasks but less efficient in information tasks.

A third goal was to observe the switching between interfaces, specifically the circumstances under which the switching behavior occurred (e.g., whether participants needed to stop to do so).

Setting and apparatus

The research prototype consisted of an 8-inch compact tablet (nVidia SHIELD K1), the SSH Glove, a headset, a pocket for storing the tablet when not in use, and a photo camera. VAR interface was presented on the tablet, while HAR interface was presented on the SSH Glove and via the headset. In the control group, participants were endowed with the tablet running the geo-localized Google Maps application loaded with the same set of POIs as in the experimental group (See Fig. 3).

Figure 3. Left: The apparatus employed for the experiment. a) The shoulder pouch for carrying the mobile device. b) The SSH Glove. c) Headset. d) The mobile device. e) The camera. f) The shoulder pouch for carrying the camera. Right: A participant with all the apparatus.

	Experimental Group			Control Group
	VAR	HAR	VAR/HAR	2D Map
Location Task	1	1	1	3
Information Task	1	1	2	4

Table 2. The study design. The table shows the number of location and information tasks that participants were asked to perform in the different conditions.

Experiment Design

The study had a mixed design. The interface modes (VAR only, HAR only, and both VAR and HAR) were treated as a within-subject variable. The separation of modalities would help us understand what kind of augmentation is helpful to a given activity. The experiment was conducted in three nearby squares that enabled the separation of the three interface modes (See Fig. 4). On the other hand, the presence of augmentation (VAR/HAR vs. 2D map) was treated as a between-subject variable. This is due to the need for contextualizing the assessment of a new prototype by comparing it with the technical solution that represents the current standard. Participants in both groups executed the same total number of tasks (See Table 2).

Data

Visiting Experience. Visiting experience was measured using a post-experience questionnaire that included 18 items to be answered on a 6-point Likert scale (See Table 3). The pleasantness of the visit (i.e., the extent to which the experience was enjoyable, amusing, and fun) was assessed by 4 items (adapted from [22]). The interference or distraction from the system was assessed by 2 items (adapted from [19]). The capability of the interface to build a sense of presence[5] in the augmented environment was assessed by 4 items (adapted from [9]). Finally, seven items aimed at evaluating the usability of the system, namely the comfort of use (3 items), the usefulness (4 items), and its responsiveness (1 item). Participants were also asked to comment their experience by answering four questions in a

[5]Sense of presence refers to the extent to which the user feels directly immersed in the surroundings compared to perceiving a tool mediating experience of the surroundings. We investigated whether the augmented devices improved the sense of immersion compared with the baseline or rather diminished in the short-term type of experience.

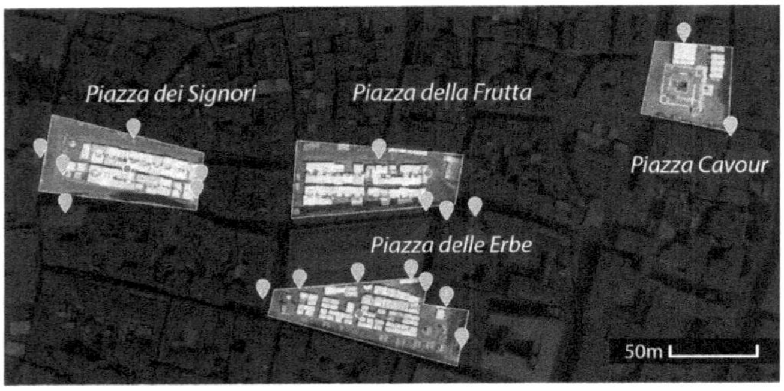

Figure 4. The experiment took place in three nearby squares. An additional smaller square on the top right corner was used for training. Predefined POIs are marked in pink labels. The red dots indicate the starting location on each square.

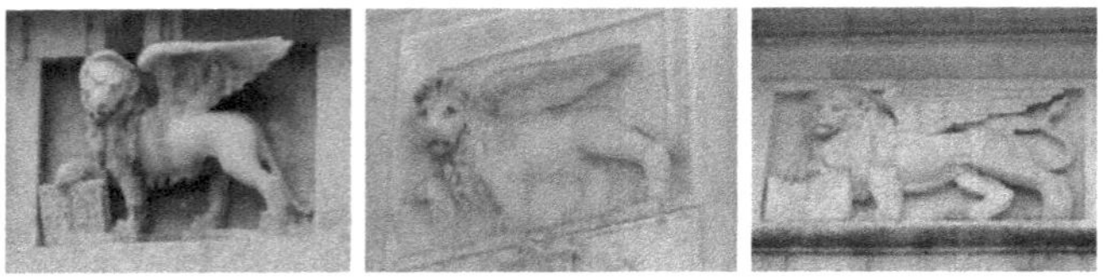

Figure 5. A set of three pictures for recognizing the target POI in the learning test.

Visiting Experience
- Overall, the visit was pleasant
- Overall, the visit was amusing
- Searching for the POIs was enticing
- Using the system was amusing
Connection with the environment
- Using the system distracted me from the surroundings
- Using the system interfered with the main task
Presence
- I had the impression that the information provided by the system were well integrated with the surroundings
- I had the impression that the system built an environment rich of information
- The system did not hamper the observation of the elements in the surroundings
- When I was using the system I had the impression that I was interacting directly with the POI
Usability
Responsiveness - The system promptly responded to my input
Comfort of use - When I was using the system I felt observed
Comfort of use - The system is bulky
Comfort of use - Using the system had limited my movements
Usefulness - The system helped me identifying the PoI around me
Usefulness - I learnt a lot of new things about the landmarks of the city
Usefulness - This system can be a valuable support for tourists
Usefulness - I would like to use this system for other visits in the future

Table 3. The post-experience questionnaire for measuring visiting experience.

semi-structured interview. More specifically, they were asked what impressed them about the experience, what were the strengths and weaknesses of the application, what were the most innovative elements and whether they had the feeling to be more focused on the devices.

The visiting experience was additionally measured using a learning test in which participants were asked to recognize the target POI from three similar pictures (See Fig. 5). Among which, only one was taken from the target POI in the location task. We assume that using VAR/HAR interfaces (focusing on the target landmarks) to explore the environment would result in participants memorizing more details regarding the viewed subjects than using touchscreen-based 2D map (focusing on the touchscreen) [13].

Efficiency. The task completion time was extracted from the synchronized video recordings, while the number of POI selections in each task was derived from system log. Efficiency might not be the most relevant index in the context of urban exploration. However, if the time to complete the same task between two different interface is very different, this may indicate that one of them requires much more effort to use.

Switching. The video recordings were analyzed to identify the occasions and the circumstances (still or on the move) when interface switching took place in the combined VAR/HAR condition.

Procedure

Preparatory phase. The participants were first debriefed on the overall experimental purposes and procedure, signed an informed consent form, and answered a brief questionnaire for background information. Then they were trained to use the devices and practiced both location and information tasks until they were confident in using the interfaces. To remove the bias of participants' prior knowledge about the city, we included in the POI selection several unpopular POIs that are least cited by most tourism apps and websites. The participants were shown the POI list from which they selected for each square a POI that was both unknown to them and seemingly of some interest. The selected POIs (that are unknown to the participant) were to be used as target POIs in the location tasks. The participants were then assigned to a starting condition, either with VAR or HAR, and a starting square (See Fig. 6), both in counterbalanced order.

Experimental phase. The participants were walked to a predefined starting point in the square. They were asked to locate the POI that was selected in the preparatory phase, walk to it, and indicate it to the experimenter (location task). Continuing to the information task, they were asked to explore the available POIs and find information about a specific POI of their choice. When the POI was determined and selected, they again walked to it to indicate it to the experimenter, and finally took a picture of it with the camera provided. After completing both tasks, the participants were asked to answer the post-experience questionnaire and to take the learning test. Then, the participants moved to the second square and repeated the same procedure but with the other interface mode.

	Experimental Group		Control Group					
	M(SD)	*Mdn*	*M(SD)*	*Mdn*	*U*	*z*	*r*	*p*
Visiting Experience	4.78(0.91)	5.00	4.82(1.25)	5.12	78.5	-.558	-0.09	0.58
Connection	4 16(0.78)	4.50	4.95(0.72)	5.00	3.0	-4.22	-0.01	0.021
Presence	4.28(0.93)	4.25	4.30(1.05)	4.37	88.00	-.096	-0.47	0.94
Usability	4.22(0.48)	4.38	4.80(0.65)	5.00	30.00	-2.87	-0.70	0.03

Table 4. Results for the Mann-Whitney test. For the reader's convenience, means, standard deviations, and medians are reported with respect to the dimensions assessed by the post-experience questionnaire for both the experimental and control groups.

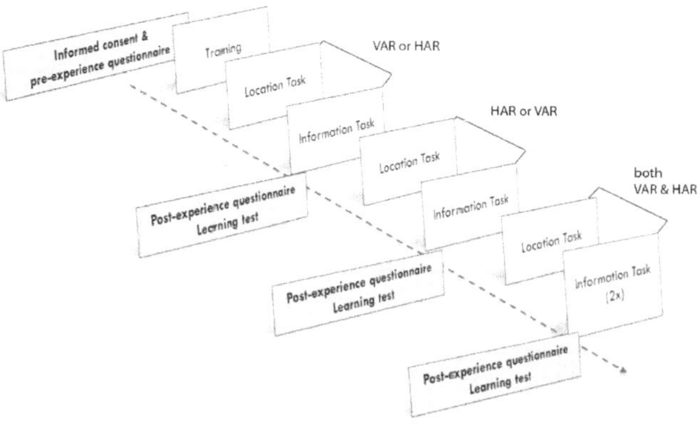

Figure 6. Steps composing the study procedure, with the three stages of the study plus the training.

Finally, the participants moved to a third square where they were free to choose which interface to use as well as switch interfaces during the tasks. When the information task was completed, the participants were forced to switch from the current (favored) interface to the other (less favored) and perform again the information task with a different target. This way, we assured we could observe whether using the less favored interface hampered the performance. At the end, they answered the questionnaire, took the learning test and answered a brief interview. The whole procedure took about 1 hour and 15 minutes per subject.

Participants in the control group performed the same sequence of location and information tasks in the three different squares, always using the same 2D map application.

Participants

A total of 36 volunteers were randomly divided into two groups. The mean age was 25.3 years (*SD* = 2.3) in the experimental group (18 participants, 9 women) and 25.1 years (*SD* = 3.2) in the control group (18 participants, 9 women). All participants reported having never or rarely used any vibrotactile or VAR device and usually relied on guidebooks (30), apps (26), or guided tours (3) when visiting a city. All participants were recruited by word of mouth and through advertising on University pages and social networks. Participants' prior knowledge of the city was not an exclusion criterion, as target POIs were not main city landmarks.

Analysis

The video of participants recorded by a trained experimental assistant and the video of the tablet screen recorded by AZ Screen Recorder[6] were synchronized and embedded into a single video clip. The video analysis followed a top-down approach based on a coding scheme previously agreed upon by three of the authors [33] and was performed by one person who was not in the development team to avoid unconscious bias. Event types were marked by explicitly observable cues. The video clips were analyzed offline using The Observer XT 12 by Noldus to annotate the time during which participants were actively engaged with each task (all conditions), favorite interface mode on the third square (VAR/HAR combined condition), and the episodes when they switched from one interface to the other in VAR/HAR condition. Specifically, the time to complete a task was measured starting from the moment when the participants raised the tablet (when using VAR or 2D map) or the gloved arm (when using HAR) to the moment when they approached the POI and identified it to the experimenter. Walking time was included in the measure because searching for the POI on the site (by the given information) was part of the task. Moreover, participants were also using the system while wandering between the starting point and the target. The switching occurrences were further analyzed in order to identify their circumstances and the modalities that were switched.

The items in the post-experience questionnaire were grouped based on the visiting experience dimension they were supposed to measure (i.e., pleasantness of the visit Cronbach's α = .937, connection with the environment Cronbach's α= .649, presence in the digital information space created by the application Cronbach's α = .72, and usability Cronbach's α = .584); the average score of each dimension was calculated.

Visiting Experience. To compare the visiting experience (H1), a Mann-Whitney test was run, which compared the signed-ranks of the scores at the post-session questionnaire in both groups. Here, the scores refer to the first time participants had experienced each system (i.e., after the first stage for the control group and after the third stage for the experimental group). The scores from the learning test for both groups were also compared. Finally, the ratio between the time spent by participants gazing at the tablet screen and the task duration was calculated and compared with a Mann-Whitney test for VAR and 2D map conditions.

Efficiency. To test the efficiency of the interface modes in the different tasks (H2), the time to complete the location task and the number of POIs selected to complete the task in VAR and HAR conditions were compared with a Wilcoxon test.

[6] https://az-screen-recorder.en.uptodown.com/android

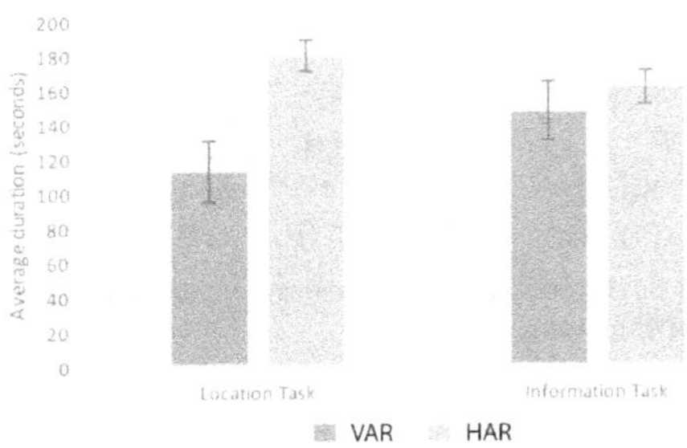

Figure 7. Average time to complete the location and information tasks using VAR and HAR. Bars indicate the standard error.

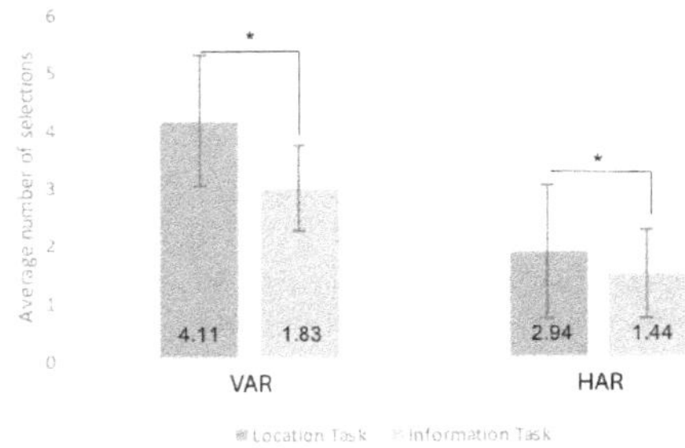

Figure 8. The average number of selections made while performing the location and the information tasks using VAR and HAR. Bars indicate the standard error. *$p < .05$

Switching. To investigate the efforts in switching between VAR and HAR, we observed the switching episodes presented in the video-recordings, especially whether they needed to stop to perform the switching.

RESULTS

Visiting Experience (H1)

The questionnaire scores regarding pleasantness and presence do not seem to differ between the two groups (See Table 4). The only noticeable difference resides in the dimensions of connection and usability. The control group declared they experienced the system as significantly less distracting and interfering, whereas the experimental group found the system easy to use. To see whether the lower scores from the experimental group in these two dimensions were to be attributed to a particular mode, the difference between the three interface modes was analyzed. No significant differences emerged.

As for the learning test, all conditions gave very good results with percentages close to the maximum (respectively, 94% in VAR, 89% in HAR, 94% in combined VAR/HAR, and 89% in the control condition); hence, no further statistical analysis was run.

Efficiency (H2)

Of the two efficiency measures, task completion time (See Fig. 7) and the number of selections made (See Fig. 8), differences in VAR and HAR were found only in the latter. Contrary to the hypothesis, for the location task, a higher number of selections was found in VAR ($M = 4.11$, $SD = 3.02$, $Mdn = 3.5$) than in HAR condition ($M = 1.83$, $SD = 1.15$, $Mdn = 2$), $Z = -2.579$, $p = .010$. Conforming to H2, for the information task, fewer POI selections were made when using HAR ($M = 1.44$, $SD = 1.04$, $Mdn = 1$) than VAR ($M = 2.94$, $SD = 2.5$, $Mdn = 2$), $Z = -2.417$, $p = .016$. In synthesis, regardless of the task, using VAR led to more POI selection than using HAR but with similar task completion time.

Switching

When using both VAR and HAR combined, the participants spontaneously switched interfaces more frequently from HAR to VAR (16) than the contrary (9). Switching interfaces required participants to stand still in the majority of the cases (20 out of 25). No difference was found between the task completion time when using the preferred ($M = 136.18$ seconds $SD = 34.58$) and less preferred ($M = 124.11$ seconds $SD = 27.20$) interface, suggesting that participants could effectively use both modes despite their preferences.

Participants were inquired in the final interview about the reasons why they spontaneously switched interface. Four of the participants switching from VAR to HAR reported that they preferred to listen to the audio rather than reading the textual description of the POIs (3):

> *"This coupling was ideal (VAR+HAR). You can scan the points of interest with the tablet and then listen (to the description) with the headsets, so you can look directly at the point of interest [P11]"*

> *"If possible I would have used only the glove (HAR) ... but since I arrived in a place with many things I didn't know, I wanted to get an overview first ... at that point it is less intrusive to point and listen instead of reading [P33]"*

On the other hand, participants who switched from HAR to VAR mentioned that they wanted to verify the directions provided by HAR (4), to better localize the POI (4), to get information faster (1), to be more in control of the application (1) or because they found VAR more intuitive (1). For example:

> *"(With HAR) my hands were free. I could move more easily ... (I switched to VAR because) I wanted to have a confirmation that I had found the right monument [P31]"*

> *"I like the glove better. I find it easier to use and less bulky ... At some point I could not find a point of interest, but with the tablet (by switching to VAR) I managed [P47]"*

When asked about the strengths of each AR mode, participants seem to find that VAR enables the syncretic overview of all POIs available in the surroundings (3), with an accurate localization of the landmarks (2), while HAR is considered more amusing (5), innovative (3), and able to get information without a screen interposed between them and the environment, enabling a head-up interaction (7):

> *"(The glove) is less bulky... You don't even feel like you are using a tool and even the vibration was pleasant... It felt as if it was an extension of your body [P16]"*

> *"(With the glove) you can interact directly with the environment... you get a concise description of what you see.*

> *Sometimes you visit places and see things and wonder what they are. Here you only need to make a simple pointing gesture and you get to know the basic info [P27]"*

> *"You can use it (VAR) by just turning around and see in real-time all the points of interest [P52]"*

> *"The tablet is good to see where are the points of interest. With the glove if there are more hidden or small points of interests is difficult to find them. I think the glove is better to find bigger monuments and landmarks ... if used together (with VAR) is helpful [P47]"*

Other qualitative remarks

To better understand how the system affected the general visiting experience it is interesting to look at some more qualitative remarks. In particular we asked about perceived weaknesses of the VAR+HAR interface. Here participants mainly complained about the discomfort caused by the too many devices:

> *"The bulkiness. Having to carry the tablet and the glove with this warm weather... [P28]"*

> *"You have to handle many things and your hands are always busy [P44]"*

Additionally some participants reported to be very focused on the technology and that caused some distraction:

> *"At some point I was very focused on the glove ... I was focused on where my finger was pointing ... I was thinking at how to use my glove, I mean, my hand, as a pointer... but after a while it became comfortable and natural [P27]"*

Other times the system was found difficult to use due to the noise of the external environment:

> *"Sometimes the noise from the crowd didn't allow me to hear the audio descriptions [P32]"*

In general, however, the system was well accepted:

> *"I feel this system is very innovative. You can use an object absolutely not bulky as a glove and another very common as a tablet to get the maximum of AR ... I mean I don't have to go around and look tons of things on my guide, but I can use this special audio-guide (HAR) to see what's around me and only use the tablet to go to a specific place. [P52]"*

> *"Even though physically bulky (VAR+HAR), you are still aware of what's going on around you, at safety level also ... You can easily notice other things (from the environment) while receiving the suggestions of the interface [P44]"*

DISCUSSION

VAR and HAR interfaces have complementary strengths in helping users interact with information while maintaining focus on the environment. In this study, we explored the effect of providing users with an urban explorer interwoven with both VAR and HAR. We discussed how participants develop their strategies in using these interfaces in response to the immediate situation as well as providing insights into how each interface could be improved. The observed spontaneous switching confirmed the usefulness for a multi-interface system in a dynamic environment.

Visiting Experience

In terms of visiting experience (H1), the multi-interface system did not differ from the more popular 2D map system even though the former was perceived as more distracting and more difficult to operate. This "distractibility" was probably due to both the number of devices to be managed and the novelty of the system. The lower usability scores of the multi-interface system are consistent with the sensation of being focused on the system itself. However, it is interesting that the other scores were not affected, and the system was considered pleasant and allowed a sense of presence in the information space.

Results from the learning test showed that both groups had high accuracy, indicating that the distinguishability between the pictures was too high. Even though no further insights were gained, we reported this test for the record and the community may find this method useful.

Efficiency of different modalities

Regarding efficiency, H2 was partly confirmed: the different interface modes were indeed used differently, although this did not depend on the task. Basically, VAR always led to selecting more POIs than HAR. Although this did not lead to longer task completion time. While filtering for wanted information through HAR requires some time to listen to the audio information for each selection, skimming for information on VAR, due to the high bandwidth in processing textual information visually, could be quickly done by repeating the following: POI selection, information skimming, quitting, and selecting the next. Timewise, the cost of selecting a wrong POI on VAR was lower than in HAR. So in VAR the time wasted in opening wrong PoIs was eventually compensated by the higher speed at which they could be found compared with HAR. Hence the higher number of selections did not result in longer task completion time.

Switching between modalities

Spontaneous interface switching during the exploration revealed the usefulness of providing complementary interfaces on one system. Although interface switching causes participants to stop, sacrificing both time and physical effort, the majority of the participants spontaneously switched an interface when they felt the other interface was more suitable for a concurrent situation. The situation, be it subject feeling or environmental factors, could be so dynamic that it drove participants to switch to the other interface in the next moment. Equally important to be considered in the decision making is the effort required from the interface switching mechanism. This observation shows that the proposed switching mechanism did not present a high cost which could stop participants from switching interfaces. Moreover, the result corresponds to previous research on users' behavior in urban exploration, where their needs are dynamic and evolving, and the tools should support switching between interfaces [37]. As praised by participants, these two interfaces are complementary and it was easier to locate POIs with them working together.

Effects of Interaction on Strategy Development

The fundamental differences between the modalities have an impact on participants' decision making in choosing which interface to use. People seem to be more comfortable and confident in using visual interfaces than non-visual ones. Some of the participants switched from HAR to VAR because they wanted to check the direction given by VAR, to better localize the POIs, or to be more in control of the application. However, none of these was the reason why people switched from VAR to HAR although direction misalignment due to sensor error is pervasive. This could result from the fact that people are more familiar with and confident in using visual interface, hence more comfortable with certain errors. On the other hand, HAR did provide unique experience in the exploration that a VAR cannot achieve. Some participants developed a strategy that they localized a POI through VAR but switched to HAR because they wanted to listen to, instead of read, the description of the POI while visiting it. Most of all, although both VAR and HAR enabled head-up interaction, HAR was preferred for it did not interpose a screen between the participants and the surroundings.

The ratio between the number of selections made and the total time also suggests something that is aligned with the above observation: VAR is mainly employed for fast access to information, while HAR serves purposeful exploration of a given POI. While using VAR, participants tended to select multiple POIs for fast access to information. Although the title of the POIs was visible on the billboard, participants skipped reading the title. Instead, they simply selected POIs one after another and examined each POI's detailed view on the pop-up window until the correct one was found. This could result from the fact that the positions of POI billboards (where the title was) reacted to the tablet movement, while on the pop-up window, the title was always displayed on the same position. Participants might have preferred monitoring the same position for POI title, although with extra clicks, than tracing the moving titles. On the other hand, the selections made with the HAR interface seemed to be more purposeful, as participants tended to pay attention to the spoken title and select only when the title matches the target. Participants confirmed this strategy when they were interviewed, reporting that VAR served as a probe of the indications provided by HAR. In addition, HAR mode seems to be less suitable for supporting the search of a specific POI. Even though the difference is not statistically significant, the time required to complete a location task with HAR is higher than using VAR and with both.

Overall, VAR was chosen for faster access to information because it was perceived more precise and could display multiple POIs at once. HAR was chosen for a more purposeful exploration and experience because it did not interpose a screen between the user and the surroundings.

Limitations

In contrast to our expectations, users reported that the multi-interface application demanded more attention as compared to the 2D map application. Despite the scores recorded by the post-experience questionnaire for the experimental group being overall positive, they were indeed lower as compared to the control group. It should be considered that there were more devices to be handled in the experimental group than in the control group, which also explains why the multi-interface system was perceived as more bulky. Moreover, while most people were familiar with the 2D map application, all participants were novice users of the multi-interface system. Interestingly, participants' subjective reports are in contrast with objective observations: VAR users did not spend more time looking at the screen than 2D map users. Nevertheless, the behavioral difference was obvious: VAR users continued a head-up interaction, whereas baseline users used the tablet with heads down.

Some device-specific limitations on the interaction might affect the overall experience in urban exploration. For example, the glove could be made with more flexible fabric to be more comfortable and robust. Using wireless headsets would also reduce the physical constraints in mobility, especially when there are more than one device to manage. Choosing a more compact mobile device could also improve the mobility. However, a smaller screen limits the amount of information that could be displayed at the same time and the comfort of reading.

Both the hand gestural interaction and the switching of interface could suffer from false positives/negatives that are common on sensor-based interaction. Although we have designed the horizontal pointing gesture as the initiation of the interaction, false positives are still possible on various occasions. Similarly, the mobile device may be held in different poses under various conditions. More careful design is needed for interpreting users' intentions effectively through the sensors as well as the activation and closure of the interaction.

CONCLUSION

We investigated how VAR and HAR interfaces could coexist on one urban explorer system to allow easy adaption to a highly dynamic environment. A research prototype equipped with both interfaces was implemented for studying people's preferences in using either interface under different circumstances, how people manage multiple interfaces, and how the switching of interfaces can be designed. We found that VAR was preferred when faster access to information was desired, while HAR was preferred for a more purposeful exploration. Moreover, HAR enabled users to get information without a screen interposed between them and the environment. We also observed spontaneous switching of interfaces from most participants, which indicates that the availability of both interfaces on one system assisted users to react to environmental change or personal need. The research suggests that a versatile, multi-interface urban explorer design is preferable, which enables users to easily adapt to the concurrent environment by selecting the more feasible interface while maintaining focus on the surroundings.

ACKNOWLEDGMENTS

The research leading to these results has received funding from the European Union Seventh Framework Programme (FP7/2007-2013) under grant agreement n°601139 and FCT/MCTES LARSyS (UID/EEA/50009/2013 (2015-2017)).

REFERENCES

1. Anupriya Ankolekar, Thomas Sandholm, and Louis Yu. 2013. Play it by ear: a case for serendipitous discovery of places with musicons. In *Proceedings of the SIGCHI Conference on Human Factors in Computing Systems (CHI '13)*. ACM, Paris, France, 2959–2968. DOI: http://dx.doi.org/10.1145/2470654.2481411

2. Matthias Baldauf, Peter Frohlich, Kathrin Masuch, and Thomas Grechenig. 2011. Comparing Viewing and Filtering Techniques for Mobile Urban Exploration. *Journal of Location Based Services* 5, 1 (March 2011), 38–57. DOI: http://dx.doi.org/10.1080/17489725.2010.541161

3. Michel Beaudouin-Lafon. 2004. Designing Interaction, Not Interfaces. In *Proceedings of the Working Conference on Advanced Visual Interfaces (AVI '04)*. ACM, New York, NY, USA, 15–22. DOI: http://dx.doi.org/10.1145/989863.989865

4. Mark Billinghurst and Bruce H. Thomas. 2011. *Mobile Collaborative Augmented Reality*. Springer New York, New York, NY, 1–19. DOI: http://dx.doi.org/10.1007/978-1-4419-9845-3_1

5. Anne Braun and Rod McCall. 2010 User Study for Mobile Mixed Reality Devices. In *Joint Virtual Reality Conference of EGVE - EuroVR - VEC*. The Eurographics Association. DOI: http://dx.doi.org/10.2312/EGVE/JVRC10/089-092

6. Jaewoo Chung, Francesco Pagnini, and Ellen Langer. 2016. Mindful navigation for pedestrians: Improving engagement with augmented reality. *Technology in Society* 45 (2016), 29–33. DOI: http://dx.doi.org/10.1016/j.techsoc.2016.02.006

7. Andrew Dillon, John Richardson, and Cliff McKnight. 1990. The effects of display size and text splitting on reading lengthy text from screen. *Behaviour & Information Technology* 9, 3 (1990), 215–227.

8. Peter Fröhlich, Antti Oulasvirta, Matthias Baldauf, and Antti Nurminen. 2011. On the move, wirelessly connected to the world. *Commun. ACM* 54, 1 (jan 2011), 132–138. DOI: http://dx.doi.org/10.1145/1866739.1866766

9. Maribeth Gandy, Richard Catrambone, Blair MacIntyre, Chris Alvarez, Elsa Eiriksdottir, Matthew Hilimire, Brian Davidson, and Anne Collins McLaughlin. 2010. Experiences with an AR evaluation test bed: Presence, performance, and physiological measurement. In *Mixed and Augmented Reality (ISMAR), 2010 9th IEEE International Symposium on*. IEEE, 127–136.

10. Frank A. Geldard. 1957. Adventures in tactile literacy. *American Psychologist* 12, 3 (1957), 115–124. DOI: http://dx.doi.org/10.1037/h0040416

11. Shigeru Haga, Ayaka Sano, Yuri Sekine, Hideka Sato, Saki Yamaguchi, and Kosuke Masuda. 2015. Effects of using a Smart Phone on Pedestrians' Attention and Walking. *Procedia Manufacturing* 3 (2015), 2574–2580. DOI: http://dx.doi.org/10.1016/j.promfg.2015.07.564

12. Faizan Haque, Mathieu Nancel, and Daniel Vogel. 2015. Myopoint: Pointing and Clicking Using Forearm Mounted Electromyography and Inertial Motion Sensors. In *Proceedings of the 33rd Annual ACM Conference on Human Factors in Computing Systems - CHI '15*. ACM Press, Seoul, Republic of Korea, 3653–3656. DOI: http://dx.doi.org/10.1145/2702123.2702133

13. Linda A Henkel. 2014. Point-and-shoot memories: the influence of taking photos on memory for a museum tour. *Psychological science* 25, 2 (feb 2014), 396–402. DOI: http://dx.doi.org/10.1177/0956797613504438

14. Yi-Ta Hsieh, Antti Jylhä, Valeria Orso, Luciano Gamberini, and, Giulio Jacucci. 2016. Designing a Willing-to-Use-in-Public Hand Gestural Interaction Technique for Smart Glasses. In *Proceedings of the 2016 CHI Conference on Human Factors in Computing Systems - CHI '16*. ACM Press, New York, New York, USA, 4203–4215. DOI: http://dx.doi.org/10.1145/2858036.2858436

15. Ira E Hyman, S Matthew Boss, Breanne M Wise, Kira E McKenzie, and Jenna M Caggiano. 2010. Did you see the unicycling clown? Inattentional blindness while walking and talking on a cell phone. *Applied Cognitive Psychology* 24, 5 (oct 2010), 597–607. DOI: http://dx.doi.org/10.1002/acp.1638

16. Lei Jing, Zixue Cheng, Yinghui Zhou, Junbo Wang, and Tongjun Huang. 2013. Magic Ring: a self-contained gesture input device on finger. In *Proceedings of the 12th International Conference on Mobile and Ubiquitous Multimedia - MUM '13*. ACM Press, New York, New York, USA, 1–4. DOI: http://dx.doi.org/10.1145/2541831.2541875

17. Lynette a Jones and Nadine B Sarter. 2008. Tactile displays: guidance for their design and application. *Human factors* 50, 1 (2008), 90–111. DOI: http://dx.doi.org/10.1518/001872008X250638

18. Matt Jones, George Buchanan, and Harold Thimbleby. 2003. Improving web search on small screen devices. *Interacting with Computers* 15, 4 (2003), 479–495.

19. Antti Jylhä, Yi-Ta Hsieh, Valeria Orso, Salvatore Andolina, Luciano Gamberini, and Giulio Jacucci. 2015. A Wearable Multimodal Interface for Exploring Urban Points of Interest. In *Proceedings of the 2015 ACM on International Conference on Multimodal Interaction*. ACM Press, New York, New York, USA. 175–182 DOI: http://dx.doi.org/10.1145/2818346.2820763

20. Amy K Karlson, Benjamin B Bederson, and Jose L Contreras-Vidal. 2008. Understanding one-handed use of mobile devices. In *Handbook of research on user interface design and evaluation for mobile technology*. IGI Global, 86–101.

21. Andreas Komninos, Peter Barrie, Vassilios Stefanis, and Athanasios Plessas. 2012. Urban exploration using audio

scents. In *Proceedings of the 14th international conference on Human-computer interaction with mobile devices and services - MobileHCI '12*. ACM, 349–358. DOI:http://dx.doi.org/10.1145/2371574.2371629

22. Sang-su Lee, Sohyun Kim, and Kun-pyo Lee. 2010a. How Users Manipulate Deformable Displays as Input Devices. *Methodology* (2010), 1647–1656.
23. W. Lee, Y. Park, V. Lepetit, and W. Woo. 2010b. Point-and-shoot for ubiquitous tagging on mobile phones. In *2010 IEEE International Symposium on Mixed and Augmented Reality*. 57–64. DOI: http://dx.doi.org/10.1109/ISMAR.2010.5643551
24. Charlotte Magnusson, Kirsten Rassmus-Gröhn, and Delphine Szymczak. 2010. Scanning angles for directional pointing. In *Proceedings of the 12th international conference on Human computer interaction with mobile devices and services - MobileHCI '10*. ACM Press, Lisbon, Portugal, 399–400. DOI: http://dx.doi.org/10.1145/1851600.1851684
25. Charlotte Magnusson, Kirsten Rassmus-Gröhn, and Delphine Szymczak. 2014. Exploring history: a mobile inclusive virtual tourist guide. In *Proceedings of the 8th Nordic Conference on Human-Computer Interaction Fun, Fast, Foundational - NordiCHI '14*. ACM Press, New York, New York, USA, 69–78. DOI: http://dx.doi.org/10.1145/2639189.2639245
26. David McGookin, Stephen Brewster, and Pablo Priego. 2009. Audio bubbles: Employing non-speech audio to support tourist wayfinding. *Lecture Notes in Computer Science (including subseries Lecture Notes in Artificial Intelligence and Lecture Notes in Bioinformatics)* 5763 LNCS (2009), 41–50. DOI: http://dx.doi.org/10.1007/978-3-642-04076-4_5
27. Jack Nasar, Peter Hecht, and Richard Wener. 2008. Mobile telephones, distracted attention, and pedestrian safety. *Accident; analysis and prevention* 40, 1, 69–75. DOI:http://dx.doi.org/10.1016/j.aap.2007.04.005
28. Rui Nóbrega, Diogo Cabral, Giulio Jacucci, and António Coelho. 2015. NARI: Natural Augmented Reality Interface - Interaction Challenges for AR Applications. In *Proceedings of the 10th International Conference on Computer Graphics Theory and Applications (VISIGRAPP 2015)*. SCITEPRESS, 504–510. DOI: http://dx.doi.org/10.5220/0005360305040510
29. Eamonn O'Neill. 2014. Haptic and audio displays for augmented reality tourism applications. In *2014 IEEE Haptics Symposium (HAPTICS)*. IEEE, Houston, TX, USA, 485–488. DOI: http://dx.doi.org/10.1109/HAPTICS.2014.6775503
30. Martin Pielot, Niels Henze, and Susanne Boll. 2009. Supporting Map-based Wayfinding with Tactile Cues. In *Proceedings of the 11th International Conference on Human-Computer Interaction with Mobile Devices and Services (MobileHCI '09)*. ACM, New York, NY, USA, Article 23, 10 pages. DOI: http://dx.doi.org/10.1145/1613858.1613888
31. Martin Pielot, Wilko Heuten, Stephan Zerhusen, and Susanne Boll. 2012. Dude, where's my car?: in-situ evaluation of a tactile car finder. In *Proceedings of the 7th Nordic Conference on Human-Computer Interaction Making Sense Through Design - NordiCHI '12*. ACM Press, Copenhagen, Denmark, 166–169. DOI: http://dx.doi.org/10.1145/2399016.2399042
32. Dieter Schmalstieg and Tobias Höllerer. 2015. *Augmented Reality: Principles and Practice*. Addison Wesley Professional.
33. Julia Snell. 2011. Interrogating video data: Systematic quantitative analysis versus micro-ethnographic analysis. 14 (05 2011), 253–258.
34. Mayuree Srikulwong and Eamonn O'Neill. 2011. A comparative study of tactile representation techniques for landmarks on a wearable device. In *Proceedings of the SIGCHI Conference on Human Factors in Computing Systems CHI '11*. ACM, Vancouver, BC, Canada, 2029–2038. DOI: http://dx.doi.org/10.1145/1978942.1979236
35. Ying-Chao Tung, Chun-Yen Hsu, Han-Yu Wang, Silvia Chyou, Jhe-Wei Lin, Pei-Jung Wu, Andries Valstar, and Mike Y Chen. 2015. User-Defined Game Input for Smart Glasses in Public Space. In *Proceedings of the 33rd Annual ACM Conference on Human Factors in Computing Systems - CHI '15*. ACM Press, 3327–3336. DOI:http://dx.doi.org/10.1145/2702123.2702214
36. Matthew Turk. 2014. Review Article: Multimodal Interaction: A Review. *Pattern Recogn. Lett.* 36 (Jan. 2014), 189–195. DOI: http://dx.doi.org/10.1016/j.patrec.2013.07.003
37. Tuomas Vaittinen and David McGookin. 2016. Phases of Urban Tourists' Exploratory Navigation: A Field Study. In *Proceedings of the 2016 ACM Conference on Designing Interactive Systems (DIS '16)*. ACM, New York, NY, USA, 1111–1122. DOI: http://dx.doi.org/10.1145/2901790.2901795
38. Florian van de Camp, Alexander Schick, and Rainer Stiefelhagen. 2013. How to click in mid-air. In *International Conference on Distributed, Ambient, and Pervasive Interactions*. Springer, 78–86.
39. Yolanda Vazquez-Alvarez, Ian Oakley, and Stephen A Brewster. 2012. Auditory display design for exploration in mobile audio-augmented reality. *Personal and Ubiquitous Computing* 16, 8 (sep 2012), 987–999. DOI: http://dx.doi.org/10.1007/s00779-011-0459-0
40. J. Wither, S. DiVerdi, and T. Hollerer. 2007. Evaluating Display Types for AR Selection and Annotation. In *Mixed and Augmented Reality, 2007. ISMAR 2007. 6th IEEE and ACM International Symposium on*. 95–98. DOI: http://dx.doi.org/10.1109/ISMAR.2007.4538832
41. Z Yovcheva, Dimitrios Buhalis, and C Gatzidis. 2012. Smartphone Augmented Reality Applications for Tourism. *e-Review of Tourism Research (eRTR)* 10, 2 (2012), 63–66.

Scale Impacts Elicited Gestures for Manipulating Holograms: Implications for AR Gesture Design

Tran Pham[1], Jo Vermeulen[2], Anthony Tang[1], Lindsay MacDonald Vermeulen[3]
[1] University of Calgary, Canada
[2] Department of Computer Science, Aarhus University, Denmark
[3] Alexandra Institute, Denmark
phamt@ucalgary.ca · jo.vermeulen@cs.au.dk · tonyt@ucalgary.ca · lindsay.vermeulen@alexandra.dk

ABSTRACT
Because gesture design for augmented reality (AR) remains idiosyncratic, people cannot necessarily use gestures learned in one AR application in another. To design discoverable gestures, we need to understand what gestures people expect to use. We explore how the scale of AR affects the gestures people expect to use to interact with 3D holograms. Using an elicitation study, we asked participants to generate gestures in response to holographic task referents, where we varied the scale of holograms from desktop-scale to room-scale objects. We found that the scale of objects and scenes in the AR experience moderates the generated gestures. Most gestures were informed by physical interaction, and when people interacted from a distance, they sought a good perspective on the target object before and during the interaction. These results suggest that gesture designers need to account for scale, and should not simply reuse gestures across different hologram sizes.

Author Keywords
Gestures; augmented reality; gesture elicitation; HoloLens.

ACM Classification Keywords
H.5.2 [Information Interfaces and Presentation]: User Interfaces — interaction styles, user-centered design.

INTRODUCTION
Gestural interaction for augmented reality (AR) remains idiosyncratic, where users may need to re-learn gestures and skills for each system they use. The commoditization of AR technology is making AR experiences, where people interact with virtual objects and content overlaid atop a tracked model of the world, a reality today. While many manufacturers deliver specialized handheld controllers to manipulate the virtual objects and scenes, these remain dedicated pieces of hardware with manufacturer-specific affordances. To overcome this challenge, many researchers still aim to design freehand gestures to allow users to create, modify, and interact with virtual 3D objects in physical spaces. The problem is that we do not yet have a common framework for designing gestures for such AR experiences, much less a common gesture set for this type of 3D object interaction.

To help develop a common framework for AR gestures, we are specifically interested in this paper with how different scales of AR affect people's expectations for gestures. The AR experiences we have seen over the years have varied widely in terms of the scale of the virtual objects and scenes. For instance, researchers have explored AR experiences on tabletops (e.g. [3, 63]), as mid-air holograms (e.g. [43, 60]), at room-scale (e.g. [34, 59]), and even at city- or world-scale (e.g. [29, 45, 49]). Generally, we are interested in designing easily-guessable and memorable gestures for interacting with 3D AR content. This discoverability is important for near-future AR scenarios, for example: in "walk-up and use" AR in a museum, or in casual usage scenarios such as a new home owner using a simple AR tool to explore furniture arrangement for a room. We build on prior work that has articulated several new dimensions for AR gesture design [40], where we explore specifically whether the scale of an AR experience affects gestures people expect to use. Specifically, should designers use the same gesture for (say) moving a small AR object to also move a large AR object? Or alternatively, does a designer need to account for different object sizes when designing such movement gestures? Furthermore, does this change if the object is attached to a surface such as a wall or table, and do people use different kinds of gestures if the content is room-scale?

We conducted an elicitation study to address our research question about the impact of scale on the discoverability of gestures in AR. In this study, participants were presented referents of different AR scales and asked to propose a gesture for the referent. A referent is the desired action that the proposed gesture invokes, e.g. "zoom in." We recruited 16 participants to create these gestures in response to "before" and "after" visuals of operations on 3D objects that they could view through a head-mounted AR display (each were 3D AR scenes). We used this elicitation study to understand what kind of gestures people would expect to use to enact the operations. By analyzing this data, we gain

DIS '18, June 9–13, 2018, Hong Kong

ACM ISBN 978-1-4503-5198-0/18/06…$15.00
https://doi.org/10.1145/3196709.3196719

insight into which gestures people expect to use across different scales, and insight into designing a discoverable gesture set that matches people's expectations. To explore the impact of scale, we visualized operations at three different AR scales: a small hologram floating in mid-air, a city model attached to a physical table, and another where virtual furniture was laid out in a small physical room.

To foreshadow our results: rather than relying on the same gesture at different scales, participants generated new gestures for each hologram size. We found that because the gestures people generated had a largely physical nature (i.e. rather than symbolic gestures), participants used gestures to manipulate the virtual objects' affordances. Consequently, the size of the object or scene moderated the size of the gesture they performed. Finally, we observed that for smaller objects, people moved towards the object to operate on it directly—as if to touch it (*proximally*), while for larger objects and scenes, people relied more on perspective-based gestures to operate on the object from a distance (*distally*). Our findings extend those from Piumsomboon et al. [40] by characterizing the nature of gestures in relation to scale of virtual objects, and by providing a further characterization of their "*locale*" dimension (i.e. where the gestures are performed [40]) that designers can use.

Our work contributes an additional set of considerations for designers who are building AR experiences where people interact with 3D objects and scenes. Specifically, they suggest that to design discoverable gestures for AR experiences where virtual objects are manipulated, designers need to account for scale and apparent physical affordances of the virtual objects. Additionally, where multiple scales are involved, multiple gestures may be required for the same operation at each scale of interaction.

RELATED WORK

We begin by considering how researchers have envisaged different scales of AR experiences, demonstrating that these scales are markedly different in terms of size, the envisioned use case, and how people interact with the AR content. We then discuss how freehand gestural interaction with AR remains of interest for both practical and accessibility reasons, but that gestures have still been frequently designed around recognition technologies rather than being focused on discoverability. Finally, we describe how elicitation studies have been used to addressed this "guessability" problem for gestures. We synthesize these learnings from the community, and show how our work addresses the gap between AR gestures and the wide variety of scales that we expect AR to be used.

Scale of AR experiences. Researchers and visionaries have demonstrated that AR experiences will vary widely in terms of the scale of the virtual objects and the experience. Some experiences are small, table-based experiences, where the entirety of the objects under control are the size of one's palm (e.g. [63]). Some are tabletop experiences, where objects interact with surfaces (e.g. [3, 7]). Other AR experiences are room-scale, with virtual objects attached to multiple walls and large surfaces (e.g. [19, 20, 34, 37, 59]). Finally, some AR experiences are world-scale, where the digital content is anchored to large objects in the world (e.g. landmarks [29, 45], or infrastructure [49]).

Each of these AR scales presents different interaction challenges for acting on or affecting the digital content. To some extent, this interaction is also mediated by how we view AR content. Some approaches use head-mounted glasses with digital overlay (e.g. [34, 36, 43]) or projection-based (spatial) AR [6] (e.g. [20, 59]). With handheld, see-through displays such as tablets or smartphones (e.g. [1, 9, 49]), interaction techniques rely on the stability of a handheld see-through display to facilitate mediated "touching" (e.g. as in Apple's ARKit showcase game "The Machines" [9]). For larger-scale content, we have seen ray-based interaction techniques, where people use either their fingers, arms or another device to point at the distant objects to be interacted with (e.g. [11, 35, 38, 44]).

Given the disparate range of AR scales and experiences, it seems unlikely that we can adopt a "one-size-fits-all" approach to interacting with virtual content in AR. This presents the challenge that people cannot easily reapply learnings from one experience to the next. Our work aims to understand whether this idiosyncrasy due to size is unnecessary, that is, whether we can reasonably expect that people will expect to interact with content at different scales in the same way.

Freehand Gestural Interaction in AR. Many researchers are actively seeking to develop freehand gestures for interacting with virtual content in AR, which are considered natural user interfaces [4]. Early work considered the use of tangible proxies such as cards or wands for interacting with virtual content, where manipulating physical proxies would result in similar actions in the virtual world (e.g. [5, 22, 48]). These were later augmented via multimodal approaches integrating speech and gestures (e.g. [15, 17, 23, 25, 35, 42]). Recent work on freehand gestures has been accelerated by the commoditization of depth cameras and sensing technologies optimized for hand posture and gesture recognition (e.g. [33, 24]). These freehand gestures leverage reality-based interaction mental models for manipulating virtual content [18], for instance by pushing virtual objects with one's hands (e.g. [3, 16, 41]).

The challenge is that many of these gestures are designed for optimal recognition by the sensing technologies, rather than by being motivated by human characteristics (e.g. discoverability). For instance, [10, 21, 26] rely on overhead cameras to track the position and posture of hands. This means that because of the positioning of the cameras, certain types of gestures are not accurately recognized, while some gestures are effectively impossible to detect properly (e.g. if they are obscured by other parts of one's hands) [10, 26, 27, 28]. While advances in machine learning may help to ameliorate the sensing problems, the issue remains that the underlying design of these gesture sets is mainly motivated by identifying easily distinguishable and recognizable gestures.

Elicitation Approaches for Discoverable Interaction. To design discoverable, memorable gestures for new interaction contexts, many researchers have now turned to "elicitation studies." Rather than relying on designers (i.e., experts) create gestures for actions, participants propose gestures that they would expect to use in response to system actions. Gesture elicitation has been used for many domains including surface computing [31, 62], AR [25, 40], deformable interfaces [55], TV controls [57], omni-directional video [46], multi-display environments [50], mobile motion gestures [47], back-of-device gestures [52] and above-device gestures for smartwatches [51]. Follow-up work has demonstrated that this approach generates a better gesture set than an expert-generated one [30].

Elicitation studies for AR have identified a working set of gestures for AR (e.g. [25, 40]). Piumsomboon et al. [40] focus on interactions with "table-sized" AR content, where gestures included both manipulation on the objects (e.g. resizing, moving, etc.) along with editing, simulation, browsing, selection and menu interaction. The study helped identify two new parametric categories to classify gestures unique to AR: whereas Wobbrock et al. [62] characterized gestures in terms of Form, Nature, Binding and Flow, Piumsomboon et al. [40] added two new parameters: Symmetry (i.e. how the hands are used) and Locale (where the gestures are performed). Beyond this, the authors also propose a working set of freehand gestures for AR.

Gesture elicitation studies for AR have not adequately accounted for scale of the AR experience. Critically, while the working set of gestures of Piumsomboon et al. [40] is likely to be discoverable, the gestures were elicited for "baseball-sized" referents that appeared on or just above a large table. Notably, the authors observed that the size of the AR object affected the number of hands used to manipulate the objects (e.g. for objects palm-sized or smaller, only one hand; for objects larger, two hands). Unfortunately, the study only investigated relatively small-scale AR (in comparison to bigger experiences such as [20, 34, 59]). Thus, while large portions of the proposed gesture set are likely to be effective for tabletop AR (i.e. actions that interact with AR "above" the objects themselves such as menu selection, and abstract actions such as editing or simulation), it is unclear whether they adequately account for the range of scales we have already seen AR experiences take, which we investigate in this paper.

Synthesis. AR experiences already exist that address a wide range of scales; however, we do not understand how differences in scale impact people's expectations of how to interact with holograms. Freehand gestural interaction with 3D content in AR is likely to be a common approach, as it does not require specialized external hardware. Our current understanding of how to design these gestures, based on elicitation studies leaves unclear whether the gestures should be consistent across scales, or if they should vary across scale. We address this gap in the present study, where we consider three distinct settings and scales for AR (in mid-air, anchored to a surface and at room-scale). As we will see, these settings impact the character of the gestures that participants create, and this is even more pronounced with room-scale AR, extending earlier findings in [40].

STUDY DESIGN

To understand the impact of scale on people's expectations of how to interact with gestures, we used a reformulated form of an elicitation study. As with other domains of inquiry, an elicitation method presents participants with a "before" and "after" visualization, whereupon participants are asked to design a gesture that would move the system from one state to another. Our use of this method helped us to uncover underlying mental models people have of how 3D objects and scenes would/should be manipulated using freehand gestures, thereby giving us knowledge to design learnable, memorable gestures for these situations. Whereas prior work with elicitation studies provided participants with each referent in turn, we reformulated this approach using what we called "scenarios." These scenarios asked participants to imagine themselves completing an entire series of tasks (i.e. multiple referents), so that the referents were elicited in context with one another.

Scale. Each scenario grouped together a series of referents at a specific "scale" of interaction, each with its own constraints: *Mid-Air*, *Surface*, and *Room*. The apparent visual size of the virtual objects differed in each scenario as well as the size of the scene (the volume containing all objects expressed in length × width × height). Figure 1 illustrates these scenarios within the context that the participants experienced them in the study. The "mid-air" scale of interaction, for instance, used a 14 cm × 31 cm × 25 cm model of a home. The "surface" scale of interaction used a small city model with buildings and streets on a tabletop prop (26.5 cm × 97 cm × 56 cm). This scale also afforded interaction with the tabletop, since the hologram appeared to sit on the tabletop itself. Finally, the largest scale of interaction, the "room", used a physical three walled-room (with an open side) with dimensions of (549 cm × 303 cm × 255 cm) that contained virtual furniture such as a couch, shelves, and a coffee table. Each of these scales are illustrated in Figure 1. We chose each of these scales to represent major classes of interactive AR experiences: the mid-air scale abstracts tasks that involve a mid-air hologram (e.g. a car in automotive design), whereas the surface scale maps to augmented document tasks (e.g. [56]), while the room-scale scenario abstracts furniture re-organization in a physical space.

Scenarios. To give participants a motivating purpose in the study, participants were provided with a series of tasks to accomplish within each scenario, where each referent made sense in the context of the greater scenario. Each of these

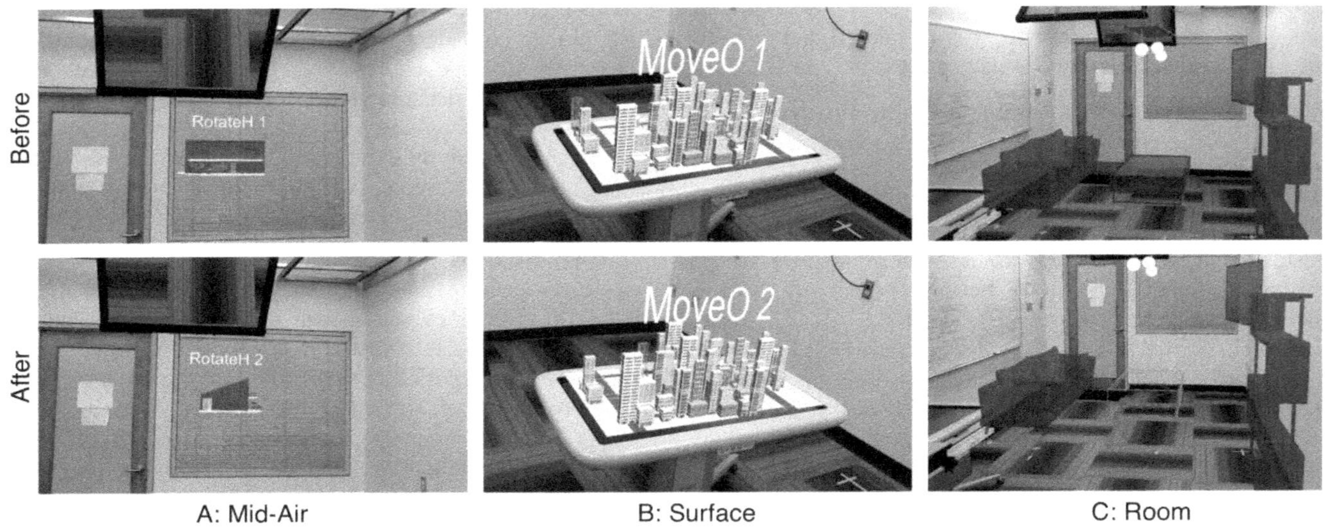

Figure 1. We used three different scenarios in our study. Illustrated here are sample before and after referents for each scenario: (A) *Mid-Air* – a virtual house model in mid-air (14 cm × 31 cm × 25 cm), "rotate scene" referent; (B) *Surface* – a small city model with buildings and streets on a tabletop prop (26.5 cm × 97 cm × 56 cm), "move building" referent; (C) *Room* – a small physical room with virtual furniture such as a couch, shelves, and a coffee table (549 cm × 303 cm × 255 cm), "select coffee table" referent.

"tasks" was represented as a referent pair of "before" and "after" scenes. Thus, the same base set of referents was presented in each scenario, and each scenario added its own set of referents that fit the scenario.

To get a sense of how the scenarios worked, we will provide an overview of the initial set of referents for each scenario (note that each scenario was considerably longer). In the *Mid-Air* scenario, the participant remodeled a house in several steps. First, they were to rotate the scene so that the home faced the right direction, then they would scale the depth of the home to fit the lot. Then, they were to move some objects out of the way before duplicating the front door, and then moving the duplicated door onto the back wall (so the home would have a back entrance). For the *Surface* scenario, participants were to change the plan for a few city blocks. Here, a participant would select a set of buildings, then, duplicate one of them. The duplicate building needed to be moved to a new block, where it would need to be rotated to fit into the block. Then, a particularly ugly building was to be deleted. Finally, in the *Room* scenario, participants were to redecorate the room they stood in. First, they were to select the bookshelf, and rotate it to create a more intimate space. Then, they were to shrink the TV on the wall so it did not occupy as much wall space, and then move the coffee table against the wall.

Referents. Each scenario enacted a different number of referents that made sense for the scenario, and all scenarios shared a common "base set" of referents. A *referent* is the desired effect of an action (e.g. zoom in) for which participants are asked to propose a gesture (e.g. pinch) [30]. We extracted 17 basic operations from 3D modelling tutorials (e.g. for SketchUp [54]) that reflected a common set of operations on 3D objects or scenes (select object, duplicate object, move object, rotate object, delete object, undo, scale x-dimension, scale y-dimension, scale z-dimension, move scene, scale scene uniformly, separate layers, select group of nearby objects, scale object uniform, select multiple objects, select layer, rotate scene). From these referents, we selected referents that were suitable for the scenario, and adapted them as appropriate; for instance, "Select object" became "Select a plant" in the *Mid-Air* scenario, "Select a building" in the *Surface* scenario, and "Select a piece of furniture" in the *Room* scenario. Not all referents were represented in every scenario (e.g. "Rotate scene" did not make sense in the room scenario). To ensure that we had a common set of referents where we could compare gestures across each scale and scenario, we identified seven referents to act as the "base set": select, duplicate, move, rotate, delete, undo, and scale (x-dimension). Each of these referents was represented in each of the scenarios, and formed the basis of our analysis.

Although some elicitation studies show a transitional animation between referents (e.g. [40]), we chose instead to "slideshow" the referents as in [50]. By presenting using a strict "before" and "after" approach, we free participants of this potential bias, allowing them to consider discrete variations if this suited their mental model. We believe the animation pre-supposes how the gesture ought to operate on the object/scene (i.e. as smooth continuous operations).

Apparatus. Participants viewed the referents using a Microsoft HoloLens head-mounted display, where the objects in the scene were anchored to fit the scenario (e.g. anchored to a physical table, the wall, or the ground). Participants could move around the scene, and the holograms would update accordingly, with the virtual objects remaining anchored to the real world. Participants were presented the start and end state in sequence.

Participants. We recruited sixteen participants (10 male, 6 female) with an average age of 23 years. Five participants had prior experience with the HoloLens (four of these had only played with demos), none of the others had prior experience. Of these 16 participants, four reported limited experience with AR/VR systems (i.e. demos at stores), while 11 reported having none. All participants were students, and their backgrounds were broad: computer science, statistics, occupational therapy, neuroscience, chemistry, engineering and kinesiology.

Method. Scenarios were presented to participants in counter-balanced order. For each referent, the participant saw the "before" and "after" scene, and was asked to generate a gesture that they expected would move the system from one state to the next. Participants could ask to toggle between the "before" and "after" scenes (controlled by the experimenter) as many times as they liked. They were then asked to rate the suitability of the gesture for the referent, and the ease of performing the gesture. Participants were given a break between each scenario.

Data Collection. We collected four sources of data: first, demographic information from a pre-study questionnaire; second, a video capturing participants' gestures created during the study; third, participants' confidence scores in the suitability and ease of use of the gestures they created (as they went), and fourth, responses to a post-study semi-structured interview. Video footage was recorded from in front of the participants.

Analysis. As we collected data, we used iterative video coding of the gestures that participants generated, identifying recurring gestures and themes, and properties that described the gestures (e.g. number of fingers used, shape of the gesture). This coding process was iterative, where we generated provisional codes, revising them as we identified better phrases and ideas to capture what we observed. We developed a tool to simultaneously view gestures across participants and scenarios and facilitate comparison. Using this tool, all co-authors viewed videos of participants' gestures to develop a coding scheme to capture and describe the gestures. We then used axial coding [8] to explain how lower level codes were related to one another. Critically, while our analytic frame was influenced by all the gestures from participants, our analysis examines *only* the base set of seven referents common to all scenarios, as these are the only ones that could be compared.

FINDINGS

We focus our analysis in this paper on the subset of seven referents that appeared across all three scenarios: select object, move object, rotate object, duplicate object, undo, delete object, scale x-dimension (which we from now on refer to as "scale" for simplicity). After describing the gestures our participants generated, we discuss the physical nature of many of these gestures and how the apparent visual affordances of the objects influenced the character of the gestures. We then describe how the size and scale of scene influenced the gestures, and how participants used perspective-based gestures for larger scenes.

Collected Gesture Data and Agreement Rate. We analyzed 261 gestures generated by the 16 participants, where we identified 64 unique gestures (some gestures were lost because they were obscured by a participant's body, or were not captured due to the camera's field of view). Participants' gestures primarily made use of their fingers, hands, arms, as well as their body position (and their body orientation). Only two participants made use of gestures where the posture of the hand was intentionally part of the gesture (e.g. using two fingers rather than one, or using their pinky and thumb). In general, participants' gestures relied on the visual position of fingers/hands in relation to one another, or on the viewing angle to the object. For instance, for the *Select* referent, some participants walked up to the object and tapped on the object (e.g. with one finger, or with an open palm). Others used what we call a perspective gesture, where they used the same tapping gesture, but rather than walk to the virtual object, changed their position or viewing angle so that their hand would appear between their eye and the object.

Table 2 shows the agreement rates (*AR*) for each of the seven common referents across the three scenarios. Based on the qualitative classification scheme from [58], most of the gestures for these referents would be considered as having medium agreement.

Gesture Themes. Rather than simply code the gestures that we observed, we saw that a coding of the *themes* underlying participants' gestures was more insightful. First, the gestures sometimes varied, but only in very minor ways, and the strict coding of the gestures distinguished between instances in ways that were not useful. Second, we found that the themes seemed to express a mental model of how the participant thought about the objects and their own role in the scene. Consequently, we found the themes to be a much more useful analytic unit in our analysis.

Gestures varied in terms of how participants executed an idea, even if thematically, the idea was the same. For instance, for the *delete* referent, one theme we observed was to squish the object, and this was performed in three

Referent	Gestures			Themes		
	Air	Surface	Room	Air	Surface	Room
Select	0.383	0.183	0.108	0.542	0.650	0.475
Duplicate	0.092	0.100	0.100	0.158	0.167	0.142
Move	0.225	0.200	0.258	0.300	0.303	0.317
Rotate	0.192	0.175	0.125	0.242	0.275	0.433
Delete	0.217	0.167	0.125	0.225	0.208	0.192
Undo	0.092	0.075	0.108	0.208	0.217	0.192
Scale	0.183	0.167	0.183	0.425	0.483	0.508

Table 2: Agreement Rate (*AR*) for referents and themes across scenarios. Shading shows low, medium, high agreement [58].

slightly different ways: one participant clapped, another pinched her fingers, while another closed his fist. Here, each of these gestures is distinct in how it is executed (and would be coded independently in our original coding process); however, given that they are conceptually similar, it makes sense to group them together in the same theme.

A gestural theme seemed to indicate a particular mental model of how the participant could operate and affect the world. For instance, with the *delete* referent, we classified three other themes: pick and throw (fingers grabbing an object and throwing; fist closing and throwing; grabbing the object with two hands and throwing), wiping the scene away (full arm wipe; one hand wipe), and symbols (drawing an X; slashing across the object). Each of these is suggestive of a different kind of mental model for the scene and the objects in the scene: whereas the "squish" implies a certain omnipotent strength, pick-and-throw implies a certain strength to the viewing perspective of the user (i.e. that throwing the object out of the view deletes it rather than throwing it behind oneself), the wiping theme implies a "scene"-based approach (e.g. as an image in a slideshow viewer), whereas the symbolic theme takes on a more conventional "operation on an object" model.

Table 3 summarizes the 33 themes that we identified. As illustrated in Table 2, our coding for the themes that underlie the gestures shows a considerably higher rate of agreement than the gestures themselves, where we counted each gesture uniquely when different body parts were used (e.g. fingers vs. hands vs. fists vs. arms).

Nature of Gestural Themes: Physical Interaction

The nature of most gestural themes was physical: participants visibly seemed to act on the objects themselves—virtually grabbing, touching, and pushing the objects in various ways. These are reminiscent of ideas from Reality-Based Interaction [18], where the themes of body awareness and environmental skills seemed to underlie many gestures (e.g. tossing an object to delete it, pushing an object to move it, stretching sides of an object to scale it, squishing an object to delete it, and so on).

Theme	Variants	Referents
Tap	With fingers, step forward and use finger, with palm	Select
Grab	With finger and thumb, as a fist	Select, Delete
Circle	Finger (pointing), using finger and thumb (to draw a selection area)	Select
Pulling it apart	Two finger tips pulled apart, hand to hand pulling it apart, two handed grab and pull, upside-down U-shape, hold original and pull a second hand out	Duplicate, Scale
Double pinch and pull	Two finger pinch, then pull apart	Duplicate
One handed tap and move over	Using fingers to tap, using palm to tap	Duplicate
Point at object, then point at second location	Using fingers	Duplicate, Move
Pick up and place in new location	With fingers, with arms, with whole body (i.e. walk)	Duplicate, Move
Grab, pull over and release	Twist hand sideways	Move
Pinch and move	Using fingertips, using fist, using finger and pinching with thumb	Move
Push with open hand	One hand, two hands	Move
Pick up and toss	Physically move, using only arms	Move, Delete
Twisting like a lightbulb	Twisting like a handle	Rotate
Hands on front and back, twist both (like a box)	With thumb and pinky, with thumb and index	Rotate
Point and twist hand		Rotate
Twist body (as if body is object)		Rotate
One point to anchor, other finger to twist around	With finger, with hands/fists	Rotate
Grab corner or edge, and move	Arm or body	Rotate
Push aside	Toss away, toss behind, upside down U	Delete
Squish	Clap with hand, with fist, double fist, twist and fist, push into ground	Delete
X symbol	Make a crossing gesture	Delete
Wipe	Using forearm	Delete, Undo
Cross off (like a straight stroke)		Delete
Backward arrow	Drawn with finger, arm, or point with thumb	Undo
Tap in top left		Undo
Reverse action		Undo
Three finger swipe		Undo
Double tap on object		Undo
Hands at sides of object and symmetric pull/squish (squeeze)	Pointer fingers, hands, fingers, palms, fists	Scale

Table 3. Each of the 33 gesture themes we observed from our participants, their variants, and the referents for which they were generated.

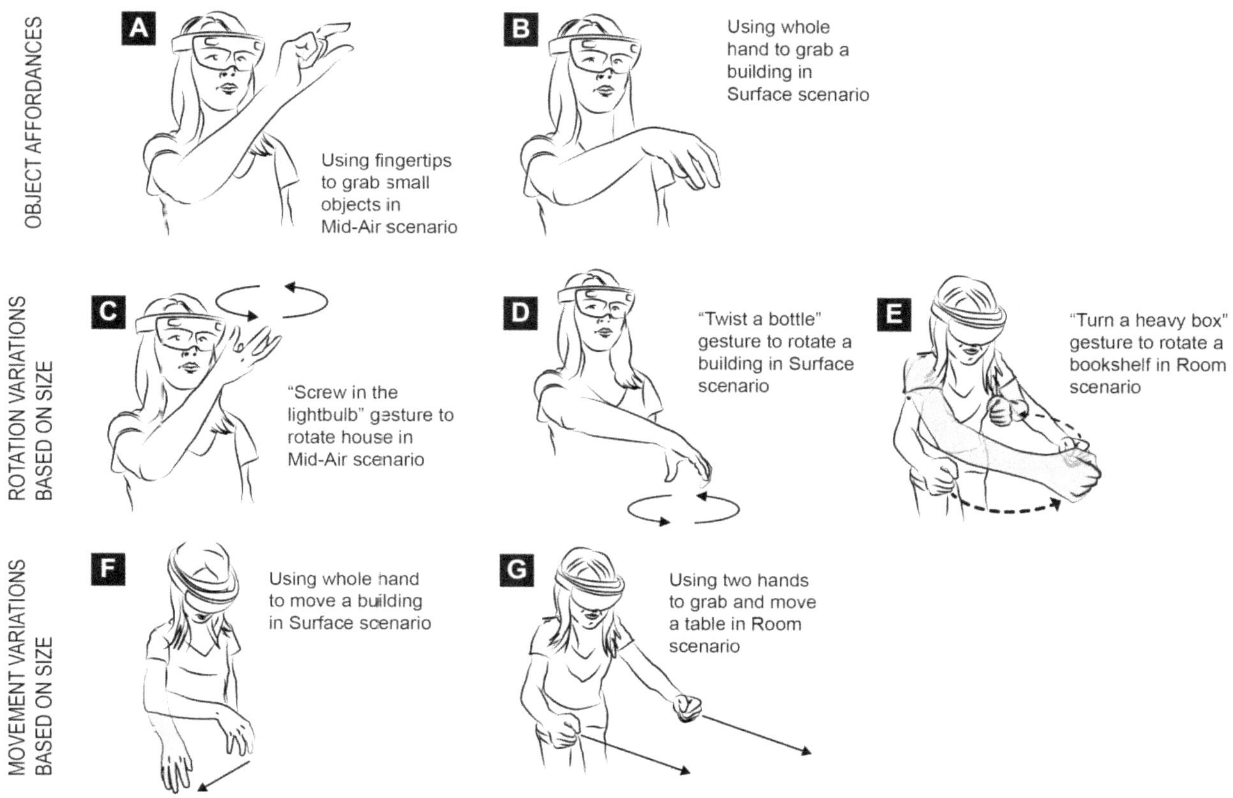

Figure 2. Examples of gestures that we observed, illustrating: (A-B) Variations for grabbing objects based on physical features (affordances); (C-E) Variations based on size for the *Rotate* referent; and (F-G) Variations based on size for the *Move* referent.

Our results indicate that 79% of the gestures were physical in nature, and this is in variance to Piumsomboon et al. [40], who report a more balanced percentage of physical gestures (only 39% of the gestures). We suspect that this is due to the nature of the referents that we selected in our study, where all referents strictly operated on the virtual objects in the holographic scene, whereas Piumsomboon and colleagues [40] also explored menu-based interaction. We offer here a more detailed exploration of the nature of these gestures, and how the participants executed these gestures within the context of the virtual objects.

Participants' gesture choices were influenced by the physical features of the virtual objects they were manipulating. As illustrated in Figure 2, peculiarities of specific models themselves would change the gestures, where participants would grab protruding parts of objects (e.g. six participants grabbed tall buildings as handles, as shown in Figure 2-B), or used finger tips to pick up small objects (rather than trying to grab it with a whole-hand grip), shown in Figure 2-A. For instance, participants generated gestures for the *Rotate* referent with small conceptual variants on the theme of turning the virtual object. Three participants in the *Mid-Air* scenario rotated the house with their wrist, as if twisting a lightbulb from a ceiling (Figure 2-C). In the *Surface* scenario, two participants rotated buildings by placing their hand on the top of a building and twisting it, like with a bottle placed on a table (Figure 2-D), while in the *Room* scenario three used a two-handed twisting gesture to rotate the bookshelf (as if to grab and rotate a heavy box), illustrated in Figure 2-E.

Participants maneuvered themselves into positions where they could easily see large parts of objects they were trying to manipulate. As with physical objects, being able to grab an object is easier when large parts of the object are visible, rather than when visibility is limited. When target objects were obscured by other virtual objects (as in the *Surface* scenario, where some buildings obscured others), people walked around the table, craned their heads or physically moved towards objects to get a better view of the target object before enacting a gesture. One reason this might have happened was to give themselves a better "target area" to gesture at. This relates to another peculiar result, where most participants (13/16) *never* touched the table surface for any referent in the *Surface* scenario (the remaining three only touched it once for the *Move* referent). This is in line with our observation of gestures being dependent on the virtual objects' affordances, where people's behaviour seems to reflect real life. For instance, it does not make sense to reach 'through' or 'under' a physical object on a table, so people did not do this with virtual objects either. The easiest way to grab a skyscraper in a physical city model is to grab it by the top or middle, which is what we observed people doing (Figure 2-B). P6 articulates the influence of this physicality: "*I think [for] stuff that is more relatable to the physical world, ... like moving stuff around and rotating it, you probably don't need an extra menu."*

Participants varied their gestures within an interaction theme as a response to the size of the object/scene, and their distance from an object. Notably, participants only sometimes used the exact same gesture across all scenarios for the same referent: 27 times out of 96 opportunities (16 participants × 7 referents). Most of these happened with more abstract, non-spatial referents (eight times with undo, nine times with delete, nine times with duplicate). With a given participant, we usually observed gestures that varied on the same theme for the referent across different scales (e.g. using fingers to "grab and move" a small object in the *Mid-Air* scenario, then using one hand to move an object in the *Surface* scenario, and finally using two arms to grab and move the object in the *Room* scenario (Figure 2 C, D, E).

We mainly observed non-physical gestures only when the referents did not have a clear physical analogue (e.g. abstract referents such as delete, duplicate, undo). For these, participants found it difficult to come up with gestures, and that resulted in mainly metaphorical or symbolic gestures (21% in our dataset). P6 again suggested that more sophisticated gestures might be necessary for such referents: *"If you want to duplicate [an object] or something, the gesture should be a bit more [complicated]. For example, I crossed my arms to delete stuff. I just haven't thought about anything for duplicating stuff though."* A common suggestion was to include a menu for those more abstract referents. P7: *"I like the idea of having a menu on the side, so that you can more easily [perform] undo, or delete. [...] Maybe a menu on the side to give you more flexibility with what you're doing."*

Size Matters for Spatial Operations

The size of objects and the virtual scene influenced participants' overall behaviour, including how they moved around and which gestures they performed. As shown in Figure 1, the *Room* scenario had the largest objects (furniture) and virtual scene size, followed by the *Surface* (city model) and *Mid-Air* scenario (house model). Whereas participants would use less bodily movement for the *Mid-Air* scenario, they tended to use more gross bodily movement (i.e. either physically moving, or using their hands or arms) for gestures in the *Room* and *Surface* scenarios. For instance, four participants changed from using a single-handed gesture for the *Rotate* referent in both the *Mid-Air* and *Surface* scenario to a two-handed gesture in the *Room* scenario. Similarly, for the *Move* referent, P4, P7 and P11 grabbed the virtual object of interest with both hands (Figure 2-E), and then proceeded to physically "carry" it to its new location in the *Room* scenario, but only used hand gestures for the other two scenarios. These changes were most dramatic when participants switched to the *Room* scenario compared to *Mid-Air* and *Surface*.

Most striking was that these differences persisted even in the number of fingers or hands being used: the smaller the virtual objects, the fewer fingers and hands that were involved. For the *Scale* referent, we observed 29 instances of a "squeeze" theme gesture. In the *Mid-Air* scenario, six participants created gestures that used their fingers, one used a hand, and four used two hands; in the *Room* scenario, only three used two fingers, three used one hand, seven used two hands, and one used both arms for the gesture. These differences are striking, since virtual objects do not weigh anything—they just appear larger.

Most participants (12/16) confirmed in the post-study interview that the experience of size of these objects impacted their gesture choices. For instance, P8 describes the difference between the scales as working with "*Lego versus Ikea.*" Similarly, P11 reported, "*Yes! [nodding] Yeah, I think the scale definitely matters. When it's really small, it gets awkward to handle around with [large gestures].*" We asked participants whether this was because it was hard to be precise with small objects. P4 mentioned: "*Yeah, something like a couch, I can move it like I move a couch [...]. With the model couch in that tiny house, I'd do something else.*" Participants generally talked about the room-scale scenario as having large objects and the other two scenarios as having smaller objects.

With abstract, non-spatial referents, size did not generally influence the gesture choice. For instance, for *Undo* and *Delete*, the common theme was to create a symbolic gesture (e.g. gesturing to the left to "undo" an action—much like undo icons in document editors) or a metaphorical gesture (e.g. tossing the object out of view, or "wiping" the view).

"Physically" Touching the Objects from a Distance

Although not strictly due to the size of the virtual objects, when using physical gestures, participants used both proximal gestures and distal gestures. Sometimes, participants would gesture extremely close to the target object—so close that the participant appeared to be touching the object: a *proximal* gesture (Figure 3-A). Other times, participants generated the gesture from a distant location, where the gesture was far from the virtual object (e.g. pointing at or grabbing something that was clearly out of reach): a *distal* gesture (Figure 3-B). Some gestures included a distal gesture component in addition to a proximal one (e.g. "picking up" an object using a proximal gesture and throwing it to a location using a distal gesture): a *mix* gesture. Figure 3-C shows a mix gesture where a distal and proximal gesture are combined to grab a coffee table from a distance and pull it closer. Finally, we noted that symbolic and metaphorical gestures (see [62]) did not occur meaningfully as a function of the proximal/distal dichotomy, thus we coded them in a separate category.

Distal gestures where still physical in nature, and operated on objects that were out of reach, and relied heavily on the participant's view and perspective on the object. As illustrated in Figure 3-B, participants lined up their perspective so that their hands or fingers appeared in line with their view of the object. Participants seemed to interact

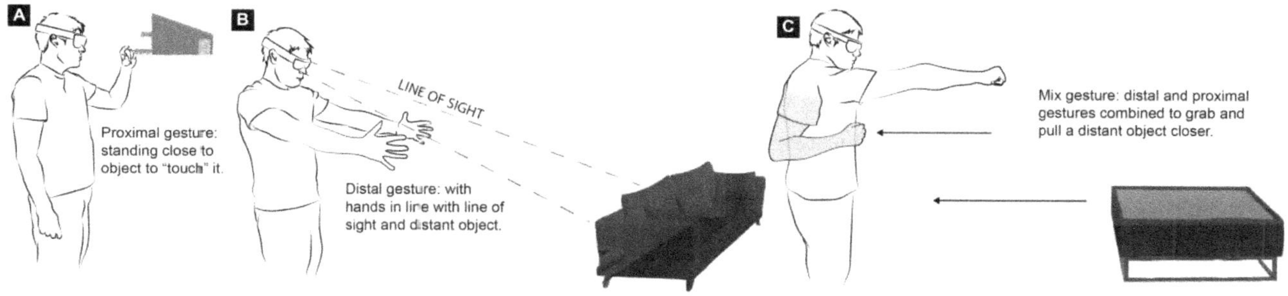

Figure 3. We saw three kinds of object interactions: (A) *proximal*, where people seemed to touch the object directly, (B) *distal*, where they interacted from a distance with a good perspective on the object, and (C) *mixed* approaches combining both aspects.

with the 2D projection that the 3D object made on the headset's image plane (e.g. as in [39]). This perspective issue is significant, as it meant that participants would change either their head position or their physical position to give them a good perspective on the object before enacting the gesture. We observed three kinds of reasons for head and physical movements: first, to reduce occlusion by other virtual objects; second, so that the virtual object was visually "large" in the headset (as opposed to being too small to interact with), and third, the opposite—to reduce the visual size of the object by moving one's head away from it (get too close, and it is hard to see anything else).

Participants moved away from the objects only rarely, but when they did, it was due to a poor field of view. In the *Room* scenario, the scene extended beyond people's viewing angle (i.e. when standing in the middle of the room, one needs to explicitly turn one's head to see all the furniture). Within this scenario, five participants stood near the back of the room—just so they could see the entire scene without needing to move around (or move their heads). We also observed that participants did this to allow them to see the object's entirety (e.g. for a *Rotation* referent), or the origin and the destination at the same time (in a *Move* referent). What is striking here is that this type of movement occurred far less for smaller scenes (i.e. the *Mid-Air* and *Surface* scenarios); rather, for these scenarios, we suspect that the movement was mainly to reduce occlusion (e.g. of the target virtual object by another).

This issue of field of view was also identified by participants in the post-study interview. P3: "*I think [with larger scenes make it] harder to see everything at once. [...] Instead of seeing everything on [the display], you have to move your body [...] to look at certain places to actually see what you're talking about.*" Similarly, P7 mentioned: "*I think if it's confined to an area, then you're more easily able to manipulate and see the changes. If you're needing to back up and look around and figure out what's going on, it's not as straightforward as if it was a confined [space].*"

Besides physically moving in the space (i.e. walking around) to get a better perspective on the objects before enacting the gestures, we also observed many instances where participants used movement as a part of the gesture itself. As discussed earlier, three participants walked from one location to another as part of a *Move* referent in the *Room* scenario. This suggests that the physical location is an enactment of the overall gesture (i.e. rather than the gesture simply being a function of hand movements).

The distribution of proximal, distal and mixed gesture locales varies and is related to the size of the virtual objects and scenes. Figure 4 illustrates the relative distribution of each gesture type across each referent and scenario. For *Mid-Air* scenarios, participants were generally proximal to the target, many appearing to carefully touch the objects with their fingers, whereas as the scale of the scene grows larger (i.e. into *Surface* and *Room* scenarios), the relative frequency of distal gestures increases fairly dramatically.

Our characterization of the "locale" of the gesture extends the articulation in [40], as it explains why some of these gestures happen *distally* (i.e. "in-the-air" in [40]) and also shows that this changes as a function of scale. Whereas with prior work [40], the percentage of "in-the-air" gestures might be explained as a function of menu interaction, we observe that these distal gestures in our study also occur for practical reasons such as ease of interaction (i.e. being able to see origin and location at the same time, or being able to see the objects of interest, both of which become more important at larger scales). We also see that many of these gestures incorporate movement within them.

DISCUSSION

Our interest is in designing gestures for 3D objects/scenes in augmented reality, and our findings show that the scale

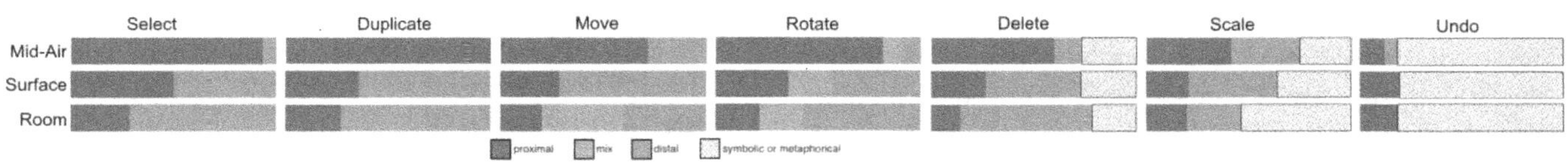

Figure 4. The relative distribution of proximal, mixed, distal and symbolic gestures in our dataset.

of the holographic AR objects and scene clearly impact how people expect to interact with them. The findings suggest that deriving a unified gesture set in this context is probably inappropriate: participants acted on the virtual objects in the scene as if they were physical, thus the gestures need to account for the apparent affordances of the objects, their size, and the person's perspective on the objects and the scene. This has implications for how we design systems that interpret gestures—particularly, that they need to account for the way that the scene is visualized, and the nature of the scene itself.

Physicality. Participants interacted with the virtual objects as they would with physical objects in the real world. They used the object's available affordances, and when objects became larger, increased the size of their gestures accordingly. The effect we observed appears to be in line with Aslan et al.'s observation that object semantics such as perceived physical weight impact the size of people's touch gestures on a tablet [2], which replicated earlier findings from neuroscience on how object semantics activated related motor tendencies [13, 14]. These findings suggest that scale matters for interaction and extends prior work around gestures for AR in more confined spaces. People's tendency to act with virtual objects in a physical way suggests that gestures that account for people's environmental skills and appreciation for naïve physics [18] will be easiest to adopt. Thus, rather than designing a unified AR gesture set, a possible approach may be to use aliasing [12, 61] (i.e., having multiple 'gesture synonyms' that people can use), to address the common gestural themes that we observed. This would address discoverability, since these themes were primarily comprised of different gestures for different scales of objects and scenes in a logical progression.

Proximal and Distal Interactions. Participants interacted with objects in two distinct ways: proximally, moving towards the target object to operate on it directly, and distally, positioning themselves with a good perspective on the object to interact from a distance. This type of interaction has already been foreshadowed to some extent by techniques that make use of perspective (e.g. [53]); however, we believe there is far more at work here. While our results suggest that designers should support both ways of interaction, we observed that a few participants always interacted from a distance, or always up close, hinting at the fact that personal preferences may play a role here.

Legacy Bias. A common issue with gesture elicitation studies is legacy bias [30], where participants propose legacy-inspired interactions. We observed this phenomenon too. Many participants used a "squishing" theme for scaling that looked like pinch-to-zoom in mobile devices. We also saw whole-arm "swipe" gestures to move objects, like gestures in contemporary sci-fi movies. Finally, many of the gestures had a corresponding action in the real world. We were somewhat less concerned about legacy bias in our study: we were interested in discoverability. It should not be surprising that legacy plays into people's first "guesses" into how they can interact with the scene.

Applicability. We are not implying that every AR application should support the gestures we extracted from our data, nor that these gestures are the most effective or efficient. Our interest was in investigating gestures people would propose in AR experiences for casual use (e.g. discoverable gestures that people could remember even when they used the AR experience once or twice a year) at different interaction scales. We envision this work being applicable to situations as using an AR application for redecorating one's home, or to repair a leaky faucet. Thus, we were focused on understanding the straightforward ways people would propose to interact with 3D AR content.

Freehand vs. Instrumented. Because we do not know whether freehand gestures will be the most dominant form of interaction for AR, it is difficult to predict the applicability of our findings beyond freehand gestures. Many consumer-grade VR and AR systems now make use of instrumented interaction, where users hold a specialized controller with buttons and manipulators (i.e. traditional 3DUI in Billinghurst's classification [4]). While we see these as a crutch (i.e. owing to poor sensing for freehand gestures), we cannot be sure whether our findings will ultimately apply to these kinds of instrumented interactions.

Limitations and Future Work. Some of our findings may be tied to the hardware limitations of the HoloLens, e.g., its limited field-of-view (FOV) [32]. People may have tried to keep larger holograms in the FOV by interacting distally. An interesting direction for future work is replicating this study for future and improved headsets and for different AR experiences such as handheld AR (e.g. with ARKit [1]) or spatial AR (e.g. RoomAlive [20]). Follow-up studies can explore if people's use of proximal vs. distal gestures would change, and if the physical nature of interaction still holds.

CONCLUSIONS

This paper explored whether people expect to use the same gesture across AR experiences at different scales. In an elicitation study with an AR headset, we asked participants to generate gestures in response to referents in three different scenarios, each at a different scale. The three main findings from our study are: (i) for most gestures, participants seemed to use physical interaction to operate on the virtual objects; (ii) the size of the virtual objects and the scene influences the gestures people perform; and (iii) people tend to touch smaller objects but increasingly interact from a distance as the size of the objects and scene grows larger. Our results suggest that AR designers ought to consider the delivery context and affordances of their AR content when designing gestures for easy discoverability.

ACKNOWLEDGEMENTS

We thank our anonymous participants and NSERC for their support.

REFERENCES

1. Apple. ARKit. Accessed September 9th, 2017. https://developer.apple.com/arkit/
2. Ilhan Aslan, Martin Murer, Verena Fuchsberger, Andrew Fugard, and Manfred Tscheligi. 2013. Drag and drop the apple: the semantic weight of words and images in touch-based interaction. In *Proceedings of the 7th International Conference on Tangible, Embedded and Embodied Interaction* (TEI '13). ACM, New York, NY, USA, 159-166. DOI: https://doi.org/10.1145/2460625.2460650
3. Hrvoje Benko, Ricardo Jota, and Andrew Wilson. 2012. MirageTable: freehand interaction on a projected augmented reality tabletop. In *Proceedings of the SIGCHI Conference on Human Factors in Computing Systems* (CHI '12). ACM, New York, NY, USA, 199-208. DOI: http://dx.doi.org/10.1145/2207676.2207704
4. Mark Billinghurst, Adrian Clark, and Gun Lee. 2015. A Survey of Augmented Reality. *Found. Trends Hum.-Comput. Interact.* 8, 2-3 (March 2015), 73-272. DOI: http://dx.doi.org/10.1561/1100000049
5. Mark Billinghurst, Hirokazu Kato, and Ivan Poupyrev. 2001. The MagicBook: a transitional AR interface. *Computers & Graphics*, *25*(5), 745-753. DOI: https://doi.org/10.1016/S0097-8493(01)00117-0
6. Oliver Bimber and Ramesh Raskar. 2005. *Spatial Augmented Reality: Merging Real and Virtual Worlds*. A. K. Peters, Ltd., Natick, MA, USA.
7. Volkert Buchmann, Stephen Violich, Mark Billinghurst, and Andy Cockburn. 2004. FingARtips: gesture based direct manipulation in Augmented Reality. In *Proceedings of the 2nd international conference on Computer graphics and interactive techniques in Australasia and South East Asia* (GRAPHITE '04), Stephen N. Spencer (Ed.). ACM, New York, NY, USA, 212-221. DOI: http://dx.doi.org/10.1145/988834.988871
8. Juliet Corbin and Anselm Strauss. 2015. Basics of Qualitative Research: Techniques and Procedures for Developing Grounded Theory. Sage. ISBN: 9781412997461.
9. Directive Games. The Machines. Accessed January 5th, 2018. http://themachinesgame.com/
10. Bruno Fernandes and Joaquin Fernández. 2009. Bare hand interaction in tabletop augmented reality. In *SIGGRAPH '09: Posters* (SIGGRAPH '09). ACM, New York, NY, USA, , Article 98 , 1 pages. DOI: http://doi.acm.org/10.1145/1599301.1599399
11. Tiare Feuchtner and Jörg Müller. 2017. Extending the Body for Interaction with Reality. In *Proceedings of the 2017 CHI Conference on Human Factors in Computing Systems* (CHI '17). ACM, New York, NY, USA, 5145-5157. DOI: https://doi.org/10.1145/3025453.3025689
12. G. W. Furnas, T. K. Landauer, L. M. Gomez, and S. T. Dumais. 1987. The vocabulary problem in human-system communication. *Commun. ACM* 30, 11 (November 1987), 964-971. DOI: http://dx.doi.org/10.1145/32206.32212
13. Maurizio Gentilucci, Francesca Benuzzi, Luca Bertolani, Elena Daprati, and Massimo Gangitano. 2000. Language and motor control. *Experimental Brain Research*, 133(4), 468-490.
14. Scott Glover, David A. Rosenbaum, Jeremy Graham, and Peter Dixon. 2004. Grasping the meaning of words. *Experimental Brain Research*, 154(1), 103-108.
15. Gunther Heidemann, Ingo Bax, and Holger Bekel. 2004. Multimodal interaction in an augmented reality scenario. In *Proceedings of the 6th international conference on Multimodal interfaces* (ICMI '04). ACM, New York, NY, USA, 53-60. DOI: http://dx.doi.org/10.1145/1027933.1027944
16. Otmar Hilliges, David Kim, Shahram Izadi, Malte Weiss, and Andrew Wilson. 2012. HoloDesk: direct 3d interactions with a situated see-through display. In *Proceedings of the SIGCHI Conference on Human Factors in Computing Systems* (CHI '12). ACM, New York, NY, USA, 2421-2430. DOI: http://dx.doi.org/10.1145/2207676.2208405
17. Sylvia Irawati, Scott Green, Mark Billinghurst, Andreas Duenser, and Heedong Ko. 2006. "Move the couch where?": developing an augmented reality multimodal interface. In *Proceedings of the 5th IEEE and ACM International Symposium on Mixed and Augmented Reality* (ISMAR '06). IEEE Computer Society, Washington, DC, USA, 183-186. DOI: http://dx.doi.org/10.1109/ISMAR.2006.297812
18. Robert J.K. Jacob, Audrey Girouard, Leanne M. Hirshfield, Michael S. Horn, Orit Shaer, Erin Treacy Solovey, and Jamie Zigelbaum. 2008. Reality-based interaction: a framework for post-WIMP interfaces. In *Proceedings of the SIGCHI Conference on Human Factors in Computing Systems* (CHI '08). ACM, New York, NY, USA, 201-210. DOI: https://doi.org/10.1145/1357054.135708
19. Brett R. Jones, Hrvoje Benko, Eyal Ofek, and Andrew D. Wilson. 2013. IllumiRoom: peripheral projected illusions for interactive experiences. In *Proceedings of the SIGCHI Conference on Human Factors in Computing Systems* (CHI '13). ACM, New York, NY, USA, 869-878. DOI: https://doi.org/10.1145/2470654.2466112
20. Brett Jones, Rajinder Sodhi, Michael Murdock, Ravish Mehra, Hrvoje Benko, Andrew Wilson, Eyal Ofek, Blair MacIntyre, Nikunj Raghuvanshi, and Lior Shapira. 2014. RoomAlive: magical experiences

enabled by scalable, adaptive projector-camera units. In *Proceedings of the 27th annual ACM symposium on User interface software and technology* (UIST '14). ACM, New York, NY, USA, 637-644. DOI: https://doi.org/10.1145/2642918.2647383

21. Ed Kaiser, Alex Olwal, David McGee, Hrvoje Benko, Andrea Corradini, Xiaoguang Li, Phil Cohen, and Steven Feiner. 2003. Mutual disambiguation of 3D multimodal interaction in augmented and virtual reality. In *Proceedings of the 5th international conference on Multimodal interfaces* (ICMI '03). ACM, New York, NY, USA, 12-19. DOI: http://dx.doi.org/10.1145/958432.958438
22. Hirokazu Kato, Mark Billinghurst, Ivan Poupyrev, Kenji Imamoto, and Keihachiro Tachibana. Virtual object manipulation on a table-top AR environment. In *Proceedings of the IEEE and ACM International Symposium on Augmented Reality* (ISAR 2000). IEEE, 111-119. DOI: https://doi.org/10.1109/ISAR.2000.880934
23. Mathias Koelsch, Ryan Bane, Tobias Hoellerer, and Matthew Turk. 2006. Multimodal Interaction with a Wearable Augmented Reality System. *IEEE Comput. Graph. Appl.* 26, 3 (May 2006), 62-71. DOI: http://dx.doi.org/10.1109/MCG.2006.66
24. Leap Motion. Accessed January 3rd, 2018. https://www.leapmotion.com/
25. Minkyung Lee and Mark Billinghurst. 2008. A Wizard of Oz study for an AR multimodal interface. In *Proceedings of the 10th international conference on Multimodal interfaces* (ICMI '08). ACM, New York, NY, USA, 249-256. DOI: http://dx.doi.org/10.1145/1452392.1452444
26. Jae Yeol Lee, Gue Won Rhee, and Dong Woo Seo. 2010. Hand gesture-based tangible interactions for manipulating virtual objects in a mixed reality environment. *The International Journal of Advanced Manufacturing Technology*, *51*(9), 1069-1082. DOI: https://doi.org/10.1007/s00170-010-2671-x
27. Taehee Lee, and Tobias Hollerer. 2007. Handy AR: Markerless inspection of augmented reality objects using fingertip tracking. In Proceedings of 11th IEEE International Symposium on Wearable Computers (ISWC '07). IEEE, 83-90. DOI: https://doi.org/10.1109/ISWC.2007.4373785
28. Taehee Lee and Tobias Höllerer. 2009. Multithreaded Hybrid Feature Tracking for Markerless Augmented Reality. *IEEE Transactions on Visualization and Computer Graphics* 15, 3 (May 2009), 355-368. DOI: http://dx.doi.org/10.1109/TVCG.2008.190
29. Blair MacIntyre, Alex Hill, Hafez Rouzati, Maribeth Gandy, and Brian Davidson. 2011. The Argon AR Web Browser and standards-based AR application environment. In *Proceedings of the 2011 10th IEEE International Symposium on Mixed and Augmented Reality* (ISMAR '11). IEEE Computer Society, Washington, DC, USA, 65-74. DOI: http://dx.doi.org/10.1109/ISMAR.2011.6092371
30. Meredith Ringel Morris, Andreea Danielescu, Steven Drucker, Danyel Fisher, Bongshin Lee, m. c. schraefel, and Jacob O. Wobbrock. 2014. Reducing legacy bias in gesture elicitation studies. *interactions* 21, 3 (May 2014), 40-45. DOI: https://doi.org/10.1145/2591689
31. Meredith Ringel Morris, Jacob O. Wobbrock, and Andrew D. Wilson. 2010. Understanding users' preferences for surface gestures. In *Proceedings of Graphics Interface 2010* (GI '10). Canadian Information Processing Society, Toronto, Ont., Canada, Canada, 261-268.
32. Microsoft. Hologram Stability. Accessed March 23rd, 2018. https://docs.microsoft.com/en-us/windows/mixed-reality/hologram-stability
33. Microsoft. Kinect for Windows. Accessed January 3rd, 2018. https://developer.microsoft.com/en-us/windows/kinect
34. Microsoft. Skype for HoloLens. Accessed January 3rd, 2018. https://www.microsoft.com/en-us/hololens/apps/skype
35. Alex Olwal, Hrvoje Benko, and Steven Feiner. 2003. Senseshapes: Using statistical geometry for object selection in a multimodal augmented reality. In *Proceedings of The Second IEEE and ACM International Symposium on Mixed and Augmented Reality* (ISMAR '03). IEEE. 300-301. DOI: https://doi.org/10.1109/ISMAR.2003.1240730
36. Sergio Orts-Escolano, Christoph Rhemann, Sean Fanello, Wayne Chang, Adarsh Kowdle, Yury Degtyarev, David Kim, Philip L. Davidson, Sameh Khamis, Mingsong Dou, Vladimir Tankovich, Charles Loop, Qin Cai, Philip A. Chou, Sarah Mennicken, Julien Valentin, Vivek Pradeep, Shenlong Wang, Sing Bing Kang, Pushmeet Kohli, Yuliya Lutchyn, Cem Keskin, and Shahram Izadi. 2016. Holoportation: Virtual 3D Teleportation in Real-time. In *Proceedings of the 29th Annual Symposium on User Interface Software and Technology* (UIST '16). ACM, New York, NY, USA, 741-754. DOI: https://doi.org/10.1145/2984511.2984517
37. Tomislav Pejsa, Julian Kantor, Hrvoje Benko, Eyal Ofek, and Andrew Wilson. 2016. Room2Room: Enabling Life-Size Telepresence in a Projected Augmented Reality Environment. In *Proceedings of the 19th ACM Conference on Computer-Supported Cooperative Work & Social Computing* (CSCW '16). ACM, New York, NY, USA, 1716-1725. DOI: https://doi.org/10.1145/2818048.2819965
38. Wayne Piekarski and Bruce H. Thomas. 2002. Using ARToolKit for 3D hand position tracking in mobile

outdoor environments. In *Augmented Reality Toolkit, The first IEEE International Workshop*. IEEE. DOI: https://doi.org/10.1109/ART.2002.1107003

39. Jeffrey S. Pierce, Andrew S. Forsberg, Matthew J. Conway, Seung Hong, Robert C. Zeleznik, and Mark R. Mine. 1997. Image plane interaction techniques in 3D immersive environments. In *Proceedings of the 1997 symposium on Interactive 3D graphics* (I3D '97). ACM, New York, NY, USA, 39-ff.. DOI: http://dx.doi.org/10.1145/253284.253303

40. Thammathip Piumsomboon, Adrian Clark, Mark Billinghurst, and Andy Cockburn. 2013. User-Defined Gestures for Augmented Reality. In *IFIP Conference on Human-Computer Interaction* (INTERACT '13). Springer, Berlin, Heidelberg. 282-299. DOI: https://doi.org/10.1007/978-3-642-40480-1_18

41. Thammathip Piumsomboon, Adrian Clark, Atsushi Umakatsu, & Mark Billinghurst. 2012. Poster: Physically-based natural hand and tangible AR interaction for face-to-face collaboration on a tabletop. In *Proceedings of IEEE Symposium on 3D User Interfaces* (3DUI '02). 155-156. IEEE. https://doi.org/10.1109/3DUI.2012.6184208

42. Thammathip Piumsomboon, David Altimira, Hyungon Kim, Adrian Clark, Gun Lee, and Mark Billinghurst. 2014. Grasp-Shell vs gesture-speech: A comparison of direct and indirect natural interaction techniques in augmented reality. In Proceedings of the *IEEE International Symposium on Mixed and Augmented Reality* (ISMAR '14). IEEE. 73-82. DOI: https://doi.org/10.1109/ISMAR.2014.6948411

43. Christina Pollalis, Whitney Fahnbulleh, Jordan Tynes, and Orit Shaer. 2017. HoloMuse: Enhancing Engagement with Archaeological Artifacts through Gesture-Based Interaction with Holograms. In *Proceedings of the Eleventh International Conference on Tangible, Embedded, and Embodied Interaction* (TEI '17). ACM, New York, NY, USA, 565-570. DOI: https://doi.org/10.1145/3024969.3025094

44. Ivan Poupyrev, Mark Billinghurst, Suzanne Weghorst, and Tadao Ichikawa. 1996. The go-go interaction technique: non-linear mapping for direct manipulation in VR. In *Proceedings of the 9th annual ACM symposium on User interface software and technology* (UIST '96). ACM, New York, NY, USA, 79-80. DOI: http://dx.doi.org/10.1145/237091.237102

45. Gerhard Reitmayr, and Dieter Schmalstieg. 2004. Scalable techniques for collaborative outdoor augmented reality. In *Proceedings of the 3rd IEEE and ACM international symposium on mixed and augmented reality* (ISMAR'04). IEEE.

46. Gustavo Alberto Rovelo Ruiz, Davy Vanacken, Kris Luyten, Francisco Abad, and Emilio Camahort. 2014. Multi-viewer gesture-based interaction for omni-directional video. In *Proceedings of the SIGCHI Conference on Human Factors in Computing Systems* (CHI '14). ACM, New York, NY, USA, 4077-4086. DOI: https://doi.org/10.1145/2556288.2557113

47. Jaime Ruiz, Yang Li, and Edward Lank. 2011. User-defined motion gestures for mobile interaction. In *Proceedings of the SIGCHI Conference on Human Factors in Computing Systems* (CHI '11). ACM, New York, NY, USA, 197-206. DOI: https://doi.org/10.1145/1978942.1978971

48. Christian Sandor, Alex Olwal, Blaine Bell, and Steven Feiner. 2005. Immersive Mixed-Reality Configuration of Hybrid User Interfaces. In *Proceedings of the 4th IEEE/ACM International Symposium on Mixed and Augmented Reality* (ISMAR '05). IEEE Computer Society, Washington, DC, USA, 110-113. DOI: http://dx.doi.org/10.1109/ISMAR.2005.37

49. Gerhard Schall, Erick Mendez, Ernst Kruijff, Eduardo Veas, Sebastian Junghanns, Bernhard Reitinger, and Dieter Schmalstieg. 2009. Handheld Augmented Reality for underground infrastructure visualization. *Personal Ubiquitous Comput.* 13, 4 (May 2009), 281-291. DOI: http://dx.doi.org/10.1007/s00779-008-0204-5

50. Teddy Seyed, Chris Burns, Mario Costa Sousa, Frank Maurer, and Anthony Tang. 2012. Eliciting usable gestures for multi-display environments. In *Proceedings of the 2012 ACM international conference on Interactive tabletops and surfaces* (ITS '12). ACM, New York, NY, USA, 41-50. DOI: http://dx.doi.org/10.1145/2396636.2396643

51. Shaikh Shawon Arefin Shimon, Courtney Lutton, Zichun Xu, Sarah Morrison-Smith, Christina Boucher, and Jaime Ruiz. 2016. Exploring Non-touchscreen Gestures for Smartwatches. In *Proceedings of the 2016 CHI Conference on Human Factors in Computing Systems* (CHI '16). ACM, New York, NY, USA, 3822-3833. DOI: https://doi.org/10.1145/2858036.2858385

52. Shaikh Shawon Arefin Shimon, Sarah Morrison-Smith, Noah John, Ghazal Fahimi, and Jaime Ruiz. 2015. Exploring User-Defined Back-Of-Device Gestures for Mobile Devices. In *Proceedings of the 17th International Conference on Human-Computer Interaction with Mobile Devices and Services* (MobileHCI '15). ACM, New York, NY, USA, 227-232. DOI: http://dx.doi.org/10.1145/2785830.2785890

53. Adalberto L. Simeone, Andreas Bulling, Jason Alexander, and Hans Gellersen. 2016. Three-Point Interaction: Combining Bi-manual Direct Touch with Gaze. In *Proceedings of the International Working Conference on Advanced Visual Interfaces* (AVI '16), Paolo Buono, Rosa Lanzilotti, and Maristella Matera (Eds.). ACM, New York, NY, USA, 168-175. DOI: https://doi.org/10.1145/2909132.2909251

54. Trimble, Inc.. SketchUp: 3D modeling for everyone. Accessed September 9th, 2017. https://www.sketchup.com/

55. Giovanni Maria Troiano, Esben Warming Pedersen, and Kasper Hornbæk. 2014. User-defined gestures for elastic, deformable displays. In *Proceedings of the 2014 International Working Conference on Advanced Visual Interfaces* (AVI '14). ACM, New York, NY, USA, 1-8. DOI: https://doi.org/10.1145/2598153.2598184

56. John Underkoffler and Hiroshi Ishii. 1999. Urp: a luminous-tangible workbench for urban planning and design. In *Proceedings of the SIGCHI conference on Human Factors in Computing Systems* (CHI '99). ACM, New York, NY, USA, 386-393. DOI: http://dx.doi.org/10.1145/302979.303114

57. Radu-Daniel Vatavu and Ionut-Alexandru Zaiti. 2014. Leap gestures for TV: insights from an elicitation study. In *Proceedings of the ACM International Conference on Interactive Experiences for TV and Online Video* (TVX '14). ACM, New York, NY, USA, 131-138. DOI: https://doi.org/10.1145/2602299.2602316

58. Radu-Daniel Vatavu and Jacob O. Wobbrock. 2015. Formalizing Agreement Analysis for Elicitation Studies: New Measures, Significance Test, and Toolkit. In *Proceedings of the 33rd Annual ACM Conference on Human Factors in Computing Systems* (CHI '15). ACM, New York, NY, USA, 1325-1334. DOI: https://doi.org/10.1145/2702123.2702223

59. Andrew D. Wilson and Hrvoje Benko. 2010. Combining multiple depth cameras and projectors for interactions on, above and between surfaces. In *Proceedings of the 23nd annual ACM symposium on User interface software and technology* (UIST '10). ACM, New York, NY, USA, 273-282. DOI: https://doi.org/10.1145/1866029.1866073

60. Andrew D. Wilson and Hrvoje Benko. 2017. Holograms without Headsets: Projected Augmented Reality with the RoomAlive Toolkit. In *Proceedings of the 2017 CHI Conference Extended Abstracts on Human Factors in Computing Systems* (CHI EA '17). ACM, New York, NY, USA, 425-428. DOI: https://doi.org/10.1145/3027063.3050433

61. Jacob O. Wobbrock, Htet Htet Aung, Brandon Rothrock, and Brad A. Myers. 2005. Maximizing the guessability of symbolic input. In *CHI '05 Extended Abstracts on Human Factors in Computing Systems* (CHI EA '05). ACM, New York, NY, USA, 1869-1872. DOI: http://dx.doi.org/10.1145/1056808.1057043

62. Jacob O. Wobbrock, Meredith Ringel Morris, and Andrew D. Wilson. 2009. User-defined gestures for surface computing. In *Proceedings of the SIGCHI Conference on Human Factors in Computing Systems* (CHI '09). ACM, New York, NY, USA, 1083-1092. DOI: https://doi.org/10.1145/1518701.1518866

63. Yan Xu, Sam Mendenhall, Vu Ha, Paul Tillery, and Joshua Cohen. 2012. Herding nerds on your table: NerdHerder, a mobile augmented reality game. In *CHI '12 Extended Abstracts on Human Factors in Computing Systems* (CHI EA '12). ACM, New York, NY, USA, 1351-1356. DOI: http://dx.doi.org/10.1145/2212776.2212453

Bare-Handed 3D Drawing in Augmented Reality

John J. Dudley[1] **Hendrik Schuff**[1,2] **Per Ola Kristensson**[1]
[1]Department of Engineering, University of Cambridge, United Kingdom
[2]Institute for Visualisation and Interactive Systems, University of Stuttgart, Germany

ABSTRACT
Head-mounted augmented reality (AR) enables embodied in situ drawing in three dimensions (3D). We explore 3D drawing interactions based on uninstrumented, unencumbered (bare) hands that preserve the user's ability to freely navigate and interact with the physical environment. We derive three alternative interaction techniques supporting bare-handed drawing in AR from the literature and by analysing several envisaged use cases. The three interaction techniques are evaluated in a controlled user study examining three distinct drawing tasks: planar drawing, path description, and 3D object reconstruction. The results indicate that continuous freehand drawing supports faster line creation than the control point-based alternatives, although with reduced accuracy. User preferences for the different techniques are mixed and vary considerably between the different tasks, highlighting the value of diverse and flexible interactions. The combined effectiveness of these three drawing techniques is illustrated in an example application of 3D AR drawing.

ACM Classification Keywords
H.5.1. Information Interfaces and Presentation (e.g. HCI): Artificial, augmented, and virtual realities.

Author Keywords
Augmented reality; 3D drawing; interaction.

INTRODUCTION
Drawings provide a rich means of information exchange. On paper, a rough drawing (sketch) can be constructed quickly, without requiring precision, in order to convey the key features of a concept [4]. While drawing on paper is fast and flexible, markings can only be made in two dimensions. Three dimensional (3D) objects can still be described on paper but these drawings are then projections and unavoidably result in information loss.

It is reasonable to hypothesise that drawing directly in 3D may provide a powerful means of information exchange, without the deficiencies of conventional 2D projections. However, providing a medium for performing 3D drawings is non-trivial—what is the 3D equivalent of a drawing pad? Physical 3D media are challenged by occlusion and access constraints.

Digital media presents a more viable alternative. Indeed, recent applications such as Tilt Brush and Gravity Sketch provide functionality for drawing in 3D using virtual reality (VR) and mobile-based augmented reality (AR). These applications provide creative environments for generating 3D content by removing the constraints of conventional physical media.

What drawing in immersive VR lacks, however, is environmental context. In other words, drawings are produced in a virtual environment that is separated from the physical environment of the user. This is not necessarily a problem for many use cases of 3D drawing but can be detrimental where the physical environment is an important source of reference or inspiration. For example, consider a use case in which an engineer seeks to make a preliminary drawing as part of designing modifications to an existing access platform. To complete this task, the engineer must generate a drawing that references sections of the existing platform whilst also accommodating the spatial constraints imposed by other objects in the space, e.g. pipes, structural columns, etc. AR supports such use cases by preserving environmental context and enables drawings that reference, link to or are inspired by the environment.

In this paper, we explore the provision of 3D drawing capabilities for head-mounted AR delivered through bare-handed interactions (i.e. the user does not hold an input device). Specifically, we explore 3D drawing techniques that do not require any input device other than the AR headset itself. We use a Microsoft HoloLens headset as the experimental platform for our investigation. The examination of bare-handed interaction is motivated by two key concerns. First, there are numerous industrial applications of AR drawing in industries such as construction, manufacturing and logistics. Typically workers in these industries must frequently work with hand tools and in other ways interact with the physical environment. A seamless transition between physical and virtual activities is desirable but there is no input device currently available which supports such interactions without encumbering the user. Second, even if input device interactions are preferable, it is undesirable to render a drawing application completely unusable in circumstances where the user does not have their input device. Such circumstances demand the need for a flexible fallback option when no input device is available.

We evaluate three alternative drawing techniques in a controlled user study. Our design and evaluation of these three

DIS '18, June 9–13, 2018, , Hong Kong

ISBN 978-1-4503-5198-0/18/06...$15.00

DOI: https://doi.org/10.1145/3196709.3196737

techniques is a response to the need for diversity in interactions to accommodate different user and use case requirements. These drawing techniques were developed with inspiration from the literature and designed to be complementary. Our study results will later highlight the trade-offs between them. The three interaction techniques are informed by five design principles distilled from the literature and deduced from several envisaged use cases of 3D drawing in AR. We evaluate the three interaction techniques in three distinct tasks abstracted from anticipated use cases: creating a planar drawing, illustrating a motion path, and creating a 3D drawing.

We use multiple metrics, such as completion time, template deviation, path length and perceived workload, for performance evaluation. Additionally, participant preferences and feedback was captured in a summative questionnaire.

In summary, our investigation offers the following contributions to the field of AR interface design:

- Five design principles informing the design of drawing functionality for head-mounted AR as distilled from the literature and deduced from several envisioned use cases.
- An empirical evaluation of alternative drawing techniques in three likely common use cases for 3D drawing in AR.
- A demonstration of the combined use of the three different drawing techniques in a hypothetical 3D drawing scenario.

BACKGROUND AND RELATED WORK

Ivan Sutherland pioneered the concept of computer-based sketches and drawings with Sketchpad [27]. Sutherland demonstrated both the creative and productive uses of computer-based drawings. Now virtual and augmented reality further extend our ability to generate visual content without the constraints of traditional physical media. The ability to perform 3D drawings in situ represents a fundamentally new capability and a powerful means of information exchange.

Early research into 3D drawing was typically hampered by technological difficulties in supporting the basic visual and interaction capabilities. Clark [7] explored the creation of free-form surfaces in 3D. The apparatus included an input 'wand' with a mechanical wire-based positioning system and an head-mounted display (HMD) (incidentally designed by Sutherland), using mechanical sensors to provide tracking. The user of Clark's system could manipulate the contours of the virtual surface using the wand. Clark observed that, despite the cumbersomeness of the system, the 3D visualisation and interaction capabilities were superior to traditional 2D techniques.

The work of Butterworth et al. [5] is an early example of a more complete 3D modelling application using an HMD. The system contained several tools aimed at allowing users to produce and connect 3D shapes. Importantly the system provided an undo/redo stack which Butterworth et al. [5] observed encouraged users to make "experimental changes to the model". Responding to users' feedback on the lack of modelling constraints, they propose the use of snap-to functionality on grids and surfaces.

Embodied 3D drawing applications can be delivered without the need for an HMD, as demonstrated by HoloSketch [9] and Surface Drawing [23] which employ stereoscopic 2D displays to construct the illusion that objects are floating in space. Using a similar visual setup, Keefe et al. [15] evaluate several single and two-handed drawing techniques developed for producing 3D curves. CAVE based 3D drawing experiences have also been designed and evaluated [14, 28].

The potential for hand-held devices to support drawing in through-the-screen AR has seen recent attention. Hagbi et al. [11] explore in-place drawing for AR games. However, this provides 3D augmentation of a 2D sketch rather than true embodied 3D drawing. Window-Shaping [13] is a mobile application in which users can generate virtual content based on a sketch-and-inflate metaphor. The application supports 'projective sketching', which means that users can sketch on detected surfaces to define boundaries and generate new virtual objects. These objects can then be transformed and manipulated in the scene. A key limitation highlighted in this study is the lack of precise control when the user is holding the device and drawing on it at the same time.

Recent improvements in VR hardware at the consumer level, have enabled more research examining fully immersive 3D drawing. Arora et al. [1] investigated the impact of the lack of a physical surface on drawing inaccuracies. They demonstrated that providing additional visual guidance can substantially improve drawing accuracy. McGraw et al. [18] used an HTC Vive VR system with motion controls to allow users to control Hermite splines and create swept surfaces. The system is capable of producing unusual 3D objects with unique aesthetics.

Augmenting Drawing Interactions

Delivering drawing functionality in digital media is related to the broader problem of selecting and manipulating virtual content. To perform a drawing the user must articulate the point or region in which markings should be generated. In a virtual environment the user is not beholden to conventional means of physical articulation.

An extensive range of manipulation techniques have been explored in the literature (see [21] for a useful taxonomy). In 1996, Poupyrev et al. [20] introduced the 'GoGo' interaction technique. The 'GoGo' interaction method augments the physical reach of the user by providing a virtual extension of the hand. A virtual hand is placed along the vector extending from the chest through the real hand, with depth modulated by a linear scaling below a certain reach threshold and by non-linear scaling above a certain reach threshold. Other variants of the GoGo concept have also been proposed such as 'stretch GoGo' in which regions are used to control growth or shrinking of the arm length, and 'indirect GoGo' in which stretching and retracting the virtual arm is controlled by a 3D mouse [2].

As Bowman and Hodges [3] state, "VEs [Virtual Environments] should enhance the physical, cognitive, and perceptual capabilities of the user, allowing them to do things that are impossible in the real world". This statement echos the proposals of prior work [1, 5, 9], which highlight the potential of allowing users to independently resize the drawing relative to themselves to apply detail at an appropriate scale. This concept is described in a manipulation context as "World-In-Miniature" [26]. The ability to enhance the user's capabilities while preserving an embodied interaction experience is a key advantage of drawing in digital media. Leveraging this potential does, however, present a unique design challenge.

The related work highlights a developing understanding of what makes embodied 3D drawing effective and enjoyable. Most research to date, however, has ignored the role AR can play in supporting in situ 3D drawing that references and is inspired by the user's environment. We seek to address this gap by exploring simple and efficient bare-handed interaction techniques that can support embodied 3D drawing in circumstances where mobility and manual engagement with the space are primary concerns.

DESIGNING FOR APPLIED DRAWING WITH AR HMDS

In the context of this study we focus predominantly on 3D AR drawing as an applied exercise for design, documentation and information exchange but acknowledge its potential as a means of artistic expression. This section briefly explores several envisioned use cases for applied drawing in AR and the common design principles that these imply.

Envisioned Use Cases

The provision of AR through an HMD enables high mobility and keeps the user's hands free to interact with the physical environment. These two key qualities promote use cases in which overlaid virtual content can be leveraged by a worker who must also navigate through and interact with the space. This kind of work practice is easily imagined in industries such as construction, manufacturing and logistics. The ability to quickly generate 3D drawings in situ could have many uses, e.g. documenting an issue, designing a modification to a space, and/or describing a workflow for training purposes.

In situ markup of virtual-physical models with identified issues or desired features is a high value use case of AR drawing in the construction industry. It is desirable to minimise the information loss and maximise information gain as details pass between site visits, issue tracking systems and building information models. We also envisage significant value in AR drawing as a means to unify the preliminary and detailed design process in various in situ applications. For example, a well-designed AR drawing application for use by cabinet or curtain makers could streamline the process of provisional measurement for quotation and detailed design for installation. Provisional client feedback could also be obtained in situ.

Lastly, drawings may be used as part of training delivered with an AR HMD. Allowing trainers to quickly and easily generate training content in situ provides a low overhead means to induct new workers. 3D drawings may be helpful in showing where objects should be placed, what sequences should be followed, and/or what built products should look like.

Design Principles

The following design principles are distilled from the literature and deduced from the use cases described above. Their intent is to provide a preliminary set of generalised guidance for the designer of 3D drawing applications built for head-mounted AR. They also help to contextualise the design decisions related to the drawing interactions proposed in this paper.

Minimal Viable Markings

Many uses of embodied AR drawing are likely to stem from momentary observations and encounters in the physical environment. Among many possible uses, the need to describe an identified issue and the need to document a design change inspired by the space are two obvious reasons for generating a 3D drawing. An application designed for this purpose should thus allow users to quickly and easily complete a drawing before the environment changes or other more pressing tasks dominate. The principle of *Minimal Viable Markings* suggests the provision of a low overhead means of drawing requiring limited effort and time, even when more precise but slower interactions are available. This design principle also reflects the dual purpose of some forms of sketching in that the act of drawing not only produces a visual artifact but it may also help the user document and respond to their thoughts and observations [10, 8]. The media and tools for drawing should thus allow the user to quickly respond to these potentially fleeting moments of inspiration.

Promote Spatial Awareness

Current AR HMDs provide relatively small display regions resulting in a narrow effective virtual field-of-view (FOV). The inability to see virtual content in the periphery challenges people's spatial memory. As drawings extend over larger areas, this can become particularly problematic. Visual aids can help users maintain their memory of the position of their virtual elements relative to their current position. 3D grids and snap-to behaviour for 3D grids and planes have been proposed in the literature [1, 5, 9, 14]. However, Arora et al.[1] caution that there can be a delicate balance between accuracy and destruction of visual aesthetics. An alternative to the provision of visual aids is careful design of interactions that help preserve user spatial awareness. For example, some interactions may better decouple body movement and environment inspection from the act of drawing.

Exploit the Lack of Physical Constraints

The transferal of sketching from the physical to the virtual world removes many physical constraints. This can be exploited in AR without necessarily severing the contextual association with the physical space. For example, the concept of relative growing or shrinking of virtual objects has demonstrated utility in allowing users to apply detail at appropriate scale [1, 5, 9]. The virtual hand and cursor techniques discussed previously are also examples of interaction metaphors that *Exploit the Lack of Physical Constraints*. It is easy to imagine from the use cases described that drawings may need to be completed in circumstances where physical access is challenging (see Figure 13 for an example). Augmenting the capabilities of the user may help address such challenges.

Modal Flexibility

This design principle is a reflection of diversity in user preferences and use cases when it comes to 3D drawing. We hypothesise that different drawing techniques will be preferred in different usage scenarios. This suggests that there is value

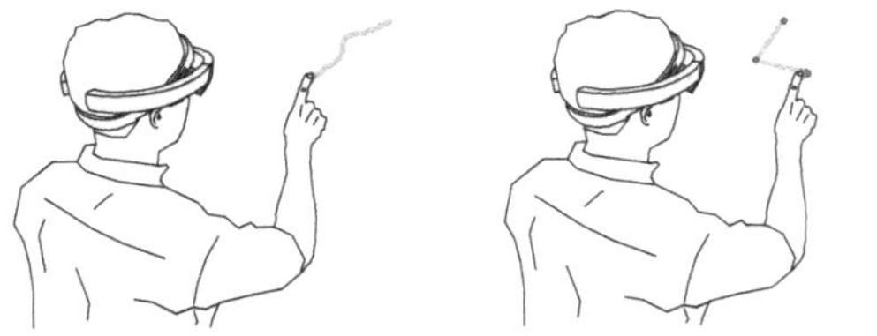

Figure 1. The Freehand (left) and Tapline (right) techniques.

in providing a correspondingly diverse range of drawing techniques which can complement each other. Importantly, there should be a high degree of fluidity when it comes to transitioning between input modes. The virtual manipulation literature has seen a variety of hybrid methods proven effective [2].

Rapid Revision

This design principle is an extension of the theory of direct manipulation [24] and an application of the golden rule "permit easy reversal of actions" [25] (pp. 71). Butterworth et al. [5] observed the value of providing an undo/redo stack in encouraging experimental behaviour. The need to provide rapid undo and revision functionality is particularly important in circumstances, such as encountered in our system, where the means of controlling the drawing cursor is noisy due to the difficulty of tracking bare hands. Furthermore, Deering [9] observes that fine motor control is harder in 3D than in 2D and Arora et al. [1] highlight that freeform drawing can be inaccurate in 3D. Therefore, embodied 3D drawing is particularly likely to require rapid means of correcting erroneous input.

DRAWING TECHNIQUES

In response to the anticipated need for quick and simple methods of generating 3D drawings in AR, we propose three alternative drawing techniques based on bare-handed interactions. These techniques leverage only the egocentric sensing capabilities of the AR headset, leaving the hands free to interact with the physical environment.

The Microsoft HoloLens supports coarse hand tracking only. Only the hand position (a point approximating the centre of the back of the hand) is reported. No other joint or articulation information is available. To deliver our bare-handed drawing techniques, we display a cursor that is directly controlled by hand movement. This cursor (subsequently referred to as the *index cursor*) is placed at a point approximating the tip of the index finger when the hand is placed in a neutral position with the index finger raised. To reiterate, since no joint or articulation information is available, the index cursor will remain in the same location if the hand/finger articulation changes but the hand position does not. The index cursor is thus a coarse approximation for the hand position but as a direct control scheme, is easily assimilated by the user. The absolute error characteristics of the device's hand tracking are not reported in the literature. Each drawing technique described is, however, subject to the same inaccuracies in hand tracking and the results reflect the summative performance incorporating device induced noise.

By default, the Microsoft HoloLens supports recognition of the *air-tap* gesture. The air-tap gesture is performed by placing the hand in the neutral position (index finger raised but all other fingers in clench), then bending the index finger at the base knuckle down and raising it again. The fact that the index cursor is not affected by finger articulation changes makes it viable to maintain relatively accurate cursor control while performing finger based gestures. The air-tap gesture is used in all the techniques to trigger line actions. Lack of a secondary default gesture lead us to use *double* air-tap as an alternative action trigger. The double air-tap is implemented simply by applying a 500 ms threshold on the time difference between sequential air-tap events. Future iterations of the HoloLens are likely to expose a broader suite of hand gestures. A more complete drawing application could exploit different gestures to deliver more seamless transitions between interaction modes in alignment with the design objective of *Modal Flexibility*.

The three different drawing techniques are described in detail below. The design of each stems from different combinations of the design principles introduced above.

Freehand

The Freehand technique allows the user to draw continuously as directed by hand movements. To start a line the user performs the air-tap gesture. The line is drawn continuously at the index cursor position until the user terminates the line by performing a second air-tap. Figure 1 illustrates the Freehand method. The Freehand technique is a response to the design principle of *Minimal Viable Markings* in that lines can be generated rapidly and easily. The interaction metaphor has strong similarities to finger painting.

Tapline

The Tapline technique allows the user to draw a line by specifying control points. Tapline seeks to accommodate the design principle of *Promote Spatial Awareness* in allowing the user to move and look around in between desinating control points. To add a control point, the user directs the index cursor to the desired location and performs an air-tap. This interaction is illustrated in Figure 1. The control points can either be connected by straight lines or by a Catmull-Rom spline [6]. The default setting produces straight polylines but users may optionally switch to splines using the drawing tool belt (introduced below). To terminate the line, the user performs a double air-tap to add a final control point.

GoGo-Tapline

The GoGo-Tapline represents an extension of the Tapline technique. The user places sequential control points to construct a line as per Tapline. However, the GoGo-Tapline control points are placed at the *GoGo-cursor* position rather than at the index cursor. The GoGo-cursor is a virtual projection of the index cursor and depends upon the user's current arm extension. If the user's hand is inside a radius of 2/3 arm length around the user's chest, the index cursor and the GoGo-cursor are co-located. Outside this radius, the cursor is extended based on the user's reach as described in [20]. We determine the virtual arm vector, $\mathbf{r_v}$ based on the real arm vector, $\mathbf{r_r}$ (and unit vector $\hat{\mathbf{r_r}}$) according to Equation 1. Here $\|\cdot\|_2$ denotes the Euclidean norm.

$$\mathbf{r_v} = \begin{cases} \mathbf{r_r} & \text{if } \|\mathbf{r_r}\|_2 < D \\ \mathbf{r_r} + k(\|\mathbf{r_r}\|_2 - D)^2 \hat{\mathbf{r_r}} & \text{otherwise} \end{cases} \quad (1)$$

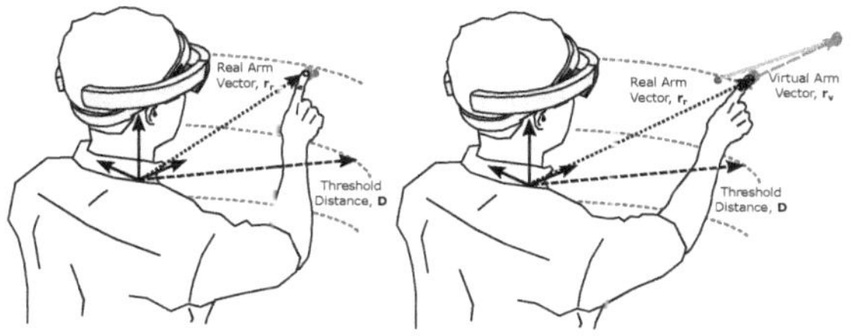

Figure 2. The GoGo-Tapline technique.

Poupyrev et al. [20] selected the scaling coefficient, $k \in [0,1]$ and found good performance choosing a threshold distance, D of $2/3$ of the user's arm length. In the implementation presented in this paper, we use $k = 1/6$ and also choose D to be $2/3$ of the distance from the shoulder joint to the middle of the right hand to be consistent with Poupyrev et al. [20]. The GoGo-Tapline drawing technique is illustrated in Figure 2. Reflecting the design principle of *Exploit the Lack of Physical Constraints*, GoGo-Tapline augments the user's ability to draw lines at distance and without moving location.

Drawing Tool Belt

The Tapline and GoGo-Tapline drawing features can additionally be adjusted in a *tool belt* implemented as a floating panel containing several buttons. The tool belt is placed at waist height and follows the user's position The tool belt allows the user to switch the line style between straight polyline and spline. The current line can also be terminated by pressing *Finish Line* instead of performing the double air-tap gesture. In a complete drawing application, a tool belt might similarly be important in promoting *Modal Flexibility*.

USER STUDY

User performance and experience was evaluated in a within-subject experiment with three interaction conditions:

- **FREEHAND**: continuous line drawing at index cursor.
- **TAPLINE**: control points placed at index cursor.
- **GOGO-TAPLINE**: control points placed at GoGo-cursor.

We recruited 18 participants (3 female, 15 male) with a mean age of 24.6 ($SD = 3.7$) by convenience sampling. Nine participants reported prior experience with the HoloLens. Participants received a briefing that introduced the headset, described how to use the drawing techniques and described the tasks they must perform. Participants were required to complete a familiarisation task at the start of the experiment and then three drawing tasks in each condition. The familiarisation task and three drawing tasks are described below.

Familiarisation Task

To reiterate, the user must perform the air-tap gesture to begin a line in FREEHAND or place a control point in TAPLINE and GOGO-TAPLINE. Prior to commencing the main drawing tasks, participants completed a gesture familiarisation task. This task was a simplified version of a circular target acquisition task, with 10 targets presented at incremental angular steps and alternating sides of a circle parallel to the participant's initial view plane. Targets were acquired by navigating the *gaze cursor* (a cursor placed at the intersection of the headset forward vector with virtual objects in the scene) to the target and then performing the air-tap gesture. Participants repeated this task, as many times as required, until they could select all ten targets within 15 s. The same task was performed with the double air-tap gesture but with a required completion time of 20 s. This procedure ensured that all participants achieved a base level of proficiency in the air-tap gesture.

Figure 3. The five 2D templates used in the Follow task.

Figure 4. The Triangle as presented in the Follow Template task.

Follow Template

The Follow Template task is derived from a simplified use case in which the user wishes to draw a planar shape at a fixed location in space. Participants were instructed to copy a 2D planar template, approximately 0.5 m × 0.5 m in size. All templates were presented in the same location in space. The template remained visible during the task and participants were free to move and position themselves as per their comfort. A standard set of 2D templates were selected from among the shapes used in the $1 gesture recognizer [29]. Figure 3 shows the five templates used in this study. Figure 4 shows the Triangle template as seen in the HoloLens by the participant. Participants were asked to draw the template as quickly and as accurately as possible using a single polyline or spline. The Triangle was used as a training task and presented first in all conditions.

Path Indication

The Path Indication task is derived from an envisaged use case in which the user seeks to indicate a motion path for an object or otherwise associate objects in the space (virtual or physical) by drawing a line. Participants were instructed to draw a path between a Start and Finish node using a single polyline or spline. The drawn path must also pass through multiple mid-point rings. This task is similar to that evaluated by Keefe et al. [15] but at room scale. Five different template paths of varying heights and orientations were constructed. The template path lengths varied between 3.51 m and 4.41 m (mean 3.93 m). Each unique template path was presented at the same location for all participants. As with the Follow Template task, the first path served as training and was presented first to all participants. This path is shown in Figure 5.

Figure 5. The Start (green), Finish (blue) and Mid-point (magenta) nodes as presented in the Path Indication task.

3D Object Recreation

The 3D Object Recreation task represents an extension of the Follow Template task into 3D. Furthermore, it introduces an element of prompted composition. Participants were instructed to draw lines to recreate a 3D object. The 3D template was presented for 10 s then the object would disappear (no drawing was permitted while the template was shown). Upon disappearing, participants were required to draw the template from memory. In this task, the participants could use multiple polylines or splines to draw the object. Four different 3D templates were used, see Figure 7. The Cube was presented first as a training task. A view of the Chair as seen through the Hololens is shown in Figure 6. To submit the completed drawing, participants press a *Done* button in the tool belt.

Procedure

The order of drawing techniques was assigned using a fully balanced design. Task order was held constant to be consistent with the increasing difficulty of the tasks from easiest (Follow Template) to hardest (3D Object Recreation). The first drawing exercise within each task was presented as a practice exercise. The practice templates in each task were held constant across conditions and participants (i.e. the Triangle, the first unique path, and the Cube). Note that the practice drawings are not included in the subsequent results as the user was encouraged to experiment and ensure they understood the interaction behaviour. The remaining templates for the drawing tasks were randomly shuffled in an effort to minimise confounding ordering effects. The experiment procedure specifically prevented editing or revision behaviour among participants in order to focus on the raw performance capabilities of the drawing techniques. In the Follow and Path Indication tasks, only one line could be drawn and the drawing was automatically submitted upon line termination. Undo or eraser functionality was intentionally removed.

Metrics

In evaluating the three alternative drawing techniques, we sought to provide resolution in the metrics of performance and user experience. These metrics are summarised below.

Completion Time

Task completion time was measured based on the elapsed time between the first and last drawing point.

Execution Accuracy

To measure how well the participants replicate the shapes in the Follow Template task we evaluate two different deviation

Figure 6. The Chair as presented in the 3D Object Recreation task.

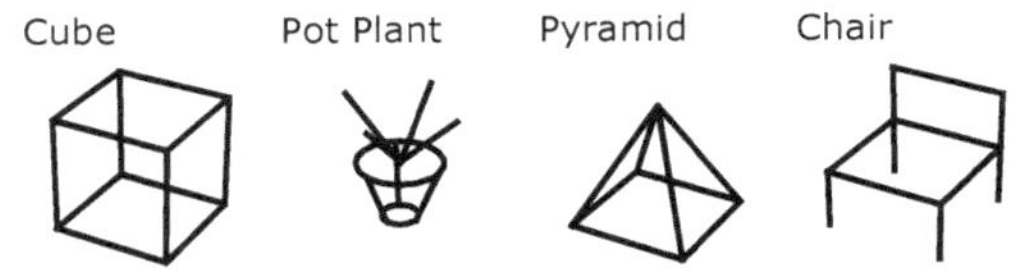

Figure 7. The four 3D Object Recreation templates.

metrics: i) proportional shape matching (psm) described in [17] and Equation 2; and ii) aggregated closest point matching (cpm) described in [15] and Equation 3. Before applying Equations 2 and 3, both polylines are resampled into N equidistant points producing temporally normalised point sequences for the drawing (D where point $d \in D$) and template (T where point $t \in T$).

$$dev_{psm} = \frac{1}{N}\sum_{i=1}^{N}\|d_i - t_i\|_2. \qquad (2)$$

$$dev_{cpm} = \frac{d_m(D,T) + d_m(T,D)}{2}, \qquad (3)$$
$$\text{where } d_m(D,T) = \frac{1}{N}\sum_{i=1}^{N}\min_{t\in T}\|d_i - t\|_2.$$

The dev_{psm} metric reflects the average spatial separation between corresponding equidistant sample points in both point sequences. It therefore captures execution direction and large discontinuities but is susceptible to error when drawing behaviour varies inconsistently with time. The dev_{cpm} metric averages the closest point fit of the drawing to the template and the template to the drawing. It reflects the mean of the shortest distance between points in the two polylines under comparison. A limitation of this metric is that it cannot discriminate between drawings performed in the reverse direction and it regularises discontinuities in the drawn line. As a summative metric of execution quality, however, this is acceptable. For all metric evaluations, the value of N was set at 100.

A secondary geometric performance metric was used to analyse the drawings completed in the Path Indication and 3D Object Recreation tasks. *Normalised line length* is the executed drawing length as a percentage of the ideal drawing length for the template.

User Experience

Before the start of the experiment, participants completed the Simulator Sickness questionnaire [16]. After completion of the three drawing tasks for a given condition, participants

Condition	*Time (s)*	Dev_{psm} *(mm)*	Dev_{cpm} *(mm)*
FREEHAND	21.6 ± 11.3	50.6 ± 27.5	21.8 ± 15.6
TAPLINE	32.5 ± 17.9	29.3 ± 16.0	19.0 ± 10.0
GOGO-TAPLINE	40.9 ± 20.7	40.4 ± 32.8	22.4 ± 14.8

Table 1. Follow Template task mean completion time and mean template deviations. Results show mean ± 1 standard deviation.

Condition	*Time (s)*	*Dev. (mm)*	*Length (%)*
FREEHAND	16.0 ± 9.1	28.7 ± 10.1	132.5 ± 32.5
TAPLINE	21.2 ± 9.1	32.1 ± 32.4	98.3 ± 3.1
GOGO-TAPLINE	30.6 ± 13.8	37.4 ± 24.7	103.8 ± 7.9

Table 2. Path Indication task mean completion time, deviation and normalised line length. Results show mean ± 1 standard deviation.

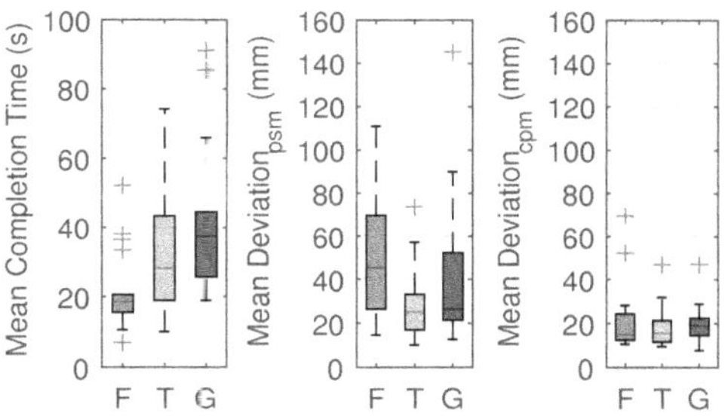

Figure 8. Boxplot of Follow Template task completion time (left), dev_{psm} (middle) and dev_{cpm} (right). The Freehand, Tapline and GoGo-Tapline are abbreviated as F, T and G respectively. Red crosses indicate outliers based on the Interquartile Range (IQR) rule, e.g. $q_3 + 1.5 \times (q_3 - q_1)$.

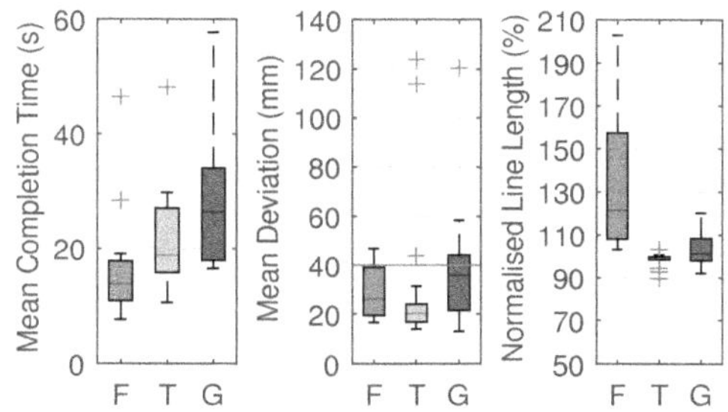

Figure 9. Boxplot of Path Indication task completion time (left), deviation (middle) and normalised line length (right). Red crosses are outliers based on the IQR rule. The red line on the deviation plot (middle) represents the node radius.

were instructed to remove the headset and fill out three questionnaires: Simulator Sickness, Flow Short Scale [22] and NASA TLX [12]. At the end of the experiment, participants completed a summative reflection questionnaire that examined their experience of the different drawing techniques and tasks. This questionnaire asked participants to rate their perceived speed, accuracy and comfort with the three drawing techniques on a five point Likert scale. Participants were also asked to provide written comments on their experience with the different techniques and to comment on their experience of the three tasks, independent of the drawing technique used. Finally, participants were asked to indicate their preferred drawing technique for each task and overall.

RESULTS

The protocol restricting drawings to a single line coupled with user error in performing the control gestures and using the tool belt meant that some drawings were prematurely terminated. Drawings in which participants either stated to have accidentally submitted the drawing or the plotted points show an obvious premature termination were removed from analysis.

Some participants also failed to understand the behaviour of splines when selecting this option to draw the curved templates. For example, several participants drew the Pigtail with control points at the start and end of the template but none in between to capture the curvature. In most cases, this mistake was only made once and participants used the spline behaviour correctly in subsequent drawings. Out of the 72 curved templates executed by participants in Tapline and GoGo-Tapline, 12 are excluded from analysis for this reason.

Follow Template

The completion time and deviation results for the Follow Task are summarised in Figure 8 and Table 1. The FREEHAND condition produced the quickest completion times, followed by TAPLINE then GOGO-TAPLINE. Repeated measures analysis of variance revealed a significant effect of the drawing technique on completion time ($F_{2,17} = 14.165$, $\eta_p^2 = 0.455$, $p < 0.001$). A Tukey post-hoc test revealed that the completion times significantly differed between FREEHAND and TAPLINE ($p < 0.05$) as well as FREEHAND and GOGO-TAPLINE ($p < 0.001$). The most accurate drawing technique based on dev_{psm} was TAPLINE, followed by GOGO-TAPLINE and then FREEHAND. We found a significant effect of the drawing technique on dev_{psm} (RM-ANOVA; $F_{2,17} = 3.767$, $\eta_p^2 = 0.181$, $p < 0.05$). A Tukey post-hoc test showed that the deviation significantly differed between FREEHAND and TAPLINE ($p < 0.05$). The dev_{cpm} values listed in Table 1 indicate only marginal differences between the three techniques. The difference observed between dev_{psm} and dev_{cpm} suggests that there are local distortions in FREEHAND that are effectively smoothed by the aggregating closest point metric.

These results indicate that the Freehand technique is an efficient method for executing planar drawings but introduces some minor inaccuracies. In contrast, the Tapline technique is on average 50% slower but produces significantly more accurate drawings. This is an intuitive result given that the Freehand technique is particularly influenced by the difficulty in fine motor control of the hand in 3D [9] and inaccuracies in the hand tracking compared with the more discrete approach of Tapline. The GoGo-Tapline was marginally slower and less accurate than standard Tapline which we conjecture is due to the additional depth control capability (of no benefit in 2D planar drawing) disrupting participants' use of the technique.

Path Indication

The Path Indication task required participants to draw a line between a Start and Finish node that also passed through all intermediary nodes. The participant mean completion times, deviations and normalised line lengths are summarised in Table 2 and Figure 9. Note that the mean deviations reported

Condition	*Time (s)*	*Line Length (%)*
FREEHAND	58.3 ± 23.7	136.4 ± 30.0
TAPLINE	87.7 ± 38.7	121.3 ± 29.8
GOGO-TAPLINE	93.7 ± 32.8	141.1 ± 52.7

Table 3. 3D Object Recreation task mean completion time and mean normalised line length. Results show mean ± 1 standard deviation.

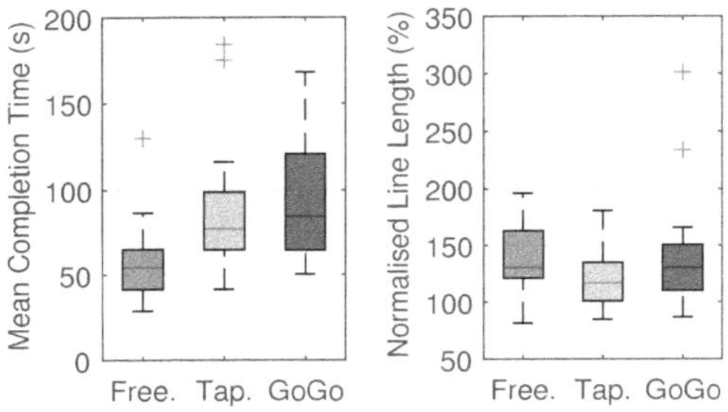

Figure 10. Boxplot of 3D Object Recreation task completion time (left) and normalised line length (right). Red crosses are outliers based on the IQR rule.

here are based only on the closest point deviation from the path nodes. The path nodes had a radius of approximately 40 mm (show as a red line in Figure 9) and so path points with deviations below this threshold can be considered as having satisfied the task requirements. The normalised line length is based on the line length drawn divided by the shortest possible line length that passes through the centre of every node.

The fastest condition was again FREEHAND followed by TAPLINE and then GOGO-TAPLINE. The effect of drawing technique was significant (RM-ANOVA; $F_{2,17} = 12.078$, $\eta_p^2 = 0.415$, $p < 0.001$). A Tukey post-hoc test revealed that the completion times significantly differed between FREEHAND and GOGO-TAPLINE ($p < 0.001$) and between TAPLINE and GOGO-TAPLINE ($p < 0.01$).

The mean deviations summarised in Table 2 indicate that all drawing techniques generally produced paths that met the task conditions (within the node radius of 40 mm). Figure 9 shows that there were several outliers in TAPLINE that exceeded the node threshold but otherwise line points were closely clustered within acceptable limits. Greater variation and a higher proportion of points exceeding acceptable limits is observable in FREEHAND and GOGO-TAPLINE.

The analysis of normalised line length indicates that significant superfluous drawing is performed when using the FREEHAND technique (RM-ANOVA; $F_{2,17} = 18.176$, $\eta_p^2 = 0.517$, $p < 0.001$). A Tukey post hoc test showed that the line lengths in FREEHAND are distinctly elevated from TAPLINE ($p < 0.001$) and GOGO-TAPLINE ($p < 0.001$), which are generally centred around the ideal line length (i.e. 100%). This behaviour in FREEHAND is also clearly visible in the produced lines, which deviate significantly from the ideal path while still passing close to the node centres. This is in part a consequence of the narrow FOV that users experience due to the small display region of the HoloLens. This makes it difficult for users to perceive the ideal path to the next node. Tapline and GoGo-Tapline techniques avoid this situation by allowing users to reposition themselves in the space and to look around, independently of executing a drawing.

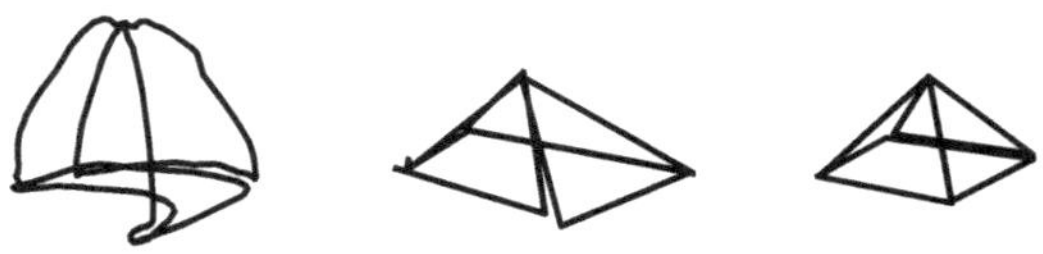

Figure 11. The Pyramid as drawn by one participant in Freehand (left), Tapline (middle), and GoGo-Tapline (right).

The results again suggest that Freehand provides a fast but sometimes inaccurate drawing method. It seems reasonable to expect that the Tapline and GoGo-Tapline techniques would be well suited to the Path Indication task given that control points can be precisely placed at the path nodes. However, Tapline and GoGo-Tapline were on average approximately 30% and 90% slower respectively than Freehand.

3D Object Recreation

The completion time and normalized line length results for the 3D Object Recreation task are summarised in Table 3 and Figure 10. The fastest drawing technique was FREEHAND followed by TAPLINE and then GOGO-TAPLINE. The condition effect on the completion time proved to be significant (RM-ANOVA; $F_{2,17} = 9.254$, $\eta_p^2 = 0.352$, $p < 0.001$). A Tukey post hoc test revealed that the mean completion times significantly differed between FREEHAND and TAPLINE ($p < 0.01$) and FREEHAND and GOGO-TAPLINE ($p < 0.001$).

The hiding of the 3D template after 10 seconds provided an aspect of prompted composition to the task. As a consequence, however, there is no appropriate template matching metric as participants drew the 3D object from their memory. Instead, we examine the total drawn line length relative to the total template line length. We found a significant effect of the drawing method on line length (RM-ANOVA; $F_{2,17} = 3.673$, $\eta_p^2 = 0.178$, $p < 0.05$). A Tukey post hoc test revealed that the line length significantly differed between TAPLINE and GOGO-TAPLINE ($p < 0.05$).

These results again favour Freehand in terms of task completion time, with participants completing the object drawings on average approximately 34% faster than with Tapline. However, Tapline produced objects with total line lengths closest to the ideal template line length.

Figure 11 shows the Pyramid as drawn by one participant using the three different techniques. The Tapline and GoGo-Tapline Pyramid drawings are considerably more precise and regular than the Freehand drawing. From this example, it is clear that interaction technique can have a significant effect on the resulting aesthetics of a drawing.

Condition Induced Discomfort

Condition induced discomfort was monitored via the Simulator Sickness Questionnaire [16]. The median responses captured prior to commencing the experiment (PRE-EXPERIMENT) and after each experimental condition are summarised in Table 4. Only the GOGO-TAPLINE condition produced marginal

Condition	Nausea	Oculo-Motor
PRE-EXPERIMENT	0.0	1.0
FREEHAND	0.0	1.0
TAPLINE	0.0	1.0
GOGO-TAPLINE	0.0	1.5

Table 4. Median response on the Simulator Sickness questionnaire prior to commencing the experiment and after completion of each condition.

Condition	Flow SS	NASA-TLX
FREEHAND	5.4	51.2
TAPLINE	5.7	53.0
GOGO-TAPLINE	5.2	67.5

Table 5. Median responses on Flow Short Scale and NASA-TLX surveys.

change in median score on the Oculo-Motor scale. In general, however, all techniques appear to have induced minimal discomfort for users. This is consistent with the qualitative feedback received from users during the study.

Flow and Perceived Workload

Participant responses to the Flow Short Scale [22] and NASA-TLX [12] surveys are summarised in Table 5 and Figure 12. These two surveys were completed at the end of each drawing condition. The differences between conditions on the Flow Short Scale responses are marginal with a slight reduction observable in GOGO-TAPLINE. This trend is also repeated in the NASA-TLX workload score where GOGO-TAPLINE is marginally elevated.

Participant Feedback

At the conclusion of the experiment, participants completed a questionnaire that targeted their experience of the drawing techniques as well as the tasks. The first part of the questionnaire asked participants to rate each of the drawing techniques on a five point Likert scale in response to three statements: 1) The technique made it easy to draw quickly; 2) The technique made it easy to draw accurately; and 3) The technique was comfortable to use. The median statement responses are listed in Table 6. A Friedman test indicated a significant difference in the responses to speed ($\chi^2(2) = 12.18$, $p < 0.01$) and accuracy ($\chi^2(2) = 10.23$, $p = 0.01$) statements. Post hoc analysis with Wilcoxon signed-rank tests was conducted with a Bonferroni correction applied, resulting in a significance level set at $p < 0.017$. It revealed significant differences

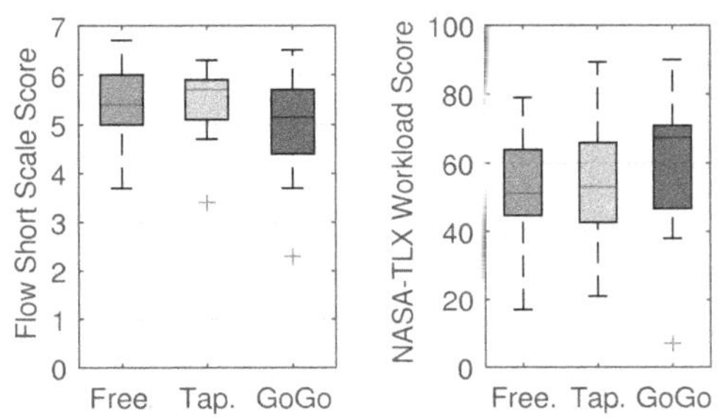

Figure 12. Boxplot of Flow Short Scale responses (left) and NASA-TLX workload (right). Red crosses are outliers based on the IQR rule.

Condition	Speed	Accu.	Comf.
FREEHAND	4.5	2.0	4.0
TAPLINE	3.0	4.0	3.0
GOGO-TAPLINE	2.0	2.5	3.0

Table 6. Median questionnaire responses assessing perceived speed, accuracy and comfort on a five point Likert scale.

Condition	Follow	Path	3D Object	Overall
FREEHAND	7 (39%)	4 (22%)	5 (28%)	7 (39%)
TAPLINE	9 (50%)	7 (39%)	9 (50%)	8 (44%)
GOGO-TAPLINE	2 (11%)	7 (39%)	4 (22%)	3 (17%)

Table 7. Count of participants' preferences for drawing technique in each task and overall.

between FREEHAND and GOGO-TAPLINE for the speed statement ($Z = -2.173$, $p < 0.05$) and between FREEHAND and TAPLINE for the accuracy statement ($Z = -2.560$, $p < 0.01$).

These results are consistent with the quantitative performance results obtained. The Freehand was fastest in all tasks and was perceived as so by participants. The Tapline technique was the most precise based on the deviation metrics and this was also reflected in participant responses to the accuracy statement. Although not statistically significant based on a Friedman test, the Freehand technique had the highest median comfort rating.

Participant Comments

Participants were invited in the questionnaire to note any perceived advantages and disadvantages of the three drawing techniques. These qualitative responses were reviewed to identify any commonality. A frequently mentioned advantage of the Freehand technique was the ability to draw fast and easily ("easy, fast"). At the same time, participants criticized that it lacked accuracy ("Hard to keep a straight line."). The Tapline technique received positive feedback regarding accuracy and expenditure of time ("Easiest to place accurately", "Quickness. [...]"). However, participants stated that it is hard to draw curved lines ("curved lines harder to get right"). The GoGo-Tapline was described as comfortable (e.g. "the most convenient, you can just stand and draw") and beneficial in maintaining an overview of the scene while drawing ("The distance allowed by the technique allowed me to see the drawings as a whole [...]"). On the other hand, the depth of the cursor was hard to perceive for multiple participants ("[...] sometimes hard to get the depth correct.").

Preferences

The final part of the questionnaire invited participants to select their preferred technique for each of the three study tasks and overall. Table 7 summarises the participant preference distribution. The Tapline technique was the most favoured drawing technique for the Follow and the 3D Object Recreation tasks. For the Path Indication task, the Tapline and GoGo-Tapline techniques were equally favoured. Overall, the two roughly evenly favoured techniques were Freehand and Tapline with GoGo-Tapline only preferred by three of 18 participants. These preference responses are interesting to interpret within the context of the performance results. Their comparatively even distribution suggests that different users appreciate different capabilities. This highlights the need to support switching between modes in a complete drawing application.

A PRACTICAL EXAMPLE OF 3D AR DRAWING

As a demonstration of the practical use of the bare-handed drawing techniques presented, one of the authors completed the 3D drawing shown in Figure 13. This drawing was created in situ based on a hypothetical scenario requiring a modification of an existing access platform to create a link to an adjoining building.

The drawing shown in Figure 13 utilises all three drawing techniques. A rapidly executed zigzag (in red) using the Freehand technique indicates the portion of railing to remove. The Tapline technique was used to accurately designate the boundary of this section. The GoGo-Tapline was essential in allowing lines to be drawn on the surface of the adjoining building. The provision of complementary interactions in this application reflects the design principle of *Modal Flexibility*.

DISCUSSION

The findings from the user study highlight the influence that task type can have on user performance and experience. Furthermore, the distribution of preferred drawing technique captured by the summative questionnaire demonstrates that different users appreciate different capabilities. Numerous participants highlighted the fact that certain operations were easier with one technique than another. It was in anticipation of this diversity that we sought to test three alternative drawing techniques with distinct advantages and disadvantages.

The Freehand technique yielded the fastest completion times throughout all tasks as well as the highest questionnaire scores regarding speed and comfort. In contrast, the Tapline method was the most precise for the Follow Template and Path Indication tasks where deviation metrics are meaningful. The GoGo-Tapline technique was developed as a demonstration of a drawing-based interaction derived from a virtual hand metaphor and reflects the design principle of *Exploit the Lack of Physical Constraints*. This was motivated by the belief that allowing users to modulate cursor depth without taking steps may be useful. In practice, the limited use of the virtual extension functionality meant that the GoGo-cursor functioned more like a generic offset cursor [19]. The additional complexity introduced by the interaction method likely confounded the performance results. Nevertheless, the technique was chosen by three of the 18 participants as their overall favourite.

If the tasks had been more demanding in terms of movement or reach, it is likely that the benefits of GoGo-Tapline would have been more clearly revealed. In terms of generating drawings as a general human-computer interaction task, there are several observations that can be made. Participants commented that they were occasionally surprised how distorted the object they were drawing looked when they viewed it from a different angle. This is consistent with observations made by Deering [9] where people had to learn to break 2D interface habits of keeping their head artificially still and instead look around the virtual world. Generally this issue relates to the difficulty of providing fine depth perception of virtual content in AR, as was commented on by several participants in this study.

Figure 13. Preliminary design drawing of a hypothetical access modification to join an existing walkway with a neighbouring building. Drawing completed in situ by one of the authors using all three of the drawing techniques. All line elements are spatially fixed to preserve references to the physical space.

Limitations and Future Work

In this paper we focus primarily on the immediate efficacy of the interaction techniques. By necessity, this ignores the common activity in drawing of revision and editing and the design principle of *Rapid Revision*. Basic line erasing and deletion functionality is provided in the application demonstration in Figure 13 but awaits user validation. Future work will examine the features necessary to provide productive and efficient drawing editing functionality.

As an initial step towards investigating the design principles set out in this paper, the study involved simplified drawing tasks. We suggest an interesting avenue for future work is to target more complicated use cases and contexts to increase the external validity of the findings.

CONCLUSION

In this paper we presented three interaction techniques supporting bare-handed drawing in AR: Freehand, Tapline and GoGo-Tapline. We studied their performance in a user study with three drawing tasks: Follow Template, Path Indication and 3D Object Recreation. We established that Freehand drawing is a fast, although not necessarily accurate, technique. Tapline, which is based on placing control points to create line segments, achieves a balance between speed and accuracy and was favoured by participants. We also introduced a novel combination of a virtual hand metaphor with the Tapline drawing technique, the GoGo-Tapline technique, which was equally most favoured in the Path Indication task.

The study highlighted the benefit of allowing users to fluidly switch between techniques to exploit the trade-offs between them. The three bare-handed drawing techniques are underpinned by five design principles, which can form a starting point for designers in developing other applications. We strongly believe that 3D drawing in AR will become a highly effective means of information exchange and will see wide use in both applied and creative applications.

ACKNOWLEDGMENTS

This work was supported by EPSRC (grant numbers EP/N010558/1 and EP/R004471/1) and the Trimble Fund.

REFERENCES

1. Rahul Arora, Rubaiat Habib Kazi, Fraser Anderson, Tovi Grossman, Karan Singh, and George Fitzmaurice. 2017. Experimental Evaluation of Sketching on Surfaces in VR. In *Proceedings of the 2017 CHI Conference on Human Factors in Computing Systems (CHI '17)*. ACM, New York, NY, USA, 5643–5654. DOI: http://dx.doi.org/10.1145/3025453.3025474
2. Doug A. Bowman and Larry F. Hodges. 1997. An Evaluation of Techniques for Grabbing and Manipulating Remote Objects in Immersive Virtual Environments. In *Proceedings of the 1997 Symposium on Interactive 3D Graphics (I3D '97)*. ACM, New York, NY, USA, 35–ff. DOI:http://dx.doi.org/10.1145/253284.253301
3. Doug A. Bowman and Larry F. Hodges. 1999. Formalizing the Design, Evaluation, and Application of Interaction Techniques for Immersive Virtual Environments. *Journal of Visual Languages & Computing* 10, 1 (1999), 37–53. DOI: http://dx.doi.org/10.1006/jvlc.1998.0111
4. R. A. Burkhard. 2004. Learning from architects: the difference between knowledge visualization and information visualization. In *Proceedings. Eighth International Conference on Information Visualisation, 2004. IV 2004.* 519–524. DOI: http://dx.doi.org/10.1109/IV.2004.1320194
5. Jeff Butterworth, Andrew Davidson, Stephen Hench, and Marc. T. Olano. 1992. 3DM: A Three Dimensional Modeler Using a Head-mounted Display. In *Proceedings of the 1992 Symposium on Interactive 3D Graphics (I3D '92)*. ACM, New York, NY, USA, 135–138. DOI: http://dx.doi.org/10.1145/147156.147182
6. Edwin Catmull and Raphael Rom. 1974. A class of local interpolating splines. In *Computer Aided Geometric Design*, Robert E. Barnhill and Richard F. Riesenfeld (Eds.). Academic Press, New York, 317–326. DOI: http://dx.doi.org/10.1016/B978-0-12-079050-0.50020-5
7. James H. Clark. 1976. Designing Surfaces in 3-D. *Commun. ACM* 19, 8 (Aug. 1976), 454–460. DOI: http://dx.doi.org/10.1145/360303.360329
8. Matthew T. Cook and Arvin Agah. 2009. A survey of sketch-based 3-D modeling techniques. *Interacting with Computers* 21, 3 (2009), 201–211. DOI: http://dx.doi.org/10.1016/j.intcom.2009.05.004
9. Michael F. Deering. 1995. HoloSketch: A Virtual Reality Sketching/Animation Tool. *ACM Trans. Comput.-Hum. Interact.* 2, 3 (Sept. 1995), 220–238. DOI: http://dx.doi.org/10.1145/210079.210087
10. Gabriela Goldschmidt. 1991. The dialectics of sketching. *Creativity Research Journal* 4, 2 (1991), 123–143. DOI: http://dx.doi.org/10.1080/10400419109534381
11. Nate Hagbi, Raphael Grasset, Oriel Bergig, Mark Billinghurst, and Jihad El-Sana. 2015. In-Place Sketching for Augmented Reality Games. *Computers in Entertainment* 12, 3 (2015), 1–18. DOI: http://dx.doi.org/10.1145/2702109.2633419
12. Sandra G. Hart and Lowell E. Staveland. 1988. Development of NASA-TLX (Task Load Index): Results of Empirical and Theoretical Research. In *Human Mental Workload*, Peter A. Hancock and Najmedin Meshkati (Eds.). Advances in Psychology, Vol. 52. North-Holland, 139 – 183. DOI:http://dx.doi.org/https://doi.org/10.1016/S0166-4115(08)62386-9
13. Ke Huo, Vinayak, and Karthik Ramani. 2017. Window-Shaping: 3D Design Ideation by Creating on, Borrowing from, and Looking at the Physical World. In *Proceedings of the Eleventh International Conference on Tangible, Embedded, and Embodied Interaction (TEI '17)*. ACM, New York, NY, USA, 37–45. DOI: http://dx.doi.org/10.1145/3024969.3024995
14. Johann Habakuk Israel, Laurence Mauderli, and Laurent Greslin. 2013. Mastering Digital Materiality in Immersive Modelling. In *Proceedings of the International Symposium on Sketch-Based Interfaces and Modeling (SBIM '13)*. ACM, New York, NY, USA, 15–22. DOI:http://dx.doi.org/10.1145/2487381.2487388
15. Daniel F. Keefe, Robert C. Zeleznik, and David H. Laidlaw. 2007. Drawing on Air: Input Techniques for Controlled 3D Line Illustration. *IEEE Transactions on Visualization and Computer Graphics* 13, 5 (Sept 2007), 1067–1081. DOI: http://dx.doi.org/10.1109/TVCG.2007.1060
16. Robert S. Kennedy, Norman E. Lane, Kevin S. Berbaum, and Michael G. Lilienthal. 1993. Simulator Sickness Questionnaire: An Enhanced Method for Quantifying Simulator Sickness. *The International Journal of Aviation Psychology* 3, 3 (1993), 203–220. DOI: http://dx.doi.org/10.1207/s15327108ijap0303_3
17. Per Ola Kristensson and Shumin Zhai. 2004. SHARK2: A Large Vocabulary Shorthand Writing System for Pen-based Computers. In *Proceedings of the 17th Annual ACM Symposium on User Interface Software and Technology (UIST '04)*. ACM, New York, NY, USA, 43–52. DOI:http://dx.doi.org/10.1145/1029632.1029640
18. Tim McGraw, Esteban Garcia, and Drew Sumner. 2017. Interactive Swept Surface Modeling in Virtual Reality with Motion-tracked Controllers. In *Proceedings of the Symposium on Sketch-Based Interfaces and Modeling (SBIM '17)*. ACM, New York, NY, USA, Article 4, 9 pages. DOI:http://dx.doi.org/10.1145/3092907.3092908
19. R. L. Potter, L. J. Weldon, and B. Shneiderman. 1988. Improving the Accuracy of Touch Screens: An Experimental Evaluation of Three Strategies. In *Proceedings of the SIGCHI Conference on Human Factors in Computing Systems (CHI '88)*. ACM, New York, NY, USA, 27–32. DOI: http://dx.doi.org/10.1145/57167.57171

20. Ivan Poupyrev, Mark Billinghurst, Suzanne Weghorst, and Tadao Ichikawa. 1996. The Go-Go Interaction Technique: Non-linear Mapping for Direct Manipulation in VR. In *Proceedings of the 9th Annual ACM Symposium on User Interface Software and Technology (UIST '96)*. ACM, New York, NY, USA, 79–80. DOI: http://dx.doi.org/10.1145/237091.237102

21. Ivan Poupyrev, Tadao Ichikawa, Suzanne Weghorst, and Mark Billinghurst. 1998. Egocentric Object Manipulation in Virtual Environments: Empirical Evaluation of Interaction Techniques. *Computer Graphics Forum* 17, 3 (1998), 41–52. DOI: http://dx.doi.org/10.1111/1467-8659.00252

22. Falko Rheinberg, Regina Vollmeyer, and Stefan Engeser. 2003. Die Erfassung des Flow-Erlebens [The assessment of flow experience]. In *Diagnostik von Selbstkonzept, Lernmotivation und Selbstregulation [Diagnosis of motivation and self-concept]*, J. Stiensmeier-Pelster and F. Rheinberg (Eds.). Hogrefe, Göttingen, 261–279.

23. Steven Schkolne, Michael Pruett, and Peter Schröder. 2001. Surface Drawing: Creating Organic 3D Shapes with the Hand and Tangible Tools. In *Proceedings of the SIGCHI Conference on Human Factors in Computing Systems (CHI '01)*. ACM, New York, NY, USA, 261–268. DOI:http://dx.doi.org/10.1145/365024.365114

24. Ben Shneiderman. 1983. Direct Manipulation: A Step Beyond Programming Languages. *Computer* 16, 8 (Aug 1983), 57–69. DOI: http://dx.doi.org/10.1109/MC.1983.1654471

25. Ben Shneiderman and Catherine Plaisant. 2010. *Designing the User Interface: Strategies for Effective Human-Computer Interaction* (5th ed.). Addison-Wesley, Boston, USA.

26. Richard Stoakley, Matthew J. Conway, and Randy Pausch. 1995. Virtual Reality on a WIM: Interactive Worlds in Miniature. In *Proceedings of the SIGCHI Conference on Human Factors in Computing Systems (CHI '95)*. ACM Press/Addison-Wesley Publishing Co., New York, NY, USA, 265–272. DOI: http://dx.doi.org/10.1145/223904.223938

27. Ivan E. Sutherland. 1963. Sketchpad: a Man-machine Graphical Communication System. In *Proceedings of AFIPS'63*. ACM, New York, NY, USA, 326–346. DOI: http://dx.doi.org/10.1145/800265.810742

28. Eva Wiese, Johann Habakuk Israel, Achim Meyer, and Sara Bongartz. 2010. Investigating the Learnability of Immersive Free-hand Sketching. In *Proceedings of the Seventh Sketch-Based Interfaces and Modeling Symposium (SBIM '10)*. Eurographics Association, Aire-la-Ville, Switzerland, 135–142. http://dl.acm.org/citation.cfm?id=1923363.1923387

29. Jacob O. Wobbrock, Andrew D. Wilson, and Yang Li. 2007. Gestures Without Libraries, Toolkits or Training: A $1 Recognizer for User Interface Prototypes. In *Proceedings of the 20th Annual ACM Symposium on User Interface Software and Technology (UIST '07)*. ACM, New York, NY, USA, 159–168. DOI: http://dx.doi.org/10.1145/1294211.1294238

Body as a Canvas: An Exploration on the Role of the Body as Display of Digital Information

Thuong N Hoang[1,2]
[1]School of Information Technology
Deakin University
Melbourne, Australia
thuong.hoang@deakin.edu.au

Hasan S Ferdous, Frank Vetere, Martin Reinoso[2]
[2]School of Computing and Information Systems,
The University of Melbourne
Melbourne, Australia
{hasan.ferdous; f.vetere; martin.reinoso}@unimelb.edu.au

ABSTRACT
The human body in HCI is often seen as an actuator for issuing commands and providing input to digital systems. We present the concept of the *body as a canvas,* in which the body acts as both an actuator and a display for information. Body as a canvas creates an interaction loop where interaction with information causes changes in the body, which in turn changes the display of information. Our qualitative study using an on-body projection system in a public exhibition investigates this concept with regards to body characteristics, types of body input, interactions between multiple bodies, and comparison to other display technologies. Findings show that body as a canvas creates connectedness between the body and information. Finally, we discuss how body characteristics and appearances can complement the information, when the body acts as a canvas.

Author Keywords
Body as a canvas; body display; augmented reality; virtual reality.

ACM Classification Keywords
H.5.m. Information interfaces and presentation (e.g., HCI): Miscellaneous.

INTRODUCTION
The human body is central to human-computer interactions (HCI), as our interactions with the world is mediated through the living bodies [6, 20]. Some ethnographers consider the body as a *site of knowing* [5] where the researcher absorbs their body into the subject culture as an instrument for fieldwork. In traditional human-machine systems, the body typically acts as an actuator, issuing commands and providing input signal through control devices (e.g. mouse) and language-based interactions (e.g. keyboard or voice) (Fig. 1a). In more advanced systems, the body can provide input through sensors that detect human movement or bio-signals (e.g. body temperature or heart beat). In each case the body is a conduit for input. The output is perceived through human senses (e.g. sight, hearing, proprioception), but it is generally rendered on an external device, such as a digital display.

Figure 1: (a) In traditional human-computer systems, the body is mostly an input channel. (b) When then body is a canvas, it acts as both input and output to the interaction.

In this paper, we present the concept of the *body as a canvas,* in which the body acts both as an actuator and a display for information (Fig. 1b). When the body is both the mechanism for activation and the surface for rendering information, a unique *interaction loop* is created. In this loop, the interaction is enacted through the body in response to the displayed information, which simultaneously changes the way the information is displayed on the body.

The use of the human body as a canvas has been explored by others, in particular by artists who practice body-painting to transform the body into new forms or make it vanish by blending it into the background. This idea is also investigated by HCI researchers working with interactive technologies related to human bodies. For example, Levisohn placed parts of the body behind a video see-through display to explore proprioceptive and kinesthetic awareness [19]. Johnson and Sun [14] projected virtual body organs on the body in an educational game. Javornik et al. [13] overlaid virtual make-up on the faces of performers through an augmented reality mirror to assist them in getting into respective character roles. In these examples, the body serves solely as a carrier of information.

Our exploration of the body as a canvas (BAAC) specifically focuses on the role of human body as both an actuator for

DIS '18, June 9–13, 2018, Hong Kong
© 2018 Association for Computing Machinery.
ACM ISBN 978-1-4503-5198-0/18/06...$15.00
https://doi.org/10.1145/3196709.3196724

input and a display for information. We investigate four issues related to body as a canvas: (i) the effect of body characteristics and appearance on the information; (ii) the type of body input signal that triggers the interaction loop; (iii) the interactions between multiple bodies as canvas; and (iv) the comparison of BAAC to other display technologies. We conducted a qualitative study of an on-body projection system in a public exhibition setting. Our findings suggest that BAAC creates connectedness between the information and the body. Body characteristics and appearances such as shape and clothing can complement the information that is displayed on it.

We begin by discussing the related work leading to our concept, and then present the findings of the study.

RELATED WORK

Body as an Actuator of Information

Perhaps the most obvious role of the human body is as an actuator, or a source of input for a computational device. HCI has contributed greatly to this perspective. Whole body interaction [7] has a holistic view of the body as a source of multiple input signals, including physical, physiological, cognitive, and emotional. Body tracking technologies capture bodily information such as movements [27] and bio signals [4], or appropriate body parts such as skin [10] or the ear [16] through on-body sensors. More recently, much of the discussion about the body in HCI has been influenced by notions of embodied interaction [6]. This perspective leverages our perception about our own body through physical and social interactions, and channels that familiarity into the interactions with and through computing devices. Taking this view, our bodily perception and actions are not separable, but always exist and evolve together.

The body as actuator can be considered both a mechanism for input and a conduit for other computations systems. For example, Mistry et al. [26] propose a technique to transfer information between different devices, using the body as a metaphoric medium to carry data in a copy and paste fashion. While the actual data is transferred in the cloud, the technique creates the illusion of using the body as a medium. In another work, Sakata et al. [30] consider the body as a conduit for emotions through dance movements and present a classification model to map the effects these dance movements in communicating emotions.

Body as a Display of Information

A less common role of the body is as a display of information. In *SixthSense* [23, 25], a neck-worn projector puts a numeric keypad on the hand of the wearer and a digital watch displayed on the wrist. Levisohn [19] uses the body as a tool to explore proprioceptive and kinesthetic awareness using a mixed reality system. He built an optical see-through interaction box that displays visual distortions of the user's hands as they interact with physical objects. Levisohn's device does not render the image directly on the hand, but overlays on a see-through screen over the hand. He discovered that delayed video and audio signal bring the user back and forth between immersion and self-awareness, or an oscillation in the user's connection with the digital information.

Johnson and Sun [14] built a game called *Augmented Anatomy* that projects virtual body organs on the body of players, who score points by correctly identifying the names of the organs. They discuss the concept of ownership of virtual artefacts through their incorporation onto the body, applied towards the context of learning in anatomy. Their study conducted with teachers and students shows an increase in the subjective level of interest in anatomy and computer science subjects. Saakes et al. [29] employ a similar on-body projection in a system called Mirror Mirror for designing t-shirts.

Instead of the whole body, Mercier-Ganady et al. [22] superimpose EEG (electroencephalography) visualization of a virtual brain on the user's head in a system called Mind-Mirror. The system uses a Microsoft Kinect camera for face and head tracking and displays a video mirror with overlay on a screen in front of the user. A pilot study was conducted to compare the system against the traditional temporal gauge visualization that displays brain concentration and relaxation levels. The result showed a comparable performance in terms of its usage as a feedback mechanism for brain computer interface.

Using a similar 'augmented mirror interface', Javornik et al. [13] developed a system that overlays digital makeup on the face using a tablet with a front facing camera. Their work aims at assisting the task of role playing, especially for theatrical performers who need to become a character through virtual make-up. An observation study in an opera dressing room with singers and make-up artists demonstrates that the visual effect makes a strong impression for the users leading to an easy and immediate transformation into the portrayed fictional character.

Displays comes in all shapes and sizes, and so do bodies. Previous work that discuss body as a display of information leave out an important discussion about the effects of body characteristics (such as size and skin tone) when considering it as a display tool. Just as Gemperle et al. [9] explain that the human form and size variations impose challenges in the design of wearable technology, we are similarly intrigued by the question of how body characteristics affects the role of the body as display of information.

Technologies for Displaying Information on the Body

In order for the body to act as a display, information needs to be placed on the body. Virtual and augmented reality technologies are most commonly used for this purpose, as they have the visualization capability to enable information to be displayed on or as a part of the body.

Virtual reality (VR) can provide a virtual environment where information can be displayed directly on the user's virtual body [12]. In order to provide the illusion that the

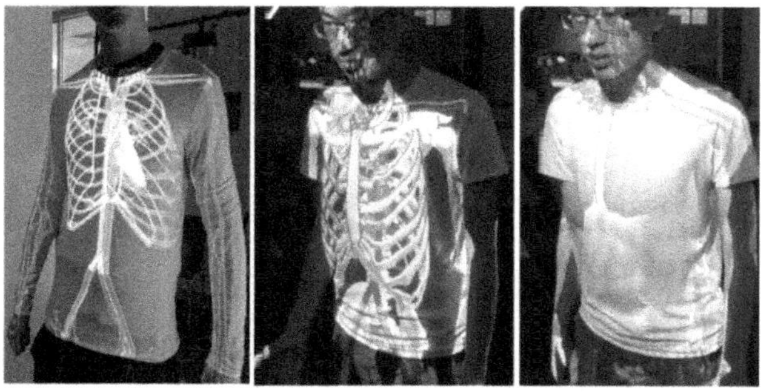

Figure 2: A demostration of the blood circulation, skeleton, and muscular system's projection on body.

information is displayed on the body, VR technology needs to recreate the body in a virtual environment [17] in such a way that there is a strong alignment between the physical and virtual bodies. A relevant project that demonstrates this concept is Onebody [12], a technology for teaching martial arts. Onebody is a VR remote posture training system that provides the student with a first-person view of their teacher's virtual body superimposed on their own virtual body. Using an immersive VR headset, the student can follow the movement as demonstrated by the teacher and match teacher's posture with their own.

Unlike VR, augmented reality (AR) systems allow the physical body to be present in the interaction. For example, screen-based AR employs cameras to track the body of a user standing in front of it, to produce an augmented mirror effect showing information overlay on the body [3]. Spatial AR [2] uses projection mapping to change the appearance of physical substrate, including the human body [11, 14]. Augmented Studio [11] is an example of a spatial AR system that projects virtual muscle and skeleton information on a volunteer student's body for physiotherapy education in a classroom. Students observe virtual anatomy mapped on the volunteer's body as a teacher explains the mechanics of body movements. In Augmented Studio, the body complements the virtual information (display) with direct coupling of body movements (input), enhancing the consumers' understanding of the information. Projection mapping on the body raises the question of how the different body shapes and characteristics impact on the display of the information. For Augmented Studio, accurate alignment of virtual muscles on the body is important for physiotherapy teaching.

Body as both Actuator and Display

Instead of constraining the roles of the body either as actuator or display, Onebody and Augmented Studio integrate both functions. Onebody takes input from the teacher's movements and displays directly on the student's body. Augmented Studio has a similar approach: it captures dynamic movements of the body as input, to couple with a virtual anatomical avatar, which is then projected back onto the same body as a display.

There is a tight coupling of the body as actuator and display of information. The body as actuator inevitably requires changes to the body, through movements or gestures. When the body also acts as a display for information, the changes enacted through body as an actuator affects the way the information is displayed on the body. Changes in the display can trigger further changes in the actuator role. We refer to this cycle as an *interaction loop*.

The interaction loop can be illustrated by a variation to SixthSense system by Mistry and Maes [24]. When the SixthSense system projects the numeric keypad on the palm and fingers of the hand, the user typically presses the buttons with the other hand. The numeric keypad projected on the hand does not change when the hand moves. If, instead, we consider the interaction on the same hand: as the thumb reaches out to touch the keypad on the fingers, the system needs to readjust the numbers as the hand moves, then we would have an interaction loop. There would be a tight coupling between the body as actuator (moving the thumb) and the display on the body (readjusting numbers). This interaction loop forms the basis for our concept of BAAC, where the body as actuator and as display are tightly coupled.

Another example of the interaction loop is a method for eye-free interaction called proprioceptive interaction [21]. A wearable bracelet captures input from the user's arm using an accelerometer and sends output to the user's arm through electrical muscle stimulations that place the wrist in certain poses. The user interacts with the input and output channel through proprioceptive sense. In this example, the interaction loop remains on the same channel (muscular actuation and stimulation). The BAAC concept in this paper further expands the input output loop from different channels, i.e. output is body surface as display, and different varieties of input, including movement and heart rate.

AIMS

Even though there are many examples of BAAC in existing literature, there are many aspects of BAAC yet to be investigated. This paper aims to address four questions:

Q1. *What are the effects of body characteristics on the display of information?* How do particular body characteristics (e.g. body size and shape, skin tone or clothing) highlight, accentuate, or detract from the role of the body as a canvas? There could also be sensitive issues related to body image and self-perception of the body, to be considered when designing with BAAC.

Q2. *What types of input signal cause interaction loop?* In addition to the body movement (physical signal), we aim to investigate how other body input signal, such as heart rate (physiological), affects BAAC.

Q3. *What are the interactions between multiple bodies as a canvas?* We extend existing works by creating a different type of third-person view, where two people can look into and interact with the body canvas of each other.

Q4. *How does body as a canvas differ from other display technologies?* We investigate the potential benefits and

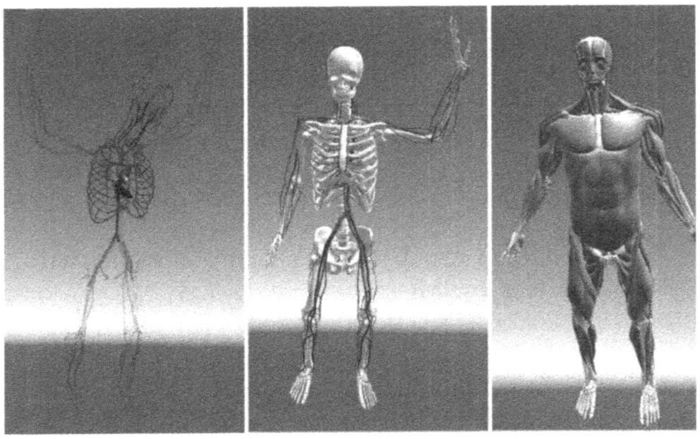

Figure 3: Views of the Inside-Out system
(a) Blood circulation, (b) Skeleton, and (c) Muscular view

challenges for using BAAC compared to traditional display technologies like television screen.

We explore these questions about body as canvas, through an on-body projection system called *Inside Out*. The system is based on the Augmented Studio [11], where a virtual musculoskeletal system is projected on the body and the projected skeleton and muscles move as the body moves. We extended it to project the blood circulatory system and an animated heart based on live pulse rate data. Thus the internal body structure and organs become visible from outside of the body (see Fig. 2 and Fig. 3).

The *Inside Out* system was deployed as an installation in a public exhibition. This provided an opportunity for us to explore the effects of different body characteristics and appearances on BAAC (Q1). To explore Q1, we used a fitness wristband to capture the heart rate of a user and map to the heart beat animation and blood circulation visualization. The heart beat information introduced a physiological input signal into body canvas (Q2). We enable projection on two bodies to explore the interactions of multiple bodies as a canvas (Q3). In the exhibition, we installed a mirror and a TV screen showing the same virtual circulatory visualization as on the body to contrast screen-based display versus body canvas (Q4).

STUDY DESIGN

The *Inside Out* Exhibition

The *Inside Out* system includes a generic virtual circulatory visualization with a pumping heart and major arteries and veins that light up in blue or red colors to indicate blood flow to and from the heart, respectively. *Inside Out* can also switch between different views (muscular or skeletal) for the visitors. We used a Microsoft (MS) Band as the fitness tracker to capture heartrate. The visitor provides bio-signal input to the system to be projected back onto their body.

We deployed the *Inside Out* system for 6 days (Monday to Sunday in one week, except Saturday) as part of a public exhibition. Visitors who came to our installation were generally interested in the larger exhibition season that we were a part of, which had the theme *blood* and its evocation

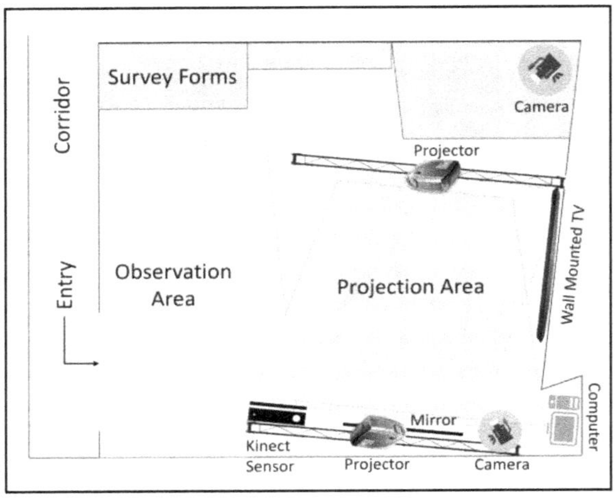

Figure 4: The Inside Out study setup.

of taboo, stigma, donation, identity, health, and sport. One member of the research team demonstrated the system and invited the visitors to try it out themselves from 12PM to 6PM Monday to Friday, and 11AM to 2PM on Sunday.

We conducted a qualitative study during this exhibition opening period to investigate the user experience with regards to the four questions mentioned above. We performed observations and interviews of visitors' experiences, collected surveys, and present our findings in this paper.

Study Protocol

As part of the BLOOD exhibition by the Science Gallery Melbourne, the *Inside Out* system was set up in a studio with projectors, television screen, and Microsoft Kinect sensors (Fig. 4). At the beginning of the exhibition, we calibrated the room using Microsoft Room Alive API [15] and placed posters in different parts of the exhibition area advertising the installation. We implemented the infrastructure as described in the Augmented Studio system [11].

The visitors would enter the room and stand in the *observation area* (Fig. 4), which was delineated by tape markings on the floor. One researcher stood in the *projection area*, wearing white clothing for maximum projection effect. The system projected a generic virtual circulatory, skeletal or muscular model onto the researcher's body and mapped to his movements. The research described the system to the visitors briefly, and then invited them to participate in the projection area. Participation was voluntary. As the participants stepped into the projection area, the researcher assisted the participant in putting on the MS Band. As the researcher stepped aside, the projection of the virtual body locked onto the participant's body instead. The research explained the circulatory system, skeletons, and muscles as it was displayed on the participant's body. The blood circulation visualization was then mapped to the participant's heart rate, as captured by the MS Band.

The system could track and project on up to two bodies in the projection area. The same anatomical model was also displayed in the large television screen (Fig. 4). Both the participants (in the projection area) and visitors (in the observation area) could watch the on-body projection and on the television screen. The participants could also see themselves in a mirror placed in front of them. The participants could move freely around the projection area. They were not asked to perform any particular task. They were allowed to explore the system in any way for as long as they wished. A researcher manually switched between different layers upon request or as needed. One researcher undertook an informal interview about the participants' experience of the system. Participant then completed a short survey upon exit.

Participants
Participants were visitors who voluntarily came to the exhibition. About 600 visitors visited the installation to watched the demonstration, among which 275 people (mostly adults, 117 male and 158 female) participated in the projection area, either alone or with another visitor. Average participation time was 2.7 minutes, with standard deviation of 1.05 minutes.

Data Collection
One researcher observed and took field-notes throughout participation. The installation area was video recorded using two video cameras – one recording the overall area including the visitors and participants, another recording the participant's activities in the projection area.

We collected observational field notes during the 33-hour deployment period, 66 hours of video recorded observations (with two cameras) that included participants interaction with the system as well as their informal interview with the research team members, and 206 survey responses. In order to avoid confirmation bias in the participants' responses, at no point during the interaction with the visitors did the researcher mention or discuss the concept of BAAC.

We designed an exit survey to capture an understanding of the user experience of the system. We asked the visitors 3 questions regarding their experience, and their connection to the information that was projected on their body. We used visual analog scale response to the questions by asking the

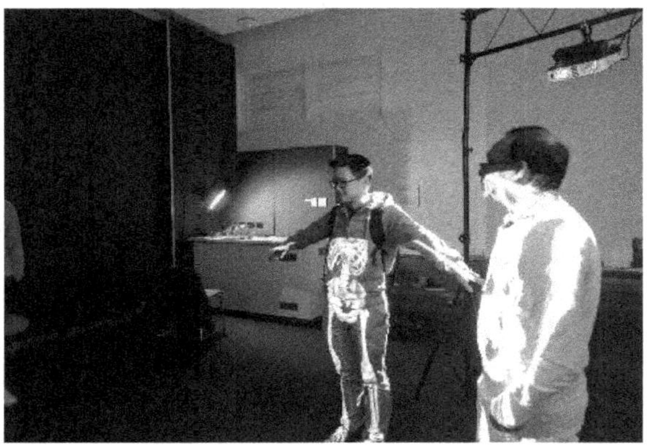

Figure 5: A participant interacting with the Inside Out system.

participants to mark their answer on a line with "Completely Agree" on one end and "Completely Disagree" on the other. Two of the questions focused on the user satisfaction metrics of user experience [1] and asked about engagement with the system and novelty of the visualization: *I find engaging with the system as good fun,* and *I feel intrigued by the system because it shows internal body organs externally.* We asked one question regarding their connection to the virtual anatomy: *I could relate to the projection as my own body systems.* The survey was conducted after their interaction and discussion with the researcher, in order not to introduce confirmation bias to the field notes and interview analysis. We also asked them to write comments on their experience.

Analysis
We performed descriptive statistical analysis on the survey data and thematic analysis on field notes, interview transcripts, and video recorded observational data to add detailed notes of all interactions with the *Inside Out* system and among the visitors themselves. These notes were coded in Nvivo and refined through discussions amongst the authors. The analysis focused on the impact of the four issues in Q1-4 above on participants interactions with the system and with one another. This analysis was done iteratively to identify common themes across participants as well as their unique activities.

FINDINGS
We present the findings based on this field study. We begin with an overview of the survey data analysis and then focus on findings based on qualitative analysis of our field notes, interviews, and video recorded observation data.

Survey Data
Out of the 206 responses, we have 148 fully completed responses. We converted the visual analog scale to a numeric value, with 0 for completely disagree and 100 for completely agree. We summarized the descriptive statistics of the three questions regarding engagement, intrigue, and relation. A high mean score of 87.37 for engagement (SD 18.3) and 69.8 for intrigue (SD 29.8) indicates a fun and engaging user experience interacting with *Inside Out.* Participants also rated that they highly relate to the projection as their own body system (mean 77.2, SD 23.2). While the survey data does not add to the core research questions, the questions were focused on measuring engagement and intrigue, which was useful information for our exhibition partner. We include in the analysis for completeness.

Interaction Loop
Inside Out is designed to explore the interaction loop concept with the heartbeat sensor as input and the virtual heart animation on body as output. Our analysis highlighted different aspects of this interaction loop related to self-reflection, connectedness, and education.

Connectedness with Information
Inside Out used generic anatomical models for projection; only two aspects were personalized: a) the heart-beat animation reflected the pulse-rate of the participant wearing

the Microsoft Band, and b) the movement of the anatomical models reflected the movement of the participants in the projection area, as tracked by the Kinect sensor. Despite such minimal personalization, many of our participants could closely connect themselves with what they saw on the screen and the image projected on their body. A common question among the participants about the projection of blood circulation system was "*Is that [emphasis] 'my' beating heart?*". Similar reaction was also observed when we projected only the heart animation. When we explained them about the generic model, some of them wished they could see their "*own*" body's internal organs. In one instance, when we switched the wristband from one participant to another, it was still showing an elevated heartrate of the previous wearer. The new participant noticed the higher heartrate and exclaimed "*That's not my heart-rate*" and when it readjusted to hers after a few seconds, she said "*That's more like me*".

In many cases (12 instances counted in the video analysis and notes) the participants tried to do some exercise on-spot to see the elevation in their pulse rates. They expressed their satisfaction when they could notice the differences both in the MS band and on their projected animation of quicker heartbeat and blood flow. This solidified their perception of the heart being their *own*.

Reflection of Body Perception

On many occasions (19 instances), participants reflected about their own body comparing to the anatomical model, when their body became a canvas for the 3D model. Most of the participants tried to flex their biceps muscles and looked at the mirror to compare it on the anatomical model on screen. One of them commented, *"My muscles are appeared (sic) large on screen than they are, but this is appreciated."* The virtual muscular model used in the exhibition was purchased from a 3D model store, which depicts an ideal human male body. Overall our participants' activities highlighted their perception of how this *ideal human body* compared to their own body and their inherent desire to achieve one.

Our participants were also aware about how their body was different from the idealized anatomy model. Many of them found humor (18 instances) about the *six-pack* abdominal muscles of the model projected on them and said, "*I don't have a six-pack*". While some of them already knew, but the rest of them found it engaging to know, through discussion with the researchers, that all humans have a six-pack muscle structure, which is often not visible or as prominent as the anatomical model shown.

Participants' reflection about the body was not limited to how their body looked, but also how it functioned. For example, when their pulse rate was a bit deviated from the typical rest heartrate, some of the participants hurriedly explained that they "*were nervous*" or expressed uneasiness about it. A male visitor in a pair said to his friend: "*your heartrate is high [pointing to screen and then gesturing on her body that her heart is moving quickly, both laughs]*". She replied: "*It looks like I am nervous [laughs]*".

Another scenario was that sometimes the *Inside Out* system appeared to single out or draw attention to the participants' physical appearance. Examples include when the system failed to track a very tall person due to its limited vertical field of view, or when the projection of the anatomy model may have highlighted obesity for some participants. These are sensitive issues related to self-reflection, equal participation, and body shaming, that needs to be considered when designing for BAAC.

Gender

An interesting contrast appeared around the perception of gender of the anatomy models used in the *Inside Out* system. We happened to purchase a male anatomy model for the project, but one of the participants noted in the survey, *"Such an interesting way to experience the biology. Muscle system was very masculine, is there male female variations?"* Some of the visitors suggested incorporating a female anatomy model too and expressed their opinion that the projection should reflect the correct gender identity. One of the visitors explained about a female participant in the projection area, "*She does not understand, underneath she is a male [in the projected skeleton model]*". Such gender related concerns around the perception of body were further highlighted when some of our female participants (sometimes jokingly) covered their chest region when the bare muscles were projected on their body. Notably here, none of the male participants exhibited such gestures.

The model used for the exhibition is from an anatomy education project [12]. We found that the female virtual model by the same designer used exactly the same skeletal, circulatory and muscular (with the exception of added breast tissues) components. There was little difference between the male and female models. We discussed this concern with a physiotherapy lecturer, who confirmed that the current model was sufficient to be used in a physiotherapy classroom. Nonetheless, we anticipate that using only the male muscular model could lead to false representation. Therefore, throughout the study, we always clarified that the virtual projection was generic and did not result from scanning their bodies, to reduce false representation.

Creating Connectedness with Others

On the other hand, the *Inside Out* system highlighted the similarity that we all share in terms of our internal body organs, despite the differences in our outward appearances. Our visitors could not help but notice the similarity when they saw the projection on multiple people (including or excluding themselves). For example, one participant said about the projected skeleton view on her, "*Now I look like everyone else. We all have skeleton inside.*"

One interesting instance involved two friends participating together in the projection area. One participant who was wearing the MS band tried to elevate her heartrate by jogging on the spot in the projection area, while her friend watched. After a while they both noticed the heart rate increasing. While the system only tracked one participant's pulse rate, the other person (who did not exercise) saw the same projection of quicker heart-beating on her body, placed her hand on the projected heart, and reported, "*I feel my heartbeat growing!*" Another participant commented about

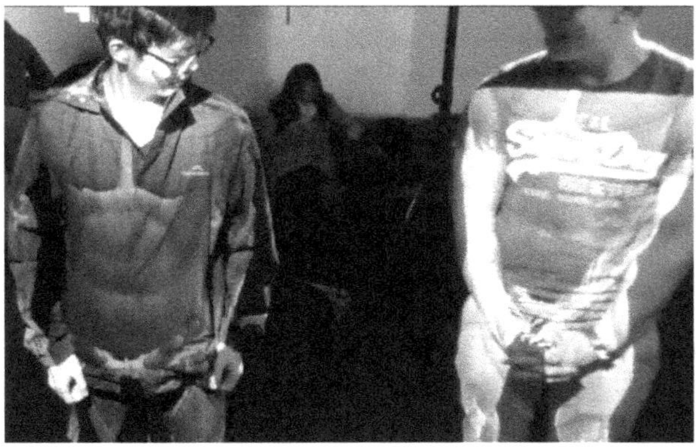

Figure 6: Two participants looking at the projection on each other.

the two of them while standing in the projection area, "*We are skeleton twins!*", thus expressing the solidarity of their relationship. This scenario was found in 13 other instances in the video analysis and observation notes.

The effect of the interaction loop can be seen here for physiological signal: by displaying an elevated heartrate on the body, *Inside Out* causes the participants to feel as if their heart rate actually increases.

Educational Reflections

While we did not have any learning objective in this public exhibition setting with this particular system, our visitors and participants noticed the potential of using it for educational purposes. While compared to another VR headset based project in the same exhibition, one participant explained that he was a teacher and thinks, "*for small group sizes, that's [VR] okay, but when you want to have a larger class size, this sort of arrangement is more practically useful*". There was a consensus that this (or similar) systems could benefit the learning experience in the classrooms at various levels of education and domains.

One participant responded in the survey: *"(the system) contextualize(s) internal body system beyond theoretical ideas and demonstrate(s) how it applies to my own body - particularly useful in classrooms and schools."* The on-body aspect of the system was interesting to the users, one of whom noted: "*I have done basic anatomy at uni, so have basic understanding. But seeing it on yourself makes it more real and relatable.*" Some of them thought similar system could be helpful in hospital settings too: "*An interesting and informative way to learn about body systems. Could be used to help explain medical conditions really well.*"

On-body projection complements the participant's understanding of the anatomy. One participant commented: "*To be able to see this system projected on to myself, was like seeing inside of my body. This perspective really helps to relate the internal to the external.*" *Another* participant reflected about the viewers' strong connection with the information presented on his/her body: "*It helped me relate the system to myself on a personal level, as opposed to learning from a text book*". Our participants expressed that such systems could benefit both the general public as well as people with extensive anatomical knowledge in disseminating their knowledge: "*By seeing my muscles and skeletons in a way I have never seen before, I gain insight into how my body looks and operates*", and "*[the system provides] clear understanding of the spatial arrangement of blood vessels, of the rate of blood flow to different regions and relationship with the skeleton.*". Another interesting response was: "*It made my previous learning feel more relevant and applicable. I didn't learn more, but learned more about what it meant.*"

Multiple Bodies as Canvas

From Spectator to Participant

There were three different ways people engaged with the system – a) as a visitor, observing others in the projection area, b) participating in the projection area alone, and c) participating in the projection area with another, thus watching the projection both on his/her body and on the other participant at the same time. These three scenarios create different types of experiences among our participants.

At the beginning, a person entering the installation area would see one of the researchers or another participant walking in the projection area and may notice that person being tracked through the anatomy model shown on the television screen. The researcher in attendance made the effort of standing in the projection area whenever there was no visitor nearby. The intention was for the eye-catching nature of the visualization to draw the attention of visitors passing by the installation area. Through observation, such practice generally prompted curious visitors to approach for a closer inspection, and the research team member would describe the system and answer their queries. Many visitors asked us about the technology, especially how the person is being tracked. Some even thought that the system was using "*X-Ray*" to detect and display internal body organs. The researcher assured them otherwise and invited them to participate by standing in the projection area.

The transition from a spectator to a participant happened in a single step. At any point that the visitor stepped into the projection area, the system would start tracking their body movement and project the virtual skeleton, muscle or circulatory system directly on their body. The system tracked up to two persons in the projection area (Fig. 6) and ignored the rest if there are more than 2 people in the Kinect's tracking range. As an example, when one visitor from a large group of friends finally joined the projection area, he exclaimed, *"Now I see what you were doing [and made various body postures while looking at the projection and TV screen]"*.

Between Visitors and Participants

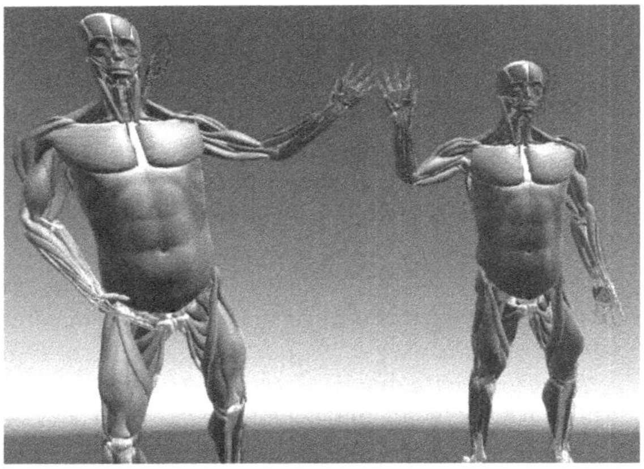

Figure 7: It was sometimes difficult to see who-is-who in the television screen.

Many of our participants visited in groups, and tested out the system in turns. Both the visualization on the body and the live tracking of the person shown on the large screen brought enjoyment to the experience for all group members. In these cases, the functionality of the system was not of much significance, but the representation on the body, as well as the awkward poses of skeleton, muscles, and blood circulatory system made it enjoyable as a group.

In one scenario, a group of 5-6 friends were trying out the system. A couple of them joined the projection area and started making some dance movements and jumps. Other group members suggested they make different body postures and everyone laughed. At one instance, the visitors of this group chanted *"muscles, muscles"* to the research team member to bring out the muscles projection. As we did so, everyone including the participant busted into laughter, possibly at the contrast to the not so well-built body of the participants. As this group were leaving, their tracked virtual bodies on the screen twisted into irregular shapes as the participants were going outside of the tracking range, and multiple audience members burst into laughter. Finally, they waved goodbye to their respective anatomical model on the television screen. Similar farewell gestures were noticed for some other participants. All these interactions highlight the lighthearted enjoyment of the visitors as a group.

Comparison between Different Display Options

Projection on Body versus Displayed on TV Screen

There was no consensus on which output is better, but our participants highlighted the general ways these two display modalities enable different experiences. While the TV screen could provide more details of the anatomical model due to the screen quality and image resolution, the on-body projection could create a sense of spatiality of the anatomical body parts among the participants.

This was evident, for example, when there were multiple people in the projection area. The participants sometimes momentarily lost the understanding of who was whom in the TV screen, and they made various hand gestures to match them with their avatars on the screen (Fig. 7). One of them explained: *"You are disconnected there [point at TV], whereas you can instantly see it [the connection with the anatomical system] on body."* In another instance, when two participants differed greatly in their heights, they explained, *"I could not see the height difference in the screen, but feels more personal on the body"*.

We placed a mirror in front of the participants to provide a viewpoint of themselves. Many participants (9 instances) commented on the mirror and the screen: *"I like the double view, people can stand there and watch you on the TV or projection and I can see myself on the mirror too. It's unlike the VR system downstairs [referring to another VR installation in the exhibition], where people can't see what I see on headset"*.

Significance of Clothes in the Body as a Canvas

There were many cases where the participants voluntarily altered their clothing to examine the projected information on their body. The exhibition occurred during the winter months where many visitors came in with layers of clothings. Without the researcher asking them to do so, many removed their coats or accessories (e.g., hand bag, scarf, etc.) to see the projection on a different layer of clothing. Some wanted to view it on different colored clothes. The visitors commented that circulatory system looked better on red clothes; the skeletal system looked great on black and the muscular system on white. The researcher often wore a white long sleeve t-shirt and white jeans on the day to demonstrate the projection on white clothing.

DISCUSSION

The themes of the finding largely address the four questions stated in the aims. Furthermore, the findings of the study highlight two effects of BAAC relating to the relationship between the consumer and information.

Connectedness

Our findings show that the *visitors had a strong connection with the information displayed on their body*. Many participants commented that when seeing the fast heartbeat animation on their body, they felt as if their heart actually beat faster. This happened especially during changeover of the MS Band when the device still showed the previous wearer's heart rate. Another observation emerged when two friends interacted in the projection space. We used a single MS band to drive two virtual bodies, resulting in a situation where a visitor would see their friend's heartbeat on their own body. After noticing the same projected animation of heartbeat on both of their bodies, many (mistakenly) exclaimed that both of them were in sync with their heartbeats, before understanding that the projection used one person's heartbeat only to project on both. The visitors in fact reached out to feel each other's heartbeats on the chest or on the wrist. We were unable to confirm if this were in fact actually happening, but we can draw the conclusion that *BAAC connects the visitors to the information and to one another*.

We argue that there are two scenarios from our study observations that demonstrated a strong sense of connectedness with the information and with one another. The first scenario relates to the contrasting observations that while the participants felt as if the virtual anatomy were their own body, it also caused them to reflect on their own physical body (*"I don't have a six-pack"*) in comparison.

The second scenario is when there are two bodies as canvas. Where two friends were interacting, both of them were told explicitly by the researcher that the visualization only shows one heart rate of whomever wore the MS band. Yet, the person, who was not wearing the band, empathized with the heartbeat animation on their body, both as their own (*"I feel my heart beat growing"*) and as the other's (*"We are skeleton twins"*).

In effect, BAAC causes the participants to have emotional responses inwards to the self and outwards to others. We observed *a meaningful connection with the information, the self, and others when one's body acts as a canvas.* We believe it was the connectedness that made the participants feel that the projection was their own skeleton, that their heartbeat was growing in tandem with the virtual heart, that their friend was their skeleton twin, that they look like everyone else because *"we all have skeleton inside"*, and that they wanted to wave goodbye to the skeletons.

We may attribute this connectedness towards the information loop and argue that the tight coupling of the interaction loop brings the body or the human closer to the information. The information in these two scenarios are visual body image and physiological signal. Through the close connection with visual body image and heartbeat, the individual reflects about themselves and connects to others.

The effects of body characteristics on information

Through *body as a canvas,* the characteristics and appearance of the human body can *change the way information is displayed by enacting changes through their bodies.* In this section, we discuss how the body's shape and clothing can affect the information.

The body effectively shapes the information. This type of interaction was only previously explored in other display technologies, including deformable [18] and shape changing display [8, 28]. Rasmussen et al. [28] approach the shape changing interface paradigm from a similar perspective as our body as a canvas: the convergence of both input and output onto the display technology. Their work outlines different types of changes in shape. We discuss the ones that apply to the human body.

Change in orientation is enacted through body movements. Change in volume applies to muscle contractions, such as arm flexing to increase the volume of the bicep muscle. We observed body flexing behaviors in many of our exhibition visitors. Even though we did not implement a proper animation of virtual muscle flexing, the visitors did report the visual illusion of seeing the virtual muscle increase in size when they flexed their arms. Shape change can be achieved through adding or subtracting units. Our BAAC concept extends to multiple bodies. There is an opportunity for further exploration of information displayed over multiple bodies. When there were two visitors in the space, we observed that many of them reach out to each other to see if the virtual avatars on the TV screen would do the same.

Compared to other display technology and methods, BAAC enriches the information. BAAC colors the information, through clothing. Participants altered their layers of clothing to see their virtual anatomy on different colored canvases, without being prompted by the researchers. BAAC complements the information, as seen by the educational reflections of *Inside Out* and as previously reported in the Augmented Studio system [11].

The exhibition setup of the current study does not allow a deeper informative analysis for research question Q4. A between-subject setup where the participants are exposed to the body projection and screen display separately would be preferred for a comparative analysis. We discuss Q4 in this study to highlight the breadth of research questions evoked by the BAAC concept. Considering the resolution of the model for instance, the projection on the body is relatively at lower resolution than the one on the TV screen (larger pixel size due to the distance between the projector and participants' bodies). How the fidelity is compensated by seeing the projection on their own body? How the on-body projection helps localizing parts of the anatomy model more accurately than when displayed on an external medium. These are some interesting questions that could inspire further studies on the BAAC concept.

CONCLUSION

Body as a canvas merges the role of input actuator and display on the human body. Interaction loop demonstrates a tight coupling of both roles, where interaction enacted through the body in response to the on-body information simultaneously changes the way the information is displayed. Through a public exhibition, we explore the concept via on-body projection of real time heartbeat animations and virtual skeletal muscular anatomy. Our findings suggest that information loop can be triggered with physiological body signal such as heart rate. Other aspects of the body characteristics and appearances such as body shape and clothing can complement the information that is displayed on it. The interactions among multiple bodies create fun and engaging experience. Body as a canvas also brings connectedness between the information and the body.

REFERENCES

1. Albert, W and Tullis, T. 2013. *Measuring the User Experience: Collecting, Analyzing, and Presenting Usability Metrics*. Newnes.
2. Bimber, O and Raskar, R. 2005. *Spatial Augmented Reality: Merging Real and Virtual Worlds.* CRC press.
3. Blum, T, Kleeberger, V, Bichlmeier, C and Navab, N. Mirracle: An Augmented Reality Magic Mirror System for Anatomy Education. *In Proceedings of Virtual Reality Short Papers and Posters (VRW),* 2012 IEEE. IEEE (2012), 115-116.
4. Chen, M, Gonzalez, S, Vasilakos, A, Cao, H and Leung, VC. Body Area Networks: A Survey. M*obile networks and applications* 16, 2 (2011): 171-193.
5. Conquergood, D. Rethinking Ethnography: Towards a Critical Cultural Politics. *Communications monographs* 58, 2 (1991): 179-194.
6. Dourish, P. 2004. *Where the Action Is: The Foundations of Embodied Interaction.* MIT press.
7. England, D. 2011. Whole Body Interaction: An Introduction. In *Whole Body Interaction*, David England (Ed.) Springer London (London), 2011, 1-5. http://dx.doi.org/10.1007/978-0-85729-433-3_1
8. Follmer, S, Leithinger, D, Olwal, A, Hogge, A and Ishii, H. Inform: Dynamic Physical Affordances and Constraints through Shape and Object Actuation. In *Proceedings of Proceedings of the 26th annual ACM symposium on User interface software and technology.* (2013), 417-426.
9. Gemperle, F, Kasabach, C, Stivoric, J, Bauer, M and Martin, R. Design for Wearability. In *Proceedings of Wearable Computers, 1998. Digest of Papers.* Second International Symposium on. IEEE (1998), 116-122.
10. Harrison, C, Tan, D and Morris, D. Skinput: Appropriating the Body as an Input Surface. In *Proceedings of the SIGCHI Conference on Human Factors in Computing Systems*. ACM (2010), 453-462. http://dx.doi.org/10.1145/1753326.1753394
11. Hoang, T, Reinoso, M, Joukhadar, Z, Vetere, F and Kelly, D. Augmented Studio: Projection Mapping on Moving Body for Physiotherapy Education. In *Proceedings of the 2017 CHI Conference on Human Factors in Computing Systems*. ACM (2017), 1419-1430.
12. Hoang, TN, Reinoso, M, Vetere, F and Tanin, E. Onebody: Remote Posture Guidance System Using First Person View in Virtual Environment. In *Proceedings of the 9th Nordic Conference on Human-Computer Interaction.* ACM (2016), 25.
13. Javornik, A, Rogers, Y, Gander, D and Moutinho, A. Magicface: Stepping into Character through an Augmented Reality Mirror. In *Proceedings of the 2017 CHI Conference on Human Factors in Computing Systems*. ACM (2017), 4838-4849. http://dx.doi.org/10.1145/3025453.3025722
14. Johnson, AS and Sun, Y. Spatial Augmented Reality on Person: Exploring the Most Personal Medium. In *Proceedings of International Conference on Virtual, Augmented and Mixed Reality.* Springer (2013), 169-174.
15. Jones, B, Sodhi, R, Murdock, M, Mehra, R, Benko, H, Wilson, A, Ofek, E, MacIntyre, B, Raghuvanshi, N and Shapira, L. Roomalive: Magical Experiences Enabled by Scalable, Adaptive Projector-Camera Units. In *Proceedings of the 27th annual ACM symposium on User interface software and technology.* ACM (Year), 637-644.
16. Kikuchi, T, Sugiura, Y, Masai, K, Sugimoto, M and Thomas, BH. Eartouch: Turning the Ear into an Input Surface. In *Proceedings of the 19th International Conference on Human-Computer Interaction with Mobile Devices and Services*. ACM (2017), 1-6. http://dx.doi.org/10.1145/3098279.3098538
17. Kilteni, K, Groten, R and Slater, M. The Sense of Embodiment in Virtual Reality. *Presence: Teleoperators and Virtual Environments* 21, 4 (2012): 373-387. http://dx.doi.org/10.1162/PRES_a_00124
18. Lee, S-S, Kim, S, Jin, B, Choi, E, Kim, B, Jia, X, Kim, D and Lee, K-p. How Users Manipulate Deformable Displays as Input Devices. *In Proceedings of the SIGCHI Conference on Human Factors in Computing Systems.* ACM (2010), 1647-1656. http://dx.doi.org/10.1145/1753326.1753572
19. Levisohn, AM. The Body as a Medium: Reassessing the Role of Kinesthetic Awareness in Interactive Applications. In *Proceedings of the 15th ACM international conference on Multimedia.* ACM (2007), 485-488. http://dx.doi.org/10.1145/1291233.1291352
20. Loke, L and Robertson, T. Moving and Making Strange: An Embodied Approach to Movement-Based Interaction Design. *ACM Transactions on Computer-Human Interaction* (TOCHI) 20, 1 (2013): 7.
21. Lopes, P, Ion, A, Mueller, W, Hoffmann, D, Jonell, P and Baudisch, P. Proprioceptive Interaction. In *Proceedings of the 33rd Annual ACM Conference on Human Factors in Computing Systems.* ACM (Year), 939-948.
22. Mercier-Ganady, J, Lotte, F, Loup-Escande, E, Marchal, M and Lécuyer, A. The Mind-Mirror: See Your Brain in Action in Your Head Using Eeg and Augmented Reality. In *Proceedings of Virtual Reality* (VR), 2014 iEEE. IEEE (Year), 33-38.
23. Mistry, P and Maes, P. Sixthsense: A Wearable Gestural Interface. In *Proceedings of ACM SIGGRAPH ASIA 2009 Sketches.* ACM (2009), 1-1. http://dx.doi.org/10.1145/1667146.1667160

24. Mistry, P and Maes, P. 2009. Unveiling the" Sixth Sense," *Game-Changing Wearable Tech*. TED.

25. Mistry, P, Maes, P and Chang, L. Wuw - Wear Ur World: A Wearable Gestural Interface. In *Proceedings of CHI '09 Extended Abstracts on Human Factors in Computing Systems*. ACM (2009), 4111-4116. http://dx.doi.org/10.1145/1520340.1520626

26. Mistry, P, Nanayakkara, S and Maes, P. Sparsh: Passing Data Using the Body as a Medium. In *Proceedings of the ACM 2011 conference on Computer supported cooperative work*. ACM (2011), 689-692. http://dx.doi.org/10.1145/1958824.1958946

27. Moeslund, TB and Granum, E. A Survey of Computer Vision-Based Human Motion Capture. *Computer vision and image understanding* 81, 3 (2001): 231-268.

28. Rasmussen, MK, Pedersen, EW, Petersen, MG and Hornbaek, K. Shape-Changing Interfaces: A Review of the Design Space and Open Research Questions. In *Proceedings of the SIGCHI Conference on Human Factors in Computing Systems*. ACM (2012), 735-744. http://dx.doi.org/10.1145/2207676.2207781

29. Saakes, D, Yeo, H-S, Noh, S-T, Han, G and Woo, W. Mirror Mirror: An on-Body T-Shirt Design System. In *Proceedings of the 2016 CHI Conference on Human Factors in Computing Systems*. ACM (Year), 6058-6063.

30. Sakata, M, Shiba, M, Maiya, K and Tadenuma, M. Human Body as the Medium in Dance Movement. *International Journal of Human–Computer Interaction* 17, 3 (2004): 427-444. http://dx.doi.org/10.1207/s15327590ijhc1703_7

Designing Interactive Visual Supports for Children with Special Needs in a School Setting

Issey Takahashi[1], Mika Oki[1], Baptiste Bourreau[1] and Kenji Suzuki[2]
Artificial Intelligence Laboratory
University of Tsukuba, Japan
[1]{takahashi, m.oki, bourreau}@ai.iit.tsukuba.ac.jp, [2] kenji@ieee.org

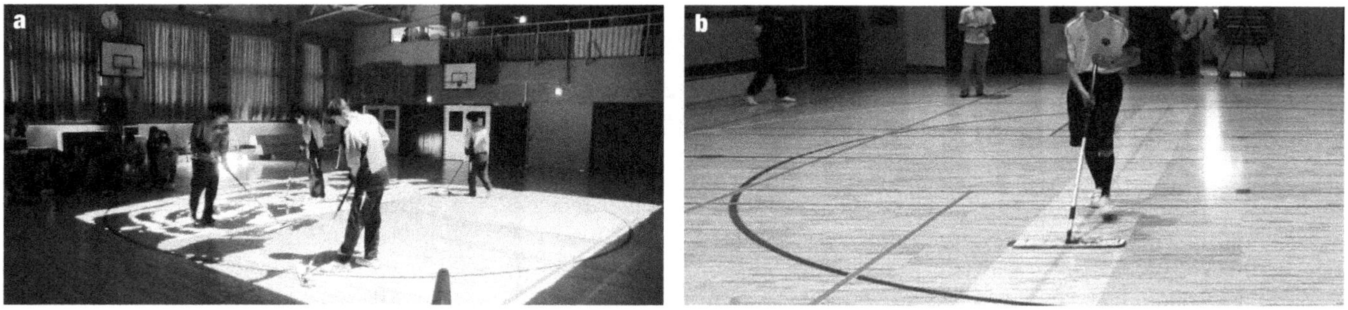

Figure 1. Interactive VS for cleaning in a special needs school. (a) Mop Game: a full-body interactive cleaning game. (b) Mop Guide: A floor-cleaning guidance tool.

ABSTRACT
Visual support (VS) is one of the effective ways of facilitating activities of children with neurodevelopmental disorder (ND). This paper reports on an interactive VS provided by a large-scale floor projection system in an augmented gymnasium called FUTUREGYM, designed for children with ND. The study focuses on students' cleaning, and two interactive VS activities—Mop Game, an exergame involving group cleaning, and Mop Guide, a VS for training about vocational cleaning—were designed with the teachers with the aim of motivating students toward cleaning and help them acquire fundamental cleaning skills. The study attempts to design a VS for cleaning that is suitable for the students by conducting an empathic design approach, which helps us understand what are the problems, obtain new perspectives, and gather ideas into demonstrative prototypes by sharing values and thoughts with the teachers and their students. This is a case study of deploying an empathic design approach in a special needs school setting.

Author Keywords
Interactive technology, Empathic design approach, visual support, autism spectrum disorder, special-needs education

DIS '18, June 9–13, 2018, Hong Kong
© 2018 Association for Computing Machinery.
ACM ISBN 978-1-4503-5198-0/18/06...$15.00
https://doi.org/10.1145/3196709.3196747

ACM Classification Keywords
H.5.3 Group and Organization Interfaces; H.5.1 Multimedia Information Systems; K.4.2 Social Issues.

INTRODUCTION
Autism spectrum disorder (ASD) is a complex neuro-developmental disorder (ND). About one in 68 children is diagnosed with ASD according to the Center for Disease Control and Prevention [12]. Children with ASD display difficulty in communication; demonstrate hardship relating to people, things, or events; and show repetitive body movements or behaviors [2]. Children with ASD have been characterized as visual learners, in that they process visual information more effectively than auditory information [31][43]. Visual supports (VS) such as pictures, lines, and spots on the floor, timers, or activity schedules are helpful in maintaining attention, clarifying the meaning of instructions by verbal communication, and preparing for an activity or transition for children with ASD [7][28][32]. In the literature review, VS using digital methods such as large group displays [41], mobile devices [11][41], or personal recording technologies [38] were reported. These digital methods are not meant to replace the analog-based methods but to complement existing methods with its usability. They help reduce caregivers' difficulties and save time spent on creating, distributing, and using analog-based methods. In recent years, Mixed Reality (MR), which makes it possible to create and develop worlds in which physical and digital elements are merged in the same space [23], has offered a new type of physical support in the sense that they integrate the benefits of both analog and digital supports [16][25][26][30]. MR can support children with ASD in a variety of ways such as to facilitate social initiation and collaborative behaviors [26], to understand that children

with ASD are challenged by a sensory overload and by unwillingness to a variety of stimuli [22], or to sustain children's selective attention [16]. Although numerous studies using MR for VS have been conducted, designing MR-based VS for physical activities in a special needs school setting is challenging. This is because designing special needs education requires a careful decision-making process involving learning about the insights, problems, needs, or abilities of users in order to provide an appropriate solution for them. The main contribution of the work is designing interactive VS in a real context, which is a special needs school setting, by involving real users who are children with ND and their teachers.

This paper reports on a case study of designing interactive VS for tool use involving a mop, which are provided by a large-scale floor projection system installed in an augmented gymnasium called FUTUREGYM for children with ND [40]. The study focuses on cleaning, because it is one of the vocational skills that either individual with or without ND should acquire as they are growing up. In addition, cleaning at the school is related to accountability and social responsibility.

An empathic design approach was deployed in a special needs school at Otsuka (Otsuka School), which is affiliated with University of Tsukuba. The school provides systematic special education courses consistent throughout preschool to high school for children with special needs, mainly ASD and/or intellectual disorders (ID). As a result of the design exercise with the teachers, the VS in Figure 1 were confirmed to help children with mild to moderate ID and/or ASD with a very low cognitive profile to:

- participate in a cleaning activity willingly
- experience cooperative behaviors in cleaning
- understand the procedure of floor cleaning
- manipulate a mop to keep it within a track for cleaning the floor

The activities listed above are difficult to instruct children with ND in using verbal or paper-based descriptions, but the interactive VS provided by FUTUREGYM helps compensate for the difficulty. The former two findings can be applied for training group cleanings (i.e., Mop Game). The latter two findings would contribute to train vocational skills in cleaning (i.e., Mop Guide) for children with ND. The case study highlights the importance of the empathic design approach for designing technology-assisted VS for children with special needs in a school setting.

This paper begins by summarizing related works on technology-based VS. Then, the design process conducted in the study is described and the viability tests of two VS, "Mop Game" and "Mop Guide," are reported. A summarized discussion and conclusions of the outcomes obtained from the study are presented. Lastly, research prospects and future works are mentioned.

RELATED WORKS

The main challenge of this study is to design interactive VS for children's physical activities in a special needs school setting. The review starts from outlining the benefits of using technologies for children with ASD. Then, the study approach is illustrated by referring to findings of the prior works using MR and interactive technologies brought into school settings.

The use of technology in the research and treatment of ASD has been increasing since a publication in 1973 [14], appearing in broad fields from social to technical, and is highly accepted among individuals with ASD due to the predictable and structured feature of computer-based systems offering immediate and consistent feedback [3]. It also provides opportunities to access abundant information from various resources and to adapt contents and tasks to the demands and capabilities of each child with tailored feedbacks [24][35]. Among the use of technology for children with ASD, spatial MR is a strong and effective tool for providing VS. It enables overlaying graphical information on real-world objects [6], and makes it possible to scale naturally up to groups of children, which allows a collective experience among children. One of the first spatial MR projects for children with ASD is "MEDIATE," which provides a sense of control for children with severe autism. A safe and controlled space using interactive rear-projection screens gives the children a chance to play and explore enjoyably [30]. An exergame, "SpaceHunters," provides foot-eye coordination exercises for children with ASD in an interactive space [13]. The game facilitates the development of social interactions by requiring collaboration among the participants to achieve a goal. A full-body serious game, "Lands of Fog," fosters social interaction for children with ASD using a large floor projection 6 m in diameter made with two projectors [25][26]. The game uses interactive virtual elements to facilitate joint attention and collaborative behaviors among children. These prior studies have demonstrated the prospects for the use of interactive projection for children with ASD to enhance positive behaviors during physical movements in a large space.

However, many of the MR projects were deployed in a laboratory setting, which is not an environment children are familiar with in the course of normal, everyday activities. Specializing in the care of children with ASD, school settings can often benefit greatly from using a smart space equipped with interactive technologies [19][41]. These environments are primarily attached to the physical domain in which the children live and interact together with the teachers providing them care and support. Therefore, solutions using MR could be useful in assisting the children's and the teachers' needs. In the literature review, numerous interactive technologies were found to be brought into school settings. Tentori et al. developed three displays and brought them to a classroom to explore ways to increase behavioral awareness, trigger social interactions, and promote group work [42]. A serious game for children with ASD called ECHOES facilitates exploration and acquisition of social interaction skills with a system based on an avatar in a multi-touch display, which can interact with the users for practicing and learning joint attention abilities in a school setting [4]. Bhattacharya et al. designed motion-based activities using an electronic whiteboard with a Kinect to engage students with ASD in classroom settings [5]. They reported that the collaborative game supports the initiation of social activities between peers, and brings out new body movements that children were not observed to make outside of gameplay. Although these projects are successfully enhancing children's positive behaviors by using interactive displays, there are few projects deploying interactive technologies in a large space in a school setting. One of the spatial MR projects brought to a large school space is "Lü" from the Canadian company SAGA [34]. The project uses large interactive walls in a school gymnasium for providing spatial games for children. It introduced the concept of interactivity and visual feedback making physical activity more fun and accessible to all types of children. However, it is not a project that is specialized in the support of children with special needs. It focuses on providing enjoyment of physical activities to neuro-typical children through games. In addition, the project attempts to ensure children's attention to virtual elements provided on walls, and deploy an intervention in the context of the virtual environment. In contrast, FUTUREGYM aims to assist children in paying attention to objects or people around them. Furthermore, FUTUREGYM provides VS from the ceiling toward the floor; therefore, individual VS can be overlaid on objects around them. It helps users navigate or be guided to a certain state as well as facilitating voluntary and wayfinding behaviors.

Designing interactive VS for children with ND that help in their physical activities in a large school space is not present in the literature. Although there are some projects in the literature that applied VS for physical coaching or training such as basketball [1], bouldering [18], or table tennis [36], projects specialized for individuals with ND in a school setting have not been undertaken yet. Especially, VS that can be applied for group activities or vocational training in a school setting are beneficial in for children's daily life and their future careers. This study shows an example of designing interactive VS that give them these benefits.

DESIGN PROCESS

The teachers at the school were habituated to current conditions, and they did not often think to ask for a new solution and had difficulty envisaging solutions due to lack of familiarity with the possibilities offered by new technologies. Therefore, an empathic design approach, which is an effective design approach for such situation [21][15], was taken in this study. An empathic design approach relies on observations that demonstrates a kind of common-sense approach, which helps inspire researchers and users involved in creative challenges [37]. "Empathize" is often adopted as the first phase in a design formulation method that aims at problem finding, because building empathy toward end users and understanding what is important to them is the foundation of the design process. Although the expression differs among researchers or designers, there are five key phases to structuring the design process: "Problem finding," "Sense-making," "Ideation," "Prototype," and "Viability test." Usually, the design process starts from obtaining an empathetic view of what the problem is, to possible new interpretations, to assembling ideas into demonstrable tests and then examining the viability in a reasonable use case [8][20][29].

Five researchers from University of Tsukuba, 21 teachers ranging from preschool to high school, and 64 students at Otsuka School were involved in the design decision-making process. The activities were organized with the approval of the ethical committee of the Education Bureau of Laboratory Schools, University of Tsukuba.

Problem finding

More than half of the study period was spent in this first phase of the empathic design approach. The researchers visited the school 20 times in seven months and conducted eight occasional observations and interviews of daily school classes in the gymnasium, five research meetings with the teachers, and seven workshops using the FUTUREGYM environment. The environment in a special needs school setting helped the researchers to identify needs that the students and teachers themselves may not recognize. It also helped the researchers to find ways to meet those needs by conducting observation in the users' own environment — in the course of normal, everyday routines. The problem-finding phase started with onsite observations and oral interviews in daily classes to pick up some issues or interests children have, and confirmed the findings during meetings with teachers. Then, workshops were organized according to the findings obtained from the classrooms. Examples of activities used in the workshops are Constellation Game (Figure 2a), a group exergame with a shared goal, and Circle-Run, involving group running with animal-shaped pacemakers (Figure 2b). Constellation Game helped us to notice that a game with a shared goal has a potential to facilitate an opportunity to trigger helping

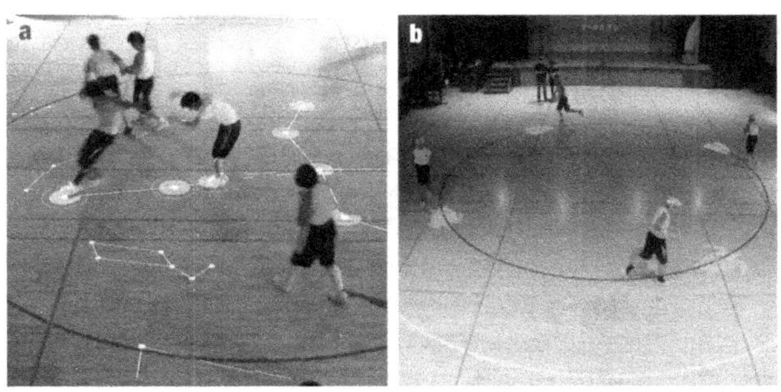

Figure 2. Examples of workshops for problem finding. (a) Constellation Game. (b) Circle-Run.

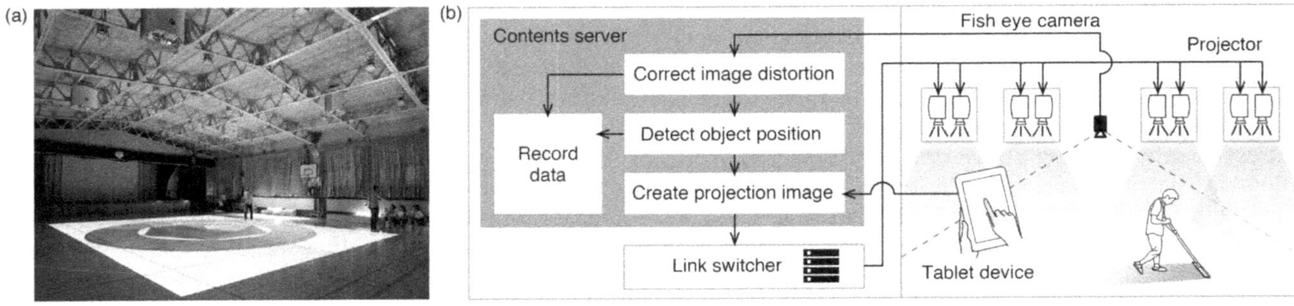

Figure 3. (a) Interactive floor projection of the FUTUREGYM (Projection size: 8 × 11 m). (b) Configuration of the interactive floor projection system.

behavior by providing a game with a shared goal. Circle-Run demonstrated the way of support in the context of interpersonal interaction among children through a group running. The visual guidance on the floor effectively escorted children to experience cooperative running. The researchers and teachers observed a trend that their running behavior improved after the experience of cooperative running with the visual guidance. More specific explanations of these activities are reported in [40].

By observing what the children do and how they interact with the FUTUREGYM environment in the workshops, the researchers and the teachers attempted to obtain clues about how the students react and feel as well as to learn their needs. Additionally, the workshops helped the researcher to show and explain the functioning of the system to the teachers and students to make them understand what can be done by the system. It also played an important role building a good partnership between the researchers and Otsuka School.

Sense-making and Ideation

In the problem-finding phase, the researchers and teachers confirmed that the students showed strong interests toward objects with various movements and colors projected on the floor. This finding made it possible to help the students practice complex actions such as moving and stopping at a certain spot or running through a zigzag course, which are difficult to instruct them in verbally. With this clue, the researchers and teachers came up with an idea to apply interactive VS for cleaning, in which the students often face difficulties.

Cleaning is an important activity not only for the students' daily lives, but also for their future careers. Many of the students at the school get a job related to cleaning after graduation. Prior studies also reported that one of the major postsecondary employment experiences among young individuals with ASD and ID is cleaning [33]. Therefore, training in cleaning skills is one of the important subjects at the school. However, the teachers encounter difficulties in teaching them cleaning skills. They require tremendous time and effort to teach and motivate them to clean using verbal and paper-based instructions at the school. Although a number of technology-based cleaning supports have been reported in the literature such as video instruction by an interactive white board [39] or cleaning training by a virtual reality system with a head-mounted display [9], the use of VS for cleaning with a floor projection system has not been investigated yet. One of the advantages of using a floor projection system is that it overlays visual aids on real objects, which creates a more intuitive VS compared to display-based applications.

In this phase of the design process, the researchers and teachers decided to develop a full-body interactive cleaning game named Mop Game (Figure 1a) and floor-cleaning guidance tool named Mop Guide (Figure 1b) using the interactive floor projection system in the FUTUREGYM. Mop Game aims to stimulate students' interests in cleaning tools and actions with a game that enables them to paint colors on the floor or erase objects on the floor with a lightning mop. Mop Guide helps the students understand the process of cleaning with a mop by providing a mop course on the floor as well as helping them manipulate a mop to keep inside a track on the floor.

The initial idea of Mop Game and Mop Guide was brought by the teachers who are responsible for vocational trainings in the school. They came up with an idea to apply the VS to cleaning after they experienced the workshops. Several idea illustrations and descriptions were made in ideate sessions with the teachers, and the prototypes were designed with their collaborative decision-making. The following sections describe prototype and viability test of Mop Game and Mop Guide.

A Prototype of Mop Game

A prototype of Mop Game was developed using the FUTUREGYM system. FUTUREYGYM has an interactive floor projection size of approximately 8 × 11 m (approx. 545 inches). There are eight digital light processing (DLP) projectors (Panasonic, PT-DW100W) equipped under the ceiling of the gymnasium (Figure 3a). Figure 3b shows the configuration of the floor projection system. The projection image created from the content server (CPU: 3.30 GHz, RAM: 16 GB, OS: Windows 8.1 Pro) is sent to the display server and monitored on a display using a graphics card (NVIDIA, NVS 510). The image on the display is projected by the projectors through a link switcher (Panasonic, ET-

Figure 4. Mop Game: erasing trash on the floor.

YFB200). A fish-eye camera (Point Grey BFLY-PGE-13S2M-CS, Lens: M13VM246) is fixed in the center of the ceiling. The images collected from the camera are used to observe children's behavior and movements. Distortion of the camera image was removed using OpenCV 3.2 in C++ (Visual Studio 2015). A router is connected to the content server; therefore, mobile devices can communicate wirelessly with the content server to control the projection images.

The mop, which is used in daily school cleaning, is equipped with an LED bar (Length: 600 mm) to increase the difference in light intensity from the surroundings in order to enhance the ceiling camera's ability to detect the mop position. The processing on the content sever is implemented as follows.

(a) Homography transformation
(b) Detection of mop position
(c) Reflecting the projection image according to the mop position

In step (a), the projection field in the camera image is cropped after binarization of the image according to the position of pylons located at the corners of the field. Then, the perspective distortion of the cropped image is corrected with a homography transformation matrix. In step (b), the contour of a moving object is detected after image frame differentiation of 10 Hz. A mop is recognized by the size of the region in the contour. The mop position is defined as the center of the contour. The projection image is projected at the mop position for the painting game and erased according to the mop position for the erasing game. These procedures were coded in Processing 3.3.1.

Although the prototype was developed by the researchers, game stories, rules, color layouts, and illustrations were designed by the teachers.

A Viability Test of Mop Game

A viability test was conducted with 24 high-school students with mild/moderate ASD and/or ID (15-18 years old) in order to confirm that they like it and it motivates them to participate voluntarily as well as facilitating social interactions. The high school students, who are taking vocational skill training classes, were selected in the test, because they are required to train cooperative working skill for their post graduation lives.

Figure 5. Examples of cooperative behaviors observed in Mop Game. (a) Sweeping a mop side by side with other members. (b) Collectively moving a mop to unswept areas.

Two types of games were organized in the test: floor painting (Figure 1a) and erasing trash on the floor (Figure 4). There were three rounds of each type of game with groups of four students. The students were instructed to paint a color all over the field (7.4 m^2) for the floor painting game or to erase the trash on the floor (500 objects) for the trash erasing game. By referring to Bratman's three features of cooperative activities [10], the game is designed as to have 1) mutual responsiveness, 2) commitment to the joint activity, and 3) commitment to mutual support, which are key elements to create a shared cooperative activity. The start and end of the game was announced to the students by a teacher's whistle. At the end of each game, the time took for the completion of the task was presented to the students.

Results

Even though many of the students have difficulty concentrating their attention on a task in daily classes, all the students completed the game tasks without giving up. Even a student with severe ID and rare interest in anything participated in the game with the other students. When changing participants between rounds, many students raised their hands to be picked. When their names were called by a teacher, they voluntarily grabbed the mops, something rarely seen in their daily cleaning situations. Moreover, soon after the time taken for task completion was announced to the students, they showed positive emotional expressions such as jumping, raising hands, or clapping. Accordingly, the game is assumed to attract the students and trigger their voluntary behaviors.

Furthermore, some social interactions were observed during the game such as sweeping a mop side by side with other members (Figure 5a) or collectively moving their mops to unswept areas (Figure 5b). These positive behaviors are important for developing their social skills, which the teachers always want to facilitate. It is considered to have been brought on by setting a shared goal in the game. The teachers were pleased with the result of the students showing positive behaviors through the game.

A Prototype of Mop Guide

The students often have difficulty remembering a mop route as well as manipulating a mop when there are no visual cues such as tapelines or spot makers on the floor. Therefore, the teachers requested the researchers to develop a function to provide mop courses on the floor.

A prototype of Mop Guide, which provides VS for learning about cleaning procedure and tool use, was developed using the FUTUREGYM system. A cleaning field was organized with a floor size of 4 × 8.7 m (Figure 6). Four pylons were placed at each corner of the field to indicate the cleaning area. A mop course was projected on the floor as shown in Figure 1b to guide students where to move the mop. The mop course was colored with white in order to increase the light intensity to have better visibility of the floor. A red line was drawn in the center of the mop course to indicate the center position of the mop head. The projection was controlled by a tablet device (Nexus 9, Android 5.1.1). An

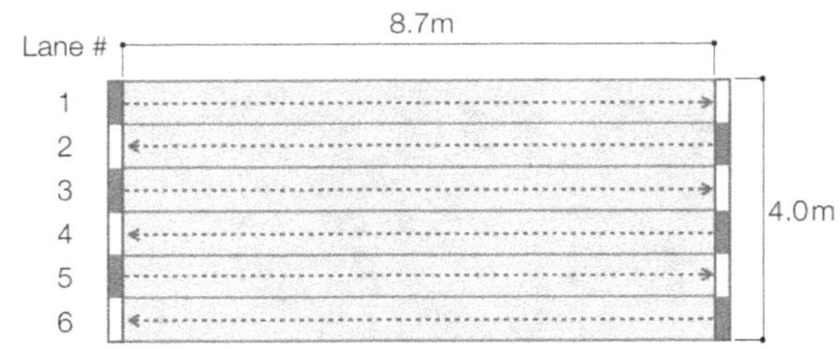

Figure 6. Size of the cleaning field and the direction of mop movement in each lane.

LED (red color) bar was equipped on the mop head in order to increase the precision of the mop position tracking for data analysis.

A Viability test of Mop Guide

In order to investigate whether Mop Guide helps them understand the procedure of cleaning and manipulating a mop to keep it inside a track for cleaning the floor, a viability test was conducted in cooperation with two male students with mild/moderate ASD and/or ID. Student A was 15 years old with FSIQ-50 and VCI-58 (WISC-IV), and student B was 16 years old with FSIQ-42 and VCI-51 (WISC-IV). They were selected as subjects of the test because they are willing to get a job related to cleaning after the graduation, but have difficulty leaning procedures of cleaning as well as tool use.

The feasibility of Mop Guide for cleaning instructions was investigated by comparing percentages of swept areas in the cleaning field before and after intervention with the VS indicating the sweeping lanes, as shown in Figure 1b. The

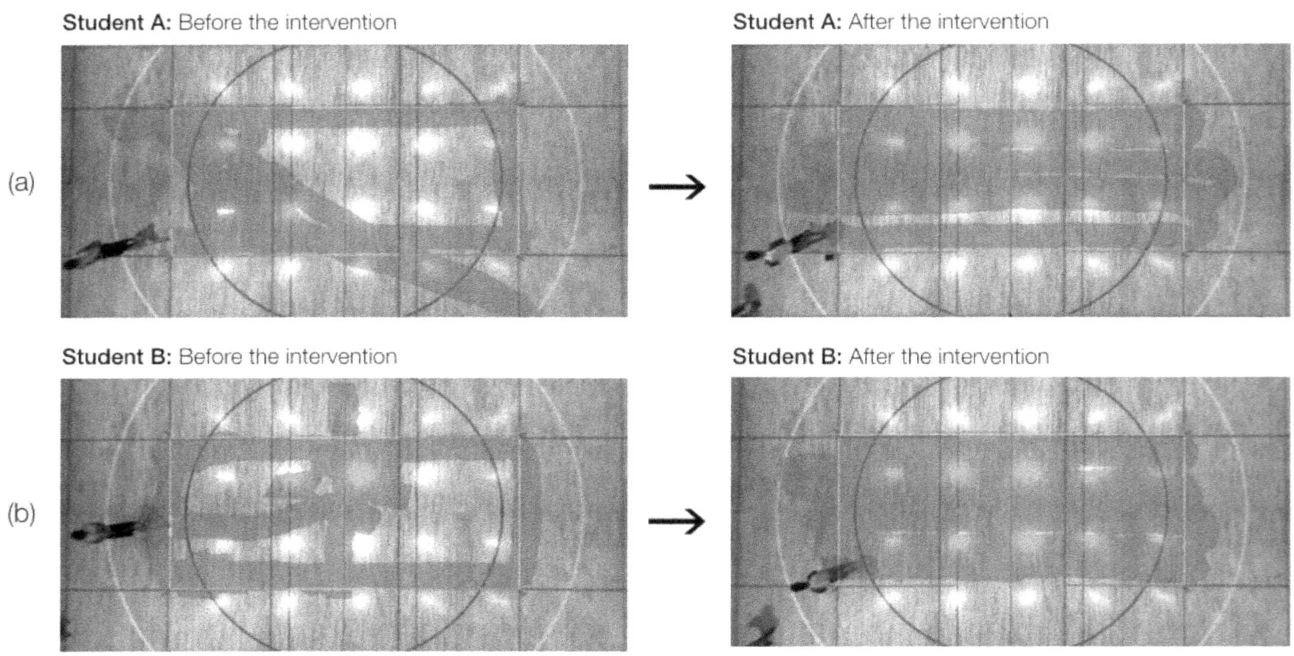

Figure 7 Trajectories of the mop in the cleaning field before and after the intervention using the VS (Red parts indicate the trajectory of the mop). (a) Student A. (b) Student B.

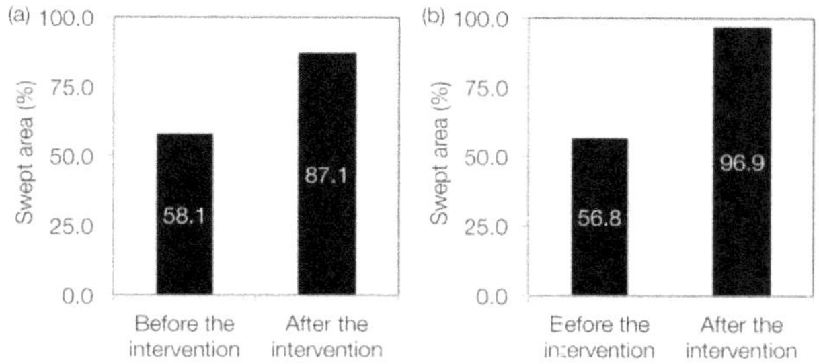

Figure 8. Comparisons of percentages of swept area between before and after the intervention with the VS. (a) Student A. (b) Student B.

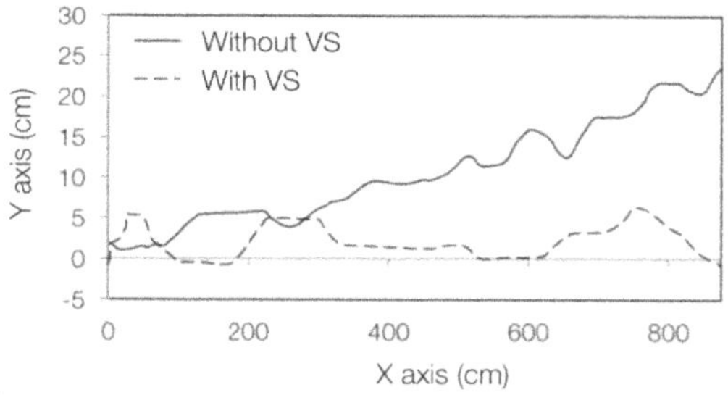

Figure 9. A representative example of walking out of sweeping lane (Student B) without the VS. Zero on the Y axis is the center of the lane.

students were verbally instructed by their teachers to sweep the whole area of the field with the mops before the intervention. The teachers instructed the students as they do in daily cleaning classes. Then, the intervention using Mop Guide was applied to the students. Each lane was highlighted on the floor one by one by the projection system with the direction indicated in Figure 6. The VS indicates the sweeping lane with a red line in the center as shown in Figure 1b. After the intervention, the students were verbally instructed to sweep the whole area of the field again. Then, the trajectories of the mop in the cleaning field and the percentages of swept areas in the field before and after the intervention were compared.

The second test, investigation of how well does Mop Guide help the students to manipulate a mop to keep in a track for cleaning the floor, was done by comparing deviations of distance between the center of a mop head and the center of the lane with (the intervention) and without (before the intervention) the VS.

Results

Figure 7 shows trajectories of the mop in the field (the highlighted parts) before and after the intervention using the VS. There are a lot of unswept areas in the field before the intervention. It is possibly because they did not understand the teachers' verbal instruction. However, the unswept areas decreased after the intervention. Figure 8 shows the comparison by using the percentages of swept areas by the mop in the field between before and after the intervention. Both students improved their coverage after the intervention using the VS. Mop Guide showed that it is potentially useful for helping the students understand a cleaning procedure compare to the instruction only with the verbal descriptions.

The viability test of the prototype also indicated that Mop Guide helps them to manipulate a mop to keep it inside a track for sweeping the floor. Figure 9 shows a representative example of walking out of a sweeping lane. The lines on the graph indicate trajectories of the center of the mop head. Zero on the Y-axis is the center of the lane. The mop head was largely driven out from the lane without the VS (solid line) compared to the trial with the VS (broken line). In the trial without the VS, the mop head

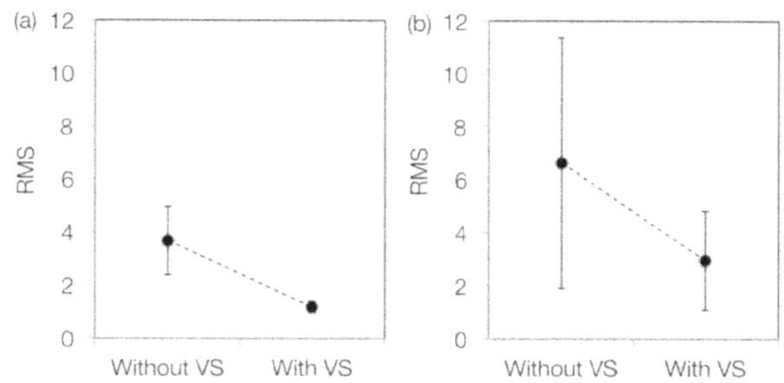

Figure 10. Comparisons of RMS with and without the VS. The bar represents the standard deviation. (a) Student A. (b) Student B.

drifted to the positive side of the Y axis, and the gap between the center of the mop head and the center of the lane was approximately 25 cm when the mop head reached the edge of the field. In order to quantify the deviation of the mop head, the RMS(i) (Root Mean Square) of the distance between the mop head and the lane for student i was calculated as follows:

$$RMS(i) = \sqrt{\frac{1}{N}\sum_{s}^{N} D_i(s)^2} \quad (1)$$

Here, $D_i(s)$ represents the distance between the center of the mop and the center of the lane at frame s. i and N indicate the number of students and number of frames in the videos from the start line to the goal line, respectively.

Figure 10 shows comparisons of RMS with and without the VS obtained from lane number 2 to 5 in Figure 6. RMS for lane numbers 1 and 6 were not included in the graph because there are straight lines beside the lanes that could affect the result. The bars on the graph represent the standard deviation. Both of the students showed smaller RMS during sweeping trials with the VS. The result indicates that the VS prevents the mop being driven out of the lane. It potentially helps the students stabilize manipulation of the mop head.

DISCUSSION

The case study represented the empathic design approach, which shifts the design process from the researchers environment to the special needs school setting for designing an MR-based VS for children with ND. The field-dependent design decision-making process helped the researchers put information in context and find contextual cues from the school environment, which is crucial to understanding figurative and literal relations between objects in the environment. The careful observations of the students and repetitive consultations with the teachers led us to design Mop Game and Mop Guide. After the prototype was built, the viability of Mop Game was tested and we confirmed that the game attracts the students' attention and triggers their active participation in the game. It has also been confirmed that Mop Game has the potential to help students focus their attention on cleaning behaviors with an element of fun as well as to facilitate social interactions such as teamwork and cooperative behavior. One of the major differences compared to related games, for example, SpaceHunter [13] or Lands of Fog [25], is that Mop Game is deployed in a special needs school setting, which is a familiar environment for the students. It is one of the best places for the students who are sensitive to unfamiliar spaces or equipment. Mop Game is also advantageous for the teachers because the game can be organized simply by overlaying projection images over daily cleaning surfaces, which allows them to include the game in their daily cleaning classes.

Mop Guide was also tested for feasibility. The result showed that it is potentially useful for instructing them in cleaning procedures. The teachers involved in the cleaning experiment were surprised to see that just one trial with the VS made them understand the procedure of mop cleaning. They told us that the clear and simple instruction helped keep their concentration and motivation. The result implies that it is not only practical for teaching the procedure of floor cleaning, but also helps them maintain motivation to clean it. It is important to note that the VS does not directly improve their cleaning skill, but guides them to experience the ideal outcome of instruction given by the teachers. It helps children eliminate or minimize taking corrective actions, which contributes to the errorless learning and eliminates or reduces errors, thereby helping children maintain their motivation and reinforcing learning [27].

The prototype test of Mop Guide also indicated that the VS helps them manipulate a mop to keep it inside a track for sweeping the floor. This is useful for coaching precise cleaning. In the daily classes, the teachers use the edges of floorboards to teach them to sweep straight, but they find it difficult. Mop Guide has the possibility of making it more intuitive and easy for the students to practice the task. The teachers requested us to project the sweeping trajectories in real time for better understanding of their task results. They also suggested us to include furniture and partitions in the field to demonstrate a room-cleaning scenario to train in various types of cleaning skills. These requirements will be considered in the next step of our research.

In this study, the FUTUREGYM environment played an important role. The researchers could not have known the problems, values, thoughts, or requirements that the teachers and their students had without the environment. The relocation of the design platform from a laboratory setting to the school setting helped us design Mop Game and Mop Guide. It also gave us a physical advantage. Both of the VS required a large space, which could not have been possible without the environment. Moreover, conducting activities in the school setting, which is the students' accustomed environment, helped them get used to the floor projection and enabled the teachers to respond immediately to some issues or difficulties that might have been faced by their students. Because the school gymnasium is bound to the physical domain in which the students learn and receive support from the teachers, it is an ideal place to deploy the VS for their needs.

Limitations

The importance of the empathic design approach has been demonstrated for designing technology-assisted VS in the special needs school setting through this case study. However, it was also found that conducting design consultations in the users' environment included some challenges. It is difficult to evaluate the impact of participation on the outcomes of the process, as shown in [17], which was represented by the impact of setting a control condition in the from of a non-empathic approach to design. In addition, it is difficult to judge how the teachers and students contributed directly to the design process and to describe how their involvement varied over the different phases of design decision-making. It is difficult to quantify if the students' engagement toward daily cleaning improved or if their ideas, opinions, or actions were incorporated in the outcome. We believe that the importance of the design approach relies more on learning about users' insights, problems, needs, abilities, strengths, and providing an appropriate solution for them with a careful decision-making process. Each of the design phases helped us understand the teachers and their students, and improved the quality of the VS. Since it is difficult to determine exactly what is the best for children with ND, careful consultations with their close teachers are a reliable way to formulate the ideal solution.

CONCLUSION

This case study highlights the importance of empathy-centered practices for designing technology-assisted VS for children with special needs in a special needs school setting. It represents an example of how technology can be designed to accommodate human behavior in a school. Mop Game and Mop Guide were designed with the teachers through the design process of Problem finding, Sense-making, Ideation, and Prototype. The careful design consultation in the school setting helped the researchers and teachers know what the problem is, obtain new interpretations, gather ideas into demonstrable prototypes, and then test the viability in a real use case. As a result of the design process with the teachers, Mop Game has been confirmed to help children with mild or moderate ID and/or ASD with very low cognitive profiles to participate in a cleaning activity voluntarily as well as to experience cooperative behaviors in cleaning. Mop Guide has been tested to have the potential to help children understand the procedure of floor cleaning and manipulate a mop to keep it inside the track for cleaning floors. These activities are difficult to instruct children with ND by verbal or analog-based graphical descriptions, but the MR-based VS helps to compensate for this difficulty. Mop Game can be potentially applied to train team workouts or group activities as well. It can contribute to vocational training in cleaning for the students' future careers.

Although Mop Game and Mop Guide are assumed to be feasible, the VS are still under design and require repetitive design cycles to improve usability. Our future research is dedicated to improving the quality of these interactive VS. In addition, there are many kinds of cleaning tasks besides mop cleaning such as table polishing, vacuum cleaning, or toilet cleaning. We are planning to develop VS for the other cleaning tasks according to the cleaning textbook provided by Tokyo Metropolitan Board of Education [44].

Furthermore, we will keep exploring the extended use of MR-based VS that enables the children to improve in their school environment using the empathic design approach.

ACKNOWLEDGMENTS

This research was supported by JST-CREST Grant Number JPMJCR14E2, Japan. The authors would like to thank the teachers and students of the special needs school at Otsuka for their participation in the design activities deployed in FUTUREGYM and the implementation of the experiments. We are grateful to Mao Asada for assistance with the development of Mop Game.

REFERENCES

1. AKQA. 2017. Nike Rise 2.0. Retrieved August 30, 2017 from https://www.akqa.com/work/nike/rise-2015/
2. American Psychiatric Association. 2013. *Diagnostic and statistical manual of mental disorders (DSM-5®)*. American Psychiatric Pub. https://doi.org/10.1176/appi.books.9780890425596.dsm01
3. Nuria Aresti-bartolome and Begonya Garcia-zapirain. 2014. Technologies as Support Tools for Persons with Autistic Spectrum Disorder : A Systematic Review. *International Journal of Environmental Research and Public Health* 11, 8: 7767–7802. https://doi.org/10.3390/ijerph110807767
4. Sara Bernardini, Kas´ka Porayska-Pomsta, and Tim J. Smith. 2014. ECHOES : An intelligent serious game for fostering social communication in children with autism ECHOES : an Intelligent Serious Game for Fostering Social Communication in Children with Autism. *Information Sciences* 264: 41–60. https://doi.org/10.1016/j.ins.2013.10.027
5. Arpita Bhattacharya, Mirko Gelsomini, Patricia Pérez-Fuster, Gregory D. Abowd, and Agata Rozga. 2015. Designing motion-based activities to engage students with autism in classroom settings. In *Proceedings of the 14th International Conference on Interaction Design and Children - IDC '15*, 69–78. https://doi.org/10.1145/2771839.2771847
6. O Bimber and R Raskar. 2005. *Spatial Augmented Reality: Merging Real and Virtual Worlds*. CRC Press.
7. Nicole Blubaugh and Joanne Kohlmann. 2006. TEACCH Model and Children With Autism. *Teaching Elementary Physical Education* 17, 6: 16–19.
8. Thomas Both and Dave Baggereor. 2017. *d.school Bootcamp Bootleg*.
9. Lal Bozgeyikli, Evren Bozgeyikli, Matthew Clevenger, Andrew Raij, Redwan Alqasemi, Stephen Sundarrao, and Rajiv Dubey. 2015. VR4VR: Vocational Rehabilitation of Individuals with Disabilities in Immersive Virtual Reality Environments. In *PETRA '15 Proceedings of the 8th ACM International Conference on PErvasive Technologies Related to Assistive Environments*, 54:1-54:4. https://doi.org/10.1145/2769493.2769592
10. Michael E. Bratman. 1992. Shared Cooperative Activity. *The Philosophical Review* 101, 2: 327–341. https://doi.org/10.2307/2185537
11. Miao-en Chien, Cyun-meng Jheng, Ni-miao Lin, Hsien-hui Tang, Paul Taele, Wen-sheng Tseng, and Mike Y Chen. 2015. iCAN : A tablet-based pedagogical system for improving communication skills of children with autism. *Journal of Human Computer Studies* 73: 79–90. https://doi.org/10.1016/j.ijhcs.2014.06.001
12. Deborah L. Christensen, Jon Baio, Kim Van Naarden Braun, Deborah Bilder, Jane Charles, John N. Constantino, Julie Daniels, Maureen S. Durkin, Robert T. Fitzgerald, Margaret Kurzius-Spencer, Li-Ching Lee, Sydney Pettygrove, Cordelia Robinson, Eldon Schulz, Chris Wells, Martha S. Wingate, Walter Zahorodny, and Marshalyn Yeargin-Allsopp. 2016. *Prevalence and Characteristics of Autism Spectrum Disorder Among Children Aged 8 Years - Autism and Developmental Disabilities Monitoring Network, 11 Sites, United States, 2012.* https://doi.org/10.15585/mmwr.ss6503a1
13. Franceli L. Cibrian, Deysi H. Ortega, Lizbeth Escobedo, and Monica Tentori. 2015. Reflections from a Long-term Deployment Study to Design Novel Interactive Surfaces for Children with Autism. In *Springer International Publishing Switzerland*. 167–176. https://doi.org/10.1007/978-3-319-26508-7

14. Kenneth M Colby. 1973. The Rationale for Computer Based Treatment of Language Difficulties in Nonspeaking Austistic Children. *Journal of Autism and Childhood Schizophrenia* 3, 3: 254–260. https://doi.org/10.1007/BF01538283
15. Lee Crossley. 2003. Building Emotions in Design. *The Design Journal* 6, 3: 35–45. https://doi.org/10.2752/146069203789355264
16. Lizbeth Escobedo, Mónica Tentori, Eduardo Quintana, Jesus Favela, and Daniel Garcia-Rosas. 2014. Using Augmented Reality to Help Children with Autism Stay Focused. *IEEE Pervasive Computing* 13, 1: 38–46. https://doi.org/10.1109/MPRV.2014.19
17. Christopher Frauenberger, Judith Good, Geraldine Fitzpatrick, and Ole Sejer Iversen. 2015. In pursuit of rigour and accountability in participatory design. *International Journal of Human Computer Studies* 74: 93–106. https://doi.org/10.1016/j.ijhcs.2014.09.004
18. Raine Kajastila, Leo Holsti, and Perttu Hämäläinen. 2016. The Augmented Climbing Wall: High-Exertion Proximity Interaction on a Wall-Sized Interactive Surface. In *CHI '16 Proceedings of the 2016 CHI Conference on Human Factors in Computing Systems*, 758–769. https://doi.org/10.1145/2858036.2858450
19. Julie A Kientz, Gillian R Hayes, Tracy L Westeyn, Thad Starner, and Gregory D Abowd. 2007. Pervasive Computing and Autism: Assisting Caregivers of Children with Special Needs. *IEEE Pervasive Computing* 6, 1: 28–35. https://doi.org/10.1109/MPRV.2007.18
20. B Lawson. 2006. *How Designers Think: The Design Process Demystified*. Elsevier/Architectural.
21. Dorothy Leonard and Jeffrey F. Rayport. 1997. Spark Innovation Through Empathic Design. *Harvard Business Review* 75, 6: 102–115.
22. M L Max and J C Burke. 1997. Virtual reality for autism communication and education, with lessons for medical training simulators. *Studies in health technology and informatics* 39: 46—53.
23. Paul Milgram and Fumio Kishino. 1994. A Taxonomy of Mixed Reality Visual Displays. *IEICE Transactions on Information Systems* E77–D, 12: 1321–1329.
24. T Mooij. 1999. Guidelines to pedagogical use of ICT in education. In *8th Conference of the European Association for Research on Learning and Instruction*, 1–15.
25. Joan Mora-guiard, Ciera Crowell, Narcis Pares, and Pamela Heaton. 2016. Lands of Fog: Helping Children with Autism in Social Interaction through a Full-Body Interactive Experience. In *IDC '16 Proceedings of the The 15th International Conference on Interaction Design and Children*, 262–274. https://doi.org/10.1145/2930674.2930695
26. Joan Mora-Guiard, Ciera Crowell, Narcis Pares, and Pamela Heaton. 2016. Sparking social initiation behaviors in children with Autism through full-body Interaction. *International Journal of Child-Computer Interaction*. https://doi.org/10.1016/j.ijcci.2016.10.006
27. Michael M Mueller, Christine M Palkovic, and Cynthia S Maynard. 2007. Errorless learning: review and practical application for teaching children with pervasive developmental disorders. *Psychology in the Schools* 44, 7: 691–700. https://doi.org/10.1002/pits.20258
28. Samuel L Odom, William H Brown, Timothy Frey, Necdet Karasu, Lora Lee Smith-canter, and Phillip S Strain. 2003. Evidence-Based Practices for Young Children with Autism: Contributions for Single-Subject Design Research. *Focus on Autism and Other Developmental Disabilities* 18, 3: 166–175. https://doi.org/10.1177/10883576030180030401
29. T Ogilvie and J Liedtka. 2011. *Designing for Growth: A Design Thinking Toolkit for Managers*. Columbia University Press.
30. Narcis Pares, Paul Masri, Gerard Van Wolferen, and Chris Creed. 2005. Achieving dialogue with children with severe autism in an adaptive multisensory interaction: The "MEDIATE" project. *IEEE Transactions on Visualization and Computer Graphics* 11, 6: 734–742. https://doi.org/10.1109/TVCG.2005.88
31. Kathleen Ann Quill. 1995. Visually Cued Instruction for Children with Autism and Pervasive Developmental Disorders. *Focus on Autistic Behavior* 10, 3: 10–20. https://doi.org/10.1177/108835769501000302
32. M. Rao, Shaila and Brenda Gagie. 2006. Learning Through Seeing and Doing : Visual Supports for Children With Autism. *Teaching Exceptional Children* 38, 6: 26–33. https://doi.org/10.1177/004005990603800604
33. Anne M Roux, Paul T Shattuck, Benjamin P Cooper, Kristy A Anderson, Mary Wagner, and Sarah C Narendorf. 2013. Postsecondary Employment Experiences Among Young Adults With an Autism Spectrum Disorder. *Journal of the American Academy of Child & Adolescent Psychiatry* 52, 9: 931–939. https://doi.org/10.1016/j.jaac.2013.05.019
34. SAGA. 2017. Lü - Interactive Playground. Retrieved August 24, 2017 from http://www.play-lu.com/
35. Ed Smeets and Ton Mooij. 2001. Pupil-centred learning, ICT, and teacher behaviour: observations in educational practice. *British Journal of Educational Technology* 32, 4: 403–417. https://doi.org/10.1111/1467-8535.00210

36. Ferdinand Streicher, Daniel Weiß, Jei Lee, Billy Boukis, and Thomas Mayer. 2017. T-T-T (Table Tennis Trainer). Retrieved August 30, 2017 from http://ttt3000.de/

37. Jane Fulton Suri. 2005. *Thoughtless acts?: Observations on intuitive design*. Chronicle Books.

38. Kenji Suzuki, Taku Hachisu, and Kazuki Iida. 2016. EnhancedTouch: A Smart Bracelet for Enhancing Human- Human Physical Touch. In *Proceedings of the 2016 CHI Conference on Human Factors in Computing Systems - CHI '16*, 1282–1293. https://doi.org/10.1145/2858036.2858439

39. Gulnoza Yakubova Teresa Taber-doughty. 2013. Brief Report : Learning Via the Electronic Interactive Whiteboard for Two Students with Autism and a Student with Moderate Intellectual Disability. 1465–1472. https://doi.org/10.1007/s10803-012-1682-x

40. Issey Takahashi, Mika Oki, Baptiste Bourreau, Itaru Kitahara, and Kenji Suzuki. 2017. FUTUREGYM: A gymnasium with interactive floor projection for children with special needs. *International Journal of Child-Computer Interaction* 15: 37–47. https://doi.org/10.1016/j.ijcci.2017.12.002

41. Monica Tentori, Lizbeth Escobedo, and Gabriela Balderas. 2015. A smart environment for children with autism. *IEEE Pervasive Computing* 14, 2: 42–50. https://doi.org/10.1109/MPRV.2015.22

42. Monica Tentori, Lizbeth Escobedo, Carlos Hernandez, Aleksandar Matic, and Gillian R Hayes. 2016. Pervasive Displays in Classrooms of Children with Severe Autism. *IEEE Pervasive Computing* 15, 3: 48–57. https://doi.org/10.1109/MPRV.2016.49

43. Catherine Tissot and Roy Evans. 2003. Visual Teaching Strategies for Children with Autism. *Early Child Development and Care* 173, 4: 425–433. https://doi.org/10.1080/0300443032000079104

44. Tokyo Metropolitan Board of Education. 2016. Text book for cleaning skills test in special needs school. Retrieved March 12, 2018 from http://www.kyoiku.metro.tokyo.jp/school/study_material/special_needs_education/cleaning_skills_test.html

Design Artefacts to Support People with a Disability to Build Personal Infrastructures

Ravihansa Rajapakse, Margot Brereton, Laurianne Sitbon
School of Electrical Engineering and Computer Science, Queensland University of Technology
Brisbane, Queensland, Australia 4000
ravihansa.r@sliit.lk, {m.brereton, laurianne.sitbon} @qut.edu.au

ABSTRACT

A person with a disability has to assemble support services and technologies from different organisations in order to live well, which may require help from family. We call this assembling of services and technologies *personal infrastructuring*, the process of learning about how to navigate the world, what support is available, and how to obtain and design new support through various organisational infrastructures. Such infrastructures include disability services organisations, the health sector, community organisations, and friend and family networks. Our vision was to explore how a person with a disability might engage in design with volunteer designers to meet their unique needs that were not met by their existing infrastructure of organisations, products and services. Through codesign with two people and their families, we developed design artefacts such as user profiles and video stories to support communication, mutual learning, need finding and need expression. We discovered that these design artefacts were used beyond their immediate purposes of design to further support their *personal infrastructuring*. In this paper, we discuss how understandings of infrastructure and infrastructuring from Science and Technology Studies and Information Systems translate into familial contexts and the concept of *personal infrastructuring*.

Author Keywords

Infrastructure; Personal Infrastructuring; Boundary Objects; Collaborations; Codesign

ACM Classification Keywords

H.5.m. Information Systems: Miscellaneous

INTRODUCTION

People with a disability often have unique needs that are not met by the marketplace. To meet such needs, they build a personal support network and adopt a variety of services and technologies. Families and caregivers often become engaged in, support or lead this process, depending on the support needed [12]. Finding suitable technologies and services usually involves significant ongoing effort, as organisations, funding policies, technologies and networks of people change over time [3,10].

We have reviewed the literature on the concept of infrastructure and infrastructuring to understand how it might be applicable and useful to the case of people with a disability building personal infrastructures. The concept of infrastructuring, developed by Star and Bowker [21] in the field of Science and Technology Studies was used to understand the nature of particular infrastructures (such as the pharmaceutical benefit scheme, railroad networks, the internet, and IT organisations) and the characteristics of how people encounter and work with these infrastructures. Here, we explore how the concepts might transfer and be adapted to *personal infrastructuring*. We introduce the term *personal infrastructuring* to refer to how people with a disability, possibly assisted by families and proxies, support their lives by using an assemblage of various organisational and societal infrastructures. These include infrastructures such as the public transport network, the health sector, disability services organisations (DSOs), community organisations, and friend and family networks. Everybody undertakes personal infrastructuring, but it is particularly salient for people with a disability because they often need to make the extra effort to construct a world that is accessible to them.

We have investigated personal infrastructuring by working with two people with a disability and their families. One participant lived with their family and needed significant family support to participate, while the other participant lived independently. We set out to explore whether individual needs of people with a disability that are not met in the marketplace could be met through a codesign project with volunteer makers from local maker communities or with university students as part of their project work.

This led us to an infrastructuring project (Figure 1) of bridging across the infrastructures of different organisations; a maker community, a university, a DSO, and the person with a disability themselves and their family, to see whether we could bring together an effective codesign approach to develop a technology or service to fill a need or desire of people with a disability.

DIS '18, June 9–13, 2018, Hong Kong

ACM ISBN 978-1-4503-5198-0/18/06 $15.00
https://doi.org/10.1145/3196709.3196749

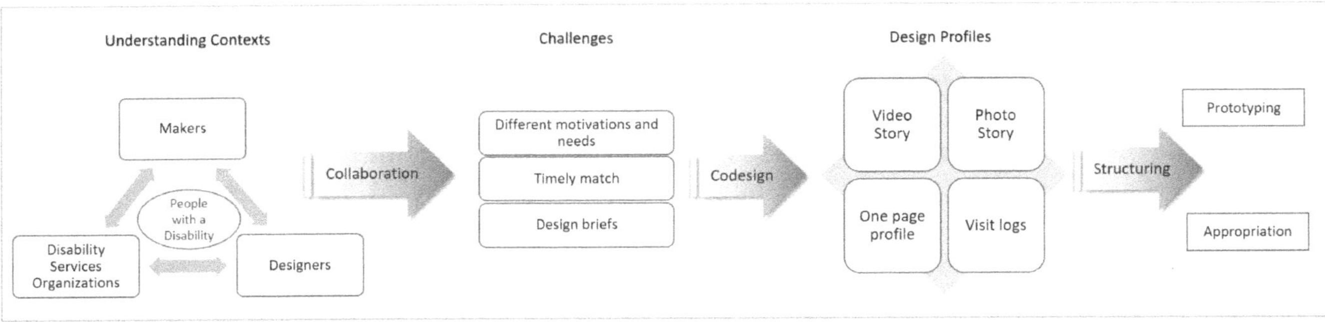

Figure 1. Phases of the collaboration to support makers, design researchers and a Disability Service Organisation to codesign with people with a disability and their family

By working with different organisations, we identified a variety of challenges that had to be overcome to initiate and sustain codesign. One challenge was that makers and university students both wanting a clear sense of a project brief before they could commit to undertaking a project, whereas the families and the DSO wanted to be sure they were engaging in a worthwhile pursuit that would benefit the person with a disability. In order to overcome this challenge of designers wanting a clear brief, and families wanting to ensure the design approach and goals were suitable, we worked with people with a disability and their families to develop some personal communication artefacts which expressed their values, challenges, needs and wishes. These artefacts included video-stories, photo-stories, personal profiles and visit logs). They subsequently became useful in communicating with other organisations.

Literature from the domain of disability studies has fostered great advances in improving the autonomy of people with a disability, by debunking deficit models and misinterpretations associated with disability and self-determination. Wehmeyer et al. [24–26] have emphasised that people with significant intellectual disabilities can be self-determined, making decisions and setting goals on their own, providing that supports and accommodations are in place. We worked to ensure that the person with a disability was in charge throughout the process, in both of our cases, we contacted the person with a disability through a family member. Also, the families played a strong role in setting up the collaboration. Our first contact with families came about because we had organised a forum about designing ICTs with people with an intellectual disability at our university. People with an intellectual disability, support workers, DSO representatives and some family members of people with an intellectual disability attended the form. Two family members of people with an intellectual disability expressed interest in codesign, and it was through them that we connected with their family member with an intellectual disability. We return in the discussion to the role of families and proxies in codesign, noting here that while many people with a disability are completely independent in choice making and living, others rely on assistance from family members, which involves negotiation within the family.

In this paper, we focus on the use of design artefacts in a process of personal infrastructuring, as little research has explored the use of design artefacts for this purpose. We proceed first by introducing the infrastructuring literature and relevant concepts. We then describe two cases of codesign in which a university student and researchers worked with two families and a maker community. We elaborate on the kinds of design artefacts produced and their role in infrastructuring. We found that design artefacts support communication, mutual learning, and negotiation. They acted as boundary objects that were worked on by the person and their family, volunteer makers/students and the research team to negotiate design pathways, supporting different kinds of activities for each party. We introduce the concept of *personal infrastructuring* and conclude the paper with a model for *personal infrastructuring*.

RELATED WORK

Infrastructure and Infrastructuring

Infrastructure is the establishment and maintenance of elements that support something to be operated on [19]. For example, a canal system is a part of the infrastructure that a farmer needs to sustain his/her cultivation but seen from the perspective of an irrigation engineer; it becomes a job. When one uses a canoe to travel on the canal, it becomes the infrastructure for one's transport. When there is a flood, it becomes a threat and hindrance in one's life. Perception of infrastructure, therefore, depends mainly on the individual and community using it, the purpose for which it was designed, and how it is being maintained. The nature of the interaction between the user and infrastructure changes with the situation, shaping the infrastructure continually. In effect, infrastructure is not merely a platform that other actions can run on top of, but rather an ongoing alignment between contexts [23]. It is a collection of social, technical and organisational elements that are shaped by or shape a community towards (a) specific goal(s) [8,14]. Star and Bowker [21] highlighted that infrastructures are dynamic, relative to the context and become visible upon breakdown.

People with a disability may encounter breakdowns in infrastructures frequently because the world is not always designed inclusively. For example, a wheelchair is a piece of infrastructure that supports a person to be mobile. A set of steps abruptly reveals a breakdown of built environment infrastructure for a wheelchair user, who then seeks an alternate accessible path, personally working out an access route for themselves. Developing a regular access route is a form of *personal infrastructuring*, finding a way to make the wheelchair infrastructure work in the built environment infrastructure. It saves time and effort for that individual the next time. Another example of a piece of personal infrastructure, often encountered as an interface to bureaucratic infrastructures, is the online or paper form that needs to be filled out to obtain a service. We use the example of a form to introduce salient aspects of infrastructure identified by Star and Bowker.

Embeddedness - infrastructure is sunk into other structures, social arrangements and technologies. (Forms gather information to keep, share and check it for relevant purposes)

Learned as a part of membership - strangers and outsiders encounter infrastructure as a target object to be learned about. (People learn how to fill out forms effectively, choosing appropriate categories to get what they need).

Reach and scope - has reach beyond a single site or practice spatially or temporally. (Forms typically are used across sites and to support diverse practices.)

Transparency - Infrastructure is transparent in that it does not have to be reinvented each time it is used (as with forms.)

Links with conventions of practice - Infrastructure shapes and is shaped by the conventions of a community of practice (as are forms.)

Built on an installed base, rather than growing from scratch. (Forms are designed to structure information needed to access an existing base of services.)

Becomes visible upon breakdown - the normal invisible quality of working infrastructure becomes visible on the breakdown. (For example, when a form does not have adequate categories to capture the information that one feels the need to offer, one is alerted to the policies and practices that underlie the form.)

We see that the humble form, so often encountered in accessing services or disability support, is a piece of the infrastructure itself that is used to interface to other infrastructures. An awareness of the concept and characteristics of infrastructure is helpful in the case of assembling services and support for a person with a disability. It alerts us to the characteristics and workings of organisations that are especially perceptible when infrastructure breaks down. It also uncovers opportunities for design and change. The concept of infrastructuring also helps us to see design, not in isolation as providing a piece of equipment or service, but in the context of its connection to other aspects of infrastructure, which may become important considerations for shaping the design at hand.

Infrastructuring involves amalgamating social, technical and organisational elements of different infrastructures to achieve a common goal [23, 25]. It often encompasses interplay between infrastructures. The goal of infrastructuring is to navigate a new form of infrastructure to support a common goal of the participating infrastructures. We set out to investigate the possibility of connecting people with a disability with students and makers organisations to codesign personalised technologies. This endeavour also involved working with universities and garnered interest from a DSO. As such, the project became one of *infrastructuring*, working out how to connect the people and the various organisations effectively to support a common goal.

Infrastructuring and Design

Whereas it has been prominently discussed in Science and Technology Studies (STS) and Information Systems (IS), the use and conceptualisation of infrastructuring in collaborative design work is emerging. Researchers are beginning to see how infrastructuring can be used to understand complexities of collaborative projects outside organisational settings [13]. Infrastructuring has been recognised as an integral part of participatory design as design work involves continuous alignment between social and technological elements and their users [4]. The use of infrastructuring has been discussed from different perspectives [7], as exemplified by the release of a special issue of the Journal of Computer Supported Cooperative Work devoted to *Infrastructuring and Collaborative Design (2017)* [13]. Karasti [7] presented a critical analysis of the different uses and conceptualisations of infrastructuring in PD. She noted that much of the design work centred on organisations and community settings utilising infrastructuring in diverse ways. She emphasised the need to embrace complex forms of inter-play, ranging from lack of interest in maintaining and sustaining, all the way to finding challenging and creative alternatives. She called for new ways of scaling-up (engaging with new communities), as distinct from traditional PD approaches that are concerned mostly with participation.

Building on Ehn's [5] view of infrastructuring as a supplement for design-for-use, Le Dantec and DiSalvo [1] conceptualised infrastructuring as the work of creating resources that both socially and technically enable adoption and appropriation. They defined infrastructuring as a mode or practice of PD that develops and provides socio-material resources and experiences, also emphasising support for the development of identity, belief systems and the struggle for predominance [2], aspects which are particularly important for people with a disability. They argued for a process that goes beyond participation, to one that encourages people to negotiate their work practices through various artefacts, e.g. the introduction of a software application in a company required its staff to re-think and re-negotiate the information flows between managerial levels. Use of infrastructuring as a lens to view design work highlights the complexities involved in the interplay between different communities.

A Framework for Infrastructuring

Pipek and Wulf [14] explored the way in which modern work environments use information systems as work infrastructures. They see infrastructuring as the successful establishment of things such as technology standards and business goals. They presented a framework for infrastructuring (Figure 2).

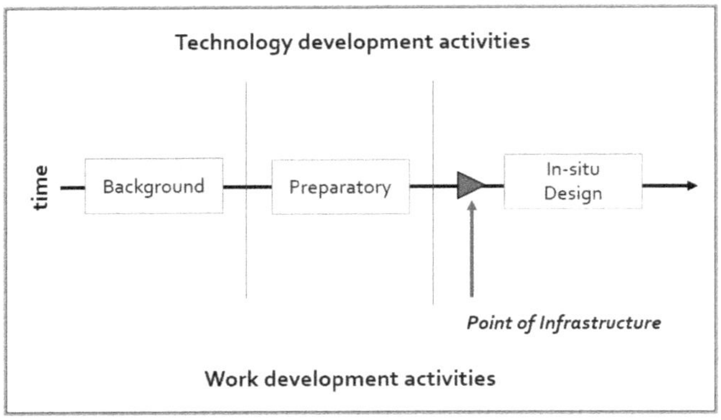

Figure 2. A simplified version of the framework for infrastructuring by Pipek and Wulf [14] **(pp 458)**

Their framework shows how people undertake a variety of background and preparatory design work before use can occur. They defined a **point of infrastructure** as occurring when an infrastructure becomes visible to its users, either because it breaks down, or during use innovation when users successfully appropriate a new infrastructure for a local context.

Understanding the role of infrastructure and infrastructuring in design helps by explicating the context and resources that designers can draw upon. The case of infrastructuring to support a person with a disability is different from the work organisation context identified by Pipek and Wolf. Most DSOs offer services but do not design technologies. The person with a disability has to navigate the various support and devices available to them from different organisations. For example, Australia recently introduced a new National Disability Insurance Scheme (NDIS) designed to enable people with a disability to choose the services that they need using financial support provided to them by the government. This "user pays" model means that individuals have to research and understand options available to them and piece together the support that they need. We call this "personal infrastructuring" because the person with a disability and family are working to understand a variety of services and infrastructures from the point of view of their personal needs, and also to draw together an infrastructure that supports themselves. They are designing in use, seeking to innovate in their life, appropriating new infrastructures into their local context and beginning to reflect on changes and innovate.

Boundary Objects

Although the ability to work across infrastructural boundaries is often discussed, the use of design artefacts as boundary objects to support infrastructuring is little explored. Boundary objects support bringing different social worlds together for a common course of action [18,22]. They are abstract or concrete things that could be adapted to suit the constraints and local needs, yet are robust enough to maintain a common identity to facilitate communication. For example, a map can aid a geologist and an ecologist to explore relationships between the local geology and ecology together. Boundary objects serve as a means of compromise where it is difficult for parties to reach consensus as they allow unique interpretations [11].

The possibility of an object being a boundary object is determined by its scale and scope [20]. Scale refers to the reach of the object, i.e. its ability to meet common grounds among diverse groups. For example, a textbook becomes a boundary object only *when* it supports different communities to interpret it in their own ways yet guides them to work around its content to achieve a common goal. Scope refers to the depth of communication supported by the object. For example, a wall notice may support communication between two parties, but it becomes a boundary object only *when* it allows itself to be worked upon by the parties to generate meaningful outcomes.

Star and Griesemer [22] defined three (3) qualities of a boundary object that qualify it as a cooperative aid: (1) The object resides between social worlds, (2) the object is worked upon by local groups who maintain its identity as a common object, while making it more specific, and (3) groups that cooperate without consensus refer back-and-forth to both vague and specific forms of the object. Star showed that standardisation or scaling-up (structuring) transforms the boundary objects from their ill-structured forms to structured forms that lead to the creation of standards, objects or processes [20].

> *"When the movement between the two forms either scales up or becomes standardized, then boundary objects begin to move and change into infrastructure, into standards (particularly methodological standards), and into things and yet other processes, which have not yet been fully studied as such" (Susan Leigh Star, 2010, pp 605).*

For example, a standardised communication protocol could be developed from a set of vague guidelines to support inter-party communication. Scaling-up involves opening boundary objects to more parties, so they could work towards the existing or a newly formed common interest, for example, by involving a new community group in a collaboration through sharing and working on a boundary object. In this paper, we will elaborate on how design artefacts aided inter-party negotiation and how they acted as boundary objects to support the work of personal infrastructuring.

OUR CASE: A COLLABORATION

We codesigned with two people with a disability, their families, student designers, makers, DSOs and academics. We will briefly elaborate on the key activities of the collaboration to convey an overall idea of the process as this has been described in prior work [15,16].

Contextual Inquiry

The first phase of the collaboration encompassed contextual inquiry with the makers, university and a DSO, to understand their unique practices and willingness to codesign with a person with a disability. This phase consisted of semi-structured interviews with 7 makers, 3 university academics and a DSO executive. We complemented the interviews by 3 on-site observations at the maker communities and DSO. The researchers attended weekly meet-ups and a maker faire (a public exhibition of designs) of the maker communities and a session of computer learning for people with a disability at the DSO's learning centre. This contextual inquiry identified key themes of their design approaches, motivations, values, challenges and factors that made the communities succeed and sustain. We found that flexible DIY practices and the supportive environments of maker communities could potentially facilitate developing design ideas for individuals into prototypes or DIY products [15]. DSOs could support designers by sharing their sector expertise and introducing potential service users. Academics and students could engage in real-world projects and explore novel design approaches. The collaboration, therefore, had the potential to benefit all the parties involved.

Inter-party discussions

After acknowledging the potential to work together, a series of five inter-party discussions was initiated to discuss possible design interventions, involving people from a maker community, a DSO, students and academics.

The first two discussions involved DSO executives and academics. The aim was to discuss possible design avenues. A DSO executive gave an example of a girl with an intellectual disability and emphasised that hardware devices could potentially ease her access to communication technologies to support her day-to-day communication better. The discussions extended to how to involve other communities such as makers in the collaboration. The principal researcher took the task of discussing with the maker communities the idea of exploring the potential for collaboration, following established ethical protocols. The aim of the third discussion, which involved academics, DSO executives and a board member of a maker community, was to explore appropriate engagement methods with service users (people with a disability and their families). Initially, we discussed the idea of exploring the settings of individuals with the aim of developing scenarios or stories. This discussion revealed that their own interests primarily drove makers in the maker community and that getting them involved and sustaining involvement would depend on whether they perceived the design activity as interesting. The fourth discussion involved university students, as there was potential to undertake codesign projects with people with a disability as part of their academic program. It became clear that students needed a reasonably clear design brief and understanding of what the project might entail for them to commit to a project. They were concerned about being able to complete a good project within the relevant academic timeframe in order to receive academic credit and to understand the kinds of learning they might undertake. In the final discussion that involved academics, students, makers and researchers, everyone agreed on the importance of spending sufficient time with the participants to develop a good sense of their settings and aspirations.

The next phase involved the researchers meeting with people with a disability and their families. We visited their homes and other places such as learning centres. In both cases, the parents of the people with a disability arranged the meeting and supported us to communicate with their adult child with an intellectual disability. These meetings served two purposes. Firstly, getting to know each other, to learn the individual needs and family contexts and for the person with a disability and their family to learn who we were, whether they trusted us and what might be possible. Secondly, finding a way to understand and express their needs in the form of design briefs that they could share with makers and students. These briefs could be shown to various makers and student groups to ascertain their interest and to spare the person with disability and family from having to meet with many different people who might not be interested in codesigning them, thus also preserving their privacy in the first instance.

Codesigning Artefacts

The research team worked with Kate, Ann and their families. Kate is a 19-year old female who likes to be social and engage in outdoor activities. She is fond of listening to music and watching TV. Kate and her younger brother live with their parents. While she likes to do many things, Kate's ability to interact is limited due to quadriplegia, cerebral palsy and microcephaly. Although she can strike objects nearby with her hands, she finds it difficult to grab, drag and type on a keyboard. She has good vision and hearing but cannot move her lower body and is non-verbal. Ann is in her early forties and lives independently in a supported living environment. She likes to be doing something all the time and to engage in outdoor activities. Due to a genetic condition, she has communication difficulties and learning difficulties, is hypersensitive and has spine and kidney conditions that need to be managed. She walks with a slight gait and can speak a limited number of words. Ann can use a computer keyboard with her limited fine hand movements but is unable to use a laptop touchpad.

The codesign projects started with discussions with the family members as they acted as the initial contacts and gatekeepers in arranging access to their adult children. We ensured that our codesign techniques enabled Ann and Kate to participate by supporting communication with visual cues such as pictures and videos, and waiting for them to take their time to take a turn in the conversation [17]. The engagement methods included activities such as using a set of pictures to ask Kate which project to choose from a set of possible design ideas [17]. Kate and Ann were able to point and choose their interests in their home contexts, and family members played a supportive role encouraging them and interpreting gestures. A set of design profiles (Figure 3) was then created to communicate the unique needs and wants of individuals to the designers.

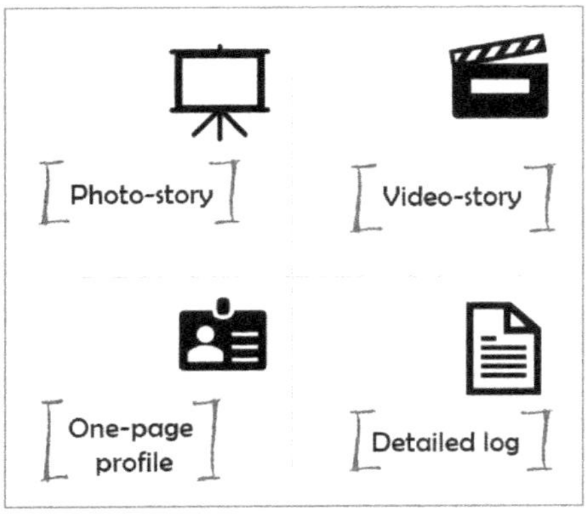

Figure 3. The set of design artefacts created. They include a photo-story, video-story, one-page profile and a detailed log.

A photo-story (Figure 4) was created with a set of real-life photographs of the individuals, with each photo accompanying a description of the story behind the picture, and challenges and opportunities associated with the story.

Figure 4. A slide from Kate's photo-story. Photo-story shows opportunities and challenges associated with different situations of the individual's life.

We codesigned a video-story (a short video clip with audio narration) to describe the interests and wants of the individuals. Following is the link to Kate's video-story (best played in Google Chrome):

https://www.dropbox.com/s/m4eazf1r1le0voz/Kate.mp4?dl=0

We also codesigned a one-page profile (Figure 5), to provide a quick snapshot of Kate's and Ann's lives.

The design profiles were crafted together with the individuals and their family members. The contents of both video and photo stories were authored by them, while the researchers acted as facilitators. The family members entirely designed the one-page profiles. Kate, Ann and their families were enthusiastic about the final video-story, photo-story and one-page profile. Every visit and activity with Kate and Ann and their families has been documented in detail as visit logs (also shared with the families), in case a designer needed to know further specifics.

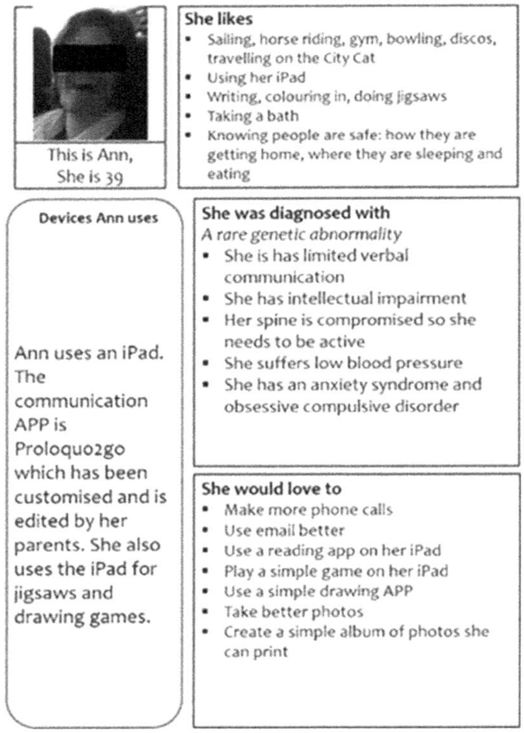

Figure 5. Ann's one-page profile

Inspiring Designers

We shared the design profiles with potential designers to inspire them to take part in design. As the university already had a working arrangement for students to engage in community projects, we shared the design profiles firstly with them. The video-stories were advertised in an information session at the university, and a student showed interest in working with Kate. We then shared the other design artefacts, enabling him to get a deeper understanding. The video stories especially were well received by the designers and families due to their engaging presentation. While Kate's design profiles were used to support the design of prototypes, Ann's design profiles were used as introductory material for future caregivers, support workers and friends. Ann's parents requested the source material of the video and photo stories, so they could keep editing them according to changes in Ann's life. When the makers were re-approached with the complete design profiles, their contribution remained uncertain due to their work commitments, hobbyist projects and logistic issues such as travel distance.

PERSONAL INFRASTRUCTURING

Most emphasis in codesign is usually placed on design engagement methods and design outcomes, once the intent to collaborate has already been established. However, a significant amount of activity may need to take place to establish a collaboration.

We found that the process by which the individuals seek to develop a support network has similarities with Pipek and Wulf's framework for infrastructuring. We, therefore, build on this framework, extending it to a framework for personal infrastructuring (Figure 6). The top sphere in this framework represents **technology and service design** activities, while the bottom sphere represents **partnership development** activities.

Background Work

Technology and service design

Background work involves appraising existing technologies and devices in the home and understanding their use. People and their families do this in an ongoing way themselves, whereas researchers need to learn this through contextual inquiry. Technology search, literature review and personal networking are also used to develop further knowledge about existing technologies and services that might be appropriated, and about potential collaborators. The aim was to explore any desire to codesign a new personalised technology to meet the aspirations of an individual.

Partnership development

Most of the collaborators were driven by intrinsic rewards, while rewards such as course completion (for students) and opportunities for research (for academics) were also present. Personnel of the DSO believed their work is a social responsibility while academics involved in the project were motivated by both the research challenge of understanding how to better support people with a disability, as well as by a desire for better social inclusion and personal connection to people with a disability. Makers were often keener to explore their own design interests, while students were interested in supporting people. These motivations, while not in smooth alignment, meant that there was a potential to collaborate and that inter-party discussions could be organised without seeking extrinsic rewards.

Respecting and moulding a partnership based on individual motivations is the key to initiating a collaboration, as also indicated by Friedman in her articulation of value sensitive design [6]. Star and Ruhleder [23] emphasised the importance of understanding the context in which an infrastructure is built and the impact that the infrastructure has on the context. Having the contextual knowledge encouraged the collaborators to think how it could impact the infrastructure and vice versa. For example, while the makers' desire to tinker meant that the design process needed to be interesting enough for them, it also needed to accommodate students by allowing them to meet their project deadlines as put forth by the university.

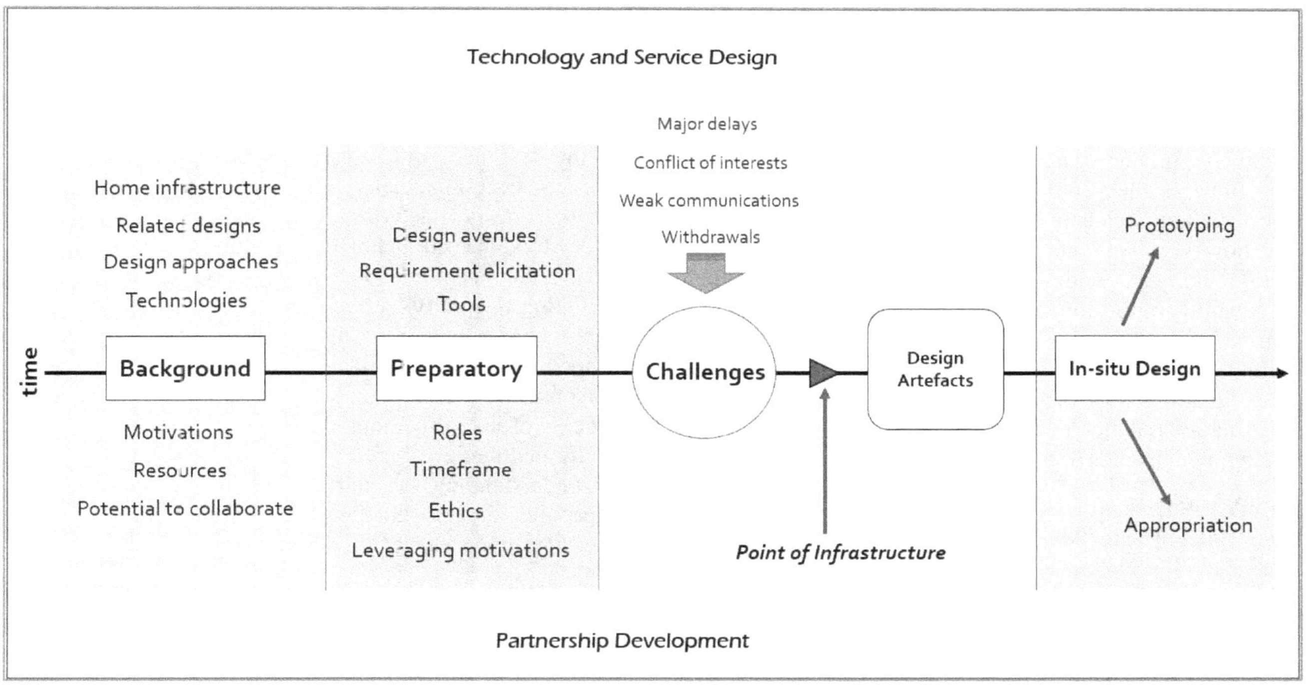

Figure 6. A framework for personal infrastructuring

Preparatory Work

Technology and service design

In a collaborative context, the preparation of the infrastructure evolves around continuous negotiation. In our case, preparatory work involved several inter-party discussions with students, maker organisations members, makers, DSO executives and managers. Having established willingness and contingencies of participation (see partnership development below), the technology and service design work involved a discussion of possible design engagement methods, designs and technologies to be used and possible design avenues.

Partnership development

Partnership development encompassed activities such as determining roles, timeframes, discussing ethical concerns, and leveraging motivations. Collaborators brainstormed possible engagement methods and tried to make provisions to fulfil their motivations. One party – in our case researchers, but alternatively, the person, their family, or a DSO – may need to act as facilitators to provide scaffolding for others to engage in active discussions. In large organisational infrastructuring, aspects such as IT training or work re-structuring may be central, but in personal infrastructuring, the work often involves finding willing parties with skills and resources and establishing conditions for collaboration.This may encompass learning oneself how to use and build with various kinds of technologies.

Identifying Challenges

The innovation or breakdown that Wulf and Pipek denote as a point of infrastructure arises when key aspects of the infrastructuring process come to the fore. In our case, this happened when the misalignment of motivations and needs of the stakeholders became evident, which made us realise how important it was to address this problem explicitly and effectively. In our case, a student group withdrew from discussions as they could not furnish a proposal for their project without a clearer design brief. Making design briefs was, however, was not possible without establishing a healthy dialogue with Kate, Ann and their families. Sustainability of the collaboration, therefore, was threatened. Significant delays, conflicts of interest and deteriorating communications may also be signs that indicate breakdown. These situations may then lead to a point of infrastructure, signalling not only the need for resolution but also a point of learning, which leads to process innovation.

Design Artefacts

Addressing the challenges of the collaboration meant that the designers required a set of design briefs. The researchers set about codesigning the design briefs with the individual and their family. Designing artefacts such as profiles and videos to communicate personal needs and context was a new experience for the people with a disability and their families, who often used verbal or written forms to communicate contact and technology requirements with often already introduced designers.

The approach to developing design artefacts was based on intimate, small activities and discussions with one or two researchers, the person with a disability and their parents, in order to build a close dialogue. In several initial discussions, one researcher met with one parent until the parent was comfortable to facilitate access to their adult child. We followed an approach built on mutual learning, respect for uniqueness and holistic participation [17]. The design artefacts enabled inter-party communication, mutual learning, negotiation and self-determination. These are discussed below.

Communication. We shared the design briefs with the potential designers to inspire them to take part. The video-stories and photo-stories inspired the designers, and detailed logs provided a deeper sense of context to those who were keen to take part. Kate's design profiles were then used, with her and her family's permission, to inspire and support the engagement with Ann and her family. Ann and her family referred to Kate's design profiles and ideated and developed their own design profiles. Design artefacts were thus used as vehicles to infrastructure in a new way, one individual appropriating the design profile of another. They provided a bridge between preparatory work and design-in-use within a collaboration. In this way, they became small pieces of infrastructure, that could inspire other similar design artefacts. The design profiles were useful in suggesting useful ideas for Ann and her family to communicate personal context to 'unknown' other parties. In future endeavours, however, researchers may ask their participants to generate their own ways of communicating context to others which may result in different kinds of artefacts.

Mutual learning. The researchers and designers were able to learn about individual needs and circumstances. Kate, Ann and their families learned about the capacity and limitations of the designers and researchers to support them. Parents learned what is actually important to their adult children through design activities. For example, Ann's parents understood that riding horses is an important activity for Ann during the making of her photo-story, as she insisted on including this activity, even though it was not one that her parents had noted. Working together on the design artefacts shaped the process until reaching the point of developing personalised prototypes or appropriations. This continuous process of learning about each other is crucial as it leads to future negotiations based on shared understanding and less misunderstanding or conflict. When one understands the capacities, dreams, challenges and limitations of another, it is easy to make room for compromises.

Negotiation. The designers and researchers referred back and forth to the design artefacts during the design engagement with individuals. For example, we asked Kate to choose from her interests showcased in her video story to scope a project. Kate was keen on developing support for her interactions on social media. She laboured for the best part of an hour to express her preference through gestures and utterances, while using a photo board, with the help of her parents. Her second choice was developing support to operate a Kettle. After re-thinking his capacity regarding timelines, knowledge and resources, the student designer opted to design support for Kate to operate a Kettle.

Kate loved the kettle because it included her in social events. Her father had developed the practice of switching on the kettle or the coffee machine as Kate squeezed his hand, empowering Kate to be the kettle controller to make friends a coffee. Kate was very excited by the idea of a switch enabling her to switch on the kettle herself, even without her father. Kate and her family understood the time limitations of the designer and agreed to work on her second choice. Such compromises are necessary for any collaboration, where each party need to understand each other's capacity. During personal infrastructuring, collaborators continuously learn how to assess and respond to such situations.

In this project, one of the principal roles of the research team was to advocate for the person with a disability to express themselves and to devise methods to support them to do so. The parents, who seemed used to often communicating for their adult children, appeared pleased to be encouraged to step back. That is, the common practice of interpreting on behalf of their adult child is at times possibly due to social expectation rather than due to a desire to control or a desire for an expedient outcome. The designer supporting the person with a disability to play the most maximal role that they can is surely the most critical part of the design work.

Self-determination. Active engagement of individuals to design the artefacts gave them a sense of control in decision making. Without self-determination, a design endeavour may be just another "design project" for a person with a disability. Much emphasis, therefore, needs to be placed on enhancing self-determination of the individuals. Both Kate and Ann were able to have control over the design process to express what they really needed, instead of others speaking on their behalf. Ann choosing pictures herself for the photo-story was a prime example.

In-situ Design

In-situ design encompassed both prototyping and appropriation during the collaboration, utilising corporeal and contextual understandings. In Kate's case, the student designer developed a high-fidelity prototype (a sensor triggered switch to turn on a kettle). Kate's ability to use her arm to push down, inspired by the discussions with her, and as illustrated in the design profiles, was a key influence in the design. In-situ codesign with a person with a disability requires designers to be considerate of individual interests and abilities. We see the intention of Ann and her parents to use design profiles as introductory material for future caregivers, support workers and friends as an appropriation of the design profiles. They would work on the artefacts to reflect Ann's future life changes. The prototyping by the student in Kate's case had a highly individual nature that was inspired by the design profiles. Prototyping or appropriation in a personal context, therefore, arises from a particularly personal and situated perspective.

DISCUSSION

Infrastructuring in Familial Contexts

The work that a person with a disability and their family undertake to assemble services, technologies and networks of people such that they can live a full life is a complex endeavour. We believe that this complex process of continuous negotiation is not well captured simply through a codesign or participatory design point of view. We rather argue for a view of infrastructuring – *personal infrastructuring* – to capture the ongoing interrelatedness of this endeavour. Personal infrastructuring highlights the value of continuous appropriation work by people with a disability and the negotiations as they venture towards codesign of new kinds of technologies and services. Personal infrastructuring as a concept brings to the fore the work done in living with a disability and the kind of design approach needed to create personal design outcomes. It also highlights the gaps between what support is available, needed and desired. On reflection, our work could have gone further in ensuring that the principal user, the person with a disability, could have been even more in charge, but we reflect that getting to this point is a learning experience for all concerned, both research team, family and individual themselves.

In STS literature, as organisations evolve their infrastructures, they often develop devices, tools, technologies, standards, conventions and protocols. People with a disability often find that standard technologies and protocols do not work for them. They, therefore, undertake personal infrastructuring to devise a personal approach to existing infrastructure. However, the more people with a disability can share their personal infrastructuring efforts, the greater opportunity there is to grow understanding, to empower and to foster inclusion and to spur on greater infrastructuring efforts. The use of Kate's design artefacts to inspire Ann, and Ann's appropriation and redesign of them is a small example of this approach at work. The vision of this work is to empower such infrastructuring further, leading to greater inclusion of people with a disability.

Recognition of challenges in amalgamating personal infrastructures, may lie in understanding and respecting individual motivations and capacities. Personal infrastructuring is, therefore, mainly a process of continuous learning of each other's capacities to shape realistic design pathways.

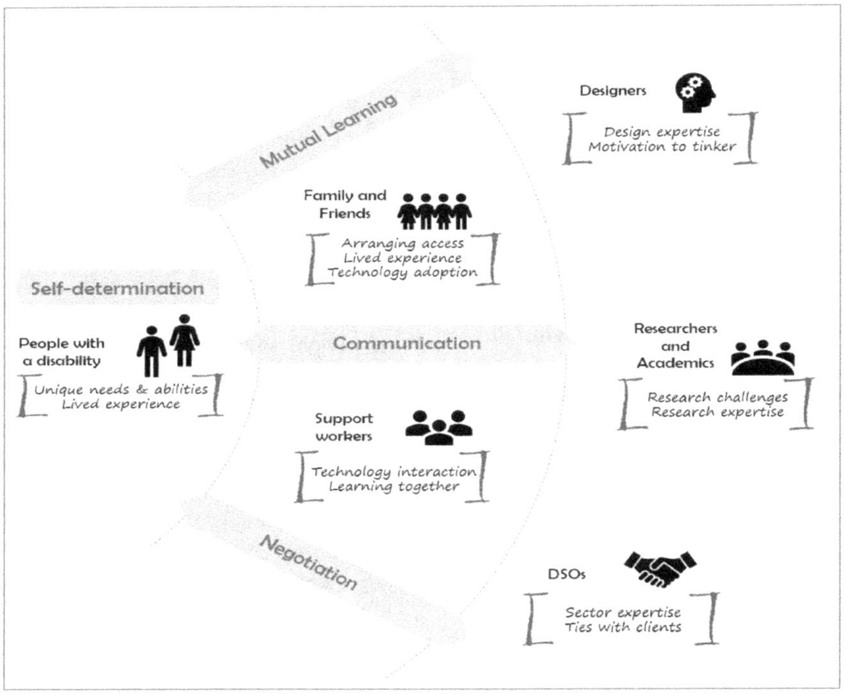

Figure 7. Design artefacts supporting communication, mutual learning, negotiation and self-determination

Utility of Design Artefacts

Design artefacts, in our case, provided scaffolds for a person with a disability to codesign with communities towards a common goal. They were vital in aiding communication, apart from supporting mutual learning, negotiation through reflection and self-determination (Figure 7). Sometimes, the items that best-supported communication, such as photos, became critical aspects of the design artefacts. Working out how best to communicate so that people with an intellectual disability participate and express themselves is important in and of itself but may also play a key role in the resulting design artefacts and designs.

Design artefacts are not the only vehicles for fostering communication and collaboration. Different forms of *things* such as a communal gathering in a community room, or an ethnographic account might also be evocative. However, tangible artefacts allow people to refer back and forth to them and to shape them as they wish in their own timeframes. This interplay between objects and other communities enables the collaborators to understand each other's capacities.

Design Artefacts as Boundary Objects

Boundary objects support bridging different infrastructures by enabling different people to work on and interpret them within their own settings and practices. We found that the design profiles showed salient characteristics of boundary objects outlined by Star and Griesemer [22]. They resided between the social worlds of researcher, families and designers, inspiring designers and supporting people and their families to communicate. Secondly, they were worked upon by the individuals, their families and the researchers to express the unique characteristics of the individuals, to help introduce them to others and supporting designers to ideate prototypes. Lee saw this augmentation of boundary objects to include contextual details as a process of making them intelligible to the receiving community [9]. Finally, the design profiles encouraged interaction by raising additional questions to guide the collaboration.

Different communities engaged in the design through scaling up and appropriating the design profiles. Unlike the traditional codesign approaches, boundary objects allow different communities to negotiate design pathways. We believe that the design artefacts had both scale (community reach) and scope (supporting meaningful dialogue). Most important was perhaps that the design artefacts created with one participant, Kate, provided inspiration and were appropriated by another participant, Ann.

CONCLUSION

We have introduced the concept of *personal infrastructuring* – the assembling of services, technologies and people to support a person with different cognitive and sensory abilities to live well and be more self-determined– to capture a broader design perspective on the life of a person with a disability than existing codesign approaches. Design artefacts and codesign can potentially facilitate further infrastructuring and inclusion of people with a disability. While acknowledging that these are very small steps, the approach, if adopted and extended, offers the further potential to support greater infrastructuring efforts.

REFERENCES

1. Christopher A Le Dantec and Carl DiSalvo. 2013. Infrastructuring and the formation of publics in participatory design. *Social Studies of Science* 43, 2: 241–264. https://doi.org/10.1177/0306312712471581

2. Maria Berghs, Karl Atkin, Hilary Graham, Chris Hatton, and Carol Thomas. 2015. Implications for public health research of models and theories of disability: A scoping study and evidence synthesis. In *Scoping models and theories of disability*. NIHR Journals Library, Southampton. Retrieved March 9, 2018 from https://www.ncbi.nlm.nih.gov/books/NBK378951/

3. Filip Birčanin and Margot Brereton. 2016. Information sharing between family members of children with intellectual disability. In *Proceedings of the 28th Australian Conference on Computer-Human Interaction - OzCHI '16*, 637–639. https://doi.org/10.1145/3010915.3011847

4. Claus Bossen, Andrew Clement, Yvonne Dittrich, and Helena Karasti. 2014. Infrastructuring, collaboration and evolving socio-material practices of changing our world. In *Workshop at Participatory Design Conference*, 221–222.

5. Pelle Ehn. 2008. Participation in design things. In *Proceedings of the Tenth Anniversary Conference on Participatory Design*, 92–101. Retrieved November 24, 2015 from http://dl.acm.org/citation.cfm?id=1795234.1795248

6. Batya Friedman. 1996. Value-sensitive design. *interactions* 3, 6: 16–23.

7. Helena Karasti. 2014. Infrastructuring in participatory design. In *Proceedings of Participatory Design Conference - PDC '14*, 141–150. https://doi.org/10.1145/2661435.2661450

8. Helena Karasti and Karen S. Baker. 2008. Community Design: Growing one's own information infrastructure. In *Proceedings of Participatory Design Conference*, 217–220. Retrieved November 19, 2014 from http://dl.acm.org/citation.cfm?id=1795234.1795280

9. Charlotte P. Lee. 2007. Boundary negotiating artifacts: Unbinding the routine of boundary objects and embracing chaos in collaborative work. *Computer Supported Cooperative Work (CSCW)* 16, 3: 307–339. https://doi.org/10.1007/s10606-007-9044-5

10. Sharon A. Livingstone-Lee, Ronald W. Skelton, and Nigel Livingston. 2014. Transit Apps for People With Brain Injury and Other Cognitive Disabilities: The State of the Art. *Assistive Technology* 26, 4: 209–218. https://doi.org/10.1080/10400435.2014.930076

11. Cliff Oswick and Maxine Robertson. 2009. Boundary objects reconsidered: From bridges and anchors to barricades and mazes. *Journal of Change Management* 9, 2: 179–193. https://doi.org/10.1080/14697010902879137

12. S. B. Palmer, M. L. Wehmeyer, D. K. Davies, and S. E. Stock. 2012. Family members' reports of the technology use of family members with intellectual and developmental disabilities. *Journal of Intellectual Disability Research* 56, 4: 402–414. Retrieved from http://gateway.library.qut.edu.au/login?url=http://search.ebscohost.com/login.aspx?direct=true&db=afh&AN=73362475&site=ehost-live&scope=site

13. Volkmar Pipek, Helena Karasti, and Geoffrey C. Bowker. 2017. A preface to "infrastructuring and collaborative design." *Computer Supported Cooperative Work* 26, 1–2: 1–5. https://doi.org/10.1007/s10606-017-9271-3

14. Volkmar Pipek and Volker Wulf. 2009. Infrastructuring: Toward an integrated perspective on the design and use of information technology. *Journal of the Association for Information Systems* 10, 5: 447. Retrieved November 19, 2014 from http://search.proquest.com.ezp01.library.qut.edu.au/docview/198832498/fulltextPDF?accountid=13380

15. Ravihansa Rajapakse, Margot Brereton, Paul Roe, and Laurianne Sitbon. 2014. Designing with people with disabilities: Adapting best practices of DIY and organizational approaches. In *Proceedings of the 26th Australian Computer-Human Interaction Conference - OzCHI '14*, 519–522. https://doi.org/10.1145/2686612.2686694

16. Ravihansa Rajapakse, Margot Brereton, Laurianne Sitbon, and Paul Roe. 2015. A Collaborative approach to design individualized technologies with people with a disability. In *Proceedings of the Annual Meeting of the Australian Special Interest Group for Computer Human Interaction on - OzCHI '15*, 29–33. https://doi.org/10.1145/2838739.2838824

17. Ravihansa Rajapakse, Margot Brereton, Laurianne Sitbon, and Paul Roe. 2017. Respectful design: Facilitating codesign with people with an intellectual disability. *CoDesign (in submission).*

18. Susan Leigh Star. 1988. The structure of ill-structured solutions: Boundary objects and heterogeneous distributed problem solving. In *Distributed Artificial Intelligence (Vol. 2)*. Morgan Kaufmann Publishers, San Francisco, 37–54.

19. Susan Leigh Star. 1999. The ethnography of infrastructure. *American Behavioral Scientist* 43, 3: 377–391. https://doi.org/10.1177/00027649921955326

20. Susan Leigh Star. 2010. This is not a boundary object: Reflections on the origin of a concept. *Science, Technology, & Human Values* 35, 5: 601–617. https://doi.org/10.1177/0162243910377624

21. Susan Leigh Star and Geoffrey C. Bowker. 2006. How to infrastructure. In *Handbook of new media: Social shaping and consequences of ICTs*. Sage.

22. Susan Leigh Star and James R. Griesemer. 1989. Institutional ecology, "translations" and boundary objects: Amateurs and professionals in Berkeley's Museum of Vertebrate Zoology, 1907-39. *Social Studies of Science* 19, 3: 387–420. https://doi.org/10.1177/030631289019003001

23. Susan Leigh Star and Karen Ruhleder. 1996. Steps toward an ecology of infrastructure: Design and access for large information spaces. *Information Systems Research* 7, 1: 111–134. Retrieved January 19, 2015 from http://citeseerx.ist.psu.edu/viewdoc/summary?doi=10.1.1.88.3121

24. Michael Wehmeyer. 2005. Self-determination and individuals with severe disabilities: Re-examining meanings and misinterpretations. *Research and Practice for Persons with Severe Disabilities* 30, 3: 113–120. https://doi.org/10.2511/rpsd.30.3.113

25. Michael L Wehmeyer. 1998. Self-determination and individuals with significant disabilities: Examining meanings and misinterpretations. *Journal of the Association for Persons with Severe Handicaps* 23, 1: 5–16.

26. Michael L. Wehmeyer and Nancy W. Garner. 2003. The impact of personal characteristics of people with intellectual and developmental disability on self-determination and autonomous functioning. *Journal of Applied Research in Intellectual Disabilities* 16, 4: 255–265. https://doi.org/10.1046/j.1468-3148.2003.00161.x

The Use(fulness) of Therapeutic Toys: Practice-derived Design Lenses for Toy Design

Peter Fikar
TU Wien
Vienna, Austria
peter.fikar@tuwien.ac.at

Florian Güldenpfennig
TU Wien
Vienna, Austria
florian.gueldenpfennig@tuwien.ac.at

Roman Ganhör
TU Wien
Vienna, Austria
roman.ganhoer@tuwien.ac.at

ABSTRACT
Early Intervention Services support children with disabilities in their development from early age on. To this end, therapeutic toys are regularly employed within training sessions. These toys often draw on interactive elements to make exercising more appealing, and hence, to motivate the children. While there is some research about interactive therapeutic toys in HCI, these works are often standalone design deployments, exploring specific health or rehabilitation applications. In contrast, this paper offers different lenses for investigating qualities of therapeutic toys to highlight the following aspects: therapeutic and playful/motivational efforts, the potential of technology in supporting suitable affordances, ease of use, flexibility and improvisation. The lenses enable guided explorations of existing toys or novel design proposals, resulting from a thematic analysis of a) in-situ observations of therapeutic exercises (n=18), b) in-depth/informal interviews with Early Intervention Specialists (combined n=16), and c) demonstrations of their favorite toys (n=21).

Author Keywords
Therapeutic toys; children; disabilities; visual impairments;

ACM Classification Keywords
• Human-centered computing~User studies • Human-centered computing~Field studies

INTRODUCTION
HCI has a long tradition in designing for and with children in the domain of education and health promotion. Much research investigated the use of toys and games to foster developmental growth, for example, [7; 16; 19; 24]. We add to the literature by investigating and reflecting the use of (interactive) therapeutic toys in supporting children with multiple disabilities in the setting of Early Intervention Services [27] with a focus on visual training. Here, we take a broad approach and explore the social relationship between therapists and children, mediated by toys. That is, we focus on the roles and qualities that toys generally have to fulfill in therapy from a social perspective and from the viewpoint of play as a motivational factor and medium for therapeutic effort in contrast to concentrating on a specific toy geared towards a specific purpose. The latter approach is common within many research efforts in HCI that led to insightful domain-specific results. However, we experience as designers and argue as researchers, that it is sometimes hard to generalize such findings to different domains. For example, while an inspirational toy design for improving fine motor skills can also be relevant for work on supporting vision training, designers might have difficulties in transferring knowledge from one toy design to their own project.

DIS '18, June 9–13, 2018, Hong Kong

ACM ISBN 978-1-4503-5198-0/18/06…$15.00
https://doi.org/10.1145/3196709.3196721

In order to provide guidance in such a situation, we interviewed and observed therapists in their daily work and synthesized our findings into five themes employing a thematic analysis approach [2]. These themes are *not* to be understood as a prescriptive model; rather we offer them as a set of analytical lenses for highlighting salient aspects of good toys that are used in therapeutic practice. The corresponding themes encourage reflection about motivational efforts in toy-mediated therapy and the role of play (see themes *Does the Toy afford the Zielreaktion*[1]*?* and *This is not Therapy, This is Play!*), the potential of technology in supporting suitable affordances (see theme *It Would be Great if it Could be Illuminated*), flexibility and improvisation in therapeutic practice (see theme *This Cannot be Planned!*), and ease of use of toys (see theme *Practicability of Toys*). While these five design lenses cannot guide *specific* actions, we argue that our findings apply across a wide range of settings and thus provide fellow researchers with entry points when conceiving novel therapeutic and interactive toys.

The insights of this paper stem from a one-year design-research endeavor with Early Intervention Specialists (abbreviated as EIS from now on). EIS are social care professionals like educators or psychologists with a special training in supporting children with (multiple) disabilities. In the context of this research, all children had a form of Cortical/Cerebral Visual Impairment, in some cases causing

[1]*Zielreaktion* translated to English: "desired reaction to be provoked".

only mild effects, in others having a more severe impact on life. In addition to vision problems, most children suffered from comorbidities such as Cerebral Palsy, which can often be found in individuals with these kinds of vision impairments due to neurological damage in related brain regions (see next section for more details) [10].

The paper is structured as follows. First, we review related work before we describe the study design. In this context, we also detail therapeutic and educational background information. Then, we provide a description of each theme resulting from the analysis and thereby communicate the 'optical properties' of our design lenses. Subsequently, we further discuss the design lenses' application and highlight the role of toys and technology in mediating therapy with toys in the context of Early Intervention. Eventually, we conclude the paper with ideas for future research.

BACKGROUND & RELATED WORK

This section entails a brief introduction to Early Intervention and the support of children with disabilities through play and toy design.

Early Intervention to support Children with Disabilities

Early Intervention Services [27] as provided by healthcare systems in many countries support children with neurological issues starting from the first weeks of life and accompanying them until about the age of six years [15]. The ultimate objective of Early Intervention Service and the EIS is to prevent or minimize developmental delays [15]. In many cases, such delays, disabilities, and syndromes stem from neurological damage, caused by lesions of the brain, resulting in complex and diverse impairments of different severities and comorbidities [15].

In the context of our research, all children suffered from Cortical/Cerebral Visual Impairment (CVI) [18] which is a frequent problem that results from such a brain-based injury. The term CVI encompasses mild to severe visual deficits causing again a vast variety of symptoms. The symptoms of CVI are affecting visual perception, like visual acuity or cortical image processing and pattern recognition, learning, mobility, development, independence and ultimately quality of life [18].

To slow down potentially degenerative effects, training and practice of vision is essential in early childhood. Training and intervention should start as early as possible and expose the affected child to appropriate sensory stimuli in order to spur growth, either on a cellular level where new synapses are established or on a personal level to foster developmental competencies [11; 15]. Moreover, additional activities are offered, such as exercising hand-eye coordination and holistic exercises (i.e., exercises addressing the whole body). Conventional tools for therapy supporting such visual training (e.g., abstract patterns of high contrast) are often described as inappropriate/uninteresting for children and the training itself as boring, repetitive or tedious [14; 32]. To make training engaging and motivating, the EIS introduce many playful elements to the training sessions. Indeed, play activities are of crucial importance for development across many domains such as cognition, language, skills and is utilized in Early Intervention to foster development [13]. The relationship between the EIS and the children (and also parents) is a central feature in Early Intervention [25; 33] as it allows them to develop a deep understanding about the characteristics of the children and their needs.

As we show in this paper, the EIS incorporate toys into therapy in order to "design" play activities that again engage the children in learning experiences. For this reason, we argue that the different roles or functions of toys and their corresponding properties should be of utmost interest for researchers who want to support Early Intervention and therapeutic play with novel (interactive) toy designs.

Toys and their Affordances & Signifiers

The Oxford dictionary defines a toy as "[...] an object for a child to play with, typically a model or miniature replica of something" [4]. In order to design toys (or other made objects in general) that can facilitate certain interactions between user and object, their *relationship* must be carefully explored and addressed. That is, the usefulness of a design is defined by its match with the potential users (are they able to comprehend the intended use and can they handle it?). The terms of *affordances and signifiers*[2] were introduced to frame this relationship. Norman [21, p.18] referring to Gibson, describes affordances as: "... the actions possible by a specific agent on a specific environment". He also explains that affordances are provided vastly but only some of them are perceivable. Signifiers, again, are signals as in terms of the perceivable part of an affordance, giving hints for interpretation and pointing to ways the object might be used.

As an example, the handle of a toy dagger, signifies where it should be held because of the way a leather band is wrapped around it at one end. Holding the dagger in the signified way, it affords to play-act a sword fight, because it can be swung around in the air, and so on. Thus, the relation between the properties of the toy dagger and the children's hand, and what the child aims to do with it is well defined. Features of toys allow for and suggest specific usage. A bouncy rubber ball invites play differently than building blocks or a toy sword. They all invite different kinds of play by providing perceivable affordances/signifiers and thus suggest opportunities for

[2]Note, in the course of this paper we will use the notions of affordances and signifiers when describing toys. In some instances, we will use the terms *cues* and *stimuli* synonymously to highlight that a therapeutic toy should not only signify its use, but also stimulate the sensory system of the children by providing appropriate cues. Moreover, we use the terms toy and therapeutic toys to denote all objects that the EIS incorporate into play activities. Accordingly, we also denote the old cans of Figure 4, e.g., as toys or therapeutic toys.

interaction. In general, designers should carefully craft meaningful signifiers and affordances to feature and support playful interactions.

Responding to these and similar considerations, researchers have created frameworks to describe and support toy design. Kudrowitz and Wallace [12] reflected on the designer's perspective and pointed to their challenge of creating affordances that users can perceive and interpret in the same way as the designers do. Their proposed framework for classifying toys and their potential play value enables designers and researchers to systematically explore toy designs and their play value. Mertala et al. [20] looked into toy preferences of young children (6-8 years old) and established a framework based on the "functional manipulation potential" of toys. That is classifying the toy's built-in affordances according to its "attractive", "pragmatic" and "adaptive" affordances when playing. Both mentioned frameworks are providing powerful tools for understanding conventional toy design and play of children *without* disabilities.

In the present paper, we elaborate design lenses by drawing on thematic analysis that consider the use of therapeutic toys in the context of Early Intervention for children aged 0-6 years. In contrast to Kudrowitz and Wallace [12] and Mertala et al. [20], we aim to create toys that *afford therapists* to design play activities for children with disabilities. Thus, our design lenses do not aim for toys and affordances addressing solely the children but also the proxies/playmakers in-between toy and child.

Play in Children with Disabilities

Brodin [3] underlines the close connection between children's play, learning and development in her work on play in children with (multiple) disabilities. She highlights that such children differ in their play behavior as they often participate rather as sole spectators and hence are often excluded from learning social play behavior. As we investigate (therapeutic) toys in this paper, we should consider that children with developmental delays are usually more passive than children without disabilities, when playing with objects. Nevertheless, they can become more actively engaged if provided with appropriate stimuli (e.g., suitable toys, other objects and materials) that are fostered through social interactions and play [3]. Therapeutic toys are designed considering these circumstances and are therefore often more beneficial in the context of therapy than commercial toys used in therapy. As we will see in the Findings, for the same reason, EIS create their own special needs toys from everyday objects.

Tangible Objects & Development

Objects play a vital role in the development of children and their construction of knowledge through play [13]. Sensory and motoric skills are crucial to establish and organize knowledge by grasping and experiencing objects. This finally leads to the ability to derive conclusions in logical and increasingly abstract ways [29].

Within HCI, the significance of objects in the development of children was utilized in the field of *tangible interaction*, connecting real world physicality and abstract digital representations in order to create computational artifacts for learning [17; 29]. The paradigm opens up a vast space for interaction design by relating the physicality of objects and their digital representation [23]. It can enrich the sensory and cognitive experiences of children as they handle and manipulate artifacts, engage in meaningful composition of tangible interactions and haptic manipulations [5]. Overall, *tangibles* are able to offer a variety of opportunities to education and have been described as beneficial when applied in the context of learning in order to gain experiences, skills and knowledge [22]. Recent examples of such tangible interaction objects are Polipo [31], ChillFish [30], BoostBeans [8], Cuebe [6], and PhonoBlocks [1].

Some researchers have conducted initial work to explicitly merge classical approaches from pedagogy to haptic and educational toys with tangible computing. Zuckerman et al. [34], e.g., imported ideas of Montessori and Fröbel and suggested that tangibles, drawing on these philosophies, might motivate children to construct objects from the real world but also model abstract concepts, enabling the child to explore, design and eventually to learn [34].

STUDY

As indicated in the introduction, we found ourselves in a situation where we had to design interactive therapeutic toys for children with disabilities, but we could not find *concrete* starting points in the HCI literature to guide our design. Accordingly, we formulated a broad research question in the beginning of the endeavor, and present it here as the challenge for this paper: *What are the properties of toys in Early Intervention and what tasks do they support?*

Participants

To this end, we recruited 24 professional therapists[3] from a local organization to be engaged in a co-design process. Four of these EIS invested a considerable amount of time (each approximately 2 hours per week), and for this effort they received financial remuneration. The remaining 20 participants were involved sporadically on various occasions, but far less time-intensively. They were compensated indirectly by donations we made to their organization from project budget (new therapeutic equipment and toys).

We then used the EIS' network and expertise to recruit twelve suitable children for our study (aged 3-6 years). Inclusion criteria for the children were approval by the parents as well as being likely to enjoy the visits of researchers and potentially benefitting from the engagement from a therapeutic perspective. The children in this study all

[3]We acknowledge that some of the participating EIS refer to themselves as *supporters* instead of *therapists* to remove deficit-centered language. For readability and to avoid confusions, we still decided to denote them as EIS and *therapists*, because in the literature their work is indeed described as *therapy*.

had disabilities related to low vision (CVI), and all of them had co-morbidities like Cerebral Palsy as described in the Background Section. As CVI is the major impairment in the target group, we focus on toys for visual training in this paper. We don't claim that the findings can be applied to artifacts for children with different disabilities. The children or their parents did not receive financial compensation, but the children received free sessions of training. In order not to distract the children or to exhaust them, only one researcher at a time came to the training sessions.

Data Collection and Analysis

All encounters with the children took place in the presence of one or two parents, in most cases at their homes, and all instructions were given by the EIS only. The researcher acted as an observer, taking field notes as unobtrusively as possible, and in rare occasions photos on the approval of the parents. All involved parties, including the researchers, signed a contract. The participants gave their written informed consent, and the researchers guaranteed not to publish any personal information without permission.

To gain insights into the practices of Early Intervention, we conducted 18 field observations of therapeutic training sessions at the children's homes (lasting 60 min each), four semi-structured in-depth interviews (60-120 min each) and twelve informal interviews (15-50 min each). In addition, we took a tour of the rooms of the Early Intervention center and investigated parts of the therapeutic equipment (lasting 90 min). Among other things, they had a large storage room with thousands of (therapeutic) toys, and so we decided to invite the individual EIS to also showcase their favorite toys for Early Intervention. Twelve participants followed this invitation and demonstrated a total of 21 toys. Additionally, the EIS provided us with short notes on these toys, detailing pros and cons of the particular pieces. We included this material in our analysis as well. When presenting the findings, we will use photographs of some of these favorite toys as illustrative examples.

During all of our observations, we considered the artifacts of therapy, in particular the toys (as their design was our primary concern), but also the surrounding social interactions, play-related facets, and the different roles of the EIS and the children.. All observations were audio-recorded when appropriate and transcribed (e.g., the in-depth interviews). When recording was not possible, we created textual field notes and an anonymized photo-documentation (e.g., in the children's homes or during some informal interviews when chatting with therapists).

In our thematic analysis, we stuck rather closely to the procedure as proposed by the well-cited article by Braun and Clarke [2, p.83]. In detail, we a) familiarized ourselves with the data corpus by reading the transcripts of the interviews and by revisiting the field-photos several times. b) Two of the authors then generated an initial set of codes (open coding) and applied them to the texts. This process was iterative and inductive, that is, codes were assigned 'bottom up' on a data-driven basis instead of being motivated by theory or pre-established coding frameworks. c) Subsequently and on a number of occasions, the same authors used these initial codes to establish an initial set of themes, primarily drawing on techniques of mind-mapping. d) Next, these initial themes were presented to the third author of this paper and in several meetings and rounds of discussion were shaped into the final theme definitions. We put particular emphasis on finding descriptive names for the themes to capture and represent salient issues in the daily therapeutic practice of the EIS.

FINDINGS

Toys had ubiquitous presence in the practices of the EIS and fulfilled a variety of different roles. Most importantly, they were used to engage children in exercising, to train vision (e.g., hand-eye coordination, fixating objects) and motor skills (fine and gross), to accentuate stimuli (i.e., to make certain objects visible for children with low vision) to exercise cognition (e.g., match patterns, understanding of cause and reaction) or to assess their skills.

In the following, we present five major themes, which relate to our research question (see previous section), and which we offer as different lenses for therapeutic toy design. They capture salient characteristics of practice, e.g., the means by which desirable reactions in the child are provoked drawing on toys and play. As we will see in the following (and elaborate in the Discussion Section), the themes when used as design lenses can add to researchers' understanding what therapists do in practice, it can support designers' understanding what kind of toys are used in which ways, and it can inspire therapists and practitioners when reflecting on their own work practice.

"Does the Toy afford the 'Zielreaktion'?"

The "Zielreaktion" theme relates closely to the therapeutic perspective, such as the therapeutic goal itself and strategies to achieve this goal. This includes elements leading to therapeutics effects such as stimulation of visual senses, motor skills and cognition, and motivational elements.

It captures how the EIS design interactions through the use of toys to achieve beneficial therapeutic effects in the children. The theme is represented by a question of central importance posed by our participants when selecting a toy for therapy, namely if it affords the desired *Zielreaktion.* We define a *Zielreaktion* as a desirable reaction invoked in a child during therapeutic session and caused by specific factors. For example, a range of exercises that we observed made children follow a specific object with their eyes. Here, tracking the object was the *Zielreaktion,* and the exercises drew on factors that motivated the child to show this desired behavior. Such factors included intentional but also unintentional affordances of a toy, for example, sensory cues or signifiers like a visually attractive cartoon character provoking being fixated with the eyes. In addition to physical toy features, other factors were integrated into practice to provoke the *Zielreaktion*, for instance, meaningful social interactions between the EIS and the child. Consequently, provoking a *Zielreaktion* was also dependent on the personal traits of the people involved, especially the EIS, as it was them who's efforts, capabilities, knowledge and experience provoked and assessed the children's' reaction.

As indicated above, there was not one particular *Zielreaktion*, but there were many desired reactions. Ultimately, it is the responsibility of the EIS to make use of different toys in order to trigger appropriate and different reactions, resulting in developmental competencies and the accomplishment of overarching goals:

"*[...] Our goals are naturally the training of visual perception, taking initiative, understanding cause-&-effect, proactivity... These are the goals, which are always present, at least for children who are able to achieve basic things. Children for whom 'seeing' is the only handicap. These are not 'complicated cases' in general. On the other hand, the main goal regarding severely disabled children is that they can do at least something on their own and maybe even enjoy doing it.* (EIS M. from Interview)

This statement exemplifies that the EIS need to design for a *Zielreaktion* based on the individual developmental status and needs of the children. It might be necessary to train a child's capability to follow a visual feature by eye or body movement, or simply to foster initiative in a child to show independent interactions. The statement also indicates that visual factors are not the only relevant stimulus in toys and that non-visual sensory cues are also of crucial importance. Auditory and haptic cues can enrich the experience of interaction and play, by extending the range of motivational features and providing multimodal elements for mixing and composing meaningful interactions.

A popular toy among the EIS, which illustrates the value of multimodal affordances and signifiers in practice, is plastic bunny "Miffy" (see Figure 1). This toy is able to playback short pieces of sound. In our field study, the EIS hid "Miffy" and asked the children to search for the sound source. The children then explored the environment by directional hearing and used their (low) vision to scan the surroundings for the bunny. The combination of cues, visual and auditive, enriched the experience by demanding the use of sensory, motoric and cognitive skills (*Zielreaktion*) in order to fulfill the task.

„*The big advantage is the strong stimulating nature of this game. Also, it is easy to judge at which distance a child is capable to visually recognize the bunny as he or she approaches the toy by foot or reaches for it by hand in a target oriented manner.*" (EIS M.O. from Favorite-Toy-Description)

This statement illustrates how the *Zielreaktion* is assessed by the EIS through observing the children's skills in multimodal interactions. While hand-eye-coordination tasks demand for visual and motor skills, cause-&-effect

Figure 1. "Miffy" toy figurine and additional game materials.

exercises require cognitive skills to understand the connection between an action set and the outcomes it produces. Emotional skills are needed to deal with failure or success regarding frustration or joy, which, in turn, affects the motivation to maintain a child's attention.

Upholding motivation is especially important when practicing an underdeveloped skill where frustration is not exceptional. Social skills are in demand as the training sessions revolve around the relationship between the child and the EIS.

"It Would be Great if it Could be Illuminated"

This theme describes the potential of technology and opportunities to manipulate stimuli that are relevant for therapy by, for example, enhancement or reduction.

It stems from efforts of our participants in rearranging or redesigning features and affordances/signifiers of toys to make them appropriate for children with disabilities. The EIS accomplished this by actively 'hacking', redesigning or augmenting toys, or by purchasing (therapeutic) toys where stimuli and affordances have been designed with special care in a particular way. In either case, enhancements and reductions of affordances/signifiers were often accomplished by drawing on technology. Hence, the theme collates instances where interaction design and technology were utilized. In line with this insight, the authors chose the subtitle of this theme *It Would be Great if it Could be Illuminated.* It was part of a remark stated by EIS M. when she was considering a yellow toy duck to be used in therapy.

We found that in a number of instances electronic lights and sounds were integrated into toys in order to add incentives for interaction and to provide more intense stimuli than passive toys. In addition, digital devices such as tablets in conjunction with specialized apps offered rich interactive features and stimuli appropriate for therapy (see Figure 2), as summarized by EIS C.R.:

"*The apps [for the tablet computers] are providing good contrast, are low cost and can be deployed at any given moment. The iPad and the projector are easy to handle, fast at hand and low on weight."* (EIS C.R. from Favorite-Toy-Description)

Moreover, devices like portable, electronic light-tables provided a flexible basis during training sessions for different types of games making use of materials such as translucent blocks, puzzle pieces and illustrations (to be placed on the light-table). As a consequence of the bright illumination of the table, the perceptibility of the objects on the table were enhanced and therefore better visible for children with low vision. Since different children required different levels of illumination, the light-tables' intensity could be either increased or reduced.

This leads to our second observation regarding the theme, namely that reductions were also relevant in the practice of the EIS and in the use of toys. Admittedly, this was rarely the case compared to enhancements. Nevertheless, this theme highlights the fact, that the EIS also made use of toy features, that allowed them to make them less bright, to switch off sounds, masking unwanted stimuli and to make the toys less intrusive not to overwhelm the children.

As indicated above, the EIS also used technology to alter existing toys and objects in novel ways. An example from practice was a big and colorful power switch that was connected to the power supply of a toy train, allowing a child to control the train with this accessible on/off switch:

"The circuit breaker and power switch can be used for a variety of battery powered games and everyday objects like fans or light sources!" (EIS C.L. from Favorite-Toy-Description)

According to our participants, a drawback of such hands-on customizations was that those were often hard to implement due to the electrical devices that were involved:

„Sometimes it is hard to attach the power switch to the train or a similar toy in a way that the battery compartment can be closed and remains functional" (EIS C.L. from Favorite-Toy-Description)

Even though technology proved to be beneficial in many ways, it was also perceived as impractical and in some cases as problematic even. Depending on the complexity, the EIS were concerned about the increased efforts coming with technologically enhanced toys. In their experience, enhanced toys were less resistant to physical force or fluids (saliva) and their energy sources needed intense maintenance. Furthermore, technology in some instances introduced a degree of complexity, which made practice overly complicated and distracting from actual therapy.

Hence, besides all advantages of "high-tech", the EIS also appreciated "low-tech" or no technology at all. Simple wooden blocks coated in primary colors or intense black and white patterns provided rich and engaging experiences, sufficient and appropriate for some of the children. These passive cues were subtler than their electrically enhanced counterparts, making them less likely to overexcite the sensory organs of the child, which could ultimately cause stress or epileptic seizures in special cases.

Figure 2. (top) Tablet computer with app showing shapes and patterns with appropriate contrast, (below) small device for projecting bright patterns of light.

"This is not Therapy, This is Play!"

This theme is elaborating the perspective of motivation through play elements, and how they are shaped by attitudes and play interactions in practice. It further elaborates the role of therapist and the children in the play process and how toys are used.

The close relationship between therapeutic practice and play was important to all participating EIS. They emphasized that without motivation their children were less likely to engage in prolonged, intense training sessions and therefore, they won't progress as effectively as possible. Hence, they named motivation as an important, if not the most crucial factor for effective training, and made play the centerpiece of their motivational strategy. Through play they were often able to motivate the children and encourage their participation in tiring, monotonous, repetitive and boring training tasks.

Consequently, the EIS highlighted play related factors within their efforts, referring to their training sessions as "units" or "sessions" and avoiding the term therapy to a certain degree. "This is not therapy, this is play!" was a remark by EIS M. when she elaborated her perspective on her training sessions and practices.

In many cases, a session started with an opening and ended with a closing ritual, comparable to entering and leaving the "Circle of Play" as conceptualized by Huizinga [9] (see also Discussion Section). For example, EIS K. reported to sing together with the child at the beginning of each session, capturing the child's attention, and also to close the unit with the ritual of tidying up the room and storing away all toys or with a rhyme spoken together:

"Most of the times, we engage in a ritual at the beginning and in the end. Some children have a greeting-song, for example - Always the same song for the same kid" (EIS K. from Interview)

In addition, the interactions between EIS and child as well as the tasks assigned to a child were often embedded in play-related narratives, providing fictional meaning. These narratives included puppets and humanoid toys, brought to life through role-play, in order to flesh out a fictional purpose for the tasks. For example, a child was motivated to solve a puzzle assembling a helicopter. To this end, the EIS communicated the task by embedding it into a short narrative about preparing the helicopter for "takeoff". By identifying the parts necessary to do so, like windows, chassis and rotors and putting the respective pieces into place, the child assisted the EIS in "repairing" the helicopter and eventually making it fly. In our observations, a puzzle was more appropriate for such forms of play when it came in puzzle pieces representing *meaningful* units. For example, a piece could be integrated better into a narrative when it contained the rotor only, compared to a piece that contained both parts the rotor and the chassis, and so on.

With such overarching stories the EIS were able to provide rich play experiences by creating additional layers of meaning and to control therapeutic efforts at the same time.

In the "helicopter" example, the EIS fulfilled a variety of roles. Initially, she chose the task of assembling a puzzle for exercising hand-eye coordination (instructor) and she selected the toy (selector), which was the medium for the playful task. In the course of the exercise, the EIS then narrated the story about the helicopter (narrator), which connected toy and task. In addition, the EIS also received instructions by the child (receiver) and acted accordingly to solve the task in a team effort partially led by the child.

The theme as a whole encompasses the relevance of play, the roles it generates and the close correlation between toys, therapeutic exercise and skills of the EIS to balance play and the therapeutic goal.

"This Cannot be Planned!"

This theme is targeting the perspective of improvisation, flexibility and changing needs. It includes challenges arising from the heterogeneity of the children, their disabilities, associated symptoms, preferences in toys, the individual traits of the EIS and their strategies for intervention. It further describes how toys are used as therapeutic tools in unanticipated ways.

Even though the EIS planned the sessions' setup in advance, the circumstances at a particular session heavily depended on a child's current condition and situation, which again heavily influenced the actual content of a session. Often, the children were cheerful and cooperative, on other occasions or days the same children however refused to engage in the exercises due to some cause of irritation in their life (e.g., physical pain, exhaustion, etc.). Thus, the EIS had to be highly flexible and improvisational when both selecting the toys for exercising and when playing with the child during a session in order to react to the child's situation appropriately. In this context, EIS K. highlighted multifaceted features of an acoustic toy, a paddle drum (see Figure 3), as follows:

"What I like best about the paddle drum is its' versatile applicability and that it is light to carry. I use it regularly as a drum for motoric play, for singing, and so on, but also for echo localization. I also use the membrane for projections, for letting lights shine through [a variety of flashlights, bicycle-lamps, etc.] and for setting additional acoustic cues. I also use it for projections from mobile projectors and put the paddle on the children's lap. In this way, I am able to project a clear and undistorted image. [...] And I use it as a bowl or container, in which I put beans, chestnuts and so on for digging around in them. Or I put other high contrast or luminous, tactually interesting things into it and offer it to the children. This again, comes with an interesting acoustic aspect, because it's a drum!" (EIS M.O. from Favorite-Toy-Description)

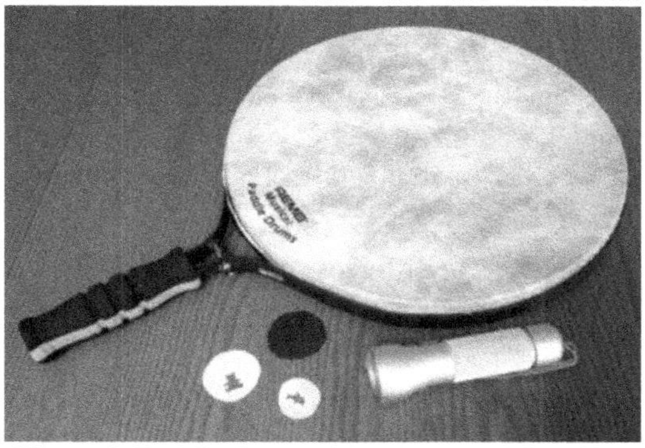

Figure 3. Paddle drum with tokens and flashlight.

This statement exemplifies how a toy was valued for the range of flexible interactions it offered. The toy provided a basis for a variety of activities, synthesizing sensory cues and signifiers of different modalities. The example of the paddle drum also shows that the intended purpose of a toy and the affordances it was designed for, are not always the single-most valued factor for therapeutic sessions. Often it is a toy's flexibility and suitability for improvised use making it an appropriate choice. To this end, supporting the personal toy preferences of the children was critical for motivation but was also posing a challenge due to their often limited communicational skills. Furthermore, the "mood" or motivation of some children changed quickly during a session, rendering planned play-activities suddenly ineffective.

In general, the varying symptoms and effects of the children's' disabilities and developmental deficits made them a highly heterogeneous group regarding their characteristics and needs. This, in turn, limited a toy's applicability and the corresponding play strategies. The EIS however anticipated these uncertainties by bringing a defined selection of toys that could be deployed in a flexible manner to match a child's preference, abilities and habits. It is the EIS' knowledge, field-experience and their careful selection of toys, which enabled them to react to changing conditions in order to keep up an effective training. Additionally, the EIS responded to this complicated situation by creating their own toy-like artifacts, which introduced another layer of flexibility to their sessions. Thereby, they created affordances and signifiers, which were appropriate for their children but not offered by stock toys. Such designs were also influenced by their in-depth knowledge of the children's characteristics and needs in order to meet their individual demands. The illustration in Figure 4a depicts such a custom-made toy, prompting the children to pick small tokens and to stick them through the small opening on the container-lid.

As the EIS possessed a variety of such containers in different sizes, in different colors and with different content, these custom-made toys enabled them to respond spontaneously and in different ways to the children:

"*I can never tell what exercise or kind of play the children will accept. But I often bring a set of old containers with me. Then I can figure out, if the child likes them, which one of them, which kind of dropping sound is fun for them, what kind of objects can be grasped with their hands. Then I make a choice dynamically. The most important thing is that I can engage them somehow.*" (EIS C.R. from Interview)

"Practicability of Toys"

This theme offers a perspective on the practicability of toys and materials used by the EIS and how these have to be designed to be applicable in daily practice.

All findings that we have reported in previous sections had a direct relation to the therapeutic efforts. The theme *Practicability of Toys*, in contrast, does not have a direct influence on therapy, but still was a salient issue in our observations. Whether a toy can be handled well or not, can at least have an indirect effect on therapy outcome, as we will outline in the following.

Practicability of Toys was especially important when it came to storing, transporting, handling and maintaining toys. EIS C., for example, provided the subsequent enumeration regarding the qualities of a ball run (see Figure 4b) when we asked her about what she liked about her favorite therapeutic toys:

"*I like the ball run because of it is low on weight and the strong colors. We can practice keeping track [of the ball] in a playful way. But the course of the track is not too long and also children with small attention spans are tracking the ball until the end... It works with different balls, and it can be used with fitting round objects from the child's home. The nice thing is that it is allowed to get wet [from salvia/disinfectants]... that it cannot break. And it can be cleaned easily. And it is a common toy. Therefore parents can buy a private ball run if they like, and they can play together with young siblings*" (EIS C. from Favorite-Toy-Description)

As evident, the toy description includes a number of physical features, which are not directly tied to therapeutic purposes, however, beneficial when transporting, handling, maintaining, cleaning and storing them. For each of these facets, specific features or aspects proved relevant. Next, we briefly describe those of most importance to the EIS.

Figure 4. a) Left: Customized containers with differently shaped lids on top, optionally painted with a pattern, and smaller objects to throw into the cans, b) Right: Ball run with modular elements and two balls.

Storage. Between sessions the toys were stored and some needed special arrangement in order to stay functional. The EIS reported that in some instances batteries leaked when left unattended in electrical toys over a longer period of time or modeling clay hardened because of bad storage.

Transportation. As training took place in the homes of the children, the EIS needed to transport the therapeutic toys to every session. In this way, the toys could be shared among all children and the EIS, but this practice introduced logistical challenges, since most therapists relied on public transportation. Still, they carried multiple toys with them when visiting a child. They described ideal toys as being light-weight, unobtrusive, and rather small than big.

Handling. The *handling* of a toy during a session was another important factor as sessions were strictly time limited (60 minutes). To minimize time-consuming in-situ preparations, the toys needed to be setup quickly. For example, putting together a racing track for slot cars would take too long, even though the toy itself could be valuable for therapeutic use.

Hygiene. Since children in Early Intervention Services are aged between 0 to 6 years, the toys must be appropriate for this age. On many occasions the children we observed put toys into their mouths; thus, a toy has to withstand saliva and has to be easy to clean. Sharp edges, spikes, etc. have to be avoided and the coatings have to be non-toxic.

Robustness was described as being important, as a child can get emotionally upset for various reasons and may start throwing the toy around or biting into it. An appropriate toy should withstand external forces to a certain degree and stay intact.

Maintenance. In order to keep their toys intact, the EIS put much effort into maintaining them. We observed the EIS cleaning toys diligently due to hygienic purposes and we saw them replacing or recharging batteries for electrical toys to avoid failure in future sessions. The EIS reported that, ideally, they want to replace or repair broken parts on their own to avoid costly repairs by professionals. Overall, the less care a toy needed, the more suitable it was for the EIS' practice.

DISCUSSION

In this discussion section, we put together the insights we gathered during the analysis and discuss how the themes can be employed as analytical design lenses for the design of novel therapeutic (and interactive) toys. Given that toys have such a prominent role in the practice of the EIS, we conclude the discussion section by reflecting on toys, play, and how this utmost important aspect of Early Intervention can be supported with technology.

Five Design Lenses for Therapeutic Toy Design, How to Use them and their Limitations

This paper investigated different properties and tasks of therapeutic toys in Early Intervention. Through a thematic analysis we identified five themes that were key in the way EIS made use of toys to foster developmental growth in children with disabilities. Given the importance of these patterns in the toy-mediated practice of the EIS, we offer them as analytical lenses for fellow researchers and designers who are interested in gaining different perspectives on this interesting design space. Each theme can be employed as a lens or entry point for designers and researchers when proposing a design idea or scrutinizing the functions of therapeutic toys.

While it was useful to separate the themes during analysis and to provide them as individual lenses, we must however consider that the themes are closely related and mutually influence each other in practice. For example, if a designer puts all their efforts in creating optimal affordances to evoke a *Zielreaktion* (*Does the Toy afford the Zielreaktion?*), they nevertheless should take the toy's practicability into account. Whenever a toy cannot be brought to the home of the clients or cannot be cleaned, it will not be used for such reasons (*Practicability of Toys*). At the same time, the children might reject the toy when the designer failed in making it playful and fun (*This is not Therapy, this is Play!*). Similarly, the designer might want to consider that EIS often embed their therapeutic toys in fantastic stories and narratives in flexible ways to motivate the child to fulfill exercises, and so on (*This cannot be planned!*). Thus, a viable toy excels in multiple themes, ideally in all of them.

As Early Intervention Service follows a holistic approach, we decided to study the practices of EIS involving toys in-situ rather than decontextualized therapeutic toys and their properties as sole objects without people's involvement. We acknowledge, however, that it might be useful in certain situations to study the toys in isolation. For example, had we been interested in supporting vision in isolation, it might have been beneficial to investigate the optical properties of the toys in close detail. We could have established a classification of color schemes in toys and asked questions like *What kind of contrasts are used? Do the toys feature patterns? Are the toys illuminated in specific ways? And so on*. Had we been interested in supporting fine motor skills in isolation, on the contrary, we might have arrived at a theoretical analysis of therapeutic toys from the perspectives of theories of tangible interaction.

However, such a research strategy has to be applied with caution. As evident from our dataset, toy-mediated therapy is a highly contextualized process with prominent actors and close social relationships. Extracting the toys or any other therapeutic/medical equipment is a delicate task, which leads to very specific results for a very specific audience. As mentioned before, one of the main reasons to conduct thematic analysis in this paper was that we found ourselves in a situation where we had to create novel therapeutic toys, but could not identify *concrete* guidance or starting points for our endeavor in the literature. Hence we argue, that our more holistic approach is justified and should be of value for fellow designers, as it can provide – drawing on its analytic lenses – an entry point for new research into therapeutic toys. While Early Intervention with a focus on vision seems to be a specific use case, it constitutes an interesting area due to its broad domain. The broad domain allows for "generalization" or transfer to related domains like toy-mediated occupational therapy [30; 31]. Departing from one of the themes, designers might want to expand on their research and explore aspects that are of their primary interest, for example, designing dedicated toys for motor rehabilitation. These explorations could then be linked back to our thematic analysis and existing frameworks [12; 20], and an interesting body of insights could be generated. It might also be fruitful to interpret existing literature through the lenses as provided by the thematic analysis in this paper.

Playing with Therapeutic Toys

According to the participants and our observations, the EIS utilize play as a powerful means to motivate the children to engage in exercises that they would otherwise not fulfill. This motivational potential of play stems in part from its transformative powers, the ability to create its own meaning. Huizinga frames play in his seminal work "Homo Ludens" as being a concealed space and time [9]. In the elaboration of the theme *This is not Therapy, This is Play!*, we provided an example where the session opened and closed with a song, sung by both the EIS and the child. In this way the therapy session has much in common with the establishment of Huizinga's "Magic Circle", which describes the separation of the sphere of play from "ordinary" life. The singing ritual is providing an entry point for entering the Magic Circle in terms of a play experience going beyond therapy, as this activity marks a clear line of separation between ordinary life and therapeutic session. It also denotes the entry point to a world of make-believe, where the EIS is able to create a new cognitive frame [28]. In their work, Salen and Zimmerman [28] exemplify this concept of framing by contrasting two ways of reading the book "Alice in Wonderland". When read and enjoyed as a fairy tale, the story can introduce a fantastical viewpoint to the reader. When read as part of an English class, in contrast, this different cognitive frame will lead to a different experience, which is probably less fantastical but more "stressful" and oriented towards a final examination about the text.

Similarly, we saw the EIS framing the training sessions in different ways, for example, by embedding toys into made-up stories, and this had consequence for how the children perceived the training sessions. This strategy enabled the EIS to build relationships with the children with different qualities. They took the role of the playmaker and the playmate (cf. theme *This is not Therapy, This is Play!* where we detailed the different roles), and thus they created a deeper connection to the children as they departed from the role of the sole therapist.

As we found, they regularly shaped the sessions around tasks with a strong narrative and role-play, putting the EIS in charge of the design of the stories. Thus, a good toy supports the EIS when shaping such a fictional frame, ideally enabling and inspiring the creation and control of interactions and also supporting the assessment of the *Zielreaktion* the EIS aim to provoke.

A good toy in this context would ideally support the EIS in designing play-related meanings for the child, by the affordances it allows to create, [28]), steering away from the therapeutic aspects of a session and from potentially difficult and frustrating experiences for the child, camouflaging boring and potentially repetitive exercises, and adding more appeal to them.

This is however a challenging task, as we outlined throughout the paper. Creating an appropriate play situation is often difficult in the setting of a time-restricted training unit. An additional challenge arises since children with (multiple) disabilities play differently compared to children developed according to their age, as elaborated by Brodin [3] (see Related Work). In this regard "passive" stimuli were described as being less attractive, as such children were rather attracted by intensified stimuli like electrical enhanced lights. Different technological enhancements may therefore provide appropriate support in this matter, and in practice the EIS make use of strong stimuli of multiple modalities to gain the child's attention. They are ever prepared to add new toys with interesting enhancements and features to their growing collection of (therapeutic) toys to be able to respond to each child's individual needs. Here, we see an opportunity for interaction design and technology to leverage toy-mediated therapy and play.

Technological Opportunities in Enhancing Toys

There are great opportunities to enrich therapeutic toys with technology. We propose that considering the findings in *It Would be Great, if it Could be Illuminated* can inspire the design of useful interactive toys. For example, visual, auditive, and tactile affordances or signifiers could be intensified by technologies in order to fit the sensorial capabilities of the children. Then again, technology could enable the EIS to reduce stimuli to prevent overstimulation of the sensory system, which is a frequent problem in their work with disabled children as reported above. However, it should be noted that in this context, technology should be utilized with care, and the EIS or the user must be in full control of the provided features to adjust the toy according to different user groups and to avoid stressful experiences.

When implemented well, technological elements like sensors and actuators might also empower the EIS to increase the possibilities to design play in novel ways. For example, a "magic wand" toy could be enhanced with bright multi-color LEDs and a touch sensor, which has an effect on the coloring. The EIS could then encourage the training of motor skills and the engagement with the light stimulus, by embedding the toy into a fantastic story, and so on. The use of smart sensors etc. could at the same time enable the implementation of novel tools for assessments. On the one hand, the current status of the children could be tested, for example, by quantifying a present tremor when holding a magic wand toy using an accelerometer. On the other hand, repeated measurements would allow for an estimation of therapy progress.

CONCLUSION

During a research project in the field of Early Intervention we had to assess and design therapeutic toys for visually impaired children. However, most of the existing literature in this and neighboring areas dealt with very *specific* use cases such as supporting fine motor control using a particular toy design. Neither could we find a general or holistic guidance, nor could we find *concrete* entry points to start our endeavor. Due to this lack in literature and guidance we conducted intensive field observations and thematic analysis on the role and functions of toys in Early Intervention to build a foundation we can base our upcoming design decisions on. Our analysis resulted in the description of five salient themes, which capture the process of toy-mediated therapy from a holistic perspective. Thus, our research complements existing HCI literature on detailed studies of existing toys, by providing more *general* design lenses for therapeutic toy design. Furthermore, the presented themes discuss five interesting entry points on which fellow designers and researchers can build upon.

ACKNOWLEDGEMENTS

This research was funded by "Gemeinsame Gesundheitsziele aus dem Rahmen-Pharmavertrag, eine Kooperation von österreichischer Pharmawirtschaft und Sozialversicherung".

We would like to thank all of our participants and the anonymous reviewers for their time and commitment.

REFERENCES

[1] Alissa N. Antle, Min Fan, and Emily S. Cramer. 2015. PhonoBlocks: A Tangible System for Supporting Dyslexic Children Learning to Read. In *Proceedings of the Ninth International Conference on Tangible, Embedded, and Embodied Interaction*, ACM, 533-538.

[2] Virginia Braun and Victoria Clarke. 2006. Using Thematic Analysis in Psychology. *Qualitative Research in Psychology 3*, 2, 77-101.

[3] Jane Brodin. 1999. Play in Children with Severe Multiple Disabilities: Play with toys - a review. *International Journal of Disability, Development and Education 46*, 1, 25-34.

[4] Oxford Dictionary. 2017. Definition for "Toy". Retrieved September 05, 2017 from https://en.oxforddictionaries.com/definition/toy

[5] Taciana Pontual Falcão. 2010. The role of tangible technologies for special education. In *CHI '10 Extended Abstracts on Human Factors in Computing Systems*, ACM, 2911-2914.

[6] Peter Fikar, Florian Güldenpfennig, and Roman Ganhör. 2018. The Cuebe: Facilitating Playful Early Intervention for the Visually Impaired. In *International Conference on Tangible, Embedded and Embodied Interactions*, 35-41.

[7] Christopher Frauenberger, Julia Makhaeva, and Katharina Spiel. 2016. Designing Smart Objects with Autistic Children: Four Design Exposés. In *Proceedings of the 2016 CHI Conference on Human Factors in Computing Systems*, ACM, 130-139.

[8] Florian Güldenpfennig, Peter Fikar, and Roman Ganhör. 2018. Interactive and Open-Ended Sensory Toys: Designing with Therapists and Children for Tangible and Visual Interaction. In *International Conference on Tangible, Embedded and Embodied Interactions*, Stockholm, 451-459.

[9] Johan Huizinga. 1971. *Homo Ludens. A Study of the Play Element in Culture*. Paladin, UK.

[10] Richard Huo, Susan K Burden, Creig S Hoyt, and William V Good. 1999. Chronic cortical visual impairment in children: aetiology, prognosis, and associated neurological deficits. *British Journal of Ophthalmology 83*, 6, 670-675.

[11] Lea Hyvärinen. 1995. Considerations in Evaluation and Treatment of the Child With Low Vision. *American Journal of Occupational Therapy 49*, 9, 891-897.

[12] Barry M. Kudrowitz and David R. Wallace. 2009. The play pyramid: a play classification and ideation tool for toy design. *International Journal of Arts and Technology 3*, 1, 36-56.

[13] Karin Lifter, Suzanne Foster-Sanda, Caley Arzamarski, Jacquelyn Briesch, and Ellen Mcclure. 2011. Overview of Play: Its Uses and Importance in Early Intervention/Early Childhood Special Education. *Infants & Young Children 24*, 3, 225-245.

[14] Conor Linehan, Jonathan Waddington, Timothy L. Hodgson, Kieran Hicks, and Robert Banks. 2014. Designing games for the rehabilitation of functional vision for children with cerebral visual impairment. In *CHI '14 Extended Abstracts on Human Factors in Computing Systems*, ACM, 1207-1212.

[15] Annette Majnemer. 1998. Benefits of early intervention for children with developmental disabilities. *Seminars in Pediatric Neurology 5*, 1, 62-69.

[16] Kevin Marshall, Gavin Wood, Janet C. Read, Svetlana Yarosh, Madeline Balaam, and Jung-Joo Lee. 2015. Supporting Children to Engage in Play for Wellbeing. In *Proceedings of the 33rd Annual ACM Conference Extended Abstracts on Human Factors in Computing Systems*, ACM, 2445-2448.

[17] Paul Marshall. 2007. Do tangible interfaces enhance learning? In *Proceedings of the 1st international conference on Tangible and embedded interaction*, ACM, 163-170.

[18] Maria B. C. Martín, Alejandro Santos-Lozano, Juan Martín-Hernández, Alberto López-Miguel, Miguel Maldonado, Carlos Baladrón, Corinna M. Bauer, and Lotfi B. Merabet. 2016. Cerebral versus Ocular Visual Impairment: The Impact on Developmental Neuroplasticity. *Frontiers in Psychology 7*, 1958.

[19] Aleksandar Matic, Gillian R. Hayes, Monica Tentori, Maryam Abdullah, and Sabrina Schuck. 2014. Collective use of a situated display to encourage positive behaviors in children with behavioral challenges. In *Proceedings of the 2014 ACM International Joint Conference on Pervasive and Ubiquitous Computing*, ACM, 885-895.

[20] Pekka Mertala, Hannele Karikoski, Liisa Tähtinen, and Vesa-Matti Sarenius. 2016. The value of toys: 6–8-year-old children's toy preferences and the functional analysis of popular toys. *International Journal of Play 5*, 1, 11-27.

[21] Donald A. Norman. 2008. THE WAY I SEE IT: Signifiers, not affordances. *interactions 15*, 6, 18-19.

[22] Sara Price. 2008. A representation approach to conceptualizing tangible learning environments. In *Proceedings of the 2nd international conference on Tangible and embedded interaction*, ACM, 151-158.

[23] Sara Price, Jennifer G. Sheridan, Taciana Pontual Falcão. 2010. Action and representation in tangible systems: implications for design of learning interactions. In *Proceedings of the fourth international conference on Tangible, embedded, and embodied interaction*, ACM, 145-152.

[24] Olga Pykhtina, Madeline Balaam, Gavin Wood, Sue Pattison, Ahmed Kharrufa, and Patrick Olivier. 2012. Magic land: the design and evaluation of an interactive tabletop supporting therapeutic play with children. In *Proceedings of the Designing Interactive Systems Conference*, ACM, 136-145.

[25] Craig T. Ramey and Sharon Landesman Ramey. 1998. Early intervention and early experience. *American Psychologist 53*, 2, 109-120.

[26] Yvonne Rogers. 2012. *HCI Theory: Classical, Modern and Contemporary*. Morgan and Claypool.

[27] Steven A. Rosenberg, Duan Zhang, and Cordelia C. Robinson. 2008. Prevalence of Developmental Delays and Participation in Early Intervention Services for Young Children. *Pediatrics 121*, 6, e1503.

[28] Katie Salen and Eric Zimmerman. 2003. *Rules of Play: Game Design Fundamentals*. Mit University Press Cambridge.

[29] Florian Scharf, Thomas Winkler, and Michael Herczeg. 2008. Tangicons: algorithmic reasoning in a collaborative game for children in kindergarten and first class. In *Proceedings of the 7th international conference on Interaction design and children*, ACM, 242-249.

[30] Tobias Sonne and Mads Møller Jensen. 2016. ChillFish: A Respiration Game for Children with ADHD. In *Proceedings of the TEI '16: Tenth International Conference on Tangible, Embedded, and Embodied Interaction*, ACM, 271-278.

[31] Victoria Tam, Mirko Gelsomini, and Franca Garzotto. 2017. Polipo: a Tangible Toy for Children with Neurodevelopmental Disorders. In *Proceedings of the Eleventh International Conference on Tangible, Embedded, and Embodied Interaction*, ACM, 11-20.

[32] Jonathan Waddington, Conor Linehan, Kathrin Gerling, Kieran Hicks, and Timothy L. Hodgson. 2015. Participatory Design of Therapeutic Video Games for Young People with Neurological Vision Impairment. In *Proceedings of the 33rd Annual ACM Conference on Human Factors in Computing Systems*, ACM, 3533-3542.

[33] Donna R. Weston, Barbara Ivins, Maty Claire Heffron, and Nancy Sweet. 1997. Formulating the Centrality of Relationships in Early Intervention: An Organizational Perspective. *Infants & Young Children 9*, 3, 1-12.

[34] Oren Zuckerman, Saeed Arida, and Mitchel Resnick. 2005. Extending tangible interfaces for education: digital montessori-inspired manipulatives. In *Proceedings of the SIGCHI Conference on Human Factors in Computing Systems*, ACM, 859-868.

Identifying Children's Fidget Object Preferences: Toward Exploring the Impacts of Fidgeting and Fidget-Friendly Tangibles

Suzanne B. da Câmara
University of California, Santa Cruz
Santa Cruz, USA
sdacamar@ucsc.edu

Rakshit Agrawal
University of California, Santa Cruz
Santa Cruz, USA
ragrawa1@ucsc.edu

Katherine Isbister
University of California, Santa Cruz
Santa Cruz, USA
katherine.isbister@ucsc.edu

ABSTRACT
Fidgeting involves interacting with objects using repetitive hand movements. Before you can study its effects, you must first study the objects with which people choose to fidget. We present the findings of our five-phase three-month study with 28 children, 24 parents, and 2 teachers examining fidget material qualities and inherent interactions children gravitate towards when fidgeting and what, if any, connections can be made between their emotional state or activity when fidgeting and their fidget interactions/materials preferences. Our study included structured interviews, observations during usage, and design workshops. We present novel insights concerning fidget object preferences, across factors including materials, interactions, stealth, durability and sound, which together can act as guidelines in the development of educational, experimental and utility tangibles for children. For example, children tend to prefer a fidget item with inherent squeezing interactions when they are angry and clicking/pressing/tapping interactions when they are bored.

ACM Classification Keywords
H.5.m. Information Interfaces and Presentation (e.g. HCI): Miscellaneous.

Author Keywords
Fidgets; Fidgeting; Self-regulation; Tangibles.

INTRODUCTION
Fidgeting and fidget-friendly tangibles have recently witnessed enormous popularity in markets and research. Though people have long been observed to fidget, dedicated products like fidget spinners, fidget cubes and other fidget items, have served to focus public attention on fidgeting and its potential benefits or disadvantages. However, whether or not fidgeting and fidget objects are beneficial or detrimental is still to be conclusively determined [23]. Popular perception of fidgeting is that it is indicative of inattention or lack of interest [4]. This is such a widely held belief that there are studies that are built on this assumption [9]. However, there is evidence that fidgeting serves various purposes and can be beneficial [25, 1, 20]. Fidgeting, in the form of hand gestures, has been shown to facilitate word retrieval when children are faced with a "tip of the tongue" situation searching for the optimal word answer to a problem [22]. Rather than being an unproductive mental-resource-wasting activity, fidgeting is postulated to regulate focus [5, 8, 19, 24] and has been shown in some cases to increase retention [1].

Research that attempts to study fidgeting often uses pre-existing fidget items that are either readily available, inexpensive, or popular at the time of the study [20, 25, 24]. We argue that alongside studying the effects of fidgeting, one must study the objects people choose to fidget with so that fidget objects suited to their general material and interaction preferences when fidgeting can be used.

We would argue that what is commonly referred to as fidgeting can be divided into two main categories. The first consists of body movements much akin to squirming or repositioning yourself in your chair. Movements in this category do not incorporate interacting with objects and consist of body movements of the head, full body, and appendages. This type of fidgeting is often linked to inattention and/or boredom [9]. The second category of fidgeting refers to repetitive activities with the hands manipulating objects, which are done without a direct purpose. To illustrate, think of the contrast between someone fidgeting in their chair during a long lecture with someone fidgeting with a pen by spinning it around with their thumb and forefinger while in a meeting or working on homework problems.

Our study focused on the material qualities and interactions that children gravitate towards when fidgeting with objects, so that these preferences can inform the design of new fidget items or the choice of existing items to incorporate in future fidgeting studies involving children. Since our goal is to analyze children's fidgeting in order to identify the kinesthetic interactions inherent in their fidgeting (i.e. squeezing, twirling, twisting, etc) and the material qualities associated with the items they choose to fidget with, we focused on the second category of fidgeting as outlined above. For the purposes of this

DIS '18, June 9–13, 2018, , Hong Kong
© 2018 ACM. ISBN 978-1-4503-5198-0/18/06...15.00
DOI: https://doi.org/10.1145/3196709.3196790

study, we define fidget items or objects as items people fidget with such as fidget spinners, pens, stress balls, etc. A fidget item can be anything that is not part of a person's body. Hence, fingers, hair, and legs though often used while fidgeting are not considered fidget items.

Fidgeting should not be confused with playing. For instance, playing catch or video games is not fidgeting as both are more mindful or intentional. Included in our definition of fidgeting are doodling, hair twisting, and repetitive movement of various other body parts. We are interested in these actions as well as the more commonly referred to "fidgeting" actions because we are interested in finding out what movements and interactions that children gravitate towards when fidgeting. For instance, hair twisting or twirling is done with a repetitive rotational motion that could be simulated with a fidget object.

In this paper, we present the details of our study and discuss the results across multiple dimensions. Our study was conducted in five phases that apart from interactions with children, also involved discussions with parents and teachers. Based on the data collected from this study, we present our findings on user fidget item preferences in terms of material qualities, inherent interactions, noise, and more such observations. In addition, we present correlations between preferred fidgeting interactions and certain emotions and activities. Through these results, we show the significance of learning fidget object characteristic preferences and how that knowledge can aid in the exploration of fidgeting and its impacts.

MOTIVATION

There is increased interest in fidgeting and its possible benefits or disadvantages. Many studies that attempt to answer these questions use existing fidget objects. We think before one can attempt to answer questions related to fidgeting, fidgeting preferences must be identified. We believe that studies that use fidget items with material qualities and interactions that people naturally gravitate towards when fidgeting, will yield organic interactions and therefore more accurate results as opposed to studies which try to encourage use of fidget objects ill suited to their participants' preferences. Therefore, identifying popular fidget item characteristics will enable informed decisions regarding which fidgets to use or make for a given study. In addition, finding connections between emotions experienced or activities engaged in when fidgeting and preferred fidget item characteristics will enable researchers to make fidget item choices aimed at answering more specific questions. Interaction and material preferences catered to the emotions or actions we want to study can be utilized. For instance, testing the effects of fidgeting on diminishing anger would make/use fidget items that incorporate fidget interactions/material qualities that people gravitate towards when angry.

Sometimes people are conscious of their fidgeting behaviors and sometimes they are not, so merely asking about fidget habits might not be sufficient. Children are a unique group to study in that there often people around them, like parents, teachers, and caregivers, who by choice or profession monitor their behavior. These additional sources of observations regarding children's fidgeting item preferences provides additional data points which help create a more complete picture of their preferences. While children will self report fidgeting that they are conscious of, it is from their parents and teachers that we are able to get information regarding fidgeting behaviours that they are not conscious of. For instance, one participant was able to show us the items that she fidgeted with in class, when she was bored or when she was studying. When asked for information regarding fidgeting item preferences and behaviors at times when she was working on a hard problem or really concentrating, she did not have an answer for us. However, her mother, who was often nearby when she was doing homework, was able to tell us easily how she fidgets during that time. We noticed the same with teachers since they are paid in part to monitor their student's behaviors. So by conducting a study around children, we were able to get more data points describing their fidgeting habits and preferences and therefore more robust conclusions.

Children are not as adept at verbalizing what they are thinking and/or feeling as adults. This, in addition to the fact that children's fidget object choices might be limited due to financial or parental constraints or even exposure, prompted us to design the study so that three different approaches were used to gather information about the children's fidget item preferences. First they were asked to show or describe the objects with which they currently fidget. Second, we brought a myriad of fidget objects to the study and encouraged them to interact with them so that perhaps they would discover new preferences. Finally, we had them design their ideal fidget with its inherent materials and interactions, so that they wouldn't be limited by the objects they had already experienced.

RELATED WORK

While research relating fidgeting to executive function and childhood developmental theories exists, the physiological, developmental or psychological reasons why people tend to fidget and the cultural differences in fidgeting frequency are outside of the scope of our research [3, 18]. Research exploring technology designed to aid in the development of executive function [26, 11] while interesting, is also outside of the scope of this work.

Popular opinion is so inclined to view fidgeting in a negative light that for research at Florida Atlantic University, a prototype was created that alerts the wearer to fidgeting actions, so that he/she can attempt to curtail them [2]. The goal of our project was the opposite of that thesis. Rather than trying to alert the user to fidgeting actions so that they can be controlled or curtailed, our project attempts to identify preferred fidgeting item characteristics so that fidget items can be chosen such that people are naturally more inclined to interact with them.

There is a limited amount of research in the area of fidget object creation. Karlesky and Isbister [14, 15, 16] created fidget objects that they referred to as Fidget Widgets. These Fidget Widgets were playful in nature and created to "selectively modulate affect and shape cognitive state to support a user's productivity and creativity". Unlike Karlesky and Isbister's Fidget Widget research, which was focused on adults, our research is focused solely on the preferences and behaviors of children.

Recent work conducted at Lund University [20], inspired by research that indicated that squeezing a small ball or walking lead to increased creativity [21, 10] postulated that fidgeting might have a similar effect on creativity and looked for a link between fidgeting and increased creativity. After using ready-made store bought fidget items for initial studies, Nyqvist made several prototypes but was unable to definitively prove that one was better than another at fostering creativity. Rather than concentrate on which interactions or materials people might gravitate towards when doing creative work, the study focused on why people fidget and identified four reasons: to focus (engage cognitively), explore (release cognitively), active (engage physically), and relax (release cognitively). Nyqvist's research did not link any of those reasons to preferred interactions or material qualities in fidget items.

In addition to the above-mentioned work, numerous fidget objects, backed by research [13], have been marketed as attention and focus enhancers (i.e, fidget spinners, fidget cubes, etc) for people with attention deficit hyperactivity disorder (ADHD). However, they lack the prior research to inform their design and ensure that they are providing interactions and experiences that children find appealing. Instead, research around these items has focused on whether or not fidgeting with them is beneficial, without ever first researching the needs and preferences of the populations they were intended for.

The primary distinction between the previously mentioned studies and our current research is that we do not seek to build a fidget object or to investigate a current fidget object but rather to inform the design of future fidgeting objects for educational, experimental, and other practical purposes.

METHODS

In collaboration with Committee for Children, we chose a convenience sample of 28 children (10 boys and 18 girls) between the ages of 6 and 11 (see Figure 1 for children's age distribution); 24 of their parents; and 2 of their teachers from two different after-school facilities to explore the following questions: Do all children fidget? When (e.g., at school, studying, when angry, sad, etc) and how (e.g., twisting, petting, bouncing, tapping, pinching, etc) do they fidget? What object properties do they gravitate towards? How does fidgeting serve the child (e.g., maintaining focus, regulating emotion, dispelling energy, etc.) What connection, if any, exists between why children fidget and preferred fidget materials and/or interactions?

The children were recruited from the two after-school programs by posting flyers in those facilities advertising the program, and directing interested children/adults to the front office, where a more detailed informational sheet was provided. If interested in having their children participate in the study, the parents then needed to turn in a signed permission form. By signing the form and having their child participate, the parent agreed to take part in two phases of the study as well, Meet & Greet and Group Session. Due to the nature of the study, we decided to allow siblings and others take part in the

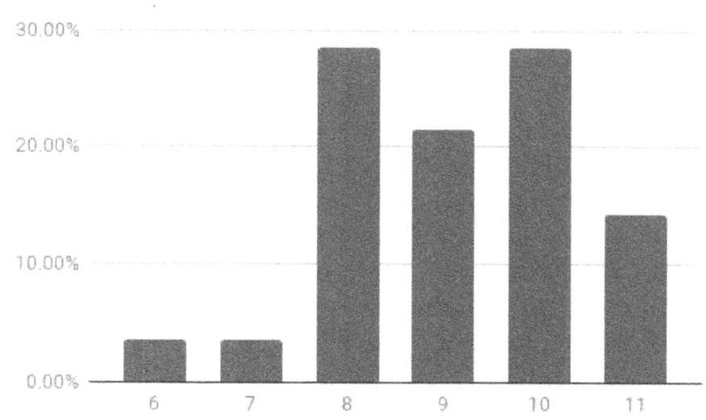

Figure 1: Age distribution of participating children (median age: 9)

process even if they were not strictly in the target age range (8-10).

While we never asked any questions directly relating to socio-economic status, parents educational background, or family makeup, through information obtained from conversations with the parents, teachers and the children themselves it became clear that we had a very diverse cross-section of children taking part in the study. For instance, at least two of the children were living in a homeless shelter with their mother at the time of the study, another was living with her mother in a trailer without running water, and several of the children were from what were clearly affluent homes. Six of the children had at least one parent who was pursuing his/her Bachelors degree at the time of the study. Several children came from one-parent homes and at least one child came from a two-parent same sex home. In addition, at least two of the students in the study have been diagnosed with ADHD.

We conducted a multi-phase study utilizing established user-centered design practices. Guided by children-specific usability testing [12, 7], we conducted a series of interviews, observation and design workshops [17] with the children to gather the necessary information to answer our research questions. Due to the often subconscious nature of fidgeting, we also chose to include the parent(s) and teachers of the children participating in this study in order to capture more complete data regarding the children's fidgeting habits and preferences.

There were five phases to the study: Exploration, Meet & Greet, Group sessions, Brainstorming, and Teacher Interview. Each phase is outlined in more detail below. The children took part in the Exploration and Brainstorming while their parents took part in Meet & Greet and Group sessions. Exploration, Meet & Greet, Group sessions, and Brainstorming were done with small groups of 5-to-8 participants. Teacher Interview was done one-on-one.

Exploration

In the Exploration phase, we obtained information from children about their fidgeting preferences and behaviors. This phase was done in two parts. During the first part, we asked each of the children whether or not they fidget and if they do, to tell us the associated times and frequency, possible reasons, and inherent materials and interactions of the fidget items that they used. If the child had the item with him/her, we took a picture of the fidget item and recorded a video of the child interacting with it. If the child didn't have the item(s) with him/her, we asked him/her to describe the item(s) in detail. During the second part, we used several bins containing an assortment of fidget items (see Figure 3). There were 29 different types of fidget items, each of which could have variations in color and shape, with a total combination of over 90 unique fidget items from which the children could choose. We instructed each child to pick a favorite fidgeting item(s) from the bin. The children had complete freedom of choice and were encouraged to touch and manipulate all of the fidgets during this exploration. At the end of the session, we asked each child to tell us what their favorite fidget item(s) were, and why and when they thought they would use them.

Meet & Greet

The main purpose of Meet & Greet was to gather some preliminary information and get parental buy-in for the field study. In order to do this, we arranged to have food and drinks at the end of the day when the parents were scheduled to pick their children up from the after-school program. While they and their children were eating, we asked the parents 4 short answer questions about their child's fidgeting habits. While speaking with the parents, we educated them on the difference between fidgeting and playing and reminded them about the group meeting scheduled for the following week.

Group Session

In the Group Session phase we obtained more detailed information from the parents about what fidgeting behavior and preferences they observed in their children. We met with the parents of the children in the study in small groups of 5 to 8 people and asked them more detailed questions about their children's fidgeting habits. The session was not a focus group in the traditional sense that a question is thrown out and the group discusses it, rather each parent was asked the same set of questions in turn with subsequent and past answers sometimes being changed upon reflection about the answers given by other parents present.

Brainstorming

During the Brainstorming phase, children designed their ideal fidget item complete with material and interaction preferences.

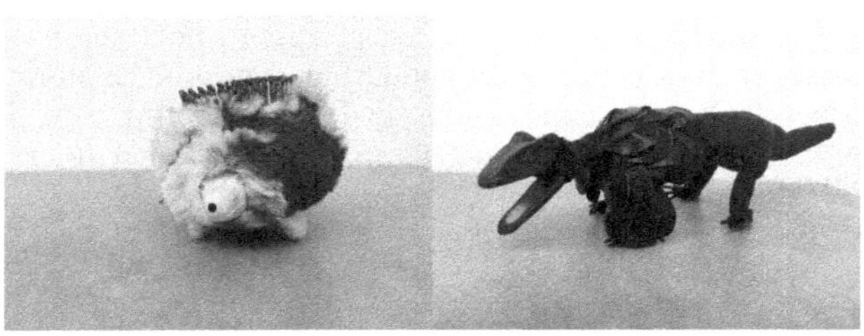

(a) Hedgehog. (b) Lizard.

Figure 2: Smart fidget prototypes shown to the children for reference.

Figure 3: Examples of some of the fidget items supplied during EXPLORATION.

This phase consisted of three activities. First, we showed the children two smart fidget prototypes (built during the work by Cottrell *et al.* [6]) and allowed them to handle and interact with them (see Figure 2). We explained the various interactions that were incorporated into each prototype (i.e., twisting, squeezing, petting, clicking, bending, etc) and then allowed each child to handle and interact with them. After that, we allowed the children to examine a variety of the materials the researchers considered when they developed the prototypes, so that they could have an idea some of the different materials that are possible. Finally, we asked the children to draw pictures of what their ideal fidget object would be and to label it, by asking them the following questions: If you could design the perfect fidget what would it look like? What would it be made of? What would the inside be made of? What things could you do with it? Like could you bounce it or roll it or twist it? Can you draw it for us and label the drawing with all of the materials it's made of along with all of the things that it does? When would you use it? What do you like about this perfect fidget item that you just drew? (see Figure 4). We encouraged them to use their imagination and incorporate any materials and/or interactions that they had been exposed to, prior to or during the study, which they would want to have in their fidget item. We then interviewed each of the children and asked them to explain their dream fidget item.

Teacher Interview

In the Teacher Interview phase, we obtained teacher observations regarding the children's fidgeting behaviors and preferences. The teachers were asked the same questions that the parents were asked in the Meet & Greet phase and the Group Session phase. The only difference was that the teachers were asked all of the questions one-on-one in a single session.

Data Handling

The video taped sessions (Exploration, Group Sessions, and Brainstorming) were transcribed. Information from the transcripts was then transferred to a spreadsheet. The spreadsheet has columns for the child associated with the fidget item, the age and gender of the child, the fidget item, whether or not

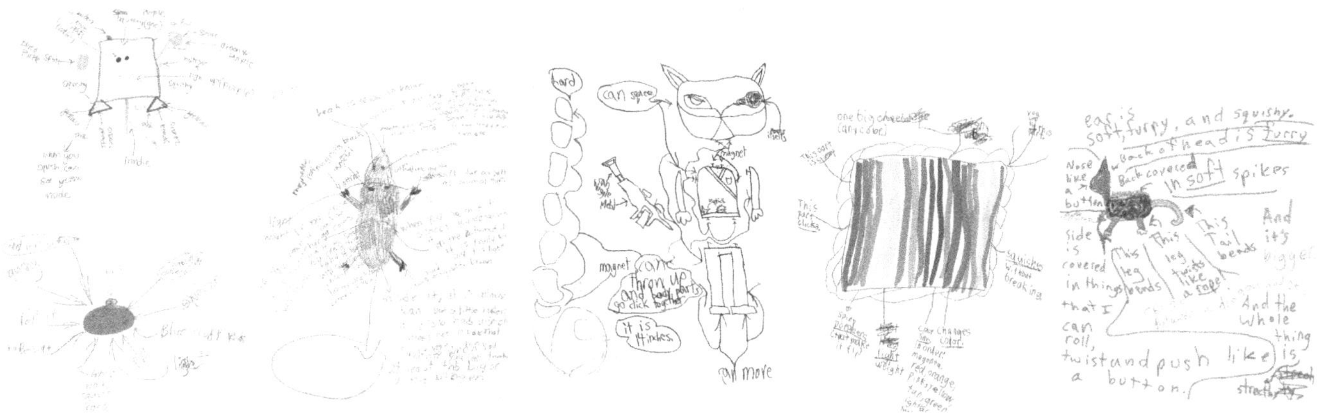

Figure 4: Drawings of the participants' ideal fidget items from BRAINSTORMING.

the fidget item is an accessible or multi-use item, whether or not it is a complex item (has multiple interactions built in), description of the fidget item with material properties, interactions inherent in the fidget item, what the child likes about that fidget item, and when or why the child uses that fidget item. In order to obtain the preferred interactions, materials and items, we input all of the fidget items (as well as the component materials and interactions inherent in each of those items) mentioned for a particular child by either the child himself/herself, the child's parent(s), or teacher. Because we realize that a child's current fidget items might be influenced or limited by financial or parental constraints, we included information on all of the fidget items that the child identified as his/her favorites during Exploration. In addition, to make sure that the child's preferences weren't unduly limited by the fidget items that we brought to Exploration, we analyzed the ideal fidget item that each child drew during Brainstorming, recording all of its component materials and interactions. The text for each fidget item was color coded to denote the source of the information about that item with the following scheme: black - fidget items that they showed or described to us during Exploration, light blue - fidget items that we provided that they spent time interacting with during Exploration, dark blue - favorite fidget items that we provided during Exploration, green - items parents mentioned, red - items teachers mentioned, and orange - ideal fidget drawing components. We then looked to see how many children in the study gravitated towards each material, object and interaction. Analysis of the reported reasons why the children fidgeted was done in a similar way. When looking for what if any connections exist between why they fidget and what materials or interactions they chose to fidget with, we were careful to look at when they said that they used or would use a particular fidget item. We initially thought that analysis of what items the children chose to interact with during Exploration in conjunction with their favorite fidget item from Exploration might yield interesting results in terms of the child being open to various types of interactions and materials or primarily being interested in certain interactions, materials or form factors, but due to time constraints and lack of initial conclusive results we chose to ignore those items in our final analysis. Thus, the light blue items in the spreadsheet were not counted towards our final results. This makes sense as they were not items for which the child declared a preference.

OBSERVATIONS

During the Meet & Greet phase, we noticed that many of the parents were not clear about what we meant by fidgeting. Several of them confused fidgeting with playing and when asked to tell us about the fidgeting items that their children used, they said things like video games. We would not consider playing video games fidgeting, because it is a purposeful activity that engages a child's full attention. As a result of this, we educated the parents about what we considered fidgeting. Later, during the Group Session phase, several of the parents mentioned that after having spoken with us a week earlier in Meet & Greet, they had noticed fidgeting behaviors and patterns in their children that they had not noticed previously.

Through interacting with the teachers over the course of the study, we realized that the teachers were aware of the differences between fidgeting and playing and further, that they had a wealth of information about the children's fidgeting habits and item preferences. This seemed especially true of fidgeting behaviors done when the children were forced to sit in one place and focus on something that was difficult for them, as is the case when they study or do school work, rather being free to move about. Consequently, we decided to expand our study to include Teacher Interview to record their responses to the same questions that the parents were asked in the Meet & Greet phase and the Group Session phase.

RESULTS

Fidgeting

All of the children in our study were found to fidget. Even if one source (a parent or the child himself/herself) responded that a particular child did not fidget, we always heard from another that said child does indeed fidget along with a description of when, why and the properties inherent in the fidget items that said child uses. Further, we observed that even when a

Category	Count	Key words
Perform Cognitive Tasks	25 (89%)	thinking, working, homework, learning, school work, when they don't know the answer, reading, studying, listening, focusing, during class
Alleviate Boredom	24 (86%)	bored, boredom, bored at home, bored in class
Regulate Emotions	22 (79%)	angry, mad, sad, frustrated, anxious, nervous, calming, soothing, unhappy, upset, discomfort, chill out, scared, happy, worried
In Class	20 (71%)	school or class are specifically stated
Dispel Excess Energy	14 (50%)	excess energy, dispel energy, can't sit still

Table 1: The reasons why children fidget.

Material	Count
Rubber	24 (86%)
Squeeze Ball	24 (86%)
Plastic	22 (79%)
Orbeez	17 (61%)
Pencil/Eraser	15 (54%)

Table 2: Materials that the participants liked.

child initially responded that he/she did not fidget, that child's teacher or teacher and parent(s) responded to the contrary.

Why They Fidget
As can be seen in Table 1, there are various reasons why children fidget. We grouped the reported reasons that they were found to fidget into five categories that are not necessarily mutually exclusive. The table shows examples of the words that the study participants used to describe when/why the children fidget that were grouped into each category. For instance, thinking, learning, reading, and focusing were some of the words that we grouped into a category called Perform Cognitive Tasks. Four of the categories (Perform Cognitive Tasks, Alleviate Boredom, Regulate Emotion, Dispel Excess Energy) are location independent. By this we mean that inclusion of a stated reason in any of these four categories is based solely on the activity or desired result and not on where it occurs, while the fifth category (In Class) is defined as any fidgeting for any reason that takes place in a school or classroom type setting. We made a separate category for this location specific fidgeting because fidgeting in this setting is often discouraged by the child's parent and/or teacher. Despite this, 71% of the children still fidget in this setting. We created a separate category for fidgeting when bored rather than include boredom prompted fidgeting in the Emotion Regulation category because it was so prevalent in the data that we felt that it warranted its own category.

Material and Object Preferences
In our study, the results show that the children gravitated towards a variety of objects and materials when fidgeting. Table 2 lists the top 5 overall material/object preferences. The table is a mix of both materials and specific objects because when a specific kind of object was prevalent in the data, we felt that it warranted its own category. Otherwise, since the variety of fidget items was so diverse, we grouped items by their component materials.

Accessible or Multipurpose Item Preferences
While the children in our study fidget with a wide assortment of fidget items, many of the fidget items, especially those employed in schools or other places with classroom like settings, are accessible or multipurpose items. For this study, we define accessible as either parts of the body (e.g., hands, fingers, hair, legs), clothing, or items that are readily at hand. We define multipurpose items as those items that have a primary purpose other than as a fidget object. Items in this category include pens, pencils, erasers, white out bottles and hair ties. Twenty-six of the 28 children (93%) fidgeted with accessible or multipurpose items.

Soft Material Preference
From among the children's material and item preferences, we found that 20 of the 28 children in the study (71%) liked fidget items that contained a material that could be considered soft. Not to be confused with smooth or pliable, items considered soft included clothes, fur, blankets, and cotton. Several of the kids who didn't even mention cloth or fur materials did mention that they liked soft exteriors (like soft rubber).

Preferred Interactions
Preferred fidget interactions can be found in Table 3. It is important to note that we differentiated between squeeze and squish. We defined squeezing as an interaction that does not alter the original form of an object. Once squeezing ceases, the object merely returns to its original shape. Squishing, on the other hand, changes the shape of the object. You can squish clay but squeeze a stress ball. The motion involved in the two interactions is the same as both involve pressing your fingers together or closing your hand into some approximation of a fist. The difference lies in how the interaction feels to the person doing it. The push back can be of varying strengths depending on how hard it is to continue to squeeze the object in question.

When collecting data in the study, we distinguished between clicking, pressing, and tapping. For the purposes of this study, we define tapping as a motion that is done on a surface that does not change as a result of the motion. So think of tapping your fingers on a table. You move your finger/fingers in a downward motion and there is no force exerted on your finger to stop its movement downward or aid its movement back up. Clicking is similar to tapping in that you move your finger/fingers in a downward motion but unlike tapping, you must exert a force in order to move your finger in that downward motion. The object that you click is then depressed and stays that way even after you stop exerting force in a downward motion. Like tapping, there is no force exerted on your finger

Interactions	Count
Squeeze	25 (89%)
Stretch	22 (79%)
Squish	20 (71%)
Click/Press/Tap	20 (71%)
Pull	19 (68%)
Roll	15 (54%)
Twist	15 (54%)

Table 3: Interactions that the participants liked.

to aid its movement back up. Pressing is similar to both tapping and clicking in that it is done by exerting a force by your finger/fingers in a downward motion. Like clicking, pressing contains a force exerted on your finger to stop its downward movement. However, unlike clicking, when you stop pressing, there is a force exerted by the object being pressed that aids your finger's movement back up. So if you pressed a button down and then stopped pressing but didn't move your finger from the button, the button would return to its original upright position the minute that you stop pressing in essence lifting your finger in the process. Due to the similar movements involved in all three, we decided to look at clicking, pressing and tapping together as one category. When considered in this way, we found that 23 of the 28 children (82%) liked objects that incorporated this interaction. Their attraction to this type of motion was further supported by the fact that 14 of the 23 children (61%) who showed a preference for this interaction built it into their ideal fidget design.

Relationships between materials/interactions and reasons to fidget

Regarding relationships between materials/interactions and reasons to fidget, we observed two things. First, every time a reason is mentioned for wanting to use an object that contains a clicky (pressing, clicking, tapping) interaction, the reasons given are primarily either that the child was bored or that the child was doing cognitive tasks such as focusing, doing homework, or thinking. Second, while squeezing is always a popular interaction regardless of the reason, when children are angry or stressed, they are more likely to want to interact with items that have squeeze or squish interactions built in than any other interaction. The same is not true in reverse. Just because children are squeezing or squishing a fidget object, does not mean that they are angry or stressed.

In addition to material and interaction preferences and social emotional ties to fidgeting, several other insights came out of the study related to durability, stealth and sound.

Rough Fidgeting

Sixty-four percent of the children in the study, 18 of the 28 participants, were observed pushing the physical boundaries of the fidget items. Many were seen to either grip the object with two hands, robustly squeezing it in an attempt to get it to burst, over-stretching to see how far they could pull one side from another, or putting all of their weight on an object while squishing it into the table.

Stealth

Children feel the need for stealth when fidgeting. Eight of the children (29%) mentioned in passing at some point during the study that they were worried that their fidget items would get taken away. This worry was exacerbated if the items were too big or looked "too much like a toy". The child's concern for stealth is further supported by the fact that many of the items that they fidgeted with at school were small or multipurpose items. When examining the fidget items that we supplied as part of the Exploration phase, some of the comments we overheard the children saying were: "probably not at school because I'd feel like they'll just take it away from me" and "Oh so it's too big to use either at school or at home". Of the participants in the study, 26 of the 28 children (93%), reported using accessible (e.g., body parts, hair, clothing) or multipurpose items (e.g., pencils, erasers, hair ties, white out bottles) that couldn't be taken away.

Sound

Children like sound. Eleven of the 28 children (39%) mentioned liking an object because of the sound that it made. An example of this is that one child liked clicking the buttons on the light switch side of the fidget cube stating 'I really like this clicking noise'. However, as was the case with fidget items looking too much like toys, children were careful not to choose items that were too loud. Among them, several liked the slight squishing sound that a gel filled squeeze ball made when it was squeezed. One of these children stated that 'if you put it up to your ear it sounds like it's really- it sounds like it's really squishy.'

Fidget Item Form

The children in our study were found to fidget with both creature-like and abstract fidget items, with creature-like items being among the fidget items of 19 of the 28 children (68%). Creature-like items refer to any item that has a face and could be anthropomorphized. 10 of the 25 children (40%) who completed ideal fidget designs in the Brainstorming phase created creature-like designs.

Parent Responses

We were able to obtain fidgeting behavior and preference information concerning 27 of the children in the study from the 24 parents who participated. This was due to some siblings being in the study. Of these 24 parents, 18 participated in both the Meet & Greet and the Group Session providing information concerning 21 of the children. Of the 18 parents who took part in both the Meet & Greet and the Group Session phases (though asked similar fidgeting related questions in the two phases), 12 parents (66%) gave much more detailed information regarding their child's fidgeting behaviors and fidget item preferences in the Group Session phase as opposed to the Meet & Greet. Of those 18, three specifically mentioned they were able to give more informed answers as a direct result of participating in the Meet & Greet phase.

Teacher Responses

Our analysis of the collected data supported our decision to expand out study from four phases to five with the inclusion of the Teacher Interview phase. The teachers gave more detailed responses in 14 out of the 20 cases where the information was obtained from both the parent(s) and teacher. In addition, teachers were often more cognizant of when and why the children fidgeted as opposed to just that they did. Further, while parents' fidgeting answers were often vague, especially when asked if they noticed any patterns to when or why the children fidgeted, teachers could often find social and emotional tie-ins as to why they were fidgeting. For instance, the teachers were more likely to link the fidgeting to a particular activity or state of mind and were better able to explain how fidgeting with that item served the child. An example of this is that while one parent was unable to cite any reasons connected to their child's fidgeting, her teacher stated that the child fidgeted to "calm and center her, and it makes her happy". Another example of this is that even though both a parent and a teacher referenced a child fidgeting with a ball, the parent stated that the child fidgeted with it when bored while the teacher said that he used it when "he's angry or needs to take a time out...I don't know if it's a control thing", it's self soothing and a mode for him to focus.

DISCUSSION

Conclusive findings and links

The Meet & Greet phase of the study was designed for two purposes: to obtain preliminary data about the children's fidgeting item preferences and habits and to get parental buy-in of the study to encourage their participation in the Group Session phase. However, during the Meet & Greet phase, we noticed that many of the parents were unaware of their children's fidgeting habits and preferences and in fact, in some cases, even of the difference between fidgeting and playing in general. This is suggestive of two additional benefits of the Meet & Greet phase of the study. First, by reminding the parents of the Group Session phase the next week and telling them that we would be asking more detailed questions about their children's fidgeting habits and item preferences at that time, we were able to focus their attention on this activity for the next week. Second, the phase provided an opportunity for us to educate the parents on the difference between fidgeting and playing and thereby ensure that their attention was focused towards the correct activity. Therefore, the main functions of the Meet & Greet phase were to educate the parents, obtain study buy-in, and focus attention on fidgeting activity.

Several of the parents mentioned during the Group Session that after having spoken with us a week earlier during the Meet & Greet, they had noticed fidgeting behaviors and patterns in their children that they had not noticed previously. The children's fidgeting habits did not change as a result of the Meet & Greet, but rather the parent's knowledge and awareness of fidgeting was raised due to their participation in the Meet & Greet.

As initially designed, our study was a four-phase study devoid of the Teacher Interview phase. However, through interacting with the teachers over the course of the study, it became clear that they were often more attuned than parents to the children's fidgeting behaviors and preferences. This seemed especially true of fidgeting behaviors done when the children were forced to sit in one place and focus on something that was difficult for them, as is the case when they study or do school work, rather being free to move about. Consequently, we decided to expand our study to include teachers' responses to the same questions that the parents were asked in the Meet & Greet phase and the Group Session phase.

Since the teachers were not only involved in the planning of the sessions but also had to be present in the room during each session that involved the children, they were already aware of the differences between play and fidgeting and their attention was already focused on those behaviors. Further, since teacher buy-in was essential in order to conduct the study in their classrooms it was obtained prior to the study. As stated previously, the primary functions of the Meet & Greet were to obtain buy-in to encourage participation in the Group Session, to educate on the differences between play and fidgeting, and to focus their attention on the children's fidgeting. Therefore, since the main functions of the Meet & Greet were already obtained with regards to the teachers, we decided to combine the two parent phases (Meet & Greet and Group Sessions) into one phase for the teachers. Consequently, the teachers were asked in one session all of the same questions that the parents were asked in the two. Analysis of the information obtained from the teachers substantiated our decision to include the teachers and combine the two phases into one for the teachers. Further, as suspected, their answers alluded to the teachers often being more aware of fidgeting that takes place when a child is bored or forced to sit in one place or work on school related cognitive tasks such as homework, learning something new, focusing, and reading.

Analysis of the data leads us to believe that the contrasting participant (parent, teacher and the child him/herself) observations regarding whether or not a child fidgets or in what situations a child tends to fidget stem not from the child him/herself rarely or sporadically fidgeting but rather from the responder not noticing it or not being around in situations where that particular fidgeting behavior is done. That a child would respond in the negative when asked whether or not they fidget and their parent(s) and teacher would respond that they did, merely underscores the thought that fidgeting is often a subconscious act rather than a conscious one. Given that several of the parents in the study held more than one job or juggled school and work, it is not unlikely that a parent would fail to notice all of their child's fidgeting given the many demands on their time and focus. In addition, many of the children finished their homework at the after school program so their parents seldom if ever witnessed them focusing on schoolwork or any fidgeting that might accompany that activity. It is important to note that the teachers interviewed never responded that a child did not fidget. We think this is because the teachers spend the majority of their time with the children in a classroom-like setting where they are watching the children while supervising their behavior and work.

We were initially concerned that showing the prototypes to the children prior to having them design their own ideal fidget item would unduly influence their designs. In order to offset this, we told them that the prototypes were a combination of all of the interactions and materials that the people who made them thought should be included in an ideal fidget item and that they (the children) should think of all of the fidget items that they already used and that we had shown them during the course of the study, in addition to the materials that we shared with them in the beginning of the session, and imagine a perfect fidget item that incorporated the materials and interactions that they liked the best. As a result of this, the drawings that the children made do not seem to have been influenced by the prototypes. The ideal fidget item drawings ranged from very complex items with multiple interactions built in to simple items with only one interaction. With the exception of maybe one dragon/cat fidget item, which is only similar to the lizard prototype in that dragons are somewhat similar to lizards, none of them looked at all similar to the hedgehog or the lizard prototypes.

The results showed that the majority of the children exhibited a tendency to test the physical limitations of a fidget item by interacting with it in a rough manner. Due to the prevalence of rough fidgeting behavior observed by the children, durability is a main concern when making or choosing fidget items for children. Perhaps the children's propensity toward what we deem as rough interactions can be attributed to their natural curiosity with regards to how things are made and what they can do. One exchange with a child during the Exploration phase that was indicative of this was as follows:

CHILD: like this one I like because, this one (blue to green squish ball with the net) it makes you want to cut it but then at the same time it doesn't want you. Like you wanna cut it but you don't want to cut it

RESEARCHER: cut it meaning get rid of the bag?

CHILD: no

RESEARCHER: cut it meaning you wanna get what's inside out?

CHILD: yeah, like (motions cutting the part sticking out of netting with finger)

Unlike adults, children must satisfy their fidgeting urges while operating within parental or teacher parameters of what is acceptable. From our observations of and interviews with the children in the study, we discovered that what they choose to fidget with is impacted by the environment in which they are fidgeting and whether or not they have to satisfy their fidgeting needs within the confines of what their parent(s) and/or teacher(s) find appropriate. Due to this adult imposed constraint, children often forgo their preferred fidget items and instead try to make-do with something that they think they can get away with. As a result of this many children choose to fidget with accessible or multipurpose fidget items that are much less likely to be taken away by parents, teachers, and/or caregivers. This is further evidenced by the fact that children try to accommodate their desire for fidgets that make noise by choosing fidget items that make subtle sounds that are less likely to be heard by anyone else. An example of this is the barely discernible squishing sound that a gel filled squeeze ball makes when squeezed.

In line with our results concerning children's need for stealth, they are very conscious of the size and conspicuous nature of things and of what they think they can get away with in different locations. One child chose a favorite fidget item in the Exploration phase and when asked where she would interact with it she said that she would interact with it at the after-school facility. When asked if she would also interact with it at home or at school, she replied 'no because it's too big.' She went on talk about another of her preferred fidget items and said that she liked it 'cuz it was more compact.'

Kids were found to value tactile sensation as the majority of children stated a preference for fidget items made of soft materials.

In a way, squeezing is similar to pressing in that both actions require force to move or change the shape of the object and both also experience a push back sensation as the object tries to return to its original shape or position. Similarly, squishing is much like clicking in that though force is required to click or squish the object, the object stays in the position that those actions put it in and there is no push back. So given the similarities between these preferred interactions, it is interesting that squeezing and pressing are not the preferred interactions for one emotion or activity and squishing and clicking are not the preferred interactions for another. All four interactions use movement of the fingers and yet the sensations they create are different. Perhaps it is because squishing and squeezing results in a clenched fist which goes better with dispelling energy when you are angry and pressing and clicking do not.

Use-Case scenarios

Future studies with children on the benefits or disadvantages of fidgeting should include fidget items that appeal to the largest subset of children. Our findings of the most popular fidget interactions and material properties can be used to inform the selection of fidget items to use in these studies. By incorporating fidget items with characteristics that appeal to a broader range of children, children are more likely to fidget with them organically rather than having to be prompted. Therefore, selecting fidget items with squeeze, squish, press, click, tap and stretch interactions and soft rubbery materials might yield more accurate results than incorporating fidget items that children do not naturally want to interact with.

Since children gravitate toward fidget items that make sound but fear of having them taken away prevents the children from either choosing them or else from using them in school and/or home settings, fidget items with either subtle sounds or sounds that can be turned off should be created or used during fidget studies. These fidget items would still satisfy their desire for noise while also making the items less distracting to those around so they will be less likely to be taken away. This will enable the children to use them in a multitude of settings that should yield better results in long term studies where the children take the fidget items home.

Further study is suggested to determine if our initial findings that a unidirectional link between anger and a preference for fidget items with a squeeze interaction exists for all or the majority of children. In addition, because our findings show that children have a propensity to gravitate toward fidget items with a squeeze interaction when angry, future studies regarding whether or not fidgeting can serve to aid in self regulation by diminishing anger might yield more accurate results by incorporating fidget items that have an inherent squeeze interaction than by using fidget items without this interaction.

Our findings also showed a link between the fidget actions of pressing, clicking, and tapping and performing cognitive tasks such as studying, doing homework, focusing, and learning. We suggest that future studies be conducted exploring this relationship to determine whether or not it holds true with other populations of children or even other populations in general. Additionally, studies interested in whether or not fidgeting aids cognitive functions such as focus, retention, or understanding could benefit from the inclusion of fidget items with inherent pressing, clicking, and/or tapping interactions. Further, since we also found a link between boredom and fidget items with those inherent interactions, studies regarding whether fidgeting could modulate boredom could potentially increase their accuracy by incorporating such items.

CONCLUSION

We conducted a five-phase field study which focused on the fidgeting habits and fidget item preferences of children between the ages of 6 and 11, for the purposes of discovering when and why they fidget, in addition to what types of fidget items they naturally gravitate towards in terms of their material properties (exterior and interior materials) and interactions.

Our findings revealed that the children in our study fidget for a variety of reasons: engaging in cognitive tasks, regulating emotion, and dispelling excess energy. Of the emotions that tend to trigger a need to fidget, boredom was the most prevalent. Top material preferences for fidget items were rubber and plastic while top fidget objects were squeeze balls, Orbeez, and pencils/erasers. Squeeze, stretch, squish and the combined category of click/press/tap were the four most liked interactions inherent in fidget items. Further, we found that stealth, durability and sound are all things that need to be considered when building fidget items.

Children are forced to satisfy their fidgeting needs within the narrow confines of what they think the adults will let them get away with using. Therefore, if a fidget item is intended to be used all the time, in order for it to be used and evaluated successfully, either the issue needs to be addressed with both the parents and the teachers of a child by educating them on the possible positive outcomes of fidgeting and fidget items or else the fidget items developed need to blend into the child's usual environment either by being or looking like multipurpose items.

We believe the results of our study are of value to anyone interested in creating tangible interfaces for children, who would like to be sensitive to the affordances of the materials and potential manipulations of those tangibles. Our own research group is currently using the results of this study to engage in the development of smart fidget objects to aid children in self-regulation and emotional management.

ACKNOWLEDGMENTS

We would like to thank the Committee for Children for their support. We would also like to thank Kyle Deino, Alicia James, Miriam del Cerro, Cora Monokandilos, Kennedy Bagnol, Alexsandrua Baltezar, and Yasunori Iwayanagi for their assistance with this project and Marily Oppezzo and Petr Slovak for information related to children's self-regulation.

REFERENCES

1. Jackie Andrade. 2010. What does doodling do? *Applied Cognitive Psychology* 24, 1 (2010), 100–106.
2. Scott A. Barnard. 2009. *The "Stop-It" Anti-fidgeting Device*. Master's thesis. Florida Atlantic University, The address of the publisher. An optional note.
3. Clancy Blair and Rachel Peters Razza. 2007. Relating effortful control, executive function, and false belief understanding to emerging math and literacy ability in kindergarten. *Child development* 78, 2 (2007), 647–663.
4. Jonathan SA Carriere, Paul Seli, and Daniel Smilek. 2013. Wandering in both mind and body: Individual differences in mind wandering and inattention predict fidgeting. *Canadian Journal of Experimental Psychology/Revue canadienne de psychologie expérimentale* 67, 1 (2013), 19.
5. John Cloud. 2009. Better Learning Through Fidgeting. (2009).
6. Peter Cottrell, April Grow, and Katherine Isbister. 2018. Soft-bodied Fidget Toys: A Materials Exploration. In *Proceedings of the Twelfth International Conference on Tangible, Embedded, and Embodied Interaction (TEI '18)*. ACM, New York, NY, USA, 42–48.
7. Allison Druin (Ed.). 1998. *The Design of Children's Technology*.
8. Stephen Garger. 1990. Is there a link between learning style and neurophysiology. *Educational Leadership* 48, 2 (1990), 63–65.
9. Nenad Gligorić, Ana Uzelac, and Srdjan Krco. 2012. Smart classroom: real-time feedback on lecture quality. In *Pervasive Computing and Communications Workshops (PERCOM Workshops), 2012 IEEE International Conference on*. IEEE, 391–394.
10. Abraham Goldstein, Ketty Revivo, Michal Kreitler, and Nili Metuki. 2010. Unilateral muscle contractions enhance creative thinking. *Psychonomic bulletin & review* 17, 6 (2010), 895–899.
11. Stuart Gray, Judy Robertson, and Gnanathusharan Rajendran. 2015. BrainQuest: an active smart phone game to enhance executive function. In *Proceedings of the 14th International Conference on Interaction Design and Children*. ACM, 59–68.
12. Libby Hanna, Kirsten Risden, and Kirsten Alexander. 1997. Guidelines for usability testing with children. *Interactions* 4 (1997), 9–14.

13. T A Hartanto, C E Krafft, A M Iosif, and J B Schweitzer. 2016. A trial-by-trial analysis reveals more intense physical activity is associated with better cognitive control performance in attention-deficit/hyperactivity disorder. *Child neuropsychology : a journal on normal and abnormal development in childhood and adolescence* 22 5 (2016), 618–26.

14. Michael Karlesky and Katherine Isbister. 2013. Fidget widgets: secondary playful interactions in support of primary serious tasks. In *CHI'13 Extended Abstracts on Human Factors in Computing Systems*. ACM, 1149–1154.

15. Michael Karlesky and Katherine Isbister. 2014. Fidget widgets: designing for the physical margins of digital workspaces. In *Proceedings of the 8th International Conference on Tangible, Embedded and Embodied Interaction*. ACM, 301–304.

16. Michael Karlesky and Katherine Isbister. 2016. Understanding Fidget Widgets: Exploring the Design Space of Embodied Self-Regulation. In *Proceedings of the 9th Nordic Conference on Human-Computer Interaction (NordiCHI '16)*. ACM, New York, NY, USA, Article 38, 10 pages.

17. Majeed Kazemitabaar, Jason McPeak, Alexander Jiao, Liang He, Thomas Outing, and Jon E Froehlich. 2017. MakerWear: A Tangible Approach to Interactive Wearable Creation for Children. In *Proceedings of the 2017 CHI Conference on Human Factors in Computing Systems*. ACM, 133–145.

18. Charlie Lewis, Masuo Koyasu, Seungmi Oh, Ayako Ogawa, Benjamin Short, and Zhao Huang. 2009. Culture, executive function, and social understanding. *New Directions for Child and Adolescent Development* 2009, 123 (2009), 69–85.

19. Malia F Mason, Michael I Norton, John D Van Horn, Daniel M Wegner, Scott T Grafton, and C Neil Macrae. 2007. Wandering minds: the default network and stimulus-independent thought. *Science* 315, 5810 (2007), 393–395.

20. Rebecka Nyqvist. 2016. *Fidgeting for Creativity*. Master's thesis. Lund University, Lund Sweden.

21. Marily Oppezzo and Daniel L Schwartz. 2014. Give your ideas some legs: The positive effect of walking on creative thinking. *Journal of experimental psychology: learning, memory, and cognition* 40, 4 (2014), 1142.

22. Karen J Pine, Hannah Bird, and Elizabeth Kirk. 2007. The effects of prohibiting gestures on children's lexical retrieval ability. *Developmental Science* 10, 6 (2007), 747–754.

23. Rachel A Schecter, Jay Shah, Kate Fruitman, and Ruth Lynn Milanaik. 2017. Fidget spinners: purported benefits, adverse effects and accepted alternatives. *Current opinion in pediatrics* 29, 5 (2017), 616–618.

24. Donald Slater and Jean French. 2010. Fidget toys in the classroom: refocusing attention. (2010).

25. Sheryl Stalvey and Heather Brasell. 2006. Using Stress Balls to Focus the Attention of Sixth-Grade Learners. *Journal of At-Risk Issues* 12, 2 (2006), 7–16.

26. Orad Weisberg, Ayelet GalOz, Ruth Berkowitz, Noa Weiss, Oran Peretz, Shlomi Azoulai, Daphne KoplemanRubin, and Oren Zuckerman. 2014. TangiPlan: designing an assistive technology to enhance executive functioning among children with adhd. In *Proceedings of the 2014 conference on Interaction design and children*. ACM, 293–296.

Designing for an other Home: Expanding and Speculating on Different Forms of Domestic Life

Doenja Oogjes
School of Interactive Arts and Technology, Simon Fraser University, Surrey, British Columbia, Canada
doogjes@sfu.ca

Pete Fung
Faculty of Design, Emily Carr University of Art and Design, Vancouver, British Columbia, Canada
peter.hoching@gmail.com

William Odom
School of Interactive Arts and Technology, Simon Fraser University, Surrey, British Columbia, Canada
wodom@sfu.ca

DIS '18, June 9–13, 2018, , Hong Kong

ACM ISBN 978-1-4503-5198-0/18/06...$15.00
https://doi.org/10.1145/3196709.3196810

Abstract
We report on the design and deployment of a probe study aimed at understanding the values, practices, and perspectives of people that actively embrace living situations that could be considered 'alternative' to normative domestic dwellings. In response to the returned probes, the pictorial describes and unpacks speculative interpretations and design responses that (i) propose alternative ways technology could be designed for the home, (ii) embody different ideas of where home is located, (iii) explore how home is constructed, re-made, curated, and pursued, and (iv) productively question material, technological, and social boundaries between the home and the outside world.

Authors Keywords
Home; Domestic Design; Probes; Design Research.

ACM Classification Keywords
H.5.m. Information interfaces and presentation (e.g., HCI): Miscellaneous.

Introduction
The DIS and HCI communities have long researched 'the home' and 'domestic life', and applied diverse methods to these investigations [6,13]. This large body of work has produced important contributions that have impacted how technology can be designed to better support the tasks, routines, and experiences of home life. However, conceptualizations of what the home is, where it resides, how it is made and by whom have arguably remained somewhat narrow in the HCI community. Whether implicitly or explicitly, 'the home' is often situated as a house and 'domestic life' is frequently cast as the social organization of collocated family members (e.g., a married couple with children). A small selection of prior work has helped expand characterizations of domestic life in HCI through exploring such issues

as: the negotiation of home-life in subsistence, off-the-grid, or co-housing communities [e.g., 11,15,26] as well as practices of making home when living in transitional situations without a central dwelling [e.g., 8,17,19,23,25]. This nascent research offers an important step toward expanding the HCI community's vision of 'the home' and developing a more diverse perspective on what constitutes domestic life. Yet, works like this remain sparse. In our view, more research is needed to further sensitize and expand approaches to designing for alternative sites of domesticity and forms of home life. On a broader level, we see our work as being in line with emerging discussions in the HCI and design communities that articulate the need to advance beyond homogenous visions of domestic technology and embrace a more diverse set of values, perspectives, and agendas in future design initiatives [1,5,10,11,12,14,16,21,24].

Our project is situated in the Greater Vancouver, Canada Metropolitan area. Like many cities worldwide, Vancouver is facing numerous challenges in the areas of affordable housing and availability of space to accommodate growing population density [2,4,22]. These issues as well as a range of social motivations has catalyzed a growing number of citizens in the Vancouver area to adopt living situations that are smaller, mobile, temporary, self-made, and/or collective. Our goal is to better understand the values, practices, and perspectives of people that actively embrace living situations that could be considered 'alternative' to normative domestic dwellings; and, to critically inquire into how such insights could inspire new ways of thinking about designing for 'the home' and what such a design practice might look like and entail.

Our design research inquiry was grounded in several key related questions (noted in the image below) and divided into two main stages: (i) cultural probes [9] and (ii) developing subsequent speculative responses and interpretations. We began our process by recruiting participants that adopted and, in several cases advocated for, alternative living situations. We recruited participants by posting flyers at various local organizations (e.g., grocery stores, coffee shops, community centers, libraries, etc.), advertising online in forums, and by word of mouth. We received notable interest and recruited a diverse set of participants that permanently lived in settings such as a van, boat, micro loft, tiny house, urban condo, collective house, and across many dwellings (as a house/pet sitter).

To better understand the lives, values, and practices our participants, we initially considered conducting an approach that combined in-person interviews with photographic inventories of the things and places that characterized their respective dwelling. However, this approach soon raised tensions. Some of our participants lived in circumstances that were in a legal grey area (e.g., in a van parked on a city street) and/or hard to access (e.g., in a tiny house on a nearby island). It was clear that they all exhibited resourceful, creative, and critical

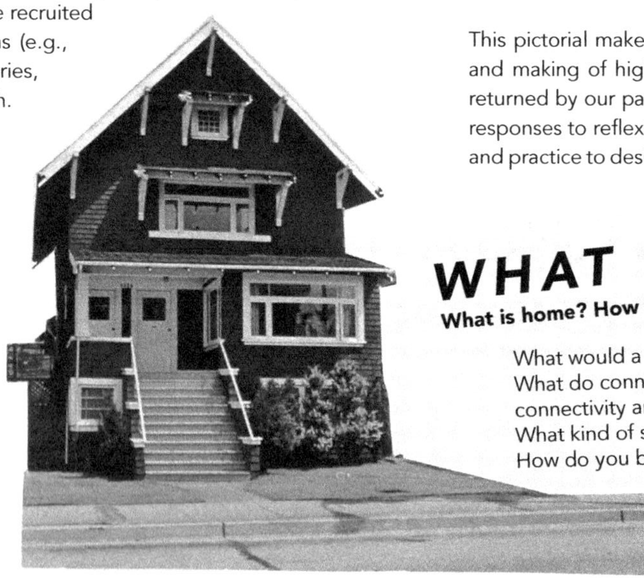

perspectives on everyday objects and dwellings. These factors made us feel they were ideal candidates for a cultural probes approach [9]. Cultural probes would enable participants to reveal to us their lives and ways of enacting domesticity on their own terms and time. Importantly, we were less concerned with collecting 'data' that would be generalizable or representative of an entire population; we wanted to use the returned probe materials for design inspiration to take a step toward speculatively engaging with diverse perspectives of domestic life, considerations of the home, and the role and place of technology within them.

Through our recruitment process, we found that several participants adopted 'zero-waste' lifestyles—a philosophy that emphasizes the reuse of materials and products to avoid their disposal. It also emerged that other participants were self-described minimalists and deeply considered their relationship to the things they possessed. These key commitments, along with the questions guiding our inquiry, highly influenced design process and decision making in creating the cultural probe kits. Collectively, the returned probe kits yielded a large amount of inspirational material that included images, audio recordings, written entries, numerous artifacts, and so on. In the second stage of our project, we chose to generatively engage with the returned probe materials by developing a series of speculative interpretations and design responses. Our aim was to explore and cultivate an attitude toward design for other, less considered forms of domestic life, and to open up a dialog about different ways that the home and domestic technology could be treated and explored in the DIS and HCI communities. The majority of this pictorial is devoted to unpacking and describing these generative interpretations and responses.

This pictorial makes two contributions. First, it offers a reflective account of the designing and making of highly finished cultural probe kits. Second, based on the probe materials returned by our participants, it proposes a series of speculative interpretations and design responses to reflexively open up different possibilities and provocations for future research and practice to design technology for other homes in the HCI and design communities.

WHAT MAKES HOME?

What is home? How is it made? Where is 'it'? How is 'it' enacted?

What would a 'smart home' be in the context of such alternative dwellings?
What do connected objects mean if you constantly move between zones
connectivity and disconnectivity? Or, if always have everything you own with you?
What kind of small luxuries are indulged in when there may be limited space for them?
How do you build a record of home over time when home is not fixed?

OUR PARTICIPANTS

In recruiting our participants, we reached out to people living in non-normative living situations. We soon realized how these living situations extended to values and lifestyles that at times overlapped. We will describe these on this page.

Zero-waste living aims to reduce landfill waste in everyday life, which entails consuming less, using less plastic, shopping packaging-free and being resourceful and thoughtful about materials in everyday life.

Zero-waste to an extent overlaps with minimalism, which some of our participants adopted as well. **Minimalism** also focuses on consuming less, but rather than being environmentally motivated, minimalism looks to establish more fulfilled lives with less stuff. The Tiny home movement is in part connected to minimalism, as an effect of space limitations and similar anti-consumerist motivations.

Other participants adopted **Urbanism** in taking maximal advantage of the city's infrastructure, e.g. bike- and car-shares and public transport. Further, our participants all advocated and promoted their living situations in response to the housing crunch in Vancouver.

The **Tiny Home Dweller** lives on Gambier Island. Her tiny home set up consists of one 16 x16 house, a separate 8x8 bathroom and a woodshed and cold room for food storage. She has lived there for 13 years. As a sustainability educator, she is knowledgeable of rules, regulations and impact around waste and specifically through living on the island where waste collection is sparse, she has over time grown into living more zero-waste. Her husband comes to the island in the weekends, and during the week works in Vancouver. He lives in a **Micro Loft Tiny Apartment**. Both of these places are considered home to the couple with an ongoing exchange between them.

The **Van Dweller** spent last year converting her second van and has been living in a van for 4 years. She organizes monthly Vehicle Dweller Meetups in Vancouver to get together with other van dwellers and to promote the van lifestyle. She works as a shuttle bus driver.

The **Boat Dweller** has been living on her boat with her family of four for several years. Advocating slow and steady living, she sails her boat to unconnected zones on local islands and the open ocean to get a break from city life.

The **Nomadic Pet/House-sitter** moves with her suitcase from one house to the next to take care of cats whose owners are away. Through word of mouth, family and friends and online platforms she has been living rent-free for more than a year. She continually adapts herself to different neighborhoods, cats and living spaces. She sometimes rearranges the furniture, and erases all her traces when it is time to leave. The Nomadic Pet/House-sitter adopts a zero-waste lifestyle and is highly connected to the cities infrastructure, e.g. through her ever-changing commute.

The **Urban Condo Dweller** lives with his five kids and utilizes the city and technology to enable his downtown family lifestyle. He is a keen promoter and self-described urbanist, minimalist and technologist and blogs about his lifestyle.

We recruited five **Collective House Dwellers** who had recently started a collective based on their shared ideas of what they wanted a house to feel like. The collective holds biweekly house meetings to continue these commitments, including maintaining a supportive community, creating a safe and inclusive space and drawing energy from each other's support.

OUR MATERIAL APPROACH

On the whole, our participants all reflected a commitment to resourceful ways of living and, albeit to differing degrees, re-use, sustainability, minimalism; on a basic level, our cultural probes kits needed to reflect this. To support this goal and empathize with our participants' commitments, we explored materials that could be adapted in the design and making of our probes. To support the sustainable and resourceful goals of our participants, we made our own paper recycled from paper scraps produced in our studio. We also used discarded fabrics such as bed sheets, old woolen sweaters and blankets to create our probe exercises. We responded to concerns of mobility and re-use by using durable materials such as metal and in creating a probe-bag that could be easily transported, passed on and be used again for next deployments.

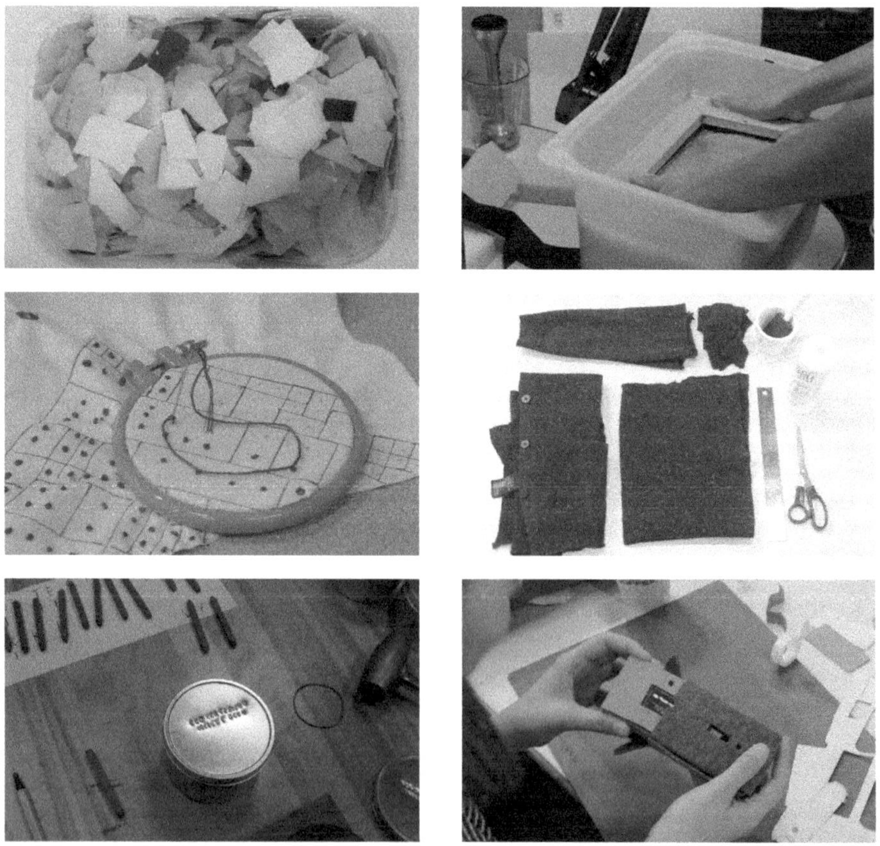

the probe kits

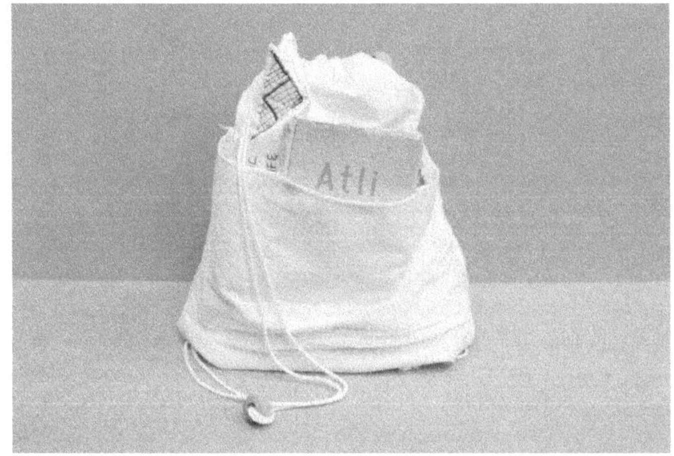

The probe exercises were organized in a canvas drawstring bag with several pockets and compartments, created out of the discarded sheets. Each probe bag was deployed with multiple participants. For each new deployment, the bag was personalized and tailored to the participants' specific living situation. At the same time, we included prompts and exercises that further emphasized the ongoing nature of the bag.

For each participant, we created a personalized invitation that exhibited her or his name on the front cover and included a brief statement about our design studio, aims of our project, and a brief summary of each probe task. We etched all writing appearing on the invitation with a laser cutter to avoid using inorganic materials that could complicate the process of composting or recycling the paper in the future. We also included a reflection booklet made out of homemade paper, with questions and prompts etched into it covering the overarching themes of the probe bags. We hoped this would give us a better understanding of their definitions of these themes. Furthermore, we wanted to give our participants a chance to share things they may not have been able to share through the other tasks.

TASKCAMS

We used TaskCams, simple digital point and shoot cameras created specifically for probe studies [3, 27], to probe into key issues, ideas and topics that we wanted our participants to respond to through photos. The TaskCams have a simple interface that allows participants to scroll through prompts displayed on an LCDscreen. We populated our TaskCams with questions (e.g. 'things that represent minimalism', 'what makes your boat home?', 'things that bring everyone together') as well as a set of more ambiguous terms and phrases (e.g., 'connection', 'disconnection', 'chaos', 'waste', etc.).

TRAVELING ROCK

The traveling rock, or 'zwerfkei' in Dutch, is a small rock with a string of homemade paper tags attached to it with yarn. Participants were invited to write the date, location and/or short messages on the small tags attached to the zwerfkei. The traveling rock was meant to evoke questions one participant might have for the other, revealing where their lifestyles overlap, what they might be curious about or even where they might misunderstand each other.

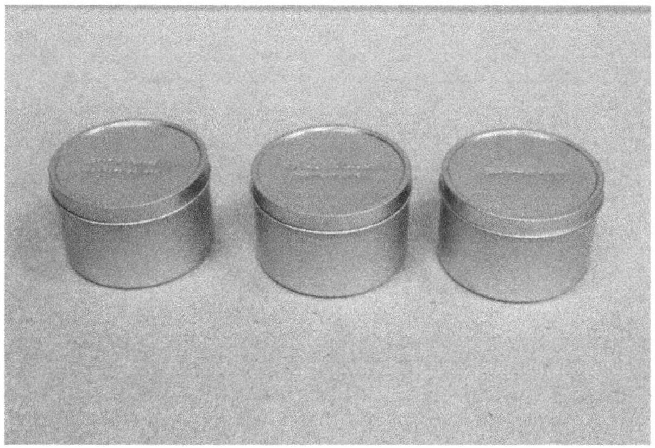

US AND THEM

This activity consisted of three metal tins with 'meme-like' statements that we stamped into each of the lids using a metalworking hammer and impress typeset. The statements were: how the mainstream thinks I live; how the cashier thinks I live; and how I actually live. We presented the tins as containers for responses of how our participants felt others viewed their lifestyle, and invited them to take their time and be creative with what to put in them. We wanted to understand how our participants might have felt their lifestyle is perhaps misinterpreted or misunderstood.

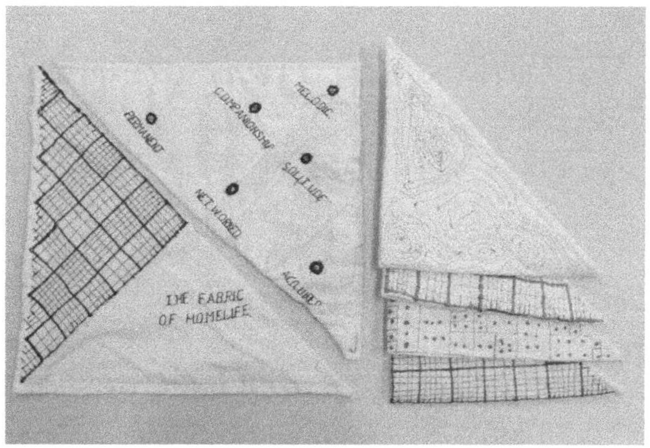

THE FABRIC OF HOME LIFE

This task consists of two triangularly shaped pieces of fabric: on one side of each fabric, two sets of six words were embroidered that represent values of home life the participant may or may not identify with, and that may or may not contradict their experience of home; for example: melodic and chaotic, free and intentional, solitude and networked. The participants were tasked to bring the textiles together with thread we provided and to sew a pathway through the terms that they felt best represented qualities of their home life. We wanted to gain insight into the subtleties, contradictions and dynamics of the values of their home life and how these differed across our participants.

PROMPTS WITH THE AUDIO RECORDER

We included an audio recorder in the bag and crafted several prompts that invited our participants to capture soundscapes and stories of their everyday life with us. With the Imagining In and Out activity, we invited participants to make use of two rolls of different colored tape to outline things, spaces or functionalities that they wish they had, as well as those that they wish were no longer there. We asked participants to take a picture of the result with the TaskCam and elaborate on their choices on the recorder. Through this activity we hoped to learn more about how things contribute to or limit the specific ways of making home of our participants. The Waste Capsule is a glass jar we asked our zero waste participants to fill with the waste they collected over the period of having the probe bags with them. The participants were asked to annotate its contents at the end, using the audio recorder. We were interested in learning how our participants considered materials of everyday life, and how their definition of and approach to waste varied.

what is the other home?

On this page, we present conceptual floorplans that are loosely based on the returned probe materials and embody aspects and values of the living situations of our participants. We aim to highlight what makes these homes different in terms of what is included in the conceptualization of home, where the home is located and how the home is enacted. These abstractions can be seen as alternative foundations of home that guided our speculative responses and design interpretations on the following pages.

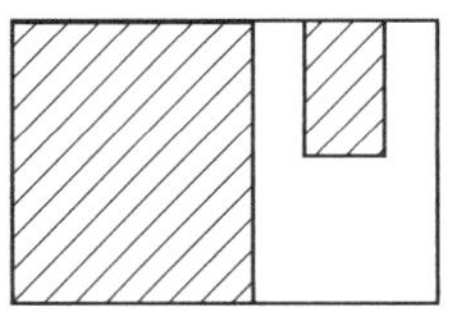

adaptable

In dwellings where space is limited (e.g. tiny homes, micro lofts, minimalist living) structures and furniture (e.g. murphy beds) often take on more than one function and/or can change states.

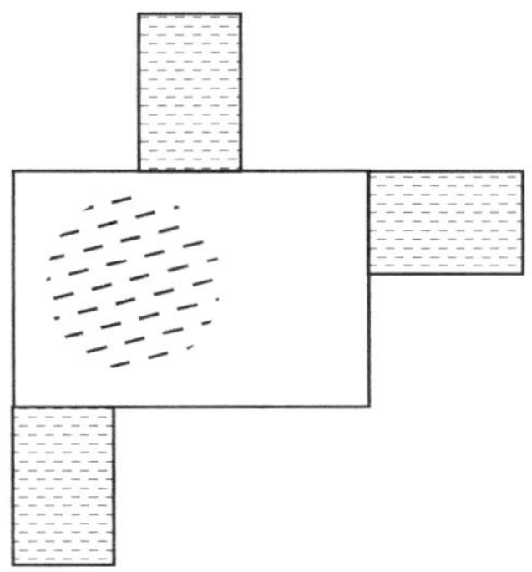

dynamic boundaries

Collective houses similarly deal with state changes in space. Where some private/shared boundaries are clearly divided (e.g. bedrooms), others are negotiable and dynamically shift between private, semi-private and shared.

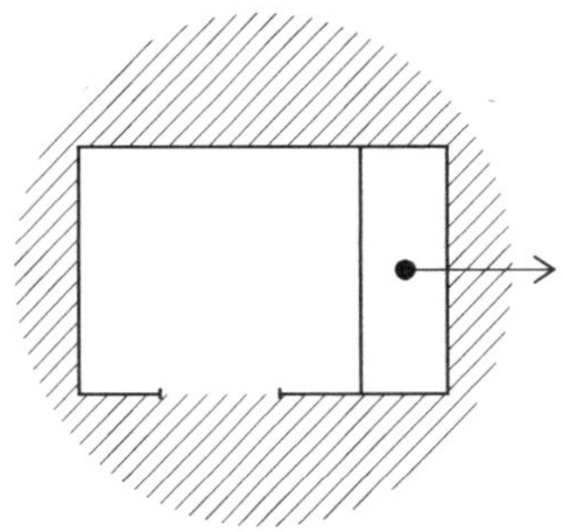

orientated

Homes like vans and boats have a "control room" that allows dwellers to adapt their orientation, location, environment and level of connectedness. The home is simultaneously fixed and dynamic, inviting the outside in.

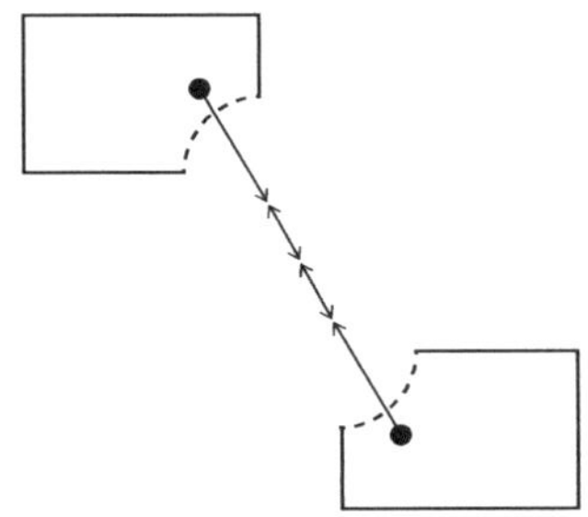

exchange

When living is distributed over multiple fixed locations, the sense of home is extended not just across these locations, but also in the back and forth between these locations (e.g. feeling at home on the ferry, exchange of things between homes, etc.).

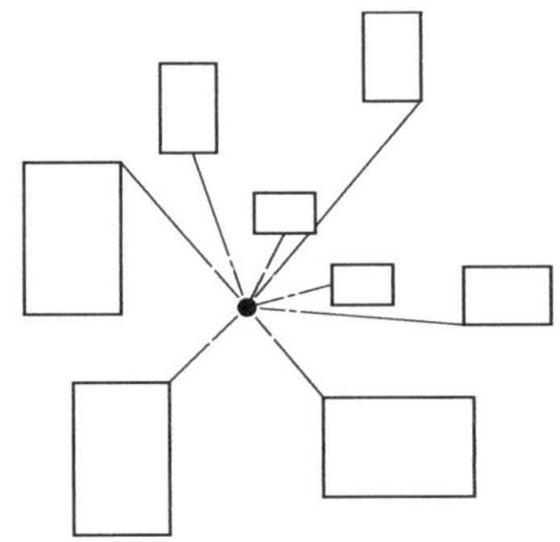

dispersed

Nomadic living is fragmented yet highly connected. Stable locations are used for work and storage, everyday living is location-less, orientation-less and traceless. What makes home is extended beyond a physical location.

Domesticating what's traditionally not considered domestic.

A set of layered window shapes that can be pulled down to connect your actual domestic location closer to fixed domestic sites in the city (e.g., one shape for the extended park kitchen in the actual kitchen, another for a few of a particular place in a city park as a part of your extended living room).

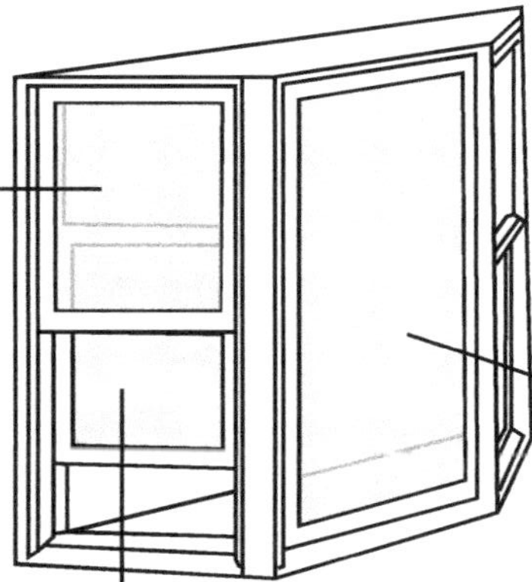

A portal or photo frame that continually shows the slowly changing landscape from the ferry's perspective as it moves back and forth between Vancouver and Gambier island.

Portholes in your boat or small windows in your van that can be configured to show prior scenes from your 'extended living room'.

the extended / distributed home

Participants expressed numerous ways in which they considered settings, places, and environments outside of their dwelling quarters to be important parts of what they conceptualized as their home. For our mobile dwellers (e.g., van and boat), the core domestic setting remained fixed, while the textures and character of their extended home continually as they moved to stopped in different locations. For our nomadic pet sitter, her fixed site of home revolved around a few core essential possessions, whereas for minimalist condo dweller 'home' extended into specific locations throughout the city (e.g., a frequently visited local park as a distributed kitchen/living room for cooking and gathering). While diverse, these responses highlight how the home can be conceptualized and designed for as a distributed relation set of fixed and dynamic points that collectively work together to evoke and enact home. Stitching together the network of relations among parts of the city, a ferry, a toiletry bag, or a scenic highway as changing facets in the fabric of everyday life opens up new possibilities to consider how technology can be designed to extend distributed, evolving spheres of domesticity.

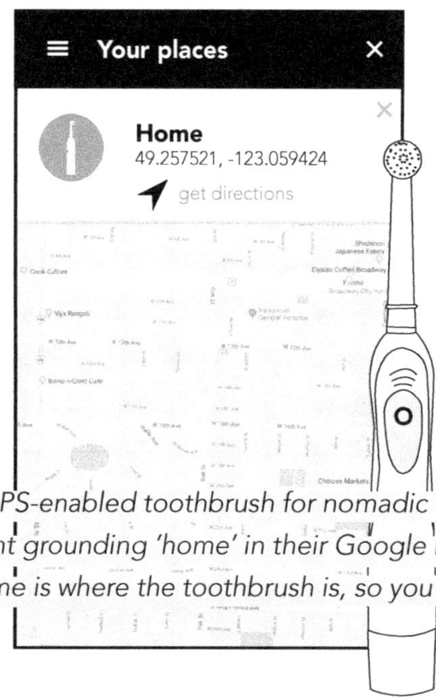

A GPS-enabled toothbrush for nomadic home dweller provides the digital anchor point grounding 'home' in their Google Maps application.
Home is where the toothbrush is, so you will never forget how to get back home.

Connected domestic objects and appliances appropriated by a van dweller that capture, amplify, and project the mundanity of her domestic practices to normalize her van as a domestic dwelling.

Participants richly expressed their material practices of making home, often celebrating their unique domestic settings.

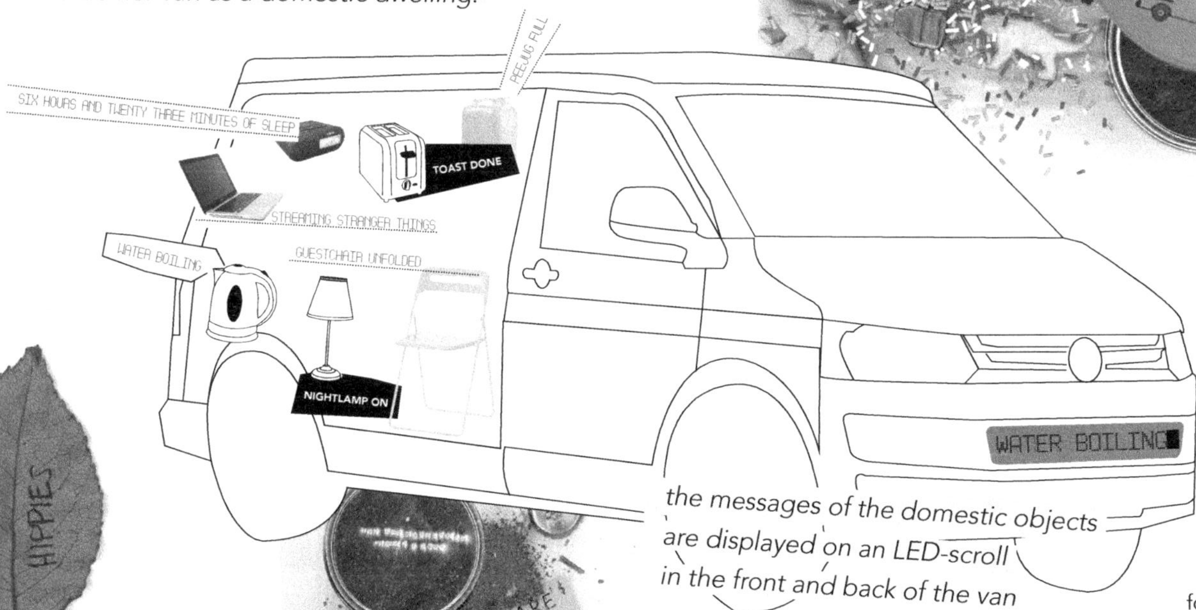

the messages of the domestic objects are displayed on an LED-scroll in the front and back of the van

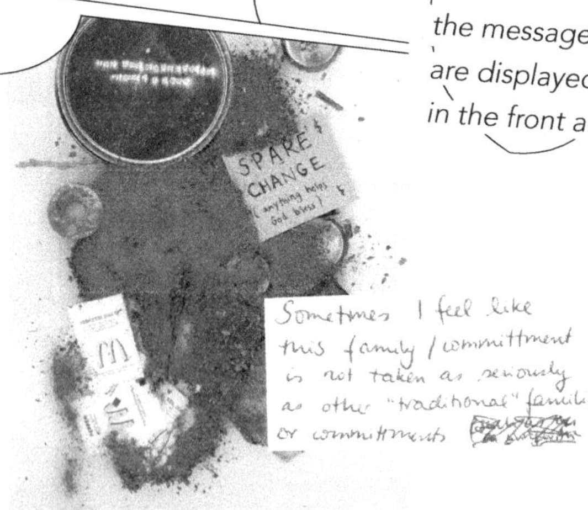

All participants expressed tensions around being viewed as non-normal, misunderstood, and not taken seriously. Consider the materials expressing a van dweller's response to 'how the mainstream views me' in the us and them activity to the materials included in her 'how I actually live' tin (shown in the top right of this page).

the making of home

Our participants responses revealed they did not view their practices of making home to be fundamentally different from house dwellers, despite living with unique and highly diverse constraints. Indeed, the making of home life is a dynamic and ongoing process for all of us. Yet, it was also clear that they frequently felt misunderstood by mainstream society and encountered tensions on being equally seen and treated as living 'normal' lives.

Recently, emerging connected domestic objects that communicate their status, such as Tweeting toasters [28], beds [29], and kettles [30], have been both lauded and highly criticized by those interested in (or concerned with) their place in in typical domestic settings. Re-appropriating such technologies in the context of our participants' lives could offer practical utility to amplify and project the status of their mundane everyday practices comprising home life to the outside world. This approach could offer an alternative critical take on such visions of emerging technologies for 'home life' by opening questions about their triviality and the underlying values they are being designed to support when situated in constrained and under-recognized domestic settings. Equally, we see value in exploring how the values, practices, and desires captured in our participants' probe responses could expand strategies for designing interactive technologies, which we explore in the following speculative proposal.

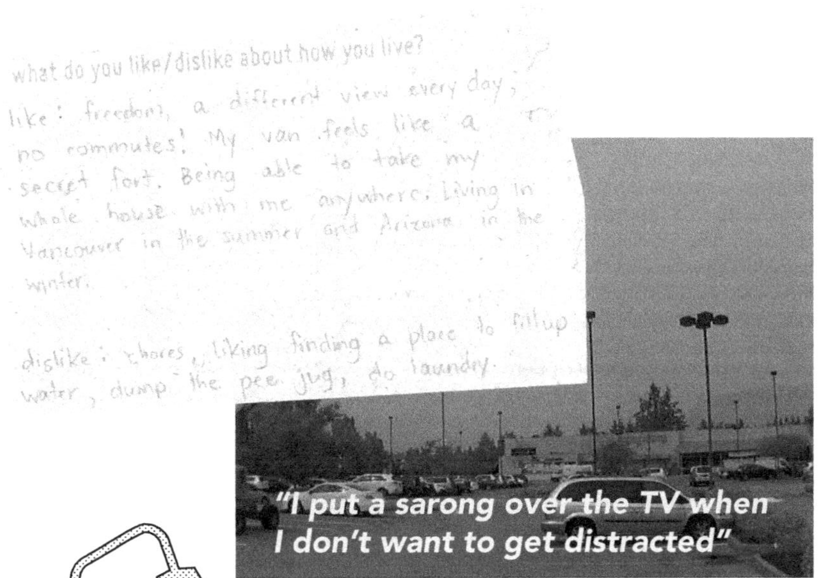

the adaptable home

While our participants are highly committed to their homes and lifestyles, they also shared with us the imperfect and unromanticised elements of their living situations. They accepted these parts of their home for other elements that they would not want to miss out on. For example, while our mobile dwellers enjoy the possibility of a new view every day, this may very well include a parking lot or another undesirable view on some days. Our van dweller accepts the compromise of missing certain infrastructural luxuries as this allows her to more freely adapt her environment. Our nomadic dweller adapts herself constantly to her changing living spaces that may or may not be her taste. She further emphasizes how while this life-style is right for her at this time, she sees it as part of a longer-term plan, saving money to travel and acquire a tiny house. These displeasures, compromises and aspirational aspects of their homes are perhaps more unique for these dwellers, yet any dwelling will prompt wishes and desires that lead to the ongoing, dynamic making of home. Rather than responding to these elements of their home as problems to fix, we see these as unique constraints that have in their actual homes already translated into spaces that are able to change states e.g. through adjustable furniture as well as in practices of making and remaking spaces. In the speculative responses on this page we explore the opportunity of technology to support adaptable, temporary and aspirational practices in the home.

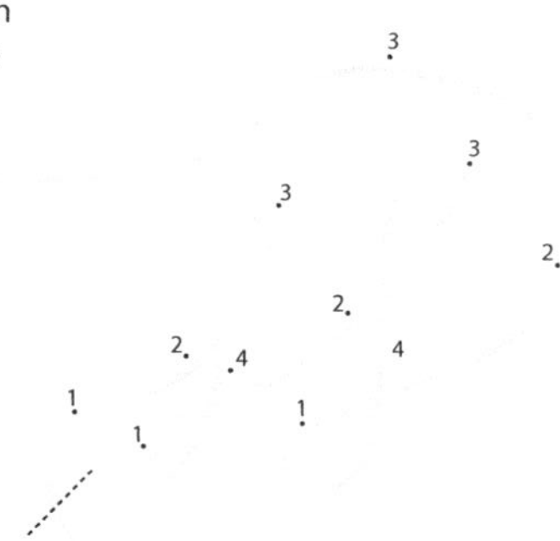

the Sometimes-Smart vacuum cleaner will do a dance when it's not connected

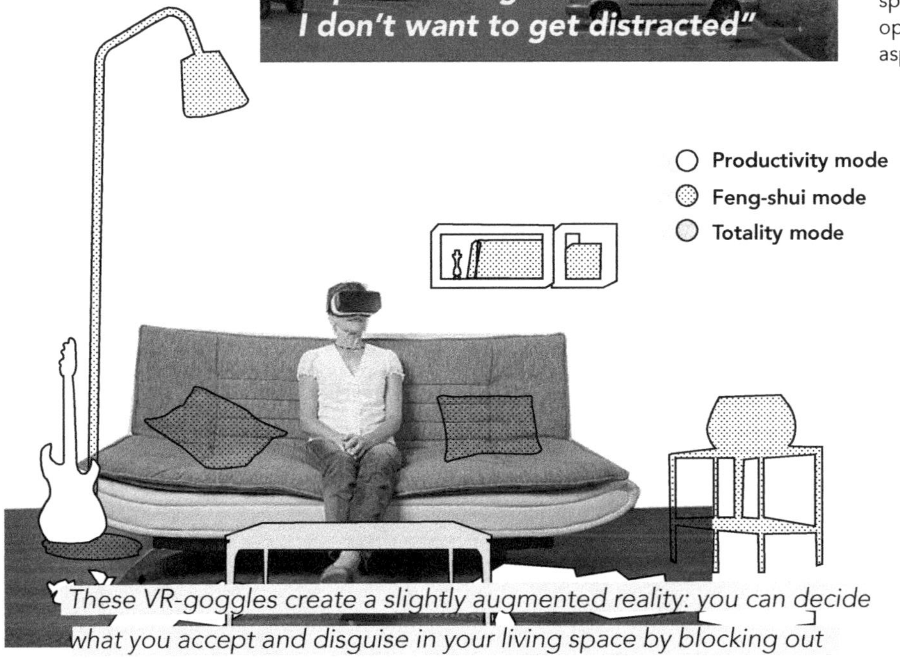

These VR-goggles create a slightly augmented reality: you can decide what you accept and disguise in your living space by blocking out elements for a while. This can be helpful to (re)create Feng-shui, to avoid distractions or to over time assess whether things still bring you joy.

When home is not fixed and you're moving between connected and disconnected zones, IoT products and smart homes can become a little dumb. To avoid useless black boxes these Sometimes-Smart Things can change states to be useful even if you're not online.

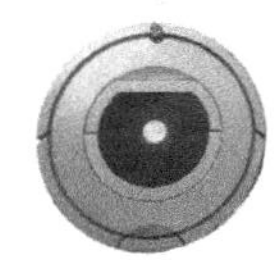

the Sometimes Smart Lightbulb goes into party-mode when it loses internet connection

tuning connectivity

Participants living in mobile, nomadic, or otherwise transitional situations as well as those living in relatively fixed domestic sites (e.g., micro loft, tiny house, collective house) expressed numerous perspectives on their respective relation to digital and network connectivity. Our mobile dwellers revealed how their movement through space to different geographic locations resulted in differing levels of connectivity as a part of daily life. In some cases, they intentionally changed their geographic location to places where they could avoid digital connectivity, only to later rejoin the digital network after moving location again. Participants that had fixed domestic sites, also expressed intentional manipulation of one's connectivity by limiting digital connectivity in the home to 'work time' during specific periods of the day or only when not co-dwelling with others in the shared domestic spaces. These instances are clearly shaped by a wide range of issues – some intentional, while others incidental or consequential of the unique constraints our participants lived with.

What we aim to draw attention to is that they suggest a continuum between neither being completely digitally connected or disconnected. We see this as inspiring a rich and intriguing design space to consider the creation of technologies that enable people with a greater capacity to manipulate and tune the granularity of digital connectivity that enshrouds our everyday home lives.

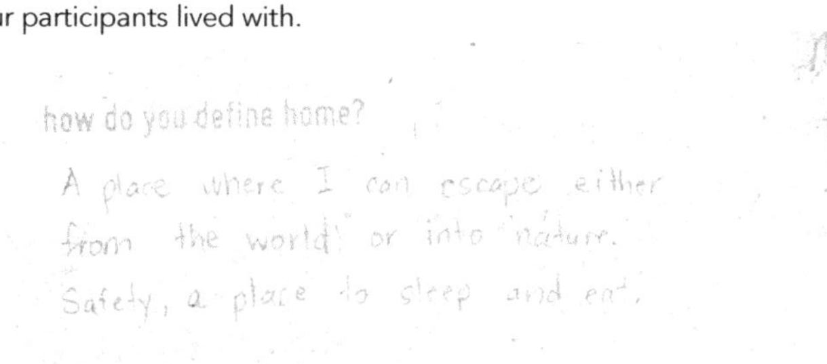

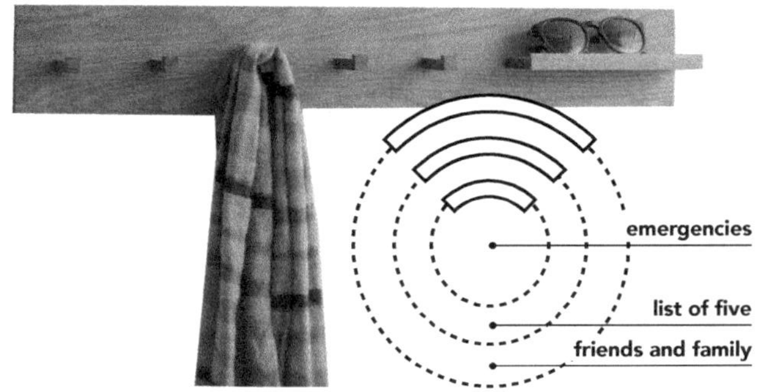

Imagine a coatrack that configures the digital permeability of the home to the outside social world. As more family members arrive home and places their hangs up their coat or scarf, the social circle of people allowed to digitally contact members in the home shrinks, increasingly restricting the intimate domestic sphere to those most intimately known by the collective family members present. This concept represents how connectivity can be configured by leveraging mundane socio-material practices by inhabitants of the home.

This set of devices proposes a vision of the connected home that treats digital network connectivity through a range of different forms that enable users to flexibly and directionally position short range Wi-Fi zones within their home. The ball form enables you to easily 'give' the one Wi-Fi position in the home to a person by merely tossing it to them; the fluffy router's speed peaks when you pet it; the rigid yet flexible textile concept enables you to mold various aesthetic forms to configure and concentrate Wi-Fi connectivity in the home. The molded form of the textile configures the relative speed and range of the Wi-Fi. For example, in a completely flat form, e.g. as a wall hanging, the speed is slow but the range is wide; in a tightly molded form like a horn or cylinder the range of very small and targeted in one direction, but the speed is high.

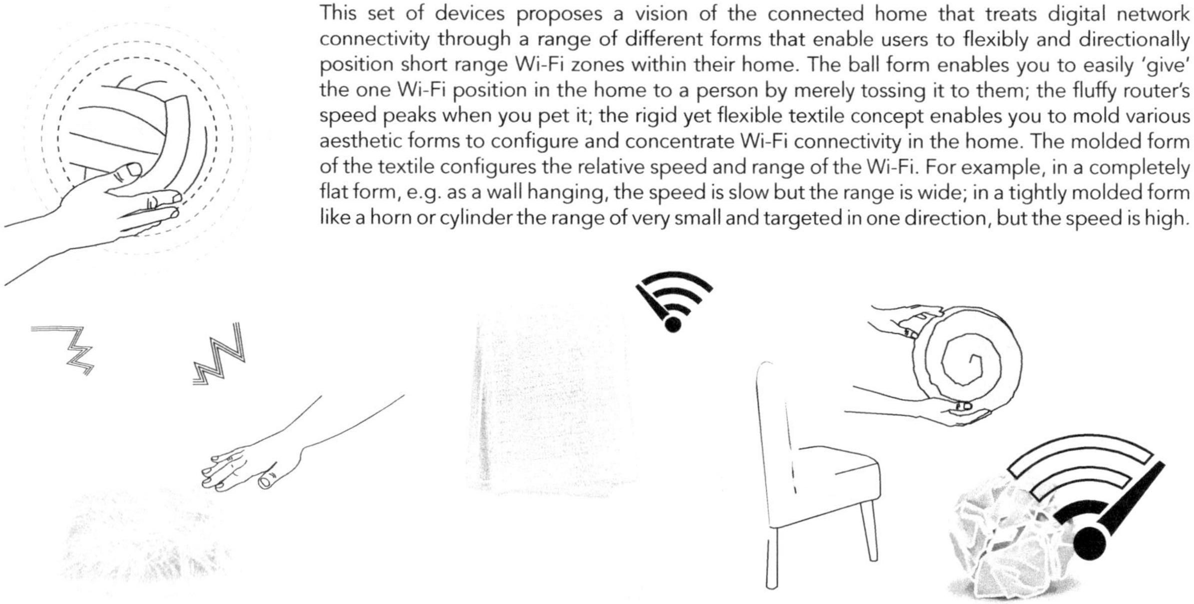

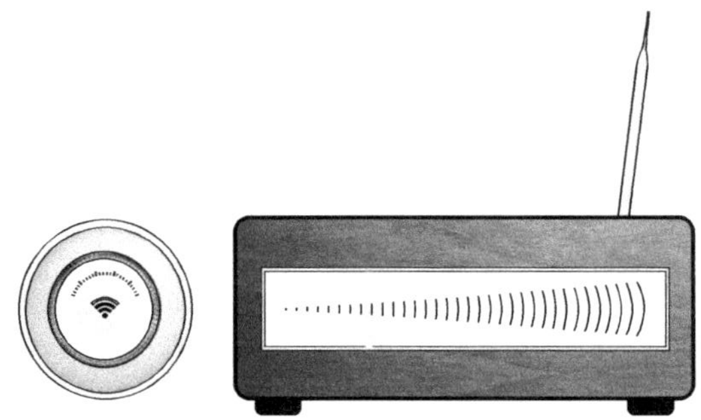

Building on the coatrack concept above, we also envision a more literal approach to enabling home dwellers to tune or 'dial in' their desired permeability of digital connectivity to the world existing outside of their domestic sphere. Embodied in the form of a circular thermostat or radio tuner, these design proposals offer direct manipulation of domestic connectivity.

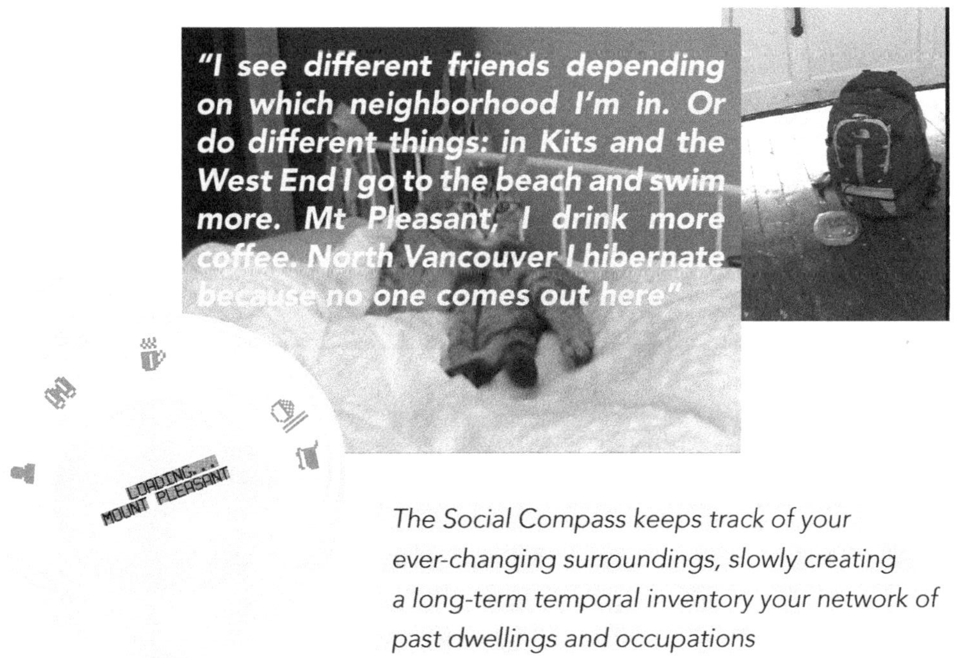

The Social Compass keeps track of your ever-changing surroundings, slowly creating a long-term temporal inventory your network of past dwellings and occupations

influence of the home on everyday life

Across their probe responses, participants expressed unique and rich connections between the lived experience of their everyday home lives and their occupations outside of home. These accounts were understandably diverse. This included a zero-waste educator noting the lessons learned from living in a tiny house on a remote island where waste removal occurs only once a year to the described satisfaction from a van dweller's day-time occupation in the somewhat similar mobile setting as a bus driver. Although there are notable exceptions [e.g., 14, 15], for the large part research in the DIS and HCI communities tend to see clear distinctions between home and work life. Our participants' responses indicated the important role that embracing lessons learned from their unique domestic situations or by virtue of the constraints they lived in played important roles in their lives outside of home and in their occupations. These responses inspired us to explore and propose alternative future possibilities in which the lived experiences of people that develop and enact diverse visions of domesticity could be more richly embraced in life outside of the home.

CLASSIFIEDS

Randomness on wheels

sales + service

Need some truly randomly generated numbers? Computers alone can't do that, but I'm about as random as it gets. Over the past four years I've been living and working on the go from my van. I've developed an algorithm that takes coordinates from my past locations and randomly assigns these to my clients. Long-term options available, please contact me for more information.

Professional Quality
IN YOUR HOME
Data Noise Provider and House Sitter

Getting bored of your targeted advertisements or recommended show?

Going on vacation soon? Maybe taking a work trip? It's the perfect time to let your devices unlearn: bring some variety to your recommendations and mix up your advertisements. Experience with all conventional browsers, streaming services and smart home providers.

references provided, rates negotiable.

CLOUD CLEANING

Hi there my name is Jen, I have been a minimalist for 6 years and love living with less. I am offering my services as a cloud cleaner in exchange for a month of unlimited internet access. I will organize, clean and label your digital files for you.

Serving all area & fully insured

Provide your cloud access

Indicate your organizational preference

Pay with internet access

conclusion

Developing approaches and strategies to design interactive systems for people's everyday lives at home continues to raise new opportunities and issues for the HCI and design communities. In this context, the overarching goal of this pictorial has been to take a modest step toward expanding how domestic life could be thought about and investigated. Design has long been regarded as an approach for framing, setting, and solving human problems, and improving the conditions of people's everyday lives. Indeed, the HCI community has a long and important tradition of developing novel technology solutions to better support people's domestic tasks, routines, and experiences.

Yet, design can also operate as an approach for critically provoking, imagining, questioning, and developing how we might treat such complex and diverse notions as 'the home' and the technologies designed in relation to it. In this way, we have sought to speculatively respond to the inspirational materials in our participants' cultural probes kits in the service of generating openings, potentials, and possibilities for engaging with a wider range of forms of domesticity. We adopted this approach to inquire into how such insights could be materially grounded through design and what it might have to offer for design practice in the future.

We proposed *adaptable, dynamic boundaries, orientated, exchange, and dispersed* as alternative foundations for conceptualizing the home, each of which offer their own unique constraints and opportunities to consider in the design of domestic interactive systems. We then described and unpacked *the making of home, the extended/distributed home, tuning connectivity, influence of the home on everyday life, and the adaptive home* as thematic collages of interpretations and speculative concepts. Taken together, these collages (i) propose alternative ways technology could be designed for the home, (ii) embody different ideas of where home is located, (iii) explore how home is constructed, re-made, curated, and pursued, and (iv) productively question material, technological, and social boundaries between the home and the outside world.

Through grounding our design research inquiry in the creation of cultural probe kits that resulted in rich materials which inspired our creation of a conceptual set of speculative proposals, our work concretely responds to growing calls in the HCI and design communities to: (a) develop alternative ways of framing and approaching the design of domestic technologies [1,10,12,14,18,21], (b) express more diverse perspectives on how 'the home' is conceptualized and how it can be researched [5,8,11,15,17,19,23], and, more broadly, (c) critically question underlying norms and values driving HCI research and practice [6,7,20,24]. Importantly, our aim is not to be prescriptive or conclusive. Rather, our pictorial aims to generatively inspire, frame, and expand future research inquiring into the fundamental questions of: What is home? How is it made? Where is it enacted? Why and by whom? And, how ought a technology be in this messy, diverse, and dynamic context?

ACKNOWLEDGMENTS

This research is supported by an Insight Development Grant from the Social Sciences and Humanities Research Council of Canada. We also thank the participants that took part in our study and the Interaction Research Studio for inviting us to use and test the TaskCam platform as a part of this project.

references

1. Ryan Aipperspach, Ben Hooker, B., and Allison Woodruff. 2008. The heterogeneous home. In Proceedings of the 10th international conference on Ubiquitous computing, pp. 222-231. ACM.
2. Luís Bettencourt, José Lobo, Dirk Helbing, Christian Kühnert, and Geoffrey B. West. 2007. Growth, innovation, scaling, and the pace of life in cities. Proceedings of the national academy of sciences 104, no. 17: 7301-7306.
3. Andy Boucher, Dean Brown, Liliana Ovalle, Andy Sheen, Mike Vanis, William Odom, Doenja Oogjes, and William Gaver. 2018. TaskCam: Designing and Testing an Open Tool for Cultural Probes Studies. In Proceedings of the SIGCHI conference on Human Factors in Computing Systems (CHI '18). ACM, New York, NY, USA, in press.
4. Grace Campagna. 2016. Linking crowding, housing inadequacy, and perceived housing stress. Journal of Environmental Psychology 45: 252-266.
5. David Chatting, Gerard Wilkinson, Kevin Marshall, Audrey Desjardins, David Green, David Kirk, and Andy Boucher. 2017. Making Home: Asserting Agency in the Age of IoT. In Proceedings of the 2017 CHI Conference Extended Abstracts on Human Factors in Computing Systems, ACM, 526-533.
6. Audrey Desjardins, Ron Wakkary, and William Odom. 2015. Investigating Genres and Perspectives in HCI Research on the Home. In Proceedings of the 33rd Annual ACM Conference on Human Factors in Computing Systems (CHI '15). ACM, New York, NY, USA, 3073-3082.
7. Audrey Desjardins, Ron Wakkary, and William Odom. 2016. Behind the Lens: A Visual Exploration of Epistemological Commitments in HCI Research on the Home. In Proceedings of the 2016 ACM Conference on Designing Interactive Systems (DIS '16). ACM, New York, NY, USA, 360-376.
8. Audrey Desjardins and Ron Wakkary. 2016. Living In A Prototype: A Reconfigured Space. In Proceedings of the 2016 CHI Conference on Human Factors in Computing Systems (CHI '16). ACM, New York, NY, USA, 5274-5285.
9. Bill Gaver, Tony Dunne, and Elena Pacenti. 1999. Design: cultural probes. interactions 6.1: 21-29.
10. Bill Gaver and Heather Martin. 2000. Alternatives: exploring information appliances through conceptual design proposals. In Proceedings of the SIGCHI conference on Human Factors in Computing Systems (CHI '00). ACM, New York, NY, USA, 209-216.
11. Tom Jenkins. 2017. Living Apart, Together: Cohousing as a Site for ICT Design. In Proceedings of the 2017 Conference on Designing Interactive Systems, pp. 1039-1051. ACM.
12. Tom Jenkins. 2015. Designing the Things of the IoT. In Proceedings of the Ninth International Conference on Tangible, Embedded, and Embodied Interaction, pp. 449-452. ACM.
13. Tejinder K. Judge and Carman Neustaedter. 2014. Studying and Designing Technology for Domestic Life: Lessons from Home. Morgan Kaufmann Publishers Inc., San Francisco, CA, USA.
14. David S. Kirk, David Chatting, Paulina Yurman, and Jo-Anne Bichard. 2016. Ritual Machines I & II: Making Technology at Home. In Proceedings of the 2016 CHI Conference on Human Factors in Computing Systems (CHI '16). ACM, New York, NY, USA, 2474-2486.
15. Gilly Leshed, Maria Håkansson, and Joseph 'Jofish' Kaye. 2014. "Our life is the farm and farming is our life": home-work coordination in organic farm families. In Proceedings of the 17th ACM conference on Computer supported cooperative work & social computing (CSCW '14). ACM, New York, NY, USA, 487-498.

16. Justin McGuirk. 2015. Honeywell, I'm Home! The Internet of Things and the New Domestic Landscape. Retrieved 11 December, 2017 from http://www.eflux.com/journal/honeywell-im-home-the-inte
17. William Odom, John Zimmerman, and Jodi Forlizzi. 2010. Designing for dynamic family structures: divorced families and interactive systems. In Proceedings of the 8th ACM Conference on Designing Interactive Systems (DIS '10). ACM, New York, NY, USA, 151-160.
18. William Odom, Abigail J. Sellen, Richard Banks, David S. Kirk, Tim Regan, Mark Selby, Jodi L. Forlizzi, and John Zimmerman. 2014. Designing for slowness, anticipation and re-visitation: a long term field study of the photobox. In Proceedings of the SIGCHI Conference on Human Factors in Computing Systems (CHI '14). ACM, New York, NY, USA, 1961-1970.
19. Marianne Graves Petersen, Aviaja Borup Lynggaard, Peter Gall Krogh, and Ida Wentzel Winther. 2010. Tactics for homing in mobile life: a fieldwalk study of extremely mobile people. In Proceedings of the 12th international conference on Human computer interaction with mobile devices and services (MobileHCI '10). ACM, New York, NY, USA, 265-274.
20. James Pierce, Phoebe Sengers, Tad Hirsch, Tom Jenkins, William Gaver, and Carl DiSalvo. 2015. Expanding and Refining Design and Criticality in HCI. In Proceedings of the 33rd Annual ACM Conference on Human Factors in Computing Systems (CHI '15). ACM, New York, NY, USA, 2083-2092.
21. James Pierce. 2016. Design Proposal for a Wireless Derouter: Speculatively Engaging Digitally Disconnected Space. In Proceedings of the 2016 ACM Conference on Designing Interactive Systems (DIS '16). ACM, New York, NY, USA, 388-402.
22. Wila Rea, Jennifer Yuen, John Engeland, and Roberto Figueroa. 2008. The dynamics of housing affordability. Perspectives on Labour and Income, 20(1), 37.
23. Irina A. Shklovski and Scott D. Mainwaring. 2005. Exploring technology adoption and use through the lens of residential mobility. In Proceedings of the SIGCHI Conference on Human Factors in Computing Systems (CHI '05). ACM, New York, NY, USA, 621-630.
24. Alex S. Taylor, Susan P. Wyche, and Joseph 'Jofish' Kaye. 2008. Pottering by design. In Proceedings of the 5th Nordic conference on Human-computer interaction: building bridges (NordiCHI '08). ACM, New York, NY, USA, 363-372
25. Jill Woelfer and David Hendry. 2011. Homeless young people and living with personal digital artifacts. In Proceedings of the SIGCHI Conference on Human Factors in Computing Systems (CHI '11). ACM, New York, NY, USA, 1697-1706.
26. Allison Woodruff, Jay Hasbrouck, and Sally Augustin. 2008. A bright green perspective on sustainable choices. In Proceedings of the SIGCHI Conference on Human Factors in Computing Systems (CHI '08). ACM, New York, NY, USA, 313-322.
27. ProbeTools: https://probetools.net
28. tweeting toaster: http://nothans.com/social-networking-for-my-toaster
29. tweeting bed: http://mashable.com/2009/12/13/twitter-bed-sex/#ljr760K_jSql
30. tweeting kettle: https://www.wired.com/2010/04/twettle-the-story-of-a-tweeting-kettle

ActuEating: Designing, Studying and Exploring Actuating Decorative Artefacts

Sara Nabil[1], Aluna Everitt[2], Miriam Sturdee[2], Jason Alexander[2], Simon Bowen[1], Peter Wright[1], David Kirk[3]

[1]Open Lab
Newcastle University
Newcastle upon Tyne, UK
{s.nabil-ahmed2, simon.bowen, p.c.wright}@ncl.ac.uk

[2]School of Computing & Communications
Lancaster University, UK
{a.everitt, m.sturdee, j.alexander}@lancaster.ac.uk

[3]Faculty of Engineering & Environment
Northumbria University
Newcastle upon Tyne, UK
david.kirk@northumbria.ac.uk

ABSTRACT

Actuating, dynamic materials offer substantial potential to enhance interior designs but there are currently few examples of how they might be utilised or impact user experiences. As part of a design-led exploration, we have prototyped (Wizard-of-Oz) an actuating, dining table runner (ActuEater1), and then developed a fully-interactive fabric version that both changes shape and colour (ActuEater2). Four in-situ deployments of 'ActuEaters' in different dinner settings and subsequent 'design crits' showed insights into how people perceive, interpret and interact with such slow-technology in interesting (and often unexpected) ways. The results of our 'ActuEating' studies provide evidence for how an actuating artefact can be simultaneously a resource for social engagement and an interactive decorative. In response, we explore design opportunities for situating novel interactive materials in everyday settings, taking the leap into a new generation of interactive spaces, and critically considering new aesthetic possibilities.

ACM Classification Keywords

H.5.m. Information Interfaces and Presentation (e.g. HCI): Miscellaneous.

Author Keywords

Shape-changing Interfaces; Organic User Interfaces; Interioraction; Multi-aesthetics; Colour-changing.

INTRODUCTION

Shape-changing interfaces (SCI) are physically, electronically, magnetically, pneumatically or mechanically capable of changing their shape as means of either input or output interaction with the user depending on shape-shifting materials or kinetic components that respond to different stimuli [5]. When situated within the built environment, SCI technology has the potential for many radically new diverse applications, e.g., dynamic artwork, shape-changing decoratives, pattern-changing fabrics, or even entire interactive interior spaces [35, 28]. Such notions of shape-changing dynamics have recently risen to prominence in both design and architecture literature. However, the 'artistic' and experiential aspects of SCI technology are rarely discussed and are thus identified as one of its main limitations [33]. Whilst many SCI explorations have focused heavily on the *development* of shape-changing materials and the *capabilities* of their interfaces, far fewer studies have considered the aesthetic value of the designs, overlooking how this might significantly influence user perception, engagement and ultimately, interaction, with such interfaces.

Figure 1. ActuEating: participants curiously exploring ActuEater2

Whilst interior decorative objects have significant potential to become dynamic, reactive and responsive, through the incorporation of Shape-Changing, Tangible and/or Organic User Interface [38] technologies [15, 23], there have, to-date, been relatively few examples of successful actuated decorative artefacts. One reason for this may be that such emerging technologies (although innovative) are struggling to find a place in our everyday environments (remaining mostly as curiosities within research labs). To help develop the conceptual design spaces from within which new and better technologies might emerge, a deeper grounded understanding needs to be developed of how people might perceive, interact with and otherwise experience such interfaces [33]. There are broad opportunities to

DIS '18, June 9–13, 2018, , Hong Kong

DOI: https://doi.org/10.1145/3196709.3196761

explore digital interfaces embedded within everyday artefacts, with the aim to make smart spaces more inhabitable, and interactive artefacts more adoptable. Such interactive artefacts should not be designed to appear 'technology-like' but could be designed and built to act like artefacts that people already admire, cherish and live with. This would extend the user experience in the built environment by adding a dynamic nature to interior design elements that match inhabitants' cultural expectations rather than appearing alien or ill-fitting. Taking shape-changing interfaces into an aesthetic design space opens up an opportunity for them to be incorporated into decorative artefacts, blending into our environments and supporting seamless transitions between physical and digital interactions.

The motivation behind our work is to 1) design exemplar interactive decorative artefacts and explore their potential, affordances, and limitations, 2) study how people interact with, interpret and experience an actuating piece of decorative fabric such as a table runner, and how it might change their experience of space and activity (in this case dining), and 3) discuss, from a user-centred perspective, possibilities and areas of future development for interactive spaces/materials.

In this paper, we present 'ActuEater1' and 'ActuEater2' as decorative centre-pieces on the dining table (see Figure 1). Utilising 'ambiguity' as a virtue [13] and 'slowness' as a value [31], our designs were created and then situated in-the-wild on four dining tables and subjected to post-study 'design crits' to drive the research forward. Our in-situ studies show how people perceive and interact idiosyncratically with a conventional decorative object that is 'actuating', yet concur when interpreting its interactions and discussing its impacts their dining experience. Furthermore, we present our reflections and discuss our main findings with regards to the overall experience of 'ActuEating' (social engagement in an interactive dining space) and the insights of people's sense-making of both ActuEaters. Furthermore, we present reflections on designing shape-changing interactive decorative artefacts.

The main contributions of this work are: 1) exploring the aesthetic design space of shape-changing interfaces in the form of decorative artefacts blending ubiquitously into our environments, rather than standing out as digital devices; 2) studying shape-change in a social event and how it affects people's experience in the space, and with each other; 3) exploring a broader interaction repertoire that is useful to learn how an SCI would be perceived and interacted with; and 4) studying how people learn and develop (individually and together) potential interactive scenarios with actuating objects.

RELATED WORK

Below we introduce some key considerations to help ground this work. Firstly, we discuss current efforts to develop shape-changing interior objects, then we discuss some aesthetic considerations of shape-changing materials before finally addressing the role of technology in supporting 'dining' experiences.

Shape-changing Interior Artefacts

Although there is some previous research around shape-changing actuation in furniture and interior objects, the work in this area is still somewhat limited. Examples of shape-changing interior objects in HCI research include the Earthquake Shelf [34], the colour-changing DigitalLace [36] and the Byobu room-divider [32]. Examples of shape-changing furniture include the colour-changing EmotoCouch [24], the shape-changing table/board [16] and coMotion [17], a horizontal shape-changing bench that changes its height and angle using 8 embedded linear actuator 'motors'. The study of coMotion gathered insights from 120 'unaware' members of the public who interacted with it (each for around 2mins). Although coMotion was remotely controlled by researchers i.e. Wizard of Oz (WoO), it enabled researchers to explore the users' interpretations, sense-making and experiences of its affordances and transitions. The pattern shape-changing (not form shape-changing), History Tablecloth [12] is a prominent example for a long-term study of situated interactive furniture. The 4-month study in a single 2-person household, provided a deeper insight into what it means to design artefacts in a real-world environment. Today still, as Gaver stated a decade ago, less purposeful, more exploratory and playful engagements that encourage people to explore, speculate and wonder, are poorly served by current technologies [12] and therefore still needs further research. Other examples of advanced shape-changing tabletops are Transform [22, 39], inForm [11] and PolySurface [9]. However, real-world applications that fit into our interior spaces are still quite limited.

Shape-changing Aesthetics

Visionary work on Radical Atoms [21] suggested that thoughtfully designed interfaces can and should be embodied in different materials and forms in our physical world. Inspired by this, some actuating interfaces were designed to explore people's experience with them and the sensational and emotional effects of such multi-aesthetic and deformable interfaces. For example, Textile Mirror [8], an actuated wall curtain, shows how interfaces can actively mirror and transform our feelings through traditional materials in our environments i.e. texture-changing fabrics can modify one's emotional state from stressed or angry to happy and calm. Similarly, Davis [7] explored a variety of different emotional expressions that can be communicated to users through texture-changing artefacts. Ueda [37] also explored actuated textiles through wrinkling shape-changing fabric as means of user interaction, and Bodanzky [2] has explored some of the potential expressive qualities of shape-changing surfaces and their actuating designs. Concepts such as Neuroaesthetics [7] and 'Aesthetic Interaction' [23] proposes how the aesthetics of visual and tactile interactivity can be used to activate not only visceral put perceptual senses, meanings and values and provoke self-reflective awareness through ubiquitous interaction with textural-changing interfaces. Proposed motivations for such interfaces include: being a conversation starter, material for storytelling, overcoming temporal blindness [6], entertainment and playfulness [26] and visualizing the unseen [28].

Interactive Eating Experiences

Previous HCI research has explored debatable ways in which digital technology should or could be used to change and/or enhance the eating experience [4, 20]. For example, in working with families, Ferdous [10] has attempted to transform the disruptive experience of mobile phone use during family meals into a positive social experience, by utilizing phones as a form of collective engagement at the table. However, Hiniker [19] has studied the challenges of using mobile phones during family mealtimes and their implications on family members' social experience. Other work [14, 29] has considered the ways in which digital technology can help connect and engage lone diners geographically dispersed. Barden [1] explored the challenge of connecting distributed diners in a Telematic-Dinner-Party using cameras and projectors exploring augmented reality that blends into the physical world. Alternatively, Mitchell [25] designed a kinetic dining table that can synchronize the eating pace of dining companions to augment their social experience with mutual alignment. This work shows that such domestic and ritual activities can be prime settings for technological explorations, and point to the entanglement of technology with the aesthetic experiences of dining.

DESIGNING ACTUEATER1

Building on previous work, most notably coMotion [17], we wanted to explore SCIs as decorative artefacts, but embedded within complex social settings. Extending typical duration of user interaction to over an hour (instead of an average of 2mins) allows people the time to observe, practice, learn and develop a variety of interaction scenarios. A richer interaction repertoire can be designed using a wider range of different shape-changing physical actuations (than controlling one parameter/dimension) by controlling the location, scale, height and speed of a fine-grained grid of embedded actuators. For our first case study, we chose ShapeClips [18] to create a rapid working prototype. ShapeClips are prototyping toolkits for creating interactive shape-changing displays using vertical actuators (stepper-motors) animated with photo-sensors using any monitor.

Making

Inspired by PolySurface [9], we re-purposed the ShapeClips to build a dynamic and customizable shape-changing prototype that fits on a dining table as a traditional table runner. As ShapeClips vary between 8 and 18 cm in height, we embedded them within the table itself to ensure an initially flat surface on our table. After the software was re-programmed and the hardware electronic components were re-structured in the desired arrangements, a full-length table runner was made as ActuEater1 (see Figure 2). Similar to PolySurface [9], we designed ActuEater1 from stretchable Spandex fabric and a uniform custom-designed pattern laser-cut on 0.8 mm thin polypropylene sheets to give it a controlled semi-flexible moving capability. After fixing it together, we lined the edges with a satin golden-beige ribbon as a finishing touch to give it an original look and an aesthetic value similar to contemporary table runners. The final runner was 93×35 cm consisting of 10 ShapeClips in a 2×5 grid to control its inner body.

Actuations

Driven using a remote WoO interface, ActuEater1 could change its shape on top of the dining table in an array of different actuations: 1) Default state (sleep mode); 2) Located actuation (using a single bit in front of a certain diner) that either moves upwards and stays for a while or vibrates up and down slowly or rapidly; 3) Two located actuations (two bits away from each other interacting with users on both sides of the table); 4) Sequential deformation from one end to the other; 5) An animated wave motion moving across the table runner; 6) All-up and all-down. Height and speed are both controlled variables that allow variation in the resulting actuation. During testing we realized that when ActuEater returns to default state, it does not become flat, but leaves 'history wrinkles' i.e. traces of previous actuations, in the form of fabric bends. Although these traces were not intentional, it was an unexpected yet interesting feature of ActuEater1, showing a 'history' of actuation which we saw as an interaction richness rather than irregular performance.

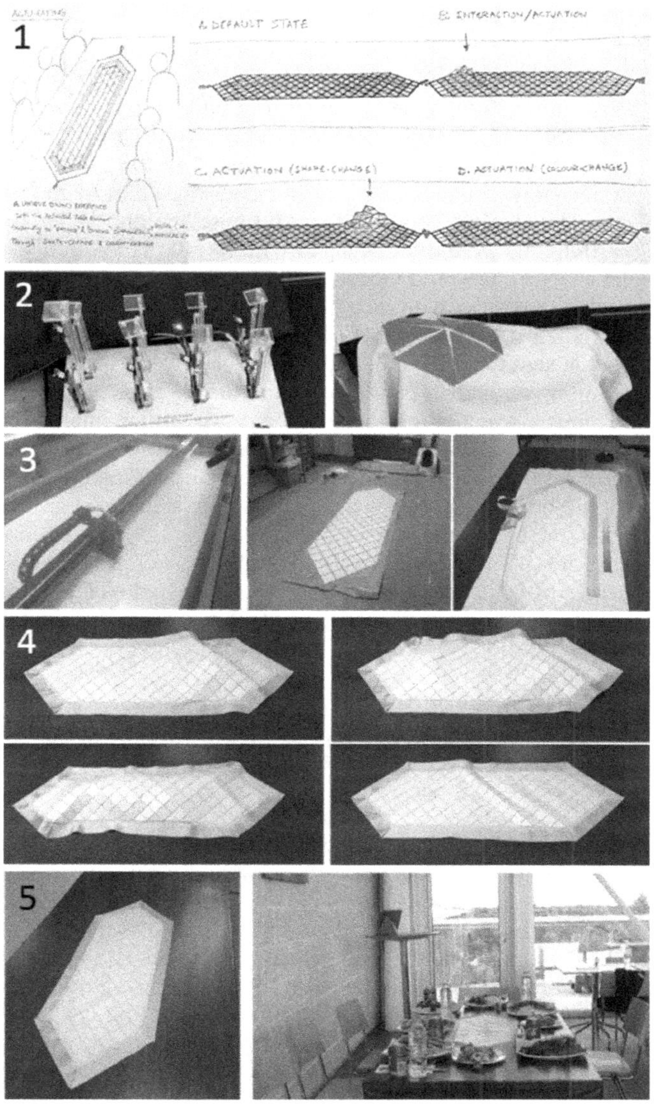

Figure 2. Designing and Making of Actuating1. 1) Ideation and Sketching. 2) Prototyping the Software and Hardware.3) Designing the Pattern. 4) Creating the Actuations. 5) ActuEater is ready and 'dinner is served'.

Interaction Repertoire

The eventual actuations performed by ActuEater1 were prototyped, live, in a WoO study (detailed below). The experimenter (first author) responded to emerging interactions and developed the following pattern of responses to users: when one participant was engaged with ActuEater1 or touched it, it vibrated (low actuation) the part in front of her/him by moving up and down in a small scale with limited height. When two participants were both engaged with it (talking about it with each other), it would vibrate in front of both of them. If two people touched it with their hands or used an object, it rose all up. Then if they tapped it, it went all down. If two or more people kept touching it, it animated in an organic wave motion going up and down from one end to the other. We were able to improvise actuations at some points to initiate interactions with one (or more) of the participants to explore the effects of this on their reactions to ActuEater1 and interactions with each other. For instance, a sequential low actuation can train from one end to the other if ActuEater1 'got bored of people ignoring it'. To allow for discoverability, we controlled the height of actuations to increase over time and usage, to see whether people will relate their interaction with the increase of deformation.

STUDYING ACTUEATER1

An initial evaluation study (A) took place in a terraced-rooftop restaurant with a group of 6 friends (P1-P6), with mixed genders (2F / 4M), age-groups and backgrounds (Media, Design, Economics, Computing, Chemistry and Psychology) who signed-up to participate in the study. Participants were not briefed as to what to expect beyond their voluntary participation in a study over a dinner meal. The meal was audio-video recorded from two different angles to capture as many of the users' expressions, interactions and conversations as possible. The dinner lasted about an hour, then we joined participants for a post-study 'design crit', a group discussion, lasting 30 mins where participants had the opportunity to express their reflections on their experience and provide us with critical feedback on our design and further design opportunities.

EVOLUTION OF THE ACTUEATER

Study A suggested a number of user-desired potential developments to ActuEater1: 1) Control: not be remotely-controlled and be legible (they assumed it was randomly actuating because human control (WoO) was not always immediate and consistent to all 6 participants); 2) Interaction: be responsive to their physical interactions (e.g. touch and physical objects); 3) Hardware: not to have such a bulky structure, loud noise or create a hole in the table; 4) Aesthetics: blend with the surrounding space and be more colourful; 5) Capabilities: colour-change was suggested to complement and enrich the shape-change; 6) Experience: be entertaining/ dancing, autonomous (have agency of its own), and interact with the surrounding space (music, objects); and 7) Meaning/ value: reveal/support further values (believing ActuEater1 had a hidden agenda of some good intention and meaningful purpose).

Therefore, we designed ActuEater2 to be a silent stand-alone fabric runner (with no motors required beneath the table) that is touch-sensitive and still has some agency designed to be more colourful with colour-changing capabilities (as well as shape-changing). Then further studies should then inform our research about how these changes affected the experience to show what meanings and values would people draw from their experience with ActuEater2. These further studies should give more insights on other findings i.e. social engagement, interaction repertoire, physical manipulations, and seamful/seamless sensing beyond interaction boundaries.

DESIGNING ACTUEATER2

In response to the suggested evolutions of ActuEater1, we developed ActuEater2 to have more organic actuations (rather than mechanical ones), direct physical interactions (rather than WoO), and richer capabilities (colour-change as well as shape-change). The redesign also shifted us away from demanding, bulky and noisy hardware (requiring a big hole in the table). Broadly speaking, ActuEater2 was intended to not be a radical departure from the design of ActuEater1, but build upon what we had learnt in terms of both design and user experience. ActuEater2 presented an organically-actuating soft decorative object which we could use to further study how multi-aesthetic interactions from a shape-changing decorative could impact people's experience of a given interior space/activity over time.

Making

ActuEater2 (see Figure 3) is a 60×40 cm cotton fabric envelope, with a stretchable spandex top holding the deformable pattern, both sandwiching a silicon rubber layer in between, holding a set of SMA (Shape Memory Alloy) wires. This layering technique was inspired by the HotFlex [15] technique for making interactive printed objects, which proved to achieve better results allowing ActuEater2 to be malleable enough to deform yet firm enough to relax again. Moreover, the layering acted as an insulating cover for the SMAs (a useful safety feature). The 9 SMAs used were each 1-inch pre-trained shape-changing 'nitinol' shape-memory springs from Kelloggs Research Labs that actuate at 'standard temperature' (45°C) or equivalent 5V and 0.7A drawn from a MOSFET transistor, pulling it back to its 1-inch spring shape from any malleable form. ActuEater2 also had capacitive sensing parts (green flowers) using 10×10 cm concealed knit conductive fabric to enable soft touch and proximity sensing through $1M\Omega$ resistors. We used an Arduino microcontroller to program ActuEater2 and control the behaviour of its interactions.

As nitinol SMA springs are not solderable, we used a crimping technique where we carefully attached to both ends of each spring a conductive (silver) crimp bead to form a connection with an insulated copper wire. Through this crimping, we were able to connect and control SMA springs through the Arduino, which was sleaved and concealed out of user sight. We found that stitching the ends of SMA carefully to the fabric gives it better grip force to 'pull' it upwards without moving freely elsewhere. As SMA 'one-way' springs work by shrinking with heat or current, it crumbles the fabric in between both ends it is stitched to creating deformations. The weight of the runner and force of gravity then brings it back slowly to the table. Working out a perfect material weight that could be light-enough to deform with SMA, but still be heavy-enough to return to flat, was key to achieving a 'two-way' actuation. Moreover, this meant that the most perceivable deformations were the ones stitched to the edges of the runner, not in the centre, where the weight is maximum, preventing visible deformation. Finally, to entirely conceal 'technology' from visibility, ActuEater2 was carefully finished using a sewing machine where we enclosed all its core components with nothing visible other than a power cable (that is replaceable with a Lipo battery).

Similar to ActuEater1, we designed ActuEater2 with a uniform custom-designed pattern laser-cut on 0.8 mm thin polypropylene sheets to give it a controlled semi-flexible moving capability. This time we optimized the pattern into triangular tessellation (instead of squares) to allow more organic deformations in different orientations. ActuEater2 was also designed to be more colourful. Thermochromic 'grey' fabric was used in some parts to add the capability of colour-change. By embedding a heating wire underneath, the thermochromic fabric was controlled to reveal a hidden pattern as an ambient display and means of richer interactivity.

Actuations

ActuEater2 changes shape more subtly, slowly and silently than ActuEater1, making it appear far more organic and less mechanical. Different parts of ActuEater2 behaved in different ways according to the affordance, stiffness and weight of the material at differing points i.e. edges deformed more freely than the centre. Touch-sensitive 'green' parts acted as ubiquitous sensing that triggered actuation of parts beside it. Agency was also enabled in the algorithm of ActuEater2 to display autonomous actuations if ignored for some time. Similar to ActuEater1, during the testing phase we realized that when ActuEater2 goes back to the default state, it also does not return entirely flat, again leaving unintentional traces showing a potentially interesting/useful 'history' of interaction.

STUDYING ACTUEATER2

We studied ActuEater2 in-situ, using methods and settings consistent with Study A (ActuEater1). We successfully ran 3 sessions with a total of 13 participants. We varied location for the meals to enhance the ecological validity of our exploration. The first (Study B) took place in a Lebanese restaurant (evening meal) with a group of 4 Middle-Eastern friends (1F, 3M) with backgrounds in Psychiatry, Health-care, Business and Biotechnology (P7-P10). The second (Study C) took place in a University cafe (lunch followed by tea and cake) with a South-Eastern Asian group of 5 female friends with backgrounds in Business, Computing, Architecture (2) and Dentistry (P11-P15). Finally, the third (Study D) was a dinner party at home (evening meal), where a group of 4 mixed international friends (2F, 2M) with backgrounds in Education, Social Work, Business and Civil Engineering (P16-P19) met at P18's home.

In all three studies, participants were not briefed about the ActuEater, or that is was an interactive artefact to give them the chance of having their meal as usual and discovering the ActuEater themselves. Although we purposely had participants from different cultures, backgrounds and age groups, we observed clear consistencies in most people's behaviour around ActuEater2 across groups. In both study B and C, the 'waiter' and 'waitress' were unexpected participants, where

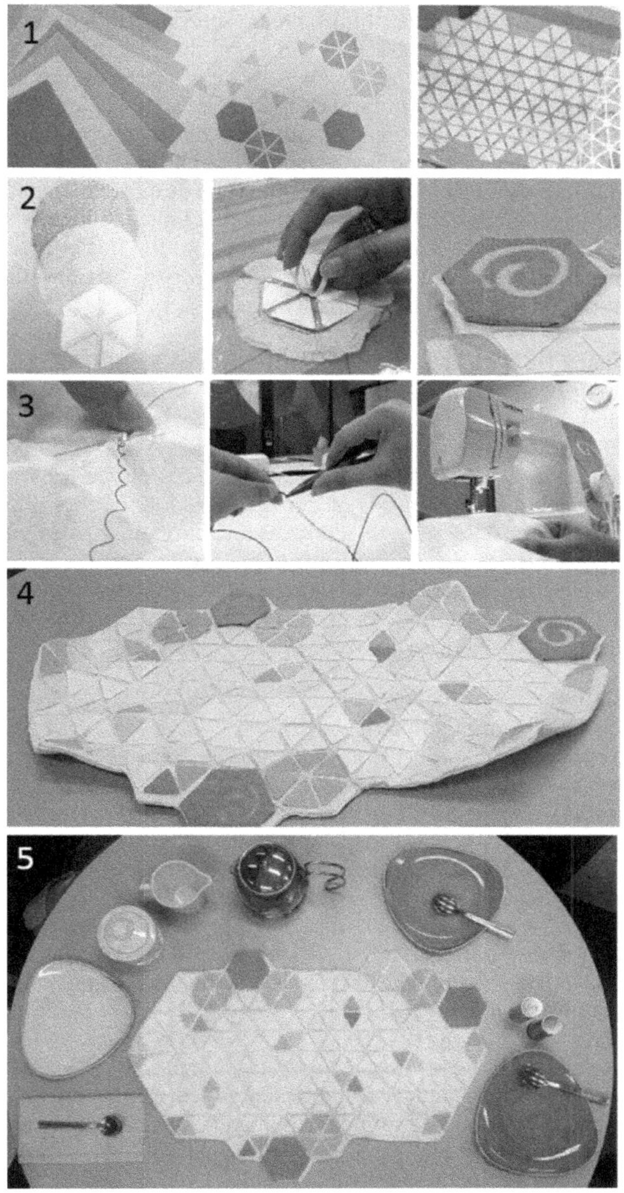

Figure 3. Designing and Making of Actuater2. 1) Designing the Pattern. 2) Making the Colour-changing parts. 3) Stitching, Crimping and Sewing. 4) Creating the Actuations. 5) ActuEater2 is ready.

the ActuEater responded to them whilst placing appetizers in the centre of the table (on top of ActuEater2). In study C, we hacked the sugar pot, plates, cinnamon and chocolate powder shakers, and the teapot, to be all capacitive, using stainless steel frames or aluminium foil bottom layer, and therefore interacting with ActuEater2. In study D, the home owner i.e. host dealt confidently with ActuEater2 in which she replaced objects and plates on top of it as she pleased, and lifted the ActuEater and re-positioned it on her dining table.

As in study A, meals were audio-video recorded from multiple angles to capture users' expressions, interactions and conversations. After each meal a design crit group discussion was held to critically evaluate the design of our ActuEaters in terms of: 1) Sense-making and interpretation (how did

ActuEater make them think? Does ActuEater look, feel and sound right?); 2) Interaction and emotional engagement they had with ActuEater, and with each other in relation to it; 3) Complex scenarios and interactions beyond expected legible interactivity; 4) Proposing possible enhancements (in terms of design, interaction, purpose, meaning/value and/or context) in light of: constructive feedback about the design itself; materiality (evaluating the material quality and finish), and pros and cons (what is bad and what is good about the design). Data from the meals and the post-meal design crits was transcribed and then subjected to Thematic Analysis [3].

UNDERSTANDING THE ACTUEATING EXPERIENCE

In this section, we discuss the results of our thematic analysis drawing on the data from all four of our in-situ studies (A-D incorporating both ActuEater 1 and 2). Our orientation to use a 'situated design crit' as an evaluatory mechanism means that the emphasis of our results is less on the 'dining experience' and more on a critical reflection on the design of the ActuEater. Accordingly, the themes we discuss unpack the ActuEating experience, exploring how users made sense of both ActuEaters, and how they imagine they could be better designed, used or employed.

Experience Sense-Making

Describing the Experience

People made sense of our actuating decoratives in various ways. While ActuEater1 was described as *"an attention seeker, not distracting in a bad way, it's more of an interesting distraction."* (P4), ActuEater2 was more *"subtle, it can take the attention, but not all the attention."* (P7) described: *"like a cherry on top, just a nice part of our conversation, but not focus demanding"* (P10). Variously, the ActuEaters were seen as conversation-starters, e.g. *"an ice-breaker* (P13) and *"an interesting talking piece"* (P5). But some focused more on its enigmatic qualities framing it as *"very creative and interesting"* (P8), *"revolutionary"* (P7), *"mysterious, quite alive"* (P19), *"unbelievable"* (P17) and *"an object of curiosity"* (P16). However, we understand how this was largely driven by its novelty effect. Nevertheless, some saw immediately entertaining qualities in the ActuEater suggesting it was playful like a *"treasure box"* (P12), a board game and generally *"fun and entertaining"* (P11). Whilst others saw it as something more meditative *"like a water fountain"* (P1) and *"calming like ocean waves"* (P8), and *"great to meditate or gaze at, like a fireplace"* (P7). When describing some of the deformations and interactions of ActuEater1, participants used more mechanical terms like *paused, rested, nudging, popping and poking, all go up, moving across and slow down*. Whilst, ActuEater2 was defined in perhaps more fluid terms as *changing, moving, crumbling, dancing* and *"it's almost like breathing!"* (P18).

Understanding the WHY

Understanding interactions with the ActuEater had clearly occupied a great portion of the conversation among participants over their meal. Some discussed how it might be proximity/motion sensing, and not any touch, but the way they touch it *"that's why when I touch it, it goes brighter than when you touch it, you have to calm down P12, see, if you're gentle to it, it responds"* (P13). Also, sound-sensing was frequently suggested and tested with its different versions: *voice*, *volume* or *conversation engagement*, *restaurant music*, *cutlery sound*, *noise in the environment*, or even *keywords*, all assuming it is *"physicalizing it (sound)"* (P2). Although it responded to their touch and physical interactions, some suggested further para-sensing beyond that, wondering if it picked up their *"heat, or energy"* (P19), *"mood"* (P12), *"stress"* (P13), *"brain waves or heartbeat"* (P16). To validate their theories, participants tested their ideas in different ways: group D gathered around it covering it up to warm it with their hands in a spiritual manner, group B and C 'clicked' it together on different parts simultaneously, while group A patted it together like a pet.

Perceiving the Meaning & Value

Besides its entertaining aspects, participants were keen to give ActuEater further values believing it had a hidden agenda of some good intention and meaningful purpose. Group A questioned *"Was it to do with how engaged you are in the conversation?"* (P2), *"or is it kinda 'stop eating' and 'talk to people'?"* (P1), *"It did try to nudge me because I was so focused while eating."* (P6), *"or maybe it's just trying to bring us all together"* (P2). Likewise, group B suggested how it could be a good conversation starter if people are not quite friends, group C also expressed it is a way to help people interact with each other, and group D argued that: *"it could be interactive with people who speak the most or speak the least, because I finished my food, that's why it is reacting more on my side"* (P19). Through conversations, participants were building assumptions that ActuEater was a resource for social engagement. Participants' responses implied how they thought ActuEater 'wanted' them to engage with each other and sought to develop a deeper social interaction amongst them.

Envisioning the Concept

The overall experience of ActuEating helped us better understand how decorative artefacts, or 'decoractives', can uplift the state-of-the-art to a new level. Envisioning decoractives in general can be drawn from participants' comments about the ActuEaters in the design crits as an abstract concept for interactive decorative artefacts in general, not specifically a table runner. For instance, participants' thinking about the broader relevance and use of decoractives was describing in study C as *"the fun part of the boring life"* (P11) elaborating on how such aesthetic interaction allows people to have fun with objects that they might not actually take notice of on a daily basis. In study B, P7 also ensured that the ActuEating experience changed his perspective about decorative objects, furniture and aesthetics in general. Moreover, in study D, P16 highlighted how *"the best value is the merge of technology where everyday objects can do more things and react to our presence and actions"*. In this sense, we need to start exploring other decorative objects and investigate ways they can be of further purposes, meanings and values to people beyond their static aesthetics.

Evolution of Interaction

Users' Roles

Participants' desire to interact with the ActuEater ranged from reluctant to frequent. During the 4 studies, participants created similar scenarios, engaging with ActuEaters through three different roles: 1) the 'explorer' role who was actively engaging and frequently interacting (9/19 participants); 2) the 'observer' closely watching in a spectator role and occasionally interacting with ActuEaters (6/19 participants), and 3) the 'bystander' role of those who rarely touched it and were reluctant to take part in 'physically' exploring it (4/19 participants). Particularly one in each group was a bystander/reluctant to touch it or look at it, yet still reflecting on it and analyzing its behaviour. Observers analyzed every interaction and assumed meanings and interpreted its actuations. Despite their different roles and positions, all participants at some point during the 4 studies attempted to explore ActuEaters either physically, by finger touching, poking, hand patting, lifting up the fabric off the table, or looking down under the table to realize what is causing the shape-change.

Social Engagement

The way participants responded to and interacted with the ActuEater varied over time and for different situations, bringing opportunities for rich social engagement. They frequently exchanged eye-contact when it moved, especially those adjacent to the moving part, expressing it felt as a personal message for them, while exchanging smiles, laughs and jokes about it, acknowledging their amusement, surprise and enjoyment of its unexpected behaviour. Four female participants were observed taking photos of their ActuEating experience using their smart phones to share on social media. Three or more participants often physically explored the ActuEater together, which made them establish social engagement around it. For example, both P2 and P5 kept their hands on ActuEater1, together, while smiling for a while, as it was actuating, enjoying the feeling of it going up and down. With ActuEater2, several participants touched 'similar' parts simultaneously to explore it together imitating each other's interactions from gentle touches to firm pressing strokes. As actuations varied, participants were developing interactions together in a self-learning exploratory process, learning from each other in playful ways, collaborating and exchanging techniques. E.g. *"wait, if we touch one by one together, what will happen?"* (P13), *"let's press it together at the same time"* (P10 to P7). On a few occasions, some would interact on behalf of others when they felt that the ActuEater needed to be responded to but was being ignored.

Physical Manipulations

Once ActuEater1 had gained users attention it attracted their touch interactions (first fingertip touch, then hand and palm touch), initially passive (responding to) then active (initiating) interaction. Then interactions went beyond touch into more physical 3D manipulations according to the shape, material and its affordance (such as grasp, pat, squeeze, bend, etc), see Figure 4. After thoroughly exploring direct physical interactions, participants became more creative. For instance, P1, P3 and P5 used water bottles, salt shakers and mobile phones to place onto ActuEater1 to explore its response. Further exploration with ActuEater2 brought richer physical manipulations to the table. For example, many participants frequently touched the coloured 'felt' parts with a brushing stroke on its soft texture, although these elements weren't sensitive. 'Hover' hand in-air gestures above sensitive parts were used by all groups when proximity-sensing was realized. Some covered up thermochromic parts with both hands to 'feel the heat'. Some lent forward or backwards in their seats to test proximity. Some repositioned physical objects (that were initially placed randomly) precisely on particular parts of ActuEater2 to test them. Many were observed 'tracing' the colour-changing pattern with one finger in a continuous satisfying way.

Figure 4. Interactions with ActuEater1 (left) and ActuEater2 (right)

Physical interactions were quite directly proportional with actuations in terms of scale. That is, we noticed that they responded to located (small) low actuations of ActuEater1 by one fingertip, higher ones with their three middle fingers, and when it was all up, they used their whole palms. ActuEater2 was definitely manipulated more intensely, it was flipped over or pulled off the table, bent, felt and squeezed, and perceived more like a 'fabric' runner than as a shape-changing device like ActuEater1. This reflects how people develop their own interactions based on their own perceptions, interpretations, backgrounds and instincts. Yet, people learn together and from each other, developing their ideas, perceptions and engagements with a certain artefact.

A Complex Behavioural Repertoire

Beyond the Boundaries

Several participants had an irresistible urge to 'tidy up' both ActuEaters after actuations by flattening the 'history wrinkles' that were created by its actuation. This physical interaction (maybe due to neatness or maybe expecting a default state of being totally flat) triggered more actuations thereafter. Observing how participants took extra effort to interact with it (e.g. stretch out their arms to reach it, put down cutlery, etc) shows their 'willingness' to physically engage with it. Interacting blindly with it (without even looking at it) shows 'expertise' and confidence. Participants not only interacted with the actuating parts of ActuEaters, but they tended to explore the boundaries of sensitivity to discover the edges of 'seamless and seamful' interaction, evident by manipulating even the satin ribbon edge of ActuEater1 and the plain senseless petals of ActuEater2.

'Interaction Boundaries' were even crossed to explore other potential means of engagement. For example, ActuEater2 received several 'voice commands' to test speech as possible input interaction: *"Hi" (P12, P13), "Move" (P13), "By the power in me, rise!" (P8)*. At the end of study B, P10 held its edge with a firm grip and shook hands with ActuEater2 saying *"nice to meet you"*. Participants often felt an urge to initiate interaction with ActuEaters deliberately, when they were not actuating, driven by an inner desire to have fun through playing and to find out more about how it works. This creates space for contradicting scenarios where they want to stop it when it's up/active, and yet they wanted it active when it sleeps. Such complicated behaviour resembles typical interactions with pets or children: when quiet, we want to play with them, but when they are manic, we wish them calm. It can also explain participants' tender 'pat' interaction, as their way to calm it down, revealing a zoomorphic interpretation of the actuations. *"stroke it carefully, it's like your pet!"* (P13). Others showed further 'empathy' towards it: *"you should just touch it, not squeeze it like that"* (P7 to P10).

Curiosity and Mystery

Curiosity was evident in all four studies, where participants explored and talked about how it works, and sneaked a peek underneath. Every participant at some point picked the table runner up from the table, pressed it to feel its inner body, or bent downwards to look underneath the table. ActuEater1 obviously had the shape-changing mechanism under the table and participants commented on how it would be more practical not to have a hole in the table *"and keep all the mystery alive, because you look under the table and oh no, it must be in the runner!"* (P4), *"what kind of sorcery would this be!"* (P6).

Accordingly, we designed ActuEater2 to be self-actuating using SMA wires which caused participants to flip it, bend it and pull it off the table to ensure there is nothing underneath, then squeeze it and press it to feel what is inside. P10 put his hand underneath the table below ActuEater2 testing if the capacitive sensing would work through the glass downwards. P17 'rolled' it firmly to realize its affordance and materiality when others wondered whether there was something inside it. Participants expressed a mysterious aspect not just in the movement but also in the colour-change: *"notice those colouring spirals again, it doesn't look like an electrical light"* (P18), *"It is totally unexpected, it would never cross my mind that a table fabric can actuate like this. I wonder how it changes? what causes the colour-change? and how does this pattern reveal?"* (P7). This shows us how people think about inter-weaving technology into everyday objects in a hidden way and how it is more 'magical' from a user perspective.

Discoverability and Illegibility

Designing for discoverability by 'hiding the interaction' creates a variable and playful repertoire of behaviours, while designing for illegibility (non-obvious and inconsistent) by 'hiding the logic' creates a sense of autonomy and a spatio-temporal aspect of 'Interioraction' [27]. In our research we wanted to explore these design directions where discoverable and illegible systems could be perceived as mysterious and magical. During the initial study, participants criticized ActuEater1 for not having an immediate consistent response to their actions. Although there was a specific pattern mapping inputs to outputs, participants expressed how they still require an explicit cue to fully understand. Apparently, ActuEater1 made participants of study A feel unconfident about its illegible and discoverable interactions, when some autonomous interactions were perceived as random. Participants not only expressed how legibility is easier to relate to, but also how a level of control over ActuEater1 was desirable.

As a result, we designed ActuEater2 to be both sensing (and reacting) and autonomous at the same time, which was appreciated in the design crits: *"It's nice to have some control of it and it is also nice that it does its own thing by itself as well"* (P18). In addition to direct and immediate input-output relationships, we explored participants' view of the artefact's behaviour that evolves with their interactions over time and usage, instrumenting discoverable interaction as an adventure: *"was it moving that much from the beginning?"* (P10), *"as we talk about it more, it moves more"* (P9), *"we'll keep playing with it and at the end we'll find out it's a Jumanji!"* (P13), *"or find the treasure"* (P12). *"it could evolve more over our dinner party and break out a dance at the end to celebrate!"* (P16). This shows how people were readily orienting to a world where objects known to be static cannot only change over time, but can change unexpectedly and in an adventurous manner with different paces, taking various forms, that could be ultimately rewarding.

Design Explorations

During their group discussion in the design crits, participants suggested many enrichments to both ActuEaters and proposed other functional and aesthetic possibilities. They also proposed different artefacts that could be similarly interactive and suggested other types of spaces where they believed it might be interesting to interact, adopt and utilize such technology.

Proposed Functions

Participants focused their suggestions of potential functions on three main themes: 1) extending, 2) engaging, and 3) entertaining. 1) 'Extending' decorative objects by augmenting them with further capabilities was suggested as an alternative to smart devices and gadgets, e.g. *"now we're getting into an era where we expect objects to be that smart and you can just talk to them and tell them what to do"*, *"so Alexa should be part of my decor and have more interactive capabilities than activating heating or obeying commands"* (P16); 2) 'Engagement' was frequently mentioned for i) bringing people together and provoking social engagement, or ii) occupying people waiting for something or feeling lonely, iii) engaging children in different situations such as doctors' waiting rooms, and iv) creating an ice-breaking object for those meeting for the first time; and 3) 'Entertainment' and stimulating was also discussed as a useful purpose for such an object as: *"it is great for an absent mind to meditate or gaze at"* (P10), *"gives a sense of calmness.. I can keep looking at it for hours"* (P7), *"it reduces stress, like a fidget-spinner"* (P12) and *"stimulating curiosity of children, how is it moving and changing colour?"* (P7). P13 expressed a similar functional quality of keeping children entertained without a digital screen i.e. a display-less display, and P18 suggested a changing wall-art that entertains, but unlike a TV set, is not focus demanding. All these functions represent the value of non-demanding and non-disrupting technology (people aspire for) that keeps the essence of social quality time and adds a bonus dessert to it.

Proposed Artefacts

As they perceived it as a gaze-drawing object, some participants suggested other artefacts that could be similarly (or more) interesting. Some suggested other flat surfaces such as *"colour-changing coasters or placemats that entertain me until the next course, or warms my plate"* (P10), *"a mat or a rug on the floor that we sit on and crumbles when one moves away"* (P11), *"a seat that changes colour the more you stay sitting down too long then moves urging you to get up"* (P15) and *"a mirror or a painting"* (P4). P7 imagined wall-art that gives different shadows or shapes responding to proximity and an entire wall that autonomously reveals and moves parts such as butterfly wings decorating the wall to actuate his home decor. Moreover, others suggested 3D objects such as *"a playful sculpture"* (P16), *"a moving vase"* (P9), *"a pillow to help my neck problems"* (P11), *"a lampshade that starts dancing like this when I'm in a 'dancey' mood"* (P7), *"a coffee table itself"* (P18, P5), *"a blanket that crumbles around you would be great to give you warmth"* (P7).

Proposed Interactive Aesthetics

A crucial aspect of decorative artefacts is their need to blend-in to complement an interior style and are usually matching other objects in the same space. Therefore, we were keen to choose settings where the ActuEaters could fit-in and complement those spaces with matching objects, such as matching tableware, interior colour-scheme and style (as much as possible): *"I didn't notice anything weird at first as it had the same colours of the restaurant chairs and napkins, and petals shape are the same as the table glass engravings."* (P7). However, more tailored design for all details has to be carried out for each individual space, e.g. *"It looks elegant and the colours are matching but the shape has to be round because the table is round"* (P13), while some saw it as a *"futuristic design"* (P10, P17) preferring more traditional aesthetics.

Although we carefully eliminated any LEDs from ActuEater1 to keep it as normal and traditional as possible, 4 of our 6 participants expressed how they expected/wanted ActuEater1 to have 'lights'. This indicates how they do not entirely perceive it as a (normal) table-runner, but as a 'digital' object. When they were asked about colour-changing capabilities instead of lights (e.g. using thermochromic inks), they showed excitement and suggested that colour-change could complement and enrich the shape-change, adding *"a more interesting layer"* (P3). When we enabled thermochromic colour-change in some parts of ActuEater2, they suggested that all petals should change colour and recommended hydrochromics as well *"if it responds to water or spilt liquids, it would turn an embarrassing bad situation into an interesting conversation re-starter"* (P9). Other richer multi-aesthetic interactions suggested that petals could move freely and blossom in 3D, or it plays music and amplifies itself with the volume to *"hit as many senses as possible"* (P16).

Proposed Environments

In terms of spaces, participants proposed different environments in which they envisioned such technology. Restaurants and silent spaces such as libraries, museums, clinics, waiting rooms and specifically waiting areas at the doctors' surgeries to entertain people while waiting, were proposed by several participants across the 4 studies. Other proposed environments, included classrooms as a board that *"attracts focus of students"* (P12), toilets *"instead of reading the shampoo ingredients if you forget your smart phone"* (P6) and office spaces *"to distract from work, to refresh, take a breath and de-stress"* (P12), but *"not in a formal setting as meeting rooms, it becomes distracting"* (P11). Alternatively, having them in homes was debatable. Some expressed their worry about the finite number of actuations that wear its novelty out too quickly for home occupants, but still found it exquisite and delightful for their guests. So careful design should create actuating capabilities that makes it 'sustainably interesting'. Others saw it *"as a creative or a special object that you'd like to display"* (P8) and saw opportunities in which a domestic artefact can change colour based on ambient temperature or display household data such as water or energy consumption.

DESIGN OPPORTUNITIES

Our exploration of critical responses to the ActuEater has suggested a number of key learnings which we highlight below in the form of a set of design opportunities to consider when designing interactive decoratives. We should *design for*:

- Meaningfulness: Although people acknowledge that decorative objects are for aesthetic purposes, not necessarily functional, they still give them purpose in terms of *meanings* and *values*. This applies to 'decoractives' as well where people interpret their *overall experience* in deeper meanings and give a purposeful value to the actuations often beyond what was designed for (in either positive or negative ways), which is a design feature to be exploited.
- Spatiality: When technology blends into our daily environment, people perceive it as part of their overall *spatial experience* and expect it to interact with the space, relating shape-changes to factors beyond their direct input such as music, conversation topics, space occupancy, weather, etc. This does not apply to digital devices that do not blend in, but stand out, requiring full attention of users.
- Sociability: *Social engagement* around an actuating artefact is rich in terms of the noticeable exploratory, collaborative and playful nature of how people interact with such technology together. This should inspire designers investigating this design space, shaping how interactive interior elements might be dealt with to utilize and support sociability.
- Tactility: Evident by how ActuEaters attracted touch, hand manipulations and *physical interaction* through other objects, designers should seize this opportunity to design for tactility utilizing the intuitive affordance of different material textures and physical objects already in the space.
- Seamlessness: People anticipate shape-changing interfaces that are portable, weavable and seamlessly hidden (instead of bulky, cabled and demanding machines), stimulating their sense of *curiosity and mystery*, believing it would be magical and more efficient in terms of everyday use in their normal environments. There is a great opportunity to augment existing artefacts with shape-changing materials instead of embedding mechanical solutions within them.
- Beyondness: Actuating decoratives are explored *beyond the boundaries* of designed interactions, where people navigate

away from observed sensors and cruise through new possibilities, from voice and gestures to shaking hands. Unlike robotic SCIs, when designing organic actuations (smooth and malleable), people will tend to develop a notion of empathy and tenderness in their interactions with it, even with no designed zoomorphic shape, texture or sound, people still believe it has a body, mood and intentions.

- Discoverability: Systems that are not consistent and obvious, but enable actuations to evolve over time or usage can be misleading, incomprehensible, or perceived as random. However, careful iterative design and the use of situated studies (beyond minutes) can create opportunities for designers to explore novel possibilities and *mysterious designs* that promote discoverability in actuating interiors, to increase *adventurous exploration* of artefacts.
- Significance: Designing decorative objects that are useful through *potential functions*, creates a greater value to them. Through slow interaction and calm technology, we can (and should) make decoractives with 'extended' functionalities, beyond their aesthetics, 'engaging' people together through artefacts and 'entertaining' them with their multi-aesthetics in diverse and novel ways.
- Match-making: As decorative objects usually have other matching items in the same interior space (to blend and complement the space aesthetics and style), people relate these relationships intuitively. Therefore, when designing 'decoractives', we can utilize such relationships in developing spatial interactions (with different elements in the space) such as our *proposed artefacts* creating a rather richer experience, e.g. a matching cushion and throw, or a curtain with a rug, can interact together or through each other.
- Colourfulness: People expect shape-changing interfaces, especially decorative ones, to be colour-changing as one of their main *proposed aesthetics*, even through lights. A good design practice to create *display-less displays* is to embed colour-changing properties in the material itself instead of using lights (e.g. thermochromic or photochromic inks) as means of both sustainable actuation and spatial interaction.
- Blending-in: Shape-changing interfaces can enhance the social experience of a group of people in different *potential environments*. In a given context, when designed to blend into their environment (instead of standing out as a separate device), people can choose when to ignore it and when to use it together as a social probe, to talk about, interact with, and engage together through it.

DISCUSSION & CONCLUSION

In this paper, we presented a series of design explorations, critically examining the potential use of shape-changing materials in the design of interactive decorative artefacts. We believe our work provides an inspiring case-study supporting others who might wish to design and develop actuating decorative artefacts for different contexts and cultures. The ActuEating study offered an open-ended set of observations in terms of user behaviour, interpretation, reactions and expectations. The intention wasn't studying the dining experience in itself, but to explore the design of interactive artefacts and how people may perceive, interact with and experience such technologies in relevant settings and to gain deeper knowledge and insight into designing interactive everyday objects as decorative artefacts.

As with both coMotion [17] and the History-Tablecloth [12], the improvised interactivity and often confusing behaviours, added value and richness to the ActuEating experience in ways that had not been anticipated, allowing for complex interpretations. While controlling ActuEater1 from behind the scenes, we learnt how participants collaborated to realize how to control it themselves, not just theorizing what triggers it, but by testing different input interactions beyond our expectations. We then designed ActuEater2 to be both physically-interactive and autonomous. From voice commands, knocking on the table and observing music patterns, to stroking, patting and using other objects (e.g. teapots, salt, sugar and phones) on top of it, participants developed interactions themselves through social engagement to explore its potentials, interaction boundaries and limitations. Despite the 'engaging' and 'entertaining' benefits realized by the ActuEating studies, we understand the limitations in terms of the effect of 'novelty' on user experience, and are planning to address this in our future work.

The challenges we faced to conceal technology within an everyday fabric artefact ubiquitously, were aimed at experimenting how hidden interactivity in objects (that blend into the space design) could be of value, meaning and significance to space occupants over an in-situ social event (in a restaurant or at home). We emphasize on how weaving technology into real-world objects, specifically decorative ones, can deliver a rather richer 'spatial experience' in a given contextual setting. By taking previous work further, we were able to explore new territories of this design space. However, the design constraints we set included studying only actuating table runners in dining settings. Further research should explore other artefacts, in other contexts, to realize the latent and intrinsic potentials of extending their capabilities, seamlessly. Although ActuEaters were designed as non-functional artefacts, their aesthetic qualities as decorative objects are rather useful as they don't need constant attention, which aligns well with slow and calm technology concepts [30].

This work will help advance and continue the research commenced by the HistoryTableCloth [12] and coMotion [17] around shape-changing interfaces and interactive spaces, furniture and everyday objects. The beauty of interactive decorative objects (unlike novel gadgets) is that whether they interact (accurately or entirely) or not, the object still has value. Its failure to interact at any time will not lead to a crisis of affordance [12], as it remains a decorative aesthetic artefact in its own right. Our work points to the future potential of new materialities, merging interaction design with interior design.

ACKNOWLEDGEMENTS

We would like to thank all our participants who volunteered to this study. This research was partially-funded by the UK's EPSRC MORPHED Project (award EP/M016528/1) and Newcastle University SAgE DTA programme.

REFERENCES

1. Pollie Barden, Rob Comber, David Green, Daniel Jackson, Cassim Ladha, Tom Bartindale, Nick Bryan-kinns, Tony Stockman, and Patrick Olivier. 2012. Telematic Dinner Party: Designing for Togetherness through Play and Performance. In *Proceedings of the 2012 Conference on Designing Interactive Systems (DIS'12)*. Newcastle, UK, 38–47. https://doi.org/10.1145/2317956.2317964
2. Alice Bodanzky. 2012. Exploring the Expressiveness of Shape-Changing Surfaces. In *Proceedings of the Sixth International Conference on Tangible, Embedded, and Embodied Interaction (TEI'12)*. Kingston, ON, Canada, 403–404. DOI: http://dx.doi.org/10.1145/2148131.2148235
3. Virginia Braun and Victoria Clarke. 2006. Using Thematic Analysis in Psychology. *Qualitative Research in Psychology* 3, 2 (2006), 77–101. DOI: http://dx.doi.org/10.1191/1478088706qp063oa
4. Jaz Hee-jeong Choi, Marcus Foth, and Greg Hearn. 2014. *Eat, Cook, Grow: Mixing Human-Computer Interactions with Human-Food Interactions.* https://mitpress.mit.edu/books/eat-cook-grow
5. Marcelo Coelho and Jamie Zigelbaum. 2011. Shape-changing Interfaces. *Personal and Ubiquitous Computing* 15, 2 (2011). DOI: http://dx.doi.org/10.1007/s00779-010-0311-y
6. Nicholas S Dalton, Emily Collins, and Paul Marshall. 2015. Display Blindness? Looking Again at the Visibility of Situated Displays using Eye Tracking. In *Proceedings of the 2015 CHI Conference on Human Factors in Computing Systems*. ACM, Seoul, Republic of Korea, 3889–3898. DOI: http://dx.doi.org/10.1145/2702123.2702150
7. Felecia Davis. 2015. The Textility of Emotion: A Study Relating Computational Textile Textural Expression to Emotion. In *C&C'15*, Vol. 2. Glasgow, United Kingdom, 1977–1982. DOI: http://dx.doi.org/10.1145/2702613.2732739
8. Felecia Davis, Asta Roseway, Erin Carroll, and Mary Czerwinski. 2013. Actuating Mood: Design of the Textile Mirror. In *Proceedings of the 7th International Conference on Tangible, Embedded and Embodied Interaction (TEI'13)*. Barcelona, Spain, 99–106. DOI: http://dx.doi.org/10.1145/2460625.2460640
9. Aluna Everitt and Jason Alexander. 2017. PolySurface: A Design Approach for Rapid Prototyping of Shape-Changing Displays Using Semi-Solid Surfaces. In *Proceedings of the 2017 Conference on Designing Interactive Systems (DIS'17)*. Edinburgh, UK, 1283–1294. http://dx.doi.org/10.1145/3064663.3064677
10. Hasan Shahid Ferdous, Frank Vetere, Hilary Davis, Bernd Ploderer, Kenton O Hara, Rob Comber, and Geremy Farr-wharton. 2017. Celebratory Technology to Orchestrate the Sharing of Devices and Stories during Family Mealtimes. In *Proceedings of the 2017 CHI Conference on Human Factors in Computing Systems (CHI '17)*. Denver, CO, USA, 6960–6972. https://doi.org/10.1145/3025453.3025492
11. Sean Follmer, Daniel Leithinger, Alex Olwal, and Akimitsu Hogge. 2013. inFORM: Dynamic Physical Affordances and Constraints through Shape and Object Actuation. In *Proceedings of the ACM Symposium on User Interface Software and Technology (UIST'13)*. St. Andrews, UK, 417–426. DOI: http://dx.doi.org/10.1145/2501988.2502032
12. William Gaver, John Bowers, Andy Boucher, Andy Law, Sarah Pennington, and Nicholas Villar. 2006. The History Tablecloth: Illuminating Domestic Activity. In *Proceedings of the 2006 Conference on Designing Interactive Systems (DIS'06)*. University Park, Pennsylvania, USA, 199–208. DOI: http://dx.doi.org/10.1145/1142405.1142437
13. William W Gaver. 2003. Ambiguity as a Resource for Design. In *Proceedings of the ACM Conference on Human Factors in Computing Systems (CHI'03)*. Ft. Lauderdale, Florida, USA, 233–240. DOI: http://dx.doi.org/10.1145/642611.642653
14. Catherine Grevet, Anthony Tang, and Elizabeth Mynatt. 2012. Eating Alone, Together: New Forms of Commensality. In *Proceedings of the 17th ACM international conference on Supporting group work (GROUP '12)*. Sanibel Island, Florida, USA, 103–106. http://dx.doi.org/10.1145/2389176.2389192
15. Daniel Groeger and Elena Chong Loo. 2016. HotFlex: Post-print Customization of 3D Prints Using Embedded State Change. In *Proceedings of the ACM Conference on Human Factors in Computing Systems (CHI'16)*. San Jose, CA, USA, 420–432. http://dx.doi.org/10.1145/2858036.2858191
16. Jens Emil Grønbæk, Henrik Korsgaard, Marianne Graves Petersen, Morten Henriksen Birk, and Peter Gall Krogh. 2017. Proxemic Transitions: Designing Shape-Changing Furniture for Informal Meetings. In *Proceedings of the ACM Conference on Human Factors in Computing Systems (CHI'17)*. Denver, CO, USA, 7029–7041. http://dx.doi.org/10.1145/3025453.3025487
17. Erik Gronvall, Sofie Kinch, Marianne Graves Petersen, and Majken K. Rasmussen. 2014. Causing Commotion with a Shape-Changing Bench. In *Proceedings of the ACM Conference on Human Factors in Computing Systems (CHI'14)*. Toronto, ON, Canada, 2559–2568. DOI:http://dx.doi.org/10.1145/2556288.2557360
18. John Hardy, Christian Weichel, Faisal Taher, John Vidler, and Jason Alexander. 2015. ShapeClip: Towards Rapid Prototyping with Shape-Changing Displays for Designers. In *Proceedings of the ACM Conference on Human Factors in Computing Systems (CHI'15)*. Seoul, Republic of Korea, 19–28. DOI: http://dx.doi.org/10.1145/2702123.2702599

19. Alexis Hiniker, Sarita Y Schoenebeck, Ann Arbor, and Julie A Kientz. 2016. Not at the Dinner Table: Parents' and Children's Perspectives on Family Technology Rules. In *Proceedings of the 19th ACM Conference on Computer-Supported Cooperative Work & Social Computing (CSCW '16)*. San Francisco, CA, USA, 1376–1389. https://doi.org/10.1145/2818048.2819940

20. Annika Hupfeld and Tom Rodden. 2012. Laying the Table for HCI: Uncovering Ecologies of Domestic Food Consumption. In *Proceedings of the SIGCHI Conference on Human Factors in Computing Systems (CHI '12)*. Austin, Texas, 119–128. http://dx.doi.org/10.1145/2207676.2207694

21. Hiroshi Ishii, David Lakatos, Leonardo Bonanni, and Jean-Baptiste Jb Labrune. 2012. Radical Atoms: Beyond Tangible Bits, Toward Transformable Materials. *Interactions* XIX, February (2012), 38–51. DOI: http://dx.doi.org/10.1145/2065327.2065337

22. Hiroshi Ishii, Daniel Leithinger, and Sean Follmer. 2015. TRANSFORM: Embodiment of "Radical Atoms" at Milano Design Week. In *CHI'15 Extended Abstracts*. Seoul, Republic of Korea. DOI: http://dx.doi.org/10.1145/2702613.2702969

23. Young Suk Lee. 2015. Spiky Starfish: Exploring 'Felt Technology' Through a Shape Changing Wearable Bag. In *Proceedings of the 9th International Conference on Tangible, Embedded, and Embodied Interaction (TEI'15)*. Stanford, CA, USA, 419–420. DOI: http://dx.doi.org/10.1145/2677199.2690878

24. Sarah Mennicken, A.J. Bernheim Brush, Asta Roseway, and James Scott. 2014. Finding Roles for Interactive Furniture in Homes with EmotoCouch. In *Proceedings of Ubicomp'14 Adjunct*. Seattle, WA, USA, 923–930. DOI: http://dx.doi.org/10.1145/2638728.2641547

25. Robb Mitchell, Alexandra Papadimitriou, Youran You, and Laurens Boer. 2015. Really Eating Together: A Kinetic Table To Synchronise Social Dining Experiences. In *Proceedings of the 6th ACM Augmented Human International Conference (AH'15)*. ACM, Singapore, Singapore, 173–174. http://dx.doi.org/10.1145/2735711.2735822

26. Nadia Mounajjed and Imran A Zualkernan. 2011. From Simple Pleasure to Pleasurable Skin: An Interactive Architectural Screen. In *DPPI '11*. Milano, IT, 30–37. DOI:http://dx.doi.org/10.1145/2347504.2347537

27. Sara Nabil, David Kirk, Thomas Ploetz, Julie Trueman, David Chatting, Dmitry Dereshev, and Patrick Olivier. 2017a. Interioractive: Smart Materials in the Hands of Designers and Architects for Designing Interactive Interiors. In *Proceedings of the 2017 Conference on Designing Interactive Systems (DIS'17)*. Edinburgh, UK, 379–390. http://doi.acm.org/10.1145/3064663.3064745

28. Sara Nabil, Thomas Ploetz, and David S Kirk. 2017b. Interactive Architecture: Exploring and Unwrapping the Potentials of Organic User Interfaces. In *Proceedings of the 11th International Conference on Tangible, Embedded, and Embodied Interaction (TEI'17)*. Yokohama, Japan, 89–100. DOI: http://dx.doi.org/10.1145/3024969.3024981

29. Mamoun Nawahdah. 2013. Virtually Dining Together in Time-Shifted Environment: KIZUNA Design. In *Proceedings of the 2013 conference on Computer supported cooperative work (CSCW '13)*. San Antonio, TX, USA, 779–788. https://doi.org/10.1145/2441776.2441863

30. William Odom, Richard Banks, Abigail Durrant, David Kirk, and James Pierce. 2012. Slow Technology: Critical Reflection and Future Directions. In *Proceedings of the 2012 Conference on Designing Interactive Systems (DIS'12)*. Newcastle, UK, 816–817. DOI: http://dx.doi.org/10.1145/2317956.2318088

31. William T. Odom, Abigail J. Sellen, Richard Banks, David S. Kirk, Tim Regan, Mark Selby, Jodi L. Forlizzi, and John Zimmerman. 2014. Designing for Slowness, Anticipation and Re-visitation: A Long Term Field Study of the Photobox. In *Proceedings of the SIGCHI Conference on Human Factors in Computing Systems (CHI'14)*. Toronto, ON, Canada, 1961–1970. DOI: http://dx.doi.org/10.1145/2556288.2557178

32. Roshan Lalintha Peiris, Jeffrey Tzu Kwan Valino Koh, Mili John Tharakan, Owen Noel Newton Fernando, and Adrian David Cheok. 2013. Ambi kraf byobu: Merging technology with traditional craft. *Interacting with Computers* 25, 2 (2013), 173–182. DOI: http://dx.doi.org/10.1093/iwc/iws013

33. Majken K Rasmussen, Esben W Pedersen, Marianne G Petersen, and Kasper Hornbæk. 2012. Shape-Changing Interfaces: A Review of the Design Space and Open Research Questions. In *Proceedings of the 2012 ACM Annual Conference on Human Factors in Computing Systems (CHI'12)*. Austin, Texas, 735–744. DOI: http://dx.doi.org/10.1145/2207676.2207781

34. Mark Selby and David Kirk. 2015. Experiential Manufacturing: The Earthquake Shelf. In *RTD2015*. Cambridge, UK, 25–27. DOI: http://dx.doi.org/10.6084/m9.figshare.1327994

35. Miriam Sturdee, John Hardy, Nick Dunn, and Jason Alexander. 2015. A Public Ideation of Shape-Changing Applications. In *Proceedings of the International Conference on Interactive Tabletops and Surfaces (ITS'15)*. Madeira, Portugal, 219–228. DOI: http://dx.doi.org/10.1145/2817721.2817734

36. Sarah Taylor and Sara Robertson. 2014. Digital Lace: A Collision of Responsive Technologies. In *Proceedings of the 2014 ACM International Symposium on Wearable Computers (ISWC'14 Adjunct)*. New York: ACM, 93–97. DOI:http://dx.doi.org/10.1145/2641248.2641280

37. Kentaro Ueda, Tsutomu Terada, and Masahiko Tsukamoto. 2016. Input Interface Using Wrinkles on Clothes. In *Proceedings of the 2016 ACM International Symposium on Wearable Computers (ISWC'16)*. Heidelberg, Germany, 56–57. DOI: http://dx.doi.org/10.1145/2971763.2971782

38. Roel Vertegaal and Ivan Poupyrev. 2008. Organic User Interfaces. *Commun. ACM* 51, 6 (2008), 26. DOI: http://dx.doi.org/10.1145/1349026.1349033

39. Luke Vink, Viirj Kan, Ken Nakagaki, Daniel Leithinger, Sean Follmer, Philipp Schoessler, Amit Zoran, and Hiroshi Ishii. 2015. TRANSFORM as Adaptive and Dynamic Furniture. In *Proceedings of CHI EA '15*. Seoul, Korea, 183–183. DOI: http://dx.doi.org/10.1145/2702613.2732494

Designing the IoT Sandbox

Joep Frens
Future Everyday Group - Eindhoven University of Technology - Dept. of Industrial Design
P.O.Box 513, 5600MB, Eindhoven, the Netherlands
j.w.frens@tue.nl

Mathias Funk
Future Everyday Group - Eindhoven University of Technology - Dept. of Industrial Design
P.O.Box 513, 5600MB, Eindhoven, the Netherlands
m.funk@tue.nl

Bastiaan van Hout
Eindhoven University of Technology - Dept. of Industrial Design
P.O.Box 513, 5600MB, Eindhoven, the Netherlands
vanhoutbastiaan@gmail.com

Joep Le Blanc
Eindhoven University of Technology - Dept. of Industrial Design
P.O.Box 513, 5600MB, Eindhoven, the Netherlands
joep@owow.io

DIS 2018, June 9–13, 2018, Hong Kong.

ACM ISBN 978-1-4503-5198-0/18/06...$15.00.
https://doi.org/10.1145/3196709.3196815

Abstract
This pictorial describes the design and design process of the IoT Sandbox: a (scale model of a) smart home which is equipped with actuators and a modular interface that controls the smart home. This modular interface can respond to changes in the functionality of the smart home whereby it offers unique possibilities for designers to explore different avenues of physically rich interaction in domestic personal spaces. We demonstrate that also physically rich interfaces can respond adequately to the dynamics of home IoT systems. We conclude with insight from the design process and a concise discussion and outlook to future work.

Authors Keywords
Physical Interaction, Internet of Things, Interface Design, Interactive Architecture

ACM Classification Keywords
H.5.2 User Interfaces

Introduction
Resonating with the various systems concepts from literature (e.g., ubiquitous computing [21], pervasive computing [20], ambient intelligence [1]) the 'Internet of Things' (IoT) is a recently booming technological undercurrent of innovation [15]. Much effort is spent to understand supportive design materials for IoT (e.g., Machine Learning [5], Voice Interaction [18], and Home Automation [14]) but human-product interaction [6]

(on the level of interface design for systems) receives comparatively little attention, while the need for it is clear [13]. This is the primary interest of this pictorial.

We are interested in interaction with home IoT and observe that the dominant interaction styles are (touch) screen interaction and speech interaction (e.g., Philips HUE [17], Reality Editor [19], IFTTT [11], Amazon Echo [2]). There seems to be little variation, suggesting that there is not much room for a more physically rich interaction style. We think this is ill-conceived; the narrow focus on only a few interaction styles stems from a large-scale platformization trend that leverages screens and a few additional voice-enabled home appliances.

IoT revolves around connected ‘things’: artifacts that can be seen as part of the tradition of the objects that we already used before the world was growing more and more interactive (e.g., coffee mugs, kitchen appliances, lamps or stereo equipment). Things can certainly inherit interaction styles from this tradition; interaction styles that are familiar, situated and that resonate with specific people because of their aesthetics in interaction. As electronic ‘intelligence’ pervades our living rooms through home IoT we can and should capitalize on these qualities that speak to our intuition and explore a physically rich interaction matching the promises of IoT systems. At the same time, we consider home IoT to be an inherently complex phenomenon and see opportunity to help people make sense of it by adopting a more physically rich interaction style. In summary, there is a lot of untapped value in exploring a more physically rich interaction style for home IoT.

The IoT Sandbox challenge and aims

We took a research-through-design approach [12] towards designing a physically rich interface for a smart home (named the IoT Sandbox). While it might seem straightforward to solve this challenge by designing different interactive artifacts, it is more complex than that. Two core challenges need to be addressed. The first challenge concerns the openness of the design task at hand. To design for (home) IoT systems is to take into account that IoT artifacts are distributed and connected and make heavy use of (big) data. Moreover, these systems are inherently dynamic; the composition of a home IoT system might change substantially as new artifacts are added, as software is updated or as outdated devices drop out; a home IoT system is a ‘growing system’ [7][8]. The challenge is to make an interface respond to this dynamism in a feasible and convincing manner while offering aesthetic qualities through a physical, growing design. Second, the combination of a physical interface and a contextual representation of the state, in which the space is, pose both conceptual and technical issues that also have an impact on the design process itself. As such, our approach in designing the IoT Sandbox aims to explore, harness and communicate complexity through demonstrating that also physically rich interfaces can be designed to control IoT systems and that those physically rich interfaces can be made as dynamic as the IoT systems that they control.

Contribution

The IoT Sandbox is part of a multi-year research-through-design project focused to generate knowledge on how to design for growing systems with high complexity and rich, potentially distributed interfaces. The results inform design researchers and students by (1) situating their designs in a tangible, connected real-life context,

(2) generating and deepening design challenges through complexity inherent in the sandbox, and (3) allowing for exemplifying and thus communicating rich interfaces as research products (that are not meant to be on the market) as experienceable carriers of information [9]. As such the IoT sandbox is both a synopsis of earlier research on 'designing for systems' [7][8] and also a starting point for new research as well as an instrument to sensitize our students to the sort of qualities that we seek in their designs.

The smart home and the growing interface

For the IoT Sandbox to convince it needs to be more than just an interface design, it needs situatedness in the form of a compelling (scaled) smart home to demonstrate the result of user action on the interface. Besides this, the house needs to be complex enough to warrant a growing interface and the interface needs to be dynamic enough to accommodate a growing house. As it would go too far to make the IoT Sandbox completely open we designed the house to be complex but scripted the growth for the time being. The design challenge was therefore subdivided to: (a) the smart home and (b) the growing interface, see figure 1. In what follows we first dig a bit deeper into the functionality and the scenario for growth that we support in our IoT Sandbox. We continue with presenting the smart home and its design processes as well as the growing interface and its design process. We finish this section by presenting the combination in a series of scenarios.

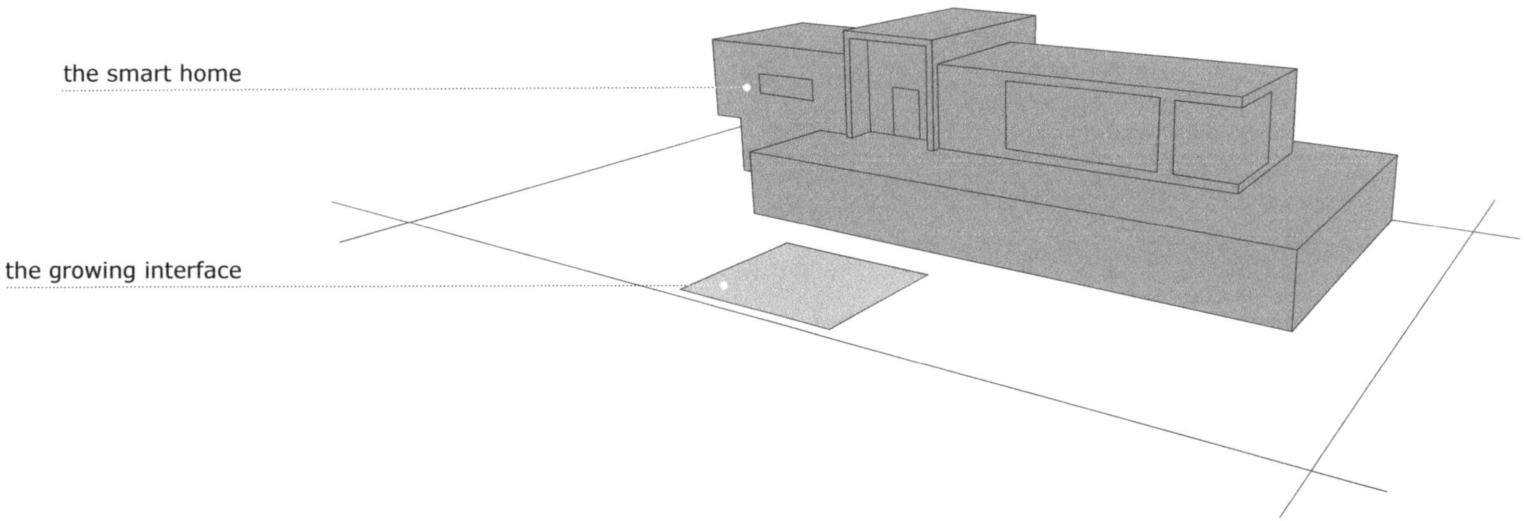

Figure 1: a sketch of the IoT Sandbox

A scenario of 'growth'

To highlight the dynamic qualities of home IoT and the physical growing interface we decided to take a scenario of 'growth' as the starting point for the IoT Sandbox design challenge. The smart home would gain new functionality over time and consequently require new control elements. The growing functionality of the IoT Sandbox consists of both 'core functionality' and 'emergent functionality'. Table 1 was used to conceptualize the emergent functionalities by combining four core functionalities. It proved to be a balancing act between far-fetched and desirable emergent functionality. Not every combination of core functionalities proved to be suitable for meaningful functionalities to emerge as shown by the 'X'.

	Light Positionable light throughout the house	Blinds Actuated blinds	Audio Different streaming audio zones in the house	TV Streaming video on a screen
Light	Grouped light Groups of light fixtures under a single control	Privacy preset Low light at the dinner table while the blinds shield the diners from outside visibility	Disco! The intensity of the light responds to the streaming audio	Light dimming The light dims automatically when the TV is switched on
Blinds			X...	Daylight shielding* The blinds take a position to shield the TV from direct daylight *not implemented
Audio				Surround sound The TV utilizes the audio speakers for surround sound
TV				

Table 1: overview of core and emergent functionality

Core functionality

Core functionality is functionality that is associated with a discrete IoT artifact (or service) and that is available to control. The IoT Sandbox supports four core IoT functionalities that are commonly available in today's smart homes: targetable light, actuated blinds, streaming audio and streaming video. In our scenario this core functionality becomes gradually available over time (initiated by the installation of new IoT artifacts).

Emergent functionality

Emergent functionality emerges in between different core functionalities. It is a relation between core functionalities resulting from user needs. To give a general example: in between the core functionalities of a smart television and that of a connected camera, videophone functionality can emerge. This emergent functionality is neither part of the television nor is it part of the camera; it exists in between. In conventional smart homes, such relations might be captured as a programmed scenario. In the IoT sandbox we can go further and first define, then parameterize and physicalize the relation in the growing interface. In the current version of the IoT sandbox, we chose to implement only 'presets', a very basic form of emergent functionality. The IoT Sandbox supports five different emergent functionalities: grouped lights, a privacy preset, disco!, light dimming and surround sound.

Figure 2: two mood-boards

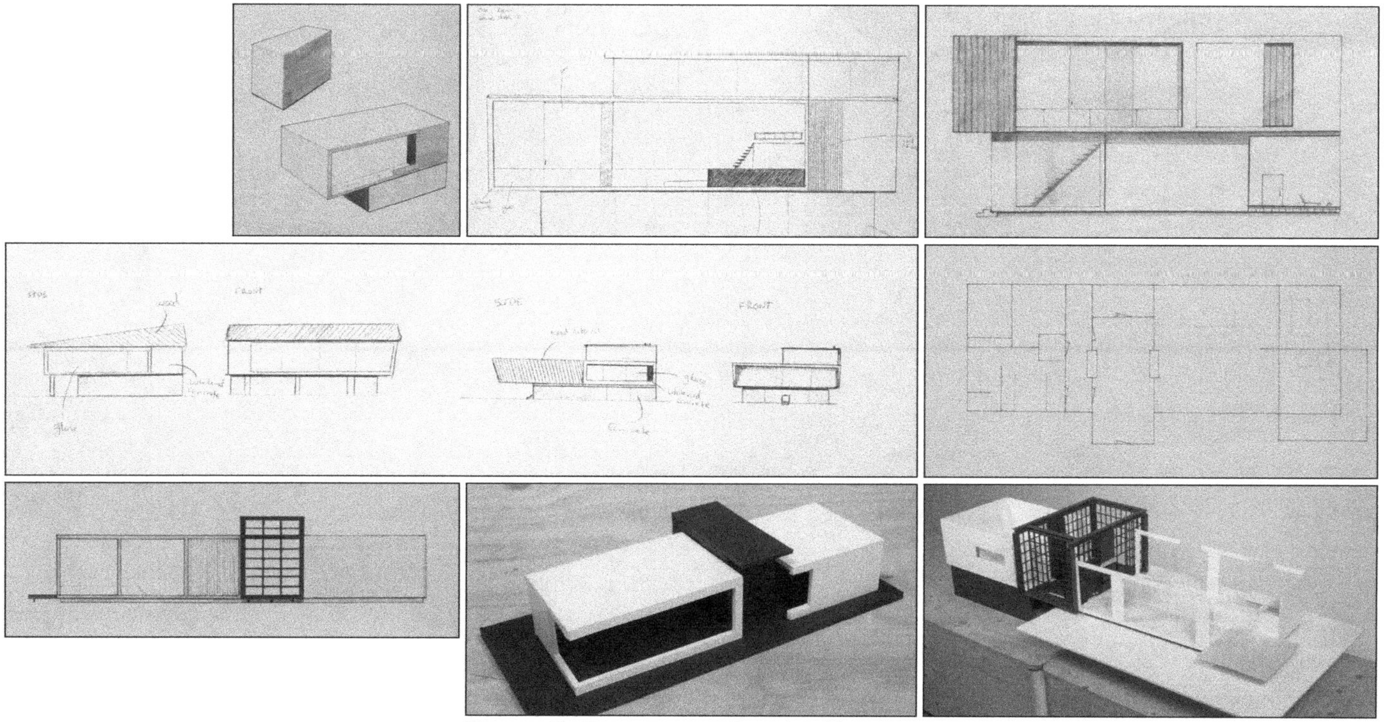

Figure 3: the process of exploration

Designing the house

The design of the house was guided by three success criteria:

1. It needs to demonstrate the operation of the interface and communicate the state of the environment as a result of interaction.
2. It needs to offer a visually compelling smart home, contextualizing otherwise abstract relations.
3. It needs to offer visual access from multiple viewing angles, creating and harnessing a feedback loop from interface to house and back.

Iterative design process

The design process of the house took off with the creation of two mood-boards: one for the exterior and one for the interior (figure 2). After this, it followed an iterative design process with ever increasing fidelity (figure 3). Each iteration involved both sketching and model making. Early models were on a very small scale. Before the final house was built a life-size mock up was created to evaluate the qualities of the house.

Presenting the house

The house is designed as a modern, open home (figure 4). It features working lights, a working television screen, streaming audio and actuated blinds. A scale model of the growing interface is placed on the table.

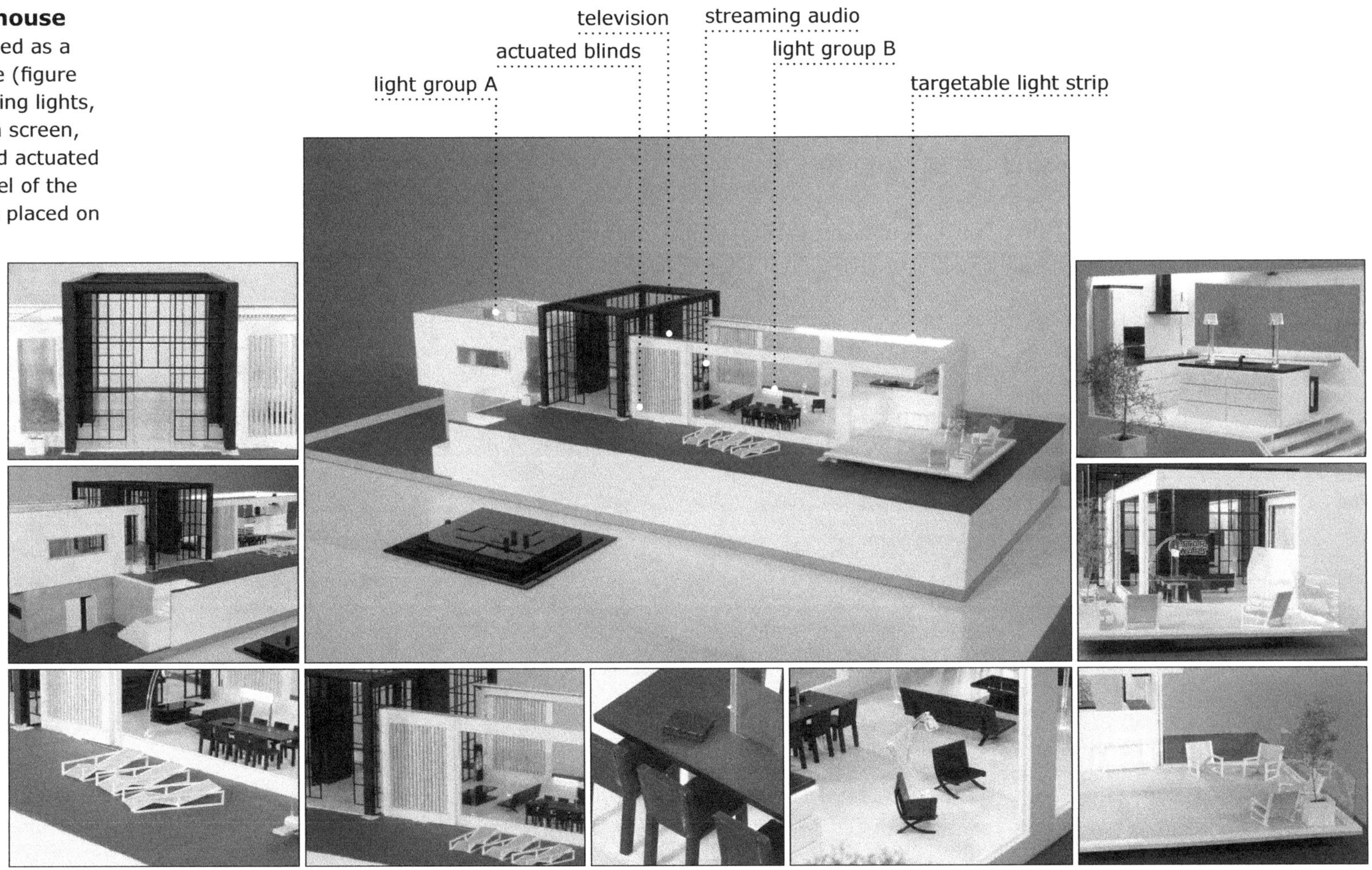

Figure 4: the smart house

Technology

The house runs on two embedded Arduino Mega boards. One controls the streaming audio and video presentation, the other the lights and the blinds. The physical interface runs on another Arduino Mega board. The house and the physical interface are connected by means of serial over USB through a RaspberryPi board that acts as a hub.

Designing the interface

The design of the interface was guided by three success criteria:

1. The interface needs to be able to 'grow'.
2. The interface needs to be completely physical.
3. The interface needs to support parameterized mappings between core functionalities (i.e., emergent functionality).

The design process of the interface was a struggle with the concept of growth. Inspired by earlier work on mechanisms for growth [8] we decided to focus on a central interface to accommodate the growing functionality. The design process started with an exploration of complete concepts. After this proved to be a dead end, a series of design principles was explored (figure 5). These design principles were used to design a modular tray with dedicated 'interactables'. These interactables became 'tiles' that can be mounted in the tray (figure 6).

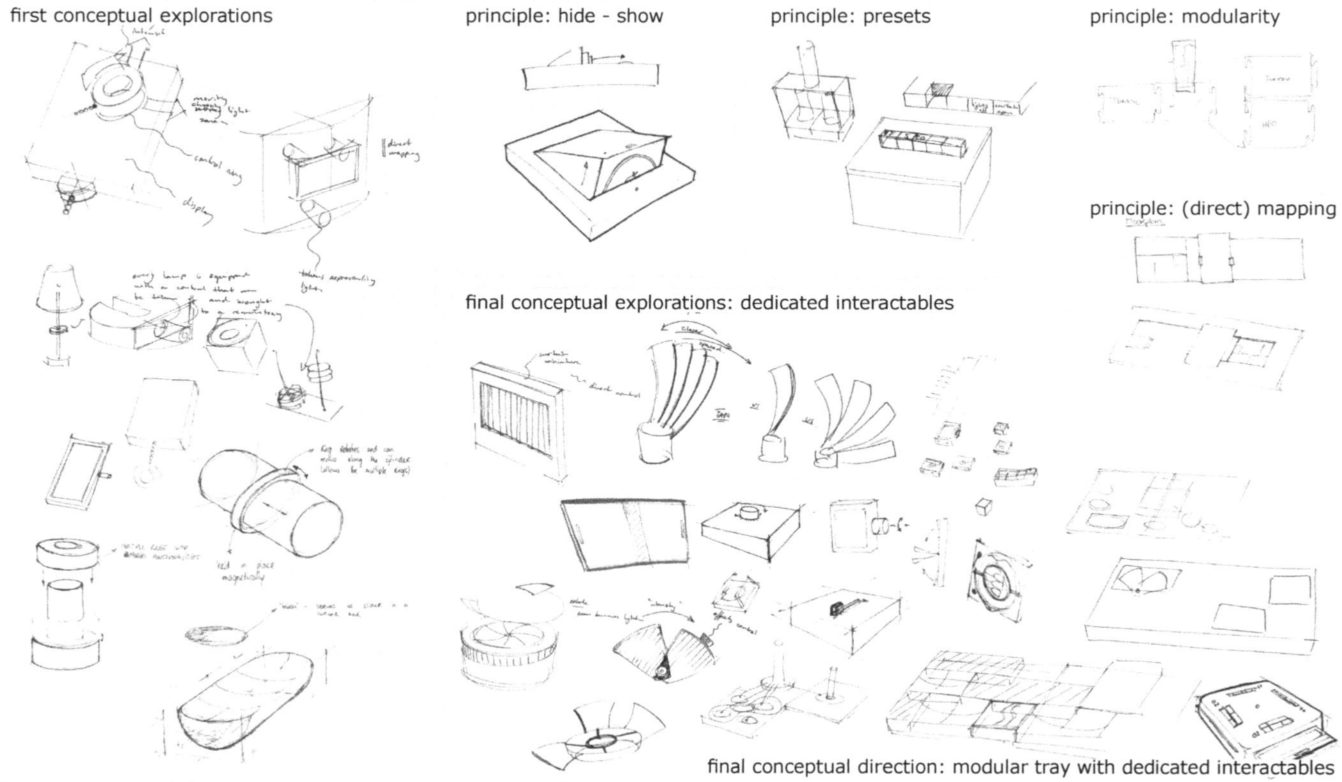

Figure 5: the design process in sketches

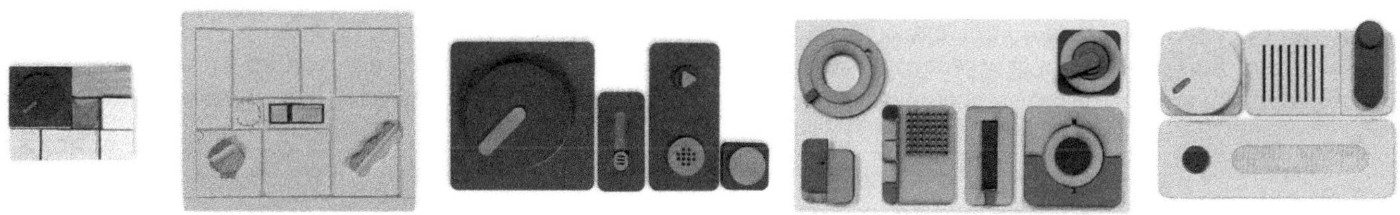

Figure 6: the design process in models

Presenting the growing interface

The growing interface comprises a modular tray in which tile modules can be mounted (figure 7). The modular tray is completely empty at the start and is populated over time – as house and interface grow. Each new IoT artifact (or service) comes with its own dedicated tile that can be installed in the tray at a position that is appropriate according to its user. In this manner the growing interface accommodates growth of core functionality. Emergent functionality that combines core functionality as a physicalization of a mapping is supported through a customization strategy. The LEDs in the top-right corner of the tiles play a role in programming those custom tiles. This is all explained in more detail in the next section.

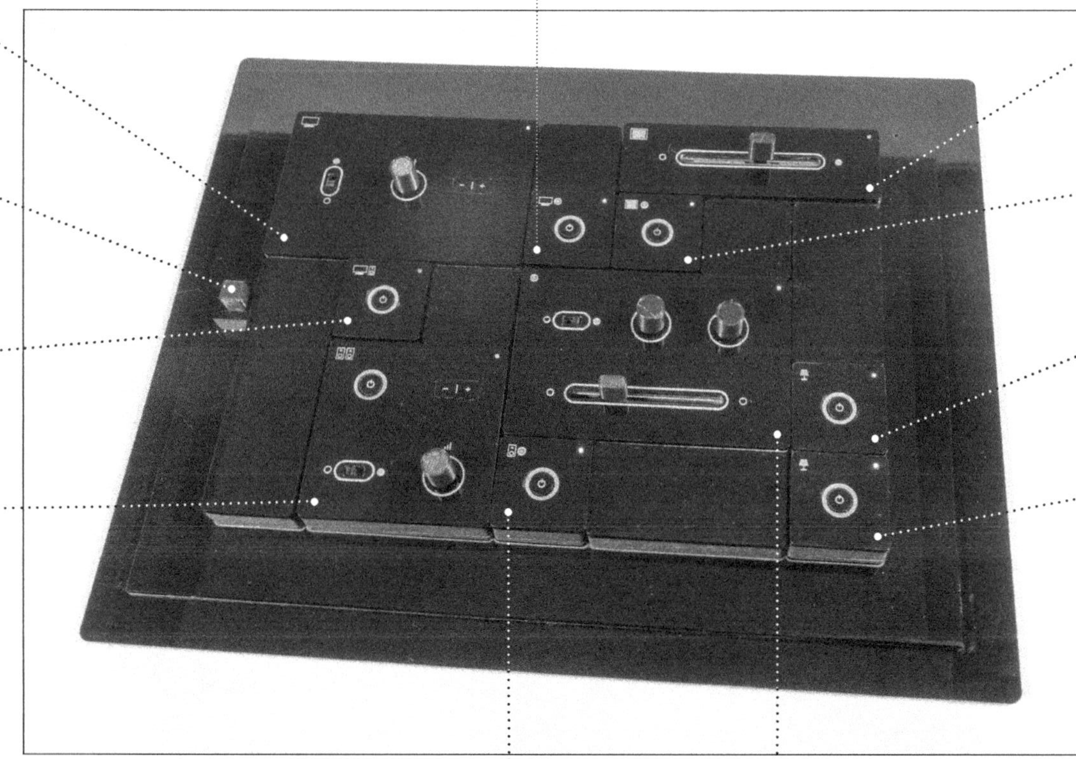

Figure 7: the growing interface

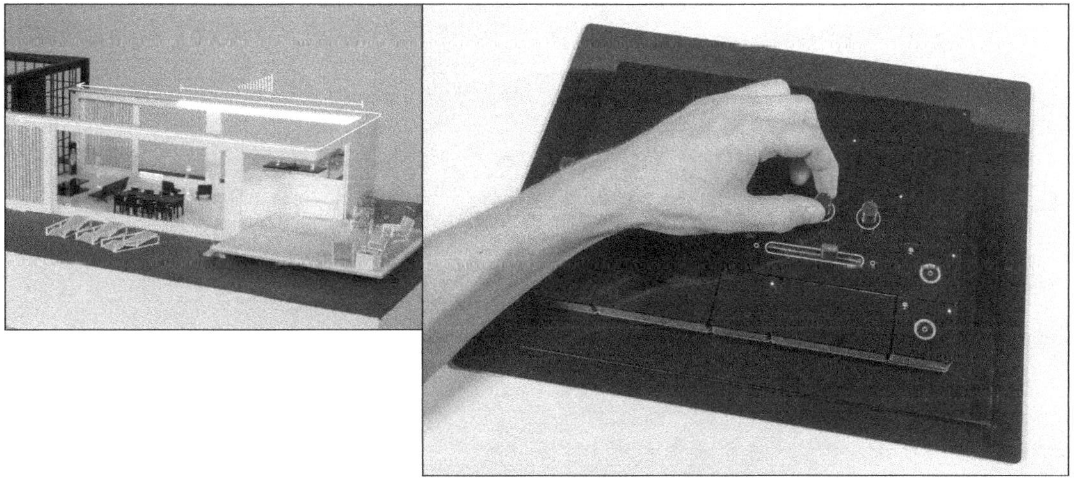

Figure 8: controlling targeted light

Controlling targeted light

This tile allows the user to control the targeted light installation in the house (figure 8). The tile features four controls: an on/off switch (partially obscured by the hand), a brightness control (left rotary control), a position control (right rotary control) and a light amount control (linear slider). This tile is connected through the tray to the respective controllers in the house, resulting in a fully operational control surface.

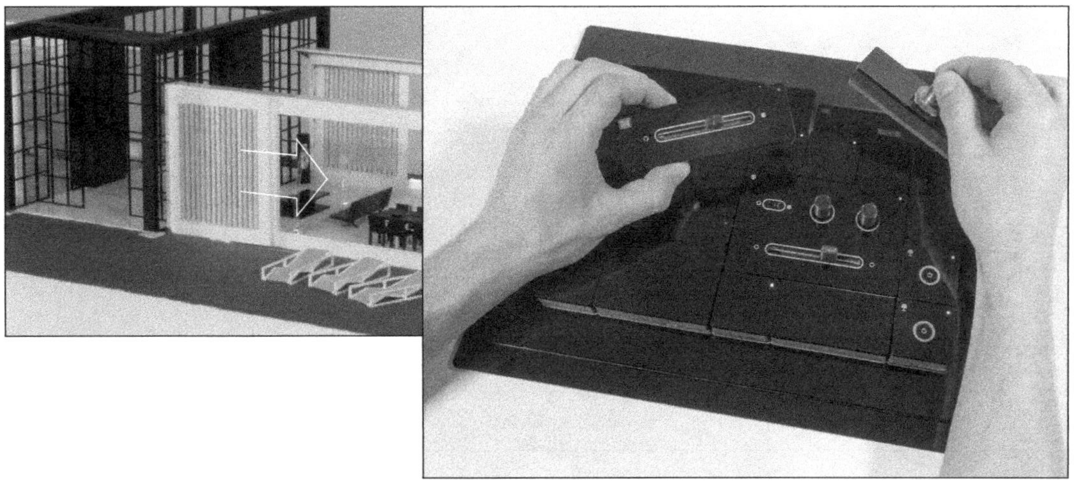

Figure 9: adding an actuated blinds tile

Adding a tile for controlling the blinds

When the desire arises to have actuated blinds in the house these can be installed. In this concept every IoT installation comes with its own tile. This tile can be placed in the modular interface (figure 9) after which it be used to control the blinds.

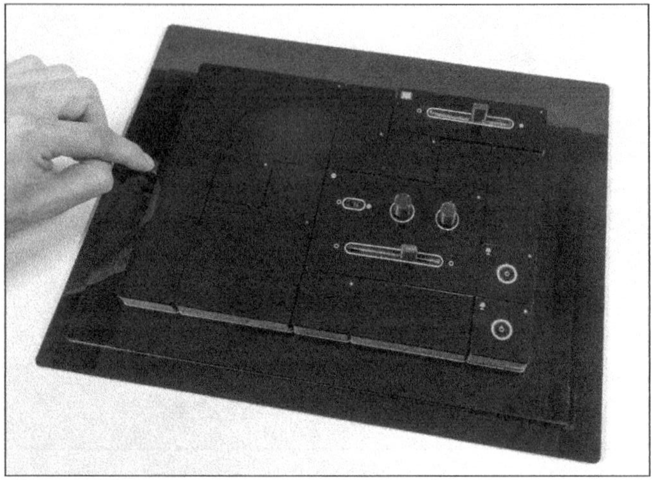

Figure 10: starting programming mode

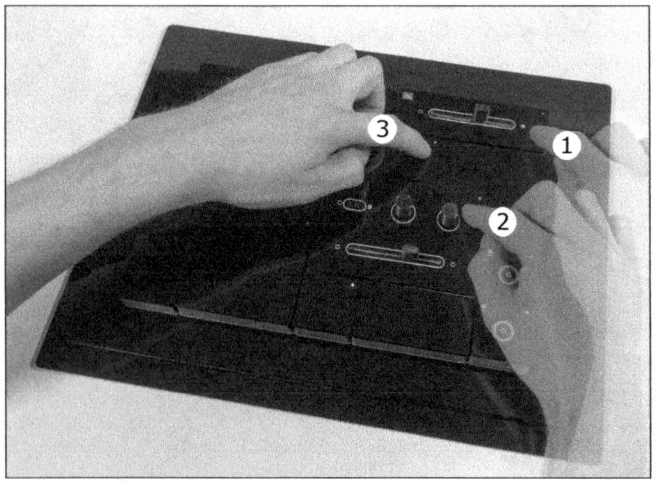

Figure 11: programming a preset

Customizing the growing interface

Perhaps even more interesting than controlling the individual smart objects in the home is the idea that their functionalities can be combined to form new, emergent functionality. A basic version of this idea is implemented in the growing interface by means of programmable presets that can be used to customize the interface towards individual preferences.

To program a preset, the programming mode is entered by pushing the control at the left side of the tray (figure 10). To indicate the program mode the lights in the top corners of the tiles turn green.

Let's consider the scenario where a user wants to set the stage for an intimate dinner. First the lights are set to project a dimmed spot of light at the dinner table and the blinds are positioned such that they give the diners privacy. This relation of direct functionalities is a proportional mapping and can be parameterized as such. To further physicalize the mapping, it is programmed in three steps (figure 11):

1. The blinds tile is selected and pushed. The light in the top corner of the tile turns red to indicate that a first selection is made.
2. The light tile is then selected and pushed and also here the light in the top corner of the tile turns red to indicate that the second selection is made.
3. The combination of blinds and lights are projected onto an empty tile. An appropriate (to the preference of the user) empty tile is selected and pushed. The three tiles blink green and the preset is programmed.

Lastly, the growing interface is taken out of program mode by pressing the button at the left side of the tray again. The newly programmed tile can now be used to set the position of the blinds and dim the lights in one go.

Figure 12: receive and install a customized tile

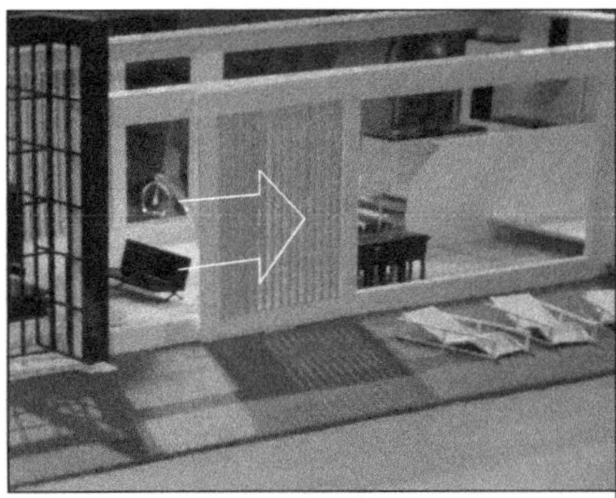

Figure 13: use the customized tile

Generic vs. customized tiles

When a mapping is programmed and projected in an empty tile, it is generic and does not give much information for use. When left to that a user would have to rely on memory alone when operating the growing interface. This will soon become problematic, particularly when many generic tiles are programmed. In the growing interface concept the mapping between direct functionalities is cast into different interaction styles: e.g., buttons for binary full on or off, sliders and rotary dials for more nuanced control, or even more expressive controllers allow to interact with emergent functionality in more expressive ways. Emergent functionality tiles are different depending on the functionality they offer and the preference for interaction of its user. We have conceptualized several approaches of how this could happen to demonstrate feasibility. However, as the IoT Sandbox is meant to be a carrier of information and a vehicle for our research (rather than a product on the market) we have not developed these approaches further.

Approaches towards creating customized tiles

After new functionality is projected in an empty tile that tile needs to be replaced by a customized tile. This new tile features a custom interface that fits the design language of the specific growing interface and has the right functionality embedded in its integrated electronics. It could be designed based on templates or by means of parametric design software. It could be manufactured as a service but it could also be 3D printed at home. When it is finished it is installed in place of the generic tile (figure 12). After it is installed it can be used to control the emergent functionality (figure 13).

Figure 17: DDW exhibition

Dutch Design Week

The IoT Sandbox was presented at the 2016 Dutch Design Week (DDW). Our IoT Sandbox attracted hundreds of interested visitors who checked out and played with the installation. We received praise, helpful suggestions and critical questions. We found that many people were open to the idea that interactions styles could differ and that also physical interaction styles might be feasible. For us this was proof that our research has value beyond the lab but more importantly it was a signal also to our students that it is important to look beyond the obvious when designing for interaction in home IoT.

Insights from the design process

At first we struggled with the challenge of designing for growth. It proved to be difficult to design a complete concept that solved everything at once. Only after we decided to temporarily constrain the challenge through a scenario of growth and define the 'core functionality' and the 'emergent functionality' separately were we able to conceptualize the dynamic and fully interactive IoT Sandbox. The openness of the challenge proved to be a paralyzing factor in the design process. It is worth mentioning that when the constraints are lifted our growing interface does solve the original challenge; it can deal with the increasing functionality of the smart home, arguably also with new functionality. To accomplish this two strategies from earlier research [8] were combined: The modular approach is most visible but there is also the service approach that was used to create customized tiles. It is in the combination of these approaches that the growing interface can handle both growth of 'core functionality' as well as 'emergent functionality'. We cannot overstate the importance of having a fully functional demonstrator: the proof of the pudding is in the eating.

Conclusion and future work

The IoT Sandbox set out to demonstrate that physically rich interfaces can be designed to control IoT systems and that those physically rich interfaces can be made as dynamic as the IoT systems that they control. It is clear that the IoT Sandbox can do this for the scenario of 'growth' that we formulated at the start. Arguably the growing physical interface is flexible enough to accommodate growth beyond this intentionally limited scenario. As such this installation is an important milestone in our research as it comprehensively summarizes our past work in a beautiful demonstrator, making the underlying concepts insightful and (literally) graspable for our students. But it also opens new research opportunities both as a vehicle for experimentation as well as more conceptually as a starting point for reflection. Below we present the result of that reflection and talk about our next steps.

The IoT sandbox was designed to be a strong concept [10] rather than a research product [16] in the sense that it extends over particular instances and exists not only as the polished demonstrator as shown above; the sandbox is also a template and tool for our students: every semester between 25 and 35 students receive the flat-packed building blocks of a sandbox, assemble, furnish it and then use it throughout the semester as a scaled live context for their designs. This scales up to the point where multiple student teams create designs that "clash" within the house and result in emergent design complexity that needs to be addressed creatively. A second avenue of future work is working towards rich and embodied interaction. We see the current physical interface as this as a stepping-stone towards a rich [6] and embodied [4] interaction interface, where we capitalize on the physicality of the interface and the situatedness of user actions [3]. Finally, we use the IoT sandbox to research, design, and communicate distributed approaches to interacting with 'things' in a highly connected context where multi-user and multi-activity scenarios inform our designerly actions.

Acknowledgements

We are grateful for the funding that we received from Design United to build the IoT Sandbox. We wish to acknowledge Taco Sieben who provided a last minute extra pair of hands necessary to meet the DDW deadline.

References

1. Emile Aarts and Stefano Marzano. 2003. *The new everyday: Views on ambient intelligence*. 010 Publishers.
2. Amazon Echo. Retrieved January 8, 2018 from https://www.amazon.com/echo
3. Jelle van Dijk. 2013. *Creating traces, sharing insight: explorations in embodied cognition design*. Unpublished Doctoral Dissertation, Eindhoven University of Technology, Eindhoven, the Netherlands
4. Paul Dourish. 2004. *Where the action is: the foundations of embodied interaction*. MIT press.
5. Graham Dove, Kim Halskov, Jodi Forlizzi, and John Zimmerman. 2017. UX Design Innovation: Challenges for Working with Machine Learning as a Design Material. In *Proceedings of the 2017 CHI Conference on Human Factors in Computing Systems (CHI '17)*. ACM, New York, NY, USA, 278-288. https://doi.org/10.1145/3025453.3025739
6. Joep Frens. 2006. *Designing for Rich Interaction: Integrating Form, Interaction, and Function*. Unpublished Doctoral Dissertation, Eindhoven University of Technology, Eindhoven, the Netherlands.
7. Joep Frens, and Kees Overbeeke. 2009. Setting the stage for the design of highly interactive systems. in *Proceedings of International Association of Societies of Design Research*, 1-10.
8. Joep Frens. 2017. Designing for Embodied and Rich Interaction in Home IoT. In *Proceedings of the Conference on Design and Semantics of Form and Movement-Sense and Sensitivity (DeSForM 2017)*. InTech, 2017.
9. Bart Hengeveld, Joep Frens, and Eva Deckers. 2016. Artefact Matters. *The Design Journal*. 19, no. 2, 323-337.
10. Kristina Höök and Jonas Löwgren. 2012. Strong concepts: Intermediate-level knowledge in interaction design research. *ACM Trans. Comput.-Hum. Interact.* 19, 3, Article 23 (October 2012), 18 pages. https://doi.org/10.1145/2362364.2362371
11. IFTTT, retrieved January 8, 2018 from https://ifttt.com
12. Ilpo Koskinen, John Zimmerman, Thomas Binder, Johan Redstrom, and Stephan Wensveen. 2011. *Design Research Through Practice: From the Lab, Field, and Showroom* (1st ed.). Morgan Kaufmann Publishers Inc., San Francisco, CA, USA.
13. Michal Luria, Guy Hoffman, and Oren Zuckerman. 2017. Comparing Social Robot, Screen and Voice Interfaces for Smart-Home Control. In *Proceedings of the 2017 CHI Conference on Human Factors in Computing Systems (CHI '17)*. ACM, New York, NY, USA, 580-628. https://doi.org/10.1145/3025453.3025786
14. Sarah Mennicken, Jo Vermeulen, and Elaine M. Huang. 2014. From today's augmented houses to tomorrow's smart homes: new directions for home automation research. In *Proceedings of the 2014 ACM International Joint Conference on Pervasive and Ubiquitous Computing (UbiComp '14)*. ACM, New York, NY, USA, 105-115. https://doi.org/10.1145/2632048.2636076
15. Daniele Miorandi, Sabrina Sicari, Francesco De Pellegrini, and Imrich Chlamtac. 2012. Internet of things: Vision, applications and research challenges. *Ad Hoc Networks,* 10, no. 7, 1497-1516.

16. William Odom, Ron Wakkary, Youn-kyung Lim, Audrey Desjardins, Bart Hengeveld, and Richard Banks. 2016. From Research Prototype to Research Product. In *Proceedings of the 2016 CHI Conference on Human Factors in Computing Systems (CHI '16)*. ACM, New York, NY, USA, 2549-2561. https://doi.org/10.1145/2858036.2858447

17. Philips Hue, retrieved January 8, 2018 from http://www2.meethue.com/

18. François Portet, Michel Vacher, Caroline Golanski, Camille Roux, and Brigitte Meillon. 2013. Design and evaluation of a smart home voice interface for the elderly: acceptability and objection aspects. *Personal Ubiquitous Comput*. 17, 1 (January 2013), 127-144. http://dx.doi.org/10.1007/s00779-011-0470-5

19. Reality Editor, retrieved January 8, 2018 from http://www.realityeditor.org

20. Mahadev Satyanarayanan. 2001. Pervasive computing: Vision and challenges. *IEEE Personal communications,* 8, no. 4. 10-17.

21. Mark Weiser. 1991. The computer for the 21st century. *Scientific american,* 265, no. 3, 94-104.

Exploring *Hygge* as a Desirable Design Vision for the Sustainable Smart Home

Rikke Hagensby Jensen [1], Yolande Strengers [2], Dimitrios Raptis [1], Larissa Nicholls [2], Jesper Kjeldskov [1], and Mikael B. Skov [1]
[1] Human-Centred Computing, Department of Computer Science, Aalborg University, Denmark
[2] Centre for Urban Research, RMIT University, Melbourne, Australia
{rjens, raptis, jesper, dubois}@cs.aau.dk {yolande.strengers, larissa.nicholls}@rmit.edu.au

ABSTRACT
In this paper, we present an exploratory study of *hygge* as a low-energy design vision for the smart home. *Hygge* is a Danish concept that embodies aesthetic experiences related to conviviality, often shaped by orchestrating atmospheres through low-level lighting. To explore this vision, we probe two Australian households that already live with smart home lighting technology. We report on household reflections of embedding *hygge* into everyday life. We conclude by outlining future directions for exploring desirable and sustainable smart home visions.

Author Keywords
Smart home; sustainability; design visions; aesthetics; smart lighting; hygge; energy consumption.

ACM Classification Keywords
H.5.m. Information interfaces and presentation (e.g., HCI): Miscellaneous;

INTRODUCTION
Currently, two HCI research discourses shape the design visions for the smart home. First, the *desirable* smart home, as a home that enhances people's experiences of comfort, convenience, and security through pervasive technologies [2]. This vision has been supported [9,12,38,40] and challenged [24,32,39] by HCI researchers and practitioners for decades. Second, the ongoing pursuit of the *sustainable* smart home [1,18,19,31,40]. In most smart home research these visions have been pursued separately and potentially undermine each other. For example, recent studies have shown that the pursuit of desirable smart home 'enhancements' may increase consumption and outweigh energy efficiency benefits [15,17,20].

In this paper, we approach this emerging dilemma by bringing desirability and sustainability together to explore ways of steering everyday life towards desirable, lower-energy visions. We build on past work, which identified an energy-intensive aesthetic vision of 'pleasance' [36] and householders' different desires or 'desiderata' [20] for the smart home. This research suggests that one possible approach for HCI designers is to identify desirable low-energy visions for the smart home and explore ways of embedding these into devices and households' everyday practices.

DIS '18, June 9–13, 2018, , Hong Kong

ACM ISBN 978-1-4503-5198-0/18/06...$15.00
https://doi.org/10.1145/3196709.3196804

Towards this end, we turn to the popular and less energy intense concept of *hygge* emerging from Denmark. *Hygge* has taken up a desirable position in contemporary visions for everyday life in several westernised countries [27,37]. The Danish concept of *hygge* reflects a romanticised Scandinavian lifestyle featuring cosiness and companionship. While not directly marketed as 'low energy', the vision embodies ideas of low-level lighting, minimal engagement with technology, and 'traditional' ways of keeping warm, such as using blankets or drinking hot cups of tea. *Hygge* contrasts with the energy-intensive vision of pleasance currently permeating smart home marketing [36], where new smart devices, sensors and functions (e.g. mood lighting) are embedded into practices and parts of the home, potentially creating new energy demands and outweighing any energy efficiencies [20].

Focusing specifically on *hygge*'s potential relationship with smart lighting, this paper reports on a deployment of explorative *hygge* probes in two Australian households as part of a larger study on the smart home. Through the deployment, we sought to circulate different ideas about desirable ways of life within the smart home and identify how designers can embed these into devices to help steer emerging smart home practices in more sustainable directions.

WHY HYGGE?
Most HCI efforts to design for sustainable outcomes have either looked for ways to do this as efficiently and effortlessly as possible via intelligent and automated technology [1,19,33], or advocated for desirable 'Going Green' visions [25] that aim to engage people with sustainable choices, either by informing and educating [5], suggesting greener alternatives [21], or proposing alternative lifestyles e.g. 'voluntary simplicity' [13]. These approaches envision sustainability as something that is desirable by assuming that people aspire to 'do the right thing' either via optimisation or by actively pursuing a 'sustainable'

lifestyle. In this paper, we experiment with a different approach for envisioning sustainability and desirability in the smart home. Specifically, we turn to *hygge*.

Lighting is central to *hygge* where natural daylight, candles, and electrical lighting all play important roles in orchestrating *hygge* atmospheres [4]. As Bille [4] demonstrates, *hygge* orchestrates desirable atmospheres of intimacy, informality, belonging, togetherness, equality, and secureness that shapes interior and exterior spaces of the home and relationships between people and things. In this way, *hygge* has parallels to the energy-intensive aesthetic vision of pleasance [36] that embeds desirable expectations of comfort, relaxation, and peace of mind into the smart home. Like pleasance, comfort and relaxation are central to *hygge*, but in contrast to it, creating the calm and convivial atmosphere associated with *hygge* tends to involve less use of electrical lighting and technology. As a result, *hygge* can be 'naturally' less energy intensive, but not generally promoted as such. This means *hygge* could appeal to a wide range of smart home adopters, including those for which environmental issues are of little interest and/or saving energy is not desirable.

In this paper, we explore whether *hygge* can engage early adopters of smart homes in a lifestyle vision and aesthetic experiences which use less energy. We explore this in a country where *hygge* is not widely understood but is gaining some traction as 'hip' and 'cool' – or desirable.

RESEARCH DESIGN

In the first phase we drew on qualitative research (photography, semi-structured interviews, and informal home technology tours [6]) with 23 Australian households that used smart lighting and other smart home technology. The main objective was to understand how smart home technology was incorporated into the everyday lives of early smart home adopters, and the energy implications [see 20].

The purpose of the second (*hygge deployment*) phase was to probe ideas of *hygge* to encourage lower energy usage without explicitly discussing energy. We designed an exploratory probe pack (Figure 1) consisting of: a digital

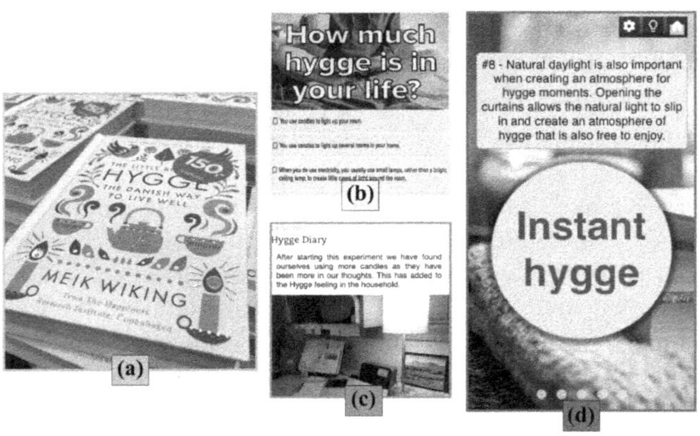

Figure 1: The explorative probes; a) *hygge* book; b) *hygge* quiz; c) snippet of a digital *hygge* diary; d) *hygge* app

diary, a coffee table *hygge* book, a *hygge* quiz, and a *hygge* app for the Philips Hue smart light system. The app was built by the researchers and included possibilities to create and select *hygge* mood scenes which involved minimal and soft lighting (instead of their existing lighting arrangements of mood scenes involving multiple colours). The *hygge* book and quiz also provided information on how to create *hygge* through (smart) lighting and other materials. The diary contained open-ended questions that allowed our participants to reflect on *hygge* and to share, through text and photos, their *hygge* 'moments'.

As lighting infuses a range of household practices, the probe pack design was inspired by Shove et al.'s [34] theory of social practice change. Shove et al. argue that one way in which practices change is by mixing up the elements (material, meanings, and competences) of practices in different ways. Thus, the purpose of the probe pack was to circulate *hygge* practice elements that would encourage participants to experiment in playful and provocative ways. More specifically, the probe pack was intended to engage householders with new (or old): 1) materials such as new scenes of smart lighting and the use of candles and natural lighting 2) meanings about what is cosy, warm, and aesthetically pleasing, and 3) competencies on how to create atmospheres, connect with others, or calm down.

Two households interviewed in phase one used the Hue system extensively and were recruited for the *hygge deployment phase* – Adam and Natalie (a couple) and Tony. Adam was an IT specialist and keen amateur photographer, while Natalie worked as a nurse. The couple had designed the lighting for their new house to include 19 smart light bulbs, two smart lighting strips, and non-smart spot lights in the ceiling throughout the house. Tony was an academic with a keen recreational interest in design. Tony's home was equipped with seven smart bulbs and one smart lighting strip. Tony's smart bulbs were placed in decorative lamps in different rooms, while spot lights were placed throughout the home.

This part of the study was conducted over four weeks in June/July 2017 (winter) and involved two interviews with each household. In the first interview, questions were directed towards their use of smart lighting. Households were also introduced to the probe pack and given the opportunity to ask questions about the probes, *hygge* and the study. In the second interview participants were asked about their understandings of *hygge* and how they used the concept/probes in the past month. Both interviews were audio recorded and professionally transcribed. The transcriptions were subsequently analysed using an emergent coding approach [23] resulting in four themes discussed below.

FINDINGS

Aesthetically pleasing experiences and smart lighting

Prior to introducing the *hygge* probe pack, households were using their lights for functional, decorative, and aesthetic outcomes. Direct electrical lighting (particular non-smart spot lighting) was mostly used to provide better visibility for chores such as cooking and cleaning. In contrast, colourful and dimmable smart lights were typically used to create attractive and comforting atmospheres via smart mood scenes. This finding reflects the dilemma of having competing desirability and sustainability visions for the smart home. One reason that households chose to install a smart light system was because the smart bulbs and strips were low energy LEDs. However, the smart lights also infused additional household practices for reasons other than functionality. Householders desired to aesthetically enhance practices such as reading, dining, cooking, television watching, and bathing with smart lights, which added beauty, nourishment, uniqueness, and playfulness to the experience. This often involved the use of more lights (lamps and strips) for more time (Figure 2 & 3) and therefore could undermine the energy efficiency benefits of LED technology.

Figure 2: Colourful LED strips in the dining room

Figure 3: Smart LED used when watching television

After circulating ideas of *hygge* through the probes, participants approached their smart lighting system differently to create atmospheres that emphasised happiness, cosiness, relaxation, and warmth. In particular, Adam and Natalie engaged extensively with the probes and aspired towards *hygge* as a way of creating aesthetically pleasing experiences through lighting.

> Adam: I have actually played with the setting of the lights more than I normally do... Just thinking about it [hygge] has actually made quite a big difference in terms of my desire, real drive to create atmosphere even more.

Interestingly, these *hygge* atmospheres were mostly created by exploring scenes in their smart lighting system that dimmed or turned off electric lights. This echoes Bille's [4] finding that soft and minimal *hygge* light shapes aesthetic, ambient, and emotional experiences. These findings are encouraging because they suggest that circulating alternative design visions for the smart home can help lower electricity consumption.

Hygge and non-electrical materials

Participants also associated *hygge* with the use of non-electrical and 'dumb' materials. Tony, for example, associated light from his fireplaces as a source of *hygge*.

> Tony: Really hygge, it's also when you've got light from the fire.

Candles were also associated with *hygge* and used in both households as a decorative light source to create *hygge* atmospheres. Candles were used as a supplement to dimmed electric smart lights as seen in Tony's home (Figure 4), while Adam and Natalie explored using candles as the only light source in some practices, e.g. bathing (Figure 5).

Figure 4: Mood setting with different lighting sources

Figure 5: Candles used during bathing time

The *hygge* probe pack also made Natalie consider using natural light for situations she thought embodied *hygge*:

> Natalie: I looked outside for a while, knitted for a bit, and then looked outside, and I was just so happy, and warm, and cosy. I like the natural light, so all the blinds were up... I think it's, for me it leads to that whole feeling of hygge. Because I tend to have a blanket and I have a drink.

This shows how participants started to use or associate different materials (e.g. light, drinks, blankets) with aesthetically pleasing experiences in existing practices (e.g. knitting, cooking, entertaining). These findings demonstrate promise for the idea that non-electric materials can be used to either reduce or replace use of smart technologies, while still maintaining expectations of experiencing the smart home as a pleasurable and nourishing space. These expectations have strong parallels with the desirable vision of pleasance [36] but without the same energy-intensive implications. Moreover, these findings open up new possibilities to design smart technology that takes advantage of these (or other) new meanings of aesthetically pleasing *hygge* experiences (e.g. blinds that automatically go up when natural light is available, heating turning down when people are cooking or snuggling up underneath a blanket).

Slowing down in the smart home

Because *hygge* promotes minimal engagement with technology, interacting with smart home technologies (e.g. smart lighting) to create *hygge* atmospheres might be understood as counterintuitive. This aspect was picked up by Tony, who felt distracted by smart phone notifications when changing light settings. Natalie and Adam, on the other hand, found it easier and more convenient to change light scenes from their smart phones when immersed in *hygge* moments because they did not have to get up from the *hygge* 'nest'. Participants also associated pursuing *hygge* with slowing down daily routines to allow oneself to be 'in the moment', suggesting that *hygge* competences were infusing several practices.

> Natalie: Just do you chores, maybe in a slow way, rather than in a frantic [way]... Mindful, present, happiness, and just relaxed enjoyment, of where you are at that moment.

These qualities reflect related ideas of slow technology [14] and slow energy [28] that Katzeff et al. [21] have explored as a positive framing for 'shifting' intensive energy activities in time [29]. Our findings suggest *hygge* could also be explored as productive and desirable design vision for framing slow energy.

The dark side of hygge

The above findings demonstrate how probing participants about *hygge* might be a promising design path for mixing up elements of practices in new and 'naturally' less energy intensive ways. However, given that *hygge* is also associated with meanings of cosiness and warmth, particularly in the winter period, circulating these ideas may introduce new expectations of comfort that could further increase energy demands. For example, Adam despised feeling cold and used his automatic heating system to ensure his house was always warm.

> Adam: I'm emotionally uncomfortable with being cold.

Introducing the *hygge* concept confirmed and encouraged Adam to maintain this expectation of thermal comfort. As reflected by Natalie, this expectation was not the norm in Australia – heating tended to be used on an 'ad hoc' basis instead of on a thermostat-controlled regular basis:

> Natalie: Australians try to avoid putting the heat on at all costs, so kind of cultivating that warm, cosy environment [through *hygge*], I think they'd use more heating, the general Australian.

These findings stress that designers should be wary of romanticising *hygge* as a design vision for the smart home because it could also embed new meanings and expectations of comfort that may increase energy use.

DISCUSSION AND FUTURE IMPLICATIONS

Designing desirable low-energy ways of life

A major question guiding our work is how to envision a smart home that challenges aesthetic expectations in lower energy ways, while still upholding the idea that living in a (smart) home should be desirable, pleasurable and comfortable. We are aware that (smart) lighting does not necessarily constitute a large proportion of a household's electricity usage, but this study is a step towards positioning the smart home as desirable *and* sustainable, without explicitly promoting 'Going Green' visions or invoking 'negative' connotations (e.g. 'we have to make do with less') embedded in visions like 'voluntary simplicity' [13].

Did we then succeed in probing *hygge* as a design vision for the smart home that brings desirability and sustainability together? Our findings show that the explorative *hygge* probe pack did challenge expectations of aesthetic experiences by mixing up the elements (materials, meanings, and competences) of practices related to smart lighting that could result in less energy usage. An important contribution for future designers and researchers is that interventions, which promote desirable design visions (in contrast to specific outcomes such as lower energy demand) can be useful for studies that aim to 'trigger' reconfigurations [22] of household practices, even without introducing a prototype.

Our findings also highlight the importance of understanding the different kinds of desires [26] that shape early adopters' use of smart technologies (also reported in [15,17,20]), which may be differently from the designed purpose [10,16]. The unforeseen ways that people combine elements of practice need to be considered when designing interactions that aim to steer towards sustainability [34,35]. However, we also need to be careful with the interpretation of our findings, as *hygge* may also lead to unsustainable expectations (e.g. using more lights that are dimmed or heating more) and new needs and desires (e.g. bringing more interactive energy-consuming technology into the home), which may lead to an increase in overall interactivity and electricity consumption that contradict *hygge's* 'naturally' using less approach.

Hygge, research through design, and provocation

We consider this research an initial step towards unpacking the relationship between desirability and sustainability in the design of smart technology. A suggested next phase is to attempt to 'trigger' [22], through *hygge*, everyday practices towards sustainability. For this, we draw inspiration from provocative design approaches such as critical and speculative design [3,11] to create interventions in the form of provotypes – prototypes that use provocation to explore design possibilities for the future [7]. Other research through design studies have illustrated that speculative [8] or provocative [30] designs can be used to steer practices towards sustainability.

We suggest using provotypes and provocation (on all three levels; conceptual, aesthetic and functional [3]) to further explore visions and designs for the smart home. In this study, we provoked aesthetic expectations of living in a smart home through the *hygge* probe pack. However, we also conceptually provoked, since *hygge*, to some extent, already promotes the idea of 'suppressing' the use of technology (for example, to switch off the lights and use candles to achieve *hygge* atmospheres). For future work, we suggest provoking functional aspects too, as a way forward for 'triggering' reconfigurations of household practices.

CONCLUSION

In this short paper, we have argued that HCI designers and researchers interested in pursuing sustainability through smart home technologies should pay closer attention to the visions of desirability that underpin them. We introduced the popular and lower energy aesthetic concept of *hygge* to disrupt and reorient ideas about desirability and sustainability in the smart home. Using an explorative probe pack, we selected two households from our larger smart home study to engage with *hygge* through their smart lighting system. Our findings show that *hygge* introduces new meanings, materials and competencies about comfortable and cosy atmospheres that can reconfigure everyday practices in less (and more) energy-intensive directions. These ideas provide a fruitful area of exploration for HCI designers interested in reducing energy consumption in households, and one which is ripe for provocation and experimentation.

REFERENCES

1. Alper T Alan, Enrico Costanza, Sarvapali D Ramchurn, Joel Fischer, Tom Rodden, and Nicholas R Jennings. 2016. Tariff Agent: Interacting with a Future Smart Energy System at Home. *ACM Transactions on Computer-Human Interaction* (TOCHI) 23, 4. https://doi.org/10.1145/2943770
2. Francis K. Aldrich. 2006. Smart homes: past, present and future. In *Inside the smart home*, Richard Harper (ed.). Springer Science & Business Media.
3. Shaowen Bardzell, Jeffrey Bardzell, Jodi Forlizzi, John Zimmerman, and John Antanitis. 2012. Critical Design and Critical Theory: The Challenge of Designing for Provocation. In *Proceedings of the Designing Interactive Systems Conference* (DIS '12), 288–297. https://doi.org/10.1145/2317956.2318001
4. Mikkel Bille. 2015. Lighting up cosy atmospheres in Denmark. *Emotion, Space and Society* 15: 56–63. https://doi.org/10.1016/j.emospa.2013.12.008
5. Jon Bird and Yvonne Rogers. 2010. The pulse of tidy street: Measuring and publicly displaying domestic electricity consumption. In *workshop on energy awareness and conservation* (Pervasive 2010).
6. Mark Blythe, Andrew Monk, and Jisoo Park. 2002. Technology Biographies: Field Study Techniques for Home Use Product Development. In *CHI '02 extended abstracts on Human factors in computing systems* (CHI EA '02), 658. https://doi.org/10.1145/506443.506532
7. Laurens Boer and Jared Donovan. 2012. Provotypes for Participatory Innovation. In *Proceedings of the Designing Interactive Systems Conference* (DIS '12), 388–397. https://doi.org/10.1145/2317956.2318014
8. Loove Broms, Josefin Wangel, and Camilla Andersson. 2017. Sensing energy: Forming stories through speculative design artefacts. *Energy Research and Social Science* 31, (2017): 194–204. https://doi.org/10.1016/j.erss.2017.06.025
9. A.J. Bernheim Brush, Bongshin Lee, Ratul Mahajan, Sharad Agarwal, Stefan Saroiu, and Colin Dixon. 2011. Home automation in the wild. In *Proceedings of the SIGCHI Conference on Human Factors in Computing System* (CHI '11), 2115. https://doi.org/10.1145/1978942.1979249
10. Paul Dourish and Genevieve Bell. 2011. *Divining a digital future: Mess and mythology in ubiquitous computing*. MIT Press.
11. Anthony Dunne and Fiona Raby. 2013. *Speculative everything: design, fiction, and social dreaming*. MIT Press.
12. W. Keith Edwards and Rebecca E. Grinter. 2001. At Home with Ubiquitous Computing: Seven Challenges. *Proceedings of the 3rd international conference on Ubiquitous Computing* (UbiComp '01): 256–272. https://doi.org/10.1007/3-540-45427-6_22
13. Maria Håkansson and Phoebe Sengers. 2013. Beyond being green: simple living families and ICT. In *Proceedings of the SIGCHI Conference on Human Factors in Computing Systems* (CHI '13), 2725. https://doi.org/10.1145/2470654.2481378
14. Lars Hallnäs and Johan Redström. 2001. Slow Technology – Designing for Reflection. *Personal and Ubiquitous Computing* 5, 3: 201–212. https://doi.org/10.1007/PL00000019
15. Tom Hargreaves, Charlie Wilson, and Richard Hauxwell-Baldwin. 2018. Learning to live in a smart home. *Building Research & Information* 46, 1: 127–139. https://doi.org/10.1080/09613218.2017.1286882
16. Marc Hassenzahl, Kai Eckoldt, Sarah Diefenbach, Matthias Laschke, Eva Lenz, and Joonhwan Kim. 2013. Designing moments of meaning and pleasure. Experience design and happiness. *International Journal of Design* 7, 3: 21–31.
17. Sergio Tirado Herrero, Larissa Nicholls, and Yolande Strengers. 2018. Smart home technologies in everyday life: do they address key energy challenges in households? *Current Opinion in Environmental Sustainability* 31: 65–70. https://doi.org/10.1016/j.cosust.2017.12.001
18. Chuan-Che (Jeff) Huang, Rayoung Yang, and Mark W. Newman. 2015. The Potential and Challenges of Inferring Thermal Comfort at Home Using Commodity Sensors. In *Proceedings of the 2015 ACM International Joint Conference on Pervasive and Ubiquitous Computing* (UbiComp '15), 1089–1100. https://doi.org/10.1145/2750858.2805831
19. Rikke Hagensby Jensen, Jesper Kjeldskov, and Mikael B. Skov. 2016. HeatDial: Beyond User Scheduling in Eco-Interaction. In *Proceedings of the 9th Nordic Conference on Human-Computer Interaction* (NordiCHI '16). https://doi.org/10.1145/2971485.2971525
20. Rikke Hagensby Jensen, Yolande Strengers, Jesper Kjeldskov, Larissa Nicholls, and Mikael B Skov. 2018. Designing the Desirable Smart Home: A Study of Household Experiences and Energy Consumption Impacts. In *Proceedings of the 2018 CHI Conference on Human Factors in Computing Systems* (CHI 18). https://doi.org/https://doi.org/10.1145/3173574.3173578
21. Cecilia Katzeff, Stina Wessman, and Sara Colombo. 2017. "Mama, It's Peacetime!": Planning, Shifting, and Designing Activities in the Smart Grid Scenario. *Proceedings of the Conference on Design and Semantics of Form and Movement - Sense and Sensitivity* (DeSForM 2017). https://doi.org/10.5772/intechopen.71129
22. Lenneke Kuijer. 2017. Practices-oriented design. In *Design for behaviour change: Theories and practices*

of designing for change, K. Niederer, G. Ludden and S. Clune (eds.).

23. Jonathan Lazar, Jinjuan Heidi Feng, and Harry Hochheiser. 2010. *Research Methods in Human-Computer Interaction.* Wiley Publishing.
24. Sarah Mennicken, Jo Vermeulen, and Elaine M Huang. 2014. From Today' s Augmented Houses to Tomorrow' s Smart Homes: New Directions for Home Automation Research. In *Proceedings of the 2014 ACM International Joint Conference on Pervasive and Ubiquitous Computing* (UbiComp '14), 105–115. https://doi.org/10.1145/2632048.2636076
25. Susie Moloney and Yolande Strengers. 2014. "Going Green"?: The Limitations of Behaviour Change Programmes as a Policy Response to Escalating Resource Consumption. *Environmental Policy and Governance* 24, 2: 94–107. https://doi.org/10.1002/eet.1642
26. Harold G. Nelson and Erik Stolterman. 2012. *The Design Way: Intentional Change in an Unpredictable World.* MIT Press.
27. Oxford University Press. 2017. Oxford Dictionaries Word of the Year 2016 is... Retrieved November 28, 2017 from https://www.oxforddictionaries.com/press/news/2016/12/11/WOTY-16
28. James Pierce and Eric Paulos. 2012. The Local Energy Indicator: Designing for Wind and Solar Energy Systems in the Home. In *Proceedings of the Designing Interactive Systems Conference* (DIS '12), 631–634. https://doi.org/10.1145/2317956.2318050
29. James Pierce, Diane J. Schiano, and Eric Paulos. 2010. Home, Habits, and Energy: Examining Domestic Interactions and Energy Consumption. In *Proceedings of the SIGCHI Conference on Human Factors in Computing Systems* (CHI '10), 1985–1994. https://doi.org/10.1145/1753326.1753627
30. Dimitrios Raptis, Rikke Hagensby Jensen, Jesper Kjeldskov, and Mikael B. Skov. 2017. Aesthetic, Functional and Conceptual Provocation in Research Through Design. In *Proceedings of the 2017 Conference on Designing Interactive Systems* (DIS '17), 29–41. https://doi.org/10.1145/3064663.3064739
31. Tom A. Rodden, Joel E. Fischer, Nadia Pantidi, Khaled Bachour, and Stuart Moran. 2013. At Home with Agents: Exploring Attitudes Towards Future Smart Energy Infrastructures. In *Proceedings of the SIGCHI Conference on Human Factors in Computing Systems* (CHI '13), 1173–1182. https://doi.org/10.1145/2470654.2466152
32. Yvonne Rogers. 2006. Moving on from Weiser's Vision of Calm Computing: engaging UbiComp experiences. In *Proceedings of the 8th international conference on Ubiquitous Computing* (UbiComp '06). https://doi.org/10.1007/11853565
33. James Scott, A.J. Bernheim Brush, John Krumm, Brian Meyers, Michael Hazas, Stephen Hodges, and Nicolas Villar. 2011. PreHeat: Controlling Home Heating Using Occupancy Prediction. In *Proceedings of the 13th international conference on Ubiquitous computing* (UbiComp '11), 281. https://doi.org/10.1145/2030112.2030151
34. Elizabeth Shove, Mika Pantzar, and Matt Watson. 2012. *The dynamics of social practice: Everyday life and how it changes.* Sage.
35. Yolande A.A. Strengers. 2011. Designing Eco-feedback Systems for Everyday Life. In *Proceedings of the SIGCHI Conference on Human Factors in Computing Systems* (CHI '11), 2135. https://doi.org/10.1145/1978942.1979252
36. Yolande Strengers and Larissa Nicholls. 2017. Aesthetic pleasures and gendered tech-work in the 21st-century smart home. *Media International Australia*: 1329878X1773766. https://doi.org/10.1177/1329878X17737661
37. Claire Thomson. 2016. The Danish concept of "hygge" – and why it's their latest successful export. *The Conversation.* Retrieved January 8, 2018 from https://theconversation.com/the-danish-concept-of-hygge-and-why-its-their-latest-successful-export-67268
38. Mark Weiser and John Seely Brown. 1996. The coming age of calm technolgy. *Beyond Calculation*: 75–85. https://doi.org/10.1007/978-1-4612-0685-9_6
39. Charlie Wilson, Tom Hargreaves, and Richard Hauxwell-Baldwin. 2015. Smart homes and their users: a systematic analysis and key challenges. *Personal and Ubiquitous Computing* 19, 2: 463–476. https://doi.org/10.1007/s00779-014-0813-0
40. Rayoung Yang, Mark W. Newman, and Jodi Forlizzi. 2014. Making Sustainability Sustainable: Challenges in the Design of Eco-interaction Technologies. In *Proceedings of the SIGCHI Conference on Human Factors in Computing Systems* (CHI '12), 823–832. https://doi.org/10.1145/2556288.2557380

Generating Mobile Application Onboarding Insights Through Minimalist Instruction

Brendan Strahm
Purdue University
West Lafayette, IN, USA
bstrahm@gmail.com

Colin M. Gray
Purdue University
West Lafayette, IN, USA
gray42@purdue.edu

Mihaela Vorvoreanu
Purdue University
West Lafayette, IN, USA
mihaela@purdue.edu

ABSTRACT
Mobile application designers use onboarding task flows to help first time users learn and engage with key application functionality. Although some guidelines for designing onboarding flows have been offered by practitioners, a systematic, research-informed approach is needed. In this paper, we present the creation of a method for designing mobile application onboarding experiences. We used the minimalist instruction framework to engage twelve university students in an iterative set of design and evaluation activities. Participants interacted with a physical prototype of an educational badging mobile application through a semi-structured exploration and reflection activity, bookended by structured mini-interviews. We found that this method facilitated engagement with participants' meaning-making processes, resulting in useful design insights and the creation of an onboarding task flow. Research opportunities for integrating instructional design and learning approaches in HCI in the context of onboarding are considered.

Author Keywords
Onboarding; minimalist instruction; user experience; design methods; mobile.

ACM Classification Keywords
H.5.2. Information interfaces and presentation: User Interfaces. - Evaluation/Methodology.

INTRODUCTION
A user's first interaction with an application frames their future interactions, enculturating the user into a complex array of interface and system components [1,4,25]. If new users are unable to understand these components and how they might be used to address personally relevant goals, the application is likely be uninstalled or ignored [19]. While learnability and usability of application interfaces has been at the core of HCI scholarship for decades [e.g., 2,4], the rapid adoption and evolution of mobile applications may present new challenges. In this paper, we focus on the *onboarding* process as a key aspect of the user experience that allows users to discover application functionality in a timely manner and identify how this functionality might allow them to achieve their personal goals. Many applications use onboarding task flows such as instructional text, just-in-time hints, or interactive tutorials to help new users learn the application's key benefits and guide new users toward meaningful engagement with those benefits, yet there is scarce methodological or theoretical guidance to inform onboarding design decisions.

ACM ISBN 978-1-4503-5198-0/18/06…$15.00
https://doi.org/10.1145/3196709.3196727

Past scholarship on the learnability of applications and interfaces has focused primarily on large or relatively stable application environments (c.f., "training wheels" instruction [1,6]), but this guidance is more difficult to apply to rapidly evolving mobile applications where users often have a multiplicity of choices. There is a need for a systematic, research-informed method for generating design insights that inform the creation of effective onboarding task flows. Some guidelines for designing onboarding have been created by industry practitioners [e.g., 10,11,12,15,19], but these guidelines are often framed separately from generative user research and neglect engagement with instructional design theory and the ways that users learn to use and engage in new technological environments.

In this paper, we propose a design method that fills this gap by using Carroll's minimalist instruction framework [4,5] to generate onboarding design insights by leveraging users' meaning-making processes. The method consists of an iterative set of design and evaluation activities, wherein participants are engaged in structured mini-interviews surrounding a mediated interaction with a physical prototype. To create and validate this method, we engaged 12 participants in the design of onboarding task flows for an existing educational badging mobile application, identifying relevant and generative design insights that resonate with the theory of minimalist instruction.

The contributions of this paper are two-fold: 1) We propose a systematic, research-informed design method for generating insights for mobile onboarding, which provides guidance to practitioners that design mobile experiences; and 2) We connect learning and instructional theory to the design of onboarding experiences using minimalist instruction as a theoretical framework, informing a learning-focused view of technology adoption and use. These contributions benefit the HCI community by cross-pollinating research on learning from the instructional design domain and reframing onboarding task flows as an opportunity to engage in minimalist instruction. This method addresses a gap identified and only partially filled by practitioners, providing opportunities for future research on onboarding and learning as part of the user experience.

RELATED WORK

To frame our research approach, we describe the work of practitioners who have identified nascent generalized approaches for user onboarding and summarize the findings of researchers who have identified situated approaches for user onboarding. We then situate our method development in relation to minimalist instructional approaches that have previously found resonance in the HCI community.

Practitioner Approaches to Onboarding

Onboarding has been a topic of great interest in the UX practitioner community, but we have been unable to identify research guidance on how designers should create user onboarding experiences through support from a research or prototyping method. Therefore, we will begin with what is known from the practitioner literature, and then move outward to document learnability and onboarding implementation more broadly in the HCI literature in the next section.

According to UX practitioner Samuel Hulick, user onboarding is "...the process of increasing the likelihood that new users become successful when adopting [a mobile application]" [10]. Onboarding task flows are comprised of instructional interface elements located at critical points throughout the application, collectively functioning as a built-in application tutorial for new users. Onboarding can be relevant as users learn to use new applications in general, additional applications within a known and specific genre (e.g., task management, puzzle games), or new versions of known applications. Examples of onboarding design patterns include: instructional text, tours, progress bars, just-in-time hints, tips placed in feeds of user-generated content, and interactive tutorials [11,15].

The majority of practitioner sources propose highly general onboarding design recommendations, including connecting specific onboarding patterns to specific types of applications based on induction from existing mobile applications. This approach positions onboarding as a drop-in solution for specific problems with a focus on design refinement rather than designing based on generative research and learning insights. However, the work of Higgins [11,12] and Hulick [10], both UX practitioners, provide a more substantive set of guidelines and process moves to engage with the challenges of onboarding.

Higgins [12] differentiates herself from other practitioners by explicitly invoking learning in her onboarding design strategy, using instructional design concepts as a foundation of her approach. She advocates for three principles of onboarding: 1) instruction should be presented contextually through guided interaction to provide a space for learning through exploration; 2) users should be presented with a limited subset of the application's functionality before being required to create an account in order to build trust and feelings of reciprocity; and 3) onboarding should focus on personalization and facilitating user tasks in order to emphasize the priority of user needs. Higgins [11] has also proposed a participatory design exercise called *Coaching Cadence* to prototype the steps in a guided walkthrough onboarding section. This method is noteworthy as it represents the only generative research method of its type proposed by a practitioner. The exercise is a dialogue where the researcher plays the part of the application onboarding and the participant describes the actions they would like to take. While this method is an effective way to engage potential users in the broad design of an initial onboarding flow, user interaction is removed from actual use of a prototype, and is geared toward identifying pacing issues rather than learnability issues.

Another substantive practitioner perspective comes from Hulick [10], who proposed an onboarding strategy focused on the user journey rather than directly on the onboarding task flow. This approach focuses on two meaningful points that ideally occur early in the user's journey: the *"aha!" moment* and the *quick win*. While these points in the user journey have not been empirically validated, they serve as a helpful frame for the present study and method design.

The Aha! Moment

Hulick calls the first point in his strategy the "aha!" moment [10], which comprises a moment of realization where new users identify personal benefits to using the application that help organize and cohere their perception of the application. Without onboarding, users might make this realization after investing significant effort, if they are willing to persevere. The purpose of onboarding could then be stated as clearly and efficiently guiding users to their "aha!" moments. Generating these moments is situational, and it is recommended that new users be provided with a rational explanation of the mobile application's purpose and an emotional reason to be interested in it.

The Quick Win

The second point in Hulick's strategy is called the "quick win" [10]. In order to achieve meaningful progress before new users lose interest, Hulick recommends that designers focus on helping the user achieve one core benefit. For example, a quick win in the Twitter onboarding flow is to follow a few people, thereby populating the user's timeline. Not only does this deliver on a core benefit in a personal way—feeling connected to interesting people—but it is also easily attainable in the first session of use due to the availability of user recommendations. This provides closure and a positive conclusion to the user journey.

Learnability of Applications

Learnability of interfaces and application systems has long been at the core of HCI theory and practice, impacting the design of systems and their usability as experienced by the anticipated end user [e.g., 2,5,17]. In the design of computing systems in the 1980s, philosophies of application design and usability such as "training wheels" [1,6] ensured that users would be able to effectively explore and use applications in a scaffolded manner, with clear instructional aids and limited functionality to guide potential actions. Other scholars have engaged in various aspects of the learning process users undergo when using a new application, generally building in some way upon learning or instructional theory. Yi and Davis [27] described how users build skills within a software environment, and identified the role of observational learning processes (attention, retention, production, and motivation) in this skill acquisition process. Haramundanis [9] identified key aspects of learnability in information design, focusing on visual consistency and usability as key drivers of creating learnable materials. Finally, Leutner [13] built on the "training wheels" approach, using detailed guidance in conjunction with limiting application functionality to create "double fading" of support, thereby increasing user acquisition of application knowledge.

Onboarding has been addressed in a limited number of HCI publications, but always in relation to specific products, contexts, or learning outcomes rather than being oriented towards a general method for producing effective onboarding experiences. One common area for onboarding study is the open-source software community, where technical and conceptual barriers to collaboration are addressed, with a limited analysis of the interaction design of the system that may promote effective onboarding (e.g., [23]). In parallel, Fraser et al. [7] and Cardoso [3] have addressed onboarding in crowdsourcing communities, focusing on the retention benefits of effective onboarding. Fraser et al. [7] addressed onboarding in the context of a photo manipulation extension, while Cardoso [3] presented in-progress work on a citizen science online platform. Other scholars have addressed onboarding in specific domains such as gaming [26] and education [14]. Petersen et al. [26] used surveys and physiological response to analyze the onboarding experiences of existing free-to-play mobile apps, while Lochrie et al. [14] documented the creation of a companion mobile application to allow children to productively engage with physical computing devices in an educational setting. While these onboarding implementations have generative and theoretical value, no prior scholarship has proposed a content- or context-free method for generating onboarding interactions, and further, no extant scholarship has engaged with instructional design and learning theory to inform onboarding design decisions.

Minimalist Instruction

Minimalist instruction (MI) is an instructional design framework developed in the 1980s by Carroll [4] as an alternative approach to hierarchical software training manuals. Its main goals were to give users more to do, less to read, and help users recover quickly from errors; this was made possible through the production of non-linear, goal-driven instructional materials that served as flexible instructional scaffolding. Carroll codified and operationalized this approach, resulting in the principles and heuristics of minimalist instruction shown in Figure 1 [25]. These principles support onboarding goals, and serve as a theoretical framing for the development of our method. While it is possible that these principles are tacitly in use in existing onboarding sequences or practitioner guidance, our focus in this study is on how MI can be used to inform onboarding-focused user research, not to explain or evaluate the presence of MI principles in existing products.

Principle 1: Choose an action-oriented approach
1.1: Provide an immediate opportunity to act.
1.2: Encourage and support exploration and innovation.
1.3: Respect the integrity of the user's activity.

Principle 2: Anchor the tool in the task domain
2.1: Select or design instructional activities that are real tasks.
2.2: The components of the instruction should reflect the task structure.

Principle 3: Support Error Recognition and Recovery
3.1: Prevent mistakes whenever possible.
3.2: Provide error-information when actions are error-prone or when correction is difficult.
3.3: Provide error-information that supports detection, diagnosis and recovery.
3.4: Provide on-the-spot error-information.

Principle 4: Support reading to do, study, and locate
4.1: Be brief; don't spell out everything.
4.2: Provide closure for chapters.

Figure 1. Minimalist Instruction Principles and Heuristics (adapted from [25]).

Using an *action-oriented approach* focuses on engaging the learner in activity to build and sustain engagement, with an implicit argument that effective learning must be situated in action meaningful to the learner. Carroll [4] identified that new users feel an urge to make tangible progress toward their goals, and this principle engages users in that active learning early, balancing their need for information with their need to experiment and produce, giving learners a sense of confidence and control. In a direct parallel to the "quick win" of onboarding design [10], Van der Meij and Carroll [25] connect this principle to creating a series of short-term goals to reflect rapidly changing learner goals.

Anchoring the tool in the task domain reinforces that the tasks presented in minimalist instruction should be real and meaningful, not imaginary, scenarios. Tasks should be immediately understandable by the learner and easy to complete in order to provide an attainable and personally

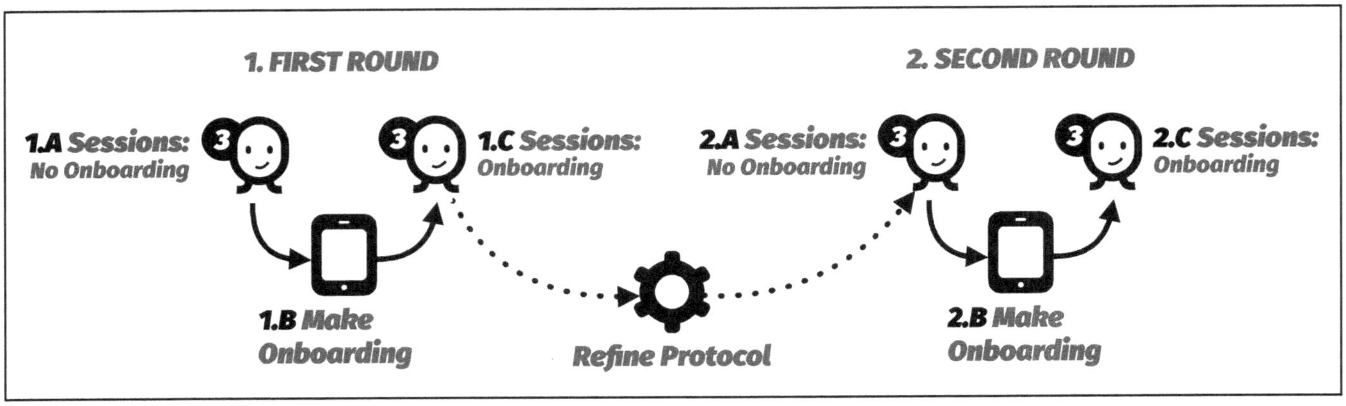

Figure 2. Iterative protocol structure.

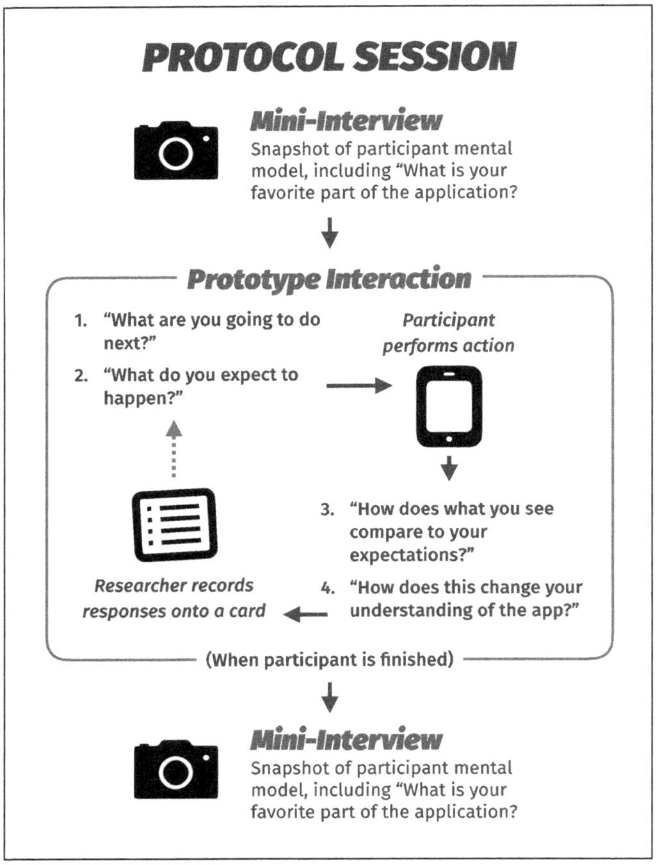

Figure 3. The process for conducting a session.

relevant reward [25]. This task-oriented approach supports experimentation and also provides common tasks using terms and descriptions that are natural for users instead of system-oriented language.

Supporting error recognition and recovery holds that the best way to fix a mistake is to prevent it from happening, while acknowledging that demanding an error-free system is unreasonable and unrealistic [4]. Designers should work to prevent common mistakes and provide contextual error information to opaque or critical tasks, while also providing clear recovery paths when errors do occur. Good error information allows users to qualify these experiences as aberrant and maintain confidence and motivation.

Supporting reading to do, study, and locate recognizes that instruction must be direct, concise, and contextual. [25] recommend designing prompts that allow users to infer missing detail, as the bulk of instruction should be mediated by interaction and context. Designers should make instructions as self-contained as possible, grouping related skills together into "chapters" with a distinct start and end.

STUDY FOCUS

When creating onboarding experiences, designers must identify which tasks and features to onboard, which design patterns to use to accomplish these goals, and how and where the onboarding fits into the rest of the application. Because onboarding task flows are inherently instructional in nature, we posit they should be grounded in insights from user research in order to substantively support situated user goals during the first session of application use.

The focus of this study is to create and validate a design method to provide further guidance to designers as they specify appropriate onboarding task flows. While the resulting method may be broadly applicable to onboarding experiences for new apps or versions of existing applications, in our validation, we focus primarily on an application type that is new to users. To evaluate our method, we will answer the following research questions:

1. What design insights can UX designers generate in guiding new users through the method?
2. What are the characteristics of "aha!" moments, as experienced by new users in the method?
3. How do design insights and the "aha!" moments inform the design of an onboarding experience?
4. How does the onboarding method facilitate the verbalization of meaning-making by new users?

METHOD

To address our study focus, we conducted a design protocol study [8], engaging 12 participants in an iterative set of design and evaluation activities in order to generate onboarding insights and design onboarding task flows for an

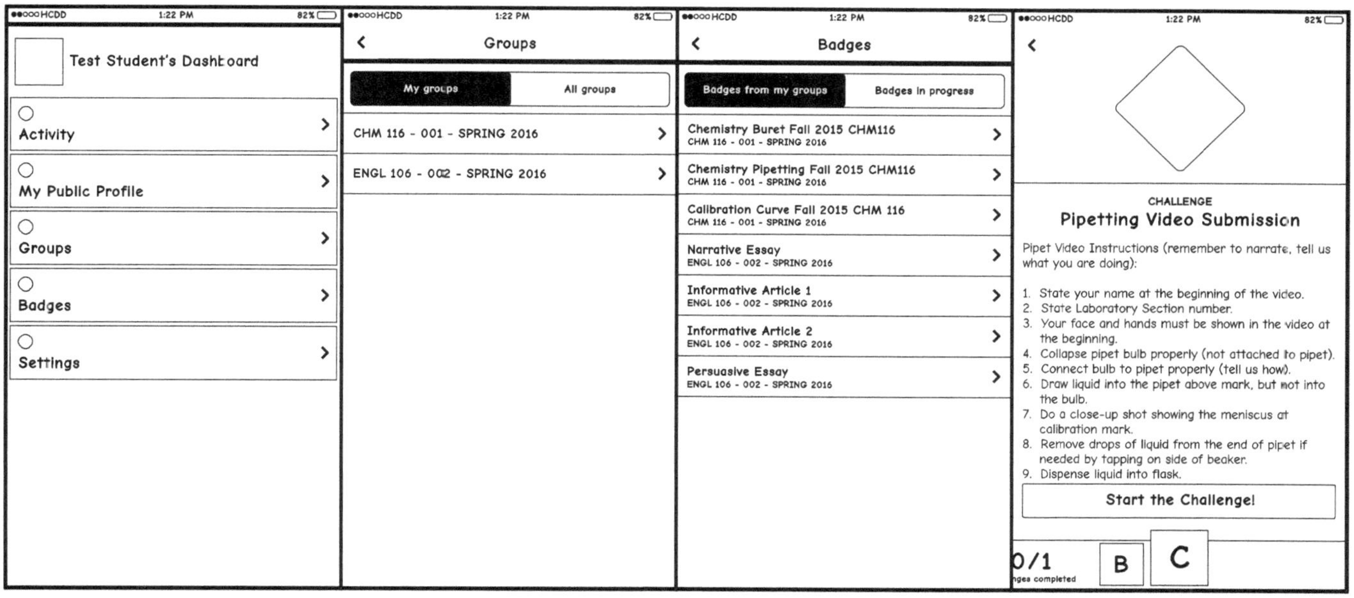

Figure 4. The main menu, groups, badges, and challenge screens from the interactive prototype.

educational badging mobile application. The app uses educator-generated badges to denote levels of competence in a topic. Badges are populated with challenges, such as quizzes, writing assignments, and video reflections, which facilitate instruction and assessment of students in an active learning setting. The lead researcher was a developer on this app, thus lending authenticity to the design task where the results guided future development [20]. Users interacted with a low-fidelity, phone-based, clickable prototype of the main screens of the application. We conducted a pilot study with six participants in order to refine the method procedure and then used the refined protocol with an additional six participants. For clarity, this paper only addresses data gathered using the refined protocol.

The researchers used minimalist instruction as a theoretical framework and generative design resource to inform the generation of onboarding insights and data collection methods. The principles and heuristics of minimalist instruction were used to guide the choice and implementation of onboarding design patterns. Data collection was structured around capturing participants' meaning-making processes, with the assumption that minimalist instruction should encourage continuous interpretation and sensemaking as users explore the space.

The method uses an iterative design (Figure 2) in keeping with minimalist instruction practice [4]. In this study, we conducted data collection and analysis sessions with three participants in order to generate onboarding design insights using a prototype with no onboarding (A). Then we made onboarding for the prototype based on the collected results from the session (B). Finally, we performed data collection and analysis with three new participants using the prototype with onboarding (C). We compared the insights generated by the two prototypes to evaluate the effect the onboarding had on the participant meaning-making process. The method was designed to support continued iterations in order to continue refining the onboarding design.

Participants

We recruited 12 participants (M=5; F=7) through email blasts to student lists, flyers, and face-to-face recruiting. All participants were undergraduate students and represented the primary user group for the badging application under study. No participants had prior experience with this application, but they displayed basic knowledge of learning management systems. Based on iterative analysis of data throughout the study period and findings from the pilot study, we found that six participants across two iterative sessions was sufficient to reach data saturation due to the richness of qualitative data we were able to collect, a key criterion for rigor in qualitative research [18]. Because the goal of the evaluation of this design method is validating pragmatic utility, our aim is not to show deep generalizability, but rather demonstrate that deep and actionable insights can be gained with relatively few participants. Additional research is needed to identify the limitations of sample size in relation to design outcomes.

Data Collection

The method protocol engaged participants in a structured set of activities, allowing consistent forms of data generation and researcher-participant interactions (Figure 3). Data collection was centered on participants' interaction with a clickable wireframe prototype, which drew inspiration from the single-person variant of the CARD method [24]. We also collected demographic information from all participants and conducted a short entry and exit interview.

Interactive Prototype

Participants were asked to interact with a prebuilt wireframe prototype, delivered as a clickable and frameless application on a smartphone (Figure 4). These interactions were captured through audio and video recording, and all generated artifacts were retained for further study (Table 1).

	Video & Audio	Card Artifacts	Survey
Prototype Interaction	●	●	
Entry & Exit Interviews	●		
Demographic Survey			●

Table 1. Sources of data collected during the protocol.

In order to engage with the participant meaning-making process, the prototype interaction was mediated using a semi-structured process to capture progression through the application. The researcher asked participants questions off of cards (Figure 5) and summarized the salient points of their answers onto the card itself, so that each card encapsulated one step in a larger meaning-making process. The first two questions on each card asked about the participant's next action and their expectation of its result, and participants were asked to perform the action after answering these two questions. The last two questions elicited the participant's perception of the result of their action as shown in the prototype and prompted them to reflect on its possible meaning in the larger application.

1. What are you going to do next?
2. What do you expect to happen?
3. How does what you see compare to your expectations?
4. How does this change your understanding of the mobile application?

Figure 5. The four questions on each card elicited participant expectations of an action and reflection on its results.

Participants were asked to explore the mobile application step-by-step through this questioning process until they notified us that they were ready to stop. Without this mediation, participants would have been more likely to proceed through the application without giving expectations and be unable to accurately remember their reactions to events during the interaction. Because these questions were asked during prototype exploration, they created a step-by-step record of the expectation and rationalization in the participant meaning-making process.

Demographic Survey and Interviews

Participants were asked to complete a demographic survey which detailed their smartphone use. These results were captured and transcribed after the protocol session. This was followed by a short interview that captured an initial summary of participant perceptions of the purpose and audience of the mobile application under study. The primary researcher read participants a short description of the mobile application, which provided information similar to a cursory look at an app store page, and asked participants a set of predefined questions which documented their perceptions of the application's purpose and intended use. At the conclusion of the participant's interaction with the prototype, we conducted a second short interview to capture how their perceptions of the mobile application had changed through prototype exploration. Questions from the entry interview were repeated; in addition, participants were asked to explain the mobile application as if they were talking to their past self at the start of the session. Both interviews were audio recorded and transcribed for further analysis.

Analysis and Onboarding Design

Analysis took place iteratively after each group of three participants completed their sessions. Each round of analysis only considered data from the current round of participants. The primary researcher first reviewed the video recordings and transcribed the interaction sections into a spreadsheet for identification and tracking of salient concepts. He then laid out the card task flow and interview responses for each participant, providing an overview of their meaning-making process. The researcher identified participants' perceptions of the main sections of the mobile application and their use, situations where the participants' understanding of the application or underlying system was challenged, and how the participants reconciled new and unexpected information with their understanding of the mobile application.

After completing analysis on the participant level, the primary researcher compared insights across participants to identify common insights, filtering out insights that were not shared by a majority of participants. Then the primary researcher identified a common "aha!" moment and quick win by comparing answers from the post mini-interviews across participants to identify perceived strengths of the experience as a whole, reviewing the prototype exploration for relevant individual experiences that resulted in expressed realization or understanding (indicating "aha!" moments) or expressed satisfaction or closure (indicating quick wins), and synthesizing the posthoc narratives and exploration experiences together into a coherent and consistent narrative of a common "aha!" moment and quick win.

Following these two levels of analysis, the insights were used to inform the design of an onboarding experience. The goal of the onboarding approach was to 1) promptly guide participants through the "aha!" moment to a quick win; and 2) help to minimize disruptions or barriers that may impede users' progress towards these goals. Relevant onboarding design patterns from practitioner sources that fit the identified insights were used.

After the creation of an onboarding experience, onboarding wireframes were added to the initial prototype. A second group of participants then used the same protocol in order to evaluate the efficacy of the onboarding experience.

The results from this group was compared to the previous group to identify how onboarding had addressed onboarding barriers and delivered on the "aha!" moment and quick win.

RESULTS

In order to provide a real-world example of how onboarding was conceptualized, created, and assessed using this method, in this section we present a selection of results across all stages of the protocol. The results presented here focus on the identification of the aha moment and quick win and the creation of onboarding directly related to those central moments.

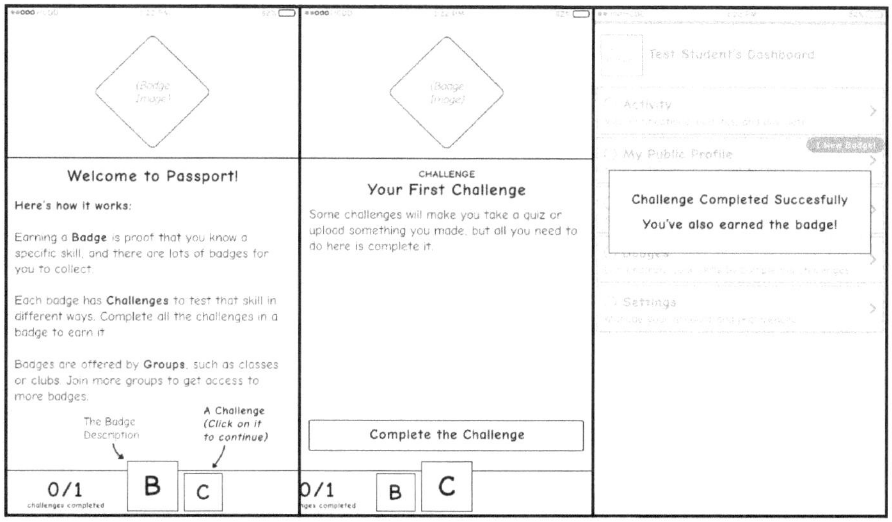

Figure 6. The "welcome" onboarding badge created using the Playthrough tutorial design pattern.

The "aha!" moment and quick win we identified were related to badges and challenges. The intended functionality of this system was for users to earn badges representing mastery of a specific subject by completing predefined learning challenges related to that badge.

RQ1: Design insights from new user interaction

The first step in analysis was to identify aspects of the participant meaning-making process shared among the majority of participants and use them to generate design insights. All three participants explored and referenced badges and the badge concept frequently during their interaction with the prototype and their post mini-interviews, which was later found to be relevant to the "aha!" moment. These frequent interactions led to the generation of five design insights, presented here along with exemplary participant quotes.

1. All three participants thought badges were achievements, functioning as a metric of accomplishment: *"*somewhat sarcastic* [Going to a badge page will] show you a star saying "Good job! You did it!" *exaggerated fist pump* ... and you got 10 extra credit points and you're not going to fail Chemistry."*
2. All three participants thought that badges were earned by completing challenges: *"It seems like when you take challenges, you'd earn the badges, and then the badges would show up on your profile."*
3. Two participants indicated that badges shouldn't function as containers for grouping challenges: *"I really like the idea of badges. I really don't like the idea that they are the completed activities themselves. ... I really like [them as a] reward system."*
4. All three participants referred to badges and challenges as activities, tests, and quizzes: *"[Maybe the app] is for you to go into the activities ... to practice for your tests and quizzes, to get better in your knowledge if you're having struggles."*
5. Two participants thought the Badge/Challenge navigation menu was unintuitive: *"*after tapping on the chemistry quiz badge screen a few times* Maybe there was supposed to be some other button to click? ... That'd be my only guess because it seems like a dead end [...]"*

These insights contributed to the onboarding design process in different ways. Insights 1 and 2 encompassed perceptions that participants used as premises for reasoning about how application systems functioned and what screens might contain. While the conclusions participants arrived at were not completely accurate, these design insights indicated what participants were able to learn about badges from the application in its barest form and what aspects of badges would need additional onboarding to be instilled. Insight 3 referenced a value judgment that participants made upon reflection, either indicating that the relationship between badges and challenges should be changed or that it should be introduced to participants earlier and more explicitly. Insight 4 highlighted a difference of vocabulary between participants, which on the surface indicates that the terminology for app systems was unclear, but could also imply that participants had different conceptions of how the badge and challenge system worked. Finally, Insight 5 indicated an area of the application where participants were unable to successfully interact with the interface, indicating that the interface should be changed if possible.

RQ2: Identifying characteristics of an "aha!" moment

We identified a shared "aha!" moment to use as a focus for onboarding design by reviewing a combination of the post mini-interviews and prototype explorations. One of the questions in the post mini-interview was designed to direct researchers toward "aha!" moments by asking participants about what they thought was their favorite part of the application. All three participants answered that their favorite part was either challenges, badges, or both, and briefly explained why they thought so. As one participant stated: *"Because the learning challenges are specific to a group or class in general, it can be a potential help... It's not as if you're going in there just to do a learning challenge, you're going in there for a purpose... and if that's a way to benefit an eventual test grade, then I don't see why you wouldn't do it."* This pointed to an "aha!" moment occurring while participants were interacting with the badge and challenge system. Our next step was to review those sections of the prototype exploration to identify specific "aha!" moments related to badges and challenges.

We identified each participant's "aha!" moment by reviewing all sections of prototype exploration where badges or challenges were mentioned. Upon first navigating to the main menu, all participants went to sections of the application that involved the badge and challenge system. Participant reflections quickly shifted to talking about badges and challenges as systems instead of interfaces, and they began speculating about the purpose of the systems:

"Now that I'm looking at it—it might [...] link what your professor wants and what you are supposed to [do]. I see Collaborative Curve Quiz here for [a chemistry course], so maybe the professor can upload quizzes for you to take on your phone. Or maybe it's just [...] for quizzes and tests and activities [...]. It might be for in-class activities, too, so the professor might be like, 'Everybody pull up your phone, go to [the app...] do this activity in class'."

Participants also began speaking in a more animated manner, connecting the value of the badge and challenge system to their lived experiences: *"...[if I were practicing for freshman math] I would have gotten a badge for it, which would have helped me through my emotional turmoil."* The combination of the abrupt integrative shift in the perception of badges and challenges and the reflection on the system's personal utility indicated that these instances were "aha!" moments.

We then reviewed the post mini-interview responses once more in order to reinterpret them in light of these specific participant experiences and synthesize them into one shared "aha!" moment for use in onboarding design. In considering which parts of the application were most meaningful to them, Participant A was most interested in earning badges and Participant C was most interested in completing quizzes, but Participant B bridged the two by connecting completing challenges and earning badges together as parts of a process. Their specific experiences during prototype exploration supported the common thread in their posthoc narratives that working to earn badges has intrinsic value while also benefiting extrinsic goals, like improving course outcomes. Therefore, we identified that the shared "aha!" moment took place when participants internalized the process of completing challenges to earn badges and thereby succeed in their courses.

RQ3: Using the design insights and "aha!" moment to inform the onboarding experience

Once we identified our shared "aha!" moment, we began designing an onboarding task flow to guide participants to that moment and reify some of its benefits in a quick win. Our design for the quick win was inspired by participant B theorizing that *"If you joined a class you [might get] a welcome badge."* We used the Playthrough onboarding pattern to create an introductory badge that would facilitate early engagement and encourage interaction with the system (Figure 6). The design leveraged the insights that badges were achievements and were earned by completing challenges by introducing those concepts to new users in their authentic task domain, in keeping with minimalist instruction principles.

The badge description framed the essential information about groups, badges, and challenges for a new user. The challenge screen was intended to guide new users through the process of completing a challenge, reinforcing the badge earning process before users arrive at the main menu. Upon completing the challenge, users were shown an overlay saying that they earned their first badge and were taken to the main menu. This part of the onboarding design integrated all four minimalist instruction principles.

RQ4: Impact of onboarding on users' meaning-making

The final step in analysis was to generate design insights from shared aspects of the participant meaning-making process during the session using the prototype with onboarding and compare them to the insights from the previous session, which used a prototype without onboarding. Participants once again referenced badges frequently, and we generated three design insights from their interaction with the onboarding badge and five relating to badges in general.

1. All three participants thought the onboarding badge was a tutor: *"This is an introduction screen that tells you the basics behind the purpose of the mobile application. It's basically... a guide."*
2. All three participants identified that you earned badges: *"[I learned] that you have these challenges. So it's basically testing your knowledge on each of these tasks and testing you if you have mastery of them."*
3. One participant connected the onboarding badge to later badges and challenges. This is significant because it explicitly validated one of our intentions for the onboarding badge: *"[This screen] has the same layout on the bottom as the original challenge, so it's taken me to another challenge."*
4. All three participants thought that badges were collectible: *"[Tapping on the badge] will show a list of what you should do to collect the badge."*

5. All three participants connected badges with challenges: *"It will show a list of what you should do to collect the badge."*
6. All three participants expected the Badges screen would contain a list of badges: *"[Badges would contain] the listing of badges."*
7. All three participants connected the Badges screen with showing homework: *"I think it's like a list of more... *pauses and raises eyebrows* homework to complete. ... [Tapping one] will show a list of what you should do to collect the badge."*
8. All three participants thought that challenges test your knowledge and mastery of skills. They talked about quizzes, activities, homework, and assignments as types of challenges: *"Okay. It's a description up top and then a video submission, so I guess you complete the challenge that way. You submit whatever assignment or whatever it is into the mobile application and then I guess you're finished with the quiz."*

Our assessment was that the onboarding improved the perception of badges and challenges. Unlike with the initial prototype, all participants learned the main features of badges and challenges and connected them together without issue. Participants also demonstrated good knowledge of the Badges section.

DISCUSSION

We have presented our method and explored its value for identifying insights that may lead to effective scaffolding of the user's journey through onboarding. In this section, we synthesize and discuss opportunities to connect learning and instructional theory to the design of onboarding experiences, describing implications of this cross-pollination of theoretical constructs for HCI practice.

Minimalist Instruction as an Onboarding Framework

Our review of onboarding best practices resulted in the identification of a nascent area of UX practice. While practitioner efforts towards the generation of onboarding design patterns have been useful and generative in contrast to the relative vacuum of scholarly guidance, these practitioner-led approaches have frequently lacked the guidance of instructional design and learning theory to engage with onboarding design—problematic in a process that is inherently about learning.

Our experience in developing and validating a method to identify design insights to guide onboarding design indicates that minimalist instruction may be an extremely valuable and relevant tool in building an onboarding framework vocabulary, both for practitioners and for the HCI community. Using minimalist instruction as an analytic and design framework shaped how we approached our research goal by situating onboarding as part of a new user's meaning-making or interpretive process. Findings from our method underscored the importance of engaging users in interaction with a prototype of the actual application in order for meaning to be co-constructed similarly to how it would be with a finished application. In this sense, we concur with existing co-design and participatory approaches [e.g., 21,22], which could be extended in future iterations of the onboarding method.

The principles and heuristics of minimalist instruction provide a language that foregrounds learning processes when critiquing and comparing onboarding task flow alternatives. Viewing existing onboarding design patterns through the lens of minimalist instructional principles and heuristics illuminates their relative strengths and weaknesses and provides guidance on how designers might productively address learning gaps or misconceptions. For example, the deferred account creation pattern serves a structural purpose, allowing new users to explore a portion of an application's content without needing to create an account. Viewing the pattern through the lens of minimalist instruction reveals that the pattern is not focused on the content of the instruction, and thus should be paired with other onboarding design patterns that focus on presenting content. Using minimalist instructional principles and heuristics as a common language for critiquing and comparing onboarding design patterns fills a gap in practitioner onboarding design knowledge, providing useful and pedagogically-sound alternatives to the current standard of inferential and largely incomparable tips and tricks.

Carroll's principles and heuristics may also inform data analysis resulting from user interactions when reframed as questions to be answered about the onboarding experience. For example, if onboarding is intended to respect the integrity of the user's activity, what tasks were the users trying to perform and where did those tasks conflict with the intentions of the application systems? As another example, if onboarding is supposed to provide enclosed, self-contained sections, where did users draw on prior or outside knowledge, especially in unintended ways? In this way, the principles and heuristics function as a lens to examine the application as users perceived it. This lowers a possible barrier to practitioner design research and provides opportunities for further investigation by the HCI community into refining, extending, and codifying useful avenues of inquiry for onboarding design research.

The results of this study indicate that even a low-fidelity prototype can elicit many meaningful and useful insights for onboarding design, consistent with prior research and conventional design wisdom regarding low-fidelity prototypes. We were able to readily identify insights about *participant behavior*, such as when participants consistently visited the Activity section first from the main menu; insights about *perception*, such as that participants all initially thought that Groups contained social aspects and tried to persist that belief even in the face of contradictory evidence; and insights into *participant mental models*, such as identifying that participants used their current class experiences as a proxy mental model for groups, badges, and challenges in the app through their use of words like "class," "assignment," and "quiz." These results demonstrate the value of combining minimalist instruction with design insights generated from user interaction.

The "Aha!" Moment as a Threshold Concept

Identifying an "aha!" moment to convert into a quick win is a central part of the analysis procedure of this method, and appeared to be a key conceptual framing of the practitioner guidance. This term is not found in existing research literature, yet we believe it has great value for understanding the initial stages of the learning process as experienced by new users. One possible conceptual analog in the educational literature is the *threshold concept*. Meyer and Land [16] describe threshold concepts as "a transformed way of understanding, or interpreting, or viewing something without which the learner cannot progress." Threshold concepts have five defining characteristics, including the following: 1) transformative, marking a radical shift in the learner's perspective; 2) irreversible, in that the new knowledge cannot easily be unlearned, if at all; 3) integrative, creating previously unknown connections between concepts; 4) bounded to a specific conceptual area; and 5) troublesome until understood [16]. The "aha!" moment appears to take on many of these characteristics, in that it represents a transformative, irreversible shift in the user's perception of an application, integrating previously arbitrary facts and features into a mental model that is newly situated towards personal and purposeful use. The troublesome aspect resolved by the moment includes a recognition from the educational literature that facts and features of the application are inert or disconnected knowledge until integrated into a coherent mental construct [16]. This is consistent with previous understandings by HCI and cognitive science scholars, which positioned the user's mental model in relation to the system model; however, the educational literature provides additional grounding to describe what defines users' transition from disconnected to "aha!," in addition to guidance on how to scaffold these learned behaviors (e.g., minimalist instruction).

IMPLICATIONS AND FUTURE WORK

While this study is limited in impact due to the small number of participants and specific prototype used, our results strongly suggest the value of leveraging user experiences and instructional theory in the design of onboarding task flows.

Extending the Onboarding Method

In future studies, differing contexts of use and user groups may indicate additional areas where minimalist instruction or a revised protocol may support the generation of onboarding insights. This may also productively include applications that serve multiple user types, where issues of how to prioritize among conflicting groups may arise. This would require sufficient specialization of the onboarding for each persona to complete a meaningful quick win. Additionally, while this study did achieve data saturation, we do recommend that groups of 4-5 participants be used in the future, in order to make the delineation between common insights and edge cases clearer. Finally, in this study we conducted the protocol with a low-fidelity clickable wireframe prototype of the app. Performing additional studies with different types of mobile applications, different types of prototypes, and different levels of fidelity would further validate the method.

Integrating Instructional Design in HCI Scholarship and Practice

This work opens up questions for further investigation of the "aha!" moment. While the work of Carroll and others in the 1980s and 1990s—bridging instructional theory and HCI—appears to have continuing value, further connections among learning and instructional theory and HCI methods and practices would likely be beneficial to future design practice. While this may open many disparate threads of integrative, multi-disciplinary research, we will propose a few opportunities for future work specific to onboarding. The presence of the learning jump, articulated as the passing of a learning threshold, indicates a potentially fruitful area for deeper investigation. This may include the identification of salient learning- and interaction-mediating characteristics, and the opportunities to refine and extend instructional design theory and existing HCI methods to effectively design for these thresholds in onboarding and other types of instruction.

Our analysis and protocol also provides significant contributions to instructional design scholarship by connecting it to onboarding and the practical concerns of interface design in a mobile context. Some researchers, such as Carroll, have explored learning outside of traditional educational areas, but more work is needed in applying instructional design theory outside of the classroom and traditional learning contexts. This study reveals numerous opportunities for instructional design and HCI scholars to align theory and knowledge bases with onboarding-focused practitioners, thereby advancing scholarship in research and practice.

CONCLUSION

In this paper, we have presented a method for designing and validating mobile onboarding task flows, building on minimalist instructional design principles and existing practitioner guidance. We found that focusing on the evolution of participant sensitivity to elements of the application allowed for the collection of useful insights for onboarding content, placement, and form. Using minimalist instruction as a lens for designing onboarding provided a helpful and validated set of user-centered instructional design principles. This study contributes a research-informed design method that can be leveraged in the creation of onboarding experiences by design practitioners, leading to generative insights.

REFERENCES

1. Maria Bannert. 2000. The effects of training wheels and self-learning materials in software training.

Journal of Computer Assisted Learning 16, 4: 336-346. http://doi.org/10.1046/j.1365-2729.2000.00146.x

2. Susanne Bødker and Marianne Graves Petersen. 2000. Design for learning in use. *Scandinavian Journal of Information Systems 12*, 1: Article 5.
3. Marina Cascaes Cardoso. 2017. The Onboarding Effect: Leveraging User Engagement and Retention in Crowdsourcing Platforms. In *Proceedings of the 2017 CHI Conference Extended Abstracts on Human Factors in Computing Systems* (CHI EA '17). ACM, New York, NY, USA, 263-267. DOI: https://doi.org/10.1145/3027063.3027128
4. John M. Carroll. 1990. *The Nurnberg Funnel: Designing minimalist instruction for practical computer skill*. MIT Press, Cambridge, MA.
5. John M. Carroll. 2014. Creating minimalist instruction. *International Journal of Design for Learning* 5, 2: 56–65. https://doi.org/10.14434/ijdl.v5i2.12887
6. John M. Carroll and Caroline Carrithers. 1984. Training wheels in a user interface. *Communications of the ACM* 27, 8: 800-806. DOI: https://doi.org/10.1145/358198.358218
7. C. Ailie Fraser, Mira Dontcheva, Holger Winnemoeller, and Scott Klemmer. 2016. DiscoverySpace: Crowdsourced Suggestions Onboard Novices in Complex Software. In *Proceedings of the 19th ACM Conference on Computer Supported Cooperative Work and Social Computing Companion* (CSCW '16 Companion). ACM, New York, NY, USA, 29-32. DOI: https://doi.org/10.1145/2818052.2874317
8. John S. Gero and Thomas Mc Neill. 1998. An approach to the analysis of design protocols. *Design studies* 19, 1: 21-61. https://doi.org/10.1016/S0142-694X(97)00015-X
9. Kathy Haramundanis. 2001. Learnability in information design. In *Proceedings of the 19th annual international conference on Computer documentation*, 7-11. DOI: http://doi.org/10.1145/501516.501519
10. Samuel Hulick. The elements of user onboarding. Retrieved from https://www.useronboard.com/training/
11. Krystal Higgins. 2016. *Evaluating onboarding experiences*. Retrieved September 19, 2016 from http://www.kryshiggins.com/evaluating-your-new-user-experience/
12. Krystal Higgins. 2015. *Engaging new users: Guided interaction*. Retrieved November 3, 2015 from http://www.kryshiggins.com/guided-interaction/
13. Detlev Leutner. 2000. Double-fading support—a training approach to complex software systems. *Journal of computer assisted learning* 16, 4: 347-357. DOI: http://doi.org/10.1046/j.1365-2729.2000.00147.x
14. Mark Lochrie, Glenn Matthys, Adrian Gradinar, Andy Dickinson, Onno Baudouin, and Paul Egglestone. 2016. Co-designing a physical to digital experience for an onboarding and blended learning platform. In *Proceedings of the The 15th International Conference on Interaction Design and Children* (IDC '16). ACM, New York, NY, USA, 660-665. DOI: https://doi.org/10.1145/2930674.2936002
15. Ty Magnin. 2016. *We categorized 327 user onboarding experiences into 9 UI patterns (Find out which you should use)*. Retrieved from http://www.appcues.com/blog/we-categorized-327-user-onboarding-experiences-into-9-ui-patterns/
16. Jan H. F. Meyer and Ray Land. 2003. Threshold concepts and troublesome knowledge (2): Epistemological considerations and a conceptual framework for teaching and learning. In *Improving Student Learning Theory and Practice: 10 Years On*, Chris Rust (ed). Oxford Centre for Staff & Learning Development, Oxford, UK, 412-424.
17. Jakob Nielsen and Raluca Budiu. 2013. *Mobile usability*. New Riders Press, San Francisco, CA.
18. Benjamin Saunders, Julius Sim, Tom Kingstone, Shula Baker, Jackie Waterfield, Bernadette Bartlam, Heather Burroughs, and Clare Jinks. 2017. Saturation in qualitative research: exploring its conceptualization and operationalization. *Quality & Quantity: International Journal of Methodology*. DOI: http://doi.org/10.1007/s11135-017-0574-8
19. Justin Singer. 2011. *Onboarding: The first, best chance to make a repeat customer*. Retrieved November 3, 2015 from http://justin-singer.com/post/2684064738/onboarding-the-first-best-chance-to-make-a
20. David J. Roedl and Erik Stolterman. 2013. Design research at CHI and its applicability to design practice. In *Proceedings of the SIGCHI Conference on Human Factors in Computing Systems* (CHI '13). ACM, New York, NY, USA, 1951-1954. DOI: https://doi.org/10.1145/2470654.2466257
21. Elizabeth B.-N. Sanders and Pieter J. Stappers. 2008. Co-creation and the new landscapes of design. *Co-design* 4, 1: 5-18.
22. Elizabeth B.-N. Sanders and Pieter J. Stappers. 2014. Probes, toolkits and prototypes: Three approaches to making in codesigning. *CoDesign 10,* 1: 5-14.
23. Igor Steinmacher, Tayana Uchoa Conte, Christoph Treude, and Marco Aurélio Gerosa. 2016. Overcoming open source project entry barriers with a portal for newcomers. In *Proceedings of the 38th International Conference on Software Engineering* (ICSE '16). ACM, New York, NY, USA, 273-284. DOI: https://doi.org/10.1145/2884781.2884806

24. Leslie Gayle Tudor, Michael J Muller, Tom Dayton, and Robert W Root. 1993. A participatory design technique for high-level task analysis, critique, and redesign: The CARD method. In *Proceedings of the Human Factors and Ergonomics Society Annual Meeting*, 295–299.

25. Hans van der Meij and John M. Carroll. 1995. Principles and heuristics for designing minimalist instruction. *Technical communication 42*, 2: 243–261.

26. Falko Weigert Petersen, Line Ebdrup Thomsen, Pejman Mirza-Babaei, and Anders Drachen. 2017. Evaluating the Onboarding Phase of Free-toPlay Mobile Games: A Mixed-Method Approach. In *Proceedings of the Annual Symposium on Computer-Human Interaction in Play* (CHI PLAY '17). ACM, New York, NY, USA, 377-388. DOI: https://doi.org/10.1145/3116595.3125499

27. Mun Y. Yi and Fred D. Davis. 2003. Developing and validating an observational learning model of computer software training and skill acquisition. *Information Systems Research* 14, 2: 146-169. DOI: http://doi.org/10.1287/isre.14.2.146.16016

How Do Sketching and Non-Sketching Actions Convey Design Intent?

Senthil Chandrasegaran
College of Engineering
University of California, Davis
schandrasegaran@ucdavis.edu

Devarajan Ramanujan
Department of Engineering
Aarhus University, Denmark
devr@eng.au.dk

Niklas Elmqvist
College of Information Studies
Department of Computer Science
University of Maryland, College Park
elm@umd.edu

Figure 1. Designers use more than sketches and annotations to express intent. Our observational study revealed three main ways (along with speech) in which designers express intent: (a) on-the-surface "pointing" actions to indicate parts of a design, (b) above-the-surface gestures with fingers or pencils to show movement, shape, or area, and (c) away-from-the-surface gestures, using their hands or other objects as proxies for components or assemblies.

ABSTRACT
Sketches are much more than marks on paper; they play a key role for designers both in ideation and problem-solving as well as in communication with other designers. Thus, the act of sketching is often enriched with annotations, references, and physical actions, such as gestures or speech—all of which constitute meta-data about the designer's reasoning. Conventional paper-based design notebooks cannot capture this rich meta-data, but digital design notebooks can. To understand what data to capture, we conducted an observational study of design practitioners where they individually explore design solutions for a set of problems. We identified sketching and non-sketching actions that reflect their exploration of the design space. We then categorized the captured meta-data and mapped observed physical actions to design intent. These findings inform the creation of future digital design notebooks that can better capture designers' reasoning during sketching.

Author Keywords
Sketching; ideation; observational study.

ACM Classification Keywords
H.5.2 Information Interfaces and Presentation: User Interfaces—*Interaction styles*

DIS '18, June 9–13, 2018, , Hong Kong

 ISBN 978-1-4503-5198-0/18/06. . . $15.00
DOI: https://doi.org/10.1145/3196709.3196723

INTRODUCTION
Design is not just a mental process for the designer: it also involves physical actions, such as drawing depictions on paper, making movements of a pencil or hands without creating physical depictions, and looking at existing depictions to interpret them [38]. These physical actions give insight into the designer's thought process, and help other collaborators (and sometimes the designers themselves) understand the rationale behind their decisions. The design notebook is typically the designer's medium of choice for recording ideas. However, paper notebooks can only capture actions that mark the paper, i.e. the depictions themselves. With the recent proliferation of handheld computing devices, there is a rising trend in digital applications to replace the design notebook, but these tend to still mostly emulate paper without fully transcending the medium to also capture the rationale behind the pen marks.

Hand-held personal computing devices such as smartphones and tablets are typically used as digital design notebooks by using their touch screen as a proxy for paper, along with the user's finger, a capacitive touch pen, or a dedicated stylus as a substitute for a pencil. However, these devices are capable of much more than capturing depictions on "paper." Studies of design processes have shown that the act of design ideation is multimodal in nature: designers *sketch* on paper, *point* to or *gesture* over parts of their sketch, and *speak* to describe their ideas, raise questions, and evaluate ideas. Capture of designers' actions has typically involved using overhead cameras that can record the sketches as well as the designers' movements, which requires cumbersome equipment. When considering digital interfaces to capture these modes of interaction, studies have suggested that encouraging and capturing speech while sketching was useful as it kept visual attention on the sketch, at the same time allowing the designer to convey useful information [14]. Recent developments in personal computing devices have made speech-based interfaces commonplace thanks to digital voice assistants such as Alexa, Cortana, and Siri. Additionally, research directions in HCI have explored the combination of touch and in-air gestures on hand-held devices [9], the use of above-the-surface sensing to anticipate user interactions [21], and the use of 3D input with a custom stylus that enables spatial interactions around a device [46]. Still, these novel technologies have yet to be employed for capturing meta-data and design rationale. Part of the reason for this gap in the literature may be that it is still not clear *which* meta-data to capture, and *how* to present it back to the designer to best support the creative process.

In order to exploit the growing sensory capabilities of hand-held devices in ways that aid the design process, one needs to first understand designers' actions and underlying intents. In this paper, we address this need by conducting an observational study of 6 experienced practitioners engaged in design ideation tasks. We focus on individual designers rather than teams, as we are interested in what actions of designers can be used to *store* their ideas. Participants followed a think-aloud protocol, exploring solutions to a given design problem using a traditional pen-and-paper medium. We video and audio-recorded the participants, and qualitatively coded all occurrences of physical actions: actions that produced marks on paper (such as sketching and annotating), as well as actions that did not (such as pointing and gesturing). We also coded all occurrences of the designer's *intent*, which referred to what the designer was trying to do: searching for solutions, describing a design solution, or analyzing a design. By identifying co-occurrences between the designer's intent and the physical actions, we determine the actions designers use to express their intent. Based on this intent-to-action mapping, and based on our observations from the study, we then formulate a set of implications for those seeking to create the next generation of digital design notebooks that offer rich interaction modalities.

The contributions of this paper are: (1) a review of research in design methods and digital support for design to identify potential research areas to capture and record designers' intent, (2) a map of designers' actions to designers' intent based on observational studies conducted with design practitioners, and (3) a set of implications for HCI designers and engineers for capturing designers' intent.

BACKGROUND

Donald Schön, in his paper on the challenges of computer support for design knowledge capture [33], states, "The designer designs not only with the mind, but with the body and senses, a fact that poses an interesting challenge to computers." Yet, studies of designers' behavior has largely focused on uncovering their cognitive actions. While there are a few bodies of work that also emphasize designers' physical behavior, the typical focus is on design methods, and not on digital support. Research on multimodal interactions for design has highlighted the importance of using speech and actions along with sketches, but typically use video and audio to capture these actions. The recent developments in non-traditional interaction techniques that include tangible, haptic, verbal, and even full-body interactions, have created an opportunity to provide computational support for designers by capturing their intent and rationale through their actions, speech, and sketches. In this section, we review work in the fields of design research, HCI support for ideation, and research on multimodal interactions for design.

Sketching in Design Ideation

Sketching during design ideation typically involves quickly drawn, loosely structured visual representations concerned with broad features rather than detail [27]. Sketches serve as an extension to working memory, reducing the burden of storing and simultaneously operating on content [41]. In such contexts, sketches can convey both, geometric and symbolic information about a designers' idea [28]. The role played by sketches in design ideation can be broadly classified into three themes [43], (1) "thinking sketches," that support cognitive aspects of idea generation, exploration, and evaluation, (2) "talking sketches," that serve as a means for communicating ideas, and (3) "storing sketches," that act as an external memory aid.

Understanding designers' cognitive processes has been an important focus area for previous research in this domain. An early instance of such work is Goldschmidt's [17] analysis of "study sketches"—quick-and-dirty sketches that help the designer reason their way through a design space. In this work, Goldschmidt models the design process as a dialectic process between "seeing as"—seeing figural properties in a sketch *and* "seeing that"—eliciting non-figural properties from the sketch. Studies by others [16, 34] also suggest that visual display of information through sketching allows reinterpretation, a vital component of design ideation. While these studies discuss designers' physical actions, they do so with the primary motive of mapping them back to their cognitive processes. Suwa et al. [38] extend earlier work by Suwa & Tversky [39] and create a coding scheme for representing designers' physical and non-physical actions. While their work provides insights into the types of physical actions used and relationships among them, it does not discuss means for supporting them.

Studies on design ideation indicate that, apart from sketching, designers use a diverse set of verbal and visual strategies for conveying ideas [35], such as pointing and verbal utterances [45]. Digital design notebooks have brought a renewed focus on supporting such physical actions [26], but doing so requires an understanding of both the *spatiotemporal properties* as well as the *intent* of the designer's actions.

Digital Support for Design Ideation

Sutherland's SketchPAD [37] remains the seminal work in interactive design applications, paving the way for Computer-Aided Design (CAD) systems and digital sketching interfaces. Since then, the increasing use of digital devices in design ideation has now made it possible to record and share one's voice and physical actions along with sketches. Such actions have been shown to be useful for communication, both with other designers and with one's "future self", who may refer to these sketches in the future for inspiration.

Computer support tools for creative design should thus support both individuals and teams [36]. Yet, digital support tools for ideation that goes beyond capturing sketches has typically focused on idea sharing via sketches, such as computer-mediated group ideation [10, 19], team-based approaches to sketching [30, 31, 47], and immersive environments for collaborative sketching [13, 15]. Computer support for individual exploration of design spaces has primarily focused on implementing algorithmic approaches to design, such as the Theory of Inventive Problem-Solving (TRIZ) [11], or aiding synthesis through shape grammar and analogy-based design [8].

In addition, observational studies focusing on designer's expression typically focus on the sketching activity. Studies of gestures and other forms of communication are conducted in the context of collaborative work. For instance, a study by Tang [40] on collaborative work found that hand gestures are often used to communicate significant information, and that the *process of creating drawings* conveys much more information than the drawings themselves. Similarly, an analysis of face-to-face interactions in design teams by Bekker et al. [6] reveals that designers typically use *kinetic* gestures to enact interactions between users and products, *spatial* gestures to show distances, sizes, and shapes, and finally *pointing* gestures to refer to objects/persons/places, to list items, and to contrast two entities. There are fewer instances of computer support tools that emulate a communication between a designer sketching an idea and the *same* designer interpreting that idea. This notion, called "representational talkback" has been simulated in the form of digital sketching applications that preserve the ambiguity of the sketches [22]. Thus, while studies have shown that the act of sketching and the gestures that accompany it are important, little work on digital support for design ideation focuses on understanding and capturing these forms of expression. Some instances of digital support for multimodal capture of designers' actions are listed in the following section. While most of these systems also simulate collaborative work, they highlight the importance of multimodal capture of designers' actions, and the need for a systematic mapping of actions and intent.

Multimodal Interfaces for Sketching

Multimodal interfaces for sketching have been researched for over two decades. Speech was considered a natural accompaniment to the sketching action as it occurred over an auditory channel, thus allowing visual attention to remain on the sketch [14]. Gross et al. [18] developed a system they called *the design amanuensis* that captured and associated co-occurring sketch strokes and speech to be played back together, in an imitation of how design researchers go over design protocol data. Adler et al. [3] also supported speech and sketching as a major aspect of multimodal interfaces for early design, but sought to aid collaboration by having one designer "explain" their sketches while sketching to another designer who may not be physically present, but can play back the explanation when needed. They identified "trimodal" interactions of speech, sketch, and gesture that would be necessary to communicate ideas, and suggested ways in which speech and gestures can be used to both convey additional information over the sketch, and in some instances, modify the sketch to reflect designers' intent [2]. In a later work, Adler [1] uses this approach in a multimodal interactive dialogue system (MIDOS) that takes sketching and speech inputs from the user, uses a physics simulator to interpret the sketched structure, and interactively asks the user to resolve ambiguities. Similarly, Bischel et al. [7] use speech features, specifically (spoken) descriptions of actions, to separate sketch strokes that portray structure from explanatory strokes, such as arrows indicating motion or circles that draw focus to specific parts of the sketch.

While most speech-based sketching technologies use the scenario of collaborative work to capture speech, studies have shown that such technology allows users to replay the audio from previous ideas, and develop variations, which leads to better creative outcomes [32]. The notion of a designer talking by herself or to her device may have been strange in the past, but recent proliferation in digital voice assistants such as Alexa, Siri, and Google Assistant have made the act of speaking to one's devices more commonplace. While most of the work discussed in this section uses cumbersome laboratory setups, this is no longer necessary: the smartphone and tablet, with its capacitive sensors, camera, microphone, inertial measurement unit, and other sensors is increasingly better equipped for multimodal interactions such as the ones described above. Interaction modalities that use touch, grip, and in-air gestures have been suggested for context-sensitive interactions [9, 21]. Design and HCI research is thus at a stage where the capability of sensing, understanding, and capturing a designer's intentions based on their actions and context is rapidly being realized. To this end, we intend to understand *what* a designer expresses in the act of designing, and *how* they express them, with the goal of providing a set of implications for engineers and researchers seeking to create the next generation of digital design notebooks. Our motivation behind this study is to support HCI researchers who are starting to look at around-the-device interactions [20] as part of the multimodal interaction set, which can be a less intrusive and more intuitive way to capture the designer's actions.

OBSERVATIONAL STUDY

In order to understand the way designers express their intent, we need to observe them in a real-world problem-solving scenario. Protocol analysis—qualitative analysis of a series of temporal observations—has been used to analyze such behavior [38]. Since we are looking at design problem-solving behavior, we adapted Structural Analysis [5], a systematic approach for analyzing verbal protocols that reveals the subject's problem-solving approaches and thought processes.

For this analysis, we first conducted a *observational study* using a think-aloud protocol, where the participant is given a design task, and asked to verbalize their thought process. The study was set up to mimic a digital design notebook capable of capturing voice and physical actions in real time in order to associate actions to intent. A microphone and camera (pointed at the notebook) were used to capture audio and physical interactions. The recorded video was qualitatively coded along two main categories: *designers' intent*, i.e. behaviors or utterances that reflected a specific intent pertinent to the design task, and *designers' actions*, i.e. nonverbal actions performed by the designers during the task. We focused on individual designers as opposed to a team because (a) we are interested in the reflective conversation between the designer and their sketch [4], and (b) our goal is to envision a system where individual designers can use multimodal interactions (including speech) to store their ideas.

Participants

We recruited six paid participants (3 female, 3 male, age 18–40), five of whom were Ph.D. students in mechanical engineering, and one a postdoctoral researcher in mechanical engineering with a design major. One participant was left-handed, and all participants had normal or corrected-to-normal vision. We chose experienced participants for this study to lend higher ecological validity to the identified behaviors. Experienced participants would also show lower variability and thus even 6 participants can provide reliable data.

Tasks

Participants were given one of two design tasks:

T1 Design a bicycle rear suspension such that the horizontal distance between the front and the rear wheels does not vary when the suspension is engaged.

T2 Design a coffee container that allows astronauts to drink hot coffee safely under zero(micro)-gravity conditions.

The two tasks were chosen to observe how designers approach a problem from a familiar domain, and one from an unfamiliar domain. We were also interested in learning if there is a difference in designers' actions when designing in varied domains. T1 was adapted from a case study by Ullman [42], and focused on mechanical design, a domain familiar to the participants, yet challenging enough to require iteration. T2 was chosen to take participants outside their comfort zone with a non-traditional mechanical design problem. The task lasted 20 minutes, during which the participant generated solutions for the given design problem. We asked participants to generate a minimum of three concepts for a given design task, to push their exploration beyond common solutions [25].

Searching for existing designs also forms a primary component of the design process. However, in order to keep the study focused on the act of designing, we discouraged participants from searching for existing designs at the very beginning. However, if they felt they were stuck, or were unclear about the appearance of a component or mechanism, we allowed them to use online search for reference. We also asked participants to follow up their sketching with explanations of their designs (~5 mins). This paper focuses on understanding the designer's thought process *during design* and not on the designs themselves. We therefore decided not to code the final explanations. However, we did use their gestures during the explanations to verify they were a subset of the gestures they made while designing.

Conditions & Equipment

All participants were remotely located, and the tasks were thus conducted via a videoconferencing setup. Participants used webcams pointing down toward their table, to stream their design activity. For the task itself, all participants used white U.S. letter paper (8.5in × 11in), with pencils, erasers, and markers for sketching. They were audio and video recorded at the researcher's end, and all sketches created by participants were scanned and retained for the study.

Analysis

In order to identify categories of designers' actions and verbalizations that describe designers' intent, we coded the video recording of the design tasks. The six resulting videos were coded by two of the authors of this paper, with an overlap of one video (~17%) between them. To do this, one coder initially created a set of memos for one design task, identifying a set of actions and intent categories. Both coders discussed each category to finalize a codebook. The final set of codes used, their descriptions, and samples from the data are provided in Table 1. Both coders then independently coded the same video. Using five-second windows to compare codes, they reached an agreement Cohen's kappa ( ) of 0.83, $p < 0.001$. A sample set of codes (by one coder) for a ten-minute segment of one participant's video is shown in Fig. 2.

In order to identify the actions that accompany a particular intent, we created a coding co-occurrence matrix between the codes categorized under "designer intent" and those under "designer action". For the scope of this study, our interest lies primarily in understanding how different designers may express similar intents. Each cell of our co-occurrence matrix (Table 2) thus reflects the number of participants observed using an action to reflect an intent, rather than the number of co-occurrences coded across participants.

RESULTS & DISCUSSION

The results from the protocol analysis exhibit distinct as well as common actions across designers. We discuss the results from our analysis from two perspectives:

- ***Diversity of Actions:*** First, our analysis focuses on identifying the *diversity* in physical actions used to convey design intent. This provides an understanding of the kinds of interactions that future digital design notebooks need to support.
- ***Intent Expressed:*** Next, we discuss the use of physical actions during different cognitive episodes (periods of designer behavior that reflect an intent). Understanding such co-occurrences can enable identification of design intent through combinations of utterances, marks on paper and gestures. This in turn can provide vital insights for creating systems that can capture designers' physical actions without intrusion into their cognitive episodes, such as synthesizing a solution or analyzing a design.

Diversity of Physical Actions

To understand the diversity in physical actions used we explore diversity in (1) physical realization and (2) representation. Both these facets provide vital insights to researchers interested in supporting such physical actions through HCI interfaces. Diversity in physical realization is discussed in Table 3. In this table, we map distinct physical actions to the intent we observed when designers performed these physical

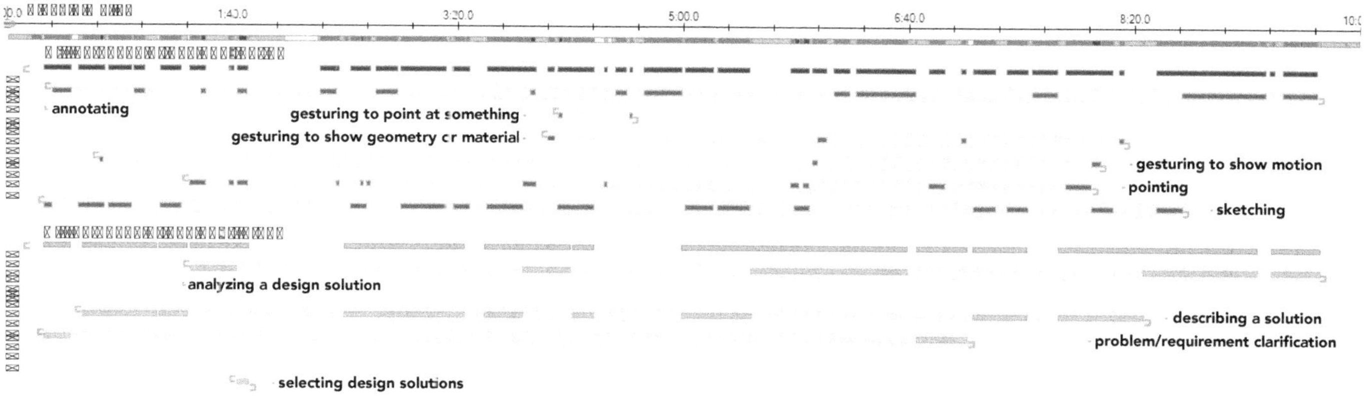

Figure 2. Screen capture of a ten-minute coded segment of one participant video, showing all instances of designer actions (blue) and designer intent (orange). Designer actions such as pointing and gesturing are discrete events that mostly co-occur with, or closely precede/succeed sketching and annotating actions. Coding designer intent based on verbalizations and context helps understand the purpose behind these actions.

Coding Category	Description	Coded Examples
Designer Intent		
Problem or requirement clarification	Participant expresses their understanding of the design requirements	*"That means somehow we need to attach this wheel with a suspension system that only moves in this direction"* (gestures)
Searching for solutions	Participant searches externally (online/books) for solutions to the design problem	*"I'm searching for"* (types on computer as he speaks) *"straight... line... mechanism..., and the first one that comes up is actually different than what I had seen before."*
Describing a solution	The participant describes a solution to the design problem as they are thinking through the solution	*"It should have a temperature sensor in here... "* (starts sketching) *"so this one shows the — whether the — how hot the cup is..."*
Analyzing a design solution	Participant analyzes a solution to find advantages, shortcomings, or limitations.	*"We could do a... Hamster bottle, um,"* (starts sketching) *"so it will... oh, but there's zero gravity. So that won't work."*
Selecting design solutions	Participant selects potential solutions from a set of candidates they have generated.	*"So, at least one is this,* (draws arrow to point at a concept) *another is this... "* (draws arrow to point at another concept)
Describing a hypothetical design scenario	Participant discusses a hypothetical scenario in which s/he is solving the given design problem	*"I'll need to go back and ask the customer"* (writes note on sketch) *"if this is okay."*
Designer Action		
Sketching	Participant makes a mark on the paper that represents form, geometry, locations, or lines of action.	*"It also... "* (sketches as he talks) *"is connected... "* (keeps sketching) *"to another piece from the main chassis... "*
Annotating	Participant makes marks such as text, numbers, and symbols.	*"... it will continue to go through these small, thin, tubules"* (writes 'tubules' and draws an arrow indicating part of sketch)
Pointing	Participant points to one or more parts of the sketch or specific artifact with one or more fingers(s), pencil(s), and/or other objects.	*"The system between the axle"* (points with right index finger to axle on sketch) *"and the pedals"* (points with left index finger to pedals) *"is the same length... "*
Gesturing to point	Participant indicates a part of a sketch or artifact, but uses a non-static gesture to point.	*"... and that's going to make this mechanism"* (makes circular gesture over the mechanism) *"pretty small, most likely."*
Gesturing to show geometry or material	Participant makes a gesture with hand(s) and/or pencil(s) to show shape, orientation, distance, or material.	*"... and then this hydraulic system kind of working to maintain this distance (makes back-and-forth movement with pen) here... "*
Gesturing to show motion	Participant makes a gesture with hand(s) and/or pencil(s) to show movement of a component or assembly.	*"This will give us our full vertical deformation"* (makes oscillatory motion with pencil over corresponding part of sketch)

Table 1. Coding categories, descriptions, and examples

actions. We also further classify each action into "marking" and "non-marking" actions, based on whether the pencil makes a mark on the paper while performing an action.

The significance of the table is apparent when studying the variety of sketches drawn by participants (Fig. 3). Some sketches are heavily annotated, while others are not annotated at all. Similarly, some sketches show a high-fidelity representation of the concept, while others show the concept as an abstract,

Designer Intent	Sketching	Annotating	Pointing	Gesturing to point	Gesturing to show geometry/material	Gesturing to show motion
Problem/requirement clarification	4	2	3	1	3	1
Searching for solutions	1	0	1	0	0	0
Describing a solution	6	5	6	6	5	5
Analyzing a design solution	6	3	4	4	2	2
Describing a design scenario	0	1	1	0	0	0
Selecting a design solution	0	1	1	0	0	0

Table 2. Number of participants (max: 6) that used an action (columns) to express a particular intent (rows) at least once.

formal mechanism diagram. Table 3, shows the various ways in which participants expressed their intent. The combinations of physical actions described in the table, provide an understanding of how sketching and non-sketching actions are used to convey intent in design ideation. Table 3 also highlights the extent of *marking* actions whose meanings are lost without the accompanying verbalizations, and *non-marking* actions that are lost entirely without a means to record them.

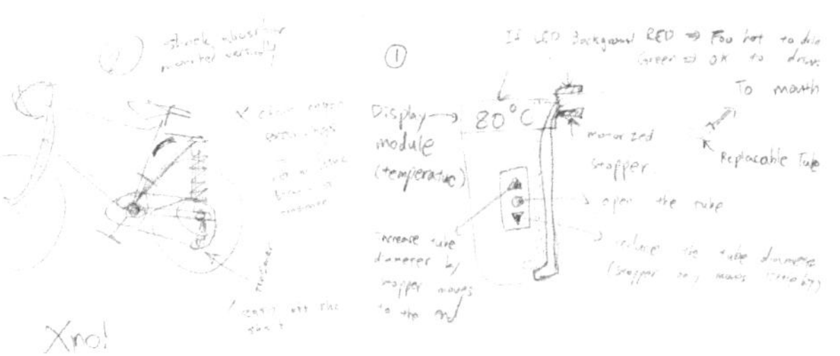

Figure 3. Sample sketches of a bike suspension (Task T1) and a microgravity coffee container (Task T2). The sketches show the variety of abstraction in the sketches, and the variation in their annotations.

These sections below discuss *prevalent* as well as *unique* means used for representing each of the coded physical actions. We also highlight the challenges/opportunities they present for creating future digital design notebooks.

Sketching: True to the notion of sketching in design ideation being "quick and dirty," participants did not spend any time on beautifying their concept sketches. We also noticed that participants did not focus on the expressiveness of their strokes. Thick lines and shading were primarily used for emphasizing components that were either thin/small or contained complex geometry, such as when sketching a one-way valve in a mouthpiece, or insulation around the cups. We also noticed that designers used "datum features" (ground, center lines) to reference the spatial location of sketch components. Such features can provide vital clues for inferring implicit intent including relational attributes among sketch components (e.g. A is contained by B), symmetry, and trajectories.

We noticed two kinds of erasing actions for editing marks on the paper: (1) corrections made when the mark was significantly different from what was intended, and (2) modification of drawn geometric features when refining or adding new ideas to the sketch. The latter is particularly important as information about the evolution of ideas is lost by this physical action. This limitation is inherent to paper-based design notebooks. Recent digital design frameworks such as skWiki [47] partly address this issue by storing sketch histories through explicit user interactions. Capturing and representing metadata associated with these actions of erasing and editing can further capture the rationale behind these changes.

Annotating: We also noticed that text annotations were primarily used for explaining mechanisms and interface elements (such as buttons). Thus, they act as a "user manual" that helps resolve ambiguities when such sketches are reused in the future. However, there were significant differences in the usage of sketch annotations between participants. P1 had the highest code coverage for annotation at 29% (percentage of overall task time spent annotating), while P5 had the lowest (3%). This represents the total time spent annotating, not the number of instances of annotation observed.

We also observed some variations in the nature and manner of the annotations made. There were instances of "floating annotations," which were not in physical proximity of, or linked to sketch elements. There were also instances of "crossed annotating," or annotations spaced temporally, in which designers paused while annotating one part of a sketch to draw an arrow to a previous annotation. Without observing the designers actually creating these annotations, it would be difficult to unambiguously resolve the information they represent. Other variations in annotating included directional inconsistencies where annotation arrows sometimes pointed at the sketch, and sometimes at the text, and finally occluding annotations that were made on top of sketch elements (see Table 3).

Pointing: Pointing was the second most common action observed, following sketching. This makes sense, given the think-aloud nature of the study: participants would often talk about their sketch and point to components and assemblies to explain what they are doing. The most common mode of behavior observed for pointing was using the pencil or the finger of either hand (see Table 3). We also observed participants using a combination of pencil and a finger, or two fingers, for pointing at two or more portions in the sketch, often to indicate relative positions of components. Sometimes, pointing was also done by creating marks on the paper, such as arrows (without annotations), or marking over a spot on the sketch, typically to refer to a point, axis, or center. An interesting behavior we observed was designers pointing to items that do not exist in the sketch, but are important considerations for the overall idea (e.g. amount of coffee in the cup). In such instances, verbal utterances are the only sources of information that tell us about the object to which the designer refers.

The duration of pointing varied significantly between occurrences as well as participants: the pointing action that lasted the shortest (0.4 sec) occurred when a participant (P1) pointed

Observed Action	Observed Intent	Type	Spatial Classification		
			On the Surface	Over the Surface	Away from the Surface
Sketching					
Marking strokes with variable line thickness	Emphasizing parts of sketch	Marking	✓	–	–
Marking strokes to create datum features	Establishing spatial relationships among components in sketch	Marking	✓	–	–
Editing strokes	Refining ideas represented in sketches	Marking	✓	–	–
Annotating					
Text annotations	Resolve ambiguities in sketch for future reuse	Marking	✓	–	–
Floating annotations	Linking ideas to non-sketched elements	Marking	✓	–	–
Crossed annotations	Refer to previous annotations in sketch	Marking	✓	–	–
Occluding annotations	Clarify components of the sketch using annotations on top of sketch components	Marking	✓	–	–
Pointing					
Pointing to sketch with pencil	Refer to sketch and non-sketched elements	Non-marking	–	✓	–
Pointing to sketch with finger	Refer to sketch and non-sketched elements	Non-marking	✓	✓	–
Pointing to sketch with finger + pencil	Refer to sketch and non-sketched elements	Non-marking	✓	✓	–
Pointing by drawing an arrow or a dot	Refer to sketch and non-sketched elements	Marking	✓	–	–
Gesturing to Point					
Marking on the sketch	Refer to an assembly or an area	Marking	✓	–	–
Tracing over the sketch (hover)	Refer to an assembly or an area	Non-marking	–	✓	–
Hand pose & gestures based on sketched geometry	Design moves [33]	Non-marking	–	✓	–
Gesturing to describe geometry/material					
Tracing over the sketch (hover)	Refer to distance, orientation, or material	Non-marking	–	✓	–
Gesture using 2 fingers (same or different hand)	Refer to distances and orientations	Non-marking	–	✓	✓
Gesture using 1 finger and pencil	Refer to distances and orientations	Non-marking	–	✓	✓
Hand as a proxy (using a specific pose)	Proxy for a component or assembly, refer to a shape	Non-marking	–	✓	✓
Gesturing to describe motion					
Tracing over the motion trajectory using finger(s) on or over the paper	Describe a motion of a component	Non-marking	–	✓	–
Indicating the motion trajectory using pencil on or over the paper	Indicate translation, rotation, or deformation	Marking	✓	✓	–
Hand as a proxy	Show (complex) movement of components	Non-marking	–	✓	✓

Table 3. Types of coded physical actions observed for P1-P6. Intent was interpreted based on accompanying verbalizations (see Table 1).

to a component *while* he was sketching it. The pointing action that lasted the longest (11 sec) happened when another participant (P2) pointed to a component with his non-dominant hand for reference, and considered the geometrical constraints in the rest of the assembly, using the pencil in his dominant hand to point to the corresponding features. Separating the intent of such simultaneously occurring pointing actions requires access to the sketch and verbalizations at the same time.

This same participant also often pointed to earlier sketches he had made to compare and contrast features with his current design. Such pointing actions indicate that ideas in the older sketch are being used as a reference for the new sketch. If captured, such actions can provide a richer understanding of *lateral transformations* [16] in design ideation.

Gesturing to Point: There is a subtle difference between "gesturing to point" and "point", in that the intent is similar, but the object and the mechanism are different. Pointing is often a more precise and discrete act: the designer points or jabs with his finger, keeps it stationary for a short while, and moves it away. Gesturing to point, on the other hand is a less precise, and more continuous act: it occurs when referring to a more general object such as an assembly or an area, and the hand/pencil is in motion for the duration of the gesture.

Table 3 shows the various forms of gesturing-to-point observed with the participants. As with pointing, there are *marking* and *non-marking* gestures. The marking gestures take the form of drawing over an existing line, feature, or component, to refer to it. We also observed a corresponding non-marking gesture where the participant traced out the rough shape of the line, feature, or component in the air just above the paper. A rougher, more approximate version of this has already been discussed above, where the participant makes a circular motion above the area of interest to indicate an assembly or region (see "Gesturing to point" in Table 1 for an example).

A less-common gesture in this category was the use of the thumb and forefinger spaced out over a component or feature of the sketch. The space between the thumb and forefinger now represented the component of interest, and the participant could then "place" the component at other locations to explore different scenarios or alternatives. These are indicative of "design moves" [33] where the designer explores configuration changes in a design. Capturing such moves not only keeps a record of the scenarios considered, but also gives us insight into the designer's creative and analytical processes.

Gesturing to Describe Geometry/Material: Table 3 shows that "gesturing to describe geometry/material" is unique: no version of it produced marks on paper. Main uses of this gesture referred to situations where participants indicated distance, orientation, or in some cases, material. Participant P1, for instance, worked on the coffee container task (T2), and used a rapid series of diagonal strokes above the paper to indicate the amount of coffee (full/half full) he considers to be in the container. Another participant (P5) used a tracing-over gesture in the air to indicate an insulated region in her design.

Participants also used combinations of two fingers (same hand), two fingers (both hands), or pencil and finger (both hands) to indicate distances and orientations above the sketch. This is similar to the "gesturing to point" with the thumb and forefinger discussed above, but the intent here is to describe a property rather than to explore scenarios. Multiple participants also showed distances and orientations using a finger or pencil by rapidly moving it back and forth between two points.

Finally, two participants used their hands as a proxy to indicate the shape of a component. P2 used both hands to indicate the shape of mechanism linkage used in a bicycle design, while P3 shaped her dominant hand to show the geometry of the cup when discussing the need for insulation. These gestures, where the hands are used as a proxy for a component or assembly, are more difficult to track and understand, but for the designer, it is a convenient abstraction to visualize their concept.

Gesturing to Describe Motion: The most common gesture to describe motion was observed to be using the pencil tip over the paper to show the motion trajectory of a component. Some alternatives to this action were the use of a finger instead of the pencil (touching or not touching the paper), and in some cases, showing movement with the pencil tip, but occasionally touching the paper to create a mark.

Multiple fingers were used together on or above the paper to indicate translation, rotation, or deformation. Participant P2 used two fingers touching the paper at two sketched features, and moved them to show a pivoting movement of a bicycle swingarm. P6 used her finger and thumb to indicate mounting points of a spring, and performed a squeezing gesture above the paper with those fingers to indicate spring compression.

Finally, some participants used their hands as proxies while verbally referring to the design to show movements. Participant P5 used both hands to show an opening/closing motion of a lid after sketching it out, to visualize and talk about how it would work, while P3 used her hand to show a squeezing motion to indicate deformation of a coffee container design. There is a significant overlap of gesturing modes with showing geometry and gesturing to point, with the differentiating factor being the intentionality behind the act. This is revealed chiefly through context and verbalizations.

Action vs. Intent: Co-occurrence Cases

All activities under *designer intent* were coded based on a combination of verbalizations and observed actions from the video data. Table 2 shows correlations between designer intent and actions through a frequency analysis of co-occurrence among the 6 participants. We noticed that actions were often repeated across the coded intent categories. This reduces their use as a method for discerning between intents. However, the lack of "intent–action" pairs can provide interesting clues about the state of the ideation process. For example, while searching for solutions, designers shifted their focus to the laptop, and therefore very little actions was performed on or above the design notebook. Similarly, activities such as "describing a design scenario" and "selecting a design solution" also seemed to move designers' focus away from the notebook.

From a study of the code coverage, it became apparent that the primary activities reflecting designers' intent during the design tasks were *describing solutions* (average 44% of participant time) and *analyzing solutions* (average 13% of participant time). Note that "describing a solution" does not just stand for the description of a solution after the fact; it includes the designer thinking through the solution as well. Temporal analysis of the codes shows (Fig. 3) that designers frequently switched-back-and-forth between the two activities. This behavior is indicative of the designer having a dialogue with their design sketch [17]. Table 2 shows individual participant actions for these two primary activities. The table shows that most of the designers' actions occur when they are either describing a solution, or analyzing a solution. This is partly because these two activities dominate the duration of the task, but also because of the reflective dialogue mentioned above. We found that, apart from sketching, the use of physical actions significantly varied across participants for both intents. For example, P6 had very few (N=3) annotations actions across the two tasks in comparison to P1 (N=37). Similarly, even though P2 and P4 worked on the same design problem, the number of pointing-related actions ("pointing" & "gesturing to point") used by them varies significantly (N=35 and N=6 respectively). Our analysis of the participants suggests that the use of non-sketching actions in depends on the design problem, designers' habits, and the artifact being created.

To get a better understanding how each action is used in the context of these two activities, we explored episodes of designers' activity in detail. Figure 4 illustrates two such episodes, which were among the most densely-coded periods. Such periods are characterized by multiple physical activities, with designers rapidly switching between them. As discussed earlier, we found that similar actions were repeated across the two intents. We could not observe any specific temporal pattern of actions in these two intents. We also analyzed whether the observed actions made marks-on-paper to understand whether they were captured in the design notebooks used. In the episodes shown in Figure 4, we see that 6/14 coded actions for "describing a sketch" and 6/12 coded actions for "analyzing a sketch" do not create marks on paper. Such actions provide vital clues about decision-making processes in design ideation. To illustrate, consider the following excerpt from P2's analysis, "*one problem... no matter how we do this (points to rear wheel)... the reason that bicycles have a bar (points to bicycle pedals)... this is what pivots (gestures to show how it pivots using his hand as a proxy)... and the reason for that is that we*

	Intent: Describing a Solution						Intent: Analyzing a Solution					
	Sketch	Annotate	Point	Gesture: to point	Gesture: geom./mat.l	Gesture: motion	Sketch	Annotate	Point	Gesture: to point	Gesture: geom./mat.l	Gesture: motion
P1	26	34	32	5	3	0	4	1	2	3	1	0
P2⋆	22	5	13	3	1	2	6	11	14	5	4	3
P3	13	19	3	2	1	1	1	0	0	0	0	0
P4⋆	24	0	2	4	0	3	2	0	0	0	0	0
P5	12	5	11	2	3	8	2	2	5	3	0	1
P6⋆	14	3	6	6	2	4	1	0	1	1	0	0

NOTE: Participants marked with ⋆ worked on the bike suspension design task (T1), while the rest worked on the coffee container task (T2)

Table 4. Number of coded instances of designer action for each participant (P1–P6) for the two most-observed instances of designer intent

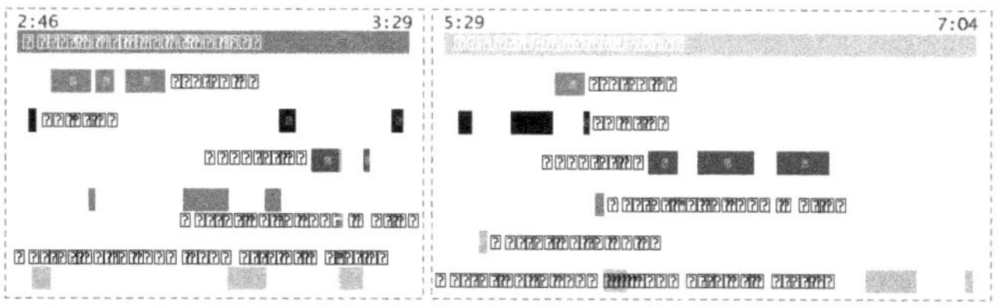

Figure 4. Sample coded segments with time stamps for "describing a solution" and "analyzing a solution". Actions that marked the paper are indicated using boxes with a white vertical line in the center.

do not actually want the distance for the chain to increase." Herein, he highlights vital considerations using a combination of utterances and non-marking gestures. These considerations form the basis for all designs he subsequently creates. Paper design notebooks cannot capture this rationale without the use of accompanying audio and video data.

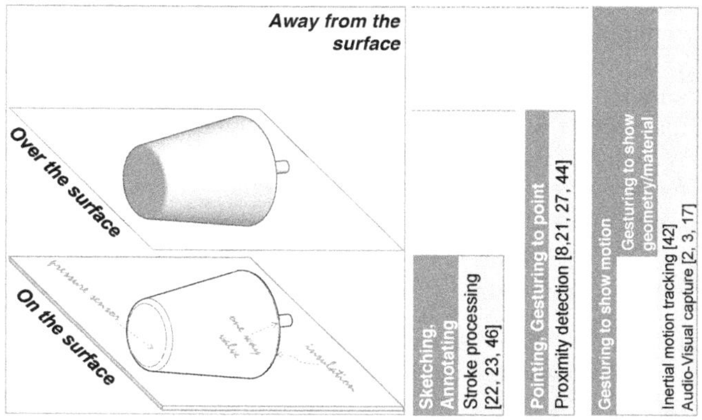

Figure 5. Spatial classification of coded physical actions observed in the studies, and typical research/technological developments that can be used to capture these actions.

IMPLICATIONS

Our results suggest that HCI research on creating digital design notebooks should not treat sketches as the *sole* focus of design ideation. This focus on sketches has already led to a fixation on creating tools for (1) easing creation, storage, & sharing of sketches, and (2) enriching sketches through multimedia data such as images, sound, and animation. Results from our analyses show that while designers primarily use sketches and annotations to express themselves, they also use actions such as pointing and gesturing, which, along with verbalizations, could help capture their intent, process, and rationale. Our review of multimodal interfaces for sketching has shown that speech-based and multimodal interfaces are typically designed for collaborative scenarios. With recent developments in voice-based interactions, there is potential for the designer, even when working alone, to verbalize, capture, and contextualize their thought processes. Here we will suggest directions, based on our results, for designing digital design notebooks that capture the designers' intention as well as the designed artifact.

Expanding the Sensory Envelope: Typically, tablet-based sketching interfaces rely on a "sensory envelope" that is limited to the capacitive field over the device surface. Interactions are thus constrained to pen and touch. Typically, existing sketching systems merely capture the digital equivalent of "marks on paper"—sketches, annotations, and gestures that leave marks on paper, as seen in Table 3. However, they are capable of capturing sketching, annotating, pointing, and gestures that occur just over the surface of the paper. In addition, we recorded other actions, such as using hands as a proxy for an object, mechanism, or deformation of the design, that occurred "away from the surface." We thus group the observed actions into three categories based on their relation to the sketching surface: *on-the-surface*, *above-the-surface*, and *away-from-the-surface* actions. Interaction modalities such as FingerIO [29] and Expressy [44] are already capable of capturing these and other around-the-device interactions. With the recent proliferation of wearable devices, especially smartwatches, the ability to sense, anticipate, and interpret physical actions has been significantly augmented. For instance, inertial measurement units on smartwatches have been used in combination with touchscreens to interpret the intention behind various touch events [44]. Gesture-based interfaces are becoming more portable thanks to devices like the Leap Motion. Prior work has also used speech to distinguish the intention behind sketch strokes [7]. A similar setup can be used to identify the intention behind on-the-surface and above-the-surface interactions, and through the use of voice recording or transcribed text, associate them with sketched features. Figure 5 maps different on-, over- and away-from-surface actions to related technologies that can be used to capture them.

Capturing Contextual Information: While coding the participant videos to identify designers' intention, it became clear that voice, sketches, annotations, or gestures in isolation cannot provide sufficient information. In fact, it was sometimes necessary to look at a window of time preceding and/or following the episode of interest, in order to establish context.

While there were dominant actions observed across participants for each identified intent, there was also a fair amount of variations between participants (Table 4). Personal voice assistants such as Alexa and Siri have developed a combination of data mining and machine learning techniques to infer context from a record of user utterances. While such assistants are now built into most handheld devices, issues such as anaphor resolution—identifying what a user refers to when they use a pronoun—still remains an open problem. Augmenting these systems with touch and gesture will, in the context of design ideation, help resolve these issues. For instance, a designer may say while sketching or pointing, "...and then this hydraulic system kind of working to maintain this distance". A synchronized record of speech and pointing actions will resolve what they mean by "this" in each context. Similarly, annotation and sketching processes take longer to complete than accompanying verbalizations, which explains why the verbalizations tend to be spaced out. Keeping a temporal record of verbalizations that co-occurred with the creation-to-completion time of a sketch can help associate sketches with verbal descriptions, and help identify higher-level processes such as the designer switching between synthesis and analysis modes. Speech, sketch, and gesture have indeed been identified as the "trimodal" interactions of designers [3], as we saw in the background section, early approaches to capture multi-modal design interactions use a combination of audio, video, and stroke records to interpret designer intent. This does not stop at capture: researchers envision sketching interfaces for design to be able to recognize, capture, and support the kinds of visual reasoning that designers perform [12]. In our study, our mapping of action, mode, and intent (Table 3) was possible only through the accompanying speech (see Table 1). Multi-modal interaction systems that aim to capture design intent will thus need to be able to "understand" the designers' speech and use accompanying actions to establish context.

Representing Metadata: For our study, we used video recordings of participants, and qualitative analysis software to identify and code actions and intent. However, playing back relevant video for a sketch is cumbersome and time-consuming in a design scenario. On-the-surface and above-the-surface gestures can be represented as animated traces on top of sketches. Gestures to indicate motion can use similar traces, or be used to animate parts of sketches, similar to tools such as Draco [24] and Kitty [23], though inferring relevant sketch segmentation could be a challenge. As mentioned earlier, verbalizations are critical to establish context, and a combination of sketch clustering techniques (e.g. Zhao et al. [48]) and voice annotation can be used to provide relevant data at different levels of resolution.

LIMITATIONS

While our study helped understand the actions through which designers express their intent, it has a few associated limitations. Firstly, it may be argued that the think-aloud protocol is not indicative of a designer's actual process (they would not talk aloud when designing by themselves). A limitation of using a think-aloud study is that in episodes with prolonged silence, we were unable to infer intent. In a couple of instances, the researcher reminded the designer to verbalize his/her intent, which may have affected their thought process. However, there are few alternatives to gain an insight into the designer's thought process. As we saw in the results, verbalizations, while not sufficient, are necessary to obtain context and rationale for a particular design decision. It can also be argued that if the goal is to suggest interactions that can store rich metadata, then speech needs to be one of them. This may not me a great hurdle considering the average users' increasing comfort with digital voice assistants.

Secondly, the design tasks themselves are focused on (1) conceptual design, and (2) come from the domain of physical products. However, the overlap in the types of actions and intents we observed (across the six participants) indicates that they represent common, consistent patterns. We do acknowledge that a follow-up study with a more comprehensive set of design tasks, spanning multiple domains such as interaction design, industrial design, and graphic design, will need to be considered to identify a more diverse set of actions.

Finally, the qualitative coding was more detailed when it came to actions, and less so when it came to designers' intent. For instance, "describing a design solution" can further be divided into stages such as "exploring alternatives", "modifying existing designs", and "creating a new design" etc. However, the focus of the study was on designers' actions reflecting their intent, and less on the design process. We believe that the scope and the depth of the study was sufficient to glean useful insights from the participants' actions.

Paper-based studies such as ours also have the limitation that they do not anticipate new forms of interactions, such as using the device itself as a proxy (to show movement, orientation etc.) for the sketch it contains. However, our goal with this study is to develop a better understanding of how designers express themselves through a medium with which they are familiar and comfortable. Future iterations of this study can accommodate how designers develop new ways to express themselves with digital media.

CONCLUSION

We have presented results from an observational study of designers engaged in design tasks. Our goal was to understand the role of both sketching and non-sketching actions in expressing the designer's intent. To do this, we categorized the physical actions of the designers under sketching, annotating, pointing, and various gesturing actions, and based on these actions and their verbal utterances, identified their intent. Through our analysis, we understood the importance of preserving "non-marking" actions—actions that do not create a mark on paper—and preserving the context of "marking" actions, in capturing the reasoning behind the designer's actions. Finally, we discuss implications for recording and representing designers' actions in order to capture designers' intent in the next generation of digital design notebooks.

ACKNOWLEDGMENTS

This work is supported by the U.S. National Science Foundation under grant IIS-1422341. Any opinions, findings, and conclusions expressed in this material are those of the authors and do not necessarily reflect the views of the sponsors.

REFERENCES

1. Aaron Adler. 2010. Reasoning About Sketches Using Context, Domain Knowledge, and Interaction with the User. In *Proceedings of the AAAI Conference on Visual Representations and Reasoning*. 2–5.
2. Aaron Adler and Randall Davis. 2007. Speech and Sketching for Multimodal Design. In *ACM SIGGRAPH Courses*. DOI: http://dx.doi.org/10.1145/1281500.1281525
3. Aaron Adler, Jacob Eisenstein, Michael Oltmans, Lisa Guttentag, and Randall Davis. 2004. Building the design studio of the future. In *AAAI Symposium on Making Pen-Based Interaction Intelligent and Natural*. 1–7.
4. Geeta Arjun and Jim Plume. 2006. Collaborative architectural design as a reflective conversation: an agent facilitated system to support collaborative conceptual design. In *International Conference of the Arab Society for CAD*.
5. Wayne A. Bailey and Edwin J. Kay. 1986. Structural Analysis of Verbal Data. *ACM SIGCHI Bulletin* 18, 4 (1986), 297–301. DOI: http://dx.doi.org/10.1145/1165387.275646
6. Mathilde M. Bekker, Judith S. Olson, and Gary M. Olson. 1995. Analysis of Gestures in Face-to-face Design Teams Provides Guidance for How to Use Groupware in Design. In *Proceedings of the ACM Conference on Designing Interactive Systems*. 157–166. DOI: http://dx.doi.org/10.1145/225434.225452
7. David Tyler Bischel, Thomas F Stahovich, Eric Jeffrey Peterson, Randall Davis, and Aaron Adler. 2009. Combining Speech and Sketch to Interpret Unconstrained Descriptions of Mechanical Devices.. In *Proceedings of the International Jont Conference on Artifical Intelligence*, Vol. 9. 1401–1406.
8. Amaresh Chakrabarti, Kristina Shea, Robert Stone, Jonathan Cagan, Matthew Campbell, Noe Vargas Hernandez, and Kristin L Wood. 2011. Computer-based design synthesis research: an overview. *Journal of Computing and Information Science in Engineering* 11, 2 (2011), 021003.
9. Xiang 'Anthony' Chen, Julia Schwarz, Chris Harrison, Jennifer Mankoff, and Scott E. Hudson. 2014. Air+Touch: Interweaving Touch & In-air Gestures. In *Proceedings of the ACM Symposium on User Interface Software and Technology*. 519–525. DOI: http://dx.doi.org/10.1145/2642918.2647392
10. Andrew Clayphan, Anthony Collins, Christopher Ackad, Bob Kummerfeld, and Judy Kay. 2011. Firestorm: A Brainstorming Application for Collaborative Group Work at Tabletops. In *Proceedings of the ACM Conference on Interactive Tabletops and Surfaces*. 162–171. DOI: http://dx.doi.org/10.1145/2076354.2076386
11. Marco Aurélio de Carvalho, Jônathas Gobbi Benazi Grillo, and Rodolfo Krul Tessari. 2015. Methodology and Software for New Product Ideation. *Procedia Engineering* 131 (2015), 352 – 358. DOI: http://dx.doi.org/10.1016/j.proeng.2015.12.414
12. Ellen Yi-Luen Do. 2002. Drawing marks, acts, and reacts: Toward a computational sketching interface for architectural design. *Artificial Intelligence for Engineering Design, Analysis, and Manufacturing* 16, 3 (2002), 149–171.
13. Tomás Dorta. 2007. Implementing and assessing the hybrid ideation space: a cognitive artefact for conceptual design. *Moon* 61 (2007), 77.
14. Kenneth D Forbus, Ronald W Ferguson, and Jeffery M Usher. 2001. Towards a computational model of sketching. In *Proceedings of the ACM conference on Intelligent user interfaces*. 77–83. DOI: http://dx.doi.org/10.1145/359784.360278
15. Florian Geyer, Jochen Budzinski, and Harald Reiterer. 2012. IdeaVis: A Hybrid Workspace and Interactive Visualization for Paper-based Collaborative Sketching Sessions. In *Proceedings of the ACM Nordic Conference on Human-Computer Interaction*. 331–340. DOI: http://dx.doi.org/10.1145/2399016.2399069
16. Vinod Goel. 1995. *Sketches of thought*. MIT Press, Cambridge MA.
17. Gabriela Goldschmidt. 1991. The dialectics of sketching. *Creativity Research Journal* 4, 2 (1991), 123–143. DOI: http://dx.doi.org/10.1080/10400419109534381
18. Mark D Gross, Ellen Yi-Luen Do, and Brian R Johnson. 2001. The Design Amanuensis: An instrument for multimodal design capture and playback. In *Computer Aided Architectural Design Futures*, Vol. 1. 1–13.
19. Joshua Hailpern, Erik Hinterbichler, Caryn Leppert, Damon Cook, and Brian P. Bailey. 2007. TEAM STORM: Demonstrating an Interaction Model for Working with Multiple Ideas During Creative Group Work. In *Proceedings of the ACM Conference on Creativity & Cognition*. 193–202. DOI: http://dx.doi.org/10.1145/1254960.1254987
20. Chris Harrison. 2010. Appropriated Interaction Surfaces. *Computer* 43, 6 (2010), 86–89.
21. Ken Hinckley, Seongkook Heo, Michel Pahud, Christian Holz, Hrvoje Benko, Abigail Sellen, Richard Banks, Kenton O'Hara, Gavin Smyth, and William Buxton. 2016. Pre-Touch Sensing for Mobile Interaction. In *Proceedings of the ACM Conference on Human Factors in Computing Systems*. 2869–2881. DOI: http://dx.doi.org/10.1145/2858036.2858095
22. A. Hoeben and P.J. Stappers. 2005. Direct talkback in computer supported tools for the conceptual stage of design. *Knowledge-Based Systems* 18, 8 (2005), 407–413. DOI: http://dx.doi.org/10.1016/j.knosys.2005.07.003 Computational Approaches for Early Stages of Design.

23. Rubaiat Habib Kazi, Fanny Chevalier, Tovi Grossman, and George Fitzmaurice. 2014a. Kitty: Sketching Dynamic and Interactive Illustrations. In *Proceedings of the ACM Symposium on User Interface Software and Technology*. 395–405. DOI: http://dx.doi.org/10.1145/2642918.2647375

24. Rubaiat Habib Kazi, Fanny Chevalier, Tovi Grossman, Shengdong Zhao, and George Fitzmaurice. 2014b. Draco: Bringing Life to Illustrations with Kinetic Textures. In *Proceedings of the ACM Conference on Human Factors in Computing Systems*. 351–360. DOI: http://dx.doi.org/10.1145/2556288.2556987

25. Barry Kudrowitz and Caitlin Dippo. 2013. Getting to the Novel Ideas: Exploring the Alternative Uses Test of Divergent Thinking. In *Proceedings of the ASME International Design Engineering Technical Conferences and Computers and Information in Engineering Conference*. V005T06A013. DOI: http://dx.doi.org/10.1115/DETC2013-13262

26. Guang Li, Xiang Cao, Sergio Paolantonio, and Feng Tian. 2012. SketchComm: A Tool to Support Rich and Flexible Asynchronous Communication of Early Design Ideas. In *Proceedings of the ACM Conference on Computer Supported Cooperative Work*. 359–368. DOI: http://dx.doi.org/10.1145/2145204.2145261

27. Robert McKim. 1972. Experiences in visual thinking. (1972).

28. Alexandre Menezes and Bryan Lawson. 2006. How designers perceive sketches. *Design Studies* 27, 5 (2006), 571–585. DOI: http://dx.doi.org/10.1016/j.destud.2006.02.001

29. Rajalakshmi Nandakumar, Vikram Iyer, Desney Tan, and Shyamnath Gollakota. 2016. FingerIO: Using active sonar for fine-grained finger tracking. In *Proceedings of the ACM Conference on Human Factors in Computing Systems*. 1515–1525. DOI: http://dx.doi.org/10.1145/2858036.2858580

30. Cecil Piya, Vinayak , Senthil Chandrasegaran, Niklas Elmqvist, and Karthik Ramani. 2017. Co-3Deator: A Team-First Collaborative 3D Design Ideation Tool. In *Proceedings of the ACM Conference on Human Factors in Computing Systems*. 6581–6592. DOI: http://dx.doi.org/10.1145/3025453.3025825

31. Ugo Braga Sangiorgi, François Beuvens, and Jean Vanderdonckt. 2012. User Interface Design by Collaborative Sketching. In *Proceedings of the Designing Interactive Systems Conference*. 378–387. DOI: http://dx.doi.org/10.1145/2317956.2318013

32. Linda C Schmidt, Noe Vargas Hernandez, and Ashley L Ruocco. 2012. Research on encouraging sketching in engineering design. *Artificial Intelligence for Engineering Design, Analysis, and Manufacturing* 26, 3 (2012), 303–315. DOI: http://dx.doi.org/10.1017/S0890060412000169

33. Donald A Schön. 1992. Designing as reflective conversation with the materials of a design situation. *Knowledge-based systems* 5, 1 (1992), 3–14. DOI: http://dx.doi.org/10.1016/0950-7051(92)90020-G

34. Donald A Schön and Glenn Wiggins. 1992. Kinds of seeing and their functions in designing. *Design studies* 13, 2 (1992), 135–156. DOI: http://dx.doi.org/10.1016/0142-694X(92)90268-F

35. Stephen Scrivener and Sean Clark. 1994. Sketching in collaborative design. In *Interacting With Virtual Environments*, Lindsay W. MacDonald and John Vince (Eds.). John Wiley & Sons, New York, NY.

36. Ben Shneiderman, Gerhard Fischer, Mary Czerwinski, Mitch Resnick, Brad Myers, Linda Candy, Ernest Edmonds, Mike Eisenberg, Elisa Giaccardi, Tom Hewett, Pamela Jennings, Bill Kules, Kumiyo Nakakoji, Jay Nunamaker, Randy Pausch, Ted Selker, Elisabeth Sylvan, and Michael Terry. 2006. Creativity Support Tools: Report From a U.S. National Science Foundation Sponsored Workshop. *International Journal of Human-Computer Interaction* 20, 2 (2006), 61–77. DOI: http://dx.doi.org/10.1207/s15327590ijhc2002_1

37. Ivan E Sutherland. 1964. Sketchpad a man-machine graphical communication system. *Transactions of the Society for Computer Simulation* 2, 5 (1964), R–3.

38. Masaki Suwa, Terry Purcell, and John Gero. 1998. Macroscopic analysis of design processes based on a scheme for coding designers' cognitive actions. *Design studies* 19, 4 (1998), 455–483. DOI: http://dx.doi.org/10.1016/S0142-694X(98)00016-7

39. Masaki Suwa and Barbara Tversky. 1996. What Architects See in Their Sketches: Implications for Design Tools. In *ACM Conference Companion on Human Factors in Computing Systems*. 191–192. DOI: http://dx.doi.org/10.1145/257089.257255

40. John C. Tang. 1991. Findings from observational studies of collaborative work. *International Journal of Man-Machine Studies* 34, 2 (1991), 143–160. DOI: http://dx.doi.org/10.1016/0020-7373(91)90039-A

41. Barbara Tversky. 2002. What do sketches say about thinking. In *AAAI Spring Symposium on Sketch Understanding*, T. Stahovic, J. Landay, and R. Davis (Eds.). 148–151.

42. David G Ullman. 2009. *The Mechanical Design Process*. Vol. 4. McGraw-Hill, New York.

43. Remko Van der Lugt. 2005. How sketching can affect the idea generation process in design group meetings. *Design studies* 26, 2 (2005), 101–122. DOI: http://dx.doi.org/10.1016/j.destud.2004.08.003

44. Gerard Wilkinson, Ahmed Kharrufa, Jonathan Hook, Bradley Pursglove, Gavin Wood, Hendrik Haeuser, Nils Y. Hammerla, Steve Hodges, and Patrick Olivier. 2016. Expressy: Using a Wrist-worn Inertial Measurement Unit to Add Expressiveness to Touch-based Interactions. In *Proceedings of the ACM Conference on Human Factors in Computing Systems*. 2832–2844. DOI: http://dx.doi.org/10.1145/2858036.2858223

45. Anthony Williams and Robert Cowdroy. 2002. How designers communicate ideas to each other in design meetings. In *DS 30: Proceedings of DESIGN 2002, the 7th International Design Conference, Dubrovnik*.

46. Sang Ho Yoon, Ke Huo, and Karthik Ramani. 2016. TMotion: Embedded 3D Mobile Input Using Magnetic Sensing Technique. In *Proceedings of the ACM Conference on Tangible, Embedded, and Embodied Interaction*. 21–29. DOI: http://dx.doi.org/10.1145/2839462.2839463

47. Zhenpeng Zhao, Sriram Karthik Badam, Senthil Chandrasegaran, Deok Gun Park, Niklas Elmqvist, Lorraine Kisselburgh, and Karthik Ramani. 2014. skWiki: A Multimedia Sketching System for Collaborative Creativity. In *Proceedings of the ACM Conference on Human Factors in Computing Systems*. 1235–1244. DOI: http://dx.doi.org/10.1145/2556288.2557394

48. Zhenpeng Zhao, William Benjamin, Niklas Elmqvist, and Karthik Ramani. 2015. Sketcholution: Interaction histories for sketching. *International Journal of Human-Computer Studies* 82 (2015), 11 – 20. DOI: http://dx.doi.org/10.1016/j.ijhcs.2015.04.003

Designing for Situational Visual Impairments: Supporting Early-Career Designers of Mobile Content

Garreth W. Tigwell
g.w.tigwell@dundee.ac.uk
[1]University of Dundee
Dundee, UK

Rachel Menzies
r.menzies@dundee.ac.uk
University of Dundee
Dundee, UK

David R. Flatla[1]
dflatla@uoguelph.ca
University of Guelph
Guelph, Canada

ABSTRACT
Mobile devices are a substantial part of our lives, supporting communication, work, and play. However, situational visual impairments (SVIs) can make completing tasks a challenge (e.g., browsing online in bright sunlight) and poorly designed content can cause or exacerbate SVIs. We surveyed 43 mobile content designers and ran four follow-on interviews to understand what designers currently do regarding SVIs, what resources they know of, and what is required to best support them in designing to reduce SVIs. Our findings highlight key similarities and differences between accessibility and designing to reduce SVIs. Our participants requested improved guidelines, education, and digital design tools for SVIs. To accommodate the growing number of people affected by SVIs and improve the inclusion of accessibility in design, we introduce recommendations that leverage the overlap between accessibility and SVIs to minimise the effort required in extending current design processes.

ACM Classification Keywords
H.5.m. Information Interfaces & Presentation: Miscellaneous

Author Keywords
Situational impairments; accessibility; mobile content design.

INTRODUCTION
Mobile devices are appealing for their portability, while enabling us to conveniently complete many tasks. Mobile shipment sales have overtaken desktop computers [19] and US consumers spend an average of five hours per day on mobile devices [24]. Furthermore, mobile devices are also beneficial within the workplace [2, 6, 13]. However, people using mobile devices can find themselves in challenging contexts that impede usability. These problems are called *situational impairments* – a context-dependent phenomenon that poses challenges for users while carrying out a task they would normally have no difficulty completing.

Previous work in HCI has discussed situational impairments caused by the *Environment* [38], and Sears et al. [47] further identified *Application* and *Human* factors as additional

DIS'18, June 09–13, 2018, Hong Kong

ACM ISBN 978-1-4503-5198-0/18/06.
DOI: http://dx.doi.org/10.1145/3196709.3196760

Figure 1. A smartphone in a bright environment. The low-contrast text is difficult to read, and is one example design choice that can cause SVIs.

contributing dimensions. As a response to this growing phenomenon, Wobbrock [53] called for a re-emphasis of mobile device research towards "on-the-go" use. There are many types of mobile device situational impairments, however, in this paper, we focus on *situational visual impairments (SVIs)* – visual impairments arising from a user's context (e.g., using Google Maps under bright sunlight) – and we investigate how to improve design processes to address this problem, since content design can cause or contribute to SVIs (Figure 1).

SVIs threaten advances in mobile device use. Mobile device screens are difficult to use as ambient light intensity increases [18]. As a result, recent research has questioned the suitability of mobile devices in medical settings due to SVIs [31]. In general day-to-day use, common design choices, such as Apple's use of low-contrasting font, introduces new challenges and this has been criticised for making reading difficult for people with typical vision [39]. Support exists to help designers identify potential SVIs [15, 33], yet there are no explicit guidelines or purpose-made design tools for accommodating SVIs when designing.

We investigated what designers currently do regarding SVIs, what resources they know of, and what is required to best support them design for SVIs. We surveyed 43 designers using an online questionnaire to understand current design processes for accessibility and SVIs. Four of our survey respondents took part in a follow-on semi-structured interview, allowing us to: 1) further understand typical design processes, 2) engage in a deeper discussion regarding accessibility and SVIs, and 3) to identify effective support for designing to reduce SVIs.

Our survey indicated several similarities and differences between designing for accessibility and SVIs. Our participants reported positive connections between accessible design and designing to reduce SVIs. Both were perceived to benefit a broader set of users, and that designing for one often resulted in at least partial inclusion of the other. Reasons for not designing to reduce SVIs were: 1) it is often not in the design scope or part of the designer's current practice, 2) there are limited resources available (e.g., time, money, tools) to design for SVIs, 3) the designers are unaware or have not considered SVIs before, and 4) SVIs can be viewed as a minor issue.

Our surveyed participants recommend that existing accessibility guidelines, education, and design tools be extended to include support for designing to reduce SVIs. During the interviews, our participants recognised the value of both 'simplified' industry guidelines (e.g., Android Material Design) and more thorough guidelines (e.g., WCAG 2.0) for guiding design, as well as using the documentation for convincing clients of the necessity of accessibility. However, both types of guideline need extending to include SVIs. Future studies are required to construct SVI guidelines for mobile content. Design tools must incorporate the SVI guidelines to double as a platform that improves understanding of designing for SVIs. In addition to improving formal education, our participants emphasised targeting popular design websites (e.g., medium.com) and online self-learning courses (e.g., Udemy.com).

This paper makes three contributions. First, we present survey results from 43 designers of mobile content highlighting similarities and differences between designing for accessibility and SVIs. We found most designers are not considering SVIs and many demonstrated misunderstanding about SVIs. Second, we present a thematic analysis of follow-on interviews with four designers, used to identify how to integrate the SVI support requested by our participants. Third, we suggest how to extend guidelines and revise education, and we outline requirements for digital design tools to support designing to reduce SVIs.

BACKGROUND AND RELATED WORK

Situational Impairments, Technology and Perception

Situational impairments are a context-dependent phenomenon that make it difficult for users to complete tasks that they would usually not find difficult. Situational impairments are known within HCI [38] and result from many factors [47]. Recently, Mauderer et al. [35] discussed moving beyond accessibility to address perceptual limitations experienced by everybody. Focusing on supporting all people is an approach also promoted by Universal Design [9] and Universal Usability [51].

There are many types of situational impairments, for example, research has investigated the challenges walking can have on being able to read text on a mobile phone [37] and how some input errors on small devices compare with errors from people with a motor impairment using a desktop [57]. There have been investigations into solutions for mobile device text entry and interaction while walking [17, 23]. Yeilsada, Brajnik and Harper [54] found commonalities between accessibility issues for people with low vision and people using a mobile device.

In this paper we focus on *situational visual impairments (SVIs)* and how design can be utilised to address this problem. The typical transmissive displays used in mobile devices require a backlight to display content on the screen [7]. Increasing ambient light reduces the image quality on the display [26, 25, 30] and the issue remains with newer screen technology, such as IPS and AMOLED displays [18]. Although anti-glare layers help, they can degrade image quality [40] and cause users to experience "visual sparkle", which is a perceived glittering effect on the display [8]. Improvements have been utilised to brighten screens (e.g., One Glass Solution [20]) and some Nokia devices use ClearBlack Displays [16], which have polarising layers under the screen to block ambient light. Yet, focusing on ambient light levels only addresses one cause of SVIs. If screen brightness is reduced to conserve power, a similar problem to viewing a screen in a bright environment occurs. Sarsenbayeva et al. [46] indicates there is limited research looking into ambient light SVIs and suggests auto-brightness may be why few studies on SVIs exist. More research is required to fully understand the factors involved and the frequency of experiencing SVIs.

Reinecke et al. [45] and Huang et al. [22] both demonstrate variations in people's perceptions under different lighting. Using ~30k web participants, Reinecke et al. found that both increasing ambient brightness and decreasing monitor brightness reduce colour differentiation abilities. Huang et al. used a smaller sample to look at visual comfort when reading on a mobile device. Higher contrasts were preferred by older participants, and female participants (particularly young female participants) preferred less contrast.

Current Support For Designers

Designers can employ a more inclusive approach to design by considering potential SVIs that a user might experience.

The W3C website includes a page called "Shared Web Experiences: Barriers Common to Mobile Device Users and People with Disabilities" [56] that lists examples of how accessibility issues such as the use of colour and font size can also be a problem for all mobile users without disabilities.

The current version (29th July 2008) of the Mobile Web Best Practice (1.0) [44] aims to improve Web browsing user experience on a mobile device. For checking colour contrast, the human test recommends shining a strong light on the screen of the mobile device while browsing the page. Instead, it may be better to develop a tool that is similar to ColorCheck [45], which supports designers by highlighting how their colour choices are difficult to distinguish for different proportions of the population. Using an automatic tool would meet the Mobile Web Best Practice machine test recommendation and to our knowledge no purpose-made SVI design tool currently exists for this to be achieved. The Mobile Web Best Practice document is now ten years old and mobile technology has changed. In addition to issues with suggested contrast ratios, it does not give sufficient SVI support regarding font style or what to consider when designing icons.

Furthermore, a working draft paper by the W3C highlights how current accessibility guidelines apply to mobile [41]. It draws attention to the issue that mobile devices are used in a range of lighting situations that can reduce usability – something not explicitly addressed in WCAG 1.0 [14] or 2.0 [12]. A limitation of the working draft is that the suggested contrast guidelines are based on calculations from WCAG 2.0, which were calculated for desktop only [41]. Although WCAG warns of the limitation, a designer is left to decide how best to proceed, which is concerning for mobile app design because the iOS [4], Android [3], and Universal Windows Platform [36] design guidelines suggest using WCAG 2.0 contrast ratios.

In addition to guidelines, there are also design toolkits to be used as part of the design process to help designers consider user behaviour in different settings [15, 33]. A workbook by HaptiMap [33] motivates designers to think about the many situations in which a user may find themselves using a system. There are also accompanying 'context cards' that have a variety of context and environmental prompts (e.g., 'pushing a stroller', 'bright light') that are used to help designers think about the implications of those conditions. 'Inclusive: A Microsoft Design Toolkit' (microsoft.com/en-us/design/inclusive) serves a similar purpose. However, these toolkits do not provide specific guidelines to help designers make informed decisions about how to reduce SVIs.

Current resources may not suitably support designers in designing to reduce SVIs. We do not know what designers currently do regarding SVIs, what resources they know of, and what is required to best support them in designing for SVIs. To gather this information, we distributed an online questionnaire.

ONLINE QUESTIONNAIRE

Material and Procedure

Our questionnaire (provided in supplementary materials) comprised of 22 close-ended and 16 open-ended questions. We distributed the questionnaire among Scottish universities and design companies, and for a wider audience used social media (e.g., Facebook, Twitter), Reddit's r/samplesize, r/designthought, and r/UI_Design; asking for designers who have released mobile content publicly or commercially.

As per our REB approval, participants first read through an information page and consented to taking part. The questionnaire was expected to take five to ten minutes to complete depending on the responses given. After submitting, the participants were debriefed and could enter into a prize draw for one of four $50 USD (or equivalent) Amazon vouchers.

Participants

Forty-four participants completed our questionnaire. One participant was removed from the analysis because he did not design any mobile content. The remaining 32 male and 11 female participants were aged 18 to 52 (Mean = 27.15, SD = 7.18; three did not respond). Twenty-two participants (51.16%) were living in the UK, with 48.84% living outside the UK (11 in the US, three in Canada, two in India, and one in Senegal, The Netherlands, Turkey, Philippines, and Australia).

Our participants indicated that they had varied design training backgrounds (multiple responses were allowed): 'Undergraduate level university' (23 participants), 'No formal training' (10), 'College' (8), 'Apprenticeship' (8), 'Postgraduate level university' (8), and 'Other' (2 – P11 wrote "*personal projects*", P21 wrote "*general assembly (the education startup)*").

We asked our participants what best described their design career; 24 participants said 'Working for a company', followed by 'Self-employed' (8), 'Hobby' (8), 'Other' (3 – "*Design researcher and practising Architect*" (P1), "*Designed as part of coursework*" (P8), "*Company owner*" (P13)).

Our participants created a range of mobile content (28 participants designed more than one type of content); our participants reported 'Mobile friendly websites' (32), 'Mobile apps' (26), 'Advertising' (12), 'Games' (7), 'Books' (5), and 'Other' (4 – "*data UI/UX*" (P2), "*brand identity*" (P32), "*branding, video graphics, magazines*" (P41), and "*Logo & Branding*" (P43)).

We asked how many years the participants had publicly or commercially released mobile content and found 42 participants had up to 15 years of experience (M = 3.71, SD = 3.64, Median = 2). Indicating that our sample is predominately made up of designers early in their design careers.

Results

Accessibility

We first asked accessibility questions to check that our sample are representative of those previously reported in the literature.

The participants were provided with a brief definition of accessibility taken from Henry et al. [21] "*'Accessibility' has historically referred to design that enables people with disabilities to interact with buildings, products, services, etc.*" and asked if they include accessibility in their design process. The responses were: 'Always' (13), 'Sometimes' (24), and 'Never' (6). For the 24 participants who indicated 'Sometimes', two-thirds only include accessibility in 40% or few projects. Overall, the proportion of our participants who include accessibility in any or all of their designs (~86%) is somewhat higher than in previous research (75%) [50], which could be due to the different recruitment mechanisms and our study focusing on mobile content designers.

Our participants who 'Always' and 'Sometimes' include accessibility typically do this 'From the beginning' (13 participants) and 'During the process' (19), while some only included accessibility 'When a design is complete' (5). We found that guidelines (e.g., WCAG) were used by 27 participants, accessibility-focused design tools (e.g., WAVE: wave.webaim.org) were used by 19 participants, and accessibility user evaluations were carried out by 14 participants. Among the types of user evaluations reported, there was evidence of evaluating without impairment (e.g., P18: "*Best guess. We do not have people come in to test it*"), recruiting people (e.g., P21: "*User testing with users who are sight-impaired for TTS*"), and evaluating with design tools (e.g., P30: "*With the use of site's like colorhexa.com*"). The six participants who never include accessibility were aware of at least one of the following: accessibility guidelines (four participants), accessibility design tools (2), and accessibility evaluation techniques (4).

We were also interested in why designers do or do not include accessibility to identify any overlaps between accessibility and SVIs. The reasons given **for** including accessibility are combined responses from participants who 'Always' or 'Sometimes' include accessibility. These reasons were: there is a moral obligation (16 participants), it was a requirement of the project (10), it improves the usability and UX (6), there is a recognised value in accessibility (3), a legal obligation (2), time was available (2), it does not require much effort (2), and pushing for accessibility will change perceptions (1). The reasons given **for not** including accessibility are combined responses from participants who 'Sometimes' or 'Never' include accessibility. These reasons were: limited resources

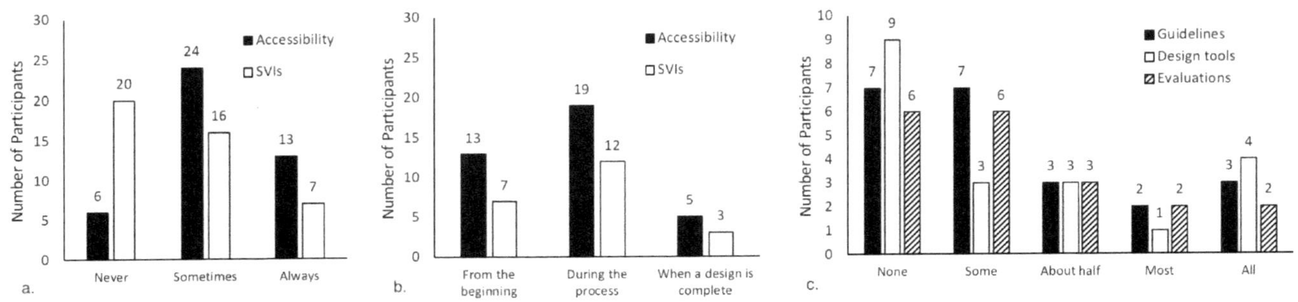

Figure 2. A) A summary of how many participants include accessibility and design to reduce SVIs. B) A summary of when accessibility and SVIs are part of the design process. C) A summary of how many participants use guidelines, design tools, and evaluations to reduce SVIs from occurring.

(e.g., time, money) (14 participants), it is not within the scope of the project (10), accessibility restricts design (2), achieving 100% is challenging (2), disinterest in accessibility (1), unpopular with management (1), and personal preference (1).

Situational Visual Impairment

We provided our participants with the definition "*situational impairments are usually caused by environment conditions that negatively affect a person's ability to complete a task when they would otherwise not have a problem*" and listed three examples: 1) standing in a noisy crowd on the phone (situational hearing impairment), 2) carrying shopping bags and trying to compose an SMS (situational mobility impairment), and 3) wearing glasses with coloured lenses, while trying to identify colours on a screen (situational visual impairment). We only provided a few examples to help reduce biasing participants. We asked if our participants design to reduce situational impairments to lead into focusing on SVIs.

We first asked our participants if they design to reduce SVIs. All forty-three participants responded to this question with 'Always' (7), 'Sometimes' (16), and 'Never' (20). There is a noticeable change (see Figure 2a) in distribution compared to the counterpart accessibility question – SVIs are not considered by the majority of the participants. A McNemar-Bowker test indicates a significant difference ($p = .007$) between the distributions. Bonferroni corrected post-hoc tests identified a significant difference between 'Never' and 'Sometimes' ($p = .024$).

For the 16 participants who sometimes design to reduce SVIs, we wanted to see how often this occurs in their design projects. Responses were: 'Rarely (Less than 20%)' (7 participants), 'Occasionally (20-40%)' (6), 'About half (40-60%)' (2), and 'Often (60-80%)' (1). A similar decreasing trend was also present in the counterpart accessibility question.

We asked our participants what types of SVIs they try to reduce occurring through design. Sixteen participants responded but only six participants listed genuine causes for SVIs such as reading at night, unusual interior/exterior lighting, bright situations, wearing tinted glasses, being far from a screen, being in a moving vehicle. Four mentions of colour vision deficiency demonstrated potential misunderstandings of SVIs.

Twenty-two participants told us the earliest point at which they design for SVIs: 'From the beginning' (7 participants), 'During the process' (12), and 'When a design is complete' (3). This distribution is similar to the counterpart accessibility question (see Figure 2b). Most participants consider accessibility and SVI 'during the process', suggesting a fluid design approach rather than focusing on all details from the outset.

Twenty-two participants told us what proportion of projects used SVI guidelines: 'None' (7 participants), 'Some' (7), 'About half' (3), 'Most' (2), and 'All' (3) (see Figure 2c). Out of seven responses to the follow-on question there were no mentions of guidelines that highlight the issue of SVIs (such as "Shared Web Experiences" [56] and Mobile Accessibility [41]) – P19 said "*can't find any*", while P4 and P41 mentioned colour vision deficiency (CVD), thus providing further evidence that designers misunderstand SVIs. P29 responded "*clear and large fonts*", which is likely to be easier to see when in a bright environment, however it is not clear what guideline this idea originates or if the designer has determined this on their own.

Twenty participants told us what proportion of projects used SVI design tools: 'None' (9 participants), 'Some' (3), 'About half' (3), 'Most' (1), and 'All' (4) (see Figure 2c). Out of five responses listing tools, there were three mentions of tools for CVD. Either this is a misunderstanding or they are using CVD tools because no alternatives exist. One comment was "*N/A*" (P40) and the other was "*Color contrast buttons*" (P6).

Nineteen participants told us what proportion of projects ran evaluations with people experiencing SVIs. 'None' (6 participants), 'Some' (6), 'About half' (3), 'Most' (2), and 'All' (2) (see Figure 2c). Out of 12 follow-on requests to list evaluation techniques, there was a range of approaches. We found four mentions of self-testing, four mentions of in-house testing, two mentions of external testing, one mention of simulating the environment, and three other mentions related to: 'user testing environments', 'usability test', and 'direct observation'.

*What reasons were given **for** designing to reduce situational visual impairments?* We combined responses from the participants who said they 'Always' or 'Sometimes' design to reduce SVIs. Reasons given were: benefits everybody (8), for improved accessibility (3), project requirement (2), sufficient budget and time (2), for completeness (1), and moral obligation (1). We found that there are some similarities and differences between designing to reduce SVIs and including accessibility. Moral obligation, requirement of project, and having time were present in both. Having a sufficient budget was mentioned as a reason for designing to reduce SVIs, but it was not mentioned as a reason for including accessibility, although budget was listed as a reason for not including accessibility. There was no mention of a legal obligation, but, this is unsurprising since we are unaware of any laws for situational impairment. Discussion of designing to reduce SVIs benefiting everybody, for completeness, and improving accessibility, are similar to the 'improving usability and UX' reasons given for why designers include accessibility. Interestingly, while one participant said that pushing for accessibility will change perception, this did not occur for SVIs and is likely due to situational impairments not being widely discussed or understood. The fact that everyone is affected by SVIs could be used to positively change perceptions.

*What reasons were given **for not** designing to reduce situational visual impairments?* We combined responses from the participants who said they 'Sometimes' or 'Never' design to reduce SVIs: it is not in the design scope or their current practice (13 participants), limited resources (e.g., time, tools, money) (13), the participants are unaware of or had not considered SVI (5), and SVI is viewed as a minor issue (4). There are some similarities and differences between not designing to reduce SVIs and not including accessibility. Not within the project scope and limited resources were present in both. However, the responses for not designing to reduce SVIs also pointed towards it not being a part of current practice, which means we need to find ways to ensure that designers do adopt this in their design process. Differences in responses further highlight the uncertainty about SVIs and situational impairments in general. SVIs being viewed as a minor issue echo some of the opinions presented about accessibility (P17: "*It is not usually considered a priority due to the [percentage] of people it would affect*"), however, this is not the case with accessibility when considered on a global scale, and with the increase in mobile device use we expect SVIs to be increasingly prevalent. Several participants stated they were unaware of or had not previously considered SVIs, highlighting the need to investigate how this is approached during education. The remaining responses for not including accessibility were the challenges (e.g., it restricts design), the disinterest in accessibility, and the personal preference of not including accessibility; these could equally apply to SVIs. In fact, we asked the participants to tell us if they distinguish between a visual impairment and a situational visual impairment and seven participants indicated 'Yes', five indicated 'No', and P19 responded "*yes and no*". This further underlines the perceived similarities and differences between accessibility and SVIs.

Finally, we wanted to know what would best help designers create content less susceptible to SVIs. All the participants responded and were allowed to indicate more than one response. In order of most requested: 30 participants wanted 'Guidelines', followed by 'Education' (25), 'Digital design tools' (20), 'Support service' (13), 'Physical design tools' (9), and P42 said: "*Understanding the context of use. That is always the biggest hurdle. After that, design becomes a lot easier.*"

Summary

Our results illustrate similarities and differences between accessibility and SVIs, and was integral in providing us with information regarding current practice and the type of support designers want. We conducted follow-on interviews to identify how SVIs are handled in design (if at all) and how to effectively integrate SVI support into design processes.

INTERVIEWS

We conducted follow-on semi-structured interviews: 1) to further understand typical design processes, 2) to have a more in-depth discussion regarding accessibility and SVIs, and 3) to identify effective support for designing to reduce SVIs.

Method

The interviews were semi-structured using an interview guide (supplementary materials), with two occurring over Skype. The interviews were audio recorded for later transcription. The shortest interview was 38 minutes and the longest interview was 1 hour (M = 50 minutes). The participants were reimbursed with a £10 GBP (or equivalent) Amazon voucher.

Participants

Twenty participants from the questionnaire provided their contact details so we could invite them to the follow-on study. When contacted, four participants consented to take part in an interview (Table 1 summarises their backgrounds). All the participants reported experiencing SVIs. However, when it comes to designing to reduce SVIs, Max does not usually consider SVIs. Jo sometimes considers SVIs, especially if time permits, while Ron is always considering SVIs. Ann has worked on a project where an SVI feature was implemented. Since taking part in the questionnaire, there were no reported changes in considering SVIs during their design process.

Phases of Thematic Analysis

We closely followed the six phases of thematic analysis, as outlined by Braun and Clark [10]. First the audio recordings were listened to in full, then transcribed, anonymising places and names as we went. The transcripts (in supplementary materials) were checked against the audio recordings to ensure accuracy. RQDA (rqda.r-forge.r-project.org) was used to support the process of thematic analysis (e.g., the coding of interesting features). We provide the initial thematic map in supplementary materials. We reviewed and removed themes that did not reflect the aims for this study, and further refined the thematic map. This refinement was done with a Level 1 analysis (each code was discussed in relation to the thematic map) and a Level 2 analysis (checking that the themes suit the entire data set). Inter-rater reliability did not take place because it is not part of Braun and Clark's recommended process for thematic analysis, and there is debate as to whether it is suitable for this type of research approach [5, 34]. The completed thematic map is shown in Figure 3.

Results

Discussion on accessibility is prominent because SVIs are not something some of our participants often include when designing. We let our participants reflect on accessibility to learn how to support their practice. We found three themes (with nine sub-themes): *Design Practices Will Vary*, *Achieving Accessibility is Complex*, and *One Solution Does Not Fit All*.

ID	Age	Gender	Experience and Education
Jo (P3)	23	F	*Jo has been releasing mobile content for 1.5 years.* She has an Environmental Engineering undergraduate degree. She is currently undertaking a Masters degree and has taken part in workshops run by app developers and self-learns (e.g., using Coursera.org).
Max (P17)	28	M	*Max has been releasing mobile content for 2-3 years.* He has an Applied Computing undergraduate degree and is a games designer with no formal training – he describes it as a "*learn as we go*" job. The company creates their own games and perceives the customer as the client.
Ann (P19)	26	F	*Ann has been releasing mobile content for 2.5 years.* She has an Applied Computing undergraduate degree and a MSc in User Experience Design. She is employed as a mobile designer making native apps and hybrid apps (i.e., applications built with Web technologies to run on multiple platforms).
Ron (P30)	19	M	*Ron has been releasing mobile content for 3 years.* He had previously attended a design school and at the time of the interview had a few weeks left of his degree at a different school in the Netherlands. He was also working at a company as an intern designer.

Table 1. Participant demographics with descriptions of education, training, and work experiences. Each participant has been assigned a pseudonym.

Design Practices Will Vary

Our participants discussed their general design practices and, predictably, design does not have a one-size-fits-all approach. The design approaches can be adaptive, iterative, and unstructured. Some treat guidelines as suggestions rather than following them precisely. Being able to work quickly and efficiently is important to our participants, who recognised that involving more people in a design process can be detrimental. Within this main theme there were four important sub-themes.

Challenges of Client Involvement

Several different challenges were highlighted across participants with regards to dealing with clients throughout the design process. Client involvement can be a positive thing and participants viewed it as important, however, it was evident that there are negative experiences too.

> Ron: "*I've spent hours [with] clients [who] have just pointed...'I want that to move one pixel to the right, I want it to move one pixel.' It was really one pixel!*"

In general, the challenges faced were often because the design brief was incorrect (e.g., not making requirements clear).

> Ron: "*That's most of the time I think [the design brief] is missing something.*"

Clients can also have a negative attitude towards accessibility, often not requesting the inclusion of accessibility.

> Ann: "*A lot of clients think that [accessibility] takes longer for us to do and no-one is going to use it.*"

Clients may have brand colours that are problematic from an accessibility point of view. When designers raise accessibility concerns, the client can become distrustful and overbearing, often needing convincing about why certain requests are not suitable for the product. When designers want to design to reduce SVIs, clients may react in a similar way, but unlike when focusing on disability, designers can make a strong argument reasoning that *all* users can experience SVIs.

Perceptions of Design Guidelines

The participants discussed various positive and negative opinions regarding design guidelines. In general, guidelines help designers with a starting point for good design. Recent design guidelines, such as Google's Material Design and Apple's iOS design guidelines are perceived as being well suited. There is also trust in guidelines because they are understood to be vetted by others over time:

> Jo: "*I think that nowadays there are the guidelines when designing and you should follow them because [the guidelines are] something proven.*"

Guidelines that are associated with a well-known or large company (e.g., Apple) are used to discourage clients' poor or inaccessible design suggestions. Such guidelines are also appealing because they are often written using less technical language compared to other guidelines (e.g., WCAG). However, guidelines are not always seen as a positive resource. Guidelines can contain far too much content. At a minimum, designers want to find the key points quickly:

> Ann: "*Have you seen the meme of...the big JavaScript book? And then it's like JavaScript the good parts...the guidelines need that!*"

There is also the risk that guidelines can be distrusted if they are not written in a way that is expected by designers:

> Ann: "*We don't link anyone to WCAG because it doesn't look...trustable. They need to be completely rewritten, not like changed but just, there's so much needless text!*"

Approaches to Evaluating

Our participants discussed their opinions of feedback on design and their different evaluation approaches.

Two designers (Max and Ann) recognised the importance of evaluating a design early, with Max elaborating that user feedback is useful because usability issues can be identified early. In addition, Jo spoke about the importance of evaluating with a diverse group of people.

Evaluating with people is viewed as important, but sometimes the people used for those evaluations are not the target audience. Participants mentioned evaluating with the intended user group (Max), but also staff (Max) and students (Jo).

It is possible to run evaluations for SVIs. Sometimes designers are unable to evaluate under real-world conditions and so need

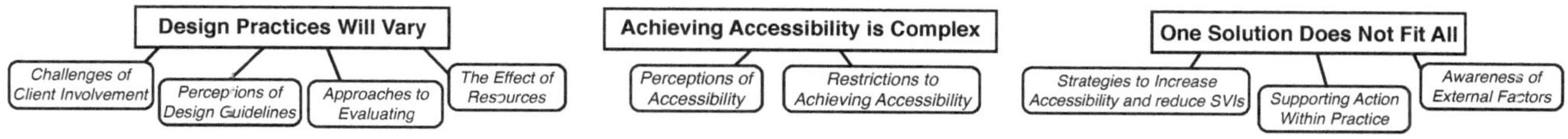

Figure 3. The thematic map with the final themes (*Design Practices Will Vary*, *Achieving Accessibility is Complex*, and *One Solution Does Not Fit All*).

to get creative. Jo and Ann discussed altering the environment to conduct evaluations:

> Jo: "*We changed the parameters like [room] lighting, and stuff like that.*"
>
> Ann: "*[We] tested it by shining [flashlights] on the phone to see if it worked because it wasn't sunny outside so – (Ann laughs) – there wasn't a lot we could do.*"

While this is commendable, providing clear SVI guidelines would increase the designers confidence that they are creating the best designs to reduce the occurrence of an SVI.

The Effect of Resources

Our participants also discussed the ways in which available resources (e.g., guidelines, time, money) can affect design.

Sometimes our participants will use design tools and they are positive towards these. For example, using a design tool that simulates colour vision deficiency helps show why designers need to consider colour more carefully (Ron). A tool that can do this for SVIs would support the designer, while increasing awareness of any nuances SVIs have in a similar way that there are different types of colour vision deficiency [48].

There was evidence of our participants trusting particular resources. For example, academic research findings that inform good design practice and trusting default designs from major OS platforms (e.g., fonts) because they will have been sufficiently verified and so save the designer time. There was uncertainty among all four participants as to the existence of guidelines for SVIs and Ron was unsure of the content of the accessibility section to Google's Material Design documentation. We know that some guidelines highlight SVIs (e.g., "Shared Web Experiences" [56] and Mobile Accessibility [41]), and the participants not mentioning this suggests that they need to be promoted more, however, based on Ron's point it is also important that guidelines be designed in a way for more rapid comprehension as discussed in the *Perceptions of Design Guidelines* sub-theme (above).

Finally, a lack of resources (e.g., time, budget) affected all of our participants. Jo mentioned facing a lack of resources and explained that "*One perception was to do it for free or not do it at all, so we preferred not to do it at all.*" In game development, Max said that a game never truly ships in a finished state because there is "*always more stuff*" to do.

Achieving Accessibility is Complex

Jo, Ann, and Ron all include or have included accessibility in their design process. All our participants were familiar with accessibility, but the amount of focus given to accessibility varied. Max and Ann had similar, quite extensive exposure to accessibility through their undergraduate degrees. However, while Ann includes accessibility during work, Max does not, highlighting how different industries can dictate accessibility adoption. Max does believe it "*would be nice to do*".

Perceptions of Accessibility

There are similar and contrasting perceptions that our participants presented towards accessibility, as well as their positive and negative attitudes towards accessibility.

The perceptions of accessibility range from negative to positive. During the discussion with Ann and Ron, there was a sense that accessibility is an afterthought for some designers. The negative perceptions towards accessibility that were offered as reasons for it not being done was that it took time to implement and it only benefits a small number of people – suggesting great effort required (in time and money) for little reward. Furthermore, requirements of implementing accessibility were seen as compromising design. The positive perceptions of accessibility were that it was not only important for people with disabilities but for all users because they benefit from accessibility (Jo and Ann). Ann also commented that because accessibility improves usability and user experience it would increase the likelihood of people returning to a product.

Similar contrasting views were present when commenting on SVIs. Jo said, "*No, it's not a small issue at all. [Using] an application [on] your mobile phone...you're not at home [in a controlled environment]...you go everywhere.*" However, Max did not consider it to be an important problem.

Restrictions to Achieving Accessibility

Our participants emphasised several reasons for designers not including accessibility when designing, which can provide insights into issues for promoting the consideration of SVIs.

Accessibility within education can vary. Two of our participants (Max and Ann) found there was a major focus on accessibility within their education, while Ron said accessibility was only given a minor focus, if any at all. Jo was introduced to accessibility, but it is unclear how much focus it was given. Restrictions to achieving accessibility may be due to designers themselves having a lack of awareness, particularly if they are early in their design career and therefore are unsure how to go about designing accessible content. Their lack of knowledge means it does not get done:

> Ann: "*They've come from being a pure graphics designer and moved in, and there's a lot of considerations that they just don't have.*"

In addition, limited exposure to accessibility is not limited to formal education; online courses, for example online UX courses "*barely mention accessibilty*" (Ann).

Max suggested that accessibility would be included if it was requested by the game players, thus reasoning his games do not require accessibility because there is no demand. However, by offering an inaccessible gaming experience, the players that require accessibility could be looking elsewhere. It is estimated that in the US alone, 6.2 million people are unable to play games due to a disability [61]. Max also suggested that the function of a product can determine if accessibility should be considered, believing that *"accommodat[ing] a lot of accessibility options in games kind of compromises, well it can compromise the actual gameplay."*

There is also the problem that current accessibility solutions are not adequate to support accessible design:

> Ann: *"I think a lot of the limitations of them is that they're terribly designed – (Ann laughs)."*

To ensure adoption of any solutions, such as design tools for SVIs, development must closely involve input from designers.

One Solution Does Not Fit All

There are different ways in which the inclusion of accessibility and designing to reduce SVIs can be increased. We report what support is required and the need to raise awareness about other factors that contribute to SVIs.

Strategies to Increase Accessibility and reduce SVIs

Our participants discussed ways in which awareness and understanding of accessibility and SVIs can be increased. It is clear that talking about these problems is not enough:

> Jo: *"There is no point of talking and talking about an issue without doing anything, [give designers] something because designers want to have something."*

Time was a recurring theme; designers require strategies that will save them time by supporting quick accessible design. Furthermore, considering the budget constraints faced by designers, any solution must be affordable (preferably free). There should be effort among the design community to create a dialogue discussing SVIs and accessibility in general:

> Jo: *"I think that we should, actually, all of us, we should try and make [designers] understand."*

Although Max equates education as similar to what guidelines are doing, educational settings can be used to scaffold the learning process of why guidelines are important and how they can be used. Since SVIs are *"never mentioned"* (Ron), it is important to target education and run tutorials or workshops, because learning extends beyond formal education.

It is also important to disseminate research outside of academia to increase awareness and understanding (e.g., Ron suggested a marketing campaign), and increase presence on popular websites used by designers. Ann felt that inclusion of a case study would be helpful. Since major OS platforms have some influence on designers, it was recommended that change could occur if the OS companies push for designing to reduce SVIs. Max mentioned that one way to increase accessibility within the games industry is for the app store companies (i.e., Apple and Google) to *"push for [accessibility]"* by saying a game can only be featured or promoted if it is accessible.

Finally, for some designers they may only be willing to rely on automated solutions handed by the mobile device. Max spoke positively about *"[Getting] saved a lot by the OS you know, like that colourblind mode and things like that."*

Supporting Action Within Practice

There are different ways that we can help designers implement accessibility and, in particular, design to reduce SVIs. Evaluations with people are important, however, recruiting people can be difficult. Jo suggests using incentives for getting people to take part, although this can become costly. It is important that the guidelines are *easy to understand* by the designer, but also for the client because designers are able to use design guidelines as leverage when the client is adamant that the design must meet a particular request. However, it is important that the solutions offered do not restrict design too much. We could achieve this with flexible guidelines to help maintain the designer's creativity:

> Max: *"As long as they weren't too restrictive then we'd probably be quite happy to just do that all the time."*

Offering design tools will be helpful and can reduce the reliance of reading guidelines. Max and Ann both felt that simulations would be useful to enhance the designer's understanding of SVIs, and simulations can be incorporated into design tools. However, a design tool must fit within the design process. This is a challenge since we know that designers do not follow the same design process, and even for an individual designer, approaches can vary according to the project requirements:

> Ann: *"I think that a lot of [the accessibility tools] are very much designed for specific use cases...but as part of a design flow, it sits by itself and it's very isolated."*

This presents an interesting challenge where there is a need for adaptable accessibility and SVI design tools that meet the needs for many different designers and their projects.

Finally, various techniques were discussed by our participants throughout the interview, either when discussing accessibility for visual impairments or SVIs, and these can be used to improve content visibility overall: increase brightness, increase contrast, increase font size or zoom in to the content, increase line thickness and weight of an element. Although guidelines exist for accessibility, we need to investigate what contrast ratios and font size are appropriate for SVIs. Jo suggested that applications should adapt to the environment.

Awareness of External Factors

There are also external factors that designers should be considering so that alternative modes of interaction can be implemented. One participant raised the point that external factors contribute to situational impairments:

> Ann: *"If [a user is] outside, there's a couple more things we need to be looking at, things like: Can they actually see it? Are they gonna be wearing gloves? [Will they] be touching the screen?"*

Although the full set of factors that contribute to SVIs is currently unknown, any solution must be flexible both in terms of design process and its outcome. Using resources such as the Haptimap Context Cards [33] are a good starting point, although they do not easily lend themselves to solutions.

DISCUSSION

Through surveying designers we found that there are striking similarities between the challenges faced when designing for accessibility and for SVIs – particularly when considering past issues surrounding accessibility. It appears as though SVI design is understandably 'behind' accessibility design: designing to reduce SVIs is often not in the design scope or part of the designer's current practice, there are limited resources available (e.g., time, money, tools) to design for SVIs, some designers are unaware or have not considered SVIs before, and SVIs can be viewed as a minor issue. However, our participants also reported positive connections between accessibility and SVI design. Both were perceived to be of benefit for a broader set of users than the target audience, and it was recognised that designing for one often resulted in at least partial inclusion of the other.

Our participants reported a *legal* obligation to incorporate accessibility in their designs, whereas this was not evident when discussing SVIs. Instead, motivation can come from *financial* gain through increasing market share by considering SVIs because people are more likely to return to apps with increased usability in different contexts. Furthermore, our participants incorporate accessibility due to moral convictions, suggesting a sense of *sympathy* for users with disabilities and arguing it is unethical to exclude accessibility. Impairment simulations can help designers build understanding of the importance of accessibility both in education [59] and a broader context [32], but these can be difficult, expensive, or time-consuming to prepare. In contrast, consideration of SVIs is likely coming from a feeling of *empathy* because designers, having experienced SVIs, can relate more easily. The 'empathic' understanding designers have of SVIs can be leveraged to enhance awareness of the importance for SVIs and accessibility, which should help to increase the inclusiveness of design. In our recommendations section for education, we further discuss increasing inclusivity and accessibility through designing to reduce SVIs in the context of related literature.

Compared to accessibility, less is known about particular situational impairments, such as SVIs, and what design guidelines are required [46]. Previous work has demonstrated the limitations imposed by hardware (e.g., screen technology [18]). Better displays and using auto-brightness only partially address the problem. More research is required to understand all the factors involved when experiencing SVIs. It is important to investigate how users currently deal with SVIs, which may result in alternative solutions not yet considered. However, we know that design can both cause and exacerbate SVIs.

Overall, there were fewer designers considering SVIs than accessibility. In addition, some participant responses showed a misunderstanding of what SVIs are, likely artificially inflating the numbers of designers who reported that they feel they are designing to reduce SVIs. Our participants requested support in the form of 'Guidelines', 'Education', and 'Digital Design Tools' and we ran follow-up interviews to identify the best way to integrate this support within current design processes.

From our interviews, we identified three themes providing us with greater insight into supporting designers in designing to reduce SVIs. The themes were *design practices will vary*, *achieving accessibility is complex*, and *one solution does not fit all*. In light of our findings, we next discuss and make recommendations on how to extend each of the following: Guidelines, Education, and Digital Design Tools.

Recommendations

Guidelines – We recommend that existing accessibility guidelines be extended to include SVIs. Industry guidelines (e.g., Android Material Design (material.io/guidelines) and WCAG 2.0 [12]) should be extended to help designers to increase luminance contrast for reduced screen brightness (e.g., due to low-battery) or bright sunlight situations. Huang et al. [22] have made progress in outlining mobile interface guidelines for comfortable reading, however, their study was run in a controlled indoor environment with ambient illumination levels much lower than those expected outside [1], thus further research is required. It is important to revise contrast ratios with data gathered on a large scale from typical real-world conditions and investigate guidelines for design elements such as font type, style, size, and weight, as well as icon designs.

Through discussion during the interviews, it became clear that there are both positive and negative attitudes towards guidelines. Criticism about accessibility guidelines (e.g., WCAG) being too verbose and dense is not new [11, 49], however we did discover that there are also positive attitudes towards guidelines (e.g., using them to support an argument against a client's design request, trusting the content designed will be of a high standard). Ultimately, we must create guidelines that are easy to understand and allow for a degree of flexibility (Ann: "*...a number but with a tolerance level...*") so creativity is not restricted. Allowing for flexibility is important: P15 (questionnaire) reported "*often picking colors is limited*", and during the interview Ann discussed the challenge of having to use company brand colours (echoing previous research [50]).

Education – During the interviews, Ron explicitly said SVIs were not part of his education and the other three participants discussed ways of increasing awareness and understanding of SVIs without mentioning their own education.

Youngblood et al. [58] argue that the ethical reasons for implementing accessibility are not effective, and so more should be done to emphasise the legal implications of not creating accessible content. However, as we found in our study, legality does not factor into designing to reduce SVIs at all because it is not required by law. Instead, we could potentially further increase the motivation to include accessibility by arguing that the population affected by SVIs is much larger and broader. This approach is not new; both Universal Design [9] and Universal Usability [51] promote designing for a broad range of users and situations. This idea persists in the academic community – a panel discussion led by Gavin Lew suggests that addressing accessibility for people with a disability will lead to designs that are universally beneficial [28]. This opinion is also supported by Petrie et al. [42] and Yesilada et al. [55]. However, based on the results of our study, it seems that this knowledge is not being passed on to designers.

There has been research looking at the pedagogical culture for accessibility in computer science programs [29], and suggestions on how to instil best practice in higher education classrooms [43, 58]. However, in addition to formal education, other methods of design training were discussed such as using online courses and learning best practice approaches promoted at conferences. Our participants discussed a range of resources available for people to learn from (e.g., online courses such as Coursera.org and Udemy.com, case studies on medium.com, blogs). In addition to formal education, targeting design websites (e.g. dribbble.com, medium.com) and online self-learning courses to address SVIs can further raise awareness and help to forge an inclusive design culture.

SVIs provide the benefit of helping designers to *empathise* first, rather than be *sympathetic*. Leveraging the conceptual and practical overlap between accessibility and SVIs, this empathy can increase accessible design. However, it is important to recognise that situational impairments are a temporary experience, therefore we must be careful not to equate situational impairments with congenital and acquired disabilities as they are fundamentally different [21].

Digital Design Tools – Digital design tools are one method of supporting action in practice, and this was the third most requested solution to support designing to reduce SVIs. A design support tool can serve as a platform for understanding how best to design for SVIs and the tool should incorporate the extended guidelines we suggest above.

Max discussed being more willing to rely on automated accessibility options provided by the mobile device's OS, thereby reducing the responsibility of the designer to create accessible content. Jo discussed applications that can adapt to the environment. Adapting content under variable lighting has been researched before [27, 60, 52]. However, this passes the responsibility to either the user to install an app, or the manufacturer or OS creators to implement the setting on the device. By automating the feature, there is additional processing power (resulting in lower battery life) and, more importantly, the designer no longer has control over their design's look.

During our interviews, Ann explained that accessibility design tools tend to be inadequate either by not fitting within the designer's design process or needing to be used when a design has been finished, thereby making accessibility checking more of an afterthought. Tigwell et al. [50] found similar issues with online tools for supporting designers to choose accessible colours for people with colour vision deficiency, yet demonstrated that by including designers in the creation of such tools, focus can be placed on designing with accessibility in mind, rather than restricting creativity for accessibility. SVI design tools must be developed with a user-centred design approach.

Our participants discussed increasing contrast to reduce SVIs caused by bright environments. In particular, Ann discussed implementing a high-contrast version of an interface, however, this addition was late in the design process and was only achieved because her design team had time while another feature was being developed. Considering that common issues reported by the participants were *working towards a deadline* and *not having enough time*, the design tool should support rapid designing, and be implemented to fit within the designer's typical work environment. The benefit of this approach is that the designer has control over the look and feel of the high-contrast design. Furthermore, it would be beneficial if the design tool allowed designers to interact with the interface layout to alter other design elements (icons, font, etc.).

Limitations and Future Work

First, many of our participants were early-career designers. However, early-career does not mean little design experience. We asked how long our participants had publicly or commercially released content, but we recognise this time does not account for prior experience refining their skills. Mobile content designers further into their career may have a greater awareness of SVIs and use of guidelines or tools that our participants are unaware of. Future work will look to understand how the results in this study compare with designers further into their career. However, it is concerning that designers who have experienced current education and training are mostly unaware of SVIs and the few support resources available. Therefore, it is important that we address this early rather than wait for designers to learn to design for SVIs through trial and error.

Second, only four designers responded to our request for a follow-on interview, yet each participant was at different points in their design careers, had different exposures to accessibility, and varied in the mobile content that they designed, which resulted in diverse information and opinions. All were able to discuss how to address SVIs. The sample size is small, however, the larger sample responding to the questionnaire provides us with the broad overview of designing to reduce SVIs, whereas the interviews were used as a means of discuss certain points more deeply. We will continue to work with a diverse range of mobile content designers to add to the findings of this work. Running a focus group would allow further reflection on these finding and provide an opportunity to outline an approach to creating new guidelines and tools.

CONCLUSION

Many people rely on their mobile devices for both personal and professional use. However, people experience SVIs when using these devices and content design can exacerbate SVIs. We surveyed 43 mobile content designers and ran four follow-on interviews to identify how often SVIs are considered and how we can provide effective support. We found key similarities and differences between accessibility and designing to reduce SVIs. Our participants requested guidelines, education, and digital design tools for improved SVI design support. Consequently, we make recommendations to shape the future of mobile design. (1) Current guidelines need to be extended to include validated SVI guidelines. (2) Information about SVIs must be included within formal education and online popular professional development resources. (3) New design tools, co-developed with designers to fit within their design process, will support rapid designing to reduce SVIs.

ACKNOWLEDGEMENTS

We thank our study participants. This work is part of Tigwell's PhD funded by an EPSRC DTP grant (EP/M506497/1).

REFERENCES

1. Gregg D Ander. 2003. *Daylighting performance and design*. John Wiley & Sons.
2. John P Andrawis, David A Muzykewicz, and Orrin I Franko. 2016. Mobile device trends in orthopedic surgery: rapid change and future implications. *Orthopedics* 39, 1 (2016), e51–e56. DOI: http://dx.doi.org/10.3928/01477447-20151228-01.
3. Google Android. n.d. Material Design Guidlines: Accessibility. (n.d.). https://material.io/guidelines/usability/accessibility.html Accessed: 2018-01-07.
4. Apple. n.d. Human Interface Guidelines: Visual Design. (n.d.). https://developer.apple.com/ios/human-interface-guidelines/visual-design Accessed: 2018-01-07.
5. David Armstrong, Ann Gosling, John Weinman, and Theresa Marteau. 1997. The place of inter-rater reliability in qualitative research: an empirical study. *Sociology* 31, 3 (1997), 597–606. DOI: http://dx.doi.org/10.1177/0038038597031003015
6. Orly Avitzur. 2010. In Practice: How Neurologists are Using the Newest Tablets – In and Out of the Clinic. *Neurology Today* 10, 24 (2010), 22–24. DOI: http://dx.doi.org/10.1097/01.NT.0000393332.57261.72
7. Kwang-Soo Bae, Uiyeong Cha, You-Jin Lee, Yeon-Kyu Moon, Hyun Chul Choi, Jae-Hoon Kim, and Chang-Jae Yu. 2011. Single pixel transmissive and reflective liquid crystal display using broadband cholesteric liquid crystal film. *Optics express* 19, 9 (2011), 8291–8296. DOI: http://dx.doi.org/10.1364/OE.19.008291
8. Michael E Becker and Jürgen Neumeier. 2011. 70.4: Optical Characterization of Scattering Anti-Glare Layers. In *SID Symposium Digest of Technical Papers*, Vol. 42. Wiley Online Library, 1038–1041. DOI: http://dx.doi.org/10.1889/1.3620997
9. Eric Bergman, Alistair Edwards, Deborah Kaplan, Greg Lowney, T. V. Raman, and Earl Johnson. 1996. Universal Design: Everyone Has Special Needs. In *Conference Companion on Human Factors in Computing Systems (CHI '96)*. ACM, New York, NY, USA, 153–154. DOI: http://dx.doi.org/10.1145/257089.257893
10. Virginia Braun and Victoria Clarke. 2006. Using thematic analysis in psychology. *Qualitative research in psychology* 3, 2 (2006), 77–101. DOI: http://dx.doi.org/10.1191/1478088706qp063oa
11. Catherine M. Brys and Wim Vanderbauwhede. 2006. Communication Challenges in the W3Cs Web Content Accessibility Guidelines. *Technical Communication* 53, 1 (2006), 60–78. https://www.ingentaconnect.com/content/stc/tc/2006/00000053/00000001/art00007
12. Ben Caldwell, Michael Cooper, L Guarino Reid, and Gregg Vanderheiden. 2008. Web content accessibility guidelines (WCAG) 2.0. *WWW Consortium (W3C)* (2008).
13. Hung-Lin Chi, Shih-Chung Kang, and Xiangyu Wang. 2013. Research trends and opportunities of augmented reality applications in architecture, engineering, and construction. *Automation in construction* 33 (2013), 116–122. DOI: http://dx.doi.org/10.1016/j.autcon.2012.12.017
14. Wendy Chisholm, Gregg Vanderheiden, and Ian Jacobs. 1999. *Web Content Accessibility Guidelines 1.0*. https://www.w3.org/TR/WCAG10/wai-pageauth.pdf. Accessed: 2017-03-04.
15. John Clarkson, Roger Coleman, Ian Hosking, and Sam Waller (Eds.). 2007. *Inclusive design toolkit*. Engineering Design Centre University of Cambridge.
16. Steve Clayton. 2012. Explaining NokiaâĂŹs ClearBlack display technology. (Feb 2012). https://blogs.microsoft.com/ai/explaining-nokias-clearblack-display-technology/. Accessed: 2018-03-21.
17. Mayank Goel, Leah Findlater, and Jacob Wobbrock. 2012. WalkType: Using Accelerometer Data to Accomodate Situational Impairments in Mobile Touch Screen Text Entry. In *Proceedings of the SIGCHI Conference on Human Factors in Computing Systems (CHI '12)*. ACM, New York, NY, USA, 2687–2696. DOI: http://dx.doi.org/10.1145/2207676.2208662
18. Rui Gong, Haisong Xu, Binyu Wang, and Ming Ronnier Luo. 2012. Image quality evaluation for smart-phone displays at lighting levels of indoor and outdoor conditions. *Optical Engineering* 51, 8 (2012), 084001–1. DOI: http://dx.doi.org/10.1117/1.OE.51.8.084001
19. GSMArena 2011. *IDC report says smartphones outsell computers for the first time*. GSMArena. http://www.gsmarena.com/idc_report_says_smartphones_outsell_computers_for_the_first_time-news-2303.php. Accessed: 2017-09-10.
20. Eric Hawkins. 2017. OGS: One Glass Solution touch panels Q&A. (Nov 2017). https://focuslcds.com/journals/ogs-one-glass-solution-touch-panels-qa/. Accessed: 2018-03-21.
21. Shawn Lawton Henry, Shadi Abou-Zahra, and Judy Brewer. 2014. The Role of Accessibility in a Universal Web. In *Proceedings of the 11th Web for All Conference (W4A '14)*. ACM, New York, NY, USA, Article 17, 4 pages. DOI: http://dx.doi.org/10.1145/2596695.2596719
22. Hsin-Pou Huang, Li-Chen Ou, and Yinqiu Yuan. 2017. Effects of age and ambient illuminance on visual comfort for reading on a mobile device. *Color Research & Application* 42, 3 (2017), 352–361. DOI: http://dx.doi.org/10.1002/col.22089

23. Shaun K. Kane, Jacob O. Wobbrock, and Ian E. Smith. 2008. Getting off the Treadmill: Evaluating Walking User Interfaces for Mobile Devices in Public Spaces. In *Proceedings of the 10th International Conference on Human Computer Interaction with Mobile Devices and Services (MobileHCI '08)*. ACM, New York, NY, USA, 109–118. DOI: http://dx.doi.org/10.1145/1409240.1409253

24. Simon Khalaf and Lali Kesiraju. 2017. *U.S. Consumers Time-Spent on Mobile Crosses 5 Hours a Day*. http://flurrymobile.tumblr.com/post/157921590345/us-consumers-time-spent-on-mobile-crosses-5. Accessed: 2017-09-12.

25. Youn Jin Kim, M Ronnier Luo, Wonhee Choe, Hong Suk Kim, Seung Ok Park, Yeseul Baek, Peter Rhodes, Seongdeok Lee, and Chang Yeong Kim. 2008. Factors affecting the psychophysical image quality evaluation of mobile phone displays: the case of transmissive liquid-crystal displays. *JOSA A* 25, 9 (2008), 2215–2222. DOI: http://dx.doi.org/10.1364/JOSAA.25.002215

26. Youn-Jin Kim, M Ronnier Luo, Peter Rhodes, Won-Hee Choe, Seong-Deok Lee, Seung-Sin Lee, Young-Shin Kwak, Dus-Sik Park, and Chang-Yeong Kim. 2007. Image-color-quality modeling under various surround conditions for a 2-in. mobile transmissive LCD. *Journal of the Society for Information Display* 15, 9 (2007), 691–698.

27. Myong-Young Lee, Chang-Hwan Son, Jong-Man Kim, Cheol-Hee Lee, and Yeong-Ho Ha. 2007. Illumination-level adaptive color reproduction method with lightness adaptation and flare compensation for mobile display. *J Imaging Sci Techn* 51, 1 (2007), 44–52. DOI: http://dx.doi.org/10.2352/J.ImagingSci.Technol.(2007)51:1(44)

28. Gavin Lew, Marc L Resnick, Bo Campbell, Astrid Weber, and Sanjay Batra. 2015. Connecting Accessibility and User Experience in the Mobile Age. In *Proceedings of the Human Factors and Ergonomics Society Annual Meeting*, Vol. 59. SAGE Publications, 1120–1123. DOI: http://dx.doi.org/10.1177/1541931215591162

29. Sarah Lewthwaite and David Sloan. 2016. Exploring Pedagogical Culture for Accessibility Education in Computing Science. In *Proceedings of the 13th Web for All Conference (W4A '16)*. ACM, New York, NY, USA, Article 3, 4 pages. DOI: http://dx.doi.org/10.1145/2899475.2899490

30. Po-Hung Lin and Wen-Hung Kuo. 2011. Image quality of a mobile display under different illuminations. *Perceptual and motor skills* 113, 1 (2011), 215–228. DOI: http://dx.doi.org/10.2466/01.24.PMS.113.4.215-228

31. Peter Liu, Fahad Zafar, and Aldo Badano. 2014. The effect of ambient illumination on handheld display image quality. *Journal of digital imaging* 27, 1 (2014), 12–18. DOI: http://dx.doi.org/10.1007/s10278-013-9636-1

32. Rhouri MacAlpine and David R. Flatla. 2016. Real-Time Mobile Personalized Simulations of Impaired Colour Vision. In *Proceedings of the 18th International ACM SIGACCESS Conference on Computers and Accessibility (ASSETS '16)*. ACM, New York, NY, USA, 181–189. DOI: http://dx.doi.org/10.1145/2982142.2982170

33. Charlotte Magnusson. 2011. *Design for Dynamic User Experiences*. http://www.haptimap.org/designtools/due.html Accessed: 2016-02-23.

34. David F Marks and Lucy Yardley. 2004. *Research methods for clinical and health psychology*. Sage.

35. Michael Mauderer, Garreth W Tigwell, Benjamin M Gorman, and David R Flatla. 2017. Beyond Accessibility: Lifting Perceptual Limitations for Everyone. *arXiv preprint arXiv:1709.08957* (2017).

36. Microsoft. n.d. Universal Windows Platform App Developer: Accessibility. (n.d.). https://docs.microsoft.com/en-gb/windows/uwp/design/accessibility/accessibility Accessed: 2018-01-07.

37. Terhi Mustonen, Maria Olkkonen, and Jukka Hakkinen. 2004. Examining Mobile Phone Text Legibility While Walking. In *CHI '04 Extended Abstracts on Human Factors in Computing Systems (CHI EA '04)*. ACM, New York, NY, USA, 1243–1246. DOI: http://dx.doi.org/10.1145/985921.986034

38. Alan F Newell. 1995. Extra-ordinary human-computer interaction. In *Extra-ordinary human-computer interaction*, Alistair D. N. Edwards (Ed.). Cambridge University Press, Cambridge New York, NY, USA, 3–18.

39. Don Norman and Bruce Tognazzini. 2015. How Apple Is Giving Design A Bad Name. (Nov 2015). https://www.fastcodesign.com/3053406/how-apple-is-giving-design-a-bad-name. Accessed: 2017-06-25.

40. AM Nuijs and JJL Horikx. 1994. Diffraction and scattering at antiglare structures for display devices. *Applied optics* 33, 18 (1994), 4058–4068. DOI: http://dx.doi.org/10.1364/AO.33.004058

41. Kim Patch, Jeanne Spellman, and Kathy Wahlbin. 2015. *Mobile Accessibility: How WCAG 2.0 and Other W3C/WAI Guidelines Apply to Mobile* (w3c first public working draft 26 february 2015 ed.). https://www.w3.org/TR/mobile-accessibility-mapping Accessed: 2017-03-04.

42. Helen Petrie, Andreas Savva, and Christopher Power. 2015. Towards a Unified Definition of Web Accessibility. In *Proceedings of the 12th Web for All Conference (W4A '15)*. ACM, New York, NY, USA, Article 35, 13 pages. DOI: http://dx.doi.org/10.1145/2745555.2746653

43. Cynthia Putnam, Maria Dahman, Emma Rose, Jinghui Cheng, and Glenn Bradford. 2016. Best Practices for Teaching Accessibility in University Classrooms: Cultivating Awareness, Understanding, and Appreciation for Diverse Users. *ACM Trans. Access. Comput.* 8, 4, Article 13 (March 2016), 26 pages. DOI: http://dx.doi.org/10.1145/2831424

44. Jo Rabin and Charles McCathieNevile. 2008. *Mobile web best practices 1.0*. http://www.w3.org/TR/2008/REC-mobile-bp-20080729. Accessed: 2017-06-20.

45. Katharina Reinecke, David R. Flatla, and Christopher Brooks. 2016. Enabling Designers to Foresee Which Colors Users Cannot See. In *Proceedings of the 2016 CHI Conference on Human Factors in Computing Systems (CHI '16)*. ACM, New York, NY, USA, 2693–2704. DOI: http://dx.doi.org/10.1145/2858036.2858077

46. Zhanna Sarsenbayeva, Niels van Berkel, Chu Luo, Vassilis Kostakos, and Jorge Goncalves. 2017. Challenges of Situational Impairments During Interaction with Mobile Devices. In *Proceedings of the 29th Australian Conference on Computer-Human Interaction (OZCHI '17)*. ACM, New York, NY, USA, 477–481. DOI: http://dx.doi.org/10.1145/3152771.3156161

47. Andrew Sears, Min Lin, Julie Jacko, and Yan Xiao. 2003. When computers fade: Pervasive computing and situationally-induced impairments and disabilities. In *HCI International*, Vol. 2. Lawrence Erlbaum Associates, Mahwah, N.J, 1298–1302.

48. Lindsay T Sharpe, Andrew Stockman, Herbert Jägle, and Jeremy Nathans. 1999. Opsin genes, cone photopigments, color vision, and color blindness. *Color vision: From genes to perception* 351 (1999).

49. David Swallow, Christopher Power, Helen Petrie, Anna Bramwell-Dicks, Lucy Buykx, Carlos A Velasco, Aidan Parr, and Joshue O Connor. 2014. Speaking the Language of Web Developers: Evaluation of a Web Accessibility Information Resource (WebAIR). In *International Conference on Computers for Handicapped Persons*. Springer, 348–355. DOI: http://dx.doi.org/10.1007/978-3-319-08596-8_54

50. Garreth W. Tigwell, David R. Flatla, and Neil D. Archibald. 2017. ACE: A Colour Palette Design Tool for Balancing Aesthetics and Accessibility. *ACM Transactions on Accessible Computing (TACCESS)* 9, 2, Article 5 (Jan. 2017), 32 pages. DOI: http://dx.doi.org/10.1145/3014588

51. Gregg Vanderheiden. 2000. Fundamental Principles and Priority Setting for Universal Usability. In *Proceedings on the 2000 Conference on Universal Usability (CUU '00)*. ACM, New York, NY, USA, 32–37. DOI: http://dx.doi.org/10.1145/355460.355469

52. Gregory Ward, Hyunjin Yoo, Afsoon Soudi, and Tara Akhavan. 2017. 75-3: Reducing Glare from Reflected Highlights in Mobile and Automotive Displays. In *SID Symposium Digest of Technical Papers*, Vol. 48. Wiley Online Library, 1105–1107. DOI: http://dx.doi.org/10.1002/sdtp.11840

53. Jacob O Wobbrock. 2006. The future of mobile device research in HCI. In *CHI 2006 workshop proceedings: what is the next generation of human-computer interaction*. 131–134.

54. Yeliz Yesilada, Giorgio Brajnik, and Simon Harper. 2011. Barriers common to mobile and disabled web users. *Interacting with Computers* 23, 5 (2011), 525–542. DOI: http://dx.doi.org/10.1016/j.intcom.2011.05.005

55. Yeliz Yesilada, Giorgio Brajnik, Markel Vigo, and Simon Harper. 2015. Exploring perceptions of web accessibility: a survey approach. *Behaviour & Information Technology* 34, 2 (2015), 119–134. DOI: http://dx.doi.org/10.1080/0144929X.2013.848238

56. Yeliz Yesilada, Alan Chuter, and Shawn Lawton Henry. 2013. Shared web experiences: barriers common to mobile device users and people with disabilities. (2013). https://www.w3.org/WAI/mobile/experiences.html. Accessed: 2017-12-17.

57. Yeliz Yesilada, Simon Harper, Tianyi Chen, and Shari Trewin. 2010. Small-device Users Situationally Impaired by Input. *Comput. Hum. Behav.* 26, 3 (May 2010), 427–435. DOI: http://dx.doi.org/10.1016/j.chb.2009.12.001

58. Norman E Youngblood, Lakshmi N Tirumala, and Robert Anthony Galvez. 2017. Accessible Media: The Need to Prepare Students for Creating Accessible Content. *Journalism & Mass Communication Educator* (2017), 1–12. DOI: http://dx.doi.org/10.1177/1077695817714379

59. Susan A Youngblood. 2013. Communicating web accessibility to the novice developer: From user experience to application. *Journal of Business and Technical Communication* 27, 2 (2013), 209–232. DOI: http://dx.doi.org/10.1177/1050651912458924

60. Jiadi Yu, JIaming Zhao, Yingying Chen, and Jie Yang. 2015. Sensing Ambient Light for User Experience-Oriented Color Scheme Adaptation on Smartphone Displays. In *Proceedings of the 13th ACM Conference on Embedded Networked Sensor Systems (SenSys '15)*. ACM, New York, NY, USA, 309–321. DOI: http://dx.doi.org/10.1145/2809695.2809709

61. Bei Yuan, Eelke Folmer, and Frederick C Harris. 2011. Game accessibility: a survey. *Universal Access in the Information Society* 10, 1 (2011), 81–100. DOI: http://dx.doi.org/10.1007/s10209-010-0189-5

From Hyperlinks to Hypercues: Entity-Based Affordances for Fluid Information Exploration

Khalil Klouche[1,2], Tuukka Ruotsalo[1], Giulio Jacucci[1]
[1]Helsinki Institute for Information Technology HIIT, Department of Computer Science, University of Helsinki, Finland
[2]Aalto University, School of Arts, Design and Architecture, Department of Media, Espoo, Finland
first.last@helsinki.fi

ABSTRACT

We introduce the concept of hypercue, a complement to hyperlinks in the form of an interactive representation of real-world entities (e.g., persons, places, concepts) providing personalized access points to information. Hypercues create opportunities to flexibly discover, store, and share information; organize one's thoughts; and gain insights from the data.

We explore the design space of interaction techniques supporting entity-based information exploration by reviewing recent examples of such work. We reflect on these through the lens of eight essential features of exploratory search systems to devise generalizable design principles. Our main contribution is a design template describing the hypercue, which consists of a minimal set of affordances that ensure all important features for supporting exploratory search can be addressed while leaving enough design space to facilitate integration with a variety of systems. Finally, we describe the rationale behind the design template and discuss its implications.

ACM Classification Keywords

H.5.m Information Interfaces and Presentation (e.g. HCI): Miscellaneous; H.5.2 User Interfaces: Prototyping; H.3.3 Information Search and Retrieval: Search Process

Author Keywords

entity search, interaction design, information exploration, fluid interaction

DIS '18, June 9–13, 2018, Hong Kong
© 2018 ACM. ISBN 978-1-4503-5198-0/18/06... $15.00
DOI: https://doi.org/10.1145/3196709.3196775

INTRODUCTION

The amount of available information keeps growing exponentially, and the access points provided by query-and-response search engines – the ten blue links – are too narrow to offer a sensible overview of available material related to a given query. We need options for broader and more personalized access to information, and help making sense of it. Thankfully, new technologies in information retrieval have created opportunities to address these problems and rethink online media access and structuring. As entity search and recommendation become a reality and as recommender algorithms become pervasive, users' information trails rely less on documents linked explicitly by content creators.

Current work on search and recommendation technologies is mostly focused on the development of adaptive and autonomous user interfaces that ease the search process by reducing explicit user inputs at the expense of transparency and user control. An opposite approach would be to reinforce user control through the use of direct manipulation and rich user interfaces that provide users with a feeling of accomplishment and increased responsibility over the search process, as advocated by Ben Shneiderman [29]. Development of such systems is not new [1] but their reliance on filtering methods often limits them to homogeneous datasets and specific use cases (e.g., movie exploration and product finding) that limit opportunities for discovery and generalization.

However, as contemporary search and recommendation is fueled by extremely complex data structures, the same technologies create the opportunity to develop interactive systems that provide users with the ability to finely steer their progression within the information space in accordance to their immediate needs, understanding and inspiration. Related information and overview of the data can be computed on the fly to suit the very specific needs of each user at any time during the exploration, providing constant access to more detailed or more general information, new directions and branching topics. To enable such possibilities, we need visualizations and affordances that do not rely on preestablished criteria to further the exploration.

The need for supporting information exploration has been demonstrated by studies and models of information-seeking behaviors. Features of such support have been described, and most information tools (e.g., websites and browsers) al-

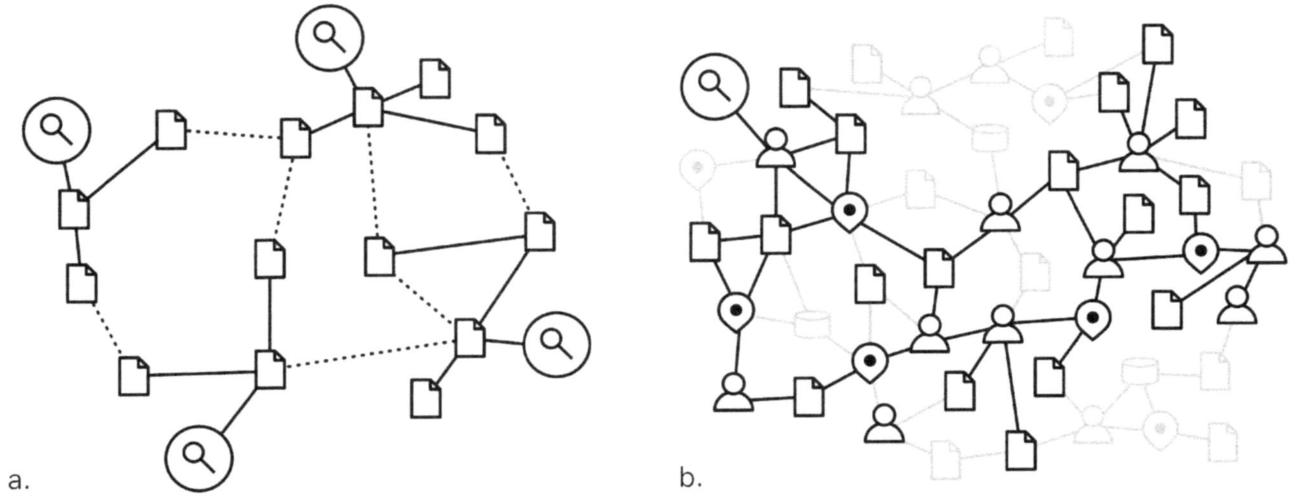

Figure 1. Information exploration is often compared to a journey through the information space. In practice, however, text-based querying and the limited overview force users to take multiple discrete steps inside the information space to make sense of it (a). In our research, we aim to utilize the underlying data structure to help users make sense of the information space and foster insights (b).

ready implement such features by providing shortcuts to quick lookup, related items or info boxes when relevant. Our research builds upon such streams of work to develop actionable solutions for implementing said features. However, instead of taking an additive design approach that would consist of bundling together multiple widgets, each addressing a specific task, we are more interested in the exploration of alternative interaction paradigms and the discovery of novel key affordances to take full advantage of the volume and complexity of the data available today. Although entity-based exploration has been studied and is already commonplace, it mostly consists of following information paths provided by successive single recommended items, like following a path of hyperlinks. Such an approach can lead to enjoyable serendipity, but it lacks the means to show the personalized results that a typed query can provide. As for typed queries, recalling search terms to formulate and reformulate queries (especially when exploring an unfamiliar information space), is not as easy as following visible items. Moreover, although information exploration is often compared to a linear journey through an information space (e.g., the information foraging theory [23] or the berrypicking model [3]), in practice, text-based querying and limited overviews force users to take multiple discrete steps inside the information space, as seen in Figure 1a, instead of utilizing the data's rich underlying structure as seen in Figure 1b. Our work suggests that a few key affordances, such as the ability to compose queries by grouping multiple entities and then refine it as new entities are discovered, provide a compelling and efficient way to explore a large information space while taking advantage of its entity-based structure.

This conceptual work is a reflection on our exploration of interaction techniques designed to support entity-based information seeking, grounded in available literature. Our main contribution is a design template describing the hypercue, an interactive representation of entities that provides personalized access points to information and serves as a complement to hyperlinks. Hypercues create opportunities to flexibly discover, store, and share information, and to gain insights from the data. The hypercue design template consists of a minimal set of affordances that ensure all important features for supporting exploratory search can be addressed while leaving enough design space to facilitate integration with a variety of systems. We describe the rationale behind the design template and discuss its implications.

BACKGROUND

A large body of work builds upon what seems to be a human propensity to consider the information space as a physical space in which we move, progress and discover. Bates' berrypicking approach to search [3] and the information foraging theory [23] describe users' information-seeking behavior through the metaphor of a physical journey. With the "information flaneur", [6] Dörk et al. go deeper into the physical metaphor by comparing information spaces to the 19th-century city in terms of growth, cultural significance, and being the place for social struggle and negotiation, and they use such parallels to envision "positive" approaches to information practice. Such models have all contributed to shift the emphasis from a mostly technical consideration of information retrieval toward human processes [14]. We see the present work as the design counterpart of such a framework, providing actionable principles toward implementation of systems supporting and based on observed human behaviors.

In this work, we utilize entity search as technical opportunities supporting fluid information exploration as a goal. Here, we clarify these two essential notions.

Fluid Information Exploration

When we discuss interactions and user interface design, fluidity is often cited as a goal [10, 25]. White and Roth [31] mention fluid interactions as an important feature of future search systems when discussing novel interaction paradigms. They link that notion to human-machine symbiosis and interactions through fluid hand gestures, citing the fantasy user interface from the movie *Minority Report* as an example of what a truly fluid interface could look like. However, that notion is not theoretically defined and is generally used while relying on the reader's intuitive understanding of the metaphor, something that flows continuously, naturally making its way around obstacles and adapting its pace to the environment.

A satisfying operational definition is proposed by Elmqvist et al. [7], who work around the difficulty of defining fluidity theoretically by focusing on the properties we can expect from fluid systems. These properties are grouped into three sets:

Fluid interactions support direct manipulation: Direct manipulation describes an interaction paradigm in which digital representations of objects behave as objects themselves [28]. Direct interaction with these objects is enabled by reducing indirections between input and output spaces. For example, the touch-sensitive layer of a touch device is confounded with its display and calibrated so that inputs are registered precisely at the display location. The paradigm relies on a preference for physical actions, and immediate visible effects allowing rapid course adaptation [13].

Fluid interactions promote flow: Flow is a mental state induced by immersion in one's activity, characterized by a loss of sense of time. The main actionable property for inducing flow relies on letting users feel in control, and employ just the right amount of skills to let them progress in their tasks at a pace that will feel neither too slow nor too fast, accommodating a person's continued and deepening enjoyment as skills grow [20].

Fluid interactions minimize the gulfs of action: The gulfs of action are a notion introduced by Donald Norman [21], who uses it to describe the gap between a user's expectation of a system and the system's actual state.

A limitation of this definition is that these properties are not complementary, as they seem contained in Shneiderman's advocacy for comprehensible, predictable and controllable user interfaces through direct manipulation [29]; however, it provides various approaches to the implementation of such a goal.

Our focus on fluidity is not exclusively motivated by performance or the sole objective of making the user more efficient in accomplishing her task. Fluidity conveys open-endedness and the consideration that the process itself, through the potential discoveries it may yield, is often just as valuable as the end product. The information flaneur [6] offers an inspiring model of information seeking centered around positive information practices, as opposed to considering information seeking the fulfilling of an information need or addressing of a deficiency. The information flaneur's implications for research and design offer design goals for fostering or enabling such experiences by considering explorability principles (e.g., orientation, visual momentum, and opportunities for serendipity) and bridging gaps between information spaces, contexts, and conceptual levels by exploiting scalable or generalizable rules and common patterns. This focus on continuity and momentum of the exploration experience complements the operational definition of fluidity.

The present work reflects our commitment to such an approach to information practices, as we strive to design interactions that do not induce specific behaviors nor limit their utility to very specific scenarios. Given a specific scenario or task, dedicated tools might undoubtedly outperform a more generalist approach applied in a monolithic system. However, we envision a future of information exploration where users' interfaces of choice are not constrained by the data but by personal preferences that could indifferently and seamlessly be used to navigate academic literature, a movie streaming catalog, the news or social media posts, allowing the transfer of any progress from one tool to another thanks to a set of standard affordances like the ones described in the present work. We work toward that goal by implementing the principles of fluidity mentioned above. We support direct manipulation by enabling direct interactions with every bit of displayed information that is relevant to the user. As a result, we design for touch-enabled displays, and present information in the form of objects that can be manipulated. We build interfaces around small sets of simple rules that are consistent across a given system, which we achieve by limiting the amount of widgets and separate views and preferring single workspaces. Through these principles, we attempt to facilitate memorization regarding operations while enabling creative strategies and behaviors leading to potentially complex results.

Entity Search

In the information search field, entities are references to real-world objects or concepts (e.g., persons, places, movies, topics, and products). Entities are linked with typed relationships. For example, "Tom Hanks (actor)" and "*Forrest Gump* (movie)" are linked via "stars in". Together, they form a graph in which entities are nodes and relationships are the edges. Such graphs are known as *knowledge graphs* and generally stored within *knowledge bases*.

In web searches, a majority of emitted queries pivot around a specific entity [24]. Knowledge bases are useful to providing additional information around an entity and recommending additional entities. In conventional web search engines, queries pointing toward an entity will usually trigger a first result that points to the information source with the most general information about the entity (typically, the corresponding Wikipedia entry), which in turn requires the system to be able to match the typed query to the corresponding entity.

Entity-Based Exploration

Google Search provides for most entity-based queries not only a relevant entry but a knowledge graph with relevant information about the entity and recommended related entities in the case of an actor, name, age, and lists of movies and costars. Miliaraki et al. [18] studied the behavior of users of Yahoo Spark, a system that recommends related entities alongside Yahoo Search results; the users take advantage of the system to engage in explorative entity search by discovering information through successive clicks on recommended entities. Such cases exemplify why entity-search is considered an ideal paradigm for exploratory search and an important topic in information retrieval and semantic web communities. A large body of recent research work addresses challenges

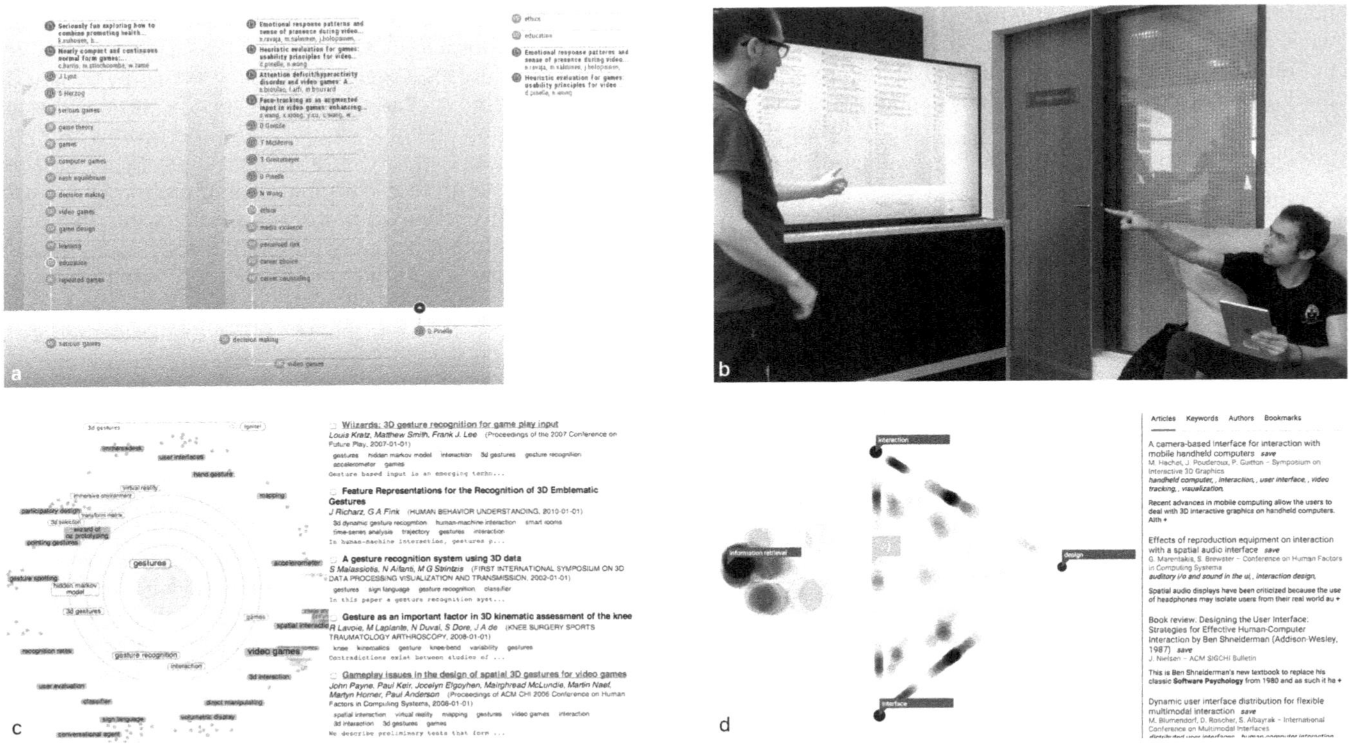

Figure 2. We have explored the design space of entity-based systems supporting information exploration through the development and evaluation of multiple prototypes: (a) ExplorationWall, (b) QueryTogether, (c) SciNet/IntentRadar, and (d) RelevanceMap.

regarding the computation necessary for entity search, such as the finding and ranking of related entities, matching entities with occurrences in free text queries and completion of entity lists based on given entity examples. However, as techniques improve, it is difficult to find research addressing interaction techniques that enable end-users to access and benefit from such rich information in a wide variety of activities, as examples usually target very specific scenarios and tasks. Several such entity-based exploration systems have been designed to support expert investigators in making sense of a corpus of documents [4, 30, 5].

As entity search becomes a reality, it creates plenty of opportunities for exploration, not only in the way relevance and ranking are computed but in how we will interact with information within the new paradigm. Once available information is meaningfully structured, the information space becomes a high-dimensional medium ready to be unfolded as explorers pull its various threads in various directions and discover content according to their needs, inspiration or chance. The goal of entity-based fluid information exploration requires substantial thinking about the way we display and interact with entities and come up with fundamental principles that are generalizable to any search contexts (e.g., academic publications, social media, movie database and personal emails).

EXPLORING THE DESIGN SPACE

We have had the opportunity to explore the design space of systems that support fluid information exploration through the design, development and evaluation of several functional prototypes. These prototypes each addressed different aspects of information exploration (e.g., facilitating query formulation, facilitating query refinement, providing insights from the data and supporting collaboration). Through user studies, we have been able to demonstrate improvement of these various aspects over conventional approaches and identify design principles that were responsible for these improvements. We have also been able to observe how these principles affected user behaviors and search strategies. The next challenge was to use this collection of observations on individual systems, to extract fundamental actionable principles that would outline a paradigm for fluid information exploration.

ExplorationWall

Figure 2a. shows ExplorationWall's interface [15]. This work initially addresses challenges in performing exploratory search tasks using touch-based devices, such as formulating queries in unknown information spaces, identifying new search directions, and going through long lists of results with low information gain. Those challenges are all made more difficult on conventional user interfaces by the lack of physical text-input or text-selection peripherals.

A single workspace allows for the simultaneous display of several parallel search streams, each consisting of a vertical organization of entities as queries and search results. Each result set consists of multiple entities of varying types (i.e., documents, persons and keywords) and each entity can in turn be used as a query or part of a query in an existing search stream or in a new one. Entities can be easily manipulated (e.g., moved, stored, or combined) and can provide content to be browsed, such as articles or insights to extend exploration(e.g., new topics or authors).

ExplorationWall has demonstrated substantial improvement over regular interfaces in exploratory search tasks [15]. Results showed a higher amount of relevant information retrieved by participants explained by a much more active behavior and measured in the search trail analysis in number of queries, as well as revisit and branching rates. In the end, participants that were given a topic to explore with which they were unfamiliar, covered much more of all available relevant information by making better use of multiple search sessions.

QueryTogether

QueryTogether has been designed to support exploratory search in a collaborative and spontaneous search setting, as shown in Figure 2b. To do so, we have adapted ExplorationWall's interface so we could use it across multiple devices (e.g., laptops, tablets, and large touch displays) and support both private sharing of information and broadcasting to all users.

The reading list has been adapted to feature saved and received entities in a scrollable list and a user panel, which shows what users are active in the system. Users are identified by the name they entered at login and their status, either *private* if they are using a private device or *public* if they act as a session moderator on a large screen available to all participants.

Sharing is performed by dragging an entity over to the chosen user. The recipient will instantly receive a new instance of the sent entity in her side panel. If the side panel is closed, a visual notification in the corner informs the user of the number of new entities received. Next to each user label, a "Message" icon allows the user to send a short message along with an entity. The reading list can be filtered with respect to a chosen collaborator and will subsequently show only entities and documents sent to or received from that user. Filtering based on one's own ID will display only entities that have been saved locally and ignore anything sent or received remotely.

SciNet/Intent Radar

SciNet/Intent Radar is a search system for information exploration that builds a user intent model to better adapt returned results to a user's needs [8, 26]. To do so, the system enables relevance feedback on a visualization of the user's intent, which is here visualized separately from the result list through the use of weighted keywords, as seen in Figure 2c. The benefits of a separate visualization are a higher cue density, a comprehensive overview of the current intent, the opportunity to provide suggestions for future intents and the practicality of being an add-on widget to familiar search interfaces. In this case, a user provides an initial query, which yields a regular result list, plus a set of the most central keywords extracted from the results, visualized on a radar (closer to the center meaning more central). This interface offers an overview of how the system perceives the query. The user can then adjust the weight distribution by sliding individual keywords closer to or farther from the center, and the result list will refresh accordingly. Another one of the system's important features is the visualization in the radar's outer ring of a variety of secondary keywords, chosen for their diversity, providing the user with insights about future search directions and a way to redirect the search incrementally without having to change the initial query. The system has been shown to improve users' task performance in complex search tasks in which conventional query-response systems failed to help users direct their search [26].

RelevanceMap

RelevanceMap [16] provides the user with an interactive map of the whole document space with respect to the positions of multiple query phrases visualized as mobile markers on a 2-D workspace, as seen in Figure 2d. The map allows for visualization of variations in information density with respect to elements of the query, even with large amounts of returned documents, which enables quick evaluation of the query and the resulting data. Browsing is performed through a pointing gesture on the map, which re-ranks the whole document collection according to the location of interest. The corresponding result list appears in a conventional layout next to the map. The quick re-ranking interaction enables exploration of the multi-dimensional data structure.

This work is another example of visualization taking advantage of direct manipulation to interact with the data for sensemaking purposes. In this case, however, manipulation of the map allows the user to determine the scope of the higher level search task by outlining the whole document space using multiple queries and visualizing the whole set (i.e., thousands of documents instead of a small selection). The exploration is then performed through a re-ranking interaction over areas of interest on the relevance map. The user can now precise or change the focus of her exploration and refresh the result list with a pointing gesture instead of reformulating the query. This ability allows the user to explore large amounts of relevant information without interruption, while still permitting changes in the query at any time, thus adapting fluidly to the user's immediate needs.

RelevanceMap showed significant support in how users perceived the information space with respect to topics of interest and in retrieval of information relevant to complex criteria [16].

FEATURES OF EXPLORATORY SEARCH SYSTEMS AS A LENS

In our exploration of the design space of systems that support information exploration, we have often taken advantage of the work of White and Roth [31] as a frame to ground our designs and explain their effects on user behavior and performance. Their work includes a list of features of exploratory search systems that exemplify essential aspects of supporting information exploration. These features have been an important source of inspiration as they bring attention to various fundamental areas of exploration.

We reflect on our work through the lens of these eight features of exploratory search systems to identify fundamental principles at work in our various systems and new opportunities for entity-based exploration.

Support Querying and Rapid Query Refinement

Search tasks are commonly addressed by inputting queries in a search system, which then yields a set of related results. However, conventional text-based queries are mostly user-defined. Relying on the user's existing knowledge to formulate satisfying search directions limits the range of incrementation in the iterative exploration process. Support for querying is commonly addressed by providing the user with ideas for new queries or additional terms. Even auto-completing text entries with popular queries has been shown to facilitate the querying phase.

When entity search is available, supporting querying and query refinement is readily achieved by augmenting conventional expression-based querying methods through entity recommendation by enabling the use of entities as queries, to provide a set of related entities as a result. A document, a person, a place or a movie can each be used as a query and can yield a variety of related new entities of various types.

ExplorationWall showed how users embrace such support for exploration over text-based querying and how that support improves the overall exploration [15].

Facets and Metadata-Based Result Filtering

Being able to navigate a large result set according to personal needs and preferences is a central requirement of fluid information exploration. That is why this ability – to narrow down such results according to a variety of criteria that are representative of what is available in the data and complementary enough to provide a meaningful choice of search directions – is an important feature to support.

Facets and metadata-based parameters are an attempt to structure information by linking documents semantically through common features (e.g., an author, a title, a date or a location). Entity search is the ideal paradigm for result filtering, given the richness and complexity of readily-linked data. From an initial query entity, a system would retrieve the most central neighboring concepts or elements and provide them as related entities to chose from. The initial result set can then be narrowed down or re-ranked with respect to the relatedness or dependency of each element to the chosen related entity.

Each result set in ExplorationWall displays facets in the form of recommended keywords related to the query. Adding such keywords to the initial query narrows down the results. For example, we have observed a user initiating a search with the query "rosetta". Results were related to the ancient translation stone and the recent European mission to land a probe on a comet. By moving the recommended keyword "probe" to the query, the result set was then focused on the space mission. Then, after the user added the recommended keyword "instruments" to the query, the result set became a catalog of Rosetta's on-board systems.

Leverage search context

A substantial part of context can already be harnessed by accessing contextual data provided by sensors (e.g., GPS signal or personal account informations). From our interaction design perspective, we are more interested in techniques enabling inference of context through users' input, either explicit or implicit.

Explicit input of context implies providing a user with the ability to critique encountered information by providing relevance feedback that informs the system of the user's intent. SciNet implements such principles and has demonstrated substantial benefits for exploratory tasks.

Implicit input of context relies on inferences made from the user's behavior. What information is being saved for later, liked, or shared is often implicitly considered relevant to a user's interest. The songs the user put together in a playlist and the movies she has watched or positively rated are primary actions with implicit implications that create an opportunity to improve any associated recommendation or retrieval process. In systems where users can freely position selected information on a workspace, such as RelevanceMap, the layout and proximity factors can be used to infer a user's intent for disambiguation and to improve the results.

Visualizations to Support Insight and Decision Making

Interactive information visualization is an important tool for sense making. Being able to encode data visually and to play with various parameters is a powerful way of discovering trends, understanding relationships, gaining insight from the data and ultimately informing decisions. Entities in knowledge graphs generally make for inspiring material regarding visualization techniques such as node-and-link diagrams and adjacency matrices.

The challenge with information visualization is that the most appropriate form of visualization is highly dependent on the task and the data. In that respect, it is crucial to be able to adapt when necessary through various techniques.

RelevanceMap uses user-driven mapping to enable multi-aspect search. Having multiple queries distributed on a surface makes it possible to consistently map a whole information space using dimensionality-reduction techniques. RelevanceMap provided users with sensible insights from the data and with the ability to explore tradeoffs with respect to multiple criteria, thus supporting decision-making [16].

Support Learning and Understanding

As it is necessary to offer some result-filtering ability for the user to take better advantage of a large set of results by narrowing down a list, it is also important to provide the user with access to more general knowledge when necessary. Support of learning and understanding implies that a user is given the means to find information that is adapted to his current level of understanding. This is typically achieved through recommendation of related material. For example, any modern browser or eBook reader provides the ability to look up the definition of a word or to link a concept with its corresponding Wikipedia entry.

More elaborate solutions consist of yielding a variety of recommended concepts or documents related to the information at hand, which provides the user with a conceptual overview of the topic with multiple options to gain knowledge directly useful to understanding the information at hand.

SciNet, in addition to visualizing the current intent through the outer rings, displays there a variety of diverse keywords, providing the user with options for future search directions, as a way to expand the information space without having to change the initial query.

As a second example, in the same way that ExplorationWall enables facets and the narrowing down of the result set through multiple queries, similar techniques can be used to expand the result set by adding new entities to the query, this time from external sources (i.e., another result set or a typed expression).

Facilitate Collaboration

Collaborative information exploration is a common strategy to tackle large information spaces through the sharing of ideas and allocation of search tasks [11]. Collaboration can take multiple forms, with settings in which collaborators either share or do not share the same space (i.e. colocated or distributed collaboration), either synchronously or asynchronously.

Methods that support collaboration when searching or interacting with information are very diverse but often share the common goal of avoiding wasteful overlaps in labor between collaborators. This problem can be tackled at the start of a search session, through mechanisms supporting division of labour by systems such as SearchTogether [19] or Cerchiamo [9], which allocate defined search areas to each collaborator. However, the same problem can also be alleviated during the search/exploration by promoting awareness of collaborators' activities, by providing a communication channel allowing participants to share their progress in the form of interesting information snippets and sources and by making their search trails visible, as CoSense [12] and CoSearch [2] do.

Entity search creates opportunities for collaborative exploration, as the information unit of reference shifts from the sole document to a variety of references to real-world objects (e.g., persons, places, concepts, and expressions – or any combination of these). We can therefore envision systems in which users have finer control over the types of information and amounts of context saved and shared.

For example, using QueryTogether, users shared various entities to facilitate task allocation and find common ground in collocated collaborative exploratory tasks. We can imagine implementing the exchange of whole workspaces and search histories as a way to share not only bits of information but whole contexts.

Histories, Workspaces, and Progress Updates

Information exploration is a sense-making activity [17]. As such, it is open-ended, potentially long-term, and changes continuously as the information need evolves [22]. The process often produces long and complex search trails with multiple branches and revisits. In this context, it is important for a user to be able to take advantage of previously encountered information and to keep track of past activity to more efficiently recognize new and interesting information.

Entity-centric information presents an opportunity to highlight updated and visited information at a finer level than documents and in overall areas of the information space. In visualizations taking advantage of the node-and-link structure, it is possible to use color to highlight visited or new areas in the knowledge graph as we implemented in later versions of RelevanceMap, where visited areas of the information space were colored in a purple shade, as is traditional for visited links.

One of ExplorationWall's central features is the endless horizontal workspace that allows users to freely move and position parallel streams (i.e., query plus corresponding result set) and to create additional space in between streams. We noticed that not only did users take advantage of such features to thematically organize multiple search directions; their natural tendency to add new elements to the right systematically resulted in naturally grown chronological search histories.

Support Task Management

As Information Exploration is potentially long-term, it is important for users to have the ability to interrupt and resume their activity and to carry it over time and across devices. This require the ability to not only save selected information but to provide future access to whole workspaces, including histories and information configuration with which a user has engaged.

An important criticism of the way we commonly search for information is the general ephemeral and secondary perceptions of the search process. Users often invest a great deal of time and effort finding information, and the process itself, including intermediate queries and results, is often lost after an endpoint has been reached. As we advocate for improved user control over the search process, often at a higher interaction cost, it is crucial to recognize its value. This improvement implies ubiquitous computing solutions to enable the saving and resuming of search sessions across time, space, and devices. We implement such features in our systems by saving workspaces to the cloud and, in the case of QueryTogether, porting the system to multiple platforms.

THE HYPERCUE TEMPLATE

A cue is a stimulus and a signal for action. We propose the notion of a hypercue as a complement to the hyperlink. A hypercue is an interactive representation of a real-world entity; it offers affordances (i.e. possibilities for action) for the user to explore, share and organize her thoughts. Systematic inspection and exploration of the design space of each feature of exploratory search systems allowed us to identify three complementary affordances that are responsible for enabling these features and that together constitute a minimal design template for implementing hypercues. The following template aims to guide the creation of future interfaces for exploration without overconstraining the design of such systems, or hindering the ability to address specific cases through the choice of a specific form of visualization. The proposed affordances can also be implemented in most existing media-handling applications (e.g., in browsers and in PDF and e-book readers). From the user's perspective, the following template provides a base set of rules and expectations to facilitate users' engagement in complex information behavior.

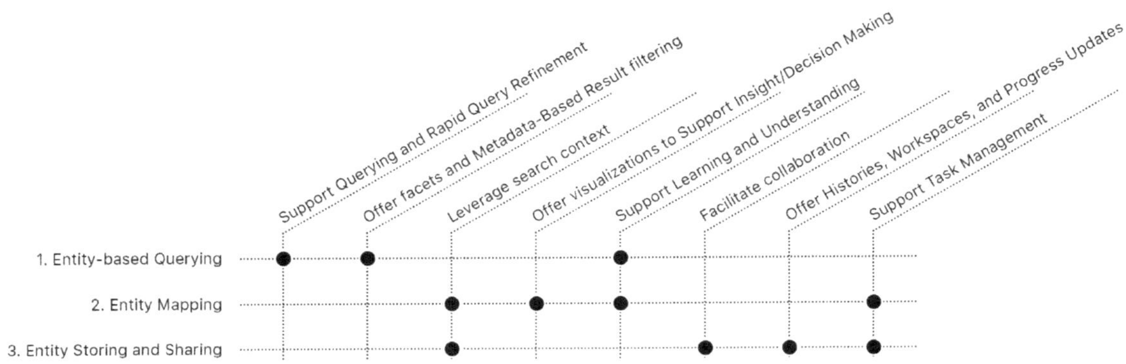

Figure 3. The three entity-based affordances for fluid information exploration together create opportunities for implementing each of the eight features of exploratory search systems that White and Roth described [31].

Entity-Based Querying

Each entity or combination of entities yields various new related entities, thus providing an overview of the respective information space.

Providing the ability to create queries through the direct manipulation of recommended entities can **support query formulation and facilitate query refinement**. The ability to add more entities to an initial query makes it possible to refine it by narrowing down or expanding the result set. Adding external entities (e.g., from somewhere else in the article or page being consulted, or from another source) results in the expansion of a query, thereby **supporting learning and understanding**. Adding an entity to the query from the result set **enables facets and metadata-based result filtering**.

Entities become resources for users to express their information interests and search intents. Sets of related or previously observed entities can be used to collect feedback from users on their current reliance, which would support advanced personalization in iterative user modeling where the exploration system presents predictions of user intent through sets of entities helping the user to discover and formulate her current intent.

Modern browsers and operating systems already implement affordances to inspect the definition of an expression, its corresponding Wikipedia entry or related search engine results. Such affordance is here generalized, using entity search to yield a crop of related entities from any selected object (e.g., an expression, article, or link).

Entity Mapping

Entities can be moved around, and users are provided with the spatial freedom to organize the entities of interest in a layout that reflects their understanding and their mental representation of the information space.

Spatial organization of thoughts is a common behavior. We draw mind maps, we make piles of documents, we organize sticky notes, and store documents within directories or under consistent tags. Sense-making is an important part of exploratory search [31], and as such it relies on users building a mental representation of the state of the world (i.e., the information space at hand) and then iteratively contrasting this representation against the real world (i.e., new information) to update it and acquire a progressively more accurate understanding of the information space [27].

Entity mapping provides support for mind mapping, which **supports learning and understanding**. It provides an implicit input channel for **leveraging the search context**. It also allows for creating **visualizations that support insight and decision-making** by enabling multi-aspect search, as well as for addressing the need for **histories, workspaces, and progress updates**.

Entity Storing and Sharing

Entities and groups of entities can be easily saved for later use and easily shared with collaborators.

Documents often serve as units of information. Users search for, bookmark, and share such documents. Such actions are not sufficient, however. The user often forgets the intent behind the bookmarking and thus loses the utility of the stored document. Some additional action is required, such as giving each bookmark a context-relevant title or organizing bookmarks within theme-specific directories. Sharing requires the use of messaging channels, as text messages are necessary to convey context and intent. Entity-centric information enables the use of variable and personalized units of information. Users can search for, store, and share references to persons, media, excerpts, and organizations. Taking advantage of affordances 1 and 2, the exchange of information involves potentially sharing – and collaborating on – whole contexts in the form of organized entities, which **facilitates collaboration**. The same principle gives access to these contexts across devices, providing flexible **support for task management** and **enabling histories, workspaces, and progress updates**. Stored or saved information also provides an implicit input channel for **leveraging the search context**.

Summary

Figure 3 shows how the hypercue template, which is based on the three proposed design principles above, creates opportunities for addressing each of the eight features of exploratory search systems.

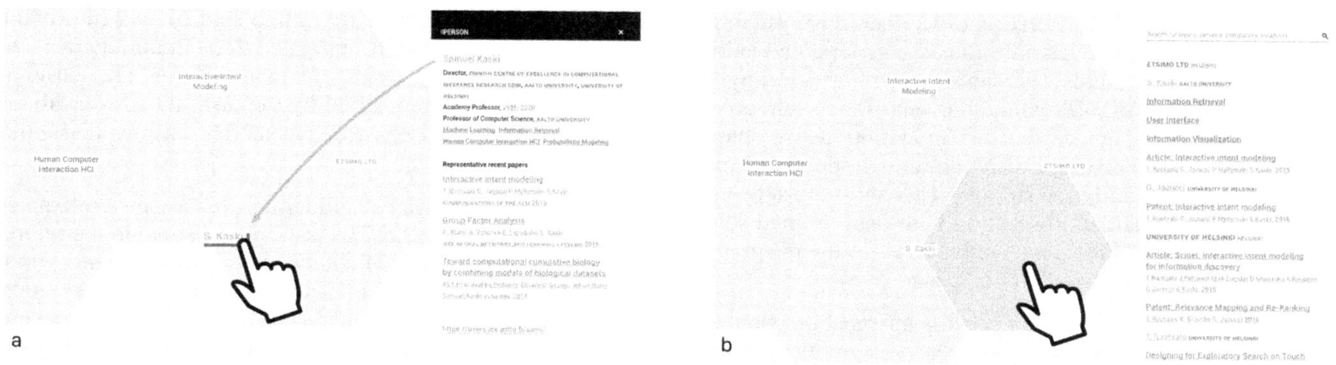

Figure 4. InnovationMap is designed for innovation exploration and discovery, and implements the three principles of the Hypercue template. (a) A user inspects the entity of a researcher in the right panel. If it is of interest to her, she drags it towards the map. (b) The right panel now displays the search results corresponding to the (blue) cell selected by the user, which has two entities as a compound query. As results are saved in the cloud, the user can resume her exploration later on a different device.

Example

To illustrate our approach to designing systems that support information exploration, and to show the hypercue's role in enabling relevant features, we describe and discuss the case of InnovationMap, a system that was designed following these principles. It is currently being implemented in partnership with the University of Helsinki to support innovation exploration and discovery.

User Interface

The workspace consists of a map, with a panel on the right, as seen on Figure 4. The map is based on a grid of hexagonal cells. The scale of the map is changeable through the use of the mouse wheel or through pinch gestures. The companion panel has a text-input field at the top, inviting typed queries, and the corresponding result set is displayed under it. Results consists of entities of various types (i.e., documents, persons, workplaces and topics). An initial text-based query yields a ranked set of mixed-type entities. Each entity can be inspected with a click or a tap, at which point the panel displays all the information about the selected entity (i.e., the full metadata) to provide a preview of the content – and access to it, if applicable, through available links such as dedicated websites, Wikipedia entries, or social media contacts. Each entity can also be dragged towards the map, where it will position itself at an intersection of the grid. The darker cells on the map are representations of the various result sets yielded from all adjacent entities. Tapping on a cell highlights it in blue, signifying that the corresponding result set is displayed in the panel. By dragging more entities to the map, users can search for information related to up to six entities for each cell. Users can freely drag entities to other parts of the map and can thus explore the information space in multiple directions.

InnovationMap does not include methods to share specific entities or entity structures with an other users. However, it is designed to remotely save the state of each session for later access, potentially on another device. As a result, even without features designed specifically for collaboration, sharing access to a session with another user is possible, thus allowing users to provide others with the information they have found, including the context of their multiple search directions and points of interests.

Scenario

An innovation manager for a foreign company is looking for partnership opportunities in Helsinki. She uses InnovationMap, an online tool for exploring research work, provided by the local university. Although she does not have academic expertise, she starts by inputting an umbrella term that roughly covers her fields of interests (i.e., "Big Data"). The system returns a variety of related fields, as well as keywords, academic articles, patents, and names of researchers and entrepreneurs, all of which are representative of the local research work. She consults the profile of some of the recommended persons and inspects a few recommended fields. Soon, she's able to drag "Human Computer Interaction (HCI)" towards the map, thus refreshing the search results. She then adds an article that describes a user-modeling technique for search systems. The results now show a startup based on the technology of interest, among other related elements. Inspection of the entity provides necessary information on the young company, including a link to its website and contact information. In parallel, she drags "Information Visualization" to the map, next to "Human Computer Interaction (HCI)", and starts exploring the intersection of these topics in the information space (in a separate cell). Progressively, and without having to recall any technical terminology or read through pages of material unrelated to the topic of interest, she not only collects useful information but also builds a representation of the whole process, thus gaining an understanding of the information space that accurately reflects the data.

DISCUSSION AND CONCLUSIONS

The present template consists of fundamental principles aimed at guiding the design of future systems and supporting information exploration while also limiting the number of constraints imposed on the overall design space. In this section we discuss aspects that are not addressed by the template, and attempt to outline the remaining design space.

Hypercues are designed to be identified and defined by users (although they could also be recommended within contents).

For instance, in the latest iteration of its operating system for tablets (iOS 11), Apple has introduced a generalized ability to drag and drop. Pictures, text snippets, news articles, hyperlinks, and other bit of information pop out of the environment with a gesture of the finger, thus becoming interactive objects that can be dragged across applications and dropped into messages, notes, or cloud-based storage. This ability lets the user interact with predefined object and with user-defined selections, and it offers an ideal interactive base for the integration of the affordances proposed in this paper.

Although the template does not provide information about the shape and size of displayed hypercues, it is useful to discuss the requirements and provide some recommendations based on our experience. The first requirements of the hypercue marker is for the represented entity to be identifiable and placed in a space that allows it to be moved and positioned in relation to other entities. A constant challenge when designing entity-based interfaces balancing the amount of information conveyed through the entity marker against the number of entities that can be comfortably displayed. In any case, it is necessary to provide the option to quickly inspect the entity, so that the user can access a comprehensive overview of the entity through linked content and related material. However, it is also essential to show enough information up-front to trigger the user's recognition and incite her interest. Modern desktop-based operating systems offer a good model for representing files and directories as manipulable objects using an icon and one or two short lines of text. The most useful information depends on the task and on the information space. Although movies are usually displayed with a poster, a title and a release year, finding the most relevant movie in a set could depend on other information, such as the cast or the rating. Likewise, finding useful academic articles can require variable criteria (e.g., authors, venue or citations). The solution might lie in a balance between user-defined preferences and automated, context-sensitive, and adaptive interface settings.

These guidelines' reliance on direct manipulation and spatial layouts makes the hypercue a potentially interesting candidate for integration with the physical world through playful tangible interactions. Registering an entity or a set of entities as physical objects allows users to combine and share such objects to playfully discover information through machine vision or sensing surfaces.

The hypercue template consists of a minimal set of affordances for the interactive representation of real-world entities. It ensures that all important features for supporting exploratory search can be addressed while still leaving enough design space to facilitate integration within a variety of systems, and it baseline rules and expectations to facilitate users' engagement in complex search behavior. The template has various potential implications regarding how people search for information. An important implication is that all interactions proposed in the present work require substantially more effort from the user than present methods require, as users have grown accustomed to content feeds and to the simplicity and immediacy of today's search engines. We advocate information practices in which users are more active, and we posit that this is the cost of providing greater transparency and control over information. However, this cost can be mitigated through fluidity by having every interaction serve an informational goal and letting the user become truly absorbed by the task, thus rewarding her with persistent and constructive search sessions that remain useful in the long run.

In this work, we propose guidelines that are generalizable to every information space. We can imagine that, in the future, a user's search interface of choice will be independent from the data being explored. As a result, a user could apply one tool to discover information of interest within news posts, academic articles, music, movies, and social media posts, thus increasing the potential for serendipity and creative solutions.

ACKNOWLEDGMENTS

This work has been supported by the Academy of Finland (D4Health 295506, 313610 and 312274). The data used in the experiments is derived from the ACM Digital Library. We would like to thank Luana Micallef for helpful discussions and valuable suggestions.

REFERENCES

1. Christopher Ahlberg and Ben Shneiderman. 1994. Visual Information Seeking: Tight Coupling of Dynamic Query Filters with Starfield Displays. In *Proceedings of the SIGCHI Conference on Human Factors in Computing Systems (CHI '94)*. ACM, New York, NY, USA, 313–317. DOI:http://dx.doi.org/10.1145/191666.191775

2. Saleema Amershi and Meredith Ringel Morris. 2008. CoSearch: a system for co-located collaborative web search. In *Proceedings of the SIGCHI Conference on Human Factors in Computing Systems*. ACM, 1647–1656.

3. Marcia J Bates. 1989. The design of browsing and berrypicking techniques for the online search interface. *Online review* 13, 5 (1989), 407–424.

4. Eric A Bier, Stuart K Card, and John W Bodnar. 2008. Entity-based collaboration tools for intelligence analysis. In *Visual Analytics Science and Technology, 2008. VAST'08. IEEE Symposium on*. IEEE, 99–106.

5. David Carmel, Naama Zwerdling, and Sivan Yogev. 2012. Entity oriented search and exploration for cultural heritage collections: the EU cultura project. In *Proceedings of the 21st International Conference on World Wide Web*. ACM, 227–230.

6. Marian Dörk, Sheelagh Carpendale, and Carey Williamson. 2011. The information flaneur: A fresh look at information seeking. In *Proceedings of the SIGCHI conference on human factors in computing systems*. ACM, 1215–1224.

7. Niklas Elmqvist, Andrew Vande Moere, Hans-Christian Jetter, Daniel Cernea, Harald Reiterer, and TJ Jankun-Kelly. 2011. Fluid interaction for information visualization. *Information Visualization* 10, 4 (2011), 327–340.

8. Dorota Głowacka, Tuukka Ruotsalo, Ksenia Konuyshkova, Samuel Kaski, Giulio Jacucci, and others. 2013. Directing exploratory search: Reinforcement learning from user interactions with keywords. In *Proceedings of the 2013 international conference on Intelligent user interfaces*. ACM, 117–128.
9. Gene Golovchinsky, John Adcock, Jeremy Pickens, Pernilla Qvarfordt, and Maribeth Back. 2008. Cerchiamo: a collaborative exploratory search tool. *Proceedings of Computer Supported Cooperative Work (CSCW)* (2008), 8–12.
10. François Guimbretière, Maureen Stone, and Terry Winograd. 2001. Fluid Interaction with High-resolution Wall-size Displays. In *Proceedings of the 14th Annual ACM Symposium on User Interface Software and Technology (UIST '01)*. ACM, New York, NY, USA, 21–30. DOI:`http://dx.doi.org/10.1145/502348.502353`
11. Marti A Hearst. 2014. What's missing from collaborative search? *Computer* 47, 3 (2014), 58–61.
12. Samuli Hemminki, Kai Zhao, Aaron Yi Ding, Martti Rannanjärvi, Sasu Tarkoma, and Petteri Nurmi. 2013. Cosense: A collaborative sensing platform for mobile devices. In *Proceedings of the 11th ACM Conference on Embedded Networked Sensor Systems*. ACM, 34.
13. Edwin L. Hutchins, James D. Hollan, and Donald A. Norman. 1985. 1.1 direct manipulation: astep beyond programming languages. *Human-Computer Interaction* 1, 4 (1985), 311–338. DOI: `http://dx.doi.org/10.1207/s15327051hci0104_2`
14. Andruid Kerne and Steven M Smith. 2004. The information discovery framework. In *Proceedings of the 5th conference on Designing interactive systems: processes, practices, methods, and techniques*. ACM, 357–360.
15. Khalil Klouche, Tuukka Ruotsalo, Diogo Cabral, Salvatore Andolina, Andrea Bellucci, and Giulio Jacucci. 2015. Designing for exploratory search on touch devices. In *Proceedings of the 33rd Annual ACM Conference on Human Factors in Computing Systems*. ACM, 4189–4198.
16. Khalil Klouche, Tuukka Ruotsalo, Luana Micallef, Salvatore Andolina, and Giulio Jacucci. 2017. Visual Re-Ranking for Multi-Aspect Information Retrieval. In *Proceedings of the 2017 Conference on Conference Human Information Interaction and Retrieval*. ACM, 57–66.
17. Gary Marchionini. 2006. Exploratory search: from finding to understanding. *Commun. ACM* 49, 4 (2006), 41–46.
18. Iris Miliaraki, Roi Blanco, and Mounia Lalmas. 2015. From "Selena Gomez" to "Marlon Brando": Understanding Explorative Entity Search. In *Proceedings of the 24th International Conference on World Wide Web (WWW '15)*. International World Wide Web Conferences Steering Committee, Republic and Canton of Geneva, Switzerland, 765–775. DOI: `http://dx.doi.org/10.1145/2736277.2741284`
19. Meredith Ringel Morris and Eric Horvitz. 2007. SearchTogether: an interface for collaborative web search. In *Proceedings of the 20th annual ACM symposium on User interface software and technology*. ACM, 3–12.
20. Jeanne Nakamura and Mihaly Csikszentmihalyi. 2014. *The Concept of Flow*. Springer Netherlands, Dordrecht, 239–263. DOI: `http://dx.doi.org/10.1007/978-94-017-9088-8_16`
21. Don Norman. 2013. *The design of everyday things: Revised and expanded edition*. Basic Books (AZ).
22. Peter Pirolli and Stuart Card. The sensemaking process and leverage points for analyst technology as identified through cognitive task analysis.
23. Peter Pirolli and Stuart Card. 1999. Information foraging. *Psychological review* 106, 4 (1999), 643.
24. Jeffrey Pound, Peter Mika, and Hugo Zaragoza. 2010. Ad-hoc Object Retrieval in the Web of Data. In *Proceedings of the 19th International Conference on World Wide Web (WWW '10)*. ACM, New York, NY, USA, 771–780. DOI: `http://dx.doi.org/10.1145/1772690.1772769`
25. Gonzalo Ramos and Ravin Balakrishnan. 2003. Fluid Interaction Techniques for the Control and Annotation of Digital Video. In *Proceedings of the 16th Annual ACM Symposium on User Interface Software and Technology (UIST '03)*. ACM, New York, NY, USA, 105–114. DOI: `http://dx.doi.org/10.1145/964696.964708`
26. Tuukka Ruotsalo, Kumaripaba Athukorala, Dorota Głowacka, Ksenia Konyushkova, Antti Oulasvirta, Samuli Kaipiainen, Samuel Kaski, and Giulio Jacucci. 2013. Supporting exploratory search tasks with interactive user modeling. *Proceedings of the American Society for Information Science and Technology* 50, 1 (2013), 1–10.
27. Daniel M Russell, Mark J Stefik, Peter Pirolli, and Stuart K Card. 1993. The cost structure of sensemaking. In *Proceedings of the INTERACT'93 and CHI'93 conference on Human factors in computing systems*. ACM, 269–276.
28. Ben Shneiderman. 1993. 1.1 direct manipulation: astep beyond programming languages. *Sparks of innovation in human-computer interaction* (1993), 17.
29. Ben Shneiderman. 1997. Direct manipulation for comprehensible, predictable and controllable user interfaces. In *Proceedings of the 2nd international conference on Intelligent user interfaces*. ACM, 33–39.
30. John Stasko, Carsten Görg, and Zhicheng Liu. 2008. Jigsaw: supporting investigative analysis through interactive visualization. *Information visualization* 7, 2 (2008), 118–132.
31. Ryen W White and Resa A Roth. 2009. Exploratory search: beyond the query-response paradigm (Synthesis lectures on information concepts, retrieval & services). *Morgan and Claypool Publishers* 3 (2009).

Designing Connected Resources for Older People

Iohanna Nicenboim
Delft University of Technology,
Dept. of Industrial Design
Delft, The Netherlands
i.nicenboim@tudelft.nl

Elisa Giaccardi
Delft University of Technology,
Dept. of Industrial Design
Delft, The Netherlands
e.giaccardi@tudelft.nl

Lenneke Kuijer
Eindhoven University of Technology,
Dept. of Industrial Design
Eindhoven, The Netherlands
s.c.kuijer@tue.nl

DIS '18, June 9–13, 2018, , Hong Kong

ACM ISBN 978-1-4503-5198-0/18/06 $15.00
https://doi.org/10.1145/3196709.3196808

Abstract
In this pictorial, we illustrate steps towards a novel approach that situates connected technologies for older people as resources. In contrast to mainstream approaches in gerontechnology that consider elderly as frail and passive, we aim to complement older people's vital competences by designing technologies that can be used in less prescriptive, and broader ways. The pictorial describes our design process in which resourceful strategies were identified through thing ethnography and used as inspiration to create a series of new connected objects conceived as resources.

Authors Keywords
Resourcefulness; thing ethnography; IoT; RtD; gerontechnology.

ACM Classification Keywords
H.5.m. Information interfaces and presentation (e.g., HCI): Miscellaneous.

1. Introduction
Houses of older people are becoming increasingly connected, as more and more smart devices are entering the home. This creates interest in how to design connected objects for older people; and especially, how to foster valuable activities for them, in contrast to the current approach that focuses on physical decline. In that mainstream approach, technologies for older people are conceived within narrow-scripted scenarios which fail to address the variety of situations elderly encounter [17,19]. These scenarios are especially problematic when they are

based on poor conceptions of older people, framing them as passive recipients of technology [15–17].

Studies in social gerontechnology have shown that rigidly scripted products can become inappropriate very quickly, as they fail to match the design intentions with actual use [7,15,16]. For example, a medicine dispenser that is designed for indoor use only, fails to address that many older people spend a lot of time outdoors [14]. These products can not only become inappropriate, but even limit meaningful activity of elderly people, and suppress their creativity and autonomy [11–13,16].

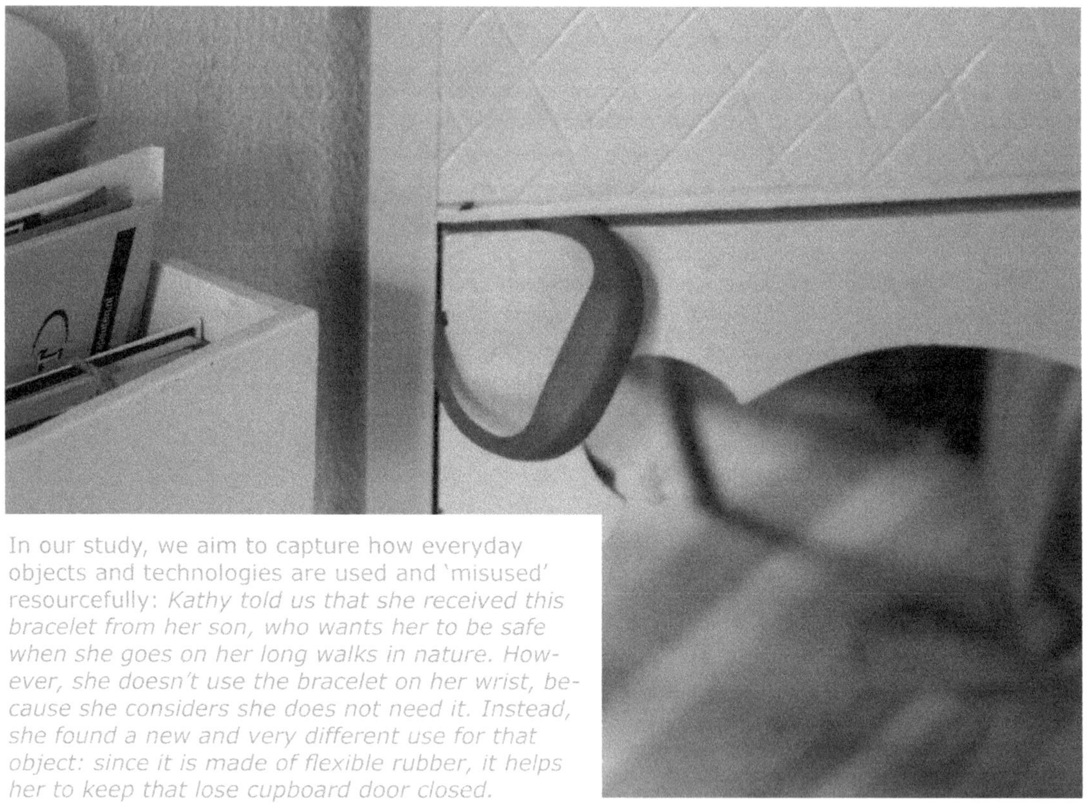

In our study, we aim to capture how everyday objects and technologies are used and 'misused' resourcefully: *Kathy told us that she received this bracelet from her son, who wants her to be safe when she goes on her long walks in nature. However, she doesn't use the bracelet on her wrist, because she considers she does not need it. Instead, she found a new and very different use for that object: since it is made of flexible rubber, it helps her to keep that lose cupboard door closed.*

Thus, there is a need for new design approaches, which step away from the stereotype of elderly as frail, passive and technologically incompetent, and see them as well capable of dealing with the challenges they encounter as they age [11]. In the interdisciplinary research project Resourceful Ageing, we focus on designing technologies that can empower elderly people, by *learning from the ways in which they creatively deal with challenges* [12]. This innovative approach proposes to position connected technologies as resources: tools that can "complement the ageing competences of older people and be adapted in a variety of ways" [11].

This pictorial focuses on the question: How to design connected objects as resources for elderly?. In order to explore that question, we worked within a research-through-design process [18], in which we used design tools and prototypes to further understand what are elderly's existing competences of resourcefulness, how to support these competences with new designs, and how to encourage use in a variety of ways. We developed the design tools in a series of iterations, feeding the insights from every step back into the design process – impacting on the brief, ideation tool, and informing esthetical and functional decisions in the design of the prototypes.

2. Thing-centered Ethnographic Study

In order to understand older people's resourceful competences, we conducted an ethnographic study. Since resourcefulness is a dispersed practice, which occurs spontaneously in everyday situations, it is particularly difficult to capture [12]. To tackle this challenge, we applied a thing-centered approach to our ethnographic study: considering both elderly as well as their everyday things as participants [10,12]. This method was particularly suitable to uncover resourceful strategies, as it revealed how things were used across practices in unexpected ways.

We conducted the study in the homes of older people living independently. The study was conducted by a social scientist, accompanied partly by a design researcher. We visited four homes of female participants between 65 and 78 years old [24]. Three of them lived alone, and one lived with her spouse. We conducted semi-structured

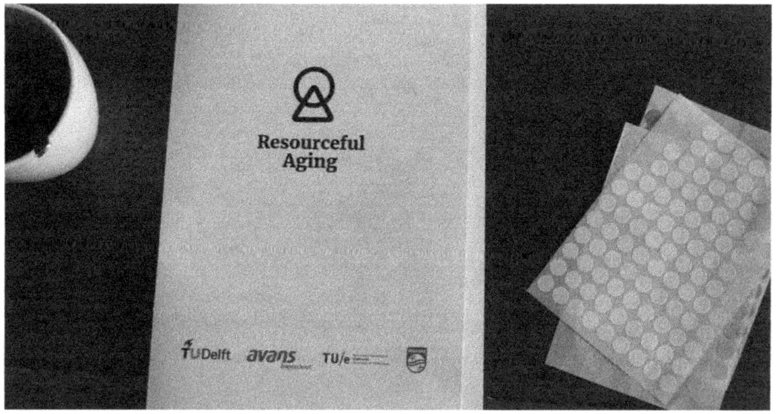

One crucial aspect of the study was to start from resourceful practices in activities older people valued, rather than from problems. To do that, we asked participants to tag with different colors objects they frequently used, objects they used in activities they value, as well as objects they valued even if they were not strictly "used", such as a picture on a wall.

interviews, and a one-week home assignment with a booklet [9,20]. In the assignment, participants were asked to tag objects they frequently used in activities they valued. Once the exercise was completed, the ethnographer and the designer visited the homes, asking participants to walk them through a home tour. The tour consisted in pointing at the tagged objects and explaining the reasoning behind their choices and how they were meaningful for them. Using those tagged objects as a starting point, together with participants, we were able to recognize and better *define resourceful practices in valuable activities*. Once a common understanding was established, participants were able to show us additional examples of resourcefulness, which we documented with photos.

3. Resourceful Repertoire

Data from the thing-centered ethnographic study were clustered into what we call the *resourceful repertoire*: a non-exhaustive collection of elements we found in elderly's existing practices of resourcefulness. We did that by coding the photos and organizing them in three categories: resources, capabilities, and strategies. The idea of a repertoire was inspired by the *resilient repertoire* [8], but instead of focusing on efficiency and safety at work, we focused on creativity and resourcefulness at home.

We recognized eight strategies, sixteen resources and sixteen capabilities. Resources included physical materials and everyday objects. Capabilities included abilities that resources presented. Although resources and capabilities were relatively simple to spot, strategies demanded to look for *know-hows*, high level plans, or emergent systems which participants developed over time [19] in order to achieve a goal or just make do. Strategies also showed combinations with immaterial resources, such as getting help from the family or their social connections. We present here the eight strategies, and a few examples of capabilities and resources.

RESOURCEFUL STRATEGIES

Having more than one object, to find always one at hand *Many participants keep multiple pairs of glasses - for example Inge told us she has more than ten pairs. Toothbrushes were also duplicated in Maria's house, one on each floor. Minnie reported having multiple agendas, including digital and physical ones, as well as personal and shared.*

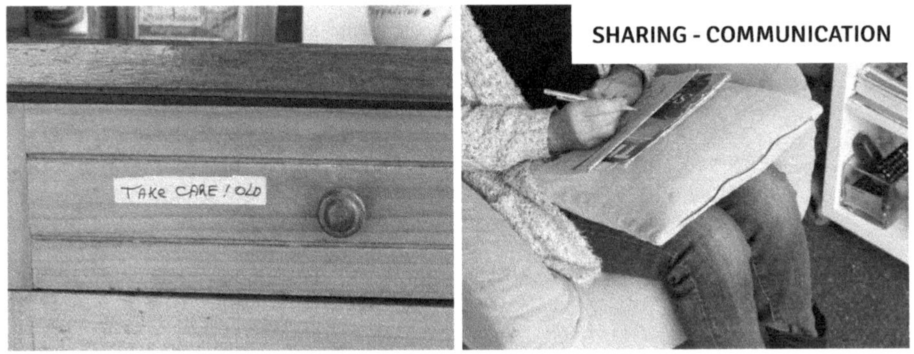

Communicating with others through objects *Inge shares a newspaper subscription with her daughter, and brings it to her every afternoon. In that way, her daughter knows she was there: "If she does not receive it, they know something is going on." This practice serves both of them to keep an eye on each other in a non-intrusive way. Another example of communication through objects is from Minnie: she placed a sticker in a drawer to remind guests that rent her home sometimes, to be careful with the old piece of furniture.*

Sorting by type or purpose *Items are commonly arranged in groups according to their function, use or shape. These clusters seem to be sometimes intentional, when things are placed in drawers; and some other times unintentional, when a collection of items that don't have a specific place, ends up in a sort of container.*

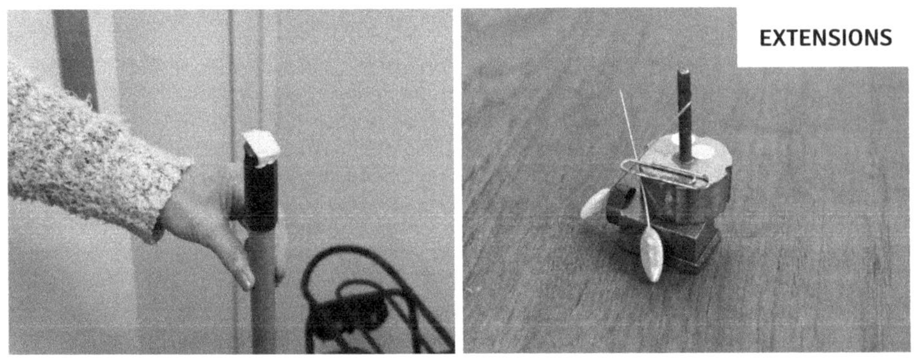

Extending physical capabilities, to reach where we cannot *In order to reach higher, Inge placed double-side tape on a broomstick. She uses this to kill spiders in the ceiling. Kathy also showed us how a magnet helps her to pick up small metallic items, which she cannot grab with her hands anymore.*

RESOURCEFUL STRATEGIES

Combining unusual elements to form something new *Kathy adapted her pans by wrapping the handles with thread, in order to avoid burning her hands, especially since she prefers grabbing close to the pan, as it gives her a stronger grip. Inge created a wooden cube wrapped with leather to block the garden door. This is her own "low-tech" system to avoid theft, and feel safe.*

Arranging related things close to each other *Many people keep things together next to the door, for example, to remember them before leaving the home. Many participants keep the remote controls next to the television. When Minnie is knitting, she leaves the unfinished parts and needles together -normally on this decoration plate- so she can easily continue knitting later.*

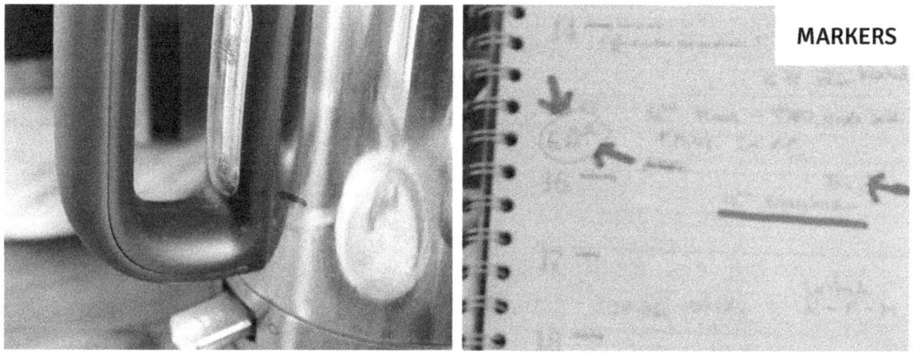

Highlighting or emphasizing physical elements *Inge uses this strategy around the kitchen: she placed a red mark in her kettle, to make the minimum water level more visible. She also showed us how in order to avoid missing important events from the agenda, her system was to highlight them with a red marker.*

Organizing actions in a temporal order *All participants follow steps more or less in the same order, while doing a recurring practice. For example, Minnie described her morning routine, which starts by turning on the radio, and then making cereal in a sequence that involves several steps.*

Most of the resources we found in the ethnographic study were in between products and raw materials. For instance, clips and elastic bands, which were very common amongst our resourceful examples, are mass produced objects, but have a mundane character.

Regarding capabilities, although we saw in the ethnographic study that our participants use digital devices frequently, we didn't encounter resourcefulness using digital means, and especially not in combination with physical ones.

RESOURCES

Clips and bands were used to keep parts together, either a door or a curtain, or a cover on a garden bench. Magnets were extensively used to stick papers and photos in metallic surfaces.

CAPABILITIES

Some capabilities included for example: hanging a garbage bag from the handle, or a plug in a hook for towels; inserting photos behind sockets and other tight spaces; or wrapping a handle or a broken hinge with threads.

4. Design Process

One of the aims of our project was to use the resourceful competences of older people as an inspiration for the design of new connected objects. For this purpose, we used the resourceful repertoire as a generative tool by translating its items into cards. Every item was represented in a card with its name and an icon. The items were organized in groups according to the categories we had in the repertoire (resources, capabilities and strategies) and had different colors.

Since we wanted to create not only new resources but technological ones, we added a new category of digital capabilities, which included twenty four cards. The items of this group were defined during the kick off session (see 3.1).

The card set was used in a series of workshops with a design team –composed by one design researcher, three design master students, and one computer science student. Then it was evaluated in two sessions with professional designers. The process is briefly described in the following sections.

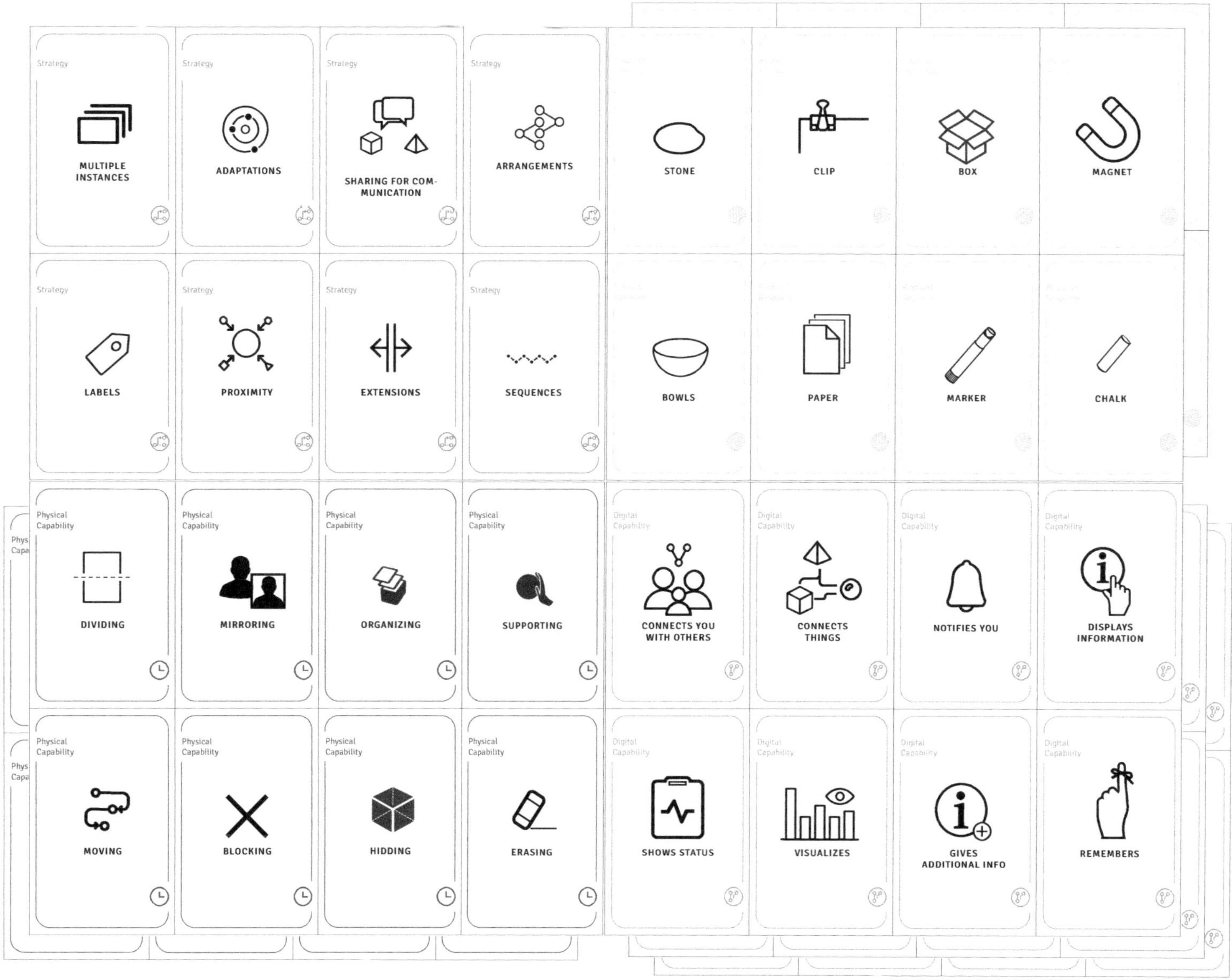

4.1. Kick off session

A design team brainstormed initial ideas of "connected objects to empower elderly to age resourcefully". The cards were not used yet as such, but examples from the repertoire were shown to the team before the brainstorming exercise. After the team presented ideas for new connected objects, we noticed they all included extra capabilities, such as visualizing information, saving information, or showing notifications. Thus we made a list of what we called 'digital capabilities', which was added as a new group in the card set.

4.2. Design session

The card deck was printed in a draft version and used in an ideation session with the design team. We presented the following brief: "Using the set of cards, design connected resources for elderly, that can be configured in their everyday practices, in a variety of ways". After the researcher introduced the card set, and presented the brief, the team was divided into two groups and provided with a deck of cards and physical resources (such as clips, elastic bands, fabric, etc.). Since we had a collection of physical resources in that meeting, we skipped the cards 'resources' and worked directly with physical elements.

At every round, someone picked a card of each category, and a physical resource. Then we sketched as many ideas as possible. We noticed that physical capabilities and resources were sometimes overlapping, and either one or the other was chosen as a starting point. However, later the group agreed that it was useful to have more than one option to choose from. The resulting ideas were a combination of a physical resource –or capability, with a digital capability, to support a certain strategy. Several proposals were presented per group, and three concepts were selected, according to the student's interests (see section 3.4).

4.3. Feedback session

The card set was evaluated later at the design studio The Incredible Machine, and at Philips Design (partners in the

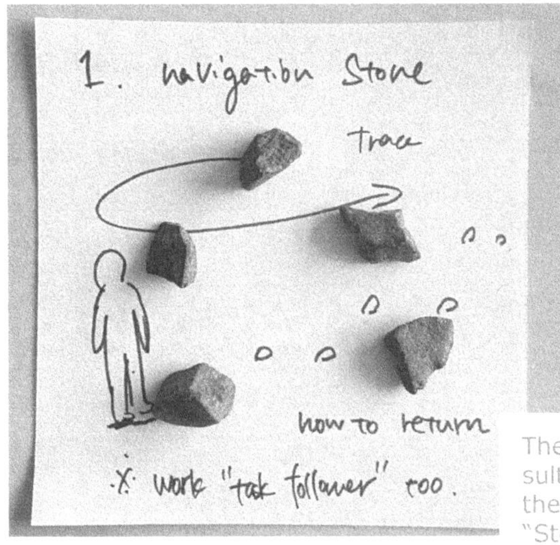

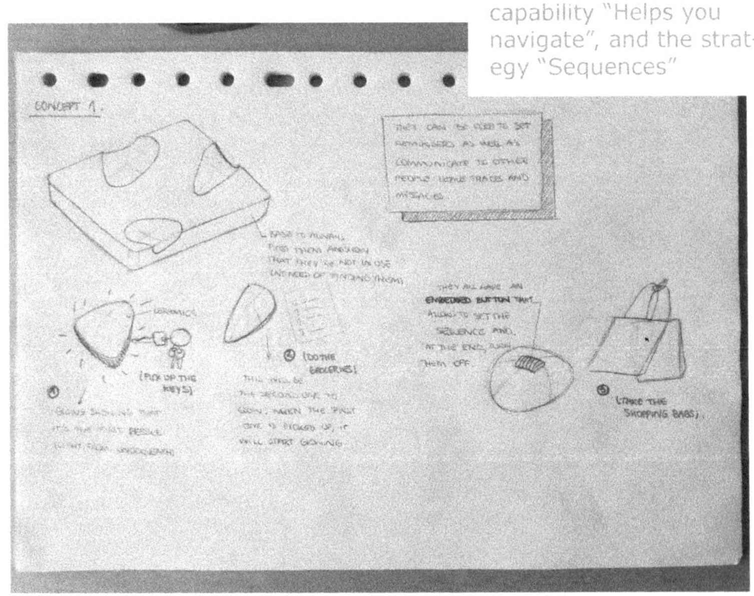

These sketches resulted from combining the physical resource "Stones", with the digital capability "Helps you navigate", and the strategy "Sequences"

Resourceful Ageing project). In both sessions, we played some rounds and then reflected on the card set as a generative tool. The feedback focused around how the card set could be scaled for other projects and other user groups.

4.4. Design and Prototyping

The three initial ideas selected at the design session evolved with a series of iterations to three final concepts:

1- Connected Stones

2- Connected Bell

3- Connected Magnets

The three concepts were prototyped in several iterations. The design and making of these prototypes included: defining their shape and interaction based on existing objects/ metaphors in elderly's homes; deciding and trying different materials, including 3D printing in PLA and porcelain; and developing electronics and connectivity, which included a custom board and the design of a website. For technical details of the prototypes see [23].

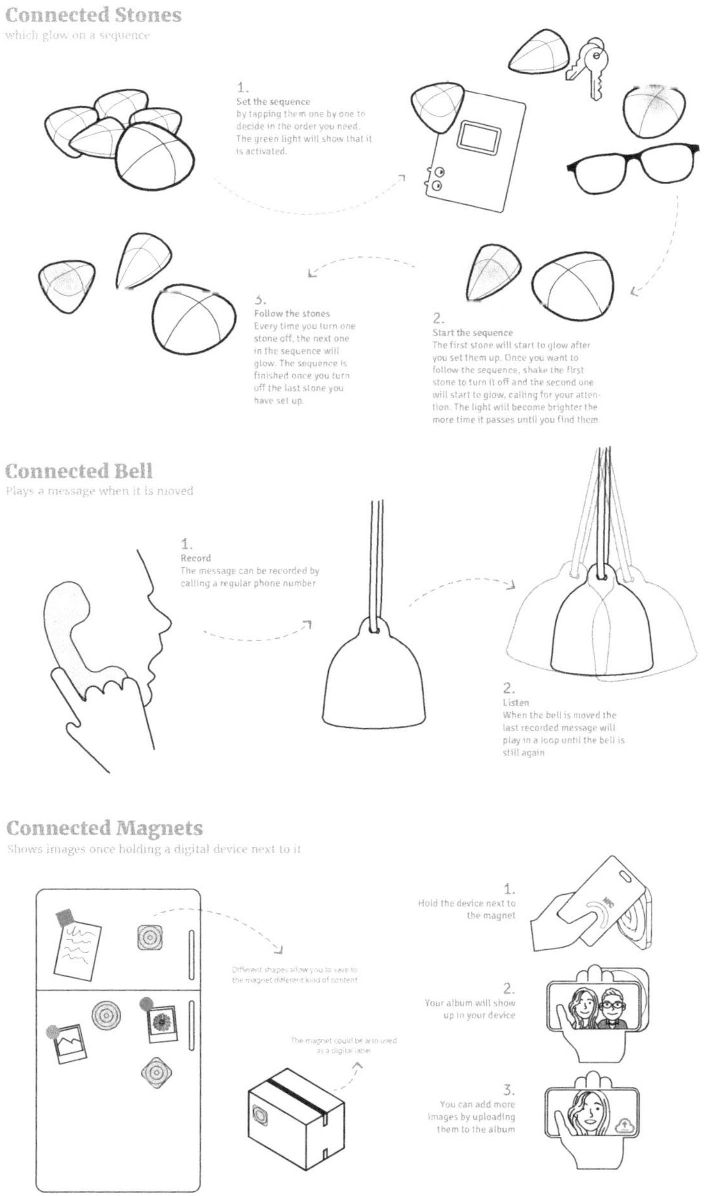

4.5 Presentation

Although the final prototypes weren't deployed yet, we photographed them in a home to better explain their context for an exhibition at the Dutch Design Week.

Connected Stones

Inspired by the idea of leaving a trail with crumbs, this series of stones glow in a sequence. The interaction is very simple: once the first pebble is turned off by shaking it, the second stone starts to glow; once the second one is turned off, the third stone glows; and so on. We imagined these objects could be used to make sequences more visible, to light up a path at night, to leave a step-by-step instruction, message or reminder. As we observed, participants leave objects together to easily find them, so this tool could facilitate that strategy without the need of taking objects out of their context. Thus, keeping them together "virtually".

Connected Bell

This bell plays a recorded voice message when it is moved. The message can be recorded by calling a regular phone number, and plays in a loop until the bell is still again. We found interesting that the message can be intentionally or unintentionally triggered depending or where it is placed: it can be triggered by opening a door, or by the wind for example. We imagined this tool not only to leave or receive messages from others, but also to leave messages to oneself.

Connected Magnets

These magnets open a digital album once a device is placed close to them. Every magnet has an NFC tag, which links to an online album that supports images and videos. Since the album is online, it can be shared by more than one person. The magnets might be used to access personal or shared content in a situated way, by storing a collection of photos and videos about a topic in a relevant place.

5. Discussion

Designing connected objects as resources demanded a shift in focus, from solving specific problems of older people, to conceiving technologies that can support their strategies of resourcefulness, and be used in a variety of ways. This shift implied a different design process. Even though the connected resources have so far not been deployed in the homes of our target audience, we can reflect on the design process and how these objects can be positioned as resources.

The connected objects we created can be positioned as resources firstly because they are conceived to support, and inspired by, older people's competences of resourcefulness. In order to understand what were these competences, we used a *decentered* 'thing perspective' [10] to identify the possible strategies, capabilities, and materials that play a key role in shaping elderly's resourceful arrangements. We first organized these strategies, capabilities, and materials in a repertoire, and then translated them into an ideation card set, which was used to generate ideas for connected objects.

Secondly, we position these connected objects as resources because they don't try to solve one specific problem, but are designed to be used in multiple ways. Since resourcefulness is not a property of a person or a technology alone but the result of how they work together [5,22], connected resources let users decide how and why to use them in a situated way [11]. To avoid rigidly scripted scenarios, one necessary step was to keep the purpose of these objects as *underdesigned* [6] as possible. However, while some *dimensions* [12] had to be open in order to make these objects suitable across practices; others needed to be closed to make them familiar and easy to use.

In summary, these objects can be positioned as resources because they (i) complement the resourceful competences of older people, and (ii) can be used in a variety of ways.

Positioning technologies as resources opens new design opportunities in the space between digital and physical, as well as between products and materials. Although our participants used digital devices frequently, we didn't encounter instances of resourcefulness that combined both digital and physical capabilities. Thus we wanted to explore how elderly could use digital capabilities as everyday resources in a simple and playful way. We explored this by adding digital capabilities to existing physical resources. The assumption was that the familiarity that older people have with these physical resources, as well as their everyday character, might help to perceive them as materials for adaptation [1,12,22]. Additionally, we observed that resources such as clips and elastic bands seem to be somewhere in between products and raw materials. This space seemed refreshing, since technologies are commonly divided into high-tech smart products, or smart materials.

In a previous publication [12,] we have uncovered some of the characteristics of resourcefulness as a dispersed practice. However, still many questions remain open regarding how resourcefulness manifests differently in older people versus other groups. Long-term deployment and further studies are needed to identify how different groups may relate to these objects, and whether they support or inspire new strategies of resourcefulness.

6. Conclusion

Designing connected resources instead of scripted products is not an easy task. We, as designers, tend to start from personas or scenarios [2,3]. Designing resources required a different approach. In this pictorial we presented the alternative process we followed, which included organizing elderly's competences of resourcefulness in a repertoire, by analyzing data from a thing-centered ethnographic study. We also showed how we used those competences as inspiration for the design of new technologies by translating them into a card set, which was used in the design of three prototypes. Finally, we reflected on our design process by discussing how these prototypes can be positioned as resources, and what new design spaces are opened with a resourceful approach.

7. Acknowledgements

We would like to thank the design team: Masako Kitazaki, Tomo Kihara, Ana Torralba, and Xin Liu. We would like to also thank the Resourceful Ageing team, esecially Ivo Maathuis and Tjeerd Stamhuis, the reviewers, and the participants of the study. We want to thank as well Martin Havranek, Aadjan van der Helm, and Thomas van Arkel for helping with the prototypes. Finally, we want to thank the partners of the project Philips Design and The Incredible Machine for their feedback. This research is part of the project 'Resourceful Ageing' funded by STW under the Research through Design program (2015/16734/STW).

8. References

1. U. Brandes, S. Stich, and M. Wender. 2009. *Design by Use: The Everyday Metamorphosis of Things*. Birkhäuser, Basel. Retrieved from https://books.google.de/books?id=yGRIunROBoUC
2. John M. Carroll. 2000. *Making Use: Scenario-Based Design of Human-Computer Interactions*. The MIT Press. Retrieved from https://dl.acm.org/citation.cfm?id=517699
3. Alan Cooper, Robert Reimann, and Hugh Dubberly. 2003. *About Face 2.0: The Essentials of Interaction Design*. John Wiley & Sons, Inc., New York, NY, USA. Retrieved from https://dl.acm.org/citation.cfm?id=862232
4. Alan Costall and Ole Dreier. 2006. *Doing Things with Things: The Design and Use of Everyday Objects*. Ashgate Publishing, Aldershot, UK.
5. Audrey Desjardins and Ron Wakkary. 2013. Manifestations of Everyday Design: Guiding Goals and Motivations. In *Proceedings of the 9th ACM Conference on Creativity & Cognition (C&C '13)*, 253–262. https://doi.org/10.1145/2466627.2466643
6. Gerhard Fischer and Elisa Giaccardi. 2006. Meta-design: A Framework for the Future of End-User Development. In *End User Development*, Henry Lieberman, Fabio Paternò and Volker Wulf (eds.). Springer Netherlands, 427–457. https://doi.org/10.1007/1-4020-5386-X_19
7. Hysse Birgitte Forchhammer. 2006. The Woman who used her Walking Stick as a Telephone: The Use of Utilities in Praxis. In *Doing things with things: the design and use of everyday objects*, Alan Costall and O. Dreier (eds.). Ashgate Publishing, Aldershot, UK, 131–157. Retrieved July 22, 2016 from http://eprints.port.ac.uk/5453/
8. Dominic Furniss, Nick Barber, Imogen Lyons, Lina Eliasson, and Ann Blandford. 2014. Unintentional non-adherence: can a spoon full of resilience help the medicine go down? *BMJ quality & safety* 23, 2: 95–98. https://doi.org/10.1136/bmjqs-2013-002276
9. Bill Gaver, Tony Dunne, and Elena Pacenti. 1999. Design: Cultural Probes. *Interactions 6*, 1: 21–29. https://doi.org/10.1145/291224.291235
10. Elisa Giaccardi, Nazli Cila, Chris Speed, and Melissa Caldwell. 2016. Thing Ethnography: Doing Design Research with Non-Humans. In *Proceedings of the 2016 ACM Conference on Designing Interactive Systems*, 377–387. https://doi.org/10.1145/2901790.2901905
11. Elisa Giaccardi, Lenneke Kuijer, and Louis Neven. 2016. Design for Resourceful Ageing: Intervening in the Ethics of Gerontechnology. In *Proceedings of DRS 2016*, Design Research Society 50th Anniversary Conference.
12. Lenneke Kuijer, Iohanna Nicenboim, and Elisa Giaccardi. 2017. Conceptualising Resourcefulness As a Dispersed Practice. In *Proceedings of the 2017 Conference on Designing Interactive Systems (DIS '17)*, 15–27. https://doi.org/10.1145/3064663.3064698
13. Stephen Lindsay, Daniel Jackson, Guy Schofield, and Patrick Olivier. 2012. Engaging Older People Using Participatory Design. In *Proceedings of the SIGCHI Conference on Human Factors in Computing Systems (CHI '12)*, 1199–1208. https://doi.org/10.1145/2207676.2208570
14. Daniel López Gómez. 2015. Little arrangements that matter. Rethinking autonomy-enabling innovations for later life. *Technological forecasting and social change* 93, Supplement C: 91–101. https://doi.org/10.1016/j.techfore.2014.02.015
15. Louis Neven. 2015/4. By any means?

Questioning the link between gerontechnological innovation and older people's wish to live at home. *Technological forecasting and social change* 93: 32–43. https://doi.org/10.1016/j.techfore.2014.04.016

16. Alexander Peine, Ingo Rollwagen, and Louis Neven. 2014/2. The rise of the "innosumer"—Rethinking older technology users. *Technological forecasting and social change* 82: 199–214. https://doi.org/10.1016/j.techfore.2013.06.013

17. Alessandro Soro, Aloha Hufana Ambe, and Margot Brereton. 2017. Minding the Gap: Reconciling Human and Technical Perspectives on the IoT for Healthy Ageing. *Proceedings of the International Wireless Communications & Mobile Computing Conference 2017*, Association for Computing Machinery. https://doi.org/10.1155/2017/7439361

18. Pieter Stappers and Elisa Giaccardi. 2017. Research through Design. In *The Interaction Design Foundation*.

19. Kate Vaisutis, Margot Brereton, Toni Robertson, Frank Vetere, Jeannette Durick, Bjorn Nansen, and Laurie Buys. 2014. Invisible connections: investigating older people's emotions and social relations around objects. In *Proceedings of the 32nd annual ACM conference on Human factors in computing systems*, 1937–1940. https://doi.org/10.1145/2556288.2557314

20. Froukje Sleeswijk Visser, Pieter Jan Stappers, Remko van der Lugt, and Elizabeth B-N Sanders. 2005. Contextmapping: experiences from practice. *CoDesign 1*, 2: 119–149. https://doi.org/10.1080/15710880500135987

21. Ron Wakkary and Leah Maestri. 2007. The Resourcefulness of Everyday Design. In *Proceedings of the 6th ACM SIGCHI Conference on Creativity &Amp; Cognition (C&C '07)*, 163–172. https://doi.org/10.1145/1254960.1254984

22. Ron Wakkary and Leah Maestri. 2008. Aspects of Everyday Design: Resourcefulness, Adaptation, and Emergence. *International Journal of Human–Computer Interaction* 24, 5: 478–491. https://doi.org/10.1080/10447310802142276

23. Iohanna Nicenboim, *Masako Kitazaki, Tomo Kihara, Ana Torralba and Martin Havranek, to appear in* CHI'18 Extended Abstracts, April 21–26, 2018, Montreal, QC, Canada, https://doi.org/10.1145/3170427.3186527

24. Neven, L. and Maathuis, I. Resourceful Ageing: Countering the Paternalistic Stance By Viewing Older People As Innovators *ISA World Congress of Sociology*, International Sociological Association, Toronto, 2018

Conducting Qualitative Fieldwork with Ageing Saudis: A Visual Diary

Soud Nassir, Tuck Wah Leong
Interaction Design and Human Practice Lab
Faculty of Engineering and Information Technology
University of Technology Sydney, Australia
soud.a.nassir@student.uts.edu.au, tuckwah.leong@uts.edu.au

Abstract
This pictorial offers a visual diary of our qualitative fieldwork to understand ageing people's experiences in Saudi Arabia. It provides insights gained through conducting qualitative fieldwork with ageing Saudis. We present a range of cultural considerations that shaped the design of the fieldwork and highlight opportunities, challenges, and issues that we faced when conducting interviews and deploying research probes. In particular, we highlight the power and effectiveness of using probes to elicit participants' values, views and desires when working within the sociocultural norms of Saudi Arabia.

DIS '18, June 9–13, 2018, Hong Kong

ACM ISBN 978-1-4503-5198-0/18/06...$15.00
https://doi.org/10.1145/3196709.3196820

Authors Keywords
Methods; interviews; probes; ageing; Saudi Arabia; HCI; cultural considerations; privacy; gender; social media.

ACM Classification Keywords
H.5.m. Information interfaces and presentation (e.g., HCI): Miscellaneous.

Cross-Cultural HCI Research
While HCI has in recent years extended its western-centric focus through efforts such as cross-cultural design and HCI for Development (HCI4D) [1-3], current HCI research methods are not culturally universal [4]. Researchers have highlighted the need to adopt, tune and even develop new methods when conducting qualitative fieldwork in different cultural context [5]. Ways to explore, interact and design technologies with people who live in non-Western contexts require a degree of translation that must consider local culture, gender, religion, education, politics and environment. Despite the various efforts to adopt and develop new research methods across the globe, we found very little guidance as to how to conduct HCI research in countries such as Saudi Arabia, where its religion and particular cultural values have heavily shaped the sociocultural practices and norms of people's everyday lives, activities and practices [6].

Conducting Qualitative Fieldwork in Saudi
This pictorial presents a collection of the visual elements, designed to offer glimpses into our experiences of

[A]

[A] Jeddah, Saudi Arabia
This photo captures the heritage buildings in the old part of Jeddah (Al-Balad), the city where we conducted most of our fieldwork. Jeddah is the 2nd largest city in Saudi Arabia.

Traditional homes in the Gulf Arab Countries *"are typically designed with an inward-facing center to protect the family from the public eye. The idea is to maintain the sanctity of the home, which is considered sacred and pure, which must be guarded from the gaze or intrusion of non-family members."* [Sobh & Belk, 2011 cited in 9, p674].

conducting qualitative fieldwork with ageing people in Saudi Arabia. The aim is to provide insights gained when conducting interviews with older Saudis and deploying research probes for them to use. We present a range of the cultural considerations that shaped how we approached and designed the fieldwork, and highlight opportunities, challenges, and issues that we faced when conducting the fieldwork. In particular, we highlight the usefulness of probes in helping us to traverse some of the cultural boundaries we encountered during our fieldwork in Saudi.

Challenges to Conducting Qualitative Fieldwork in Saudi Arabia

Our search and review of research literature revealed a lack of resources about culturally sensitive methods and tools that can be used when conducting qualitative research in Saudi Arabia. From the limited available resources, we realised that conducting qualitative research in Saudi Arabia can be problematic to researchers [7. 8]. This is mainly due to challenges associated with issues of privacy and cross-gender communications.

To Saudis, privacy is associated with honour. It extends beyond personal boundaries to one's family and community. This means that one is protective not only of one's personal privacy but of others within the community. This includes preventing or limiting discussions of personal life and views with 'strangers' [8, 9]. This maintenance of privacy is further heightened when communication is conducted with a non-familial individual, especially of a different gender [8]. Cross-gender communications - male-to-female conversations (and vice versa) - are often mediated through a proxy, i.e. a chaperon/guardian [10, 11]. Traditionally, this chaperon/guardian is a male relative who is tasked with the role of maintaining this privacy. This heightened privacy concerns impacts significantly on the recruitment of participants for interviews. Although researchers have reported the challenges associated with privacy, surprisingly little have been discussed as to how we could mitigate them.

The Fieldwork (The Background)

This fieldwork is the first part of a larger ongoing research project that seeks to design ICTs to support older people in Saudi Arabia to age-well. The aim of this fieldwork is to develop local (and culturally situated) understandings of ageing in Saudi. This is because current ageing research has been developed primarily through work conducted in the West [11]. In addition, the fieldwork seeks to explore how ageing Saudis use digital technologies in their everyday lives to support their experiences of ageing. It is hoped that the insights gained could offer inspirations into how technology could be designed in culturally appropriate and meaningful ways to support the aspirations of ageing Saudis. This pictorial only reports on the methods and tools used in the fieldwork as well as the methodological challenges and issues encountered conducting fieldwork with older Saudis.

When designing our fieldwork, we drew what we could from these limited sources. More importantly, we relied upon the

[B] Research Timeline

first author's understanding of the local culture. Soud was born and raised in Saudi Arabia. He spent the first 18 years of his life in Saudi before moving to Australia to pursue further studies. Soud is bilingual and is accustomed to the traditions of everyday life in Saudi. Having lived away from Saudi for the past 8 years, except for occasional short visits, has given Soud some 'distance' and sense of being a 'familiar outsider' when he returned to Saudi to conduct this fieldwork.

Participants and Recruitment

We recruited 14 Saudi individuals (6 females, aged from 55 to 71). We conducted the study mainly in the Western region of Saudi where gender segregation laws are more relaxed [8]. We were particularly interested in participants who were literate, because the probes used in this fieldwork involve some reading and writing. Likewise, we recruited individuals living at home because generally, older Saudis live with their families in the same household and prefer informal home care [12, 13].

Just like [8, 14], snowballing sampling method was used to recruit participants, starting from our own social circle of friends. This form of personal referral helps generate a sense of trust in participants because this referral somehow provides a personal vouch for the researcher. Furthermore, this form of chain referrals also grants the investigator "insider or group member" access [15].

During recruitment, we did not initiate any direct contact with potential female participants. Instead, we relied on their kin to mediate negotiations. This is because Saudi males are socially responsible to provide for and to 'protect' their female family members [16]. As noted earlier, protection can include mediating non-familial cross-gender negotiations. After the initial interview, we exchanged contact information with the participants so that they could communicate directly with us (during research period).

Research Timeline

For each participant, the research spanned over 10 days. Figure [B] highlights the overall research timeline starting with the initial interview, where we get to know the participant, introduce the research, get them to sign the consent forms, conduct the interview and present the probe kit. Throughout the research period, we maintained periodic contact with our participants through social media applications.

Interviews

We conducted face-to-face semi-structured interviews, which lasted between about 40 – 90 minutes. The open-ended questions sought to elicit a range of information, including the participants' background, their everyday activities, their state of health and if they receive any care. We were also interested in their social lives, their social participation, their sense of self and identity, and their use of technology. Finally, most interviews were conducted at participants' homes to learn more about their domestic settings and particular circumstances.

We were aware of various cultural factors that may impact face-to-face communications. Non-familial cross-gender communication is considered culturally inappropriate and thus male-to-female conversations are often mediated through a chaperon who is an immediate male relative [16]. Consequently, participants may behave differently or offer answers that are not necessarily of their own volition [10]. Therefore, we used probes to supplement our interviews.

Probes

Probes allow a desirable minimal external influence on participants' action compared to different research methods [17, 18]. While probes have been previously used to elicit older people's views and perception (e.g. [19, 20]), we have not found any reports of its deployment in Saudi Arabia.

We designed our probe pack (see Figures C & D) so that participants have a number of tasks to complete over the span of seven days. The probe kit consisted of a diary, a map and a set of postcards. The diary contains "how to use" instructions on the front cover and the contact details of the researcher at the back cover. The postcards contained printed instructions for participants to complete different tasks for seven days. They included activities whereby participants had to take photos, for example, of something they value the most; use stickers to map places of interests, such as places that they like, e.g. socialize. Other activities included drawing a family tree and naming any technologies they have used during the day.

[C] The Probe Pack

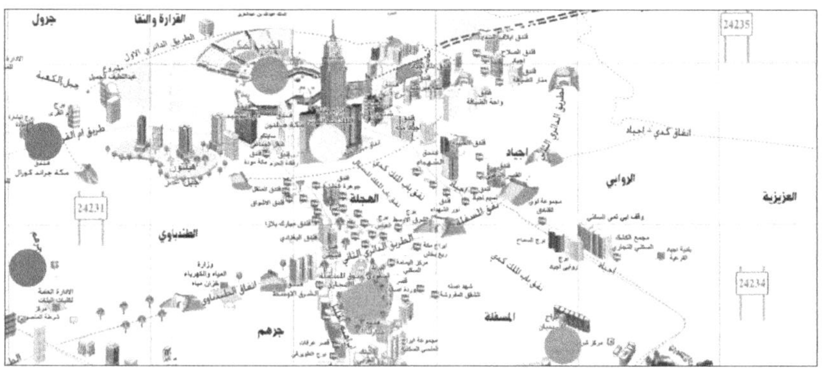

[D] We included a mapping activity in our probe

Being culturally aware of Saudi people's heightened concerns about the sanctity of privacy, especially of their own homes [8], we decided not to include a disposable camera in the probe pack. This is because participants may feel that they have limited control over what they capture or inadvertently capture since they cannot review, edit or delete the content. For example, it may not be appropriate to share photographs of adult females who are not fully or partially covered. As an alternative, we encouraged participants to share their daily activities with us through various online social media apps using their smart phones. The use of these chat apps allows participants flexibility in self-reporting and have full control over the content they share.

[E] The initial 'Mood Box'

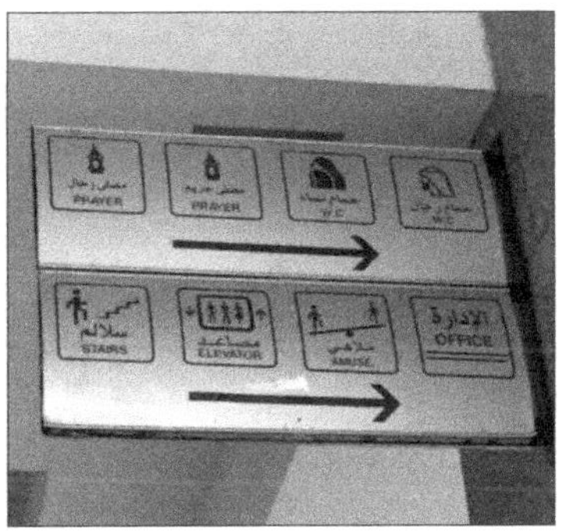

[G] A public directional sign

Early in the research process, we piloted our probe kit with potential participants to ensure its cultural appropriateness and to evaluate its effectiveness in eliciting participants' responses. This has led to changes to our design of the probe kit. For example, participants were provided with a printed 'mood box' at the beginning of each diary entry and were instructed to draw a face that describe how they felt most of the day. This was used as a trigger to encourage participants to write about their feelings as well as their daily activities. However, we found that the mood box we used was confusing. For example, one participant initially wrote 'happy' in the mood box and then later drew a smiley face (as show in Figure E). So, we decided to instead use a Likert scale (as shown in Figure F).

[F] The updated 'Mood Box' with Likert scale

Similarly, we used various icons in the cover page of the diary as triggers to the different activities participants can talk about, such as going to the mosque, eating habits as well as physical activities (Figures H&I). We also included icons that represented people such as family, friends and others to capture social interactions. Public directional signs, e.g. at the local shopping mall (Figure G), prompted us to reflect back on our design and ensure that chosen icons are not revealing in any way and do not, for example, show the female body. Overall, we were mindful of our participants when designing the probes.

[H] The initial design of the cover page

[I] The final printed design of the diary with updated icons

[J] A photo of our interview with a female participant taken by her chaperon

[K] Some of the sweet treats that was served to the guest (the researcher in this case)

Reflections About the Fieldwork

Interviews

Our experiences of interviewing in Saudi homes differed from the interviews we are familiar with in the West. Traditionally, older Saudis live with their family, which often includes children and grandchildren and other extended family member (as well as foreign maids). So, Saudi homes are often very busy and filled with many family members, often present at the same time. Most of our participants preferred interviews to take place during late afternoons, in the evenings, or weekends because they are often busy during the day. However, we discovered that this was also a busy family time, with children and many members of the extended family present. Saudis also often receive visitors over weekends. As a result, our interviews often took place in noisy settings with constant interruptions by various family members or carers.

We found that chaperons or kin were often present, seated with the participants during the interview. As such, our interviews in Saudi homes were hardly ever conducted in private with the participant alone. Conducting interviews in busy Saudi homes meant that besides the presence of chaperons, anyone else could sit and listen to the unfolding interview. Occasionally, two or more chaperons were present at the same time during the interview. Figure J shows an example of interview we conducted with a female participant. In this particular instance, we moved between three rooms in order to find a quieter room to conduct the interview with minimal interruptions. Nonetheless, a chaperon was present at all times, listening in, taking photos (Figure J) and even asking questions.

Furthermore, Day One of the research turned out to be longer than we expected. This is because the researcher was considered a guest and hence, provided hospitality. For example, we were served coffee/tea, sweets (Figure K) and even dined in with the participant and their (male) family members (Figure L). The researcher also attended the daily prayers with the participants at their local mosque (Figure M). This first meeting is, as [7] noted, a part of developing a participant-researcher relationship, where participants asked about the researchers' origin, studies, work and other personal matters. The researcher did his best to answer the questions freely and openly in order to develop trust and rapport.

[L] Dining in with a participant and his 'male' family members

[M] Walking to the local mosque with a participant to attend the daily evening prayer

Probes

Our participants were generally active in reporting their daily experiences. The following figures (N, O, P, Q & R) show examples of the returned probes we received from our participants.

Our use of probes has led us to explore alternative and maybe more productive means of data collection. We also found that the use of probes allowed us to mitigate some of the challenges we encountered when conducting interviews, e.g. chaperon external influences on participants.

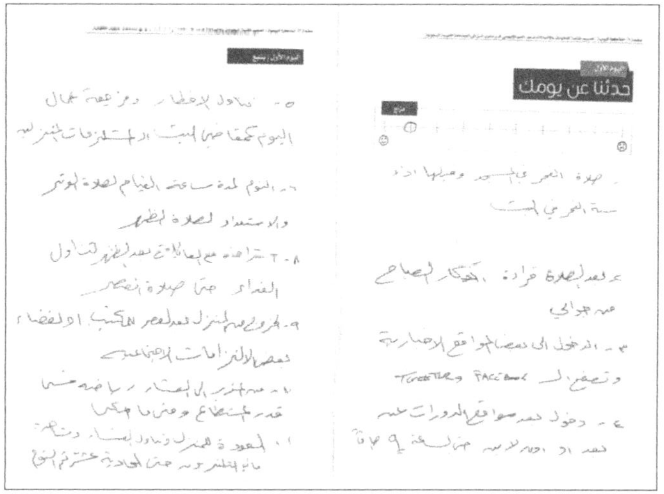

[N] A participant's diary entry. The participant appears to lead a very busy and family-oriented life.

[O] The probe kit in setting

[P] A female participant's creative craft of her family tree. The name tags have been covered to maintain anonymity

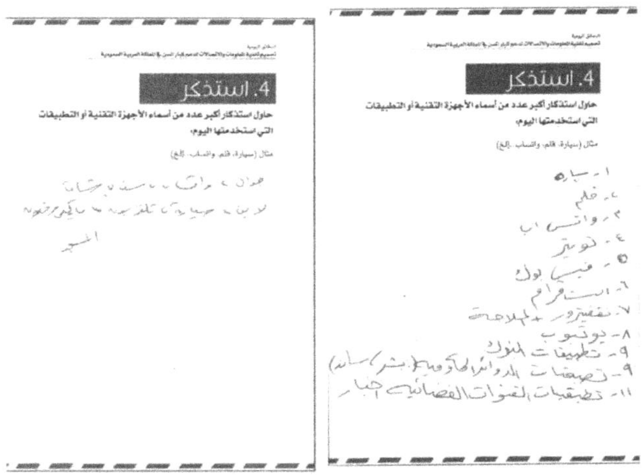

[Q] A postcard activity whereby participants name any technologies they have used during the day.

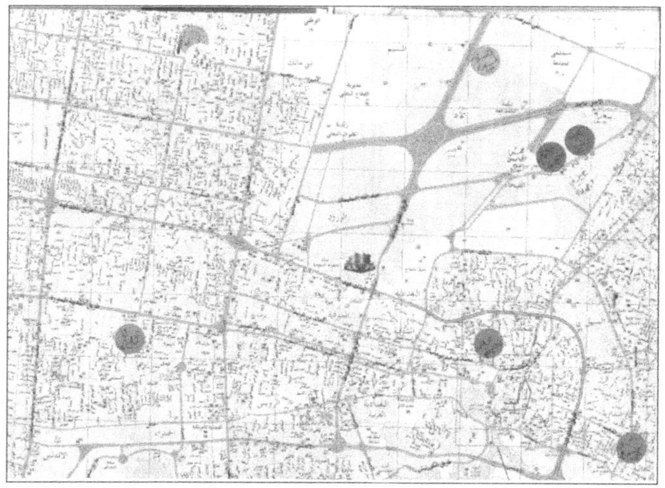
[R] A returned map activity highlighting the various areas that our participant enjoys going to, spending time at and even avoiding. Here, the participant marked his local mosque, gym and the beach as places of frequent visit.

The Use of Social Media

We encouraged participants to share aspects of their everyday lives with us using social media technologies such as WhatsApp. This is because WhatsApp is one of the most popular social media applications in Saudi Arabia. Our participants were very active in sharing their lives with us through this platform, revealing the potentials for using social media technologies when conducting fieldwork in Saudi.

The use of social media in this fieldwork allowed us greater access to domestic spaces beyond the guest room, where interviews were often conducted. This technology offers almost 'live' insights into participants' lives because messages or media are created and captured just before they are sent. The use of WhatsApp, in our research gave us a kind of vicarious snapshots into participants' daily lives as it unfolded often close to real time (Figure T). WhatsApp also allowed us to engage the participants in bursts of ongoing conversations, giving us opportunities inquire further about their current contexts and particular situations (Figure S).

Introducing flexibility of reporting, including drawing and use of social media, have given us deep insights into our participants' lives. For example, we learned more about one participant's hobbies and passion to gift handcrafted items to family friends (see Figure T - Far Right).

[S] A participant sharing his daily activity through WhatsApp

[T] Participants' use of Social Media platforms to take photos, record videos, add filters and captions as well as emoticon.

[T] Cont.

The following collection of photos provide glimpses into our participants' daily lives. For example, the top row of photos highlights many of our participants passions for handcraft and cooking, while the 2nd and 3rd row show the various domestic activities of our participants' daily lives. This includes spending the evening with family members; watching TV, chatting and having dinner together (2nd&3rd row - left). The photos also provide insights into the roles participants play in their domestic settings. Despite their authoritative roles as elders, our female participants, appear to be heavily involved in carrying out their domestic 'duties'. This is because traditional roles, where by females look after children and the housework, remain strong in Saudi Arabia. A female participant wrote on a photo she shared of the laundry machine (bottom-right) "I have prayed, cooked and cleaned the house. I am now doing the laundry."

[U]

[U] "My son is travelling, and I am currently helping prepare his luggage"

Furthermore, the ability to use emoticons afforded certain participants the ability to express emotion. As seen in Figure U, a participant was sad because her son is travelling overseas to pursue further studies. She shared a photo of her son's luggage and wrote about her son's departure with a 'crying face' emoticon. She also shared a picture of the laundry (Figure W) and annotated how overwhelmed she was with the housework. Just like the use of the mood scale, social media afforded some of our participants opportunities to express emotions and feeling that might have been difficult to surface during interviews.

With our participants, we found that once trust has been established, cross-gender communication and privacy concerns did not become a problem during online conversations. This contrasts strongly with physical face-to-face interviews where there is still a strong barrier during cross-gender communications. The male researcher could contact the female participants directly using WhatsApp without the need for a chaperon to mediate the conversation. In our research, the use of social media was also useful in fostering the ongoing development of researcher-participant rapport.

[W]

[X]

[V]

[W, X & V] A female participant expressing her emotions via captions and emoticon. She shared photos and videos with us; noting how overwhelmed she was with the housework. She writes in Figure W (after sharing Figure X), "I am now doing the laundry, may God aid the housewives"

Considerations for Future Research

Traversing boundaries through Social Media

The capacity to collect ongoing streams of data through using social media in our research have yielded surprising benefits. This platform allowed us direct access to communicate with participants, without the presence of chaperons/kin or others, such as what we encountered during interviews at homes. Using social media allowed us to have direct access and ongoing conversations, which provided more immediate opportunities to follow up with questions, receive visual/audio media, clarify media that were shared with us, and so on. Once trust has been established, participants, especially females, were able to use social media to communicate directly with us without having to use the chaperon/kin to mediate conversations and to pass on information. In other words, we found that social media was able to help traverse strong boundaries that are particular to cross-gender communications in this qualitative fieldwork. Through the use of social media, female participants in our research were certainly more forthcoming in sharing their thoughts, emotions and experiences with the male researcher. Despite this, we see great possibilities to explore how social media can be used more productively when conducting fieldwork in general in Saudi.

Interviews as an occasion to build trust

Certainly, conducting interviews in busy domestic spaces brought about unexpected and unforeseen challenges. Despite this, we realized, after the initial interview, that this first contact is also as much as an occasion to build trust with the participants, as it is to gather research information. Face-to-face communication, whereby the participants learn more about the research and the researcher and vice-versa, was crucial to establishing direct online communication with our participants. In fact, we found during our research that the opportunities afforded by the use of social media for research purposes is likely to be dependent on the initial meeting and interviews.

Limitation

This study is limited in the range of ageing people we recruited in our research. For example, we were particularly interested in literate participants as the probes involve reading and writing activities. Similarly, we conducted most of our fieldwork in the Western religion of Saudi Arabia where segregation laws are more relaxed. We can imagine that conducting fieldwork beyond this region, where cultural norms and social practices are more strictly observed will pose greater challenges in all aspect of the research. Similarly, we can imagine that face-to-face cross- gender communication might be more problematic for female researchers. This is because female researchers themselves are likely to be expected to have a chaperon with them when conducting interviews with males.

Conclusion

This pictorial seeks to provide visual a dairy of experiences of conducting qualitative research with ageing people in Saudi Arabia. The aim is to provide insights gained about conducting interviews and probes with older Saudis. The pictorial describes some of the challenges and cultural consideration that influenced our approach and research design. More importantly, it highlights the effectiveness of using probes, particularly social media, to elicit users' experiences, values and aspiration. Finally, the experiences of using interviews and probes in conducting qualitative research in Saudi Arabia, including the practical challenges, and methodological considerations have been discussed at length in our earlier work [21]. As HCI expand its boundaries, we hope that this paper contributes to the growing body of cross-cultural research.

References

1. Margot Brereton, Paul Roe, Thomas Amagula, Serena Bara, Judy Lalara and Anita Lee Hong. 2013. Growing Existing Aboriginal Designs to Guide a Cross-Cultural Design Project. in Kotzé, P., Marsden, G., Lindgaard, G., Wesson, J. and Winckler, M. eds. Human-Computer Interaction – INTERACT 2013: 14th IFIP TC 13 International Conference, Cape Town, South Africa, September 2-6, 2013, Proceedings, Part I, Springer Berlin Heidelberg, Berlin, Heidelberg, 323-330.
2. Neha Kumar, Susan Dray, Andy Dearden, Nicola Dell, Melissa Densmore, Rebecca E. Grinter, Zhengjie Liu, Mario A. Moreno Rocha, Anicia Peters, Eunice Sari, William Thies, Indrani Medhi-Thies, William D. Tucker, Elba Valderrama Bahamondez and Susan Wyche. 2016. Development Consortium: HCI Across Borders Proceedings of the 2016 CHI Conference Extended Abstracts on Human Factors in Computing Systems, ACM, Santa Clara, California, USA, 3620-3627.
3. Susan P. Wyche. 2011. Designing for everyday interactions in HCI4D. interactions, 18 (2). 52-56. 10.1145/1925820.1925832
4. Lilly Irani. 2010. HCI on the move: methods, culture, values CHI '10 Extended Abstracts on Human Factors in Computing Systems, ACM, Atlanta, Georgia, USA, 2939-2942.
5. Helma van Rijn, Yoonnyong Bahk, Pieter Jan Stappers and Kun-Pyo Lee. 2006. Three factors for contextmapping in East Asia: Trust, control and nunchi. CoDesign, 2 (3). 157-177. 10.1080/15710880600900561
6. David E. Long. 2005. Culture and Customs of Saudi Arabia. Greenwood Press, Westport, Connecticut - London.
7. Sana Hawamdeh and Veena Raigangar. 2014. Qualitative interviewing: methodological challenges in Arab settings. Nurse Researcher, 21 (3). 27-31. 10.7748/nr2014.01.21.3.27.e357
8. Norah Abokhodair and Sarah Vieweg. 2016. Privacy & Social Media in the Context of the Arab Gulf Proceedings of the 2016 ACM Conference on Designing Interactive Systems, ACM, Brisbane, QLD, Australia, 672-683.
9. Bronislaw J. Verhage, Ugur Yavas and Robert T. Green. 1990. Perceived risk: A cross-cultural phenomenon? International Journal of Research in Marketing, 7 (4). 297-303. http://dx.doi.org/10.1016/0167-8116(90)90007-A
10. Mohammad Zafir Al-Shahri. 2002. Culturally Sensitive Caring for Saudi Patients. Journal of Transcultural Nursing, 13 (2). 133-138. 10.1177/104365960201300206
11. Soud Nassir, Tuck Wah Leong and Toni Robertson. 2015. Positive Ageing: Elements and factors for design Proceedings of the Annual Meeting of the Australian Special Interest Group for Computer Human Interaction, ACM, Parkville, VIC, Australia, 264-268.
12. M. H. Mufti. 2002. A case for community and hospital-based long-term care facilities in Saudi Arabia. Annals of Saudi Medicine, 22 (5-6). 336-338.
13. Sulaiman Al-Shammari, Jamal S. Jarallah and Ferial Felimban. 1997. Long-term care experience in Saudi Arabia. Social Science & Medicine, 44 (5). 693-697. http://dx.doi.org/10.1016/S0277-9536(96)00196-7
14. Graham Mytton, Peter Diem and Piet Hein van Dam. 2016. Media Audience Research: A Guide to Professionals. Sage Publishing.
15. R Atkinson and J Flint. 2001. Accessing Hidden and Hard-to-reach Populations: Snowball Research Strategies. Social Research Update, 33.
16. Tamara Alsheikh, Jennifer A. Rode, Si, #226 and n E. Lindley. 2011. (Whose) value-sensitive design: a study of long- distance relationships in an Arabic cultural context Proceedings of the ACM 2011 conference on Computer supported cooperative work, ACM, Hangzhou, China, 75-84.
17. William W. Gaver, Andrew Boucher, Sarah Pennington and Brendan Walker. 2004. Cultural probes and the value of uncertainty. interactions, 11 (5). 53-56. 10.1145/1015530.1015555
18. Connor Graham, Mark Rouncefield, Martin Gibbs, Frank Vetere and Keith Cheverst. 2007. How probes work Proceedings of the 19th Australasian conference on Computer-Human Interaction: Entertaining User Interfaces, ACM, Adelaide, Australia, 29-37.
19. Joseph Wherton, Paul Sugarhood, Rob Procter, Mark Rouncefield, Guy Dewsbury, Sue Hinder and Trisha Greenhalgh. 2012. Designing assisted living technologies 'in the wild': preliminary experiences with cultural probe methodology. BMC Medical Research Methodology, 12.

188-188. 10.1186/1471-2288-12-188

20. Bill Gaver, Tony Dunne and Elena Pacenti. 1999. Design: Cultural probes. interactions, 6 (1). 21-29. 10.1145/291224.291235
21. Soud Nassir and Tuck Wah Leong. 2017. Traversing Boundaries: Understanding the Experiences of Ageing Saudis Proceedings of the 2017 CHI Conference on Human Factors in Computing Systems, ACM, Denver, Colorado, USA, 6386-6397.

Designing the Lost Self: Older Adults' Self-representations in Online Games

Romina Carrasco, Jenny Waycott, Steven Baker, Frank Vetere
Interaction Design Lab, School of Computing and Information Systems, The University of Melbourne,
Melbourne, Australia
rcarrasco@student.unimelb.edu.au, jwaycott, steven.baker, f.vetere [@unimelb.edu.au]

ABSTRACT
Older adults are increasingly engaging in online activities, including games, with other people. Many online environments require the user to create some form of self-representation, ranging from a simple user name through to a full body avatar. These self-representations not only enable access to online activities, but also provide an opportunity for expressing both the real and ideal identity. We wanted to better understand the impacts of later life on the construction of self-representations when playing online games. Our study used gameplay observations and semi-structured interviews with 10 older adult gamers aged from 65 to 95 years. We found they designed their player self-representations to project aspects of their lost (former) self and to embrace their present older selves. This engagement with self-representations as a form of self-expression suggests that designers need to consider older gamers, and their diverse preferences, when creating tools for customizable self-representations in online games.

Author Keywords
Older adults; self-representation; design; online games; avatar; aging; identity.

ACM Classification Keywords
H.1.2 [User/Machine Systems]: Human Factors;

INTRODUCTION
Craig plays as *Kowalski the shooter* in Battlefield, a Massively Multiplayer Online Game (MMOG). Craig is 82 years old and has been playing online games for the last 16 years, almost 6 hours every day. This is one example that challenges stereotypes of older adults using technology. Like Craig, other older adults are using social media [1], online communities [7, 8, 25], dating sites [50], and games [1, 28]. In fact, recent reports indicate that the fastest growing segment of the online gaming population new to games is older adults over 65 years of age [5].

DIS '18, June 9–13, 2018, Hong Kong

ACM ISBN 978-1-4503-5198-0/18/06…$15.00
https://doi.org/10.1145/3196709.3196773

As many gaming environments involve social interactions online, users require a digital self-representation (e.g., *Kowalski the shooter*) in order to be identified by others. Online self-representations range from simple nicknames to full body depictions of a character. These self-representations are critical elements of social interaction as they project information about the self, helping to create initial impressions [19]. This information can be so significant that some authors state that meeting an individual online can be more informative than meeting that person face to face [23]. But these self-representations do not act as mere representational elements; they also allow a "construction and reconstruction of the self" [47] supporting in many cases the enhancement or idealization of the self in virtual environments.

To understand the role of self-representations in older adults, this study investigated the question: how do older adults represent themselves in online games? In this paper, we focus in particular on aspects of self-representation significant to later life. We conducted semi-structured interviews and gameplay observations with 10 older adults (65-95 years old) playing online games with other people. Though our findings depict great diversity in player representations, they also highlight the potential of self-representations in projecting aspects of the self that had been lost during the lifetime and that are still considered important for the individual acting as a tool of reminiscence. In addition, some participants designed self-representations that embraced aspects of their current experiences as older adults. Our analysis provides a case for designers to expand the possibilities of customization of player representations, especially for older adult gamers, while contributing to the growing literature that aims to understand the benefits online technologies can provide for people as they age.

PRIOR WORK

Self-representations in Play
When meeting a person face to face, we construct our impressions by looking at their body appearance, body language and even their clothing. However, in online environments we do not have all these visual cues to learn about someone's identity. For some this relative anonymity achieved in online environments provides more freedom in expression [3, 35]. For example, online environments enable users to experiment with self-representations portraying different genders or races [47]. Moreover, recent

studies have shown that online self-representations can be use for self-disclosure [52] or creativity [13, 24].

Depending on the online environment, self-representations can range in complexity from text-based nicknames to avatars. Despite the simplicity of nicknames, they can depict individual traits of the user, personal interests [13] or indicate belonging to a particular group [2]. An early study of online player nicknames found that 45% of 260 nicknames included some feature of the self, such as references to physical or psychological character traits [2]. As online self-representations become more complex they can provide more information about the individual.

In virtual worlds users adopt an avatar in order to interact with each other and their surroundings. Avatars provide a richer way to present the self as they provide a depiction of a full body character [45]. The use of an avatar may go beyond static self-representations. The avatar is a medium to express gestures and actions, and can potentially denote values and behaviors in the virtual world. McDonough says that the actions build an identity; suggesting a 'performative' identity on the online world that is made of what you do, not only what you are [34]. Some authors state that the visual depiction of an avatar influences the personality that the user attaches to the avatar in the virtual world [52]. Others state that the personality of the player is usually maintained through his or her avatar [14]. What is important is that when creating an avatar, users customize visual traits but also attach a personality to the character.

In addition, in online games the narrative and features of the game influence avatars' depictions [14]. Users embody roles and characters that are linked to the game. For example, Craig in Battlefield can choose an avatar from a set of characters such as shooters or medics. The visual features of the characters are also representative of this context of use and therefore the characters wear uniforms and use tools such as guns and war vehicles typical of this setting. Even though some of these visual characteristics of the avatars come from the game and not from the user, Turkle argues that users are what they play, suggesting that the selection of a specific type of game may be already depicting an aspect of the self [48].

Projecting an Ideal Self

Self-representations also give an opportunity to project personal ideals or aspirations [2, 3]. Studies have shown that these aspirations are influenced by societal norms such as standards of beauty [14, 37]. When customizing their avatars, users in these studies created an idealized avatar applying Western aesthetic features to make them younger, thinner, and fashionable. Scholars believe that avatars can be used to go beyond the specific body appearance and hide traits that Western culture often views in negative terms [37]. Users can create avatars of how they desire to look, representing their ideal self [47], which may not align to their physical appearance but to the one they want to show to others. For example, the use of certain outfits in a digital avatar can provide status that cannot be afforded in physical life [30]. Avatars may constitute a way to be portrayed according social expectations, achieving new representations that may not be possible in the physical environment. It is through these idealizations that the user can also feel identification with the avatar.

Identification with Online Self-representations

Identification is the degree to which individuals empathize with a character, perceiving it to be similar to themselves [4]. This similarity can be achieved projecting actual or ideal traits of the self [52]. In fact, greater identification between the avatar and the user can lead to more enjoyment, autonomy, immersion and positive affect [4]. Furthermore, Yee (2014) states that avatar identification can be used as a persuasion tool to change the player behavior [52]. In his experiments, Yee blended the characteristics of the avatars with the participant's traits showing that users were more motivated to perform the actions that the avatar was doing if they perceived more identification.

However identification between the user and the avatar may not be achieved if the options to customize the avatars do not represent the intentions of the user. For example, researchers have argued that in many character creator interfaces there are visual features such as gender and ethnicity that are depicted in a restricted mode [27, 32]. These systems mediate self-representation practices in a socially exclusive way limiting how minorities are represented in virtual environments [32].

Investigators have addressed these design limitations of character creator interfaces in different ways. Taylor (2003) and McDonough (1999) interviewed designers of virtual environments to have a better understanding of the processes behind the creation of these systems. While some designers highlighted the importance to embrace "... diversity of people and experiences" [44], both studies suggest that the software of virtual environments is designed with intended visions of identities [34, 44]. Authors suggest that these designs respond to hegemonic views of an industry mostly dominated by males [20, 34]. Utilizing another approach, McArthur et al. propose an avatar affordance framework to understand the representational options of customization systems [33]. In her studies, she recommends practices to help designers to make socially inclusive games focusing in the selection of avatar features [32]. Instead, Taylor suggest the use of participatory design methods to reproduce visual traits that represent a wider set of social values in character creation systems [44]. While researchers had pointed to the constrained representations of race and gender in character creation interfaces, there is not much research in relation to the presence of ageing features in these customizations systems.

Older Adults' Self-representations

Older Adults' Offline Self

The changes that older adults experience in later life may impact how they project their identity and how others view them. In later ages, the roles people play in their family, work and other environments frequently become less clear as the circumstances change [51]. For example, older people's roles as parents may be less demanding as they get older; roles as spouses may disappear as they have more probability to lose their partners. Additionally many older adults stop executing their professional roles when they retire. These changing circumstances may influence identity, making it harder for an individual to understand their new place in society, thus impacting on their self-perception and self-esteem [26]. In addition, older adults may experience changes in the appearance and functionality of the body that may not correspond with their personal image of themselves [18]. The different domains that construct an individual's identity become less visible as people grow older Online self-representations can serve to visualize these hidden aspects of past identities.

Online Self-representations of Older Adults

There is very little research exploring the use of online self-representations by older adults. Recent research on self-representations of older adults in dating sites (where users are searching for a potential partner) suggest that they depict themselves as being active, productive, healthy, accentuating their positive approach to life [50]. These portrayals are made by older adults using static elements such as nicknames, slogans and photographs to highlight a positive image in relation to their age, finding that suggests that this may be a way to override negative stereotypes attached to older age [50]. This may influence not only how others see them but also how they perceive themselves.

In relation to the use of avatars, previous research suggests that avatars may be attractive for older populations as they provide the opportunity to embody younger bodies that hide their age [11, 39, 43]. Adults aged 55+ stated that being portrayed in a younger body expanded their possibilities of social interactions as they could blend with younger populations [43]. On the other hand, when participants exposed their real age, some felt that their presence was unwelcome by younger users. The perception of the body must also be highlighted, as some older adults who had physical limitations suggested that avatars removed the restrictions of their physical bodies allowing them to enjoy 'outdoor activities'. In a recent survey of video game preferences among 100 older adults (60+), they marked that the less important feature of a video game was to have a character that looked like themselves [41]. This finding suggests that they may not be attracted by the idea of having an avatar that depicts their actual self. Finally the idea that older adults prefer to create an avatar with a younger body was confirmed in a recent study with a group of older adults (70+) designing avatars in a workshop setting [9]. Even though this study does not report on the use of avatars in online environments, it does suggest that older adults enhanced their depiction with healthier, stronger and younger traits illustrating a desire for an augmented physical condition. However, other participants in this study also depicted the desire to mirror their actual selves using ageing feature, which may suggest an acceptance of the older self. These findings may sound contradictory, but they also depict the range of preferences found among this population, highlighting the importance of recognizing the diversity among this group [49]. In order to address the diversity and avoid stigma, previous research has involved older adults in discussions of technology designs, expanding the design considerations to respond to specific needs and fit with older adult's active lives [29].

Considering the influence that character creator interfaces can have on the presentation of the self in online environments, we wanted to learn from the actual choices of older adults (65+) designing online self-representations (including avatars) outside a lab setting and in a real context of use. As older adults are increasingly using online games as a medium to engage online and it is where users will commonly use avatars, we chose gaming as a context for observing the design and use of self-representations among this population.

Older Adults and Online Games

Older adults are increasingly engaging in online games. In Australia more than 40% of older adults (65+) are playing online games. More first-time players are in this group than in any other age group [5]. This incremental participation of older adults, is expected to continue to rise as baby boomers achieve later age [5, 10].

It seems that older adults have very heterogeneous preferences in online games. While some older adults prefer casual games, such as *Candy Crush* or simple games that replicate traditional table board games such as card games [42], others state that baby boomers are interested in engaging in fantasy worlds and are playing through MMOGs [38].

Online games can have collaborative possibilities that allow users to interact with each other individually or by creating teams, bringing possibilities for social interactions. This may be an important trend at a time where there are strong initiatives to promote social participation among this population [12, 51]. In a report of gamers, older adults state that they play online to keep the mind active, to pass time, to have fun, to relax and to be challenged [5]. These experiences had shown to be beneficial among older people increasing mental stimulation, fighting dementia and augmenting mobility [5, 25]. As these systems become more pervasive in older adults' lives, it is important to understand how older adults want to be represented in online games.

Among the limitations found in this literature review, is the lack of research with older adults over 65 years old. Even though some studies state that they target older adults, the participants of these studies were under 65 years old, age bracket defined by the World Health Organization for older adulthood [51]. Further research is needed in order to understand the social, mental and emotional implications of older adults over 65 years old when using self-representations and specifically avatars in online environments.

AIMS

This study aims to understand how older adults are using self-representations in online games. This understanding will contribute to the growing academic literature about older adults and technology use, providing a more nuanced view of how older adults embrace online social environments. This may challenge the stereotyped views that are often expressed in discourse about older age and technology [49].

METHOD

This study used an exploratory research approach as it is recommended when scarce knowledge is available about a topic [36]. We know very little about the use of player self-representations by older people (65+) explaining also why we did not restrict our observation to the use of a specific type of self-representation such as avatars. Instead, we extended the type of player self-representations to include a wider variety such as nicknames, static pictures and full body animated avatars.

Participants

We conducted semi-structured interviews and gameplay observations with ten participants aged 65 to 95 years, 5 women and 5 men, 1 couple (see Table 1 for detailed demographics). We recruited older people above 65 years old who were playing online games with other people. The participants were recruited via purposive sampling in two countries, the country of residence (Australia), and nationality (Ecuador) of the first author. The recruitment process combined online and offline advertising and snowball sampling. The online advertising was done in online communities of older adult gamers such as the 'The Older Gamers', local Facebook groups and networks of people who work with older adults. The offline advertising was done with flyers displayed on noticeboards at community centres such as libraries, universities, retirement villages and seniors activity clubs. The ethics office of our university approved this study, and informed consent was obtained from all participants.

The involvement in online games among our participants is quite diverse in time playing games, frequency, types of games (see Table 1) and type of technology used to practice this activity. Participants have been involved in computer games (not always online games) from 3 to approximately 30 years. Most of the participants play daily and there are some who play up to 6 hours per day. In addition, most of our participants play more than one online game and in some cases have developed multiple online self-representations. However for the purpose of this research we only focused on one game. Participants selected their favorite social online game to play during the study. The devices that they used in the gaming session were also varied among the group including iPhone (1), iPad (1), desktop computer (6) and laptop computer (2).

Data Collection

We conducted in-depth semi-structured interviews and observations of game sessions with each of the participants. The study prioritized face-to-face sessions at 'normal place of play' of participants. However, alternate options were used in order to adapt to the participants' preferences: 5 sessions were conducted at the home of the participants, 3 at an alternate location and 2 through videoconferencing. The sessions started with a short interview that asked about the demographic characteristics, technical skills and experience playing online games. Then participants were asked to play their favorite online game they play with other people. All the games are social and require an element of self-representation. While playing, participants were asked to "think aloud", a technique in which participants describe out loud their thinking while performing an activity [36].

The observation of the players interacting in the game gave a further understanding of the role of self-representations in the context of use, as these customizations seem to be influenced by online social interactions in which the participants are situated. After the game session, the researcher initiated a discussion to understand the meaning behind the process of creating their self-representations and the relation between the online representation, the offline self, and online social contexts in which they play.

The data included audio recording of the interview and video recording of the game playing behavior. Additionally, the researcher made field notes during the whole session, photographs to record the context of playing and screenshots of the players' online self-representations.

Data Analysis

The data were transcribed and three of the game player sessions and interviews were translated from Spanish to English. The first author conducted all the interviews and made the required translations. Participants' names and nicknames used in online games were anonymized. The first author started analysis by closely reading the transcripts to become familiar with the data, then classifying and reiteratively coding the data using thematic analysis [6]. The codes and themes were discussed and refined in multiple sessions with all the authors. This process offered insights of patterns found across self-representations and the ageing self, in which we focused our attention.

Game	Participant pseudonym	G	Age	Years playing computer games	Favourite actual online game	Hours playing favourite online game per day	Type of self-representation of favourite online game
Casual Games	Albert	M	76	3 years	Words with Friends	1	Nickname
	Belinda	F	74	3 years	Words with Friends	<1	Nickname
	Elly	F	68	11 years	Bridge Base online	3	Nickname, flag
	Grace	F	66	9 years	RedDeLetras	2	Nickname, photograph, quotation of the day
	Francis	F	95	6 years	Casino Online	1	Nickname
	Ivan	M	65	5 years	Antike Duellum	2	Nickname
MMOGs	Craig	M	82	16 years	Battlefield	6	Nickname, Supporter avatar
	Danny	M	76	30 years	Guild Wars II	2	Nickname, 6 avatars
	Hannah	F	68	26 years	Guild Wars II, Final Fantasy*	4	Nickname, 7 avatars
	Jacob	M	68	30 years	World of Warcraft	2	Nickname, 33 avatars

Table 1: Participants demographics, gaming profile and type of self-representations.
*** Hannah also talked about a self-representation she had in a game she played in the past**

FINDINGS

The types of self-representations that our participants use are diverse, ranging from simple usernames through to full-body avatars controlled by the user. These are influenced by the characteristics of the game, with avatars only available in MMOGs and more limited, static self-representations used in casual games. Therefore, the findings will be analyzed in relation to these two categories: casual and MMOGs. Despite this diversity, our participants all used self-representations in online games to project aspects of the past they have lost or to embrace their current older self.

Self-representations of Older Adults in Casual Games

Six participants (4 female and 2 male) play casual games, digitalized versions of offline games. These games in our study usually restricted participants to create simpler online self-representations such as a nickname that sometimes was presented together with a flag, a portrait or a quotation of the day (see Table 1).

Portraying Places from the Past

Albert (male, 76) and Belinda (female, 74) are a couple who daily play *Words with Friends,* a multiplayer crossword game similar to the classic game *Scrabble.* In the game, Albert uses as a self-representation the name of the place where he was born saying that it reminds him of home. When asked what he would like in case of using an image as a self-representation in the game, he stated that: "*I will prefer perhaps a photo of the house we lived in ...*" mentioning that this house had been in the family for many generations. Likewise, Belinda uses the name of the farm where the couple lived and worked until they retired. Both of their nicknames use the postcode of these places as a suffix.

Elly (female, 68) plays *Bridge Base Online,* an online version of the traditional card game that her family played when she was a child. Elly uses her home country flag as part of her self-representation. Even though she had live 40 years in another country, she still prioritizes her original nationality.

Connecting through Self-Representations

Elly's self-representation has allowed her to recover communication with family members and friends that she lost contact 40 years ago when she moved from her home country. Elly adds, "*I like my name as I do not have anything to hide. I love that people can identify me rather than being an incognito.*" Because her last name is very common in her birthplace, many conversations started when people tried to identify her.

Likewise, Grace (female, 66) plays *ReDeLetras*, a popular (Spanish) online version of a word game similar to *Scrabble.* Like Elly, Grace uses her flag and family name, but in addition she also expresses herself through a short quotation of the day that is part of her self-representation. After a stroke that she had three years ago, she started following spiritual guides that had supported her emotional recovery. As part of her self-representation in the game, she posts quotations of her spiritual guides, which had prompted players with similar interests to contact her, and develop meaningful friendships in this phase of her life. In fact, nowadays online games are her main medium for socializing.

Albert and Belinda mostly play within themselves, and are not interested in playing with unknown people. Albert says that he does not "bother" to reply to strangers who want to play with him. Belinda on the other hand says that it is "too risky". In fact, they state that it does not matter that other players cannot familiarize with their self-representations. Both players may be using names of places that other players may find difficult to relate to on purpose, as they do not want to attract social interactions with unknown people in the game.

Maintaining the Prior-Self

As part of her self-representation in the online word game, Grace had chosen to use a photograph of herself that was made 4 years ago. Three years ago she had a stroke that changed her health situation. When asked about this photograph, she started describing how she used to be: "I was very friendly, like partying, drinking, not anymore, I've retired from the madding crowd..." The stroke affected her life drastically and now she feels frail and prefers to stay at home. Grace's hands tremble and she stutters when taking to strangers. Grace self-representation may be a way to remind herself and others of the person she was prior to the stroke.

From the six participants who play casual games with other people, four interviews related to self-representations. The other two participants described their games in relation to social interactions and the association with their self-representation was not clear: Francis (female, 95) plays *Casino Online*, a machine slot game that reminds her offline visits to the local casino. She enjoys sharing the online game with her children and grandchildren. In contrast, Ivan (male, 65) plays online table board games as *Antike Duellum,* a map-based game where the user has to conquer cities. He is housebound due to an illness and uses the online games to socialize with family members that live in other cities.

Self-representations of Older Adults in MMOGs

Four participants (1 female and 3 males) play MMOGs to get immersed in battles, adventures, and fantasy worlds such as *Battlefield or Guild Wars* (see Table 1). In contrast to the simple self-representations of casual games, in these MMOGs participants can choose a full body character to use in the online environment. These types of games offer more possibilities of self-representation as users can continually customize and experiment with the features and tools of the avatar. Most of these participants play with more than one character, Jacob may be an extreme example as he had customized 33 avatars in *World of Warcraft*. It is through these avatars that our participants took the advantage of embodying a new digital body to perform roles and leisure activities of their past, to reclaim youth and to embrace their current older self.

Embodying Careers and Roles from the Past

Jacob (male, 68) has been playing *World of Warcraft*, a MMOG of role-playing characters set in a fantasy universe. Jacob is bringing his engineer role through one of his favorites avatars mentioning: *"I've chosen [avatar name] as a very, very important person to me, because he is an engineer, and I'm an engineer"* (see Figure 1). Nowadays, Jacob is not able to execute his profession explaining *"...the reason that I'm a security guard, after being an industrial chemist, with postgraduate chemical engineering, is that people don't want to hire older people."* *World of Warcraft* provides Jacob the opportunity to embody an engineer role through a virtual avatar.

Figure 1. Jacob embodying his former career as an engineer through one of his favorite's avatars in *World of Warcraft.*

Likewise, Hannah (female, 68) states that one of her initial roles in online games was connected to her previous work as a nurse. During 8 years she played *Final Fantasy XI*, a game that focuses on fantasy role-playing characters who fight against an evil. While playing this game, she embodied the role of a healer, a character that can restore the health of other characters when they had been injured allowing them to keep playing. Remembering what she thought when she discovered this role she mentions: *"Oh wow I can be a healer!, I can keep people alive, I can help people..."* Hannah mentions that embodying this role was connected with her career as a nurse as she enjoys giving support to people online as in real life.

Danny (male, 76) also commented on the personality he attaches to his avatars while recalling a character he created in the past and that may have represented a previous role he had in his family. This is the first character of six he had designed in *Guild Wars* and may be linked to his family social context as he was playing with his two adult children at that time. When describing his character, Danny says: "*... is a tough older ... military kind of guy, and I played him as sort of serious and responsible for the other characters [children avatars] ...*" Through this avatar Danny may be depicting a protective and hierarchical role that he had in the family as a father when he was younger.

Performing Leisure Activities from the Past

Craig (male, 82), who was introduced in the Introduction, plays *Battlefield*, a first person shooter game characterized on large maps, war vehicles and team-based interaction. When Craig was younger, he used to compete in shooting, representing his country. As he cannot practice shooting in real life anymore, this activity motivated him to embody avatars with shooting roles on *Battlefield* (see Figure 2). Explaining what he likes about the game, he mentions: "*It's a shooting game because that is what I did years ago…you know, it is not the same. I was good at that, I'm not at this [laugh].*"

Figure 2. Craig playing a supporter role with a machine gun to increase his shooting speed in *Battlefield.*

In the game he can choose among different shooting roles. Some of these make him feel vulnerable as the roles are involved in exposed activities in which the avatars can be killed very fast. Craig explains that when he plays he is not as fast as younger players stating: "*my reflexes are not quite fast. The young ones… go bang bang and put you strike on with a couple of shots.*" This is the reason why Craig prefers to choose a 'support' role that provides opportunities of hiding and do not require his avatar to be so visible (see Figure 2). Craig also customizes his avatar with a machine gun that allows him to "*spray*" bullets to the enemy providing more possibilities to reach the target compared to other types of guns that require more accuracy. The role of Craig's avatar and type of gun he uses are the result of an exploration of character's features that can enhance his speed and accuracy while reducing his exposure in the game. In addition, Craig's avatar nickname: Kowalski is inspired in another element of his past, the nickname of a famous wrestler that he admired and used to impersonate when he was younger.

Reclaiming Youth

Some participants use their avatars as a way to reclaim a lost youth. Hannah (female, 68) currently is playing Guild Wars II, where she had designed seven avatars to represent herself. Her favorite avatar is a younger representation of herself stating: "*I think when I made her… I was thinking of me as I been in Guild Wars. One of the strange things about aging, you still remember you as you are… it doesn't really matter if I get grey hair, or if I am finding harder to shoot weight. You still retain the memory of what makes you, you… I always had very, very long hair, my character has very long hair here.*" (see Figure 3). She concludes by saying that this character is: "*All I ever wanted to be*".

When using this avatar in the game, Hannah prefers to use a bow and arrow, which helps compensate her slow manipulation of weapons. In relation to this, she says: "*because of my hand injury.. I am better at shooting or operating instruments from a distance because I don't have to move my hand so much.*" (see Figure 3). By using these types of weapons, her character can still participate in the battle while maintaining a distance and not being up front in the middle of the fight, which she considers, requires to be very proactive. The customization of the weapons of her avatar compensates her lost speed abilities allowing her to maintain her accuracy while playing the game.

Figure 3. Hanna's portrait (left) and favorite avatar in *Guild Wars* (right): a younger version of herself shooting a bow and arrow to compensate for her lost speed skills.

Jacob (male, 68) had created 33 avatars in *World of Warcraft*. When commenting on the younger look of his characters, he says: "*There's something really nice, when you're old, to create a 20-ish character… it's like you're reliving your life, through your avatars.*" It seems that Jacob may feel that he is actually embodying younger bodies when experimenting in the online world.

All the previous findings suggest that older adults are using self-representation to depict elements that had been lost throughout the lifetime. In the next section, we will detail findings that also suggest that self-representations are use to portray the current older self.

Embracing the Current Older Self

Danny created his latest character (of six he has created) explaining that he plays it with a comedian personality (see Figure 4). He described this avatar with reference to his current role as a grandparent: "*...is one of [granddaughter's] favorite's characters because he[avatar] interacts with [granddaughter's] characters and they will dance together and you know laugh, imitate each other and do all kinds of things.*" The avatar is therefore a way to attract his granddaughter's attention who nowadays is also playing online as part of Danny's guild.

There may be another way in which Danny's current older self had influenced the decisions in relation to the development of his latest avatar. Danny has been playing as part of a family guild participating in battles and missions as a team. During the gaming session that we observed, one of Danny's family members made a comment about his avatar: "*he [Danny's avatar] is slow, so when you are in a group, everyone is waiting for you*". In relation to this avatar, Danny commented: "*he [avatar] is going to make a career decision which is going to take him out of the action entirely, ... he is going to retire of combat and follow a different career or path which you can in Guild Wars, you can become for example completely devoted to making things which is was he plans to do...*" These two comments suggest that Danny is feeling the pressure of the other players of the family to move faster and is thinking about developing his character toward roles that do not demand a fast pace. This may be a way in which Danny plans to counteract his slower interactions in the game and still play as part of the family guild.

Associating with Older Adults Groups

Craig and Hannah play MMOGs as members of 'The Older Gamers' (TOG), an online international community of mature gamers. As its Code of Conduct states, TOG rejects "...the abusive, disruptive and disrespectful behavior displayed by many but often attributed to younger players that are so often encountered when gaming online" [21]. In fact, this group requires that participants apply to a membership with a public thoughtful motivation that has to be approved. After joining the TOG the nicknames that the players use in their games include the acronym TOG displaying the membership to the community. When comparing his community with younger players, Craig mentions that TOGs "*...don't play any mysterious stuff in the games. It is all fair and above board and if they are good it is because they are good*". He contrasts his comment in relation to younger players who often use technology tricks (hacks) to win the game. Craig finally comments that he has been interviewed on many occasions by the media as he is one of the oldest players of the community. He proudly shares with us the publications that mention his gaming activity as a TOG member.

Figure 4. Danny customizing his latest avatar in *Guild Wars*: a comedy character, which is his gran daughter's favorite.

Hannah also plays in this community and says that TOGs are an empathetic group of gamers who provide support to each other adding: "*Because people are older, have families or had families, they much, can understand...*" The TOG association is linked to a set of morals of mature players that these two participants value and are proud to represent.

In contrast, Jacob has not found a gaming group that depicts values of mature players. Jacob has been rejected from many guilds because of his slower pace making him feel disowned: "*Now, I'm 68. I'm a disabled person, disabled not that I've got anything wrong with me, but I cannot keep up with the pace expected on the computer games. So there's a rejection and you're going to find, if you're dealing with elderly people that this is common everywhere.*" As a way to embrace this challenge he proposes the creation of guilds with names that are inclusive to older people: "*the guilds are the answer for elderly. I would like to see Aged Care groups...*" Interestingly, Jacob did not explore ways to improve his speed but proposed ways to embrace his slower speed through a group nickname self-representation.

DISCUSSION

The interviews and game observations that we conducted revealed that player self-representations both mediate the player experience and provide opportunities for older adults to express aspects of their past and present identities. Although this study examined a broad range of games, we found that player self-representations played an important role in both casual and MMOGs. While self-representations in casual games were mostly static and consisted of simple names or images, participants still chose these carefully to represent meaningful aspects of the self. Meanwhile, self-representations as avatars in MMOGs were customizable and provided opportunities for participants to explore how they wanted to project themselves in their gaming environments.

Our analysis of participants' self-representations revealed two trends that seem particularly poignant in light of the changes people experience as they age: 1) self-representations were used to illustrate elements of participants' previous lives that they felt they had lost as they had grown older and 2) self-representations were used to define and embrace the present older self. While the first involves a more nostalgic reflection on one's lifetime, the second is linked to an acceptance of participants' current identities as older members of their families and communities. Both these trends align with theories from psychologists and social gerontologists about the ageing process [16, 17, 22, 26], and research within the HCI literature on how older people construct online identities [e.g., 7, 9]. These findings also point to a need for designers to create more inclusive customization options in online games, as discussed below.

Nostalgic Reflection of Loss

According to Erikson's (1963) psychological stages, adults tend to evaluate their life stories when they retire and reduce their productivity [16, 17]. This may explain why older adults in our study use elements of the past as important parts of their self-representations. Participants' self-representations encompassed reminiscence about place, past activities and roles, and youthful appearance.

For example the portrayal of a farm or a country flag among people who no longer live in these places may be a way to remember life stories linked to that location. The affinity people express about place translates into the perception that in those places they are "known and know others" [37:303]. This may be what Elly is achieving with the use of the flag, as she has been able to reconnect with friendships and family that she knew in her childhood. Another reason for projecting places from the past may be that familiar places provide an ongoing sense of belonging [40]. The notion of place as a site of sociality and belonging has been explored by human-computer interaction researchers seeking to design tools that encourage older people to engage in local social activities [31]. Our analysis of older adults' self-representations in online games suggests that place is not only a site of local community interactions, but is also associated with older adults' life histories. Place can therefore be used as a tool for reminiscence and to represent aspects of one's younger self – for example, the place where someone grew up, or the house in which they raised a family.

People's former roles in life can also be a central focus of nostalgic reflections and reminiscence as people age. Many older adults, for instance, still consider their professional roles to be a key aspect of their identity (that is, who they are), even long after retirement [46]. Research has shown that people create an identity in relation to the work they do and that these identities persist after retirement: they will be forever 'ex' doctors, ex-teachers and so on. This aligns with our observations, our participants designed self-representations that portrayed elements of their previous career roles even though they did not practice them anymore. For example, Hannah (a former nurse) represented herself as a healer and Jacob (a former engineer) as an engineer. These self-representations provided an opportunity to reminisce about, and identify with, a role they enjoyed earlier in their lives.

Previous roles include not only past careers, but also roles within the family. One of our gamers (Danny) represented himself as a character who provides protection for the other characters. This bears similarity to Danny's role as a father, although now that his children are grown, Danny no longer plays such a protective role in real life. In this way, the gaming environment provides an opportunity to play a role he used to have earlier in his life. Meanwhile, Craig chose to play as a shooter, an activity that he enjoyed when he was younger. It may be that the elements that participants bring into their digital self-representations are linked to the level of satisfaction with those aspects of their identities in the past [46].

The participants who used avatars to represent themselves usually preferred characters that were younger than their current selves. This finding aligns with previous studies where older adults created avatars with idealized younger bodies [9]. Previous studies have shown that avatar depictions can change an individual's body perception [14]. That is, if someone represents themselves as a younger person, they may start to perceive themselves as younger. While we do not have data to support this assertion, it is interesting to note that none of our participants customized self-representations that depicted ageing features. It may be that the customization options in the games played did not provide enough features to create an older depiction of the self [9]. However, Hannah did mention that even though she can grey the color of the hair of the avatar, she preferred to portray a younger self. The portrayal of a younger avatar may have different meanings. First, it may be a response to social norms such as Western ideals of beauty that value youth in physical appearance. Second, these avatars may also depict the acquisition of physical condition which could be a way of eliminating constraints for some ageing bodies. Finally, younger avatars may provide some level of anonymity in the online game.

Self-representations in online games can be a way for older adults to share aspects of former identities with people in the present. In this way these important aspects of their identities are no longer hidden but available for family, friends and strangers. Moreover, the recreation of self-representations with aspects of the past may provide a sense of continuity on what can be passed to the future [40].

Designers of virtual worlds should consider how to support the inclusion of nostalgic elements in online self-representations to expand the possibilities of self-expression. This is important as greater identification with the online self-representation could foster more immersion, autonomy or enjoyment in the virtual environment [3]. While previous research has suggested that younger populations enhance their self-representations with idealistic features [2, 14, 37, 47], our research suggest that older adults (65+) include more nostalgic elements. Further research should be done to gain a more comprehensive understanding of these design patterns across age groups.

The Present Older Self in Self-representations

In some cases, our participants' self-representations incorporated their current life roles and their experiences as older adults. In Danny's case, for example, these roles influenced his avatar design choices. His latest avatar depicts personality features that provide a playful way to engage with his granddaughter.

The references to older gamer communities in player's nicknames were considered important by two of our participants. Even though this may be connected to their sense of belonging to a community, it may also be a demonstration of their pride in being recognized as gamers. Further, strong identification with the older gamers' community may be a way to challenge the stereotypical perception of online gamers as being young and male. Age in this group may be valued and perceived as something that provides wisdom. These findings suggest that our participants want to project some aspects of their ageing self and that these features do not always need to depict visually aspects of an ageing body but values such as wisdom.

The reflections on players' pace of gameplay influenced the customization of self-representations in different ways. Hannah and Craig had appropriated tools and roles that supported their participation in battles through features other than a faster pace. Danny was looking for ways to develop his character into roles that do not require a fast pace, while Jacob considered that groups that represent older adults should be created in order to support his participation in the game at a slower pace. These examples suggest that designers of virtual worlds should create alternatives ways to respond to the speed requirements of online games by creating roles and tools that respond to other skills.

Customizing Older Adults' Self-Representations

When players start building their avatar, they are often offered many visual options to customize their character, for example, a menu of diverse hairstyles or eye colors. In this creation process, users do not always have a clear model in mind of what they are creating and the options of the interface guide the design of their avatars. As McArthur and others point out, an avatar is "the result of a dialogue between user and interface" [33]. This can be challenging if the options of the interface do not offer a diverse set of features that represent all the ranges of human bodies such as ageing features.

The study of customization of ageing features through character creation interfaces had not received much study. This is particularly urgent because the requirements of older adults and their self-representations may be depicted according negative stereotypes of elderly already found in Human Computer Interaction [15, 49]. These stereotypical views may influence self-representations projecting older adults as disengaged and lonely [49]. Moreover, recent initiatives such as 'Healthy Ageing', are based in strengthening individual choices as a way to recognize diversity and avoid stigmas related to later age [51]. We should consider the consequences that character creation interfaces can have among older adults, because through their affordances they co-construct the online identity of the user [33].

The findings of this paper have some implicit implications of design. First, game designers should explore designing characters that encompass elements of diverse life histories. This diversity may be favorable not only for older adults but for other populations who are experiencing changes in their lives. Second, designers should explore the representations of older age by including alternatives to depict features of an ageing body through visual options in character creation interfaces. In addition, the representation of older age should include a wider set of attributes not only linked to the physical characteristics of ageing bodies but to personality values typical of those in later life such as wisdom. Third, online self-representation systems should support a wider range of features and roles to embrace the diversity among human beings and also depict inclusive social values as these will provide alternatives that may be more suitable when choosing a self-representation. Finally, future research should involve older adults' voices in the design of systems of online self-representation such as character creator interfaces.

CONCLUSION

In this paper we analyzed how older adults (+65) are using self-player representations in online games with other people. Our participants illustrated great disparities in the games and types of self-representations they use. However through the use of the diverse elements of their self-representation they portrayed two main inclinations: 1) aspects of their past that have been lost as they have grown older, and 2) embracing their present older self. While the first suggests a reflection of the lifetime in a nostalgic way, the second suggests that older adults may be accepting the present older self, and the roles they play in their families and communities. Considering the impact that online self-representations can have on older adults' perceptions of the self, we suggest that designers of online games should embrace this diversity in the design of systems to include characters of older age.

ACKNOWLEDGMENTS

This research is supported by the Australian Research Council and the Microsoft Research Centre for SocialNUI.

REFERENCES

1. Monica Anderson and Andrew Perrin. 2017. Tech adoption climbs among older adults. *Pew Research Center*, May: 1–22. Retrieved from http://www.pewinternet.org/2017/05/17/technology-use-among-seniors/

2. Haya Bechar-Israeli. 1995. FROM 〈Bonehead〉 TO 〈cLoNehEAd〉 : Nicknames. Play, and Identity on Internet Relay Chat. *Journal of Computer-Mediated Communication* 1, 2: 1–30. https://doi.org/10.1111/j.1083-6101.1995.tb00325.x

3. Katherine Bessière, A. Fleming Seay, and Sara Kiesler. 2007. The Ideal Elf: Identity Exploration in World of Warcraft. *CyberPsychology & Behavior* 10, 4: 530–535. https://doi.org/10.1089/cpb.2007.9994

4. Max V. Birk, Cheralyn Atkins, Jason T. Bowey, and Regan L. Mandryk. Fostering Intrinsic Motivation through Avatar Identification in Digital Games. In *Proc. - CHI 2016*, ACM Press (2016), 2982–2995.

5. Jeffrey Brand, Stewart Todhunter, and Jan Jervis. 2017. *Digital Australia 2018*. Eveleigh, NSW.

6. Virginia Braun and Victoria Clarke. 2012. Thematic analysis. *APA handbook of research methods in psychology, Vol 2: Research designs: Quantitative, qualitative, neuropsychological, and biological.* 2: 57–71. https://doi.org/10.1037/13620-004

7. Robin Brewer and Anne Marie Piper. 2016. "Tell It Like It Really Is": A Case of Online Content Creation and Sharing Among Older Adult Bloggers. *American Journal of Orthodontics and Dentofacial Orthopedics* 150, 4: 563. https://doi.org/10.1016/j.ajodo.2016.08.001

8. Oliver Kisalay Burmeister. 2012. What Seniors Value About Online Community. *The Journal of Community Informatics* 8, 1: 1–12.

9. Romina Carrasco, Steven Baker, Jenny Waycott, and Frank Vetere. Negotiating stereotypes of older adults through avatars. In *Proc. OZCHI 2017, ACM Press (2017),* 218–227.

10. Neil Charness and Walter R. Boot. 2015. Technology, Gaming, and Social Networking. In *Handbook of the Psychology of Aging* (Eighth Edi). K.W. Schaie and S.L. Willis (eds.). Elsevier Inc., Tallahassee, 389–407. https://doi.org/10.1016/B978-0-12-411469-2.00020-0

11. Wei Lun Cheong, Younbo Jung, and Yin-Leng Theng. Avatar: A Virtual Face for the Elderly. In *Proc. VRCAI 2011, ACM Press (2011),* 491–498.

12. Commissioner for Senior Victorians. 2016. *Ageing is everyone's business: a report on isolation and loneliness among senior Victorians*. Melbourne Commissioner for Senior Victorians.

13. Nicole Crenshaw and Bonnie Nardi. What's in a name? In *Proc. CHI PLAY 2014,* ACM Press (2014), 67–76.

14. Nicolas Ducheneaut, Ming-Hui "Don" Wen, Nicholas Yee, and Greg Wadley. Body and Mind: A Study of Avatar Personalization in Three Virtual Worlds. In *Proc. CHI 2009,* ACM Press (2009), 1151-1160.

15. Jeannette Durick, Toni Robertson, Margot Brereton, Frank Vetere, and Bjorn Nansen. Dispelling ageing myths in technology design. In *Proc. OzCHI 2013,* ACM Press (2013), 467–476.

16. Erik H Erikson. 1964. *Childhood and society.* New York, Norton.

17. Erik H Erikson, Joan M Erikson, and Helen Q Kivnick. 1986. *Vital involvement in old age.* New York : Norton.

18. Mike Featherstone. 2003. Post-Bodies, Aging and Virtual Reality. In *Images of Aging: Cultural Representations of Later Life*. Routledge, 231–248.

19. Katrina Fong and Raymond A. Mar. 2014. What Does My Avatar Say About Me? Inferring Personality From Avatars. *Personality and Social Psychology Bulletin* 41, 2: 1–13. https://doi.org/10.1177/0146167214562761

20. Janine Fron, Tracy Fullerton, Jacquelyn Morie, Ford, and Celia Pearce. The Hegemony of Play. *Situated Play, In Proc.DIGRA 2007,* 1–10.

21. The Older Gamers. About The Older Gamers (TOG); Code of Conduct. Retrieved March 28, 2018 from https://www.theoldergamers.com/threads/about-the-older-gamers-tog-code-of-conduct.644520/

22. Christopher Gilleard and Paul Higgs. 2000. *Cultures of Ageing Self, Citizen and the body*. Pearson Education.

23. Samuel D. Gosling, Sam Gaddis, and Simine Vazire. Personality impressions based on Facebook profiles. *ICWSM 2017,* 1–4.

24. Jérôme Guegan, Stéphanie Buisine, Fabrice Mantelet, Nicolas Maranzana, and Frédéric Segonds. 2016. Avatar-mediated creativity: When embodying inventors makes engineers more creative. *Computers in Human Behavior* 61: 165–175. https://doi.org/10.1016/j.chb.2016.03.024

25. Dave Harley and Geraldine Fitzpatrick. 2009. YouTube and intergenerational communication: The case of Geriatric1927. *Universal Access in the Information Society* 8, 1: 5–20. https://doi.org/10.1007/s10209-008-0127-y

26. Nancy R. Hooyman and H. Asuman Kiyak. 2008. *Social Gerontology: A Multidisciplinary Perspective*. Pearson Education.

27. Yasmin B Kafai, Melissa S Cook, and Deborah A Fields. 2010. "Blacks deserve bodies too!": Design and discussion about diversity and race in a tween virtual world. *Games and Culture* 5, 1: 43–63. https://doi.org/10.1177/1555412009351261

28. David Kaufman, Louise Sauvé, Lise Renaud, Andrew Sixsmith, and Ben Mortenson. 2016. Older Adults Digital Gameplay: Patterns, Benefits, and Challenges. *Simulation & Gaming* 47: 1–25. https://doi.org/10.1177/1046878116645736

29. Amanda Lazar, Hilaire J. Thompson, Anne Marie Piper, and George Demiris. Rethinking the Design of Robotic Pets for Older Adults. In *Proc. DIS 2016, ACM Press (2016), 1*034–1046.

30. Christine Liao. 2013. Art Medium Too: Avatar, Art, and Assemblages. *Journal Of Virtual Worlds Research* 6, 2: 1–13.

31. Ann Light, Kate Howland, Tom Hamilton, and David A. Harley. The Meaning of Place in Supporting Sociality. In *Proc. DIS 2017,* ACM Press (2017), 1141–1152.

32. Victoria McArthur and Jennifer Jenson. E is for Everyone? Best Practices for the Socially Inclusive Design of Avatar Creation Interfaces. In *Proc. IE 2014,* ACM Press (2014), 1–8.

33. Victoria Mcarthur, Robert J Teather, and Jennifer Jenson. The Avatar Affordances Framework: Mapping Affordances and Design Trends in Character Creation Interfaces. *In Proc. CHI PLAY 2015,* ACM Press (2015), 231–240.

34. Jerome P McDonough. 1999. Designer selves: Construction of technologically mediated identity within graphical, multiuser virtual environments. *Journal of the American Society for Information Science* 50, 10: 855–869. https://doi.org/https://doi.org/10.1002/(SICI)1097-4571(1999)50:10<855::AID-ASI3>3.0.CO;2-6

35. Katelyn Y. A. McKenna and John A. Bargh. 2000. Plan 9 From Cyberspace: The Implications of the Internet for Personality and Social Psychology. *Personality and Social Psychology Review* 4, 1: 57–75. https://doi.org/10.1207/S15327957PSPR0401_6

36. W. Laurence Neuman. 2014. *Social Research Methods: Qualitative and Quantitative Approaches*. Pearson New International Edition. https://doi.org/10.2307/3211488

37. Carman Neustaedter and Elena Fedorovskaya. Presenting identity in a virtual world through avatar appearances. In *Proc. Graphics Interface 2009,* 183–190.

38. Celia Pearce. 2008. The Truth About Baby Boomers Gamers: A Study of Over-Forty Computer Game Players. *Games and Culture* 3, 2: 142–174. https://doi.org/10.1177/1555412008314132

39. Mark Rice, Ranieri Koh, Quintessence Lui, Qixiang He, Marcus Wan, Vanessa Yeo, Jamie Ng, and Wah Pheow Tan. 2013. Comparing avatar game representation preferences across three age groups. *Ext. Abstracts CHI 2013, ACM Press (2013),* 1161–1166.

40. Graham D. Rowles. 1983. Place and personal identity in old age: Observations from Appalachia. *Journal of Environmental Psychology* 3, 4: 299–313. https://doi.org/10.1016/S0272-4944(83)80033-4

41. Joshua P. Salmon, Sarah M. Dolan, Richard S. Drake, Graham C. Wilson, Raymond M. Klein, and Gail A. Eskes. 2017. A survey of video game preferences in adults: Building better games for older adults. *Entertainment Computing* 21: 45–64. https://doi.org/10.1016/j.entcom.2017.04.006

42. Bob De Schutter and Steven Malliet. 2014. The older player of digital games: A classification based on perceived need satisfaction. *Communications* 39, 1: 67–88. https://doi.org/10.1515/commun-2014-0005

43. Panote Siriaraya, Chee Siang Ang, and Ania Bobrowicz. 2014. Exploring the potential of virtual worlds in engaging older people and supporting healthy aging. *Behaviour & Information Technology* 33, 3: 282–293. https://doi.org/10.1080/0144929X.2012.691552

44. T. L. Taylor. 2003. Intentional bodies: Virtual environments and the designers who shape them. *International Journal of Engineering Education* 19, 1: 25–34.

45. T L Taylor. 2002. Living Digitally : Embodiment in Virtual Worlds. In *The Social Life of Avatars Presence and Interaction in Shared Virtual Environments*. 40–62. https://doi.org/10.1088/0957-4484/16/9/062

46. Ursina Teuscher. 2010. Change and persistence of personal identities after the transition to retirement. *International Jeeournal of aging & human development* 70, 1: 89–106. https://doi.org/10.2190/AG.70.1.d

47. Sherry Turkle. 1994. Constructions and reconstructions of self in virtual reality: Playing in the MUDs. *Mind, Culture, and Activity* 1, 3: 158–167. https://doi.org/10.1080/10749039409524667

48. Sherry Turkle. 1995. *Life on the Screen. Identify in the Age of the Internet*. London : Weidenfeld & Nicholson, 1996,c1995.

49. John Vines, Gary Pritchard, Peter Wright, and Patrick Olivier. 2015. An Age-Old Problem : Examining the Discourses of Ageing in HCI and Strategies for Future Research. *Tochi* 22, 1: 1–27. https://doi.org/10.1145/2696867

50. Mineko Wada, Laura Hurd Clarke, and W. Ben Mortenson. 2017. "I am busy independent woman who has sense of humor, caring about others": older adults' self-representations in online dating profiles. *Ageing and Society*: 1–26. https://doi.org/10.1017/S0144686X17001325

51. World Health Organization. 2015. *World report on Ageing And Health*. Luxembourg. https://doi.org/10.1007/s13398-014-0173-7.2

52. Nick Yee. 2014. *Proteus paradox : how online games and virtual worlds change us, and how they don't*. Yale University Press.

Investigating Gamification for Seniors Aged 75+

Maximilian Altmeyer
DFKI GmbH
Saarland Informatics Campus
maximilian.altmeyer@dfki.de

Pascal Lessel
DFKI GmbH
Saarland Informatics Campus
pascal.lessel@dfki.de

Antonio Krüger
DFKI GmbH
Saarland Informatics Campus
krueger@dfki.de

ABSTRACT
Gamification, the use of game elements in non-game contexts, has been successfully used to motivate people to reach their goals more efficiently or turn unpleasant tasks into fun ones. However, most gamified systems are conceptualized for a younger audience and do not account for age-specific changes in the motivation to play or the perception of game elements. To inform the design of gamified applications targeting elderly people (aged 75+), we investigated their gaming experiences, what affects them positively while playing and their attitudes towards the most commonly used game elements. We report findings from semi-structured interviews and a storyboard-based game element assessment (N=18, mean age=84.61), indicating that the main motivation to play is socializing, that participants avoid competition and prefer collaboration and care-taking as well as that badges and points are considered meaningless and provide a level of visibility that puts participants under pressure.

ACM Classification Keywords
H.5.m. Information Interfaces and Presentation (e.g. HCI): Miscellaneous

Author Keywords
Older adults; game elements; interviews

INTRODUCTION
Gamification, the use of game elements in non-game contexts [7], has been frequently used as a motivator, e.g. to help people to reach their goals [28], to make unpleasant tasks fun [1] or to engage users in sustainability projects [19]. However, most of those systems do not account for age-related changes [17] and are designed for a young audience [28], even though there might be a huge potential in designing gamified systems supporting seniors: besides the fact that playing digital games was shown to be associated with successful aging [21], gamified systems may help seniors to remain physically, cognitively and socially active [9], which has positive effects on health and well-being [18]. This is further enhanced by the demographic transition leading to a drastic increase

DIS 2018, June 9–13, 2018, Hong Kong.

ACM ISBN 978-1-4503-5198-0/18/06 ...$15.00.
http://dx.doi.org/10.1145/3196709.3196799

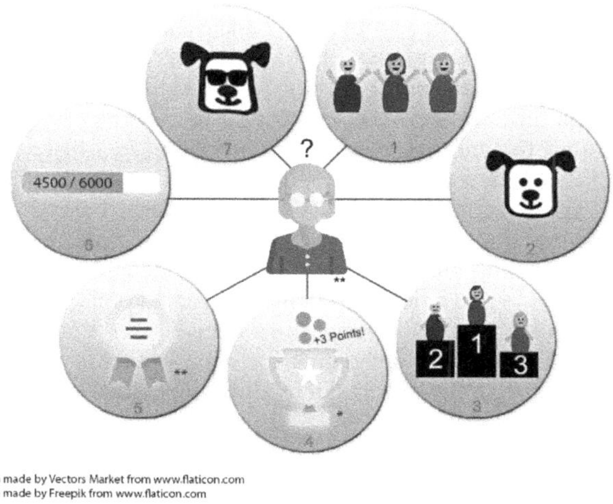

Figure 1. Stylized, frequently used, game elements in gamified systems (collaboration, virtual characters, leaderboards, points, badges, progress bars, customization (from 1-7))

of the group of seniors in the near future [8], implying that a rapidly growing number of people can benefit from research in this domain.

Elderly people are most often not used to game mechanics applied in digital games and might have different assumptions [10], which makes it essential to account for their experience with games, their sources of fun as well as any physical or mental limitations in order to conceptualize a successful and suitable gamified intervention. Moreover, goals and priorities differ between younger and older people [13] which might have an impact on what motivates or affects seniors and what is considered to be fun while playing. Past research explored the motivations of older adults to play [2, 6, 27], the design space of exergames targeting seniors [3, 10], issues related to the accessibility of games [10, 15] and exercise motivations of older adults to inform the design of technologies supporting physical activity [16, 26] revealing that older adults have specific needs regarding all these aspects. However, there is a lack of research targeting motivations of seniors (aged 75+) to play games, their perception of single game elements and the role of social factors for them while playing games.

In this paper, we contribute to the aforementioned points by investigating game experiences of seniors, what motivates and affects them positively when playing, social aspects and how certain game elements are perceived in order to inform the design of gamified interventions for seniors.

RELATED WORK

The perception of digital games for older adults as well as their motivations to play have been researched in different domains. We summarize core findings from related work and discuss their implications for and differences to our work.

Older Adults' Motivations to Play

De Schutter et al. [6] conclude that a playful activity is considered meaningful if it fosters connectedness, cultivation and contribution. Interestingly, playing multiplayer games was rare among the participants, even though connectedness was one core factor for meaning. Similarly, Nap et al. [23] found that staying in touch with society and escapism are strong motivations to play. In line with [6], there was a strong indication that participants prefer solitary over multiplayer play, even though they appreciate socialization in general. As potential reasons, the authors mention the increased fear of failure seniors have and the unwillingness to be dependent on other players and their availability. Furthermore, Birk et al. [2] showed that motivations to play change with increasing age from focusing on performance towards focusing on completion, choice, and enjoyment (which is, for example, manifested by preferring casual over performance-related games). This is explainable by older adults focusing on goals supporting emotional stability and social relationships rather than striving to learn new skills.

Encouraging Older Adults Through Technology

Kappen et al. [16] emphasize the need to consider the life stage of older adults without exploiting fears, to explore ways to provide meaningful and engaging feedback to the users as well as to support socialization around physical activity. The authors note that social sharing needs to be used carefully as some participants reported feelings of self-consciousness when confronted with persons who are more active than themselves. Results from Romero et al. [26] show the fear of elderly people for being stigmatized when using technologies that emphasize their need for help. However, using new ways of interaction may raise acceptance issues and lead to seniors rejecting the technology. Therefore, technologies should support familiarity and promote participation. Another important aspect to design playful systems encouraging physical and social activity is mutually using social (sharing of activities) and physical (monitoring one's own activities) motivators.

Implications and Differences

Older gamers play games to relax and have fun [23] and value choice, enjoyment [2] and meaningful play, i.e. they appreciate social interaction, teaching or learning and contributing to society [6]. We elaborate further on this (**RQ1**) and aim to elicit game elements to satisfy the need for purpose and meaning as this link is currently missing. Interestingly, even though social interaction was shown to be a core motivation to play in most of the presented papers [6, 16, 23, 26], older gamers strongly indicated a dislike of multiplayer games [6, 23]. To get more insights about this, we investigate fears and motivations related to social game elements (**RQ2**). Related to this, we want to explore the perception of most commonly used game elements [28] (**RQ3**). Worthwile to mention is also that the age at which participants were considered to be "elderly" is reasonably lower than in our sample: 45 years in [6], 50 years in [16], 55 years in [2] and 65 years in [23, 26]. For the other presented papers the minimum age was either not reported or there was no user study conducted.

STUDY

We investigate the following research questions ("RQ"), which are based on the findings from related work:

RQ1: *Reasons for playing games:* What are underlying factors that motivate seniors to play games?

RQ2: *Social play:* What social game elements are suitable for seniors? What do they fear or appreciate in competitive/cooperative settings?

RQ3: *Perception of game elements:* How are frequently used game elements perceived by seniors?

Procedure and Method

We recruited participants from nursing homes and participants living on their own. To ensure that they do not suffer from mental diseases, we consulted the nursing management. The study started with a short questionnaire covering demographical data. A semi-structured interview followed to learn more about their gaming experience and their motivation for playing games. The semi-structured interviews were directly transcribed and were conducted in face-to-face conversations with the participants in separate rooms (in the nursing homes) or in participants' apartments (for those living on their own). We followed a directed content analysis approach [14], i.e. we went through the transcripts to find themes related to each of the RQs (e.g. themes for **RQ1** included "socializing", "watch others play", and "cognitive benefits"). We then counted for each theme how many participants mentioned it and exemplary reported statements of participants related to the theme [5]. All questions can be found in the supplementary materials.

Afterwards, we adapted the procedure of Orji et al. [24]: participants were shown seven storyboards, each explaining one game element in the scenario *"Motivate yourself to go for a walk"*. We decided to use a concrete scenario since context is crucial for a proper imagination of game concepts among older adults [26]. The scenario was chosen based on a literature review of persuasive systems [12] showing that a huge majority are conceptualized in the exercise domain. For the scenario to be relevant, we ensured that all participants were able to walk on their own. We also limited the amount of storyboards so as not to overwhelm them (cf. [29]) and chose the game elements points, badges, virtual characters, unlockables, competition, collaboration and progress bars, as they are frequently used [28]. For every storyboard, we asked questions like *"What is awarded to the person on the storyboard?"*, *"What does the person on the storyboard need to do to get the reward?"* to make sure that the participants understood the underlying game elements. We then assessed for each game element whether it is considered to be motivational using 5-point Likert scales. To improve older participants' abilities to respond adequately [29] and to get insights about reasons why participants like or dislike different elements, we discussed

Figure 2. The translated storyboard showing the concept of competition

their decisions in a semi-structured way. Exemplary, the storyboard for "competition" is shown in Figure 2. All other storyboards can be found in the supplementary materials. The study was approved by our Ethical Review Board[1].

Results and interpretation

18 German participants took part in the study (10 female, 8 male – 13 living in nursing homes and 5 living on their own) aged 84.61 years on average (Mdn=86, Min=75, Max=93). They reported not to be familiar with technology (M=1.5, SD=1.01, Mdn=1) but agreed to being interested in accumulating more experience with technology (M=3.83, SD=1.12, Mdn=4). In addition, participants reported playing parlor games multiple times a week (M=3.72, SD=0.80, Mdn=4) but never play video games (M=1.39, SD=0.83, Mdn=1).

RQ1: *Reasons for playing games*

All participants emphasized to value the time spent playing: *"After playing games I have the feeling of accomplishment, that time was not wasted"*[2] **(P3)**. Even those that do not play regularly stated that this is mostly because they do not have people to play with: *"When my children were younger we used to have a whole cupboard full of games and played really a lot. Today I don't have people to play with. [...] I would definitely like to play more games again"* **(P16)**.

The main reason to play (mentioned by all), is socializing with others (*"In first place we meet to communicate. Playing games supports this by inducing a good mood"* **(P14)**). They also reported seeing games as a starter for conversations (*"The Bingo evenings here helped me to get in touch with other seniors living here"* **(P2)**). We furthermore found evidence that elderly people have fun watching others play and use the occasion to get in touch with them (reported by 5): *"Sometimes I just sit there and watch others playing. It is fun to see their reactions and it offers me the opportunity to talk to them"* **(P9)**. Despite socializing, 12 participants stated to value the perceived cognitive benefits that arise from playing games (*"A nice side effect of playing games is that I keep mentally fit"* **(P10)**).

RQ2: *Social play*

Most participants (16) reported not to be driven by winning the game in first place but instead enjoy spending time with others: *"It is not about winning at all, it's about spending time together"* **(P3)**. While for 6 participants winning does not matter at all, 10 participants stated that they also like to win, but that is not most important: *"The main reason [to play] for me is to avoid being alone and enjoy time with others. However, winning a game is also nice sometimes"* **(P10)**. We also found that nearly all participants (17) prefer collaborating: *"We sometimes do teamwork when playing Skip-Bo. [...] Winning as a team makes me much happier than winning on my own"* **(P6)**. Since Skip-Bo is a competitive game, this statement underlines the strive for collaboration even more. In addition, the aspect of taking care of others was mentioned by almost all (17). They indicated to have a better experience when all players are satisfied: *"It is not too much about winning, it is more about ensuring everybody has a good time"* **(P9)**.

15 participants reported that they were more inclined to competition at younger ages: *"When I was young I was a swimmer and very ambitious [...]. Today I don't want to compete against others, those times are over"* **(P5)**. In addition, there is less pressure to win a game and a more relaxed atmosphere during play: *"I think what has changed is that we don't take things too seriously when playing"* **(P4)**. A majority (14) of participants stated that they value social contacts and communication with others much more than in their younger years: *"Once you are old and live alone you realize that having people around you is the most valuable thing you can have"* **(P18)**.

RQ3: *Perception of game elements*

Considering the storyboards representing different game elements, participants rated both collaboration, i.e. working as a team to reach a goal together, and caring for a virtual character (we showed them a virtual dog), i.e. reaching a goal to make a virtual character happy, to be most motivational (see Table 1). When discussing what participants like about collaboration, reasons were related to statements mentioned in the interview. In addition, most of the participants (10) reported that collaboration includes all players when winning a game, regardless of their abilities, which is especially important at older ages: *"When collaborating, those that are not as fit as others also participate in winning the game, which is important as age brings disabilities that you cannot control. Being confronted with others reaching scores you will never be able to reach because of your disabilities is very demotivating"* **(P5)**. 12 participants reported that the virtual character provides a meaningful incentive for them, since they felt responsible for it: *"I would definitely do my best to make it [the dog] feel good"* **(P1)**. **P15** has some reservations and remarks that the character should not try to imitate a real pet too much, but should *"look like in a cartoon for example"* to be more authentic.

Customizing the virtual character, i.e. collecting/unlocking gifts for it, was considered to be slightly motivational. 8 participants liked this idea as they perceived it as a way to care for it, but on the other side four of them reported that the motivational impact strongly depends on the gift itself (*"Of course I would like to collect gifts or things for it, but I really need to have the feeling that the gift makes it happy and that the gift is suitable for it"* **(P16)**) and that they like to be able to decide what kind of gift is given to their virtual character (*"I want to be able to decide what gift is given to my pet [...] just like in real life I don't want to give generic presents, they need to be personal"* **(P6)**). Seeing the current progress towards a goal was considered neutral regarding its motivational effect.

[1] https://erb.cs.uni-saarland.de/, last accessed March 21, 2018
[2] All statements were translated from German to English

Game element	M	STD	Mdn
Collaboration	4.22	0.71	4
Virtual Characters	4.17	1.01	4
Unlockables/ Customization	3.39	0.89	3.5
Progress Bars	3.39	0.68	3
Badges	1.67	0.82	1.5
Points	1.56	0.83	1
Competition	1.44	0.60	1

Table 1. Perceived motivational effect of game elements, rated using 5-point Likert scales.

Asked for reasons, participants most of the time appreciated seeing their current progress towards a goal, but also reported that they are afraid not to be able to reach the goal, which would make them feel discouraged or sad.

Interestingly, points, badges and leaderboards were negatively perceived (see Table 1). Participants (14) stated that they do not see the benefit of earning points or emphasized that they miss the feeling of reaching something that is meaningful: *"I don't have the feeling of having reached something that has value. I don't see the benefit of collecting points"* **(P7)**. Concerning badges, they had similar concerns, with 8 participants that additionally disliked the visibility badges provide: *"I don't want to show these badges to anyone, I don't like putting myself in the foreground"* **(P3)**, *"Having those badges would put me under pressure. I would have the feeling that others expect me to perform even better"* **(P12)**.

The competitive aspect of leaderboards was criticized by all of our participants, stating that they prefer playing for fun and leisure and do not want to make other players feel sad. Digging deeper into that, we also found that a reason to avoid competition comes from a fear of failure: *"I am afraid that people will think I am not fit anymore"* **(P16)**. **P15** adds that reasons or explanations for failures changed compared to when he was younger: *"When I lost a competition at a younger age, there were various reasons [...] you just had a bad day or something. When I fail today, people often attribute this to my age which is quite frustrating."* Participants additionally often stated being tired of competition: *"I don't want to compete against others, I had enough competition in my life"* **(P1)**.

Discussion and Limitations

We found that besides leisure and fun, socializing is a core motivator for participants to play games. This may come from the demand to socialize that was found to be higher among seniors [4]. We also found that collaboration and care-taking are motivating factors to reach certain goals, which may be explainable through research done by Cornwell et al. [4] showing that age is positively related with socializing and volunteering. Another explanation for this might be related to the fact that a huge majority of participants were recruited from nursing homes, as this might affect participants' attitude towards collaboration and social aspects during play.

Points, badges and leaderboards, which are widely used in gamified interventions [28], are negatively perceived by the participants. Concerning points, the main reason for the low motivational influence on elderly people was found to be the lack of value, which is explainable by findings from [30] and [22], showing that elderly people are more inclined to value meaningfulness. Besides that, badges were often reported to harm motivation as they provide a certain level of visibility, i.e. participants complained that badges put them in focus. A potential explanation for this might be lower self-esteem among elderly people: Robins et al. [25] investigated self-esteem during the life span and found that self-esteem sharply decreases in old age. Keeping in mind that elderly people like collaborating and care-taking, the low motivational effect of leaderboards is not very surprising. Reasons include the fear of failing, the fear of making other players feel sad and of compromising harmony or starting arguments.

Findings related to the game elements have two limitations: First, they were not based on interventions in which these game elements were applied but on subjective assessments of the participants. Second, we used only one specific context and did not investigate the game elements in other contexts as well. Addressing the first limitation, we decided to use storyboards over a software prototype due to similar reasons as mentioned in [24]: To avoid inducing confounding variables (visual attractiveness of the prototype, usability issues, issues related to the lack of experience with technology, concrete implementation details) as well as to provide a common visual language that is easier to understand and does not involve game- or technology-specific knowledge. Concerning the second limitation, we decided to use only one scenario so as not to overwhelm participants (which was shown to be especially important for seniors [29]) and because research exists indicating that the perception of single game elements does not significantly change between different scenarios [20]. Participants' little to no experience with digital games is another limitation which may have an impact on the transferability of our findings to digital games. However, low experience with digital games is very common in this age group [11]. Moreover, the design of the storyboards themselves may have also had an effect on the perception of the game elements, which is why we attached them as supplementary material.

CONCLUSION

Although seniors could benefit from gamified systems [9], these mostly are designed for a young audience [28]. To inform the design of such systems, we investigated game experience, reasons to play, social aspects and how popular game elements are perceived. We considered a notably older sample than previous work (aged 75+) and found that participants are experienced in playing analog games and that their main motivation to play is socializing. Moreover, we add to the body of knowledge that they avoid competition and strive for collaboration and care-taking to ensure all players enjoy the game equally and because they are afraid to fail. Badges and points are considered meaningless and provide a level of visibility that puts participants under pressure. On the other side, virtual characters are perceived as meaningful, as participants felt responsible for them.

Future work should validate findings from this paper in other contexts as well. Morever, concrete implementations of game elements (that were outlined in this paper) should be evaluated.

REFERENCES

1. Luis Von Ahn, Ruoran Liu, and Manuel Blum. 2006. Peekaboom: A Game for Locating Objects in Images. *Proceedings of the SIGCHI Conference on Human Factors in Computing Systems* (2006), 55–64.
2. Max V. Birk, Maximilian A. Friehs, and Regan L. Mandryk. 2017. Age-Based Preferences and Player Experience: A Crowdsourced Cross-sectional Study. *Proceedings of the Annual Symposium on Computer-Human Interaction in Play - CHI PLAY '17* (2017), 157–170. DOI: http://dx.doi.org/10.1145/3116595.3116608
3. Philipp Brauner, Andre Valdez, Ulrik Schroeder, and Martina Ziefle. 2013. Increase Physical Fitness and Create Health Awareness through Exergames and Gamification – The Role of Individual Factors, Motivation and Acceptance. *Human Factors in Computing and Informatics* (2013), 349–362.
4. Benjamin Cornwell, Edward O Laumann, and L Philip Schumm. 2008. The Social Connectedness of Older Adults: A National Profile. *American Sociological Review* 73 (2008), 185–203.
5. J. R. Curtis, M. D. Wenrich, J. D. Carline, S. E. Shannon, D. M. Ambrozy, and P. G. Ramsey. 2001. Understanding physicians' skills at providing end-of-life care: Perspectives of patients, families, and health care workers. *Journal of General Internal Medicine* 16, 1 (2001), 41–49. DOI: http://dx.doi.org/10.1046/j.1525-1497.2001.00333.x
6. Bob De Schutter and Vero Vanden Abeele. 2010. Designing Meaningful Play Within the Psycho-Social Context of Older Adults. *Proceedings of the 3rd International Conference on Fun and Games - Fun and Games '10* September (2010), 84–93. DOI: http://dx.doi.org/10.1145/1823818.1823827
7. Sebastian Deterding and Dan Dixon. 2011. From Game Design Elements to Gamefulness: Defining Gamification. *Proceedings of the 15th International Academic MindTrek Conference. ACM, 2011.* (2011), 9–15. DOI: http://dx.doi.org/10.1145/2181037.2181040
8. Luciano Gamberini, Mariano Alcaniz, Giacinto Barresi, Malena Fabregat, Francisco Ibanez, and Lisa Prontu. 2006. Cognition , Technology and Games for the Elderly: An Introduction to the ELDERGAMES Project. *PsychNology Journal* 4, 3 (2006), 285–308.
9. Kathrin Maria Gerling and Maic Masuch. 2011. Exploring the Potential of Gamification Among Frail Elderly Persons. *Proceedings of the CHI 2011 Workshop Gamification: Using Game Design Elements in Non-Game Contexts* (2011), 1–4.
10. Kathrin Maria Gerling, Frank Paul Schulte, Jan Smeddinck, and Maic Masuch. 2011. Designing and Evaluating Digital Games for Frail Elderly Persons. *Proceedings of the 8th International Conference On Advances In Computer Entertainment Technology* (2011).
11. Kathrin Maria Gerling, Frank Paul Schulte, Jan Smeddinck, and Maic Masuch. 2012. Game Design for Older Adults : Effects of Age-Related Changes on Structural Elements of Digital Games. *International Conference on Entertainment Computing* (2012), 235–242.
12. Juho Hamari and Harri Sarsa. 2014. Does Gamification Work? - A Literature Review of Empirical Studies on Gamification. *Hawaii International Conference on System Sciences.* (2014), 3025–3034. DOI: http://dx.doi.org/10.1109/HICSS.2014.377
13. Jutta Heckhausen and Richard Schulz. 1995. A Life-Span Theory of Control. *Psychological Review* (1995), 284. DOI:http://dx.doi.org/10.1037/0033-295X.102.2.284
14. Hsiu-Fang Hsieh and Sarah Shannon. 2005. Three Approaches to Qualitative Content Analysis. *Qualitative Health Research* 1 (2005), 1277–1288. DOI: http://dx.doi.org/1049732305276687
15. Wijnand Ijsselsteijn, Henk Herman Nap, Yvonne Kort, and Karolien Poels. 2007. Digital Game Design for Elderly Users. *Proceedings of the 2007 conference on Future Play* (2007), 17–22.
16. Dennis L Kappen, Lennart E Nacke, Kathrin M Gerling, and Lia E Tsotsos. 2016. Design Strategies for Gamified Physical Activity Applications for Older Adults. *Hawaii International Conference on System Sciences* (2016), 1309–1318. DOI: http://dx.doi.org/10.1109/HICSS.2016.166
17. Jonna Koivisto and Juho Hamari. 2014. Demographic Differences in Perceived Benefits From Gamification. *Computers In Human Behavior* 35 (2014), 179–188. DOI: http://dx.doi.org/10.1016/j.chb.2014.03.007
18. Bruce W Lemon, Vern L Bengtson, and James A Peterson. 1972. An Exploration of the Activity Theory of Aging: Activity Types and Life Satisfaction among In-Movers to a Retirement Community. *Journal of Gerontology* 27, 4 (1972), 511–523.
19. Pascal Lessel, Maximilian Altmeyer, and Antonio Krüger. 2015. Analysis of Recycling Capabilities of Individuals and Crowds to Encourage and Educate People to Separate Their Garbage Playfully. *Proceedings of the SIGCHI Conference on Human Factors in Computing Systems. ACM, 2015.* (2015), 1095–1104. DOI: http://dx.doi.org/10.1145/2702123.2702309
20. Pascal Lessel, Maximilian Altmeyer, Marc Müller, Christian Wolff, and Antonio Krüger. 2016. Don't Whip Me With Your Games - Investigating Bottom-Up Gamification. *Proceedings of the SIGCHI Conference on Human Factors in Computing Systems. ACM, 2016.* (2016), 2026–2037. DOI: http://dx.doi.org/10.1145/2858036.2858463

21. Anne Collins Mclaughlin and Maribeth Gandy. 2013. Successful Aging Through Digital Games: Socioemotional Differences Between Older Adult Gamers and Non-Gamers. *Computers In Human Behavior* December 2016 (2013). DOI: http://dx.doi.org/10.1016/j.chb.2013.01.014
22. Anne-Sophie Melenhorst, Wendy Rogers, and Evan Caylor. 2001. The Use of Communication Technologies by Older Adults: Exploring The Benefits From The User's Perspective. *Proceedings of the Human Factors and Ergonomics Society Annual Meeting* (2001), 221–225.
23. H.H. Nap, Y.a.W. De Kort, and W.a. IJsselsteijn. 2009. Senior Gamers: Preferences, Motivations and Needs. *Gerontechnology* 8, 4 (2009), 247–262. DOI: http://dx.doi.org/10.4017/gt.2009.08.04.003.00
24. Rita Orji, Julita Vassileva, and Regan L Mandryk. 2014. Modeling the Efficacy of Persuasive Strategies for Different Gamer Types in Serious Games for Health. *User Modeling and User-Adapted Interaction* (2014), 453–498. DOI: http://dx.doi.org/10.1007/s11257-014-9149-8
25. Richard W Robins, Kali H Trzesniewski, Jessica L Tracy, Samuel D Gosling, and Jeff Potter. 2002. Global Self-Esteem Across the Life Span. *Psychology and Aging* 17, 3 (2002), 423–434. DOI: http://dx.doi.org/10.1037//0882-7974.17.3.423
26. Natalia Romero, Janienke Sturm, Tilde Bekker, Linda De Valk, and Sander Kruitwagen. 2010. Playful Persuasion to Support Older Adults' Social and Physical Activities. *Interacting with Computers* 22, 6 (2010), 485–495. DOI: http://dx.doi.org/10.1016/j.intcom.2010.08.006
27. Bob De Schutter. 2010. Never Too Old to Play: The Appeal of Digital Games to an Older Audience. *Games and Culture* (2010), 1–16. DOI: http://dx.doi.org/10.1177/1555412010364978
28. Katie Seaborn and Deborah Fels. 2015. Gamification in Theory and Action: A survey. *International Journal of Human-Computer Studies* 74 (2015), 14–31. DOI: http://dx.doi.org/10.1016/j.ijhcs.2014.09.006
29. Jan Smeddinck, M Herrlich, and M Krause. 2012. Did They Really Like the Game?–Challenges in Evaluating Exergames with Older Adults. *CHI 2012 Workshop on Game User Research: Exploring Methodologies* (2012).
30. Hartmut Wandke, Michael Sengpiel, and Malte Sönksen. 2012. Myths About Older People's Use of Information and Communication. *Gerontology* (2012), 564–570. DOI: http://dx.doi.org/10.1159/000339104

An Annotated Portfolio on Doing Postphenomenology Through Research Products

Sabrina Hauser[1], Doenja Oogjes[1], Ron Wakkary[1,2], Peter-Paul Verbeek[3]
[1]School of Interactive Arts and Technology, Simon Fraser University, Surrey, BC, Canada,
{shauser, doogjes, rwakkary}@sfu.ca; [2]Eindhoven University of Technology, Netherlands;
[3]University of Twente, Netherlands, p.p.c.c.verbeek@utwente.nl

ABSTRACT
In this paper, we argue for framing the crafting and studying of research products as *doing philosophy through things*. We do this by creating an annotated portfolio of such Research through Design (RtD) artifact inquiries as postphenomenological inquiries. In our annotated portfolio, we first provide an account of the postphenomenological commitments of 1) taking empirical work as the basis of the inquiry, 2) analyzing structures of human-technology relations and 3) studying technological mediation Secondly, we trace these commitments across six RtD artifact inquiries. We conclude with a discussion on how research products can be seen as an *experimental way of doing postphenomenology* and how HCI design researchers can work with that. As a result, the presented philosophical framing can be leveraged in HCI research to form a deeper and more dimensional understanding of the human-technology relations we craft and study. This also adds a methodological path to moving beyond foci of use, utility, interaction, and human-centeredness.

Author Keywords
Research through Design; Annotated Portfolios; Research Products; Material Speculation; Postphenomenology.

INTRODUCTION
Over the past several decades, research in the Human-Computer Interaction (HCI) community has largely focused on utilitarian technological advancements. However, there have been steadily growing concerns about the limitations that such a strong focus on utility and functionality can introduce. In particular, researchers have articulated a dominantly utilitarian focus can obscure efforts to fully account for the relations humans have with technology; and, how technology shapes human experiences in the world. As a result, there has been emerging interest in the HCI community in expanding focus beyond interaction and functionality. Design approaches, such as ludic design [e.g., 11] and slow design [e.g., 32], are emerging as alternatives to goal-driven, feature-laden, and productivity-oriented digital technologies. These works and other recent studies in HCI have shown that a move to a more contemporary philosophical orientation is needed to design novel and concrete interventions that theoretically account for the complexity of human-technology relations. As a step in this direction, postphenomenology, and its underlying concepts, have been utilized as a productive theoretical perspective in the HCI and design communities [e.g., 8,30,36,40,55,60,65,68]. Postphenomenology, a contemporary strand of philosophy of technology that views technology as mediators of human-world relations rather than as separated functional or instrumental objects, has been useful in pursuing these theoretical framings. The migration towards this philosophical perspective shifts the emphasis of design research to explore the relations between humans and things, rather than human behavior or qualities of things in and of themselves. In recent works, postphenomenological framework have been helpful in understanding and analyzing human-technology relations in design-oriented HCI research [14,40,65,66]. Postphenomenology brings powerful analytical concepts to HCI and Research through Design (RtD). RtD, in turn, as an approach and set of commitments holds potential to ground and make concrete postphenomenological concepts.

There are similarities and a mutual interest between RtD inquiries and postphenomenological ones. Both approaches at their core investigate technologies and the relationships humans have with them. Further, RtD offers a promising methodological path to uncovering and investigating mutual concerns of postphenomenology, to look beyond use, interaction, and human-centeredness, to form a deeper understanding of people's experiences and relations with technology. The making and studying of research artifacts provide concrete ways to advance new knowledge on how complexities of human-technology relations can be productively approached [14,43,66]. We particularly focus on RtD artifact inquiries that are able to generate speculation through their actuality and materiality (e.g., [34]). In line with work that has come before [43], we see the inquiries of such speculative design artifacts as an *experimental way of doing postphenomenology* or in other words *doing philosophy through things*.

In this paper, we want to take a step towards generative engagements with this conceptual framing through the creation of an annotated portfolio and subsequent reflection. Annotated portfolios [5,9] is an emerging method in design-oriented HCI research that in our case helps bring together a collection of known designed and studied RtD artifacts exploring human-technology relations to show how they align with postphenomenological commitments.

DIS '18, June 9–13, 2018, Hong Kong

ACM ISBN 978-1-4503-5198-0/18/06…$15.00
https://doi.org/10.1145/3196709.3196745

This work is motivated by two of our previously conducted RtD artifact inquiries. Our investigations with and through *table-non-table* [14] and *Tilting Bowl* [66] are early explorations with the conceptualization of our inquiries as postphenomenological. We provide details of these two inquiries and their expressions of postphenomenological commitments as introductory examples. Motivated by these works, we set out to develop an annotated portfolio of six other RtD artifact inquiries.

In what follows, we describe related work and detail our methodological and analytical approach highlighting our commitments to RtD and postphenomenology. We then explore postphenomenological commitments in design research artifacts alongside three themes through an annotated portfolio. Lastly, we reflect on what our approach holds for future work in the HCI community.

POSTPHENOMENOLOGY

Postphenomenology is the concrete and empirical study of the social and cultural roles of technologies in human existence and experience practiced by an expanding group of different scholars. This school of thought was initially developed as a contemporary and empirical strand of philosophy of technology [17–19,45,51,52,56,59,60]. In postphenomenological studies, philosophy and empiricism blend, marrying approaches of more traditional philosophy of technology including phenomenology and American pragmatism as well as Science and Technology Studies [50]. The postphenomenological approach sees technology as *transformative mediators* of human-world relations rather than separated functional or instrumental objects or alienating entities [56]. Technologies mediate humans' experiences and perceptions in and of the 'world'. The 'world' here can be seen as a placeholder for a situational holistic context such as an environment like a home. It could also be an interpretation framework, or one's understanding of the self. Through *technological mediation*, humans and technological artifacts co-shape or *co-constitute* human *subjectivity* and the *objectivity* of their 'world' in any given situation [50]. In postphenomenological studies, concrete case examples of technologies are investigated in terms of the relations humans have with them and the implications technologies have for the relations between humans and their world. Examples of studies are investigations of imaging technologies such as Verbeek's study of obstetric ultrasound [57,50]; where he shows the technology's impact on the relations between parents' and the fetus and on the parents' moral decision-making because the ultrasound *co-constitutes* the fetus as a patient, parents as decision-makers and mothers as environments. Other study examples are the impact of mobile phones while driving [46] and the mediation of implanted technologies [1]. In all of these cases, technologies help to shape both the 'subjects' that use them and the 'world' they live in.

Towards Postphenomenology in HCI

As focus expanded beyond the office and technologies were increasingly becoming part of people's leisure times, there was a growing need for an alternative value set to guide the design of technology for everyday life [29,53,61,63]. Emphasis was put on the need to understand the messiness of everyday life (e.g., emotions, experience, values, new contexts outside of the office, etc.). In this context, new frameworks for understanding human "experience" [28] and "interaction" [7] provided an important foundation. In recent years, the focus on interaction and the underlying notion of functionality however has been seen as limiting, not fully accounting for unpacking the relations humans have with technology, and also how technology shapes human's existence and experiences in the world [8]. As a result, the HCI community has been expanding its focus beyond interaction and functionality, and design approaches such as ludic design [12], slow design [13,32], and undesigning [37] have been developed opposing a utility-oriented, feature-laden, and productivity-enhancing development of digital technologies. A move to a more contemporary philosophical orientation promises to support the development of theoretical framings for design that accounts for the complexity of human-technology-world relations to create novel and concrete interventions. For example, [8] discussing Borgmann's notion of the device paradigm [2] and the idea of the non-neutrality of technology-mediated experience [16,69]—a key point in postphenomenology—raises issues within guiding visions and values in HCI. Odom et al. [30] grounded in concepts of the philosophy of technology describe attachment as a key factor in human-technology relations for future design implementations. Pierce & Paulos [40,41] informed by phenomenological accounts and a defined set of human-technology relations [17] analytically uncover and describe new ways of relating to and experiencing electricity and also explore electric materiality. Furthermore, concepts like personal informatics [35] have been analytically re-examined through the utilization of the postphenomenological framework to discuss the changing agency of users. Wiltse and Stolterman [68] use the framework to analyze the interaction architectures of instant messaging and file sharing to reveal how these interactive spaces mediate human activity.

Collectively, these emerging works illustrate that philosophy of technology is becoming utilized as a productive theoretical perspective in HCI and interaction design research. Despite these developments, there is a lack of work that draws on postphenomenology in a generative way for design. Within philosophy of technology, efforts exist to make postphenomenological ideas, concepts, features, characteristics, and methodology more accessible [37]. There is now an opportunity to bring these new developments back to HCI, which is a goal of this paper. We believe a reflexive engagement with a postphenomenological framing of RtD inquiries can help with that, given the postphenomenological focus on the roles technology can play in human-world relations; and in turn, research artifacts and their resulting evaluations help advance new knowledge on human-technology relations [23,24,38]. In this paper, we focus on RtD artifact inquiries that share commitments to two of our own RtD studies that we have come to see as postphenomenological inquiries. We describe these as introductory exemplars to our annotated portfolio next.

INVESTIGATIONS OF THE TABLE-NON-TABLE AND TILTING BOWL: INTRODUCTORY EXAMPLES OF POSTPHENOMENOLOGICAL INQUIRIES

In two of our own RtD artifact inquiries [14,66] we went through processes of framing, reframing and productively working with viewing them as postphenomenological inquiries. In this section, we elaborate on elements of the studies of the *table-non-table* that allowed us to arrive at that point. We will also briefly sum up how this framing developed in our study of the *Tilting Bowl.*

Figure 1. A cat examining the table-non-table, b. A Tilting Bowl filled with fruit on a household table. © Everyday Design Studio

We see both, the *table-non-table* and *Tilting Bowl*, as *material speculations* [64], which is an RtD approach that centers on the crafting of a *counterfactual artifact* to carefully and precisely inquire into research questions. A counterfactual artifact is a fully realized system or object that in a use-context may contradict what would normally be considered logical.

The *table-non-table* is a table-like structure made of approximately 1000 sheets of stacked common stock paper. Each sheet of paper measures 17.5 inches by 22.5 inches with a square hole die cut in the middle to allow it to stack around a solid aluminum square post that holds the sheets in place. Almost entirely hidden, an aluminum chassis holds the stacked paper about half an inch from the floor, which gives the structure a floating appearance. When plugged into an electrical outlet, the *table-non-table* moves one to two times per day, at random times, very slowly and for less than ten seconds. The *table-non-table* diverts from assumptions around use-centric, utilitarian ideas of technologies and technology design, while retaining subtle design qualities that could enable it to easily fit in everyday domestic settings.

Over the course of four and a half years, we conducted iterative field studies, reflections, and conceptualizations that, over time, helped us to better make sense of our research artifact and the relations that emerged with and through it. After this lengthy period of time, we came to see the *table-non-table* as a successful postphenomenological inquiry. We drew on postphenomenology to productively shape our capacity to theoretically and empirically articulate key qualities of the *table-non-table*. This allowed us to look past *useful use* to uncover key empirical experiences of living with the table-non-table and see the more subtle and diffuse mediations of the *table-non-table*. The utilization of postphenomenology in our studying and conceptualizing of the *table-non-table* enabled us to frame our RtD inquiry to develop precision and language for non-utilitarian notions of interaction and uncommon assumptions of human-technology relations.

In a concurrent research project, we designed and studied the *Tilting Bowl* [66], which is a ceramic double-walled bowl with a hidden motor that lets the bowl tilt occasionally. It is similar to any other ceramic bowl in that it is food safe and washable. The *Tilting Bowl* is counterfactual in that it looks and functions like a regular bowl except that counter to what is common to bowls, it tilts. By defamiliarizing such a familiar artifact through digital technologies, the *Tilting Bowl* specifically inquiries into the types and qualities of relationships beyond use and functionality that may emerge. We generatively worked with our previously articulated non-utilitarian notions of interaction, such as *intersections* and *ensembles* [33,62], to guide the design of the *Tilting Bowl.* We have been deploying six bowls in the households of philosophers to inquire into postphenomenological topics and questions. From this study, novel and rich descriptions have been emerging with respect to alterity and background relations with the *Tilting Bowl* in particular.

Our two investigations offer empirical and reflexive accounts of human-technology relations and technological mediations with counterfactual RtD artifacts. Both contribute argumentative exemplars for the value and use of postphenomenological concepts and concerns for considering RtD artifacts in HCI. This helped us see the productive postphenomenological framing of RtD-inquiries and made us aware of the similar interest between postphenomenology and RtD artifact inquiries; and further it motivated us to explore whether other RtD projects could similarly be seen as postphenomenological inquiries.

OUR METHODOLOGICAL APPROACH

In developing an annotated portfolio of RtD artifact inquiries, we aim to bring out particularities of enacted postphenomenological dimensions. A first selection criterion was that the RtD artifact inquiries were in line with two methodological commitments to RtD pursued in the crafting and studying of *table-non-table* and *Tilting Bowl*: *Material Speculation* and *Research Products*.

To further elaborate, in *material speculations* [64], artifacts are designed to be lived with over long periods and are crafted to embody research questions or propositions through what we call counterfactual artifacts. A counterfactual artifact is a fully realized functioning product or system that intentionally contradicts what would normally be considered logical to create given the norms of design and design products. This countering of norms, opens the possibilities to empirically investigate multiple alternative existences (or what-ifs) as lived-with realities of the counterfactual artifacts. In addition to counterfactuality, material speculations rely on crafted research products to perform the inquiry.

Odom et al. [34] describe *research products* through four qualities of *inquiry driven, finish, fit,* and *independent*. The artifacts are designed to drive a research inquiry; they have a high quality of finish such that people engage with them as they are, rather than what they might become and such that they can fit among other things and into everyday environments; and lastly, they operate independently in everyday settings over time. The term and concept of research products "emphasizes the actuality of the design

Figure 2. The Selected Research Products. Top, Middle, & Bottom (L to R): T1&2. Greenscreen Dress; T2&3. Obscura 1C Digital Camera; M1&2. Indoor Weather Stations; M3&4. Morse Things; B1&2. Photobox. B3&4. Datacatcher. Image credits: T1&2 ©Angella Mackey, T3&4 ©James Pierce; M1&2, B3&4 ©Interaction Research Studio; M3&4 ©Everyday Design Studio; M3&4; B1&2 ©William Odom.

artifact helping to overcome the limitations of prototypes when investigating complex matters of human-technology relations over time, which is of growing interest in the HCI community" [34:2550].

Our selection process began by first collecting RtD artifacts without specific curation criteria. We searched for published articles, images and videos of them and ended up with over thirty artifacts. We then determined which held up against the criteria of research products and material speculation. We made sure that there were published articles or videos of them reporting on real-world placements or experiences with the artifacts (e.g., participant deployments or auto-ethnographic self-deployments). We also wanted our chosen RtD projects to be from various sources, including different design research studios [70,71] and design researchers [e.g., 27,43].

The Selected Research Products

Next, we offer brief descriptions of our final choices of RtD inquiries and refer to publications that report on each project in more detail.

Greenscreen dress (T1&2) is a long-term investigation into the wearing of dynamic textiles [26,27]. With the use of a chroma key mobile application, content is digitally displayed on green fabric. The design researcher, Mackey started with wearing a green dress and expanded this to other green garments she bought or made. Mackey et al. report on her day-to-day experiences of wearing green dynamic clothing for ten months.

Obscura 1C Digital Camera (T3&4) is a camera with a concrete housing that would have to be destroyed in order to view the pictures [42–44]. The designer-researchers Pierce and Paulos have reported on Pierce's own experiences of using the *Obscura 1C*. They produced around 20 cameras of which 10 were distributed purposefully through craigslist ads, bulletin boards and local stores. They did not follow up on the deployment of these design artifacts.

Indoor Weather Stations (M1&2) is a set three objects aimed at playfully exploring environmental awareness of the home [6,11,22]. The *Wind Tunnel* measures gusts of air near the device and visualizes these through a small fan that creates storms through paper film trees. *Temperature Tape* resembles a measuring tape but visualizes different temperatures within the home through screen-printed stripes that change color from yellow, orange, red and black corresponding with temperature. The *Light Collector* measures and recreates the color of the ambient light in the home. Over 20 sets were batch-produced and deployed to more than 20 households over the course of a year.

Morse Things (M3&4) are sets of connected cups and bowls that communicate solely to each other in Morse Code and over Twitter [65]. They were deployed for six weeks with designers and design researchers with an interest in the IoT.

Photobox (B1&2) is an antique chest that prints four or five randomly selected photos its owner's Flickr collection at random intervals each month [31,32]. Three *Photoboxes* were created and then deployed in three households for 14 months respectively.

Datacatchers (B3&4) are mobile devices that collect and display topical information about their surroundings (e.g., house prices, typical incomes, etc.) [3,4,10]. Scrolling the wheel one way will display messages and turning the other way accesses a poll. 100 *Datacatchers* were deployed for two months. Two filmmaking teams collected over 2 hours of footage of the participant's lived experiences of the devices in context.

Creating the Annotated Portfolio

Annotated portfolios are "a means for capturing the family resemblances that exist in a collection of artifacts, simultaneously respecting the particularity of specific designs and engaging with broader concerns" [5]. In the context of our work, the utilization of annotated portfolios provides us with a concrete way of showing conceptual themes we viewed as generalizable to other designs (based on prior work). As Bowers describes further, "Annotated portfolios are *descriptive* (of past occurrences) and intended to be *generative-inspirational* (of future possibility) with their primary business constituting a portfolio in close contact to [...] the actual artifacts themselves" [5:76]. Annotated portfolios allow for a way to explore what postphenomenology holds for design researchers by not simply giving prescriptions.

Alongside concept-driven interaction research [54] and strong concepts [15], annotated portfolios [5] offers a method for theorizing in interaction design research. These approaches are related in their goal of supporting the development of design knowledge that lies between theories and instances. Höök and Löwgren [15] explicitly characterize this as *intermediate-level knowledge*. Bowers [5] and Löwgren [25] define annotated portfolios as offering intermediate-level knowledge for design research. Our work extends these approaches by providing an interpretive account of methodological commitments through annotations of RtD artifact inquiries.

Annotation Themes of Postphenomenological Commitments

For our annotation process, we developed three themes based on descriptions of how postphenomenological studies methodologically operate [50]:

1) Empirical work as the basis of the inquiry
2) Structures of human-technology-world relations as a starting point
3) Technology co-constitutes objectivity and subjectivity of any given situation (mediations or implications)

For our annotated portfolio, we analyzed how the selected research products express these commitments by going through their respective published works and annotating them in a lengthy process. From this, we developed our final annotated portfolio of postphenomenological research products, which we describe next.

ANNOTATED PORTFOLIO OF POSTPHENOMENOLOGICAL COMMITMENTS IN RESEARCH PRODUCTS

For each of the three annotation themes, we first describe the postphenomenological commitment and key examples; and, then describe how the selected research products express it.

1) Empirical work as the basis of the inquiry

Central to postphenomenological studies is that empirical work is the basis for the philosophical reflection. Rather than applying philosophical work to technology in a broader sense, postphenomenological insights are derived from actual experiences with certain technologies. As Rosenberger and Verbeek describe, the purpose of the empirical work is "to investigate the character of the various dimensions of the relations between humans and these technologies, and their impact on human practices and experiences" [50:31]. Empirical work in postphenomenological investigations can include both self-conducted studies and first-person experiences and studies conducted by others. Frequently the two types of investigations are combined.

First Person Experiences

Investigating the implications of a technology through a first-person experiential account is most common in postphenomenology. Ihde has reported on his experience with hearing aids [20] and a heart stent [21]; Verbeek on his and his wife's experience with obstetric ultrasound [57,59].

Self-conducted studies

An example of a postphenomenological investigation basing its philosophical reflections on self-conducted study data is Rosenberger's investigations of the politics of park benches and other public-space objects [47,48]. Over several years, he has collected several hundreds of pictures of public-space objects from all over the world [49], which he argues are being designed against homeless populations.

Empirical Work by Others

Many postphenomenological investigations are based on empirical work by others or at least involve such data alongside self-gathered data. In his investigation, Rosenberger [46] studies data gathered by cognitive scientists to make an argument around the mediation of cell phones while driving including when on speaker phone and against the use of cell phones in any way while driving. Although using empirical work by others, Rosenberger additionally brought in his own first-person experiences in the study. Wellner [67] also conducts a postphenomenological inquiry into cell phones, however on a broader level looking back at the history of cell phones studying the role they play in contemporary everyday life.

Next, we discuss how research products represent this theme by describing: *What kind of empirical work is done with and through the selected research products?*

Empiricism in Research Products

The Datacatchers [10] were batch-produced and deployed to around 100 participants. The researchers were specifically interested in semi-random approaches to the deployment to be able to get responses from a broad demographic. They commissioned a service consultancy to form a deployment team, who recruited participants at local markets. Once participants agreed to be part of the study, a package containing a manual, a charger and a Datacatcher was given to the participants on the spot. The participants lived with the devices for two months, after which filmmakers (briefed by the research team) made a short documentary (1-5 minutes) of each participants' experience with the devices.

The *Indoor Weather Stations* [11] were also batch-produced and deployed in 20 homes. The researchers recruited participants that lived near the research studio through posters in the area and websites of local interest. Participants first participated in a cultural probe study to encourage reflection on their indoor climate [6]. After this, the packaged *Indoor Weather Stations* were given to participants either at group events, at the research studio or during individual drop-offs. Data collection included home visits and prompts. During the study, the researchers created a web-platform for visualizing the data of the *Indoor Weather Stations* of participating households to enable further engagement between participants and the devices.

Approximately 20 *Obscura Digital Camera 1C*'s [44] were created, including packaging and instructional material that allowed the camera to be stand-alone: they can be understood and used without scaffolding or interference of a research team. In such, the empirical account builds on the specific actuality of this counterfactual and counterfunctional artifact. In addition, 10 packages were distributed through approaches such as bulletin boards, local stores, and craiglist ads. Pierce [39] also reflects on his own experience with the *Obscura 1C*.

Participants for the *Morse Things* [65] were recruited through personal contacts of the research team. The team was looking specifically for trained designers and researchers with an expertise in the area of connected things. The participants received a box containing a manual, instructions for deployment, a router and three *Morse Things* (one red, one yellow, one blue). Participants were asked to describe what it is like to live with the *Morse Things* from the perspective of the things and to create design proposals for things that could co-exist with the *Morse Things*. After living with the artifacts for six weeks and self-reporting on the experiences, and sharing and discussing the experiences and design proposals in a workshop, the participants and researchers were able to speculate on new types of connected things in the home.

The *Greenscreen Dress* [26] was studied for seven months as an autobiographical design and auto-ethnographic study. The first author incorporated green clothing in her outfits daily during this time and took pictures and videos that she shared on social media. The actuality of wearing the dynamic fabric daily allowed the authors to reflect on real-life implications of such a technology, e.g. the possibilities and limitations in expressing personal style.

With the aim of exploring topics such as anticipation, reflections and re-visitation, *Photobox* was part of a long-term deployment in which three nearly identical photoboxes were deployed in three households for fourteen months respectively [32]. The participants were recruited with the requirement of having a large Flickr account. *Photobox* was described to participants only briefly to allow for them to create their own interpretations over time. To collect these temporal accounts, home visits and interviews were conducted bi-monthly. This longitudinal study allowed the researchers to reflect on the mediations *Photobox* brought forward with the Flickr archive and on how the artifact took on different roles over time.

Concluding Remarks about Empiricism in Research Products

The RtD artifacts that we have discussed are bespoke to the inquiry and counterfactual in nature. Studies of them rely on the actual existence of the artifacts and the fact that they can be taken as is. Through these combined commitments it becomes possible to study not merely a new artifact, but also the newly constituted world in which this artifact exists. The presented studies enable the researchers to inquire into the lived experiences of this new world. These experiences can form the basis of uncovering mediations and relativistic accounts. We will elaborate on how this is the case in our selected RtD works in the forthcoming sections.

2) Structures of Human-Technology Relations as Starting Points

Postphenomenological studies begin their analyses with particular technological encounters and the structure of human-technology relations at play. They then usually move into an analysis of technological mediations in human-technology-world relations (theme 3). Ihde, a key pioneer of the postphenomenological school of thought, argues that we encounter technologies through four bodily-perceptual relationships [17]: as an *embodiment*, as an *alterity*, through a *hermeneutic*, or a *background* relation. In the next sub-sections, we will work our way through these four relationships, which are neither exhaustive nor mutually exclusive.

The Embodiment Relationship

A technology is being *embodied* when a part or an aspect of the world is experienced or perceived *through* the technology. Classic examples that postphenomenological philosophers have examined are glasses or wearable technologies such as hearing aids [20]. The mobile phone, for instance, enables a person to experience a conversation through a phone; in this case, the phone is embodied and almost moves into the background [46]. In embodiment relations, technologies, or aspects of them, fade to a certain degree in the background. Ihde describes this as *transparency*. For example, if someone has grown very accustomed to their glasses, they may be barely noticed [50].

The Hermeneutic Relationship

When a technology is hermeneutically encountered it is '*read*' and reveals a certain aspect of the world to humans who *interpret* it. For example, a thermometer lets humans hermeneutically know that it is cold or hot. Through such technological encounters, humans receive access to an aspect of the world by being provided with a representation of it, which then requires interpretation to be made sense of.

The Alterity Relationship

When a technology is *being interacted with* and becomes '*quasi-other*' or '*quasi-autonomous*' postphenomenologists characterize this as an alterity relation. In this case, humans interact with a technology whereas the world moves in the background. Examples that have been used in postphenomenology include GPS navigation systems and ATM machines.

The Background Relationship

A background relation is at play when a technology is operating but not calling for focal attention; nevertheless, it is still shaping people and their surroundings or contexts [17]. Ihde calls this *contextual* state an '*absent presence*' when a technology is not directly used but still being experienced becoming "a kind of near-technological environment" [17:108]. We are typically not aware of such technologies when they function or are in operation (e.g., much like today's smart technologies, IoT devices, or cloud technologies). The technological mediation of background technologies is often more through the "indirect effects upon the way a world is experienced" [17:112]. Key examples in this context that postphenomenologists draw on are semi-automatic machines, such as a fridge or a heating system.

Collectively, these bodily perceptual relationships that come about between humans and technology show how technologies in such structural relationships can go from being very close to the body, i.e. embodied, towards moving further, i.e. hermeneutic, and further, i.e. alterity, away from the body towards being unnoticed and moving into the background.

Cyborg Relations

Verbeek extended these relationship structures with three more *cyborg* relationships [58] to cover additional contemporary human-technology structures. First, in the *Fusion Relationship*, a technology merges with the human in a way that is more intimate than an embodiment relation. Examples of this relation are implanted technologies like brain implants. Second, in an *Immersion Relationship*, a technology merges with the environment in a way that they are in the background not for our existence but also interactive contexts. Examples of this relation include ambient technologies that detect human presence or smart toilets that generate health reports. Third, *Augmentation Relationship* is an embodiment relation and a hermeneutic relation combined which is the case with, for example, Google Glass.

Next, we show how research products represent this theme by describing: *What structures of relationships are at play?*

Relationship Structures in Research Products

Photobox can be seen as dominantly in a background relation; (indeed, Odom et al. describe the *Photobox* as a "background device"). For example, consider the following quotes from Odom et al.'s participants in which they reflect on living with *Photobox*: *"[It's] in the backdrop of our life, not distracting, just there. ...like many of the things we keep out on the mantle or put up on the wall"* [32:1968]. Another participant described the fading into and out of the background: *"it's awesome to find new photos, but [Photobox] doesn't make me crazy to run over and check it every time I get home. [...] I can walk past it. I can come back later. [...] in that way it has quite a different character"* [33]. Importantly, there was a period of time participants needed to get used to the *Photobox* in their life and as it is. Odom et al. describe this in their study: "*Despite the relative simplicity of the Photobox, it provoked a range of reactions across households—many of which were characterized by initial frustration and disappointment, which slowly shifted towards acceptance, and pleasurable anticipation"* [32:1965]. After several months of living with it, a participant described the technology as *"one that could be closed up and fade away, not demanding nor requiring the owners' attention"* [32]. Lastly, human-technology relations with *Photobox* being somewhat uncommon in that users cannot control how often or when it is printing photos can be seen as entailing alterity aspects.

The *Indoor Weather Stations* were designed to be part of a hermeneutic relation. Gaver et al. describe that they "*reveal the home's microclimate by highlighting small gusts of wind, the colour of ambient light, and temperature differentials within the home*" [11:3451]. More specifically, *"[t]he temperature measure [...] tells you something about your energy use. In my room I was quite shocked at the temperature difference from one end of the room to the other, how cold it was in the middle of the room with the central heating on*" [6:7]. Similar as with the *Photobox*, there was a time period in which participants had to get adjusted to the new (and different) design artifacts in their lives. A participant described that the constant whirring of one of the weather stations changed from being irritating to soothing, something he only noticed in its absence [11]. Another participant made the remark that she loved things that *"haven't quite settled down yet into what they are going to be"* [11:3455].

In another remark Gaver et al. [11] describe that they thought their design artifacts were failing because their participants were not engaging with them. However, they realized that there was an attachment that had built while the devices had found a place in the background: "*Moreover, even though it was not uncommon for participants to tell us that they no longer engaged with the devices after a month or two, they were still adamant that they did not want to return them, but preferred for the devices to stay in their homes. They had become part of the home's 'background' and in a desirable way*" [11:3458].

Morse Things operate mainly in the background but also have alterity aspects to them. For example, participants thought of them as having human qualities and as being like pet cats: present and interactive but not always interested in humans. One participant "*thought the Morse Things would be happy with their new home, and as [they] made sounds when she and Noah entered the house, she imagined them to be happy to see them: 'they were here and they spoke a little bit and then we went out for dinner [...] we came back [...] and as we entered the door, someone, one of them was like bipbipbip, and I was like, Oh! He's so happy to see us!"* [65:508].

Greenscreen Dress can be seen as becoming part of a fusion relationship. Mackey et al. describe how Mackey responded to the merging of the green garment and her body from her first-person perspective: "*I observed that being completely covered in the green fabric from my neck to my knees was too strong in that I felt overpowered by the complete digital transformation of most of my body. Some days I only wanted a pocket or collar that was green, a green-striped print or just green pants*" [26:55]. While physically arguably less intrusive as brain implants, the fusion of the green garments was obvious and even overwhelming to Mackey. Her reflections on responses of the select group of people who were aware of the study illustrate further the intimate relation with and through the garments that goes beyond embodiment: *"Only colleagues, friends and family members intimately aware of this study recognized the greens I wore as 'active' and were able to experience the live, AR [augmented reality] versions of the clothing through my smartphone. Mostly, this awareness provoked a heightened attention to what I wore each day and sometimes a question like 'Oh, you're not wearing green today?' would bring attention to this. I would respond by pointing to the subtle green leaves within the pattern of my shirt, or the green hue in my 'blue' pant"* [26:57].

Datacatchers give access to an aspect of the world by providing a representation of information about the near environment which users then interpret. This represents a hermeneutic relation. Additionally, users can move around with the device in hand and see added aspects of their environment through the devices through an additional layer of information. This can be seen as combining an embodiment, hermeneutic and even augmentation relation.

Lastly, the *1C Camera* is mainly a background relationship. With the use being limited towards not being able to access or experience the images taken with the camera, the 1C has an absent presence in the life of its user.

Concluding Remarks about Relationship Structures in Research Products

Collectively, through our annotations we described the structures of human-technology relations across our selected research products. We have shown that artifacts can become part of several relationship structures and can further entail subtle relational aspects. Importantly, the novelty in research products commonly results in relationships and their dynamics to evolve over time. This way, research products may, unlike the commonly studied things in post-phenomenology, cause a low sedimentation or transparency in relationships. Additionally, research products can also challenge common postphenomenological understandings of human-technology relations.

While it is true that any technology can be analyzed for their relational aspects, we believe that such analyses for RtD artifacts specifically hold promise for HCI. Postphenomenological structures can bring new insights into future RtD analyses. Traditionally, in HCI there is a focus on alterity relations. The presented nuanced structures give ways to the more complex and meaningful relations coming about between humans, technologies, and the world.

3) Technology Co-Constitutes Objectivity and Subjectivity of any Given Situation (Mediations)

In addition to the structure of relations at play between humans and technologies, postphenomenology looks at the accruing implications or *mediations*. Verbeek [56] describes mediations happening on an *existential* level meaning "[h]ow humans appear in their world" or their actions and practices, and on a *hermeneutic* or experiential level meaning "[h]ow reality [or the world] appears to humans" or their perception and experience [56:196] (see Figure 3). In this, technologies work to *amplify* and *reduce* human perception and experience, and *invite* and *inhibit* human action and practices. In other words, this part of an investigation focuses on how, in the relations that arise around a technology, a specific "world" or objectivity and a specific "human" or subjectivity is constituted; and what are the implications of that?

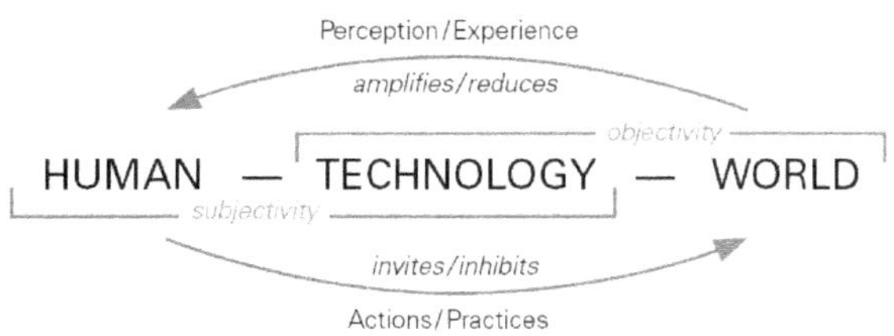

Figure 3 Technological mediation (based on Verbeek's descriptions)

In the previously mentioned study of obstetric ultrasound [57,50], Verbeek shows how the mediating effect of this technology can impact parents' access to the fetus and, in doing so, shape their moral decision-making. His analysis also reveals how this technology *co-constitutes* the fetus as a patient, parents as decision-makers (subjectivity) and mothers as environments (objectivity). The questions guiding our analysis of the research products for this theme are: *What are mediations of the technology in people's lives? What kind of 'world' (objectivity) and what kind of 'human' (subjectivity) is co-constituted by the technology?*

Mediations of Research Products

Odom et al. share a vast amount of insights about the mediating or co-constitutional dimensions of *Photobox*: *"While households were initially frustrated by the slow rate of photos being printed, over time they appreciated how this pace created time to reflect on an individual image and the memories it triggers [...] participants described how, over time, the relative slowness of our prototype provoked them to consider the rate at which other domestic technologies operate"* [32:1966]. Further, Photobox *"provoked some participants to critically consider the role of technology in their everyday lives"* [32:1968] as one of their participants took a break from Facebook.

Odom et al. specifically speak to the changes in the experiences and perceptions across Photobox owners describing *"how [their] participants' perceptions of the Photobox changed over time as it transitioned from a perplexing and, at times frustrating, device, to one that was eventually understood and integrated into the home"* and thereafter *"how, over time, the Photobox supported experiences of anticipation, reflection, and meaningful interactions with participants' Flickr archives"* [32:1967].

Pierce shares his own account of living with an *Obscura 1C* describing a co-constituted subjectivity of himself: *"In my own use of the Obscura 1C, I have occasionally sat and held the camera while I vaguely imagined what might be inside. I also have distinct memories of images I believe I captured but that I know I may never actually see. In several instances, I consciously chose not to capture a corresponding image with a conventional camera* [39:126]. When sharing a post on craigslist to offer the *Obscura 1C* as a form of distribution [43], Pierce and Paulos also created a reality or world (objectivity) with the *Obscura 1C* existing in other people's lives. In the post, they asked people to motivate why they wanted to own *an Obscura 1C* and how they envisioned using it. The received responses further support the legibility of the world created through the artifact.

The *Indoor Weather Stations* emphasize that the home can be seen as a microclimate, changing the perception of this environment. One participant shared: "*My lightbulb moment was when I thought about the house as being an ecology – that it's not a sealed homogeneous box* "[6:7]. In terms of implications around the subjectivity of their participants, Gaver et al. also share unexpected implications: *"While the stations only marginally aroused the kind of investigative curiosity of the microclimate of the home we had expected, we found participants using them to make sense of their homes in other ways–particularly when they could see their own data over more extended time periods than the device's replay buttons allowed"* [11:3455].

The Datacatchers short statements reveal information about the surrounding area appearing every few seconds. The statements are on topics like average housing prices, typical incomes, and the number of pubs or GP surgeries nearby [10:1598]. Gaver et al. describe that the statements "*simultaneously draw attention to the sociopolitical topology of the lived environment and to the nature of big data itself* [10:1597]. The *Datacatchers* were seen by many of Gaver et al.'s participants as *"extending the environment, however, by adding 'a new layer to the city with the data and information that you can't really see when you walk around'"*[10:1603]. This had an effect on their user perceptions of the environment. For example, one participant of Gaver et al. shared: "*I think the thing that really shocked me first was what a depressing area I live in, because all the statistics are about crime and health and how unhealthy the people are in my neighbourhood and in my community. You know that immediately starts you thinking: 'Is this the place that I live in'"*[10:1604].

Participants of the *Morse Things* study experienced tensions with making sense of the non-human-centeredness of the artifacts. Their perspectives of the cups and bowls shifted back and forth between anthropomorphized and withdrawn: *"While Olivia 'loved imagining' that the Morse Things talked and cared for her and her partner, she realized that 'that's not what they're saying at all, and they don't care about us at all'"*[65:510]. Another participant described how he did not perceive the *Morse Things* as different from other cups and bowls, yet mentioned that it may take more time to understand them and considered learning Morse Code to follow their conversations. Although the *Morse Things* were used in households among other bowls and cups, to hold food, liquids and trinkets, they garnered special attention. One participant reported: *"I continue to keep trying to grab the bowls while they are "tweeting." I don't know why I'm doing this, because I can just wait and check Twitter to see which bowl it was ... guess I feel like I might be able to learn if they have different sounds? Maybe I'll be able to tell them apart eventually."*[65:509]. Further, in their proposed design concepts, the things supposedly co-existing with the *Morse Things* were often more human-centred and connecting with human practices. Through both study engagements, participants were trying to find new ways to constitute the relationship between them and the *Morse Things*.

In the *Greenscreen Dress* study, Mackey et al. report on how Mackey's perception of and experiences with the system moved from being "gimmicky" to an exploration into regaining control and expressing identity. In her study, the color green is constituted as something with virtual potential. Through this, and through her commitment of wearing a dynamic fabric every day, Mackey built her wardrobe with green as a main consideration: *"The resulting wardrobe was a product of rebuilding my personal identity through clothing that confronted the constraint of green fabric and allowed for the chroma-keying action to happen"*[26:55]. This process allowed her and her co-authors to further understand the nuances of green fabrics in combination with the interaction possibilities of the mobile application: *"She used the sensitivity slider in the application interface to render fabrics less "effective" to the keying-out, so that shadows and textures could remain. She found that dark greens and pastel greens gave a "grainy" effect to the digital content. She found that sheer materials worked in surprising ways whereby they could hold a faint layer of the digital content while still remaining transparent"*[27:449].

Mackey et al. [26,27] further report on how most of the digital content Mackey 'wore' came from captures from her surroundings. They describe how she collected and stored these images and videos as 'things to wear'. They elaborate on how she started thinking of these as patterns, similar as how one would think of patterned fabric. In such, her environment was constituted as wearable through the system of *Greenscreen Dress*.

Concluding Remarks about Mediations of Research Products

Through our annotations we have described how the selected research products mediate people's lives and worlds, i.e. shape new subjectivities and objectivities. Investigating these mediations allows researchers to holistically inquire into the role of technology in people's lives. Another important aspect that the notion of mediation offers is being able to look beyond human-centeredness. While within postphenomenology, artifacts are indeed seen for their mediations rather than their mere instrumental or functional purposes, the studied technologies do also have clear functionalities with at times close-ended purposes. This further highlights the potential we see for RtD approaches to engage in philosophical work. Where postphenomenological studies report on the role and implications of functional technologies in people's life, e.g. mediations of existing ultrasound technology, RtD artifacts are often more open-ended and therefore able to forecast with detailed descriptive accounts. Importantly, this entails how research products shift not only existing relations to digital technologies but may even challenge them and shape *new mediations* given their novelty (e.g. new ways of experiencing archived photos with *Photobox*, new ways of relating to clothing through *Greenscreen Dress*, or new ways of seeing an urban environment through *Datacatcher*).

DISCUSSION

Thus far in this paper we have described and unpacked an annotated portfolio of research products or RtD artifact inquiries revealing how they align with key postphenomenological commitments. We described empirical approaches across the research products, structures of human-technology relations they become part of, and, emphasized that they mediate human-world relations in any given situation. In this, we have established a postphenomenological vocabulary and concepts in the context of HCI and RtD, and sought to make the argument that research products can be seen as *doing postphenomenology* albeit in a more experimental way. Next, we discuss this in more detail and describe the constructive roles HCI researchers can take on in their RtD inquiries.

RtD as Doing Experimental Postphenomenology

First, we can consider RtD as an 'experimental' way of doing postphenomenology specifically due to its main commitment of the *crafting* of an artifact being an integral part of the inquiry. The actuality and high level of finish of research products allows them to be encountered and taken 'as they are' which means, in postphenomenological terms, that they mediate or co-constitute subjectivity and objectivity in any given situation. The crafting of research products allows HCI design researchers to investigate human-technology-world relations and technological mediations by not only studying them but also taking part in creating them. In this, research products can also challenge common postphenomenological understandings of human-technology relations and subjectivity and objectivity.

Second, the context in which research products are *studied* is co-constructed by the *choices* made around deployments, which extends postphenomenological ways of studying. Postphenomenological studies take empirical accounts of existing artifacts as the basis for their philosophical reflections. This offers a variety of existing contextual settings to be studied that have evolved around an artifact. Postphenomenological accounts often take on first person perspectives and, in a philosophical nature, are highly interpretative. This is in contrast to many HCI works that aim to produce a more objective account of the crafted and studied artifacts. The artifacts that we have discussed are unique to the inquiry and counterfactual in nature. In such, it is not merely a new artifact that is studied but, with it, usually a newly mediated *'world' (objectivity)* and *'human' (subjectivity)*. Based on our annotated portfolio of six research products, we aim to offer an exemplifying (but not definite) account of how HCI design researchers can take on the co-constructive and multifold roles in their inquiries (Fig.3).

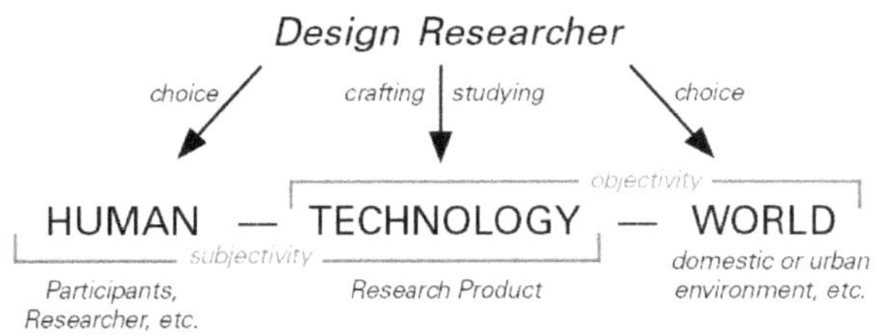

Figure 4 Constructive roles of HCI design researchers in their RtD inquiries

The design researcher can intentionally *choose* an environment *(world)* for the artifact to exist in (e.g., a domestic environment with the *Photobox* and *Morse Things* or an urban environment with the Datacatchers). The researcher's choices also determine who encounters the technology. An empirical account can, for example, come from deployment studies with participants. As described, this can involve researchers choosing specifically skilled or trained participants (e.g., design experts in the *Morse Things* study, or philosopher households living with a *Titling Bowl*) or through introducing an additional interpretive voice (e.g. the service-design team for recruitment and the documentary moviemakers for data collection with the *Datacatchers*). Further, the researcher can choose to analyze her/his own experiential accounts as a *researcher-participant* (e.g., Pierce's experiences with the *Obscura 1C* and Mackey's experiences with the *Greenscreen Dress*), which further entangles empirical accounts, design artifacts, and theory. We believe this type of *interpretive empiricism* can better support efforts in the HCI community to reflexively report on lived experiences, relativistic accounts and mediations.

In summary, research products and their commitments to the *crafting* and *deploying* of artifacts is a generative, bespoke, and more experimental way of investigating into human-technology-world relations and technological mediation. RtD artifact inquiries allow for philosophical reflection similar to postphenomenological inquires; and, they are also able to extend postphenomenological methodology in two ways. First, through their ability to *craft the object of inquiry*. Second, through their unique approach to studying technological mediation, and as a result creating inquiries that are experimental, generative, constructive, and anticipative. Accordingly, HCI design researchers can be seen as performing a kind of *radical empiricism* through the design and study of research products.

Through our annotations and further discussions, we hope to have created a more graspable, design-oriented way of understanding postphenomenological commitments and concepts, which can further aid in this process of purposefully crafting technologies that mediate and become part of human-world relations. The theoretical nature and abstract concepts of postphenomenology as well as the novel way we used this framing impelled us to create a rather text-heavy annotated portfolio; although we had initially anticipated it to be more visual. We see an opportunity for future work to engage with the theoretical foundation and language we have laid out in a more visual way.

CONCLUSION

In this paper, we have offered an account of postphenomenological commitments and concepts through an annotated portfolio describing and articulating how they are expressed across a number of RtD artifact inquiries. Our goal was to advance the idea of seeing the empirical efforts of research products as an *experimental way of doing postphenomenology* or in other words *doing philosophy through things* by making this theoretical framework more intelligible and actionable to other HCI researchers. Particularly, the utilization of annotated portfolios enabled a concrete way of showing conceptual themes that we found could be scalable to HCI research. As a result, these philosophical concepts can be better leveraged in future HCI research inquires, particularly with attention to forming a deeper understanding of people's "interactions" with technology and looking beyond human-centeredness. Moreover, the demonstrated value of postphenomenology advances HCI particularly in the way it speaks to the understanding, discussions, and positioning of RtD and more generally human-technology relation studies.

ACKNOWLEDGEMENTS

We thank all the design researchers for allowing us to use their images of their projects, William Odom for his comments and help with editing, and our reviewers for their comments. This research was funded by SSHRC and NSERC.

REFERENCES

1. Kirk Besmer. 2012. Embodying a Translation Technology: The Cochlear Implant and Cyborg Intentionality. *Techné: Research in Philosophy and Technology* 16, 3: 296–316. https://doi.org/10.5840/techne20121 6319
2. Albert Borgmann. 1984. *Technology and the character of contemporary life: a philosophical inquiry*. University of Chicago Press, Chicago.
3. Andy Boucher. 2016. The Form Design of the Datacatcher: A Research Prototype In *Proceedings of the 2016 ACM Conference on Designing Interactive Systems* (DIS '16), 595–606. https://doi.org/10.1145/2901790.2901907
4. Andy Boucher and William Gaver. 2017. Designing and Making the Datacatchers: Batch Producing Location-Aware Mobile Devices. In *Proceedings of the Eleventh International Conference on Tangible, Embedded, and Embodied Interaction* (TEI '17), 243–251. https://doi.org/10.1145/3024969.3024971
5. John Bowers. 2012. The Logic of Annotated Portfolios: Communicating the Value of "Research Through Design." In *Proceedings of the Designing Interactive Systems Conference* (DIS '12), 68–77. https://doi.org/10.1145/2317956.2317968
6. David Cameron, Nadine Jarvis, and Andy Boucher. 2014. Designing Deployment: a visual paper of the batch deployment of research prototypes. In *Proceedings of DRS 2014: Design's Big Debates*. Retrieved from http://www.drs2014.org/en/presentations/252/
7. Paul Dourish. 2001. *Where the action is: the foundations of embodied interaction*. MIT Press, Cambridge, Mass.
8. Daniel Fallman. 2011. The New Good: Exploring the Potential of Philosophy of Technology to Contribute to Human-computer Interaction. In *Proceedings of the SIGCHI Conference on Human Factors in Computing Systems* (CHI '11), 1051–1060. https://doi.org/10.1145/1978942.1979099
9. Bill Gaver and John Bowers. 2012. Annotated portfolios. *interactions* 19, 4: 40–49. https://doi.org/10.1145/2212877.2212889
10. William Gaver, Andy Boucher, Nadine Jarvis, David Cameron, Mark Hauenstein, Sarah Pennington, John Bowers, James Pike, Robin Beitra, and Liliana Ovalle. 2016. The Datacatcher: Batch Deployment and Documentation of 130 Location-Aware, Mobile Devices That Put Sociopolitically-Relevant Big Data in People's Hands: Polyphonic Interpretation at Scale. In *Proceedings of the 2016 CHI Conference on Human Factors in Computing Systems* (CHI '16), 1597–1607. https://doi.org/10.1145/2858036.2858472
11. William W. Gaver, John Bowers, Kirsten Boehner, Andy Boucher, David W.T. Cameron, Mark Hauenstein, Nadine Jarvis, and Sarah Pennington. 2013. Indoor Weather Stations: Investigating a Ludic Approach to Environmental HCI Through Batch Prototyping. In *Proceedings of the SIGCHI Conference on Human Factors in Computing Systems* (CHI '13), 3451–3460. https://doi.org/10.1145/2470654.2466474
12. William W. Gaver, John Bowers, Andrew Boucher, Hans Gellerson, Sarah Pennington, Albrecht Schmidt, Anthony Steed, Nicholas Villars, and Brendan Walker. 2004. The Drift Table: Designing for Ludic Engagement. In *CHI '04 Extended Abstracts on Human Factors in Computing Systems* (CHI EA '04), 885–900. https://doi.org/10.1145/985921.985947
13. Lars Hallnäs and Johan Redström. 2001. Slow Technology – Designing for Reflection. *Personal and Ubiquitous Computing* 5, 3: 201–212. https://doi.org/10.1007/PL00000019
14. Sabrina Hauser, Ron Wakkary, William Odom, Peter-Paul Verbeek, Audrey Desjardins, Henry Lin, Matthew Dalton, Markus Schilling, and Gijs De Boer. 2018. Deployments of the table-non-table: A Reflection on the Relation Between Theory and Things in the Practice of Design Research. In *Proceedings of the SIGCHI Conference on Human Factors in Computing Systems (CHI '18). In Press.*
15. Kristina Höök and Jonas Löwgren. 2012. Strong concepts: Intermediate-level knowledge in interaction design research. *ACM Trans. Comput.-Hum. Interact.* 19, 3: 23:1–23:18. https://doi.org/10.1145/2362364.2362371
16. Don Ihde. 1979. *Technics and praxis*. Reidel, Dordrecht.
17. Don Ihde. 1990. *Technology and the lifeworld: from garden to earth*. Indiana University Press, Bloomington.
18. Don Ihde. 1993. *Philosophy of Technology: An Introduction*. Paragon House Publishers, New York, NY, USA.
19. Don Ihde. 1995. *Postphenomenology: Essays in the Postmodern Context*. Northwestern University Press.
20. Don Ihde. 2007. *Listening and voice: phenomenologies of sound*. State University of New York Press, Albany.
21. Don Ihde. 2008. *Ironic Technics*. Automatic Press/ VIP, Kopenhagen.
22. Nadine Jarvis, David Cameron, and Andy Boucher. 2012. Attention to detail: annotations of a design process. In *Proceedings of the 7th Nordic Conference on Human-Computer Interaction: Making Sense Through Design*, 11–20. https://doi.org/10.1145/2399016.2399019
23. Tom Jenkins, Kristina Andersen, William Gaver, William Odom, James Pierce, and Anna Vallg\a arda. 2016. Attending to Objects As Outcomes of Design Research. In *Proceedings of the 2016 CHI Conference Extended Abstracts on Human Factors in Computing*

Systems (CHI EA '16), 3423–3430. https://doi.org/10.1145/2851581.2856508

24. Ilpo Koskinen, John Zimmerman, Thomas Binder, Johan Redstrom, and Stephan Wensveen. 2011. *Design Research Through Practice: From the Lab, Field, and Showroom*. Morgan Kaufmann, Waltham, MA.
25. Jonas Löwgren. 2013. Annotated portfolios and other forms of intermediate-level knowledge. *interactions* 20, 1: 30–34. https://doi.org/10.1145/2405716.2405725
26. Angella Mackey, Ron Wakkary, Stephan Wensveen, and Oscar Tomico. 2017. "Can I Wear This?" Blending Clothing and Digital Expression by Wearing Dynamic Fabric. *International Journal of Design* 11, 3: 51–65.
27. Angella Mackey, Ron Wakkary, Stephan Wensveen, Oscar Tomico, and Bart Hengeveld. 2017. Day-to-Day Speculation: Designing and Wearing Dynamic Fabric. In *Proceedings of the 3rd Biennial Research Through Design Conference*, 438–454. https://doi.org/DOI: 10.6084/m9.figshare.4747018.
28. John McCarthy and Peter Wright. 2004. *Technology as experience*. MIT Press, Cambridge, Mass.
29. Harold G. Nelson and Erik Stolterman. 2012. *The Design Way: Intentional Change in an Unpredictable World*. The MIT Press.
30. William Odom, James Pierce, Erik Stolterman, and Eli Blevis. 2009. Understanding why we preserve some things and discard others in the context of interaction design. In *Proceedings of the SIGCHI Conference on Human Factors in Computing Systems (CHI'09)*, 1053–1062. https://doi.org/10.1145/1518701.1518862
31. William Odom, Mark Selby, Abigail Sellen, David Kirk, Richard Banks, and Tim Regan. 2012. Photobox: on the design of a slow technology. In *Proceedings of the Designing Interactive Systems Conference (DIS '12)*, 665–668. https://doi.org/10.1145/2317956.2318055
32. William T. Odom, Abigail J. Sellen, Richard Banks, David S. Kirk, Tim Regan, Mark Selby, Jodi L. Forlizzi, and John Zimmerman. 2014. Designing for Slowness, Anticipation and Re-visitation: A Long Term Field Study of the Photobox. In *Proceedings of the 32Nd Annual ACM Conference on Human Factors in Computing Systems* (CHI '14), 1961–1970. https://doi.org/10.1145/2556288.2557178
33. William Odom and Ron Wakkary. 2015. Intersecting with Unaware Objects. In *Proceedings of the 2015 ACM SIGCHI Conference on Creativity and Cognition* (C&C '15), 33–42. https://doi.org/10.1145/2757226.2757240
34. William Odom, Ron Wakkary, Youn-kyung Lim, Audrey Desjardins, Bart Hengeveld, and Richard Banks. 2016. From Research Prototype to Research Product. In *Proceedings of the 2016 CHI Conference on Human Factors in Computing Systems* (CHI '16), 2549–2561. https://doi.org/10.1145/2858036.2858447
35. Fredrik Ohlin and Carl Magnus Olsson. 2015. Beyond a Utility View of Personal Informatics: A Postphenomenological Framework. In *Adjunct Proceedings of the 2015 ACM International Joint Conference on Pervasive and Ubiquitous Computing and Proceedings of the 2015 ACM International Symposium on Wearable Computers* (UbiComp/ISWC'15 Adjunct), 1087–1092. https://doi.org/10.1145/2800835.2800965
36. Doenja Oogjes and Ron Wakkary. 2017. Videos of Things: Speculating on, Anticipating and Synthesizing Technological Mediations. In *Proceedings of the 2017 CHI Conference on Human Factors in Computing Systems*, 4489–4500. Retrieved June 7, 2017 from http://dl.acm.org/citation.cfm?id=3025748
37. James Pierce. 2012. Undesigning Technology: Considering the Negation of Design by Design. In *Proceedings of the SIGCHI Conference on Human Factors in Computing Systems* (CHI '12), 957–966. https://doi.org/10.1145/2207676.2208540
38. James Pierce. 2014. On the Presentation and Production of Design Research Artifacts in HCI. In *Proceedings of the 2014 Conference on Designing Interactive Systems* (DIS '14), 735–744. https://doi.org/10.1145/2598510.2598525
39. James Pierce. 2014. Working by Not Quite Working: Designing Resistant Interactive Proposals, Prototypes, and Products. Carnegie Mellon University, Human-Computer Interaction Institute, School of Computer Science.
40. James Pierce and Eric Paulos. 2011. A Phenomenology of Human-electricity Relations. In *Proceedings of the SIGCHI Conference on Human Factors in Computing Systems* (CHI '11), 2405–2408. https://doi.org/10.1145/1978942.1979293
41. James Pierce and Eric Paulos. 2013. Electric Materialities and Interactive Technology. In *Proceedings of the SIGCHI Conference on Human Factors in Computing Systems* (CHI '13), 119–128. https://doi.org/10.1145/2470654.2470672
42. James Pierce and Eric Paulos. 2014. Counterfunctional things: exploring possibilities in designing digital limitations. In *Proceedings of the 2014 Conference on Designing Interactive Systems (DIS 2014)*, 375–384. https://doi.org/10.1145/2598510.2598522
43. James Pierce and Eric Paulos. 2015. Obscura 1C Digital Camera. In *Proceedings of the 2nd Biennial Research Through Design Conference*, Article 6. https://doi.org/DOI: 10.6084/m9.figshare.1328005
44. James Pierce and Eric Paulos. 2015. Making Multiple Uses of the Obscura 1C Digital Camera: Reflecting on the Design, Production, Packaging and Distribution of a Counterfunctional Device. In *Proceedings of the 33rd Annual ACM Conference on Human Factors in*

Computing Systems, 2103–2112. https://doi.org/10.1145/2702123.2702405

45. Robert Rosenberger. 2009. The Sudden Experience of the Computer. *AI Soc.* 24, 2: 173–180. https://doi.org/10.1007/s00146-009-0190-9
46. Robert Rosenberger. 2012. Embodied technology and the dangers of using the phone while driving. *Phenomenology and the Cognitive Sciences* 11, 1: 79–94. https://doi.org/10.1007/s11097-011-9230-2
47. Robert Rosenberger. 2014. Multistability and the Agency of Mundane Artifacts: from Speed Bumps to Subway Benches. *Human Studies* 37, 3: 369–392. https://doi.org/10.1007/s10746-014-9317-1
48. Robert Rosenberger. 2017. *Callous objects: designs against the homeless*. Univ Of Minnesota Press.
49. Robert Rosenberger. 2018. Personal communication.
50. Robert Rosenberger and Peter-Paul Verbeek. 2015. A Field Guide to Postphenomenology In *Postphenomenological investigations: essays on human-technology relations*, Robert Rosenberger and Peter-Paul Verbeek (eds.). Lexington Books, Lanham, 9–41.
51. Robert Rosenberger and Peter-Paul Verbeek. 2015. *Postphenomenological Investigations: Essays on Human–Technology Relations*. Lexington Books.
52. Evan Selinger (ed.). 2006. *Postphenomenology: A Critical Companion to Ihde*. State University of New York Press, Albany.
53. Phoebe Sengers and Bill Gaver. 2006. Staying Open to Interpretation: Engaging Multiple Meanings in Design and Evaluation. In *Proceedings of the 6th Conference on Designing Interactive Systems* (DIS '06), 99–108. https://doi.org/10.1145/1142405.1142422
54. Erik Stolterman and Mikael Wiberg. 2010. Concept-Driven Interaction Design Research. *Human–Computer Interaction* 25, 2: 95–118. https://doi.org/10.1080/07370020903586696
55. Nynke Tromp, Paul Hekkert, and Peter-Paul Verbeek. 2011. Design for Socially Responsible Behavior: A Classification of Influence Based on Intended User Experience. *Design Issues* 27, 3: 3–19. https://doi.org/10.1162/DESI_a_00087
56. Peter-Paul Verbeek. 2005. *What Things Do: Philosophical Reflections on Technology, Agency, and Design*. Penn State Press.
57. Peter-Paul Verbeek. 2008. Obstetric Ultrasound and the Technological Mediation of Morality: A Postphenomenological Analysis. *Human Studies* 31, 1: 11–26. https://doi.org/10.1007/s10746-007-9079-0
58. Peter-Paul Verbeek. 2008. Cyborg intentionality: Rethinking the phenomenology of human–technology relations. *Phenomenology and the Cognitive Sciences* 7, 3: 387–395. https://doi.org/10.1007/s11097-008-9099-x
59. Peter-Paul Verbeek. 2011. *Moralizing technology: understanding and designing the morality of things*. The University of Chicago Press, Chicago ; London.
60. Peter-Paul Verbeek and Petran Kockelkoren. 1998. The things that matter. *Design Issues* 14, 3: 28–42.
61. Ron Wakkary. 2005. Framing complexity, design and experience: A reflective analysis. *Digital Creativity - DIGIT CREAT* 16, 2: 65–78.
62. Ron Wakkary, Audrey Desjardins, and Sabrina Hauser. 2015. Unselfconscious Interaction: A Conceptual Construct. *Interacting with Computers* 28, 4: 501–520. https://doi.org/10.1093/iwc/iwv018
63. Ron Wakkary and Leah Maestri. 2007. The Resourcefulness of Everyday Design. In *Proceedings of the 6th ACM SIGCHI Conference on Creativity & Cognition* (C&C '07), 163–172. https://doi.org/10.1145/1254960.1254984
64. Ron Wakkary, William Odom, Sabrina Hauser, Garnet Hertz, and Henry Lin. 2015. Material Speculation: Actual Artifacts for Critical Inquiry. *Aarhus Series on Human Centered Computing* 1, 1: 12. https://doi.org/10.7146/aahcc.v1i1.21299
65. Ron Wakkary, Doenja Oogjes, Sabrina Hauser, Henry Lin, Cheng Cao, Leo Ma, and Tijs Duel. 2017. Morse Things: A Design Inquiry into the Gap Between Things and Us. In *Proceedings of the 2017 Conference on Designing Interactive Systems* (DIS '17), 503–514. https://doi.org/10.1145/3064663.3064734
66. Ron Wakkary, Doenja Oogjes, Henry Lin, and Sabrina Hauser. 2018. Philosophers Living with the Tilting Bowl. In *Proceedings of the SIGCHI Conference on Human Factors in Computing Systems (CHI '18). In Press.*
67. Galit P. Wellner. 2016. *A postphenomenological inquiry of cell phones: genealogies, meanings, and becoming*. Lexington Books, Lanham.
68. Heather Wiltse and Erik Stolterman. 2010. Architectures of Interaction: An Architectural Perspective on Digital Experience. In *Proceedings of the 6th Nordic Conference on Human-Computer Interaction: Extending Boundaries* (NordiCHI '10), 821–824. https://doi.org/10.1145/1868914.1869038
69. Langdon Winner. 1986. Do Artifacts Have Politics? In *The whale and the reactor: a search for limits in an age of high technology* (Nachdr.). Univ. of Chicago Press, Chicago, 19–39.
70. Interaction Research Studio, Goldsmiths, University of London. *Goldsmiths, University of London*. Retrieved January 4, 2018 from https://www.gold.ac.uk/interaction/
71. Everyday Design Studio, School of Interactive Arts & Technology at Simon Fraser University. Retrieved January 4, 2018 from http://eds.siat.sfu.ca/

Understanding Craft-Based Inquiry in HCI

Raune Frankjaer
Aarhus University
Aarhus, Denmark
frankjaer@cc.au.dk

Peter Dalsgaard
Aarhus University
Aarhus, Denmark
dalsgaard@cavi.au.dk

ABSTRACT
Over the last decade, a number of craft-based approaches to research have emerged within the field of Human-Computer Interaction (HCI). In this paper, we examine the roots of crafting as they apply to these approaches, which blend analog crafts with digital technology, and we outline three defining characteristics: the integration of analog and digital crafting processes, the creation of highly refined products, and the creation of a deep and embodied knowledge. Moreover, we demonstrate how Richard Sennett's tripartite deconstruction of the crafting process can be applied to support analysis of the types and processes of knowledge generated in craft-based approaches to HCI.

Author Keywords
Hybrid Craft; Digital Craft; Technocraft; Tangible Computing; Wearable Computing; Human-Computer-Interaction; Research Methodology; Knowledge Creation; Craft; Craft-based research.

ACM Classification Keywords
H.5.m. Information interfaces and presentation (e.g., HCI): Miscellaneous.

INTRODUCTION
Recent years have seen a growing interest in craft-based approaches within research in the design and use of interactive systems. Craft-based approaches offer new ways of thinking about both the process and outcomes of research and design. They resonate with the overarching topic of diversity at this year's DIS conference by expanding the field in terms of understanding of what digital artifacts are and could be, how these artifacts are perceived and put into use, and how we create new insights and knowledge. These approaches represent an emergent and evolving field, and as of yet we do not have a clear overview of the field, neither a common language for presenting and discussing the different strands that form the field.

DIS '18, June 9–13, 2018, Hong Kong

ACM ISBN 978-1-4503-5198-0/18/06…$15.00
https://doi.org/10.1145/3196709.3196750

While there is a growing appreciation of novel, craft-based approaches, there are therefore also ongoing discussions about which practices constitute the field, which types of knowledge are generated through them, how they fit into research on designing interactive systems, how they fit into pre-existing paradigms of inquiry, and by which standards should we evaluate them.

To move towards a better understanding of these approaches and the potentials they hold for research into Human-Computer Interaction (HCI), we address two interrelated research questions in this paper:

1) What are the defining characteristics of craft-based inquiry in HCI?

2) How can we understand and analyze the types and processes of knowledge creation that they entail?

To address these questions, our objective is to first offer an overview of craft-based approaches to designing interactive systems, and to identify their key characteristics. We demonstrate that insights from craft research [1, 15, 28, 33, 43, 57], with a particular focus on Richard Sennett's work on crafting and his tripartite deconstruction of the crafting process into questioning, localizing and opening [57], can form the basis for understanding knowledge generation through craft-based HCI. We argue that craft research has much to offer in terms of understanding digital craft-based approaches in HCI, since this field has historically had a strong focus on the interrelation between the crafting process and knowledge production. For instance, Nimkulrat asserts that craft is a way of thinking through the senses, a method of knowing which is deeply entangled with the crafting process: "craft practice in a research context can facilitate the reflection and articulation of knowledge generated from within the researcher-practitioner's artistic experience" [43]. For Adamson crafting is "a way of thinking through practices of all kinds" [1 p.7], whereas Gray and Burnett defines crafting as "a dynamic process of learning and understanding through material experience" [28 p.51], and Sennett describes how "thinking and feeling are contained within the process of making" [57 p.7].

The intended audience of the paper is twofold. Firstly, researchers and practitioners who integrate craft-based approaches in their work, for whom both the overview of the field and the deeper understanding of the epistemic value of these processes as modes of inquiry may be of value. Secondly, researchers engaged in the ongoing debate about forms of knowledge and knowledge generation in HCI, e.g. [22, 30, 67]. We consider our work here an open invitation to the community to develop the discourse on craft-based approaches to knowledge creation in HCI.

STRUCTURE OF THE PAPER

Our main objective is to examine and articulate knowledge creation that result from emergent craft-based approaches to HCI research. To position and frame our work, we first offer an overview of the literature on craft-based approaches in HCI, namely Hybrid, Digital, Computational and Technocraft. We then identify and analyze the distinguishing traits of craft-based research in HCI through an array of examples from the existing literature from the field, supported by observational studies and interviews of practitioners engaging in these practices. Since craft approaches in HCI research are relatively new phenomena, there are yet no integrative frameworks by which to analyze their knowledge generation processes and outcomes. However, the realm of traditional craft research examines these issues [1, 57]. We therefore use craft research to understand these modes of inquiry. Here we in particular found Sennett's tripartite deconstruction of the crafting process fruitful for achieving a deeper understanding of the value of crafting processes within HCI. We therefore extend the three core components of Sennett's deconstruction of *localization, questioning*, and *opening,* into three guiding questions for evaluating craft-based research inquiries in HCI. We subsequently use these questions to analyze three examples of craft-based HCI research, the *Bamboo Whisper* by Flanagan and Frankjaer, *Stiching Worlds*, by Kurbak and Posch and the *Hamefarers Kist* by White. We have chosen these examples due to a) their diversity, representing a wide range of craft-based approaches to HCI, and b) the availability of the authors' descriptions of their creative processes, which are necessary for the particular forms of in-depth analysis we carry out in this paper.

We consider this a contribution to the ongoing discussion in the HCI community to explore if and how design-oriented research approaches can contribute to academic knowledge generation. This is evident in the emergence and development of e.g. Research through Design [68] as a legitimate research approach, and of novel formats for representing and communicating research outcomes, e.g. in the shape of Pictorials [9]. However, as pointed out by several recent contributions e.g. [3, 16, 26] many central issues regarding designerly knowledge production in HCI are still contested and not fully developed. In this light, we will end the paper with a discussion on how craft-based approaches provides opportunities to explore novel forms of knowledge creation within HCI.

BACKGROUND: HYBRID, DIGITAL, COMPUTATIONAL AND TECHNOCRAFT

Several definitions have been attempted in this nascent field, which spans a wide range of practices from digitally assisted design of physical artifacts [9, 33, 46, 52], fashioning of computational physical artifacts and materials using traditional craft practices [12, 33], production of digital artifacts, e.g. code [8], merging of digital and physical media and practices [27, 33, 63] as well as artifacts emerging from within Maker and DIY culture [3, 53]. Terms such as Hybrid Craft, Digital Craft, Technocraft, and Computational Craft are used to describe this somewhat fuzzy area often used interchangeably, sometimes describing distinct areas. The ambiguity in HCI of what precisely constitutes Hybrid, Digital, Technocraft or Computational Craft, seems to at least partly stem from discrepancies of the definition of craft itself, which is at times interpreted as denoting traditional, i.e. pre-industrial fabrication methods [12], sometimes as signifying any kind of physical making, extending to simple manipulation and reassembling of physical objects [27], application of software in the fabrication process [46], to constituting a particular methodological approach and way of thinking in a creative context [23]. These discrepancies also mean that it is hard to establish a common frame of reference. We are well aware of the heavy female bias in the field, the analysis of which lies outside the scope of this paper, as our focus here lies with the possibilities for knowledge creation inherent in craft-based processes within HCI.

Hybrid Craft

Golsteijn, van den Hoven, Frohlich and Seller define Hybrid Crafting as "everyday creative practices of using combinations of physical and digital materials, techniques or tools, to make interactive physical-digital creations" [27]. In spite of the broadly encompassing definition the authors' focus lies with the incorporation of digital audio-visual media, e.g. movie, image, and audio files into interactive physical constructions, where craft denotes "making [anything] which is novel in that context" [27]. Buechley and Perner-Wilson use the term Hybrid Craft as denoting the integration of electronics with traditional, low-tech crafts in what they describe as Blended Practices, e.g. painting. One of their many projects, the Living Wall can be seen in fig. 1a. Buechley and Perner-Wilson place great importance on the activity of constructive making of electronics framed specifically within a certain craft context. Different craft methods and their inherent materials provide different affordances, which shape the expression and construction of the technology, diversifying not just the possible outcomes within the crafts themselves, but also the types of engaging with practitioners and public reach [12].

Digital Craft

Another prominent term, Digital Craft, is generally applied to denote the design and fabrication of physical artifacts by the use of digital tools, such as CAD, digital clay, 3D printing and CNC laser cutting, as shown in fig 1b. These tools merge the traditionally distinct practices of design generation and fabrication. In this context crafting signifies material selection, fabrication methods and assembly logic, not the fabrication process in itself [46]. Similar use of Digital Crafting can be observed coming from within traditional craft practice when embracing the use of digital tools [13]. In contrast, Nitsche et al., discussing approaches

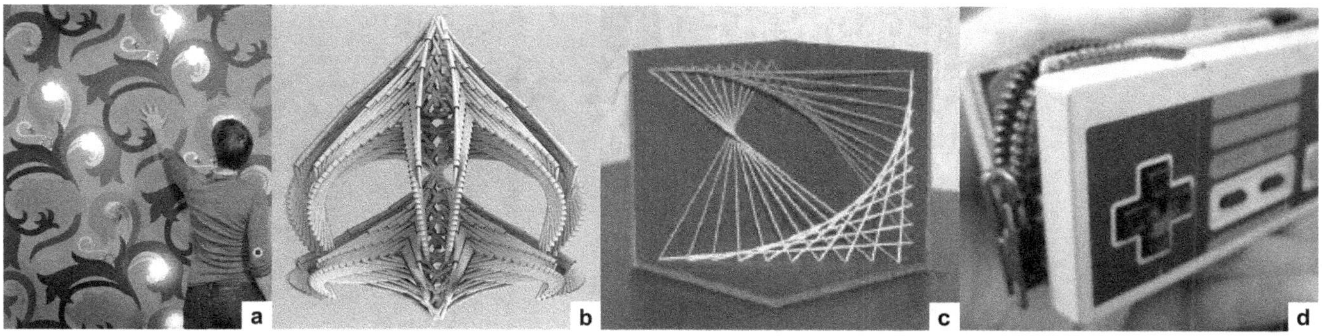

Figure 1. Hybrid, Digital, Computational and Technocraft, image examples from a.[12] ©Leah Buechley, b.[46] ©Neri Oxman, c.[8] ©Glenn Blauvelt, d. [24] ©Zenilorac. The various terms are often used interchangeably, with divergent definitions.

within university and design school curricula to Digital Craft, define it as the combination of digital media, physical computing, and traditional craft approaches [44]. Jacobs et al. apply the term Digital Craftsmanship very broadly, encompassing computer-aided design, electronic crafts, procedural design, and hybrid human-computer digital fabrication [33]. Exploring digital fabrication methods in the production of ceramics, Rosner, Ikemiya and Regan use Hybrid Craft and Digital Craft interchangeably as the use of computational resources within and around traditional modes of craft activity [53]. Likewise working with ceramics and digital fabrication techniques, Zoran and Buechley, explore the inherent incompatibilities and possibilities of crafts and digital fabrication around the notion of artifact uniqueness. Here the authors suggest the notion of Hybrid Reassemblage, i.e. repairing broken handcrafted artifacts with 3D printing techniques [69].

Computational Craft

Blauvelt, Wrench and Eisenberg use the term Computational Crafts to describe the then nascent field, exemplified with computer generated patterns for realizing handcrafts as seen in fig. 1c., but also recognize the notion of Computational Crafting to suggest a certain way of approaching immaterial computational production [8], as explored thoroughly by McCullough in [41], representative of the general understanding of Computational Craft in HCI today. In contrast, Vallgårda and Redström speak of Computational Composites, referring to combining physical and digital materials [63], albeit not necessarily in a craft-based context.

Technocraft

The term Technocraft, emerges from craft practice with relations to Maker culture, taken loosely to mean a crafting approach to digital technology, i.e. crafting with technological objects, e.g. repurposing old gaming console controllers, as seen in fig. 1d., or integrating craft with digital technology [4, 24, 37, 58, 64]. At first glance, this usage reflects common understandings of technology as something of a modern or contemporary nature, usually electrified and/or digital, and craft as analog and preindustrial applied practices. We are however somewhat partial to the notion of Technocraft, due to its allusion to the word technê, the etymological stem of technology. Although often translated to mean mere skill or craft, technê is not merely applied practice, but denotes a state were knowing and making are inextricably linked. Techné reveals the ontological status of a thing through the disclosure of its epistemic value [25 p.23]. The focus on process, skill and knowledge as inseparable components as part of craft practice is what we explore in this paper, more so than referring to the involved materialities, i.e. analog/digital/hybrid, or a particular material outcome, such as the creation of novel products. As Hamilton notes in a response to Nitsche et al. in Teaching digital craft "[the] focus on creating alternative input devices or output devices points to a narrow definition of craft [that] fits well with current cultural pre-occupations with small-scale production, but not with the larger, much older questions about craft as a matter of process, epistemology, and conversation between form and content" [Hamilton in 44].

METHODOLOGY

To arrive at a coherent understanding of craft-based research approaches to enquiry in HCI, we have carried out a situational analysis mapping [16] of 1) examples of craft-based research, 2) observational studies of the work processes of the Connected Textiles research group which is part of the Design Research Lab at the Berlin University of the Arts, in the area of e-textiles and smart clothing, and 3) semi structured interviews with an array of experts within electronic textiles and wearable technology. Situational Analysis creates analytic maps of heterogeneous data by using principles from grounded theory, where analysis, coding, and memo writing begin at the same time as data collection. Theoretical sampling then guides further data collection. As a qualitative method, in Situational Analysis the researcher is seen as a 'research instrument' [16 p.85], hence, the resulting analysis is strongly reflexive and informed by a number of different types of data. Our analysis resulted in three main characteristics: *1. Combining, aligning, and integrating analog and digital crafting techniques and processes. 2. Creating highly*

Figure 2. Illustrating the three characteristics from 1 -3. a. Various handcrafted circuit samples by Perner-Wilson exploring an array of materials and crafting techniques ©Raune Frankjaer, b. Krakow, a color changing printed tapestry ©XS Labs, c. Frankjaer in the process of crafting the Bamboo Whisper ©Nick Ashby.

refined artifacts, defined by attention to detail and aesthetics. 3. Creating knowledge through deep, embodied engagement. We then examined these three characteristics through theoretical sampling, i.e. observations and further readings. We will describe our analysis in more detail below, keeping in mind that due to the intertwined nature of these practices the characteristics are closely interrelated, e.g. the integration of analogue and digital crafting techniques both influences, and is in turn influenced by, the creation of knowledge through embodied engagement, which again is both result and driver of the creation of highly refined artifacts.

At this point we wish to stress that we do not see our work here as exhaustive, but rather as proposing common definitions and methods of analysis for furthering research in this field.

THREE CHARACTERISTICS OF CRAFT-BASED RESEARCH IN HCI

1. Combining, aligning, and integrating analog and digital crafting techniques and processes

Crafting in HCI can be understood as an extension of traditional crafting, in which novel techniques and processes for shaping digital technologies, i.e. embedding digital abilities into physical materials, are integrated into the creative process as means of exploration and expression. This area has been thoroughly covered by several practitioners, in particular in some of the early explorative works, of which many grew out of the MIT research Group High-Low Tech led by Buechley. Initially a response to the cumbersome, fragile and uncomfortable devices of 1990s wearable computing, as well as a way of transcending seemingly antithetical, juxtaposed worlds, such as fabrics, stereotyped as handcrafted, decorative and feminine, and computer technology, seen as mass-produced, functional, and masculine, HCI researchers such as Berzowska and Orth, began integrating traditional fiber-technology into their work [6, 7, 45, 51, 65]. Researchers such as Buechley, Pernier-Wilson and Satomi have extensively explored a wide array of analog materials including textiles, wood, paper, paints and gold, even seashells, as well as a plethora of techniques such as carving, sewing, embroidering, knitting, drawing, crochet, painting, hand-printing, and origami [10-12, 48], examples of which can be seen in fig. 2a. Here the goals are wider than material exploration and extend into the cultural and social. Blending digital technology with traditional craft fosters diversity on a number of levels, and is seen as an approach, which provides a unique and promising way to increase technological literacy and broaden technology culture, in addition to developing new kinds of devices. Expanding and diversifying the processes that are used to build electronics, naturally expands and diversifies the electronics which are created and the communities of people who build them [12]. Craft is not merely a method of working, a set of fabrication techniques but a way of thinking about and understanding the material landscape on a very intimate and refined level, which does not stop at material boundaries but transcends into computational logic. As Adamson and Csikszentmihalyi have noted, another distinct trait of craft is the small-scale undivided fabrication process [1, 18], i.e. the crafter is in control of all the elements of the process through which a given artifact is created, if not directly then through close cooperation with others. The work in the Connected Textiles research group is characterized by a remarkably low division of labor, where the designer-researchers perform tasks such as crafting, programming, inventing use scenarios, debugging electric circuits, creating analogies, searching for images online, mashing up different ideas in sketches, creating various types of models etc. on a daily basis, offering a rare opportunity to study the same actors working on very different problems, with entirely different means of work within the same project [34]. It also enables the crafting researcher to explore the meanings and aesthetics of the interaction through a unified vision even though the practitioner may not always be conscious or appreciative hereof. During one of our observations of the Connected Textiles research group, one of the groups' leaders was working with a small group of researchers on a capacitive carpet for a smart home exhibit, and almost apologetically explained they had to hand weave the sample as they did not have enough time to "have it made properly". During an interview, another researcher explained how handcrafting practice often constituted a pragmatic choice, due to production tools not being accessible or viable in small scale productions.

2. Creating highly refined objects, defined by attention to detail and aesthetics

In Sennett's view, craft enables the expression of an innate creative urge, which drives the crafter to produce the best possible work by providing the practitioner with a profound feeling of satisfaction when producing quality results [57], furthermore craft traditionally places great importance on the finish of the crafted artifact, with quality and individuality constituting two of its hallmarks [13]. Whilst this urge to perfection, may also constitute an impulse for researchers who adopt craft-based approaches to inquiry, we propose that there may be other important factors at play in explaining the researchers' choice in producing such elaborate prototypes. One of the experts, a sociologist who has studied the Connected Textiles research group extensively, deduced their practice of producing elaborately crafted products, to three main factors, 1. 'Handwerker Stolz' (eng.: crafter's pride), which relates to Sennett's notion of the desire to do a job well for its own sake, 2. developing and experiencing haptic objects being a very bodily process, 3. majority of the researchers having a background in fashion and textiles, where this is "just how they are trained". In contrast objects fashioned within HCI research are often prototypes rapidly produced as means to an end, with little regard to pleasing aesthetics or haptic. Lim et al. refer to this as the economic principle of prototyping, defined as "the best prototype is one that, in the simplest and most efficient way, makes the possibilities and limitations of a design idea visible and measurable" [40]. Going counter to the economic principle of prototyping, craft-based inquiry often produces elaborate objects, resembling works of art or finished products, e.g. the color-changing wall-hanging by Berzowska seen in fig. 2b. Characterized by their integration of materials with diverse properties, this can be seen as the explicit outcome of these approaches and in most cases, constitutes the main focus of the researchers' academic contributions and has been extensively covered elsewhere, e.g. [2, 5, 6, 45, 51].

3. Creating knowledge through deep, embodied engagement

Crafting is a mode of inquiry that generates knowledge as an intrinsic outcome through deep, embodied engagement. The emergence of craft-based modes of inquiry in HCI raises questions of whether this practice of high level attention to detail and application of developed skills and laborious practice, stems from a mindset inherent to the practitioners, or arises out of the agency of the applied materials, e.g. as in fig. 2c. where Frankjaer is in the process of crafting and programming the Bamboo Whisper. In their work on Hybrid Craft, Buechley and Perner-Wilson write that in contrast to the traditional crafters, the electronics makers were the only group in their study, which did not mention aesthetic nor meditative qualities as a characterizing part of their practice, in their survey results [12]. Similarly, Nitsche et al. note the 'taken for grantedness' of the aspect of material construction of physical computing in academia, resulting in "numerous Arduino classes but a gaping absence of courses on welding, pottery, or woodworking" [44]. Carter offers the concept of Material Thinking, where materials are active components in creative processes. They interact with the maker's artistic intelligence when his or her hands, mind, and eyes are connected in a creative process [15]. Posited outside the limitations of linguistics and reasoning, the creative practitioner must be attuned to an aesthetic awareness and refined perceptional sensing ability, articulated through material affordances, which facilitate comprehension and knowledge transfer inaccessible through discursive methods [26]. In a 2016 TEDx talk, Papadopoulos refers to this as the "synesthetic materiality of ideas" and explains how, as her work evolved, as she "kept weaving technology in ideas and ideas in technology", she realized that the very act of making, translating ideas into wearable artifacts, sparked a critical conversation between what materials could do, and the shape ideas could take and became a metaphor for a whole array of profound philosophical questions, inquiring to the nature, narratives, relationships and purpose of wearable technology, humans and society [47]. This characteristic constitutes the main focus in this paper. In order to better understand the processes and outcomes of knowledge generated in craft-based inquiry, we turn to craft research, with a particular emphasis on Sennett's tripartite deconstruction of the crafting process, which we apply as a lens to unfold and understand the creation of knowledge through deep, embodied engagement within HCI as shown in fig 3.

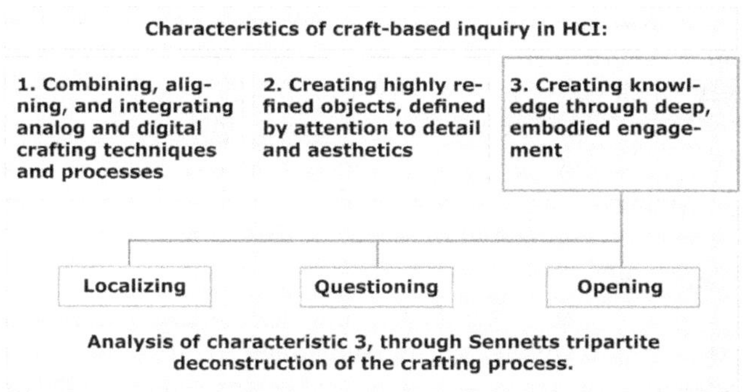

Figure 3. Analyzing characteristic no. 3, through Sennett's deconstruction of the crafting process.

UNDERSTANDING CRAFT-BASED RESEARCH IN HCI THROUGH SENNETS MODEL OF CRAFTING

Craft scholars offer numerous interpretations of the term 'craft': Risatti states that craft denotes workmanship of a refined quality [55], whereas Adamson and Csikszentmihalyi perceive a small-scale undivided fabrication process as distinctive [1, 18]. For Pye, craft is procedural and related to risk [50 p.4] and Sennett emphasizes that craft practice entails "the desire to do a job well for its own sake", which he believes to denote an innate human impulse [57 p.9]. Sennett furthermore extends the concept of craft practice to signify a condition of deep engagement, more than being bound to a particular practice. The material consciousness of the crafting practitioner, emerges from an inner curiosity of the material at hand and fuels a desire to create high quality objects, whilst striving towards ever evolving perfection [57 pp.119-120,241-242]. According to Sennett, the intimacy and dedication which characterizes the work processes of the crafter, dwell in the acts of metamorphosis and manifestation, and rests on three abilities: to localize, to question, and to open up, requiring the brain to simultaneously process visual, aural, tactile and language-symbol information [57 p.227]. As skills progress they become increasingly problem attuned, sustaining a constant dialogue between concrete practice and reflexive thought, evolving into established rhythmical thinking of problem solving and finding [11, 23]. Similar concepts can be found in the works of Schön, who, building on Dewey [20, 21] defines design as a "reflective conversation with the materials of the situation" [55]. Schön asserts that "competent practitioners usually know more than they can say" [56 p. 8] and further argues that reflection "is susceptible to a kind of rigor that is both like and unlike the rigor of scholarly research and controlled experiment" [56 p. ix]. Reflection-in-action, i.e. listening to the 'talk-back' of the situation and its materials, is at the core of 'professional artistry' where doing and thinking is seen as complementary.

In the section below, we explore the crafting process through Sennett's model of localization, questioning and opening, and relate it to processes of craft-based inquiry in HCI, with the caveat that just as with the three characteristics discussed previously, this kind of division will always be somewhat artificial due to the integration and intertwinement inherent in craft processes. Nevertheless, we have found it useful for getting a clearer understanding of how these processes unfold. Subsequently, we apply the model to three selected examples of contemporary craft-based HCI research in the section *Analyzing Craft-Based Research In HCI.*

Localization

Localization, makes a matter concrete [57 p.277]. It is the skill of identifying where something of importance is happening through the analysis of sensory input. As shown in the previous section *Understanding Craft-Based Research In HCI Through Sennett's Model Of Crafting,* localization is prompted by an inner curiosity of the material at hand by the crafting practitioner, and marks the beginning of a movement of enquiry into material properties and situational affordances [57 pp.119-120].

When practicing a craft, this thinking locates where a material, a practice, or a problem is significant [57 p.278]. The time-consuming and laborious process of a crafters skill development leads to a state of attunement to the qualities of given material, and allows the practitioner to access tacit knowledge that exists beyond the boundaries of language [49]. When crafting with digital and physical materials this means identifying when and how particular digital technologies can form a significant focal point in the creative process, which in turn requires a deep understanding of the qualities and potentials of these technologies, as well as of the analog materials in use. Humans naturally tend to focus on 'cognitive dissonances', i.e. difficulties and contradictions. These complicated experiences can be traced directly to animal behavior, consisting of the capacity to attend to a here or this, as parallel processing in the brain activates different neural circuits to establish attention. Digital technology provides many opportunities of dissonant experiences, where naturally inert materials behaves beyond its usual capabilities as computational composites [63]. Embedding the computational abilities into the physical material in the crafting process enables the researcher to intervene intuitively at a structural level of the emerging artifact and cause the composite to emerge as an integrated whole. This procedural approach of 'feeling one's way' is one of the distinctive traits of "the workmanship of risk" as Pye, defines craft, where the qualities of the emerging artifact is continuously renegotiated throughout the creation process [50 p.4]. Buchley and Zorat [69], citing Turkle and Papert [61], refer to this kind of approach as 'soft'. A Soft Approach denotes a loose framework of tools to be deployed at the discretion of the researcher, and uses concrete forms of reasoning. Theories are constructed by arranging and rearranging, negotiating and renegotiating with a set of well-known materials. The Soft Approach stands in opposition to the Hard Approach, an analytic, engineering mindset, which by default is built in to the standard tools and techniques of electronics [61]. The Hard Approach favors intellectual planning and directing a problem before initiating action. It describes that before any action is carried out a cognitive map is assembled laying out the objects, their properties and locations as well as the relations between them, in a given environment. Ingold uses the notion of Navigation as opposed to Wayfinding [31 p.219], where upon determining the current position and desired destination, the individual navigates along a plotted route to carry out the intended action.

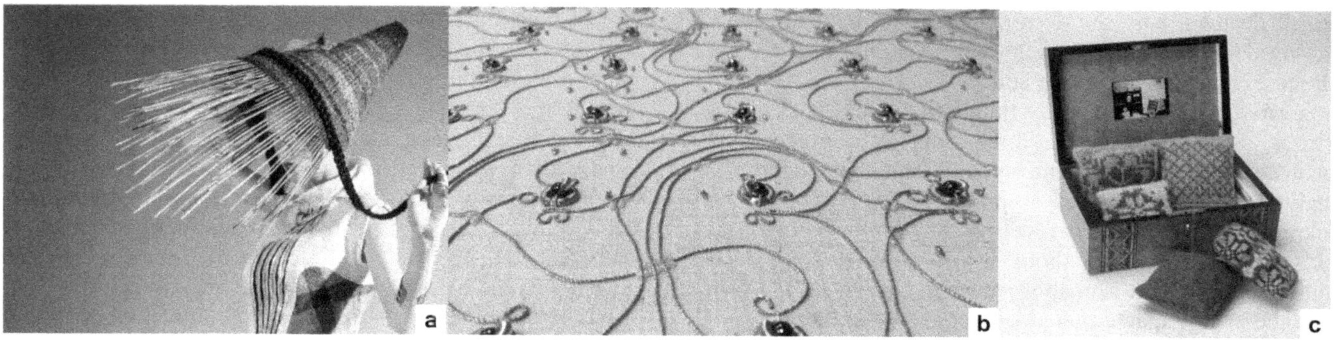

Figure 3. From a – c. The Bamboo Whisper ©Patricia Flanagan, Stitching Worlds ©Irene Posch, and the Hamefarers Kist ©Hazel White

In contrast, an adherent to a Soft Approach is more of a builder or assembler, finding their way throughout the process, i.e. localizing points of interests as they move through the material landscape.

Questioning

According to Sennett, the act of questioning reflects on the qualities of the matter at hand [56 p.277]. It arises out of the the experience of curiosity, where resolution and decision is suspended in order to probe. In the enquiring movement, the act of questioning signifies a moment of stillness, often too brief to be perceptible to an observer or even to the crafting practitioner, however this moment of reflexivity allows the crafter to compare the newly acquired sensory knowledge with existing knowledge, tacit as well as explicit. The process follows a time-based rhythm, where action leads to suspension whilst the results are questioned. Upon analysis the action resumes, now calibrated to incorporate the new knowledge. This rhythm of action-rest/question-action marks the development of complex hand skills. In contrast, mere mechanical activity, without the development of technique, is simply movement [57 p.279]. Ingold discerns between interation and iteration, illustrated as the difference between the act of hand-sawing through a wooden log and the workings of a metronome. The back-and-forth motion of the saw, although seemingly constant in its repetitions much like the ticking of a metronome, is continuously adjusted to the structure of the wood, and so the movements are never identical [32]. Questioning implies a desire to understand and according to Sennett the crafting process is a way of intellectual thinking, where touch delivers unbounded data and the eye supplies framed and contained images [57 p.152]; a view in line with Dewey's, who stresses the correlation between hands and eyes, which operate both doing, and perceiving "[a]s we manipulate, we touch and feel, as we look we see; as we listen, we hear" [19 p.51]. However, only the hands can effect changes within the material world. Tallis asserts that the simultaneously perceptive and manipulative abilities of the human hand is at the core of the evolution of human consciousness, as the "instrument of transcendence required to bring us out of nature sufficiently to manipulate it beyond the kind of manipulations that are available to animals" [60 p.324]. In a craft-based approach to inquiry within HCI, questioning moves beyond adapting a process to an inconsistent material or physical landscape, and requires knowing on the one hand how the digital technology itself can be examined and inquired into; and on the other hand, knowing how a digital technology can help the crafter examine and question other components in the creative process.

Opening

Sennett describes the capacity to opening up, or solving a problem, to draw "on intuitive leaps, specifically on its powers to draw unlike domains close to one another and to preserve tacit knowledge in the leap between them" [57 p.277]. In opening, the movement of inquiry commences, adapting and appropriating the newly gained insights into the materials at hand. Problem solving generally relies on one of two strategies. The first is analytical processing, such as the standard scientific method that is adopted in many approaches to research. Another method lies with fostering insights, a key aspect to creative thought. Phenomena such as serendipity, hunches and sudden insights are often perceived as luck or mere coincidence. But rather than accidental these occurrences denote an ability to combine disparate parts. This ability is associated with a propensity toward diffuse rather than focused attention and an enhanced awareness of peripheral environmental stimuli, capable of triggering remote associations [38, 39]. The repetitive movements and tactile stimuli of any crafting process, in conjunction with the semi-focused attention necessary to produce a quality product, creates a fertile environment for exactly the kind of resting-state of mind necessary to peripheral thought processes, informed and supported by the tacit knowledge and agency communicated through the materials in use [14, 26]. In the crafting process, this means acknowledging that digital technologies are malleable and full of potential to become something else, and integrating this knowledge into the creative process so there are prompts and opportunities to see the technology in a new light, and to establish surprising connections. During our observational study of the Connected Textiles research group, we asked one of the project leaders, why she does not plan out the process and end-product before commencing the creation of an artifact. She responds with economic concerns: “That could get very expensive, there are so many things that could possibly go wrong”, implicating that the cyclical process of localization, questioning and opening to her is superior to analytical preplanning of a process, due to the many unknowns inherent to her research. As an afterthought, she adds “also if I think about it too much before I do something it would probably get very boring, most of the time the unanticipated that emerges is the exciting part”. In other words, based on her prior experience she expects that new knowledge will be created as an emergent aspect of the embodied process and material engagement.

ANALYZING CRAFT - BASED RESEARCH IN HCI

One of the signifiers of craft practice is the intense engagement with the artifact by the practitioner. This aspect of craft on the one hand facilitates the formation of deep embodied knowledge, on the other hand this trait can become problematic in a research context if the artifact and its visceral qualities assume such importance that they become goals in themselves and the research objectives subsequently become secondary. The desire for a job well done which according to Sennett drives crafting practice as a motivator for the investment necessary to produce great results, has the potential of obsession. Sennett invokes the somewhat drastic example of the creation of the atom bomb as a cautionary tale, where the pride of creating an outstanding product overrides the implications of the developed artifact, “They [the creators of the bomb] had taken pride in making something that, after the work was done, caused many of these makers great distress” [57 p.295]. Granted, most HCI today is far away from creating weapons of mass destruction and craft-based-approaches in particular are generally centered around ‘soft’ aspects of technology; still we feel it should be of concern in the evaluation of these kinds of research, whether the visceral bias towards high quality finishes distracts from actual research results. One approach for evaluation we have found useful is to apply the tripartite model of localization, questioning and opening, extended into three leading questions encompassing the digital technology with which to approach and analyze craft-based inquiries as presented in table 1, and exemplified by three examples: the *Bamboo Whisper* by Flanagan and Frankjaer; *Stiching Worlds* by Kurbak and Posch; and the *Hamefarers Kis*t by White. We have chosen these three examples due to their diversity and the availability of the authors’ description of, and focus on, their creative processes. Below we briefly describe the three projects and our analysis based on Sennett’s deconstruction. of the crafting process, extended into three guiding questions, which can be seen in table 1.

Example 1: Bamboo Whisper

The Bamboo Whisper, pictured in fig. 3a. is a headdress fashioned of woven Bamboo Reeds. The device reacts to sonic input by agitating the protruding brim-sticks. The project found its shape through an unfolding process of exploration of possible percussive expressions, achieved by running a vibrating motor attached to the emerging artifact during the crafting process. Different algorithms, in conjunction with the qualities of the bamboo reeds bound in a particular weave structure, engendered expressions of varying characteristics [26]. The most interesting effect, the artifact ’talking back’, emerged from an unanticipated delay in the code. Instead of correcting the delay caused by the structure of the algorithm, the authors instead allowed it to question the desired qualities of the artefact and consequently used the glitch as a shaping material [26].

2: Stiching Worlds

In the *Stitching Worlds* project, pictured in fig. 3b., Kurbak and Posch attempt to build a handcrafted computer, thereby questioning how computing technology would unfold if approached through crafting, rather than from an engineering mindset, i.e. the project “questions whether ‘what’ we make is really more important than ‘how’ we ‘what’ we make is really more important than ‘how’ we make things” [66]. Electronic components such as resistors, capacitors, inductors are created through knitting, weaving, embroidery and crochet, based on the premise that the patterns used in these practices are equal to digital code, as they can be saved, copied, distributed and manifested as textiles, at differing times and places, in unlimited numbers [66]. Equating fiber-based, domestic crafts with computing logic may at first seem controversial, however it is interesting to note that modern computing has its origin in fiber craft. The first modern computer is generally accepted as to a punch-card loom, constructed by Joseph Jacquard in 1804 [29 p.45], and in the 1960s, NASA used Rope Core Memory, handwoven computer programs, constructed of rings and string fitted inside metal tubes, to guide the Apollo missions [42].

Example 3: The Hamefarers Kist

In Handle with Care, White describes the process of creating the *Hamefarers Kist*, pictured in fig. 3c., a wooden ‘memory box’, for sharing online photo streams with distant, aging relatives, who do not use digital devices [62]. The finely crafted wooden box contains an array of small knitted cushions of differing patterns, each symbolizing a certain person. Placing the cushion on a special shelf inside the box connects to a photo stream created by the associated person, displayed on a screen on the inside of the lid of the box, which is actually a concealed iPhone. White, citing Dunne, describes the device as a genotype, i.e. as the embodiment of an idea, created by a hybrid design and crafting process, where material and technical explorations produce speculative objects that can suggest how the physical world can be used to access the digital world. The craftsperson, according to White, “pulls out particular qualities of a material, whether that is through knitting or a smartphone…taking the huge mass of technological possibility and taking a small sliver of it to create meaning through evocative objects” [62 p. 83].

Crafting Process	Opening	Questioning	Opening
Guiding Question / Example	When and how can/does the digital technology and physical materials form a significant focal point in the creative process?	How can/does the digital technology help the researcher examine and question digital and physical components in the creative process and vice versa?	What are the potentials of the physical technology and physical materials to establish new and surprising connections?
Bamboo Whisper Explores how wearable technology could unfold if crafted from organic materials.	Different algorithms, in conjunction with the bamboo reeds bound in a particular weave structure, engendered expressions of varying characteristics.	Instead of correcting the unintended delay caused by the structure of the algorithm, the authors used it to question the desired qualities of the artifact.	A glitch can be used as a shaping material, i.e. the prototype was molded around the affordances of both the code and those of the bamboo reeds.
Stitching Worlds Examines 'crafted logic', by fashioning embroidered computers.	The patterns used in fiber-based crafts are equal to digital code.	How can computing components be created through various fiber-based crafting techniques.	Computing and fiber crafts are closely related, original computers were based on fiber technology.
Hamefarers Kist Explores the use of physical artifacts to share online content with populations devoid of digital skills.	Extracting one single technological function from a multifunctional device and making it meaningful through its physical embedding.	How can traditional artifacts be used to allow aging populations to operate digital devices?	Old, traditional knitted patterns can be used as a filing system.

Table 1. Three leading questions to approach analyze and evaluate craft-based inquiries in HCI, exemplified through analysis of the creative processes of the three examples.

DISCUSSION: KNOWLEDGE CREATION THROUGH CRAFT-BASED HCI

In this paper, we have chosen to examine HCI practice from a craft perspective as we believe that craft, with its strong focus on the interrelation between the crafting process and knowledge production can inform HCI into forms of insight into knowledge creation through embodied engagement. As Sennett's three-step process of localization, questioning and opening indicates, craft practice is a complex system, moreover when extended to include computational technologies it is not a simple matter to align and integrate digital and physical crafting processes; it goes well beyond learning to code and solder, and is as much, if not more-so, a question of how the crafting researcher perceives and approaches the use of materials and techniques. In design research, the importance of experiential material engagement is widely recognized. Karana and Giaccardi suggest designing for 'materials experience'. A particular material, whether analog, digital or both, is deployed as the point of departure in the design process. The material and its unique qualities becomes co-performers, leading the way in the potential unfolding between material and practitioner [35]. Karana writes: "Materials are like words: The richer one's vocabulary (in materials), the larger is the number of design solutions that can be seen and expressed" [36] and asserts that intellectual knowledge, or acquaintance with virtual materials data is insufficient, as material engagement plays a unique role in the process of thinking and reflecting [19]. The notion of Somatic Connoisseurship, as proposed by Shiphorst, "highlights the significance of somatic facilitation" and "characterizes expertise that is developed, expressed, and passed on through the constantly refining process of practice", which "develops expertise that can access and train experiential acuity including observation, discernment, synthesis, empathy, and focus [54]. These statements effectively mirror craft practice and demonstrate the value of bringing craft research into dialogue with HCI. We have chosen here to focus on exploring the potentials of Sennett's tripartite model, since this offers a well-developed theoretical foundation for establishing such a dialogue, and enables us to compare and contrast craft-based approaches in HCI to craft-based approaches from other disciplines.

The deep engagement and absorbed concentration which forms the basis of any crafting process, the multi-modal perceptive abilities that time-consuming craft-based practices foster and hone, enable the crafter with an acute sensitivity to the affordances and qualities of materials and the artifacts they create. The mastery of any skill, i.e. for "complex skills to become so deeply ingrained that these become readily available, tacit knowledge" takes about ten thousand hours [57 p.127]. This is a time through which the practitioner, struggling with the properties of the chosen materials and the available tools becomes intensively attuned to the properties and idiosyncrasies of the material at hand. Merleau-Ponty describes this immersive experience as 'being as a thing', whilst Polanyi calls it 'focal awareness' and exemplifies with the act of hammering a nail: ''When we bring down the hammer we do not feel that its handle has struck our palm but that its head has struck the nail. . . I have a subsidiary awareness of the feeling in the palm of my hand which is merged into my focal awareness of my driving in the nail', to which Sennett adds that "we are now absorbed in something, no longer self-aware, even of our bodily self. We have become the thing on which we are working" [57 p.174]. In relation to HCI this means that to engage in research through craft-based practices, necessitates an appreciation of the value inherent in the time spent acquiring skills and engaging in material practices, as a prerequisite to access the tacit knowledge intrinsic to these processes.

CONCLUSION

Several contributions have argued that design is a particular paradigm of inquiry [57, 59]. One of the particulars seem to be the development of experiential knowledge, or 'first order knowledge' [17]: subjective insights and understandings pertaining to particular situations explored through craft-based approaches in HCI and the design of interactive systems. However, addressing this form of knowledge in research can be problematic. While it might be articulated and documented, this for better or worse transforms the experiential knowledge into knowledge of a different nature.

To gain a better understanding of these approaches and the potentials they hold for research in HCI, in this paper we have addressed two questions: 1) What are the defining characteristics of craft-based inquiry in HCI? 2) How can we understand and analyze the types and processes of knowledge creation that they entail?

To do so, we have provided an overview over different strands of craft-based research in HCI and highlighted three characteristics we have observed to signify approaches to scientific inquiry: *1. Combining, aligning, and integrating analog and digital crafting techniques and processes; 2. Creating highly refined artifacts, defined by attention to detail and aesthetics; 3. Creating knowledge through deep, embodied engagement.* We have used insights from craft research and in particular Richard Sennett's tripartite deconstruction of the crafting process, as a lens to understand crafting and the kinds of knowledge emerging from such processes. One of the crucial challenges for crafting as a research approach in HCI is to examine and further develop ways of addressing how, when, and why such processes of knowledge translation are viable and productive. We have introduced an extended version of Sennett's tripartite model localization, questioning and opening as an approach to understand crafting in HCI. We see our research here as an invitation to the DIS community to engage in and develop better understanding of craft-based research practices, which exhibit substantial potential to unlock tacit, embodied and material forms of knowledge.

REFERENCES

1. Glenn Adamson. 2007. *Thinking through craft*. Berg Oxford.
2. Sara Adhitya, Beck Davis, Raune Frankjaer, Patricia Flanagan and Zoe Mahony. 2016. The BIOdress: A Body-worn Interface for Environmental Embodiment. In *Proceedings of the TEI'16: Tenth International Conference on Tangible, Embedded, and Embodied Interaction*, ACM, 627-634.
3. Morgan G. Ames, Jeffrey Bardzell, Shaowen Bardzell, Silvia Lindtner, David A. Mellis and Daniela K. Rosner. 2014. Making cultures: empowerment, participation, and democracy-or not? In *CHI'14 Extended Abstracts on Human Factors in Computing Systems*, ACM, 1087-1092.
4. Rowan Bailey and Katherine Townsend. 2015. Craft and the handmade: Making the intangible visible. *Craft Research*, 6 (2). 157-163(157).
5. Steve Benford. 2015. Of Guitars, Stories, Luthiery and Hybrid Craft. In *Proceedings of the 2015 ACM SIGCHI Conference on Creativity and Cognition*, ACM, 1-1.
6. Joanna Berzowska. 2005. Electronic textiles: Wearable computers, reactive fashion, and soft computation. *Textile*, 3 (1). 58-75.
7. Joanna Berzowska. 2010. XS Catalogue, Concordia University.
8. Glenn Blauvelt, Thomas Wrensch and Michael Eisenberg. 2000. Integrating craft materials and computation. *Knowledge-Based Systems*, 13 (7). 471-478.
9. Eli Blevis, Sabrina Hauser and William Odom. 2015. Sharing the hidden treasure in pictorials. *interactions*, 22 (3). 32-43.
10. Leah Buechley. 2010. New Twists. Retrieved September 18, 2017 from http://highlowtech.org/?p=537
11. Leah Buechley. 2011. How to "sketch" with electronics. Retrieved January 05, 2017 from https://www.ted.com/talks/leah_buechley_how_to_sketch_with_electronics
12. Leah Buechley and Hannah Perner-Wilson. 2012. Crafting technology: Reimagining the processes, materials, and cultures of electronics. In *ACM Transactions on Computer-Human Interaction (TOCHI)*, 21.
13. Katie Bunnell. 2004. Craft and digital technology. In *World Craft Council 40th Annual Conference.*
14. Paul Cairns and Anna L Cox. 2008. *Research methods for human-computer interaction.* Cambridge University Press New York (NY).
15. Paul Carter. 2004. *Material thinking: The theory and practice of creative research.* Melbourne University Press.
16. Adele E Clarke, Carrie Friese and Rachel S Washburn. 2017. *Situational analysis: grounded theory after the interpretive turn.* SAGE Publications.

17. Mihaly Csikszentmihalyi and Isabella Selega Csikszentmihalyi. 1992. *Optimal experience: Psychological studies of flow in consciousness.* Cambridge University Press.
18. Mihaly Csikszentmihalyi and Eugene Halton. 1981. *The meaning of things: Domestic symbols and the self.* Cambridge University Press.
19. John Dewey. 1934. *Art as Experience*. Perigee Trade, New York.
20. John Dewey. 1933. *How we think*. D.C. Heath & CO. Publishers, Boston.
21. John Dewey. 1930. The quest for certainty: A study of the relation of knowledge and action. *The Journal of Philosophy*, 27 (1). 14-25.
22. Daniel Fallman and Erik Stolterman. 2010. Establishing criteria of rigour and relevance in interaction design research. *Digital Creativity*, 21 (4). 265-272.
23. Jodi Forlizzi, John Zimmerman and Shelly Evenson. 2008. Crafting a place for interaction design research in HCI. *Design Issues*, 24 (3). 19-29.
24. Sally Fort. 2007. *UK DIY Craft research report.* National Lottery, Arts Council. .
25. Kenneth Frampton. 1985. *Studies in tectonic culture.* Harvard University Graduate School of Design.
26. Raune Frankjaer, Patricia J. Flanagan and Daniel Gilgen. 2013. Employing creative practice as a research method in the field of wearable and interactive technologies. In *International Conference on Human-Computer Interaction*, Springer, 31-35.
27. Connie Golsteijn, Elise van den Hoven, David Frohlich and Abigail Sellen. 2014. Hybrid crafting: towards an integrated practice of crafting with physical and digital components. *Personal and ubiquitous computing*, 18 (3). 593-611.
28. Carole Gray and Gordon Burnett. 2009. Making sense: An exploration of ways of knowing generated through practice and reflection in craft. In *Proceedings of the Crafticulation and Education Conference*, 44-51.
29. Eric Hobsbawm. 2010. *Age of revolution: 1789-1848.* Hachette UK.
30. Kristina Höök, Peter Dalsgaard, Stuart Reeves, Jeffrey Bardzell, Jonas Löwgren, Erik Stolterman and Yvonne Rogers. 2015. Knowledge Production in Interaction Design. In *Proceedings of the 33rd Annual ACM Conference Extended Abstracts on Human Factors in Computing Systems*, ACM, 2429-2432.
31. Tim Ingold. 2000. *The perception of the environment: essays on livelihood, dwelling and skill.* Psychology Press.
32. Tim Ingold. 2009. The textility of making. *Cambridge Journal of Economics*, 34 (1). 91-102.
33. Jennifer Jacobs, David Mellis, Amit Zoran, Cesar Torres, Joel Brandt and Joshua Tanenbaum. 2016. Digital Craftsmanship: HCI Takes on Technology as an Expressive Medium. In *Proceedings of the 2016 ACM Conference Companion Publication on Designing Interactive Systems*, ACM, 57-60.
34. Valentin Janda. 2015. The means of design work. Models, sketches, and related objects in the creation of new technologies. Retrieved September 13, 2017 from https://www.ts.tu-berlin.de/fileadmin/i62_tstypo3/TUTS_WP2015_3_means_of_design_work.pdf
35. Elvin Karana, Elisa Giaccardi, Niels Stamhuis and Jasper Goossensen. 2016. The Tuning of Materials: A Designer's Journey. In *Proceedings of the 2016 ACM Conference on Designing Interactive Systems*, ACM, 619-631.
36. Elvin Karana, Owain Pedgley and Valentina Rognoli. 2013. *Materials Experience: fundamentals of materials and design.* Butterworth-Heinemann.
37. Brian Kennedy, Jackie Cooper and Bruce James. 1999. *Techno craft: the work of Susan Cohn, 1980 to 2000*. National Gallery of Australia.
38. John Kounios and Mark Beeman. 2009. The Aha! Moment the cognitive neuroscience of insight. *Current directions in psychological science*, 18 (4). 210-216.
39. John Kounios, Jessica I. Fleck, Deborah L. Green, Lisa Payne, Jennifer L. Stevenson, Edward M. Bowden and Mark Jung-Beeman. 2008. The origins of insight in resting-state brain activity. *Neuropsychologia*, 46 (1). 281-291.
40. Youn-Kyung Lim, Erik Stolterman and Josh Tenenberg. 2008. The anatomy of prototypes: Prototypes as filters, prototypes as manifestations of design ideas. *ACM Transactions on Computer-Human Interaction (TOCHI)*, 15 (2). 7.
41. Malcolm McCullough. 1998. *Abstracting craft: The practiced digital hand.* MIT press.
42. NASA. 2018. Computers in Spaceflight: The NASA Experience. Retrieved January 04, 2017 from https://www.hq.nasa.gov/office/pao/History/computers/Ch2-5.html
43. Nithikul Nimkulrat. 2012. Hands-on intellect: Integrating craft practice into design research. *International Journal of Design*, 6 (3). 14 pp.
44. Michael Nitsche, Andrew Quitmeyer, Kate Farina, Samuel Zwaan and Hye Yeon Nam. 2014. Teaching digital craft. In *CHI'14 Extended Abstracts on Human Factors in Computing Systems*, ACM, 719-730.
45. Maggie Orth. 2009. 100 Electronic Art Years. Retrieved September 15, 2017 from http://www.maggieorth.com/art_100EAYears.html
46. Neri Oxman. 2007. Digital craft: Fabrication-based design in the age of digital production. In *Workshop Proceedings for Ubicomp 2007: International Conference on Ubiquitous Computing*, 534-538.
47. Despina Papadopoulos. 2016. From Thinking to Making: Weaving Technology in Everyday Life. Retrieved September 18, 2017 from

http://www.tedxvilnius.com/2016/speakers/Despina-Papadopoulos
48. Hannah Perner-Wilson, Leah Buechley and Mika Satomi. 2011. Handcrafting textile interfaces from a kit-of-no-parts. In *Proceedings of the fifth international conference on Tangible, embedded, and embodied interaction*, ACM, 61-68.
49. Michael Polanyi. 1966. *The Tacit Dimension*. Peter Smith, Gloucester, Massachusetts.
50. David Pye. 1968. *The nature and art of workmanship*. Cambridge UP.
51. Bradley Quinn. 2013. *Textile visionaries: Innovation and sustainability in textile design*. Laurence King Publishing.
52. Daniela K. Rosner, Miwa Ikemiya and Tim Regan. 2015. Resisting Alignment: Code and Clay. In *Proceedings of the Ninth International Conference on Tangible, Embedded, and Embodied Interaction*, ACM, 181-188.
53. Daniela K. Rosner and Kimiko Ryokai. 2009. Reflections on craft: probing the creative process of everyday knitters. In *Proceedings of the seventh ACM conference on Creativity and cognition*, ACM, 195-204.
54. Thecla Schiphorst. 2011. Self-evidence: applying somatic connoisseurship to experience design. In *CHI'11 extended abstracts on human factors in computing systems*, ACM, 145-160.
55. Donald A Schön. 1992. Designing as reflective conversation with the materials of a design situation. *Knowledge-based systems*, 5 (1). 3-14.
56. Donald A Schön. 1983. *The reflective practitioner: How professionals think in action*. Basic books.
57. Richard Sennett. 2008. *The craftsman*. Yale University Press, New Haven.
58. Danny Sinopoli. 2008. The 'smart' set's new pastime: technocrafting. Retrieved January 05, 2017 from https://www.theglobeandmail.com/life/the-smart-sets-new-pastime-technocrafting/article17971052/
59. Erik Stolterman. 2008. The nature of design practice and implications for interaction design research. *International Journal of Design*, 2 (1).
60. Raymond Tallis. 2003. *The Hand: a Philosophical Enquiry Into Human Being*. Edinburgh University Press.
61. Sherry Turkle and Seymour Papert. 1990. Epistemological pluralism: Styles and voices within the computer culture. *Signs*, 16 (1). 128-157.
62. Louise Valentine. 2013. *Prototype: Design and Craft in the 21st Century*. A&C Black.
63. Anna Vallgårda and Johan Redström. 2007. Computational composites. In *Proceedings of the SIGCHI conference on Human factors in computing systems*, ACM, 513-522.
64. Victoria. 2017. Technocrafting & The Maker Movement. Retrieved January 04, 2017 from http://www.sumopeanut.com/crafting-the-maker-movement-science-technology/
65. Rachel Won. 2008. Photonic-bandgap fibre: Colour-tunable textiles. *Nature Photonics*, 2 (11). 650-650.
66. Stitching Worlds. Research Topic Retrieved January 05, 2017 from http://www.stitchingworlds.net/abstract/
67. John Zimmerman, Jodi Forlizzi and Shelley Evenson. 2007. Research through design as a method for interaction design research in HCI. In *Proceedings of the SIGCHI conference on Human factors in computing systems*, ACM, 493-502.
68. John Zimmerman, Erik Stolterman and Jodi Forlizzi. 2010. An analysis and critique of Research through Design: towards a formalization of a research approach. In *Proceedings of the 8th ACM Conference on Designing Interactive Systems*, ACM, 310-319.
69. Amit Zoran and Leah Buechley. 2013. Hybrid reassemblage: an exploration of craft, digital fabrication and artifact uniqueness. *Leonardo*, 46 (1). 4-10.

Bricks, Blocks, Boxes, Cubes, and Dice: On the Role of Cubic Shapes for the Design of Tangible Interactive Devices

Kevin Lefeuvre, Soeren Totzauer, Michael Storz, Albrecht Kurze, Andreas Bischof, Arne Berger
Chemnitz University of Technology, Chair Media Informatics
Chemnitz, Germany

ABSTRACT

Cubic shapes play an astonishing role in the design of tangible interactive devices. Due to our curiosity for this widespread design preference lasting over thirty years, we constituted a literature survey of papers, books and products since the late 1970s. Out of a corpus of fourty-seven papers, books and products that propose cubic shapes for tangible interactive devices we trace the origins of cubicle tangibles and highlight the rationale for their application. Through a comparative study, we analyze the properties of this shape for tangible interaction design and classify these along the themes of: Manipulation as Input, Placement in Space as Input, Arrangement, Multifunctionality, Randomness, Togetherness & Variations, Physical Qualities, Container, and Pedestal for Output. We propose a taxonomy for cubic shaped tangible interactive devices based on the reviewed contributions, in order to support researchers and designers in their future work of designing cubic shaped tangible interactive devices.

Author Keywords

Literature Survey; Interactive Tangible Device; Cube; Design;

ACM Classification Keywords

H.5.2. Information interfaces and presentation: User Interfaces: Miscellaneous;

INTRODUCTION

Cubes seem to be ubiquitous when investigating related work for tangible input devices and IoT devices. We noticed this in our search for related work when we were developing our own tool for co-design sessions aimed at ideating scenarios for IoT devices in the home [22]. By looking at the references cited by these papers we tried to trace the origin and the evolution of this phenomenon. However, we did not find a satisfying rationale for this design choice, yet collected a notable quantity of papers and books on cubic shaped tangible interactive devices developed over the past thirty years and noted a continuity for this design choice.

DIS 2018, June 9–13, 2018, Hong Kong.

ACM ISBN 978-1-4503-5198-0/18/06…$15.00
https://doi.org/10.1145/3196709.3196768

Most of these papers do not explicitly refer to a framework, classification, or taxonomy that has supported their design process. Yet many quote related cubical devices as an inspiration. As such we looked at the reasons cited by the designers and researchers to justify their design choice for a cubic shape and how they have taken advantage of the benefits of this shape for their own interactive tangible artifacts. All these works provide a rich history of the evolution of design approaches, that aim to exploit the properties of the cubic shape for interaction design in various ways. Yet, they lack an established global taxonomy of these properties to guide the design of such devices.

We wanted to better understand why this design choice is so prevalent. In order to offer a theoretical backdrop for future design, we conducted a non-exhaustive representative survey, that includes a diversity of projects on cube shaped tangible interactive devices.

As a result of this survey, we propose a non-exhaustive taxonomy of design properties of cubic shaped tangible interactive devices for supporting the future development of such devices.

This paper is structured as follows: First, we present our methodological process to search, extract, collect and classify the design properties of cubical shapes for tangible interactive devices, discovered and used by the devices we met. Second, we look at three papers [12,17,39] that we consider ultimately relevant because they highlight the advantages of a cubical shape for tangible interactive devices from three very different perspectives. We begin with a short presentation of their approaches on “natural affordance of a cube” [39], “spatial awareness between cubes” [12], and “container of bits” [17]. Third, we present two main categories, in which we classify the extracted design properties. Based on those, we propose a set of nine design properties for cube shaped tangible interactive devices.

We argue that these highlight the particular advantages of cube and thus elucidate the main reasons of its popularity.

This also serves as a taxonomy for helping designers to make informed choices during the development of future artifacts. In our discussion we also confront this particular shape with other platonic shapes, and discuss its limitations in comparison with other related shapes. We hope this encourages designers to extend their design choices to other shapes, because particular needs may greatly benefit from choosing different platonic solids.

METHODOLOGY

Research Question

Cubes seem to be ubiquitous when investigating related work for tangible input devices and IoT devices. We noticed this in our search for related work for a project when we were developing our own tool for co-design sessions aimed at ideating scenarios for IoT devices in the home.

Confronted with such a widespread phenomenon, we expected to find a well-established taxonomy that details the main benefits of a cubical shape for tangible interactive tools, on which other researchers have based their artifacts. But we found none. Except for a framework from Sheridan et al. that focuses on basic manipulations that can be done with a cube in one or two hands and on how some characteristics of a cube does affect these manipulations [39]. Although this framework details many advantages of a cube for designing tangible devices, its field of study does not encompass all the advantages. This posed the question: *How did so many other researchers come to choose the shape of a cube for designing interactive artifacts if this is not suggested by a common taxonomy, given larger design guidelines or rationales?* In order to get a better understanding of the success of a cubical shape in interaction design, we analyzed how other researchers took advantage of cubical shapes for designing tangible interactive artifacts, and why they chose this shape and not others. Based on an analysis of these advantages, we propose nine design properties of cubic shapes for tangible interaction design.

Search Strategy

We began building the corpus by searching via keywords related to the form of “cube”, “cubic”, “block”, “brick”, “square”, or “dice” in the ACM Digital Library. We sharpened our search strategy and corpus of papers by adding keywords related to common features of tangible interactive devices like “interactive”, “tangible”, “wearable”, “learning”, “interface”, “communicative” and “connected”.

As many product designers and interaction designers are not accustomed to publish their work through academic papers, we also extended our search to other publication media, including crowdfunding platforms, professional portfolios, companies and personal websites (e.g. *Light Cube* [54], *Fidget* [55], or *Beatdice* [56]). We became also aware of other devices by visiting researchers in their universities (e.g. *Hikari Tsumiki 2.0* [57]).

When one of these search strategies did not yield any more outcomes, we proceeded to a second step. Here, we looked at references cited in the original articles.

As we wanted to keep a reasonably sized and manageable corpus, we limited our final corpus of selected papers to approximately fifty articles and products and limited our direct searches in the acadamic field to the ACM-Library. We met some papers from other libraries by looking at the references of papers found in the ACM-Library. Instead of an exhaustive list we aim to propose a relevant sample of projects for a representative analysis of the contribution of cube-shaped devices in the research field of tangible interaction design.

Search Filtering/Inclusion – Exclusion Criteria

Papers were selected if their abstract was considered relevant, when the paper presented a tangible and cube-shaped device or dealt with the properties of the cubical shape for tangible interactive devices (e.g. Sheridan et al. [39]). As we focus on the properties of tangible, cubic shaped interactive devices only, papers that present non-physical/material cubes (e.g. cube-shaped digital-virtual representations and interaction models) were excluded from our selection. Products and devices were included, if their physical shape was a regular cube with six regular, rectangular faces. Products which did not adhere to these criterias were excluded, e.g. *Siftables* [28]. An exception was made for *MediaBlocks* [46] and *Bricks* [8] because of their particular importance in our survey. We selected fourty-three papers and books in total, that seems us to be relevant and representative, presenting cubic shaped devices and another four products from outside academic research. Overall the list of devices for our taxonomy consists of fourty-one cube-shaped tangibles.

Data Collection

In order to have a better overview of the selected papers and products, a compilation in form of a chart was built. This chart consists of each presented product, its main functionality, its main interactions, how the device takes advantages of its cubical shape and if that was the case, how its authors justified their design choice. Papers that explicitly discussed the properties, advantages or disadvantages of cubical shapes were added to the chart as well. By giving us a more restrictive but clearer data base, this compilation process of the collected information was our first step towards a deep analyzing process.

Data Coding and Data Synthesis

We used an affinity mapping process to classify the cubic devices in accordance to their similarities and differences. In this way categories of design properties started to emerge, and we began to build a taxonomy and to formulate hypotheses that could explain the impressive presence of cubical shaped tangible interactive devices. As subsequent papers and products surfaced, the chart grew and categories were revised. As such our methodological process can be related to a grounded theory process. Then, we conflated all derived explicit and implicit design choices for cubical shapes. We categorized them in nine design properties that are further subdivided in formal and abstract design properties.

FINDINGS

In what follows we present these categories of design properties, and propose an illustration for each them.

We will first relate to three especially relevant papers. In many of the papers we analyzed, a frequent citation is Sheridan et al. *"Exploring Cube Affordance: Towards a Classification of non-verbal Dynamics of Physical Interfaces for Wearable Computing"* [39]. We also relate to Ishii et al. *"Tangible Bits: Towards Seamless Interfaces between People, Bits and Atoms"* [17], arguably one of the most influential paper found. It does not discuss the implications of a cubic shape as explicitly, but it is also cited by many of the papers reviewed. We also chose Goh et al. *"The i-Cube: Design Considerations for Block-based Digital Manipulatives and their Applications"* [12]. Although not cited as often as Sheridan et al. and Ishii et al., it highlights several formal implications for interactive tangible systems based on the arrangement of multiple cubic shaped devices. After this, we will discuss the two meta categories formal and abstract design properties and will further present nine properties of cubic shaped interactive tangible devices that emerged from our survey.

Influential Papers and Previous Taxonomies

Although we did not find any paper that claims to be a general taxonomy for cube-shaped interactive tangible devices, two papers are prominently cited within our corpus [17,39]. Many researchers use them as reference or inspiration for their design choice, as for example, the creators of *Z-agon* [26,44] or *Display Cube* [23].

The first paper, Sheridan et al., focused on the "natural affordance of a cube" [39] for tangible interaction design research. The authors in this case chose a cubic shape to study the properties of grasping tangible interactive devices. They did so in order to explore "the possible non-verbal dynamics that a user can perform with a cube" [39]. For this study, Sheridan et al. built various cubes that differed in size, weight, surface texture, color, sound and shape. For their design study exploring affordance, they chose "the shape of a cube as an example" [39]. Notably, this choice resulted in subsequent enthusiasm for this shape. Many other researchers [1,18,27,36,43] relate their design choice to the results of this paper.

Whereas Sheridan et al. focus on the manipulation of one cube, Goh et al. [12] propose a study on the "spatial awareness between cubes" in order to explain the design goals of their own cubic device, called *i-Cube*. Goh et al. [12] explain that interactive cubes can be spatially arranged in 1D, 2D and 3D space. And that if each interactive cube in addition can detect whether other interactive cubes are in contact with its faces, can identify which of their faces, and how these are oriented, then this opens more possibilities for building of interactive tangible interactions within three-dimensional space.

The third paper [17], one of the most prominently cited within our corpus, presents "tangible bits" – "making digital information (bits) tangible" – and introduces the concepts of "physical icons" and "container of bits". In this paper the authors refer, among others, to the project *Bricks* [8]. These are small physical graspable blocks that can be linked to virtual objects, in order to access and manipulate these in the physical world [17]. "Physical icons" do not physically contain information, but only virtually [46], and their shape is in principle not limited to a particular form. In another paper [46] the authors use such "physical icons" as tokens "for the containment, transport, and manipulation of online media" and give them a shape closely resembling a cube. An interesting notion in these papers is the symbolic and semantic meaning around the words: blocks, bricks, bits, icons, container, that seem to be intuitively associated to the shape of a cube.

These papers highlight important advantages of cubical shapes for tangible interactive devices. However, neither propose a proper taxonomy of design properties, nor an encompassing rationale for choosing the right platonic solid for a particular interactive device. Also, a lot of others implications of the cube as a particular elementary shape must be highlighted. In the next section we summarize and discuss the explicit and implicit advantages of cubes that have been raised within the corpus of our literature survey.

Design Properties

Although the design properties that emerged from the literature survey are numerous, we found the following nine recurring themes: *Manipulation as Input, Placement in Space as Input, Arrangement, Multifunctionality, Randomness, Togetherness & Variations, Physical Qualities, Container, and Pedestal for Output.* Those can be further divided into two main categories. The first category includes *formal properties*, resulting directly from the geometrical characteristics and from the configuration of a cube in the 3D space, and its relation to corresponding cubes. This category also includes material characteristics like weight, size, material, surface, and softness and derived haptic and visual properties. The second category encompasses more *abstract properties*. By this, we mean symbolic and semantic properties that exist due to the meaning humans relate to cubic shapes.

Formal Properties

A cube is the second of the five platonic solids, which are classified by the number of sides: four, six, eight, twelve and twenty: tetrahedron, cube, octahedron, dodecahedron and icosahedron. A platonic solid is a convex regular polyhedron, which is a solid made of regular flat faces, that are regular polygons of equal size, shape, angles and length [53]. As commonly known, a cube consists of the following geometrical characteristics: ninety degree angles, six equally sized faces paired opposite each other, twelve edges of the same length, and eight vertices. These properties have direct consequences for the configuration of a cube in 3D space.

First, on its disposition: a cube can be rotated in ninety degree steps, and second on its orientation: a cube has three orientation axes (x, y, and z), by which its state can be unambiguously defined [48]. Third, modification in the geometry of a cube could be easily measured with the help of a shape-deformation sensor [30].

Manipulation as Input: Sheridan et al. [39] have shown that a cube has a natural affordance for manipulation. This leads to the widespread adoption of cubes as input devices by means of manual manipulation with one or two hands and one or more cubes. By tracking each manipulation in rotation and displacement, cubes can easily be used as navigation tools in virtual 3D environments [48]. In comparison with spherical or other platonic shapes, because of its ninety degree angles, the cubic shape clearly represents the three spatial axis (x, y, z) and therefore enables checking and performing orientation in space [48]. Triple-axis accelerometers provide the possibility to measure both accelerations and tilts in all directions [7]. Gyroscopes check rotation [48], compasses map the magnetic orientation and barometers measure the elevation in comparison with the sea level [7].

This means it is possible to exactly know the state of a cube and to measure each change of it on all three axes in 3D space. Therefore, it is possible not only to transcribe a cube's position, orientation and movement within virtual space but also to convert intentional gestures like shaking or twisting into particular inputs [48]. These properties are involved in many works on the development of three-dimensional input devices [11]. Many added additional sensors to their cubes, such as capacitive sensors [48], buttons and rotary encoders [34], or buttons and linear potentiometers [11], in order to increase input possibilities.

Cubik [24] for example is a tangible tool for 3D-modeling. Although this tool is not equipped with position or rotation sensors, and therefore it is not possible to apply displacements and rotations to the virtual cube by moving and rotating the tangible cube, it enables applying changes to the 3D-Model of its virtual counterpart. This tangible cube is equipped with one push-pull button on each of its faces. When two buttons on opposite faces are simultaneously pushed or pulled, the virtual cube is expanded or retracted on the respective axis.

Rubikon [34] is a similar device which looks like a Rubik's cube. It can detect user actions such as rotation, as well as additional manipulations thanks to five rotary encoders/buttons distributed on the five sides. These rotary encoders are equipped with RGB LEDs to display information. Among various examples of applications for their tool, Roudaut et al. propose to use *Rubikon* as authentication tool. By rotating the cube along a particular choreography and confirming by pressing one of the buttons, the user can, for example, unlock a computer or a user session.

For *Do-It* [30], the cubic device is considered as a unique shape-deformation sensor. The panel of processed deformations is going from global to local pressures and from local lifts to global release and thereby deforming a real shape in order to model a virtual one. It is made of an electrically conductive polyurethane foam, enables fine operating deformations of its 3D shape. The possible input gestures are intuitive and multiple.

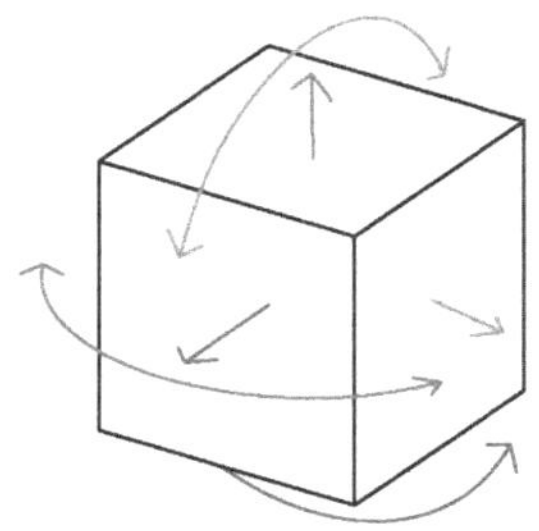

Figure 1. Illustration of the design property: Manipulation as Input.

Placement in Space as Input: The orientation and spatial placement of a cube as input device in relation to other cubes are also useful. In fact, the configuration of cubes in the space of a system can be used as input. By adding, displacing, or removing cubes from a spatial arrangement, users can modulate output. *AudioCubes* [36], handle audio signals through their positioning on a plane. They can be coupled together over distance, thus enabling continuous spatial configurations. Each *AudioCube* can send or receive signals through four of its faces to neighboring cubes using light of different colors. Depending on their spatial relationship a musical composition can be created and freely modified by rearranging the cubes.

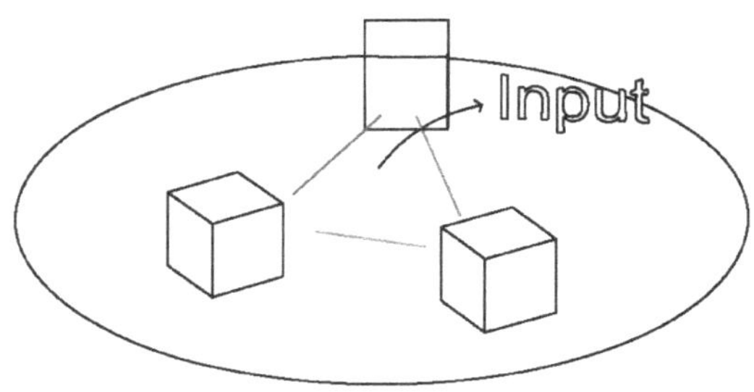

Figure 2. Illustration of the design property: Placement in Space as Input.

Arrangement: A cube presents more practical implications for interaction design than solids, that do not present opposite parallel faces. In contrast to them, cubes can be arranged together in an easy way, e.g. stacked or juxtaposed. As the authors of *i-Cube* [12] demonstrated, this allows for seemingly endless manual arrangement possibilities, e.g. 1D-linear [42,49], 2D-planar [18,51], full 3D-arrangements [5,12,37,50,57]. Bigger cubes or complex forms can even be created from smaller cubes, like pixels form an image. Through the pairing of cubes within such an arrangement, an interaction can be established. Two building cubes systems, *Cuboino* [14] and *Hikari Tsumiki 2.0* [57], consist of single usage cubes (like for example sensor cubes, logic cubes, energy cubes, wireless communication cubes, actuators cubes) which, once assembled, create an autonomous tangible interaction. These systems enable the creation of 3D-arrangements.

Once interaction patterns are constructed by the users, little modifications within the 3D-arrangement, like interchanging one cube with another or flipping a particular cube by 180 degrees, can easily modify interaction [12]. The authors of *i-Cube* [12] point out the "block face and orientation awareness" in cube-based building systems by citing an example where flipping a cube by 180 degrees inverses the meaning of the global interaction. They integrate this rotation property in a musical application of their *i-Cubes*, where a cube can be rotated by 90° degrees steps for changing the length of a pause in a musical sequence composed by the arranged cubes.

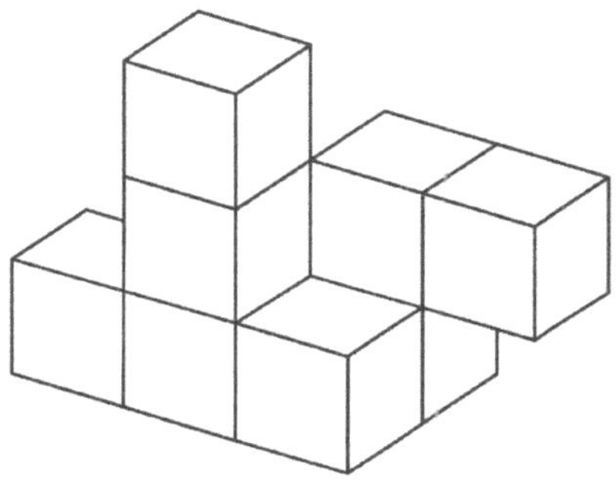

Figure 3. Illustration of the design property: Arrangement.

Multifunctionality: Having six distinct faces without a dominant one makes a device a formally equal distribution system. Multiple functionalities can be equally offered to the user by distributing them on the respective faces of the cube-shaped device. We consider this to be the key property of multifunctionality. For example, *Loaded Dice* [22] is a pair of interactive cubes that dedicate a different functionality to each of its faces. *Fidget* [55] places one different anti-stress feature on each of its sides, like click, glide, breathe, roll, spin and flip. *CubeLendar* [27] is presented as "an interactive calendar", which offers different displays with information on three of its faces: time and date, weather forecast and work details respectively. Rotating the *CubeLendar* by 45° to the left or right allows for switching the days. Rotating it up or down allows for scrolling appointment information of a given day. *Cueb* [13] are "interactive photo cubes", that can be shaken for showing random photos on their six faces. Although this does not offer different functionalities – except for showing pictures – we include it in this category, because each displayed image is different from the five others, and thus employs multiple facets.

To distinct multifunctionality further, we classify single devices that combine multiple forms of input [48] without employing multiple facets but manipulation properties of the cubic shape as Gesture as Input. Additionally cube-based systems [16] that distribute their functionality to multiple cubes instead of multiple faces would be classified in our following property of Togetherness & Variations.

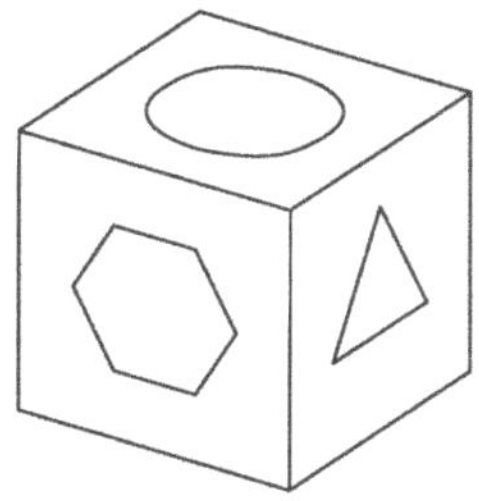

Figure 4. Illustration of the design property: Multifunctionality.

Randomness: As a consequence from the implication of Multifunctionality, a cube that offers six different functions or variations of a function distributed along its six faces can work as a formidable tool for supporting serendipity in interaction design by generating random combinations. In fact, a cube, or rather a dice, thanks to its geometry, can been rolled to randomly choose a side and thus a feature. This serendipity adds benefits like playfulness to cubic tools for exploring and learning. *Loaded Dice* [22] for example, consists of two wireless connected cubes, one with six sensors distributed along its six sides, and the other with six actuators. As only the sensor/actuator on the top side is activated, a random pairing between one sensor and one actuator could be created by rolling both dice [21].

Figure 5. Illustration of the design property: Randomness.

Togetherness and Variations: From a more distant perspective, if a system includes multiple cubes, another expected phenomenon plays an important role for interaction design. A cube-based system constitutes a familiar resemblance. In turn, these emergent properties have direct consequences for the usability of interactive devices. Embedding such devices in a simple cube shape increases accessibility for people that otherwise might refrain from using more common computer interfaces [3].

Arguably, learning tools for children often come in the shape of cubes. Many of these toys were developed and introduced in the hands-on pedagogy of Fröbel [10] and Montessori [29] and have become commonplace. Cubes are easily manipulable and users are accustomed to usage of: grasping, rotating, stacking etc. Also, having a set of identically shaped devices allows the introduction of variation of their functions without changing the main way of using them. Possible variations comprise self-describing and self-demonstration of sensors or actuators [14,16,22,57], using transparent material showing the inner working of the cubes [5,20,32], employing visual properties on the sides like with colors [16] or words [3].

A family of cubes does not necessarily lead to interaction between them. Each cube could be used as a standalone device. *Cubes* [32], for example, work in self-contained interaction, with instructions on the required input being clearly shown on the top surface, while the user has to discover what the genereated output is. All *Navigational Blocks* [3] work as a "physical icon" and embody a particular question (When, Where). This interacts with a data space for supporting visitors in exploring tourist spots by providing historical information. Once the main function of one cube as a stand-alone device is discovered, the user can easily switch to another cube without having to learn completely new ways of interaction.

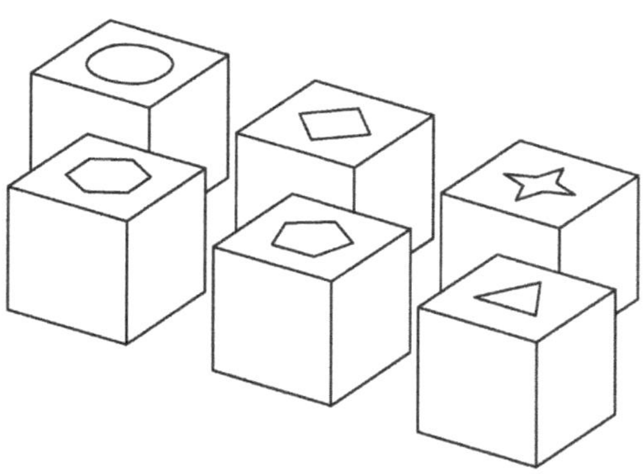

Figure 6. Illustration of the design property: Togetherness & Variations.

Physical Qualities: Thanks to its geometrical properties, choosing a cubic shape for a tangible interactive device shell yields additional advantages considering production processes. Thanks to the faces being arranged in ninety degrees angles, cubic shells can be easy built from rectangular cut sheets (e.g. acrylic glass, plywood). *ConnectUs* [20] for example are made of cut acrylic glass and *Topaoko* [51] of cut plywood. For a tangible interactive device, a cubic shape not only presents advantages for the built of its shell but also for the prototyping of its electronic system. For the same reasons as for a the building of shell, ninety degrees angles make building of a 3D-shape made of Printed Circuit Boards (PCB) easier. PCBs are made of epoxy sheets of different thickness and are CNC cut. *ConnectUs* [20], made of six PCBs stacked together, is a perfect example to illustrate.

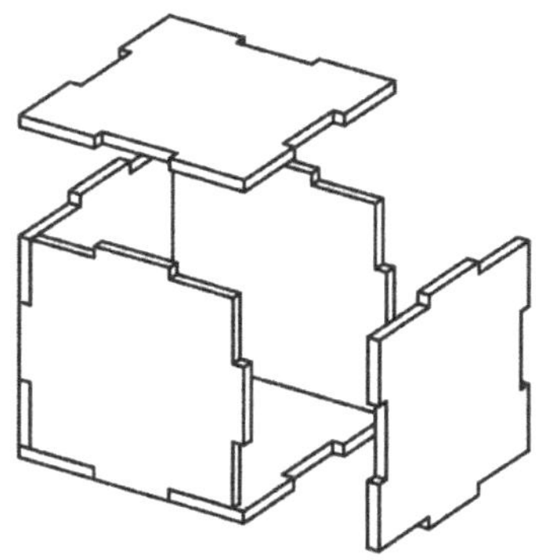

Figure 7. Illustration of the design property: Physical Qualities

Abstract Properties

A cube, one of the most common platonic shapes, is etymologically related to words like "brick, block, box, stone, dice" [58]. That's probably why most of the devices we met have a name that includes or variates one of these words. The semiotic meaning transported by all these words plays a role in the way we perceived cubical shaped devices and have implications as the functions we give them. In what follows we argue that this has a variety of meaningful implications for tangible devices that contain a digital information or communicate a function.

Container: One abstract implication of the shape of a cube for interaction design research is a symbolic one. The term "container" has been introduced by Ishii and Ullmer [17,46] as a symbolic, yet tangible, token [47] to hold other un-tangible artifacts, like data. As such the prevalent notion of "GUI (Graphical User Interface)-based boxes" [17], can also be extended to the physical/material world of tangible user interfaces.

Tangible interactive cubes are often used for representing digital information in the physical world. A common purpose of token devices is, for example *Navigational Blocks.* They embody information for an easier manipulation of complex digital information and enable a palpable interaction with the data space [3].

MediaBlocks, are presented "as physical icons ("phicons") for the containment, transport and manipulation of online media" [46]. Each of these little blocks contains an ID tag, associated with online media elements. These "containers" can virtually transport media between different devices (e.g.

display devices like projectors or printers, media interfaces like browsers) or graphical user interfaces [46].

As such, "container" represents the symbolic quality of a tangible to hold representations of in-tangible artifacts, for example information or data. We consider any cube a container that virtually holds information, being part of a data space external to the cube. A cube that is a container does not outsource the information itself. This data or information could, for example, be shown through an external GUI or an auditory device.

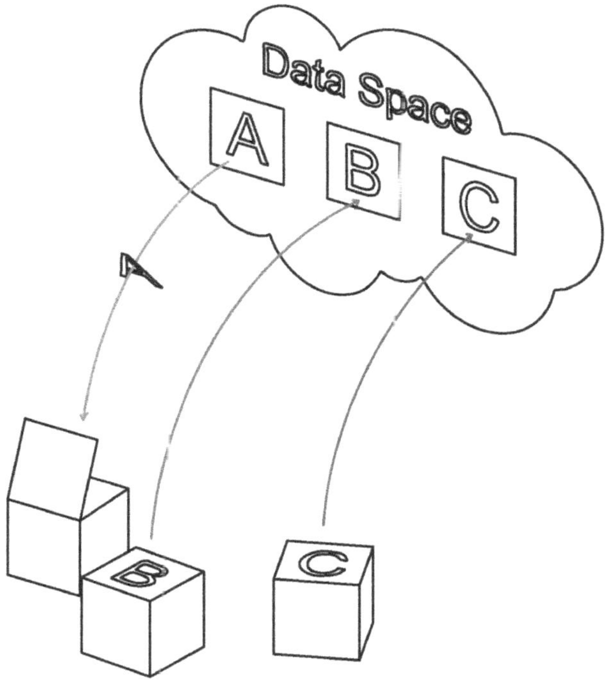

Figure 8. Illustration of the design property: Container.

Pedestal for Output: This usage of cubes as output devices is more idiosyncratic. Its role is very similar to that of a pedestal, encapsulating and highlighting the actual output device without distracting the observer. An output device would thereby be any actuator creating, for example sounds, lighting, vibrations, temperature, or air flows. Since most outputs are self-describing, the output device shell does not need to visually or haptically describe their function.

Physikit [16] illustrates this pedestal purpose. It is a set of explorative tools for visualizing sensor data through physical actuators. Besides environmental sensors and a web-based configuration tool, *Physikit* consists of four single output blocks which visualize data of the environmental sensors using light, movement, vibration and airflow [16]. By using the same shape for all output device shells, it allows the user to focus on the output signals instead of focusing on the shell shape as a crucial part.

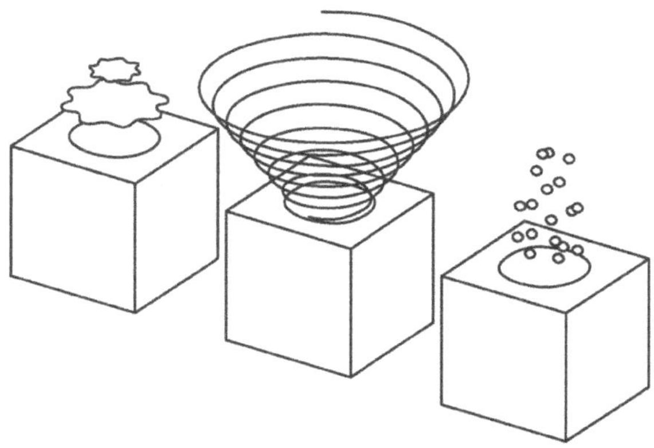

Figure 9. Illustration of the design property: Pedestal for Output.

OVERVIEW

The properties Arrangement and Placement in Space as Input arguably overlap. However, in cases, where the cubes are not in contact with each other, but where their placement in space needs to respect a strong spatial arrangement, like for example *BlackBlocks* [1], we consider it as Arrangement.

Some properties are dependant of others. The Randomness property exists only if the cube also has the property Multifunctionality. Here, rotating a cube selects a random function, as a kind of a manipulation as input. In this case we consider that the cube only partially fits the property Manipulation as Input, because rotating is only a way to access the main function.

The property Togetherness & Variations is present only if there are multiple cubes. Consequently, it often correlates with the property Arrangement or Placement in Space as Input. But how much a cube system fulfills this category, depends on how evident it is to understand the independent functions of the cubes.

The property Manipulation as Input was evident only with cubes that are involved in 3D modelling, but actually each cube that create an input through a gesture like shaking enters totally or partially in this category, depending on the diversity of the inputs.

The property Container is also often linked with the property Placement in Space as Input. In fact many of the devices configured spatially in order to generate output are connected to an external data space. The output (visual or auditory) is not generated by the cubes themselves, but by an actor external to the cubes. Some devices that interact with a GUI could also be considered as a container. But as we consider the concept of container in a symbolic way, cubes that are not strong representatives of an external information are not considered containers.

	Manipulation as Input	Placement in Space as Input	Arrangement	Multifunctionality	Randomness	Togetherness & Variations	Physical Qualities	Container	Pedestal for Output
Active Cube [50]	XX		XX			X			XX
AlgoBlock [42]			XX			XX	X?	XX	
AudioCubes [36]		XX				X	XX	X	
Autonomous Cube [48]	XX			XX			X?	X?	
Beat Dice [56]	X	X?		XX	X?	XX	XX		XX
BlackBlocks [1]			XX			XX		XX	
Boda Blocks [2]			XX			XX			XX
Bricks [8]		XX				XX	X	X?	
Captive [4]	XX								
ConnectUs [20]	X	X				X	XX		XX
CubeBrowser [52]	XX			XX					XX
Cube-in [31]			X			X	XX		XX
CubeExplorer [40]	X?						XX		
CubeLendar [27]	X			XX			X		XX
Cubement [5]			XX			X	X		XX
Cubes [32]	X					X	XX		XX
Cubik [24]	X								
Cuboino [14]			XX			X	XX		XX
CubTile [33]	X								
Cueb [13]	X			XX	X?		XX		XX
Cupa [25]									XX
Display Cube [23]	X			XX			XX		XX
Do-It [30]	XX								
E-Block [49]			XX			XX	XX	XX	
Fidget Play Cube [55]				XX					
Hikari Tsumiki 2.0 [57]			XX			X	XX		XX
i-Cube [12]	X		XX	XX		XX	X?	XX	XX
InterCube [35]	XX						XX		
Light Cube [54]		X?							X?
Loaded Dice [21,22]	X			XX	XX	X			XX
mediaBlocks [46]			X?			XX		XX	
Navigational Blocks [3]	X?		X?	XX		XX	XX	XX	X?
pCubee [41]	XX								XX
Physikit [16]						XX	X		XX
roBlocks [37]			XX			X			XX
Rubikon [34]	XX			X			X?		
SIG-Blocks [18,19]	XX		XX			XX		XX	
The Cubic Mouse [11]	XX								
Three Design Probes [15]	X					X	XX		XX
Topaoko [51]			XX			X	XX		X
Z-agon [26,44]	X			X?					XX

Table 1. Mapping of the cubical interactive tangible devices along the design properties. XX: fit this category. X: partially fit this category. X?: disputably fit this category.

The property Physical Qualities is certainly the most subjective, as the authors do not systematically communicate on the materials and manufacturing processes of their cubes. And if that influenced their choice for a cubic shape.

DISCUSSION & CONCLUSION

Taken by so many designers and researchers in the HCI-field, the choice to build an interactive tangible device seems to have be supported by Ishii et al. papers. Also, the choice to give it a cubical shape, especially for cubes that have to generate inputs through gestures, by Sheridan et al. paper. Finally, also earlier works [9,42] proposed the cubic shape for interactive tangible devices and are often cited as examples. John Frazer presents for example in his book "An Evolutionary Architecture" [9] cellular computing tangible system, developed during the late 70's, that use the shape of a cube for theirs cells. Schaer et al. [38] point in their survey "Tangible User Interfaces: Past, Present, and Future Directions" at the Ullmer et al. [47] classification of tangible user interfaces along three categories: "tangible objects on interactive surfaces, constructive assemblies of modular connecting blocks, and token-constraint systems." [38] This categories are respectively similar to our categories: Placement in Space as Input, Arrangement and Container. Ullmer et al. [45] presented one of the first frameworks for tangible devices regardless of their shape in 2000. Yet, many of the examples cited by Ullmer et al. for illustrating their categories [45] are cubic devices. As we have shown, also 18 years later, cubes continue to be a very popular choice for tangibles. Thus it only seems normal that the taxonomy on cubic shaped devices presented here shares some of these properties presented by Ullmer et al..

Cubical shaped tangible interactive devices do not have the monopole of this properties. The functions of tangible controllers on a surface, of tokens, and even of arranged interactive modules, are tangible devices that present other shapes than a cubical one. But the main reason for the popularity of this design choice is probably that this platonic solid appears to HCI-researchers and designers as the form that could best support their respective project specifications. Such a shape has already proven advantages. It could be easily used to build sides of a shell and electronic boards. Its natural affordance can fill many tangible specifications. Also, it intuitively reminds of mechanisms known from childhood like arrangements of blocks. Indeed many of the researchers that developed interactive tangible learning tools, often coming in the form of building blocks, mentioned the works of Fröbel and Montessori for the advantages of building block systems in teaching.

And it is full of semantic meaning that inspire additional usages like, for example, the roll of a dice. In comparison to other platonic solids, cubes offer significant advantages. A cube can roll much better than a tetrahedron. It can be stacked with its counterparts, which an octahedron or icosahedron do not allow for, but a dodecahedron does.

Sheridan et al. demonstrate that "the rhombus fit comfortably in the hand" because of its curviness [39]. In others words: platonic solids and other convex polyhedrons, that are regular or not, with more than six faces, fit better in the palm of the hand, due to faces joined with angles over 90°.

As an example of this advantage, *Oto-No-Katachi* [59], a midi multimedia and sound controller with the shape of an icosidodecahdron (thirty-two faces: twenty triangles and twelve pentagons). Thanks to its multifaceted shape, this device offers a lot of features, some of which can be distributed over its faces. A multi-axis control enables to control features like fade or filters by turning or displacing the device laterally, and its faces could be programmed to be used as separated touch interfaces. Thanks to its many faces, this product fits better in hand than a cube. And although a cube indicates the three axis of the 3D-space much better, we can easily imagine it could be used for a navigational tool in the 3D-space.

We can expect that the development of soft PCBs like *Fingies* [6,60] opens new possibilities for the building of electronic devices with more complex shapes. We can expect that these new PCBs can be folded and therefore platonic solids with more than six sides can be built, as well as more freely shaped forms. In combination with 3D-printed shells, this new technologies gives designers and researchers the possibility to deviate from the design of cubic shapes for future tangible interactive devices.

But soft PCBs do not reduce all the complexity of an electronic circuit. Devices that offer features distributed over their faces could offer more features if they have more faces, and could been equally well rolled to offer a random selection feature. But more faces and thus more features mean in many cases more complexity on the electronic side.

AKNOWLEDGMENTS

The authors would like to thank Eva Hornecker for her valuable feedback and contribution. This research is funded by the German Ministry of Education and Research (BMBF) under grant number FKZ 16SV7116.

REFERENCES

1. Wafa Almukadi and A. Lucas Stephane. 2015. BlackBlocks: Tangible Interactive System for Children to Learn 3-Letter Words and Basic Math. In *Proceedings of the 2015 International Conference on Interactive Tabletops & Surfaces* (ITS '15), 421–424. https://doi.org/10.1145/2817721.2823482
2. Leah Buechley and Mike Eisenberg. 2007. Boda Blocks: A Collaborative Tool for Exploring Tangible Three-dimensional Cellular Automata. In *Proceedings of the 8th International Conference on Computer Supported Collaborative Learning* (CSCL'07), 102–104. Retrieved from http://dl.acm.org/citation.cfm?id=1599600.1599618
3. Ken Camarata, Ellen Yi-Luen Do, Brian R. Johnson, and Mark D. Gross. 2002. Navigational Blocks: Navigating Information Space with Tangible Media. In *Proceedings of the 7th International Conference on Intelligent User Interfaces* (IUI '02), 31–38. https://doi.org/10.1145/502716.502725
4. Arpan Chakraborty, Ryan Gross, Shea McIntee, Kyung Wha Hong, Jae Yeol Lee, and Robert St. Amant. 2014. CAPTIVE: A Cube with Augmented Physical Tools. In *CHI '14 Extended Abstracts on Human Factors in Computing Systems* (CHI EA '14), 1315–1320. https://doi.org/10.1145/2559206.2581340
5. Jeeyong Chung, Kyungeun Min, and Woohun Lee. 2013. CUBEMENT: Democratizing Mechanical Movement Design. In *Proceedings of the 8th International Conference on Tangible, Embedded and Embodied Interaction* (TEI '14), 81–84. https://doi.org/10.1145/2540930.2540933
6. Johannes Deich, Michael Markert, Jens Geelhaar, Martin Schied, Jens Hammerschmidt, and Gabriel Rausch. 2013. Form & Function Toolkit: Printed Electronics for Unconventional Interface. In *Proceedings of the 8th International Conference on Tangible, Embedded and Embodied Interaction* (TEI '14), 365–368. https://doi.org/10.1145/2540930.2567900
7. Richard Feynman, Michael Gottlieb, and Richard Leighton. 2013. *Feynman's Tips on Physics, A Problem-Solving Supplement to the Feynman Lectures on Physics.* Basic Books; 2nd Revised ed. edition.
8. George W. Fitzmaurice, Hiroshi Ishii, and William A. S. Buxton. 1995. Bricks: Laying the Foundations for Graspable User Interfaces. In *Proceedings of the SIGCHI Conference on Human Factors in Computing Systems* (CHI '95), 442–449. https://doi.org/10.1145/223904.223964
9. John Frazer. 1995. *An Evolutionary Architecture.* Architectural Association Publications.
10. Fröbel, Friedrich. 1826. *On the Education of Man (Die Menschenerziehung)*. Keilhau/Leipzig: Wienbrach.
11. Bernd Fröhlich and John Plate. 2000. The Cubic Mouse: A New Device for Three-dimensional Input. In *Proceedings of the SIGCHI Conference on Human Factors in Computing Systems* (CHI '00), 526–531. https://doi.org/10.1145/332040.332491
12. Wooi Boon Goh, L. L. Chamara Kasun, Fitriani, Jacquelyn Tan, and Wei Shou. 2012. The i-Cube: Design Considerations for Block-based Digital Manipulatives and Their Applications. In *Proceedings of the Designing Interactive Systems Conference* (DIS '12), 398–407. https://doi.org/10.1145/2317956.2318016

13. Connie Golsteijn and Elise van den Hoven. 2013. Facilitating parent-teenager communication through interactive photo cubes. *Personal and Ubiquitous Computing* 17, 2: 273–286. https://doi.org/10.1007/s00779-011-0487-9

14. Felix Heibeck. 2013. Cuboino. Extending Physical Games: An Example. In *CHI '13 Extended Abstracts on Human Factors in Computing Systems* (CHI EA '13), 2813–2814. https://doi.org/10.1145/2468356.2479525

15. Trevor Hogan, Uta Hinrichs, and Eva Hornecker. 2017. The Visual and Beyond: Characterizing Experiences with Auditory, Haptic and Visual Data Representations. In *Proceedings of the 2017 Conference on Designing Interactive Systems* (DIS '17), 797–809. https://doi.org/10.1145/3064663.3064702

16. Steven Houben, Connie Golsteijn, Sarah Gallacher, Rose Johnson, Saskia Bakker, Nicolai Marquardt, Licia Capra, and Yvonne Rogers. 2016. Physikit: Data Engagement Through Physical Ambient Visualizations in the Home. In *Proceedings of the 2016 CHI Conference on Human Factors in Computing Systems* (CHI '16), 1608–1619. https://doi.org/10.1145/2858036.2858059

17. Hiroshi Ishii and Brygg Ullmer. 1997. Tangible Bits: Towards Seamless Interfaces Between People, Bits and Atoms. In *Proceedings of the ACM SIGCHI Conference on Human Factors in Computing Systems* (CHI '97), 234–241. https://doi.org/10.1145/258549.258715

18. D. Jeong, K. Endri, and K. Lee. 2010. TaG-Games: Tangible geometric games for assessing cognitive problem-solving skills and fine motor proficiency. In *2010 IEEE Conference on Multisensor Fusion and Integration*, 32–37. https://doi.org/10.1109/MFI.2010.5604479

19. Donghwa Jeong, Endri Kerci, and Kiju Lee. 2010. Sensor-integrated geometric blocks: towards interactive play-based assessment of young children. In *Proceedings of First International Workshop on Interactive Systems in Healthcarethcare* (WISH 2010).

20. Zuzanna Lechelt, Yvonne Rogers, Nicolai Marquardt, and Venus Shum. 2016. ConnectUs: A New Toolkit for Teaching About the Internet of Things. In *Proceedings of the 2016 CHI Conference Extended Abstracts on Human Factors in Computing Systems* (CHI EA '16), 3711–3714. https://doi.org/10.1145/2851581.2890241

21. Kevin Lefeuvre, Arne Berger, Albrecht Kurze, Sören Totzauer, Michael Storz, and Andreas Bischof. 2016. Smart Connected Sensations: Co-Creating Smart Connected Applications Through Distributed Serendipity. In *Proceedings of the 9th Nordic Conference on Human-Computer Interaction* (NordiCHI '16), 88:1–88:4. https://doi.org/10.1145/2971485.2996723

22. Kevin Lefeuvre, Sören Totzauer, Andreas Bischof, Albrecht Kurze, Michael Storz, Lisa Ullmann, and Arne Berger. 2016. Loaded Dice: Exploring the Design Space of Connected Devices with Blind and Visually Impaired People. In *Proceedings of the 9th Nordic Conference on Human-Computer Interaction* (NordiCHI '16), 31:1–31:10. https://doi.org/10.1145/2971485.2971524

23. K. Leichtenstern, E. Andre, E. Losch, M. Kranz, and P. Holleis. 2007. A Tangible User Interface as Interaction and Presentation Device to a Social Learning Software. In *2007 Fourth International Conference on Networked Sensing Systems*, 114–117. https://doi.org/10.1109/INSS.2007.4297402

24. Surapong Lertsithichai and Matthew Seegmiller. 2002. CUBIK: A Bi-directional Tangible Modeling Interface. In *CHI '02 Extended Abstracts on Human Factors in Computing Systems* (CHI EA '02), 756–757. https://doi.org/10.1145/506443.506582

25. Chin Chooi Liew. 2017. CUPA: Cube Pal for Developing Children's Emotional Intelligence and Parent-Child Relationship. In *Proceedings of the 2016 CHI Conference Extended Abstracts on Human Factors in Computing Systems* (CHI EA '17), 124–129. https://doi.org/10.1145/3027063.3048423

26. Takashi Matsumoto, Daisuke Horiguchi, Shihori Nakashima, and Naohito Okude. 2006. Z-agon: Mobile Multi-display Browser Cube. In *CHI '06 Extended Abstracts on Human Factors in Computing Systems* (CHI EA '06), 351–356. https://doi.org/10.1145/1125451.1125528

27. Andrii Matviienko, Sebastian Horwege, Lennart Frick, Christoph Ressel, and Susanne Boll. 2016. CubeLendar: Design of a Tangible Interactive Event Awareness Cube. In *Proceedings of the 2016 CHI Conference Extended Abstracts on Human Factors in Computing Systems* (CHI EA '16), 2601–2608. https://doi.org/10.1145/2851581.2892278

28. David Merrill, Jeevan Kalanithi, and Pattie Maes. 2007. Siftables: towards sensor network user interfaces. In *Proceedings of the 1st international conference on Tangible and embedded interaction*, 75–78.

29. Maria Montessori and Anne E George. 1964. *The Montessori method.* Schocken Books, New York.

30. Tamotsu Murakami, Kazuhiko Hayashi, Kazuhiro Oikawa, and Naomasa Nakajima. 1995. DO-IT: Deformable Objects As Input Tools. In *Conference Companion on Human Factors in Computing Systems* (CHI '95), 87–88. https://doi.org/10.1145/223355.223442

31. Hyunjoo Oh and Mark D. Gross. 2015. Cube-in: A Learning Kit for Physical Computing Basics. In *Proceedings of the Ninth International Conference on Tangible, Embedded, and Embodied Interaction* (TEI '15), 383–386. https://doi.org/10.1145/2677199.2680597

32. Michal Rinott, Shachar Geiger, Eran Gal-Or, and Luka Or. 2013. Cubes. In *Proceedings of the 7th International Conference on Tangible, Embedded and Embodied Interaction* (TEI '13), 397–398. https://doi.org/10.1145/2460625.2460711

33. Jean-Baptiste de la Rivière, Cédric Kervégant, Emmanuel Orvain, and Nicolas Dittlo. 2008. CubTile: A Multi-touch Cubic Interface. In *Proceedings of the 2008 ACM Symposium on Virtual Reality Software and Technology* (VRST '08), 69–72. https://doi.org/10.1145/1450579.1450593

34. Anne Roudaut, Diego Martinez, Amir Chohan, Vlad-Stefan Otrocol, Rupert Cobbe-Warburton, Max Steele, and Ioana-Madalina Patrichi. 2014. Rubikon: A Highly Reconfigurable Device for Advanced Interaction. In *Proceedings of the Extended Abstracts of the 32Nd Annual ACM Conference on Human Factors in Computing Systems* (CHI EA '14), 1327–1332. https://doi.org/10.1145/2559206.2581275

35. Benjamin Salem and Harold Peeters. 2007. InterCUBE: A Study into Merging Action and Interaction Spaces. In *Human-Computer Interaction – INTERACT 2007*, Cécilia Baranauskas, Philippe Palanque, Julio Abascal and Simone Diniz Junqueira Barbosa (eds.). Springer Berlin Heidelberg, 57–70. https://doi.org/10.1007/978-3-540-74800-7_5

36. Bert Schiettecatte and Jean Vanderdonckt. 2008. AudioCubes: A Distributed Cube Tangible Interface Based on Interaction Range for Sound Design. In *Proceedings of the 2Nd International Conference on Tangible and Embedded Interaction* (TEI '08), 3–10. https://doi.org/10.1145/1347390.1347394

37. Eric Schweikardt and Mark D. Gross. 2006. roBlocks: A Robotic Construction Kit for Mathematics and Science Education. In *Proceedings of the 8th International Conference on Multimodal Interfaces* (ICMI '06), 72–75. https://doi.org/10.1145/1180995.1181010

38. Orit Shaer and Eva Hornecker. 2010. Tangible User Interfaces: Past, Present, and Future Directions. *Found. Trends Hum.-Comput. Interact.* 3, 1–2: 1–137. https://doi.org/10.1561/1100000026

39. J. G. Sheridan, B. W. Short, K. Van Laerhoven, N. Villar, and G. Kortuem. 2003. Exploring cube affordance: towards a classification of non-verbal dynamics of physical interfaces for wearable computing. In *IEE Eurowearable, 2003*, 113–118. https://doi.org/10.1049/ic:20030156

40. Hyunyoung Song, François Guimbretière, Michael A. Ambrose, and Carl Lostritto. 2007. Cubeexplorer: An Evaluation of Interaction Techniques in Architectural Education. In *Proceedings of the 11th IFIP TC 13 International Conference on Human-computer Interaction - Volume Part II* (INTERACT'07), 43–56. Retrieved August 16, 2016 from http://dl.acm.org/citation.cfm?id=1778331.1778337

41. Ian Stavness, Billy Lam, and Sidney Fels. 2010. pCubee: A Perspective-corrected Handheld Cubic Display. In *Proceedings of the SIGCHI Conference on Human Factors in Computing Systems* (CHI '10), 1381–1390. https://doi.org/10.1145/1753326.1753535

42. Hideyuki Suzuki and Hiroshi Kato. 1995. Interaction-level Support for Collaborative Learning: AlgoBlock—an Open Programming Language. In *The First International Conference on Computer Support for Collaborative Learning* (CSCL '95), 349–355. https://doi.org/10.3115/222020.222828

43. Lucia Terrenghi, Matthias Kranz, Paul Holleis, and Albrecht Schmidt. 2006. A Cube to Learn: A Tangible User Interface for the Design of a Learning Appliance. *Personal Ubiquitous Comput.* 10, 2–3: 153–158. https://doi.org/10.1007/s00779-005-0025-8

44. Junya Ueda, Takashi Matsumoto, and Naohito Okude. 2004. Cubic Display Device "Z-agon": a movie to design Z-agon. In *Adjunct Proceedings of Ubicomp 2004 - Videos.*

45. B. Ullmer and H. Ishii. 2000. Emerging Frameworks for Tangible User Interfaces. *IBM Syst. J.* 39, 3–4: 915–931. https://doi.org/10.1147/sj.393.0915

46. Brygg Ullmer, Hiroshi Ishii, and Dylan Glas. 1998. mediaBlocks: Physical Containers, Transports, and Controls for Online Media. In *Proceedings of the 25th Annual Conference on Computer Graphics and Interactive Techniques* (SIGGRAPH '98), 379–386. https://doi.org/10.1145/280814.280940

47. Brygg Ullmer, Hiroshi Ishii, and Robert J. K. Jacob. 2005. Token+Constraint Systems for Tangible Interaction with Digital Information. *ACM Trans. Comput.-Hum. Interact.* 12, 1: 81–118. https://doi.org/10.1145/1057237.1057242

48. Kristof Van Laerhoven, Nicolas Villar, Albrecht Schmidt, Gerd Kortuem, and Hans Gellersen. 2003. Using an Autonomous Cube for Basic Navigation and Input. In *Proceedings of the 5th International Conference on Multimodal Interfaces* (ICMI '03), 203–210. https://doi.org/10.1145/958432.958472

49. Danli Wang, Yang Zhang, Tianyuan Gu, Liang He, and Hongan Wang. 2012. E-Block: A Tangible Programming Tool for Children. In *Adjunct Proceedings of the 25th Annual ACM Symposium on User Interface Software and Technology* (UIST Adjunct Proceedings '12), 71–72. https://doi.org/10.1145/2380296.2380327

50. Ryoichi Watanabe, Yuichi Itoh, Masatsugu Asai, Yoshifumi Kitamura, Fumio Kishino, and Hideo Kikuchi. 2004. The Soul of ActiveCube: Implementing a Flexible, Multimodal, Three-dimensional Spatial Tangible Interface. *Comput. Entertain.* 2, 4: 15–15. https://doi.org/10.1145/1037851.1037874

51. Kuan-Ju Wu and Mark D. Gross. 2010. TOPAOKO: Interactive Construction Kit. In *CHI '10 Extended Abstracts on Human Factors in Computing Systems* (CHI EA '10), 3619–3624. https://doi.org/10.1145/1753846.1754028

52. Ludwig Zeller and Lasse Scherffig. 2009. CubeBrowser: A Cognitive Adapter to Explore Media Databases. In *CHI '09 Extended Abstracts on Human Factors in Computing Systems* (CHI EA '09), 2619–2622. https://doi.org/10.1145/1520340.1520366

53. 2018. Platonic solid. *Wikipedia*. Retrieved from https://en.wikipedia.org/w/index.php?title=Platonic_solid&oldid=832467181

54. Light Cube. Retrieved February 8, 2017 from https://www.behance.net/gallery/32910829/Light-Cube-Panta-Rei

55. Fidget. Retrieved February 8, 2017 from https://www.thefidgetcube.co/

56. Beatdice. Retrieved February 8, 2017 from http://www.tobyk.com.au/beatdice_vivid2015_1/

57. Hikari Tsumiki 2.0. Retrieved February 8, 2017 from https://gugen.jp/entry2016/2016-121

58. http://www.thesaurus.net/cube. Retrieved from http://www.thesaurus.net/cube

59. Oto-No-Katachi. Retrieved February 8, 2017 from https://otonokatachi.com/

60. Fingies. Retrieved February 8, 2017 from http://www.fingies.de/

Making Things Apart: Gaining Material Understanding

Martin Murer
Center for
Human-Computer Interaction
University of Salzburg
martin.murer@sbg.ac.at

DIS '18, June 9–13, 2018, , Hong Kong

ACM ISBN 978-1-4503-5198-0/18/06...$15.00
https://doi.org/10.1145/3196709.3196806

Abstract
This pictorial explores the material resources that can unfold through taking things apart. We describe a workshop program and according exercises designed around four particular modes of disassembling (interactive) artefacts. These exercises aim to provide low-threshold engagements with artefacts and the materials those artefacts are composed of. Based on a series of workshops we conducted following this program, we depict nine different forms of material resources that are unveiled through taking things apart. With this distinction we aim to contribute to the understanding of how the material histories of components and the rules that were governing their previous relations, are carried over to new compositions during reuse or reinterpretation.

Authors Keywords
Design Exercises; Disassembly; Un-Crafting; Material; Material Understanding; Making;

ACM Classification Keywords
H.5.m. Information interfaces and presentation (e.g., HCI): Miscellaneous.

Making Things Apart as a Material Practice

While research into making typically emphasizes the synthesizing, the constructing, the putting things together, recent research has foregrounded the relevance of the de-constructive counterpart: For instance, research on practices around repair and obsolescence [6], material literacy [7], playful hacking [5], un-crafting [9], and the collaborative act of taking things apart as means to create shared material knowledge [10] has provided several related approaches.

In the context of interaction design research, those de-constructive encounters with materials – as integral part of many making practices – can be related to experimental engineering, as coined by Vallgårda and colleagues. While their concept of experimental engineering is not "a radically new way of working in design" it is about articulating "the value of open-ended technological experiments as a legitimate design research practice." [13, p. 199] They distinguish three types of experimentation (i.e., recombining, reconfiguring, and recontextualizing technology); all three of which might be well supported or unleashed by deliberately taking existing technology apart.

While studies on taking things apart often depart from existing works in the realm of (mainly engineering or STEM) education, we see *making things apart* as an approach that is not limited to material literacy in education. Rather, we interpret it as a practice of engaging with technology that unfolds particular material resources. In order to unveil the characteristics of those resources, we created a dedicated workshop program around the theme of *making things apart* and conducted a series of according events. In the remainder of this pictorial we will detail the program and procedure, and provide nine categories of material resources and knowledge we saw unfold.

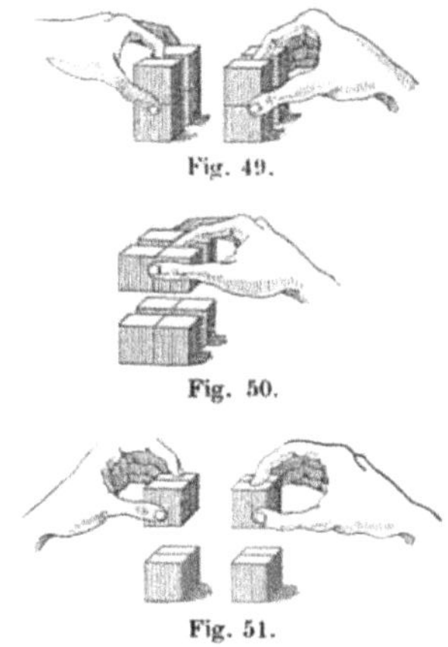

"One whole—two halves."
"One half—two quarters (or fourths)."
"Two quarters—one half."
"Two halves—one whole."

Taking things apart has a long history in education, *starting with Fröbel's Third Gift. As part of a series of educational toys created in the early 19th century, the third gift is composed of eight cubes, accompanied by instructions for the educator to facilitate the development of early number concepts through taking apart and putting back together. While a plethora of related building block kits has found its way into education, and eventually into making and design, tools that specifically facilitate learning through deconstruction are less visible than their constructive counterparts. Image taken from [14, p. 100].*

Un-Crafting as Guiding Framework

The workshops discussed in this pictorial are conceptually based on an organizational framework for un-crafting [9], i.e., taking (interactive) things apart as part of a design, research or making activity. This framework differentiates four modes of un-crafting that are distinct in their focus and orientation.

The un-crafting framework targets two applications: *analytical,* in order to render visible and describe how un-crafting is inherent to manifold making and design processes, and *constructive*, as a means to create material knowledge by engaging with interactive artefacts through disassembling them. For the workshop program described in this pictorial we instantiated the four modes provided by the un-crafting framework in concrete exercises.

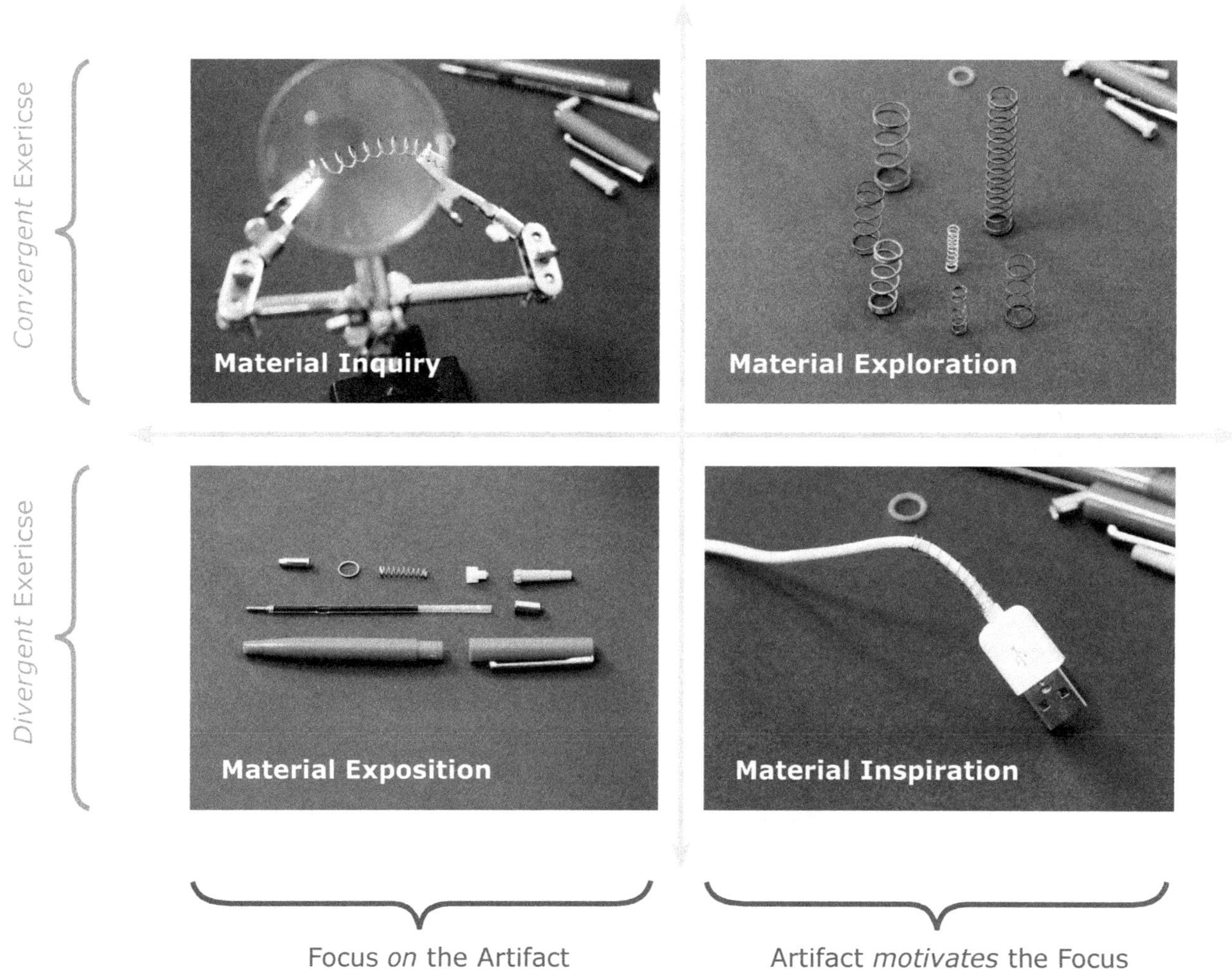

The organizational framework for Un-Crafting [9]. De-constructive activities (or exercises) are distinguished by their focus and orientation. Divergent Exercises are open-ended and characterized by questions about the "What?" (e.g., what is it made of), while convergent exercises are about (design) rationales and attributes ("Why?"). The second dimension of the framework allows to differentiate whether the artifact is in focus or motivates the focus of the exercise.

Making Things Apart – A Workshop Program

In order to explore what material resources unfold through taking things apart we created a workshop program that consists of four stages, organized by the un-crafting framework described above. While not mutually exclusive, the four stages allow to focus on specific aspects of taking things apart. As disassembling and reverse engineering are used in various – mainly educational – settings, the individual exercises were not developed from scratch but are based on or inspired by existing approaches (e.g., [2,3,11]).

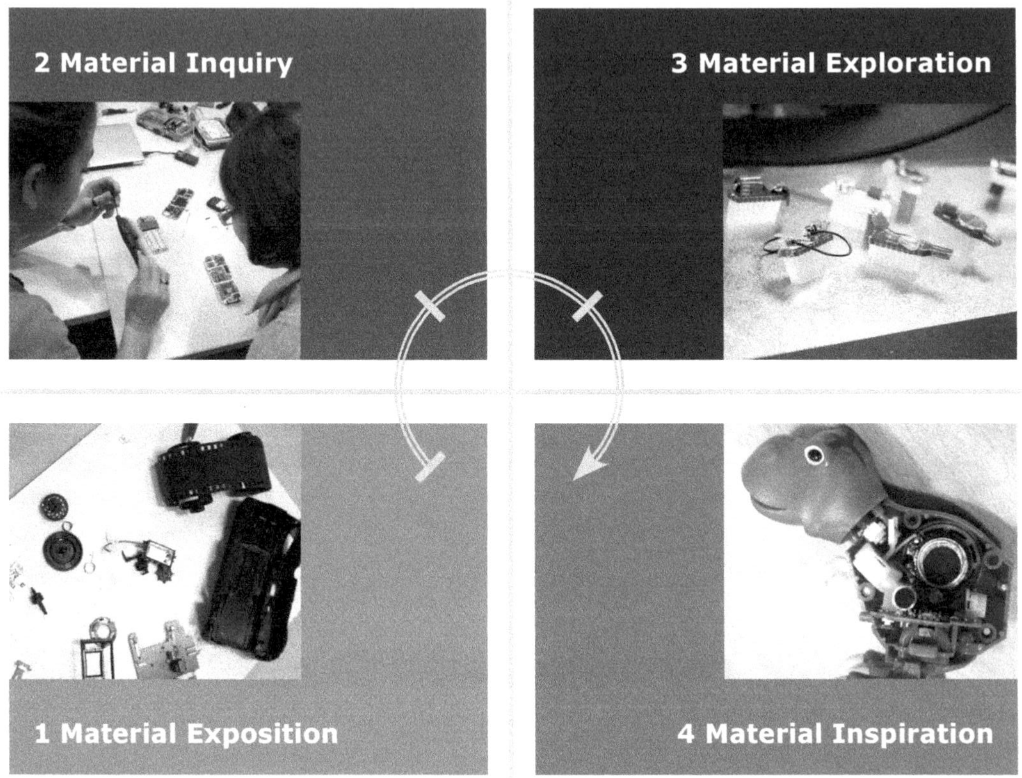

Stage 1 – Material Exposition

The first phase of the workshop focuses on basic principles of taking something apart. To kickstart the workshop, push-button, screw-apart ballpoint pens, are the disassembled and analyzed. (See [3] for a thorough guideline on applying this particular process in engineering education.) As a second exercise, participants take apart an object of their choice from a pile of prepared artifacts, aiming to disassemble as much as possible without breaking individual components.

Stage 2 – Material Inquiry

The second stage draws attention to the specifics of a material. For this exercise, the participants are asked to find the component that makes a mobile phone vibrate (i.e., its vibration motor) by taking the phone apart.

Stage 3 – Material Exploration

For the third stage the participants are introduced to bristlebots, a design that utilizes vibration to provide propulsion to tiny bots made from toothbrushes. While there is some controversy [11] about their original invention, bristlebots gained a lot of attention both as DIY and commercial educational materials. Taking apart further mobile phones allows to compare and contrast vibrating motors with different characteristics.

Stage 4 – Material Inspiration

In the final stage of the workshop the participants take apart functioning devices and create new compositions based on the material gathered from all preceding exercises. This exercise is inspired by several existing programs for taking apart toys, such as the one hosted by the Tinkering Studio of San Francisco's Exploratorium [2].

Workshop 1

Setting: International Conference (TEI 2015)
Participants: 8 Design Research Experts
Duration: one-day workshop (8h)
Program: Integration of artifact dissection, open ended experimentation, reflection, and discussion

The initial workshop of this series was conducted with experts in Design Research to inform the conceptualization of the making things apart workshop program.

Workshop 2

Setting: STEM event as part of a promotion of excellence program during an international technology forum
Participants: 25, aged 13 - 18
Duration: one-day workshop (8h)

The second event followed exactly the workshop program outlined above. As accompanying inspiration, photos and videos from related work in the arts was used (e.g., Todd McLellans fabulous photographic work on disassembled technology [8], or videos form Simone Giertz, the self-entitled "Queen of Shitty Robots" [4]).

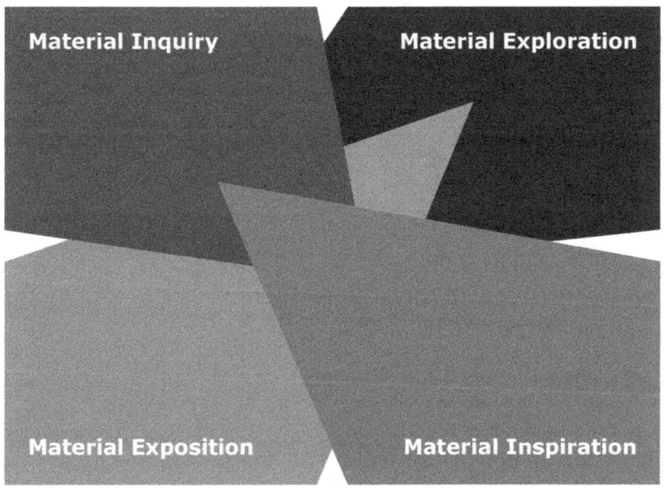

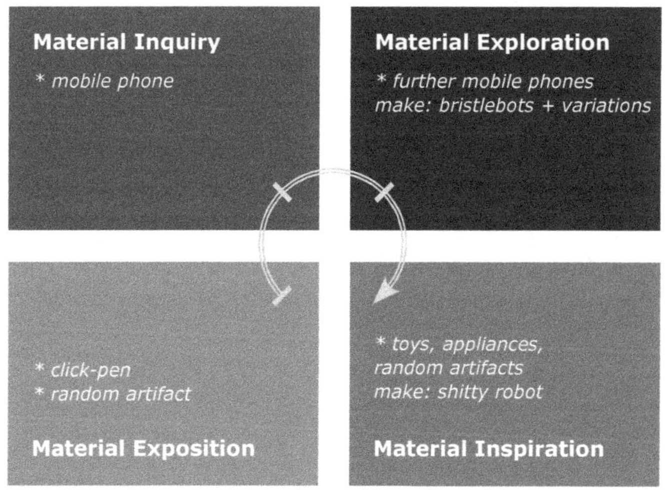

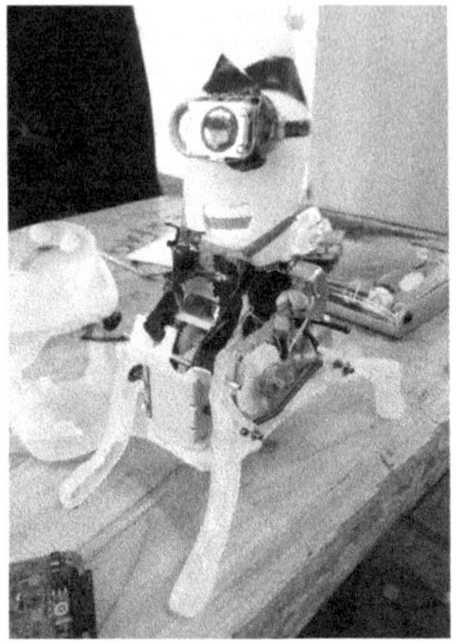

Workshop 3

Setting: public workshop as part of *Schmiede 2016,* an annual media art festival in Hallein, Austria
Participants: 28, aged 4 - 59, children, their parents, artists, makers, designers
Duration: one-day workshop (8h)

Material Inquiry
* mobile phone

Material Exploration
* further mobile phones
make: bristlebots + variations

* click-pen
* random artifact

Material Exposition

* toys, appliances, random artifacts

Material Inspiration

make: hebocon contestant

Hebocon*

This workshop was organized in coordination with a hebocon taking place the following day at the same festival. Working towards a *crappy robot* for the hebocon created a productive balance between goal-oriented and material-driven modes of making during the final phase of the workshop.

*Hebocon - A robot contest for the ungifted

Hebocons are robot sumo-wrestling competitions for crappy robots. The Hebocon format was envisioned by Daiju Ishikawa in 2014 after realizing "... that the way people fail in engineering is very interesting and entertaining." [1] Since then, hebocons got pervasive at, e.g., makerfairs and media art festivals as well as in manifold educational contexts as a low-threshold, engaging and fun way of approaching technology. In the context of creating a hebocon contestant, reusing broken or decommissioned hardware is almost self-evident.

The hebocon battlefield and audience during *Schmiede 2016*. *Schmiede* is an annual media art festival in Hallein, Austria.

Workshop 4

Setting: STEM event as part of a promotion of science and technology week
Participants: 26, aged 13 - 14
Duration: half-day workshop (4h)

Due to a limited duration of 4 hours, the workshop program was adapted: Instead of creating functioning (crappy) robots in the concluding material inspiration exercise, we asked the students to create scale models of imaginary buildings based on the material gathered.

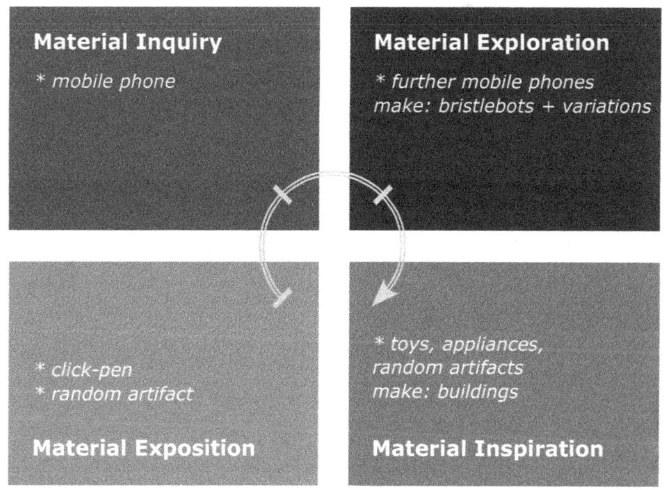

Material Resources

During all workshops, photos were taken to document the processes and outcomes. Afterwards, photos that expose some sort of material resource were annotated and clustered based on similarities. On the following pages we depict exemplars of the nine categories of material resources we saw unfold through the exercises. The categorization provided here is not to be understood as exhaustive or mutually exclusive, i.e., a single material component might as well fall into several classes of material resources simultaneously.

The Totality of Components as Material

The wholeness of an artefact bears its own distinct quality; even in its disassembled state.

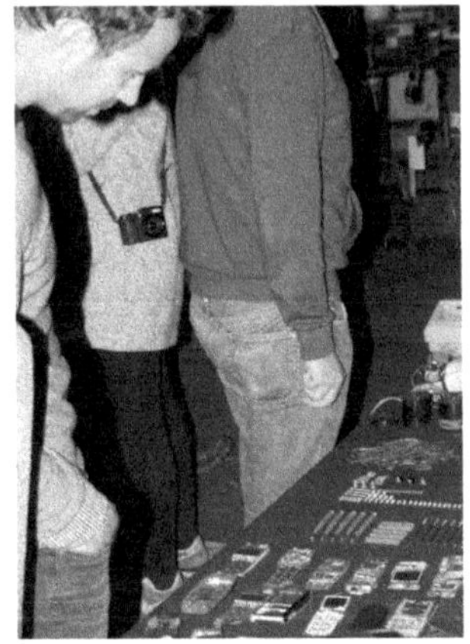

A Treasury of Components as Material

Through dissecting one or multiple artifacts, the maker gains a treasury of components as a source for, e.g., a subsequent bricolage (see e.g., [12]).

A Quantity of Components as Material

Certain components do occur in groups and thus create a stock of new material to work with.

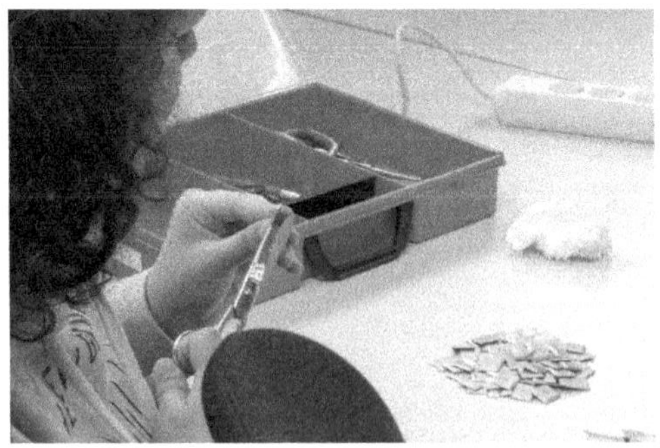

Movement as Material

Movements of (parts of) artifacts can be conserved, reused or reinterpreted as a material of its own. For instance, here the movement of a remote controlled plush dog got reinterpreted as a "mars rover". Subsequently, the preceding "mars rover movement" was reinterpreted as a "horse", carrying a minion knight.

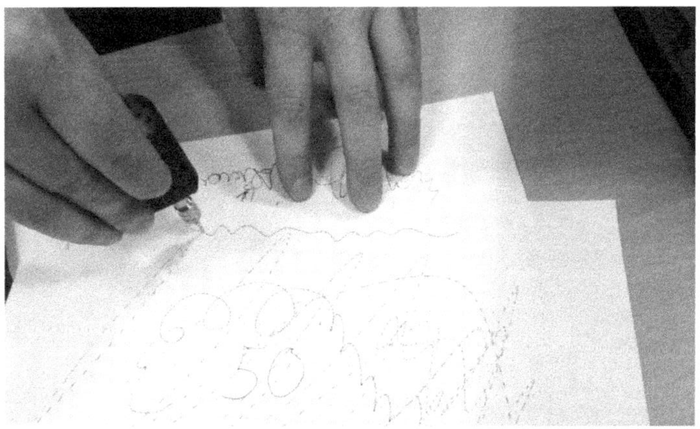

Function as material

The function of individual components provides a material resource to be reinterpreted by creating new expressions. For instance, the rotation of a small handheld power drill, refactored into a pen drawing dashed lines.

The Unfamiliar as Material

Being unfamiliar with the qualities of material components can create suspenseful mysteries and new connections.

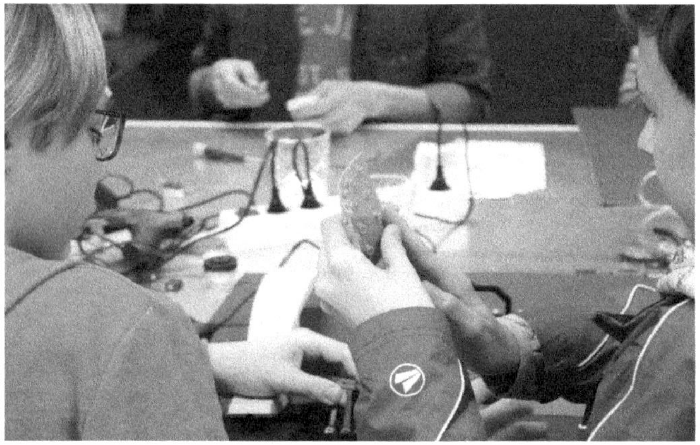

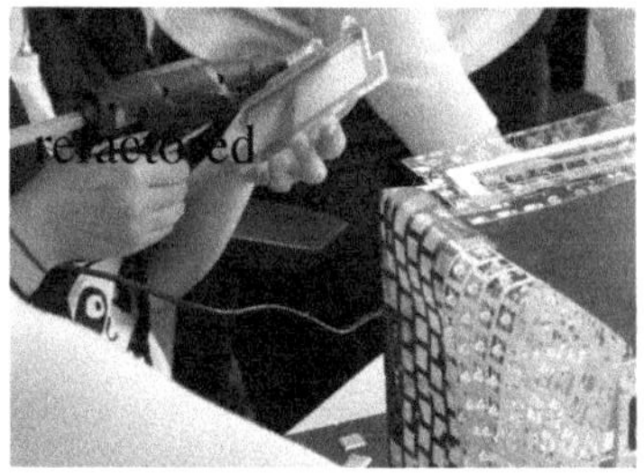

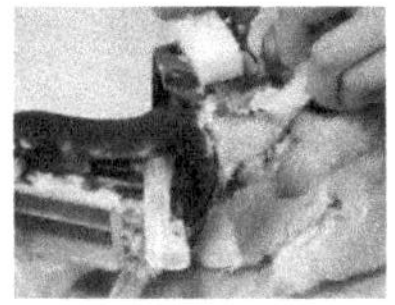

Retained Expressiveness as Material

Material gathered from decomposition can carry on some of the expressiveness of its donor, even when the physical configuration and composition is altered.

Shape as Material

The shape of components can be reinterpreted in a new composition. For instance, here what used to be an industrial keyboard's casing and keys are refactored into a facade.

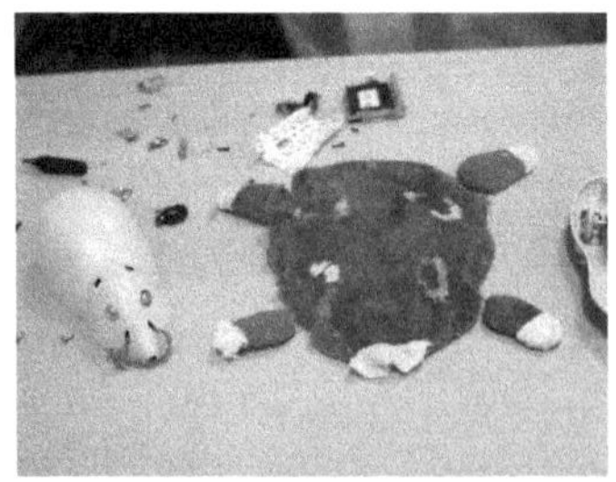

Performance as Material

Entire artifacts can become materials by taking apart and remixing its performative structure.

Bim Bim the Nutty Squirrel™, a plush toy. Squeeze it, and it starts shaking and bouncing while emitting a nerve-racking, boisterous laughter.

The final design, entitled "trumpster", is still nervously jumping up and down and emitting its annoying laughter, while the iPod touch, reinterpreted as a banner, displays a video loop of the then presidential candidate Donald Trump. Trumpster was a result of remixing not only the original toy's physical parts but its whole performance into a new composition, based on the toy's physical appearance, its movement, and its sound.

After full disassembly and reassembly of the toy, the squirrel's tail got chopped off and reattached horizontally on the head, mocking a contemporary prominent hair flip.

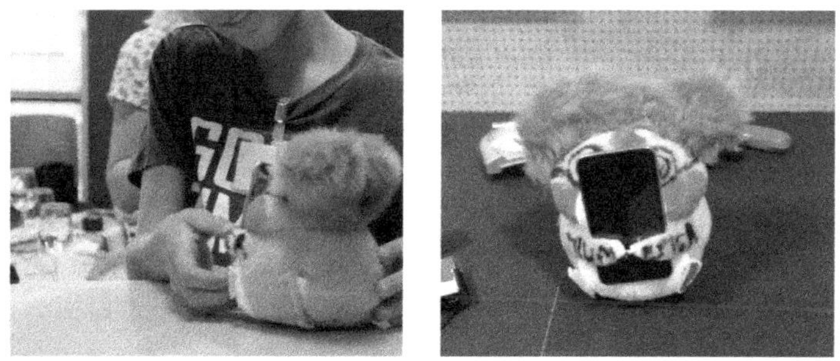

The redesign got further extended by the addition of an iPod Touch and some makeup.

Conclusions

In this pictorial we presented a workshop program for *making things apart* that aims to harvest the potential of an un-crafting practice for experiential engagement with the materials (technological) artifacts are composed of. The material resources gained are essentially based on, constrained and shaped by the particular artifacts taken apart. Thus, making things apart is not to be understood as method to be applied in conceptual design, but rather as a tool that provides points of departure for engaging with materials in making and design (education).

Those in-situ constraints imposed by the specific nature of a given artifact might moreover be used in a productive way by deliberately selecting objects and technologies to start from, and, thus, providing a targeted material grounding to an open ended, exploratory journey.

While we were not specifically targeting collaborative practices, the greater part of the exercises conducted almost naturally grew into collaborative endeavors. Making things apart as a team effort not only benefits from an extended set of preconceptions and skills, it also has the potential to create shared conceptualizations about the material gathered to be subsequently used in a collaborative construction activity.

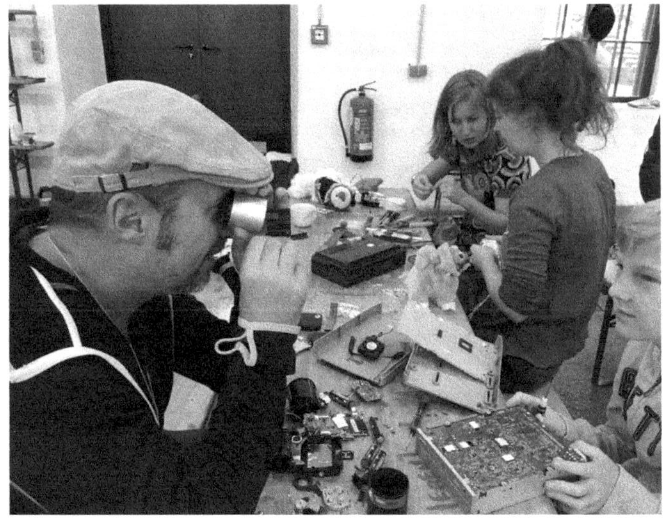

The set of nine material resources we derived from a series of workshops provide a glimpse into how the material resources gained are accompanied by material knowledge that is constructed through the act of disassembling. This material can be seen as inherently distinct from material gathered from other sources as each harvested component stays tightly connected to its material history: It carries on the rules that were governing its previous relations to other components. It is this material history that provides starting points for reconfiguration and reinterpretation when disassembling is incorporated in design, making or experimental engineering practices. We hope the nine categories of material resources presented in this pictorial can help to better articulate the relations between material and material knowledge we gain by taking things apart.

Acknowledgements

I would like to thank the following people for their manifold contributions to the preparation, organization, and documentation of the workshops described in this pictorial: Verena Fuchsberger, Thomas Grah, Mattias Jacobsson, Alina Krischkowsky, Bernhard Maurer, Dorothé Smit, Anna Vallgårda, and Rüdiger Wassibauer. Special thanks to all the workshop participants as well as to the organisations hosting them, i.e., TEI 2015, Schmiede (www.schmiede.ca), Wissensstadt Salzburg, The European Forum Alpbach, and the Center for Human-Computer Interaction at Salzburg University.

References

1. Evan Ackerman. 2017. Hebocon: The Best Worst Robot Competition. (2017). https://spectrum.ieee.org/ automaton/robotics/diy/hebocon-the-best-worst-robot-competition
2. Exploratorium. 2014. *Toy take apart*. (2014). http://tinkering.exploratorium.edu/sites/default/files/Instructions/toy_take_apart_0.pdf
3. Tufts University Center for Engineering Educational Outreach. 2016. *Hands-on Activity: Disassemble a Click Pen.* (2016). https://www.teachengineering.org/activities/view/disassemble_a_click_pen
4. Simone Giertz. 2017. *Simone Giertz*. personal webpage. (2017). http://www.simonegiertz.com
5. William Goddard and Robert Cercos. 2015. Playful Hacking Within Research-through-Design. In *Proceedings of the Annual Meeting of the Australian Special Interest Group for Computer Human Interaction* (OzCHI '15). ACM, New York, NY, USA, 333–337. http://dx.doi.org/10.1145/2838739.2838802
6. Steven J. Jackson and Laewoo Kang. 2014. Breakdown, Obsolescence and Reuse: HCI and the Art of Repair. In *Proceedings of the SIGCHI Conference on Human Factors in Computing Systems* (CHI '14). ACM, New York, NY, USA, 449–458. http://dx.doi.org/10.1145/2556288.2557332
7. Sophie Landwehr Sydow, Jakob Tholander, and Martin Jonsson. 2017. "It's a Bomb!" – Material Literacy and Narratives of Making. In *Proceedings of the 2017 CHI Conference on Human Factors in Computing Systems* (CHI'17). ACM, New York, NY, USA, 121–132. http://dx.doi.org/10.1145/3025453.3025529
8. Todd McLellan. 2013. *Things Come Apart: A Teardown Manual for Modern Living*. Thames & Hudson.
9. Martin Murer, Verena Fuchsberger, and Manfred Tscheligi. 2017. Un-Crafting: De-Constructive Engagements with Interactive Artifacts. In *Proceedings of the 11th International Conference on Tangible, Embedded, and Embodied Interaction.* http://dx.doi.org/10.1145/3024969.3024993
10. Martin Murer, Mattias Jacobsson, Siri Skillgate, and Petra Sundström. 2014. Taking Things Apart: Reaching Common Ground and Shared Material Understanding. In *Proceedings of the SIGCHI Conference on Human Factors in Computing Systems* (CHI '14). ACM, New York, NY, USA, 469–472. http://dx.doi.org/10.1145/2556288.2557267
11. Daniel Terdiman. 2009. *Controversy surrounds 'Bristlebots' book*. (2009). https://www.cnet.com/news/controversy-surrounds-bristlebots-book
12. Anna Vallgårda and Ylva Fernaeus. 2015. Interaction Design As a Bricolage Practice. In Proceedings of the Ninth International Conference on Tangible, Embedded, and Embodied Interaction (TEI '15). ACM, New York, NY, USA, 173–180. http://dx.doi.org/10.1145/2677199.2680594
13. Anna Vallgårda, Erik Grönvall, and Jonas Fritsch. 2017. Experimental Engineering: Articulating and Valuing Design Experimentation. In *Proceedings of the 2017 ACM Conference Companion Publication on Designing Interactive Systems* (DIS '17 Companion). ACM, New York, NY, USA, 197–201. http://dx.doi.org/10.1145/3064857.3079145
14. Edward Wiebé, Milton Bradley, and Henry Wolcottt Blake. 1907. *Quarter century edition of The paradise of childhood: A practical guide to kindergartners*. Milton Bradley Company.

Words Become Worlds: The LIT ROOM, a Literacy Support Tool at Room-Scale.

George J. Schafer, Susan King Fullerton, Ian Walker, Amith Vijaykumar
Clemson University, Clemson SC, USA
{gschafe, susanf, iwalker, amithmv}@clemson.edu

Keith Evan Green
Cornell University
Cornell, NY, USA
keg95@cornell.edu

ABSTRACT
Illiteracy is a global problem impacting the growth and development of individuals and society. Studies indicate that picturebook reading within a facilitated storytime setting is an important tool for children's language acquisition. In the research reported here, we hypothesized that literacy, in an increasingly digital society, can be cultivated in a robot-embedded environment that is physical, digital and evocative of the picturebook being read. *Words become worlds.* To test our hypothesis, we designed, prototyped, and implemented the LIT ROOM, a cyber-physical room for literacy. As a *Research through Design* [RtD] exemplar for interactive systems at habitable scale, the LIT ROOM featured a multi-phase, iterative process of design and evaluation for usability and efficacy. Evaluations with 35 children and 6 librarians in a public library serving a population with grave literacy challenges suggest that our reconfigurable learning environment facilitates a diversity of children's literary responses during the dialogical reading of picturebooks.

Author Keywords
Computer Support Tools; Children; Emergent Literacy; Intelligent Environments, Architecture, Design; Human Factors, HRI.

ACM Classification Keywords
H.5.2 [Information Systems]: User Interfaces—*Theory and methods, and* H.1.2 User/Machine Systems—*Human factors;* K.3.1 [Computers and Education]: Computer Uses in Education—*collaborative learning.*

INTRODUCTION
According to an UNESCO study, roughly 20% of the world's population is illiterate [35]. In the United States, 14% of the nation's residents are illiterate; 32 million Americans cannot read the directions on a medicine bottle, and 50 million Americans cannot read above the 5th grade (ten-year old) level [24]. The cost of illiteracy to society, not to mention the cost to the individuals who can't read, is staggering [19]. Efforts to enhance early literacy are necessary to address the significant societal problems that illiteracy poses [24]. As such, public libraries direct much of their resources toward literacy acquisition programming, especially for at-risk children [17]. There is evidence that public libraries effectively leverage technologies (physical and digital) to reduce illiteracy in their communities [17]. There is also a body of literature focused on the usability and efficacy of technology-enhanced tools and texts for children, including electronic books (e.g. [8, 23]), augmented books (e.g. [4, 36]), multi-media tools (e.g. [3, 14]), robotic-enhanced literacy tools (e.g. [29]), and technology-enhanced story rooms (e.g. [5, 7]). But despite the efforts of libraries and technologists, little is known about how technology, particularly when deployed at larger physical scales, may be leveraged to augment children's literacy during *read-alouds* [17], even though these instructional events, where adults read books aloud to children, have been shown to be essential for children's literacy attainment [9, 10, 16, 17, 37].

Figure 1. The LIT ROOM, from inside.

In response to this shortcoming, we designed, implemented and evaluated the LIT ROOM (Figure 1), a cyber-physical room set within a public library. In a typical LIT ROOM activity, a librarian and a group of 4-8 children engage in a multi-sensory read-aloud of a printed picturebook. Prior to reading the text, librarians program wall and ceiling-mounted robotic panels by selecting, on a tablet computer, from a wide palate of lighting, sound and shape/movement

DIS '18, June 9–13, 2018, , Hong Kong
© 2018 Association for Computing Machinery.
ACM ISBN 978-1-4503-5198-0/18/06···$15.00
https://doi.org/10.1145/3196709.3196728

effects to create "scenes" that they imagine are evocative of key aspects of a picturebook they select from the library collection. Multi-sensory scenes are saved into the system and replayed in sequence during an interactive read-aloud. When activated, each scene enhances the text and serves as a spatial prompt, providing the adult reader an opportunity to elicit children's literary responses and facilitate reader-child dialogue. This type of *scaffolding*, where the adult reader actively guides the discourse – is critical for children's meaning-making during interactive read-alouds [33]. In the LIT ROOM, the adult works in tandem with the lighting, sounds and shape/movement effects to facilitate connections between children's understandings, the multisensory environment and the text.

As a story-extension tool, the LIT ROOM system also provides opportunities for adult readers to engage children users as co-creators of their learning environment, which is very motivational to children [13]. The ideas, understandings and connections of these young readers shape their physical surroundings, *giving form* to their ideas about the text. When the form of the picturebook offered by the adult reader's pre-programmed scenes fails to match those envisioned by the children, they are afforded the opportunity to make visible and tangible their own imaginations for inspection by themselves and others. Using the touchscreen tablet to manipulate the environmental effects, children can increasingly assume ownership of the environment, providing real-time feedback for their creative expressions. The broader aim of this exemplar of interdisciplinary "Research through Design" [12, 38] is to successfully leverage technology in the creation of a reconfigurable environment augmenting the dialogical reading of picturebooks within an engaging, exploratory space for the advancement of literacy – one that facilitates a wider range of children's literary responses and scaffolds a diversity of textual interpretations.

Informed by new thinking about literacy that recognizes knowledge as "situated," the LIT ROOM may be understood "in terms of a relationship between an individual with both a mind and a body and an environment in which the individual thinks, feels, acts and interacts" [13]. The LIT ROOM's wide-ranging pallet of lighting, sound, form, and movement at room-scale finds inspiration in Gee's argument that "people are smarter when they work in smart environments; that is, environments that contain, integrate, and network a variety of tools, technologies, and other people, all of which store usable knowledge [13]. Similarly, the LIT ROOM's reconfigurability is inspired by *embodied interaction* in children which foregrounds the body of a child in a physical environment that affords "multiple spatial configurations," thereby advancing the "child's grasp of our universe through active, creative exploration" [2]. An elaboration of our motivations for the LIT ROOM including our review of the literature on literacy support tools can be found in our foundational publications [30, 31].

ITERATIVE DESIGN

The LIT ROOM was developed and evaluated by a research team of architectural and interaction designers, roboticists, a literacy expert, and a library scientist. Conceptualization of the LIT ROOM followed its pilot project, the LIT KIT (Figure 2—left) – essentially a LIT ROOM reduced to a low-cost, compact, and easily transportable box that supports multi-sensory picturebook read-alouds in classrooms and private dwellings [31]. While the LIT KIT offers a compelling facsimile of the LIT ROOM experience, the LIT KIT amounts to a lesser social, lesser spatially-rich literacy support tool.

LIT ROOM Conceptualization and Early Prototyping

The conceptualization of the LIT ROOM benefited from the team's extensive, iterative development and evaluation of LIT KIT as reported in [31]. Our early photo collage established the LIT ROOM's key components, including a reconfigurable ceiling, represented in the collage by our photo of a matchbook manipulated to show different physical configurations (Figure 2—center). Other key components include: a transportable superstructure that defines the read-aloud context and supports the robotic elements; wall and ceiling-mounted robotic elements containing integral lighting, sound, and actuated panels that transform the environment, and a touchscreen tablet that serves as the interface for read-aloud design and activation.

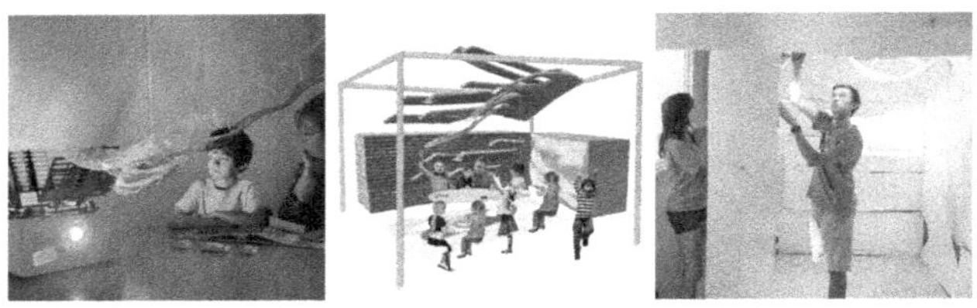

Figure 2. The LIT ROOM collage; LIT KIT; early prototype.

To "make mistakes faster" [21] in our early prototyping and evaluation activities, we cobbled together a full-scale prototype of the LIT ROOM (Figure 2—right) using Bosch aluminium framing [6], polyethelene foam actuated by a pulley and tendon system, digital projectors, and audio speaker. Physical reconfigurations were operated manually to simulate a full-function system following the "WoZ" method [11]. Low-fidelity prototypes like this one were developed using design and engineering principles developed in our laboratory [15], evaluated by usability methods common to the design and evaluation of interactive technologies for both adults [25] and children [20]. Multiple, formative evaluations provided information that guided design decisions as the project developed from small and full scale, low-fidelity prototypes to the full-scale, robotics embedded LIT ROOM implemented in the children's room of our public library test-bed.

Phase-1 Evaluation: Heuristic Evaluation & Co-Design

We performed heuristic evaluations and co-design activities on low and high-fidelity prototypes of the LIT ROOM, and report here on overall results.

Heuristic Evaluations

Heuristic evaluations were performed in order to: (1) identify usability errors impacting the technical design (such as lag time between motor activation and panel actuation); and (2) identify usability errors impacting the educational context (such as the need for task light sufficient for reading the picturebook balanced against a space dark enough for the LIT Room's environmental effects). Additionally, the evaluation served as a pilot for procedures used to gather usability data for the children participants.

Co-design Activities with Children and Librarians

Three studies engaged children and librarians as co-designers of the LIT ROOM. A focus group of six children's librarians used task analysis and paper prototypes of three touchscreen formats to reveal preferences for both the format and functionality of the LIT ROOM interface. Another focus group of librarians co-designed lighting, sound, and moving panel designs for picturebooks included in the study, revealing preferences for the multi-media effects in the space. Finally, sixteen second-grade children (typically seven and eight-year olds) co-designed scenes from picturebooks with team members. These studies built upon established participatory design techniques that have proven effective with children [22].

Development of the Fully Functioning Prototype

For library implementation, the LIT ROOM prototype was assembled to partial completion in our lab where it was evaluated and refined to address issues related to constructability and technical functionality. The prototype was then disassembled and installed in the children's reading room at Richland Library [27] in Columbia, South Carolina – the largest public library in the state, located approximately 100 miles from our lab.

LIT ROOM Superstructure

The LIT ROOM superstructure inscribes a twelve-foot square in plan. The primary frame defining the vertical walls is eight feet high. For ease of assembly and disassembly, the superstructure is reduced to the fewest structural members required to both create a rigid frame and to structurally support the weight of the wall and ceiling-mounted robots. Black, extruded plastic conduits are attached to the superstructure at the top of the beams, facilitating power distribution to the four robots.

All connectors and fasteners are either flush with the extruded profiles or hidden, resulting in a clean, sleek appearance. The installation is clad with white and red, aluminium-composite panels, digitally fabricated using CNC routers, creating two distinctly visual elements (Figure 3). The horizontal, overhead portion of the red arch serves as an electrical plenum, concealing wiring running from the main control cabinet (located in the white tower) to the extruded plastic conduit connecting to the individual robots. Aesthetically, the red archway spatially defines the entry to the LIT Room, serving as the threshold between the ordinary space of the library and the extraordinary world within. The archway also houses a bookshelf to hold a small collection of picturebooks for read-alouds.

Figure 3. LIT ROOM in the library – front façade.

LIT ROOM Robotic Components

What was a reconfigurable ceiling in our photo collages (Figure 2) became one of four identical robotic modules (Figures 4 and 5) in the fully-functioning prototype. Each robotic module contains integral lighting, sound, and a motor assembly for actuation. Three of these robotic modules are mounted within the wall frames; the fourth is suspended from the ceiling frame. Each robotic module measures three feet, four inches horizontally and seven feet, four inches vertically. The four-inch margin around each robotic module allows for connection to the superstructure.

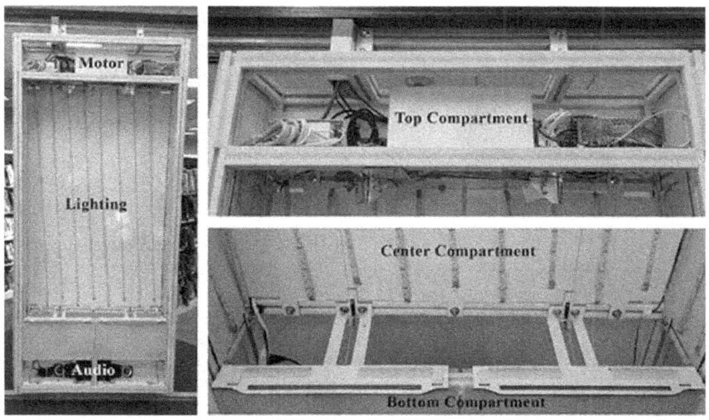

Figure 4. Details of one of four identical robotic modules.

Aesthetically, this gap creates the appearance that the robotic modules are "floating" within the structural frame. The modularity of their design is intended to create the suggestion that the LIT ROOM could be populated by additional robotic components, resulting in a variety of enclosure conditions. The depth of each robot, ten inches, is a function of the dimension of the technological components housed within, and the depth required for adequate panel deformation.

Each robotic module is faced with translucent, 4mm thick, light-weight, corrugated plastic, digitally cut and scored using a CNC router fitted with a drag-knife attachment. A library of such corrugated panels is provided with the LIT ROOM (Figure 5 shows examples). Within each robotic module, a plastic pulley system guides a nylon cable connecting the motor to each plastic panel. When actuated, the plastic panels create abstract shapes, shadows, patterns and/or movements inside the LIT ROOM. Adhesive Velcro, attached to tabs at the top and bottom of each plastic panel, secures the plastic panel to the robotic panel, allowing the librarians and children to easily change-out plastic panels to achieve different formal possibilities (Figure 5). The Velcro can also be repositioned on either side of the panel, resulting in a wider variety of potential profiles. For example, a panel that creates a concave arc will create a convex arc when the Velcro is repositioned on the opposite side. We created approximately thirty pairs of panels for the initial study. Many panels were designed with librarians and children, inspired by picturebooks used in the participatory studies (elaborated here, later).

Figure 5. Four different corrugated panel designs, actuated.

LIT ROOM Interface

A touchscreen tablet (Figure 6) serves as the interface for the LIT ROOM. The interface facilitates the design of a multi-media, environmentally-situated read-aloud and allows adult readers to replay saved scenes while reading the picturebook to children. A home screen (Figure 7—top-left) displays an image of a three-dimensional model of the LIT ROOM installation, and contains two buttons: "Start," which guides users into the system, and a "Sleep" button, which provides a real-time demonstration of the lighting, sound and movement effects.

Figure 6. The LIT ROOM GUI interface in use with children.

By touching the "Start" button, users advance from the "home" screen to the "My Read Aloud Library" screen (Figure 7—top-center). This screen displays a listing of pre-programmed picturebooks. The initial LIT ROOM prototype contained six pre-programmed read-alouds designed in collaboration with the children's librarians. The cover and title of each picturebook is displayed in a list that is navigated by a standard, vertical swiping motion on the interface. The library can hold an infinite number of programmed read-alouds, with new picturebooks added to the listing in simple, sequential order using the "Create New" button. When users press the "Create New" button, t-he interface advances to a "Create New Read Aloud" screen, where users are prompted to enter the name of the picturebook into the system. By tapping on the entry field, a keyboard appears. Pressing "Go" saves the title into the system, and returns users to the "My Read Aloud Library" screen. The new read-aloud is populated into the system at the bottom of the picturebook listing.

Pressing a saved read-aloud on the library listing screen allows users to access design and reading features for that picturebook. Upon touching the desired picturebook, the interface advances to a screen that lists the text title, displays an image of the cover, and indicates how many (and if any) scenes have been programmed for the read-aloud. On the picturebook screen (Figure 7—top-right), four options are provided to users: "Create New Scene" which allows users to add a new scene to the read-aloud; "Edit Scene" which provides access to existing scenes for revision; "Read" which advances to the screen that activates the multi-media read-aloud, and "Delete Book" which allows users to delete a read-aloud from the library.

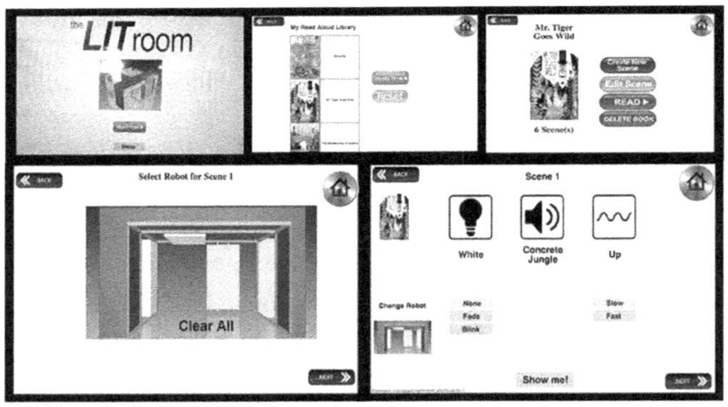

Figure 7. Screen shots of the LIT ROOM tablet interface.
***Top row:* Home, Library, and Read/Create/Edit Scene**
***Bottom row:* user-controls of lighting, sound, form/movement**

To add a new scene to a read-aloud, users touch "Create New Scene." The interface advances to a robot selection screen (Figure 7—bottom-left) that depicts a three-dimensional image of the LIT ROOM. Prior to selection, the robots are depicted in their resting state as solid white elements. Touching a robot selects it for activation during the scene. The interface provides visual confirmation by highlighting selected robots in bright green. Users can select one, two, three, or all four robots for activation for a scene. All robots selected for the scene will activate in unison and will display the same choices for lighting, sound, and movement effects. A "Clear All" button is provided so that users can reselect and revise choices during the robot selection process. Designers save their robot selections by touching "Next," which also advances the interface to the effects customization screen.

Users can select lighting, sound and movement settings on the effects customization screen (Figure 7—bottom-right). This screen orients the user to the read-aloud (an image of the picturebook is depicted in the upper left-hand corner) and the scene being designed (listed at the top-center). A small image depicting the robot selection made on the previous screen is displayed in the bottom left-hand corner. Users are also afforded the opportunity to change their robot selection by touching the "Change Robot" button above the image. Lighting, sound, and movement settings are accessed through three, large icons in the center of the display. Touching on an icon activates a listing of options for that effect. For example, pressing the light bulb icon results in a listing of lighting options directly below the icon. A standard, vertical swiping motion on the interface navigates the list of color options. Users select a color option (the color "Red," for example, is displayed using red text). Upon selection, the listing of options disappears and the color selection populates the space beneath the light bulb icon. Designers are also given three options for light timing effects ("None," which results in continuous light in the robot, "Fade," and "Blink") after making a color selection.

The LIT ROOM effects library includes: nine standard options for color, three options for light timing; fifty-five options for sound including contextual sound files such as "Tiger Roar," "Train" and "City Night Crowd," music sound files such as "Melancholy" and "Tango" named to suggest their inherent emotional quality, and ambient sound files with the least specificity such as "Hum," "Danger," "Alien," and "Static;" and three options for panel actuation including "Down" which leaves panels dormant in the resting position, "Up" which raises panels to the maximum vertical position emphasizing the shapes created by panel scores and perforations, and "Up/Down" which activates panels in a continuous motion from resting position to the maximum vertical position, emphasizing movement over shape.

A "Show Me" button is provided on the effects customization screen, allowing users to see their choices in real-time within the LIT ROOM. When pressed, the button turns from grey to green, indicating that the real-time feedback feature is activated. The "Show Me" feature is provided in the interface as an option. Frequent users who are familiar with the lighting, sound and motion effects after repeated use may prefer to opt out of the real-time feedback feature. Novice users, however, are likely to desire environmental feedback as they customize scenes and explore options provided in the effects library.

Pressing "Next" on the effects selection screen saves the choices made for the new scene, and advances the interface to the scene-listing screen for the picturebook (Figure 8—left). This screen displays the title and an image of the picturebook as well as a listing of scenes designed for the read-aloud. For each designed scene, the choices for lighting, sound, and movement effects are displayed. Users have the option of adding additional scenes for a read-aloud (a maximum of six scenes can be designed for each picturebook), or pressing the "Home" button to return to the read-aloud library screen.

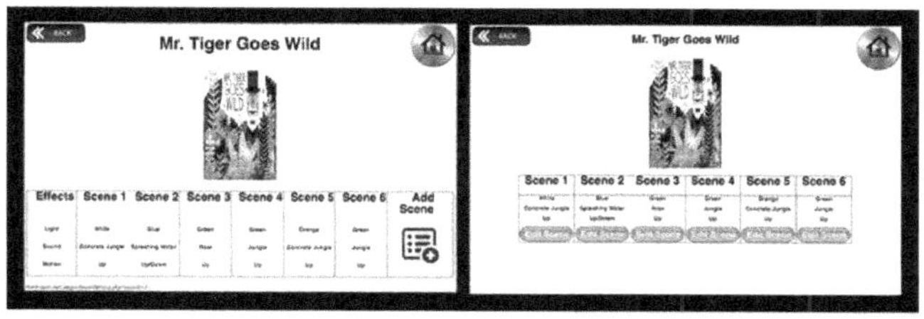

Figure 8. Tablet interface: Save Scene and Edit Scene pages.

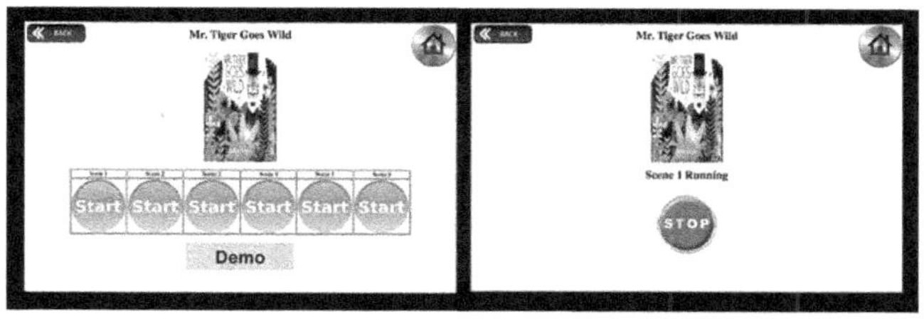

Figure 9. Tablet interface – Read and Stop pages.

Once all of the desired read-aloud scenes have been designed and saved for a specific picturebook, users can easily access them for refinement through the "Edit Scene" feature. The edit read-aloud screen (Figure 8—right) displays the title and image of the picturebook, and a horizontal listing of the scenes saved into the system for the read-aloud. Saved settings for lighting, sound and movement effects are displayed for each scene, and users can access saved settings for revision by touching the "Edit Scene" button under the desired scene. The interface then advances to the standard effects customization screen, where saved settings are displayed and desired changes can be implemented.

In order to play-back scenes during a LIT ROOM read-aloud, users press "Read" on the picturebook screen. The interface advances to the read-aloud screen (Figure 9—left), which displays the title and cover of a picturebook as well as a horizontal listing of its pre-programmed scenes. Each scene is activated by a "Start" button, which, when pressed, activates the lighting, sound, and movement effects in the LIT ROOM. The interface guides users through the read-aloud by only allowing for sequential scene activation (only one "Start" button is active at a time). This ensures that the effects of the LIT ROOM track sequentially with the picturebook as read, protecting readers (for example) from mistakenly activating "Scene 3" when they intend to activate "Scene 2." Visually, the "Start" button for a scene that is available for activation displays bright green, while non-available scenes are grey.

Activating the effects for a scene advances the interface to a blank screen containing a large "Stop" button (Figure 9—right). When a scene is activated, the lighting, sound, and movements transform the LIT ROOM for thirty seconds, providing the adult and children an opportunity to engage in discourse and make connections to the text. The "Stop" button allows adult readers to adjust to the discourse and return to the picturebook sooner, if necessary, to ensure optimum pacing for the read-aloud.

A "Demo" button is also provided on the bottom of the read-aloud screen. This button activates a pre-set demonstration of the environmental effects, creating an opportunity for adults to prime children adequately for the LIT ROOM experience. The standard demo plays for ninety seconds, during which an adult reader can engage with children in a discussion about the technology before the read-aloud begins. During the demo, children can comment on the lighting, sounds and movements, touch and inspect the robotic panels, and ask questions about how the system functions. The demonstration feature hypothesizes that children who are adequately acclimated to the LIT ROOM effects are more likely to attend to the picturebook during the interactive read-aloud in this setting.

The interface also includes buttons for ease of navigation and troubleshooting on most screens. The "Back" button, located in the upper left-hand corner of each screen, allows users to move back to the previous screen. The "Next" button, located in the bottom right-hand corner of screens, advances the system forward and. in some instances, saves selections into the system. The home button, located in the upper right-hand corner of the interface and represented by a house icon, returns users to the read-aloud library screen. A "Reset" button is also provided as a safety measure for when the LIT ROOM system is malfunctioning. Pressing the "Reset" button arrests the effects (lighting and sound) in the LIT ROOM, returns the moving-panel actuators to their resting position ("Down"), and navigates the interface back to the home page.

SCENARIO (DIRECTLY FROM OUR TRANSCRIPT)

Barbara, a children's librarian, is planning a storytime program in the LIT ROOM for a small group of second graders. Barbara selects the picturebook *Little Beauty,* written and illustrated by Anthony Browne [41], about a gorilla in captivity that can communicate using sign language. Barbara aims to design a read-aloud in the LIT ROOM that leverages the lighting, sound, and moving panels to emphasize the emotional aspects of the book. Barbara is intrigued by the book's use of pattern to create the background for Gorilla's home, and by the book's use of wordless spreads, especially one that depicts Gorilla and Beauty swinging from a chandelier. She decides to emphasize these features for the "happy" scene during her LIT ROOM read-aloud.

On the LIT ROOM tablet, Barbara presses "Start Now" which brings her to the "Read-aloud Library." As *Little Beauty* is not yet in the library, Barbara presses "Create New." As she selects the three wall panels for Scene 1, the tablet provides visual feedback to confirm her selection by changing the panels from white to bright green. Barbara presses the "Next" button, and the tablet displays options for lighting, sound, and movement. For Scene 1, Gorilla is sad, so Barbara selects the color "blue" in the "fade" setting, the sound "melancholy," and decides to leave the panels in the "down" position. She presses "Show Me," and the LIT ROOM activates. Pleased with her selections, she presses "Next," saving Scene 1 into the read-aloud library. Barbara repeats this process to design and save Scenes 2-5.

Next, Barbara browses through the plastic panels provided with the LIT ROOM. As Barbara wishes to scaffold the book's use of pattern, she selects pairs of panels with different perforations that match her vision for the scenes of the book. Barbara attaches each plastic panel to its robotic panel with Velcro, and marks her printed copy of *Little Beauty* with adhesive tabs to reminder her to activate the scene on the touchscreen after reading the page.

The children arrive for storytime, intrigued. Barbara asks them to seat on the floor at the center of the installation.

Barbara: "Today we are going to be sharing a book together." [Barbara touches the "Demo" button on the interface. The panels on the wall and ceiling robots begin to slowly move up and down. Their lighting fades from color to color, and an ambient tone fills the room].

Children: [Laughing, looking around and pointing at the environmental effects, and displaying interest and curiosity.] "Whoa! Cool! What's happening?"

Barbara: " What are you noticing?"

Tony: "The walls are changing colors!"

Allison: "I see this wall moving up and down."

Barbara: [Presses the "Demo" button again, halting the lighting, sound, and movement.] "As we read the book in this space, there will be moments when the room will change color, play sounds, and change shape!" [Picks up the picturebook and displays its cover.] "Today, we'll be reading *Little Beauty*, [...]. "'Once upon a time there was a very special gorilla who had been taught to use a sign language'" [...] [Points to the illustration.] "What are you noticing here?"

Tony: [Laughs and points to the illustration.] "I'm noticing the gorilla is watching TV and eating a hamburger! That's funny!" [...]

Allison: "Maybe he's watching a sad movie."

Barbara: "He could be watching something sad, that's a good thought." [Focusing the children on the illustrator's style, pointing at the background.] What are you noticing on this page about the wall and the chair?"

Allison: "It's really colorful and looks like trees and flowers."

Barbara: "It's kind of like a floral pattern, isn't it? Can anybody tell me what a pattern is?"

Ellie: "Um, a pattern is like, when there's lots of lines and stuff, like plaid is a pattern, but it's not like trees and flowers like that." [Points at the illustration.]

Barbara: "That's right. A pattern is like a design when something is repeated. Let's keep reading and see how Gorilla might be feeling." [Turns page and notices a tab indicating Scene 1.] "'But the gorilla was sad.'" [Touches the "Start" button for Scene 1. The walls glow blue, fading gently; light shines through the perforated, patterned panels. Melancholy piano music plays.] "What are you noticing?"

Tony: "The walls are blue. And music is playing."

Barbara: "The walls are blue. Why do you think they're blue?"

Fatima: "Well, sometimes people say that they're blue when they're sad. That's what I think." [...]

Barbara: "That's a good connection, Fatima. [...] What are you guys noticing about the walls other than the color?"

Allison: "They kind of have patterns. That one [points to left wall] kind of looks like stars, and..." [...]

Barbara: [Pressing the "Stop" button to arrest the effects.] "Patterns? Kind of like the patterns the illustrator is using in the book. Great observations. Let's keep reading."

Barbara continues through the remainder of *Little Beauty*, pausing for discussion, and scaffolding the children's discourse, particularly related to the emotional arc of the characters, for each of the LIT ROOM's transformations. After a brief discussion of the book, Barbara begins a story-extension activity using the LIT ROOM by engaging the children as co-designers of the environment. She begins by redirecting discussion to address one of Tony's comments following the reading of Scene 1 when Gorilla was sad. With help from his peers, Tony, by touchscreen, fine-tunes the LIT ROOM so that its effects better match his vision for how the LIT ROOM should look, sound, and move.

The LIT ROOM serves to facilitate a diversity of children's literary responses and encourage diverse meaning-making strategies as they make connections to the text during the read-aloud. Additionally, the LIT ROOM functions as an "object-to-think-with" [26] by engaging children as co-designers during the story-extension activity.

USABILITY AND EFFICACY EVALUATIONS

Installed in Richland Library, the fully functioning LIT ROOM underwent Phase-2 (a formative usability evaluation) and Phase 3 (concurrent summative evaluations of usability and efficacy) of our evaluation cycle. Participating children were drawn from two public elementary schools identified as "Title 1" where high numbers or high percentages of students are from low-income families. Phases-2 and 3 aimed to understand: (1) the preferences of librarian and children participants for the design of the LIT ROOM; (2) how users rate the LIT ROOM on measures of usability as a context for an interactive picturebook read-aloud; and (3) the nature of literary understanding exhibited by children during shared picturebook reading in this context.

For these evaluations, as reported in this section, the two picturebooks used were *Mr. Tiger Goes Wild* by Peter Brown [39] and *Gorilla*, by Anthony Browne [40]. In order to ensure fidelity of the read-aloud protocol across the two texts, librarians were assigned to read one of these titles in both the control (a traditional storytime room, Figure 10—left) and treatment (the LIT ROOM, Figure 10—right) settings. The two picturebooks were pre-programmed into the tablet to match the librarians' specifications for the effects (lighting, sound, and actuated panels) identified during previous participatory design sessions. The librarians followed a protocol (script) for administering the interactive read-aloud for the picturebooks that was designed and piloted by members of the research team with an expertise in children's literacy. The scripts were designed to ensure fidelity to the read-aloud protocol across readers and settings (control and treatment). For a short video depicting scenes from a LIT ROOM read-aloud of *Gorilla*, see https://www.youtube.com/watch?v=SjH-mNwzi7k#t=220.

For the various evaluations reported here, interactive read-alouds and the customization sessions were audiotaped and videotaped. Focus group sessions were audiotaped. Approval for all evaluations was obtained from the appropriate institutional review boards and parental permission was provided.

Phase-2 (Formative) Evaluation for Usability

Our research team evaluated the LIT ROOM with respect to usability through one formative cycle. (A summative usability cycle is presented in the next section devoted to Phase-3). Twelve children participants (six males and six females), ages seven and eight, were from three second-grade classrooms. Prior to the study, children participants were divided into two groups, randomly determined by one of the classroom teachers. In lieu of Measures of Academic Progress (MAP) scores, the school categorized each child as (L) low, (M) medium or (H) high "literacy level." Additionally, some of the children were differentiated by classroom type, such as (SN) special-needs or (M) Montessori. The classroom teacher was instructed to create two groups that, to the extent possible, represented a cross-section of learner characteristics. Each group was evenly split along gender.

A convenience sample of four children's librarians from Richland Library participated in the evaluation. The librarians were members of the core focus group that was integral to the research activities spanning the three-year iterative design, installation and evaluation of the LIT ROOM. During the study, two of the children's librarians facilitated the interactive picturebook read-alouds in both settings, while two functioned as observers.

The study featured the following activities: two small-group interactive picturebook read-alouds for two texts (one per group) in the LIT ROOM; a customization activity in the LIT ROOM with one group; piloted participatory design sessions and usability assessments (via facilitated questionnaire) with all children following their LIT ROOM read-alouds; and a focus group with the children room's librarians after all activities were completed.

Group 1 engaged in a read-aloud in the LIT ROOM using *Mr. Tiger Goes Wild* [39]. Following the read-aloud, children individually (1) completed a facilitated questionnaire (with Likert "Smileyometer" scales and open-ended questions) to assess usability and satisfaction [20]; and (2) participated in a story-extension design activity which, from a printed image of the LIT ROOM, asked participants to draw their favorite scene from the book supported by LIT ROOM effects, and offer an explanation for why this was their favorite. Group 2 followed the same procedure with *Gorilla* [40]. Concurrent with the participatory design and usability assessment activities for Group 2, the children in Group 1 were provided an opportunity to customize scene effects for the LIT ROOM and interact with the tablet interface for a third picturebook, *Little Beauty* [41]. Guided by a children's librarian, the children were asked to collaboratively design lighting, sound, and actuated panel effects to represent the emotional arc in the text. After reading the book aloud to the children, the children took turns making selections to evoke an environment that, *to them*, represented sadness, happiness and anger. A member of the research team with an expertise in engineering observed the session and notated errors [34] in the interface. At the end of the study, a brief focus group was conducted with the children's librarians who participated as readers and observers. We asked open-ended questions regarding the usability and effectiveness [34] of the tablet interface, and facilitated a discussion about their experience reading a book and customizing scenes with children using the LIT ROOM.

Results

The results focus on three main areas: an analysis of observed or reported usability errors and preferences related to the LIT ROOM's tablet interface (and the refinements made to the system as a result); an analysis of observed or reported usability errors and preferences related to the LIT ROOM as an effective system for reading picturebooks and customizing scenes with children; and findings on the validity of the protocols used during the piloted participatory design and usability assessment sessions with children.

Overall, the technology in the LIT ROOM functioned as expected. The research team, however, observed librarians struggling to resolve a system error using the tablet. The tablet did not adequately provide the librarian user with information about the type of problem that was occurring, nor did it guide the user as to how to resolve the system error. Nielsen would identify this as a feedback error [25]. The research team subsequently identified the system error (i.e. when a scene mistakenly replayed) to be related to a "bug" in the coding (one that occurred randomly and unpredictably). Because the issue could not be fixed by a revision in the code, the tablet was augmented to allow users to quickly and efficiently replay a scene when this system error occurred. A "Reset" button was also added to the interface on every screen where the room effects could be activated. The team also observed that the length of each pre-programmed scene (the length of time that the lighting, sound, and panels were actuated), originally set at fifteen seconds, was not enough time for the children to adequately experience and identify the effects, discuss them with the adult reader, and make connections to the text. The system was redesigned to set the scene time to thirty seconds.

All of the librarians reported being surprised that the children did not seem distracted by the environmental effects in the LIT ROOM. We meanwhile found that written responses and drawings offered by the children could not be productively leveraged for useful, specific data that might guide the design team on preferences for the affordances of the LIT ROOM effects; according to [20], this was not an unexpected outcome from young participants.

Phase-3 Evaluation for Usability and Efficacy

Our research team conducted a usability and efficacy evaluation of the LIT ROOM in one summative cycle. In the study conducted over two days, 17 second-grade children from two local classrooms participated, as did six children's librarians from the core focus group. Nine children (6 males, 3 females) participated on the first day and eight (5 males, 3 females) participated on the second day. Participants engaged in interactive read-alouds in two settings: the traditional storytime room (Figure 10—left) and the LIT ROOM (Figure 10—right).

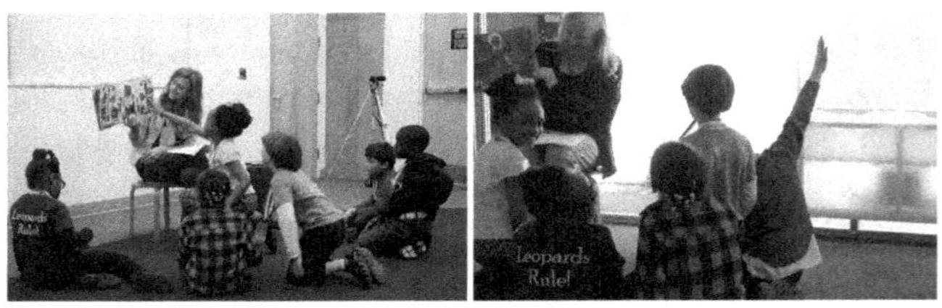

Figure 10. Storytime room and LIT ROOM read-alouds.

The procedures for the summative usability evaluation follow closely the procedures for the formative usability evaluation elaborated in the previous section: (1) we conducted four small-group interactive picturebook read-alouds – two for each group – for the same two texts, with each group exposed to both texts in the control and treatment settings (a traditional storytime room and the LIT ROOM); (2) we conducted usability evaluations via facilitated questionnaire with all children participants; and (3) we conducted a focus group with the children's librarians focused on measures of usability.

In order to better understand the efficacy of the LIT ROOM as a context for children's literacy, we also conducted an initial analysis of children's literary understandings during picturebook read-alouds in the LIT ROOM. To report on how the multi-media effects were influencing children's meaning-making in the LIT ROOM setting, we categorized children's response initiations guided by seminal research in children's literary response [18, 32]. Maloch and Beutel's study on meaning-making strategies framed our coding of instances where children seemed to be leveraging the environmental effects: to make *connections* between their personal experiences and the picturebook being read; to make *predictions* about the text; to clarify information in the text; to make *observations* about the text; and to *enter the story world* as co-participants or co-authors [18]. These meaning-making strategies built upon Sipe's seminal study identifying five primary categories of initiations for children responding to fiction texts: the *analytical* response, the *personal* response, the *intertextual* response, the *transparent* response and the *performative* response. [32]. While a comprehensive, descriptive statistical analysis was conducted to determine the frequency and percentage for each category of response, we focused on two of Sipe's five categories of literary understanding [32] – the *transparent* and *performative* – in order to consider how the LIT ROOM multi-media and architectural robotics effects might influence children's *aesthetic* responses. Finally, we conducted an initial descriptive analysis of the differences between the children's literary responses (and specifically, their *aesthetic* responses) in two settings for two of the small groups (N=8), comparing those observed in the LIT ROOM to those observed in the traditional storytime room. For these analyses, the discourse was transcribed according to a methodology devised by [32] in his seminal study of children's literary responses.

Overview of Results

From the summative usability testing, we learned that the LIT ROOM functioned largely as expected. We therefore focus the reporting of results on our summative efficacy evaluation – far more illuminating – for three main areas: (1) an analysis of children's responses to two picturebooks within the LIT ROOM installation to describe how the environment and its multi-media, architectural robotics [15] effects were influencing the strategies the children utilized for connecting to the text; (2) an analysis of the frequency of responses mediated by the specific effects deployed in the LIT ROOM environment, including elaborations on how the lighting, sound, and moving panels were influencing their strategies for making connections to the text and their aesthetic response initiations; and, (3) a comparative analysis of the children's aesthetic responses (*transparent* and *performative*) observed in the traditional storytime room and in the LIT ROOM for one of the picturebooks. Our analyses of the efficacy studies are far too detailed to present in the limited space of this paper; we therefore present the key results in the form of a narrative.

Results-1: Impact of LIT ROOM on connecting with text

Children exhibited a wide range of strategies for making connections to the text while the LIT ROOM environmental effects were activated [18]. Some children leveraged the effects to make *connections* between their personal experiences and the picturebook being read, while others made *predictions* about the text, *clarified* information in the text, made *observations* about the text, or *entered the story world* as co-participants or co-authors [18, 32].

The initial analysis of children's responses suggests that the LIT ROOM effects figured prominently in the discourse and influenced the strategies and response types exhibited by the participants. Nearly half (48%) of the children's responses were identified as having been mediated by the effects of the LIT ROOM. A "response" was identified as being influenced by the LIT ROOM if the child mentioned the specific effect in his/her response (such as by saying "blue," in reference to the lighting); if the comment referenced a transformation in the space but did not name a specific effect (such as "It looks like he's going to come at all of us!" when a child referred to the "gorilla" wall-mounted robotic panel); and for responses where no specific effects were named but the child was gesturing towards or visually attending to a specific area of activation (such as "To the forest," where a child was predicting the actions of Mr. Tiger while gesturing to a wall robot). Non-specific verbal utterances where children were reacting to the effects (such as "Oh!" when a child reacted to the ceiling robot immediately upon activation) were also included as an example of an effect-mediated response.

The results also indicate that for the instances where a response was associated directly with the LIT ROOM effects, children exhibited a wide variety of strategies [18] while transacting with the picturebook in this setting. Some children leveraged the effects to make *connections* to the text (such as "I play around in water sometimes," a *personal* response to the ceiling robot evoking waves), while others made *intertextual* connections (such as a child sing-talking "Superman!" while the ceiling robot above resembled a red, flying cape and played movie-music sounds). An example of the *analytical* response, other children made *predictions* about the text using the LIT ROOM effects, (evidenced by a child pointing at the "wilderness" wall-mounted robotic panel while answering, "To the forest" when the librarian reader asked where Mr. Tiger was going to go next). Many children made *observations* about the environment while relating to the picturebook (evidenced by a child stating: "I notice the lights—the lights is [sic] acting like, when, uh, the tiger is swimming in the water"), and others clarified and extended the effects and how they relate to the inner life of the characters (such as the comment: "It sounds like he's lonely and it's raining," referring to the scene where Mr. Tiger is in the wilderness, alone). The LIT ROOM effects also served as a conduit for children to *enter the story world* [18, 32]. During an interactive read-aloud for *Gorilla*, for instance, one child repeatedly monitored the "gorilla" wall-mounted robotic panel behind him as if it was alive. Sipe [32, 33] would identify this instance as a *transparent* response, an example of Rosenblatt's "lived through experience" [28] where a child becomes one with the story world. This initial analysis of the children's responses suggests that the LIT ROOM effects created a threshold between the imaginary and the real, and allowed the world of the picturebook to become transparent to the children's world, if only momentarily [32].

Results-2: Frequency of responses mediated by LIT ROOM
Following Sipe's elaboration of "aesthetic impulses" [32, 33], we counted the frequency of both *transparent* responses (where children enter the world of the book, even responding to characters from the book as if they were sharing the physical space with them), and *performative* responses (where children leverage the text to express their own creative impulses, often evidenced by dramatic interpretations, characterizations, embodied gestures and vocal intonations [1]). Among the children's response initiations that were identified as being directly influenced by the LIT ROOM effects during scene activation, approximately 38% of them were categorized as transparent responses, while approximately 20% of them were categorized as performative responses. The instances of aesthetic impulse therefore comprised over half of the responses analyzed for this study. By comparison, in Sipe's seminal study of first and second-grade children's literary understanding during interactive picturebook read-alouds in traditional classroom settings [32], the aesthetic impulse comprised only 7% of children's responses: 2% categorized as transparent responses, and 5% categorized as performative responses. This comparison suggests that the LIT ROOM, as compared to a traditional storyroom, could hold promise for facilitating more diverse categories of children's literary responses by providing opportunities for children to explore the text as a launching pad for their own creative and aesthetic expression.

Results-3: Children's responses in LIT ROOM vs storyroom
While in Sipe's seminal study, as just considered, the aesthetic impulse in a traditional story room comprised only 7% of children's responses, the interactive picturebook read-alouds analyzed for this study resulted in higher frequencies *for both* the traditional story room setting *and* the LIT ROOM setting (28% and 29%, respectively). Moveover, while the results indicate no significant difference between the overall frequency of aesthetic response initiations across the control and treatment settings, children's *transparent* response, where they entered the story world, was observed at greater frequency in the LIT ROOM installation. Further, there were also differences in the nature of transparent responses in the two settings. In the traditional storytime setting, children were observed entering the story world through primarily verbal responses, by speaking directly to a character (such as "What are you doing, mister?" when a child confronted Mr. Tiger about being wild), or spontaneously assuming the role of the character (such as "I'm free!", when a child expressed Mr. Tiger's feeling of being in the wilderness). In comparison, children in the LIT ROOM were more likely to "act out" Mr. Tiger's transformation by crawling around the installation and roaring like tigers. This suggests that the LIT ROOM may encourage more full-bodied (*embodied*) performative response styles.

Sipe argues that interactive read-aloud settings, such as the multi-sensory LIT ROOM, should be designed to facilitate the entire range of dialogue, and in particular, children's aesthetic responses [32, 33]. By blurring the lines between the picturebook and the real world, the LIT ROOM may even support a transformation in the way we think about children's performative and transparent responses to picturebooks, resulting in a "blended" aesthetic response category – the "transformative response."

CONCLUSION

While there is evidence that public libraries effectively leverage technologies – physical and digital – to reduce illiteracy in their communities [17, 22], there are significant gaps in the research on effective interventions in children's libraries, especially in the realm of employing interactive technologies for early literacy skill development [16]. This research sought to fill this gap through a reconfigurable, cyber-physical environment in which *words become worlds*. In the LIT ROOM, children leverage cognitive, embodied processes to foster early literacy skills.

Supporting a variety of programming beyond that reported here, the LIT ROOM proved robust and engaging to library patrons for over one year following the conclusion of our formal studies. We recognize such cyber-physical systems at room scale, like the LIT ROOM, as a new frontier for designing interactive systems. As offered in this paper via our RtD reporting, the LIT ROOM represents an exemplar for designing and studying interactions within interactive systems at habitable scale – an inevitable future for the field.

ACKNOWLEDGMENTS

The authors gratefully acknowledge support for this research from the U.S. National Science Foundation (#IIS-1352992).

REFERENCES

1. D. S. Adomat, Dramatic interpretations: Performative responses of young children to picturebook read-alouds. Children's Literature in Education, 41, 207-221.
2. Alissa. N. Antle. 2009. Embodied child computer interaction: Why embodiment matters. *Interactions,* 16, 2: 27-30.
3. M. Ananny. 2002. Supporting children's collaborative authoring: Practicing written literacy while composing oral texts. In *Proceedings of the 2002 Conference on Computer Supported Collaborative Learning*, Boulder, Colorado, 595-596.
4. M. Back, J. Cohen, R. Gold, S. Harrison, and S. Minneman. 2001. Listen reader: An electronically augmented paper-based book. In *Proceedings of the 2001 Conference on Computer Human Interaction* (CHI '01), 23-29.
5. A. F. Bobick, S. S. Intille, J. W Davis, F. Baird, C. S. Pinhanez, L. W. Campbell, and A. Wilson. 1999. The KidsRoom: A perceptually-based interactive and immersive story environment. In *Presence: Teleoperators and Virtual Environments,* 8, 4: 367-391.
6. Bosch Rexroth Corporation. Retrieved August 17, 2017 from http://www.boschrexroth.com.
7. J. Cassell and K. Ryokai. Making space for voice: Technologies to support children's fantasy and storytelling. *Personal and Ubiquitous Comput*, 5: 169-190.
8. A. Chang and C. Breazeal. 2011. TinkRBook: Shared reading interfaces for storytelling. In *Proceedings of the 2011 Conference on Interaction Design for Children* (IDC 2011), 145-148.
9. C. Crain-Thoreson, C. and P. S. Dale. 1992. Do early talkers become early readers? Linguistic precocity, preschool language, and emergent literacy. *Developmental Psychology,* 28: 421–429.
10. D. Dickenson and R. Keebler. 1989. Variation in preschool teachers' styles of reading books. *Discourse Processes*, 12: 353-375.
11. S. Dow, J. Lee, C. Oezbek, B. MacIntyre, J. D. Bolter, and M. Gandy. "Wizard of Oz Interfaces for Mixed Reality Applications," in *Proceedings of the 2005 Conference on Human Factors in Computing Systems, Extended Abstracts* (CHI '05), 1339–1342
12. C. Frayling. 1993. Research in Art and Design. *Royal College of Art Research Papers* 1, 1: 1–5.
13. J. P. Gee. 2008. A sociocultural perspective on opportunity to learn. Retrieved August 15, 2017 from http://jamespaulgee.com/pdfs/Opportunity%20to%20Learn.pdf.
14. J. W. Glos and J. Cassell. 1997. Rosebud: A place for interaction between memory, story, and self. In *Proceedings of the 1997 Conference on Computer Human Interaction: Late-Breaking/Short Talks*, 359-360.
15. Keith Evan Green. 2016. *Architectural robotics: ecosystems of bits, bytes and biology.* The MIT Press.
16. C. N. Jensen, W. Burleson, and J. Sadauskas. 2012. Fostering early literacy skills in children's libraries: Opportunities for embodied cognition and tangible technologies. In *Proceedings of the 2012 Conference on Interaction Design and Children* (IDC 2012), 50-59.
17. Lora, P. 1990. Libraries and literacy in America 1985–2000. *Public Libraries, 29*, 6: 354–362.
18. B. Maloch and D. D. Beutel. 2010. "Big loud voice. You have important things to say": The nature of student initiations during one teacher's interactive read-alouds. *Journal of Classroom Interaction, 45*(2), 20-29.
19. Erin N. Marcus. July 27, 2006. The Silent Epidemic—The Health Effects of Literacy. The New England Journal of Medicine 355: 339-341.
20. P. Markopoulos, J. Read, S. MacFarlane, and J. Hoysniemi. 2008. *Evaluating children's interactive products: Principles and practices for interaction designers*. Morgan Kaufmann Publishers.
21. Bruce Mau. An Incomplete Manifesto for Growth. Retrieved August 17, 2017 from http://www.manifestoproject.it/bruce-mau/
22. J. Montemayor, A. Druin, A. Farber, S. Simms, W. Churaman, and A. D'Amour. 2002. Physical programming: Designing tools for children to create physical interactive environments. In *Proceedings of the SIGCHI Conference on Human Factors in Computing Systems* (CHI '02), 299-306.
23. K. Mori, R. Ballagas, G. Revelle, H. Raffle, H. Horii, and M. Spasojevic. 2011. Interactive rich reading: Enhanced book reading experience with a conversational agent. In *Proceedings of the 2011 Conference on Multimedia*, November 28 – December 1, Scottsdale, Arizona, 825-826.
24. The National Center for Education Statistics (NCES). The National Assessment of Adult Literacy (NAAL). 2017. Retrieved August 14, 2017 from https://nces.ed.gov/naal/.
25. J. Nielsen. 1993. *Usability Engineering.* Academic Press.
26. S. Papert. 1993. *Mindstorms: Children, computers, and powerful ideas*. Basic Books.
27. Richland Library. LIT Room ignites young minds. April 28, 2015. Retrieved August 17, 2017 from http://www.richlandlibrary.com/inform/lit-room-ignites-young-minds.

28. L. M. Rosenblatt. 1994. The transactional theory of reading and writing. In *Theoretical models and processes of reading* (4th ed.), R. B. Ruddell, M. R. Ruddell and H. Singer (eds International Reading Association, 1057-1092

29. K. Ryokai, L. Jongseon, and J. M. Breitbart. 2009. Children's storytelling and programming with robotic characters. In *Proceedings of the 2009 Conference on Creativity & Cognition* (ACM C&C 2009), 19-28.

30. G. Schafer, K. E. Green, I. D. Walker, S. K. Fullerton, and E. Lewis. 2014. An interactive, cyber-physical read-aloud environment: results and lessons from an evaluation activity with children and their teachers. In *Proceedings of the ACM Conference on the Design of Interactive Systems* (DIS 2014), 865-874.

31. G. Schafer, K. E. Green, I. D. Walker, and E. Lewis. 2012. A networked suite of mixed-technology robotic artifacts for advancing literacy in children. In *Proceedings of the 11th International Conference on Interaction Design and Children* (IDC 2012), 168-171.

32. L. R. Sipe. 2000. The construction of literary understanding by first and second graders in oral response to picture storybook read-alouds. *Reading Research Quarterly, 35*(2), 252-275.

33. L. R. Sipe. 2008. *Storytime: Young children's literacy understanding in the classroom*. Teachers College Press.

34. D. Stone, C. Jarrett, M. Woodroffe, and S. Minocha. 2005. *User interface design and evaluation*. Morgan Kaufmann Publishers.

35. UNESCO. The Global Literacy Challenge. 2017. Retrieved August 14, 2017 from unesdoc.unesco.org/images/0016/001631/163170e.pdf.

36. S. Uras, D. Ardu, and M. Deriu. 2012. Do not judge an interactive book by its cover: a field research. In *Proceedings of the 2012 Conference on Advances in Mobile Computing and Multimedia*, 17-20.

37. B. A. Wasik and M. A. Bond. 2001. Beyond the pages of a book: Interactive book reading and language development in preschool classrooms. *Journal of Educational Psychology,* 93: 243–250.

38. J. Zimmerman, J. Forlizzi, and J. Evenson, Research through Design as a Method for Interaction Design Research in HCI. In *Proceedings of the SIGCHI Conference on Human Factors in Computing Systems* (CHI '07), 493–502.

PICTUREBOOK REFERENCES

39. Peter Brown. 2013. *Mr. Tiger Goes Wild*. Little, Brown and Company / Hachette.

40. Anthony Browne. 1983. *Gorilla*. Candlewick Press.

41. Anthony Browne. 2008. *Little Beauty*. Candlewick Press.

Deepening Visitor Engagement with Museum Exhibits through Hand-crafted Visual Markers

Susan Ali, Boriana Koleva, Ben Bedwell, Steve Benford
School of Computer Science, University of Nottingham
Nottingham, UK
{firstname.lastname}@nottingham.ac.uk

ABSTRACT

Visual markers, in particular QR codes, have become widely adopted in museums to enable low cost interactive applications. However, visitors often do not engage with them. In this paper we explore the application of visual makers that can be designed to be meaningful and that can be created by visitors themselves. We study both the use of these markers as labels for portraits that link to audio recordings and as a mechanism for visitors to contribute their own reflections to the exhibition by drawing a marker and linking an audio comment. Our findings show visitors appreciated the use of the aesthetic markers and engaged with them at three levels – physical placement, aesthetic content and digital content. We suggest that these different levels need to be considered in the design of future visiting systems, which make use of such markers, to ensure they are mutually supporting in shaping the experience.

Author Keywords

Visual markers; mobile interaction; museums; galleries; visitor interpretation

ACM Classification Keywords

H.5.m. Information interfaces and presentation (e.g., HCI): Miscellaneous;

INTRODUCTION

Visual markers, particularly QR codes, are widely adopted in museums and galleries as a way to exploit the capabilities of mobile devices carried by visitors to augment exhibits with digital content. An online survey conducted in 2013 by the Museum Association for the UK reported that 50% of those taking part had a mobile offer, with QR codes being the most popular technology deployed (63%), followed by museum-provided audio-tours (46%), mobile-optimised websites (45%), and smartphone apps (39%) [3].

DIS '18, June 9–13, 2018, Hong Kong

ACM ISBN 978-1-4503-5198-0/18/06…$15.00
https://doi.org/10.1145/3196709.3196786

The appeal of QR codes is that they provide a low-cost way to deliver a broad range of applications. Simply by scanning a marker with their smartphone, visitors can get access to additional multimedia information about artefacts, play games such as treasure hunts and puzzles, and even contribute to the exhibition's interpretation by leaving comments and feedback. At the same time, visual markers are relatively cheap and easy to deploy, as no new technical infrastructure needs to be installed; visitors use their own devices to interact and only new labels need to be added.

However, visitor engagement with QR codes in museum settings can often be low. A study by Wein [34] found that QR codes were the least preferred mechanism by visitors for accessing background information on artworks with ease of use, enjoyability and distance identified as the main contributing factors. QR codes might not only be aesthetically unappealing, but also lead to a shift of attention away from the artwork [37]. Schultz [26] found that visitors at the Ryerson University Library and Museum of Inuit Art had an awareness of QR codes, but usage was observed to be low. The author suggests that a lack of perceived usefulness and misconceptions about ease of use might explain the low adoption. The study also reveals an assumption by staff and visitors that QR codes are only used for one-way provision of information, and highlights the opportunity of using the technology to initiate a conversation, as well as to personalize a visit to an institution.

In this paper we explore how visitors engage with a visual marker technology where the codes can be designed to be more aesthetic and meaningful, and can be created by the visitors themselves to contribute their own reflections to the exhibition. We chose Artcodes (previously known as Aesthticodes) [2, 21] as the approach for the authoring and recognition of aesthetically-pleasing patterns, as previous research has shown that people can easily understand the drawing rules and create interesting designs [21, 33].

The paper presents a study of the use of Artcodes to link audio recordings to photographic portraits exhibited in an art gallery. We also explore how visitors engaged with contributing their own reflections to the exhibition by drawing a marker and linking an audio comment. These hybrid artefacts were then displayed within the exhibition space. Our findings show that participants were positive about these kinds of markers as a means of providing additional information. They particularly appreciated the use of audio as media to augment their engagement with the portraits. However, we found that they became really enthusiastic when they were able to successfully draw their own code and link it to content. Subsequent visitors also really enjoyed viewing the codes left by previous visitors and interacting with this user contributed content. Our study revealed that visitors engaged with the aesthetic markers at the three levels of *physical placement*, *aesthetic content* and *digital content*. We suggest that these different levels need to be considered in the design of future visiting systems, which make use of such markers, to ensure they are mutually supporting in shaping the experience.

USE OF VISUAL MARKERS IN MUSEUM SETTINGS

There is a lot of interest by museums and cultural heritage sites in using mobile technologies to enhance visitor engagement [3]. Visual markers, usually in the form of QR codes, are most commonly used to provide additional information about exhibits, as this is a low-cost mechanism to overcome the space restrictions of text labels and enable the incorporation of multimedia (audio, video, animations) in an easily updatable form. Examples of this include the QR codes placed next to artworks in The Los Angeles County Museum of Art and Fort Wayne Museum of Art [4] to reveal biographical information about the artist, as well as QR codes linking to audio and video explanations of the objects on exhibit as shown in a early demonstration by the Museum in Urk, Holland [5].

QR codes can also be used to add more visitor interactivity through quizzes and treasure hunts. For example the Oslo Norsk Telemuseum enabled visitors to engage with the museum objects through solving a series of riddles and identifying the right answer by scanning the appropriate QR code [9]. Similarly a quiz and QR codes were used in an Art Gallery for students to identify correct paintings [22]. On the other hand, the exhibit on the 100th anniversary of the Boy Scouts in America across the Smithsonian National Museums in DC used QR codes to challenge visitors to a scavenger hunt to uncover links between scouting and some great national treasures [7]. Kuflik et al. describe the Treasure Hunt Game Generator System that was developed at the Hecht Museum to enable the museum staff to create new versions of treasure hunt games based on QR codes for special events, as well as for regular visits [20].

Going further, QR codes can also be used to enable visitors to contribute to exhibitions by sharing their own stories, interpretations, reflections and feedback. Although less explored, this application addresses recent museum concerns to support visitors in engaging with multiple interpretations, and creating, sharing and connecting with each other [39, 27]. The Tales of Things platform [29], which enables users to tag objects with stories through QR codes, has underpinned two notable examples. Workshops and events held at the National Museum of Scotland where visitors were encouraged to attach a QR code to an object and to 'record' a memory of using such an object [28] and the QRator project implemented at the Grant Museum of Zoology, which engaged visitors in meaning-making by asking them to respond to questions about different issues at exhibits [15]. Similarly, QR codes were installed to accompany objects at the Imperial War Museum with visitors being able to join the conversation by adding text comments to any item in the collection and reading what other people have to say [18].

However, while QR codes can be used to cost effectively support a range of relevant application in museums, visitor engagement with these markers is often low [26]. Previous research suggests that this might be because QR codes are aesthetically unappealing [37] and visitors are not aware of their usefulness [26]. Schultz also suggests that the most promising application of visual markers might be to personalize visits to institutions and to enable a conversation with visitors.

In this paper, we explore how visitors engage with handcrafted visual makers that can be designed to be more aesthetic and meaningful. We study both the use of such markers as labels for artefacts to provide complimentary information and as a mechanism for visitors to contribute to the exhibition themselves by creating physical as well as digital content. Our findings reveal (1) how museum visitors engaged with markers provided by the gallery versus those contributed by museum visitors, (2) provide detailed observation of how visitors interact with visual markers in galleries/museums (which is not detailed in previous literature) and (3) show what impact the use of more visually meaningful codes has on the experience.

APPROACH

We chose to augment the "Uncovering the Invisible" photography exhibition, which was due to be displayed at the Nottingham Lakeside Arts gallery. Created as a collaboration between British-Mexican photographers Pablo and Roxana Allison, it focuses on the diversity of backgrounds and life stories of the people that make up the Latin American community in the UK. Each portrait presents a photograph of a person and a label with a short description about them. In addition, audio recordings were available of the migrants featured in the photographs talking about their experiences of living in the UK. This presented us with an opportunity to explore the use of more aesthetic and meaningful visual markers as a mechanism for visitors to access the voice of each person featured on a portrait. Gallery staff and the photographers also saw the benefit of enabling the visitors to contribute to and grow the exhibition by sharing their own stories of life in the UK and reactions to the portraits. This enabled us to explore how visitors would engage with a visual marker technology, which allows them to design the visual appearance of the marker as well as the digital content it links to, and then how subsequent visitors interact with these additions to the exhibition.

Implementing Interaction with Visual Markers

Recently, there has been growing interest in vision technologies that can recognize more aesthetic or natural images. Various approaches have been proposed to creating markers that contain the correct balance of features to make them recognizable by an image processing algorithm. These involve the designer selecting an existing image that fits requirements (e.g. Blippar [6], Vuforia [36]), modifying an image (e.g. ARTcodes [40], PiCode [17]) or drawing a new pattern following a set of rules (e.g. ARTTag [16], D-touch [13] and Artcodes [21]).

We chose to use Artcodes as the visual markers in our study as the drawing approach promotes visitor creativity and previous research has shown that the rules are easy to understand and follow, with a variety of interesting designs created [21, 33]. The technology involves recognizing topological structures in a live video, where a code is determined by the number of connected regions (which gives the number of digits in the code) and the number of blobs contained within each region (which gives the value of each digit). These are then written in ascending order (see Figure 1 for an example). The shapes of the regions and blobs, and ordering on the page are not considered, giving designers great flexibility to create varying designs. Thresholding to black and white is performed on the images before recognition, so color can be used in designs as long as there is sufficient contrast (as seen in Figure 2).

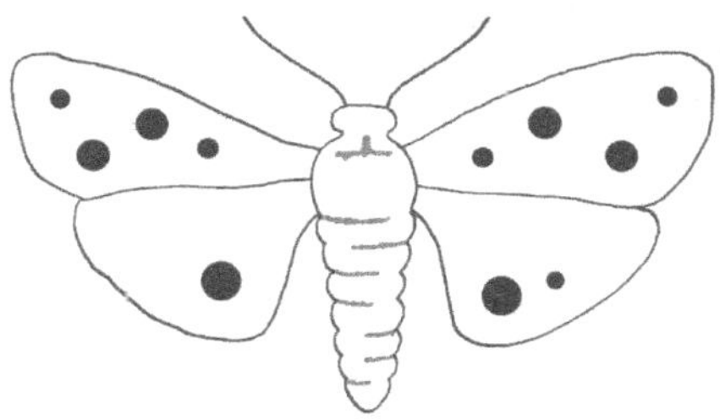

Figure 1. Artcode with 5 regions with the code 1:1:2:4:4

The "Uncovering the Invisible" exhibition consists of 22 portraits and we augmented 12 of them with Artcodes to trigger the associated audio recordings. The markers were created by a professional designer to represent the maps of the countries where the people came from. Figure 2 shows two examples and Figure 3 shows their placement.

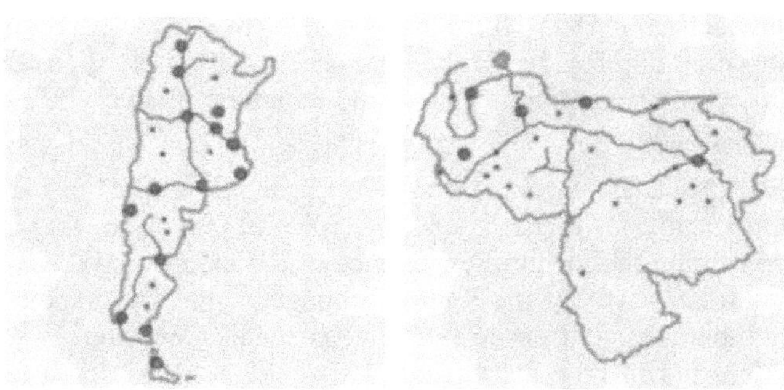

Figure 2. Artcodes representing the maps of Argentina and Venezuela

Figure 3. Placement of the markers in the gallery

We used the publicly available Artcodes app [2], which allows experiences to be created by specifying a set of codes and linking each one to a URL. We defined the "Uncovering the Invisible" experience and linked each of the 12 codes to the corresponding audio file on YouTube (where the voice recordings were already publicly available). By using the app and scanning an Artcode while browsing the exhibition, visitors could access the associated audio (see Figure 4).

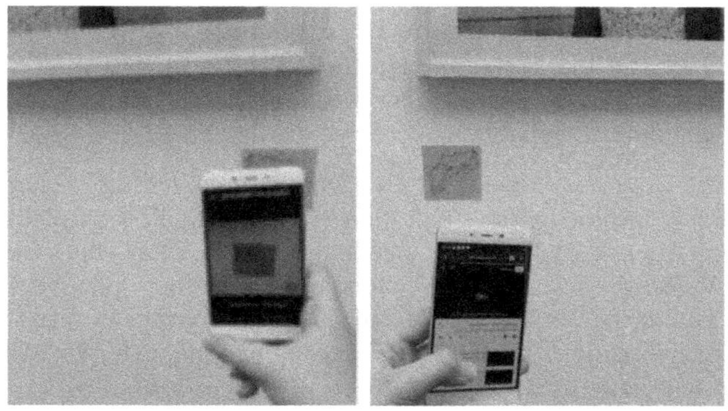

Figure 4. Scanning an Artcode label (left) and voice recording on YouTube (right)

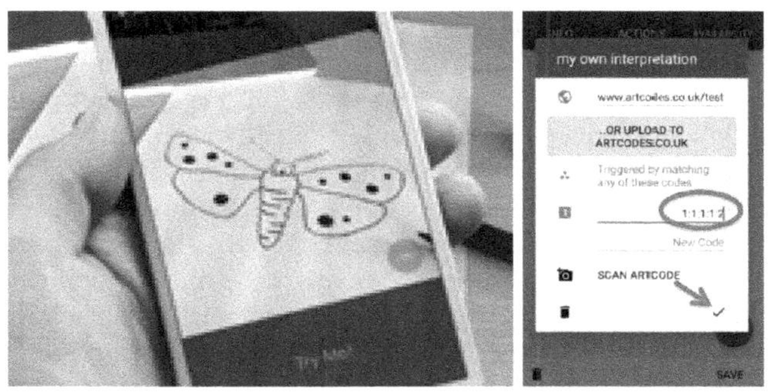

Figure 5. Testing an Artcode (left) and associating an audio file with a code (right)

The app also supported participants in drawing their own Artcode and linking this to digital content. To create their own drawing, which incorporates a valid code, visitors could use the Artcodes app functionality for testing (Figure 5, left), which highlights the detected regions and displays the code. They could record their audio comment through an audio recording app on the smartphone and then upload it in the Artcodes app, associating it with an Artcode (Figure 5, right) either by manually writing the code or scanning the picture (which automatically detects and displays the code). The user could choose to share their contributions publicly or with selected people through SMS or social media (the audio file is uploaded on to a server in either case).

Study Procedure

Participants

Participants were recruited by advertising through the mailing lists and websites of the Nottingham Lakeside Arts gallery and the University of Nottingham Mexican society, as well as on physical notice boards around the University. 28 participants (11 male and 17 female) took part in the study. Of these 14 were aged (20-29), 11 (30-39), 2 (40-49) and 1 was over 60 years old. Participants came in groups of 2 or 3 friends apart from 4 who came alone. Only one of the participants was already familiar with the Artcodes technology.

Study Structure

The participants were split across 4 evaluation sessions each lasting approximately 2 hours. On arrival participants were briefly introduced to the exhibition, the aims of the study and the app (although they were not taught how to use it), asked to complete a consent form and provided with headphones. Then there were two distinct phases.

The first part (around 40-50 minutes) involved the visitors freely exploring the exhibition (with researchers available to offer assistance if needed), which after the first evaluation session also included contributions by visitors (Figure 6). This was followed by a focus group to discuss their experiences and views on augmenting exhibits with visual markers like Artcodes.

The second phase began with a demonstration of how to draw Artcodes and how to use the Artcodes app to create their own hybrid artefact comprising a visual code and audio recording. Participants were then provided with a worksheet to structure their creation process into the following sequence of activities: identify the aim of the artefact and who it is for (public, for specific people or private), plan the Artcode design and digital content and reflect on why they have been chosen, draw the code, record the audio, create the experience in the app and finally share it. This was followed by a focus group session to gather feedback on how participants felt about contributing to the exhibition in this way.

After we ran the first evaluation session, however, we found that participants spent a lot of time on drawing and experimenting with different Artcode designs. Consequently, even though they had all planned appropriate digital content (based on the worksheets), 11 out of 16 (that took part in the first evaluation session) only recorded audio as a means of testing that they had a working experience (e.g. "Hello" or "Testing"). We contacted these participants to ask them if they would like to send us the planned recording, so that it could be included in the exhibition and 7 of them provided this to us. For the remaining sessions, we swapped the order of drawing and recording audio, to check if this would make a difference and indeed, all subsequent participants made meaningful voice recordings. The hybrid artefacts were added to the exhibition space after each session for subsequent visitors to explore (see Figure 6). The choice of exhibiting all visitor contributions on one wall was made by the gallery staff who wanted to retain curatorial control of the presentation of the portraits.

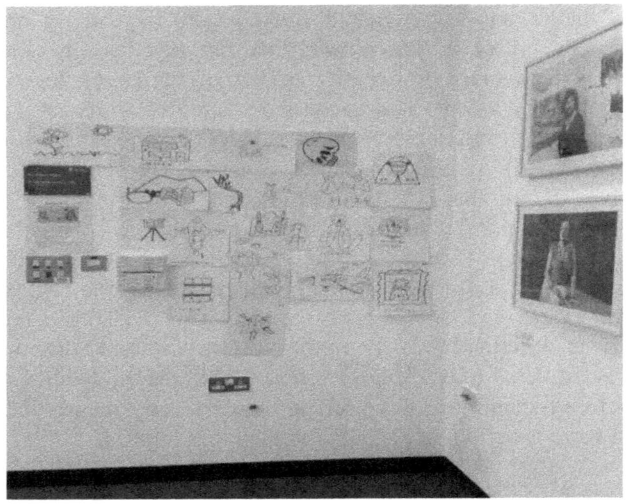

Figure 6. Exhibition of visitor contributed markers

Data capture and analysis

Data was collected through field notes, photographs, video recording of the visitors' interaction with the exhibition in phase 1 (a video camera was placed in a corner of the gallery), audio recording of the focus group sessions and the completed worksheets. The video recordings were qualitatively analyzed to understand how visitors interacted with the Artcodes accompanying the portraits and those created by previous participants, as well as with each other. The audio recordings of the focus group sessions were transcribed and thematically analyzed by two researchers through an active and reflexive process [8]. Data from the phase one focus group was used to complement observations with what participants' said about their interactions. Data from the phase two focus group, information provided in the worksheets and observations of this phase were combined to build a picture of what visitors created and why.

FINDINGS

Our analysis focused on the role of the markers in enhancing the visitors' experience of the exhibits. We were interested in how the visitors engaged with the markers, photographs and associated digital media. We were also interested in how the capabilities of the markers could be used to extend the experience beyond passive consumption to involve participants in a creative process to convey their reflections as part of the exhibition.

Engagement with the Provided Exhibits and Markers

Participants' experiences where broadly structured around three distinct phases. An initial engagement with the photograph and Artcode was followed by scanning the code and then a longer engagement with both the photograph and digital content.

After the initial brief engagement, all 28 participants scanned all 12 Artcode labels that had been provided. The scanning phase raised a number of issues that were often manifest in terms of the physical position of participants and markers. Uncertainty in code recognition led to users reconsidering the best position and distance to scan the image. For example, delays in recognition for two markers made some participants unsure about the best distance to scan from. They were observed stepping back and forth while scanning and in the focus group P9 (female, 20-29) reported:

"It seems that it will scan when focus like camera so you try to help camera to focus image so that is why."

Positioning was also significant in another way. The physical markers were placed in relation to the photographs being exhibited, with the photographs being the focus for visitor engagement rather than the markers. As a result markers that were placed lower could also be more challenging to scan in terms of finding an appropriate position to hold the phone (see Figure 7).

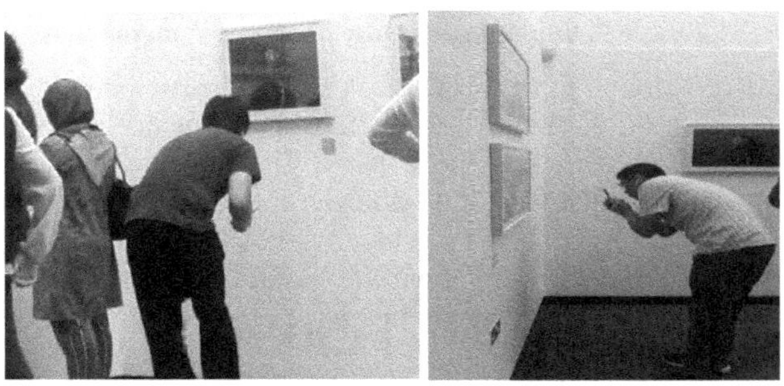

Figure 7. Participants trying to scan labels

Once participants had successfully scanned a marker and accessed the corresponding voice recording, they started a deeper engagement with the photograph and digital content. This was often marked by a change in orientation to the photograph and the marker, with the photograph often becoming the principle focus for participants. The majority of visitors (20 out of 28) moved back away from the marker to a position where they could still keep eye contact with the portrait (e.g. see Figure 8) and disengaged with the marker. This behavior was predominately observed in the first evaluation session when the largest number of participants (16) took part. In the focus group, visitors reported that they acted in this way because they were mindful of the presence of others and wanted to make space for them to interact while they were still engaged with the portrait, e.g. P1 (male, 30-39):

"You want to still keep eye contact with the person you are listening to but you do not need to distract other visitors. So you step back, you know, you still get this content to remember who you are listening to but to let other people get close and see the photo in more detail."

Figure 8. Scanning an Artcode from a close distance (left) and then moving back (right)

Few of the participants (6 out of 28) remained in place close to the portrait to listen to the audio after scanning. This was during the less busy sessions when there were not many other visitors around. The remaining 2 participants moved around the space after scanning while listening to the voice recording. They explained that they were looking for the next portrait to engage with.

The photograph was the dominant focus of engagement for participants. Engagement with the visual representation of the code tended to be determined by the extent to which participants recognized the image. The design of the markers was effective for those who were familiar with the shapes of Latin American countries and could recognize that the labels represented maps. In these cases the markers themselves conveyed an additional piece of information and this was appreciated. Some visitors, however, did not know what the pictures were meant to represent, e.g. P21 (male, 20-29):

"The people [who are] like good in geography ok, but for people like me, it was just like image not map."

Engagement with the Provided Digital Content

Audio was chosen as the media for the digital content to allow users to focus on the photographs in the exhibit. However, as participants moved from scanning the marker to a deeper engagement with the photograph, most participants looked at the phone screen when the voice recording started to play. They reported that this was to confirm that they had the right audio for the portrait they had selected.

We then observed that most participants (18) listened to the recording at the same time as they were looking at the portrait. They did this to observe the person in more detail, get a better understanding of them and feel more connected, e.g. P28 (female, 20-29) stated:

"So I said I will enjoy the photos because that is what I am meant to look at. But also I think when you got a voice and you are looking at photo, you kind of make more of emotional link between them."

In the focus groups there was general agreement that audio works well because it compliments the visual information from the portraits. It was suggested that text would be distracting and tiring to read. 4 from the 28 participants also thought that video would be an engaging format for the digital content, providing further information about the person depicted in the portrait. The others, however, strongly disagreed, arguing that it would take away from the engagement with the artworks, e.g. P27 (female, 20-29) reported:

"Video, for me is like losing the point because the art is there, so if you have a video or another picture in the app, maybe you going to look at that instead of the art."

On the other hand, the other (10) participants appeared more disengaged from the portraits as they were looking at the phone screen or other portraits rather than the one that they were listening to. They explained they were looking at the phone to check how long the audio is and then to focus on listening rather than attend to the portrait. This effect was amplified for some participants as the YouTube interface led them to expect a video instead of only audio.

Design of the User Generated Hybrid Artefacts

In general, participants wanted to design their hybrid artefact to express something personal about themselves or to add comments related to the exhibition. Most participants (18) focused on personal expression, with 15 planning their contribution to be about their own experience of living in the UK, or about their home country or other countries that they visited and 3 wanting to share their interests. On the other hand, 6 participants planned to comment on the exhibition and their experience of it.

The majority of participants (19) designed their artefact for the public, 8 for family and friends, who they hoped would visit the exhibition, and 1 participant had no target audience in mind. Half of those that focused on creating an artefact for a specific person (4 participants) specifically mentioned that their design would address the interests/preferences of the recipient.

Crafting of Markers

All participants were provided with the materials (paper and marker pens) to create Artcodes and were not restricted to specific codes or numbers of regions. Following instructions on how to draw (which were also provided as a printed sheet), all participants managed to create a valid marker within 15 minutes. A few of them drew more than one Artcode and some designed draft versions to learn how to draw valid patterns before designing the final marker.

Most Artcode designs (23) fitted the overall concept that participants had for their contribution as stated in the worksheets. For example, P17 (female, 20-29) designed a map of India (Figure 9, top left) to share her experience of leaving India and living in the UK to study. A picture of a house (Figure 9, top right), designed by P18 (female, over 60) was inspired by the exhibition and was used to leave a comment about the lives of people who come to the UK, while a skeleton (Figure 9, bottom left) designed by P11 (male, 30-39) was linked to information about Mexican illustrations. P23 (female, 40-49) created an airplane (Figure 9, bottom right) to symbolize travel but also because her son loves them, thus personalizing the illustration as her hybrid artefact was intended for a specific person – her son.

Figure 9. Example Artcodes created by participants

As mentioned in the previous section, 4 participants did not record a purpose for their artefact so it was not possible to make a judgement in those cases. The Artcode that did not appear to match was of a butterfly, designed by P8 (female, 30-39) (Figure10, left) whereas the stated purpose and recorded content were about life in the UK (without making a reference to the butterfly imagery).

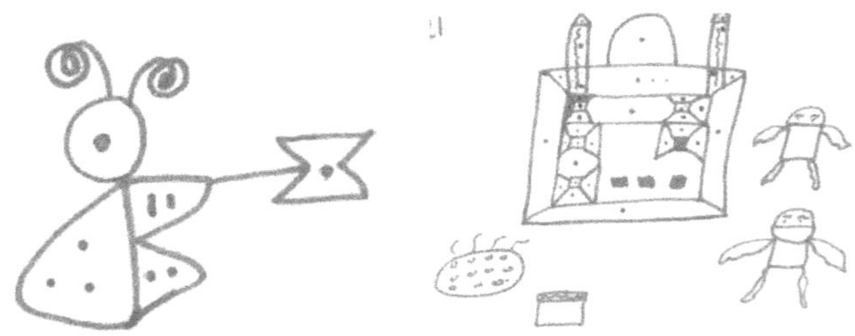

Figure 10. Marker not related to the content (left) and difficult to scan (right)

Only two participants struggled to get their Artcodes to scan and needed a lot of help from the workshop facilitators to make working versions. The technical issue with these designs was that there were a lot of blobs inside the regions, with most of them too close to the border to be recognized robustly by the app (e.g. Figure 10, right) designed by P21 (male, 20-29) showing a Hyderabad temple. P23 (female,

40-49) was able to identify the issue with P21's Artcode – that he struggled because he drew a complicated picture:

"It will be hard to start with complicated drawing but if you start with simple drawing, with the explanation that she gave it, will not be difficult".

Recording of Digital Content
All participants recorded their voice using a recording app on the smartphone. As discussed in the Study Structure section, during the first evaluation session 11 of the 16 participants did not initially record meaningful content. Although most provided content after the session when we invited them to send us the planned contribution, so that it could be included in the exhibition. During the subsequent 3 evaluation sessions, all participants recorded the intended digital content, resulting in 24 audio recordings in total. Their length ranged from 0:40 to 4:18 minutes.

The content of each audio recording either shared personal experiences associated with the themes of the exhibition or commented on the content of the exhibition. The former included reflections on life in the UK, the participant's home country and visiting other countries. For example, P7 who drew the house marker (Figure 9, top right) recorded a comment about family life in the UK:

"What I love about this country is a way they prioritize the family matters, so developing the work life and family. This one I love most in this country".

While another participant P15 (female, 30-39) designed a "teddy bear" Artcode to symbolize social relationships and reflected on her experience of this in her home country and in the UK:

"Nigeria is bubbly and lively place, the people there are full of energy, and passion and creativity and they show it. I have lived in the UK for sixteen years now. One major difference I would say that I find between people who live in the UK and Nigeria is that over here in the UK, people are a lot more conservative in terms of the social side...".

On the other hand others more directly responded to the exhibition with their contribution building upon the content of the exhibits. One example of this is the use of a skeleton marker (Figure 9, bottom left) by F11 where the audio comment recorded by the participant explains:

"Happy skeleton is about the Mexican tradition of drawing funny skeletons on the 2nd of November that is the Day of the Dead."

An example of the ways in which participants reflected on their experience of the exhibition itself is shown below by P28 (female, 20-29):

"Today I found through the use of Artcode app I was able to put a voice to the faces and that was really interesting to hear their experiences and created an emotional bond to the photos as you looked at them. You could gain more understanding of how people feel living here and what they experience being in this country. I also quite like the visitors' opinions of the art exhibition and their experiences in their country too... "

Participants also differed in how they began the audio recording with over half providing a brief biographical introduction to themselves and giving some background information, e.g. P8 (female, 30-39):

"Hi, I am X, a PhD student in computer science at the University of Y. I came from Bangladesh, a South Asian country... "

Whereas the others just provided a name or started to talk about their experiences straightaway, e.g. P21 (male, 20-29):

"Hi, I would like to talk about Hyderabad..."

All participants in the first evaluation session (initially) recorded their voices in the workshop room, whereas in the other three sessions only 3 participants did so, with the others asking if they could go outside for this. Participants gave a number of reasons for this behavior. Some were worried about noise from other participants interfering with their audio recording. Others felt embarrassed to record their thoughts in the presence of other visitors, e.g. P28 (female, 20-29):

"I am shy to take phone calls in front of people so recording my voice to me is quite unnatural thing. I think if you are in a museum or something like that you can normally find a quiet corner to talk and then come back but I don't think I would record my voice in a middle of a gallery."

This was particularly the case if they were not native speakers, as they wanted some privacy to prepare, e.g. P27 (female, 20-29):

"And I wanted to express what I have in my mind. And another issue of because English is my second language I think in Farsi and then translate what I have in Farsi..."

Despite these issues that some participants experienced with recording their voices, everyone highlighted that audio was the most suitable format to associate with the Artcode markers in museum and gallery settings. Participants felt that the audio medium compliments the visual information conveyed by the markers and enables them to communicate emotion in their reflections. It was suggested that providing a booth for audio recording in the museum or allowing visitors to complete the digital part of their artefact at home would address the privacy issues. There was agreement between all participants that they would prefer not to communicate their message through text. Video was suggested as an alternative, but some participants stated they would be too shy to make a video of themselves. It was proposed that providing the choice of audio or video recording might be a good solution.

Engagement with the Visitor Generated Artefacts

Participants were highly engaged with the hybrid artefacts created by previous visitors (Figure 11). These were displayed within the gallery setting as part of the overall exhibition. In the three evaluation sessions where these were exhibited, we found that participants spent more time with them than interacting with the more formal Artcode labels provided with the portraits. In the focus group discussion they reported a number of reasons for this. All participants found the design of the visitors' markers to be meaningful and to relate to the digital audio content. They also felt a connection to these artefacts because they were created by visitors like them who had already experienced the exhibition and were curious to hear their experiences and reflections on the topic of the exhibition. The participants also appreciated points of view from different cultures and countries.

The visitors' markers also (unintentionally) turned out to be easier to interact with. The participants found the interface for playing the voice comments, which was directly integrated in the app, more convenient than the YouTube interface used for accessing the voices of the portraits. The visitors' markers were also more quickly recognized by the app due to their larger size and higher contrast. Unlike the labels, which were placed alongside exhibits, these markers were exhibits in their own right. Consequently, their position invited easy scanning. The codes replaced the photographs as the focal point for interaction. All visitors looked at the Artcode design while listening to the associated voice recording.

Figure 11. Participants interacting with the visitors' markers

As with the portrait markers, the behavior of scanning and moving back was also observed. This happened more frequently, usually when there was more than one other participant nearby, as the visitor markers were all placed on one wall close to each other and adjacent standing space was limited (see Figures 6 and 11).

Social Interaction

Although not designed for collaboration, the system enabled participants to engage in social interaction, with the overall experience being an inherently social activity. This was manifest in a number of ways during the visiting experience. People would observe others' interaction with the Artcodes and use the opportunity to help each other in scanning codes. The system was also appropriated to allow shared listening of the audio content. For example, a group of three friends visited the gallery together. This group stayed close to each other throughout the visit experience. They enthusiastically engaged with the Artcodes and the digital content. They approached the scanning of the codes collectively and at times they even shared the headphone earplugs to ensure they were listening to the recorded voices synchronously (Figure 12).

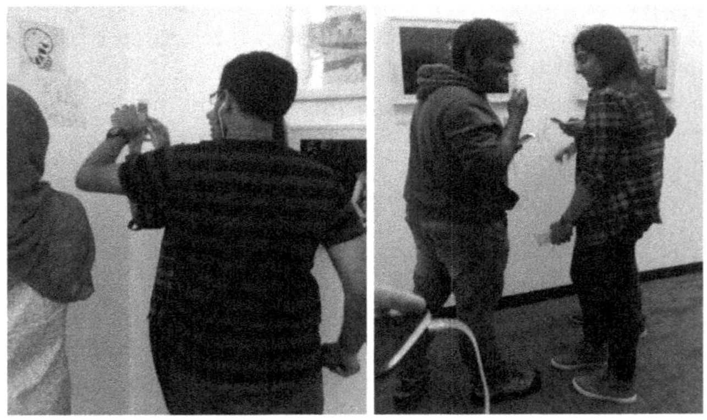

Figure. 12 Participants sharing the visiting experience

The process of designing the markers was also engaged with as a social activity promoting collaboration between visitors. Participants were actively engaged with the others' images during the drawing process and most of them (even those who came alone and did not know the others previously), talked, looked at other participants' designs, asked questions and helped each other (Figure 13). They reported that the activity was interesting and enjoyable, e.g. P19 (female, 20-29):

"It's nice like a puzzle and I really enjoy drawing things."

Figure 13. Participants engaged with drawing markers

DISCUSSION

Based on our study findings, we reflect on the lessons for using aesthetic meaningful markers as labels for exhibits and as a mechanism for visitors to craft a hybrid artefact that encapsulates a contribution to the exhibition.

Augmenting Exhibits through Labels

The placement of markers within the exhibition and their augmentation with audio commentary were viewed positively. We found that users successfully self-managed access to markers by being mindful of the presence of others and repositioning. This is in contrast to Wein [37] who suggests that visitors may be reluctant to engage with visual markers, such as QR codes, because they need to be able to get close to them in potentially crowded spaces. However, our study also highlights considerations for the use of this form of label as a technique for constructing visitors' experiences that exploit their mobile devices.

Our study revealed that visitors engaged with the aesthetic markers at three levels – *physical placement*, *aesthetic content* and *digital content* – that are mutually supportive in shaping the experience. Issues with any single level undermine the overall experience. This effect was notable in our study in terms of the challenges for some visitors arising from the positioning of labels and the legibility of the aesthetic content. It is also important that visitors can readily engage at multiple levels and shift their focus between these levels at low cost.

Interaction with the Physical Placement of Markers

Although it may seem an obvious point, placement needs to be considered carefully. It is critical to shaping the engagement across the other levels of interaction. Exhibitions are carefully curated and significant thought is given to the placement of artefacts in the space [39], and labels are often positioned such that they do not distract from the exhibit. One consequence of this is that labels might not be in a position that invites users to scan them easily. The ability to design markers that are aesthetically pleasing and complementary to the exhibits can potentially alleviate this problem by allowing such labels to be more prominent than QR codes. However, we still found that the positioning of labels would occasionally offer challenges for scanning. Ng and Shaikh also previously note issues with users having to scan labels from awkward positions when they were deployed in a botanical garden in Malaysia [23]. This arose from the placements of some of the labels, which were too far from the walkway. They suggest careful design of the physical labels, use of mounting stands to provide an optimum scanning distance for users, and real-world testing to reveal how real users will physically engage with the markers.

Interaction with the Aesthetic Content of Markers

Users also engaged at the level of the aesthetic content of markers. The images within the markers themselves can be used to add value to the experience of the exhibition. In our case they conveyed information about which country the person depicted on the portrait came from. However, the visual content needs to be designed with care to ensure that it is meaningful to users and supportive of the other levels. We found that a number of visitors were not able to interpret the images as country maps. It can be a challenge to strike a balance in the design of labels so that they convey additional information and/or imply their function, but are also sufficiently abstract to pique visitors' curiosity and encourage experimentation. The visual design of the label needs to be considered carefully in terms of its function in inviting visitors to scan it to engage with the digital content.

Interaction with the Digital Content.

The augmentation of this exhibition involved the assembly and linking of digital media hosted on a commodity service. Audio was presented to users through the interface provided by YouTube rather than by a dedicated functionality in the app. This form of construction is likely to be common for marker based mobile experiences. For example, there are a number of QR code based museum applications that link to Wikipedia [24]. However, this also introduces an interactional cost – that of understanding the change in interface, and switching back from the YouTube app or website to the Artcodes app – that makes it harder for visitors to shift their focus between the different levels involved. As we saw in our study, there is potential for confusion or distraction that arises through the presentation of digital media through a third party interface and there is a need for the careful assembly of the experience.

Visitor Crafted Hybrid Artefacts

As museums increasingly recognize the value of engaging visitors in a dialogue and enabling them to contribute their own interpretations [26, 36], a range of mechanisms to support visitor contributions have been explored. These include use of social media to encourage visitor engagement [35, 19, 38], tagging of exhibits [1, 11, 34] and specially developed interactive displays [12, 31]. Previous research projects, such as Retracing the Past [14] and Reminisce [10], have shown that allowing visitors to record voice messages is a particularly effective way of sharing memories and opinions with others in the museum setting.

We build on these mechanisms with our approach of visitors crafting hybrid artefacts that comprise both a voice recording and a hand drawn physical label. The ability to generate hybrid artefacts in reaction to the exhibition proved popular as a means of visitor expression and as an extension of the exhibition in its own right. It is interesting to note that all visitors chose to contribute new content (in effect creating a new exhibit), as outlined in the section Design of the User Generated Hybrid Artefacts, rather than offer reflections focusing on a specific portrait. Our results raise the possibility that hybrid contributions are more rewarding for the visitor than digital tags, which previously have been predominantly used to comment on existing exibits [11, 32]. In turn, participants who visited the gallery when the visitor-generated artefacts were displayed, found the hybrid contributions as engaging as the curated content.

However, unlike digital tags, it is important to note that hybrid contributions consume the museum's physical space. In our study, gallery space was kindly dedicated to participants to use, but for many museums space may be considered too valuable to spare for visitor contributions. Longer-term studies of hybrid artefacts as visitor contributions will need to consider how long the lifespan of a contribution should be, and strategies for rotating or retiring contributions to ensure that they do not overwhelm the museum.

Supporting Multi-Level Crafting of Hybrid Artefacts

The importance of the interplay between the multiple levels of interaction was evident as visitors recorded *digital content*, created *aesthetic content* by drawing labels and *physically placed* these in the exhibition in relation to other content. People expressed themselves through a combination of the physical image and the associated digital recording. As presented in the Findings section, most Artcode designs fitted the overall concept that participants had for their contribution, with the image linked in some way to the digital content.

The crafting of hybrid artefacts required effort and creativity and we suggest that consequently visitors put in more thought in the process, resulting in the generation of more interesting contributions than are usually found in an equivalent visitors' book or systems that allows objects to be tagged with text comments. Studies of maker communities have revealed that members value the pleasure of making and personal expression [30]. Allowing museum visitors to craft hybrid artefacts as a means of contributing to the museum can enable them to tap into these feelings. Our findings also contrast with those of Thom-Santelli at al's study [32], which found difference in engagement between expert and novice users in leaving digital tags. Arguably this lends further support for the value of drawing (and physical crafting more generally) in engaging visitors in making meaningful contributions.

However, the fact that the creation of hybrid artefacts requires a significant commitment from visitors also means that this process will require some form of scaffolding. It is important that support for crafting addresses the need to work at each of the three levels: people need to be supported in drawing the labels, linking the digital content and potentially placement in the space. We have seen from our study that dedicated sessions, facilitated by staff, work successfully. Alternatively, support for self-led creative activities could be provided in the form of a workstation with worksheets and instructions. However, the challenge of embedding sufficient contextual knowledge of the exhibit and how people relate to it, must not be underestimated.

Another direction for future research is to explore the placement of visitor contributions within the exhibition. In our study visitor drawings were displayed on one wall allocated by the gallery. These placements, worked well as all visitors chose to extend the exhibition with new drawings and voice comments rather than reflections focusing on a specific portrait. This was also the case for the 16 visitors in the first sessions, who at the point of creation, had not seen how their contributions would be displayed. In future research it would be interesting to explore if and how visitors can be allowed to be involved in the placement of their contribution within the exhibition and if this would affect what visitors create. This would further extend the role of visitors in shaping museum content but must be balanced against the need for museums to maintain overall curatorial control and moderation of content [25, 27].

Scheduling within the Overall Visiting Experience

The drawing of markers takes time, with participants experimenting with designs and then producing a final working version. It is important that this time commitment is designed for and managed as part of the overall visitor experience. It is important that this should reflect the creation of aesthetic and digital content and the physical placement in the setting. In our case, we found that the scheduling of marker drawing before the audio recording activity led participants to spend most of the available time on it, causing the remaining parts of the experience to be rushed, undermining the value of the hybrid artefact.

Finally, we would also suggest that people need space to generate images and audio commentary. It is worth noting that, although many museum visits are social, people often felt the need for privacy when recording audio content. Future work can also explore what the impact would be of allowing visitors to complete their hybrid artefacts at home.

CONCLUSION

Our study has shown that visual markers, such as Artcodes, which can be designed to convey visual meaning, can be combined with mobile devices to enhance the visitor experience of exhibits, especially when linked to complimentary audio content. Issues, such as the interface for accessing the digital media, appropriate marker design and marker placement, however, need to be considered carefully to ensure smooth interaction.

We have highlighted directions for future work on the use of visual markers, which can be crafted by the visitors, as a valuable mechanism for contributing new content to an exhibition. In our study the participants generated hybrid artefacts that were well thought-out and engaging for subsequent visitors, consisting of an image and audio comment. We raised the question of where these contributions might be embedded in the museum, how visitors can be involved in the process of placing their contributions in the museum, and what strategies for rotating and recycling contributions need to be implemented. We suggest that the drawing activity, which took time and effort, encouraged participants to reflect more deeply on the theme of the exhibition and focus on content that other visitors could relate to. To utilize visual markers in this way, however, requires further consideration of how, when and where to scaffold creative visitor activities.

ACKNOWLEDGMENTS

This work was supported by UK Engineering and Physical Sciences Research Council grant EP/M02315X/1 and by the EU Horizon 2020 grant 727040 (the GIFT project).

REFERENCES

1. Ahern, S., Davis, M., Eckles, D., King, S., Naaman, M., Nair, R., ... & Yang, J. 2006. Zonetag: Designing context-aware mobile media capture to increase participation. In *Proceedings of the Pervasive Image Capture and Sharing, 8th Int. Conf. on Ubiquitous Computing, California*, .
2. Artcodes website. Retrieved December 2017 from http://www.artcodes.co.uk/
3. Atkinson, R. 2013. Museum Practice: How are museums using mobile, from Museums Association. Retrieved December 2017 from https://www.museumsassociation.org/museum-practice/mobile-in-museums-2013/15102013-mobile-survey-2013-results
4. BeQRious. Fort Wayne Art Museum Uses QR Codes To Educate Visitors. Retrieved December 2017 from http://beqrioustracker.com/fort-wayne-art-museum-uses-qr-codes-to-educate-visitors/
5. BeQRious. Museum Urk First Dutch Museum to use New Media. Retrieved December 2017 from http://beqrioustracker.com/museum-urk-first-dutch-museum-to-use-new-media/
6. Blippar website. Retrieved December 2017 from https://blippar.com/en/
7. Boy Scouts of America. Boy Scouts of America Takes Center Stage in Nation's Capital to Celebrate 100th Anniversary. Retrieved December 2017 from http://www.prnewswire.com/news-releases/boy-scouts-of-america-takes-center-stage-in-nations-capital-to-celebrate-100th-anniversary-99133979.html
8. Braun, V. and Clarke, V. 2006. Using thematic analysis in psychology. Qualitative Research in Psychology, 3 (2). pp. 77-101. ISSN 1478-0887
9. Ceipidor, U. B., Medaglia, C. M., Perrone, A., De Marsico, M., and Di Romano, G. 2009. A museum mobile game for children using QR-codes. In *Proceedings of the 8th International Conference on Interaction Design and Children* (IDC '09), 282-283 http://dl.acm.org/citation.cfm?doid=1551788.1551857
10. Ciolfi, L. and McLoughlin, M. 2011. Challenges for the technological augmentation of open-air museums: Bridging buildings, artefacts and activities. *Nordisk Museologi*, (1), 15.
11. Cosley, D., Baxter, J., Lee, S., Alson, B., Nomura, S., Adams, P., Gay, G. 2009. A Tag in the Hand: Supporting Semantic, Social, and Spatial Navigation in Museums. In Proceedings of the 27th International Conference on Human Factors in Computing Systems (CHI'09), 1953–1962. http://doi.acm.org/10.1145/1518701.1518999
12. Cosley, D., Lewenstein, J., Herman, A., Holloway, J., Baxter, J., Nomura, S., ... & Gay, G. 2008. ArtLinks: fostering social awareness and reflection in museums. In *Proceedings of the SIGCHI Conference on Human Factors in Computing Systems* (CHI '08), 403-412.
13. Costanza, E. Huang, J. 2009. Designable visual markers. In Proceedings of the SIGCHI conference on Human Factors in Computing Systems (CHI '09). http://dx.doi.org/10.1145/1518701.1518990
14. Ferris, K., Bannon, L., Ciolfi, L., Gallagher, P., Hall, T., & Lennon, M. 2004. Shaping experiences in the hunt museum: a design case study. In *Proceedings of the 5th conference on Designing interactive systems: processes, practices, methods, and techniques* (pp. 205-214). ACM.
15. Gray, S., Ross, C., Hudson-Smith, A., Warwick, C., and Terras, M. 2012. Enhancing Museum Narratives with the QRator Project: a Tasmanian devil, a Platypus and a Dead Man in a Box. In Proc. *Museums and the Web* (MW 2012).
16. Higashino, S., Nishi, S., & Sakamoto, R. 2016. ARTTag: aesthetic fiducial markers based on circle pairs. In *ACM SIGGRAPH 2016 Posters* (p. 38). ACM.
17. Huang, W., & Mow, W. H. 2013. PiCode: 2D barcode with embedded picture and ViCode: 3D barcode with embedded video. In*Proceedings of the 19th annual international conference on Mobile computing & networking* (pp. 139-142). ACM.
18. Imperial War Museum. Social Interpretation. Retrieved December 2017 from http://blogs.iwm.org.uk/social-interpretation/
19. Kidd, J. 2014. Museums in the New Mediascape: Transmedia, Participation. Ethics. New York: Routledge.
20. Kuflik, T., Rokeah, O., Salman, S. 2014. The Treasure Hunt Game Generator – a system and its application at the Hecht Museum. *MW2014: Museums and the Web 2014.* Available online: http://mw2014.museumsandtheweb.com/paper/the-treasure-hunt-game-generator-a-system-and-its-application-at-the-hecht-museum/
21. Meese, R., Ali, S., Thorne, E. C. et al. 2013. From codes to patterns: designing interactive decoration for tableware. In *Proceedings of the SIGCHI Conference on Human Factors in Computing Systems* (CHI '13), 931-940 http://dl.acm.org/citation.cfm?id=2466119
22. Mikalef, K. and Chorianopoulos, K. 2011. Game playing in the field: Effects of interactivity on learning and museum experience. In *Proceedings of the DEG workshop on Involving End Users and Domain Experts in the Design of Educational Games.*
23. Ng, K. H., & Shaikh, S. P. 2016. Design of a mobile garden guide based on Artcodes. In *User Science and Engineering (i-USEr), 2016 4th International Conference on* (pp. 23-28). IEEE.

24. Ross, Claire Bailey. 2012. What does success look like for museum QR code usage? Retrieved December 2017 from: https://claireyross.wordpress.com/tag/qr-codes/
25. Russo, A., Watkins, J., Kelly, L., & Chan, S. 2008. Participatory communication with social media. Curator: The Museum Journal, 51(1), 21-31
26. Schultz, M. K. 2013. A case study on the appropriateness of using quick response (QR) codes in libraries and museums. *Library & Information Science Research*, 35(3), 207-215.
27. Simon, N. 2013. *The Participatory Museum*. Museums 2.0, 2010.
28. Speed, C and McDonald, J. 2013. TOTeM (Tales of Things and Electronic Memory). Retrieved December 2017 from: http://www.omnimuseum.org/id21.html
29. Tales of Things. Retrieved December 2017 from http://talesofthings.com
30. Tanenbaum, Joshua G., et al. 2013. "Democratizing technology: pleasure, utility and expressiveness in DIY and maker practice." *Proceedings of the SIGCHI Conference on Human Factors in Computing Systems*. ACM.
31. Taylor, N. 2014. Supporting community participation in interactive exhibits. In *Proceedings of The International Symposium on Pervasive Displays* (p. 74). ACM.
32. Thom-Santelli, J., Cosley, D., & Gay, G. (2010). What do you know?: experts, novices and territoriality in collaborative systems. *In Proceedings of the SIGCHI Conference on Human Factors in Computing Systems* (CHI '10), 1685–1694. http://doi.org/10.1145/1753326.1753578
33. Thorn, E. C., Rennick-Egglestone, S., Koleva, B., Preston, W., Benford, S., Quinn, A., & Mortier, R. 2016. Exploring large-scale interactive public illustrations. In *Proceedings of the 2016 ACM Conference on Designing Interactive Systems* (pp. 17-27). ACM. https://doi.org/10.1145/2901790.2901826
34. Trant, J., & Wyman, B. 2006. Investigating social tagging and folksonomy in art museums with steve. museum. In *Collaborative Web Tagging Workshop at WWW2006, Edinburgh, Scotland.*
35. Von Appen, K., Kennedy, B., & Spadaccini, J. 2006. Community sites & emerging sociable technologies. In *Museums and the Web* (pp. 197-206).
36. Vuforia website. Retrieved December 2017 from https://www.vuforia.com/
37. Wein, L. 2014. Visual recognition in museum guide apps: do visitors want it? In *Proceedings of the SIGCHI Conference on Human Factors in Computing Systems* (CHI '14), 635-638. http://dl.acm.org/citation.cfm?doid=2556288.2557270
38. Weilenmann, A., Hillman, T., & Jungselius, B. 2013. Instagram at the museum. *In Proceedings of the SIGCHI Conference on Human Factors in Computing Systems* (CHI '13), 1843. http://doi.org/10.1145/2470654.2466243
39. Whitehead, C. 2012. Interpreting art in museums and galleries. Routledge,
40. Zhe Yang, Yuting Bao, Chuhao Luo, et al. 2016. ARTcode: preserve art and code in any image. In *Proceedings of the 2016 ACM International Joint Conference on Pervasive and Ubiquitous Computing* (UbiComp '16), 904-915. http://dx.doi.org/10.1145/2971648.2971733

TouchBranch: Understanding Interpersonal Touches in Interactive Installation

Seungki Kim[1], Jiwoo Hong[1], Jaeyeon Lee[2], Hyun-Sook Choi[3], Geehyuk Lee[2] and Woohun Lee[1]

[1] Department of Industrial Design, KAIST, Daejeon, South Korea {seungki.kim, jwhong10, woohun.lee}@kaist.ac.kr

[2] HCI Lab, KAIST, Daejeon, South Korea jaeyeonlee@kaist.ac.kr, geehyuk@gmail.com

[3] Exhibition Service Division, National Science Museum, Daejeon, South Korea hschoi1@korea.kr

ABSTRACT
Interpersonal touch, one of the most primitive social languages, is an excellent design element frequently used in interaction design. In this paper, we present a richer understanding of it by using spatial factors and social relations among people, which has rarely been explored in interactive systems. We designed an interactive installation called "TouchBranch" where players can move light between branches placed at various distances by connecting their bodies. The user studies were conducted with 21 groups consisting of intimates, acquaintances, and strangers. We observed a change in the interpersonal touch pattern and touch tolerance according to each factor. Interestingly, the effect of the social relation was dramatic, but that of the spatial factor was not quantitatively significant. Nevertheless, we discovered that spatial factor can influence the interpersonal touch experience. Based on the results, we discuss in this paper the influence of two factors on the interpersonal touch that stands out in the context of interactive systems.

Author Keywords
Interpersonal touch; TouchBranch; Social relationship; Spatial factors; Distance; Touch tolerance; Types of Interpersonal touch; Interactive installation;

ACM Classification Keywords
H.5.m. Information interfaces and presentation (e.g., HCI): Miscellaneous;

INTRODUCTION
Interpersonal touch is one of the most natural social languages that exists among people. It has been used extensively in fields where social factors are important,

DIS '18, June 9–13, 2018, , Hong Kong

ACM ISBN 978-1-4503-5198-0/18/06...$15.00
https://doi.org/10.1145/3196709.3196740

Figure 1. A couple is playing an interpersonal touch game using a TouchBranch

such as interactive advertisement and entertainment, because it greatly affects the user's emotional and social behavior[1,4,9,15,16,20].

Interpersonal touch must be deeply understood to be effectively used in an interactive system. Social factors, such as gender, relationship, and age have been suggested as elements affecting interpersonal touch [5,8,9,13,18,25]. In interactive systems, however, designing interpersonal touch is a more complex and challenging issue. More than social factors, the interpersonal touch behavior of users can be affected by external factors, such as hardware, which detects interpersonal touch. In addition, the known social factors can also be further understood with regard to how they function in interactive systems using interpersonal touch.

In this study, we investigate how the relationship between users and the distance between them, which has been less explored among various interpersonal touch elements, affects interpersonal touch by research through design approach[29]. We designed a playable interactive installation called "TouchBranch" where players can move light between branches by connecting their bodies. In the user study, we teamed up with intimates, acquaintances, and strangers to explore the effects of the social relation on interpersonal touch behavior. We also observed changes due to distances by providing branches placed at various distances. In this way, we forced users to stretch their bodies to touch others, or we placed users close enough to one another.

This paper presents three major findings and discusses about them.

1. The change in touch tolerance before and after using TouchBranch, based on the distances and relationships between users

2. Interpersonal touch behavior patterns and the differences in their frequencies according to distance and relation

3. An understanding of how these factors influence the interpersonal touch experience in interactive systems

The findings of this study will be design guidelines for constructing interactive system with interpersonal touch technology.

RELATED WORKS

Interpersonal Touches in Interactive Systems

Interpersonal touch is not a novel technology that has never been used in interactive systems. Many academic research studies, advertisements, and artworks have engaged users via interpersonal touch. The types of hardware used have been diverse, so the users' touch behaviors have been immensely different.

Hobye discusses the five key qualities that appear when interpersonal touch is applied to interactive systems through several case studies[14]. These key qualities, including sparking curiosity and norm bending intimacy, can be useful for understanding the interpersonal touch experience. However, we need to look further to see which design factors affect these experiences of interpersonal touch. Especially, in many cases, the distance between users has been fixed via hardware design. However, the influence of the distance is not yet clear.

Interpersonal Touch in Close Distance

In most studies, interpersonal touch interaction takes place at a close distance. In general, the touch distance is shorter than 1m long. In the case of Freqtric Drum[2] or Touch-O-Matic[20], the electrodes are exposed on one device, and touch is detected through them. In some cases, such as Fingle[31] and Intangle[10], the interface does not recognize the interpersonal touch, but simply induces it. These cases are very close to each other because they are tangled with a shared device like Twister. The Sensation[4] that verifies the emotional and hedonic effects of interpersonal touch interaction is developed as a wearable device that can widen the touch distance. However, the touch occurs at a close distance because the interface uses one stand screen that forces participants to stand nearby. An interactive game even exists that uses a hug, a touch behavior at an extremely close distance, such as Musical Embrace[16].

Regarding the use of these systems at a close distance, the use of the hands, arms, and torso is outstanding. In general, because the body parts used for touch recognition are fixed, the movement of the legs is limited, and the touch frequently occurs by hands. Therefore, hand-to-hand interpersonal touch can be observed in various systems, such as Freqtric Drum[2], Touch-O-Matic[20], and EnhancedTouch[26].

However, it is also possible to observe a touch used to express intimacy or pleasure, such as twisting or softly hitting a face at a close distance [20]. In the case of an interface with a different sound depending on the touch area, such as Mediated Body[15], various touch behaviors using various body parts, such as the cheek, arm, hand, and even lips, are explored. Of course, these touches may be intimately related, but the possibility still exits to explore the intimacy further while interpreting interpersonal touch interactive systems.

From these studies, the use of the hand and torso is predominant in a touch at a short distance, and the behavior is limited, but touch regions vary. Even if the touch distance is close, the interpersonal touch behavior becomes more dynamic as more space elements are provided. In addition, the touch behavior patterns may vary depending on the social relationship between the users. Further exploring the touch that appears at various distances is necessary.

Interpersonal Touch in Far Distance

An example of an interpersonal touch occurring at a farther distance than the previous example is Moment of Warmth [6], an interactive advertising installation for Duracell. In this installation, the electrodes are installed at opposite ends of a bus shelter so that when users connect each other with their hands, the heater is activated. Because the two ends of the bus shelter are far apart, several people must extend their arms far away. A similar example is Milka's "tender chain" advertisement[21]. The advertisement uses an interactive vending machine that provides chocolates freely when users connect with each other between a vending machine and a cow sculpture. As the cow sculpture continues to move backward, the distance required to be interpersonally connected becomes longer, so the participants must connect with more people to fill it.

In an interactive system featuring a long distance, a relatively large number of people are involved, and the social element is emphasized. Therefore, it is often used as a public advertisement. People who do not know each other naturally engage because they can touch other people with their hands from long distances.

By contrast, some systems provide spatial interactions with small groups of people. These include Balance of Power [19], a game that uses the physical contact that occurs when two people are bumping against each other;

B.U.T.T.O.N[28], where body naturally becomes entangled, and SoundTag[27], which combines touch and musical elements in a tag game. These examples use vision technology, wearable devices to detect interpersonal touch, or the rules of games to derive interpersonal touches. In these cases, the touch areas are more diversified, and the touch behaviors are more active than in the systems that provide shorter distances.

In previous studies, the possibility of various behaviors depending on the distances between users when interpersonal touch occurs was mentioned, but this type of research has not been done systematically yet. Therefore, it is necessary to find out how users' interpersonal touch behavior varies according to the distance, and to derive design guidelines.

Understanding Interpersonal Touch

The understanding of interpersonal touch has been widely explored. Because interpersonal touch is anthropologically and psychologically important, many researchers in social science and psychology have understood interpersonal touch[5,8,9,13,18,25]. However, it is difficult to apply this understanding directly to HCI. Interpersonal touches in interactive systems can be multi-modally reinforced with touch feedback, unlike naturally occurring interpersonal touches. Because the system senses the touch, the way in which the user perceives the touch may vary depending on the sensing sensitivity or the sensing range. In addition, the motivation for an interpersonal touch is different from that of the natural communication situation.

Marshall and Tennent[20] conducted a long-term in-the-wild experiment to understand interpersonal touch in interactive systems. Marshall understands the value of touch interaction as an element of the game interface, the differences in touch by gender and age, and the relationship among the interface, player, and spectator on the interpersonal touch interface. Garner et al.[10,11] argue that ambiguity is important for inducing more interpersonal touch in interactive systems.

In addition to the gender, age, spectator elements, and ambiguity, various factors such as the number of people engaging, spatial factors, temporal factors, and relationships among people can affect interpersonal touch[9,25]. Especially, social relations among people have been mentioned as important factors in existing psychological studies. However, no study has been conducted on how this social relationship works in interactive systems. However, we predicted that interactive systems would display a different pattern from those of previous studies because these systems have a different purpose and motivation for interpersonal touch.

In this study, we attempted to explore interpersonal touch using social relations and spatial elements among people. It is difficult to know the effects of social relations by studying only intimate relationships or conducting in-the-wild studies that cannot control social relations among participants. Thus, we studied their influence on interpersonal touch by dividing the intimate and stranger as well as the acquaintance group, which has rarely been explored. We also adjusted the proximity between the participants, which is an important factor of social interaction, by adjusting the touch distance[3,12,22,23]. Participants were placed at various proximities with other participants and naturally induced social interaction.

DESIGN

To understand the effects of distance and relationship on interpersonal touch behavior in an interactive system, we follow the Research through Design approaches[29]. As a design artifact, we constructed an interactive installation called TouchBranch.

Game Scenario

TouchBranch is a playable interactive installation that can be installed in public spaces. Users create a light by rotating the handle on the start branch. They can transfer the light through the connection branches to the end branch by connecting their bodies interpersonally.

Users rotate the handle next to the start branch to generate light in the start branch. When the light is fully generated, the light is turned to white and blinks. At this moment, when the knob of the start branch is connected to the knob of the other connection branch using the body, the light is moved. When the user moves the light between the connection branches and moves it to the end branch, the light comes out with the wind at the kinetic part next to the end branch.

Game scenarios that have been implemented on the TouchBranch include game modes where the time limit and the goal of the game are fixed, and a free-play mode that allows a user to freely explore the game. In game modes, a time limit exists after the light is generated in the start branch, and the branch to be connected is determined. If the user generates light, the knob to be connected in the connection branches will blink with a shining orange light. The user has to connect their body between the knobs with the orange light and the knob of the start branch as soon as possible. If the user successfully transfers the light to the connection branch, the next knob to be connected will be turned on with orange color.

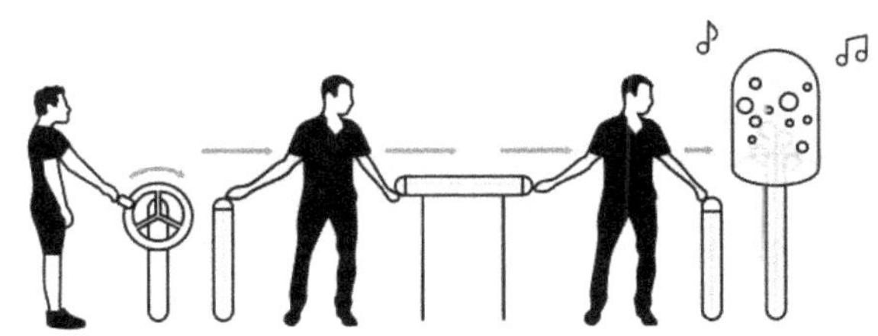

Figure 2. The quick overview of TouchBranch game scenario

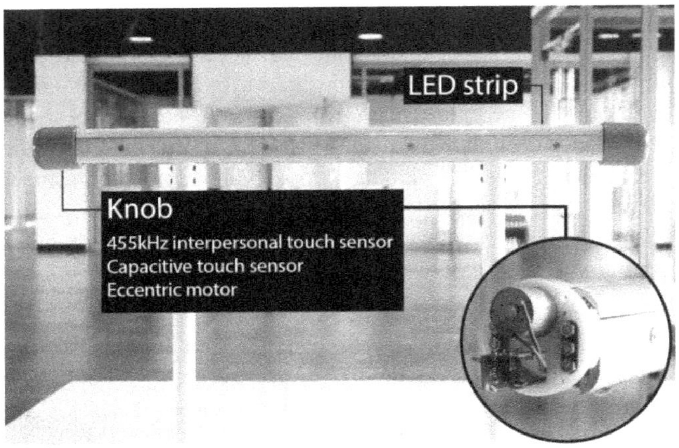

Figure 3. The design and components of connecting branches

Figure 4. The design of end brach and its kinetic parts

The routes are pre-defined, and they must be connected within the time limit. If the user fails to connect all in time, the light will disappear, and the user should try the game again from the beginning.

In addition, to understand the effect of distance elements on the interpersonal touch experience, we produced two scenarios in the game mode: a long-distance game in which the average distance between the knobs to be touched is maximized, and a short-distance game in which the average distance to be touched is minimized. In the game mode, all routes were created using a pseudo-random sequence with fixed frequency ratios such that the ratio of the long distance (or short distance) and the middle distance is 2:1.

In the free-play mode, no restriction of time and goal exists. Users can freely move the light between branches and try various distance, including moving light from the start branch to the end branch at once. Moreover, users can generate multiple lights in one game by regenerating light after transferring light to connection branches.

In this study, we implemented non-screen games, such as Intangle[10], EnhancedTouch[26], and Moments of Warmth[6], rather than screen-based interpersonal touch games, such as Touch-O-Matic[20], Sensation[4], and Musical Embrace[16].

The screen-based game provides a rich game experience and can enhance immersion by using graphic elements. However, in this study, using the screen was not feasible because the TouchBranch system deals with interpersonal touch using the whole body at various distances. In addition, because the touch behavior itself becomes the main modality of the game, the non-screen based interaction is assumed to yield users to focus on the interpersonal touch experience. We used an array of NeoPixel LED strips to enhance scarce visual feedback and improved user recognition of the interpersonal touch by providing vibrotactile feedback from the touch area of the developed system.

Branch Design

Because the branch is the part that the user touches directly and where the direct feedback appears, the most important consideration is the touchability of various parts of the body, feedback with various modalities, and the stability of sensors.

The height of the branch was determined to be 900 mm, which is the natural height for touching the knob with the hands and even with other body parts including legs. The LED strip passes in the middle of the branch. It displays the transferred light on the branch and visualizes the movement of the light. It also provides visual feedback when the two branches are connected through the user's interpersonal touch.

At the end of the branch is a painted aluminum knob that recognizes the user's touch. The knob is coated with paint to protect it from noise, such as static electricity. In the knob is a sensor that senses the interpersonal touch between branches and a capacitive touch sensor that senses simple touch behavior. An eccentric motor is embedded in the knob, and when the user connects the branch through bodies, the vibrotactile feedback is given (Figure 3).

We designed the connection branch as a horizontally lying column because we wanted to make sure that it is a pathway to the ends. In the contrast, the start and end branches are in the form of vertical columns. Unlike the connection branch, the start and end branches have only one knob. The height is the same as the connection branch. Turning the handle next to the start branch will generate the light that can be transferred to the other branch. A final kinetic part is located next to the end branch. If the light is transferred to the end branch, the light transferred to the kinetic part and winds blow out from the air pump under the kinetic part. The winds hit small balls inside of the kinetic part, and the lights blink by flowing movements of balls (Figure 4).

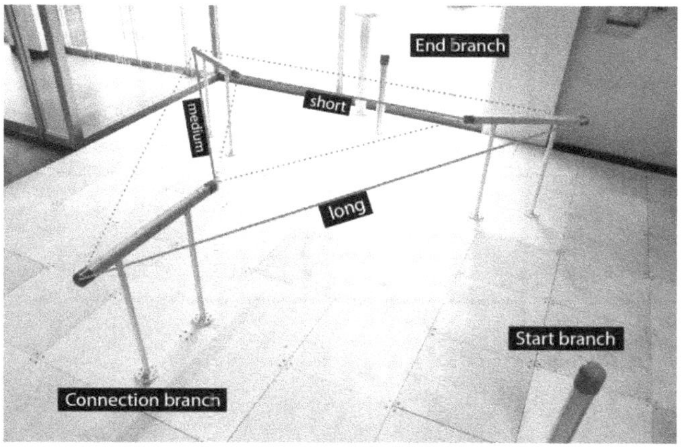

Figure 5. Layout of TouchBranch. It looks distorted by perspective, but equilateral triangles share the same center

Layout of TouchBranch

In this study, we tried to understand interpersonal touch under various distances, especially the proximity between the participants[3,23]. Although we could provide many distances through various arrangements, in this study, we decided to narrow down the connectable distance to three distances to obtain clear results. The criteria of the three distances are as follows: 1) a short distance that is difficult for one person to connect by two hands but is very close for two people; 2) a long distance that is difficult for two people to connect only via their hands; and 3) a medium distance that two people can naturally connect by their hands. Based on the anthropometric data, especially the height, of South Korea[30], the distances were set to a short distance: 1850, long distance: 3400, and medium distance: 2700 mm respectively.

The final layout is the form of two equilateral triangles (Figure 5). The longest distance that can be made is one side of a large equilateral triangle, the shortest distance is one side of a small equilateral triangle, and the medium distance is the line connecting the vertexes of the large and small triangles.

IMPLEMENTATION

Our system has two kinds of touch sensors; one detects a simple touch by using a capacitive touch sensor, and the other detects interpersonal touches. The interpersonal touch is sensed by detecting a 455-kHz AC signal transferred between the metal knobs of two branches. We selected the frequency of 455 kHz because it was high enough to use an AC capacitive coupling and it was easy to get parts. A person senses at least 1 mA (RMS) of electric current. Because a typical body resistance of dry skin is 300 kΩ, and the RMS current is approximately 0.01 mA.

In a knob, as shown in Figure 1, transmitting and receiving modules of a 455-kHz signal share an electrode, and the state of a knob (transmitting or receiving) can be set by an Arduino board connected to each knob. The transmit module consisted of a 455-kHz crystal. The receive module consisted of a 455-kHz filter (LTM455DU).

In an interpersonal touch-sensing cycle, we set a knob as the transmit mode and the others as the receive mode. Then we checked every knob set as the receive mode if it detected a 455-kHz signal. We iterated the cycle n times (n=the number of knobs) by changing the transmit knob, and then, we could figure out which of the knobs were connected together. The whole interpersonal touch-sensing process was designed to be done in 300 ms with eight knobs.

USER STUDY

To understand the effects of distance and social relations on interpersonal touch in interactive systems, we conducted a user study with TouchBranch. We recruited participants in various social relationships and arranged sessions to allow interpersonal touch at various distances. The process using TouchBranch was video recorded, and the interview was audio recorded.

Participants

Participants consisted of a total of 21 teams with seven teams of intimates, acquaintances, and strangers according to social relations. The each team members consisted of two people for manageable research. The participants consisted of 22 males and 20 females as well as same-sex teams: 11 teams and different-sex teams: 10 teams. In the case of the same-sex team, the number of male–male teams was six teams, and that of the female–female team was five teams. The average age of the participants was 25.3. The average height of female participants was 163.3, and the average height of male participants was 176.2, which is 1 cm taller than the average height of men in South Korea[30]. The stranger group randomly matched among participants recruited on the Internet, and they were cross-checked so that they did not know one another before the experiment. The acquaintance group was recruited through Internet and offline recruitment and was defined as people who belonged to the same job or group but did not communicate privately. The intimate group was recruited through online and offline recruitment and consisted of roommates, couples, husbands and wives, and close friends.

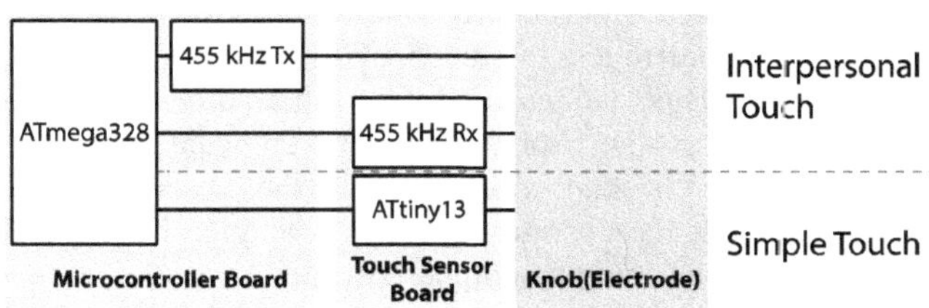

Figure 6. Block diagram of TouchBranch sensor part

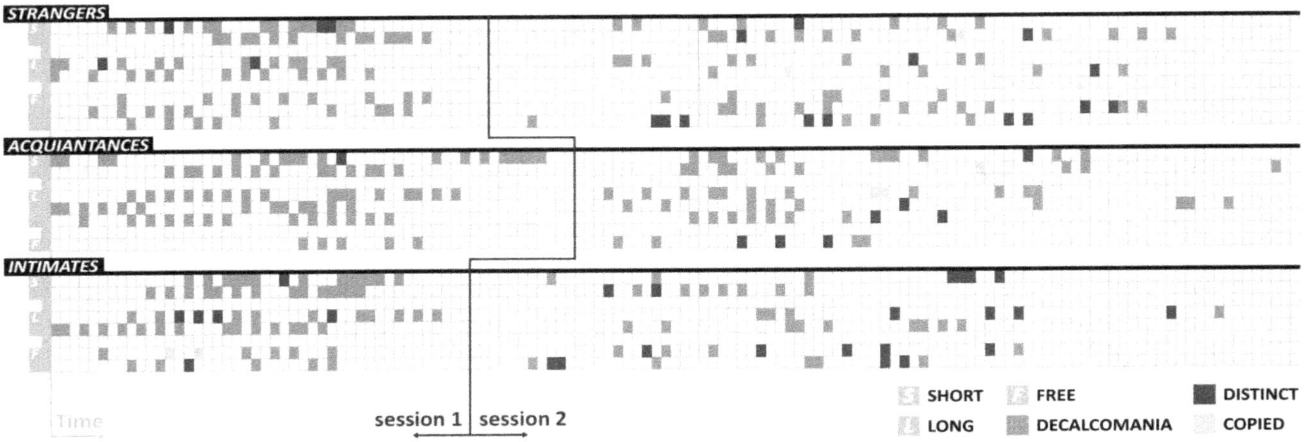

Figure 7. A timeline showing the interpersonal touch of each type. Based on the middle line, the left side is the first session, and the right side is the second session. One cell takes five seconds.

User Study Sessions

The experiment consisted of two sessions.

The first sessions were divided into long-distance games, short-distance games, and free play to adjust the distance between participants when they played TouchBranch as mentioned in the design session.

In a second session, we provided a free-play mode for every team that allowed all participants to freely move light between connected branches without restrictions. Through this session, we wanted to observe whether the distance elements experienced in the first session affected the free-play situation in the second session.

In terms of the time spent in the experiment, a simple experiment instruction took five minutes, and 20 minutes of the main experiments were conducted (10 minutes for the first session and 10 minutes for the second session). Then, an interview was conducted for five to 10 minutes, and a total of 30 to 40 minutes of experiments were conducted.

Questionnaire and Interview

Participants were asked to rate their familiarity with the team members on a 5-point Likert scale and to define their relationship in one word or sentence. Through this, we checked whether the social relationships of the groups we recruited differed significantly. Participants then checked the interpersonal touch tolerance of the face, neck, arms, hands, belly, legs, ankles, and feet when others touched theirs or touched others' on a 5-point Likert scale. The same question was checked after the all the sessions were finished so that the changes of touch tolerance before and after the sessions could be compared.

The interviews were conducted after both the experiment and the questionnaires were completed. The interviews were semi-constructed interviews with the overall experience of the game, interpersonal touch, differences between sessions, questions about communication with the partner, and considerations behind the gameplay. All the interviews were audio recorded and scripted after the experiment

ANALYSIS

All questionnaire data were analyzed by one-way analysis of variance (ANOVA) through SPSS. First, the intimacy scale that the participants checked was analyzed to see if the social relations of the recruited groups were significantly different. Then, one-way ANOVA analysis was performed for differences in the touch tolerance scores before and after the experiment.

All the scenes where participants used the TouchBranch were video recorded and all the process was mapped and coded in a timeline using Microsoft Excel by 3 coders. We focused on the interpersonal touch that occurred between the participants. The coding schemes were when the interpersonal touch occurred, whether the touch was successful, which part of body region was used by the two participants and what verbal & non-verbal communication was used to touch. We checked when an unrelated conversation with an interpersonal touch occurred and what kind of conversation took place. Three types of interpersonal touch types were derived by analyzing the total 21 timelines collected and analyzed again by mapping them to the timeline (Figure 8).

Interview data were used to more qualitatively support the analysis of the timeline, and was not coded separately because it was a semi-constructed interview.

	First Session 10min	Second Session 10min
Short Distance Game	S: 2 A: 2 I: 3	Free play All teams
Long Distance Game	S: 2 A: 3 I: 2	
Free play	S: 3 A: 2 I: 2	

S: Number of Stranger group/ A: Number of Acquaintance group/ I: Number of Intimate group

Figure 8. The arrangement of user study sessions

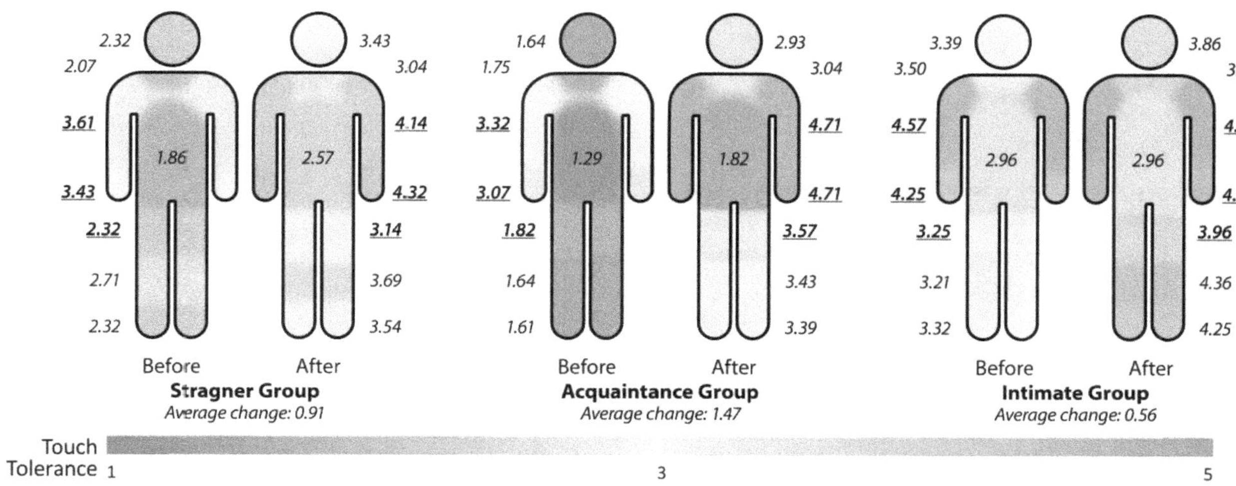

Figure 9. Average changes in interpersonal touch tolerance according to social relations. Red indicates an unnatural contact area due to low touch tolerance, and green indicates a natural contact area with high touch tolerance. The arm, hand, and legs in bold numbers also showed significant differences when analyzed separately

RESULT

The intimate group had the highest intimacy score of 4.64, the acquaintance group had an intimacy of 2.57, and the stranger group had an intimacy of 1.00. This confirms that there is a clear difference between the recruited groups' relations.

As a result of the touch tolerance evaluation by the bodily region through the questionnaire, we found that the degree of touch tolerance change before and after the experiment was different according to the participants' social relations. In all experimental groups, regardless of intimacy or distance, the change in touch tolerance was significantly affected according to bodily regions (F = 2.658, p = 0.011). The change of the touch tolerance of the ankle was the highest among the whole region (2.52→3.92), followed by the change of the foot. Many participants expected that their feet and ankles would be easily rejected, but they felt that the touch of the foot and ankle was comfortable because the areas were less sensitive than the hands were.

"I was surprised to feel less of an ankle or foot touch. So I felt more comfortable than my hands." –P3

Tolerance Changes with Social Relation and Spatial Elements

Impressively, the change in touch tolerance did not show a significant difference by distance experienced by the participants. However, there was a difference due to social relations among participants.

The social relations have a significant effect on the change of touch tolerance. (For all body regions, F = 16.186, p = 0.000) The acquaintance group showed the largest changes significantly (Post-hoc test with Turkey HSD p = 0.001, average tolerance changes, stranger: 0.91 (2.65 → 3.56), acquaintance: 1.47(2.04 → 3.51), intimate: 0.56 (3.53 → 4.09)). In the case of intimate group, the touch tolerance before the experiment showed an average of 3.53 already high, so the change of the score seems not to be big. In the case of the acquaintance group, the average touch tolerance before the experiment was 2.04, which was lower than 2.65 for the stranger group. However, the change in the touch tolerance of the acquaintance group was the highest, which can be inferred from the interview of subject P6.

"Normally our relationship was little bit awkward, but could potentially be friendly. But during the game our relationship was not awkward, but familiar. "-P6

Paradoxically, the initial touch tolerance of the stranger group was higher than that of the acquaintance group because there will be no personal contact after the experiment. The acquaintance group, on the other hand, had a lower touch tolerance, while the change of tolerance through games seemed to be more dramatic.

However, the actual interpersonal touch appearance was the most monotonous in acquaintance group. In the stranger group, interpersonal touch using body regions except for hands and feet was 10.2%. 6.0% in the acquaintance group and 10.0% in the intimate group used various body parts in addition to hands and feet among total 408 touches. The acquaintance group showed the most monotonous tendency, even in the type of interpersonal touch discussed in the next part. Nevertheless, it is very interesting that the change in touch tolerance is the largest.

By body region, touch tolerance changes were significant in the arm, hand, and leg. In the case of the belly, the change was not large, and the face, neck, ankle, and foot showed a similar increase in touch tolerance in all groups. In the arms, hands, and legs, the social relations have significant effects on the touch tolerance changes (arm: F = 5.016, P = 0.012, hand: F = 5.092, P = 0.011, leg: F = 6.270, P = 0.004, Figure 8).

Figure 10. Types of interpersonal touch

TYPES OF INTERPERSONAL TOUCHES

Based on the coding of interpersonal touch behavior, we classified the types of interpersonal touch. First, we categorized the interpersonal touch behavior according to the body region that the two participants used for interpersonal touch. With the result, we conducted affinity diagraming with featured conversation, and represented pictures of interpersonal touch events. As a result, we extracted three different types of interpersonal touches.

Decalcomania Type

The decalcomania type refers to the type of interpersonal touch in which two people make the same pose symmetrically, as in a mirror (Top pictures of Figure 10, Decalcomania: symmetrical painting drawn by half-folded paper with paint). At this time, not only poses but also bodily regions that touched each other are symmetrically identical. In addition to holding hands together or ankle-to-ankle, poses such as pinching each other's face by hand also belong to the decalcomania type. This type is the most common among all interpersonal touch types, as indicated in the timeline (Fig. 5), with 348 of the total 408 touches (85.3%) being the most common. According to the social relationship, the decalcomania type was found to be 125 times (85.0%) in the stranger group, 129 times (92.1%) in the acquaintance group and 94 times (77.7%) in the intimate group.

The decalcomania type seems to be the easiest and most natural type considering that it is the most dominant of all touch types. One of the reasons the decalcomania type is easily seen is due to the sharing of senses.

"*The touch that I could afford would be okay for my partner.*-P33"

Participants in the decalcomania type thought their partners were feeling the same feeling because the contact areas were same. This made the decalcomania type feel comfortable.

Interestingly, the decalcomania type not only mirrors the parts of the body that are touched but also the other parts of the body. For example, when one participant leaned and grabbed a knob and stretched out his leg, the other participant could easily reach it, even if he reached straight for his leg, but he leaned and stretched out his leg to create a perfect symmetry. This symmetrical state can be seen as balancing the load that each person owns by sharing the physical sensation felt by the other person.

Decalcomania is the most common type to appear regardless of social relations, and this type is easily visible in video or photographs of existing interpersonal touch interface studies[6,7,15,17,20].

Copied Type

The copied type is similar to the decalcomania where participants are posing in the same poses, but the parts touching each other are asymmetric (Middle of Figure 10). It is easy to relate it to a train or a chain. This type has the same posture as holding one's hand or holding one's shoulder, but the area one touches is completely different.

This type occurred the least, which included a total of 7 cases throughout the entire user study processes. In the stranger, acquaintance, and intimate groups, the number of these types was 2, 3, and 2 respectively. In this type, the leading person and the follower were very clearly defined. One person led and directed actions and goals, and others followed directions unilaterally. Because the two people do not face each other but rather face the same direction like a chain, the person in front is touched by the person behind.

Distinct Type

The distinct type refers to a case where two persons' postures or touch areas are completely different (Bottom of Figure 10).

The distinct types accounted for 13.6% in the stranger and 5.7% in the acquaintance group. In the intimate group, the rate was as high as 20.7%. The distinct type appeared when each person took a desired posture and then touched or when a person took a specific posture but the partner did not respond to it and touched a completely different part. This type also appeared in the case of one-sided touch that did not depend on the will of the other person, which is a touch where one person performs most of the touching and others the least.

This distinct type of touch seems to be more common in intimate cases where there is a minimal courtesy to others' opinions. For example, in couples, when a woman extended her feet, the man grabbed her feet without any hesitation, and while the man extended his hand, the woman ignored his hand and caught the man's ankle.

DISCUSSION

From the results, we discussed how distance factors and social relations play a role in the interactive system, and why the influences are different from previous studies.

The Screened Influence of Distance and Its Possibility

We have been able to speculate that different interpersonal touch behavior patterns will appear depending on the distance between people. Particularly in the experiment, in the case of long-distance games, there were many tasks that could not be done using only hands, so the legs and other parts of the body were frequently used. Therefore, it was predicted that the touch tolerance change of various body parts would be different from other condition, but there was no significant effect. Two main reasons exist for why the influence of the distance element does not appear.

First, the touch tolerance of the entire body was increased only by performing the interpersonal touch irrespective of the body part where the touch was performed. For example, in the case of group 2, that did not touch using the legs at all, the touch tolerance of the legs and feet increased by 3. The touch tolerance of the parts that were not directly involved in the touch changed, and it seems that the touch tolerance change did not have a major influence even if the dominant touch region was changed due to the distance.

Second, the influence of the social relationship was dominant that the effect of distance was obscured by the screening effect. This applies not only to non-touch tolerance, but also to the frequency of interpersonal touch types. However, 21 groups and 42 participants were not enough to know the effect of distance in the same social relation situation.

Although we could not quantitatively study the difference, we could see that the distance factor had enough potential from the interview.

"If the distance is too long, it is not good because I can only use my hands and legs to touch the knobs as long as possible." – P11 experienced long-distance game, stranger group

"I can't think of using any other part of my body because it's a totally touchable distance with my hands." – P38 experienced short-distance game, stranger group

To verify this, more systematic interviews and analyzes are needed, but there is plenty of possibility. Therefore, adjusting the distance factor within the same social relation may provide interesting findings. The results also indicated that the social relationship among users is more dominant in interpersonal touch experience and behavior pattern than distance and proximity are.

Influence of Social Relation and Design Guideline

As discussed, the social relation was a very important element in the interpersonal touch. Not only the change of touch tolerance but also the type of interpersonal touch varies depending on the relationship. This is consistent with the results of research in the psychology studies[9,24]. On the other hand, we could also observe the unique findings of interpersonal touch in the interactive installation, which was not explored in the previous research.

Distinguishable Influence of the Social Relation in Interactive System

First, the most representative example is the lowest initial touch tolerance of the acquaintance group. In existing psychology studies, touch tolerance to acquaintances was higher than to strangers because it assumed touch in daily situations [9,24]. However, in the interactive game situation, the touch tolerance to the stranger is high. In the special situation of games, it seems that the instant relationship to play the game together only once has made the touch easier. In the same context, the decalcomania type with the lowest mental load was the most frequent in the acquaintance group.

Second, because touch tolerance depends on social relationships, even if users explore the same interface, their core experience differs. The change in touch tolerance was the largest in the acquaintance group and the smallest in the intimate group. As mentioned above, in the intimate group, the interpersonal touches are very natural, so the hedonic value of the touch and its perception are low. In these groups, they were often focused on the challenges presented by the game, not interpersonal touch experience.

"It was more important to me to touch within the time limit. So even though my partner was not ready, I snatched his hand unilaterally."-P21

On the other hand, acquaintance and stranger groups often talked about the unfamiliarity and enjoyment of the touch itself rather than the challenge.

"Because we don't know each other, I never imagined grabbing her hands or holding her ankle. It was more fun than I thought when I touched."- P12

The perception of touch and naturalness have influenced the way in which people experience the interface.

Third, the ratio of interpersonal touch type was changed according to the relationship, as communication for touching was different. A lot of verbal and non-verbal communication occurs before the touch occurs, as no natural contact takes place while the interactive system is being used. Decalcomania type is symmetrical with each other, so users feel the same feeling and have less mental load.

"When we took the same posture, the partner was recognized like a mirror or an avatar of me. So I was comfortable when I touch the partner." -p1

In this case, the majority of cases occurred through simple non-verbal communication, such as reaching out the hands or legs. However, in copied and distinct types, a lot of verbal communication occurs and there is consensus about which body regions to use. In an intimate group that does not need to care about each other, verbal communication is much simpler, and distinct types appear to be easier.

Design Recommendations by Target Group's Social Relation

In the case of entertainment interaction, which is mainly studied by interpersonal touch, intimate users are more likely to use it. In the case of public installations, this is also highly likely to be used by intimate users, and the probability also exists that strangers will use it.

When the main target group is an intimate group, it is easy to use various body parts because of the high touch tolerance for most of the body parts. Therefore, the intimate group was less aware of the interpersonal touch and concentrated on the game challenge than the touch experience. Therefore, it is necessary to enhance the hedonic aspects of the touch by emphasizing the experience of the interpersonal touch. For example, providing users with different feedback based on different body regions of touch is a good strategy for enhancing the awareness of touch and making them to explore more dynamic interpersonal touch.

On the other hand, it is also a good idea to forcibly set the early touch body regions for the stranger group. The stranger group had a relatively high touch tolerance and showed various touch types compared to the acquaintance group. However, unlike the intimate group, they tend to focus on the experience of interpersonal touches, so it is easy to induce various interpersonal touches at the beginning and it improve the touch experience.

Acquaintance groups show the most dramatic changes in touch tolerances, but they are less exposed to interactive systems for entertainment. Of course, simple games for icebreaking can be applied for this group. However, many opportunities exist to be exposed to work situations such as interactive groupware. Using interpersonal touch interaction, such as transferring data using interpersonal touch, can create a more intimate work situation. At this point, if the interface allows users to touch symmetrically like the decalcomania types, they will be able to create a natural social group work without being too rigid.

Analysis Guide for Interpersonal Touch Interface

The various interpersonal touch types selected in this paper and the process patterns in which these touches occur can be used as user action analysis frames of interactive systems using existing interpersonal touches. The researchers can estimate the intimacy level through the ratio of the touch type used by the users and confirm that the touch behavior is changed by the interface. Researchers can also analyze the communication patterns that occur during the interaction by analyzing the invitation or response from the interpersonal touch.

LIMITATION

In this study, we limited the spatial aspect of the interpersonal touch to a touch distance for adjusting the proximity of participants. As a result, touch distance did not significantly change the touch tolerance or interpersonal touch pattern. If there were three dimensional spatial elements, such as height, the interpersonal touches that appeared to have the effect of increasing the distinct type due to the physical constraints or the more collaborative ones would have appeared. In future research, it is necessary to explore more spatial aspects in addition to distance elements between touch points or proximity.

In addition, if the social relations between participants are set the same, the influence of spatial factors can be understood more deeply. In this study, we tried to examine the two factors of social relations and spatial factors independently, but the influence of social relations was very strong, so distance factors did not appear well. Therefore, controlling the distance factor between the same social relations is necessary.

In many studies, the cultural aspect has been mentioned as an important factor in interpersonal touch. In this study, however, participants from different cultures were not searched and compared. Among the considerations of interpersonal touch, the cultural norm is a very important factor, and consideration may change the entire interpersonal touch process, further research on the cultural aspect seems necessary.

CONCLUSION

This study provided a rich understanding of interpersonal touch in interactive systems with the social relationship between users and touch distance as design elements. We designed an interactive installation called TouchBranch and conducted a user study. As a result, we have found the changes of touch tolerance according to the each elements and classified interpersonal touch types, such as decalcomania, copied, and distinct types. Based on the results, we discussed the influence of physical distance and social relationship between users on the interpersonal touch that were different from previous studies because they were used in interactive systems. Through the understanding of interpersonal touch, this study provided a design recommendation for interactive systems using interpersonal touch and an analysis guide to analyze such a system.

ACKNOWLEDGEMENTS

This work was supported by the National Research Foundation of Korea(NRF) grant funded by the Korea government(MSIP; Ministry of Science, ICT & Future Planning) (No.2015M3C1B4024732)

REFERENCES

1. Leonardo Angelini, Omar Abou Khaled, Maurizio Caon, Elena Mugellini, and Denis Lalanne. 2014. Hugginess: encouraging interpersonal touch through smart clothes. *Proceedings of the 2014 ACM International Symposium on Wearable Computers Adjunct Program*, ACM Press, 155–162. http://doi.org/10.1145/2641248.2641356
2. Tetsuaki Baba, Taketoshi Ushiama, and Kiyoshi Tomimatsu. 2007. Freqtric drums: a musical instrument that uses skin contact as an interface. *Proceedings of the 7th international conference on New interfaces for musical expression*, ACM, 386–387. http://doi.org/10.1145/1279740.1279827
3. Till Ballendat, Nicolai Marquardt, and Saul Greenberg. 2010. Proxemic Interaction : Designing for a Proximity and Orientation-Aware Environment. *Proceedings of the 24th annual ACM symposium on User interface software and technology*, ACM, 315–326.
4. Mert Canat, Mustafa Ozan Tezcan, Celalettin Yurdakul, et al. 2016. Sensation: Measuring the Effects of a Human-to-Human Social Touch Based Controller on the Player Experience. *Proceedings of the 2016 CHI Conference on Human Factors in Computing Systems*, ACM Press, 3944–3955. http://doi.org/10.1145/2858036.2858418
5. April H. Crusco and Christopher G. Wetzel. 1984. The Midas Touch The Effects of Interpersonal Touch on Restaurant Tipping. *Personality and Social Psychology Bulletin* 10, 4: 512–517. http://doi.org/10.1177/0146167284104003
6. Duracell. 2014. .@Duracell (Canada) Moments of Warmth (surprise bus shelter) #PowerWarmth - YouTube. Retrieved September 18, 2017 from https://www.youtube.com/watch?v=-mQZqKLiMIg
7. eharmony AU. 2016. Human Touch at Vivid Sydney 2016 - YouTube. Retrieved September 18, 2017 from https://www.youtube.com/watch?v=yYXC5I8irm4
8. Jeffrey D. Fisher, Marvin Rytting, and Richard Heslin. 1976. Hands Touching Hands: Affective and Evaluative Effects of an Interpersonal Touch. *Sociometry* 39, 4: 416. http://doi.org/10.2307/3033506
9. A Gallace and C Spence. 2010. The science of interpersonal touch: an overview. *Neuroscience & Biobehavioral Reviews*.
10. Jayden Garner, Gavin Wood, Sandra Danilovic, Jessica Hammer, and Florian Mueller. 2014. Intangle: exploring interpersonal bodily interactions through sharing controllers. *Proceedings of the first ACM SIGCHI annual symposium on Computer-human interaction in play*: 413–414. http://doi.org/10.1145/2658537.2661306
11. William W. Gaver, Jacob Beaver, and Steve Benford. 2003. Ambiguity as a resource for design. *Proceedings of the SIGCHI Conference on Human Factors in Computing Systems*, ACM, 233–240. http://doi.org/10.1145/642611.642653
12. Edward T. (Edward Twitchell) Hall. 1966. *The hidden dimension*. Doubleday.
13. MJ Hertenstein and SJ Weiss. 2011. *Tactile Traditions. In The handbook of touch: Neuroscience, behavioral, and health perspectives*. Springer.
14. Mads Hobye, Nicolas Padfield, and Jonas Löwgren. 2013. Designing social play through interpersonal touch: An annotated portfolio. *Nordic Design Research Conference*, Kunstakademiets Arkitektskoles Forlag.
15. M Hobye and J Löwgren. 2011. Touching a stranger: Designing for engaging experience in embodied interaction. *International Journal of Design*.
16. Amy Huggard, Anushka De Mel, Jayden Garner, Cagdas "Chad" Toprak, Alan Chatham, and Florian "Floyd" Mueller. 2013. Musical embrace: exploring social awkwardness in digital games. *Proceedings of the 2013 ACM international joint conference on Pervasive and ubiquitous computing*, ACM Press, 725. http://doi.org/10.1145/2493432.2493518
17. Yuhwan Kim, Seungchul Lee, Inseok Hwang, et al. 2014. High5: promoting interpersonal hand-to-hand touch for vibrant workplace with electrodermal sensor watches. *Proceedings of the 2014 ACM International Joint Conference on Pervasive and Ubiquitous Computing*, ACM Press, 15–19. http://doi.org/10.1145/2632048.2632072
18. JW Lee and LK Guerrero. 2001. Types of touch in cross-sex relationships between coworkers: Perceptions of relational and emotional messages, inappropriateness, and sexual harassment. *Journal of Applied Communication*.
19. Joe Marshall, Conor Linehan, and Adrian Hazzard. 2016. Designing Brutal Multiplayer Video Games. *Proceedings of the 2016 CHI Conference on Human Factors in Computing Systems*, ACM Press, 2669–2680. http://doi.org/10.1145/2858036.2858080
20. Joe Marshall and Paul Tennent. 2017. Touchomatic: Interpersonal Touch Gaming In The Wild. *Proceedings of the 2017 Conference on Designing Interactive Systems*, ACM, 417–428. http://doi.org/10.1145/3064663.3064727
21. Milka. 2013. Milka Vending Machine Makes You Work Hard for the Chocolate - Print (video) - Creativity Online. http://creativity-online.com/work/milka-tender-chain/32511

22. Florian "Floyd" Mueller, Martin R. Gibbs, Frank Vetere, and Darren Edge. 2017. Designing for Bodily Interplay in Social Exertion Games. *ACM Transactions on Computer-Human Interaction* 24, 3: 1–41. http://doi.org/10.1145/3064938

23. Florian Mueller, Sophie Stellmach, Saul Greenberg, et al. 2014. Proxemics play: understanding proxemics for designing digital play experiences. *Proceedings of the 2014 conference on Designing interactive systems*, ACM Press, 533–542. http://doi.org/10.1145/2598510.2598532

24. JT Suvilehto, E Glerean, and RIM Dunbar. 2015. Topography of social touching depends on emotional bonds between humans. *Proceedings of the National Academy ofSciences of the United States of America*, 122,45: 13811-6. http://doi.org/10.1073/pnas.1519231112

25. Juulia T Suvilehto, Enrico Glerean, Robin I M Dunbar, Riitta Hari, and Lauri Nummenmaa. 2015. Topography of social touching depends on emotional bonds between humans. *Proceedings of the National Academy of Sciences of the United States of America* 112, 45: 13811–6. http://doi.org/10.1073/pnas.1519231112

26. Kenji Suzuki, Taku Hachisu, and Kazuki Iida. 2016. EnhancedTouch: A Smart Bracelet for Enhancing Human-Human Physical Touch. *Proceedings of the 2016 CHI Conference on Human Factors in Computing Systems*, ACM Press, 1282–1293. http://doi.org/10.1145/2858036.2858439

27. R Ueoka and M Hirose. 2008. SoundTag: children's interactive play based upon RFID employed wearable computer. *Digital Creativity*. Retrieved September 18, 2017 from http://www.tandfonline.com/doi/abs/10.1080/14626260802312699

28. D Wilson. 2011. Brutally unfair tactics totally ok now: On self-effacing games and unachievements. *Game Studies*. Retrieved September 18, 2017 from http://gamestudies.org/1101/articles/Wilson

29. John Zimmerman, Jodi Forlizzi, and Shelley Evenson. 2007. Research through design as a method for interaction design research in HCI. *Proceedings of the SIGCHI conference on Human factors in computing systems*, ACM Press, 493. http://doi.org/10.1145/1240624.1240704

30. Average Male Height | height and weight for men & women. Retrieved September 18, 2017 from http://www.averageheight.co/

31. 2012. Fingle - Official Trailer - YouTube. Retrieved March 27, 2018 from https://www.youtube.com/watch?v=ff0fku1r-gU

Unlocking the Interactive Office: Concurrent Prototyping Approach

Tomasz Jaskiewicz
Delft University of Technology
Landbergstraat 15
2628 CE Delft NL
J.J.Jaskiewicz@tudelft.nl

Aadjan van der Helm
Delft University of Technology
Landbergstraat 15
2628 CE Delft NL
A.J.C.vanderHelm@tudelft.nl

DIS 2018, June 9–13, 2018, Hong Kong.

ACM ISBN 978-1-4503-5198-0/18/06...$15.00.
https://doi.org/10.1145/3196709.3196821

Abstract
In this pictorial we present a project case, where an interactive office environment was designed following a concurrent prototyping approach embedded in an iterative design process. The case illustrates how concurrent prototyping supports designing complex interactions between multiple people and multiple interactive objects, while innovating in both social and technological realm. Identified variables of the involved process allow steering the design towards a variety of possible solution qualities. We propose this approach as a viable strategy for dealing with the complexity of designing in the domain of Human-Building Interaction.

Authors Keywords
Iterative prototyping, programmable office, interactive environments, smart environments, socio-technical systems, maker culture, agile design.

ACM Classification Keywords
H.5.m. Information interfaces and presentation (e.g., HCI): Miscellaneous.

Introduction
Office environments are an example of a design context that involves high social and technological complexity. Increased mobility of knowledge workers leads to new forms of shared office work organization, incorporating trends such as flexible working [13], activity-based working [16] and co-working [9]. Flexible

Figure 1: The existing central shared workplace of the IDE faculty at the TU Delft illustrates the office design trend, where desks are not permanently assigned to individuals and flexible furnishing can be used to create work areas of various characteristics, specific to the activities performed individually and in groups by office users at a given moment.

and shared office environments are increasingly common in corporate, governmental or university buildings, as exemplified in Figure 1. Mobile technology allows people to perform most of their typical office work tasks from any place with internet access. Because of that, face-to-face collaborations, social interactions and serendipitous knowledge exchange between office workers are becoming the main reasons to be physically present at the office. At the same time, catering to employees' physiological and psychological comfort and well-being becomes a priority for many employers, despite striving for cost and energy efficiency of office building operation. Modern office buildings, such as the Edge building designed by the PLP Artects for Delloite [14], are embedded with high-tech installations, services and furnishings to support work flexibility. However, the resulting work environments are often frustrating for their users due to, for example, mutual disturbances between people, time wasted looking for a desk, difficulties in finding colleagues, as well as lack of privacy, personal storage and ability to personalise the work setting [2]. The failure of modern office buildings to leverage the opportunities of technologies such as the Internet of Things to deal with such problems can be seen as a challenge for the Human-Computer Interaction community and for the emerging field of Human-Building Interaction [1] to develop new methods to deal with the involved socio-technical complexity.

Figure 2: The TU Delft Facility Management department commissioned the presented case to explore radically innovative furnishing alternatives for the context of an under-development open space building called "Pulse", the design of which is shown in the picture.

Figure 3: The case study was performed by 26 students with mixed design, engineering and other educational backgrounds over the course of 5 months using a dedicated prototyping studio (in the picture) and workshop.

Figure 4: Process data was collected using the "progress card" format used by project participants to document generated project knowledge and prototypes, which in aggregation allowed extensive process analysis.

Case

The project presented in this pictorial followed a brief to design a part of a shared workspace to be located within the upcoming student workspace building shown in figure 2, to be located at the campus of the Delft University of Technology (TU Delft). The brief included provisions for the desired workspace flexibility, adaptable indoor climate, stimulation of social relationships among workspace users, preference for non-screen interactions between users and the building, and considerations for environmental impact of users' activities in the building.

The project team involved 26 student participants with mixed educational backgrounds including industrial design, architecture, computer science, mechanical engineering, aerospace engineering and psychology. It lasted for a total of 61 workdays spread over the duration of 5 months, and was supported by a variety of additional skill-building activities. For the duration of the project the participants had exclusive use of a prototyping studio, shown in Figure 3, and had access to an adjacent prototyping workshop.

Throughout the project its participants were required to document their process using "progress cards" [6] in weekly intervals. The documentation included an overview of the latest prototype and reflection on generated or acquired project knowledge in the form of new insights, ideas or know-how. In addition, data about the project process was collected through notes from non-directive interviews performed per team during biweekly coaching sessions, approximately 500-word long individual participant reflections on the design process in an essay format, individual retrospective survey performed after the project was completed, and evaluation of intermediate project outcomes performed by a team of 4-6 external experts at the end of each project phase.

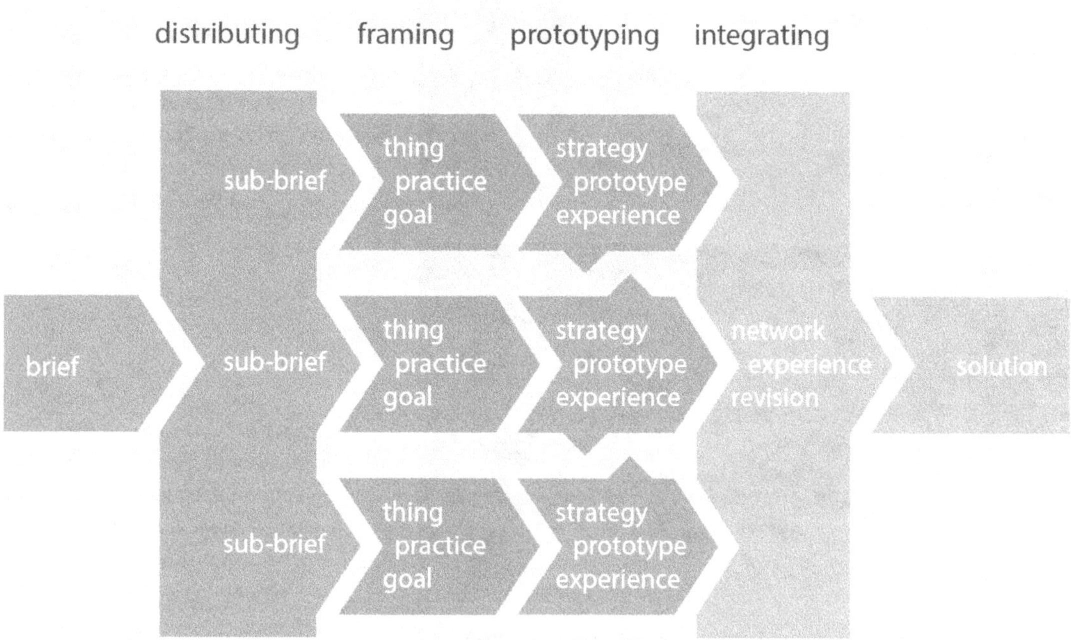

Figure 5: The concurrent prototyping approach consists of parallel tracks containing framing and prototyping activities, which are initiated by defining and distributing project sub-briefs at the outset of each iteration and integrating of developed complementary designs at the end of each iteration

Figure 6: We envision that iterations containing complementary tracks can be combined in various configurations.

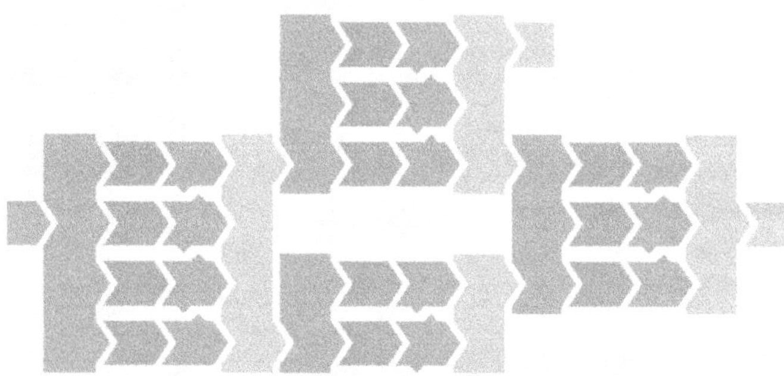

Concurrent prototyping approach

The "concurrent prototyping" approach introduced in this pictorial builds on the qualities of iterative design practices such as the Lean Startup [15], Google Ventures Design Sprint [12] or Tom Chi's workshops [5], which involve fast prototyping and frequent "pivoting" of concept direction, while performing multiple design iterations. Such agility can be achieved through various forms of low-fidelity prototyping involving "hacking, mashing and gluing"[10] and sketching with technology [4], where interactive prototyping platforms such as Arduino lend themselves to building standalone and networked interactive devices [11]. Concurrent prototyping further extends the principles of an iterative design process by involving simultaneous generation of multiple designs and prototypes, such that they are complementary to each other. By this, we mean that concurrently developed solutions should be able to coexist, connect to each other and mutually enhance each others' functionality in ways meaningful to their users. Concurrent prototyping is not synonymous, but also not mutually exclusive with "parallel prototyping" [8], where multiple prototypes are created simultaneously as instantiations of alternative, not complementary, solutions to the same design problem.

Based on the above principles, we have defined the main project iteration as consisting of 4 distinguishable steps of "distributing", "framing", "prototyping" and "integrating", as shown in figure 5. The two middle steps are prescribed to be performed in concurrent tracks by sub-teams of designers, while the distributing and integrating steps are to be performed jointly. We have further envisioned that such iterations could be combined over time in various configurations, as shown in figure 6. Eventually, the case project was executed in 7 iterations, and each iteration contained between 4 and 6 concurrent prototyping tracks.

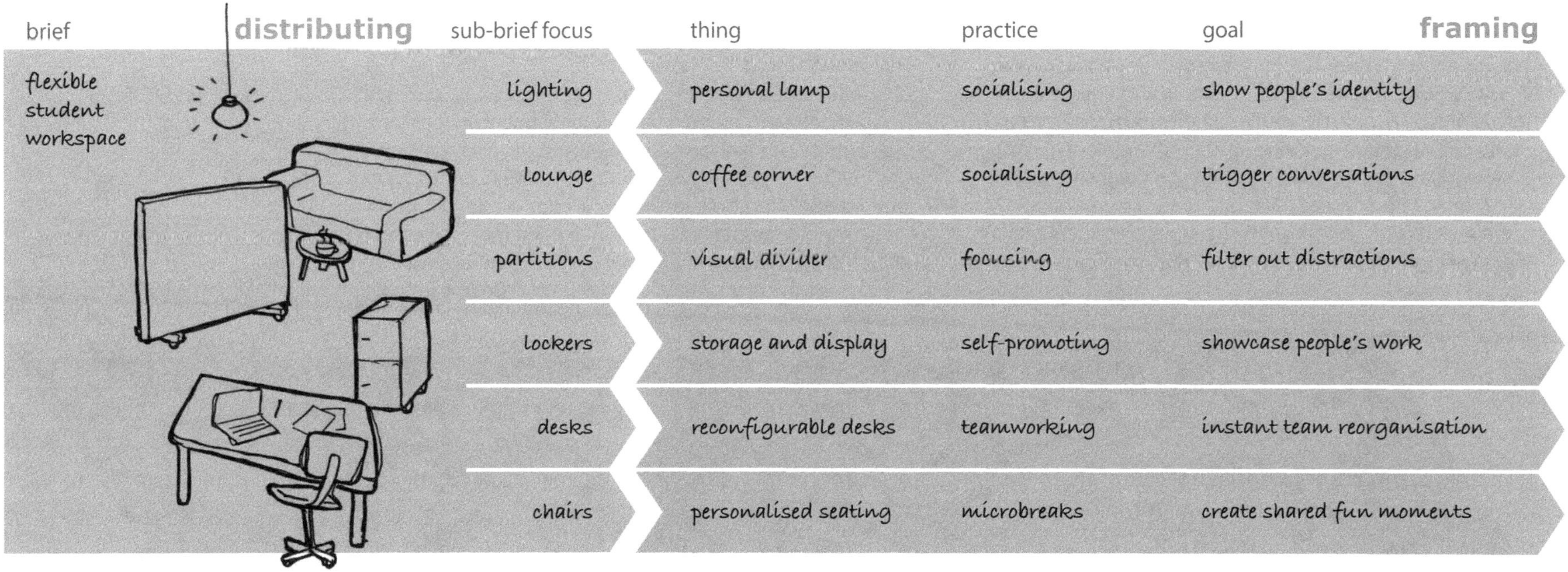

Figure 7: The project brief was divided into sub-briefs and distributed into individual tracks by using different furniture types as differentiators.

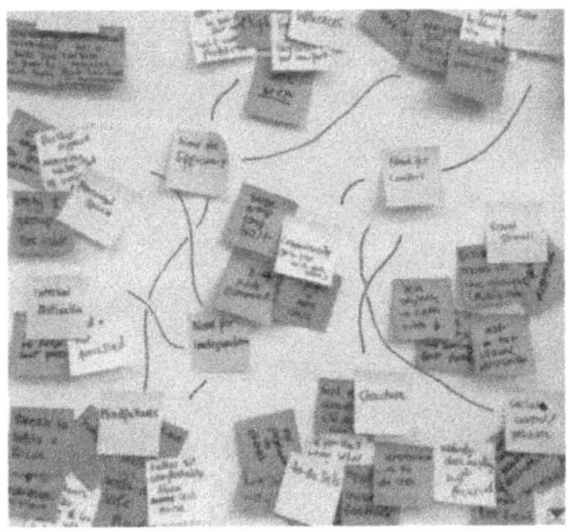

Figure 8: During the distributing and framing steps, designers mainly discussed using abstract, generalizable terms.

Distributing

The distributing step of each iteration involves subdividing the general brief of the entire project into sub-briefs for complementary tracks, illustrated in figure 7. For the first iteration of the presented case we chose to prescribe such subdivision based on the furniture types expected in the commissioned office setting, namely lighting, lounge, space partitions, lockers, desks and chairs. The resulting sub-briefs were provided to project participants during the first "distributing" step of the first project iteration. Participants were encouraged to further reinterpret the assigned sub-brief in their respective teams, while maintaining consistency with the global brief. In each of the following iterations the sub-briefs were defined and distributed by participant teams themselves.

Framing

The framing step encompasses the broadly understood "problem framing" [7] for each of the concurrent tracks. In our case the framing consisted of defining the type of the designed "thing", the practice in which office users were envisioned to engage with that thing, and the goal of the respective design. The order in which the thing, practice and goal were defined was not prescribed, and the framing was encouraged to be revised throughout the track. To give an example, framing of the sub-brief for designing a lighting solution resulted in the designed thing being defined as a personal, carry-on lamp, with a goal of showing the person's work identity in order to trigger the practice of casual social encounters in the workplace, as shown on the top of figure 7.

Figure 9: Prototyping has been the central design activity in the presented case.

Prototyping

The prototyping step involved generation of thee different outcomes, namely the strategy, prototype and experience. Strategy can be seen as an actionable translation of the problem framing, describing how the design aims to solve the problem. The prototype instantiates the strategy in a preliminary and incomplete version of the designed solution, which can be used to "prototype the experience" [3]. Although the three outputs of our prototyping step appear as sequential, this step of the process has shown to be a messy affair, involving frequent revisions of the strategy, changes to prototypes, and various forms of staging the experience. Such staging included quick trials and self-testing, as well as well-organised user tests.

The prototyping process substantiated Shön's reflective conversation with the design material, with designers "making moves" by modifying the strategies and prototypes and subsequently "looking" at their own or other people's experiences with the prototypes [17]. Since designers from all teams shared the studio space and workshop facilities, the experience of prototypes was both intentionally and accidentally shared, resulting in mutual influences of teams and enriching their "reflection in action", as shown in figures 10 a-h. On the other hand, the regular, obligatory activity of joint filling in of progress cards by teams served as a stimulus for performing "reflection on action".

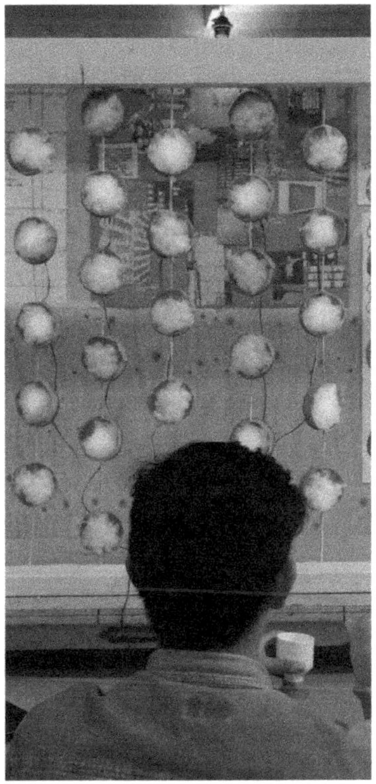
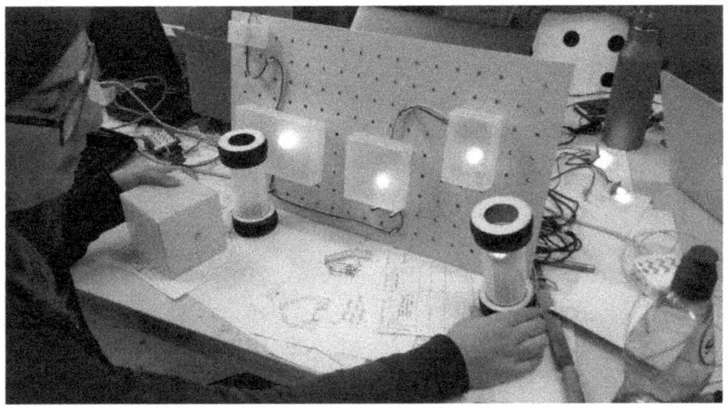

Figures 10 a-h. The prototypes developed throughout the project varied in fidelity, used technology and construction time. The fidelity of prototypes gradually increased within and across project iterations. Being immersed in a workshop setting, designers rarely resorted to making detailed conceptual or technical drawings of their designs. Instead, the prototypes served as immediate articulations of designers' insights and ideas. This supported internal communication within each team, communication to other teams, coaches, clients or casual spectators. Many old prototypes were kept and displayed in the design studio, even if the idea behind them was no longer being developed.

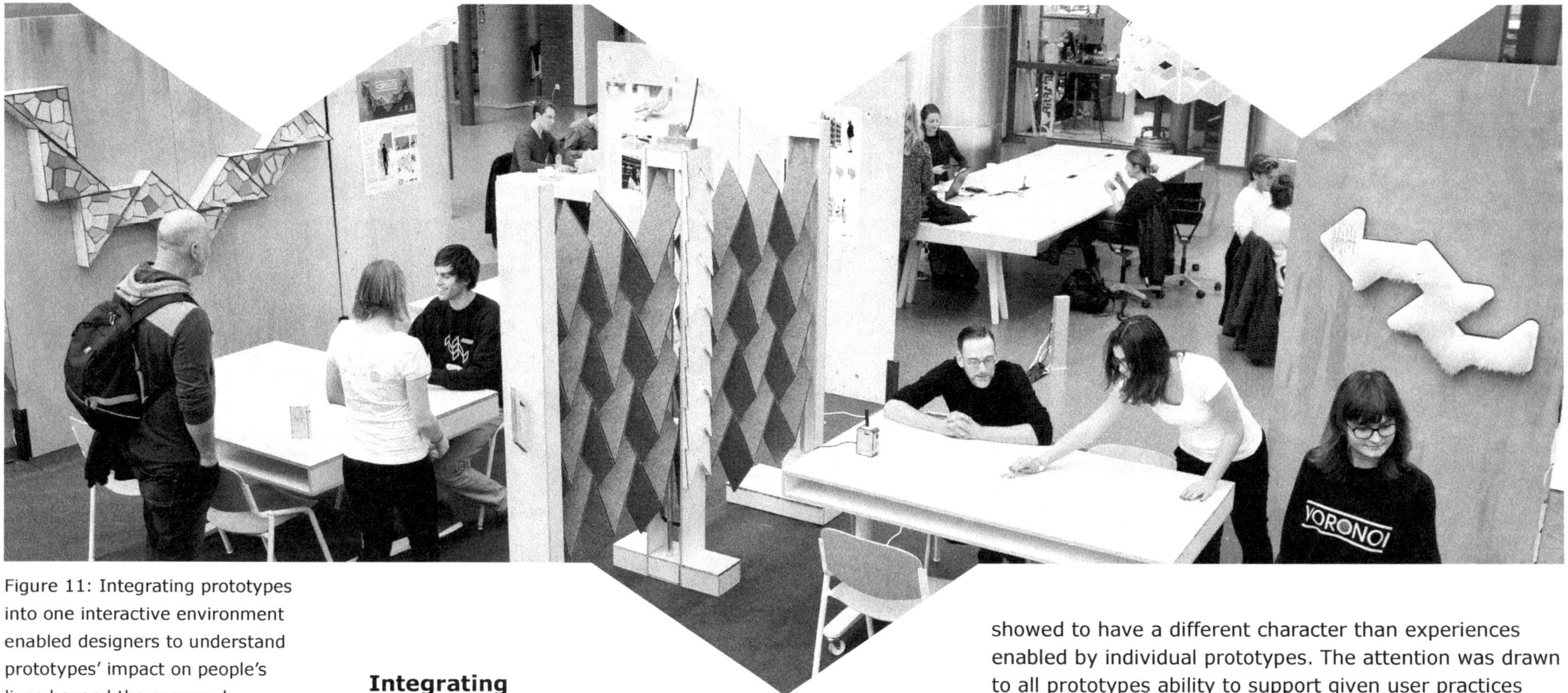

Figure 11: Integrating prototypes into one interactive environment enabled designers to understand prototypes' impact on people's lives beyond the assumed problem framing, while revealing how prototypes could support one another through connected services and by engaging people in social practices involving multiple prototypes at once.

Integrating

Each project iteration was concluded by selecting one prototype per track and team, and setting up all prototypes in an exhibition. This involved attempting to integrate all prototypes into one functional office environment, and creating interactive connections between prototypes wherever envisioned and technically possible. The integration of prototypes during early iterations failed, as prototyped designs showed to be contradicting or overlapping with each other. In later integrations, experiencing the exhibition as one interactive environment became possible. The integrated experiences showed to have a different character than experiences enabled by individual prototypes. The attention was drawn to all prototypes ability to support given user practices in synchrony, as well as transitions between enabled practices. For example, charging a phone in a DC socket, could send a signal to attract the charging person to take a relaxing micro-break with help of interactive wall panels, or to combine both activities. Identifying such transitional practices of users, enabled teams to discover and further explore the meaning and purpose of networking their prototypes into one system. In this way, integrating prototypes served as a tool to make a transition from designing interactions between things and people, towards interactions between networks of things and people.

Figures 12 a-g. The final prototypes included

- a kinetic sit-stand table supporting time-boxing of team work activities,
- a system of DC power sockets communicating in a playful way the moments to charge devices when locally sourced power is available, while triggering spontaneous social interactions,
- a system of kinetic wall panels triggering people to take micro-breaks and engage in random encounters,
- a folding visual and acoustic partition wall, indicating the qualities of spaces it separated, and sending notifications to users of those spaces.

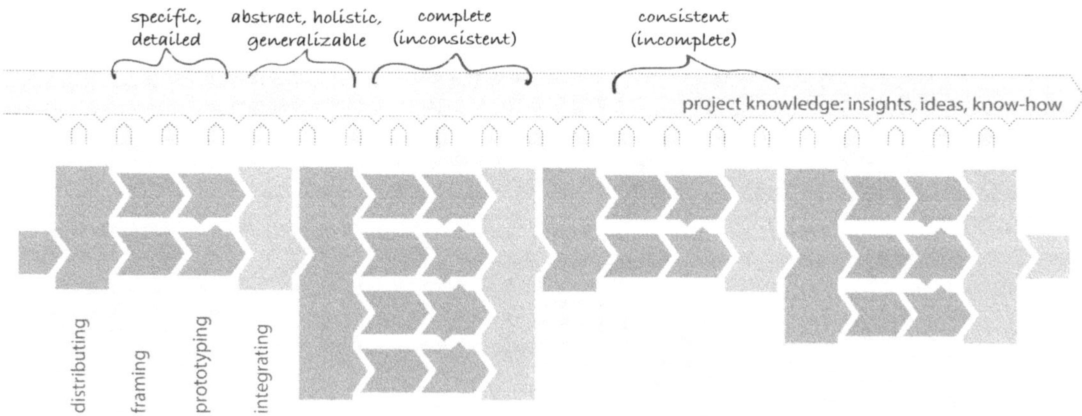

Figure 13: Identifying characteristics of knowledge obtained by designers throughout the project has allowed us to evaluate the parameters of the concurrent prototyping process, showing a simplified example for clarity.

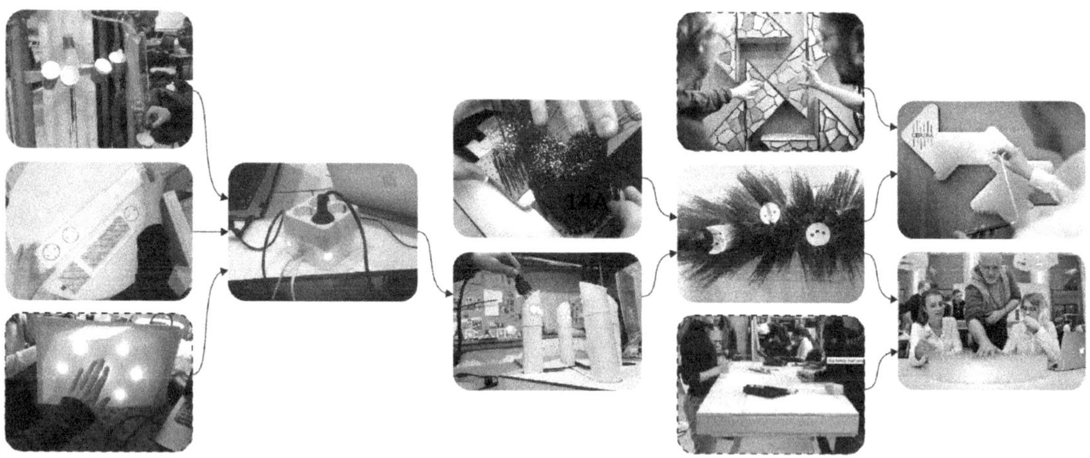

Figure 14: Assessing the qualities of prototypes across iterations and across teams revealed the evolutionary character of concurrent prototype development.

Process evaluation

The collected data allowed us to evaluate the design process from two perspectives. First, we have analyzed the characteristics of the "project knowledge" generated by designers in the process, as conceptually illustrated in figure 13. Second, we have assessed the qualities of prototypes developed by all teams across all iterations, as exemplified in figure 14. We have used the identified qualities to reflect back on the organization of the design process, in order to identify parameters which have had an impact on the knowledge outcomes, as follows:

- During the "framing" and "prototyping" steps, the generated project knowledge was specific to the sub-brief and limited in scope. In "integrating" and "distributing" steps designers were generating more abstract, generalizable and holistic project knowledge.
- The iterations with a higher number of concurrent tracks led to integrated solutions with more diverse functionalities than in the case of fewer tracks. However, more diversity also meant contradictions between prototypes, making the track integration difficult or impossible. On the other hand, iterations with fewer concurrent tracks delivered more consistent, but less comprehensive final results.
- The increased duration of the "framing" steps promoted more radical solutions, while longer "prototyping" steps promoted design of more conservative solutions, only incrementally improving functionalities of established types of office objects.
- Multiple short iterations led to explorations of a wide spectrum, yet typically cliché or superficial design solutions. Long and fewer iterations promoted a deeper focus on selected aspects of the brief.

Assessment of qualities of created prototypes revealed the non-linear nature of design progress across the entire process. Features of prototypes from one iteration were often carried on to next iterations, both within and across teams. In several cases, a distinguishable feature of form, interaction or material use was not continued in the next iteration but was reintroduced in a later iteration. When describing this process, we used an analogy to natural selection and evolution, as prototypes from past iterations would appear to combine to form new "specimens" with shared features in later iterations. For example, features of a power socket prototype of one team were combined with features of interactive tiles of another team, and became integrated in a table design of yet a different group, as shown in figure 14. Further analysis of progress cards has also shown that the observed evolutionary process also took place in the area of project knowledge. Alongside prototypes, insights, ideas and know-how were passed on across iterations and between teams. In this process, prototype features appeared to function as carriers of that knowledge. For example, the insights regarding "short social breaks" practice, originated in one team an proliferated to four other projects through similarly employed interaction patterns involving lights.

The integration of solutions from different tracks has shown to be an important step in the process, revealing to designers how an office work practice of several users would involve interactions with multiple products. For example, breaks triggered by the sit-stand table, required the partition wall to be opened and change the indicated status, allowing users to reach the kinetic wall panels. Understanding the interactions between groups of users and multiple prototypes in the context of various involved office work practices has led to further development of ideas for implementing interactions between products.

Conclusions

The presented case study allowed us to investigate design of shared office environments approached as systems of connected interactive products and people through the process of concurrent prototyping. First, this case has allowed us to asses how the concurrent prototyping approach can help in designing for situations involving high technological and social complexity. Second, setting up and assessing the case study led to identifying the key variables of a concurrent prototyping process, including the number of tracks, their duration and relative duration of track steps (distributing, framing, prototyping and integrating) within each iteration. We could preliminarily infer the influence that each of these variables had on the qualities of the concepts and project knowledge developed in the process. Based on these findings, we can further speculate that increasing the number of concurrent prototyping tracks while assigning more time and designers' effort to the framing and integrating steps in the process can be expected to promote further increase of innovation in respect to how products and services are interconnected, cross-dependent and used in a social setting. We also envision that the prescribed process can be further modified, for example by introducing a different division of steps, or by encouraging the use of specific methods within steps in order to improve process efficiency or stimulate specific qualities in obtained results.

The presented case study had an explorative character, and the proposed concurrent prototyping approach requires further research. We hope that the insights from this explorative work will help in finding new ways to unlock designers' ability to create rich, meaningful and innovative interactions involving multiple products, services and people, both within and beyond the context of shared office environments.

Acknowledgements

We would like to thank the following people involved in the project for their work, energy and commitment. The students: Alice Coey, Babette van Schaik, Bart van Dijk, Carmen Pepping, Charlotte Middelveld, Danilo Dumeljic, Daniël Hesselman, Daniël van den Broek, David van der Blonk, Elias van der Linden, Felix Kwa, Fergus Mckenzie, Floortje Lycklama à Nijeholt, Irene van der Blij, Jimmy Iliohan, Judith Cohen, Kati de Jong, Maaike de Wit, Marijke Blom, Marleen Dohmen, Matthijs Jansen, Max van Manen, Milada Speet, Oliver Damian, Patrick Keesmaat, Roy Graafmans, Sami Hurwitz, Sarah De Herde, and Thomas Bakker. Experts: David Keyson, Jakob Lehr, Marco Rozendaal, Huib de Ridder, Ianus Keller, Peter Kun Coaches: Wouter van der Hoog, Martin Havranek Student Assistants: Roy Graafmans, Charlotte Middenveld, Thomas Bakker, Ties Luiten. Photographer: Guus Schoonewille.

References

1. Hamed S. Alavi, Denis Lalanne, Juliet Nembrini, Elizabeth Churchill, David Kirk, and Wendy Moncur. 2016. Future of human-building interaction. In *Proceedings of the 2016 CHI Conference Extended Abstracts on Human Factors in Computing Systems* (pp. 3408-3414). ACM.
2. Iris De Been, Marion Beijer, and Dorieke Den Hollander. 2015. How to cope with dilemmas in activity based work environments-results from user-centred research. In 14th EuroFM Research Symposium Proceedings. (pp. 1-10). EuroFM research papers
3. Marion Buchenau, and Jane Fulton-Suri. 2000. Experience prototyping. In Proceedings of the 3rd conference on Designing interactive systems: processes, practices, methods, and techniques (pp. 424-433). ACM.
4. Bill Buxton. 2010. Sketching user experiences: getting the design right and the right design. Morgan Kaufmann.
5. Tom Chi. 2013. Fast solutions for a brighter future - rapid prototyping entrepreneurship: Tom Chi at TEDxKyoto 2013. YouTube Video, 14:13, Published on October 31, 2013 by "TEDx Talks", Retrieved December 1, 2016 from https://www.youtube.com/watch?v=DkyMCCnNI3Q.
6. Tomasz Jaskiewicz and Aadjan van der Helm. 2017. Progress Cards as a Tool for Supporting Reflection, Management and Analysis of Design Studio Processes. In DS 88: Proceedings of the 19th International Conference on Engineering and Product Design Education (E&PDE17)
7. Kees Dorst. 2015. Frame innovation.
8. Steven P. Dow, Alana Glassco, Jonathan Kass, Malissa Schwarz, Daniel L. Schwartz, Scott R. Klemmer. 2012. Parallel prototyping leads to better design results, more divergence, and increased self-efficacy. In *Design Thinking Research* (pp. 127-153). Springer.
9. Alessandr Gandini, 2015. The rise of coworking spaces: A literature review. ephemera, 15(1), p.193.
10. Bjorn Hartmann, S. Doorley, and Scott R. Klemmer. 2008. Hacking, mashing, gluing: Understanding opportunistic defsign. In IEEE Pervasive Computing 7, no. 3. IEEE. 46-54.
11. Karl A. Hribernik, Zied Ghrairi, Carl Hans, and Klaus-Dieter Thoben, 2011. Co-creating the Internet of Things—First experiences in the participatory design of Intelligent Products with Arduino. In Concurrent Enterprising (ICE), 2011 17th International Conference on (pp. 1-9). IEEE.
12. Jake Knapp, John Zeratsky and Braden Kowitz. 2016. Sprint: How to solve big problems and test new ideas in just five days. Simon and Schuster.
13. Lilian M. De Menezes, and Clare Kelliher. 2011. Flexible working and performance: A systematic review of the evidence for a business case. International Journal of Management Reviews, 13(4), pp.452-474.
14. PLP Architecture, the Edge. Retrieved March 28, 2018 from http://www.plparchitecture.com/the-edge.html
15. Erik Ries. 2011. *The lean startup: How today's entrepreneurs use continuous innovation to create radically successful businesses*. Crown Books.
16. Philip Ross. 2010. Activity based working. The hybrid organisation: Buildings. Microsoft.
17. Donald A. Schön. 1987. *Educating the reflective practitioner: Toward a new design for teaching and learning in the professions.* Jossey-Bass.

"It's hard to argue with a computer:" Investigating Psychotherapists' Attitudes towards Automated Evaluation

Tad Hirsch
Department of Art + Design
Northeastern University
Boston, MA
tad.hirsch@northeastern.edu

Christina Soma
Department of Educational Psychology
University of Utah
Salt Lake City, UT
christina.soma@utah.edu

Kritzia Merced
Department of Educational Psychology
University of Utah
Salt Lake City, UT
k.mercedmorales@utah.edu

Patty Kuo
Department of Educational Psychology
University of Utah
Salt Lake City, UT
patty.kuo@utah.edu

Aaron Dembe
Department of Educational Psychology
University of Utah
Salt Lake City, UT
aaron.dembe@utah.edu

Derek D. Caperton
Department of Educational Psychology
University of Utah
Salt Lake City, UT
derek.caperton@utah.edu

David C. Atkins
Department of Psychiatry and Behavioral Sciences
University of Washington
Seattle, WA
datkins@uw.edu

Zac E. Imel
Department of Educational Psychology
University of Utah
Salt Lake City, UT
zac.imel@utah.edu

ABSTRACT

We present CORE-MI, an automated evaluation and assessment system that provides feedback to mental health counselors on the quality of their care. CORE-MI is the first system of its kind for psychotherapy, and an early example of applied machine-learning in a human service context. In this paper, we describe the CORE-MI system and report on a qualitative evaluation with 21 counselors and trainees. We discuss the applicability of CORE-MI to clinical practice and explore user perceptions of surveillance, workplace misuse, and notions of objectivity, and system reliability that may apply to automated evaluation systems generally.

Author Keywords

Mental health, machine learning, psychotherapy, design.

ACM Classification Keywords

H.5.m. Information interfaces and presentation (e.g., HCI): Miscellaneous; I.2.1. Artificial Intelligence: Applications and Expert Systems; J.4 Applications: Social and Behavioral Sciences: Psychology; Design.

DIS '18, June 9–13 2018, Hong Kong

ACM ISBN 978-1-4503-5198-0/18/06…$15 00
https://doi.org/10.1145/3196709.3196776e.

INTRODUCTION

In 2015 over 5 million Americans accessed mental health services [47], and mental health and addiction problems are among the most common causes of disability in the U.S. [49].

Psychotherapy – a conversation between a client (or a group of clients) and counselor – is an effective treatment across a broad range of mental health and addiction problems [28]. Among approaches to psychotherapy, Motivational Interviewing (MI) is effective in promoting behavior change, particularly for addiction and behavioral health problems [35]. MI is explicit in its reliance on the therapeutic relationship (e.g., empathy, collaboration) and promotes specific counselor relational strategies such as the use of open-ended questions and making high-quality reflections of what the client has said.

Although MI has demonstrated efficacy in many research-based clinical trials [32], the quality of MI delivered in real-world settings can be highly variable, due to heterogeneity in the quality of training and supervision [40]. Gold-standard training and supervision involves recording sessions, deriving performance-based feedback from session recordings, and providing expert consultation and coaching. Unfortunately, this approach is time consuming, expensive, and does not scale up to real-world settings [1, 23]. Due to time, resources, and confidentiality issues, in many clinics supervision either does not occur or is often based upon the self-report of the counselor rather than independent observation of clinical sessions [17]. Independent, performance-based feedback is key to promoting and maintaining counselor skills [46], and so relying on retrospective self-report as the sole source of supervision data limits supervisors' ability to provide constructive, actionable feedback.

Advances in machine learning (ML) and natural language processing (NLP) offer computational methods to automatically map spoken language in psychotherapy sessions to quality indicators and performance-based feedback [38]. Recent work has demonstrated that MI sessions can be evaluated using ML and NLP methods, and that machine-coded sessions can be comparable with human-coded sessions [1] for both specific, granular techniques (e.g., the quality of individual counselor reflections [8]) and for broad evaluations of an entire therapy session (e.g., how empathic the counselor is toward their patients [51]). These results suggest that NLP and ML may be used to offer counselors fast, reliable, objective feedback to support high-quality therapy.

In this paper, we describe Counselor Observer Ratings Expert for Motivational Interviewing (CORE-MI), an automated performance-based feedback system for MI, and report results from a qualitative evaluation with 21 counselors and trainees. We offer two contributions to the field of interactive system design. We present the first study of perceived applicability of automated evaluation software for psychotherapy, an under-studied but potentially important domain for interaction design research. We also identify challenges for user adoption of, trust in, and satisfaction with automated evaluation systems that may apply to machine learning systems generally.

RELATED WORK

There is growing interest among interaction design researchers in bringing computation to bear on problems associated with mental health. For instance, there have been recent efforts to automatically identify and diagnose suicidal ideation [15], insomnia [25], and other mental health disclosures [33] by analyzing social media [3] and mediated speech [10].

In a more interventionist vein, researchers have explored the potential for interactive games to teach users about anxiety disorders [48] and treat geriatric depression [30], while others have investigated the potential for mobile technologies to support users to monitor and reflect on symptoms of bipolar disorder [4], anxiety, and autism [41]. There have also been experiments in using augmented and virtual reality environments to offer exposure therapy to sufferers of PTSD [42] and phobia [50].

In the psychotherapy domain, there are several commercially-available systems that provide automated therapy, particularly cognitive behavioral therapy (CBT), a widely-used evidence-based therapeutic practice. Interestingly, a recent evaluation of automated CBT systems found that users fared poorly if they didn't also receive human support [39], a need that has been well-documented in the eMentalHealth literature (e.g., [26]). There are also established services that provide mediated counseling via the Internet and telephony networks (e.g., [29]), although prior work has found high attrition rates among users of these services [12].

While prior work has often emphasized supporting clients and promoting wellbeing, our work focuses on enhancing the work of professional counselors. Although less developed, there have been recent efforts in this area, including tools for counselors to construct therapeutic game environments for clients [13], and mobile phone applications that enable adolescents who experience mental health disorders to monitor their symptoms for later review with healthcare providers [34].

Despite this flurry of activity, there remains a dearth of research into computer support for training and evaluation of mental health practitioners. One notable exception has been the development of virtual standardized clients, which are conversational agents that simulate symptoms of various mental health conditions [27]. We believe that the relative lack of attention given to training and assessment is an unfortunate oversight, because most psychotherapy will continue to be delivered by human counselors for the foreseeable future, and at present, the quality of psychotherapy in the community is highly variable [22].

CORE-MI OVERVIEW

The Counselor Observer Ratings Expert for Motivational Interviewing (CORE-MI) is an automated coding and visualization system that provides report-card like feedback on psychotherapists' adherence with MI [24]. CORE-MI combines speech and language processing with automated coding and interactive visualization to help counselors and trainers identify strengths and areas for improvement (Figure 1).

Speech and Language Processing

CORE-MI utilizes foundational speech signal processing methods to translate an audio-recording of an MI session into a numeric representation of semantic and vocal acoustic data, which are in turn used as features in machine learning predictive models. Key processing steps include: voice activity detection (i.e., is someone speaking or not?), speaker segmentation (also called "diarization"; i.e., which person is speaking?), role identification (i.e., is the speaker the counselor the client?), and automated speech recognition (i.e. what is being said?) [51]. Additionally, paralinguistic information such as prosody, pitch, speech rate, and intensity are all estimated. A variety of machine learning approaches have been used to take these speech and language derived inputs and predict MI-relevant features of the session.

CORE-MI makes use of the Barista open-source speech processing framework [14].

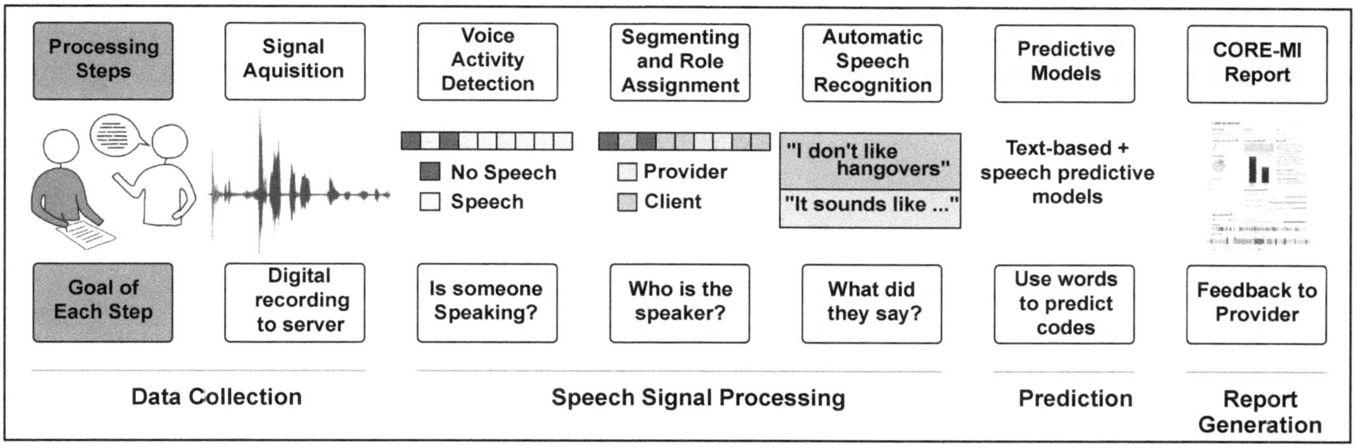

Figure 1: CORE-MI system architecture

Automated Coding

CORE-MI provides feedback on standard MI quality measures described in the Motivational Interviewing Treatment Integrity Scale [37].

Summary Measures

The report presents users with an overall MI fidelity score: a composite metric of the six standard summary measures of MI quality: empathy, MI spirit, reflection-to-question ratio, percent open questions, percent complex reflections, and percent MI adherence. Overall MI fidelity is rated on a 12-point scale; in each of the six domains, counselors can receive one point for passing basic proficiency benchmarks and two points for passing advanced competency benchmarks, where these benchmarks have been defined by the treatment developers.

The second measure is MI adherence, a percentage-based metric, that divides the total number of MI-adherent utterances (e.g., asking open questions, making complex reflections, supporting and affirming patients, and emphasizing client autonomy) divided by the sum of MI adherent and MI non-adherent counselor behaviors. Therefore, any score less than 100% indicates a session where the counselor used at least some non-adherent behaviors (e.g., being confrontational or giving unsolicited advice).

MI spirit and empathy are additional global ratings that capture the "gestalt" of the session. MI spirit assesses the overall competence of the counselor along dimensions of collaboration, evocation, and autonomy. Empathy measures the extent to which the counselor makes an effort to understand the client's perspective. Both are rated on a 1-5 Likert scale.

Behavior Counts

CORE-MI also tracks three "behavior count" measures that characterize the quantity and quality of questions and reflections in the discourse. Questions and reflections are key discursive elements in MI. Behavior count quality metrics include:

1. Reflection to question ratio: the total number of counselor reflections divided by the total number of questions. MI developers have set a 1:1 ratio to indicate basic proficiency and a 2:1 ratio to indicate advanced competence.
2. Percent open questions – open questions (as opposed to closed questions) are preferred as they allow a wide range of possible answers. The percent open questions metric is the number of counselor open-ended questions divided by the sum of the counselor's open and closed questions. Fifty percent open questions indicates beginning proficiency and advanced competence is earned at 70% open questions.
3. Percent complex reflections: the percentage of all counselor reflective utterances that are "complex" rather than "simple". Complex reflections add meaning to client utterances or summarize what they client has said across previous statements, whereas simple reflections may be mere restatements. Basic and advanced proficiency levels are achieved at the 40% and 50% levels, respectively.

Interactive Visualization

CORE-MI provides a report card-like, visual summary of counseling sessions (figure 2). The visualization is implemented in HTML and JavaScript, and makes use of the D3 visualization library. It is accessible through standard web browsers on a variety of devices and platforms, but the design is optimized for tablet-like devices.

At the top of the CORE-MI summary report page is information identifying the session, the counselor, and the client. The feedback portion is organized with the highest-level, summary data at the top and shows progressively more specific metrics throughout the page. Near the top-right of the page is a Notes section, which offers a free-field text entry box for trainees and supervisors to add comments on a session.

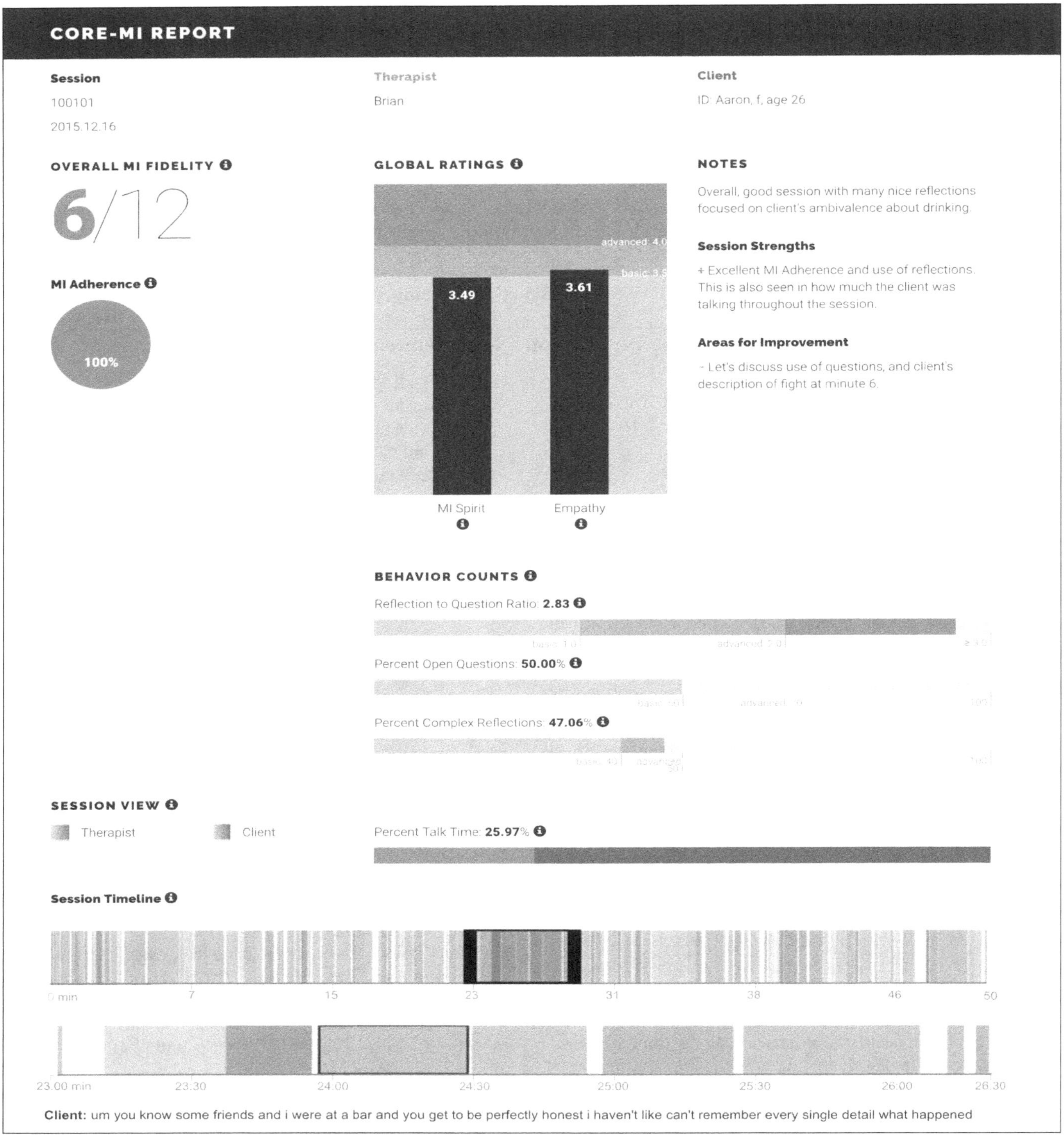

Figure 2: CORE-MI summary report

Interactive "information buttons" are available throughout and can be selected by users to view detailed information about particular measures. For example, a user might select the button next to the MI Adherence title to read about the how that measure is calculated, and desired competency thresholds.

The report prominently features an Overall MI fidelity score that aggregates all measures to give an impressionistic view of the participant's general level of adherence to MI principles. MI adherence, another summary rating, is depicted as a pie chart.

Bar charts indicate global measures (MI spirit, empathy) on a 1-5 scale where 3.5 – 4 indicates basic proficiency, and advanced competency is indicated by scores of 4 or greater. Changes in color highlight the counselor's level of proficiency. MI spirit characterizes the general therapeutic style of a session, captured by how collaborative, accommodating, and supportive the counselor is. Empathy is the degree to which the counselor makes efforts to see and understand their client's worldview.

The behavior counts section of CORE-MI provides finer grained feedback, focusing on summaries of specific types of counselor statements. Like the global ratings, each behavior count is visually depicted as a horizontal bar graph with colors changing as different levels of proficiency are reached.

The session view displays percentage of counselor and client talk time as a bar chart, and includes a session timeline that illustrates turn taking, with counselor and client speech indicated in different colors. Color intensity is mapped to vocally-encoded arousal, such that dark hues indicate a speaker speaking intensely – perhaps in anger, frustration, surprise, or joy. The top section of the session timeline represents the entire session and contains a moveable window that can be stretched and dragged over the bar to focus in on specific sections, shown in the bottom section at a larger scale. Hovering over specific talk turns brings up a transcription of the utterance and how the system coded it (e.g., as a counselor's open question). In this way, the session view provides an overview of key session dynamics, directs the user's attention to areas of greatest interest, and enables her to review key exchanges.

System Reliability

CORE-MI evaluates counselor fidelity to MI via the motivational interviewing skill code (MISC) [36], which is a gold-standard, human-based rating system. The ML / NLP system in CORE-MI was trained on a dataset of 300K utterances from 356 MI session recordings, which were hand labeled by an 8-person coding team using established MISC coding protocols [31]. Various machine learning models have been evaluated for predicting MISC codes (i.e., MI quality metrics) from word-based and paralinguistic (e.g., tone) features [9][45][51]. Averaging over all counselor codes, the correlation of model-based predictions with human-generated codes was found to be 93% of human reliability (SD = 16%) [7]. It is worth noting that, because human ratings are measured with error [i.e., inter-rater reliability is < 1.0], machine learning based predictions can never be higher than human reliability).

Overall, common codes and session summary codes (e.g., different types of counselor questions and reflections; empathy) are strongly predicted by ML/NLP models. Infrequent codes (e.g., confront) are more challenging for human and machine coding.

STUDY DESIGN

Counselors in community clinical practice are rarely evaluated, and never by an automated system. As such, we anticipate that CORE-MI may be disruptive to typical clinical workflows and may not be acceptable to all users. To better understand these concerns, we conducted a study of likely users' attitudes towards automated evaluation. We were particularly interested in three questions:

1. Receptivity: How open are counselors to the concept of automated evaluation?
2. Workflow: What role, if any, can counselors imagine automated evaluation playing in their clinical practice?
3. Concerns: What concerns, if any, do counselors have about introducing automated evaluation into their practice?

Participants

To evaluate potential users' perceptions of CORE-MI, we conducted a study with 21 counselors who were recruited at or nearby a large, North American university. 18 clinicians identified as White, two as Hispanic/Latinx (n = 2), and one as Asian American/Pacific Islander. The mean age of participants was 42.1 (*SD* = 11.7).

Counselors were sampled from two training categories. Clinicians-in-training (n = 10) were recruited from master's (n = 8) and doctoral (n = 2) level clinical training programs, and all clinicians-in-training were enrolled in introductory counseling training courses. The trainees reported having either no training or experience with MI (n = 4), or some familiarity, but no training, with MI (n = 5). One participant did not provide information on their experience in MI.

Experienced counselors (n = 11) were recruited from local community mental health sites. Contact information for experienced counselors was obtained via a snowballing sample where individuals within the mental health community spread information about the study via word of mouth. Seven of the experienced counselors were doctoral level practitioners who have been licensed for more than two years (n = 7), and four of the experienced counselors were licensed master's level practitioners. Regarding training experience, participants reported that they received training MI training and integrate MI in their practice (n = 2), are members of an MI organization (n = 1), have familiarity with and formal training in MI (n = 7), or have familiarity with, but no formal training, MI (n = 1).

Methods

This was a qualitative, mixed-methods study. Participants conducted brief counseling sessions with standardized clients, which were analyzed by CORE-MI. Participants were shown their results and interviewed by the research team. Interviews were recorded and transcribed, and thematic analysis was employed to analyze transcripts.

Standardized Patients
Each counselor participated in a 10-minute mock counseling session with a single graduate student, who was trained to portray a client seeking substance abuse treatment. This approach is often called a standardized patient (SP), and is a well-established research technique among psychotherapy researchers (for an example, see [2]). The SP profiles included an individual who was addicted to methamphetamines, and two college aged individuals seeking treatment for their alcohol usage. The SP profiles were randomly assigned to participants and enacted by four different graduate students.

Semi-structured interviews
SP sessions were recorded and analyzed by the CORE-MI system. Counselors received an email containing a URL to a password-protected CORE-MI summary report of their session. After the counselor had an opportunity to independently review his or her results, a semi-structured interview was conducted by a member of the research team. During the interview, the researcher presented the report on a laptop and used a think-aloud protocol as the counselor navigated the report, asking clarifying questions when necessary. Participants were also asked about their perceptions of the report, and to provide feedback on each report section. Researchers probed on counselors' responses to receiving automated feedback on their clinical work, thoughts on incorporating CORE-MI into their clinical or training practice, and about the counselor's comfort and experience with MI.

Thematic analysis
Interview sessions were video recorded and transcribed verbatim. Following transcription, a team of eight researchers used thematic analysis [5] to identify common themes in participant interviews. First, each researcher read four transcripts and created their own code-books of salient themes. After independent coding, researchers convened to compare themes. The researchers reached consensus on common themes, and developed domain categories: higher-level codes that describe similar themes [11]. Finally, researchers created a master codebook based on the generated domains and themes. All of the transcripts were then coded using the master codebook. To increase the trustworthiness and dependability of the findings, the researchers engaged in consensus coding throughout the study [18]. Each feedback session was coded four times by different researchers, and researchers met weekly to resolve disagreements and reach agreement on codes until all transcripts were analyzed. The researchers shared their rationale for specific codes and discussed how their codes may have been influenced by their views and biases.

RESULTS
Participants generally provided two categories of responses. The bulk of each interview was dedicated to providing specific responses to the CORE-MI summary report. However, participants also speculated on CORE-MI's applicability to clinical practice. For clarity, we report these responses separately.

Reactions to the CORE-MI summary report
Three major themes emerged in participants' discussions of the CORE-MI summary report: user interface, quantitative measures, and personal reflections. The user interface codes encapsulated participants' comments about layout, usability, accessibility of information, and aesthetics. The quantitative measures theme referred to the different MI quality metrics and language summaries presented by the tool. Personal reflections pertained to participants thinking about their own clinical work with patients, prompted by the CORE-MI report.

User Interface
Participants provided substantial feedback on the user interface. Much of this is specific to the CORE-MI report and may not be easily generalizable to other systems. We report these results in the interest of completeness, and to aid the reader in determining what if any influence user interface may have had on participants' overall impressions of CORE-MI.

Upon opening the feedback tool, many (10) participants said the layout was clean, uncluttered, and simple, though three participants attributed overlooking some information due to the simplicity of the layout. One participant found the amount of information initially overwhelming and difficult to navigate. Twelve participants described initially looking at the fidelity and adherence scores or the global ratings graphs and moving across the interface from left to right and then up to down. If the graph was viewed first, two participants noted that it was because it was in the middle of the page. Eight people found the bar graph benchmarks to be visible, eye-catching, and a familiar and easy way to assess proficiency, although some reactions were mixed regarding the ultimate meaning of these benchmarks and the information they conveyed. Participant 2E noted that the graphs "present nice and look really good."

16 participants used information buttons to gather information from the written statements, when they were feeling confused, and to retroactively confirm their assumptions about definitions and interpreting scores. As noted by participant 8E, "the info boxes were helpful," and the 16 participants indicated that they were intuitive to find.

CORE-MI presents detailed information on the Session Timeline, including talk-turns, vocally-encoded arousal, transcription, and behavioral codes linked to transcript. Participants described scrolling through the timeline in conjunction with reflecting on their session, examining the transcript as an indicator of their performance, and using the timeline transcript to confirm the accuracy of other measures. The participants also scrolled over the color blocks and saw the transcription and behavioral codes. There were concerns with the accuracy of the computer-generated transcript, but participant 14N noted that "eighty percent of it made sense." Three participants did not interact with the Timeline.

Different colors throughout the layout represented different concepts, and participants described a variety of thoughts surrounding the colors. Participant 5N noted the colors were, "calm…not passive." Nine participants used the colors to distinguish between counselor and client utterances on the session timeline as well as to distinguish between basic, intermediate, and advanced competency levels. Five participants noted that they recognized the change in color as a metric for proficiency (basic to advanced), though there were mixed feelings about how to interpret these findings. These participants described their interpretations of the competency metrics in conjunction with their personal feelings of their performance during the session.

Five participants did not notice varying color intensity on the session timeline. This may be due to relatively consistent levels of arousal during the SP sessions, and the corresponding consistency in color intensity across the session timeline.

Overall, participants found the interface usable and demonstrated basic competency with the system, including the ability to access information, interpret their scores, and generally understand how automated evaluation related to their sessions.

Quantitative Measures

Overall MI fidelity was described as a salient measure. Six participants indicated they looked first at fidelity and considered this metric as important when interpreting the feedback page overall. Participant 10E, a novice counselor, noted that they looked to see whether they got a "passing grade." Novice counselors seemed to interpret these scores as academic ratings, possibly due to the majority of their professional development occurring through classes. Alternatively, participant 3E, an experienced counselor, reflected on what this number meant for their performance and professional development. Participants, both novice and experienced, expressed a desire to see how their scores changed over time, broadly and with particular clients.

Several participants indicated they struggled to understand some of the measures. This was particularly true for global ratings (empathy and MI spirit) as well as overall evaluations of fidelity and adherence. Seven participants, a majority of novice counselors, reported not fully comprehending the meaning of MI Fidelity score; perhaps due to a lack of experience in the field and not having a more practical understanding of fidelity that might be held by experienced counselors. Nonetheless, these participants expressed confidence in the accuracy of the scores.

Four participants who said they didn't understand some of the measures wanted to know more about their definitions or calculations. This desire seemed primarily motivated by participants seeking to improve their scores.

Several counselors commented on the apparent objectivity of quantitative data and automated systems. Five participants preferred the simplicity of behavioral count data to interpretive measures because it was "raw" and "objective." The same general attitude held for percent talk time.

Several novice counselors cited objectivity as contributing to their willingness to accept automated evaluation. For example, participant 16N said it was "hard to argue with a computer," and that the feedback data was objective because it was computationally derived instead of human evaluated. Participant 9E said it was in some ways easier to accept automatic feedback because it was "objective" and did not generate defensiveness in the same way as a human supervisor might when delivering critical feedback.

Overall, participants accepted the accuracy of the measures. Sixteen participants, both novice and experienced counselors, expressed a general acceptance of the accuracy of the measures despite not knowing how some constructs were defined, and in some cases, questioning transcription accuracy.

Experienced counselors were more likely to question the accuracy and calculation of feedback. For example, participant 1E expressed skepticism about how the computer program coded specific utterances and questioned the accuracy of his scores.

In summation, counselors were receptive to automated feedback, and were generally confident in the accuracy of CORE-MI measures despite not fully understanding how they were derived. Several explicitly invoked notions of objectivity as underlying CORE-MI's appeal.

Personal Reflections

The majority of participants (18) reflected upon how they interact with clients and their use of particular techniques, while they examined the CORE-MI report from their session with the standardized patient. Participants were particularly aware of how personal experience influenced their approach therapy. For example, participant 3E shared, "I think we all internally have a sense of space and how dominant we are in the room but that's I think so contingent upon your history and your family…so actually [the percent talk time] was a really helpful number for me to look at."

Nine participants compared scores from measures on the CORE-MI with their perceptions of how they conducted therapy. In particular, participants described how their CORE-MI scores were consistent with their therapeutic style or experience level. For example, participant 1E indicated that, "I tend to ask a lot of questions and that is my form of directiveness in session which is something that in the past I've tried to curb…and this just really brought out to me that I'm still being pretty directive." In addition, participant 6N indicated that, "I'm on a good course you know I'm just under basic and given my level of experience I think that's fine."

Seven participants reported that the software sparked reflection on areas of improvement, and that the CORE-MI offered an objective measure of skills to improve upon. Quantitative measures on the CORE-MI helped participants focus upon different domains and explore alternative ways of implementing techniques in therapy. For example, participant 14N shared that, "I felt like it…just clarified my own thoughts about my skills…it was nice to have maybe a professional opinion about what I needed to develop". Participant 3E stated that, "looking at these ratings…my sense is okay…like proficient like consistent enough…but potentially really looking at what are the things that I could be doing that [are] more in line with the overall spirit of MI…and empathy."

Clinical uses

Participants also speculated about CORE-MI's suitability for clinical use. Three subthemes emerged in these discussions: personal data benchmarks, supervision and training, and workplace concerns.

Personal Data Benchmarks

Throughout the interviews, participants seemed particularly contemplative about how to internalize feedback and curious about how scores were generated in order to integrate the feedback into practice. Participants expressed the desire to make personal improvements based upon the feedback provided. As was mentioned above, participants' questions about how measures were calculated appeared to be motivated by the desire to improve their scores (rather than, say, to challenge an assessment, or to simply understand how the system worked).

Many participants expressed interest in using CORE-MI to monitor how their practice evolves over time. Both novice and experienced counselors projected using this tool across multiple sessions with multiple clients to examine trends and patterns and study their counseling style with different clients.

Participants were curious about including information related to the counselor's progress in fidelity and adherence scores across multiple sessions. Two suggested including a personal average (based on the average across one's clients), as opposed to only comparing scores to a normative sample. Two others (8E and 9E) mentioned tracking how their practice evolved with particular clients. Participant 9E noted that "is not only how do I measure compared with the general (normative sample), but how do I compare myself with that particular client." The same participant (9E) referred to this concept as "personal data benchmarks"; they explained that this information could provide "longitudinal information of what's going on with a specific client", thus, suggesting the system's use for treatment plan and recommendations.

Three participants suggested additional behavioral count data such as amount of silence, and total time spent on reflections and questions, and imagined using these raw, basic numbers to gauge their own performance over time, or compare themselves to other practitioners. Participants also wondered about a method of continuously interacting with the feedback by adding comments about their clinical work. For example, participant 7E was curious about the tool's possibility to generate specific strengths and growth areas based on the computer-generated feedback. They indicated that an overview of these might better contextualize the information about the scores and the presented information.

One participant (15N) expressed her interest in delivering specific psychotherapy training before and after the implementation of the tool, as a way for counselors to stay current. Participant 12E recommended the use of alternate data to verify the tool's assessment; he noted that "it would be cool if it had physiological data (e.g. heart rate, skin response) to rate the session."

Training and Supervision

All the participants noted the potential use of the feedback tool in their clinical practice and supervision. A novice counselor (15N) stated "I could see it being used with therapy sessions being recorded and then using this tool to provide feedback. I could see a supervisor reviewing it first and then adding notes here." Eleven participants talked about the value of the tool within a training context, particularly noting the potential for supervisors to monitor trainees' progress.

Eight participants described how the CORE-MI could be integrated into the supervision and training of new counselors by generating detailed feedback for trainees and opening discussion of development of specific skills. In particular, they suggested that CORE-MI could be used to give quick, immediate feedback after sessions and could help counselors objectively see how they are interacting with clients. Participant 9E stated that "if I was doing this with someone, like a supervisee…we can visit numbers and I think they would be really good talking points. You know, like data that we can really reflect on." Similarly, participant 3E indicated that, "a lot of times in supervision we're looking at these more global things around content and really drilling down into the phrasing of questions and so on, [CORE-MI] would be really valuable I think." Eight participants also described how the notes section could be helpful by being used to give feedback of strengths and weaknesses to providers. Notes could be linked to specific instances in therapy sessions to explore ways that counselors could improve. For example, participant 10E shared that, "I think it would be useful for the clinician as well to jot down things that they thought were good that they did, areas for growth." Finally, seven participants indicated that CORE-MI could establish benchmarks for whether providers are meeting adequate standards. Participants discussed how CORE-MI could be particularly useful in evaluating providers after they graduate. For instance, participant 9E stated that "at some level this could be used as a performance evaluation for an experienced counselor. Because once you become licensed you literally don't have to be supervised."

Workplace concerns

Several experienced counselors (n=3) expressed concern about the unintentional consequences of including this automated tool in clinical practice.

Experienced counselors mentioned worries about workplace surveillance, and the possibility of the CORE-MI serving as a benchmarking tool to penalize providers. Participant 18E said, "I would be open to [CORE-MI] but I'm concerned about, you know, like, is my performance based on the tool and then I would be evaluated by my boss. Is it gonna lead to getting fired... I don't know if that's the idea." Another participant (19N) raised concerns about the possibility of misusing the tool to rate a clinician's performance in contexts outside the individual therapy format, referring to intake assessments (initial interviews), psychological testing, and group therapy.

Three participants highlighted the need for training on how to use and interpret the different measures included in the feedback tool, both to enhance their own understanding and as a bulwark against misuse.

DISCUSSION

Our findings demonstrate that counselors are generally receptive to introducing a computer-generated assessment and evaluative technology into clinical settings. Trainee participants generally perceived the application as usable, and professional participants seemed genuinely excited about its potential to enhance clinical practice, promote skill development, and improve the quality of supervision.

Further, CORE-MI seems to encourage psychotherapists' self-reflection on their practice, which we take as a good indicator that the system can play a role in ongoing skill development. Participants drew links from the CORE-MI report to clinical activities and their approach to therapy, with little prompting from investigators. As described above, several participants described CORE-MI as offering a quantitative perspective on their implicit beliefs about therapeutic style and areas for improvement.

We also note that novice and expert counselors alike expressed interest in using CORE-MI to monitor changes in their practice over time, and to use CORE-MI for training and supervision. This suggests that counselors of varying levels of expertise are generally interested in continuing to improve their practice and see a role for automated evaluation in ongoing education and skill development.

However, we did observe differences in how novice and expert counselors perceived the system. Trainees generally accepted the accuracy of CORE-MI scores (regardless of whether they understood how those scores were generated, or what they meant), while experienced counselors were more likely to question the validity of scores that did not match their subjective perceptions of their own performance. It may be the case that experienced counselors have a better understanding of the nuances of motivational interviewing and are thus able to probe more deeply into the meaning of particular scores. It might also be the case that novice counselors are more habituated to receiving performance evaluations, and thus are more accepting of this kind of feedback than their more experienced counterparts.

This study also suggests several challenges and opportunities for future development of CORE-MI. The first of these stems from the surprising finding that participants expressed great enthusiasm for and general trust in CORE-MI, even as they acknowledged they did not fully understand how feedback was derived or what precisely it meant. This tension applied to the application as a whole, and also to specific measures: as described above, participants relied on MI Fidelity as a primary performance measure and reflected on its implications for professional development, while simultaneously expressing a lack of understanding of the components of their score.

From one perspective, it may seem encouraging that participants were willing to accept feedback results as valid, as future iterations of similar tools may not struggle overmuch to establish legitimacy. However, this also raises concerns that counselors and supervisors could uncritically accept machine-generated ratings. It may become necessary to provide additional information to ensure users' interpretations of automated ratings matches their intended meaning and actual system capabilities as closely and reliably as possible.

We suspect that these findings may be at least partially attributable to general enthusiasm for the CORE-MI system, and to a broader cultural valorization of quantification and machine learning. We also hypothesize that recruiting participants with limited MI training may explain some of the misunderstandings about standard MI evaluation measures. Nonetheless, users' ability to trust in a system that they don't understand has been previously observed [21], and is endemic to ML systems—particularly when system predictions are based on trained non-linear ML models rather than on theoretical models. This is not to say that users will blindly trust ML systems. But, prior work suggests that evaluations of a system's reliability are based on subjective perceptions of its output and the perceived "soundness" of its reasoning rather than on statistical evidence of its accuracy [43]. The implication for system designers is that users' willingness to trust and ultimately adopt ML systems is dependent on perceived "legibility," meaning, the degree to which system behavior seems to "make sense" to its users, regardless of its mechanism or statistical accuracy [19].

We also uncovered apprehension among potential users, including concerns about surveillance and misuse in the workplace. Several participants expressed concern that CORE-MI assessments might be adopted by supervisors and administrators as performance benchmarks, with at least one participant expressly invoking the possibility of "getting fired" based on a CORE-MI evaluation.

These concerns were particularly pronounced among expert counselors, who presumably have more professional experience than their less experienced counterparts and are thus more sensitive to workplace issues.

We think there is an interesting link between these concerns, and the perception that CORE-MI provides objective assessments of counselor performance. As has been previously shown, ML systems can inherit biases implicit in their design and in the data sets upon which they are trained [6][44]. Nonetheless, they are often perceived as and valued for their apparent lack of prejudice.

Participants in our study suggested that automated evaluation's perceived objectivity might facilitate better, more open reflection and communication, because counselors might be less defensive receiving critical feedback from a machine than from a human supervisor.

Most notably, automated assessment was also seen as more definitive than human evaluation. This could be taken to suggest that CORE-MI predictions will lead to greater acceptance of counselor's shortcomings, and thus will promote learning and enhance performance. Viewed through the lenses of workplace justice, though, this observation takes on a darker hue. As system designers, we acknowledge the very real potential for CORE-MI to be adopted as a performance evaluation and selection tool. At the same time, we also recognize the inherent fallibility of machine learning systems. As such, we understand the possibility that decisions about counselor performance may be based on mistaken predictions made by machines, whose very status as machines simultaneously render them unassailable even as they make mistakes. While it may be "hard to argue with a computer," as designers it is our responsibility to create mechanisms that enable users to do precisely that – particularly when the predictions that our systems make have the potential to adversely impact human welfare [19].

We believe that concerns about system fallibility, perceived objectivity, and workplace justice may be broadly applicable to the design of ML-based automated evaluation systems for human service and other contexts. This suggests a vital new research area for research.

Prior research on interaction design and machine learning often focused on consumer applications (e.g., recommender systems), and much of it was conducted at a time when ML systems were relatively uncommon. In recent years, these systems have increasingly "become real" [20], finding widespread adoption and media attention. At the same time, they are finding their way into human service domains, including healthcare [52], public safety [16], and transportation planning. With these applications, ML is being used not simply to predict user preferences, but to anticipate and evaluate human performance in contexts involving human life, livelihood, and well-being. These are high-stakes applications where trust and perceptions of accuracy have significant consequences for end-users, and for the lives that depend on the decisions they make. As researchers, we have an important role to play in understanding these implications, and hopefully, helping to mitigate these risks.

LIMITATIONS AND FUTURE WORK

We acknowledge the limitations of our recruiting methods. Half of our study sample consisted of psychotherapy students, who are accustomed to having their counseling sessions recorded and evaluated. As such, they may be unusually willing to adopt an automated assessment system. Similarly, using snowball sampling may have biased our study sample of experienced counselors towards those who are generally accepting of automated evaluation. We look forward to evaluating CORE-MI with populations who are more representative of professional clinicians.

We also recognize inherent limitations of our study design. While this study has provided useful insights into users' initial impressions of CORE-MI's potential utility, usability, and desirability, we expect that these perceptions may change with ongoing use of the system. We look forward to evaluating users' actual experience with the system in clinical settings, over prolonged periods of time.

ACKNOWLEDGMENTS

Funding for the preparation of this article was provided by the National Institutes of Health/National Institute on Alcohol Abuse and Alcoholism (NIAAA) under award R01/AA018673 and National Institute on Drug Abuse under award R34/DA034860. In addition, David C. Atkins time was supported in part by K02 AA023814. The content is solely the responsibility of the authors and does not necessarily represent the official views of the National Institutes of Health. The funders had no role in study design, data collection and analysis, decision to publish, or preparation of the manuscript. Drs. Atkins, Hirsch, and Imel are co-founders with equity stake in a technology company, Lyssn.io, focused on tools to support training, supervision, and quality assurance of psychotherapy and counseling.

REFERENCES

[1] Atkins, D.C., Steyvers, M., Imel, Z.E. and Smyth, P. 2014. Scaling up the evaluation of psychotherapy: evaluating motivational interviewing fidelity via statistical text classification. *Implementation Science*. 9, 1 (Dec. 2014). DOI:https://doi.org/10.1186/1748-5908-9-49.

[2] Baer, J.S., Wells, E.A., Rosengren, D.B., Hartzler, B., Beadnell, B. and Dunn, C. 2009. Agency context and tailored training in technology transfer: A pilot evaluation of motivational interviewing training for community counselors. *Journal of Substance Abuse Treatment*. 37, 2 (Sep. 2009), 191–202. DOI:https://doi.org/10.1016/j.jsat.2009.01.003.

[3] Bagroy, S., Kumaraguru, P. and De Choudhury, M. 2017. A Social Media Based Index of Mental Well-Being in College Campuses. *Proceedings of the 2017*

CHI Conference on Human Factors in Computing Systems (2017), 1634–1646.

[4] Bardram, J.E., Frost, M., Szántó, K., Faurholt-Jepsen, M., Vinberg, M. and Kessing, L.V. 2013. Designing mobile health technology for bipolar disorder: a field trial of the monarca system. *CHI '13 Proceedings of the SIGCHI Conference on Human Factors in Computing Systems* (2013), 2627.

[5] Boyatzis, R.E. 1998. *Transforming qualitative information: thematic analysis and code development*. Sage Publications.

[6] Caliskan, A., Bryson, J.J. and Narayanan, A. 2017. Semantics derived automatically from language corpora contain human-like biases. *Science*. 356, 6334 (Apr. 2017), 183–186. DOI:https://doi.org/10.1126/science.aal4230.

[7] Can, D., Atkins, D.C. and Narayanan, S.S. 2015. A dialog act tagging approach to behavioral coding: a case study of addiction counseling conversations. *INTERSPEECH* (2015).

[8] Can, D., Georgiou, P.G., Atkins, D.C. and Narayanan, S.S. 2012. A case study. *Detecting counselor reflections in psychotherapy for addictions using linguistic features*. 2251–2254.

[9] Can, D., Marín, R.A., Georgiou, P.G., Imel, Z.E., Atkins, D.C. and Narayanan, S.S. 2016. "It sounds like...": A natural language processing approach to detecting counselor reflections in motivational interviewing. *Journal of Counseling Psychology*. 63, 3 (2016), 343–350. DOI:https://doi.org/10.1037/cou0000111.

[10] Chang, K., Chan, M.K. and Canny, J. 2011. AnalyzeThis: unobtrusive mental health monitoring by voice. *CHI EA '11 CHI '11 Extended Abstracts on Human Factors in Computing Systems* (2011), 1951.

[11] Charmaz, K. 2006. *Constructing grounded theory*. Sage Publications.

[12] Christensen, H., Griffiths, K., Groves, C. and Korten, A. 2006. Free range users and one hit wonders: community users of an Internet-based cognitive behaviour therapy program. *Australian and New Zealand Journal of Psychiatry*. 40, 1 (Jan. 2006), 59–62. DOI:https://doi.org/10.1111/j.1440-1614.2006 01743.x.

[13] Coyle, D., Doherty, G. and Sharry, J. 2010. PlayWrite: end-user adaptable games to support adolescent mental health. *CHI EA '10 CHI '10 Extended Abstracts on Human Factors in Computing Systems* (2010), 3889.

[14] D. Can, J. Gibson, C. Vaz, P. G. Georgiou and S. S. Narayanan 2014. Barista: A framework for concurrent speech processing by USC-SAIL. *2014 IEEE International Conference on Acoustics, Speech and Signal Processing (ICASSP 2014): Florence, Italy, 4 - 9 May 2014* (Piscataway, NJ, May 2014), 3306–3310.

[15] De Choudhury, M., Kiciman, E., Dredze, M., Coppersmith, G. and Kumar, M. 2016. Discovering Shifts to Suicidal Ideation from Mental Health Content in Social Media. *CHI '16 Proceedings of the 2016 CHI Conference on Human Factors in Computing Systems* (2016), 2098–2110.

[16] Emerging Technology from the arXiv 2016. Neural Network Learns to Identify Criminals by Their Faces. *MIT Technology Review*.

[17] Falender, C.A., Cornish, J.A.E., Goodyear, R., Hatcher, R., Kaslow, N.J., Leventhal, G., Shafranske, E., Sigmon, S.T., Stoltenberg, C. and Grus, C. 2004. Defining competencies in psychology supervision: A consensus statement. *Journal of Clinical Psychology*. 60, 7 (Jul. 2004), 771–785. DOI:https://doi.org/10.1002/jclp.20013.

[18] Hill, C.E. ed. 2012. *Consensual qualitative research: a practical resource for investigating social science phenomena*. American Psychological Association.

[19] Hirsch, T., Merced, K., Narayanan, S., Imel, Z.E. and Atkins, D.C. 2017. Designing Contestability: Interaction Design, Machine Learning, and Mental Health. *ACM Conference on Designing Interactive Systems (DIS'17)* (2017), 95–99.

[20] Höök, K. 2000. Steps to take before intelligent user interfaces become real. *Interacting with Computers*. 12, 4 (Feb. 2000), 409–426. DOI:https://doi.org/10.1016/S0953-5438(99)00006-5.

[21] Höök, K., Karlgren, J., Wærn, A., Dahlbäck, N., Gustaf Jansson, C., Karlgren, K. and Lemaire, B. 1996. A glass box approach to adaptive hypermedia. *User Modeling and User-Adapted Interaction*. 6, 2–3 (Jul. 1996), 157–184. DOI:https://doi.org/10.1007/BF00143966.

[22] Imel, Z.E., Baldwin, S.A., Baer, J.S., Hartzler, B., Dunn, C., Rosengren, D.B. and Atkins, D.C. 2014. Evaluating therapist adherence in motivational interviewing by comparing performance with standardized and real patients. *Journal of Consulting and Clinical Psychology*. 82, 3 (Jun. 2014), 472–481. DOI:https://doi.org/10.1037/a0036158.

[23] Imel, Z.E., Steyvers, M. and Atkins, D.C. 2015. Computational psychotherapy research: Scaling up the evaluation of patient–provider interactions. *Psychotherapy*. 52, 1 (2015), 19–30. DOI:https://doi.org/10.1037/a0036841.

[24] James Gibson, Geoff Gray, Tad Hirsch, Zac E. Imel, Shrikanth Narayanan and David C. Atkins 2016. Developing an Automated Report Card for Addiction Counseling: The Counselor Observer Ratings Expert for MI (CORE-MI). (San Jose, CA, 2016).

[25] Jamison-Powell, S., Linehan, C., Daley, L., Garbett, A. and Lawson, S. 2012. "I can't get no sleep": discussing #insomnia on twitter. *CHI '12 Proceedings of the SIGCHI Conference on Human Factors in Computing Systems* (2012), 1501.

[26] Johansson, R. and Andersson, G. 2012. Internet-based psychological treatments for depression. *Expert*

Review of Neurotherapeutics. 12, 7 (Jul. 2012), 861–870. DOI:https://doi.org/10.1586/ern.12.63.

[27] Kenny, P., Parsons, T.D., Gratch, J. and Rizzo, A.A. 2008. Evaluation of Justina: A Virtual Patient with PTSD. *Intelligent Virtual Agents*. H. Prendinger, J. Lester, and M. Ishizuka, eds. Springer Berlin Heidelberg. 394–408.

[28] Lambert, M.J. ed. 2013. *Bergin and Garfield's handbook of psychotherapy and behavior change*. John Wiley & Sons.

[29] Lederman, R., Wadley, G., Gleeson, J., Bendall, S. and Álvarez-Jiménez, M. 2014. Moderated online social therapy: Designing and evaluating technology for mental health. *ACM Transactions on Computer-Human Interaction*. 21, 1 (Feb. 2014), 1–26. DOI:https://doi.org/10.1145/2513179.

[30] Li, J. 2014. Examining the impact of game interventions on depression among older adults. *CHI PLAY '14 Proceedings of the first ACM SIGCHI annual symposium on Computer-human interaction in play* (2014), 291–294.

[31] Lord, S.P., Can, D., Yi, M., Marin, R., Dunn, C.W., Imel, Z.E., Georgiou, P., Narayanan, S., Steyvers, M. and Atkins, D.C. 2015. Advancing methods for reliably assessing motivational interviewing fidelity using the motivational interviewing skills code. *Journal of Substance Abuse Treatment*. 49, (Feb. 2015), 50–57. DOI:https://doi.org/10.1016/j.jsat.2014.08.005.

[32] Lundahl, B. and Burke, B.L. 2009. The effectiveness and applicability of motivational interviewing: a practice-friendly review of four meta-analyses. *Journal of Clinical Psychology*. 65, 11 (Nov. 2009), 1232–1245. DOI:https://doi.org/10.1002/jclp.20638.

[33] Manikonda, L. and De Choudhury, M. 2017. Modeling and Understanding Visual Attributes of Mental Health Disclosures in Social Media. *CHI '17 Proceedings of the 2017 CHI Conference on Human Factors in Computing Systems* (2017), 170–181.

[34] Matthews, M. and Doherty, G. 2011. In the mood: engaging teenagers in psychotherapy using mobile phones. *CHI '11 Proceedings of the SIGCHI Conference on Human Factors in Computing Systems* (2011), 2947.

[35] Miller, W. and Rollnick, S. 2012. *Motivational Interviewing*. Guilford.

[36] Miller, W.R., Moyers, T.B., Ernst, D. and Amrhein, P. 2008. *Manual for the Motivational Interviewing Skill Code (MISC), Version 2.1.* University of New Mexico Center on Alcoholism, Substance Use, and Addictions.

[37] Moyers, T.B., Martin, T., Manuel, J.K., Miller, W.R. and Ernst, D. 2010. Revised Global Scales: Motivational Interviewing Treatment Integrity 3.1.1 (MITI 3.1.1). University of New Mexico Center on Alcoholism, Substance Abuse and Addictions (CASAA).

[38] Pace, B., Tanana, M., Xiao, B., Dembe, A., S Ba, C., Soma, C., Steyvers, M., Narayanan, S., Atkins, D. and Imel, Z. 2016. *What About the Words? Natural Language Processing in Psychotherapy*.

[39] Rennick-Egglestone, S., Knowles, S., Toms, G., Bee, P., Lovell, K. and Bower, P. 2016. Health Technologies "In the Wild": Experiences of Engagement with Computerised CBT. *CHI '16 Proceedings of the 2016 CHI Conference on Human Factors in Computing Systems* (2016), 2124–2135.

[40] Schwalbe, C.S., Oh, H.Y. and Zweben, A. 2014. Sustaining motivational interviewing: a meta-analysis of training studies. *Addiction (Abingdon, England)*. 109, 8 (Aug. 2014), 1287–1294. DOI:https://doi.org/10.1111/add.12558.

[41] Simm, W., Ferrario, M.A., Gradinar, A., Tavares Smith, M., Forshaw, S., Smith, I. and Whittle, J. 2016. Anxiety and Autism: Towards Personalized Digital Health. *CHI '16 Proceedings of the 2016 CHI Conference on Human Factors in Computing Systems* (2016), 1270–1281.

[42] Simms, D.C., O'Donnell, S. and Molyneaux, H. 2009. The Use of Virtual Reality in the Treatment of Posttraumatic Stress Disorder (PTSD). *Virtual and Mixed Reality*. R. Shumaker, ed. Springer Berlin Heidelberg. 615–624.

[43] Stumpf, S., Rajaram, V., Li, L., Burnett, M., Dietterich, T., Sullivan, E., Drummond, R. and Herlocker, J. 2007. Toward harnessing user feedback for machine learning. (2007), 82.

[44] Sweeney, L. 2013. Discrimination in Online Ad Delivery. *Queue*. 11, 3 (Mar. 2013), 10. DOI:https://doi.org/10.1145/2460276.2460278.

[45] Tanana, M., Hallgren, K.A., Imel, Z.E., Atkins, D.C. and Srikumar, V. 2016. A Comparison of Natural Language Processing Methods for Automated Coding of Motivational Interviewing. *Journal of Substance Abuse Treatment*. 65, (2016), 43–50. DOI:https://doi.org/10.1016/j.jsat.2016.01.006.

[46] Tracey, T.J.G., Wampold, B.E., Lichtenberg, J.W. and Goodyear, R.K. 2014. Expertise in psychotherapy: an elusive goal? *The American Psychologist*. 69, 3 (Apr. 2014), 218–229. DOI:https://doi.org/10.1037/a0035099.

[47] Treatment Episode Data Set (TEDS): Substance Abuse Treatment Admissions by Primary Substance of Abuse, According to Sex, Age Group, Race, and Ethnicity among admissions aged 12 and older Year = 2015, UNITED STATES: 2015. *https://wwwdasis.samhsa.gov/webt/quicklink/US15.htm*.

[48] Wehbe, R.R., Watson, D.K., Tondello, G.F., Ganaba, M., Stocco, M., Lee, A. and Nacke, L.E. 2016. ABOVE WATER: An Educational Game for Anxiety. *CHI PLAY Companion '16 Proceedings of the 2016 Annual Symposium on Computer-Human Interaction in Play Companion Extended Abstracts* (2016), 79–84.

[49] Whiteford, H.A., Degenhardt, L., Rehm, J., Baxter, A.J., Ferrari, A.J., Erskine, H.E., Charlson, F.J., Norman, R.E., Flaxman, A.D., Johns, N., Burstein, R., Murray, C.J. and Vos, T. 2013. Global burden of disease attributable to mental and substance use disorders: findings from the Global Burden of Disease Study 2010. *The Lancet*. 382, 9904 (Nov. 2013), 1575–1586. DOI:https://doi.org/10.1016/S0140-6736(13)61611-6.

[50] Wrzesien, M., Burkhardt, J.-M., Alcañiz Raya, M. and Botella, C. 2011. Mixing psychology and HCI in evaluation of augmented reality mental health technology. *CHI EA '11 CHI '11 Extended Abstracts on Human Factors in Computing Systems* (2011), 2119.

[51] Xiao, B., Imel, Z.E., Georgiou, P.G., Atkins, D.C. and Narayanan, S.S. 2015. "Rate My Therapist": Automated Detection of Empathy in Drug and Alcohol Counseling via Speech and Language Processing. *PLOS ONE*. 10, 12 (Dec. 2015), e0143055. DOI:https://doi.org/10.1371/journal.pone.0143055.

[52] Yang, Q., Zimmerman, J., Steinfeld, A., Carey, L. and Antaki, J.F. 2016. Investigating the Heart Pump Implant Decision Process: Opportunities for Decision Support Tools to Help. (2016), 4477–4488.

Grounding Interactive Machine Learning Tool Design in How Non-Experts Actually Build Models

Qian Yang[1] Jina Suh[2] Nan-Chen Chen[3] Gonzalo Ramos [2]
Human-Computer Interaction Institute, Carnegie Mellon University [1]
Microsoft Research [2]
Human-Centered Design & Engineering, University of Washington [3]
yangqian@cmu.edu jinsuh@microsoft.com nanchen@uw.edu goramos@microsoft.com

ABSTRACT
Machine learning (ML) promises data-driven insights and solutions for people from all walks of life, but the skill of crafting these solutions is possessed by only a few. Emerging research addresses this issue by creating ML tools that are easy and accessible to people who are not formally trained in ML ("non-experts"). This work investigated how non-experts build ML solutions for themselves in real life. Our interviews and surveys revealed unique potentials of non-expert ML, as well several pitfalls that non-experts are susceptible to. For example, many perceived percentage accuracy as a sole measure of performance, thus problematic models proceeded to deployment. These observations suggested that, while challenging, making ML easy and robust should both be important goals of designing novice-facing ML tools. To advance on this insight, we discuss design implications and created a sensitizing concept to demonstrate how designers might guide non-experts to easily build robust solutions.

ACM Classification Keywords
H.5.m. Information Interfaces and Presentation (e.g. HCI): Miscellaneous

Author Keywords
Interactive Machine Learning; End-user Machine Learning; Machine Teaching; Empirical Study; User-Centered Design; Sensitizing Concept.

INTRODUCTION
Machine learning (ML) promises data-driven insights and solutions for a wide variety of domains and people from all walks of life, but crafting these solutions generally requires knowledge that is possessed by only a few. Emergent ML and HCI research aims to make solutions easy to build and accessible, enabling more people to build ML solutions for their respective domains of interest [21, 24].

DIS '18, June 9–13, 2018, , Hong Kong

ISBN 978-1-4503-5198-0/18/06...$15.00

DOI: https://doi.org/10.1145/3196709.3196729

Making ML accessible to people beyond formally trained data scientists is a reality that some researchers are focused on achieving. Technical ML community has worked to improve amateurs' efficiency and reliability in labeling, aiding feature engineering and error-proving, for instance [17]. HCI researchers have created interactive machine learning (iML) tools for developers and end users [9, 16, 29, 7]. Many in the industry even promote the idea of "ML for everyone", creating tools that amateurs could walk up and use [3, 14, 26, 27].

Given the potential benefits and rapid growth in the work that makes ML accessible, it seems that understanding how amateurs build ML solutions for themselves should be a part of iML research and tool design. Interestingly, such investigation is rare. Extensive prior work instead focused on lab studies, where crowd workers accomplish pre-identified ML tasks following preset procedures (i.e. [5, 6, 17]). Some HCI researchers noted a lack of user understanding in the design of these systems and called for "power to the people" in ML [1, 12, 20].

To bridge the gap between accessible iML technology and its intended users, we conducted an empirical study. We focused on those whom we call "non-experts" – *people who are not formally trained in ML, and are actively building ML solutions to serve their needs in the real world* (e.g., a corporate recruiter who built a job candidate profile classifier to aid his decision; or a hobbyist developer who built a signal classifier for her context-aware mobile app). We wanted to understand how they built ML solutions in real-life contexts, including their goals, their approaches to ML and the challenges they encountered. We wanted to identify opportunities where accessible ML tools might help.

We interviewed 24 non-experts who were building ML models and the ML consultants some of them hired to help. We surveyed another 98 non-experts to collect more diverse ML experiences. The study revealed that non-experts are more satisfied and trusting toward the learning results than their professional counterparts. However, they were also susceptible to several technical pitfalls. For example, they tend to perceive percentage accuracy as a sole measure of model performance, thus problematic or even invalid models sometimes proceeded to deployment.

These observations helped us shift the focus away from thinking of non-expert ML as being simply a problem of facilitating the needs of data scientists, or one of reducing tool complexities. While challenging, making the process of building ML models easy, flexible, and robust should be an important goal of designing accessible ML tools. But how? The design seems inevitably need to trade off achieving one goal against interfering with another. [20]. To help both ourselves and fellow designers address this challenge, we designed a new interaction flow for accessible iML tools, namely *Test-Driven Machine Teaching*, exemplifying one possible solution. It functions as a sensitizing concept [31], informing and inspiring HCI researchers of the rich opportunities in this open design space. We discuss its design implications and other open research questions the empirical findings inspire.

This work makes three contributions. 1) Our empirical study provides a rare description of how non-experts actually build ML solutions in the real world. 2) This work provides an alternative perspective to the common assumption that novice-facing tools are GUI tools that reduce or hide ML complexities. An ML tool might better support non-experts if it considered their unique mental model of ML and guided them to build more robust models. 3) Our sensitizing concept exemplifies one possibility in this new design space, offering a starting place for future design innovation.

RELATED WORK

Understanding People in Interactive Machine Learning

In HCI and ML literature, people who build ML models fall into three categories: experts, intermediate users of ML [16], and amateurs. This work focuses on the latter two populations; together we refer to them as "non-experts".

Interestingly, it remains unclear how much ML knowledge qualifies one as an "intermediate user", and what level of ML knowledge stratifies across intermediate and expert users. Researchers defined intermediate users as those "who have *some* experience with ML, but without a *deep* knowledge the experts have" [7, 16]. Without a clear-cut definition, some researchers identified intermediate users based on the tools they use: Those who use graphical user interface (GUI) tools or libraries like Weka are intermediate users; Those who implement their own algorithms are experts [16].

Little to no research has investigated how intermediate users work with ML empirically. A related strand of work has looked at how software engineers build applications that use ML [12, 20]. HCI researchers have also shared their own experiences [9, 10, 29]. Together they revealed many challenges of applying ML in software applications. For example, they had difficulties in understanding the limits of what can be learned; in exploring different formulations of an ML problem, and in evaluating model performance in the context of its application.

Extensive research has investigated ML amateurs–those who interact with ML systems but have no knowledge of ML, such as some domain experts and end users. They typically are engaged in ML when automatic ML approaches fail or deliver unsatisfactory results [1]. Through various crowd-sourcing systems, amateurs help label data, repair data flaws, reason about data, test and troubleshoot learning algorithms. Research has created many techniques that improve crowd workers' efficiency and reliability in these distinct steps of ML pipelines [5, 6, 8, 18, 25, 28].

HCI researchers pointed out that some design of these systems failed to account for users; that the role of amateurs in ML should not be finite state machines that repeatably tell algorithms what is right versus wrong [1]. They called for increasing collaborations across the fields of HCI and ML, and for bringing "*Power to The People in iML*" [1, 20]. They found that integrating user understanding into crowd-sourced ML systems can improve both crowd-workers' experience and efficiency [1, 25].

While making important contributions, these crowd-sourced systems remain focused on predefined ML problems and pipelines. We are not aware of studies that investigated how amateurs build learning algorithms in real-world contexts.

Designing Accessible iML Tools

By accessible iML tools, we refer to tools that enable non-experts to build ML models. Interestingly, most academic iML systems do not specify the amount of ML knowledge required for proper use, making it practically impossible to differentiate accessible ML tools from expert-facing ones. Few other tools, such as Gestalt [19], supported the integration of ML and larger software development workflows. While making ML more accessible, these tools assumed sufficient ML knowledge among their users, therefore fall out of the purview of this work.

When designing explicitly for non-experts, researchers removed complex steps and interactions in the ML process. These tools uniformly adopted GUI designs, eliminating the need for users to write code (i.e. [7, 9, 16]). In addition, some tools became focused on particular application domains and limited the types of input a user can provide [7, 21]. Users have little or no recourse if their problem does not conform to the assumptions made by the tool. Researchers concluded this design choice as the trade-off between generalizability and accessibility. To make accessible ML tools, designers had to sacrifice flexibility for ease of use [20].

There is a noticeable lack of connection between these designs and the work that investigated non-experts. Accessible iML tools in HCI research rarely came out of an elaborate understanding of their users, or the challenges they face in real-world situations. Commercial iML tools that promote the idea of ML for everyone did not document how their design choices support their diverse users [11, 14]. Bridging these two threads of research, this work brings a user-centered lens to the currently technology-driven iML tool design and research.

EMPIRICAL STUDY DESIGN

We aimed to investigate how non-experts actually build ML models for their own purposes in real-world contexts. We aimed to identify opportunities where accessible ML tools might help. Towards these goals, we chose to conduct a qualitative study consisting of interviews and an open-question

Non-Experts			Supporting Experts*
Profession	**Example ML Problem**	**count**	**count**
Professional Software Engineer	Bug report classifier	4	2
Project Manager	User feedback classifier	2	2
Manager	HR Policy Q&A bot	2	1
Business Analytics	Predictive machine maintenance	1	2
Artist	Emotion classifier for wearables	1	
Botanist	Predictive plant nutrient management	1	1
Academic Researcher	Sensor signal classifier	1	
Clinical Researcher	Prognostic classifier	1	
Mechanical Engineer	Insurance risk estimate	1	1

Table 1. Interview study participants. We focused on non-experts, those who are not formally trained in ML, and are actively teaching learners to solve particular problems. [*] We also interviewed the ML consultants whom the non-experts hired to help.

survey. We chose interviews because we wanted to capture in rich detail the thought processes of the non-experts when building ML models. We used an online survey because we wanted to collect more narratives of such processes from a broader population.

Participants
Previous research offered us no clear division between experts and non-experts. In this study, we chose to use their educational degree as approximation. We had two criteria when screening non-expert participants: 1) Participants do not have a degree in ML, statistics, mathematics or artificial intelligence; 2) Participants are pro-actively building one or more ML models for his/her own purposes. Our interviews and survey were then devised to probe participants' specific knowledge and skillset, including subject domain knowledge, statistics and ML knowledge, programming skills, etc.

Field Interviews
We conducted semi-structured interviews with users of four consumer-facing ML services. The four services are an iML tool for building ML and deep learning applications, a consulting service for ML analytics, a consulting service for data-driven business decision making, and a chat-bot-building framework. We recruited an initial set of participants through our professional networks in these ML teams, and later expanded via snowball sampling.

We interviewed 14 non-expert users of these services. We asked participants to walk us through in detail the problems had and how they solved or failed to solve the problems with ML. Several participants also offered to share with us their data schema, iML tool workbench status, documents, or notes. All interviews were audio-recorded and transcribed for analysis. Table 1 provides a summary of the participants' profession and the type of projects they described in our study.

During these interviews, we found that some of the non-experts hired ML consultants to help. In order to better understand where and how they sought help, we also interviewed 10 of these consultants. We were also invited to observe two of the clients' meetings with their ML consultants for ongoing projects. The consultants are professional data scientists trained in ML, mathematics or statistics. In the data analysis and the rest of the paper, we strictly differentiate the narratives of non-experts and ML consultants.

Online Survey
We then sought to collect more diverse ML experiences through an online survey. The survey centered on one open question: "*Describe in detail a recent project where you built or attempted to build an ML model*". Follow-up questions inquired about this model's inputs and outputs, data, tool use, code functionality (if applicable), participants' expectations, frustrations and results. We publicized links to the survey on two *Reddit* boards for ML hobbyists. We also promoted it via ML-related mailing lists of a large-scale technology company and of two universities. We collected 98 valid survey responses from self-identified non-experts.

We analyzed both survey responses and interview transcriptions using affinity diagrams [2] and sequence-flow models. We created multiple affinity diagrams based on ML workflow, the expertise participants have, the problems they encountered, the application domains, etc. We discussed patterns in non-expert ML as they emerged.

EMPIRICAL FINDINGS
We organized our empirical findings around four themes: non-experts' motivations to build ML models, their overall experience, their knowledge of ML and their blind spots.

Motivation Toward Machine Learning
A majority of non-experts began to experiment with ML because they had a dataset at hand, rather than a clear ML goal in mind. ML consultants shared that a vast majority of their clients come with available data, and may "*want ML but do not yet know exactly what for*" (P9,10,23).

Many non-experts built ML models solely for gaining data insights (Figure 1b). A model's accuracy or related metrics

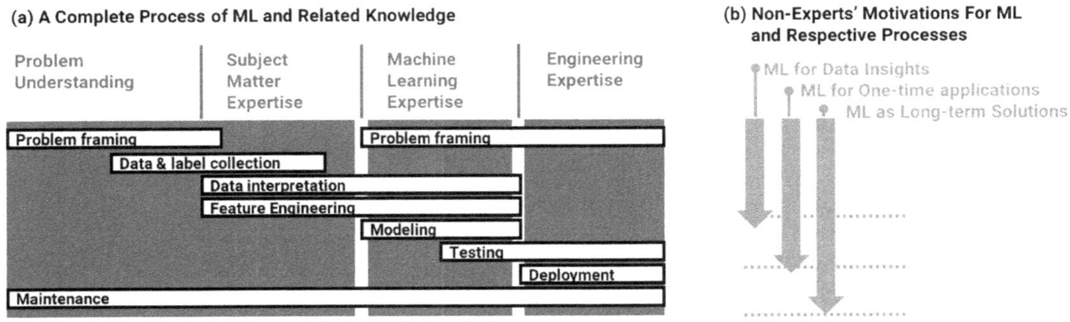

Figure 1. (a) A consolidated ML process and the four fields of expertise involved; (b) non-experts' varied goals. Their goals anchored the fractions of an ML pipeline they need to implement, and frequently veered them away from some of the thorny challenges of ML.

was not their focus. Rather, they value the byproducts of the ML model: the choices of features that generated the best-performing model. For example, a mortgage website manager (P9) applied ML to the web log data, in searching for insights on why the users drop their mortgage applications halfway.

> *Tell me what I don't know about the data.* (P24)

> *The fun part was seeing what a most predicted phrase would be.* (Survey respondent #37, building a chatbot)

Others who build models for intelligent applications evaluated ML success as a matter of improvement; their goal was to build a good enough model that improves the current manual or heuristic-based solution. Very few of them had a predefined learning problem in mind that must be modeled as accurately as possible.

> P4 (artist who creates wearable robots): *it doesn't need to be a perfect algorithm for that (my art) to work. It's nice if it is. The algorithm is not the important part of that, it was the demonstration of the wearable and my ideas.*

> *Machine learning is just a chainsaw in a workshop. I'd love to work in a workshop that has a chainsaw, but I don't necessarily need it.* (P2, developer, building a smart sensor for his home):

Experience of Machine Learning

Non-experts in our study were able to build models that they perceive as satisfactory. They first formulated a task for the ML system to perform based on the data they have. When the available data is insufficient for the problem, they adjusted their expectations and designed a new model to build. As such, non-experts did not need to acquire additional data or labels. Other participants who did not have a ready dataset at hand took a similar approach. They started with a vaguely defined problem space and searched for publicly available ML tutorials or scripts that solve comparable problems. The search results provided non-experts with possible ML problem formulations and solutions. They then implement the fledgling problem-solution and iterate, until they arrived on a matching problem-solution pair.

> *I don't understand the frustrations yet.* (#28)

> *This is my fist project with ML, due to its success I'm planning to create my next project in one month.* (#50)

Non-experts implemented learning models by showing desired outputs and inputs. They understood an ML algorithm as an input-output (I/O) mapping mechanism; a mechanism in which data inputs go in, and the prediction and a performance score come out. They tweaked the algorithms that their tools offered until the accuracy was good enough; otherwise, they adjusted their ML goal and iterated on this experimental process.

> *I need to be see what the model looks like so I can be sure of what I'm building, and can modify and adjust details.* (Survey respondent #93)

In our interviews, all non-experts expressed no doubt on validity of the models they built, regardless of their level of ML experience or the interpretability of the model. They trusted their ML results more than their consultant collaborators.

Non-experts' level of trust, in the ML consultants' opinion, depends on the extent to which they are engaged in the building process. In order to gain their clients' trust on their ML model, ML consultants frequently reported data insights to the clients, presented the models built in every debugging iteration, and kept the algorithms explainable even at the cost of model performance. This interactivity in this process made the non-experts trust the result models.

Knowledge of Machine Learning and Tool Use

How did non-experts build satisfying and trustworthy models by merely mapping in/outputs? To take a closer look, we created a sequence-flow map, detailing the knowledge and skills that our participants utilized at different stages of the process. This surfaced four fields of expertise instrumental for the success of ML: problem understanding, subject matter expertise, engineering expertise and ML expertise (Figure 1a). Drawing on them, we note non-experts' skillset and discuss the challenges they knowingly or unknowingly experienced.

Problem Understanding and Subject Matter Expertise

Problem understanding is the in-depth knowledge about what predictions could be valuable to a real-world situation, and how the prediction would be used in that context. All of the non-experts in our study have profound problem understandings as they built models for their work or hobbies.

Subject matter expertise includes the abilities to explain jargon and nominate possible feature interrelations, and a detailed understanding of how the data is collected in the field and its potential flaws. Most of the non-experts in our study are subject matter experts too. Even when collaborating with ML consultants, they played leading roles in interpreting data, guarding against insensible data maneuvers, suggesting important features to include, and directing how to visualize and use ML outputs.

Engineering Expertise

Engineering expertise includes the skills to write code, and the knowledge of software engineering best practices.

Non-experts did not perceive programming as a challenge. Formally trained software engineers make up a majority of the non-expert participants. Only one of the 98 survey respondents had no programming skills at all and s/he managed to build the model using GUI tools (Excel and Weka). Others relied on publicly available scripts and learning from online working examples. They expressed frustration that they felt limited by the possibilities these tools offer, but none cited inability to write code as barrier to their ML success.

It is worth noting that, even among those who do have a degree in computer science, many did not write code at all. More than half of them wrote less than a hundred lines of code. When building models for personal use or for hobby projects, they only wrote code to prepossess data or craft features.

Machine Learning Expertise

Beyond the ability to build a working model, ML expertise also includes a variety of aspects of practical data science knowledge: 1) the statistical knowledge, such as processing data based on descriptive statistics and interpreting algorithm performances based on visualizations and performance matrices; 2) topical knowledge such as "X model works well with Y kind of data"; and finally, 3) procedural knowledge of ML, such as how to assemble multiple components of an ML solution via large masses of "glue codes".

Non-experts learned how to build an ML model by reading the documentation of iML tools/APIs, at the time when they started building a model. One ML consultant shared that, across all her clients, "*how well they build a model depends on how much effort they put into reading documentations*".

Interestingly, non-experts rarely read API documentation at all, unless pushed by their consultants. Non-experts instead simply relied on pivoting publicly-available working ML examples, re-purposing these scripts toward their needs. The knowledge and reasons underlying these working examples remained unknown to the them.

> *The main challenge along the way was the problem domain and the nature of the data were quite unique – no publicly available analogous datasets or literature.* (Survey respondent #42)

Non-experts rarely attempted to introspect the internal mechanism of learning algorithms. They did not attempt to use data visualization or descriptive statistics to understand their data or introspect their models. None of them has mentioned any consideration about unintelligible features, unseen data or model generalizability.

The characteristics of different learning algorithms were not in non-experts' sphere of knowledge either. Among the survey respondents, nearly half non-experts have only explored one algorithm throughout their ML processes; Another 10% of the survey respondents either "*tried all algorithms that I could think of*" or "*simply followed system recommendation*" when building models. ML consultants described this topical knowledge as undocumented "*or on the fringes of ML textbooks*", and could only be acquired via years of ML experience.

Non-experts did not mention the procedural knowledge of ML either. Contrarily, ML consultants often preserved and reused the structure of their previously built ML solutions, and considered the pipeline design an important part of their expertise. This difference led to their distinct preferences for ML tools.

Preference for Machine Learning Tools

ML consultants uniformly and strongly preferred GUI-based, drag-and-drop tools that allow them to reuse their ML pipeline setup and application deployment codes, for example, knowledge-flow tools and scripting tools that support movable code sections. They thus could focus on implementing their learning algorithms with minimal code changes in other parts of the application.

In contrast, most non-experts expressed a strong preference for iML tools that take the form of a code editor. Except the one participant who does not program at all, non-experts prefer text-editor tools so that they can more easily re-use online scripts and ML solutions. Non-experts with formal training in software engineering particularly preferred these tools. Code-versioning and collaboration features of these tools (i.e. Git integration) enabled them to easily integrate various APIs, control versions, track bugs, and collaborate in real-time. They described these features as essential parts of their work. These observations are very different from the assumptions in previous literature, that non-experts are those who use GUI tools, while experts write customized code and use "*expert tools*" [16].

> *Writing code is just so much faster, more efficient. [...] After my consultant did all the exploratory work in [a knowledge-flow GUI tool], I always re-wrote them all in my [code] editor.*

Pitfalls of Machine Learning

Many non-experts successfully built ML solutions; they mapped algorithm in/outputs and groped their way towards a better model performance. This was effective in many modeling tasks, particularly the ones that do not require statistical reasoning or model generalizability. For example, P2 built an application that recognizes environmental noises and alerts ongoing events at home (i.e., microwave finished and made a "ding" noise). He recorded microphone stream data, labeled segments of the stream with event names, and trained the model. The model functioned well only at his home, and this was good enough to be useful for him.

In other application domains, however, non-experts' I/O mapping approach seeded frustrations and performance problems. With little to no understanding of a learning algorithm's internal mechanism, non-experts were more often baffled when model performance stalls, and more often abandoned their tasks.

Designing an Achievable Learning Task

A vast majority of non-experts are unaware of the complexities in translating a problematic real-world situation into a feasible ML problem (namely, "problem design"). Often, they directly map the high-level goal they have in mind into the ML problem they have to design: "When I put in X, the application should return Y" (Figure 2). The data inputs in this scenario are the training data, and the output is the labels.

This strategy for problem design did not pertain to a particular learning algorithm's capability or the available data, and thus sometimes led to difficult or unrealistic learning goals. For example, P6 (a botanist) planned to build a signal classifier that detects plants' health status. She presumed to collect video streams of her plants as training data, and her strategy was to *"just collect the data that we (biologists) use now"*.

In contrast, most of the ML consultants stated that formulating the right ML problem to solve is the greatest challenge in the whole process. They carried out *"long and difficult processes"* to gradually identify and articulate a meaningful and achievable goal.

They first exhausted simpler analytic methods: they ran various analyses to gain insights into the data, and then arrived on *"a decision point whether to proceed to ML"*. If they decided to proceed, they then extensively investigated what real-world problems were worth solving and solvable by ML. When building a user-feedback classifier, for example, one ML consultant interviewed multiple levels of enterprise leadership to understand how the ML result would be used, how long it would stay active and the benefit it could generate. She factored these observations into the design and the evaluation criteria of her model.

Finally, ML consultants put explicit efforts in weighing *"how deep the learner can and should go"* (P5). In the previous analytic stage, they have accumulated some understandings of the data; at this stage they more carefully investigated data

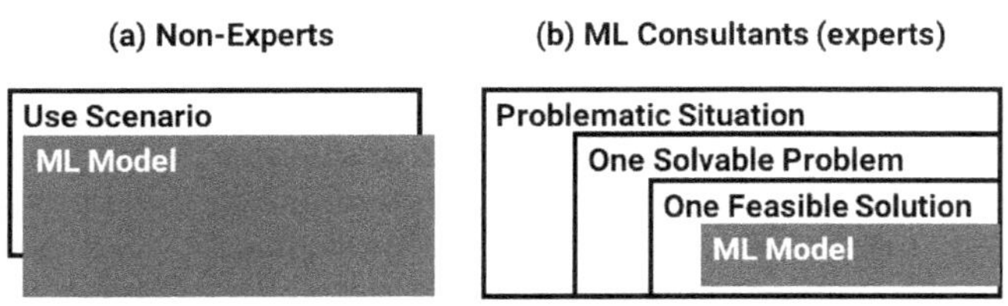

Figure 2. Non-experts' and their consultants' (experts) approaches to formulating an ML problem.

distribution and the extent of missing values. In dealing with familiar problems, consultants applied tried-and-true measures to quickly estimate the feasibility of their learning goal. For example, *"if a human cannot tell apart the intention of this sentence (class value), you have set the classes too fine-grained"* (P12). In dealing with more complex ML systems, participants also weighed the resources required before they start to build a model:

> *If I can predict 20% of these failures, that can save you how much. Is that gonna be worth our time and effort? If I can only predict 10%, is that enough to prove to you that you can invest a little bit more so that we can improve?* (P24, building predictive maintenance solution)

> *I estimated the amount of labeled sample data that we will need to accurately predict [topics]. There is a formula to calculate that [labeled data needed].* (P16, building text topic classifier)

In sharp contrast to non-experts' approach, ML consultants factored in all of the above considerations–the real-world situation, available data, resources and intended investments, and the capability of ML techniques–in their problem design. Their investigative processes took up to two months.

Debugging Strategically

Debugging refers to the iterative testing and revision of an ML model toward a certain level of performance [17]. Most non-experts' only strategy to improve a model's performance is to *"add more data"*. Across all of the non-experts in our interviews and survey, none has ever removed or simplified any features while debugging. Very often non-experts ask their consultants "The model is not doing well. Should I add more instances or add more features?" As one ML consultant concluded: *"They just expect a white list of examples improves model performance."*(P12)

Assuming adding more data directly improves performance, non-experts started training a model with all data and features available. When the performance stalled, they added more training inputs or turned to more complex models. After they exhausted both options, *"the next step is experimenting (with) deep learning"* (P3,18).

Some non-experts turned to API documentation to seek additional actions that they could take. However, many struggled with understanding the abstract concepts in the documents. One most-mentioned such concept is *feature*. Non-experts conceptualized features as concrete entities, such as columns of data in spreadsheet, or certain words and phrases to match in a text. We observed that this method frequently failed when the model involved composite or hierarchical features, or features that are difficult to interpret.

> *Whoever started using [an iML tool] that doesn't have ML background doesn't understand what a feature means, [...] to grasp the idea behind features.* (P12, ML consultant)

Although unclear about what a feature exactly is, non-experts examined the value of features by its impact on model performance. If the performance gets better, they added more

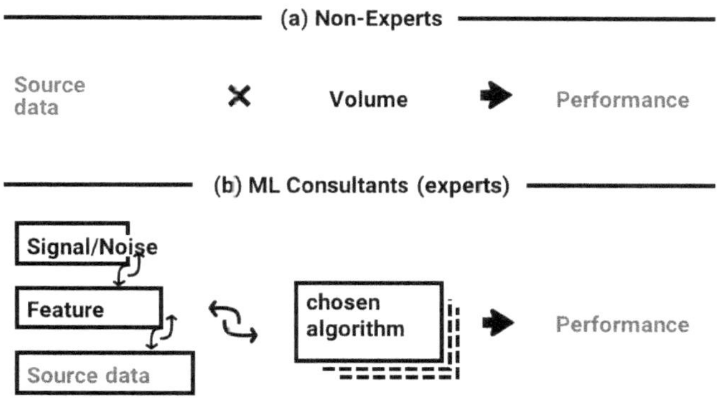

Figure 3. Non-experts' and their consultants' (experts) approaches to improve model performance.

features. Otherwise, they gave up on feature engineering altogether.

> *Feature is magic. I don't know what exactly is happening, but I can feel its impact.* (Survey response)

> *I wasted a week on it. It doesn't change anything. Feature is useless.* (P26, software engineer)

Contrarily, ML consultants starting model building with a "*solid, basic model*". As they evaluated the model solution, they weighed and decided whether to "*fancy it up or to add another component*". This incremental approach allowed them to debug only one component of the model in every iteration, "*so when it breaks you know why*". The most frequently mentioned debug "components" include: the choice of learning algorithm and its parameters, the choices of including a signal or not ("*is this information a signal or a noise?*"), the representation of the signal (using what and how many features?), and the design of a feature (Figure 3).

> *We used a very basic set of features there and there was a question, do we continue to make a fancier and fancier feature, or do we go after new signal. We weigh that constantly: Am I getting the right signal or wrong signal from the data source I have? If I am, should I add on another one, or should I continue trying to extract signals from the same set of information?* (P17, ML consultant)

While debugging, ML consultants constantly judged whether the power of a feature, signal or algorithm of certain complexity "*has saturated*", and took actions accordingly. They made these judgments based on an understanding of the affordances and limitations of the chosen algorithm, as well as monitoring metrics regarding data distribution and model performance. These knowledge and tools helped them probe into the interplay between different components of the model and improve its performance in a systematic manner.

Measuring and Interpreting Model Performance

Most non-experts consider their task completed once their model reached a "good enough" percentage accuracy. They expressed no concern over how well their solution generalizes to new data. None mentioned any over-fitting issues: The need of considering new, previously unseen data instances is not an activity non-experts actively engage. Some shared that they struggled with grasping unseen data in general, "the data that don't fit into my memory".

Almost all non-experts viewed percentage accuracy as the only measure of ML success. Our interviews captured a number of cases where non-experts deployed their ML application once the percentage accuracy "*looked good*", unaware of the likely problems and risks in their models such as bias and overfitting.

ML consultants, in contrast, expressed a constant alertness to the possible breakdowns of their ML solutions. "*Things can go wrong with no obvious reasons in ML,*" one ML consultant said. With such a mindset, almost all ML consultants inserted "*checkpoints*" and "*gates*" into their processes, and closely monitored potential problems in the data or model. They regularly briefed each step of their ML process to subject matter experts or problem owners to assure their every step was statistically and practically valid. After deployment, they closely monitored incoming data and model performance for weeks "*just to see if it (the model) actually works*".

> *You shouldn't proceed to train the model if the quality of your data doesn't meet certain requirement, say, the percentage of missing data and so on.* (ML consultant)

DESIGN IMPLICATIONS AND TRADE-OFFS

We have depicted how non-experts build ML models for their respective purposes in real life. We intend to draw implications from these observations to inform future iML tool design and research. Yet we were alerted to the fact that participants in our study used publicly available toolkits rather than state-of-art iML systems in academic research. In this light, we searched HCI, ICML and AAAI publications for systems and techniques that intend to facilitate non-experts. We reflected on whether and how these tools and techniques could have improved non-expert ML. After much discussion, we found three issues where prior research and the empirical findings seem to be in conflict.

The first issue concerns non-experts' role in building ML models. Accessible iML tools to date are mostly intended to increase performance of a given model. This somewhat conflicts with the observation that non-experts proactively build models for their own purposes. We found their overall approach to be similar to that of a reflective practitioner [23]. They use their repertoire of ML knowledge to experiment with ML solutions for solving issues of practice. They continually assess the viability of the solution, and pivot when it seems to fail.

The second issue regards non-experts' knowledge of ML and tool use. Previous HCI research identified those who use GUI tools as non-experts [16]. Accessible ML tools also uniformly took the form of GUIs. Our empirical study provided an alternative perspective on these commonly held assumptions: Many non-ML experts used scripting tools to more easily make use of publicly available ML solutions. These solutions embedded implicit knowledge that non-experts find valuable, such as data pre-processing procedures and model evaluation methods. GUI tools do not offer such embedded knowledge, thus were unattractive to many non-ML experts, especially to those who are proficient programmers. On reflection, we should not equate users' ML expertise with programming skills. Instead, we need to more carefully examine their needs in both ML and programming tasks respectively.

Lastly, ML tools should guide and safeguard users to build robust models. Our study revealed several technical pitfalls non-experts are susceptible to. This is a missing perspective in prior research on accessible ML, which has instead been focusing on making ML easily accessible to everyone. Guided by this framing, accessible ML tools frequently adopted simplified interfaces and functionality, hiding ML's complexities. The critical role of model quality control is left to the users. Such tools are unlikely to prevent the technical pitfalls of ML. When blindly used, they could even increase the risk of misleading or erroneous results.

These observations helped us shift the focus away from thinking of non-expert ML as being simply a problem of facilitating the needs of data scientists, or one of reducing tool complexities. While challenging, we need to make the process of building ML models *flexible*, *easy* and *robust*. Taking a lesson from the HCI work on end-user programming, we need to make tools for non-experts based on how they react to ML challenges, instead of by simplifying or appropriating expert tools for them.

This new framing led us to look for ideas where non-experts gained awareness of ML's technical pitfalls, and for opportunities to guide and safeguard non-experts to easily build robust models. But how? The trade-off between functional elasticity and ease of use poses a fundamental challenge for designing general-purpose, accessible iML tools [22]. To help both ourselves and fellow designers and researchers, we created an iML tool design as a sensitizing concept [31], demonstrating one possibility of creating novice-friendly yet robust iML processes.

A SENSITIZING CONCEPT

In the second stage of our work, we set out to design a sensitizing concept for accessible iML tools. We deliberately broke the norm and chose to create a sensitizing concept rather than elaborating on a set of discrete design implications. This is because our goal is to inform the HCI community of the *ready* opportunities in this research space, and to offer a starting place for future innovation. We had three goals for this design:

- Grounding its interaction design in non-experts' intuitive approach to ML;
- Scaffolding and safeguarding a robust model building process;
- Supporting users of various needs and skillsets, both in terms of ML knowledge and programming skills.

Toward these goals, we sketched various possible iML tool forms and functions. We also synthesized technical advances in HCI and ML research. We mapped them onto the workflow and pitfalls our empirical study has revealed and discussed how they might benefit non-experts. This process resulted in a new design, namely "*Test-Driven Machine Teaching*".

The Concept of Test-Driven Machine Teaching

Test-driven machine teaching is the interaction flow of an iML tool. It takes inspirations from two technical concepts: "Machine Teaching" [24] and "Test-Driven ML" [4].

With *Machine Teaching*, we refer to a human-centered perspective to the process of ML [24]. While ML focuses on improving the accuracy of "learners" (learning algorithms), machine teaching focuses on improving the efficacy of "teachers" –people who interact with data and "teach" how algorithms should behave. We adapted this focus in the design of our iML tool. Instead of aiming to better explain algorithm behaviors to users, our design aims to help users better express their expectations towards ML, and guide users towards features and algorithms that match their expectations.

Test-Driven ML is the practice of defining test cases *before* model building. Users first define examples of model inputs and outputs as test cases, then build a simple model to get one test to pass, and then improve the model until passing all tests [4]. This approach has several benefits: 1) It documents how the models are intended to work; 2) It reduces user errors; 3) It helps novices learn to start with simple solutions and improve incrementally [15]. Given these potential benefits for non-experts, we designed the iML tool to scaffold a test-driven ML process.

Interaction Flow (Figure 4)

Before training learning models, the iML tool displays data and *requires* users to elicit a set of observations as test cases. Users curate a test set that encapsulates their ML goals and priorities. This hand-picking process forces users to examine their data, grounding their ML goals in concrete data instances. It also facilitates those who "*want ML but do not know what exactly for*" to crystallize their expectations.

Accordingly, the iML tool alerts users of the potential skews and biases in their selections, guiding them to understand their data more comprehensively and to curate a statistically representative test set. For example, our empirical study showed that non-experts tend to select a "white list" of test cases (cases whose class values are uniformly positive). The iML tool could remind the user to also provide negative examples.

Next, the iML tool recommends features and learning algorithms that are likely to work well with the characteristics of the data, the prediction task, and user priorities captured from the test set. It also alerts users of significant data quality flaws. For small datasets, the iML tool may automatically run multiple basic algorithms, and suggests a subset based on standard performance measures such confusion matrix and F score. We imagine ML best practices and existing mixed-initiative ML techniques could be leveraged in support of this (i.e. [6, 28, 32]).

After a model is built, the iML tool shows model predictions on all test cases. In contrast to statistics and visualizations whose interpretation requires additional know-how, these hand-picked test cases provide concrete, direct probes into the data and the model performance. They also represent the subset of data instances that the user understands and cares

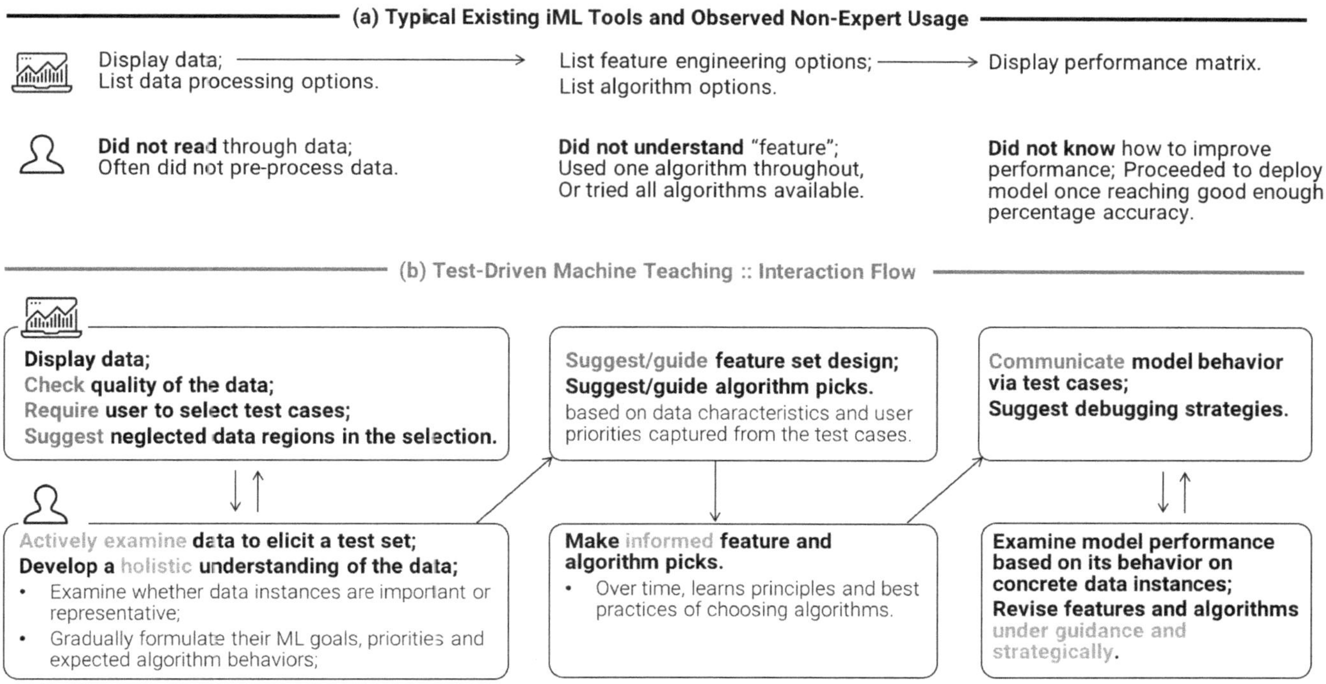

Figure 4. Test-driven machine teaching workflow. It uses user-selected test cases as the major interface between participants and learning algorithms. Central to this design is the idea that novice-facing iML tools should not only make it easy to teach ML models, but also actively and intelligently support robust teaching processes and activities.

about. We imagine users are more likely to engage with and be able to understand algorithm behaviour through these test cases. Central to this design is to prevent users from taking percentage accuracy as the sole performance measure.

While communicating model behaviours, the iML tool also suggests debugging strategies and actions for users to take. One simple way to generate these suggestions is to automatically run principal component analysis, informing users of strongly relevant features. Previous research on explanatory debugging, mixed-initiative ML and automatic ML techniques can inform more sophisticated debugging suggestions [6, 13, 17, 32].

This interaction flow can take various UI forms. Designers may choose one or more interface manifestations of this interaction flow, based on their intended users or typical ML tasks.

Actualizing the Design Implications

Test-driven machine teaching (TDMT) functions as a sensitizing concept for designing accessible ML tools. It exemplifies one concrete solution for the design trade-offs among functional flexibility, ease of use and robust ML results. It embodies three implications for mediating these trade-offs in the design of accessible ML tools.

1. *Test cases as the interface between non-experts and learning models*: TDMT captures how users expect the algorithms to behave via test cases, helping users better articulate these expectations. Such articulation enables the iML tool to offer personalized, in-situ safeguard mechanisms and guidance in the modeling process.

   This design is rooted in the observation that non-experts understand model behaviour by mapping inputs and outputs. Test cases as a form of model input-output pairs fit how non-experts intuitively understand ML.

   Moreover, the process of hand-picking test cases invites users to carefully examine their data and their expectations toward ML. The empirical study showed that non-expert ML is highly experimental and exploratory. TDMT thus guides users to examine their data and formulate ML goals that should be part of the ML process. At a higher level, accessible ML tools should support non-expert ML as a co-evolution of problem and solution, rather than as a gradual procession to an optimum in the loss function.

2. *Scaffolding and safeguarding a robust ML process by blending user and machine intelligence*:

   Clearly, there are opportunities in embedding data-driven techniques in iML tool design to make non-expert ML more robust. Research has produced many techniques that improve amateurs' ML reliability and efficiency [30, 6, 8]. Previous crowd-sourcing work [1, 20] as well as our empirical study have offered observations of how non-experts work with ML. IML tool design can be a perfect fusion point of these parallel research efforts in making ML accessible to non-experts.

   TDMT offers one example of this. It leverages test cases to capture user expectations toward ML. The iML tool thus can deliver personalized, ad-hoc suggestions targeted to a user's goal and the dataset in-use. Future research is necessary to evaluate this concept, and more importantly, to explore solutions to bridge user and machine intelligence via the design of iML tool.

3. *Adaptive interfaces to support users with various needs and background knowledge*: Previous iML research claimed that general-purpose ML tools require complex functionality and interactions; thus they are difficult to design for non-experts [22]. We see opportunities in adaptive user interfaces (UI) and interactions to help with this challenge. As an example, TDMT offers intelligently pliable functions, surfacing only the data procedures and algorithm choices that are relevant to the user task at the moment.

   TDMT is also pliable for various UI forms. As the empirical study showed, we cannot assume ML novices are those who use GUI tools [16]. Designers should deliberately choose one or more interface forms based on their target audience's tooling, mental model, data types and ML tasks they are likely face. At a higher level, there needs be a more reflective and principled discussion on the relationship between ML tools for those who are not experts in ML and tools for those who do not code.

DISCUSSION

ML promises powerful data-driven insights and solutions for people from all walks of life. Emergent ML and HCI research aim to make ML solutions easy to build and accessible to non-experts. Adding to this growing body of research, this work investigated how non-experts build ML solutions for themselves. We further suggested that iML tools might play a more vital role in making ML accessible if it helps non-experts prevent technical pitfalls. We put forward a sensitizing concept to exemplify one near-future solution in this new design space. We encourage the HCI community to join us in evaluating and evolving this design, and more importantly to innovate on more creative forms of user-centered, accessible iML tool designs. Here, we also want to more broadly reflect on our work and the idea of *ML for everyone*.

Making Machine Learning Accessible

The idea of human-centered ML is not new to the research that aims to make ML available to non-experts. Yet this field has largely focused on technical advances. The major vehicle that drives the work to understand end users is the need for more efficient and reliable "human oracles" that compliment automatic ML methods [1, 18, 24].

Through the empirical study and the sensitizing concept, we hope to formulate some changes to the research on accessible ML. We hope to start a discourse centered on how to help people better build learning algorithms, rather than how to enable the algorithms to learn better. We hope more human-centered ML research not only focuses on non-experts' affordability and objective efficiency, but is rooted in an elaborate understanding of their goals, needs, and the contexts in which they use ML.

An elaborate understanding of non-experts could not only make ML more accessible, but inspire creation of new ML applications. For example, our empirical findings suggested that the interactive process of building ML models might have lead to non-experts' greater trust in the learning results. We see critical value in evaluating this observation, as it could potentially open up a new path to improving end-users' trust in ML.

Risks and Limits of Non-Expert Machine Learning

In parallel to the work that makes ML accessible, there should be research to better understand the risks and limitations of non-expert ML. This work has illuminated some signs of ML misuse and its preliminary breakdown by type. Accessible ML tools, if used blindly, could cause perplexities.

One straightforward solution is to embed additional corrective measures in these tools, as we have shown via the sensitizing concept. Future research could extend, evaluate and improve these measures to safeguard the validity and quality of ML models. Additionally, when creating an accessible ML tool, we HCI researchers could more explicitly document its intended users, intended ML tasks, as well as the situations in which its use is not recommended.

As the industry is increasingly calling for "*ML for everyone*", HCI research could provide a reflective and principled discussion on whether this vision is achievable or desirable. Can we identify some general criteria such that, if satisfied, we would agree this is an ML task no longer achievable for a non-expert? Can we identify some basic principles of designing novice-facing ML tools, to more easily and objectively identify the level of ML knowledge needed for their proper use? These are important issues for our community to grapple with and debate moving forward.

Non-expert ML is an exciting area in both industry and HCI research. Having a reflective discussion on the potentials, risks, and limits of non-expert ML would be a vital next step in our collective endeavor to make ML accessible in moving forward. This work serves as one step into this direction.

REFERENCES

1. Saleema Amershi, Maya Cakmak, William Bradley Knox, and Todd Kulesza. 2014. Power to the People: The Role of Humans in Interactive Machine Learning. *AI Magazine* 35, 4 (2014), 105–120. DOI: http://dx.doi.org/10.1609/aimag.v35i4.2513

2. Hugh Beyer and Karen Holtzblatt. 1999. Contextual design. *interactions* 6, 1 (1999), 32–42.

3. Bonsai. 2017. *BONSAI WHITEPAPER: A fundamentally different approach for building intelligent industrial systems*. Technical Report. https://bons.ai/resources.

4. Justin Bozonier. 2015. *Test-Driven Machine Learning*. Packt Publishing Ltd.

5. Joseph Chee Chang, Saleema Amershi, and Ece Kamar. 2017. Revolt: Collaborative Crowdsourcing for Labeling Machine Learning Datasets. In *Proceedings of the 2017 CHI Conference on Human Factors in Computing Systems*. ACM, 2334–2346.

6. Justin Cheng and Michael S. Bernstein. 2015. Flock: Hybrid Crowd-Machine Learning Classifiers. In *Proceedings of the 18th ACM Conference on Computer Supported Cooperative Work & Social Computing - CSCW '15*. ACM Press, New York, New York, USA, 600–611. DOI: http://dx.doi.org/10.1145/2675133.2675214

7. Jerry Alan Fails and Dan R Olsen Jr. 2003. Interactive machine learning. In *Proceedings of the 8th international conference on Intelligent user interfaces*. ACM, 39–45.

8. Matthias Feurer, Aaron Klein, Katharina Eggensperger, Jost Springenberg, Manuel Blum, and Frank Hutter. 2015. Efficient and robust automated machine learning. In *Advances in Neural Information Processing Systems*. 2962–2970.

9. Rebecca Fiebrink, Perry R. Cook, and Dan Trueman. 2011. Human model evaluation in interactive supervised learning. In *Proceedings of the 2011 annual conference on Human factors in computing systems - CHI '11 (CHI '11)*. ACM Press, New York, New York, USA, 147. DOI: http://dx.doi.org/10.1145/1978942.1978965

10. Marco Gillies, Bongshin Lee, Nicolas D'Alessandro, Joëlle Tilmanne, Todd Kulesza, Baptiste Caramiaux, Rebecca Fiebrink, Atau Tanaka, Jérémie Garcia, Frédéric Bevilacqua, Alexis Heloir, Fabrizio Nunnari, Wendy Mackay, and Saleema Amershi. 2016. Human-Centred Machine Learning. In *Proceedings of the 2016 CHI Conference Extended Abstracts on Human Factors in Computing Systems - CHI EA '16*. ACM Press, New York, New York, USA, 3558–3565. DOI: http://dx.doi.org/10.1145/2851581.2856492

11. Mark Hall, Eibe Frank, Geoffrey Holmes, Bernhard Pfahringer, Peter Reutemann, and Ian H Witten. 2009. The WEKA data mining software: an update. *ACM SIGKDD explorations newsletter* 11, 1 (2009), 10–18.

12. David J Hand. 1998. Data mining: Statistics and more? *The American Statistician* 52, 2 (1998), 112–118.

13. Andreas Holzinger, Markus Plass, Katharina Holzinger, Gloria Cerasela Crişan, Camelia-M Pintea, and Vasile Palade. 2016. Towards interactive Machine Learning (iML): applying ant colony algorithms to solve the traveling salesman problem with the human-in-the-loop approach. In *International Conference on Availability, Reliability, and Security*. Springer, 81–95.

14. IBM Watson Machine Learning: Machine Learning for everyone 2016. (2016). http://datascience.ibm.com/blog/machine-learning-for-everyone/

15. David Janzen and Hossein Saiedian. 2005. Test-driven development concepts, taxonomy, and future direction. *Computer* 38, 9 (2005), 43–50.

16. Seungjun Kim, Dan Tasse, Anind K Dey, S Kim, D Tasse, and A K Dey. 2017. Making Machine-Learning Applications for Time-Series Sensor Data Graphical and Interactive. *ACM Trans. Interact. Intell. Syst* 7, 8 (2017). DOI:http://dx.doi.org/10.1145/2983924

17. Todd Kulesza, Margaret Burnett, Weng-Keen Wong, and Simone Stumpf. 2015. Principles of explanatory debugging to personalize interactive machine learning. In *Proceedings of the 20th International Conference on Intelligent User Interfaces*. ACM, 126–137.

18. Besmira Nushi, Ece Kamar, Eric Horvitz, and Donald Kossmann. 2017. On Human Intellect and Machine Failures: Troubleshooting Integrative Machine Learning Systems.. In *AAAI*. 1017–1025.

19. Kayur Patel, Naomi Bancroft, Steven M. Drucker, James Fogarty, Andrew J. Ko, and James Landay. 2010. Gestalt: Integrated Support for Implementation and Analysis in Machine Learning. In *Proceedings of the 23nd annual ACM symposium on User interface software and technology - UIST '10*. ACM Press, New York, New York, USA, 37. DOI: http://dx.doi.org/10.1145/1866029.1866038

20. Kayur Patel, James Fogarty, James A. Landay, and Beverly Harrison. 2008. Examining difficulties software developers encounter in the adoption of statistical machine learning. In *23rd AAAI Conference on Artificial Intelligence and the 20th Innovative Applications of Artificial Intelligence Conference*. Chicago, IL, United States, 1563–1566.

21. Kayur Dushyant Patel. 2012. *Lowering the Barrier to Applying Machine Learning*. Ph.D. Dissertation. University of Washington.

22. Kayur Dushyant Patel. 2013. *Lowering the Barrier to Applying Machine Learning*. Ph.D. Dissertation.

23. Donald A Schon. 1984. *The reflective practitioner: How professionals think in action*. Vol. 5126. Basic books.

24. Patrice Simard, Saleema Amershi, Max Chickering, Alicia Edelman Pelton, Soroush Ghorashi, Chris Meek, Gonzalo Ramos, Jina Suh, Johan Verwey, Mo Wang, and John Wernsing. 2017. *Machine Teaching: A New Paradigm for Building Machine Learning Systems*. Technical Report. Microsoft Research. https://arxiv.org/pdf/1707.06742

25. Simone Stumpf, Vidya Rajaram, Lida Li, Weng Keen Wong, Margaret Burnett, Thomas Dietterich, Erin Sullivan, and Jonathan Herlocker. 2009. Interacting meaningfully with machine learning systems: Three experiments. *International Journal of Human Computer Studies* 67, 8 (2009), 639–662. DOI: http://dx.doi.org/10.1016/j.ijhcs.2009.03.004

26. TensorFlow: Smarter machine learning, for everyone 2016. (2016). https://www.google.com/intl/en/about/main/tensorflow/.

27. Udemy Online Course: Applied machine learning for Everyone 2017. (2017). https://www.udemy.com/applied-machine-learning-for-everyone/.

28. Steven A Wolfman, Tessa Lau, Pedro Domingos, and Daniel S Weld. 2001. Mixed initiative interfaces for learning tasks: SMARTedit talks back. In *Proceedings of*

the 6th international conference on Intelligent user interfaces. ACM, 167–174.

29. Qian Yang, John Zimmerman, Aaron Steinfeld, and Anthony Tomasic. 2016. Planning Adaptive Mobile Experiences When Wireframing. In *Proceedings of the 2016 ACM Conference on Designing Interactive Systems - DIS '16*. ACM Press, Brisbane, QLD, Australia, 565–576. DOI:http://dx.doi.org/10.1145/2901790.2901858

30. Xiaojin Zhu. 2015. Machine Teaching: An Inverse Problem to Machine Learning and an Approach Toward Optimal Education. In *Proceedings of the Twenty-Ninth AAAI Conference on Artificial Intelligence (AAAI'15)*. AAAI Press, 4083–4087. http://dl.acm.org/citation.cfm?id=2888116.2888288

31. John Zimmerman, Erik Stolterman, and Jodi Forlizzi. 2010. An analysis and critique of Research through Design: towards a formalization of a research approach. In *Proceedings of the 8th ACM Conference on Designing Interactive Systems*. ACM, 310–319.

32. Martin Zinkevich. 2017. Rules of Machine Learning: Best Practices for ML Engineering. (2017).

Investigating How Experienced UX Designers Effectively Work with Machine Learning

Qian Yang[1] Alex Scuito[1] John Zimmerman[1] Jodi Forlizzi [1] Aaron Steinfeld[2]
HCI Institute[1] Robotics Institute[2]
Carnegie Mellon University, Pittsburgh PA, USA
{yangqian, steinfeld}@cmu.edu {scuitoalex, johnz, forlizzi}@cs.cmu.edu

ABSTRACT
Machine learning (ML) plays an increasingly important role in improving a user's experience. However, most UX practitioners face challenges in understanding ML's capabilities or envisioning what it might be. We interviewed 13 designers who had many years of experience designing the UX of ML-enhanced products and services. We probed them to characterize their practices. They shared they do not view themselves as ML experts, nor do they think learning more about ML would make them better designers. Instead, our participants appeared to be the most successful when they engaged in ongoing collaboration with data scientists to help envision what to make and when they embraced a data-centric culture. We discuss the implications of these findings in terms of UX education and as opportunities for additional design research in support of UX designers working with ML.

Author Keywords
User Experience Design; UX Practice; Machine Learning; Design Material; Interaction Design.

ACM Classification Keywords
H.5.m. Information Interfaces and Presentation (e.g. HCI): Miscellaneous

INTRODUCTION
Machine learning (ML) plays an increasingly important role in improving a user's experience. From mundane spam filters to personalized newsfeeds to conversational agents like Alexa to the promise of driverless cars, many products and services now improve user experience (UX) with algorithms that learn from an underlying data source. This growing reliance on ML somewhat implies that UX designers have become quite skilled at envisioning new products and services that leverage ML's capabilities. Interestingly, recent research indicates that many UX designers are unprepared to effectively leverage ML capabilities [9, 32]. For example, a recent survey showed that many UX designers struggle to understand the capabilities and limitations of ML. Also, they typically joined projects towards the end, after the functional decisions had been made. "*Design teams are simply putting lipstick on the pig*" [9]. Other work showed designers often fail to notice obvious places where ML could improve UX [32].

DIS '18, June 9–13, 2018, , Hong Kong

ISBN 978-1-4503-5198-0/18/06...$15.00
DOI: 10.1145/3196709.3196730

Recently, design researchers and educators began taking actions to address this problem. A few have developed designer focused education materials, meant to teach the technical concepts of ML [13, 14, 15]. This work implies that designers should understand the mechanics of algorithms in order to work effectively with ML. Other researchers created design patterns to help practitioners recognize common situations where ML can improve UX [32]. Others organized workshops, bringing together groups of artists, designers, and technologists to collectively explore how ML might function as a creative material [11, 16].

The work to make ML more accessible to designers has led some to discuss *ML as a design material* [31]. Our research adds to this growing area of inquiry. Instead of investigating problems designers face when working with ML or working on tools meant to make ML more accessible to designers, we chose to investigate the design practices of some of the few UX designers who regularly create new products and services that use ML to enhance UX. We hoped that their approach and reflections would reveal new insights around UX design education and insights on the kinds of tools needed for enhancing UX with ML.

We interviewed 13 designers who all had at least four years of experience designing ML enhanced UX. The interviews produced several interesting findings: 1) Designers shared that they knew very little about how ML works, and this was not a priority for them. They instead used designerly abstractions and popular exemplars to explain what ML is and to communicate design ideas with each other. 2) ML projects are longer in preparation and scope than other design projects. During the preparation stage, designers evolved their ideas in close collaboration with data scientists; They did not deliver fully formed designs to a technical team. 3) Designers "play" with quantitative data during all phases of a design project. Our findings suggest an alternative to the common assumption that teaching designers how ML works as the most effective way of helping them engage with it as a design material. Instead, design researchers hoping to aid practitioners might focus on providing abstractions, exemplars, and new tools and methods that support designers collaborating with data scientists.

This paper makes two contributions. First, it presents a rare description of how experienced designers effectively worked with ML. It offers a point of reference for UX education; equipping novice designers with knowledge and skills needed for the best practice in industry. Second, this work illuminates many open research questions in understanding and supporting UX design of ML. It suggests an agenda for important future research topics.

RELATED WORK

Making Machine Learning Available to Designers

Design researchers investigating ML noted 1) designers overlook simple opportunities to utilize ML and that 2) design-led innovation of ML is rare [32]. In a recent survey, practitioners stated they could not easily envision novel and interesting uses of ML. While they understood how ML worked broadly, they did not understand what was needed to design with it [9]. Based on observations of these challenges, design researchers and practitioners have begun making efforts to help UX designers work with ML as a design material. These efforts advanced in a variety of directions, but they typically fall into two broad characterizations.

One characterization presumes that designers cannot work with a material they do not fully understand, redirecting designers' focus away from the interactive artifact towards the statistical processes of ML products [6, 27]. Several books, courses and online collections of materials help designers learn about ML (i.e. [5, 13, 14, 15]). The book *Machine Learning for Designers*, for example, reviews concepts of supervised and unsupervised learning, as well as common analogies of how ML works [14]. This is quite different from the traditional ways of moving new technology from research to design practice, which assume designers do *not* need to understand the technical specifics of the materials they use to design.

A second characterization, less popular than the first, works to demonstrate divergent ways of designing ML, sensitizing designers to its rich design possibilities. Yang et al. developed a set of design patterns and a boundary object to help designers better communicate their designs to data scientists [32]. Other researchers have explored various themes related to the interaction design challenges ML imposes, such as intelligibility [18], animistic design [19], and design for the peace of mind [12]. An university design course asked students to create a "useless artificial intelligence" product, encouraging students to engage with ML through a making process that probes affordances, capabilities, and limitations of this technology [29]. Instead of teaching designers what ML is, this approach challenges designers to envision applications technologists would likely never imagine.

Design Practice and Collaboration with Data Scientists

Designing a partially known material for uncertain situations is a common task for any interaction designer [24, 17]. To envision things that have never before existed, designers engage in reflective conversations with design materials [10, 23]. Understanding how designers engage in this conversation and how the materials "talk back to the designer" is an important component in understanding design practice [23].

Research about design practice has shown that designers can handle complex design materials by using simple methods, such as sketching, brainstorming, body-storming, and diagramming with sticky notes [24]. HCI research on UX practitioners discussed software as a design material, noting that designers often need to use developers as a proxy in conversations around the possibilities of software design [21].

With the increasing use of ML to enhance UX, there has been speculation that data scientists and ML will decrease the need for UX design [5, 8]. Girardin and Lathia's investigation of the designer-data scientists collaboration within their own organization seems to confirm this speculation [12]. Additionally, some HCI researchers observed that when developers use statistics to make design decisions, the role of designers can diminish [2]. As AI becoming the new UX [4, 32], some even claimed that "data scientists are the next UX designers" [8]. In spite of this speculation, we found no work investigating how design practitioners collaborate with data scientists in industry.

We see a need for more studies UX practice as it relates to ML. The HCI and IxD communities have learned over time that the effectiveness of design research depends on its fit with the nature of design practice [1, 24]. In the midst of diverse orientations and approaches to moving ML to practice, we need to understand how UX practitioners actually work with ML. We need to understand not only the challenges, but also the successful attempts in designing with ML that have produced the many ML products people now use every day. This paper takes a step towards addressing this need.

METHOD

We wanted to understand the current practices used by UX designers who regularly design ML products and services. Previous work focused on the struggles that less experienced designers often face. We were interested in how designers with lots of experience designing with ML work compared to traditional UX design. We hoped to identify opportunities for new design research that could make it easier for all UX designers to work more effectively with ML as a design material.

We conducted retrospective interviews with UX design practitioners who have played an active role in creating widely adopted ML-driven products. We recruited participants by leveraging our network of alumni who work in practice; mostly former master's students now working in industry. We then used snowball sampling, asking them to recommend other designers with experience working with ML, to grow our set of participants.

Education	Professional Role	Example Design Project	Org Size	Exp.
HCI	Design Manager	Intelligent features in multiple messaging or conversation apps	>10,000	10+ yrs
Design	Design Manager	Intelligent features in a media consumption app to better match content providers and users	>10,000	10+ yrs
Design	UX Designer	Decision support app for physicians	1,000 - 10,000	10+ yrs
Design	Designer-turned PM	Language learning app; patient coaching app.	100 - 1,000	10+ yrs
Design and HCI	Designer	Intelligent tutoring feature for education apps	<100	10+ yrs
CS and HCI	Designer-turned entrepreneur	New messaging and efficiency apps	<100	10+ yrs
Design and HCI	Designer	Recommender in a shared service app	>10,000	7-10 yrs
CogPsy	UX researcher	Intelligent reminder in a social media app	>10,000	7-10 yrs
EE and Design	UX designer	New wearable health product	>10,000	5-7 yrs
HCI	Designer	Recommender in a text processing software	>10,000	
Design	Service designer	New health coaching app	>10,000	5-7 yrs
Psychology	UX researcher	Intelligent feature in a social media app	>10,000	4 yrs
HCI	UX researcher	Intelligent content recommendation for a media consumption product	>10,000	4 yrs

Table 1. Interview Participants. We interviewed UX designers who had more than four years of experience in designing ML-enhanced products. Many had more than 10 years of related experience.

We chose retrospective interviews because observations of current practice seemed impractical. First, actual cases unfold very slowly, over many months. Second, the practitioners we encountered all worked on new projects they could not discuss for reasons of industrial competition.

We interviewed 13 participants. All had designed products and services that enhance UX with ML for more than 4 years. Most had worked on these types of products and services for more than 10 years. Nine participants designed products used by more than one billion users. Two worked on successful special-purpose ML applications: a clinical decision support systems and a wearable health coaching system. The others worked to extend existing products with new ML features. Table 1 provides a summary of the participants' background and the type of projects they described in our study.

We asked all participants to complete a pre-interview survey where they described their education and professional background, as well as their familiarity with concepts from UX design, statistics, machine learning, and data storage. We then interviewed participants, asking them to walk us through a recent design case where they used ML to improve the UX. Throughout the interviews, we probed them to get details on their process and to surface the triggers that drove specific decisions for what to do and how to work. We paid particular attention to two previously expressed challenges from the literature [9]. First, UX designers often struggle to understand the capabilities of ML, so we probed on what they did to understand these. Second, designers working on ML projects are often only included at the end of a project, so we wanted to probe on when they joined projects or if they ever initiated projects on their own.

To better understand how they perceived ML, we asked them to draw an illustration of how the systems they designed worked. We wanted to see how they represented things like data collecting, labeling, and training. At the end of the interview, we asked participants to reflect on what they viewed as the major differences between how they design when working with ML and when working on products and services that don't use ML. We asked them to share, "*the things you wish you had known about before you started your career in designing ML systems*".

We recorded and transcribed the interviews. We then reviewed the transcripts, pulled out important insights, and used affinity diagrams to synthesize across the interviews in order to identify thematic patterns. We created and consolidated process models detailing how the different projects unfolded and how the designers collaborated with data scientists. We chose affinity diagrams and models instead of grounded theory for several reasons. These methods are typically used in HCI and interaction design practice. Our intention was not to build up a detailed theory of current design practices performed by only a tiny number of designers. Instead, we chose to follow a more practice-based approach because our focus was on generating ideas that could help practitioners other than the practitioners we were studying. We wanted to inform the design of new resources and tools for less experienced practitioners by better understanding what these few experienced practitioners do.

FINDINGS

We organized our findings around three themes: work participants did to understand ML capabilities, changes to the design process that seem directly related to working with ML, and participants' acknowledgement of a data culture. These themes are not exclusive, and some aspects spill across two or all three.

We noticed two distinct work cultures that had a large impact on how participants worked. A few participants worked in large, AI-focused organizations, where designers had access to many data scientists and the companies actively promoted innovation via ML. The others worked in environments with much more limited access to data scientists. In the detailed findings below, we note where this difference impacted the work they described.

Understanding Machine Learning Capabilities

Participants almost all stated that they "*know very little*" about how ML works. They characterized their ML literacy as "*understanding at a very high level... [at the level of] knowing what a classifier is and what a label is.*" Only one participant (P6) had taken any ML course; an online course taken well after graduation. P6 was the only participant with a CS degree, and had transitioned from CS to UX while earning an MHCI degree. All other participants claimed they gained familiarity with ML mostly by reading online articles found on Medium and Reddit.

Interestingly, participants did not feel their lack of technical knowledge hindered their ability to design or to collaborate with data scientists. They shared that they worked on the design issues, not the technical issues, and that working with ML required "*... more design savvy*". Several participants claimed designing the user interaction was "*the actual challenge.*"

> *I don't think of ML as affecting my interaction designs or not. I think about it more like impacting certain algorithms that are inputs into users' experience.* (P14)

This issue often came up when they made illustrations of their ML systems. Many drew a line in the middle, creating a distinct break between the users and the technology. P10's illustration, for example, had a dense collection of design factors on the left: usage scenario, user's frustration, and "*a very simple thing*" the design team thought ML could do to aid the user. They then drew a line followed by several boxes representing the back-end mechanisms. The ML was one of these boxes, and they noted it was really not so simple.

Most claimed that they learned to work with ML similarly to how they learned to work with other interactive technologies. "*ML is just like JavaScript*", several participants claimed. They did not seem to view themselves as technology experts, but instead as UX design experts who had great comfort working with a variety of technologies, and ML was one of these.

Designerly Abstractions and Examplars

We found almost nothing in common with the way designers spoke about ML and the way education materials meant to teach ML for engineers. Participants rarely spoke of ML in technical terms. For example, they never talked about supervised or unsupervised learning (common starting point for teaching ML). Instead, they appeared to think with, and work with, abstractions; simple insights about an ML capability had had implicitly linked with generating value for users. These were much more abstract than design patterns. More similar to design patterns, they often used exemplars to communicate these abstractions.

> Q: What does machine learning do?
> P7: *Some try to recognize intent, a bit like auto-correct. Some are intent prediction like Clippy. Anyone who is working on assistive technology, is working on some class of that problem.*

In the excerpt above, P7 describes ML using abstractions of its capabilities: recognize intents and predict intents. He then ground these capabilities through the use of exemplars: auto-correct and Clippy. We found this manner of describing ML across most participants.

Participants most often described the capabilities of ML as it related to the user's utility. Their abstractions narrowly oriented towards both the users and scenarios related to their designs. They never spoke of general taxonomies of ML functionality or specific algorithms. Some examples:

> *We use machine learning so that we can build something that can personalize for a lot of people.* (P3)

> *In consumer tech, we try to raise the level of abstraction [of user commands] rather than doing everything manually.* (P7)

> *ML gets users directly into the task they really need to do.* (P1)

> *We are doing a recommendation system of sorts. As a product designer [not a technologist], I think about that as how can we show an evolving relationship between a user and our service... [I want users] foreseeing our relationship improve, where the relationship is the recommendations we are giving them.* (P14)

The abstractions almost always appeared with exemplars. The abstractions served as a general insight about an ML capability and provided an understanding of how it worked. The design exemplars provided specific interaction possibilities and a glimpse of a possible felt experience. In our interviews, participants frequently referenced widely-known exemplars including Clippy, autocorrect, email spam filtering, and Tay the Twitter bot. They used these to help describe the capabilities of ML; the form, function, and user experience; and the potential breakdowns that might occur.

Participants actively grew their working set of abstractions and exemplars. They looked for these in both online articles and in competitors' products. One participant recalled that she carried around many conversational virtual assistants so that she could learn the feedback different products gave in response to the same instruction, in different contexts.

The number and variety of exemplars participants used varied wildly, and those with the largest working sets seemed to be the most successful and comfortable at using ML to enhance UX. Participants working at AI-focused organizations had a significant advantage in building their working set of exemplars and abstractions. These organizations had data scientists frequently giving demos as one way to sensitize their design teams to emerging ML capabilities. "*So many people demo for me. I don't even know whom to call if I have an idea and want to consult a data scientist.*" Participants at smaller or less AI-focused organizations had much more limited access to data scientists. They appeared to consider and propose fewer design alternatives. They were also more likely to use only the most familiar interaction forms, such as recommender or reminder, when describing their process.

Design Process and Collaboration

Participants shared that working with ML took much longer than when designing other UX products and services. We wanted to synthesize the actual time span ML projects required. However, we found that none of our participants had worked on an ML product from its initial ideation until its final release. We could see that some ML projects had lasted for more than four years.

> *ML has a different time-frame for design iteration. Longer initial development, but then ongoing iteration. It felt like building a feature versus building a framework. When you ship it, it's not the end of it. They cycle, and data drives the next step.* (P3)

A consolidation of participants' design process narratives revealed an ML design process. It starts with a long preparatory stage (stage 1), during which designers and data scientists identify a design goal that is both technically viable and that appears to have a high likelihood of improving the user's experience. Once a team had settled on the design goal, scientists and developers developed the system and designers crafted its interaction design (stage 2). In stage 3, they together invested in frequent iterative releases and assessments in order to improve user adoption.

All participants described stage 2 in their ML projects. Stage 2 is a central stage that all projects that participants described went through. Stage 1 happened only at the large, AI-focused organizations. Few projects had made it to stage 3. Below we describe three distinct design stages.

Stage 1: Concept Development

New ML design seemed to only happen within the AI-focused organizations. It started with a long, preparatory stage involving two activities. First. participants collected log data form current services their organization provided. Participants examined the log with sensitivity to specific patterns. They often seemed to search for patterns they thought might be there more than they would data mine to discover unexpected patterns. They imagined what user behavior might be worth learning and what learned interactions might be valuable for users. One designer described this process as "*just me being really excited about the product*" (P14)

Second, participants would share these inchoate ideas with data scientists. This happened informally, outside of any specific development projects, and they had iterative interactions, where they might return to the same data scientists with new or refined ideas. They noted that the data scientists had a very different view of scenario-based design. They used scenarios to validate what an idea might be instead of using scenarios to generate and refine new ideas. "*Data scientists use scenarios to validate designers' assumptions about how the product should work, [and then] toss back ideas*".

The conversation between designers and data scientists focused on identifying a design goal worth pursuing. Often this would lead the discussion away from working with ML. The discussions focused on coming up with a "good enough" idea, and it did not address either its exact technical feasibility or experiential quality. Participants particularly pushed the data scientists to understand what might be technically possible.

> *(I) framed the questions not as do you know what would work, but in your gut, do you think this would be possible. Possible on a scale of 1-10.* (P8)

> *The level of detail I'll need to discuss with [the data scientists] is understanding the capability of what could be possible. I didn't need to get into specific detail about it.* (P3)

> *Those [design ideas] are a series of aspirations. Rather than saying what data do we have [...] Could we challenge the data team to figure out how to get close to that?* (P9)

The collaboration at this stage focused on co-evolving a shared vision between the two areas of expertise, an ideal user experience that was worth pursing and ML could potentially help achieve. This shared vision often took form of a unique abstraction of ML capabilities that emerged out of both UX and ML. Instead of saying "machine learning", designers and data scientists might select an expression better suited to the context of their product. For example, some used "affinity" to describe the match between a user and a piece of content. Others used "personalization" to describe the intended, evolution of the relationship between the product and the user. Participants characterized these discussions as a chance for both sides to learn from the others' expertise.

> *There is no such a framework or something, but I think later there is a kind of an acknowledgment when we talk about "personalization"... An acknowledgment that a more personalized experience is a better experience that one is less likely to walk away from.* (P14)

> *I gained a better understanding of the capabilities of the algorithms. The data scientist gained a better understanding of what was worth pursuing.* (P3)

Stage 2: Interaction Design and Assessment

Stage 1 produced preliminary understanding of the data, and it established a shared vision between the designers and the data scientists that met the company's goals. Stage 2 focused on refining this vision. In many organizations, this was the stage when UX designers were invited to join a project. During stage 2, participants described developing "*a funnel of visions, a funnel of what exists and what is possible in the company*" (P8). This would advance towards defining a single, valuable ML feature that was both experientially valuable and technically feasible.

> *It's definitely an ongoing process. We had a lot of basic things to get working. [...] Once we get that improved, then we will probably be adding more ML stack onto the system.* (P14)

> *Design is always about a new product and a complete, larger vision. But that doesn't make it easy to build. We chunk. We talk about stages of development.*" (P8)

Once a product idea was clearly formulated and agreed upon, participants shared that they would next put the required resources in place. Participants would start to design the interactions in parallel with the technical development. Participants explored many possibilities. They also spoke about assessing their interaction designs based on following criteria:

- *Could users produce effective labels needed to train the ML system?*
- *Could users make sense of the ML inference [or adaptation] and did they view it as valuable?*
- *Could users easily recover from ML [inference] errors?*

Participants used a combination of traditional UX methods such as user studies, sketching, and usability testing. They also engaged in continued negotiations with technologists. Collectively, these activities allowed them to craft the user experience. This iterative process continued until the interaction design had matured to a point it could be handed over to a front-end development team.

Today, most new features for online products and services only see broad release after passing a series of A/B tests, and the same process was used for ML features. These tests are meant to reduce the risk of user abandonment and/or reduction in new user conversion rates. Almost all participants spoke of A/B testing as a critical part of improving their design, and this related to both improving the algorithms' performance and improving the interaction. In most cases, the participants shared that they offered users the option to turn a new ML feature off. This appeared to help them view passing of the A/B tests as less challenging.

Stage 3 - Release and Continued Refinement

Few of the projects described by participants made it to stage 3. One notable exception was P7's worked on a message classifier. At the beginning of stage 3, they worked to improve the poor adoption rate. This became "*a really key moment in thinking about design of systems like this*". Stage 3 had to do with refinement that could make a project successful.

> *We had a classifier that predicts whether or not an incoming message is important . . . and the performance is scary good. . . . However, a vast majority of users didn't turn the feature on or soon opted out. When you dug into why that was, people would say "I don't even know what's important to me, how am I gonna trust the ML system to know it's important to me?"*

> *The core insight my research team had was that people are trying to figure out whether they are gonna trust that system, and the way they figure it out to think of it as a person. If I hand a stack of messages to a person, someone I don't know, is it possible that person could figure out with some accuracy if that message is important to me. Most people's take was "no, I barely know it myself".*

Stage 3 sent the UX designers into the field to investigate how people used their system in order to improve the design. The team improved the design by moving away from a binary classification (important or not important) to a small set of categories. The new design made it clear why something might not be important by classifying it as "promotional materials," something the team felt any human would be able to do. The new design used the same ML technology and proved to be a huge success.

The few participants who had projects reach stage 3 stated that such a re-design was inevitable because some mental model issues are difficult to catch before products launch. They felt they "*have to do this level of work on the design side*" (P2,7,13) so that users cannot only recover from the errors, but can understand the errors, and at the same time preserve some level of trust in the system.

> P1 describing why design problems for a chatbot auto-reply feature were unforeseeable: *We help you [users] say that you already gonna say. We do it a bit faster. We are actually influencing what you are saying, but not predicting what you are saying.*

Embracing a Data-Driven Culture

We probed participants on what they needed to be effective and what UX students should know in order to effectively envision ML innovations. Their responses collectively revealed an acknowledgement that they all worked in data centric environments, and that designers needed to embrace this data centricity in order to have impact. They spoke of the importance of learning to speak the language of quantitative data and data science (e.g., telemetry, analytics, A/B testing, covariance, correlation). In the pre-interview surveys, participants responded that they worked with these concepts constantly (Figure 1). "*This is how engineers measure and businesses do things. This can influence how you design.*"

To help embrace a more data-centric culture, participants shared that they engaged in new design activities. They used a combination of qualitative and quantitative methods to advocate for their design. Specifically, they developed new skills around collecting telemetry data (data remotely collected from current products and services), and they generated data visualizations as one way of making sense of their data. In addition to working with data, participants shared that their collaborating data scientists share their role as a user advocate and as facilitator of incorporating domain experts' insights; something that did not happen with other, technical development efforts.

Designing Telemetry Data

Participants frequently asked ML specialists about how people use the product, how they feel about it, and what

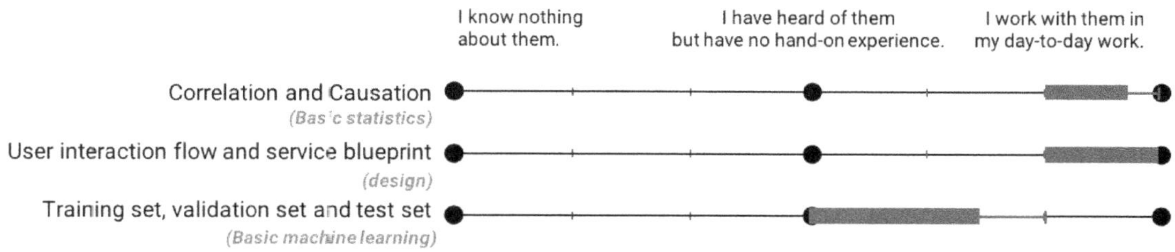

Figure 1. Participants' familiarity with concepts from statistics, UX design and machine learning.

problems they had that could be rectified by design. To help answer these questions, participants shared that they designed telemetry systems so their products can better track users' interactions. They used the data to capture meaningful and accurate snapshots of user behaviors.

Designers began to define their design goals in relation to the user behavioral data collected telemetrically, in the form of a "*matrix for a good experience*" (P2,8,12). This matrix would later be used to measure the success of their designs through a suite of A/B tests. Designers use these matrices to "*influence the engineers to think a different way, not in terms of single A/B test, but a suite of tests.*" The telemetry data thus became a space of exchange between designers and data scientists. The data helped to expand the narrow scope of A/B tests and to more holistically address user experience over a larger course of interactions.

Designing Data Visualizations

Participants worked to interpret user behavior data. Most utilized customized dashboards that translated mundane log data snapshots into user stories and insights. Several taught themselves to create data visualization tools, creating visualizations that used by data scientists, engineers, and fellow designers in their organizations. They designed dashboards and visualizations to combine an immersive and an analytical way of understanding, so that the quantitative analysis of user behavior "*do not privilege data scientists*".

> *Data scientists have their methods, and I have my bag of tricks. They have kernels and clusters, and we are good at telling rich, compelling user stories. How can we look at hundreds and thousands of attempts, and also reach out to inquire more about what happened, what the breakdown was?* (P14)

A few designers further utilized these data visualizations as vehicles for conducting user studies. One participant recalled that the first thing he did when joining the project was to list "*a series of questions about user behavior that data analytics can answer*" (P8). They then bookmarked the corresponding data matrix on the telemetry analytics tool the team used. Every morning they checked the new incoming log data against this matrix. When they noticed an intriguing user behavior, they emailed the user to inquire the back story, details, and sometimes set up follow-up interviews. They labeled this method as "*qualitative study in a quantitative scale.*"

Advocating for Users Along with Domain Experts

Besides data scientists, designers also worked closely with domain experts during all phases of a ML project, especially projects that design special-purpose applications. For example, P12 designed a reminder feature of a social network product in collaboration with psychologists who specialized in human perception and memory; P15 designed an intelligent tutoring system on biology in collaboration with middle school teachers and biologists.

While cross-disciplinary collaboration is not new nor unique to ML projects, participants suggested that when working with ML, data scientists and domain experts overlapped with the responsibility in their work to make sense of and predict user behavior. They were no longer the sole user advocates. Most participants repeatedly stressed the unique skills designers brought to the table in relation to other human-centered ML roles; some designers also adapted new methods to manage and communicate their designs:

> *I embedded an information-motivation-behavior framework (in user data analysis). It showed everyone that just (user) information is not enough.* (P8)

> *Designers have domain knowledge about how people typically respond to certain things, how easy is it to change a certain behavior. Designers helping with shaping the experience, with the missing part, the things you have not thought about.* (P9)

DISCUSSION

ML plays an increasingly important role in how new products and services deliver an improved user experience. Today, UX designers face challenges in understanding ML capabilities, in envisioning new products and services, and in collaborating effectively with data scientists. Our study of UX designers who have had years of experience designing ML enhanced products and services adds to this growing area of research. We found that these UX designers do not view themselves as ML experts, nor do they think that learning more about ML would make them better ML designers. Instead, participants appeared to be the most successful when they engaged in ongoing collaboration with data scientists to help envision what to make and when they embraced a data-centric culture and became proactive at using data in their design practice.

Below, we reflect on how these findings point to needs and opportunities related to the education of new UX designers who wish to enter a field where they can innovate with the possibilities of ML. We also reflect on opportunities for additional design research that can better inform the HCI community about the current disconnect between UX practice and innovation via ML and that can create new resources and tools that allow all UX designers to more effectively engage with ML as a design material.

Preparing UX Design Students

Like others in the HCI community [4, 9, 32], we promote the idea of ML as a design material. We hope to enable designers to leverage ML in their designs, and to conceive of entirely new ways to use ML. The practice of experienced designers provides a point of reference for this effort. We see two main ways HCI and UX educators can better prepare students to more successfully enter industry: training them to work and think with data and providing opportunities for them to collaborate with data scientists.

Designing in a Data-Driven Culture

Many education efforts aiming to improve designers' ability to work with ML has focused on teaching statistics and ML algorithms (i.e. [5, 14, 32]). Our findings suggest an additional skillset — basic interpretation and manipulation of quantitative data. Use of telemetry data and A/B tests to assess and measure user behavior is not new or unique to ML. However, we observed that ML design teams used these skills with great frequency.

Basic data literacy and the ability to draw quantitative user insights from telemetry data would benefit designers in the increasingly data-driven cooperate culture. Student designers should learn to speak the language of data, analytics, and A/B tests as an extension of their user-centered training. Existing cross-disciplinary courses such as "Data Storytelling" and "Data Visualization" could be leveraged in support of this. Learning these skill has the added benefit of help designers work on non-ML projects that also rely on analytics for insights.

Additional experience in integrating data analytics and qualitative user study methods is also likely to benefit student designers. UX education can provide a disciplined discussion on the advantages and disadvantages of each approach, and how they might best be used together. In our study, all participants used both qualitative and quantitative methods. They invented several design techniques toward this goal, for example, using telemetry data system as a way of understanding user behavior quantitatively, recruiting user study participants based on log data, and identifying design goals through a matrix of telemetry data so as to evaluate their designs through a suite of A/B tests. These methods could serve a starting point for UX courses and programs that aim to cultivate UX designers who can work with both quantitative and qualitative methods.

Collaboration with Data Scientists

Effective collaboration with data scientists was critical for all of our participants. In working with ML, participants started by establishing a shared understanding with collaborating data scientists in order to discover a goal or innovation to pursue. Participants then experimented with various design ideas, pushing the boundaries of technical constraint. Data scientists tested design ideas and fed technical limitations back to designers. Students would benefit from having some exposure to this new kind of ideation and iterative design process. This pattern of collaboration enabled our participants to play a central role in shaping both the function and form of ML applications. Our participants used data scientists as a proxy to have a conversation with the material of ML. New designs arose as a part of their design intention, rather than from the availability of data or algorithm.

This emerging form of collaboration should not yet be considered a best practice, but it was the best practice we observed. Student designers entering industry now and in the near future will need to work with data scientists in this unstructured manner, with very few boundary objects to help scaffold their collaborations. We recommend that UX and HCI educators create more ML related courses designed to attract cross-disciplinary students; for example, courses that require user researchers, designers, data scientists, and software engineers to work together. Students would benefit from experiencing this collaborative, creative approach.

Research Opportunities in Supporting UX Practice and Education

This study also surfaced many immediate research opportunities in supporting UX practice: 1) developing designerly abstractions of ML's technical capabilities, 2) developing examplars and sensitizing concepts of ML-enhanced designs, and 3) creating boundary objects that bridge UX and ML expertise.

Designerly Abstractions of ML

We advocate for research to develop resources that make the mechanisms of ML more available to designers. Previous research reported that some UX designers could fail to understand ML "specifically," even when they understand how ML systems generally work [9]. Our study echoes this. The designers comprehend ML in notably different ways than its textbook definitions; they understand ML largely through abstractions and examplars.

The abstractions served as a frame through which designers reflected on the design challenges at hand and made new assertions about how ML might provide value for users. They freed designers from grappling with technical limitations when sketching, empowering them to envision ML applications that moved beyond current archetypical forms. They served as boundary objects, allowing designers to discuss what users value with data scientists and to address issues of context. They also fostered new design ideas, serving as bridges between technical capabilities and design possibilities.

We suspect that many of the abstractions participants shared would generalize well beyond the specific applications they were working on. For example, participants stated that ML enables "*an experience personalized for everyone*" (P3), "*an evolving relationship with the users*" (P14), and "*handling more abstract user instructions*" (P7), and these typically matched with other UX values that HCI research has raised over time [12, 31]. Extending, evaluating, and documenting these abstractions offers a clear space for design research. We encourage HCI researchers aid UX practitioners to develop a large suite of these abstractions, possibly by deconstructing current products and services that employ ML. Our participants developed such abstractions over months and even years of collaboration with data scientists. A ready repository of ML abstractions could potentially expedite this process, enabling novice designers to grasp the design possibilities of ML and build a rapport with technologists much faster.

A robust set of these abstractions would help to evolve the understanding of ML as a design material. It could function as a kind of taxonomy that is likely to be radically different from ones used by data scientists; a taxonomy focused on the match of contextual capability and user value.

Design researchers could advance the abstractions by creating many instantiations of the same abstraction as a way of investigating the opportunity space. For example, P14 described how ML enables users to engage in an unfolding relationship with the service, which evolves with user interaction. Design researchers can investigate many different kinds of evolving relationships between users and ML-enhanced products, looking for the best opportunities and unintended consequences linked to different forms. These design inquiries could then function as sensitizing concepts, allowing practitioners better operationalize the suite of abstractions.

Design Examplars and Sensitizing Concepts

In addition to abstractions, our participants used examplars to comprehend and communicate ML's more nuanced design qualities. A set of widely known examplars – Clippy, Tay, auto-correct and email spam filters – codified a rudimentary set of algorithm capabilities and interactions, as well as limitations and frustrations they have personally experienced.

Interestingly, designers in our study only referenced a few classic, and some failed, designs despite the fact that many commercial applications employ ML today. They seemed to only notice successful designs when they studied competitor products, comparing multiple ML interactions across different products, users, and contexts. We suspect that designers in our study failed to recognize many ML designs that they use every day, especially the ones that have so successfully adapted to their interactions that they have become invisible or unremarkable [26].

The frequent use of exemplars suggests that they would be a great way to communicate ML capabilities and limitations to UX practitioners. To help expand designers' perceived application of ML, design researchers could assemble a collection of well-documented examplars. A wide variety of HCI technical research that uses ML could also provide a source of exemplars and this could help to transfer these ideas to practice.

We speculate that this reliance on explicitly documented exemplars points reveals a huge opportunity for sensitizing concepts; designs created to open up the space for design innovation by sensitizing researchers and practitioners to the breadth of possibility [3, 33]. Design researchers could create sensitizing concepts to communicate ML design opportunities that are not instantly recognizable. Demonstrating a functional ML system to designers might not be enough to sensitize them, as many of these systems have weak connections to divergent user experiences after repeated use. Some work is needed to explore the diverse forms of research artifacts and knowledge representations, and to deliberately choose the ones that most effectively sensitize practitioners.

Boundary Objects for UX and Machine Learning Expertise

Our interviews captured an intimate, constant, cross-disciplinary collaboration when creating ML products. This is somewhat different from the design and technical collaborations found in a traditional UX design [7], where designers typically deliver a fully formed design to a technical team to implement. We see opportunities for new collaboration tools that help designers better work with data scientists. Previous work has proposed the use of boundary objects that scaffold the conversation between UX and ML expertise in creating adaptive UIs [32]. Our findings suggest similar work to be potentially valuable for many other application domains of ML.

We also see value in data visualizations and tools that serve the particular needs of UX designers. In our study, participants taught themselves to capture "rich and compelling user stories" from telemetry data that were different from the data scientists' insights. Designers frequently ask: How do users use the system? What is the matrix for a good user experience? What are the situations where design can make things better? Data tools for UX designers could surface some answers to these frequently asked questions. The visualizations could also serve as a boundary object for discussing user behavior patterns.

Our interviews showed that designers who lacked effective access to data scientists explored fewer design ideas and more often quickly resorted to familiar designs of ML. Previous design research has focused on enabling and improving designer and data scientist collaboration, assuming that capable data scientists are readily available [12, 32]. However, our study indicates that this assumption in not always true. Many designers in our study lacked access to dedicated or even proficient data scientists, especially the ones working at startups, small technology companies, and non-IT-focused companies. Despite efforts to make ML available to everyone [28, 25], the fact that proficient data scientists were scarce might be a reality that most designers will face.

There is a real need for design tools and methodologies that support designers who lack constant access to capable data scientists. For example, ML tools for designers could simulate the role of the data scientists, enabling designers to quickly evaluate the feasibility of their ideas when sketching. We also see opportunities for constructive design research to demonstrate creative designs that use off-the-shelf, ML plug-ins; designs that do not need intensive ML development effort to implement.

Open Research Questions

We have discussed research opportunities around disseminating the current best practices in industry for UX designers working with ML. Parallel to these efforts should be work to critically examine if these are indeed the "best" practices. We highlight two key issues on which prior research in designing ML and current practice are in conflict, and therefore merit further study.

Do Designers Need Technical Machine Learning Knowledge?

Designers in this study understood ML at a high level, treating it largely as a black box. When sketching, they asked the data scientists "not whether this would work, but in your gut, whether this would be possible on a scale 1-10", acquiring only enough understanding to evoke a response to the design questions they had at that point in time. This behavior somewhat conflicts with the efforts being made to teach designers the statistical taxonomies and descriptive mechanisms of ML [13, 14, 15]. Designers instead used data scientists as a proxy for their design material.

This study showed that designers were *capable* of engaging in a reflective conversation with ML without a formal ML education. Yet it remains an open question whether a more advanced understanding of ML would inspire new design perspectives and new designs. On the one hand, design research has long promoted a "designerly way of knowing and doing" — the idea that designers can work with technologies and situations that they do not fully understand [1, 20, 23]. More investigation is needed to better define what is a "good enough" understanding of ML, and to understand when a more detailed knowledge of ML might help.

On the other hand, previous investigations of technology materials are often based on in-depth descriptions of their special properties, and then progressed to envisage a novel interaction design [30]. This approach allows designers to redirect their focus from the artifacts toward the materials from which the artifacts are built. This kind of discussion has not yet happened in designing ML. What are ML's special properties in improving UX? How do its experiential qualities differ across algorithms or datasets? Answers to these questions would allow for a more reflective and disciplined discussion of how to make ML available to design practitioners and enable design-led ML innovation. This would also inform educators whether and how ML education for designers should be different from the one for general non-ML experts.

Should the User-Centered Design Process Change?

Previous work shows some designers do not know how to bring their UX expertise to bear on ML [9]. Our study offered one possible solution, a divide-and-conquer approach. Designers first identified the right problem for ML to solve, validated its technical feasibility, and then iterated on the diverging-converging ideation process to craft the right manifestation of ML functionality. We found their overall approach to be similar to descriptions of the lean startup with a focus on making a minimal viable product [22]. They were similar in the way teams would assess the viability of an idea and pivot when it seemed to fail.

Future research should reflect on and improve the process we observed. One advantage of this process is that it did not require designers to acquire extensive ML skills, use many new tools, or radically change their familiar design activities. After a working ML application was launched, designers would go through a second design and evaluation process, fixing the design problems that the initial iteration failed to capture. However, a complete ML design process seemed to take way more time than a conventional double-diamond UX process [7]. Can the function and form of a ML design be addressed at once? Are there new ways to prototype and evaluate the technical viability and design quality before product launch? Answers to these questions have the potential to radically lower the cost of developing ML systems, and to enable many more resource-sensitive organizations to insert ML to their products and services.

At a higher level, the procedural knowledge of designing ML marks a clear space for HCI/design research. Existing work has offered valuable declarative knowledge and conceptual understandings of ML from a design perspective (i.e. [18, 19]). Embedding this growing body of new knowledge into organizational and procedural contexts opens up new research opportunities and promises real impact on UX practice.

CONCLUSION AND LIMITATION

In this paper, we report on an interview study to understand how expert designers who regularly design ML products do their work. We expanded previous work by illustrating the best practice of incorporating ML in the design process in industry. Our findings offer points of reference for design education, research and tool development with the goal of making ML available to UX practice. Through this work, we hope to start a reflective discussion around how HCI research can better support actual UX-ML design practice.

One limitation of this study is that it is exclusively from the perspective of a small and very specific sample of UX practitioners. We do not know the design process from the perspective of their data scientist or other collaborators. We do not know if or how other organizations have experienced resistance to ML approaches. We encourage the IxD and HCI research community to join us, and understand the UX practice more holistically.

ACKNOWLEDGEMENTS

This material is based in part upon work supported by the National Science Foundation under Grant Numbers SES 1734456. Any opinions, findings, and conclusions or recommendations expressed in this material are those of the author(s) and do not necessarily reflect the views of the National Science Foundation. This material is also in part based upon work supported by the National Institute on Disability, Independent Living, and Rehabilitation Research under NIDILRR 90RE5011. The first author is also supported by the Center for Machine Learning and Health (CMLH) Fellowship in Digital Health.

REFERENCES

1. Christoph Bartneck. 2007. Design methodology is not design science. In *the CHI 2007 workshop: Converging on a" science of design" through the synthesis of design methodologies, San Jose, CA.*
2. Jonathan Bean and Daniela Rosner. 2014. Big data, diminished design? *interactions* 21, 3 (2014), 18–19.
3. Glenn A Bowen. 2006. Grounded theory and sensitizing concepts. *International journal of qualitative methods* 5, 3 (2006), 12–23.
4. John Brownlee. 2015. Apple Finally Learns AI Is The New UI. (2015). https://www.fastcodesign.com/3047199/apple-finally-learns-ai-is-the-new-ui
5. Shan Carter and Michael Nielsen. 2017. Using Artificial Intelligence to Augment Human Intelligence. *Distill* (2017). DOI:http://dx.doi.org/10.23915/distill.00009 https://distill.pub/2017/aia.
6. Amber Cartwright. 2016. Invisible Design: Co-Designing with Machines. (2016). http://airbnb.design/invisible-design/
7. Design Council. 2005. The 'double diamond' design process model. *Design Council* (2005).
8. Laura Denham. 2017. Data Scientists Are The Next UX Designers. (2017). https://channels.theinnovationenterprise.com/articles/data-scientists-are-the-next-ux-designers
9. Graham Dove, Kim Halskov, Jodi Forlizzi, and John Zimmerman. 2017. UX Design Innovation: Challenges for Working with Machine Learning as a Design Material. In *Proceedings of the 2017 CHI Conference on Human Factors in Computing Systems - CHI '17*. ACM Press, New York, New York, USA, 278–288. DOI: http://dx.doi.org/10.1145/3025453.3025739
10. Daniel Fallman. 2003. Design-oriented human-computer interaction. In *Proceedings of the SIGCHI conference on Human factors in computing systems*. ACM, 225–232.
11. Marco Gillies, Bongshin Lee, Nicolas D'Alessandro, Joëlle Tilmanne, Todd Kulesza, Baptiste Caramiaux, Rebecca Fiebrink, Atau Tanaka, Jérémie Garcia, Frédéric Bevilacqua, Alexis Heloir, Fabrizio Nunnari, Wendy Mackay, and Saleema Amershi. 2016. Human-Centred Machine Learning. In *Proceedings of the 2016 CHI Conference Extended Abstracts on Human Factors in Computing Systems - CHI EA '16*. ACM Press, New York, New York, USA, 3558–3565. DOI: http://dx.doi.org/10.1145/2851581.2856492
12. Fabien Girardin and Neal Lathia. 2017. When User Experience Designers Partner with Data Scientists. In *The AAAI Spring Symposium Series Technical Report: Designing the User Experience of Machine Learning Systems*. The AAAI Press, Palo Alto, California. https://www.aaai.org/ocs/index.php/SSS/SSS17/paper/view/15364
13. Mayank Goel, Nils Hammerla, Thomas Ploetz, and Anind K. Dey. 2015. Bridging the Gap: Machine Learning for Ubicomp — Tutorial @UbiComp 2015. https://openlab.ncl.ac.uk/bridging-the-gap/. (2015).
14. Patrick Hebron. 2016a. *Machine learning for designers*. O'Reilly Media.
15. Patrick Hebron. 2016b. New York University Tisch School of the Arts Course: Learning Machines. (2016). http://www.patrickhebron.com/learning-machines/
16. Mike Kuniavsky, Elizabeth Churchill, and Molly Wright Steenson. 2017. *The AAAI Spring Symposium Series Technical Report: Designing the User Experience of Machine Learning Systems*. Technical Report SS-17-04. Palo Alto, California.
17. Bryan Lawson. 2012. *What designers know*. Routledge.
18. Brian Y Lim, Anind K Dey, and Daniel Avrahami. 2009. Why and why not explanations improve the intelligibility of context-aware intelligent systems. In *Proceedings of the SIGCHI Conference on Human Factors in Computing Systems*. ACM, 2119–2128.
19. Betti Marenko and Philip Van Allen. 2016. Animistic design: how to reimagine digital interaction between the human and the nonhuman. *Digital Creativity* 27, 1 (2016), 52–70.
20. Wanda J Orlikowski and Debra C Gash. 1994. Technological frames: making sense of information technology in organizations. *ACM Transactions on Information Systems (TOIS)* 12, 2 (1994), 174–207.
21. Fatih Kursat Ozenc, Miso Kim, John Zimmerman, Stephen Oney, and Brad Myers. 2010. How to support designers in getting hold of the immaterial material of software. In *Proceedings of the SIGCHI Conference on Human Factors in Computing Systems*. ACM, 2513–2522.
22. Eric Ries. 2011. *The lean startup: How today's entrepreneurs use continuous innovation to create radically successful businesses*. Crown Books.
23. Donald A Schon. 1984. *The reflective practitioner: How professionals think in action*. Vol. 5126. Basic books.
24. Erik Stolterman. 2008. The nature of design practice and implications for interaction design research. *International Journal of Design* 2, 1 (2008).
25. TensorFlow: Smarter machine learning, for everyone 2017. (2017). https://www.google.com/intl/en/about/main/tensorflow/
26. Peter Tolmie, James Pycock, Tim Diggins, Allan MacLean, and Alain Karsenty. 2002. Unremarkable Computing. In *Proceedings of the SIGCHI Conference on Human Factors in Computing Systems (CHI '02)*. ACM, New York, NY, USA, 399–406. DOI: http://dx.doi.org/10.1145/503376.503448

27. Mary Treseler. 2017. *Designing with Data: Improving the User Experience with A/B Testing*. O'Reilly Media, Chapter Designers as data scientists. http://radar.oreilly.com/2015/05/designers-as-data-scientists.html

28. Udemy Online Course: Applied machine learning for Everyone 2018. (2018). https://www.udemy.com/applied-machine-learning-for-everyone/

29. Philip van Allen and Ben Hooker. ArtCenter College of Design Course: Internet of Enlightened Things. (????). https://canvas.instructure.com/courses/1111888

30. Mikael Wiberg. 2014. Methodology for materiality: interaction design research through a material lens. *Personal and ubiquitous computing* 18, 3 (2014), 625–636.

31. Qian Yang, Nikola Banovic, and John Zimmerman. 2018. Mapping Machine Learning Advances from HCI Research to Reveal Starting Places for Design Research. In *Proceedings of the SIGCHI Conference on Human Factors in Computing Systems - CHI '18 (CHI '18)*. ACM.

32. Qian Yang, John Zimmerman, Aaron Steinfeld, and Anthony Tomasic. 2016. Planning Adaptive Mobile Experiences When Wireframing. In *Proceedings of the 2016 ACM Conference on Designing Interactive Systems - DIS '16*. ACM Press, Brisbane, QLD, Australia, 565–576. DOI: http://dx.doi.org/10.1145/2901790.2901858

33. John Zimmerman, Erik Stolterman, and Jodi Forlizzi. 2010. An analysis and critique of Research through Design: towards a formalization of a research approach. In *Proceedings of the 8th ACM Conference on Designing Interactive Systems*. ACM, 310–319.

Interaction Challenges in AI Equipped Environments Built to Teach Foreign Languages Through Dialogue and Task-Completion

Rahul R. Divekar[1], Jaimie Drozdal[1], Yalun Zhou[1], Ziyi Song[1], David Allen[1], Robert Rouhani[1], Rui Zhao[1], Shuyue Zheng[1], Lilit Balagyozyan[1], Hui Su[1,2]

Rensselaer Polytechnic Institute[1]
Troy, NY 12180
{divekr, drozdj3, zhouy12, songz2, allend5, rouhar2, zhaor, zhengs6, balagl}
@rpi.edu

IBM Thomas J. Watson Research Laboratory[2]
Yorktown Heights, NY 10598
{huisuibmres}
@us.ibm.com

ABSTRACT

As cities around the world become more diverse in culture and language, there is a growing need for learning foreign languages. To further this excitement, we have built a human-scale, immersive room with a virtual AI agent that aids foreign language learning. Our system aids the language learning process through task-completion exercises using multi-modal dialogue. The Cognitive and Immersive Room (CIR) is developed as an immersive Chinese restaurant to teach Mandarin, but the interaction challenges and solutions can be reasonably generalized to other languages taught using similar techniques. As users interact with the immersive environment and the virtual AI agent, they face several user interaction challenges. These challenges arise from new learners' lack of proficiency in the foreign language. By studying user interactions in the CIR, we were able to articulate some of the interaction challenges. We have enhanced the AI agent, virtual environment, and the on-boarding process for new users to mitigate these challenges. The enhancements and the results which show that they were effective are discussed here.

ACM Classification Keywords

H.5.2 Information Interfaces and Presentation (e.g. HCI): User Interfaces

Author Keywords

Language teaching; Mandarin teaching; Immersive room; Intelligent agent; Multi-modal interaction; Mandarin as a foreign language; Three dimensional virtual worlds

INTRODUCTION

In this work we are addressing a universal problem. People coming from different backgrounds want to learn a foreign language. A common and effective way to learn a foreign language, after learning the words and grammar structures, is by speaking and listening to it [35]. Practicing dialogues in the context of completing a task that one might face in real life, like ordering food at a restaurant, can help the language learning process [38]. However, the avenues to do this are limited because fluent, reliable speakers who are willing to help are hard to find.

DIS '18, June 9–13, 2018, , Hong Kong

ISBN 978-1-4503-5198-0/13/06. . . $15.00

DOI: https://doi.org/10.1145/3196709.3196717

Currently, our immersive Chinese restaurant, also referred to as the Cognitive and Immersive Room (CIR), targets college-level students who are primarily English speakers and are learning Mandarin as a foreign language. The terms *users*, *learners* and *students* are used interchangeably hereon. We refer to L1 and L2 in this paper, which are the language students know well and the language students are newly learning, respectively. In our immersive system, L1 is English and L2 is Mandarin.

In this work, we give an overview of Mandarin as a language, highlighting its complexities for learners. We discuss current state-of-the-art technology available for learning Mandarin, and we emphasize the effect, but lack of immersive, human-scale, dialogue enabled, and task-based systems. After outlining the need for an advanced system for the purpose of Mandarin learning, we define expectations of our system and discuss the interaction environment, AI agent, and task (scenario) developed.

The CIR has a special technology relationship between artificial intelligence and immersive technology. The room is equipped with a virtual AI agent that can listen, speak, and "see" its users. The intelligent and immersive capabilities serve two major purposes. The AI agent allows students to practice their language skills through conversation, and the immersive environment gives more visual context to the task they are trying to complete with the agent. In the scenario we have developed, the immersive environment resembles a Chinese restaurant. The users are guests ordering food, and the AI agent is a waiter referred to as *AI Agent*, *AI Waiter* or *waiter* hereon.

This is a new paradigm of human-scale visuals and AI agents combined in the context of language learning through task completion. However, there are gaps between the new technologies and the users that we need to fill. In this paper, we discuss two main themes of interaction challenges: the system not understanding the *imperfect* language of the students, and the students not understanding the *fluent* language of the AI agent. Both are due to the lack of L2 proficiency in the users. We address the communication gaps between the AI agent and the users by enabling multi-modal interactions and verbal help features.

We have run many beta-tests of the system on native and non-native Mandarin speakers from a local university. The core of this paper describes the details of these tests and the enhancements built as a result of them. The paper concludes with an analysis of a formal user-study. Sixteen students from a Chinese Level-1 class taught at a local university were invited to interact with the system. The observations and feedback from the students further motivate the direction for next steps in language teaching via AI and immersive technologies.

In this new learning paradigm, there still remain several other interaction challenges that are articulated here. Natural interactions do not follow a script, and therefore, it is challenging to create a system that teaches language through natural interactions. Nonetheless, these challenges are a motivation to the research community to build AI agents that, especially in the language education domain, can pro-actively mitigate the challenges between users and new technologies.

MANDARIN - THE LANGUAGE

In this section, we provide an overview of Mandarin as a language so that readers are able to understand the interaction challenges and the help functions described in later sections.

Mandarin is an increasingly popular language in the United States[44]. The Foreign Service Institute rates Mandarin as a category 5 language, making it one of five most difficult languages in the world [3]. Because of its level of difficulty and high demand for learners, Mandarin language-learning programs, now more than ever, need effective language-learning technology.

Mandarin is a complex, intricate language that can be represented by characters (*Hanzi*) or by *pinyin* [22]. *Pinyin* uses the Roman alphabet to represent Mandarin Chinese sounds and allows non-native speakers to grasp the Chinese pronunciation and tone system better [34]. Fig. 1 shows *pinyin* in red on line 1 and *Hanzi* on line 2. Understanding only one of these representations will cause a severe deficit in communication.

Mandarin is a tonal language, which means the tone of a syllable carries meaning. It is an especially difficult language for non-native speakers whose first language is not a tonal language [40]. Each syllable in Mandarin carries one of five

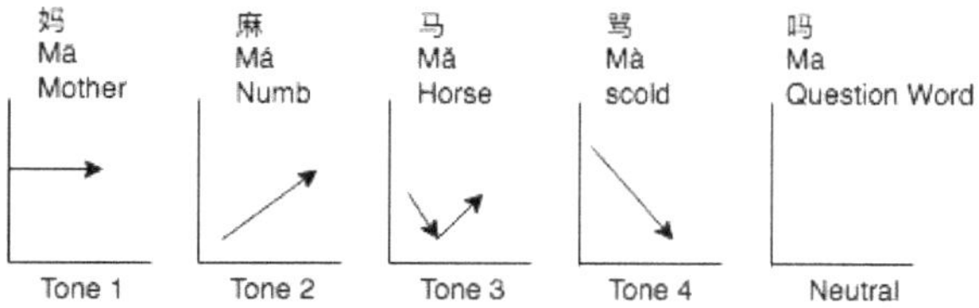

Figure 1. The Five Tones of Mandarin

possible tones, and each tone has a specific pitch, modulation, and duration. In written *pinyin*, a diacritical mark above each syllable specifies what tone is associated with the syllable [22]. As shown in Fig. 1, depending on the tone, the syllable 'ma' can translate to English as mother, numb, horse, to scold, or as a question particle. Because of these subtleties, accurate tone recognition and pronunciation are critical to Mandarin speakers and new learners. Furthermore, there are many grammatical conventions and structures that rely on tones (tone sandhi[22]) and influence the meaning of a statement.

New learners of Mandarin, especially new learners with a non-tonal first language, have a wider pitch range than native Mandarin speakers. The mispronunciations associated with their novice and inarticulate speech lead to mis-communications [26]. Only with practice and exposure to the language can a new learner of Mandarin become fluent in their tone pronunciation and recognition. For more information on Mandarin as a language see [13]

In this overview, we see the numerous ways learners of Mandarin can go wrong with communication. In the next sections, we will describe our technology which is an avenue for the students to practice spoken Mandarin. This section showed why it is easy for the building blocks of our technology such as one of the most sophisticated natural language processing systems ([18]) to misunderstand or misinterpret speech input from new learners. The challenges of learning Mandarin as a foreign language also explain why users misinterpret or completely do not understand what they hear from the system. There is clearly a communication gap between the system and the users while communicating in L2. This work aims to ease this communication gap.

REVIEW OF CURRENT TECHNOLOGY

In this section, we review the existing applications and technology methods out there to aid Mandarin language learning. We then motivate what is needed to add on top of the current state-of-the-art.

Available Applications

There are numerous mobile applications and Internet resources that new learners can utilize to practice and improve their Mandarin. The most common applications for language learning focus on vocabulary and grammar learning [1]. A student is expected to rehearse and memorize the vocabulary through simple activities and is then tested on their knowledge. This method of learning relies largely on memorization and does not provide the foreign language exchanges, specifically opportunities to engage in authentic linguistic and social practices, considered necessary for the acquisition of a second language [43][38][24][54].

Other language teaching applications allow users to interact with native speakers from all over the world. These online programs, where a new learner can chat with someone and receive feedback, have a more immersive element because the user is able to speak directly with a native speaker. Some applications ([12]) allow anyone to register as a native speaker and chat with other users. The interactions occur through a text messaging system where users can edit and provide feedback on the grammar and vocabulary of the other person's messages in the conversation.

On the other hand, there are applications (e.g. ChinesePod[9], eChineseLearning[10], busuu[7], tutor Mandarin[15]) that provide Mandarin-teaching experts, not just anybody, to interact with users. As Mandarin is a tonal language, pronunciation is a focus of many Mandarin learning applications (Wai Chinese[16]). Liao et al. [40] developed an unreleased, prototype of an adaptive Chinese pronunciation training system that analyzes a users pronunciation and provides feedback on phonetic and tonal errors. This prototype, along with many other computer-assisted pronunciation training (CAPT) systems, shows tone-analysis charts based upon the speaker's utterance. The user receives a real-time visualization of their pronunciation and can adjust their tone(s) to match a the tone-analysis chart of a native-speaker. However, unlike commercially available CAPT systems, Liao et al.'s prototype allowed for real-time feedback on pronunciation. Currently, there are no published papers on any user studies with this prototype. While these resources are beneficial in the education domain, we see an opportunity for enhancing these experiences by simulating real-word environments and scenarios.

Available Immersive Environments

Traveling to a foreign country is a highly praised approach for second-language acquisition [49]. When someone is immersed in a foreign culture, they are surrounded by and speaking the target language. Out of necessity, they will have to learn how to function in society and interact with others with a language they are newly acquiring. Studies have shown linguistic gains in people who study abroad [23][28][33][31]. However, Wright & Cong [59] reference multiple studies that show conflicting results, and they emphasize the lack of consistent methodologies in research on studying abroad. Due to geographical and financial constraints, it is often a challenge for new learners of a language to travel abroad and immersive themselves in that language. Perhaps a virtual, culturally immersive environment is the next best thing.

Lin & Lan [42] report two case studies, Vogel et al. [56] and Liao & Chen [41], that analyzed a total of 53 studies. The meta-analyses show positive findings (e.g. superior cognitive outcomes and more positive attitudes toward learning) associated with the use of interactive simulations and games compared to respective traditional teaching methods. Similarly, Cok [27] performed a meta-analysis of 37 papers and reports linguistic gains associated with using computer and Internet-based technology. She suggests that these gains result from allowing users to be in touch with authentic speaking situations and to experience interaction, neither of which can be achieved in traditional learning environments. The positive findings associated with computer-assisted language learning (CALL) highlight the potential of creating immersive, computer simulated environments for education purposes.

Virtual Worlds

In the context of this discussion, there are many ways to think of the term 'immersive' in regards to different environments. Systems that are virtually immersive are equipped with a 3D virtual world (VW) and are used across a variety of domains for multiple purposes. Berns[20], Gonzales-Pardo, & Camacho [38] define virtual worlds as '3D environments where users' graphical representations, called avatars can interact with other avatars as well as objects within the environment'. They argue that VWs are 'highly immersive' environments because of their ability to reproduce or simulate a tremendous amount of real life activities. Furthermore, VWs provide great value to foreign language learning because of the interactions and inferences they allow. A 3D world allows users to explore linguistic concepts such as 'asking for directions' or 'ordering a meal' and learning propositions, among others [57].

An example of this type of immersive environment is SAIL (situated avatar-based immersive learning), a habitable 3D virtual space where users are able to control avatars and manipulate objects in the virtual world in the context of problem solving activities [52][39]. VEC3D, a virtual English classroom, is an interactive English learning environment in which users role-play open ended scenarios. Users conduct synchronous communication and can have real-time interactions in written or spoken format [52]. Most recently, a prototype of VEC3D 5.0 was developed linking the virtual world with Web 2.0 tools, but the efficacy of this system to learners studying English as a foreign language (EFL) has yet to be studied [53]. Roger Schank's DUSTIN [50] includes a digital environment that provides non-English speakers the opportunity to practice their English in a handful of scenarios. This system was developed for new employees at the company Accenture who are non-native English speakers that attend meetings at the company's U.S. training center near Chicago. To help with encounters the employees will have, scenarios enabled in the environment include getting through U.S. customs at the Chicago O'Hare Airport, checking into a hotel, and ordering food. Instead of computer generated graphics, the digital environment consists of videos of actors in the real-world locations [48].

Two of the most popular and commercial virtual learning environment systems are Active Worlds (AW) [4] and Second Life (SL) [5][52]. These systems are both Internet-based 3D worlds that are game like and include multiple users. Users choose and control avatars that they use to meet and chat with other users. In these virtual worlds instructors can host online projects and set up classrooms. These systems are often researched in the context of language learning because of their environments and the interactions they allow. A study of new learners of Hungarian in SL showed that '...the environment can generate a large quantity of productive and genuinely communicative language by learners, far more than would be possible in the normal classroom' [43].

Many studies on Second Life have focused on collecting qualitative and quantitative data to analyze student communication and interests and motivations within the virtual world. The studies of Toyoda & Harrison [55], Peterson [47], and Deutschmann et al. [30] focused on negotiation of meaning, strategy use during task-based interaction, and participation patterns during voice chat, respectively. While these studies did not assess learning gains, they shed light on the implementation of task-based learning in virtual worlds[47]. A number of studies measure learning gains associated with 3D virtual worlds (e.g. Canto & Ondarra [24]; Guzel & Aydin [35]; Milton et al. [43]; Henderson et al. [36]; Chen [25]), and a number of those studies have found significant effects of SL on language performance (e.g. Canto & Ondarra [24]; Guzel & Aydin [35]).

Studies on virtual worlds other than SL and AW have also shown significant linguistic gains in users. Taguchi, Li, & Tang [50] developed a scenario-based interactive environment to improve student's knowledge of Chinese formulaic expressions. Results showed that students made significant gains in their knowledge of formulaic expressions after the practice, and this knowledge was retained two weeks later.

Yamazaki [61] studied Japanese learning throughout a 15-week curriculum in a 3D virtual world. Quantitative analysis confirmed statistically significant improvement in students' natural vocabulary acquisition, and qualitative analysis revealed statistically significant improvement in 'contextualized communicative competence' (e.g. persuasive talk, awareness of audience, and collaborative communication).

We plan to use these two studies, and others like these (e.g. Lan et al. [38]; Liao et al. [40]; Hismanoglu [37]), to motivate our research into applying the appropriate tools and pedagogy behind the CIR to produce language gains in the users.

Immersive Spaces

Apart from virtual worlds, immersive environments can be characterized by their physical environment and technologies. Katie Salen and David Birchfield's SMALLab (the Situated Multimedia Arts Learning Laboratory) is a room-sized interactive learning environment that integrates precise motion-capture technology and immersive floor projections. Currently, the system includes 30 scenarios, mostly related to science and mathematics, that support thousands of activities [14]. Research on this environment has linked it to student learning gains, improvement in teacher performance [14], and increase in student-led learning [21].

CAVE environments provide a high level of immersion through multi-screen projection systems that point to between three and six walls of a room-sized cube [45]. The first CAVE (Cave Automatic Virtual Environment) was developed in 1992[8], but since then many have been developed for applications in military training, medical education, manufacturing, and design. These environments are equipped with tracking systems that can track multiple users and their interactions in the environment. O'Brien, Levy, and Orich [46] compared the effectiveness of CAVE and PC technology in the language learning domain and found that complete immersion via CAVE technology did not provide significantly better experience for students. However, this study should not pose a threat to further research as linguistic gains were solely measured by the ability of a student to follow commands in the L2.

We believe that the immersive nature of virtual worlds can be enhanced by using panoramic displays and interactive 360 degree environments. The main inspiration for our CIR comes from a previous project that some members of the research team worked on. This project is an unreleased mixed-reality environment and learning game. Designed for a college-level Chinese language course, the game combines virtual reality with real props to create a mixed-reality environment where students must navigate through Beijing to find a missing book. This game provided a foundation and pedagogical backbone that inspired us to implement a new interactive scenario. Currently, we have been unable to find any other studies on rooms with immersive technologies that attempt to improve a user's Mandarin through the use of task-based scenarios in a 3D world.

In the next section we describe the room we have built and set our readers up to understand the interaction challenges in it.

THE CIR ENVIRONMENT

This section describes describes the CIR. It provides detail on the display set-up, the visuals presented to the users, and the AI capabilities.

Physical Environment

The CIR holds a 360 degree panoramic display, as shown in Fig. 2. The computer render for this configuration is shown in Fig. 3. The edges, or lines, in the image show the start and end of each projector display. However, to a user in the room, it appears as a round and seamless screen, see Fig. 2. Each projector display has a diameter of 12 m and height of 3.8 m. We use five projectors to project on to the 360 display using special warping software. This panoramic display allows us to build environments that can visually immerse users.

The CIR is equipped with several Kinects and Point-To-Zoom cameras that act as the "eyes of the room". Software that runs on top of these sensors allows the room to recognize certain gestures made by the users, such as pointing. We made the design decision to have no intrusive devices that need to be worn or hand-held/laptop devices that need to be used to interact with the room. This is to make the virtual dining experience as real as possible with only the panoramic display. The CIR is also equipped with microphones, so the users can "talk" to the system. Natural Language Processing (NLP) software interprets what the users are saying and helps the system provide an appropriate response back to the users. Specifically, we use the Watson Assistant service [17] which we trained with pre-defined intents, examples, and [18] for speech-to-text processing. The utterance from the user, after being converted to text, is mapped to one of these intents. Based on the intent received from the NLP services and other contexts maintained locally, appropriate graphical and visual responses are chosen to execute. All of these individual intelligent services coming together in context constitute the AI.

The engineering and research behind the development and integration of displays, computer vision technologies, and natural language processing technologies are massive and scalable to other use-cases. We urge the more enthusiastic readers to see [32] for a sense of the entire technology stack and [62] for specifics on computer vision systems.

Ideal User Experience

Using the described physical environment, we have completed a running and integrated system based on the beginner college level curriculum from Modern Chinese: Simplified Characters Textbook 1A[19]. This curriculum is divided into different units, each one highlighting the Mandarin Chinese vocabulary, grammar, and culture behind the unit topic. The CIR currently focuses on Unit 4: Food and specifically aims to assist a student in getting through a common restaurant dialogue

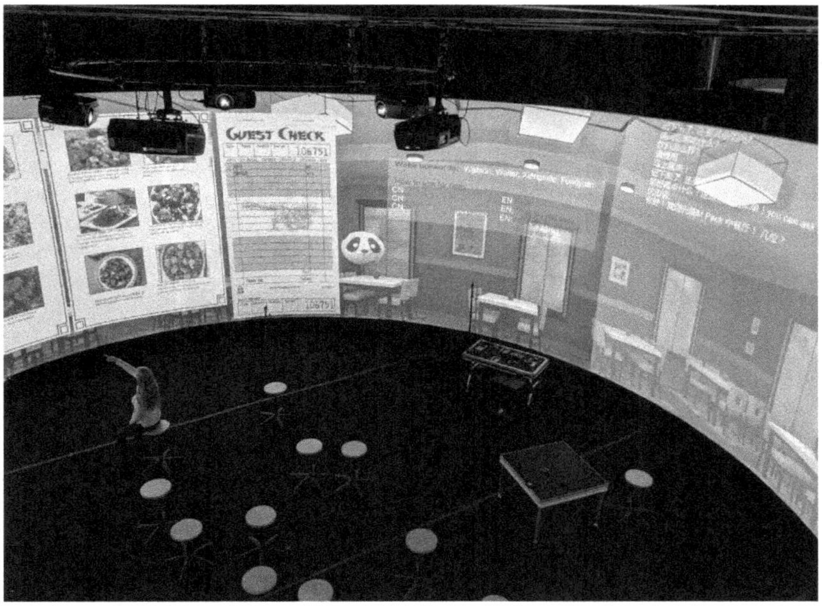

Figure 2. A user interacting with the immersive Chinese restaurant in the 360 degree panoramic display. Best view in color. Demo Video: https://youtu.be/lZWtDqhFlAc

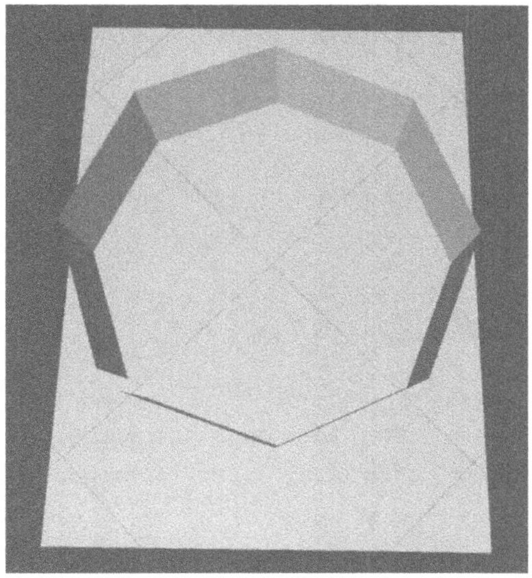

Figure 3. Computer render of the CIR display

in Mandarin. We chose this unit because Chinese restaurants are located all over the United States and can provide culturally rich environments. By increasing students' ability to successfully have a restaurant dialogue in Mandarin, they may be more comfortable or willing to carry out a similar conversation in their new language at a real Chinese-American restaurant.

Part of the curriculum as taught in the Chinese-1 class at the university involves students role-playing scenarios in pairs or groups. Specifically in Unit 4, students practice dialogues related to communication goals which represent conversations that may occur at a restaurant. These dialogue exercises are critical because they allow students to practice their pronunciation, which is critical for beginners of this tonal language, and because multi-player classroom course designs can enhance student motivation, attitude, and performance [60]. The CIR allows students to practice their dialogue through an exercise based on ordering food at a Chinese restaurant. This dialogue includes sub-tasks like asking for seating, ordering drinks and food, confirming the order for any mistakes, giving feedback on the taste of food, and paying the check. The user is not given a script to follow. To give the readers an example of what the interaction between a user and the waiter can look like a sample dialogue interaction is shown in fig. 4. A typical dialogue is longer and has more turns.

Using the L2 proficiency of the users and the capabilities of the physical environment, we have developed a cognitive and immersive system that simulates the environment of a Chinese restaurant. The waiter of the restaurant is a panda that appears to be floating. Users can have a conversation with this panda in the context of dining while they are surrounded by the visuals of the Chinese restaurant displayed on the 360 screen.

To build this experience, we carefully crafted sub-tasks, like asking for a table or ordering a menu item. Using the Modern Chinese textbook[2] and inputs from Chinese professors at a local university, we designed dialogue inputs and responses that include vocabulary and grammar at the existing language level of the new learner. The system can accept a range of inputs that map to an intent. For example, "I want water" and "Can I get some water" map to the 'ordering' intent. For each intent that is detected by the system, the system has multiple sentence variations as possible outputs, and it picks one to randomly output. All of these possible outputs for a given intent mean the same thing. E.g. "I will get your food", "Your order will be right up", etc. as output for when food is ordered. This makes the system less repetitive and adds versatility to the dialogue. To test the pedagogical value of the system, we added a few words that are outside of the new learners' known vocabulary. Even though the goal of this literature is not to validate the pedagogical model, we mention this because it is a possible hindrance for a smooth user experience.

Based on our dialogue design, our expectation is that most of the time new learners will be able to speak fluently with the waiter using sentence structures they know without needing any help. After practicing a dining scenario in the immersive Chinese restaurant using their new language, we expect the students may be more confident going to a real Chinese restaurant and having similar conversations with a human waiter.

INTERACTION CHALLENGES

To better understand how to develop our system, students from a Chinese III class at a local university were asked for their informal feedback throughout the development process. Over the period of several months, nine students visited the CIR and interacted with the system. Every time users interacted with the system, a native Mandarin speaker and the development team was standing by to help with any issues that may have arose, identify them as interaction challenges, and translate that into a technology problem.

	Mandarin	English
AI Agent	你好！欢迎光临中餐厅！你们几位？	Hello! Welcome to the Chinese restaurant! How many people?
Customer	我们两位	We are two people
AI Agent	这边请，请问您想喝点什么？	This way please. What would you like to drink?
Customer	我想要水	Can i get some water?
AI Agent	好的马上就来. 饮料怎么样？	Sure. Coming right up. How was your drink?
Customer	很好喝。	It was great!
AI Agent	你想吃点什么？这是我们的菜单。	Would you like something to eat? Here's the menu
Customer	我想要熏鱼。	I want smoked fish
AI Agent	好的。还要其他的菜吗？	Okay. Anything else?
Customer	北京烤鸭是什么?	What is the peking duck?
AI Agent	*(story about peking duck)* 你想要那个吗？	*(story about peking duck)* Do you want that?
Customer	好的.	Ok
AI Agent	好的。记下来了。	Sure. I'll put your order in
AI Agent	*(after a moment)* 菜的味道怎么样？这是您的账单，账单对吗？	*(after a moment)* Was everything okay? Here is your check, is it correct?
Customer	很好吃	Yes! it was great
AI Agent	谢谢光临	Thanks for coming to the restaurant!

Figure 4. Sample dialogue interaction. Best view in color.

The first group of students to ever test the system could not complete more than three turns of dialogue, even at their level (three) of proficiency. This was a key indicator that there were major communication gaps we needed to identify and fill. Since then, we have learned and addressed several interaction challenges and reached a level of system development where new learners are able to get through the restaurant dialogue in a reasonable time (5-10 minutes.)

Here, we describe the interaction challenges we observed through beta-tests of the system, and later, we specify the incremental enhancements made for these challenges. Although these interactions are presented in the context of a dining scenario in the immersive environment, the challenges can be generalized a good extent to other scenarios and environments where an AI teaches a foreign language through dialogue.

1. *Misrepresentations in the speech-to-text engine*
Mandarin is a complex language with tones and pronunciations different from the L1 of a majority of our intended users. Given its intricacies, a range of errors are common in new learners. We observed that even the slightest errors in users' pronunciations threw off the speech-to-text engine and led to a dead-end in their interactions. In addition to these errors, the text-to-speech engine expects continuity and fluency in user's speech. So, if the user's timing and fluency is not right, syllables that make up one word may be recognized as multiple words. This becomes more of an issue as it is common for words to have similar pronunciations but different meanings in Mandarin.

2. *New learners are used to multi-lingual communication*
In a classroom, when students learn from a teacher or role-play with their peers, they often use their L1 to help move the conversation along. A new learner may use their L1 to confirm what they understood, to correct what they meant, or to continue the conversation more comfortably. In the early stages of our environment, the system only supported Mandarin. This limited the users' abilities to complete the task if they were stuck at a stage in the dialogue. The native expert that was in the room during system tests had to give pronunciation feedback and encouragement to the students in order for them to make progress with the AI agent.

3. *Agent's response was not understood*
Although we use a standard Mandarin text-to-speech engine, it is possible that the speed of the AI agent's speech is too fast for new learners. It was clear during our beta-tests that the users either did not hear the waiter or did not understand the waiter. In these situations, the users struggled to move forward in the dialogue and had to ask the native expert and research team to reiterate what the waiter said. We did not want to slow down the speech of the waiter because in a real-world situation, new learners would be expected to understand sentences spoken at a standard pace.

4. *Words in the dialogue are outside of the new learner's vocabulary*
Words outside of the students' vocabularies were incorporated into the interactive dialogue through menu items and words spoken by the AI waiter. This was done intentionally, as mentioned earlier, and was based on the unit vocabularies from Modern Chinese textbook [2]. In the real world it is expected that the new learners will hear words they do not know. However, by using context and social interactions, the new learner might be able to understand the meaning conveyed. Yamazaki's [61] study is a successful example of this.

5. *Users do not know how to respond to the waiter*
We observed during the beta-tests that students may have understood what was said by the AI waiter, but they were unsure of what would be a good response. For example, during one interaction, the waiter asked for the user's order, but the user did not want to order anything else. The only way to move past this challenge was for a researcher in the room to suggest what the user could say. Overall, students get stuck in the interaction because they do not know what to say due to either their beginner-level language proficiency or not knowing what the AI waiter is capable of understanding.

6. *Users do not know where they went wrong in the interaction*
Especially in the beginning stages of our system, there were times when the AI agent did not respond to the users after they had spoken. This was due to the communication gap of the speech-to-text system, explained in interaction challenge 1. When this happened, students did not know what the system had heard and had no idea where the miscommunication was coming from. The system provided no feedback on what word or syllable the user mispronounced.

There was also little feedback on what the system interpreted from the user's input. The users relied on the native speakers in the room to explain their pronunciation errors.

Enhancements to Ease Interaction Challenges

This section describes help features/functions we designed and incorporated to bridge the communication gaps between the users and the system. We have been careful not to make the user interactions with the waiter too easy to the extent that there is no learning benefit. However, we still need to give the feeling of accomplishment to every student. The help functions include multi-modal interactions that feel natural to the user and the interaction at hand. Meaning, the help features are interactions that are likely to occur in the real world when there is a communication gap. We use the subsection numbers from the previous section to match the interaction challenges with the current, implemented solutions.

1. *Enabling multi-modal interactions*
Under interaction challenge 4, we discussed that the students in our beta-tests did not know how to pronounce a majority of the items on the menu. Some items themselves are popular in Chinese-American restaurants, the students did not know the Chinese names of them. Thus, in this section, we describe the two multi-modal dialogue interactions available in the room using pointing. In the real world, when one does not know how to pronounce something on the menu, they would likely point at the item on the menu and say "I want to order this" or "What is this?". This is a real-world solution to the communication gap and is common to almost all languages.
In our immersive restaurant, there is a menu on the panoramic display, as seen in fig. 2. To implement a solution to the communication gap, we enabled the room with Kinect devices and software that recognizes pointing gestures. By using this technology, we serve our aim of providing an experience without intrusive devices. Our software fuses data from multiple Kinects and multiple speech channels to interpret the menu item being referred to in the deictic speech. This is a deep research effort of its own that is not a scope of this paper. Now, users can point at an item on the menu and say "I want this" to order it.
Not only can users point at and order a dish on the menu, they can also ask for the cultural history and significance of a dish. Chinese cuisine is an important part of Chinese culture [58], and giving new learners of Mandarin the opportunity to explore the history of dishes on the menu in L1, culturally immerses them further and enhances the learning process. According to research, language and culture are inextricably linked, and Brown [29] argues that the acquisition of a second language is the acquisition of a second culture. In the case that a new learner does not know about a dish, they can point at the dish on the menu and ask "What is this?". The system then provides background information on the dish. The AI agent can also display a tone-chart to show the exact pronunciation of a dish. These two features can be utilized to introduce new words into the user's vocabulary.
The above actions, pointing and saying "I want this" or "What is this?", can alternatively be accomplished with just verbal input. Instead of saying the command and gesturing at the menu, users would say the command including the menu item, assuming they know the correct pronunciation.

2. *Allowing the users to switch between languages*
At any point in the digital dining experience, if the user is having difficulties communicating with the AI agent, they can ask the AI agent to switch from L2 to L1. In our Chinese restaurant, this means the user can switch from Mandarin to English and vice versa. The user can carry on the dialogue for as long as they like in L1, or they can switch back to L2 at any point. Again, this explicit request for help identifies areas in the language that new learners may be struggling with. Allowing the user to switch between their L1 and L2 specifically mitigates interaction challenges 1 and 2, but is a fall-back for any communication failure in Mandarin.

3. *Asking the AI agent for clarification*
To address interaction challenges 3, 4 and 5, when a user does not grasp what was said by the AI Agent, a user can ask the AI agent, in their L2 or L1, "What did you say?" and "What am I supposed to say?". Modern voice-interface devices, such as Amazon Alexa[6] and Google Assistant[11], also include the feature where a user can ask "What did you say?". However, with these systems, the user is most often looking for the device to repeat what it just said most likely because the user did not hear it or misheard it. When the user is new to a language, repetition without any further information can be useless.
Therefore, in our immersive restaurant, when a user asks the AI agent "What did you say?" the agent repeats the phrase, gives an explanation/translation of the phrase in L1, and suggests a possible response in L2 to the user. The explanation and suggested response is manually encoded in the system based on the speech input. The spoken phrase and its suggested response are displayed on the screen in *pinyin*. This visual allows the new learner to see and hear the words simultaneously. The explicit asking for help provides insight to teachers and system developers on areas of the language that new learners are struggling with.
Although a user may understand what the agent said to them, they may not know how to respond to the agent. In this case, the user can ask "What am I supposed to say?". This triggers the same response as asking "What did you say?". The user receives the phrase repeated in L2, the phrase explained in L1, and a possible response in L2.

4. *Displaying the live transcript*
As described in interaction challenge 6, users may not know where the miscommunication is in the interaction. Therefore, a transcription of the dialogue is always shown on the panoramic display. Users can reference this to see what the system thinks they said or what the AI agent said. This provides the users immediate feedback by showing that the system is listening and what the system interpreted from the speech input. The users can use this information to determine which word, or words, was mis-interpreted (if

any) and correct it. This help feature also helps mitigate challenge 1.

5. *Designing a system-initiated dialogue*

Students may not know the dialogue capabilities of the system in the immersive restaurant, and consequently, they may not know what a reasonable response in the dialogue is. Imagine the situation where a student walks into the immersive restaurant and the AI agent says "Welcome to the restaurant." At this point, the user may be unsure of what to say next. They may wonder - do I say hello?, do I say thank you?, or do I ask for a table? In our beta-tests we saw students were hesitant at points in the dialogue because of these confusions. This interaction challenge is a general UX problem in most voice-based interfaces where the entire "menu" or "capability list" is not shown or known to the user.

In a restaurant scenario where communication is limited to a specific set of vocabulary, this challenge is easier to solve than in the general voice-bot space. We address this problem by ending all agent responses with a question that hints at what response is expected. For example, if the AI agent says "Welcome to the restaurant", it does not give an indication of what answer is expected, and the branches from this turn in the dialogue could grow wild. To avoid this, the AI agent specifically says "Welcome. How many people are you?" This question indicates the user should reply back with information containing a number. Additionally, creating a system-initiated dialogue limits the scope of the dialogue that is managed on the technological end because a user-initiated dialogue could grow into a really huge space. The system-initiated dialogue was planned in collaboration with the language teachers and the textbook [2] to elicit specific vocabulary words and sentence structures in users' responses. If the dialogue needs to be expanded, we will still follow the principles of a waiter-initiated dialogue. As an example, if multiple dining options were incorporated into the immersive restaurant, then the opening question from the AI agent might be "Welcome! Would you like a table or takeout?" Each line from the waiter ends in a question, initiating a specific response from the users, as shown in Fig. 5.

Table 1 shows a mapping of challenges and solutions numbers (from the list above) to summarize the previous two sections. Once the system was enabled with these help functions, we needed to get information about these help functions to the users and set-up their expectation of the capabilities of the system. We added the three main help functions (asking for help, asking what the waiter said, and asking what can be said next) to the display so that they are always visible to the user. The help features are shown in both English and Mandarin. Currently, Mandarin and English are the two languages enabled in our immersive restaurant; however, the interaction challenges and our enhancements to mitigate these challenges are not limited to only these languages. The interaction challenges and respective help features are universal.

Table 1. Summary of interaction challenges and solutions

Interaction Challenge	Solution
Misrepresentation in Speech-to-text	2,4
Need for multi-lingual communication	2
Agent's response not understood	2,3
Words are out of users' vocabulary	1,2,3
Users do not know how to respond	2,3,5
Users unaware of what went wrong	4

USER STUDY

We invited 16 students who were taking a Chinese I course at the same university this system is being developed at to interact with our immersive Chinese restaurant. Out of these 16 students, 12 listed English as their first language, with other first languages including Spanish, Taishanese, and Cantonese. Fifteen of the 16 students indicated having friends that speak Chinese, and four of the 16 indicated having family that speak Chinese. As mentioned earlier, the content of the immersive Chinese restaurant is based on the Modern Chinese: Simplified Characters Textbook 1A [2]. This is the textbook that the recruited Chinese I class uses. In the class prior to the study, students learned the new vocabulary and grammar structures in the food unit. The following class, instead of role-playing scenarios with peers (as is usual), the students came to the CIR to practice spoken communication with the AI agent. The professor of this Chinese I class is a member of our research team and was present during the user study to provide instruction when necessary.

Set-up of the User Study

A week before coming to the CIR to experience the system, the students were e-mailed a document explaining the immersive environment and restaurant scenario. The e-mail also included a link to a video that described how to interact with the system and how to use the help features. When the students arrived at the Cognitive and Immersive Room, they were given a demonstration of how to interact with the system by members of the research team. The demo showed the students what an entire run-through of the dialogue could look like. The students were also provided with the same document explaining the system and help features that was e-mailed to them a week before the study.

After the demonstration, the students were randomly assigned into pairs. We designed the study with student pairs to promote cooperative learning because it has been shown that learners who work together acquire more language and social skills than those who work individually [63][51]. The student pairs were randomly assigned a turn number. One at a time, each pair went to the front and center of the immersive restaurant to interact with the AI agent. Because this study ran during the Chinese I class time, each pair was given five minutes to get through as much of the dialogue as possible. This time limit was specific to this user study and ensured that all pairs of students would get a chance to interact with the immersive restaurant. The students in the pair took turns talking to the waiter and ordering their drinks and dishes.

The pair's interaction ended when they completed the dialogue and the waiter said goodbye, or it ended when the five minute time limit was up.
The professor and some native speakers were present in the room to help them with any language difficulties. All students were in the CIR for the entire study and could watch the other students interact with the system. After all the pairs had completed their turn with the immersive restaurant, they were asked to fill out a questionnaire; the questions and responses are discussed in the next section. A week following the study, a follow-up questionnaire was sent to the students to fill out online.

Results and Reflections

Questionnaire Analysis

The post-study questionnaire included questions about users' age, gender, first language, and if they have friends or family that speak Chinese. They were asked to rate the available help functions on a 5 point Likert scale of very unhelpful to very helpful. The questions asked how helpful the help functions are in the real-world and in the immersive-environment (CIR). The results of this portion of the questionnaire are shown in Fig. 5. The y-axis represents the different help features, and the x-axis shows the helpfulness score from 0-5 (very unhelpful to very helpful). The results show that the users consider all of the help functions useful in a real-world scenario. Almost all of the help functions were perceived as more useful in the real world compared to the immersive environment. We believe this is because students did not use the help features in the immersive room that often. For each of the help functions, excluding pointing, only one in four students remembered that they could use that help function. This is with the help functions demonstrated before the experiment and constantly displayed in their field-of-view throughout the study. The pointing feature was remembered by 15 out of the 16 students. Because large-scale, digital, and immersive environments like the CIR are sparse and not available to most of the general public, we assume the users have not interacted with a system like the CIR. Not only are we introducing users to the immersive environment, but we are also introducing them to the restaurant dining scenario. Therefore, we need to effectively familiarize the users to the environment and the task. Before the Chinese I students came to the CIR, they were shown a video of how the system looks and how to interact with it. They were also given an information sheet that briefly introduced the system and mentioned the help functions. This gave them information on the environment and the dialogue task. The help document was given to the students during the study to use as a reference during their interactions with the system. Interestingly, during the study we did not observe any of the students looking at their help sheet during their interaction in the immersive restaurant.
Because the user study was run during class time, we were unable to give in depth questionnaires at the time of the study. We followed up via e-mail a week after the study with a questionnaire about introducing the users to the system and what additional questions about which help features they liked. Only six subjects participated in this portion of the study, but they

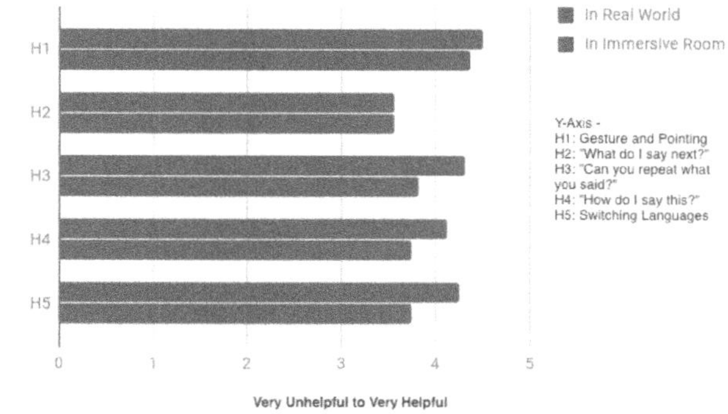

Figure 5. User ratings on helpfulness of help features in the real world vs. immersive environment

indicated that the video, the demo, and the document were helpful to them and that they liked all of the help features. Although the video, the demo, and the help document were received positively by the Chinese I students, we aim to develop more effective and efficient ways to introduce the users to the immersive restaurant. The goal is for users to need no outside help from a teacher or member of the research team to successfully communicate and interact with the system.

Evaluation of the Help Functions - Researcher Observations

The help feature that was used most frequently was the pointing gesture. Many times when a student was struggling with the pronunciation of a menu item, they would instead point to the item and order it. The students resorted to using this interactive help function on their own. Otherwise, the professor had to encourage students to try some of the help functions. For example, at one point in the dialogue a student asked the professor what to do. Instead of telling them, the professor told the student to ask the system what to say next.

Students seemed to rely on help from their professor, classmates, and members of the research team when they were stuck, instead of the help functions enabled in the system. The professor and members of the research team provided help even when the students did not explicitly ask for it. For example, a majority of the users had to repeat themselves multiple times in order for the system to pick up the correct interpretation of their pronunciation. In these instances, the professor and members of the research team would chime in with the correct pronunciation or would encourage the student to keep trying. This is typical to any language learning classroom and the native Mandarin speakers were able to guide the students on their timing and pronunciations. Our goal is to enable the AI agent to provide the same help that the professor and native speakers did. This gives us additional motivation to integrate a more a pro-active help system into the immersive restaurant.

Using video recordings of the study, we observed the help that the professor and native speakers provided to the students. From these observations we can further develop our help features. Every student was given help at some point in their interaction. The different kinds of help given were classified as the following:

- Encouraging the student to try the phrase again

- Suggesting pronunciations of words and phrases
- Suggesting the student try a different word or menu item (e.g. instead of Panda say Waiter)
- Suggesting the correct tones for the pronunciation including hand gestures of the tones
- Explaining the system bugs (usually related to timing of speech)
- Confirming they understood what the student said, although the system did not
- Repeating what the waiter said or hinting to the student what the waiter was expecting them to say

These observations motivate us to enhance the ability of the AI agent by teaching it to observe when a user needs help and what help to provide or suggest.

Other Observations

Further observations of video footage from the user study, showed the students consistently looking at the transcript to get feedback on their pronunciations and to understand the stage of interaction. We noted in our communication with some students that they found the displayed transcript of the waiter's response and their own response useful. In the future, we want to explore the pedagogical relevance of this. The students might have understood the written Chinese better than the AI agent's spoken response, or they might have used the transcript to confirm what they heard. Either way, from an interaction perspective, it made things easier for the user. However, a live transcript is not something that is available to a new learner in the real word. We would like the students to use the system without it, but in a student's initial interactions with the CIR, having the transcript available could have a positive impact or a moral boost. In future CIR developments, it may be possible for the transcript to be turned on or off by the user in order to set the difficulty level of the system.

We observed that most students used the shortest path to complete the dialogue and each step within the dialogue. Students only ordered one drink and one dish each, they always said the food was good without any additional remarks, and they did not, in general, explore dialogue paths not demonstrated to them (e.g. asking for a dish recommendation).
The goal of the immersive Chinese restaurant is to encourage students to explore and have detailed conversations in Mandarin. However, we believe that even with a sufficient demonstration of how complex the dialogue can be, students would likely take the shortest path to complete it. A further enhancement of the system is to utilize the waiter-initiated dialogue design to encourage students to expand the conversation. For example, if a user says that the food was good, the waiter could say "Did you like the spicy dish or the sweet one more?". There are many questions the waiter can ask throughout the dining experience that will challenge the new learners to expand their Mandarin skills.

We also noted that the pairs of students who interacted with the system later in the class got further in the dialogue than the pairs that went first. For example, the last two pairs of students made it farther in the dialogue than any other pair before them, and the last pair was the only pair to complete the entire dialogue in the five minute limit. This suggests that being in the CIR and watching other students had positive effects on student performance in the CIR.

Encouragements

According to the class textbook [2] and information from the professor of the class, upon arriving to the study students had not yet learned how to ask or pay for the check in Mandarin. In the open ended portion of the questionnaire, one student wrote that after their time in the CIR they knew how to pay the bill. This is an encouraging feat for the research team. Although the students were receiving some guidance from the professor and other Mandarin speakers in the room, a student learned something new through their experience with the Cognitive and Immersive Room. Another student wrote that our system is 'a good proof-of-concept', and they 'hope to see more technology like this integrated into education'.

CONCLUSION AND FUTURE WORK

In this work, we have motivated the need for an immersive room where users can practice spoken language through real-life task completion exercises. We have presented the Cognitive and Immersive Room developed as an immersive Chinese restaurant by collaborating with experts from a variety of domains (e.g. computer science, HCI, foreign language education, graphic design, game development, software development, etc.) The immersive Chinese restaurant is an environment where new learners of Mandarin can role-play with a virtual waiter. We evaluated interaction challenges of new learners and new CIR users through beta tests. These challenges motivated the development of multiple help features, including pointing at an on-screen menu item to order it. A formal user study showed the effectiveness and likability of the features developed to mitigate the interaction challenges, and the study also shed light on further developments.
Our goal is to have an immersive environment where a user can interact with the AI agent as though it were a real human. We are constantly developing new technologies in the room that we think would be helpful in bridging the communication gaps. In the future steps, the AI agent will be able to provide productive feedback to the user and help them improve their L2 proficiency. This includes integrating a pitch contour analysis graph that will show the users a plot of their tones in real time. We also plan to enable the immersive restaurant with a society of agents playing different roles (e.g. customers, chefs, etc.). Once we have confidently tackled the restaurant scenario, we hope to enable multiple scenarios in the CIR. In this direction, we hope to find and solve new interaction challenges that are not yet foreseen.

ACKNOWLEDGMENT

This work is supported by the Cognitive and Immersive Systems Laboratory (CISL), a collaboration between IBM Research and Rensselaer Polytechnic Institute, and also a center in IBM's AI Horizon Network. The authors would like to thank all of the researchers at CISL and the colleagues at IBM Yorktown Heights and IBM China for their contributions to this research. Without their help, this project would not have been possible.

REFERENCES

1. 2009. *Computer Assisted Language Learning: Critical Concepts in Linguistics*. Vol. I. Routledge.
2. 2013. *Modern Chinese Textbook 1A*. Better Chinese.
3. 2017. Effective Language Learning. (Oct 2017). http://www.effectivelanguagelearning.com/language-guide/language-difficulty
4. 2018. (2018). http://www.activeworlds.com/
5. 2018. (2018). http://secondlife.com/
6. 2018. Amazon Alexa. (2018). https://developer.amazon.com/alexa
7. 2018. Busuu. (2018). https://www.busuu.com
8. 2018. CAVE Automatic Virtual Environment. (2018). http://www.visbox.com/products/cave/
9. 2018. Chinese Pod. (2018). https://chinesepod.com
10. 2018. eChineseLearning. (2018). https://www.echineselearning.com
11. 2018. Google Assistant. (2018). https://assistant.google.com
12. 2018. Hello Talk. (2018). http://home.hellotalk.com
13. 2018. Mandarin (Chinese) | About World Languages. (2018). http://aboutworldlanguages.com/mandarin
14. 2018. Smallab Learning. (2018). https://www.smallablearning.com/
15. 2018. Tutor Mandarin. (2018). https://www.tutormandarin.net/en
16. 2018. Wai Chinese. (2018). https://waichinese.com/features.html
17. 2018. Watson Assistant. (2018). https://www.ibm.com/watson/services/conversation/
18. 2018. Watson Speech To Text. (2018). https://www.ibm.com/watson/services/speech-to-text/
19. Muna Mohammed Abbas Alkhateeb. 2017. An Analytical Approach of the Cultural Context in Language Teaching and Learning. *Journal of University of Babylon* 25, 2 (2017), 832âĂŞ840. https://doaj.org/article/d1e436f141a6483b832b2895c02dd40e?
20. Anke Berns, Antonio Gonzalez-Pardo, and David Camacho. 2013. Game-like language learning in 3-D virtual environments. 60 (01 2013), 210–220.
21. David Birchfield and Colleen Megowan-Romanowicz. 2009. Earth science learning in SMALLab: A design experiment for mixed reality. *International Journal of Computer-Supported Collaborative Learning* 4, 4 (01 Dec 2009), 403–421. DOI: http://dx.doi.org/10.1007/s11412-009-9074-8
22. Lynne Bolduc. 1997. Mastering Difficult Concepts Using Software to Support Learning: A Case Study in Teaching Mandarin Chinese. *Journal of Science Education and Technology* 6, 2 (1997), 91–102.
23. Richard Brecht, Dan Davidson, and Ralph Ginsberg. 1995. Predictors of foreign language gain during study abroad. *Second language acquisition in a study abroad context* 9 (1995), 37.
24. Silvia Canto and Kristi Jauregi Ondarra. 2017. Language learning effects through the integration of synchronous online communication: The case of video communication and Second Life. *Language Learning in Higher Education* 7, 1 (2017), 21–53.
25. Dongdong Chen. 2010. Enhancing the learning of Chinese with Second Life. *Journal of Technology and Chinese Language Teaching* 1, 1 (2010), 14–30.
26. Nancy F Chen, Darren Wee, Rong Tong, Bin Ma, and Haizhou Li. 2016. Large-scale characterization of non-native Mandarin Chinese spoken by speakers of European origin: Analysis on iCALL. *Speech Communication* 84 (2016), 46–56.
27. Tina Cok. 2016. ICT-supported language learning tools for Chinese as a foreign Language: a content review/Jezikovnotehnoloska orodja za ucenje kitajscine kot tujega jezika: pregled vsebine. *Revija za Elementarno Izobrazevanje* 9, 3 (06 2016), 103–120. http://libproxy.rpi.edu/login?url=https://search.proquest.com/docview/1799383943?accountid=28525 Copyright - Copyright Univerza v Mariboru, Faculty of Education/Pedagoska Fakulteta Jun 2016; Document feature - Tables; ; Graphs; Last updated - 2016-06-25.
28. Dan E Davidson. 2010. Study abroad: When, how long, and with what results? New data from the Russian front. *Foreign Language Annals* 43, 1 (2010), 6–26.
29. Oxana Dema and Aleidine Kramer Moeller. 2012. Teaching culture in the 21st century language classroom. *Faculty Publications: Department of Teaching, Learning and Teacher Education* (2012), 75âĂŞ91.
30. Mats Deutschmann, Luisa Panichi, and Judith Molka-Danielsen. 2009. Designing oral participation in Second Life–a comparative study of two language proficiency courses. *ReCALL* 21, 2 (2009), 206–226.
31. Wenhao Diao. 2011. Study abroad, participation and turn taking: A case study. In *Selected Proceedings of the 2010 Second Language Research Forum. Cascadilla Proceedings*.
32. Rahul R. Divekar, Robert Rouhani, Matthew Peveler, Rui Zhao, Jeffrey O. Kephart, David Allen, Kang Wang, Qiang Ji, and Hui Su. CIRA - An Architecture for Building Configurable Immersive Smart-rooms. In *To appear in proceedings of Intellisys 2018*.
33. Hang Du. 2013. The development of Chinese fluency during study abroad in China. *The Modern Language Journal* 97, 1 (2013), 131–143.
34. Michael E Everson. 2011. Best practices in teaching logographic and non-Roman writing systems to L2 learners. *Annual Review of Applied Linguistics* 31 (2011), 249–274.

35. Serhat Güzel and Selami Aydin. 2016. The Effect of Second Life on Speaking Achievement. *Online Submission* 6, 4 (2016), 236–245.

36. Michael Henderson, Hui Huang, Scott Grant, and Lyn Henderson. 2009. Language acquisition in Second Life: Improving self-efficacy beliefs. (2009).

37. Murat Hismanoglu. 2012. Integrating second life into an EFL classroom: A new dimension in foreign language learning and teaching. 3 (01 2012), 100–111.

38. Yu-Ju Lan, Yu-Hsuan Kan, Indy Y.T. Hsiao, Stephen J.H. Yang, and Kuo-En Chang. 2013. Designing interaction tasks in Second Life for Chinese as a foreign language learners: A preliminary exploration. *Australasian Journal of Educational Technology* 29, 2 (2013). DOI: http://dx.doi.org/10.14742/ajet.144

39. Mark Lee and Barney Dalgarno. 2011. *Scaffolding Discovery Learning in 3D Virtual Environments: Challenges and Considerations for Instructional Design*. IGI Global, United States, 138–169. DOI: http://dx.doi.org/10.4018/978-1-61692-825-4.ch008 Imported on 12 May 2017 - DigiTool details were: publisher = Hershey, PA: IGI-Global, 2011. editor/s (773b) = Shalin Hai-Jew; Issue no. (773s) = 8; Parent title (773t) = Virtual immersive and 3D learning spaces: emerging technologies and trends.

40. Hsien-Cheng Liao, Ying-Hua Guan, Jia-Jang Tu, and Jiang-Chun Chen. 2014. A prototype of an adaptive Chinese pronunciation training system. *System* 45 (2014), 52–66.

41. Yuen-kuang Liao and Yu-wen Chen. 2007. The effect of computer simulation instruction on student learning: A meta-analysis of studies in Taiwan. *Journal of information Technology and Applications* 2, 2 (2007), 69–79.

42. Tsun-Ju Lin and Yu-Ju Lan. 2015. Language Learning in Virtual Reality Environments: Past, Present, and Future. *Educational Technology & Society* 18, 4 (2015), 486–497.

43. James Milton, Sunniva Jonsen, Steven Hirst, and Sharn Lindenburn. 2012. Foreign language vocabulary development through activities in an online 3D environment. *The Language Learning Journal* 40, 1 (2012), 99–112. DOI: http://dx.doi.org/10.1080/09571736.2012.658229

44. Corey Mitchell. 2016. One million U.S. students could be studying Mandarin by 2020. (Aug 2016). http://www.pbs.org/newshour/rundown/2020-u-s-aims-1-million-students-studying-mandarin/

45. Max North and Sarah North. 2016. A Comparative Study of Sense of Presence of Traditional Virtual Reality and Immersive Environments. *Australasian Journal of Information Systems* 20, 0 (2016). DOI: http://dx.doi.org/10.3127/ajis.v20i0.1168

46. Mary G. O'Brien, Richard Levy, and Annika Orich. 2009. Virtual Immersion: The Role of CAVE and PC Technology. *CALICO Journal* 26, 2 (01 2009), 337. http://libproxy.rpi.edu/login?url=https://search-proquest-com.libproxy.rpi.edu/docview/750619686?accountid=28525 Copyright - Copyright CALICO Jan 2009; Last updated - 2014-12-07.

47. Mark Peterson. 2011. Towards a Research Agenda for the Use of Three-Dimensional Virtual Worlds in Language Learning. *CALICO Journal* 29, 1 (2011), 67–80. http://www.jstor.org/stable/calicojournal.29.1.67

48. Thomas C Reeves and John G Hedberg. 2003. *Chapter 1: A Pragmatic Rationale for Evaluation*. Education Technology, 7âĂŞ9.

49. Wei Ren. 2013. The effect of the study abroad on the pragmatic development in internal modification of refusals. 23 (12 2013), 715–741.

50. Roger C. Schank. 1990. Case-Based Teaching: Four Experiences in Educational Software Design. *Interactive Learning Environments* 1 (1990), 231–253.

51. Helen H Shen and Wenjing Xu. 2015. Active learning: Qualitative inquiries into vocabulary instruction in Chinese L2 classrooms. *Foreign Language Annals* 48, 1 (2015), 82–99.

52. Ya-Chun Shih. 2007. The Development of an Online Virtual English Classroom: VEC3D.

53. Ya-Chun Shih. 2017. *Weaving Web 2.0 and Facial Expression Recognition Into the 3D Virtual English Classroom*. Vol. I-III. IGI Global, 1375âĂŞ1399.

54. Naoko Taguchi, Qiong Li, and Xiaofei Tang. 2017. Learning Chinese Formulaic Expressions in a Scenario-Based Interactive Environment. 50 (10 2017).

55. Etsuko Toyoda. 2002. Categorization of Text Chat Communication between Learners and Native Speakers of Japanese.

56. Jennifer J. Vogel, David S. Vogel, Jan Cannon-Bowers, Clint A. Bowers, Kathryn Muse, and Michelle Wright. 2006. Computer Gaming and Interactive Simulations for Learning: A Meta-Analysis. *Journal of Educational Computing Research* 34, 3 (2006), 229–243. DOI: http://dx.doi.org/10.2190/FLHV-K4WA-WPVQ-H0YM

57. Airong Wang. 2017. *Learning English in a Multi-User Virtual Environment: Exploring Factors Affecting Participation*. Ph.D. Dissertation. Mid Sweden University.

58. Endymion Porter. Wilkinson. 2015. *Chinese History: A New Manual* (4 ed.). Harvard University Asia Center for the Harvard-Yenching Institute distributed by Harvard University Press.

59. Clare Wright and Z Cong. 2014. Examining the effects of Study Abroad on L2 Chinese development among UK university learners. *Newcastle and Northumbria Working Papers in Linguistics* 20 (2014), 67–83.

60. Zhou Yalun. 2016. Digital Vocabulary Competition as Motivator for Learning in CFL Classrooms. *JOURNAL OF TECHNOLOGY AND CHINESE LANGUAGE TEACHING* 7, 2 (2016), 1–22.

61. Kasumi Yamazaki. 2018. Computer-assisted learning of communication (CALC): A case study of Japanese learning in a 3D virtual world. *ReCALL* (2018), 1âĂŞ18. DOI:http://dx.doi.org/10.1017/S0958344017000350

62. Rui Zhao, Kang Wang, Rahul Divekar, Robert Rouhani, Hui Su, and Qiang Ji. 2018. An Immersive System with Multi-modal Human-computer Interaction. In *The IEEE Conference on Automatic Face and Gesture Recognition (FG)*.

63. Wenjing Zuo. 2011. The Effects of Cooperative Learning on Improving College StudentsâĂŹ Reading Comprehension. *Theory and Practice in Language Studies* 1, 8 (Jan 2011). DOI: http://dx.doi.org/10.4304/tpls.1.8.986-989

Designing for Multiple Hand Grips and Body Postures within the UX of a moving Smartphone

Rachel Eardley[1], Anne Roudaut[2], Steve Gill[1] and Stephen J Thompson[1]

[1] Cardiff Metropolitan University
Cardiff, UK
rachel@racheleardley.net, [sjgill, sthompson]
@cardiffmet.ac.uk

[2] University of Bristol
Bristol, UK
roudauta@gmail.com

ABSTRACT

In this paper we explore how screen-based smartphone interaction can be enriched when designers focus on the physical interaction issues surrounding the device. These consist of the hand grips used (Symmetric bimanual, Asymmetric bimanual with thumb, Single handed, Asymmetric bimanual with finger), body postures (Sitting at a table, Standing, Lying down) and the tilting of the smartphone itself. These physical interactions are well described in the literature and several research papers provide empirical metrics describing them. In this paper, we go one step further by using this data to generate new screen-based interactions. We achieved this by conducting two workshops to investigate how smartphone interaction design can be informed by the physicality of smartphone interaction. By analysing the outcomes, we provide 14 new screen interaction examples with additional insights comparing outcomes for various body postures and grips.

Author Keywords

Handgrip; Mobile device; Smartphone; Grasp; Body posture; Design; Interaction; Standing; Lying down.

ACM Classification Keywords

H.5.2. User Interfaces: Input Devices and Strategies.

INTRODUCTION

Hand interaction is a complex activity, one that Wilson [27] claims requires much 'skill'. These 'skills' once learned are used daily for simple tasks such as lifting a fork to our mouths to eat. The hands 'skill' as stated by Napier [21] is the use of different grips (Power, Scissor, Hook and Precision) that enable us to physically interact. Both Napier and Guiard [14] argue that using the 'skills' of both hands cooperatively allows for far more complex actions e.g. removing a lid from a jar where the non-dominant hand uses a power grip to secure the jar, while the dominant hand removes the lid through a mixture of power/precision grips.

Although we understand the hands' 'skill' well, most smartphone interactions are via touchscreen and make limited use of the physical interaction around the device. For example, no account is taken of the hand grip used, how the device tilt is affected by the user's posture (e.g. the position of the smartphone is different when the user is lying), or how the hand moves the device when physically interacting with it. All of these factors provide potential UI design opportunities, but apart from a few commercial examples (interface orientation changed from portrait to landscape when tilting or sensor-based character control in games), there is little use of physical interaction in smartphone UIs.

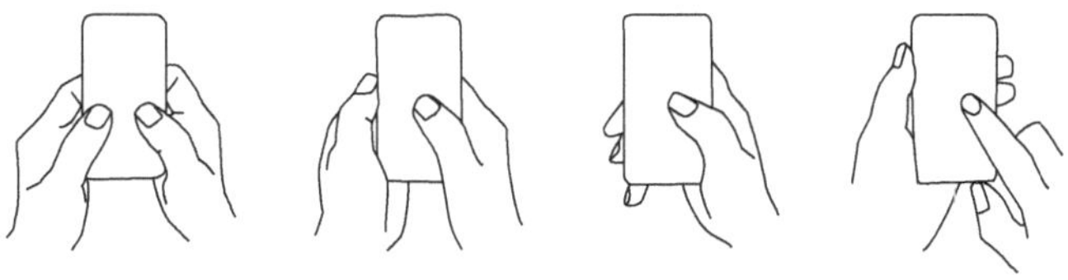

Figure 1. Four handgrips: Symmetric bimanual; Asymmetric bimanual thumb; Single-handed; Asymmetric bimanual finger. (From [9])

Figure 2. Three body postures: Sitting at a table resting arms; Standing; Lying down with the back to the floor. (From [10])

This is even more surprising given the empirical data available in the literature that describes how users manipulate their smartphones depending on hand grip, body posture or smartphone form factors. E.g. Eardley et al [9][10] systematically investigated how four hand grips (Figure 1) and three body postures (Figure 2) affect phone movements, providing a detailed table of metrics describing the different smartphone movements achieved in various interactive conditions. However, these works do not concentrate on

DIS '18, June 9–13, 2018, , Hong Kong

ACM ISBN 978-1-4503-5198-0/18/06…$15.00
https://doi.org/10.1145/3196709.3196711

using the data to generate new UIs, as we are exploring in this paper.

In order to generate new UIs that make use of available empirical data, we conducted two design development workshops. Each had the same structure but investigated different factors: the first asked participants to generate UIs for different body postures given a specific grip, while in the second we fixed the body postures and let participants generate UIs for various hand grips. In both workshops, participants were given empirical data on hand grip, body posture and the corresponding tilting range of the smartphone as extracted from empirical data in [9][10].

The outcomes of these two workshops, analyzed and summarized in this paper, allow us to expand the set of possibilities for physical interaction with a smartphone for 14 new designs, as well as providing insights on how designs differ when different postures or hand grips are used. In summary, we contribute: (1) 14 new UIs using physical interaction to enhance touchscreen interfaces; and (2) insights into how hand grip and posture affect these designs.

RELATED RESEARCH

The current knowledge of the effect of hand grip and body posture on smartphone interaction is summarized below.

Using grip for interaction

Many studies have investigated how individuals hold a smartphone via their hands. In [8] the authors mapped four grips during an observational study with three smartphone interaction types. [1] investigated three grips using a touchscreen keyboard and examined the resulting typing accuracy while [3] looked at what zone of the screen was reachable with the thumb for a static grip. Another study compared the use of a static single-handed grip in the dominant and non-dominant hand and the effect on tapping accuracy [24]. What these studies have done is highlight the ways in which people grip the smartphone the range of reach available when using these static grips as well as the accuracy that individuals have when interacting with action items. Previous work has also proposed to detect grip type and adapt the UI accordingly [28,19]. In [19], grips were used to predict the smartphone mode (e.g. camera, call, game) while in [5] the change of grip changes the screen from landscape to portrait. Researchers also proposed screen-based sensor technology to allow UIs that adapt depending on where fingers are on the screen [16]. All these approaches explore static grips rather than hand movement during interaction. However, other research looked into hand movements when using a single-handed grip by tilting the device to allow the thumb to reach more items [22,20,4], This research established a precedent of using smartphone sensors in order to further interaction experience within the physical realms. Research by Eardley et al [9,10], was the first to provide a detailed table of empirically-derived metrics of factors (hand grips, body posture, phone form factors, target position) that affect movements.

Physical body posture

Studies have investigated the influence of gender, body posture [25] or muscles used when interacting with smartphones sitting down and using single and asymmetric bimanual grips [2]. Researchers have also investigated how text entry can be affected by walking [12]. Meanwhile [22] and [18] investigated single-handed interaction in multiple body postures by comparing the thumb's biomechanical joint movement and musculature pressures for three body postures (sitting, sitting at a table and standing). [4] investigated how smartphone movement varied in various physical positions during different activities (sitting, standing, walking and sitting on a moving bus). Finally [10] looked systematically at the hand-smartphone interaction and compared body postures with multiple grips.

WORKSHOPS METHODOLOGY

The goal of the workshops was to validate the value of previously gathered empirical data by using it to develop new UI design concepts. In the first workshop, "*Fixed Grip*", we asked 13 participants to focus on one assigned hand grip (within the four shown on Figure 1), designing for three different body postures (Figure 2). In the second workshop "*Fixed Posture*", *9* participants focused on one of the Figure 2 body postures, designing for the four different hand grips shown in Figure 1. The body postures and grips were chosen based on previously gathered empirical data, on which participants of both workshops were thoroughly briefed [10]. We split in two the workshops to avoid giving too many conditions to our participants and reduce the overall workshop duration.

Workshop material pack

Each team of participants were given a material pack described below.

Figure 3: Prototyping material given to each team.

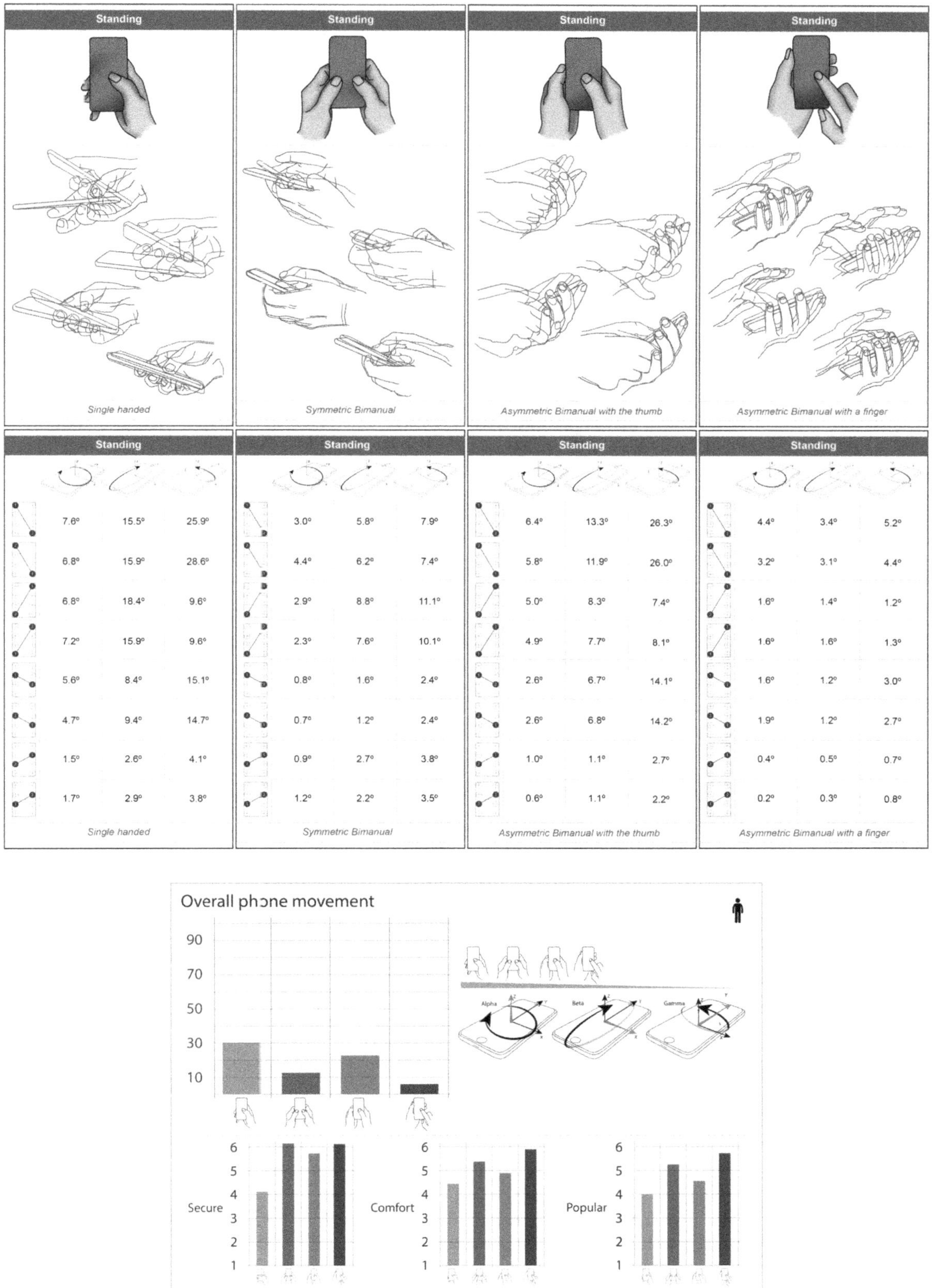

Figure 4: An example of the individual data cards given to the teams, here showing data from [10] for the four grips using the body posture standing; and the overall data presented to the team assigned standing in the 'fixed posture' workshop.

Prototyping material: (1) Physical model of the iPhone 6 constructed out of foam board with the target locations used in previous studies [9,10] printed on a transparent cover; (2) printed A4 sheets with 4 smartphone templates for sketching screen designs; (3) number cards used for team splitting (described further) ; (4) a pen (Figure 3);

Data cards: Using the data gathered from [10], where 20 participants used an iPhone 6 running a custom-built application with 8 random tapping tasks. The participants completing the tapping tasks for 4 hand grips (Figure 1) and in 3 selected body postures (Figure 2). This custom built application gathered data on the smartphone's movement along the Alpha, Beta and Gamma axis. In order to communicate this data, we created a number of cards explaining the Alpha, Beta and Gamma rotational movements corresponding to the body postures and hand grips used. The cards included: (1) Images of the four different grips; (2) Mean rotational angle of smartphone movement along the Alpha, Beta and Gamma axes for the 8 tapping tasks; (3) Overall statistical data for the individual grip/body posture that was gathered by asking the participants how they felt about the individual grips in relation to the body posture used.

Figure 4 shows an example of the cards for a group designing for the four hand grips used in the Standing posture. In summary, we gave each team a total of 4 or 5 cards depending on the workshop type: 4 hands grip cards plus the overall data card in the "fixed posture" workshop and 3 body posture cards plus the overall data cards for "fixed grip".

Structure of the workshops

Each workshop lasted for 90 minutes in five stages:

Step1: organizing the participants (5 min)

Participants were organized into teams. This was done by asking the participants of each academic year to randomly pick a card with a number between 1 and 4 printed on it for the "fixed grip" and 1 and 3 for the "fixed posture" workshop (Figure 3). The numbers corresponded to the team that each participant would be placed in, ensuring that each workshop contained a mixture of academic levels.

Step 2: informing participants of previous research (15 min)

Participants were asked about their average daily smartphone usage and the types of applications they use in an average day. The discussion then transitioned to locations in which the smartphones were used, ultimately culminating in conversations centred on the body postures participants adopted for various applications or contexts. Participants were also asked to list the top three applications that they used on a standard day, with the discussion serving an additional purpose of bonding and relaxing the group. Next, we asked each participant to imagine writing a text message on their phone. They were then asked what type of grips they used. This exercise was conducted in order to facilitate a discussion with all participants about different types of grip types (Figure 1). At this point the teams were informed about previously-gathered metrics on smartphone body postures and grip types and were told that they would be given this data to work from in the form of a 'material pack'.

Step 3: assigning factors and giving material pack (10 min)

Each team was handed a material pack that defined the grip/body posture that they would design for. The participants from the 'fixed grip' workshop had three body posture variables to design for: (Standing, Sitting at a table and Lying down). The participants from the 'fixed posture' workshop had four grip variables to design for: (Single handed, Asymmetric bimanual with finger, Asymmetric bimanual with thumb, Symmetric bimanual).

Step 4: designing new UIs (45 min)

Each team was asked to design for an existing application, chosen from among the top three applications listed in Stage 2. They were asked to create a new UI design for the application using the data provided in the material pack. They were asked to sketch the UI design and to circle the body posture and grip that they were designing for at the top of their sheet (See top of Figure 5). Participants were encouraged to assume the appropriate body posture and if possible use the selected application on their smartphone to inform their design process.

Step 5: presenting new UIs (15 min)

When the team finished their designs, they presented their UI concepts to the rest of the participants.

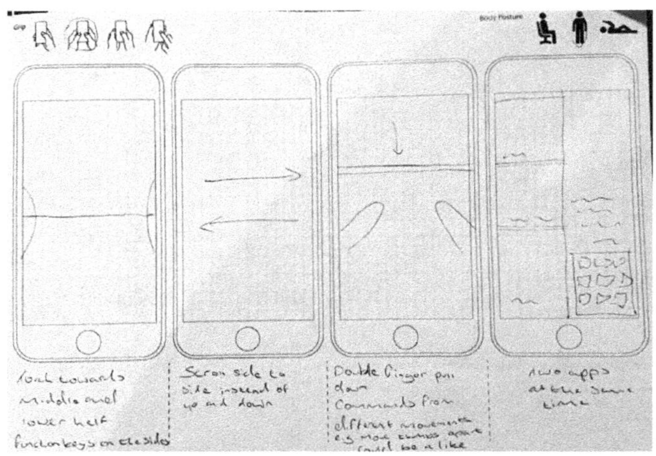

Figure 5: Example of outcomes from a team for the Grip "Symmetric bimanual" and the Body posture "Standing".

Participants

22 participants studying product design at the same university with mixed levels of education, attended one of two 90 minute design workshops.

Fixed Grip workshop: 13 participants (12 Male and 1 Female) 5 Masters, 4 third year and 4 second year product design students.

Fixed Posture workshop: 9 participants (6 Male and 3 Female) 4 Masters, 3 third year and 2 second year product design students.

Figure 6: Participants attending the workshop discussing designs ideas within their teams.

Note on pilot workshop

Prior to these workshops we conducted a pilot workshop with a slightly different structure. 20 participants were split into 8 teams with participants randomly assigned one of three body postures (Figure 2), one of four grips (Figure 1), and one of two application types (Security or Messaging). Application selection was based on previous academic research [8,29].

The pilot workshop took 55 mins and generated 22 UI concepts. Analysis showed that the workshop had succeeded in generating a number of thought-provoking concepts using the empirical data. However, we had no ability to compare the body postures or grips in order to identify if there were any overarching design themes that were grip or body posture specific. We consequently made changes to the workshop design as described below.

WORKSHOPS RESULTS

We describe and analyze the results of the two workshops but first we explained how we analyzed the sketches made by our participants. We then analyze the results first by theme, and then by body posture and hand grips.

Analysis of sketches

Of the 63 individual sketches produced, 3 were discarded as being out of scope: scrolling horizontally instead of vertically (2 sketches) and using eye tracking to select action items (1 sketch).

As shown in Table 1, the 60 sketches produced by the participants provided a mean of 5 sketches per grip/body posture. With grip Asymmetric bimanual with thumb and body posture sitting at a table having the least (2 sketches) and grip Single handed and body posture lying down having the most (8 sketches). Next the 60 individual sketches were coded on interaction methods and then categorized into groups following the categorization method [13], resulting in 5 themes that ranged from placement of action items to using the phone's movement to change the current app. During the categorization process, we additionally looked at how variation in grips or postures affected the designs and if there were any trends. A professional UX designer then solidified the concepts and created visuals for them.

	Standing	*Sitting at table*	*Lying down*
Single handed	4	5	8
Asymmetric bimanual with thumb	4	2	5
Asymmetric bimanual with finger	6	5	5
Symmetric bimanual	6	6	4

Table 1: Overall sketches broken down into grips and body postures.

Results by themes

6 of the 7 teams selected the Facebook newsfeed application and 1 chose Instagram. Five themes emerged: (1) the placement of buttons on the screens; (2) using the passive movement of the smartphone; (3) using the deliberate movement of the smartphone; (4) layout of information on the screen and; (5) areas of the screen having specific types of integration. We now explain these in more detail:

Theme 1: Placement of buttons on the screen

Of 19 initial sketches, three key concepts were formed around the action items being repositioned on the screen in order to improve reachability. For example, in Figure 7, we can see that all of the main action items have been removed from the top bar of the screen and have been placed to fit within the functional area of the thumb [3]. These concepts differed only in the location of the action items (Bottom right/left area of the screen, down the side of the screen and central area of the screen).

We analysed the grips and body postures in which the participants created the sketches for this theme (Table 2). We noticed that there were a higher percentage of sketches for Standing (10 sketches) than Lying down (7 sketches) and finally Sitting at a table (3 sketches). For the grips, we found that Asymmetric bimanual with finger and Asymmetric bimanual with thumb had the most (7 Sketches) with Symmetric bimanual next (3 sketches) and finally Single handed (2 sketches).

It is worth noting that grip Symmetric bimanual only had sketches for the UI concept with action items on the side of the screen (Figure 7b & 7c) and for body postures Standing and Lying down. Grip Single handed only had sketches for the UI concept with the action items at the bottom (Figure 7a) and for body postures Sitting at a table and Lying down. For Grip Asymmetric bimanual with finger, 5 out of the 7 sketches occurred for the body posture Standing, with 1 each for Sitting at a table and Lying down. The most sketches occurred for UI concepts that included moving action items to the bottom right of the screen (Figure 7a).

	Standing	*Sitting at table*	*Lying down*
Single handed		1	1
Asymmetric bimanual with thumb	3	1	3
Asymmetric bimanual with finger	5	1	1
Symmetric bimanual	2		1

Table 2: Showing how the 19 sketches for Theme 1 mapped between grips and body postures.

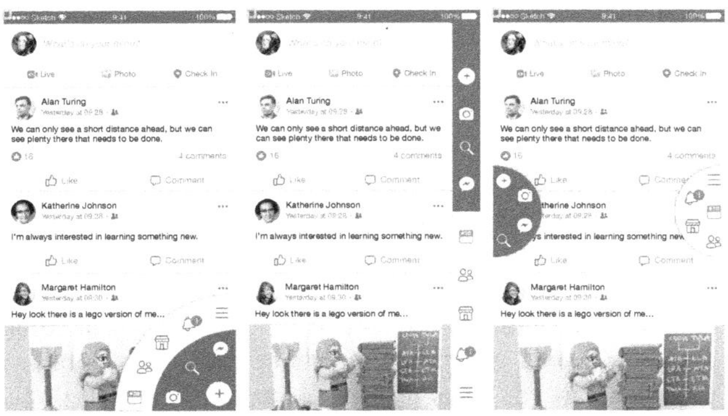

Figure 7: Changing the placement of buttons on the screen to improve accessibility for right handed users (a) Bottom right (b) Right side and (c) Middle.

Theme 2: Passive movement of the smartphone

9 sketches centred on two key concepts formed around passive movement of the phone. The first group had the action items moving around the screen so that they relocated to a more reachable area, while the second enlarged the action items so they were easier to tap.

	Standing	*Sitting at table*	*Lying down*
Single handed		2	
Asymmetric bimanual with thumb	1	1	
Asymmetric bimanual with finger		3	1
Symmetric bimanual	1		

Table 3: Showing how the 9 sketches for Theme 2 mapped between grips and body postures.

For example, in Figure 8a, as the user tilts the phone up in order for their fingers to reach the top items, the items will transition to the bottom of the screen for easier reach. For Figure 8b, the same tilting action occurs, however the action item's visual representation and touch area expand, making it easier for the user to complete their intended task.

Looking at the grips and body postures of the sketches (Table 3) we found that the body posture Sitting at a table was the most popular (6 sketches), followed by Standing (2 sketches) and finally Lying down (1 sketch). Asymmetric bimanual with finger, was the most popular grip (4 sketches). Grip Single handed only accounted for 1 moving action item concept for the body posture Sitting at a table, while sketches for grips Asymmetric bimanual with finger and Symmetric bimanual showed UI concepts involving expanding action items with a mixture of body postures.

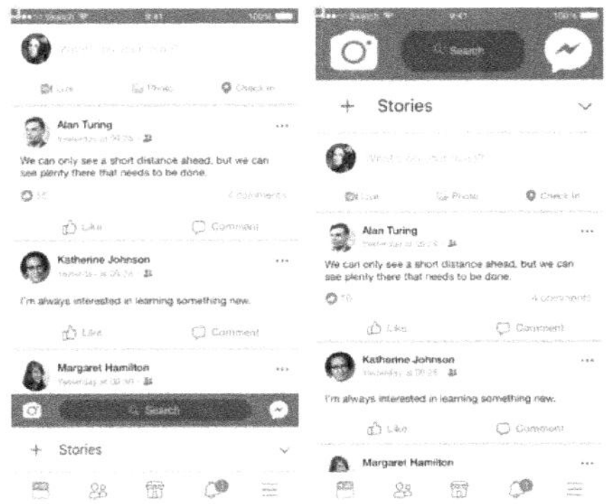

Figure 8: Concepts for passive movement updating the UI (a)

Theme 3: Deliberate movement of the smartphone

13 sketches focussed on 3 key concepts enabled via the smartphone's inbuilt sensors. The first, aspired to use the physical casing in order to identify the user's grip or position of the hand and update the screen layout accordingly, which is a similar concept to [28]. The second conceived of a screen-based sensor that traced the thumb's location and located the action items next to it, similar to previous research undertaken by [16]. The third set of concepts used the smartphone as a physical gesture device so that deliberate manipulation of the phone would update the functionalities of an application or switch the application itself.

Figure 9a illustrates a concept whereby when a user picks up the smartphone, the action items appear automatically within reach of their hand, no matter how or where they are gripping the phone. The concept in Figure 9b moves action items close to the thumb's contact point based on its proximity to the screen. In Figure 9c we see a concept that has the user flicking the smartphone in order to reveal the action items via a pop-up box.

Body posture Lying down accounted for most sketches (6), with Sitting next (4) and Standing (2). All grips were included, with Symmetric bimanual and Single handed having the most sketches (4) followed by Asymmetric bimanual with finger (3 sketches) and finally Asymmetric bimanual with thumb (2 sketches).

Grip Symmetric bimanual had the concept types shown in Figure 9b and for body postures Sitting at a table and Lying down. Grip Asymmetric bimanual with thumb concepts focused on the concept types shown in Figure 9a and for the body posture Lying down. Grip Asymmetric bimanual with finger concepts were split, 1 sketch of the Figure 9a type (body posture Lying down) and 2 sketches of the Figure 9c type (body postures Sitting at a table and Lying down).

	Standing	Sitting at table	Lying down
Single handed	2	1	1
Asymmetric bimanual with thumb			2
Asymmetric bimanual with finger		1	2
Symmetric bimanual		3	1

Table 4: Showing how the 13 sketches for Theme 3 mapped between grips and body postures.

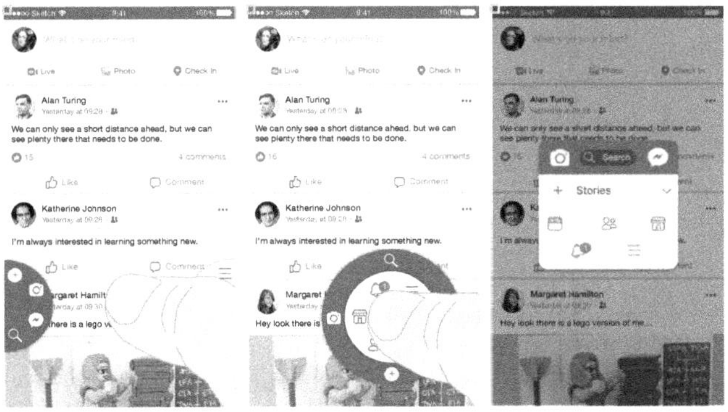

Figure 9: Concepts for physical sensors (a) Action items move position depending on the grip (b) Action items position dependent on the location of the thumb (c) Deliberately tilting the smartphone brings the action items on the screen.

Theme 4: Layout of information on the screen

The 8 concepts produced in Theme 4 can be grouped into three key concepts based on the screen layout. The first uses the phone's internal sensors to tilt screen content according to the angle at which it is being held. The second using the motions of the phone to present content in the form of a 3D scroll. In the third concept group the user taps to trigger a 3D horizontal scrolling interaction.

Figure 10a illustrates a UI screen designed for a user viewing Facebook via a smartphone while lying down. Instead of the phone transitioning directly from portrait to landscape, this UI has the screen tilt to match the angle at which the user is gripping the smartphone. In Figure 10b a 3D transition occurs when the user tilts the smartphone horizontally left or right, in order to change the application mode or move to the next application. Figure 10c shows a UI requiring the user to tap the screen to change the viewing capabilities. The action transforms the card layout to a rotary system, allowing to scroll the content by tilting the phone vertically.

By analysing the grips and body postures we see that only Lying down (5 sketches) and Standing (3 sketches) provoked concepts. The grip that triggered the most ideas was Single handed (4 sketches), followed by Asymmetric bimanual with finger and Symmetric bimanual (2 sketches). Neither the Asymmetric bimanual with thumb grip nor the Sitting at a table body posture provoked any concepts at all.

The UI concept in Figure 10a uses only the Single handed grip and incorporates the body postures Standing and Lying down. Figure 10c illustrates a concept which integrated the Asymmetric bimanual with finger grip sketches which both highlighted scrolling by tilting the smartphone.

	Standing	Sitting at table	Lying down
Single handed	1		3
Asymmetric bimanual with thumb			
Asymmetric bimanual with finger	1		1
Symmetric bimanual	1		1

Table 5: Showing how the 8 sketches for Theme 4 mapped between grips and body postures.

Figure 10: Concepts for physical sensors (a) Tilting the content of the screen to its in line with the user's physical position (b) Using the physical gestures to via a 3D effect switch to another application. (c) Using the card layout of Facebook to act as a rotary system.

Theme 5: Areas of screen with specific types of integration

The 11 sketches in Theme 5 can be categorized as being two UI approach types. The first uses a given area of the screen either as a track pad (Figure 11a) or as a more sensitive display area, allowing the user to scroll quicker (Figure 11b). The second splits the screen in half, allowing the separate content for each half of the screen to be scrolled independently (Figure 11c).

In Figure 11a we see the user using the bottom part of the screen as a touch pad to control a pointer (red circle) in order to select the required items. Figure 11b illustrates a concept where the part of the screen within the functional area of the thumb for a right-hand user is made more sensitive. Scrolling in this area speeds up the standard scroll so that the Facebook feed or photos can be viewed more quickly. The third UI concept splits the screen in two halves, allowing the user to scroll each independently of the other (Figure 11c).

The body postures, Sitting at a table and Lying down produced the most concepts (4) while Standing accounted for 3 sketches. Only grip Single handed (5 sketches) and Symmetric bimanual (6 sketches) provoked concepts.

The concepts displayed in Figures 11a and 11b worked for grip Single handed and all body postures. The concept illustrated in Figure 11c is intended predominantly for grip Symmetric bimanual although 1 concept used grip Single handed and the Lying down body posture.

	Standing	*Sitting at table*	*Lying down*
Single handed	1	1	3
Asymmetric bimanual with thumb			
Asymmetric bimanual with finger			
Symmetric bimanual	2	3	1

Table 6: Showing how the 11 sketches for Theme 5 mapped between grips and body postures.

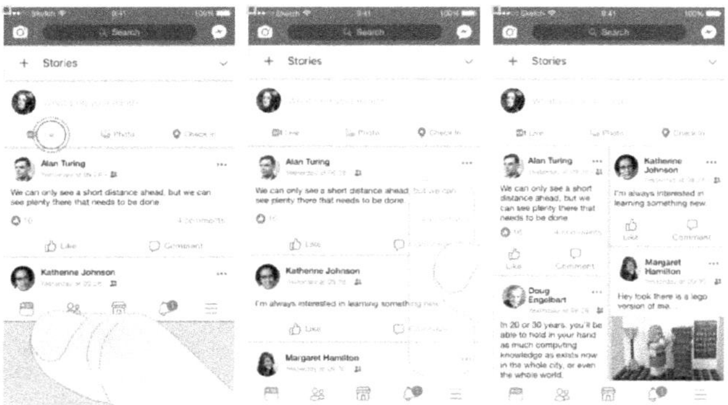

Figure 11: Concepts for physical sensors (a) A trackpad controlled icon shows the selection location (b) Area on the screen shows a more sensitive area for scrolling (c) Split screen content allows for each side of the screen to scroll.

Results by grips and body postures

We analysed the workshop results to identify any key characteristics for individual grips and body postures and made a series of findings:

Grip: Symmetric bimanual

The concepts focused around grip Symmetric bimanual incorporate 4 themes. Examples are shown in Figures 7b, 7c, 8b, 9b and 11c. Two key characteristics are true for most of these concepts:

- Action items down both sides of the screen can be used with the corresponding thumb (Figures 7c and 11c).
- Generic interaction methods allow either thumb to activate the action items (Figures 8b and 9b).

The odd concept out is Figure 7b which has the action items down the side of the screen, so it can be accessed via the dominant hand rather than both hands at the same time.

Grip: Single handed

The concepts related to grip Single handed are Figures 7a, 8a, 10a, 11a and 11b which incorporate 4 themes. These figures show three key sets of characteristics:

- Action items sit within range of the functional thumb and are either placed at or controlled from the bottom of the screen (Figures 7a, 8a, 11a).
- Action items are placed on the dominant hand side of the screen and within the functional arc of the thumb (Figure 11b).
- Designed for single-handed use, utilising the smartphone's in-built sensors to adjust the way information is viewed (Figure 10a).

Grip: Asymmetric bimanual with thumb

The concept sketches associated with grip Asymmetric bimanual with thumb focused on three themes, and are illustrated in Figures 7a, 7c, 8a, 8b and 9a. These concepts have two key characteristics:

- Action items are placed or appear near the lower end of the screen within the functional area of the thumb for the dominant hand (Figure 7a, 7c, 8a and 9a).
- Action items interactively enlarge to improve reachability (Figure 8b).

Grip: Asymmetric bimanual with finger

Grip Asymmetric bimanual with finger concepts cover four themes seen in Figures 7a, 8b, 9a, 9c and 10c. There are two key characteristics:

- Action items are revealed or manoeuvred depending on the activities or physical placement of the non-dominant hand (Figures 8b, 9a, 9c and 10c).
- Action items appear in the bottom corner (Figure 7a)

Body posture: Standing

The Standing body posture is included in all 5 themes and concepts can be seen in Figures 7a, 7c, 8a, 9b, 10c, 11b, 11c. These figures have three key characteristics:

- Action items that are positioned in or which transition to be within the functional area of the thumb (Figures 7a, 8a, 9b and 11b).
- Action items that are positioned on either or both side(s) of the screen (Figures 7c and 11c).
- The ability to interact with the smartphone's scrolling functions using its in-built sensors (Figure 10c).

Body posture: Sitting at a table

Sitting at a table is included in four themes with illustrations which can be found in Figures 7a, 7b, 8a, 8b, 9c, 11a and 11c. There are 4 key characteristics:

- Action items are positioned or actively transition to be within the functional area of the thumb (Figures 7a, 8a and 11a).
- The movement of the smartphone is used to update the content of the screen either passively or through deliberate user input (Figures 8b and 9c).
- Action items are positioned on the dominant hand side of the screen (Figure 7b).
- Content is split vertically down the middle of the screen, allowing either side to be separately activated (Figure 11c).

Body posture: Lying down

The Lying down body posture is included in all 5 themes and concepts can be seen in Figures 7a, 7c, 8b, 9a, 10a, 10c, 11a, 11b and 11c. There are three key characteristics:

- Action items are within the range the functional area of thumb and are either placed, transitioned or controlled from the bottom of the screen (Figures 7a, 11a and 11b).
- The phone's in-built sensors are used to update the controls so they are either reachable, within the functional area of the thumb or can control the viewing of information (Figures 8b, 9a, 10a and 10c).
- Action items that are positioned on either side of the screen or both (Figures 7c and 11c).

DISCUSSION

When reviewing smartphone UI designs, one must be aware that smartphone UX/UI designers have to create designs for a number of technology platforms (e.g. Apple iOS and Google Android). Whilst part of the design process gives these UX/UI designers a degree of freedom in what they create, they are limited, somewhat by the relevant platforms' design guidelines. Looking at the Apple iOS design guidelines [30] and Google Android's material design notes [31] we find that they have very distinct recommendations for the location of action items; i.e. the top and bottom of the screen. Apple call this top screen area "Navigation/Search bars" while Google refer to it as "App bar/Primary toolbar". Meanwhile, the bottom screen area is named "tab bars/Toolbars" by Apple and 'Bottom bar' by Google. Our research was focused on non-commercial consumer requirements, with design students given an open brief to investigate how they might design for the physical movement of the smartphone in terms of grips and body postures.

Our work brings a new perspective on smartphone UI design focusing not just on the screen but on the physicality of the devices. That being said we are aware that our study has limitations, in particular we only focus on a certain application and specific postures (As the previous research only had empirical data about those [10]). Additionally, we need to make sure that with these new smartphone UI concepts, we do not ignore the cognitive price that may occur for an ever changing interface. Automatic changes could be confusing and further investigations need to be done to understand this.

Insights by themes

If we look at the themes, we can see that 4 out of the 5 categories of concepts adjust the location of action items from the top of the screen area to the sides, bottom or in a dynamic position governed by the thumb's location. Additionally, 3 out of 5 themes are designs exploiting extra functionality via the phones internal sensors, something that is not currently prominent within the design guidelines.

Insights by grips and body postures

Focusing on the grips and potential locations of items, the participants' sketches showed that each grip has a preferred location for items (Figure 12). We can see that for grip Symmetric bimanual this means having items down either side or at the bottom of the screen. For grip Asymmetric bimanual with thumb, action items should appear down the dominant hand's side and on the lower part of the screen. Grip Single handed is similar but with a smaller area of action at the bottom of the screen, while the preferred area with the Asymmetric bimanual with finger grip is the lower corner of the dominant hand's side of screen.

With regard to body postures, the potential location of action items only differed for one; Standing (Figure 13). For both Sitting at a table and Lying down action items down either side and at the bottom of the screen were preferred. In the case of Standing, the preferred action items location was down the side of the dominant hand as well as on the lower part of the screen.

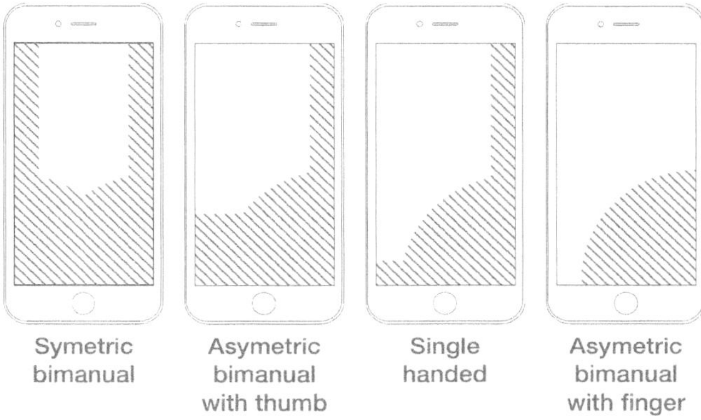

Figure 12: Main areas of action item placement from participants' sketches for each grip shown in grey.

Figure 13: Main areas of action item placement from participant's sketches for each body posture shown in grey.

CONCLUSION

We have presented the results and analysis of two workshops aimed at proving how existing empirical data relating to smartphone hand grip and posture can provide useful material for new UI concepts. We believe our work will be useful for designers, not only by providing new ideas for design approaches, but also by bringing relevant insights on how design can change through the accommodation of body posture and hand grip. Additionally, we hope our paper demonstrates the importance of gathering empirical data and how they can be a critical research source for the design of more adapted user interfaces. The next steps will be to construct clickable prototypes in order to evaluate the position of the action items and movement of the UI concepts shown in this paper. This will be done for a selection of applications such as text messaging. The usability tests will be run with end users who have a range of ages, genders and technology awareness. The aim of these usability tests is to highlight the best design approaches concerning the placement of action items and the cognitive load that the transitions may place on the user. This work will inform further iterative design development on smartphone UI.

ACKNOWLEDGEMENT We thank the participants for their time, Somo for the loan of the technical equipment and support given to RE. AR would like to acknowledge the Leverhulme Trust as well as the EPSRC EP/P004342/1 who funded part of this work

REFERENCES

1. Azenkot S., Zhai, S. 2012. Touch behavior with different postures on soft smartphone keyboards. MobileHCI '12. ACM, New York, NY, USA, 251-260.
2. Bachynskyi, M., Palmas, G., Oulasvirta, A., Steimle, J. Weinkauf, T. 2015. Performance and Ergonomics of Touch Surfaces: A Comparative Study using Biomechanical Simulation. CHI '15. ACM, New York, NY, USA, 1817-1826.
3. Bergstrom-Lehtovirta, J., Oulasvirta, A. 2014. Modeling the functional area of the thumb on mobile touchscreen surfaces. CHI '14. ACM, New York,USA, 1991-2000.
4. Chang, Y., L'Yi, S., Koh, K, Seo, J. 2015. Understanding Users' Touch Behavior on Large Mobile Touch-Screens and Assisted Targeting by Tilting Gesture. CHI '15. ACM, New York, NY, USA, 1499-1508.
5. Cheng, L.P, Hsiao, F., Liu Y., Chen, M.Y. 2012. iRotate: automatic screen rotation based on face orientation. CHI '12. ACM, New York, NY, USA, 2203-2210.
6. Corsten C., Daehlmann B., Voelker S., Borchers, J. 2017. BackXPress: Using Back-of-Device Finger Pressure to Augment Touchscreen Input on Smartphones. CHI17, ACM, New York, NY, USA, 4654-4666.
7. Dreyfuss, H. The Measure of Man: Human Factors in Design, Whitney Library of Design, 1967
8. Eardley, R., Gill, S., Roudaut, A., Thompson, S., Hare, J. 2016. Investigating how the hand interacts with different mobile phones. MobileHCI '16. ACM,
9. Eardley, R., Roudaut, A., Gill, S., and Thompson, S. J., 2017. Understanding Grip Shifts: How Form Factors Impact Hand Movements on Mobile Phones. (CHI '17). ACM, New York, NY, USA, 4680-4691.
10. Eardley, R., Roudaut, A., Gill, S., and Thompson, S. J., 2018. Investigating How Smartphone Movement is Affected by Body Posture. (CHI '18). ACM, New York, NY, USA,
11. Frameless web browser Retrieved May 3, 2016 from http://stakes.github.io/Frameless/
12. Goel, M., Findlater, L., and Wobbrock, J. WalkType: using accelerometer data to accomodate situational impairments in mobile touch screen text entry. CHI'12, ACM (2012), 2687–2696.
13. Goetz, J. & LeCompte, M. (1981). Ethnographic research and the problem of data reduction. Anthropology and Education Quarterly, 12, 51-70.
14. Guiard, Y. (1987). Asymmetric division of labor in human skilled bimanual action: the kinematic chain as a model.
15. Heads-Up webcam viewer Retrieved May 3, 2016 from https://itunes.apple.com/gb/app/headsup-webcam-viewer/id583912513?mt=12
16. Hinckley, K., Heo, S., Pahud, M., Holz, C., Benko, H., Sellen, A., Banks, R., O'Hara, K., Smyth, G., Buxton, W. 2016. Pre-Touch Sensing for Mobile Interaction. CHI '16. ACM, New York, NY, USA, 2869-2881.
17. Holz, C., Baudisch, P. 2010. The generalized perceived input point model and how to double touch accuracy by extracting fingerprints. CHI '10. ACM, USA, 581-590.
18. Kim, D.-S., and Chae, W.-S. Biomechanical analysis of a smartphone task with different postures. Korean Journal of Sport Biomechanics 22, 2 (2012), 253--259.
19. Kim, K., Chang, W., Cho, S., Shim, J., Lee, H., Park, J., Lee, Y., Kim, S. Hand Grip Pattern Recognition for Mobile User Interfaces. In Proceedings of the National Conference on Artificial Intelligence, vol 21, page 1789. Menlo Park, CA; Cambridge, MA; London; AAAI Press; MIT Press; 1999, 2006.
20. Mohd Noor, M.F., Ramsay, A., Hughes, S., Rogers, S., Williamson, J., and Murray-Smith, R. 28 Frames Later: Predicting Screen Touches from Back-of-device Grip Changes. CHI'14, ACM (2014), 2005–2008.
21. Napier, J., (1993) Hands, Published by Princeton University Press.
22. Negulescu, M., McGrenere, J. Grip Change as an Information Side Channel for Mobile Touch Interaction, CHI15, April 18-23, 2015, Seoul, Republic of Korea.
23. Ng, A., Brewster S.A, Williamson, J.H. 2014. Investigating the effects of encumbrance on one- and two- handed interactions with mobile devices. CHI '14. ACM, New York, NY, USA, 1981-1990.
24. Perry K., Hourcade, J.P. 2008. Evaluating one handed thumb tapping on mobile touchscreen devices. GI '08. Canadian Information Processing Society, Toronto, Ont., Canada, Canada, 57-64.
25. Gold, J.E., J.B. Driban 1, N. Thomas, T. Chakravarty, V. Channell, E. Komaroff, Postures, typing strategies, and gender differences in mobile device usage: An observational study, 22 June 2011, Applied Ergonomics 43 (2012) 408e412

26. Silverback 2 Retrieved May 3, 2016 from https://silverbackapp.com/
27. Wilson, F. (1998). The Hand. Published by Vintage ISBN: 0-679-74047-3.
28. Wimmer, R., Boring, S., HandSense: discriminating different ways of grasping and holding a tangible user interface, TEI09, February 16-18, 2009, Cambridge, United Kingdom
29. Mehrnezhad M, Toreini E, Shahandashti SF, Hao F. Stealing PINs via mobile sensors: actual risk versus user perception. Information Security 2017.
30. Apple iOS design guidelines, January 6, 2016 from https://developer.apple.com/ios/human-interface-guidelines/bars/toolbars/
31. Google android design guidelines, January 6, 2016 from https://material.io/guidelines/layout/structure.html - structure-ui-regions

Gestures for Smart Rings: Empirical Results, Insights, and Design Implications

Bogdan-Florin Gheran
MintViz Lab | MANSiD
Research Center,
University of Suceava
Suceava 720229, Romania
vatavu@eed.usv.ro

Jean Vanderdonckt
Louvain School of
Management, Univ.
catholique de Louvain
Louvain-la-Neuve, Belgium
jean.vanderdonckt@uclouvain.be

Radu-Daniel Vatavu
MintViz Lab | MANSiD
Research Center,
University of Suceava
Suceava 720229, Romania
vatavu@eed.usv.ro

ABSTRACT
We present empirical results about users' gesture preferences for smart rings by analyzing 672 gestures from 24 participants. We report an overall low consensus (mean .112, maximum .225 on the unit scale) between participants' gesture proposals, and we point to the challenges of designing highly-generalizable ring gestures across users. We also contribute to the practice of gesture elicitation studies by discussing how *a priori* conditions (e.g., participants' traits, such as creativity and motor skills), commitment and behavior *during* the experiment (e.g., their thinking times), but also *a posteriori* aspects (the experimenter's choice of criteria to group gestures into categories) affect agreement. We offer design guidelines for ring gestures informed by our empirical observations, and present a collection of gestures reflective of our participants' mental models for effecting commands using smart rings.

ACM Classification Keywords
H.5.2. [Information Interfaces and Presentation (e.g., HCI)] User Interfaces: *Input devices and strategies.*

Author Keywords
Smart Rings; Ring Gestures; Gesture User Interfaces; Elicitation Study; Wearables; Experiment; Design Guidelines.

INTRODUCTION
In J.R.R. Tolkien's "The Lord of the Rings" [48], extraordinary events take place as a direct consequence of the magical powers of one ring. Common in fiction, magical rings enable their owners to perform outstanding acts and gain superhuman powers, such as to control objects with a mere twist of a finger; see the "Rings" entry in Clute and Grant's "Encyclopedia of Fantasy" for an overview of magical rings imagined by the creative authors of the fantasy literature [8]. For centuries, humans could only dream of such fantastic experiences. However, recent advances in miniaturization, communications, and the richness of high-fidelity sensors have paved the way to a world in which wearables can implement spectacular visions of mobile computing [31,60]. In fact, we have reached a turning point in miniaturization where active rings, known as "smart rings," are no longer fantasy. Smart rings can be rigorously prototyped to mediate interactions with the physical objects and space around us [17,27,35,61,67,68].

DIS '18, June 9–13, 2018, Hong Kong.

ACM ISBN 978-1-4503-5198-0/18/06...$15.00.
https://doi.org/10.1145/3196709.3196741

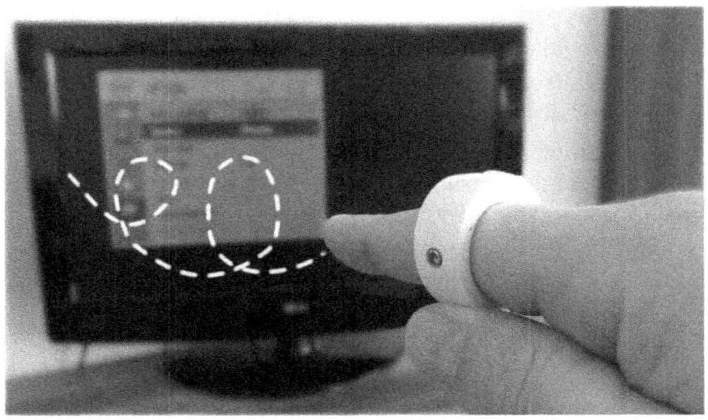

Figure 1. Smart rings afford a variety of touch and mid-air gesture input. In this work, we employ Ring Zero devices [28], as illustrated in this picture, to elicit and understand users' preferences for ring gestures.

To this end, smart rings embed a variety of electronics, such as micro-controllers, inertial measurement units, LEDs, and Bluetooth modules, and can be programmed to react to events produced by their owners or sensed directly from the context of use [36,37]. For instance, the Ring Zero device (Figure 1) enables its owners to play music on a connected smart device by recognizing gestures in mid-air [28]. Although ring technology is still in its infancy, several startups and projects are under progress at the moment of this writing, generating impressive interest on crowdfunding campaigns, such as OURA [37], ORII [36], or Nimb [34], to name just a few.

While smart ring technology is developed, the majority of effort has been put into miniaturization and industrial design [17,27,35] and algorithms to recognize ring gestures effectively [61,67,68]. However, no investigation has been conducted on *users' preferences for ring gestures* and, consequently, there is little information available to (i) *designers and practitioners* about what types of gestures to utilize in their prototypes, (ii) *manufacturers* regarding desirable features to include in the future versions of their smart rings, or (iii) to *researchers* to employ relevant criteria to analyze users' ring gestures. This work represents the first investigation to inform gesture UI design for smart rings by providing insights and implications for design resulted from an elicitation study.

The contributions of this work are two-fold:

1. We conduct the first scientific investigation to collect, analyze, and understand users' preferences for ring gestures. Our practical results consist in:
   (a) An analysis of agreement between participants' gestures for contexts of use with one and two smart rings.
   (b) A generic taxonomy for ring gestures with 5 dimensions (nature, structure, complexity, symmetry, and locale) to analyze and inform ring gesture designs.
   (c) A collection of representative gestures reflective of our participants' conceptual models for effecting commands using smart rings.
   (d) A discussion and a set of practical recommendations for designing ring gesture commands.

   We believe that these practical results will be useful to designers that wish to prototype ring gesture user interfaces tailored to and informed by actual user behavior.
2. Besides our practical findings in terms of what ring gestures are preferable, we also contribute to the generic gesture elicitation methodology [57,62,63] with insights on how various factors, related to either the participants or the experimenter, can affect the level of consensus for *any* elicitation study. To this end, we use our specific investigation on ring gestures to point the community to important aspects to consolidate the practice of conducting gesture elicitation studies.

RELATED WORK

We overview in this section prior work on smart rings with a focus on gesture input techniques. We also discuss the elicitation methodology [57,58,63] that we employ in this work to collect and analyze users' preferences for ring gestures.

Smart Ring Prototypes and Technology

The first ring device known in history, dating from the Chinese Qing Dynasty, inlaid a tiny abacus with 1 mm-wide beads operated using a pin [7]. The first electronic prototype (1997) was Fukumoto and Tonomura's "FingerRing" [12] that embedded an accelerometer to detect gesture input in the form of taps performed with the fingertips. Since then, electronic rings have elicited researchers and practitioners' imagination and creativity, and many designs emerged with various input and output capabilities [4,24,27,66,67]. Current smart ring designs typically fall into one of two categories [4,41]: *output-only* devices that notify their owners about the occurrence of predefined events (e.g., incoming messages or alerts) and *input-and-output* rings that listen to user input and effect commands (e.g., to control other devices). In this work, we are interested in smart rings of the latter kind.

Various technologies have been used to prototype ring devices. For instance, Ogata et al.'s "iRing" [35] utilized infrared reflection to detect directional gesture swipes and finger bending; "Magic Ring" [17] used an accelerometer to detect motion gestures; the rotations and sliding of "Nenya" [4] were detected via magnetic tracking; "OctaRing" [27] implemented pressure-sensing multi-touch input; the "eRing"prototype of Wilhelm et al. [61] employed electric field sensing to detect multiple finger gestures; and "LightRing" [20] used infrared proximity sensing and a gyroscope to locate the fingertip on any surface for cursor pointing and target selection.

Recognition of gestures performed with smart rings has been implemented with rule-based systems that use the orientation of the ring [17], detection of the ring's rotation and sliding directions [4], calculations on quaternions [28], nearest-neighbor classification and the dynamic time warping function to match ring gestures with templates [67], or more complex approaches, such as Support Vector Machines [67], decision trees, and neural networks [42]. As long as ring gestures can be described as time-ordered series of points in 2D or 3D [51], any state-of-the-art stroke-gesture recognition algorithm, including the recognizers of the "$-family," such as $1, $N, $P, $P+, Protractor, or $3 [3,22,25,53,55,64], to name just a few, could be employed to classify ring gestures effectively.

Interactive Techniques for Smart Rings

Smart rings afford a wide range of touch, motion, and mid-air gesture interactions. However, despite the rich literature on generic gesture input [38,43,59,63], prior work on smart rings has employed small gesture sets of simple gesture types [11,17,66]. For instance, the "Magic Ring" prototype of Jing et al. [17] employed four gestures only: pointing the finger up/down and left/right to control home appliances, such as a lamp, radio, and a TV set. "RingIoT" [11], a smart ring for controlling devices in an Internet-of-Things (IoT) ecosystem, implemented pointing, directional movements, and simple shapes, such as a "circle" drawn in mid-air. A similar vocabulary was used by Zhang et al. [66], who designed a technique to turn any uninstrumented surface into an interactive one with six gestures: four directional swipes, a "click," and the "circle" shape. Overall, for most ring gestures proposed in prior work, a very limited vocabulary of gesture types was involved.

Exceptions to this trend are creative gesture designs specific to some smart rings only, such as "i-Throw", "Nenya", "OctaRing", and "Frictio" [4,15,24,27]. The "i-Throw" ring [24] incorporated "throwing", "receiving", and "scanning" gestures for a location-based service environment. "Nenya" [4] implemented item selection from menus by twists of the ring and "clicks" by sliding the ring along the finger. Other creative gestures emerged from specific ring form factors [9]. For instance, "OctaRing" [27], with its octagonal shape, was designed to detect multi-finger pressure input on its sides; "Frictio" delivers passive kinesthetic force feedback on rotational input [15]; and "Ringteraction" [13] exploits unique biomechanical characteristics of the human hand to support micro-interactions.

Gesture Elicitation Studies

Understanding users' preferences and behavior with new interactive technology right from the early stages of design empowers designers with valuable information to shape a product's characteristics for more effective and efficient use. This process is known as "participatory design" [5,19], and its specific implementation in the gesture literature in the form of "guessability studies" [62] or "gesture elicitation studies" [57,58,63] has been extremely popular to understand users' preferences

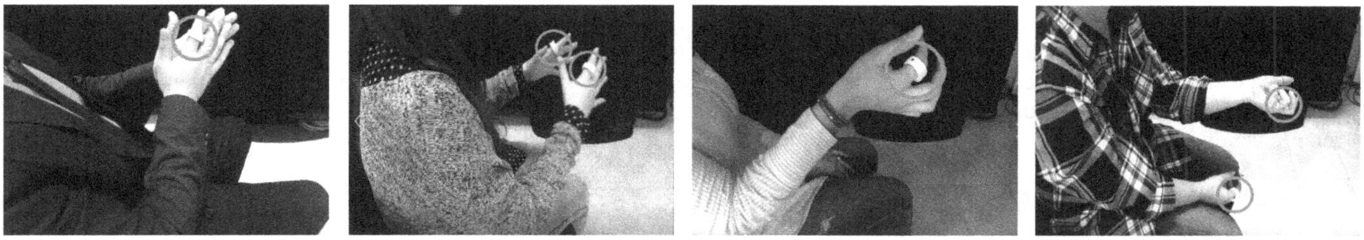

Figure 2. Snapshots from the elicitation study showing participants performing gestures using one or two smart rings (highlighted in each image).

for gesture input for a variety of application domains and devices [38,43,50,59,63]. For instance, Wobbrock et al. [63] reported users' preferences for multi-touch input on interactive tabletops; Vatavu [50,52] and Zaiţi et al. [59,65] addressed mid-air gesture input to control the TV set; Ruiz et al. [43] investigated users' preferences for motion gestures performed using smartphones; Lou et al. [30] looked at motion gestures for cyber-physical smart home environments; and Piumsomboon et al. [38] examined gesture commands for augmented reality applications, to name just a few examples. The outcome of a gesture elicitation study consists in a characterization of users' gesture input behavior with valuable information for designers and practitioners regarding the consensus levels between participants (computed as *agreement* or *coagreement rates* [57,58,63]), the most frequent (thus, generalizable across users) gesture proposals for a given task, and insights into users' conceptual models for performing tasks. The most recent formalization of the elicitation methodology was proposed by Vatavu and Wobbrock for both repeated measures [57] and between-subjects [58] experimental designs.

Summary

Ring-based gesture input has a lot of potential for a variety of contexts of use [46], from control applications, gaming, and autonomous vehicles [12,13,17] to smart spaces [11,20,24,42,49] and collaborative environments [14]. Prior work has focused almost exclusively on prototyping ring technology and neglected systematic exploration of how ring gestures can be effectively designed and mapped to commands. Thus, the community lacks relevant knowledge about *how to design intuitive ring gestures reflective of user behavior*. A solid, rigorous understanding of users' gesture preferences will unquestionably benefit all the aforementioned application domains. In this work, we make the first step towards such an understanding.

EXPERIMENT

We conducted a gesture elicitation study following the methodology from the literature [38,43,50,57,62,63] to collect users' preferences for ring-based gesture input. Before we continue, we provide our definition for ring gestures, as follows:

> A "ring gesture' is any action performed *with* or *on* a smart ring or any movement of the wearing finger and/or hand that causes a detectable change in the ring's position and/or orientation in a system of reference centered on the user's finger or body.

By adopting this definition, we follow Shilkrot et al. [46], who compiled a comprehensive survey of finger augmentation devices and made the distinction between *contact-based* and *contactless* input on smart rings. In the first case, gestures are performed on the ring surface and usually mimic interactions common on touchscreens, such as taps, pinch gestures, or directional swipes. But contact-based input on the small surface of a ring can only provide a limited vocabulary of mostly predefined gesture types. Contactless input, however, offers designers a richer design space for mid-air gestures and end-users more opportunities to customize gestures to their own preferences. In this work, we adopt a comprehensive approach, reflected in our definition of ring gestures, by examining both contact-based and mid-air input for smart rings, including combinations thereof. Thus, all the following examples are valid ring gestures for the purpose of this study:

> *Example*: Touch the ring once, twice, or multiple times in a row. Tap a rhythmic pattern on the ring's surface.

> *Example*: Rotate the ring on the finger. Rotate the finger wearing the ring. Rotate the hand wearing the ring.

> *Example*: Slide the ring along the finger. Pull out the ring. Place the ring back on the finger. Change the ring to a different finger, etc.

> *Example*: Draw a gesture in mid-air, such as a "question mark" symbol, with the finger wearing the ring. Place the finger or the hand wearing the ring in a specific position with respect to the body, e.g., near the mouth.

> Any combination of the above.

Participants

Twenty-four (24) participants (9 female), aged between 21 and 45 years old ($M = 27.5$, $SD = 7.9$ years), volunteered for our study. Participant occupations included students (Computer Science), psychologist, teacher, lawyer, police officer, interpreter, office clerk. Of all participants, 79% (19/24) had a technical background. We chose the age group of our participants to be as representative as possible for adopters of wearable technology.[1] The majority of participants ($22/24 = 91.7\%$) were right-handed. All participants owned smartphones and, thus, were accustomed with touch and gesture input.

[1] Statistics show that the percentage of individuals who use wearables is the highest for the age group 25–34 years old (30.8%), followed by the 18–25 years old age group (29.1%), and the 35–44 years old group (25.3%), according to http://www.emarketer.com/Chart/US-Wearable-User-Penetration-by-Age-2017-of-population-each-group/202360.

Apparatus

We employed two Ring Zero devices [28] (see Figure 1), which participants wore on their index fingers of each hand; see Figure 2 for a few snapshots captured during the study. Ring Zero reports changes in its orientation to a Bluetooth 4.0 connected device, such as a smartphone. The ring also features a touch button that detects short (< 2 s) and long presses (> 2 s).

Task

Participants were presented with the two rings and were given time to familiarize with the new technology (none of them had used smart rings before this study). The experiment consisted of two sessions, during which participants wore one ring and both rings, respectively. Each session implemented the gesture elicitation protocol [63]: participants were presented with *referents*, i.e., functions to control in a home environment, described next in this section, for which they proposed suitable gestures to execute those referents, i.e., gestures that fit referents well, are easy to produce and remember. We did not constrain participants' choices of gestures to any particular context of use (e.g., on the ring) or to any hardware ability (e.g., motion gestures only), as such an influence would have inconveniently narrowed the findings of this first exploratory study on ring gestures. The experimenter clarified all participants' questions before the study, e.g., regarding the type of gestures (all types were allowed) or the possibility to assign a given gesture to more than one referent (not allowed). Participants operated with the belief that any gesture they performed was recognizable.[2] The order of the referents was randomized per participant. Participants' fine motor skills and creativity levels were evaluated before the experiment, and a short questionnaire was administered after the experiment.

Design

Our study was within-subjects with two independent variables:

1. REFERENT, nominal variable with 14 conditions, representing common tasks to execute in a home environment with a smart ring: (1) turn the TV on/off, (2) start player, (3) turn the volume up and (4) down, (5) go to the next and (6) previous item in a list, (7) turn AC on/off, (8) turn lights on/off, (9) brighten and (10) dim lights, (11) turn heat on/off, (12) turn alarm on/off, (13) answer and (14) end phone call.
2. NUMBER-OF-RINGS, ordinal variable with two conditions, corresponding to two contexts of use: 1-ring and 2-rings.

Our choice of referents was inspired from other elicitation studies [23,50,59] that examined generic tasks for smart homes. Also, most of the tasks are mutually exclusive (e.g., turn on/off the TV) and, according to the context, they can be executed with the same gesture command, e.g., if the TV is on, performing the gesture will turn it off and vice versa We adopted this design approach to reduce the number of gesture commands that users would need to learn and recall. Moreover, previous studies reported users' preferences for employing the same gesture type to perform "on/off" tasks, such as turn on/off devices or pop up/hide menus [50,59].

[2] This approach enabled participants to invent gestures beyond the hardware abilities of the rings, which represents a useful result that can potentially inform new technology design for smart rings.

Measures

We employed the following measures to evaluate and understand users' preferences and cognitive and motor performance for gestures produced with or on smart rings:

1. We computed agreement rates (AR) for each REFERENT and NUMBER-OF-RINGS conditions using the formula of Vatavu and Wobbrock [57] (p. 1327), as follows:
$$AR(r) = \frac{\sum_{i<j} \delta_{i,j}}{n \cdot (n-1)/2} \quad (1)$$
where n is the number of participants from which gestures are elicited, and $\delta_{i,j}$ evaluates to 1 if the i-th and j-th participants are in agreement over referent r and to 0 otherwise.
2. Participants' creativity was evaluated before the elicitation procedure using a generic creativity test. The test is available on-line[3] and reports a score between 0 and 100 (higher scores denote more creativity) computed from answers to a set of 40 questions. We specifically chose this test due to its ease of application and large diversity of factors evaluated: *abstraction* (of concepts from ideas), *connection* (between things without an apparent link), *perspective* (shift in terms of space, time, and other people), *curiosity* (to change and improve things accepted as the norm), *boldness* (to push boundaries beyond accepted conventions), *paradox* (the ability to accept and work with contradictory concepts), *complexity* (the ability to operate with a large quantity of information), and *persistence* (to derive stronger solutions even when good ones have already been generated).
3. We measured participants' fine motor skills with a standard motor test of the NEPSY test batteries (a developmental NEuroPSYchological assessment) [21]. The test consists in touching each fingertip with the thumb of the same hand for eight times in a row. Higher motor skills are reflected in less time to perform this task.
4. THINKING-TIME measures the time, in seconds, needed by participants to propose a gesture for a given referent.
5. GOODNESS-OF-FIT represents participants' subjective assessment, as a rating between 1 and 10, of their confidence about how well the proposed gestures fit the referents.

RESULTS

We collected a total number of 672 gesture proposals from 24 (participants) $\times$ 14 (referents) $\times$ 2 (number of rings) conditions, which we clustered into groups of similar gesture types according to the following criteria:

1. *Handedness.* Gestures performed with the dominant hand are considered different from those performed with the nondominant hand, e.g., "circles" drawn with the dominant/nondominant hand fall into distinct categories.
2. *Scale.* Gestures performed at different scales go into distinct categories, e.g., a large amplitude "circle" performed with the entire arm is considered different from a small "circle" performed with the finger. For the purpose of this study, we considered three scales (large, medium, and small) corresponding to arm, wrist, and fingers' ranges of movements.

[3] http://www.testmycreativity.com/

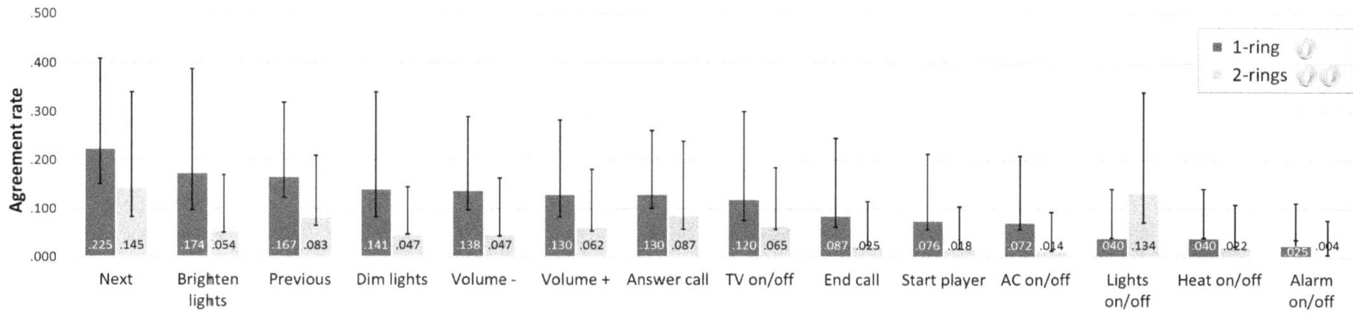

Figure 3. Agreement rates for gesture proposals elicited with one and two rings, respectively. Notes: referents are ordered on the horizontal axis in descending order of their agreement rates for the 1-ring condition; error bars show 95% CIs computed with the AGATe tool [57].

3. *Direction*. The same gestures performed in different directions are considered different, e.g., clockwise and counter-clockwise "circle" shapes drawn in mid-air.
4. *Hand pose*. We considered that specific hand poses adopted by participants during gesture articulation contain relevant information for the gestures' meaning, e.g., a "circle" performed with the open hand is considered different from the same "circle" drawn with the index finger pointed.
5. *Ring use*. We differentiated between various actions performed *on* the rings. For instance, short presses (less than 2 s) on the touch button located on the smart ring were considered different from longer presses. Also, touching the ring with the thumb of the wearing hand is a different gesture than using the index finger of the other hand.

We identified 81 distinct gestures for the 1-ring condition and 139 gestures (+72% more) for the 2-rings condition. Next, we analyze the consensus between participants' gesture proposals, and assign gesture types to meaningful categories.

Consensus between Proposed Gestures

Figure 3 shows the agreement rates obtained for each REFERENT and NUMBER-OF-RINGS conditions. Overall, agreement rates are very small in magnitude, between .025 and .225 for 1-ring gestures (M=.112, SD=.058) and between .004 and .145 for the 2-rings condition (M=.058, SD=.043). These results are very close to the lowest ever reported agreement rates in the literature of gesture elicitation; see Vatavu and Wobbrock [57] (p. 1332) that summarize agreement rates of 18 studies, for which the smallest value (.108) was reached by Liang et al. [26] and Seyed et al. [45] for motion+surface and multi-display gestures, respectively. According to the recommendations of Vatavu and Wobbrock [57] to interpret the magnitudes of agreement rates, our results fall inside or are close to the low consensus ($\leq .100$) category. These results were confirmed by Kendall's coefficient of concordance:[4] $W = .108$ for 1-ring gestures ($\chi^2(13) = 33.552$, $p < .001$) and $W = .110$ for 2-rings ($\chi^2(13) = 34.389$, $p < .001$). As Kendall's coefficient is related to the average of Spearman correlation coefficients between pairs of rankings [18] (p. 276), we can interpret the magnitude of its effect as small (close to .100) according to Cohen's suggested limits for interpreting effect sizes.

[4] Kendall's W is a normalization of the Friedman statistic used to assess the agreement between multiple raters with a number ranging between 0 (no agreement at all) and 1 (perfect agreement).

Although consensus was low overall, we nevertheless found that gestures performed in the 1-ring condition led to 93% more agreement than 2-rings gestures. A paired t-test revealed a statistically significant effect of NUMBER-OF-RINGS on AGREEMENT-RATE ($t_{(13)}$=3.985, p=.002, r = .741). We also found that the rankings of referents correlated significantly for the two conditions (Spearman's $\rho_{(N=14)}$=.556, p=.039<.05).

It is interesting at this point to look at a shortlist of gesture proposals; see Table 1. Even this shortlist of most frequent proposals includes a wide range of gesture types, ranging from touch input (such as "touch the ring once" or "touch both rings simultaneously") to hand poses (e.g., the "call me" sign performed by placing the thumb near the ear and the little finger pointed at the mouth), and to motion gestures performed in mid-air (flicks to increase or decrease volume). Inspired by the diversity of these first results, we decided to run a thorough classification of all gestures into meaningful categories.

Taxonomy of Ring Gestures

To better understand our participants' ring gesture proposals, we considered the following five dimensions of analysis, inspired by previous gesture studies [38,43,63] and informed by the specifics of ring gestures:

1. *Nature* describes the meaning of a gesture, with three categories: (a) *symbolic*, (b) *metaphorical*, and (c) *abstract*. Symbolic gestures depict commonly accepted symbols employed to convey information, such as emblems and cultural gestures, e.g., the "call me" gesture performed with the thumb and little finger stretched out to denote a phone call, or swiping the index finger from left to right, a convention on touchscreens to access the previous item in a sequence. Metaphorical gestures give shape to an idea or concept, such as using the thumb to press a button on an imaginary remote control to turn on/off the TV set or turning an invisible knob in mid-air. Abstract gestures have no symbolic or metaphorical connections to their referents, and the mapping is arbitrary, e.g., touch the ring twice to answer a phone call. We adapted the nature dimension from Wobbrock et al. [63], who used it for multi-touch gestures.
2. *Structure* characterizes the relative importance of hand poses versus hand motion in the articulation of a ring gesture, with five categories: (a) *buttons-only*, (b) *hand poses only*, (c) *hand motion*, (d) *hand poses & motion*, and (e) *mixed locales*. For instance, for the buttons-only category,

REFERENT	1-RING			2-RINGS[§]		
	AR	Most frequent	Second most frequent	AR	Most frequent	Second most frequent
1. *TV on/off*	**.120**	Press button on an imaginary remote control	Touch the ring once	**.065**	Press button on an imaginary remote control	Touch both rings simultaneously
2. *Start player*	.076	Press imaginary button in mid-air	Press button on an imaginary remote control	.018	Press imaginary button in mid-air	Flick to the right
3. *Volume up*	**.130**	Circle clockwise	Flick upwards	**.062**	Circle clockwise	Flick upwards
4. *Volume down*	**.138**	Flick downwards	Circle counter-clockwise	.047	Flick downwards using both hands	Circle counter-clockwise
5. *Next*	**.225**	Flick to the right	Flick to the left	**.145**	Flick to the right	Flick to the right using both hands
6. *Previous*	**.167**	Flick to the left	Swipe on the ring upwards	**.083**	Flick to the left using both hands	Flick to the left
7. *AC on/off*	.072	Raise hand and touch the ring	Touch the ring once	.014	Bring both hands in front and towards the body	Use the hands as a hands fan
8. *Lights on/off*	.040	Raise hand and touch the ring	Clap once	**.134**	Clap once	Raise hand and touch the ring
9. *Brighten lights*	**.174**	Flick upwards	Circle clockwise	.054	Spread palms horizontally	Flick upwards
10. *Dim lights*	**.141**	Flick downwards	Circle counter-clockwise	.047	Flick downwards using both hands	Flick downwards
11. *Heat on/off*	.040	Touch the ring once	Press imaginary button in mid-air	.022	Rub hands	Spread palms horizontally
12. *Alarm on/off*	.025	Touch the ring once	Draw letter "S" in mid-air[‡]	.004	Touch both rings simultaneously	Press several imaginary buttons in mid-air
13. *Answer call*	**.130**	Flick to the right	"Call me" sign[†]	**.087**	Flick to the right	"Call me" sign[†]
14. *End call*	.087	Flick to the left	Touch the ring once and flick to the left	.025	Flick to the left	Flick to the left using both hands

[†]Thumb placed near the ear, little finger pointed at the mouth; [‡]Letter "S" stands for "Security"; [§]Unless indicated explicitly, gestures listed in this column are performed using the ring worn on the dominant hand; Referents with agreement rates above average are highlighted for each condition.

Table 1. First and second most frequent gesture proposals for each referent using one and two rings, respectively. Note how even this shortlist of proposals spans a wide range of gesture types, from touch input to hand poses and motion gestures performed in mid-air.

the gesture employed to press the button is not important: all that matters is that the button was pressed and for how long it was pressed. The hand poses category includes gestures for which the specific configuration of the hand is meaningful, while the movement of the hand is not important (e.g., the "thumbs up" gesture), and so on. This category was inspired by the taxonomy of Vatavu and Pentiuc [56].[5]

3. *Complexity* characterizes a gesture as either (a) *simple* or (b) *compound*. We define simple gestures as gestures that have meaning on their own, e.g., drawing a "circle" in mid-air. Compound gestures can be decomposed into individually meaningful gestures, e.g., pressing a button followed by drawing a "circle." We adopted the complexity dimension from Ruiz et al. [43], who used it to describe user-defined motion gestures for smartphones.
4. *Symmetry* characterizes how the two hands are employed to produce a 2-rings gesture, with four categories: (a) *dominant unimanual*, (b) *nondominant unimanual*, (c) *symmetric bimanual*, and (d) *asymmetric bimanual*. We adopted this dimension from Piumsomboon et al. [38], who used it to characterize users' mid-air gestures for AR applications.
5. *Locale* specifies the location in space where the gesture is performed: (a) *on the ring*, (b) *on other surface*, (c) *in-the-air*, and (d) *mixed locales*, adapted and extended from [38].

[5]Vatavu and Pentiuc [56] refer to the categories of their taxonomy as "simple static", "static generalized", "simple dynamic", and "dynamic generalized" gestures. Although we adopted a different terminology here referring specifically to hand poses and motion, the categories are practically the same.

Gesture dimension	Pearson's χ^2	*p*-value	Cramer's *V*
1. *Nature*	$\chi^2(2) = 5.503$	*n.s.*	.090
2. *Structure*	$\chi^2(4) = 68.556$	$p < .001$	.319
3. *Complexity*	$\chi^2(1) = 4.154$	$p = .051$	.079
4. *Symmetry*	$\chi^2(3) = 307.575$	$p < .001$	.677
5. *Locale*	$\chi^2(3) = 27.030$	$p < .001$	.201

Table 2. The effect of NUMBER-OF-RINGS on the distribution of participants' gesture proposals for each gesture dimension.

Figure 4 (next page) illustrates the observed percentages of gestures falling in each category. Pearson Chi-Square tests showed significant effects of NUMBER-OF-RINGS on the distribution of proposed gestures for the *Structure*, *Symmetry*, and *Locale* dimensions ($p < .001$) and a marginally significant effect ($p = .051$) for *Complexity*; see Table 2. Overall, gestures performed with two rings involved more motion than 1-ring gestures (42.3% *vs.* 14.0%) due to the extra degrees of freedom afforded by the second hand. Also, there were more 2-rings gestures on a surface other than the ring than in the 1-ring condition (10.7% *vs.* 2.1%), because the nondominant hand acted as a natural surface to perform gestures on.

Gestures' Goodness of Fit

Participants rated their gesture proposals with numbers from 1 (poor fit) to 10 (excellent fit) to denote their confidence in the goodness of fit of their proposals. A Wilcoxon signed ranks test revealed a statistically significant effect of NUMBER-OF-RINGS on GOODNESS-OF-FIT

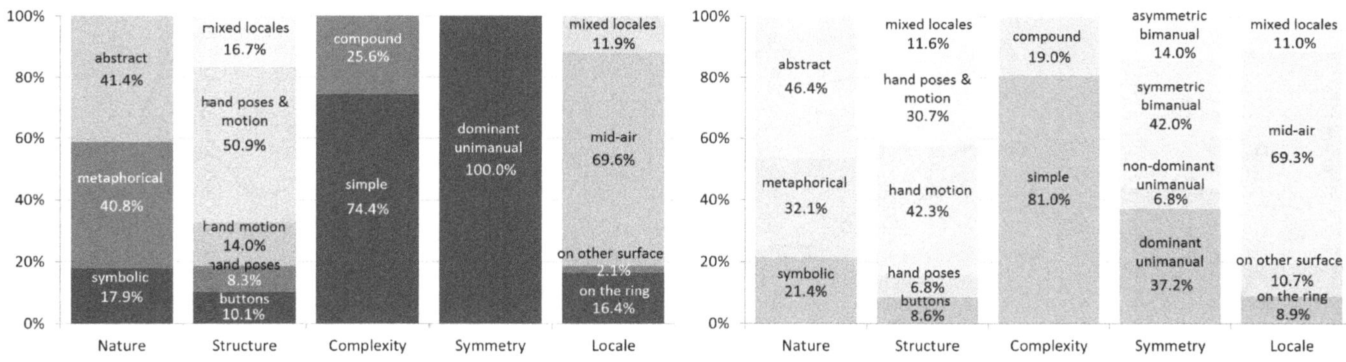

Figure 4. Observed percentages of 1-ring (left) and 2-rings gestures (right) for each category of our taxonomy.

($Z_{(N=14)} = 2.518$, $p = .012$, $r = .476$): participants rated 2-ring gestures (M=8.14, Mdn=8.00, SD=1.26) significantly higher than those produced with one ring (M=7.87, Mdn=8.00, SD=1.41). GOODNESS-OF-FIT correlated significantly with AGREEMENT-RATE for 1-ring gestures (Pearson's $r_{(N=14)}$=.685, R^2=.469, p=.007): referents that reached high agreement rates were assigned gestures that were rated a good fit. This relationship was however not met for the 2-rings condition ($r_{(N=14)}$=.150, p=.609, *n.s.*), probably because of the lower agreement reached overall for 2-rings gestures (.058).

ON THE PROCESS OF REACHING CONSENSUS

Our results from the previous section showed that the agreement rates for ring gestures and our specific set of referents are among the lowest ones ever reported in the literature. Possible explanations for this outcome are (1) the large number of degrees of freedom afforded by unconstrained finger and hand gestures, (2) our rigid criteria for clustering participants' gestures proposals into categories of similar types, and (3) the novelty of smart ring devices. Regarding the novelty aspect, ring-based gesture input represents a very recent interaction paradigm to which users will need time to accommodate before feeling confident about their preferences. In this section, we want to understand our results on agreement better by looking into how the elicitation process works. Specifically, we identified the following factors that we believe affect the magnitudes of agreement rates reported by *any* elicitation study:

> 1. *A priori* factors that relate to participants' individual traits and characteristics,

such as fine motor abilities to perform gestures, cognitive abilities to produce (sometimes abstract) associations between various categories and concepts, or previous experience with gesture input, i.e., the "legacy bias" [33]. In this section, we focus on discussing participants' creativity and motor skills.

> 2. Factors occurring *during* the study,

such as participants' commitment and dedication to the study. Elicitation studies, just like any participatory design studies, require great willingness from participants to commit to the task, disclose their views of the situation at hand, share their experience [5], and conform to the experimental setup, such as the think-aloud protocol [63]. We report in this section on the relationship between participants' thinking time to propose ring gestures and the resulted agreement rates.

> 3. *A posteriori* factors, occurring after the experiment

can influence the magnitude of agreement rates, such as the experimenter's choice of criteria to group participants' gestures into categories of similar types, which can be rigid (such as the criteria employed in this work; see the "Results" section) or relaxed (as we are about to discuss next in this section).

To our surprise, none of the above factors (except for the legacy bias [16,33,44] and thinking times [59,65]) have been considered before for gesture elicitation studies, despite the popularity of this methodology and its frequent application [26,32,38,43,44,45,50,57,58,59] over more than ten years since it was introduced [62,63]. In this context, our discussion from this section, besides unveiling interesting aspects regarding our participants' gesture input behavior with smart rings, represents a contribution to *any* gesture elicitation study and should be viewed as such.

Thinking Time, Fine Motor Skills, and Creativity Scores

RM ANOVA revealed a significant effect of NUMBER-OF-RINGS on participants' THINKING-TIME ($F_{(1,23)} = 13.697$, $p < .001$, $\eta_p^2 = .373$): our participants spent 48% more time thinking about gestures in the 1-ring condition ($M = 4.60$ s, $SD = 1.47$ s) than when using two rings ($M = 3.10$ s, $SD = 1.00$ s). We did not find any significant effect of REFERENT ($p = .075$, *n.s.*), nor an interaction between NUMBER-OF-RINGS and REFERENT ($p = .894$, *n.s.*) on THINKING-TIME.

Figure 5 shows the relationship between thinking times and agreement rates per REFERENT and NUMBER-OF-RINGS. Agreement rates decreased for longer thinking times for both the 1-ring (Pearson's $r_{(N=14)} = -.778$, $R^2 = .605$, $p < .001$) and 2-rings conditions ($r_{(N=14)} = -.336$, $p = .241$, *n.s.*), although only the former correlation was significant.

The more time participants took to think about gestures, the less agreement resulted. This finding can be interpreted in several ways. First, the more time participants allocated to the task, the more creative they presumably wanted to be and, consequently, they thought of gestures less likely to be proposed by others. Second, it is reasonable to assume that participants' first choice of a gesture (i.e., the gesture proposal coming to mind after a minimum thinking time) was likely to be found by other participants as well, probably due to some internal mechanism of understanding referents, e.g., flick to

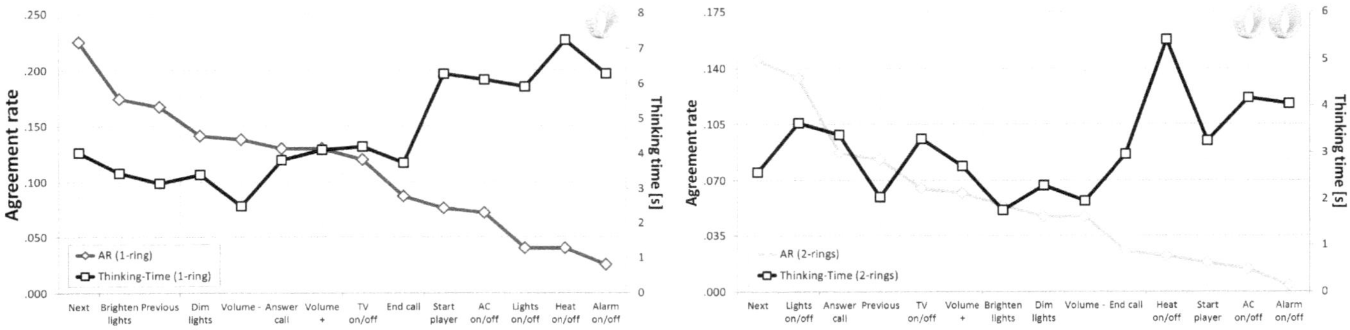

Figure 5. Relationship between AGREEMENT-RATE and THINKING-TIME for gestures performed using one ring (left) and two rings (right).

the left to advance to the next item in a list. It may also be that participants failed to produce highly similar gestures because some tasks exceeded their sensorimotor knowledge [6]. If that was the case, participants might have recurred to other types of knowledge to provide suitable gesture proposals, such as motor-intuitiveness, e.g., some gestures were proposed because of their convenient spatial or biomechanical properties. All these interpretations are interesting as a direct consequence of participants' individual traits, such as their cognitive and motor abilities to invent and articulate ring gestures.

Our participants' creativity scores varied between 46.4 and 81.6 ($M = 59.4$, $SD = 9.4$) on a scale from 0 to 100 (higher is more creative). Their fine motor skill levels varied between 7.3 and 14.1 ($M = 9.9$, $SD = 1.7$, lower is better). We found no difference in creativity between male and female participants ($t_{(22)} = -1.296$, $p > .05$, *n.s.*), but we did find that male participants performed 23% better at the motor skill test (9.0 versus 11.1, $t_{(22)}$=3.559, p=.002, r=.604). Informed by these results and our insights presented above, we computed correlations between CREATIVITY and THINKING-TIME for all participants and between MOTOR-SKILL and THINKING-TIME separately for male and female participants due to the difference in motor skill levels found between the two groups. We found a negative relationship between CREATIVITY and THINKING-TIME for both the 1-ring (Pearson's $r_{(N=24)} = -.143$) and 2-rings conditions ($r_{(N=24)} = -.150$), showing that higher creativity related to shorter thinking times to propose gestures. However, statistical significance was not achieved ($p > .05$), which prevent us to extrapolate these findings to the wider user population. We did find, however, a strong negative correlation between MOTOR-SKILL and THINKING-TIME for female participants ($r_{(N=10)} = -.748$, $R^2 = .560$, $p = .013$): higher fine motor skills in women were connected to shorter thinking times.

These results suggest that thinking time may be an important factor to the success of a gesture elicitation study: the way participants dedicate to the task may affect both consensus and the set of gestures. While we point to these aspects in the specific context of our ring gestures investigation, we believe that such interesting connections should be explored thoroughly by future work, as they apply to any gesture elicitation study.

The Gesture Pairing Criteria

The first step of the analysis process for elicitation studies consists in identifying gestures that look similar in order to compute agreement rates [62]. However, this process is inherently dependent on the designer's goals for the specific application for which gestures were elicited in the first place. Gesture pairing can be *rigid* or *relaxed* and, thus, may have an influence on the magnitudes of agreement rates.

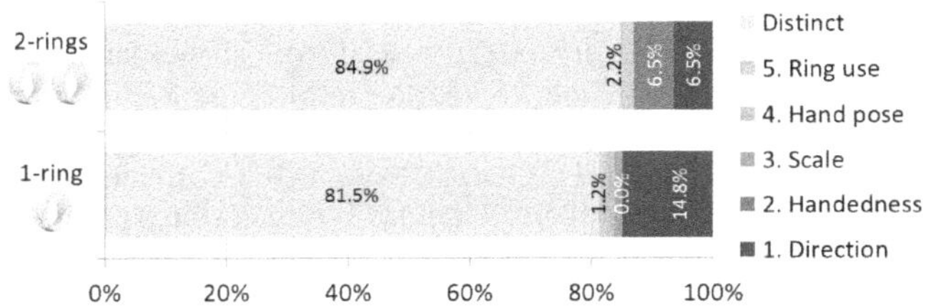

Figure 6. Percentage of gestures that become similar when relaxing grouping criteria. For example, 14.8% of all 1-ring gestures will merge into the same category if gesture *direction* is no longer important.

In this work, we adopted a set of five criteria to pair gestures into categories of similar types: *handedness*, *direction*, *scale*, *hand pose*, and *ring use*; see the "Experiment" section. It could be that our criteria were too rigid compared to other studies [43, 50,59,63], which would help explain our low agreement rates. Therefore, we wanted to see what happened when these criteria were relaxed. Figure 6 shows the percentage of gestures that merged after eliminating each of our criteria in a row. For example, by not considering gesture *direction* as important, 14.8% of the gestures in the 1-ring condition and 6.5% of the gestures in the 2-rings condition merged into the same category. In the end, the average agreement rates increased from .112 (1-ring) and .058 (2-rings) to .144 (maximum .442) and .074 (maximum .210), respectively, representing an increase of 28% on average. We can conclude that the criteria to group gestures has an influence on the magnitude of agreement rates.

Influence of the Methodology and Experiment Design

Besides the aforementioned factors, the methodology and experiment design can affect the level of agreement. For instance, we randomized the order of referents in our experiment to avoid bias and potential transfer effects from one referent to the next. However, with such an approach, it may be difficult for participants to identify relationships between referents and propose relevant gestures in consequence, e.g., brighten and dim lights are symmetrical referents, but this relationship is not explicitly presented to participants, who may or may not identify it. Presenting all the referents at once, or adopting a hybrid approach where groups instead of individual referents are randomly presented to participants may lead to different levels of agreement. Other aspects regard the possibility to propose more than one gesture for a referent (many-to-one relationship) or reusing the same gesture for more than one referent (one-to-many). In both cases, higher agreement is likely to be reached. Ultimately, such choices depend on the practitioner's goal, but we point to these aspects as we believe that they should be thoroughly examined by future work.

DESIGN GUIDELINES FOR SMART RING GESTURES

We discuss in this section some of our participants' gestures in more depth as we derive recommendations for ring gestures. However, the following should not be viewed as an absolute set of design guidelines, because of the too novel technology involved and, thus, limited time for users to become aware of their preferences, but rather as a set of proposals to inform further investigations and developments.

> ✍ Motion seems to be preferred over static gestures.

We found that static gestures (i.e., hand poses) were performed for 8.3% of all 1-ring gestures and 6.8% for 2-rings. Examples include emblems and cultural signs, such as the "thumbs up" gesture (Fig. 7f) or the "call me" sign. Motion gestures were proposed in 64.9% and 73.0% of all cases; see directional swipes (Fig. 7a,b), synchronized bimanual swipes (Fig. 7y), hands approaching or separating in space (Fig. 7n,o,p), fingers spreading (Fig. 7d,e), or relative movements of the hands, such as sliding, rubbing, or twisting (Fig. 7m,v,x).

> ✍ Users prefer "simple" gestures of the dominant hand.

Of all proposed gestures, 74.4% (1-ring) and 81.0% (2-rings) were "simple" according to our taxonomy, i.e., not reducible to simpler actions without losing meaning. Participants went for simplicity even when two rings were available: 37.2% of the 2-rings gestures involved just one hand, and only 6.8% used the nondominant hand. Also, we found that compound 2-rings gestures were less frequent than 1-ring gestures (19.0% *vs.* 25.6%), showing again a quest for simple gestures.

> ✍ Consider gesture designs that exploit the surface of the ring and/or its unique shape and form factor.

The smart rings literature has proposed some creative ring interactions, such as twisting and sliding the ring on the finger [4] or simultaneously touching parts of the ring's surface [27]. Our participants proposed gestures that not only rediscovered such expert designs, but went further. We found that participants used the ring surface in 8.9% of their 1-ring gestures and in 16.4% for 2-rings. Such gestures included taps on one ring, taps on both rings, and tapping rhythms (Fig. 7r,s), sliding the thumb along the ring's surface (Fig. 7h), closing the ring inside the fist (Fig. 7g,u), rotating the ring (Fig. 7t), pulling the ring out and putting it back on the finger, sliding the ring along the finger, or putting the two rings in contact (Fig. 7z).

> ✍ Reuse touch gestures and touch-based interaction paradigms from smartphones due to their familiarity.

We found that 30.1% of the gestures proposed in the 1-ring condition and 27.3% of the 2-rings gestures were variants of taps (performed on the ring) and directional swipes (in mid-air or on the ring's surface). The literature has documented this effect as the "legacy bias" [33]. Wobbrock et al. [63] made the observation *"It's a Windows World"* (p. 1089) in their study from 2009 when their participants often thought of the desktop paradigm when elicited for multi-touch gestures. In the nearly ten years that passed, we have witnessed large adoption of touchscreen devices.[6] We can now paraphrase Wobbrock et al. [63] and note *"It's a touch input world."* Thus, users' experience with touch gesture input should be exploited.

> ✍ Consider multiple gestures for the same command (many-to-one association), but also the same gesture for many commands (one-to-many), if permitted by context.

Prior work showed benefits of assigning more than one gesture to the same command [39] and that users perform the same gesture in many ways [2,40], at least for multi-touch input. On average, a referent received 13.3 distinct gestures (SD=3.1) in the 1-ring condition and 17.0 gestures (SD=2.9) in the 2-rings condition. It is also interesting to look at this aspect from the opposite perspective of "conflicts," i.e., the same gesture proposed for different referents by different participants. The average number of conflicts was 2.3 (SD=1.9) for the 1-ring condition and 1.7 (SD=1.1) for 2-rings. Many-to-one associations can enhance intuitiveness and "guessability" [62], while one-to-many mappings can minimize the effort to learn many gestures, provided that the context of execution is unambiguous, e.g., the gestures to turn on the TV and the AC unit can be the same, if the command to execute can be inferred from the context, e.g., the device the user is facing to.

> ✍ Favor symmetry in designing bimanual gestures.

We found that 42% of the gestures performed with two rings were symmetric, e.g., simultaneous taps on the two rings (Fig. 7s), approaching or spreading hands (Fig.s 7n,o,p), clapping, rubbing, or rotating hands (Fig. 7q,v,x).

> ✍ Gestures for operating imaginary objects in mid-air.

Some participants used gestures to manipulate imaginary objects, e.g., pushing a virtual button in mid-air (Fig. 7j) with variations (one push, two pushes, using the dominant or the nondominant hand, or both hands simultaneously), holding an imaginary remote control and pressing a button on it (Fig. 1i), or twisting a knob in mid-air (Fig. 1k). We recommend exploring such gestures to create intuitive mappings between movement and action, e.g., rotating a knob replicates a physical action with precise and unequivocal meaning.

> ✍ Design that fosters synergy with body gestures.

Some ring gestures were performed in relation to various body parts, such as placing the wearing hand close to the ear, raising the hand to the ear and touching the ring, placing both rings near the mouth (Fig. 7w), or gently blowing on the ring (Fig. 7l). We recommend investigation of such *body-referenced gestures*, which might benefit from high recall rates due to the mechanism of proprioception [29]. Body-referenced gestures could make the transition towards whole-body interaction, where rings are combined with other sensors [32,44,50].

[6] In fact, 8.4 billion smartphone units were shipped between 2009 and the time of this writing [47].

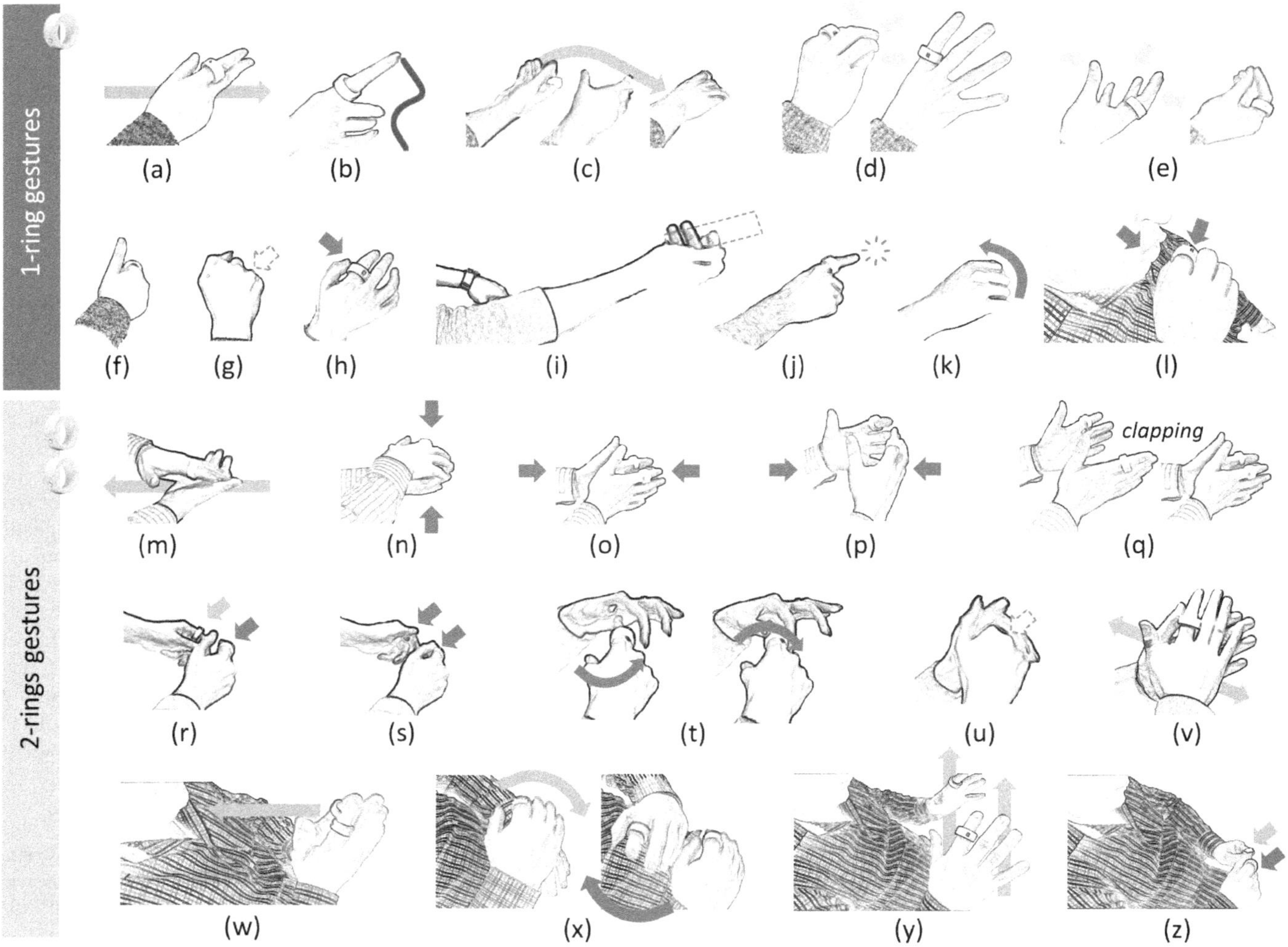

Figure 7. A selection of our participants' 1-ring (top) and 2-rings gesture proposals (bottom) illustrating various categories of mental models and articulation behavior for gesture input and smart rings. Gestures are referenced and discussed in the text.

> ✍ Design ring gestures that foster multimodal input.

One participant used voice commands in conjunction with ring gestures, e.g., raise the hand wearing the ring and say "player" out loud, while another participant placed the ring next to the mouth and blew on it. These examples suggest that multimodal input should be explored to make ring commands more intuitive and effective for various contexts of use.

CONCLUSION AND FUTURE WORK

We presented results from the first study conducted to understand users' preferences for ring gestures. We contributed a taxonomy to analyze ring gestures, a collection of gesture types, and a set of guidelines to inform further developments. Our gesture dataset can be freely downloaded and used for research purposes from `http://www.eed.usv.ro/~vatavu`.

Future work will look at the articulation details of bimanual gestures, i.e., the way the dominant and nondominant hands move to perform a ring gesture, such as by employing temporal algebra [1]. A detailed examination of participants' creativity is also envisioned by employing other, less generic tests, that look at specific aspects of creativity [10]. Allowing participants to suggest more than one gesture per referent is likely to lead to more consensus for novel technology, something to explore in the future as well. Also, connecting ring tap gestures with other gesture types, e.g., whole-body gestures, such as to deal effectively with the segmentation problem [54], is another interesting exploration. Our results on users' gesture input behavior can also be used to inform new smart ring technology, such as new sensors to embed into smart rings to detect various user actions, such as sliding, rubbing, twisting, or voice input. We leave such explorations for future work.

We believe that our investigation of user-defined ring gestures will be useful to practitioners that wish to prototype gesture interfaces for smart rings. At the same time, the factors that we outlined as important for reaching consensus in elicitation studies should be examined further by the community.

ACKNOWLEDGMENTS

This work was supported from the project PN-III-P2-2.1-PED-2016-0688 (209PED/2017) financed by UEFISCDI, Romania.

REFERENCES

1. James F. Allen. 1983. Maintaining Knowledge About Temporal Intervals. *Commun. ACM* 26, 11 (Nov. 1983), 832–843. DOI:http://dx.doi.org/10.1145/182.358434
2. Lisa Anthony, Radu-Daniel Vatavu, and Jacob O. Wobbrock. 2013. Understanding the Consistency of Users' Pen and Finger Stroke Gesture Articulation. In *Proc. of Graphics Interface 2013 (GI '13)*. 87–94. http://dl.acm.org/citation.cfm?id=2532129.2532145
3. Lisa Anthony and Jacob O. Wobbrock. 2010. A Lightweight Multistroke Recognizer for User Interface Prototypes. In *Proc. of Graphics Interface 2010*. 245–252. http://dl.acm.org/citation.cfm?id=1839214.1839258
4. Daniel Ashbrook, Patrick Baudisch, and Sean White. 2011. Nenya: Subtle and Eyes-free Mobile Input with a Magnetically-tracked Finger Ring. In *Proc. of the SIGCHI Conf. on Human Factors in Computing Systems (CHI '11)*. 2043–2046. DOI: http://dx.doi.org/10.1145/1978942.1979238
5. Jarg Bergold and Stefan Thomas. 2012. Participatory Research Methods: A Methodological Approach in Motion. *Forum Qualitative Sozialforschung / Forum: Qualitative Social Research* 13, 1 (2012). DOI: http://dx.doi.org/10.17169/fqs-13.1.1801
6. Debaleena Chattopadhyay and Davide Bolchini. 2015. Motor-Intuitive Interactions Based on Image Schemas: Aligning Touchless Interaction Primitives with Human Sensorimotor Abilities. *Interacting with Computers* 27, 3 (2015), 327–343. DOI: http://dx.doi.org/10.1093/iwc/iwu045
7. ChinaCulture.org. 2017. The Story of the Chinese Abacus. The Abacus Inlaid in a Ring. (2017). http://en.chinaculture.org/classics/2010-04/20/content_383263_4.htm
8. John Clute and John Grant. 1997. *The Encyclopedia of Fantasy*. St. Martin's Griffin, New York, NY.
9. Ashley Colley, Virve Inget, Tuomas Lappalainen, and Jonna Häkkilä. 2017. Ring Form Factor: A Design Space for Interaction. In *Proc. of the 2017 ACM Int. Symp. on Wearable Computers (ISWC '17)*. 178–179. DOI: http://dx.doi.org/10.1145/3123021.3123055
10. Eileen Cooper. 1991. A Critique of Six Measures for Assessing Creativity. *The Journal of Creative Behavior* 25, 3 (1991), 194–204. DOI: http://dx.doi.org/10.1002/j.2162-6057.1991.tb01370.x
11. Rajkumar Darbar, Mainak Choudhury, and Vikalp Mullick. 2017. RingIoT: A Smart Ring Controlling Things in Physical Spaces. (2017). https://rajkdarbar.github.io/RingIoT.pdf
12. Masaaki Fukumoto and Yoshinobu Tonomura. 1997. Body Coupled FingerRing: Wireless Wearable Keyboard. In *Proc. of the SIGCHI Conf. on Human Factors in Computing Systems (CHI '97)*. 147–154. DOI: http://dx.doi.org/10.1145/258549.258636
13. Sarthak Ghosh, Hyeong Cheol Kim, Yang Cao, Arne Wessels, Simon T. Perrault, and Shengdong Zhao. 2016. Ringteraction: Coordinated Thumb-index Interaction Using a Ring. In *Proc. of CHI EA '16*. 2640–2647. DOI: http://dx.doi.org/10.1145/2851581.2892371
14. Martin Hachet, Ryoichi Watanabe, and Yoshifumi Kitamura. 2006. A Collaborative Interface for the IllusionHole Using a Control-Ring and a Set of Mice. In *Proc. of 3DUI '06*. 66–68. DOI: http://dx.doi.org/10.1109/VR.2006.5
15. Teng Han, Qian Han, Michelle Annett, Fraser Anderson, Da-Yuan Huang, and Xing-Dong Yang. 2017. Frictio: Passive Kinesthetic Force Feedback for Smart Ring Output. In *Proc. of the 30th ACM Symp. on User Interface Software and Technology (UIST '17)*. 131–142. DOI:http://dx.doi.org/10.1145/3126594.3126622
16. Lynn Hoff, Eva Hornecker, and Sven Bertel. 2016. Modifying Gesture Elicitation: Do Kinaesthetic Priming and Increased Production Reduce Legacy Bias?. In *Proc. of the 10th Int. Conf. on Tangible, Embedded, and Embodied Interaction (TEI '16)*. 86–91. DOI: http://dx.doi.org/10.1145/2839462.2839472
17. Lei Jing, Zixue Cheng, Yinghui Zhou, Junbo Wang, and Tongjun Huang. 2013. Magic Ring: A Self-contained Gesture Input Device on Finger. In *Proc. of MUM '13*. DOI:http://dx.doi.org/10.1145/2541831.2541875
18. M.G. Kendall and B. Babington Smith. 1939. The Problem of m Rankings. *Annals of Math. Statistics* 10, 3 (1939), 275–287. http://www.jstor.org/stable/2235668
19. Finn Kensing and Jeanette Blomberg. 1998. Participatory Design: Issues and Concerns. *Comput. Supported Coop. Work* 7, 3-4 (Jan. 1998), 167–185. DOI: http://dx.doi.org/10.1023/A:1008689307411
20. Wolf Kienzle and Ken Hinckley. 2014. LightRing: Always-available 2D Input on Any Surface. In *Proc. of the 27th ACM Symp. on User Interface Software and Technology (UIST '14)*. 157–160. DOI: http://dx.doi.org/10.1145/2642918.2647376
21. M. Korkman, U. Kirk, and S. Kemp. 1998. *NEPSY: A Developmental Neuropsychological Assessment. San Antonio TX: Psychological Corporation.*
22. Sven Kratz and Michael Rohs. 2010. The $3 Recognizer: Simple 3D Gesture Recognition on Mobile Devices. In *Proc. of the 15th Int. Conf. on Intelligent User Interfaces (IUI '10)*. 419–420. DOI: http://dx.doi.org/10.1145/1719970.1720051
23. Christine Kühnel, Tilo Westermann, Fabian Hemmert, Sven Kratz, Alexander Müller, and Sebastian Möller. 2011. I'm home: Defining and evaluating a gesture set for smart-home control. *International Journal of Human-Computer Studies* 69, 11 (2011), 693–704. DOI: http://dx.doi.org/10.1016/j.ijhcs.2011.04.005
24. Jupyung Lee, Seung-Ho Lim, Jong-Woon Yoo, Ki-Woong Park, Hyun-Jin Choi, and Kyu Ho Park. 2007. A Ubiquitous Fashionable Computer with an i-Throw

Device on a Location-Based Service Environment. In *Proc. of the 21st Int. Conf. on Advanced Information Networking and Applications Workshops (AINAW '07)*. 59–65. DOI:http://dx.doi.org/10.1109/AINAW.2007.63

25. Yang Li. 2010. Protractor: A Fast and Accurate Gesture Recognizer. In *Proc. of the SIGCHI Conf. on Human Factors in Computing Systems (CHI '10)*. 2169–2172. DOI:http://dx.doi.org/10.1145/1753326.1753654
26. Hai-Ning Liang, Cary Williams, Myron Semegen, Wolfgang Stuerzlinger, and Pourang Irani. 2012. User-defined Surface+Motion Gestures for 3D Manipulation of Objects at a Distance Through a Mobile Device. In *Proc. of the 10th Asia Pacific Conf. on Computer Human Interaction (APCHI '12)*. 299–308. DOI:http://dx.doi.org/10.1145/2350046.2350098
27. Hyunchul Lim, Jungmin Chung, Changhoon Oh, SoHyun Park, and Bongwon Suh. 2016. OctaRing: Examining Pressure-Sensitive Multi-Touch Input on a Finger Ring Device. In *Proc. of the 29th Symp. on User Interface Software and Technology (UIST '16 Adjunct)*. 223–224. DOI:http://dx.doi.org/10.1145/2984751.2984780
28. Logbar. 2017. Ring ZERO. List of Actions. (2017). http://ringzero.logbar.jp/how-it-works
29. Pedro Lopes, Alexandra Ion, Willi Mueller, Daniel Hoffmann, Patrik Jonell, and Patrick Baudisch. 2015. Proprioceptive Interaction. In *Proc. of the 33rd Annual ACM Conf. on Human Factors in Computing Systems (CHI '15)*. 939–948. DOI: http://dx.doi.org/10.1145/2702123.2702461
30. Yihua Lou, Wenjun Wu, Radu-Daniel Vatavu, and Wei-Tek Tsai. 2017. Personalized gesture interactions for cyber-physical smart-home environments. *Science China Information Sciences* (2017), 60:072104. DOI: http://dx.doi.org/10.1007/s11432-015-1014-7
31. Steve Mann. 1997. Wearable Computing: A First Step Toward Personal Imaging. *Computer* 30, 2 (Feb. 1997), 25–32. DOI:http://dx.doi.org/10.1109/2.566147
32. Meredith Ringel Morris. 2012. Web on the Wall: Insights from a Multimodal Interaction Elicitation Study. In *Proc. of the 2012 ACM Int. Conf. on Interactive Tabletops and Surfaces (ITS '12)*. 95–104. DOI: http://dx.doi.org/10.1145/2396636.2396651
33. Meredith Ringel Morris, Andreea Danielescu, Steven Drucker, Danyel Fisher, Bongshin Lee, m.c. schraefel, and Jacob O. Wobbrock. 2014. Reducing Legacy Bias in Gesture Elicitation Studies. *interactions* 21, 3 (May 2014), 40–45. DOI:http://dx.doi.org/10.1145/2591689
34. NIMB. 2017. Nimb: A Smart Ring that Helps You Feel Safe and Sound. (2017). https://www.kickstarter.com/projects/1629204423/nimb-a-smart-ring-that-keeps-you-safe-and-sound
35. Masa Ogata, Yuta Sugiura, Hirotaka Osawa, and Michita Imai. 2012. iRing: Intelligent Ring Using Infrared Reflection. In *Proc. of UIST '12*. 131–136. DOI: http://dx.doi.org/10.1145/2380116.2380135
36. ORII. 2017. ORII - The Fastest Way to Send Messages Without a Screen. (2017). https://www.kickstarter.com/projects/187732114/orii-your-voice-powered-smart-ring
37. OURA. 2017. OURA ring. Improve sleep. Perform better. (2017). https://www.kickstarter.com/projects/oura/oura-ring-improve-sleep-perform-better
38. Thammathip Piumsomboon, Adrian Clark, Mark Billinghurst, and Andy Cockburn. 2013. User-defined Gestures for Augmented Reality. In *Proc. of INTERACT '13*. 282–299. DOI: http://dx.doi.org/10.1007/978-3-642-40480-1_18
39. Yosra Rekik, Laurent Grisoni, and Nicolas Roussel. 2013. Towards Many Gestures to One Command: A User Study for Tabletops. In *Proc. of INTERACT '13*. 246–263. DOI: http://dx.doi.org/10.1007/978-3-642-40480-1_16
40. Yosra Rekik, Radu-Daniel Vatavu, and Laurent Grisoni. 2014. Understanding Users' Perceived Difficulty of Multi-Touch Gesture Articulation. In *Proc. of ICMI '14*. 232–239. DOI: http://dx.doi.org/10.1145/2663204.2663273
41. Mikko J. Rissanen, Samantha Vu, Owen Noel Fernando, Natalie Pang, and Schubert Foo. 2013. Subtle, Natural and Socially Acceptable Interaction Techniques for Ringterfaces – Finger-Ring Shaped User Interfaces. In *Proc. of the 1st Int. Conf. on Distributed, Ambient, and Pervasive Interactions*. 52–61. DOI: http://dx.doi.org/10.1007/978-3-642-39351-8_6
42. Mehran Roshandel, Aarti Munjal, Peyman Moghadam, Shahin Tajik, and Hamed Ketabdar. 2014. *Multi-sensor Based Gestures Recognition with a Smart Finger Ring*. Springer International Publishing, Cham, 316–324. DOI: http://dx.doi.org/10.1007/978-3-319-07230-2_31
43. Jaime Ruiz, Yang Li, and Edward Lank. 2011. User-defined Motion Gestures for Mobile Interaction. In *Proceedings of the SIGCHI Conference on Human Factors in Computing Systems (CHI '11)*. 197–206. DOI: http://dx.doi.org/10.1145/1978942.1978971
44. Jaime Ruiz and Daniel Vogel. 2015. Soft-Constraints to Reduce Legacy and Performance Bias to Elicit Whole-body Gestures with Low Arm Fatigue. In *Proc. of the 33rd ACM Conf. on Human Factors in Computing Systems (CHI '15)*. 3347–3350. DOI: http://dx.doi.org/10.1145/2702123.2702583
45. Teddy Seyed, Chris Burns, Mario Costa Sousa, Frank Maurer, and Anthony Tang. 2012. Eliciting Usable Gestures for Multi-display Environments. In *Proc. of ITS '12*. 41–50. DOI: http://dx.doi.org/10.1145/2396636.2396643
46. Roy Shilkrot, Jochen Huber, Jürgen Steimle, Suranga Nanayakkara, and Pattie Maes. 2015. Digital Digits: A Comprehensive Survey of Finger Augmentation Devices. *ACM Comput. Surv.* 48, 2, Article 30 (Nov. 2015), 29 pages. DOI:http://dx.doi.org/10.1145/2828993

47. Statista. 2017. Global smartphone shipments forecast from 2010 to 2021 (in million units). (2017). https://www.statista.com/statistics/263441/global-smartphone-shipments-forecast/

48. J.R.R. Tolkien. 1954. *The Lord of the Rings*. George Allen & Unwin, London, UK.

49. K. Tsukada and M. Yasumura. 2004. Ubi-finger: A simple gesture input device for mobile and ubiquitous environment. *Journal of Asian Information, Science and Life* 2, 2 (2004), 111–120. http://mobiquitous.com/pub/aisl2004-ubi-finger.pdf

50. Radu-Daniel Vatavu. 2012. User-defined Gestures for Free-hand TV Control. In *Proc. of the 10th European Conf. on Interactive TV and Video (EuroITV '12)*. 45–48. DOI:http://dx.doi.org/10.1145/2325616.2325626

51. Radu-Daniel Vatavu. 2013a. The Impact of Motion Dimensionality and Bit Cardinality on the Design of 3D Gesture Recognizers. *International Journal of Human-Computer Studies* 71, 4 (2013), 387–409. http://dx.doi.org/10.1016/j.ijhcs.2012.11.005

52. Radu-Daniel Vatavu. 2013b. There's a World Outside Your TV: Exploring Interactions Beyond the Physical TV Screen. In *Proc. of the 11th European Conf. on Interactive TV and Video (EuroITV '13)*. 143–152. DOI: http://dx.doi.org/10.1145/2465958.2465972

53. Radu-Daniel Vatavu. 2017a. Improving Gesture Recognition Accuracy on Touch Screens for Users with Low Vision. In *Proc. of CHI '17*. 4667–4679. DOI: http://dx.doi.org/10.1145/3025453.3025941

54. Radu-Daniel Vatavu. 2017b. Smart-Pockets: Body-Deictic Gestures for Fast Access to Personal Data during Ambient Interactions. *International Journal of Human-Computer Studies* 103 (2017), 1–21. DOI: http://dx.doi.org/10.1016/j.ijhcs.2017.01.005

55. Radu-Daniel Vatavu, Lisa Anthony, and Jacob O. Wobbrock. 2012. Gestures As Point Clouds: A $P Recognizer for User Interface Prototypes. In *Proc. of ICMI '12*. 273–280. DOI: http://dx.doi.org/10.1145/2388676.2388732

56. Radu-Daniel Vatavu and Ştefan Gheorghe Pentiuc. 2008. Multi-Level Representation of Gesture as Command for Human-Computer Interaction. *Computing and Informatics* 27, 6 (2008), 837–851. DOI:http://dx.doi.org/ojs/index.php/cai/article/viewArticle/16

57. Radu-Daniel Vatavu and Jacob O. Wobbrock. 2015. Formalizing Agreement Analysis for Elicitation Studies: New Measures, Significance Test, and Toolkit. In *Proc. of the 33rd ACM Conf. on Human Factors in Computing Systems (CHI '15)*. 1325–1334. DOI: http://dx.doi.org/10.1145/2702123.2702223

58. Radu-Daniel Vatavu and Jacob O. Wobbrock. 2016. Between-Subjects Elicitation Studies: Formalization and Tool Support. In *Proc. of CHI '16*. 3390–3402. DOI: http://dx.doi.org/10.1145/2858036.2858228

59. Radu-Daniel Vatavu and Ionuţ-Alexandru Zaiţi. 2014. Leap Gestures for TV: Insights from an Elicitation Study. In *Proc. of the ACM Int. Conf. on Interactive Experiences for TV and Online Video (TVX '14)*. 131–138. DOI: http://dx.doi.org/10.1145/2602299.2602316

60. Mark Weiser. 1999. The Computer for the 21st Century. *SIGMOBILE Mob. Comput. Commun. Rev.* 3, 3 (1999), 3–11. DOI:http://dx.doi.org/10.1145/329124.329126

61. Mathias Wilhelm, Daniel Krakowczyk, Frank Trollmann, and Sahin Albayrak. 2015. eRing: Multiple Finger Gesture Recognition with One Ring Using an Electric Field. In *Proc. of the 2nd Int. Workshop on Sensor-based Activity Recognition and Interaction (WOAR '15)*. 7:1–6. DOI:http://dx.doi.org/10.1145/2790044.2790047

62. Jacob O. Wobbrock, Htet Htet Aung, Brandon Rothrock, and Brad A. Myers. 2005. Maximizing the Guessability of Symbolic Input. In *Proc. of CHI '05 EA on Human Factors in Computing Systems*. 1869–1872. DOI: http://dx.doi.org/10.1145/1056808.1057043

63. Jacob O. Wobbrock, Meredith Ringel Morris, and Andrew D. Wilson. 2009. User-defined Gestures for Surface Computing. In *Proc. of the CHI Conf. on Human Factors in Computing Systems (CHI '09)*. 1083–1092. DOI:http://dx.doi.org/10.1145/1518701.1518866

64. Jacob O. Wobbrock, Andrew D. Wilson, and Yang Li. 2007. Gestures Without Libraries, Toolkits or Training: A $1 Recognizer for User Interface Prototypes. In *Proc. of the 20th ACM Symp. on User Interface Software and Technology (UIST '07)*. 159–168. DOI: http://dx.doi.org/10.1145/1294211.1294238

65. Ionuţ-Alexandru Zaiţi, Ştefan Gheorghe Pentiuc, and Radu-Daniel Vatavu. 2015. On Free-Hand TV Control: Experimental Results on User-Elicited Gestures with Leap Motion. *Pers. Ubiquit. Comput.* 19, 5–6 (2015), 821–838. DOI: http://dx.doi.org/10.1007/s00779-015-0863-y

66. Boning Zhang, Yiqiang Chen, Yueliang Qian, and Xiangdong Wang. 2011. A Ring-shaped Interactive Device for Large Remote Display and Mobile Device Control. In *Proc. of UbiComp '11*. 473–474. DOI: http://dx.doi.org/10.1145/2030112.2030177

67. Cheng Zhang, Anandghan Waghmare, Pranav Kundra, Yiming Pu, Scott Gilliland, Thomas Ploetz, Thad E. Starner, Omer T. Inan, and Gregory D. Abowd. 2017a. FingerSound: Recognizing Unistroke Thumb Gestures Using a Ring. *Proc. ACM Interact. Mob. Wearable Ubiquitous Technol.* 1, 3, Article 120 (Sept. 2017), 19 pages. DOI:http://dx.doi.org/10.1145/3130985

68. Cheng Zhang, Xiaoxuan Wang, Anandghan Waghmare, Sumeet Jain, Thomas Ploetz, Omer T. Inan, Thad E. Starner, and Gregory D. Abowd. 2017b. FingOrbits: Interaction with Wearables Using Synchronized Thumb Movements. In *Proc. of ISWC '17*. 62–65. DOI: http://dx.doi.org/10.1145/3123021.3123041

Interactive and Situated Guidelines to Help Users Design a Personal Desk that Fits Their Bodies

Bokyung Lee Joongi Shin Hyoshin Bae Daniel Saakes
Department of Industrial Design
KAIST, Republic of Korea
{bokyunglee, jgshin, bluepepper, saakes}@kaist.ac.kr

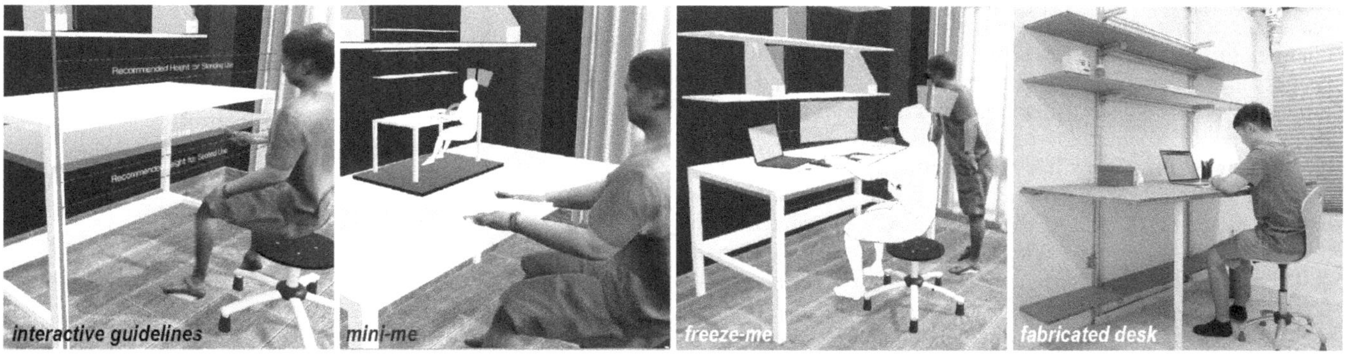

Figure 1. How can we design a desk that fits our bodies and needs? We explored interactive ergonomic recommendations for personal design applications. We developed a desk design system in VR, and evaluated it with six users through DIY design and the use of custom fabricated desks.

ABSTRACT
In this paper, we explored the application of human factor guidelines in personal fabrication. This is useful for several Do-It-Yourself (DIY) scenarios, including users adjusting workstation configurations or designing a desk to fit a single person. We identified a dependency map between the user's anthropometrics, ergonomic pose recommendations, and design dimensions. Based on this, we developed situated and interactive guidelines to assist users in design applications. We applied these guidelines in a Virtual Reality (VR) system that lets users customize their desk and provides real-time feedback and feedforward on pose and design. We evaluated the system with six participants, had each one design a personal desk, fabricated their desks, and let them work on their desks for four hours. The design and evaluation contribute to fabrication tools as it helped users be aware of their pose and ergonomic knowledge, and design for their bodies and needs.

ACM Classification Keywords
H.5.2 Information Interfaces and Presentation (e.g. HCI): Graphical user interfaces.

DIS '18, June 9–13, 2018, Hong Kong
© 2018 ACM. ISBN 978-1-4503-5198-0/18/06... $15.00
DOI: https://doi.org/10.1145/3196709.3196725

Author Keywords
personal fabrication, interactive guidelines, DIY

INTRODUCTION
Emerging technologies in *parametric design*, *personal fabrication* or *DIY toolkits* provide new opportunities for people to make products according to their specifications [28]. People take on a new role as both designer and user when they design objects for themselves. In this paper, we look into how to support people designing personal products that fit their bodies and needs.

Our motivation is based on casual observations of how people estimate comfort or good posture when buying furniture in offline stores. People test comfortable poses and simulate their use, not unlike designers employing experience prototyping [6]. They also gather information from experts, such as asking family members to measure the height up to their hands when holding a pose [31], or hiring ergonomists to adjust office desks [24]. This observations shows that selecting, adapting, and designing furniture is a process that includes information gathering and prototyping to understand personal fit, and the body plays a central role. However, those play-acting activities are difficult to perform when shopping online or using CAD or mass-customization tools. Also, personalized advice on ergonomics is an under-explored topic in personal fabrication tools.

For this reason, we looked into design guidelines that deal with the personal fit of a product. The field of *Human Factors* provides recommendations for product comfort and safety.

However, these guidelines are either aimed at professional designers who design items to fit a population of users, or at ergonomists who evaluate and recommend good postures. In this paper, we made a first step in making these recommendations applicable for personal design, and related anthropometrics, ergonomic pose recommendations, and design parameters in a dependency map. The result is a set of guidelines that provides both feedback and feedforward on design and pose.

We made these guidelines applicable for interactive design systems. Guidelines are generated based on the user's body, posture, and pair-use items, and dynamically respond to users' real-time design choices or actions. For example, if a user changes the seat height, the recommended desk and monitor heights update accordingly. Likewise, if the user makes the tabletop deeper, the shelf reachability guidelines are also updated. We implemented these guidelines in an office desk customization system: Body2Desk, that employs motion-capture and Virtual Reality (VR). We evaluated Body2Desk with six users and let them design their desk. We fabricated their desks then let them use their desk for a few hours. The results indicate that the system makes them aware of ergonomic guidelines and lets them effectively employ them. We discuss the benefits and uses of guidelines in a personal design process, and applications for future fabrication interfaces.

We selected the office desk as an application for this research because it interacts with the entire body and consists of a complex set of recommendations including pose as well as use efficiency, such as reachability. In addition, the use of computer workstations is commonly reported to contribute to back and neck pain. Also, an office can be customized by users through several fabrication services such as *Opendesk* [40], or additional accessories like monitor stands or shelves. However, the insights or interaction techniques derived from this study are not limited to desks, and can be applied to other types of products such as kitchen bars and bookshelves, or to services like furniture arrangement.

There are several limitations to this work. We employed a Kinect v2 for motion capture which has known problems with accuracy [8, 67]. We derived ergonomic guidelines from literature [7, 27, 42, 43, 61], and applied them in a novel, but untested way. By situating and visualizing human factor guidelines in design tools, we limited our focus to 1) the education of good body poses, and 2) workplace intervention. We do not claim that this approach solves discomfort or prevents musculoskeletal disorders; however, it might be part of a future solution.

This paper makes three contributions: 1) Personalizing human factor guidelines with a dependency map that relates anthropometrics, pose, and design dimensions, 2) Design considerations that deal with interaction techniques for informing guidelines in VR fabrication tools, and 3) Body2Desk system implementation and user evaluation.

RELATED WORK

Our research bridges existing work in physical ergonomics with design tools for non-professionals (casual users).

Active Posture Measuring

Musculoskeletal disorders, such as back pain caused by office work, are a common but important problem. Research in HCI has focused extensively on active posture measuring and feedback. Some projects monitor upper body posture with body-worn sensors [34, 64] or with sensors embedded in furniture, such as in chairs [38]. Other projects employ cameras [57]. Real-time feedback on posture is provided in various ways: in apps and on displays [64], through physical feedback [16] such as a bending plant, vibrotactile actuators in a chair [69], augmented mirrors [1, 57] or co-workers alerting each other [50]. These systems aim to assist users in maintaining good posture over time; however, they do not consider configurations of the workspace in conjunction with their pose.

Ergonomic Knowledge and Application

The optimal workplace setup is highly dependent on the task, and prolonged postures need to be avoided [35]. Modern office equipment is designed to adapt to the users' anatomy and needs, such as with highly adjustable chairs or configurable table heights. However, chairs are often not adjusted by users, or not adjusted to the optimal position [14, 60, 62].

Several books inform users and designers about ergonomics with practical guidelines [7, 27, 42, 43, 61] and are discussed in the next section. Education and training programs are popular approaches in companies [20], but their effectiveness is debatable [56]. Some studies show that ergonomic knowledge does not always lead to action [53] whereas other studies indicate that users changed their work practices and were able to adjust their workstations effectively [46]. Combining ergonomic furniture with office ergonomic training programs [20], on-site interventions by ergonomists [24] and follow-up was found to be effective. In this paper, we focus on education and interventions as we situate and personalize ergonomic guidelines for users who are designing and adjusting their own desks.

Interactive Simulation in Design

A large body of work on HCI aims to make geometric modeling accessible to non-professionals [12, 23, 37, 48, 65, 51]. One problem is how to ensure that the design can be made, and whether it functions as expected. Therefore, researchers recently started to include interactive physics simulations in the modeling application, to ensure the design is valid [51], stable [48] or structurally sound [59]. Sketchchair [48] for instance, lets users sketch a chair with a few strokes and generates fabrication-ready design drawings. Reference objects and a poseable mannequin help users estimate the size of the chair, and rigid body simulations predict stability. Umetani et al. [59] provides suggestions on the stability and durability of furniture based on an interactive physics simulation of the joinings between planks. Providing feedback and feedforward on the design helps users make decisions. We build upon these works but focus on ergonomic guidelines to help users design for usability, comfort, and health.

Ergonomic Simulations for Evaluating Designs

CAD systems with built-in ergonomics assessment capabilities are used to simulate complex tasks to analyze postures, forces,

Body	***Body Posture (health)***		ex. The angle between the thighs and the torso should be greater than 90 degrees.
	Body Activity		ex. For comfortable typing, the height of the desk should be 25-30cm above seat. ex. For standing worker, the room for the feet should include toe and knee space to move up close to the working surface.
	Body Clearance		ex. The clearances between the seat surface and the underside of the table should anthropometrically accommodate the thigh clearance of the person.
	Body Reachability		ex. For comfortable reach, the height of the shelf should be within the reachable range when the user is standing in front of the desk. (Maximum Shelf Height)
Object	***Object Efficiency***		ex. To design efficient and flexible storage area around a workplace, key operating objects should be in a reachable area.
	Object Use	***Visuality***	ex. The position of the monitor should be at about eye height, and keep a distance of more than 30cm from the eyes.
		Input Motion	ex. Ideally, your keyboard and mouse should be shoulder-distance apart and as level as possible.
Space	***Space Clearance***		ex. It is important to consider the circulation zone requirement for passage behind the seat at the typical workstation.The edge of this zone should take into account the movement of the chair within the chair clearance zone to avoid obstruction of any people circulation behind it.

Table 1. We collected 68 human factor recommendations related to office work, and grouped them into three categories: body, object, and space.

collisions, and visibility. Jack [4] for instance, is a virtual human model that supports anthropometric scaling, mass, and joint-limit information for given populations. Other systems let users evaluate virtual designs in Virtual Reality [2], such as automotive interiors or accessibility in factories. Although some authors reported on the advantages of co-designing ergonomics with users [15], professional ergonomics tools are used to evaluate designs to fit a population, not to generate designs for, by, or with a single user.

Rehabilitation, Sports, and Skill

Third-person feedback on pose and motion is widely used in sports training and rehabilitation. Biomechanical analysis helps optimize particular movements or adopt new techniques. Motion Capture and Augmented or Virtual Reality provided advantages over traditional video playback, as they can be real-time, situated, interactive, and allow multiple viewpoints. Marker-less motion tracking with a depth camera such as the Kinect v2 sensor is commonly applied and has advantages over systems that require markers or sensors placed on the user's body [8]. Since the Kinect was developed for playing games, the accuracy is best when facing the sensor and standing, and upper body joints are identified with less error than lower joints, especially in sitting poses such as crossed legged [67].

Various systems provide real-time, third-person avatars for training, providing feedback on poses and feedforward on how to move [1, 18, 45, 49, 58]. Other systems employ augmented reality to annotate the real world with instructions or feedback on motion [17, 52, 54]. Laplacian Vision [22] predicts the motion path of a bouncing ball and visualizes its trajectory in the Hololens. We build upon these works and included virtual avatars to provide real-time feedback from multiple views.

Design for and with the Body

Systems that let users design for their bodies have to deal with the challenges of dynamic and complex geometries. Therefore, some systems let users design directly on or with their bodies [13, 47, 68]. Lee et al. [30] let users simulate actions and pose to design furniture that fits their bodies and uses. To solve reachability issues, for instance when designing shoes or hats, other systems use a mannequin [66], or let users temporarily step out of their bodies [68]. However, most systems use augmented mirrors [10, 63]. Although these systems embody the design task, as far as we know, situated ergonomic guidelines have not been explored in a personal design context.

Augmented and Virtual Reality

Wearable displays (such as HMDs) let users design virtual objects real-scale, immersed or situated. For instance, Yee et al. [5] let users sketch objects in Augmented Reality, and Lau et al. [29] presented a system that composed objects out of primitive shapes. Instead of generic design tools, we focused on variant design [41] as we let users configure a parametric model. Designing in-situ brings similar challenges as designing on the body, as these interfaces do not support multiple or scaled views. In order to achieve an overview of the design, some systems provide a second miniature representation [55, 44], while others let users step back [30]. We employed both in our design.

GUIDELINES FOR PERSONAL COMFORT AND USE

In this study, we limit our focus to an office desk. We collected design guidelines for desks from various fields: human factors [27, 43, 61], working postures [7], furniture design [42], government regulations [21, 3], and furniture companies [25, 11, 36]. Guidelines aimed at industrial designers are mostly to fit a large percentage of an intended user population, and are indicated as a range, for instance, from the 5 percentile to the 95 percentile (e.g., *the desk height should be 610mm-711mm from the floor*). Guidelines for ergonomists are for observing people's poses and defined as angles (e.g., *the monitor should not be located lower than 45 degrees from eye level*). Both guidelines are not directly applicable in personal design tools that provide interactive design recommendations. Therefore, we first grouped the collected guidelines into three categories as shown in Table 1: related to body, object, and space.

Body-centered guidelines are related to anthropometrics and pose (Table 1-body). Several guidelines aim to prevent back and neck discomfort and carpal tunnel syndrome through good *posture*. These are typically measured as the angle between

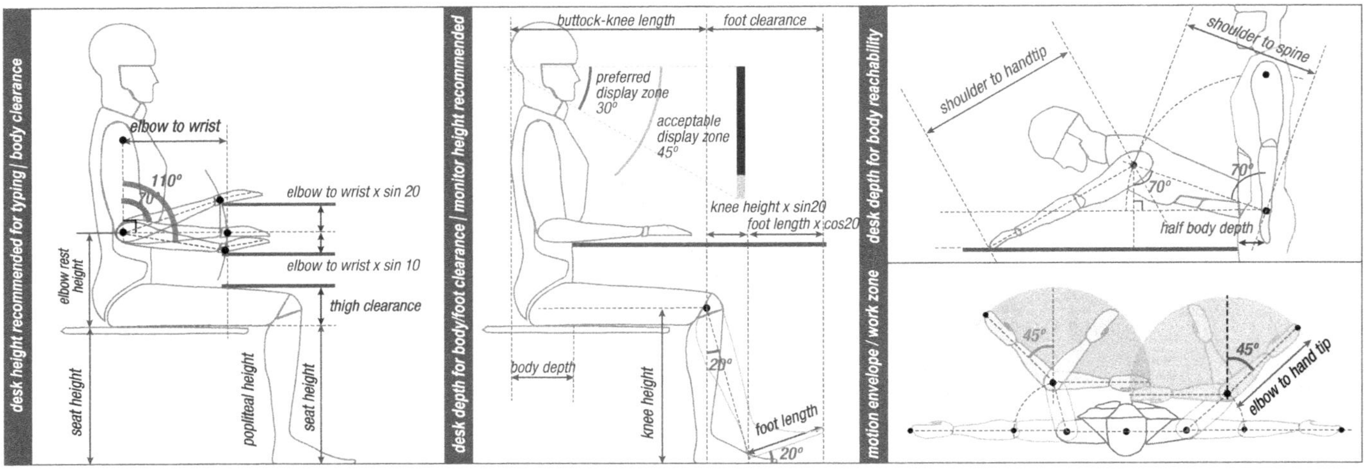

Figure 2. We redefined ergonomic guidelines for a single person and a desk; and we used anthropometrics and recommended angles for good posture.

connected bones in the sagittal plane. A second set of guidelines provides recommendations for specific *activities* such as typing or crafting. Third, *body clearance* deals with the distance between the body and the desk, while *body reachability* illustrates the limits where the desk can be used comfortably concerning the user's reach with their hands.

Object-centered guidelines are related to the objects that people use on the desk, such as a monitor or a keyboard (Table 1-object). Some inform users how to use objects *efficiently* and deal with the arrangement and reachability of frequently used items. (e.g., recommended motion envelopes are presented in the transverse plane with primary and secondary zones.) Other recommendations involve the correct *use* of objects (e.g., the height of the screen to maintain good posture while reading).

Space-centered guidelines deal with the desk in relation to the office environment. For example, the user needs to consider the minimal distance between the chair and the walls to move around freely. Proximity to other furniture (eg. the distance between the desk and storage closet) should also be considered to maintain efficient usability.

Guidelines from Population to a Person

There are no guidelines for furniture dimensions and ranges based on a single person's anthropometrics and pose. Therefore, we reverse engineered furniture guidelines from the recommended pose guidelines. For instance, there is a rule that "*good posture for typing is defined as sitting straight and keeping the elbow angle between 70 to 100 degrees,*" as illustrated in the Figure 2 on the left. We personalized the rule with seat height, elbow rest height, length between elbow to wrist, and the recommended elbow range, as shown in Equations 1 & 2.

$$\min h_{typing} = h_{seat} + h_{elbow\ rest} - l_{elbow,\ wrist} \times \sin(90 - 70) \quad (1)$$

$$\max h_{typing} = h_{seat} + h_{elbow\ rest} + l_{elbow,\ wrist} \times \sin(100 - 90) \quad (2)$$

TYPE	SAMPLE GUIDELINES	COROLLARY PERSONAL VARIABLES (static, dynamic*, body, object, desk parameter)
Body Posture	Proper back /neck angle	*back angle*, neck angle*, monitor height*, desk height**
Body Activity	Recommended desk height for typing (sitting)	*elbow rest height, elbow-wrist length, seat height*, proper elbow angle, tabletop thickness*
	Recommended desk height for typing (standing)	*elbow rest standing, elbow-wrist length, proper elbow angle, tabletop thickness*
	Recommended monitor height	*sitting eye height*, seat height*, proper display angle*
Body Clearance *(sitting)*	Desk height clearance	*thigh clearance, seat height*, desktop thickness*
	Desk depth clearance	*knee height, foot length, buttock-knee length, body depth*
Body Reachability *(sitting & standing)*	Desk depth reachability	*desk height*, shoulder-fingertip length, spine height, shoulder-spine length, body depth,*
	Shelf height reachability	*desk depth*, shelf depth*, shoulder height*, shoulder-fingertip length, body depth, shelf thickness*
	Shelf depth reachability	*desk depth*, shelf depth*, shelf height*, shoulder height*, shoulder-fingertip length, body depth*
Object Efficiency	Motion Envelope	*sitting position(x)*, elbow-fingertip length, shoulder-fingertip length, primary working angle*
Space Clearance	Chair clearance	*desk depth*, chair depth*, space (wall)*

Table 2. The dependency map illustrates how the design relates to anthropometrics, ergonomic pose, design parameters, and pair-objects.

These rewritten guidelines define ranges of recommended furniture dimensions and can be applied in personal design systems. For validation, we tested the new rules with two anthropometric indices (the fifth and 95th percentiles). When we applied our rules, the recommended ranges matched the lower and upper recommendations of the rules that fit a population.

Dependency Map for Personal Guidelines

Because dimensions and guidelines are related to each other, *e.g. the recommended tabletop height is dependent on the seat height*, we made a dependency map. As shown in the Table 2, a user's body measurements, joint position, pair-use objects, and desk dimensions all influence the guidelines.

A few rules depend on static variables that do not change, such as the length between the body joints. However, most of them need to respond to a user's real-time dynamic posture, actions or design decisions. For instance, the recommended tabletop height should be updated when the user changes the height

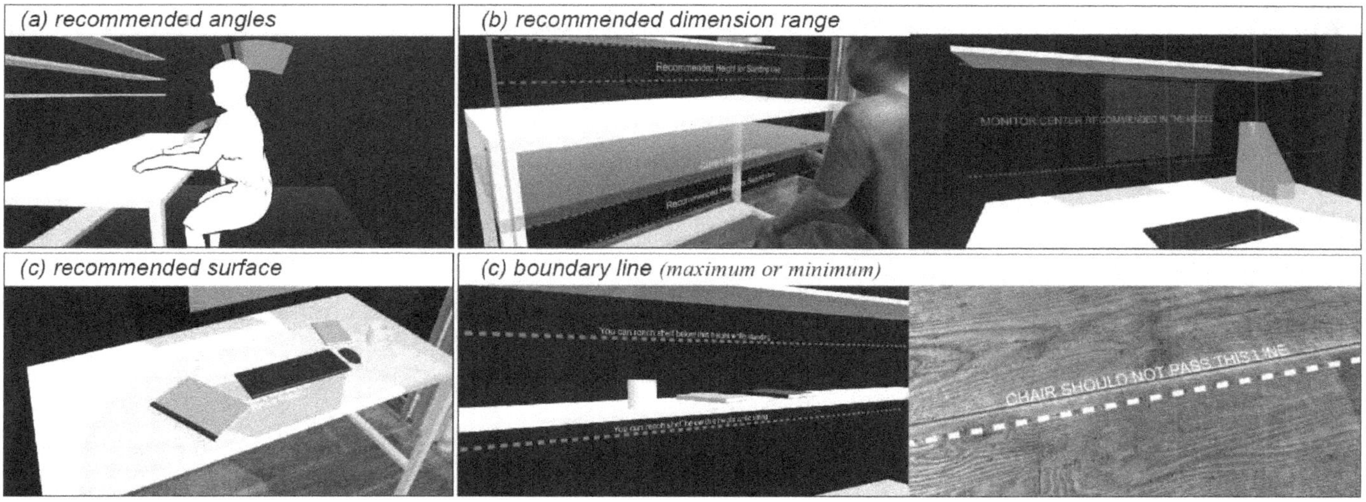

Figure 3. Different visualization approaches are required for each type of guideline. Good posture is described as an angle range and can be situated on the body. The recommended range can be illustrated with two lines on the spot, while reachable maximum guidelines can be drawn as a single line.

of their seat. Also, the desk parameters affect guidelines; for example, desk height relates to the reachability of shelves.

The dependency map also revealed conflicting dependencies between guidelines. For example, the desk depth is not only related with the tabletop itself, but also with shelf reachability. In such cases, presentation is important. Currently, we provide all the related guidelines and the user has to balance or compromise between the rules to make decisions.

DESIGN CONSIDERATIONS

In this section, we explore several design considerations for responsive and situated guidelines for interactive design systems. We highlight four: *visualization*, *feedforward and feedback*, *context-awareness*, *visualization*, and *point of view*.

Visualization

The guidelines can be provided in several ways, such as with haptic feedback. In this paper, we focused on the visualization techniques as we were inspired by the seminal book by Dreyfuss "Human Scale" who overlaid dimensions on bodies in poses, which allows to situate interactive guidelines in-place [9]. Related design interfaces that provide users with suggestions visualize design options separately on extra panels [59, 39, 19], or provide parametric design sliders with illustrations of recommended ranges [26], as it is difficult to show alternative 3D geometries in-place at the same time. By situating the guidelines near the design parameter, the users can be aware of information while making design decisions.

Guidelines regarding *posture* of the back, neck, or elbow are visualized in the form of an arc. We drew the angle range directly on the real-time body, as shown in Figure 3a. Also, the recommended range for a dimension (e.g., the recommended height of the desk or monitor) is represented with two lines and a plane in between (Figure 3b). Similarly, the *motion envelope* for object efficiency is illustrated with a highlighted surface and directly shows their primary and secondary working zones. Other guidelines are represented as a line on the limit for that dimension (Figure 3d), so the user can understand where the maximum height or depth they can reach.

In addition to these guidelines, simulation such as collision detection between furniture and the virtual body could limit a range. For example, when the user tries to lower the height of the desk below the body clearance height, the height remains unchanged at the minimum value.

Feedforward and Feedback

As guidelines are dependent on body, pose, and objects, they need to be responsive. First, guidelines provide interactive *feedback* [9] on users' posture changes or design decisions. For example, when people make the depth of a desk too deep, the system informs the user that the back of the desk is not reachable. Also, when users assume an unhealthy posture, the guideline warns them, such as their back leaning forward too much (Figure 4, top left).

Guidelines also provide recommended ranges with *feedforward* [9] interaction, which tells users the ergonomic impact of their design decision in advance. For example, guidelines indicate a range of recommended table heights, or show recommended neck, wrist, or back angles. Feedforward suggests proper posture and dimensions while designing the desk.

Context-Awareness and Dynamic

Some guidelines are context-dependent. For example, the recommended desk height for typing is different from those reading a book or writing on paper (Figure 4, bottom). Therefore, the system needs to discern a user's prime needs based on their behavior and visualize the guidelines accordingly.

Other guidelines are activity agnostic. For instance, designing the shelf heights needs to take into account both sitting and standing reachability, and both ranges should be shown at the same time. In addition, as users use their bodies for both designing and simulating, certain guidelines do not need to be responsive to the changes in posture when switching from

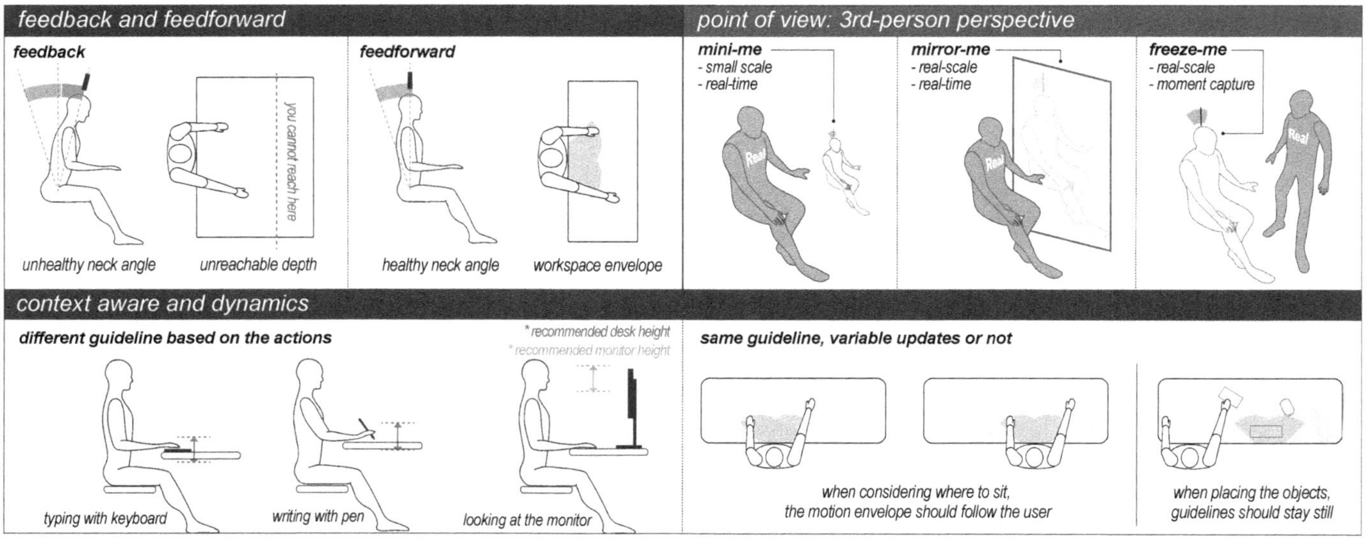

Figure 4. (top left) We provide interactive feedback on user's posture changes or design actions, and provide feedforward to show the design space and recommendations. (top right) To support third-person views, we explored avatars that copy the user's actions in time or space.

posing to design activities. For example, the motion envelope that indicates primary and secondary reachability depends on the user's position. However, when the user moves around to arrange virtual objects, the motion envelope should be frozen in the default sitting/standing pose (Figure 4, bottom).

Point of View

Designing with the body and from a first-person perspective engages users in their designs and relates their design to their needs [6, 30]. However, as people cannot see their entire body, feedback on poses is better achieved from a third-person perspective. Therefore we designed two principal ways of providing feedback: in space and in time (Figure 4, right).

The advantage of feedback in time is that the body is visualized in place and on a real scale. *Freeze-me* captures a user's pose and lets them step out of their body to examine their pose in relation to their furniture design. The advantage of feedback in space is a direct feedback on the pose while interacting with the furniture. *Mini-me* is a scaled-down avatar that can be freely positioned and oriented as any other virtual object. In that way, users can examine their pose from various angles, and move the avatar in their line of sight when posing and acting. *Mirror-me* is similar but on a real scale. By looking sideways, users observe the angle of their back and arms.

BODY2DESK

The guidelines we described in the previous sections can be applied to multiple types of interactive design systems. As an example, we developed a prototype in VR as it provides an embodied, first-person view on the design task. Body2Desk lets users customize the dimensions of a parametric desk model to their specifications by prototyping with their bodies, and provides guidelines according to the uses' pose and actions.

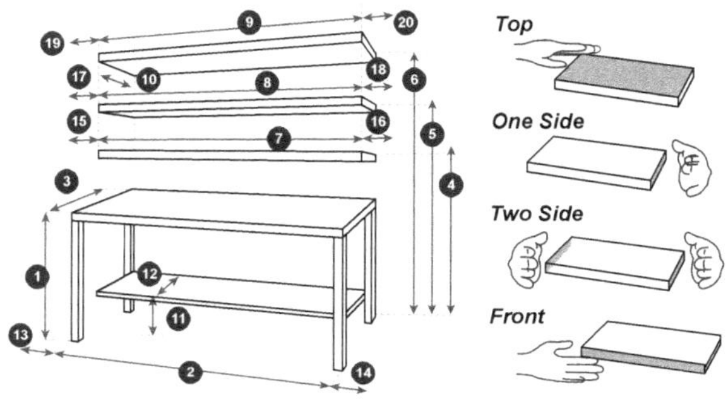

Figure 5. The parametric desk used in Body2Desk has a tabletop, footrest below, and three shelves. The position and dimension of each surface can be customized with gestures or voice commands.

System Design

Based on a typical work desk design, we prepared a parametric desk with a tabletop, a footrest, and three shelves, which can be defined with 12 parameters (Figure 5). Similar to Lee et al [30], we employed a combination of full-body gestures and voice commands. Immersed in a VR environment, users can act freely, move around in the design space, position virtual objects such as monitors or books, and set dimensions by saying *"Desk height, until here."* Voice commands were useful when users were posing and acting, or specifying dimensions with body parts other than their hands, such as their feet. However, we found that hand gestures were preferred for positioning objects. For completeness, we also implemented hand gestures for changing dimensions. We employed pinch gloves [33], and let users grab or drag a surface to manipulate dimensions (Figure 5), as well as the virtual props. An undo feature was provided with a voice command, *"undo."*

To provide a third-person perspective on the users' poses in VR, we implemented two virtual avatars: *Mini-me* and *Freeze-*

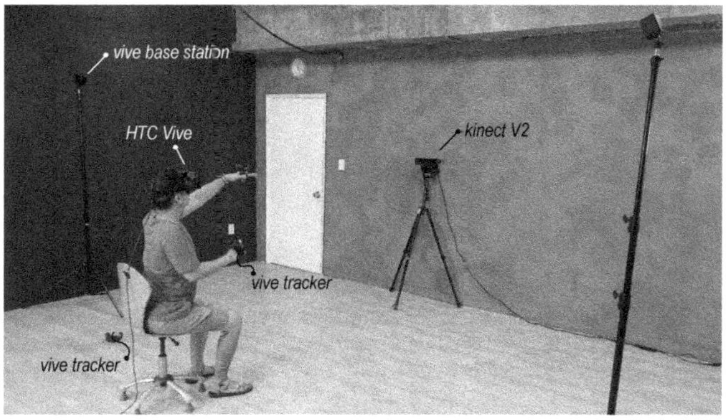

Figure 6. The user wears an HMD and a Kinect captures the user's pose. Two 3D trackers were attached to hands for pinching interaction, and 3D tracker was attached to the chair to capture the seat height.

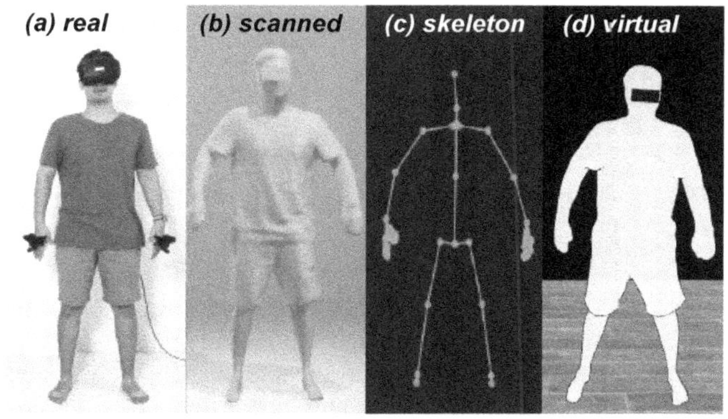

Figure 7. The user's body(a) was 3D scanned with a Kinect (b), and the skeletal joints were captured (c). Those were combined to generate a virtual human avatar, and a toon shader was applied (d).

me, based on the users' 3D-scanned bodies (Figure 1). Mini-me can be manipulated with gestures, same as manipulating the virtual props. Freeze-me was not able to move or rotate, but can be activated with voice command, *"freeze."* We generated human factor guidelines based on each user's anthropometrics (from the scanned body) and joints (captured in real time) as shown in Figure 2. For our system, we selected guidelines which were frequently mentioned in the literature (Table 2), and suitable to be captured in the Kinect. The goal of this study was not to provide accurate and complete set of guidelines, but to observe how people use interactive guidelines in their design process.

We followed the design considerations previously described, and made the guidelines context-aware with feedback and feedforward. Our system only activates the guidelines that are related to the parameter the user is changing (Table 2). For example, when the user is adjusting the seat height, information regarding the 'desk recommendation height,' 'monitor height,' and 'reachable shelf height while sitting' is visualized. This will prevent visual clutter and information overload.

System Implementation

The prototype (Figure 6) was built in Unity with SteamVR, an HTC Vive HMD and tracking system to create an immersive experience. We decorated the virtual environment to look like a room (Figure 1) and added the parametric desk. A 'store' with objects to be used as props, such as laptops, monitor of various sizes, and books is located behind the user.

A Microsoft Kinect for Windows tracked the users' joint positions. The joints were used for ergonomic measurements, as input in conjunction with voice commands, and for animating the first and third-person avatars. The Kinect was calibrated to the floor, and the Vive was calibrated to the Kinect using an affine transformation matrix calculated with OpenCV. Based on prior experience with speech recognition for non-native speakers, we used Wizard of Oz for voice commands.

Prior to a design session, we 3D scanned the user with a Kinect v1 and Skanect [32] and we recorded joint positions with the Kinect v2 as shown in Figure 7. Both model and joints were used in Maya to rig a posable virtual avatar. A toon shader is applied to make avatars less creepy.

We attached a Vive tracker to the palms of both hands to accurately track orientation and position. Two microswitches were added to create a simple pinch-glove. One of them is for grabbing and moving virtual objects (pinch gesture), the other is for resizing the virtual desk. When resizing, the hand is held parallel to the orientation of the plane that needs to be moved, as shown in Figure 5. Using the orientation allows for ambiguous voice commands such as *"until here"*. Objects collide in a rigid body simulation and can be stacked or positioned on the tabletop and shelves. We attached the third tracker to the chair and made a matching virtual model. In the virtual environment, users can find the chair and easily adjust the height.

USER EVALUATION

We conducted a small user study and let six participants design with Body2Desk. The study aimed to explore how people design a personal desk with interactive guidelines (*How do they trust, and use the guidelines? How guidelines affect design process?*). Therefore, we analyzed their design process, then we fabricated their design. We let them use it for four hours to see how their virtual design related to real comfort.

Participants

We recruited six participants (mean age=27, 3 female) through an online community board used by university students. The height of the tallest participant was about 180cm and that of the shortest participant was 151cm. Therefore, it was possible to see how the guidelines are applied to the different size of people. The participants had no experience in industrial design or ergonomics and used their desks for more than three hours per day. Half of the participants (P1, P2, and P5) worked mostly at home, while the others worked in their labs. All of the participants had unique needs and requirements for their desks.

Procedure

The study consists of four stages: *sensitizing*, *designing*, *making*, and *using* (Figure 8). The goal of the first stage was

Figure 8. The research process consisted of four stages.

to sensitize the participants and let them think about their needs before the design session. We provided probe packages with worksheets that asked participants to show their frequent working postures, likes/dislikes of their current desk, photos of objects on their desk, and a floor plan of the room. We also 3D scanned each participant's body to create their virtual avatars, and personalized the VR environment for the participant to make it look like their workspace.

In the *design* stage, we introduced the Body2Desk interface briefly. After 10-minute practice, the participants started designing with the system until they were satisfied with their desk result. We employed a think aloud protocol and captured their design activity from three different perspectives: two from virtual cameras (the participant view and the third-person view), and one from the real camera (capturing the participant from a side view). The design session was followed by a semi-structured interview regarding their design process and rationales.

We provided transportation so each participant could bring their PC, monitor(s), peripherals, and other objects they needed for their work. In the *making* stage we gave participants a break in which we quickly fabricated their design in an empty office room. We exported parameters from the Body2Desk prototype and configured an aluminum T-Slot frame, shown in Figure 10. We fabricated the desk from 16mm honeycomb cardboard and installed their personal items.

In the *using* stage and after their break, we let participants work on the fabricated desk for a minimum of four hours, doing usual activities without any interference, and gave them access and keys to the room. This stage was conducted on the same day as the *design* stage, as we wanted the participants to reflect on their design process while using the desk. The session concluded with a short interview to sample the participants' experience using their own design and any differences between their virtual and real-life design assessment.

For the analysis, we transcribed design behaviors and narrations from the interview recordings. We used open coding and axial coding methods to identify how the participants interacted with guidelines, and how they utilized them throughout the design process. Additionally, we compared the dimensions between their designs and their existing office desk.

RESULTS

All of the participants designed a desk that met their personal needs and preferences, resulting in six unique designs, shown in Figure 10. For example, P3 (Figure 9,left) designed a half-width shelf design to fit their vertical monitor and to meet both recommended monitor height and reachable shelf height while

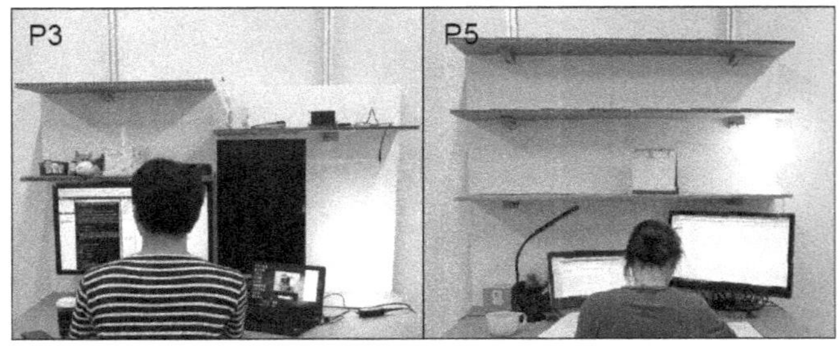

Figure 9. (left) P3's height is 172cm, and he uses 27 inch vertical monitor. (right) P5's height is 158cm, and and she uses 25 inch horizontal monitor and laptop. These leads to different fitting designs as shown here.

sitting. P6 repurposed the footrest as a secondary shelf below the tabletop, and P2 made three shelf widths, all different, and tried a creative layout for aesthetics.

All designs met the ergonomic recommendations of the guidelines. Four of six participants made the tabletop higher than their current one (average 5.4cm) to make it fit the recommended range. Five participants dramatically increased the height of their monitor by 18cm on average. P3 also mentioned that he raised his monitor (15cm) when he went back to his office after the experiment. These results indicate that the system makes users aware of ergonomics and lets them effectively apply guidelines in their designs.

Body2Desk engaged participants in an iterative design process that took 40 minutes on average. All participants revisited and adjusted parameters, and the interactive guidelines were used throughout the design process. All six participants started with adjusting their seat and tabletop height accordingly, following the recommendations. The remainder of the design process varied among the participants. P2 and P4's primary concern was to avoid back pain as they spend many hours at their desks, so they relied on the pose feedback. On the other hand, reachability and comfort were the driving design factors for others, such as for P6. All participants used the guidelines as a final evaluation check.

All six participants quickly mastered the Body2Desk interface, except P2 who required more time. All of the participants freely acted out scenarios of use, walked around to look at their desk from various perspectives, and occasionally switched from standing to sitting positions. They tried out different techniques to evaluate usability, comfort, and good posture: using their bodies, virtual avatars, virtual objects, and referring to the guidelines. Hands, feet, heels, and elbows were commonly referenced body parts to set parameters. Participants often set the initial parameter using a voice command and gesture but used the buttons for minor (re-) adjustments.

We observed users design with their bodies in two ways. Similar to experience prototyping [6], they acted out work activities and frequently used props to understand their needs. Participants also used their bodies as a tool to test reachability. P3 remarked that *"With the virtual body figure, I could test if I could grab things in the left corner."* P1 implied that whereas the guidelines provided health-related information, comfort could be tested with his body by simulating several activities.

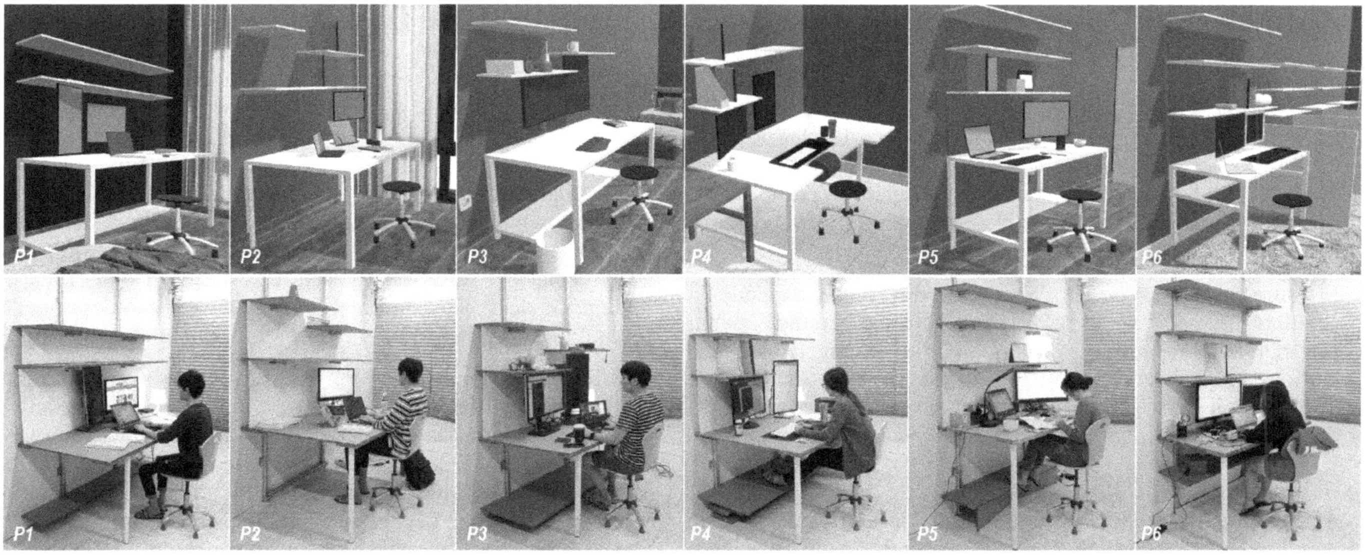

Figure 10. The research process consisted of four phases: sensitizing, designing, making, and using. We started with a probe study and prepared the personalized prototype. Then, participants designed a desk, and used it after we fabricated their design result.

Interaction with the Guidelines

Desk and monitor height recommendations guided early-stage design decisions. An initial setting based on the recommendations was typically followed by occasional minor adjustments for comfort. For example, P1 set the desk height first but later lowered it after he simulated typing. P2 first positioned the monitor in the middle of the recommended range but moved it a little bit higher because he preferred a high monitor.

All of the participants needed some time to gain confidence with the guidelines and to confirm that those were generated from their personal body measurements. Most of them confirmed the reachability guidelines by trying it out, and this process built trust between the user and guidelines.

Whereas the tabletop and monitor recommendations were strictly followed and related dimensions were set first, participants followed other guidelines more freely. Guidelines such as shelf reachability and workspace motion envelope depend on personal preference and use. For instance, although P2 checked the reachable depth range, he set the tabletop depth deeper beyond the reachable line for storage space. Similarly, the workspace guideline also indirectly helped users arrange their objects. For example, P2 mentioned, *"I used the primary zone for papers, and used the secondary zone for the keyboard. I don't use keyboard often, but it should be in my reachable range."* P6, however, stated that it was not useful as she arranges objects based on her habits.

The recommendation that dealt with space around and behind the desk was not used (Figure 3, bottom right). P4 indicated that these guidelines were only useful if she was allowed to rearrange her other furniture. Other participants mentioned they needed more information. P3 asked to *"turn on"* the monitor to estimate an appropriate distance, which could be a new guideline. P4 and P6 suggested guidelines on aesthetics such as for distribution or alignment of surfaces and objects.

In reflection, participants mentioned that context-aware feedforward interactions made the guidelines available when they needed them and were not a distraction. Only P6 said she would have liked to hide the guidelines after setting the tabletop height.

Evaluating Good Posture during the Design

When the participants designed their desks in a first-person perspective, they evaluated several usage scenarios and used and moved virtual objects to help them. They did not only design the desk as an object in space but as an object that they use in their routines. P6 stated, *"the first-person view was very comfortable because I felt like I was using this desk. I was engaged in the scenario."*

The small virtual avatar was referenced frequently. All participants grabbed, moved, and rotated the Mini-me to check their real-time posture while posing and simulating. Five participants out of six intermittently looked at the Mini-me to check the posture feedback. P2 mentioned, *"I usually sit correctly but I wanted to be convinced that I sat in a proper way while designing."* P3 and P6 used Mini-me to evaluate their posture from a third-person perspective and the immediate feedback helped them to make rapid iterations. Additionally, the Mini-me was helpful to visualize the footrest while sitting on the chair. P5, while looking at the Mini-me, moved his feet up and down to estimate the proper height and depth for the footrest.

The interaction with Freeze-me was appreciated in the later stages, when participants evaluated their designs and checked whether they satisfied the recommendations. Four people froze their design to check their pose just before finalizing their design. P2 and P6 stated, *"In the last moment, I froze my usual posture and check if the desk design fits my body. Mini-me kept moving with me, so it was hard to focus on one posture."* Participants also valued Freeze-me because it was larger than the Mini-me and provided more detail. P1 and

P3 also mentioned, *"The freezing function was particularly helpful when I wanted to see on a large scale. Regarding the footrest, I needed to accurately check if the footrest was located on my heel position, not on the ankle."* Additionally, P6 used the freezing function to check the particular posture that blocks her sight, for example: the act of taking a nap on her desk. When they activated the freezing function, participants tried various angles and positions by walking around their frozen bodies or sitting down and standing up.

In some cases, participants combined different perspectives simultaneously. Whereas participants adjusted parameters in a first-person perspective, occasionally they posed, froze their bodies, and adjusted parameters to their Freeze-me from a third-person perspective (e.g. after capturing a typing pose, they set the height that fit the fixed body's elbow position).

Reflections After Using the Desk

After using their personalized desk for four hours, participants could reflect on design and use. All six participants indicated satisfaction with their design, and four of them wanted to bring the desk to their homes. In the post-interview, they mentioned two key reasons. First, scenarios they prototyped in VR, felt very similar in reality, as their designs fit their body and the objects they use. Second, the parameters they set based on the guidelines provided more comfort than they expected from the VR environment. P6 indicated that, *"The monitor height from my design was higher than the one in my office, but it was more comfortable and reduced my neck pain."*

However, using the desk, participants found several problems that they didn't realize while designing. The materiality of the physical desk provided haptic feedback and let them experience support. For instance, P4 indicated that she had trouble setting the footrest with her feet floating in the air. Some participants re-evaluated trade-offs after using their desks. P2 and P4 wanted both a deep desk and reachable shelves; therefore they compromised on aesthetics and increased the depth of their shelves. After using the desk, they found that they could decrease the desk depth about 10 cm (and shelves accordingly) as the shelves looked too large. P5 lowered her monitor by a few centimeters because she couldn't evaluate the text size in VR (still within the recommended range).

Some participants realized they forgot to consider some usage scenarios in the VR design session. In the interview, P6 remarked that she enjoyed typing while putting her entire arm on the tabletop, but she did not test that action in VR. For other participants, using shelves (P2, P3) or a footrest (P6) was new. After using them in real life, they had more ideas on how to design them, and how to use them in the future.

DISCUSSION AND FUTURE WORK

We personalized human factor guidelines, applied them in a design system, and evaluated their use with users. The prototype posed several limitations; for instance, wrist angle could not be measured and the study was preliminary with a few participants. Nevertheless, the results indicate that the system makes users aware of their pose and lets them design a desk that meets human factor guidelines. Here, we discuss our insights and implications and challenges for future work.

Interactive personal guidelines let participants fluidly switch between being *"user"* and *"designer"* as they carefully design a desk that fits their needs. The guidelines took on the role of an expert and helped them become more aware of their comfort and health, in addition to providing professional advice. The participants trusted the interactive guidelines after informal verification with their bodies. To make sure that the design is within the recommendations, a future system could support a pre-flight check. This will help users gain a final confirmation. Additionally, future system can support earlier stage of design by automatically generating recommended configurations based on the user's initial exploration.

Future research should look into how to present conflicting recommendations, such as for reachability. Other guidelines depend on the task, such as typing or crafting. As future systems might include a more complicated set of guidelines, we need to further study interrelationships between them. Systems could prioritize certain guidelines based on importance or frequency of use, give freedom to users by mapping the conflicts, or hide guidelines that are not used.

Participants frequently used Freeze-me to evaluate their static poses in relation to their desk from a third-person view, and made changes to the desk dimensions. However, the Freeze-me did not react to design changes, so the users needed to freeze their bodies repeatedly to test resulting poses. Providing a virtual avatar with agency [4] could be a possible next step, such as making the avatar responsive to changes in the design or to playback usage scenarios.

Body2Desk could be work with Augmented Reality (AR) with the benefit of including the real contexts of the users. In the future, it could also be part the daily working environment in which posture is continuously monitored and thus fully merge use and design. On the other hand, tablet-based systems require different interactions, as they do not support embodied actions. Therefore, we can provide agency with body figures for simulations or support multi-user interactions to assess the pose and workplace of another user.

Recommendation techniques we investigated in this research can also be applied in other domains that benefit from ergonomics and personal use, such as home kitchens, car interiors, or interior layouts. Using our system augment the role of experts in the future by providing personal guidelines.

With the advent of digital fabrication and flexible manufacturing, we need to investigate interactive design systems that support tailoring designs for a unique person rather than for a population. In this paper, we made a first step toward including human factor guidelines in personal design tools. In the future, augmented and situated guidelines will not only enhance the designing of objects, but can also be part of daily life and active posture measurement.

ACKNOWLEDGEMENTS

This research was supported by Basic Science Research Program through the National Research Foundation of Korea(NRF) funded by the Ministry of Science, ICT & Future Planning(NRF-2015R1C1A1A01051808)

REFERENCES

1. Fraser Anderson, Tovi Grossman, Justin Matejka, and George Fitzmaurice. 2013. YouMove: Enhancing Movement Training with an Augmented Reality Mirror. In *Proceedings of the 26th Annual ACM Symposium on User Interface Software and Technology (UIST '13)*. ACM, New York, NY, USA, 311–320. DOI: http://dx.doi.org/10.1145/2501988.2502045
2. Susanna Aromaa and Kaisa Väänänen. 2016. Suitability of virtual prototypes to support human factors/ergonomics evaluation during the design. *Applied Ergonomics* 56, Supplement C (2016), 11 – 18. DOI: http://dx.doi.org/https://doi.org/10.1016/j.apergo.2016.02.015
3. Business Institutional Furniture Manufacturer Association. 1918. BIFMA. (1918). https://www.bifma.org/store/ViewProduct.aspx?id=1610163
4. Norman I. Badler, Welton M. Becket, and Bonnie L. Webber. 1995. Simulation and analysis of complex human tasks for manufacturing. (1995). DOI: http://dx.doi.org/10.1117/12.227222
5. Yee Brandon, Ning Yuan, and Lipson Hod. 2009. Augmented Reality In-Situ 3D Sketching of Physical Objects. In *Intelligent UI Workshop on Sketch Recognition*.
6. Marion Buchenau and Jane Fulton Suri. 2000. Experience prototyping. In *Proceedings of the 3rd conference on Designing interactive systems: processes, practices, methods, and techniques*. ACM, 424–433.
7. Nico J Delleman, Christine M Haslegrave, and Don B Chaffin. 2004. *Working postures and movements*. CRC Press.
8. Jose Antonio Diego-Mas and Jorge Alcaide-Marzal. 2014. Using KinectâĎć sensor in observational methods for assessing postures at work. *Applied Ergonomics* 45, 4 (2014), 976 – 985. DOI:http://dx.doi.org/https://doi.org/10.1016/j.apergo.2013.12.001
9. Tom Djajadiningrat, Kees Overbeeke, and Stephan Wensveen. 2002. But How, Donald, Tell Us How?: On the Creation of Meaning in Interaction Design Through Feedforward and Inherent Feedback. In *Proceedings of the 4th Conference on Designing Interactive Systems: Processes, Practices, Methods, and Techniques (DIS '02)*. ACM, New York, NY, USA, 285–291. DOI: http://dx.doi.org/10.1145/778712.778752
10. P. Eisert, J. Rurainsky, and P. Fechteler. 2007. Virtual Mirror: Real-Time Tracking of Shoes in Augmented Reality Environments. In *2007 IEEE International Conference on Image Processing*, Vol. 2. II – 557–II – 560. DOI:http://dx.doi.org/10.1109/ICIP.2007.4379216
11. Ergotron. 2016. (2016). https://www.ergotron.com/en-us/
12. Sean Follmer, David Carr, Emily Lovell, and Hiroshi Ishii. 2010. CopyCAD: Remixing Physical Objects with Copy and Paste from the Real World *(UIST)*. 381–382. DOI:http://dx.doi.org/10.1145/1866218.1866230
13. Madeline Gannon, Tovi Grossman, and George Fitzmaurice. 2016. ExoSkin: On-Body Fabrication. In *Proceedings of the 2016 CHI Conference on Human Factors in Computing Systems (CHI '16)*. ACM, New York, NY, USA, 5996–6007. DOI: http://dx.doi.org/10.1145/2858036.2858576
14. E Grandjean, W. Hünting, and M. Pidermann. 1983. VDT Workstation Design: Preferred Settings and Their Effects. *Human Factors* 25, 2 (1983), 161–175. DOI: http://dx.doi.org/10.1177/001872088302500203 PMID: 6862447.
15. M. Susan Hallbeck, Tim Bosch, Gu (J. W.) Van Rhijn, Frank Krause, Michiel P. de Looze, and Peter Vink. 2010. A tool for early workstation design for small and medium enterprises evaluated in five cases. *Human Factors and Ergonomics in Manufacturing & Service Industries* 20, 4 (2010), 300–315. DOI: http://dx.doi.org/10.1002/hfm.20222
16. Michael Haller, Christoph Richter, Peter Brandl, Sabine Gross, Gerold Schossleitner, Andreas Schrempf, Hideaki Nii, Maki Sugimoto, and Masahiko Inami. 2011. Finding the Right Way for Interrupting People Improving Their Sitting Posture. In *Proceedings of the 13th IFIP TC 13 International Conference on Human-computer Interaction - Volume Part II (INTERACT'11)*. Springer-Verlag, Berlin, Heidelberg, 1–17. http://dl.acm.org/citation.cfm?id=2042118.2042120
17. S. J. Henderson and S. K. Feiner. 2011. Augmented reality in the psychomotor phase of a procedural task. In *2011 10th IEEE International Symposium on Mixed and Augmented Reality*. 191–200. DOI: http://dx.doi.org/10.1109/ISMAR.2011.6092386
18. Keita Higuchi, Tetsuro Shimada, and Jun Rekimoto. 2011. Flying Sports Assistant: External Visual Imagery Representation for Sports Training. In *Proceedings of the 2Nd Augmented Human International Conference (AH '11)*. ACM, New York, NY, USA, Article 7, 4 pages. DOI: http://dx.doi.org/10.1145/1959826.1959833
19. Takeo Igarashi and John F. Hughes. 2001. A Suggestive Interface for 3D Drawing. In *Proceedings of the 14th Annual ACM Symposium on User Interface Software and Technology (UIST '01)*. ACM, New York, NY, USA, 173–181. DOI:http://dx.doi.org/10.1145/502348.502379
20. E Innes. 1997. Education and training programs for the prevention of work injuries: do they work? *Work* 9, 3 (1997), 221–232.
21. American National Standards Institute. 1918. ANSI/HFES 100-2007. (1918). https://www.ansi.org/
22. Yuta Itoh, Jason Orlosky, Kiyoshi Kiyokawa, and Gudrun Klinker. 2016. Laplacian Vision: Augmenting Motion Prediction via Optical See-Through Head-Mounted Displays. In *Proceedings of the 7th Augmented Human International Conference 2016 (AH '16)*. ACM, New York, NY, USA, Article 16, 8 pages. DOI: http://dx.doi.org/10.1145/2875194.2875227

23. Takashi Kikuchi, Yuichi Hiroi, Ross T. Smith, Bruce H. Thomas, and Maki Sugimoto. 2016. MARCut: Marker-based Laser Cutting for Personal Fabrication on Existing Objects. In *Proceedings of the TEI '16: Tenth International Conference on Tangible, Embedded, and Embodied Interaction (TEI '16)*. ACM, New York, NY, USA, 468–474. DOI: http://dx.doi.org/10.1145/2839462.2856549

24. Phyllis M. King, James C. Fisher, and Arun Garg. 1997. Evaluation of the impact of employee ergonomics training in industry. *Applied Ergonomics* 28, 4 (1997), 249 – 256. DOI: http://dx.doi.org/10.1016/S0003-6870(96)00067-1

25. Knoll. 2016. (2016). https://www.knoll.com/ Knoll - Modern Furniture Design for the Office & Home.

26. Yuki Koyama, Daisuke Sakamoto, and Takeo Igarashi. 2016. SelPh: Progressive Learning and Support of Manual Photo Color Enhancement. In *Proceedings of the 2016 CHI Conference on Human Factors in Computing Systems (CHI '16)*. ACM, New York, NY, USA, 2520–2532. DOI: http://dx.doi.org/10.1145/2858036.2858111

27. Karl HE Kroemer, Henrike B Kroemer, and Katrin E Kroemer-Elbert. 2001. *Ergonomics: how to design for ease and efficiency*. Pearson College Division.

28. James A. Landay. 2009. Technical Perspective: Design Tools for the Rest of Us. *Commun. ACM* 52, 12 (Dec. 2009), 80–80. DOI: http://dx.doi.org/10.1145/1610252.1610274

29. Manfred Lau, Masaki Hirose, Akira Ohgawara, Jun Mitani, and Takeo Igarashi. 2012. Situated Modeling: A Shape-stamping Interface with Tangible Primitives. In *Proceedings of the Sixth International Conference on Tangible, Embedded and Embodied Interaction (TEI '12)*. ACM, New York, NY, USA, 275–282. DOI: http://dx.doi.org/10.1145/2148131.2148190

30. Bokyung Lee, Minjoo Cho, Joonhee Min, and Daniel Saakes. 2016. Posing and Acting As Input for Personalizing Furniture. In *Proceedings of the 9th Nordic Conference on Human-Computer Interaction (NordiCHI '16)*. ACM, New York, NY, USA, Article 44, 10 pages. DOI:http://dx.doi.org/10.1145/2971485.2971487

31. Bokyung Lee, Gyeol Han, Jundong Park, and Daniel Saakes. 2017. Consumer to Creator: How Households Buy Furniture to Inform Design and Fabrication Interfaces. In *Proceedings of the 2017 CHI Conference on Human Factors in Computing Systems (CHI '17)*. ACM, New York, NY, USA, 484–496. DOI: http://dx.doi.org/10.1145/3025453.3025666

32. ManCTL. 2011. ManCTL. (2011). http://http://skanect.occipital.com/

33. Daniel P. Mapes and J. Michael Moshell. 1995. A Two-Handed Interface for Object Manipulation in Virtual Environments. *Presence: Teleoperators and Virtual Environments* 4, 4 (1995), 403–416. DOI: http://dx.doi.org/10.1162/pres.1995.4.4.403

34. Corinne Mattmann, Oliver Amft, Holger Harms, Gerhard Troster, and Frank Clemens. 2007. Recognizing Upper Body Postures using Textile Strain Sensors. In *2007 11th IEEE International Symposium on Wearable Computers*. 29–36. DOI: http://dx.doi.org/10.1109/ISWC.2007.4373773

35. S.M. McGill, N.S. Kavcic, and E. Harvey. 2006. Sitting on a chair or an exercise ball: Various perspectives to guide decision making. *Clinical Biomechanics* 21, 4 (2006), 353–360. DOI: http://dx.doi.org/10.1016/j.clinbiomech.2005.11.006

36. Herman Miller. 2016. (2016). http://store.hermanmiller.com/

37. Stefanie Mueller, Pedro Lopes, and Patrick Baudisch. 2012. Interactive Construction: Interactive Fabrication of Functional Mechanical Devices. In *Proceedings of the 25th Annual ACM Symposium on User Interface Software and Technology (UIST '12)*. ACM, New York, NY, USA, 599–606. DOI: http://dx.doi.org/10.1145/2380116.2380191

38. Bilge Mutlu, Andreas Krause, Jodi Forlizzi, Carlos Guestrin, and Jessica Hodgins. 2007. Robust, Low-cost, Non-intrusive Sensing and Recognition of Seated Postures. In *Proceedings of the 20th Annual ACM Symposium on User Interface Software and Technology (UIST '07)*. ACM, New York, NY, USA, 149–158. DOI: http://dx.doi.org/10.1145/1294211.1294237

39. Peter O'Donovan, Aseem Agarwala, and Aaron Hertzmann. 2015. DesignScape: Design with Interactive Layout Suggestions. In *Proceedings of the 33rd Annual ACM Conference on Human Factors in Computing Systems (CHI '15)*. ACM, New York, NY, USA, 1221–1224. DOI: http://dx.doi.org/10.1145/2702123.2702149

40. Opendesk. 2014. ManCTLOpendesk. (2014). https://www.opendesk.cc/

41. Gerhard Pahl, W Beitz, Jörg Feldhusen, and Karl-Heinrich Grote. 2007. *Engineering Design. A Systematic Approach* (3 ed.). Springer-Verlag, London. DOI:http://dx.doi.org/10.1007/978-1-84628-319-2

42. Julius Panero and Martin Zelnik. 2014. *Human dimension and interior space: a source book of design reference standards*. Watson-Guptill.

43. Stephen Pheasant and Christine M Haslegrave. 2016. *Bodyspace: Anthropometry, ergonomics and the design of work*. CRC Press.

44. Jeffrey S. Pierce, Brian C. Stearns, and Randy Pausch. 1999. Voodoo Dolls: Seamless Interaction at Multiple Scales in Virtual Environments. In *Proceedings of the 1999 Symposium on Interactive 3D Graphics (I3D '99)*. ACM, New York, NY, USA, 141–145. DOI: http://dx.doi.org/10.1145/300523.300540

45. Otniel Portillo-Rodriguez, Oscar O. Sandoval-Gonzalez, Emanuele Ruffaldi, Rosario Leonardi, Carlo Alberto Avizzano, and Massimo Bergamasco. 2008. *Real-Time Gesture Recognition, Evaluation and Feed-Forward Correction of a Multimodal Tai-Chi Platform*. Springer Berlin Heidelberg, Berlin, Heidelberg, 30–39. DOI: http://dx.doi.org/10.1007/978-3-540-87883-4_4

46. Michelle Robertson, Benjamin C. Amick, Kelly DeRango, Ted Rooney, Lianna Bazzani, Ron Harrist, and Anne Moore. 2009. The effects of an office ergonomics training and chair intervention on worker knowledge, behavior and musculoskeletal risk. *Applied Ergonomics* 40, 1 (2009), 124 – 135. DOI: http://dx.doi.org/10.1016/j.apergo.2007.12.009

47. Daniel Saakes, Hui-Shyong Yeo, Seung-Tak Noh, Gyeol Han, and Woontack Woo. 2016. Mirror Mirror: An On-Body T-shirt Design System. In *Proceedings of the 2016 CHI Conference on Human Factors in Computing Systems (CHI '16)*. ACM, New York, NY, USA, 6058–6063. DOI: http://dx.doi.org/10.1145/2858036.2858282

48. Greg Saul, Manfred Lau, Jun Mitani, and Takeo Igarashi. 2011. SketchChair: An All-in-one Chair Design System for End Users *(TEI)*. 73–80. DOI: http://dx.doi.org/10.1145/1935701.1935717

49. Christian Schönauer, Kenichiro Fukushi, Alex Olwal, Hannes Kaufmann, and Ramesh Raskar. 2012. Multimodal Motion Guidance: Techniques for Adaptive and Dynamic Feedback. In *Proceedings of the 14th ACM International Conference on Multimodal Interaction (ICMI '12)*. ACM, New York, NY, USA, 133–140. DOI: http://dx.doi.org/10.1145/2388676.2388706

50. Jaemyung Shin, Bumsoo Kang, Taiwoo Park, Jina Huh, Jinhan Kim, and Junehwa Song. 2016. BeUpright: Posture Correction Using Relational Norm Intervention. In *Proceedings of the 2016 CHI Conference on Human Factors in Computing Systems (CHI '16)*. ACM, New York, NY, USA, 6040–6052. DOI: http://dx.doi.org/10.1145/2858036.2858561

51. Maria Shugrina, Ariel Shamir, and Wojciech Matusik. 2015. Fab Forms: Customizable Objects for Fabrication with Validity and Geometry Caching. *ACM Trans. Graph.* 34, 4, Article 100 (July 2015), 12 pages. DOI: http://dx.doi.org/10.1145/2766994

52. Roland Sigrist, Jürg Schellenberg, Georg Rauter, Simon Broggi, Robert Riener, and Peter Wolf. 2011. Visual and Auditory Augmented Concurrent Feedback in a Complex Motor Task. *Presence: Teleoperators and Virtual Environments* 20, 1 (2011), 15–32. DOI: http://dx.doi.org/10.1162/pres_a_00032

53. S.O. Sigurdsson, M. Artnak, M. Needham, O. Wirth, and K. Silverman. 2012. Motivating ergonomic computer workstation setup: Sometimes training is not enough. *International Journal of Occupational Safety and Ergonomics* 18, 1 (2012), 27–33. DOI: http://dx.doi.org/10.1080/10803548.2012.11076912

54. Rajinder Sodhi, Hrvoje Benko, and Andrew Wilson. 2012. LightGuide: Projected Visualizations for Hand Movement Guidance. In *Proceedings of the SIGCHI Conference on Human Factors in Computing Systems (CHI '12)*. ACM, New York, NY, USA, 179–188. DOI: http://dx.doi.org/10.1145/2207676.2207702

55. Richard Stoakley, Matthew J. Conway, and Randy Pausch. 1995. Virtual Reality on a WIM: Interactive Worlds in Miniature. In *Proceedings of the SIGCHI Conference on Human Factors in Computing Systems (CHI '95)*. ACM Press/Addison-Wesley Publishing Co., New York, NY, USA, 265–272. DOI: http://dx.doi.org/10.1145/223904.223938

56. P.A. Swinton, K. Cooper, and E. Hancock. 2017. Workplace interventions to improve sitting posture: A systematic review. *Preventive Medicine* 101 (2017), 204–212. DOI: http://dx.doi.org/10.1016/j.ypmed.2017.06.023

57. Brett Taylor, Max Birk, Regan L. Mandryk, and Zenja Ivkovic. 2013. Posture Training with Real-time Visual Feedback. In *CHI '13 Extended Abstracts on Human Factors in Computing Systems (CHI EA '13)*. ACM, New York, NY, USA, 3135–3138. DOI: http://dx.doi.org/10.1145/2468356.2479629

58. Junya Tominaga, Kensaku Kawauchi, and Jun Rekimoto. 2014. Around Me: A System with an Escort Robot Providing a Sports Player's Self-images. In *Proceedings of the 5th Augmented Human International Conference (AH '14)*. ACM, New York, NY, USA, Article 43, 8 pages. DOI:http://dx.doi.org/10.1145/2582051.2582094

59. Nobuyuki Umetani, Takeo Igarashi, and Niloy J. Mitra. 2012. Guided Exploration of Physically Valid Shapes for Furniture Design. *ACM Trans. Graph.* 31, 4, Article 86 (July 2012), 11 pages. DOI: http://dx.doi.org/10.1145/2185520.2185582

60. J Verbeek. 1991. The use of adjustable furniture: evaluation of an instruction programme for office workers. *Applied Ergonomics* 22, 3 (1991), 179–184.

61. Peter Vink. 2004. *Comfort and design: principles and good practice*. CRC press.

62. P. Vink, R. Porcar-Seder, Álvaro Page de Pozo, and F. Krause. 2007. Office chairs are often not adjusted by end-users. *Proceedings of the Human Factors and Ergonomics Society Annual Meeting* 51, 17 (2007), 1015–1019. DOI: http://dx.doi.org/10.1177/154193120705101704

63. L. Wang, R. Villamil, S. Samarasekera, and R. Kumar. 2012. Magic Mirror: A virtual handbag shopping system. In *2012 IEEE Computer Society Conference on Computer Vision and Pattern Recognition Workshops*. 19–24. DOI: http://dx.doi.org/10.1109/CVPRW.2012.6239181

64. Qi Wang, Marina Toeters, Wei Chen, Annick Timmermans, and Panos Markopoulos. 2016. Zishi: A Smart Garment for Posture Monitoring. In *Proceedings of the 2016 CHI Conference Extended Abstracts on Human Factors in Computing Systems (CHI EA '16)*. ACM, New York, NY, USA, 3792–3795. DOI: http://dx.doi.org/10.1145/2851581.2890262

65. Christian Weichel, Manfred Lau, David Kim, Nicolas Villar, and Hans W. Gellersen. 2014. MixFab: A Mixed-reality Environment for Personal Fabrication. In *Proceedings of the SIGCHI Conference on Human Factors in Computing Systems (CHI '14)*. ACM, New York, NY, USA, 3855–3864. DOI: http://dx.doi.org/10.1145/2556288.2557090

66. Amy Wibowo, Daisuke Sakamoto, Jun Mitani, and Takeo Igarashi. 2012. DressUp: A 3D Interface for Clothing Design with a Physical Mannequin. In *Proceedings of the Sixth International Conference on Tangible, Embedded and Embodied Interaction (TEI '12)*. ACM, New York, NY, USA, 99–102. DOI: http://dx.doi.org/10.1145/2148131.2148153

67. Xu Xu and Raymond W. McGorry. 2015. The validity of the first and second generation Microsoft KinectâĎć for identifying joint center locations during static postures. *Applied Ergonomics* 49, Supplement C (2015), 47 – 54. DOI: http://dx.doi.org/https://doi.org/10.1016/j.apergo.2015.01.005

68. Yupeng Zhang, Teng Han, Zhimin Ren, Nobuyuki Umetani, Xin Tong, Yang Liu, Takaaki Shiratori, and Xiang Cao. 2013. BodyAvatar: Creating Freeform 3D Avatars Using First-person Body Gestures. In *Proceedings of the 26th Annual ACM Symposium on User Interface Software and Technology (UIST '13)*. ACM, New York, NY, USA, 387–396. DOI: http://dx.doi.org/10.1145/2501988.2502015

69. Ying Zheng and John B. Morrell. 2010. A vibrotactile feedback approach to posture guidance. In *2010 IEEE Haptics Symposium*. 351–358. DOI: http://dx.doi.org/10.1109/HAPTIC.2010.5444633

EMGuitar: Assisting Guitar Playing with Electromyography

Jakob Karolus[1], Hendrik Schuff[2†], Thomas Kosch[1], Paweł W. Woźniak[2‡], Albrecht Schmidt[1]
[1]LMU Munich, Munich, Germany
[2]University of Stuttgart, Stuttgart, Germany
[1]{jakob.karolus, thomas.kosch, albrecht.schmidt}@ifi.lmu.de,
[†]hendrikschuff@gmx.de, [‡]pawel.wozniak@vis.uni-stuttgart.de

ABSTRACT
Mastering fine motor tasks, such as playing the guitar, takes years of time-consuming practice. Commonly, expensive guidance by experts is essential for adjusting the training program to the student's proficiency. In our work, we showcase the suitability of Electromyography to detect fine-grained hand and finger postures in an exemplary guitar tutor scenario. We present *EMGuitar*, an interactive guitar tutoring system, that assists students by reporting on play correctness and adjusts playback tempi automatically. We report person-dependent classification utilizing a ring of electrodes around the forearm with an F1 score of up to 0.89 on recorded calibration data. Furthermore, our system was received well by neither diminishing ease of use nor being disruptive for the participants. Based on the received comments, we identified the need for detailed play accuracy feedback down to individual chords, for which we suggest an adapted visualization and an algorithmic approach.

ACM Classification Keywords
H.5.m Information interfaces and presentation (e.g., HCI): Miscellaneous.

Author Keywords
Electromyography; posture detection; fine motor tasks; assistance system.

INTRODUCTION
When interacting with the physical world we predominately use our hands to manipulate objects and tools at our disposal, yet correct execution of fine motor tasks such as learning how to play an instrument often requires training that may take up to several years depending on the student's affinity. Individual supervision by experts is often expensive and requires effort, which gives rise to the idea of sensor-based assistance systems that may alleviate the need for supervision.

DIS 2018, June 9–13, 2018, Hong Kong.

ACM ISBN 978-1-4503-5198-0/18/06 ...$15.00.
http://dx.doi.org/10.1145/3196709.3196803

Figure 1. User interacting with *EMGuitar* (chord visualization is not part of the prototype). Muscle activity is being recorded by electrodes on the forearm (red).

Such systems evaluate task execution and can provide assistance if necessary. In the domain of music education, researchers have already experimented with different modalities for feedback and assistance. In *guitAR* [5], Löchtefeld et al. showed an augmented reality approach to depict correct finger position on a guitar fretboard, while *MusicJacket* [4] employed a vibrotactile jacket to inform users of bad posture during violin play.

In this work, we evaluate the feasibility of Electromyography (EMG) as a sensing modality to detect domain-specific fine motor tasks and facilitate action detection in a guitar tutoring scenario. This concept of muscle-computer interfaces (muCIs) has already been researched in the context of gesture recognition [9]. Previous research has shown that finger movements and specific gestures can be detected effectively using Electromyography under different recording scenarios (10 electrodes setup [9] vs high-density grid with 192 electrodes [1]). We investigate if EMG is not only feasible as an explicit input method by invoking defined gestures, but can be used implicitly as well.

For this purpose, we draw on musician-instrument interaction and aim to recognize played chords during a guitar playing session. We believe that playing chords on the guitar is a representative case for many fine motor tasks, because it mainly consists of isometric muscle activation[1], which is easily recognizable with Electromyography [6, 12]. Furthermore, different playing styles allow to assess the feasibility of this technique in scenarios with high variance, i.e. achieving the same result (chord sound) with varying postures (different chord grip).

To verify the applicability of EMG in interactive assistance systems, we created the guitar tutoring system *EMGuitar* and deployed it in a study with seven participants to evaluate its accuracy in a real-world scenario including cross-session and inter-person detection of chords.

We contribute that (1) Electromyography can be used successfully and deliver real-time input for an interactive system that detects fine motor tasks, such as playing the guitar. Additionally, we found that (2) adequate and timely feedback during the learning process is desirable.

EMGUITAR: A GUITAR TUTORING SYSTEM

A guitar tutoring system should be able to assess the student's play accuracy in real-time and respond accordingly. If this is technically feasible, how can we design for adequate feedback that supports the learning process? In this paper, we want to answer the question whether such a system is able to provide automatic tempo adjustment during the learning phase or if manual adjustment is to be preferred.

Scenario

Our tutoring system detects the player's proficiency by evaluating how accurately a given chord progression was executed. If the player is comfortable with the current song tempo, chord accuracy will be high and the system increases the tempo. If the chosen tempo is too fast, the player will struggle to finger the chords correctly, hence accuracy will diminish. The system reacts by slowing the tempo for the next iteration. During the study, we analyzed how musicians interact with *EMGuitar* and which requirements and problems arose when they used the system.

Apparatus

We used the BrainVision actiCHamp EEG recorder[2] with active surface electrodes to perform EMG sensing. Individual finger movement is the result of multiple muscles working together [11], hence, we utilize a ring of electrodes around the forearm to capture the majority of the involved muscle activity. In total, we applied ten electrodes around the participants' left upper forearms. This included one ground (GND) and one reference (REF) electrode, minimizing noise levels. The remaining eight data channels were sampled at $500Hz$[3].

The electrodes were attached in a ring-like fashion around the arm using adhesive foil rings as shown in Figure 2. Afterwards, each electrode was injected with conductive gel and checked for impedance.

[1]Continuous muscle activity without visible movement.

[2]http://brainvision.com/actichamp.html

[3]The recording system is able to sample at much higher rate. However, related work [7] states that most power of the signal is within $5Hz$ and $250Hz$.

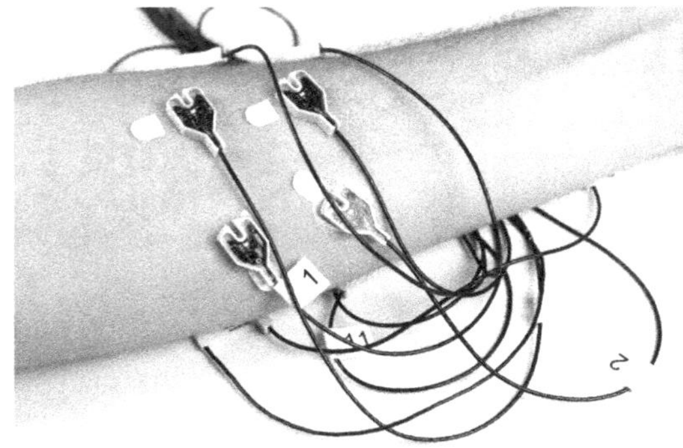

Figure 2. Electrode configuration with two rings around the forearm each consisting of five electrodes.

The recorded data was transmitted via USB to the Recording PC and redirected as a data stream into the local network. On the other side, the Stimulus PC was presenting chord patterns on a 27 inch LCD monitor, while simultaneously sending a marker stream into the network. Both streams were locally time synchronized on the Stimulus PC using the *Lab Streaming Layer (LSL)*[4] framework and saved to its hard drive.

Methodology

We closely follow related work ([6, 9]) with regard to preprocessing[5] and feature extraction[6]. In a preliminary evaluation with three participants we found that the RMS (root mean square) feature groups performed best with a given epoch size of $250ms$ when tasked with classifying seven different chords[7].

Since the system is aimed at beginner guitarists, we reduced the set of chords to C, F, Am and G. This set of chords forms the *I-V-vi-IV-progression*, which is heavily used in pop music. By including the barre chord F, we introduced a challenging chord for beginners as well.

We employed a within-subject design with two conditions; the first with manual tempo adjustments by the participants, the second with the tempo adjusted by the system. To counteract learning effects due to repetitive chord changes, we created two chord sequence patterns (A and B) out of all possible permutations of the above chords. Each chord appeared 12 times in each pattern, while their duration was randomly assigned from one to three beats. A pattern consisted of 20 bars; each containing four beats. For calibration, we tasked the participants to play two bars of each chord twice.

The tempo adjustments were made between 40 BPM and 90 BPM. Tempi lower than 40 BPM were hardly playable, while 90 BPM was challenging if chords changed as often as every beat. Based on test runs, we chose the following mapping for the new tempo: $\min(90, \max(40, p + (a - 0.5) \cdot 100))$, where p is the previous tempo and a the estimated chord accuracy of the player.

[4]https://github.com/sccn/labstreaminglayer

[5]Segmentation into epochs; Bandpass filter between $2Hz$ and $100Hz$; Bandstop filter between $49Hz$ and $51Hz$.

[6]Features are calculated as described in [9].

[7]Up to 0.87 F1 score for person-dependent classification.

Since chord changes might happen every beat, we chose to neglect one epoch ($250\,ms$) at the end of each chord change. To further counteract noise due to chord-change artefacts, we set up a majority voting as a post-processing step.

Participants

We recruited eight participants from the University of Stuttgart through mailing lists. The data of seven (1 female, $\bar{x} = 22.6\,y$, $SD = 2.3\,y$) were used for further analysis[8]. All participants were beginners on the guitar and reported normal sight and hearing. They were able to play the four chords. After the experiment, each participant was paid an allowance of 10 Euro.

Procedure

After introducing the prospective participants to our study, we handed them a detailed study description, stating that they were to play a given chord sequence with the guitar during several iterations. Playback, provided by a metronome, would be adjusted either manually by the participants or automatically by the system. Participants were made aware that adhesive electrodes would be placed on their forearm and their muscle activity would be recorded. After providing informed consent, the participants were asked to complete a demographic questionnaire, polling sex, age, work field, highest educational qualification, their eyesight and general health. The experimenter was present to answer any questions.

Before the experiment started, the experimenter placed electrodes on participants' forearms. They were then given time to familiarize themselves with the provided guitar. Subsequently, we conducted a first calibration at 40 BPM followed by a first run consisting of five repetitions of either pattern A or B and intermediate tempo adjustments between repetitions. Adjustment were either made manually or automatically. The last repetition was always executed at 90 BPM, ensuring the same end tempo for each participant. After a short break, another calibration was conducted followed by five repetitions using the other experiment condition.

At the end of the experiment, we asked the participants to fill out two identical questionnaires, one targeting the manual condition and one for the automatic condition[9]. The questionnaires contained questions (7-point Likert scale) based on the work of Yuksel et al. [14] and their piano tutoring system. These questions were aimed at the learning process and mastery of the piece (cf. Figure 3). A third questionnaire was specifically tailored to the automatic condition where we asked the participants the questions listed in Table 1 (5-point Likert scale and free text). The whole study including setup and electrode placement did not exceed 60 minutes. Ethical approval for this study was obtained from the Ethics Committee at the University of Konstanz.

Results and Discussion

In this section, we will discuss the results from our questionnaires and their implications. Additionally, we will assess classification performance and its influence on the tutoring system.

Question
Please rate your perceived accuracy of the system in evaluating your performance.
How did you perceive the tempo adjustments the system made?
How challenging were the system's tempo choices?
Did the electrodes limit you in playing the guitar?
Would you use the system to learn to play guitar? Why or why not?
Imagine the system/electrodes could be integrated into your garments. How does this change your perceived usability of the system?
Further comments

Table 1. Questionnaire for the automatic condition.

Questionnaires

We compared the answers for the automatic and manual conditions from the first two questionnaires. A Wilcoxon signed-rank test showed that the reported Likert scores for all four questions were not significantly affected by the condition the subjects were using. The results are illustrated in Figure 3.

However, the results of the first two questionnaires (cf. Figure 3), indicate that the participants were comfortable with either tempo adjustment. We believe that the automatic system gave the participants a feeling of security as it relieved them from having to choose a new tempo, which was lower on average for the automatic condition[10]. However, answers for "How enjoyable was it to learn the piece?" suggest that the manual condition was more enjoyable for the subjects. We believe, that this can be explained by the low accuracies reported by the system and might have irritated the subjects. Nevertheless, participants stated that the electrodes did not limit them during their guitar play in the third questionnaire[11].

We analyzed the textual feedback provided by the users in the third questionnaire using affinity diagramming with two researchers identifying themes in the qualitative data. We found that users perceived an increase in playing accuracy:

> *"The given tempi helped to challenge me in play more quickly but still accurately."* [P7]

Further, users were able to realize, reflect upon and rectify possible flaws in their playing style:

> *"Yes, because my own adjustment was probably too high, the system probably is more realistic."* [P2]

EMGuitar was also perceived as offering a playful experience and the opportunity to practice alone while still receiving feedback was welcomed by the users:

> *"Yes because it's fun and it has the self-learning aspect into it without having a teacher to keep telling me what to do."* [P3]

[8] We believe this to be a meaningful sample size for our formative evaluation since all participant are familiar with the instrument [3].

[9] Since the electrode cables limited their writing capabilities, we opted to get feedback at the end for both conditions.

[10] Automatic: $\bar{x} = 57$, $SD = 18$; Manual: $\bar{x} = 66$, $SD = 12$; all BPM.

[11] Only the lowest two values were given as answers.

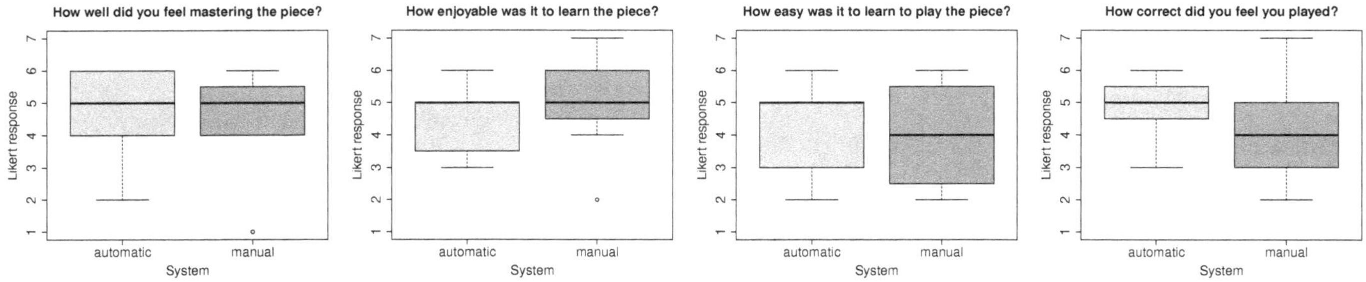

Figure 3. Boxplots illustrating the results of the first two questionnaire, reaching from lower to upper quartile. Whiskers mark the furthest observation within a distance of 1.5 times the box size. Outliers are marked with small circles. Questions are adapted from the work of Yuksel et al. [14].

In the free text comments, the subjects asked for more sophisticated feedback like chord and chord-change highlighting. This matches with our vision of the system and encourages further development. Figure 4 shows a possible visual feedback.

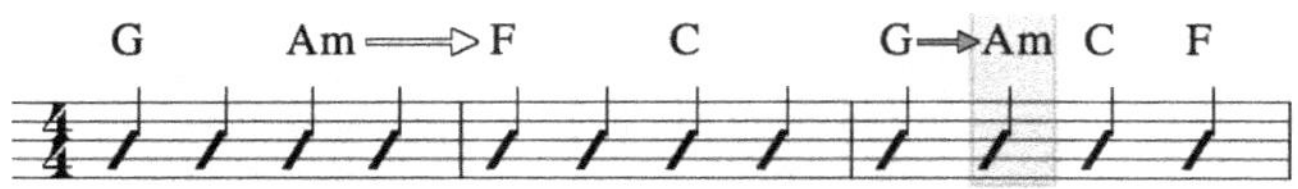

Figure 4. Possible feedback visualization for chord grips and chord changes. Colors range from green (flawless play) to red (faulty play).

Intra-Person Performance

To assess person-dependent performance during the experiment, we utilized the recorded calibration data. We report F1 scores[12] for training and testing on either calibration, respectively, yielding an average F1 score of 0.89. To evaluate the degradation of accuracy due to electrode location shift and sweating, we additionally trained on the first calibration set and tested on the second[13], only reaching an F1 score of 0.59 ($min = 0.25$, $max = 0.72$).

We have shown that detection accuracy is high when calibrating just before the evaluation. Yet it is also evident that performance can degrade quite fast after half an hour of playing time, mostly due to electrode shifts and impedance changes. Hence, repetitive calibration is necessary and hinders usability. We believe that tailored sensing wear, such as gloves and sleeves, will alleviate this issue, allowing for a tight fit.

Estimated chord accuracy when playing either pattern A or B ranges between 30% and 70%. While this can be attributed to the player proficiency, quick chord changes at high tempi introduce artefacts in the signal chain. We believe that detecting chord changes, e.g. using hidden Markov models, can remedy this problem and also provide feedback on flawed changes (as explained in Figure 4).

Inter-Person Performance

Inter-person performance was evaluated using a leave-one-subject-out approach. Furthermore, we applied a principal component analysis (PCA) before learning. This technique can help to compensate inaccurate electrode placement across participants and has been applied to EMG signals before [15].

The unmodified evaluation shows F1 scores ranging from 0.10 to 0.46, rendering the approach unusable for a tutoring system. PCA-modified evaluation shows similar values (0.10 to 0.3), yet only relying on nine principal components[14]. These findings suggest that dimensionality reduction techniques are effective and suitable for EMG-based detection, effectively reducing the feature space. However, current performance is not satisfactory for a tutoring system. A person-dependent calibration is still essential. Independent component analysis (ICA), as shown by Naik et al. [8], might be a method to tackle this challenge, revealing the contribution of specific muscle fibers and applying automatic re-calibration.

CONCLUSION

In this paper, we have showcased the feasibility of detecting fine-grained hand and finger postures using Electromyography in a guitar playing scenario. Our system *EMGuitar* was received well as it neither diminished ease of use nor was disruptive for the participants. Automatic tempo adjustment was neither better nor worse than manual adjustment by the participants. However, they expressed the need for more fine-grained feedback on play accuracy down to individual chords as opposed to mean scores per song. We conclude that it is more favorable to design for intermediate and detailed feedback. Here, we suggest an adapted visualization as well as an algorithmic approach to realize this. It remains to be researched which feedback modality – visual, audio or tactile – works best in this case to maximize the learning effect.

We envision the use of electrode bands as a natural sensing modality in tutoring systems. Especially since sensing electrodes can be easily integrated into garments and wearables, allowing for widespread deployment including playful interaction (*YouHero* [2], *Air-Guitar Hero* [10]) as well as natural interaction [13] with the instrument.

ACKNOWLEDGMENTS

This research is financially supported by the German Research Foundation (DFG) within the project C02 and task force TF3 of SFB/Transregio 161 and supported by the SimTech Cluster of Excellence. Part of this research was supported by the European Union's Horizon 2020 Programme under ERCEA grant no. 683008 AMPLIFY and the German Federal Ministry of Education and Research as part of the project KoBeLU (grant no. 16SV7599K).

[12] Grouped k-fold cross validation using an SVM classifier.

[13] Conducted approximately 20 minutes later.

[14] Instead of 36 dimensions for the unmodified version.

REFERENCES

1. Christoph Amma, Thomas Krings, Jonas Böer, and Tanja Schultz. 2015. Advancing Muscle-Computer Interfaces with High-Density Electromyography. In *Proceedings of the 33rd Annual ACM Conference on Human Factors in Computing Systems (CHI '15)*. ACM, New York, NY, USA, 929–938. DOI: http://dx.doi.org/10.1145/2702123.2702501
2. Palle Dahlstedt, Patrik Karlsson, Katarina Widell, and Tony Blomdahl. 2014. YouHero Making an Expressive Concert Instrument from the GuitarHero Controller.. In *NIME*. 403–406.
3. Wonil Hwang and Gavriel Salvendy. 2010. Number of People Required for Usability Evaluation: The 10±2 Rule. *Commun. ACM* 53, 5 (May 2010), 130. DOI: http://dx.doi.org/10.1145/1735223.1735255
4. Rose M.G. Johnson, Janet van der Linden, and Yvonne Rogers. 2010. MusicJacket: The Efficacy of Real-Time Vibrotactile Feedback for Learning to Play the Violin. In *CHI '10 Extended Abstracts on Human Factors in Computing Systems (CHI EA '10)*. ACM, New York, NY, USA, 3475–3480. DOI: http://dx.doi.org/10.1145/1753846.1754004
5. Markus Löchtefeld, Sven Gehring, Ralf Jung, and Antonio Krüger. 2011. guitAR: Supporting Guitar Learning Through Mobile Projection. In *CHI '11 Extended Abstracts on Human Factors in Computing Systems (CHI EA '11)*. ACM, New York, NY, USA, 1447–1452. DOI: http://dx.doi.org/10.1145/1979742.1979789
6. Roberto Merletti and Dario Farina. 2016. *Surface Electromyography: Physiology, Engineering and Applications*. John Wiley & Sons.
7. Roberto Merletti and Philip A. Parker. 2004. *Electromyography: Physiology, Engineering, and Non-Invasive Applications*. John Wiley & Sons.
8. Ganesh R. Naik, Dinesh Kant Kumar, Vijay Pal Singh, and Marimuthu Palaniswami. 2006. Hand Gestures for HCI Using ICA of EMG. In *Proceedings of the HCSNet Workshop on Use of Vision in Human-Computer Interaction - Volume 56 (VisHCI '06)*. Australian Computer Society, Inc., Darlinghurst, Australia, Australia, 67–72.
9. T Scott Saponas, Desney S. Tan, Dan Morris, and Ravin Balakrishnan. 2008. Demonstrating the Feasibility of Using Forearm Electromyography for Muscle-Computer Interfaces. In *Proceedings of the SIGCHI Conference on Human Factors in Computing Systems (CHI '08)*. ACM, New York, NY, USA, 515–524. DOI: http://dx.doi.org/10.1145/1357054.1357138
10. T. Scott Saponas, Desney S. Tan, Dan Morris, Ravin Balakrishnan, Jim Turner, and James A. Landay. 2009. Enabling Always-Available Input with Muscle-Computer Interfaces. In *Proceedings of the 22Nd Annual ACM Symposium on User Interface Software and Technology (UIST '09)*. ACM, New York, NY, USA, 167–176. DOI: http://dx.doi.org/10.1145/1622176.1622208
11. M. H. Schieber. 1995. Muscular Production of Individuated Finger Movements: The Roles of Extrinsic Finger Muscles. *J. Neurosci.* 15, 1 (Jan. 1995), 284–297.
12. Atau Tanaka and R. Benjamin Knapp. 2017. 2002: Multimodal Interaction in Music Using the Electromyogram and Relative Position Sensing. In *A NIME Reader*. Springer, Cham, 45–58. DOI: http://dx.doi.org/10.1007/978-3-319-47214-0_4
13. George Tzanetakis. 2016. Natural Human-Computer Interaction with Musical Instruments. In *Digital Tools for Computer Music Production and Distribution*. IGI Global, 116–136.
14. Beste F. Yuksel, Kurt B. Oleson, Lane Harrison, Evan M. Peck, Daniel Afergan, Remco Chang, and Robert JK Jacob. 2016. Learn Piano with BACh: An Adaptive Learning Interface That Adjusts Task Difficulty Based on Brain State. In *Proceedings of the 2016 CHI Conference on Human Factors in Computing Systems (CHI '16)*. ACM, New York, NY, USA, 5372–5384. DOI: http://dx.doi.org/10.1145/2858036.2858388
15. X. Zhai, B. Jelfs, R. H. M. Chan, and C. Tin. 2016. Short Latency Hand Movement Classification Based on Surface EMG Spectrogram with PCA. In *2016 38th Annual International Conference of the IEEE Engineering in Medicine and Biology Society (EMBC)*. 327–330. DOI: http://dx.doi.org/10.1109/EMBC.2016.7590706

Improvising with an Audience-Controlled Robot Performer

Claire Mikalauskas, Tiffany Wun, Kevin Ta, Joshua Horacsek, Lora Oehlberg
University of Calgary
Calgary, AB Canada
{crmikala, twwun, kta, joshua.horacsek, lora.oehlberg}@ucalgary.ca

ABSTRACT

In improvisational theatre (improv), actors perform unscripted scenes together, collectively creating a narrative. Audience suggestions introduce randomness and build audience engagement, but can be challenging to mediate at scale. We present Robot Improv Puppet Theatre (RIPT), which includes a performance robot (Pokey) who performs gestures and dialogue in short-form improv scenes based on audience input from a mobile interface. We evaluated RIPT in several initial informal performances, and in a rehearsal with seven professional improvisers. The improvisers noted how audience prompts can have a big impact on the scene — highlighting the delicate balance between ambiguity and constraints in improv. The open structure of RIPT performances allows for multiple interpretations of how to perform with Pokey, including one-on-one conversations or multi-performer scenes. While Pokey lacks key qualities of a good improviser, improvisers found his serendipitous dialogue and gestures particularly rewarding.

ACM Classification Keywords

H.5.m. Information Interfaces and Presentation (e.g. HCI): Miscellaneous

Author Keywords

Improvised Theatre; Human-Robot Interaction; Crowdsourcing; Creativity-Support Tools

INTRODUCTION

Improvised theatre (improv) gives actors the freedom to improvise the well-known or explore something new without a script, pursuing plot details of particular interest. One common practice is to gather audience suggestions, which creates engaging interaction between the audience and the actors on-stage [13]. However, the actor must find a balance between going with an obvious choice based on the suggestion, or introducing a change or conflict that is inspired by the suggestion but not directly related [13]. Audience suggestions are used in many different ways in improv games. *Ask-Fors* allow the whole audience to shout suggestions or can be used to connect personally with one random audience member. In *Audience Speak* [6], the audience must create one voice for a character, while *Moving Bodies* [6] brings audience volunteers on-stage to physically move the actors. However, there is a limit to the number of people who can meaningfully participate, or whose input becomes part of the show. For example, *Audience Speak* is most successful with a big audience, as the "funny" answers are drowned out by obvious answers. Improv is often not about being "funny" with every line, as the mundane suggestions are more relatable and playful on-stage [6].

DIS '18, June 9–13, 2018, , Hong Kong

ISBN 978-1-4503-5198-0/18/06...$15.00
DOI: https://doi.org/10.1145/3196709.3196757

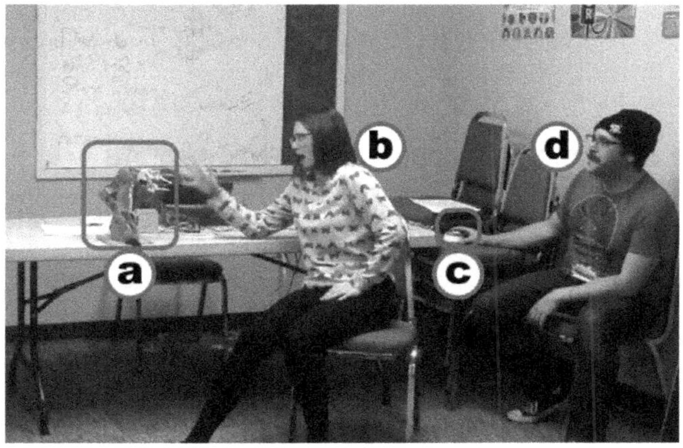

Figure 1: Improvising a scene using RIPT, with (a) Pokey, (b) an improviser, (c) the GO button, and (d) an off-stage button operator.

Technology offers one possible means of mediating audience input, and improving the quality of audience participation in improvised performance. There are several open questions on how technology might address these issues:

- *How can technology increase audience engagement through more direct participation in an improvised performance?*
- *What are effective ways to solicit audience input for an improvised scene?*
- *How do performers integrate large amounts of audience input into their improvised performance?*

We introduce Robot Improv Puppet Theatre (RIPT) (Figure 1), an improv experience where one or more improvisers perform with an Arduino Braccio robot arm, Pokey. The robot arm performs a set of pre-recorded gestures and "mouth movement" actions with its gripper, while using text-to-speech to read aloud random audience input. RIPT solicits audience input for both dialogue and gestures via a web-based application. The improviser creatively interprets the robot's dialogue and actions to construct new storylines. The robot's performance is directly based on audience participation, and offers improvisers unpredictable content to drive new, creative stories.

We offer the following research contributions: (a) the design and implementation of a system that allows an audience to control a robot actor in an improvised scene; (b) an evaluation of the aforementioned system with (i) informal performances with an amateur improviser, and (ii) a feedback session with seven professional improvisers as both performers and an "expert" audience; and (c) a discussion of how to manage audience input and how audience input impacts improvisational performance, when enacted by a performance robot.

BACKGROUND: IMPROVISED PERFORMANCE

Improv has many different styles and formats; for the purposes of this paper, we focus on *short-form improv*[1], which utilizes audience suggestions. Actors will often use a game or *ask-for* to begin their scene; the actors then respond to the rules or constraints of the game to create a new scene, on-the-fly. Key improv skills include carefully listening to fellow actors and introducing *callbacks* to previously discussed elements in the scene. The scene ends when one of the actors decides that the story has run its course or hits a strong punchline.

There are a range of ways to solicit the audience for suggestions. For example, *Bucket*[2] asks the audience to write words or phrases on slips of paper. Actors place the slips of paper in their pockets without looking at the contents; as needed throughout the scene, actors pull out a slip of paper to directly use as dialogue. Improvisers also draw "random" input from pre-existing bodies of text. In *Actor's Nightmare*[3], one actor has a script from which they must pull dialogue from one character's lines. The use of one character maintains the same perspective for the actor, while their partner contextualizes the seemingly random lines of dialogue into a cohesive scene. Games such as *Moving Bodies* rely on more active audience participation by bringing volunteers from the audience onstage to directly manipulate the body positions of the actors during the scene [6]. For RIPT, we focus on direct forms of audience participation over thematic suggestions as the audience directly contributes dialogue and movement to the scene from one character's perspective.

Although most improv games do not currently use technology, the use of technical effects in improv is not unheard of. However, the use of advanced technology in improv is rare [3] and often limited to light and sound [14]. This type of control implies an improviser is in the tech booth of the theatre; in practice, improv can be performed anywhere. We focus on technologies that are lightweight and operate independently of existing on-set theatre tech; our goal is to focus on a mediated interaction between the performers and their audience.

[1] http://improvencyclopedia.org/glossary/Short_Form.html
[2] http://improvencyclopedia.org/games/Bucket.html
[3] http://improvencyclopedia.org/games/Actor%60s_Nightmare.html

RELATED WORK

In this section, we discuss past research on robot performance, and technology-mediated audience participation in performance.

Robots and Performance

Performing robots are often operated by a human performer or act out pre-programmed behavior. There are numerous examples of theatre incorporating robots in human-to-human performance. Puppeteering is one common approach, in which robots act as a surrogate for a human puppeteer. Some examples include using the robot as a marionette operator [7] or as a hand puppet through a VR headset [12]. We are interested in what happens when performers no longer have complete control over what the robot does.

Research has also explored how robots can effectively express emotion. Through human interpretation, robots can convey emotions and intent effectively. Movement alone can elicit emotional responses from an observer despite the lack of a face or other human characteristics [4]. By expressing forethought and reaction through movement, robots can make their character more appealing [18]. Furthermore, a human performer can elicit more lifelike interpretations from a robot by allowing the robot's actions to affect the narrative and build motives through its past actions [1, 8]. Our work focuses on the robot as a surrogate for crowdsourced audience input, whose motives and goals can be creatively interpreted by other actors to drive the story.

Performing with a robot provides different opportunities for the creation of an improvised show. Improvisational TheaterSpace [15] allows a human actor to perform with a virtual actor in the form of projected text, which understands simple words and phrases. The text is intended to be the inner thoughts of the actor. The system has since been used for improv, such as a person talking to their alter ego [16]. We focus on using both the robot's dialogue and physical action as openly interpretable material for improv.

Audience Participation in Performance

The HCI community has seen an increased interest in the role that online crowds can have in creativity practices — either as a source of ideas [20, 21] or constructive critique [2, 9]. Performance, however, is a fundamentally different setting for soliciting creative input from audiences. Every audience member brings their own individuality to their responses, but when put on the spot, they may feel pressured to self-edit and give a response they think the crowd will expect [6]. While there is no "right" answer for audience suggestions, improvisers want to elicit interesting, even personal, answers from the audience [13]. With any audience, there is a chance that an audience member is too embarrassed to provide suggestions [19]. Technology offers one way to mediate anonymous audience participation, protecting individual audience members from embarrassment and rewarding multiple audience members for their participation. Theatre Engine [11] gives the audience an opportunity to provide input to the performance through smart devices. The devices are used live throughout the performance, providing engagement by letting audience members impact what occurs on-stage. However, Theatre Engine does not provide anonymity for the participants. With RIPT, we look at leveraging audience engagement, while maintaining anonymity in audience suggestions.

We are also interested in how performers adapt to technology on-stage. Honauer et al. [5] presented a scripted play to an audience, containing interactive special effects where the control is in the hands of the performers. The researchers studied how the performers adapt over the process, from rehearsals with the systems, fixes to the systems, and finally a performance. Although the audience is not in control of the interactive effects, understanding how they perceive technology is crucial to understanding its success on-stage. We extend actor-controlled technology to the stage of improvised theatre with RIPT. By gathering all input from the audience before the performance, rather than during, the input instead comes entirely from the audience.

POKEY, AN IMPROV ROBOT

Trisha arrives twenty minutes early to ensure she gets a good seat for viewing an improv show. When she walks into the lobby, she is greeted by one of the actors, and is instructed to go to a website on her phone to input dialogue and gestures for the upcoming show. Excited, Trisha pulls out her phone and visits the website. She first sees a prompt and asks the actor where the prompt is coming from. The actor explains that there is a set of prompts for each show, determined by someone who is not performing, in an attempt to get dialogue from the same perspective. Trisha asks who will be saying this dialogue, and learns that a robot arm will be performing on-stage as well. Trisha quickly enters some dialogue based on the prompt, and notices that she needs to also select a gesture. The names of the gestures are vague, but she is excited to see what it looks like on-stage. Trisha selects a gesture that seems the most interesting in combination with her dialogue. Once she hits submit, the screen confirms her submission and reloads with a new prompt and a new list of gestures. Trisha decides to submit as many entries as possible before she is asked to find her seat for the show. The show begins and Trisha is eager to hear her lines of dialogue delivered by the robot in the scene.

In the following section, we describe key RIPT system components: *Animating Pokey's Gestures and Movement* by defining and recording a library of possible gestures that the robot can perform with the "Gesture Animation Rig"; the *Audience Crowdsourcing Mobile Interface*; and the *Backstage Controller* that allows for minimal control by a behind-the-scenes "director".

Animating Pokey's Gestures and Movement

RIPT as a system facilitates the performance of dialogue and gesture by an Arduino Braccio Robot Arm ("Pokey"). First, we defined a series of gestures for Pokey to perform. To record gestures, we designed a custom animation rig that temporarily attaches to the exterior of the Braccio robot arm. The rig includes three lengths of 3D printed armatures and one base piece (Figure 2). Each joint of the animation rig has a potentiometer that adjusts its value according to the angle of the joint; as the animator moves the robot manually, the rig

Prompts *What you would say to...*
• someone cooking in the kitchen • a professional chef in a restaurant • a friend in the kitchen with you
• a manicurist doing your nails • a shop clerk selling you jewelry • a friend while getting your nails done
• a sales clerk when buying business clothing • your new boss at a part-time job • your friend shopping with you for business clothing
• a lifeguard at the beach • someone teaching you how to swim • your spouse at the beach
• the police after witnessing a petty theft • your sibling after witnessing a petty theft • to show you are a law abiding citizen
• your child when trying to get them to go to sleep • your dog when trying to calm them down • a preteen you are babysitting
• a barista in a coffee shop who sees you everyday • your sibling after not seeing them in years • your best friend while quickly grabbing coffee
• a library volunteer • your best friend while chatting on the phone • someone in a whisper
• someone giving you a tattoo • a doctor giving you a vaccination • your favourite visual artist
• your mom while shopping for your prom dress • a pushy sales associate who thinks you need help shopping • a school chaperone for a high school event
• your sassy friend when you forgot something • your sassy friend when you do something embarrassing • your sassy friend about someone else when they do something

Table 1: List of prompt sets used in RIPT.

Gestures		
Idle*	Exaggerated Yes	Head Up
Confront	Defeated	Inspect
Nod Yes	Defensive	Jump
Laugh	Sulk	Dance
Raise Head Slowly	Shake No	Lean Back Quickly

Table 2: Table of Gestures. "Idle" gesture is not selectable in the mobile interface.

produces an analog value corresponding to the angle of each joint as a keyframe. Very few of our planned gestures used the yaw rotation about the base of the Braccio; thus, we did not design a jig to capture the yaw rotation of the base. Instead, gestures with yaw base rotation had each yaw angle manually defined for multiple keyframes.

To account for any misalignment of the potentiometers during the construction of the animation rig, we calibrated the translation from analog values to angles by first collecting the analog values while the arm is fully extended (as controlled by the provided Braccio library). We then reconstructed the affine map of analog values to angles using linear regression. This allowed us to disengage the servo motors and puppeteer the Braccio arm, recording the angles at each joint over time.

We recorded and implemented 18 gestures for Pokey (see Table 2). These include gestures such as: confronting the actor, inspecting something, or dancing. We recorded an idle animation for the robot to perform when there is no user-selected animation playing. This serves the two-fold purpose of giving the audience and performer a sense that the robot is "thinking", as well as informing the RIPT operator that all systems are working as expected.

In each recorded animation file, we manually placed cues to indicate both when the gripper should start moving for speech, and when the text-to-speech module should start producing sound. Mouth movements are not coordinated with the dialogue; the grippers simply open and close while talking and mouth movements stop once the text-to-speech process is terminated. Mouth movements operate independently from the arm gestures to accommodate different lengths of dialogue.

Audience Crowdsourcing Mobile Interface

Audience members access the crowdsourcing interface (Figure 3) by visiting a web URL on their mobile devices before the start of the show. The mobile interface prompts the audience for dialogue using one of three prompts from the selected prompt set. Dialogue entries need to be between 3-35 words and must be paired with a selected gesture. We created prompts that encourage a common character perspective with audience input for a show (see Table 1). The prompts come in sets of three, where each set is a show. The interface also asks the audience to select one of three gestures to go with their line of dialogue; the three options are selected at random from the full list of available gestures (see Table 2). The set of prompts and available gestures are chosen by a behind-the-scenes director using the backstage controller.

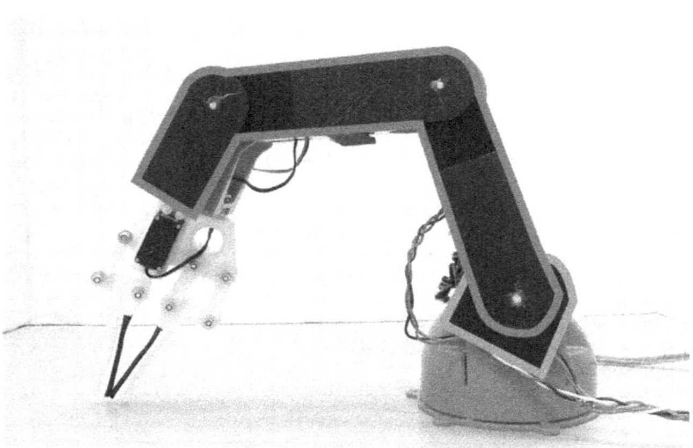

Figure 2: Animation rig. Armature is outlined in red and base piece outlined in blue. Each joint is fitted with a potentiometer to measure angles of the joint.

Backstage Controller

The backstage controller allows a director to initiate a show and collect submissions for Pokey. While the director can remove inappropriate submissions, they cannot use the back-

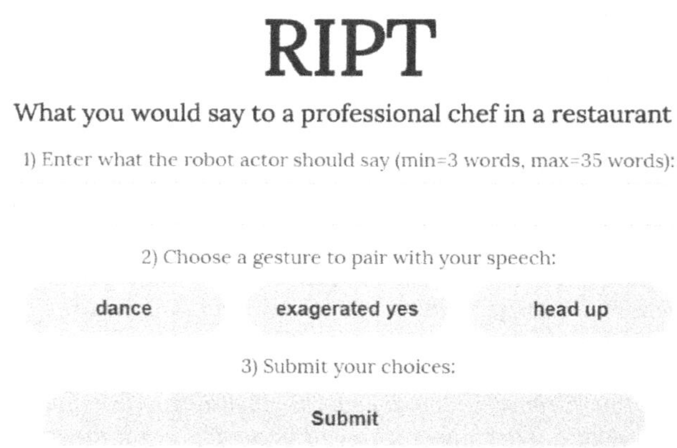

Figure 3: Audience Mobile Interface. One random prompt from a chosen set of prompts is presented per submission. The audience member supplies a line of dialogue paired with one of the three randomly presented gestures.

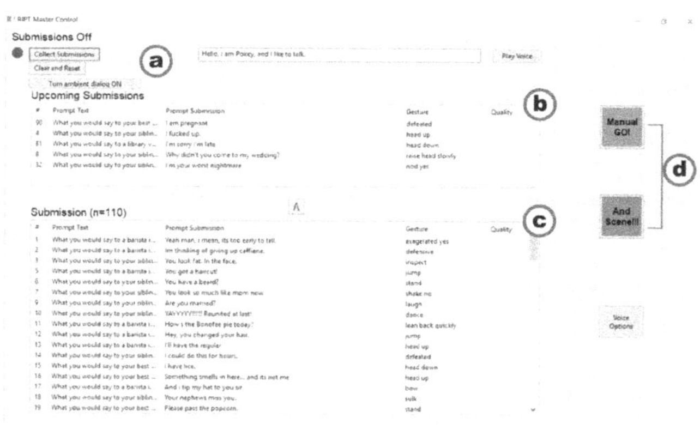

Figure 4: Backstage controller interface includes: (a) controls to initiate submission collection; (b) queue of next five submissions, to be used on upcoming GO button presses, chosen randomly from the collection; (c) the full list of submissions; and (d) manual controls for hardware buttons.

stage controller to add submissions or control the ordering of those submissions. Once a submission is removed or played through Pokey, it can no longer be played again. To collect submissions, the director selects a set of prompts and gestures to be displayed on the mobile interface. A web-server then opens the mobile interface for submissions from the audience (Figure 4). Submissions are automatically saved to a file and can be reloaded for later. Once there is a satisfactory number of submissions, the director can close the submissions and begin the show.

The backstage controller and the mobile interface connect to each other via a proxy server. Each mobile interface connects to a server, which manages all mobile interface connections and relays submissions to and from the backstage controller. The backstage controller receives submissions and updates the server (therefore the mobile interface) with prompt sets, gestures, and submission collection status. The mobile interface was written in HTML5 and JavaScript, the server with Node.js and Socket.io, and the backstage controller with Python.

Initiating Pokey's Dialogue

Once the director signals that the show is ready to start, the show begins. An audience member, or one of the actors not currently in the scene, sits off-stage with the GO button. The button operator presses the GO button each time Pokey needs to deliver a line in the scene. A green LED provides feedback for when Pokey is ready to deliver another line; this prevents Pokey from playing another submission until the current one has finished executing. The performers interpret and respond to Pokey's gestures and dialogue to integrate the robot's performance into the scene. The scene ends whenever a performer, the director, or the button operator feels the scene has come to a natural end.

We rely on human intelligence to decide the timing of when Pokey should perform its lines. This not only simplifies the implementation of the system, but also keeps either an audience member or actor engaged in performing along with Pokey.

EVALUATION

To evaluate RIPT, we first conducted proof-of-concept performances both informally and at a demo session. However, for a more in-depth evaluation we brought RIPT to a rehearsal with professional improvisers.

Preliminary Evaluation

During the development of RIPT, we conducted several rounds of improvised puppet shows. One of our co-authors is an amateur improviser and performed scenes with Pokey using a sock puppet (see Figure 5). We initially used a puppet due to Pokey's size and movements resembling a sock puppet. Meanwhile, an audience member triggered Pokey's dialogue with the GO button. Our early performances led to usability improvements for the backstage and web interface. We made minor revisions to the prompts, robot voice, and gestures to improve the cohesion of the performance.

We also participated in a conference demo session at ACM UIST 2017, where a large number of people (appx. 200) passed by a booth featuring our co-author performer. We ran four performances with Pokey during the demo session, and gathered audience contributions in the 20 minutes leading up to the show (avg. = 70). Each improvised show lasted approximately 5 minutes and used 15-20 submissions.

Naturally, performances with Pokey are unpredictable because of the randomness of the responses. While we intended for the prompts (Table 1) to guide the suggested dialogue, many audience members ignored the prompts by either inputting text copied from the internet or attempting to break the system with specific character strings. Although non-sequitur statements can be entertaining, submissions that followed the prompts provided more opportunities for a cohesive storyline. Ultimately, it is the performer's responsibility to make sense of what Pokey says and does.

In the demo session performances, the sock puppet limited the amount of emotion and movement the human performer could add to the show. Emotion can be crucial when bringing context and meaning to an improvised scene, yet Pokey's text-to-speech provided no emotion or tone. We decided to allow actors to use their bodies — instead of hand puppets — to allow them to fully emote during a scene. We brought our refined system and setup to a professional improv troupe to better understand how professional improvisers react to the audience-sourced experience. The improv troupe served as an "expert" audience, given their expertise with how audiences might behave in a performance, and as professional performers.

Professional Improvisers Evaluation

We brought RIPT to a rehearsal session with seven members from a local professional improv troupe. The actors (3 female, 4 male) had between 5 and 20 years of experience in improv, including experience in competitions, performing at corporate events, and working with multiple professional troupes.

We first demonstrated how RIPT uses the audience's input for dialogue and gestures. We stepped through how we selected the prompts and asked the actors to input dialogue as the audience for their own rehearsal performance. We demonstrated

Figure 5: Improvised puppet show performed by one of our co-authors using a sock puppet.

how the backstage controller could moderate input during a show; the actors agreed that it served a key purpose for public shows. In our study, we did not use a director to moderate submissions through the backstage controller (and informed our participants of this) as audience members themselves would take turns performing. Throughout the study, we asked the actors specifically about the usability and level of audience engagement with the prompts, gestures, and overall layout of the web interface. While they were adding dialogue, we asked them to speculate on how the audience experience of this type of performance might work out in practice. The semi-structured group interview format benefitted from the improvisers' retrospective and analytical tendencies stemming from their creative practice [10].

Once there was a sufficient amount of audience input, the actors took turns performing with Pokey, with one actor offstage to operate the button for each scene. The performers initially performed one-on-one scenes with Pokey, but eventually branched out to include multiple performers in the scene. In total, they performed seven scenes; each scene lasted approximately 3 minutes. Between scenes, the improvisers discussed how that scene went, and what worked (or did not work) with Pokey as a fellow actor; these discussions often informed how they experimented and played with Pokey in the following scene. At the end of the session, we gathered final feedback on what it is like to improvise with Pokey, and how Pokey's limitations affect the performer.

Our findings reflect actors' responses to our specific questions about the prompts, the backstage and web interface, and gestures. To understand the performance itself, we performed open coding [17] on videos of the rehearsal performances to identify emergent patterns.

FINDINGS

We discuss how RIPT solicits audience input and how a RIPT performance might be structured to coordinate audience input with the actors' performance. We then examine how improvisers crafted scenes using Pokey's random, audience-sourced dialogue and gestures. Throughout our findings we use pseudonyms to refer to our participants.

Soliciting Dialogue and Gesture from the Audience

Our improvisers were very familiar with improv performances that leverage audience input; finding ways to increase audience engagement through participation is a key challenge of their current practice.

Patty: When we do corporate shows, all of our games involve the audience, and that's to heighten the engagement of the audience. The audience loves nothing more than to hear themselves, center stage.

We asked the professional improvisers to provide feedback on how RIPT asked for audience input, given their extensive past experience with phrasing effective *ask-fors* more broadly in improv. The actors gravitated towards prompts that help the audience generate more interesting, personal answers.

Patty: When you're like "can we get a word?", you get 'dildo' or 'broccoli'. [...] When we're trying to get something a little bit more sophisticated from an audience, we're often asking "Can I"... even just an adjective, an interesting word... "Can I get- What was the toy you played with as a child?"

Overall, the improvisers approved of the prompts' level of detail. They also appreciated the attempt to generate dialogue around a common perspective to identify a consistent role for Pokey in the scene: *"[The input is] like Actor's Nightmare, it's all coming from one perspective" (Alex).* They suggested alternate ways of prompting the audience to provide dialogue from a particular character or role, by including, *"a picture of a person or an actor or, like, a role or a character, and then, like, 'things that that person would say' " (Alex).*

When selecting a prompt for their own performance, the actors discussed prompts that stood out as good or bad for a show. Good prompts bring about scenes with *"the widest variety of intimacy and casualness" (Alex)*, character qualities that *"can be played in different ways" (Leah)*, and *"more emotional content and less specific content" (Alex).*

The actors were less attracted to scenes with plot *("We don't care about plot" (Elizabeth))*, and were particularly wary of *"transaction scenes" (Patty)* — where two actors go through an established series of exchanges to reach a clear goal. For example, *"'What would you say to a sales clerk while buying business clothes?' is very specific about where the scene is going to go. It doesn't leave you a lot of space [...] It gets boring" (Elizabeth).*

Instead, the actors gravitated towards questions that can lead to multiple, emotionally-charged interpretations.

Dalton: I really like the question, "What is something you would whisper?"

Leah: What I really like about the whisper thing is, like, why are you whispering? Like, you're embarrassed of it? Or is it creepy? [...] or, like, accidentally, like, racist or something...?

The actors chose the "barista in a coffee shop" set of prompts, swapping out the "best friend" prompt for the "whisper" prompt from another set (Table 1). They ultimately recommended formulating sets of prompts that (a) defines the context, (b) maintains the perspective, and (c) provides openness.

We also asked the actors to comment on how we asked the audience to select gestures. The actors approved of offering three choices of gestures for the audience. First, they reasoned, the limited set forces the audience to make a decision more quickly than if they had to pick from a broader set. Second, the random selection offered new possible gestures with each submission that could inform or inspire the scene. Finally, the actors felt the ambiguity of the gesture descriptions would entice the audience to look forward to discovering what their gesture looks like in the performance:

Elizabeth: It makes it more fun for the audience because then they don't know exactly what the gesture is, so then they're surprised when they see it.

With the dialogue prompts and gesture options set, the improvisers provided dialogue for their own scenes. They added

(a) Pokey: "Do you have any picture books?" (b) Dalton: "Of course I have picture books, they're the best things when you're high. Take a look at this..." (c) Pokey: "We should get together like this again."

Figure 6: In this scene: (a) Pokey suggests reading a picture book; (b) Dalton pulls out an imaginary picture book; and (c) Pokey, by chance, performs inquisitive gesture, which results in him moving in to look more closely at the book before delivering his line of dialogue.

input to RIPT both before they began performing, and between scenes, submitting 163 lines of dialogue in total.

While we expected the gestures to influence what the participants input into the system, they often ignored the gestures, and focused more on the dialogue prompts themselves. While RIPT accepted dialogue entries from 3-35 words in length, the experienced improvisers only provided short lines of dialogue (avg. = 6.11 words). They considered the impact of raising the minimum word count, or setting specific word count challenges as a way of getting the audience to provide more meaningful dialogue.

Patty: I got caught up in the "Oh, I want to do another one, I want to do another one". But if I have to get to fifteen words for this one, then I'll try a little harder.

Alex: Yeah, the system makes you want to write short sentences.

The performers also adjusted their input in anticipation of what they thought might be funny in a scene — without any sense of how the scene would actually play out: *"I found myself doing a lot of gag lines off of the top" (Leah)*. Their excitement to create so much dialogue (albeit terse) was in anticipation of the performance itself:

Elizabeth: As an audience member, you want to hear what you write. You're so excited, so you're just, like, "I'm going to do as many as I can, so that I can hear my thing."

Structuring a RIPT Performance

We discussed several variations on how to run a RIPT show with the improvisers. They were hesitant to allow the audience to add dialogue to RIPT during the show, since they want the audience to focus on the performance, not their phones: *"It's just distraction-ville with all the phones out" (Patty)*. They alternately suggested pausing the show between scenes or mid-scene: dimming the lights on-stage, bringing up the house lights, and inviting the audience to add new dialogue based on what just happened in the scene.

Elizabeth: You could be in a scene, like, you and me are in a scene and we're talking [moving hands like talking heads] "duh, duh, duhh..." and [the audience] is doing their thing for a minute, and then we start the scene when the lights come up. But we're still doing the scene [...] just no verbal.

This opened up the possibility for the audience to introduce *callbacks*, as a way of responding to what the improvisers had introduced in the scene. This could also heighten audience engagement, which is strongly impacted by how "live" the performance feels. In our earlier performances, we often encountered skepticism that the scenes were indeed improvised. The professional improvisers confirmed that this is a typical response to improv, and advised ways to use the prompts themselves to emphasize spontaneity:

Alex: [Better prompts are] anything that convinces the audience that it's more in the moment and that the robot's doing it live.

Having prepared prompts can communicate pre-planning to the audience — *"The audience is like, 'Oh, they've predetermined, like, five sets'" (Alex)* — even if the performers are unprepared and the show director (a non-performer) determined the prompts.

Performing Alongside Pokey

Once the improvisers added input to RIPT, they took turns performing a total of seven scenes with Pokey. When not performing in a scene, fellow actors observed as part of the audience. We discuss key elements that influenced a performance with Pokey, such as: how the improvisers created a cohesive scene, the comedic timing of Pokey's performance, the number of actors in a scene, and the physicality of Pokey's movements in relation to the performer.

Creating Cohesive Scenes

Pokey presented an unusual challenge for our improvisers. The key to making sense of Pokey's words and actions was for the actor to do the *"emotional weight lifting" (James)* of the scene. The improvisers were able to bring more emotional weight to their performance because they interacted with Pokey as a human, instead of with a hand puppet as in our initial performances:

Alex: What we can do while we are with Pokey is we can give all that nuance, [pointing to own face] all that stuff that, like, the other sock puppet can't do. So [the sock puppet] really limits the range of expression [...] That's why Avenue Q is half-and-half, and, like, half-and-half is more interesting.

Most scenes were initiated by Pokey's first line of dialogue; the actors could then begin to contextualize what was said into a cohesive storyline. Only one scene did not begin with Pokey, where the actor struggled to incorporate what Pokey was saying; the actor often turned to clarifying the situation that Pokey's character obviously did not understand.

Patty: As an artist, what's your process? Just walk me through that.

Pokey: These elbows. A-A-A-A-A-R-P I will fight you.

Patty: Well...Well okay. You know, I know you're new to podcasts there [sigh] but can we get you some coffee?

Pokey: How was your day off?

Patty: Great, thank you. The interview is about you though.

In one of the more successful scenes, everything Pokey said was accepted as truth: Pokey's dialogue introduced a picture book, and later he gestured to "inspect" the book (Figure 6). The actor in this scene clearly used the "yes, and" principle[4] of improv to accommodate Pokey's unpredictable dialogue. While Pokey cannot "yes, and" in response, in this case the dialogue and gesture lined up such that Pokey appeared as though he had an understanding of the scene.

Timing

Pressing the GO button is another form of audience engagement — in both our early performances, and the rehearsal with professional improvisers, everyone enjoyed pressing the GO button. However, in our early performances, audience members needed a clear cue from the performer (e.g., eye contact, awkward silence) for when they should press the GO button to continue the scene. This gap between the cue and the execution of Pokey's line resulted in a more intermittent performance. In the rehearsal, the improvisers played the role of an audience member controlling the GO button — however, they advised against inviting a random audience member controlling the button, because of timing.

Patty: What's great about it is having an improviser on the GO button, because that timing is an important piece [...] As the person playing the button [in the 3 person scene] that was way more fun because I had to wait, and I was like, "where do I want it to be?" And then there were times where I was like, "talk faster, just talk over him, we don't even care what's happening anymore!"

The gestures also introduced their own performative timing — the "inquisitive" gesture stood out during the study, as it had a meaningful movement towards a specific, imaginary artifact on the table, and it delayed the dialogue by five seconds. We introduced this delay so that the gesture could carry more meaning. Due to the delay, the performer in the scene (Alex) could lean in and match Pokey's gesture, as though he were listening to a secret.

[4]http://improvencyclopedia.org/glossary/Yes_And.html

Patty: If we're starting to mimic the, uh, Pokey, then that's great. We'll do that all the time on-stage. We'll mimic each other, we'll copy each other.

Number of Actors

In our preliminary performances we only had one amateur improviser; in the rehearsal setting with professional improvisers, we were curious how RIPT might extend to a larger troupe. When we asked the actors about their expectations for the "barista in a coffee shop" scene, they clearly anticipated a two-person performance: *"It's going to be two people having a chat. Not a lot of action" (Alex); "Might be a lot of talking heads" (Elizabeth).*

While the actors mentioned the possibility of three-person scenes, no one started a scene with two human actors on-stage. However, it became clear that the scene could extend to more players, as needed. In one scene, Pokey's dialogue called for an additional character (Figure 7).

Pokey: Please pass the popcorn.

Leah: [passes mimed popcorn bowl to Pokey]

Pokey: Well, look who it is.

Leah: [makes eye contact with Dalton who is off-stage]

Dalton: [walks toward Pokey and Leah] Hey, hey guys.

Towards the end of the session, the improvisers became more playful with Pokey and decided to start a five-person scene from the start (Figure 8). This scene quickly devolved — all the performers played off of each other, while Pokey stayed in the middle of the scene interjecting non-sequitur lines that interrupted others. Pokey's character ended up being an unpleasant person at a bus stop, driving others out of the scene. In the end, Pokey was left alone to just say a few lines, creating a monologue, and finally drawing the audience in.

Leah: I was projecting so much emotion into everything he was saying. I was like, "poor guy."

Physicality of Pokey

When discussing alternative variations of RIPT, one actor suggested transforming a visual, animated character that could be projected anywhere on the stage. However, we observed that Pokey's physicality was an important element for the actors to play with during the scene. Pokey's physical presence was

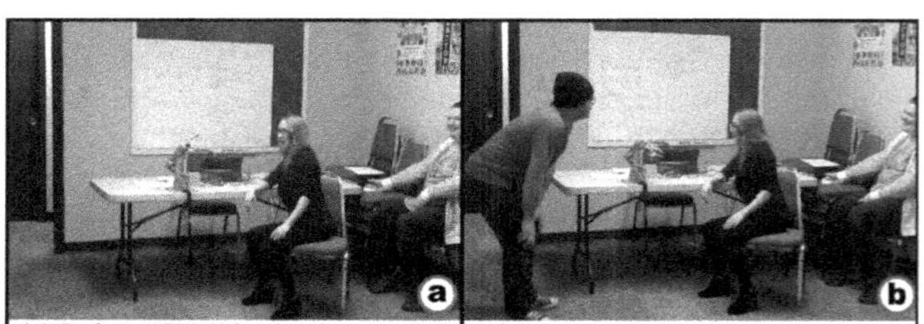

(a) Pokey: "Well look who it is." (b) Dalton: "Hey, hey guys."

Figure 7: (a) Pokey delivers a line implying a new character and (b) Dalton takes advantage of this to invite himself into the scene.

not only mimicked by actors, but expressive in themselves. The actors valued the robot's ability to communicate beyond dialogue *("So much of communication is nonverbal" (Elliot))*, particularly those actions that clearly communicated an emotional state *("The dancing one was the clearest, like, the more expressive animal ones" (Alex))*. The participants saw potential in Pokey's gestural expression that was yet untapped.

Alex: It's almost like you want a puppeteer to spend an hour with it, there's some that aren't emotional enough. There's some [gestures] that are too subtle.

The most successful gesture — the "inspection" to look closely at a picture book — was only possible because there was such a clear indication of Pokey's "gaze". The actors wished they could play more with Pokey's gaze and eye contact — which was limited based on the location of his eyes.

Alex: You want to play with eye contact when he's looking at you and looking away, and you can't when [Pokey's eyes] are on either side [of his head], because he's a bird.

Pokey's physicality brings many of the same qualities as past work on robot performance [7, 12]. Because RIPT also brings in unpredictable audience input, Pokey could bring elements of a physical performer into an improvised scene while maintaining the spontaneous spirit of live improv.

DISCUSSION & FUTURE WORK

Our implementation and evaluation highlighted several current limitations of RIPT, as well as opportunities for future design iterations, research, and performances.

Pokey's Voices. We used a single male text-to-speech reader for Pokey's voice. This resulted in referring to Pokey as a "he", even though in practice, actors will adopt different voices to communicate a range of characters. In future iterations, Pokey's voice could be selected by the director to adapt to a particular role in a given scene: man, woman, child, or non-human (e.g., a gruff "wolf" voice).

Costumes and Props. Improvisers will often grab and use props or costume elements before the beginning of a scene to help reinforce elements of their character. Our actors suggested dressing up Pokey with costumes or props that reflect a particular character while collecting audience submissions.

Figure 8: A multi-performer scene at a bus stop.

Physical Gaze Cues. Pokey currently has two googly eyes on the sides of his head — similar to a bird's eyes. However, the performers found it difficult to figure out where exactly Pokey was looking. Revisiting Pokey's design and gesture vocabulary — particularly from the perspective of a puppeteer — could improve the types of signals that Pokey gives to the actors and the audience.

Emphasize "Live" Performance. One way of emphasizing the "live" nature of RIPT would be to allow the prompts to immediately reflect audience input. For example, the director could ask the audience for a few initial elements of a scene (e.g., "What's a good Halloween costume?"; "Pirate"), and then create a set of three questions on-the-fly that reflect that prompt (e.g., three questions from the perspective of a pirate). Another way to emphasize the "live" nature of improv would be to pause the show so that the audience can provide the *callbacks* needed in Pokey's dialogue.

Audience Size. Audiences become engaged when they *"hear themselves, center stage"*; in an improv scene, an audience member's satisfaction heightens when their suggestion affects the show's outcome, such as: introducing a plot twist, making a joke, or creating a situational coincidence. When testing our system, we primarily used smaller audiences (6-20 people). However, as audiences become larger, an audience member may have increasingly lower odds of hearing Pokey perform one of their lines during a performance. While RIPT currently randomly performs input lines, greater awareness of where lines come from, or what their potential impact could be at different points in a scene, could increase the audience's satisfaction during a show.

Improv Format. RIPT was designed with short-form improv in mind; while the actors in our evaluation could imagine integrating a brief scene with Pokey in the context of a longer-format show, RIPT was designed for performances only lasting a few minutes. Due to its novelty, Pokey was generally the focus of a scene with one-on-one dialogue. However, improv troupes often include multiple performers on-stage, with new performers entering or exiting the scene as needed. While it is possible that our actors have been primed to use Pokey in one-on-one dialogue, our actors would have liked more opportunities outside of the suggested dialogue structure involving Pokey. Participant suggestions for future work include starting scenes with a second performer to break out of one-on-one conversations, or to include Pokey as a recurring character that appears periodically during a show (e.g., a landlord looking for rent money).

CONCLUSION

Is Pokey a good improviser? Clearly not. Even with the best prompts and audience input, Pokey is comedically terrible at many fundamentals of improv performance. Pokey is not aware of the scene at hand; he does not listen to his fellow actors; he does not create *callbacks*; he cannot "yes, and" in response to other actors; he does not know which actor on-stage is addressing him; and he does not know where to look on-stage. But despite Pokey's lack of fundamental improv skills, RIPT offers a way for audience input to play a larger role in short-form scenes, leading to a fascinating, compelling improvised performance. And despite his naïvité, Pokey is capable of performing serendipitously good scenes. When Pokey recites the "right" random line of dialogue and gesture at the correct time, it's magical: inviting others into the scene as an improviser would, or playing into another performer's setup to deliver a scene-ending punchline.

ACKNOWLEDGEMENTS

This research was supported by the Discovery Grant 2016-RGPIN-04240 from NSERC. The authors would like to thank the organizers of the UIST 2017 Student Innovation Contest for providing the opportunity to develop for the Arduino Braccio. We also thank our participants for lending their time and rehearsal space to conduct the study.

REFERENCES

1. Allison Bruce, Jonathan Knight, Samuel Listopad, Brian Magerko, and Illah R Nourbakhsh. 2000. Robot improv: Using drama to create believable agents. In *Proceedings of the IEEE International Conference on Robotics and Automation (ICRA'00)*, Vol. 4. IEEE, 4002–4008.
2. Steven Dow, Anand Kulkarni, Scott Klemmer, and Björn Hartmann. 2012. Shepherding the crowd yields better work. In *Proceedings of the ACM Conference on Computer-Supported Cooperative Work (CSCW '12)*. ACM, 1013–1022.
3. Dustin Freeman and Ravin Balakrishnan. 2016. Improv Remix: Mixed-Reality Video Manipulation Using Whole-Body Interaction to Extend Improvised Theatre. In *Proceedings of the ACM Conference on Designing Interactive Systems (DIS '16)*. ACM, 533–542.
4. John Harris and Ehud Sharlin. 2011. Exploring the affect of abstract motion in social human-robot interaction. In *RO-MAN, 2011 IEEE*. IEEE, 441–448.
5. Michaela Honauer, Patrick Tobias Fischer, Eva Hornecker, Julia Hahn, Bahar Akgün, Claire Dorweiler, Liese Endler, Yvonne Götzl, Muhammad Raisul Islam, Thomas Keßler, and others. 2017. Dusk: Adaption and Perception in Interactive Theatre. In *Extended Abstracts of the ACM Conference on Human Factors in Computing Systems (CHI '17)*. ACM, 1037–1045.
6. Keith Johnstone. 2014. *Impro for Storytellers*. Routledge.
7. Woong-Ji Kim, Sun-Wook Choi, and Chong Ho Lee. 2012. MARIOBOT: Marionette robot that interact with an audience. In *Proceedings of the ACM/IEEE International Conference on Human-Robot Interaction (HRI '12)*. IEEE, 409–409.
8. Heather Knight. 2011. Eight lessons learned about non-verbal interactions through robot theater. In *International Conference on Social Robotics*. Springer, 42–51.
9. Kurt Luther, Jari-Lee Tolentino, Wei Wu, Amy Pavel, Brian P. Bailey, Maneesh Agrawala, Björn Hartmann, and Steven P. Dow. 2015. Structuring, Aggregating, and Evaluating Crowdsourced Design Critique. In *Proceedings of the ACM Conference on Computer Supported Cooperative Work Social Computing (CSCW '15)*. ACM, New York, NY, USA, 473–485.
10. Brian Magerko, Waleed Manzoul, Mark Riedl, Allan Baumer, Daniel Fuller, Kurt Luther, and Celia Pearce. 2009. An empirical study of cognition and theatrical improvisation. In *Proceedings of the ACM Conference on Creativity and Cognition*. ACM, 117–126.
11. Charles B Owen, Alison Dobbins, and Lisa Rebenitsch. 2013. Theatre Engine: Integrating mobile devices with live theater. In *Proceedings of International Conference on Advances in Mobile Computing & Multimedia*. ACM, 378.
12. Mose Sakashita, Tatsuya Minagawa, Amy Koike, Ippei Suzuki, Keisuke Kawahara, and Yoichi Ochiai. 2017. You As a Puppet: Evaluation of Telepresence User Interface for Puppetry. In *Proceedings of the ACM Symposium on User Interface Software and Technology (UIST '17)*. ACM, New York, NY, USA, 217–228.
13. Tom Salinsky and Deborah Frances-White. 2013. *The Improv handbook: The Ultimate Guide to Improvising in Comedy, Theatre, and Beyond*. Bloomsbury Publishing.
14. Sally Smallwood and Cameron Algie. 2011. Unsung Heroes Of Improv: The Tech. (2011). `https://peopleandchairs.com/2014/10/06/unsung-heroes-of-improv-the-tech/`
15. Flavia Sparacino. 1996. *DirectIVE–choreographing media for interactive virtual environments*. Ph.D. Dissertation. Massachusetts Institute of Technology.
16. Flavia Sparacino, Glorianna Davenport, and Alex Pentland. 2000. Media in performance: Interactive spaces for dance, theater, circus, and museum exhibits. *IBM Systems Journal* 39, 3.4 (2000), 479–510.
17. Anselm Strauss and Juliet M Corbin. 1990. *Basics of Qualitative Research: Grounded Theory Procedures and Techniques*. Sage Publications, Inc.
18. Leila Takayama, Doug Dooley, and Wendy Ju. 2011. Expressing thought: improving robot readability with animation principles. In *Proceedings of the International Conference on Human-Robot Interaction*. ACM, 69–76.
19. Gareth White. 2013. *Audience Participation in Theatre: Aesthetics of the Invitation*. Springer.
20. Lixiu Yu, Aniket Kittur, and Robert E Kraut. 2014a. Distributed analogical idea generation: inventing with crowds. In *Proceedings of the ACM Conference on Human Factors in Computing Systems (CHI '14)*. ACM, 1245–1254.
21. Lixiu Yu, Aniket Kittur, and Robert E Kraut. 2014b. Searching for analogical ideas with crowds. In *Proceedings of the ACM Conference on Human Factors in Computing Systems (CHI '14)*. ACM, 1225–1234.

Reconfiguring the Appearance and Expression of Social Robots by Acknowledging their Otherness

Laurens Boer, Harvey Bewley
IxD Lab, IT University of Copenhagen
Copenhagen, Denmark
{laub, harb}@itu.dk

ABSTRACT
The design of social robots usually does not focus on their kinetic expression, and often follows the assumption that their appearance should be human or animal like. To encourage a broader understanding of the possibilities for design of social robots, and as an inquiry into alternative relations with them, we present two robots, the Lat-Sac and the Blo-Nut, which are purposefully moving away from typical social robot design. We present how we engaged performance experts in the choreographic sketching of their elastic expression, and how we staged the robots in a fictitious near-future scenario to create a discursive space for reflection on emerging relations. Based on these encounters we discuss how acknowledging the otherness of social robots can be valuable in designing as well as growing intriguing relations with them.

Author Keywords
Social Robots; Interactive Performance; Diegetic Prototype; Research through Design; Soft Robotics; Otherness.

ACM Classification Keywords
H.5.m. Information interfaces and presentation (e.g., HCI): Miscellaneous.

INTRODUCTION
For interaction design research, social robots are a notable category of complex computational objects. Not just the social robot as an object of design that brings together related disciplines such as mechanical and electrical engineering, computer and behavioral science, and industrial and environmental design, but also as an object of design that gives rise to new personal relations between humans and technology. Dominantly, the appearance of a social robot appears to be shaped based on a 'sameness' relation, resulting in robots that look like humans or animals, and raising expectations that their expression and modes of interaction are alike humans or animals. Even though these efforts move forward research and development in social robotics, as interaction designers (and non-roboticists), we see an important role to keep open the design space of social robots by shaping alternative designs that are inspired by aspects that are usually left out or of less concern to roboticists. As such, in this work we are motivated by what could be called a *reconfiguration of the remainder* [11, cf. 36]. This refers to stretching the boundaries of a design space in a deliberately provocative manner, to encourage a broader understanding of the possibilities for design. Following such an approach, we aim to expose perspectives and assumptions in social robot design, put forth critical and novel perspectives for the design of human-robot relations, and inspire and raise reflections on dominant trajectories in social robot design [33, 11].

As contestational objects that invert assumptions and exaggerate excluded qualities we designed the Blo-Nut and the Lat-Sac. Firstly, as an inquiry into an alternative appearance, expression and mode of interaction with social robots, and secondly to understand how it could affect and inspire different human-social robot relationships. The two social robots are purposefully moving away from typical robot designs that look like humans or animals, or a kinetic expression is driven by the achievement of specific goals. Instead, the two social robots are driven by dexterous movements, to give privilege to novel forms of expressivity. In the process of giving form to the robots, we engaged experts who are literate in an expressive language in what we call *choreographic sketching* [38] of the two robots' behavior. For this, we created an interface that non-programmers can use to easily design a dynamic expression and in real-time experience the result. Through these collaborative efforts we intended to gain a wider understanding of the qualities of expressive movement, and explore and exploit the width of design expressions that the individual robots offer. As an inquiry into the possible human-social robot relationships that emerge in interaction with the Blo-Nut and Lat-Sac, and in order to productively engage people with the social robots, we created a fictitious near-future scenario. This scenario positioned the two robots in a story world for which the robots were prototyped [25], in order to create a discursive space for imagination and reflection.

Overall, this work can be framed as a critical note to dominant appearances and expressions of social robots, and

DIS '18, June 9–13, 2018, , Hong Kong

ACM ISBN 978-1-4503-5198-0/18/06…$15.00
https://doi.org/10.1145/3196709.3196743

an encouragement of the exploration of alternative approaches, appearances and expression of their design.

SOCIAL ROBOTS

Social robotics is a growing research and design field that is recognized by dedicated journals and conferences (e.g. the International Journal of Social Robotics and the International Conference on Social Robotics) and the multidisciplinary field of Human-Robot Interaction (HRI). Social robots are distinguished from for example industrial robots or military robots by their mode of interaction and purpose of engaging in communicative exchanges with people, *to serve human needs beyond those of labor or common notions of work* [11, p.58]. Most social robots sit between industrial or academic research labs and the consumer market or make their appearance in various forms of fiction. For example, the iCat (Philips), Probo (Free University Brussels) and Huggable (MIT) are research artefacts that are used to respectively investigate robotic facial expressions [1], expression of emotions [31], and affective touch [35]; while the AIBO (Sony), PARO (AIST) and Jibo (MIT Spin off) are consumer products to respectively support companionship, elicit emotional attachment and commitment, and act as partner in the smart home. In fiction, and science-fiction in particular, films such as *I, Robot* (2004), *Ex Machina* (2015) or *Bicentennial Man* (1999) present relations with robots as helper or in adversarial or substitute roles of humans. In terms of designing and researching social robotics, all these efforts are important to explore the possible relations and form-factors of social robots, to aid developers and a wider audience in identifying and speculating about desirable relations and concerns.

Appearance

Notably, what all the above examples of social robots share, is a *visually* oriented approach that focusses on a human-like (anthropomorphic) or animal-like (zoomorphic) appearance [14]. Historically, this is not surprising as the introduction of the word *robot* in the science fiction play *R.U.R.* (1920) referred to artificial people made from synthetic organic manner. However, it is more likely that it can be attributed to an underlying assumption in robot-design, in that resembling a life form eases the acceptance of the robot as a social entity. Or, that the familiarity of appearance and behavior eases the comprehension of social signals and communication with a social robot [32]. Nonetheless, the downside of in particular an anthropomorphic appearance and expression of social robots is that people generally expect a match between a robots' appearance and behavior – it misleadingly suggests that it has the same intellectual capabilities as humans [12]. The 'uncanny valley' is a well-known concept therein, which suggests that if a robot appears and behaves too much like a human, but that it simultaneously is still clearly a robot, it will evoke a feeling of uneasiness or eeriness [27]. It is even posed that anthropomorphic appearances of social robots pose a threat to human distinctiveness, because too much similarity blurs category boundaries that undermines human uniqueness [14]. The desire to create an anthropomorphic robot imposes certain human limitations upon the robot, while alternative and perhaps more appropriate form factors and means of communication are overlooked [12, 32].

Expression

For social robots, a static human or animal like appearance itself is not required in interpreting the machine as a living and social entity. Bartneck argues that the *experience of animation* and the perception of them is crucial for successful HRI [3], while Breazeal describes social robots as the class of robots that people anthropomorphize in order to interact with them [7]. This emphasizes the character of people's relation with robots, and not the robot's appearance in itself. Many computational machines are already experienced on the border of animate and inanimate [37] as people have a tendency to anthropomorphize and to attribute feelings, thoughts and emotions to other entities, such as cars, computers and other machines [34]. Moving a robot machine into the social realm thus requires a focus on expression and not necessarily appearance. However, the expression of a robot through its movement in space is often resulting from a more *pragmatic* approach, where the expression is driven by the robot's requirements to achieve physical goals. This typically results in a mechanical expression and an appearance that looks like an assembly of electromechanical limbs [20]. Both a pragmatic and visual design approach position the design of the robots' expression later in the process. Instead, focusing on the expressive motion and the timing of a robot's motion allows for a plurality of appearances and aroused emotions [8], and for the character of the human-robot relation to develop.

In previous work we have introduced *performing objects* as a way to playfully explore provocative expressions of soft robotic objects [37]. Essentially, this was a shift from developing robots with a function in mind to developing robots with a focus on aesthetic and performative qualities. Through explorations in form, material, and movement, we designed a series of provocative performative objects to embrace aspects that are usually by-products of robot design, such as humorous, appalling, or intriguing complex movement forms. The use of soft robotics worked particularly well in designing expressions, as soft robotics use compliant materials that have similar qualities to those found in organically moving living organisms. Similar to performing objects, Hoffman and Ju [20] proposed an expressive movement centric design approach in interactive robot design, to communicate, engage and offer dynamic possibilities that go beyond the physical form factors or pragmatic motion paths. This prioritizes the communicative aspects of movement in the design of robots, to more accurately express the robot's intent, personality, and intelligence, among others [20]. With an interest in the communicative and expressive movement qualities of

Figure 1. Social Robots: a) The Blo-Nut; b) Blo-Nut actuated; c) The Lat-Sac; d) Lat-Sac removed from its base

robots, performing objects and an expressive movement centric approach both open up to the design of social robots that emphasize their movement qualities.

Modes of Interaction

Labeling a robot as social creates certain expectations about its purpose, functionality and consequent interaction. This interaction is often labelled as communication, to acknowledge the robot as an entity that can be communicated with. For human-like social robots, cybernetic, sociocultural and socio-psychological theories of communication are often employed to reinforce the idea of the robot as another human [32]. Such theories emphasize commonalities with humans, and value the use of humanlike communication channels (voice, facial expressions, bodily gestures), and value the notion of 'sameness'. Instead of this notion of 'sameness' in HRI, the notion of 'otherness' may introduce developers to new forms of robots that see and interpret the world differently, to avoid the 'reduplication of self' [28] and 'the elimination of difference' [29].

Phenomenologically, *the other* is the entity in contrast to which an identity is constructed, and thus assumes the existence of an alternative viewpoint [24]. Otherness in human-robot relations refers to the idea that the robot appears as *an other* that is different from ourselves. In Verbeek and Ihde's terms this means that the relationship with robot technology can be understood as a *quasi-alterity* relation [21, 38], where the robot appears to us as not a thing but as *a quasi-other* entity. This emphasizes the importance of a constant recognition and acknowledgement for its difference, and empowers the idea of the robot as an alive machine [32] The closest 'living non-human' – human relationship through which we can understand the qualities of such relationship is the animal – human relationship. As an alterity relation with animals, in the sense of their individual personalities and representatives of species, their behavior and demeanor can grant insight into our own experience [10, 34].

Alternative Social Robot Design

To stretch the boundaries of social robot design, it is important to expose the dominant perspectives and assumptions in their design, and to give form to excluded alternative possibilities and approaches [11]. These agonistic activities can act both as a critique and as an inquiry, keeping open a pluralism of design engagements. For this work, it means opposing social robots' common appearances and pragmatic-based expression: tempering zoo- and anthropomorphism and embracing the expressive potential of the robot as a quasi-other. As formulated by Sandy, it is often alternative designs that can push the boundaries of what is possible when humans interact with social robots that are not humanlike or animal like in appearance [33]. Our intention is to encourage, through such acts of design, the development of a broader understanding of the possible relations with social robots. We believe that this wider take on social robots is necessary, as they are increasingly imagined as solutions to various healthcare situations (e.g. care robots, therapy robots) or in domestic environments (e.g. companion robots, play robots), and thus are projected to increasingly play a role in people's lives.

Based on the above design intentions, we describe the Blo-Nut and the Lat-Sac. It is important to note both robots are rooted in and developed from our prior work on *performing objects* [37], which means that the presented robots are not emerging from a social robot community of practice. However, exactly as we take an alternative point of departure, we see potential in how they could offer novel valuable insight to social robot design.

THE LAT-SAC AND BLO-NUT

We designed the Lat-Sac and Blo-Nut as an inquiry into an alternative appearance and expression and secondly to study modes of interaction and possible relations that could emerge with the social robots. For the robot as a social entity, we were inspired by the role and related expression of a dog laying in the corner of a room, with a low, continuous murmuring sound. In line with Sparrow, who argued that the idea of robot dogs comforting and entertaining lonely older persons is both misguided and unethical [34], the idea of the dog in the corner of the room did not mean that our intention was to literally replace pets, nor that we tried to *replicate* the appearance, expression and interaction with a pet. Rather, the presence of a pet embodied qualities that we were inspired by, and following Coeckelbergh [10], it phenomenologically comes the closest through which we can understand the qualities of the relationship. It reflects an entity that plays with being in the foreground and background of the attention through minimal or sudden expressions; an entity that supports setting atmosphere in context; and an entity that offers its

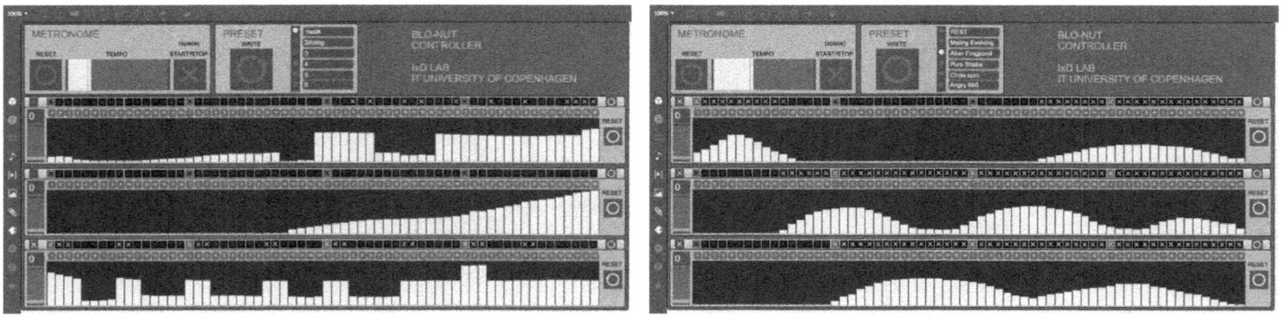

Figure 2. Examples of two designed choreographies: a) Performing artist's 'Mating Evolving'; b) Digital artist's 'The Walk'

availability as interactor. A social robot that takes on such a role allowed us to focus attention on movement expression and appearance first, opposing a more specification driven or visual oriented approach.

We deliberately worked with elasticity and air actuation as seen in soft robotics, as this combination has several benefits in terms of the variety of appearance and expression offered: appearance wise, elastic materials can handle distorting forces and return to an original shape once that force is removed, allowing for a range of different appearances; and expressivity wise, elastic material allows for a play between elastic limits and these different appearances that look and feel organic. As humans have muscles, and humans as living organisms perceive the world in terms of their own body [16], mobilizing elasticity in social robot design opens opportunities for relating to them as alive entities.

The Lat-Sac and Blo-Nut

We named our first robot the Lat-Sac (Figure 1c). The robot is made out of latex and has three plastic tubes connected to it using brass couplings. The latex sack houses three balloons that can each inflate and deflate. It has an acrylic and 3d printed base in which the Lat-Sac can be placed or be removed from (Figure 1d).

We named our second robot the Blo-Nut (Figure 1a). The robot has a shape that roughly resembles a donut, with a plastic 3d printed bottom shell, and a top made from silicone that houses three independently inflatable segments. These can be actuated by blowing air into the pockets between 3D printed inserts and the soft silicone skin. For a detailed account of the design process of the Blo-Nut robot we refer to [38].

Hardware and Interface

Both the Lat-Sack and the Blo-Nut are controlled using the same interface and hardware. One Arduino drives, for each of the three inflatable chambers, a vacuum pump, a solenoid valve, and a motor control board. Three plastic tubes are connecting the robot with this hardware setup (Figure 3a).

The interface is made in Max/MSP, which is often used as music making software, and allows for real time manipulation of the robots. It provides 64 input possibilities for sequential control for each inflatable segment (Figure 2, the 3 rows), in which the strength of the motor can be set (Figure 2, the bars), together with whether or not solenoid is open (Figure 2, the checkboxes above the bars). The overall tempo of the patch can be set to determine the time taken to execute the 64 steps (Figure 2, slider in metronome section). Up to 6 choreographies can be stored in one patch.

DESIGNING ROBOT EXPRESSIONS WITH EXPERTS

As an inquiry into the act of giving form to social robots in alternative expressive ways, we invited three experts who are literate in an expressive language: a contemporary dancer, a digital artist, and a performing artist. We asked these experts to collaboratively explore the width of communication that the Lat-Sac and Blo-Nut can offer, particularly in their physical expression using the previously described designed interface (see Figure 2). Each session took around 75 minutes, where we emphasized participants' role as experts in an expressive form language. We felt this was important in scene-setting, to direct the sessions towards playful explorations, rather than the experts feeling engaged in a formal experiment. We then demonstrated the different features of the interface and gradually left them to explore and get comfortable with these features. We recommended to keep the choreography running at all times, to merge acts of choreographing with acts of experiencing and stimulate continuous reflection. Following the emerging conversation with the design material, we asked the experts to name their designed choreography once they were satisfied with it. The creation of one choreography took approximately 20 minutes. Lastly, we discussed interactive features.

Notably, our expert engagement was deliberately *not* conducted conceptually by for example acting out expressive behaviors [cf. 30]. Instead it was done by engaging the experts directly in shaping the computational material of the robots. Through such setup we intended to avoid a replication of self in the robot's behavior, avoid an elimination of difference between humans and robots, and to embrace and exploit the opportunities offered by the design material [32].

Figure 3. Engaging experts in designing expressions: a) Setup with programming interface, hardware and Blo-Nut; choreographing session with the b) contemporary dancer and c) performing artist

Associations drive Expressions

During the three sessions many associations came up that inspired the design of the expressions. Associations ranged from things (e.g. an organ in a church, toys, a massage chair), flora and fauna (e.g. a small sea creature, an alive plant, a frog pond), activities or processes (e.g. meditation, a walk, a conversation, a mating dance, a metamorphosis of a fictitious creature), movies starring aliens and space ships, or the 'attack-decay-sustain-release' envelope as seen in electronic music making. The performance artist for example described one of his choreographies as: *It could also be a mating dance, like a mating ritual, That it blows up and shows how big it can become, and then, zjup* (making a shrinking movement with his hand), *because danger arrives or something and it cannot continue its dance...* to then name this choreography as 'mating evolving' (see Figure 2a). Similarly, the contemporary dancer described her choreography as *it's kind of like a frog pond. But like a robotic ambient frog pond. Like in the middle of the night.* The digital artist described one of his choreographies (see Figure 2b) as a conversation: *I named it 'the walk' because I wanted to explore the one-two step thing further... to make it like a three legged jumpy thing. Like a dialogue or whatever it is called when you have three partners.* The width and variety of these associations signaled firstly that the experts were able to mobilize their creativity in the shaping of the expressions, but also that the robots and technological setup had a certain openness that invited a plurality of associations.

Expressions beyond the Interface

Especially the digital artist questioned our designed interface as a means for choreographic sketching of expressions. Firstly, the interface might afford 'filling up' the three rows with bars: *You could almost be seduced by the interface and want to fill it up and draw things.* 'Filling up' was regarded as negative, as silence is a well-known affective communicative component [cf. 22] that the digital artist was actively exploring. Secondly, he saw a discrepancy between the interface and the resulting effect: *There is a difference between the pure-ness of the interface and what the thing does... Actually there is more advanced expressiveness in the physical object than that is available seen up here.* However, this discrepancy was later regarded as a playful component: *There is this playing around with the pure-ness and the trustworthiness of the interface and how the real world behaves. It's so much more fun down here* (where the object was). This showed us the important difference between the geometrical graphical representation of the whole choreography in the interface, and the actual experience of the choreography in its complexity and play between the three air chambers and their dynamic transitions. This emphasized the need for quick feedback-loops between the creation of the expression and the experience: *there is a certain friction between the command and what to expect, which is a thing to explore.* Thirdly, each air chamber could be programmed using 64 steps in total, and each of the chambers always ran at the same tempo. To have a wider and more complex expressive range that stays surprising and novel over longer periods of time, the digital artist proposed to have the ability to change the tempo and number of steps for each chamber individually: *...this is Western styled rhythm. You have three things playing in parallel, but they have the same number of steps. So you never get this phase difference going on. If it is possible to make one say 8 long, and another one 5, and 11, that don't divide easily, you can make things that do not repeat for a long while.* Combined, these comments showed how the expressive range of the choreographies could be exploited more by offering different control structures, even though the actual experience of them already offered complex expressions.

Expressions as Multisensory

The air pumps and valves that were controlling the air chambers were sealed off to block their noise, however the noise wasn't muted completely. The more voltage that ran through the pumps as set through the interface, the louder the resulting noise. Also, the valves produced a typical air releasing sound when they were opened. These sounds and the designed expression were thus tightly coupled, and it became difficult for the participants to separate it from the choreography. The performing artist found ways to actively play with the noise in the design of the expression. He tried to find a balance between the air pumped into the chambers and the amount of power needed for it to block out the noise as much as possible: *so if I do like this... it will blow up soundless*, resulting in a composition that played with the notion of aliveness: *it makes it very not-human, nor animal, but it still has life. It gets this alienated feeling, that it maybe communicates through this kind of noise that is not very organic, but it still moves organically.* He then played with the combination of the motor making a continuous noise and slowly bringing in motion by opening the valves occasionally: *With this constant drone in the background and then, suddenly, it becomes like... a soundscape and a moving thing at once.* The latter part of the first row in Figure 2a illustrates how that motor is activated (the bars) yet the valve is just occasionally opened (the x's). In one exploration the sound even became the main object of composition: *This very old movie, have you seen it? There's this big alien spaceship coming down and they have to communicate through sounds, and then they, there's this very iconic soundscape that they use for communicating with aliens. I was like, can I get that into it.* The digital artist regarded the noise as unwanted yet also tightly coupled to the designed expression: *I'm trying to avoid listening to the sounds, but it doesn't make sense not to listen to the sound.* He saw a synergy with not just the visual expression and the auditory, but also the auditory and the tactile, as articulated while holding the Blo-Nut: *You see a lot of devices move in the everyday, but you don't* feel *that many devices. So I really like the feel of it, to feel the thing. For me, the motor control is the audio part, and the tactile, the thing I feel most, is the inflation and deflation.* Even though our intention was to focus particularly on the visual expressive motion of the social robots in the expert engagements, the holistic nature of an expression became apparent through the auditory and the tactile considerations.

Performance versus Interactivity

As part of the choreographic sketching sessions we speculated about the interactive or communicative aspects of the robots. The digital artist mainly thought in terms of handling and actions, but was struggling to go beyond direct mapping especially in light of the more complex choreographies: *An almost too obvious thing would be to control the tempo based on input. If it was different, I would really love the idea of to be able to squeeze, and then somehow change what is going on.* He asked himself what the robot would be able to sense: *But still, using the sensor inside as an input. For what? If the sensor should change some behavior besides the speed, what would it be?* To then embrace other aspects of the physical design material: *As an experiment, you have three chambers in here, and if I sort of port the flow toward one chamber, that one could inflate more. How would you experience this?* As an interactive object, he struggled moving away from associations with the animal: *It's super hard for me at least, to avoid this, putting the animal into the thing. But probably as well, because even looking at it, you rarely see things bulk like this, if it is a living thing it is a living animal* to then return to his previous association of the sea monster: *...even though it is this sea monster, it has the size and a behavior a cute thing. So probably when you have this aggressive growing thing, you want to calm it down by stroking it.* The performing artist extended the idea of a performance when asked about interactivity: *it could be like integrated in some kind of costume... As in a performance where it becomes a kind of costume but it is also a performance in itself. A play between me and what it is. Is it scenography, is it a performing thing, or is it a costume?* We recognized that by focusing the inquiry on expressivity, the design and understanding of the interactive, communicative, and social aspects of the robots warranted a different design research approach.

The design session with the experts showed us how both associations and the constraints of the interface aided the shaping of a holistically perceived expression. The engagements led to six designed and articulated choreographies, which showed us the potential in the robots' expressive range. And that the involvement of expert others in the design process is needed to fully recognize alternative movement expressions. Further, the session with the digital artist led to concrete recommendations for the graphical interface that could lead to additional possibilities for expression. However, as expression was our main focus, we downplayed the object of design as a social entity. This explained why it was hard to move away from the object as a performing object, or an object of expression alone.

IMAGINING ROBOT RELATIONS

From the engagements with experts it not unsurprisingly became clear that the interactive and social aspects of the Lat-Sac and Blo-Nut were dependent on a situation of use [cf. 32, 10]. To explore possible emerging robot relationships, we thus needed to frame the robots in a role or context to understand the nature of a possible emerging relation with them. In line with our critical take on a subject matter, we borrowed from speculative approaches to design in our staging of the robots. These approaches provide concepts such as a perceptual bridge [2] to explore the desirability of relations with emerging technological possibilities, and to provoke curiosity and discussion around issues embodied by the design. To establish a discursive space we created a fictional element, a near future story world [25], that was grounded in a familiar or logical reality [cf. 2], in which the Lat-Sac and Blo-Nut were positioned.

November 2021.

The discovery by The Danish Centre for Animal Welfare (DCAW) that pets often suffer from Aboulomania* while kept in a domestic environment has led to an unanticipated and forceful societal response. Keeping for example dogs, cats, hamsters, rabbits or reptiles at home is now frowned upon in many countries.

Mo-tio Inc. are attempting to exploit this gap in the market by developing unique, responsive and expressive behaviors capable

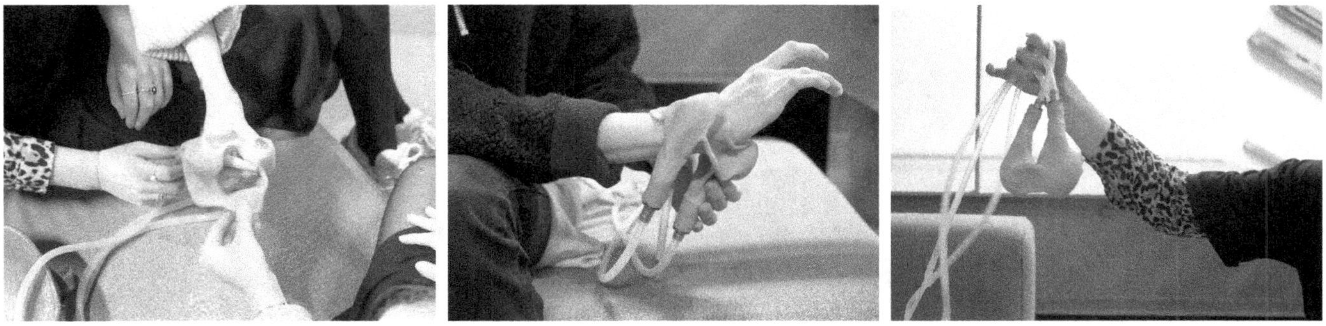

Figure 4. Study participants' engagement with the Lat-Sac.

of evoking emotional responses. The first round of Mo-tio prototypes are dubbed 'The Others'. It is expected that future customers can submit requests for their own 'Other', forming a unique blueprint to start a potentially unpredictable characterization process.

The 'Others' presented here are the first prototypes for evaluation outside the Mo-tio labs. They are beginning to develop their own body language and are starting to show signs of personality and response to human interaction...

**Aboulomania is a mental disorder in which the patient displays pathological indecisiveness. It is typically associated with anxiety, stress, depression, and mental anguish.*

This scenario speaks of 'responsive product movement', to emphasize the expressivity of the Lat-Sac and Blo-Nut and to acknowledge a certain level of interaction with them. This still is deliberately quite abstract (a human-animal relationship is highly dependent on type of animal and people's personal preferences [10]), but it allowed us to keep open a variety of possible emerging relations. Which motivates why we framed them as prototypes for future pets, and not necessarily as finished products. In relation to this setup, it is worth mentioning Dunne and Raby's technological dreams series [13], which is a collection of furniture inspired robots that have their own intelligence and capabilities, designed to stir reflection on possible and desirable relations with domestic robots. Our work also opens up and asks questions about possible relationships with social robots, however, it differs in terms of our focus on exploring these relations with a focus on kinetic expression.

We invited three groups (a total of nine participants, P1-P2, P3-P5, P6-P9) with a background in digital design or design and communication to discuss the robots. Each group session took place in a public coffee place, and took approximately 60 minutes. First, we handed over the above imaginative scenario to suspend disbelief [26], and to create a safe space for speculation and reflection [23]. Next, we handed over a description of the robot that was going to be discussed, in the format of a confidential document from the imagined company Mo-tio Inc. Even though the robots housed sensors, one of the authors live simulated the behavior of the Lat-Sac and Blo-Nut in response to how they were manipulated, without the participants knowing. This illusion of the robots being interactive offered us the possibility to use the choreographies form the experts, and to meaningfully tweak transitions between them.

Between Animal and Machine, Pet and Consumer Product

All of the participants actively contributed to the group discussion, and none of the participants seemed to be alienated by the fictitious scenario. As P2 noted in the middle of a discussion: *But I guess when you are in 2021 and you are trying to save pets from depression, then it is a different experience,* which signaled to us that the scenario was imaginable as a possible world. This could be attributed to the environment and playfulness of the of inquiry, but also as the prototypes were robust and technically working [6]. However, even though the situation was perceived as possible, it was not straightforward for the groups to conceptualize the robots.

The framing of the robots as pets raised particular expectations from the robots that were not always met. It was put forward by several participants that a pet is excited when you come home, that it can be soft and soothing to have a pet, but also that pets require feeding and care, such as walking the dog. This raised expectations with respect to handling the robots as well, e.g. P4 mentioned while P6 was pressing the Blo-Nut: *You are not supposed to do that with pets you know*, or, as P1 in first contact started to carefully handle the Blo-Nut: *the fact you frame it as a pet immediately has a connotation as something that you are gentle with.* Exactly which domesticated animal the robots resembled was source for discussion, e.g. the surface of the Blo-Nut was *like you are touching the belly of a dog* (P2), its weight was *almost too light, like these little tiny hamsters* (P1), the tubes and object combined looked like a snake (P9), or a cat *because it does take care of itself* (P7) and because it sounded like purring in one of the choreographies (P2, P6). The Lat-Sac moved away from resemblance with a pet, into an alikeness with other animals or parts thereof, e.g. a plucked chicken (P2, P4), the udders of a cow (P9, P5), the ear of a pig (P3), or a spineless sea creature like an octopus (P1). Lat-Sac's immobility in combination with its appearance also positioned it as a plant or organism, or a mix of an animal and a plant: *it has a root, a ground source, it needs to be hooked up* (P2

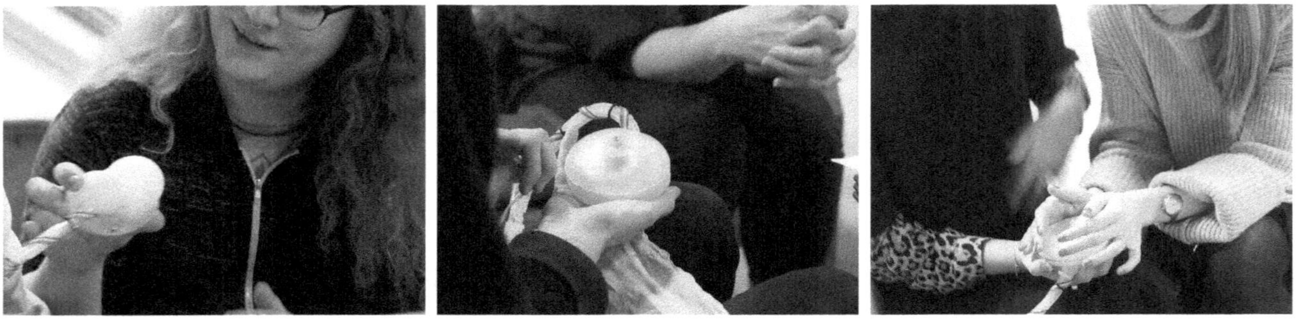

Figure 5. Study participants' engagement with the Blo-Nut.

referring to the tubes); *it's like a plant that you would see in the background of an alien movie* (P8); or, *it falls somewhere between plants and something that has a degree of agency* (P7). Besides the impressions of the robots as alive entities, the Blo-Nut in particular was at the same time seen as a gadget (P1), consumer product (P6), hospital equipment (P2, P3, P9), or laboratory prototype (P3), as *the plastic materials, and the metal, the screw, the bolt, the wires, silicone, make the appearance artificial* (P6) or for its *medical, transparency look* (P9). The Blo-Nut moved towards a machine for some participants, in particular because of its hard shell (P1), geometric appearance (P2, P6), and connotations with a respirator (P2).

The Lat-Sac and the Blo-Nut seemed hard to conceptualize, as they evoked the combination of an alive entity that is a product or machine at the same time. Or in Verbeek's terms [38], the participants both experienced an alterity relation and a hermeneutic relation with the robots. This led to on the one hand a desire to keep the robots alive, e.g. P5 when the Lat-Sac was unplugged from the tubes: *Oh! Oh it died. It's really dead now. Poor thing. Kind of disgusting*, or P2: *can I go on vacation for 14 days and then come home and it's still there?*, but on the other hand it made P6 wonder what happened when the robot was conceived as consumer product: *I would say that your relation with it depends a lot on whether you can turn it on or off. Then you choose to interact with it, so you go to turn it on and then enjoy the experience of it. But if it is always on, always expressing something, you might develop another relationship to it. It also depends if it was a house appliance. Would you just leave it around in your living room, or would you put it away in a closet and take it out whenever you need it?*

The above discussions revealed possible conceptualizations of the robots, which all inevitably lead to different emerging relationships. At a basic level, the discussions showed us that when an artefact is perceived to be alive, it can also be dead or off. We find that conceptualizing the robot as an 'alive machine' [cf. 32] captures our findings of the social robots as perceived living entities that can be switched on and off, which we believe is an inspiring notion for further exploration and design research.

Alive and Breathing

The expressions of the Lat-Sac and Blo-Nut mostly provided impressions of them being alive, as the actuation of the robots was associated with breathing, e.g. P2 with respect to the Blo-Nut: *even though this shape is not something that you would recognize from any animal like alive thing, then you can still really easily see that it is alive, because it is breathing that you can recognize*, or P5 about the Lat-Sac: *it is like suffering, or it is like really tired. And this looks like breathing now.* This perception of breathing was however not consistent and differed per choreography, e.g. P1, *it is a little bit difficult for me to associate it with breathing, because it is also not regular, it is more the way in which it is moving around* or P4 who re-enacted a dog panting and argued that the robots do not express themselves like that. Nonetheless, as potential alive entities, the Lat-Sac and Blo-Nut seemed to express emotions. For P3-P5, their expressive range was positioned on a scale from stressed to calm (e.g. as P3 was stroking the Lat-Sac, P5: *You are upsetting it,* P4: *You stress it out,* P5: *Don't kill it,* P3: *It likes me, haha, I was calming it*). Upon reflection P4 articulates that *stress contains all the negative feelings* to which P5 replies: *because it is so much about the breathing. Normally you are just able to decide if someone is relaxed or stressed by their breathing.* P1-P2 mostly talked about the robots being either more alive and independent or less alive and calm, while P6-P9 projected a wider range of states onto the robots, e.g. as excited, helpless, tired, agitated, angry, comfortable, and calm.

The use of air actuation in combination with the various designed choreographies played a big role in perceiving the robots as alive, which was attributed to the association with breathing or explained by the movement of the robots. The way in which the robots were seen alive however seemed to be restricted to a limited range of emotional or bodily states.

Reciprocity of Sociality

Before and during the sessions we deliberately did not mention our research intention in social robotics, as we were interested in how the robot's appearance and expression reinforces beliefs about what it means to be social [cf. 11]. As mentioned before, relating the robots to pets set particular expectations about the role of the Lat-Sac and Blo-Nut, and the social character of the emerging relation. This included personal preferences towards particular pets, e.g. several participants recalled what it was like having dogs, hamsters, or cats, and the role they had in their live. These were not necessarily positive memories, e.g. P2 recalled her dog running away from her just before he died, or P4's, who expressed her dislike for cats in her handling of the Lat-Sac (Figure 4c): *that's how you would hold a cat. At its tail.* The personal experiences with entities that were associated with the two robots should thus be taken into consideration in understanding emerging relations. P4, because of her dislike for cats, saw an opportunity for having the Lat-Sac at home: *You could have it at your place, to show it to people. This is my pet! I don't need like a real one, I can have this one, showing it off.* This ties into the notion of popularity as a salient source of pleasure or as a means of providing a worthwhile experience [18]. Along the same lines, P6 saw the Blo-Nut as an object that you could use to achieve a similar experience: *you could have in your purse, like a Chihuahua.* The character of the relation was dependent on what the robots did in return. Besides popularity, being stimulated was identified as another potential quality, e.g. the Blo-Nut was *better to hold in your hand, you can sit in the couch and just watch the TV or something* (P8); or P1 and P2 who mostly held the Blo-Nut with the soft part in their hands to have a *sensation* (Figure 5b); or P1 who placed the Lat-Sac around her wrist (Figure 4b): *there is something soothing wearing it, because then you can feel the inflation on both sides of it.*

However, it was still hard for participants to identify what the robots could do for them and to articulate the character of the relation, e.g. P4: *Because also, what does this give to you?*, to which P3 replied: *a pet loves you back.* This ties into the norm of reciprocity, which in social human to human interaction *may lead individuals to establish relations only or primarily with those who can reciprocate* [17, p.178]. In interaction with the robots, it was thus not entirely clear how the robots reciprocated. This can be explained by the lack of control over the robots (partially due to the live simulation) or, that the kind of control usually felt in interaction with a pet was missing, e.g. P9: *If you were able to be more aware of what it is reacting to, then you'd be more interactive with it*, and P7: *I don't really understand what I am doing that triggers it. Because I would know with a real pet what I would do to calm it, how it would react to me.* Besides the felt lack of control, it was also not clear how the robots were depending on a caretaker for their survival: *It doesn't need human care or anything, also it doesn't need food, I guess you can just count the air as food, so it can kind of take care of itself* (P3). The participant felt unsure if she was really needed and thus taking part in the relationship with the robots. As in [19], we found debate around the value of machines that are autonomous in pet like ways and that have no apparent function.

These mixed relations of the robots on the one hand providing experiences that could stimulate or enhance popularity, and on the other hand, of the robots not being able to reciprocate, showed that they were exhibiting behavior that could be understood as social, yet that the interaction with the robots was not necessarily social. This can be attributed to the live simulation of the robots' expression in the group sessions and the lack of felt control or need, or that there was only a single meeting with the robots (e.g. P3 regarding the Lat-Sac: *it grows on you. In the beginning you think it is more gross, now it is better*, or P2 upon reflection: *this is more, you experience it, you get this emotional and physical attachment*). This hints to the idea that the Lat-Sac and Blo-Nut, when confronted with new eyes, bring *closer the potentially radical Otherness of worlds to come* [9, p.134].

DISCUSSION

In designing the Lat-Sac and Blo-Nut, we have purposefully shaped an atypical, non-human nor clear animal like appearance and expression. Even though resembling a known life form could ease the acceptance of a robot as a social entity or the comprehension of social signals coming from it, we believe that designs grounded in a principle of 'sameness' unnecessarily narrow their design space. In giving privilege to novel forms of expressivity combined with an alternative appearance that is open for interpretation, we find how designs grounded in a principle of 'otherness' could overcome the duplication of self or the elimination of difference, and open up to alternative ways for communication rooted in kinetic expression. In this discussion we want to point to aspects that we found valuable therein, both in the act of giving form to the robots, and the growing of relations with them.

Acknowledging Otherness in Giving Form

Giving form to social robots and ensuring a sense of their otherness means acknowledging that they are, and have abilities that are, not clearly human or animal. In this process we found value in exploring alternative appearances and expressions that on the one hand are interpretable as alive entities, but on the other hand are provocative and invite for a plurality of associations. This requires methods and platforms for designing that go beyond the limitations of the human body, and that provide designers with more nuanced methods for creation. By enabling designers to explore the expressive range that the computational robot material affords, the motion of the robot is factored in from the onset. We found value in especially those materials that invite for playful explorations, such as elastic materials and music-making software that allow a direct experience of a sketched choreography. Additionally, the engagements of experts who are literate in an expressive language can not only inspire new associations, but also bring to the foreground how to mobilize important choreographic building blocks (e.g. the silence or pause, or the inclusion of other modalities) and inform the shaping of the methods of creation. It is in these activities that we see opportunities for recognizing that the social robot can become an alive machine that is capable of doing different things than humans or animals, inviting for a different kind of relation to grow.

Acknowledging Otherness and Growing Relations

Encountering otherness means encountering differences between the familiar and the unfamiliar. By fictitiously staging the robots in the role of pets we observed emerging relations that were curious and provoking, and not straightforward for the participants to conceptualize. The unfamiliarity of the robots resulted in a natural attempt to comprehend through known elements of the human-animal relation. Though for the participants this did not lead to satisfying conceptualizations in terms of framing the robots as an animal, pet, consumer product or machine. The 'alive machine' [cf. 32] points to an appearance and expression of robots that is open to interpretation, and therein we see an opportunity for social robot design and further design research. The playful and curious character of the relationship with such an alive machine could potentially keep open a certain width and variety of communication that leads to the robots remaining interesting over longer periods of time. Differences should then be seen as an asset rather than a difficulty that must be overcome, leading to novel intriguing relations. Short as the encounters with the robots were, there were hints of intriguing and growing relationships, as reflected in the continuous articulation of associations and the initial perceived emotional expression of the robots. However, to move the social character of the human robot relation from an exhibited behavior to an interactive behavior warrants further work in utilizing the sensing capacities of the robots, to continue the exploration of notions of control and the felt recognition of self in the emerging relationship.

Acknowledging otherness in the process of giving form to, and growing relations with social robots hopefully encourages alternative form factors and interactions. The Lat-Sac and Blo-Nut are a start in one of the many directions for design that we have found constructive, and that we hope to use as stepping stones to future designs. As such, with this work we are not just posing a critique, but also offer designs and a design direction that stimulates a playful and believable shift towards alternatives.

ACKNOWLEDGMENTS

We thank our IxD Lab manager Ben Cahill for technical support throughout, and the design of the Max/MSP interface specifically; our three performance experts for their creative input; and our nine study participants for their insightful responses.

REFERENCES

1. Albert van Breemen, Xue Yan, and Bernt Meerbeek. 2005. iCat: an animated user-interface robot with personality. In *Proceedings of the fourth international joint conference on Autonomous agents and multiagent systems*, 143-144.
2. Auger, James. "Speculative design: crafting the speculation." *Digital Creativity* 24.1 (2013): 11-35.
3. Bartneck, Christoph, et al. "Does the design of a robot influence its animacy and perceived intelligence?" *International Journal of Social Robotics* 1.2 (2009): 195-204.
4. Bewley, Harvey, & Boer, Laurens. (2018) *Designing Blo-nut*: a Soft Robot Demonstrating The Potential of Otherness in Behavioural Artefacts. In *Proceedings of the 2018 Conference on Designing Interactive Systems.* ACM.
5. Bewley, Harvey, & Anna Vallgårda. (2017). Provoking Performing Objects: Expanding the Design Space for Soft Robotics. In *Proceedings of the 2016 ACM Conference Companion Publication on Designing Interactive Systems* (pp. 243-248). ACM.
6. Boer, Laurens, and Jared Donovan. "Provotypes for participatory innovation." *Proceedings of the designing interactive systems conference.* ACM, 2012.
7. Breazeal, Cynthia. "Toward sociable robots." *Robotics and autonomous systems* 42.3 (2003): 167-175.
8. Bretan, Mason, Guy Hoffman, and Gil Weinberg. "Emotionally expressive dynamic physical behaviors in robots." *International Journal of Human-Computer Studies* 78 (2015): 1-16.
9. Candy, Stuart. "The futures of everyday life: politics and the design of experiential scenarios." *Doctorat de philosophie en sciences politiques, Université d'Hawaï à Mānoa* (2010).
10. Coeckelbergh, Mark. "Humans, animals, and robots: A phenomenological approach to human-robot relations." *International Journal of Social Robotics* 3.2 (2011): 197-204.
11. DiSalvo, Carl. *Adversarial design.* The MIT Press, 2012.
12. Djajadiningrat, Tom, Ben Matthews, and Marcelle Stienstra. "Easy doesn't do it: skill and expression in tangible aesthetics." *Personal and Ubiquitous Computing* 11.8 (2007): 657-676.
13. Dunne, Anthony, and Fiona Raby. Speculative everything: design, fiction, and social dreaming. MIT Press, 2013.
14. Ferrari, Francesco, Maria Paola Paladino, and Jolanda Jetten. "Blurring human–machine distinctions: anthropomorphic appearance in social robots as a threat

to human distinctiveness." *International Journal of Social Robotics* 8.2 (2016): 287-302.

15. Fink, Julia. "Anthropomorphism and human likeness in the design of robots and human-robot interaction." *International Conference on Social Robotics*. Springer Berlin Heidelberg, 2012.
16. Gibson, James J. *The ecological approach to visual perception: classic edition*. Psychology Press, 2014.
17. Gouldner, Alvin W. "The norm of reciprocity: A preliminary statement." *American sociological review* (1960): 161-178.
18. Hassenzahl, Marc, Sarah Diefenbach, and Anja Göritz. "Needs, affect, and interactive products–Facets of user experience." *Interacting with computers* 22.5 (2010): 353-362.
19. Helmes, J., Taylor, A. S., Cao, X., Höök, K., Schmitt, P., & Villar, N. (2011, January). Rudiments 1, 2 & 3: design speculations on autonomy. In *Proceedings of the fifth international conference on Tangible, embedded, and embodied interaction* (pp. 145-152). ACM.
20. Hoffman, Guy, and Wendy Ju. "Designing robots with movement in mind." *Journal of Human-Robot Interaction* 3 1 (2014): 89-122.
21. Ihde, Don. *Technology and the lifeworld: From garden to earth*. Indiana University Press, 1990.
22. Jensen, J. Vernon. "Communicative functions of silence." *ETC: A Review of General Semantics* (1973): 249-257.
23. Koskinen, Ilpo, et al. *Design research through practice: From the lab, field, and showroom*. Elsevier, 2011.
24. Levinas, Emmanuel. *Totality and infinity: An essay on exteriority*. Vol. 1. Springer Science & Business Media, 1979.
25. Lindley, Joseph, and Paul Coulton. "Back to the future: 10 years of design fiction." Proceedings of the 2015 British HCI Conference. ACM, 2015.
26. Markussen, Thomas, and Eva Knutz. "The poetics of design fiction." *Proceedings of the 6th International Conference on Designing Pleasurable Products and Interfaces*. ACM, 2013.
27. Mori, Masahiro (1970) The uncanny valley. Energy 7:33–35
28. Peters John Durham (1999) Speaking into the air: a history of the idea of communication. University of Chicago Press, Chicago
29. Pinchevski, A. (2005) By way of interruption: Levinas and the ethics of communication. Dusquene University Press, Pittsburgh
30. Ross, Philip, and Stephan Wensveen. "Designing behavior in interaction: Using aesthetic experience as a mechanism for design." *International Journal of Design* 4.2 (2010).
31. Saldien, Jelle, et al. "Expressing emotions with the social robot Probo." *International Journal of Social Robotics* 2.4 (2010): 377-389.
32. Sandry, Eleanor. "Re-evaluating the form and communication of social robots." *International Journal of Social Robotics* 7.3 (2015): 335-346.
33. Sandry, Eleanor. *Robots and communication*. Springer, 2015.
34. Sparrow, Robert. "The march of the robot dogs." *Ethics and information Technology* 4.4 (2002): 305-318.
35. Stiehl, Walter Dan, et al. "The huggable: a therapeutic robotic companion for relational, affective touch." *ACM SIGGRAPH 2006 emerging technologies*. ACM, 2006.
36. Suchman, Lucy. *Human-machine reconfigurations: Plans and situated actions*. Cambridge University Press, 2007.
37. Turkle, Sherry. "The second self: Computers and the human spirit." (1984): 36-45.
38. Verbeek, Peter Paul (2006). Materializing morality. Design ethics and technological mediation. *31*(3), 361-380.

Designing Expressions of Movement Qualities

Jeroen Peeters
RISE Interactive
Umeå, Sweden
jeroen.peeters@ri.se

Ambra Trotto
RISE Interactive and
Umeå School of Architecture
Umeå, Sweden
ambra.trotto@ri.se

Abstract

Tango is a form of partner dancing in which two bodies sense one another, and move accordingly, in a dynamic, physical dialogue that is known for its subtle complexities, beauty and intimate experience. In *MoCap Tango*, we explore how we can build on our skills as designers to highlight and unravel these embedded qualities and use them as inspiration in designing interactions. In this pictorial, we invite the reader to actively participate in the designerly engagement that turns objective data into subjective expressions; highlighting the qualities embedded in the movements of professional dancers.

Authors Keywords

Z	W	X	T	R	O	F	F	E	A	E	C	A	P	S	N	J	Q
I	N	T	E	R	P	R	E	T	I	N	G	N	H	S	H	D	F
A	C	T	I	V	E	P	E	R	C	E	P	T	I	O	N	C	H
Q	T	N	E	M	E	V	O	M	G	N	I	K	C	A	P	N	U
P	R	R	I	V	G	G	N	I	S	S	E	R	P	X	E	A	F
Q	I	J	K	E	M	B	O	D	I	M	E	N	T	Q	Y	Z	Y
J	W	O	L	F	S	M	A	T	E	R	I	A	L	I	T	Y	R
S	I	S	Y	L	A	N	A	Y	L	R	E	N	G	I	S	E	D
U	C	M	N	I	M	S	H	S	I	S	C	C	H	S	D	L	B
E	G	L	R	U	P	E	R	S	P	E	C	T	I	V	E	F	H
R	E	E	M	I	T	R	E	P	R	E	S	E	N	T	I	N	G
D	E	S	I	G	N	R	E	S	E	A	R	C	H	Q	P	B	L
I	R	D	V	V	I	S	U	A	L	I	S	I	N	G	Y	P	X

ACM Classification Keywords

H.5.m. Information interfaces and presentation (e.g., HCI): Miscellaneous.

DIS '18, June 9–13, 2018, , Hong Kong

ACM ISBN 978-1-4503-5198-0/18/06...$15.00
https://doi.org/10.1145/3196709.3196805

Figure 1. A still from the first *MoCap Tango* performance. The dancers move in between a set of motion-capture cameras. Some of the round trackers that reflect infrared light for the motion-capture cameras can be seen on their clothing. The captured movement data is visualised in real-time on the projection screen in the space.

Introduction

MoCap Tango is an ongoing constructive design research project that was initiated with a public performance [11]. For this performance, a team of designers, researchers, developers and dancers collaborated, using interactive technologies to visualise elements of the movements of tango dancers in real-time. The design of this performance involved custom-made wearables worn by the dancers, a motion-capture system, custom-made software for the visualisations and a projection screen. The movement of the dancers was visualised on the projection screen, providing the audience with a new perspective on the dance performance

Background

Since its inception as a performance, the *MoCap Tango* project has developed as an overarching design research endeavour in which (design) knowledge emerging from movement, is expressed and applied in other domains. In previous publications [10, 11], we have unpacked how this process unfolds: how new design programs emerge as knowledge of the topic increases, and how new application areas are identified and explored.

The value of bodily movement for the interaction design research community is clear and has been developed along many different lines of investigation [5, 7-9]. In particular, theoretical underpinnings that assert a notion of embodiment, describe the way that we make sense of the world around us as fundamentally physical and social [1]. In part, different notions of embodiment have become popular within the community because they provide designers and researchers with handles to grasp the ephemeral and subjective nature of what an experience is and how it unfolds when people interact with a design, or with eachother, through a design.

In previous work [e.g. 12], we have contributed to the existing body of work [e.g. 13] around the design of aesthetic experiences in interactions. Typically, in such work we employ used a constructive design research [6] approach to design *for* an aesthetic experience: i.e. to design, prototype and build interactive artefacts with the aim of eliciting an aesthetic experience for people using this artefact, and through this better understand the qualities that may bring such an experience about.

In the *MoCap Tango* project, we employ a similar approach in what could be considered the opposite way. Here, we design *from* an experience: the act of tango dancing. We employ the knowledge, skills, and technologies available to a group of designers, researchers, developers and dancers to jointly expose and amplify the qualities we find in this experience with the aim of better understanding what these qualities are, and how they might be transposed into other domains of design.

In this pictorial, we refine this notion. What we are addressing here specifically, is one of the activities that is part of the design process of designing *from* an experience. A form of data-based analysis, but driven by a designerly way of understanding - and giving form to - the qualities within this data. This pictorial is therefore not about what we have learned about qualities of movement in various iterations of the *MoCap Tango* project. This pictorial is about exposing about *how* we are learning by doing in giving form to movement data.

Motivation

The urge to perform this exploration stems from the difficulty embedded in describing movement-based interactions and therefore the difficulty in abstracting qualities that can be used to design for embodiment. In this pictorial, we address this issue by going back to the foundations of the project: the expressivity of the body and the way in which design can expose, amplify and unpack such expressivity.

The DIS Pictorial format is one of the examples of formal publication venues that have started to explore ways to accomodate the richness of designed artifacts and the processes in which they are developed. Of particular interest here is previous work that uses the space opened up by, amongst others, the Pictorial format, to unpack processes in design research and expose the (tacit) knowledge the design researcher generates during such a process. Examples include Karana et al. [4] that unpack in great detail the journey of a designer as she explores the performative qualities of materials in design ideation, Jarvis et al.'s photo essay that reports on detailed design decisions [3]. Or, Dykes et al. [2] who demonstrate the value of comics as a way to communicate the narrative of a design research project more effectively than text alone.

What we haven't seen yet, in how the format of the pictorial has been developed so far, is an exploration on how the reader can be engaged differently than usual. In this pictorial, we aim to convey the embodied engagement of the designer and her process of giving form to abstraction through her skills, during part of the design research process: designerly analysis and expression of data.

Figure 2.
Visualisations of the data provide new perspectives on the movement. For example, by slowing time down or by enhancing embedded qualities. Such visualisations have in this project been developed as teaching material for tango, amongst other uses.

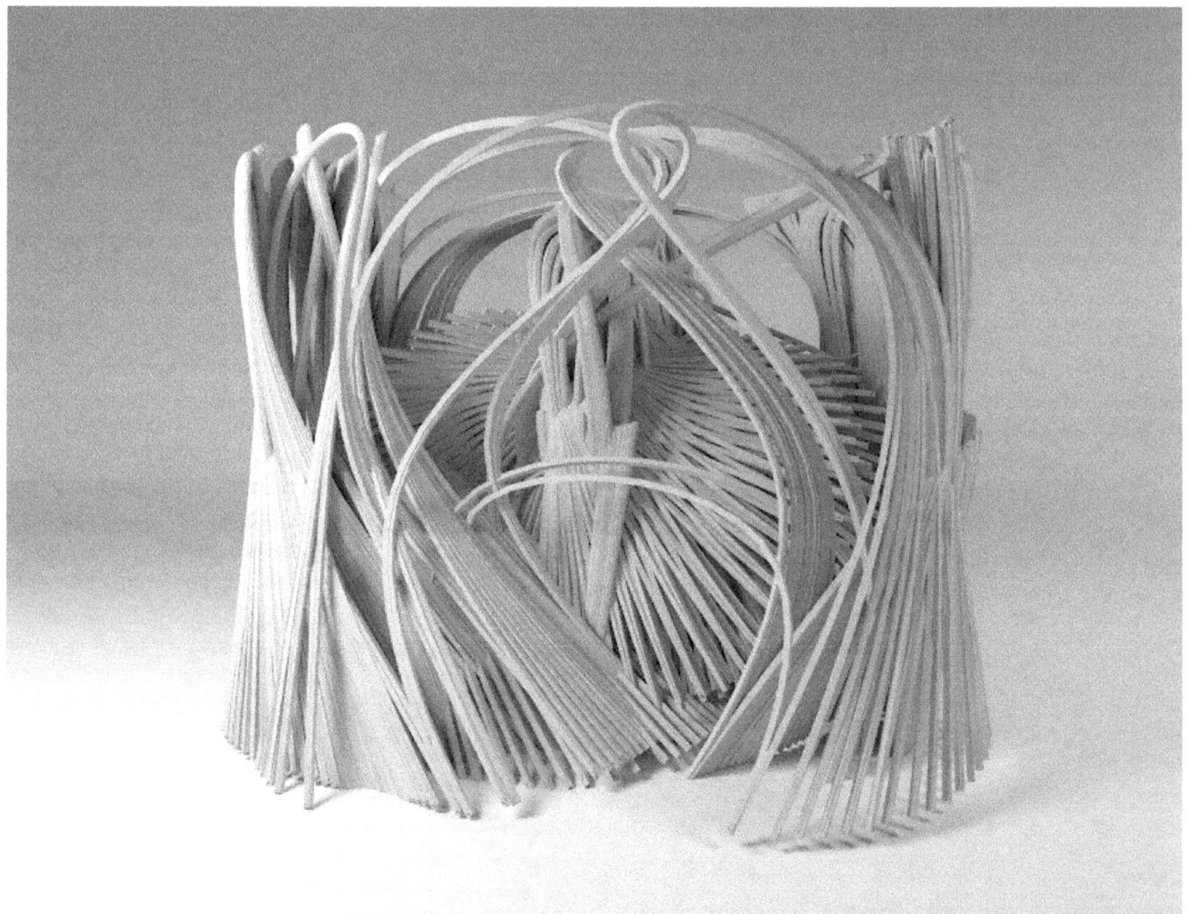

Expressing Data

This pictorial focuses on the design research activity that is the core element underpinning the *MoCap Tango* project: the design of expressions that turn captured movement data into compelling and evocative imagery with the aim of retaining the complex qualities embedded in the movements.

This is the designer's journey: seeing, understanding, and expressing the qualities embedded in data. Make design decisions that lift distant and objective abstractions of movement, documented in digital data, into the design domain by exploring evocative expressions that preserve dynamic and emotional qualities: a process to unpack movement into rich material, able to inspire and inform the design of interactions.

On the following pages, we ask of you, the reader, to become an active agent in this journey. We highly recommend physically printing these pages to maximise their use, and would like to encourage creative and expressive interpration of the tasks. Questions appear as annotations on the following pages. These are intended to provoke reflections on the expressions you will create.

packing movement into rich material able inspire and inform the design of interactions

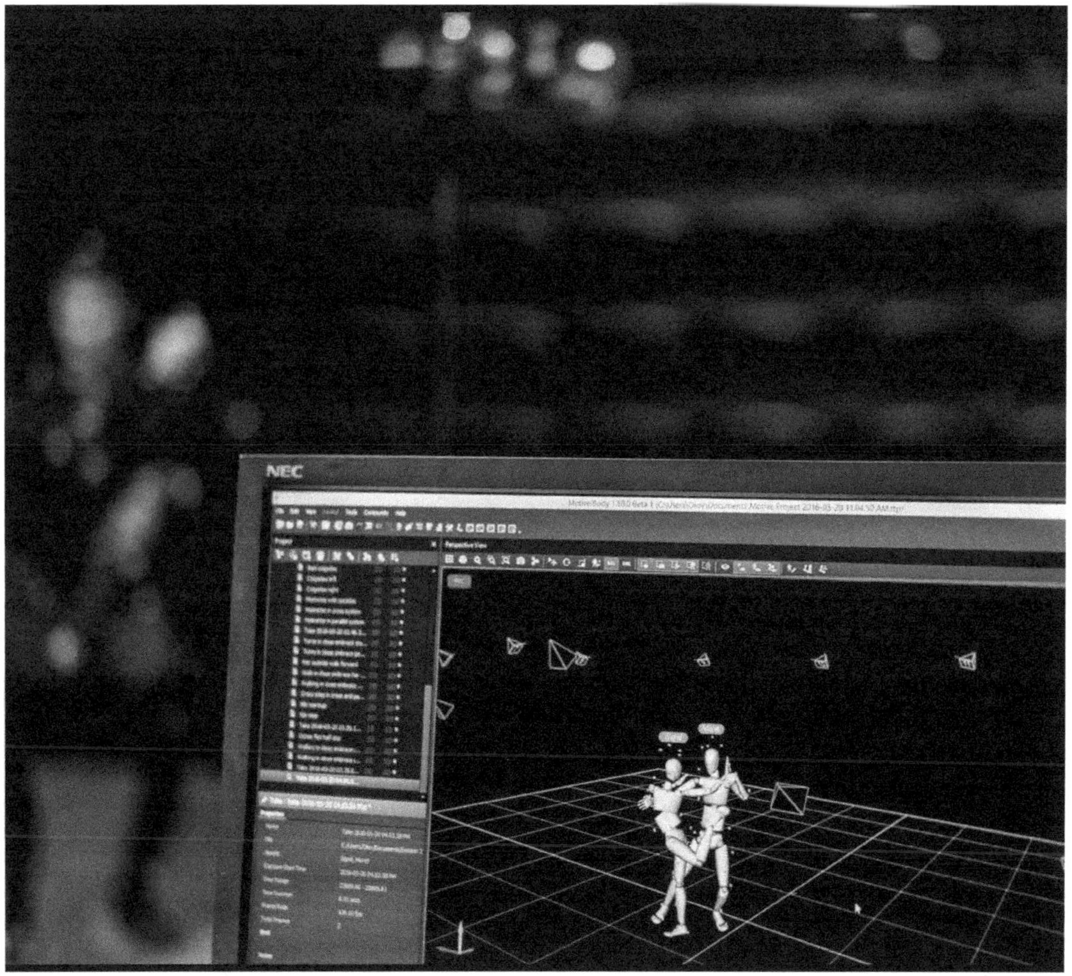

Figures 3 and 4. Small reflective spheres, trackers, are placed on the dancers' bodies. The motion capture system consists of 24 cameras that use infrared light reflected by the trackers to determine the position of the trackers in space and time.

Capturing a Body

The first step in designing with data in *MoCap Tango* is to understand the relationship between the captured data and the body. Expanding or reducing the amount of data used, is one way to emphasise or reduce the importance of one body (part) or its movement over another.

The two photographs below are stills from a couple dancing tango. On this page, we focus on motion-capture trackers worn by the female figure. The trackers are highlighted as white dots on her feet, hips, knees and shoulders. The black dots on this page have been lifted from these images: removing the presence of surrounding space and reducing two bodies in the photography to an abstraction of just one, the female figure. Use a pen, marker, pencil, brush, knife or other tool to connect the dots in order.

Or, if you so desire, explore in other ways to connect the parts of the dancer's body.

how is the body represented?

what does it say about the movement?

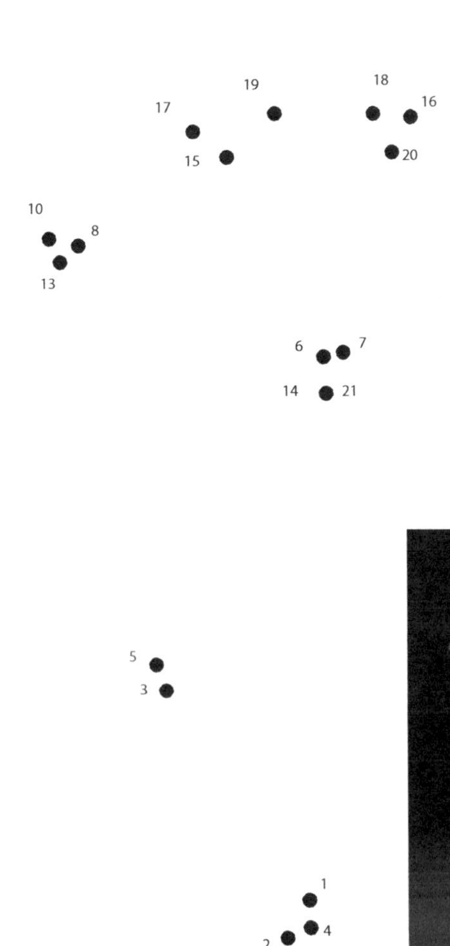

Expressing a Moving Body

The motion-capture system used for MoCap Tango has a frequency of 60Hz. This means that the position of the trackers is recorded 60 times per second. This allows the designer to work with multiple frames, showing the movement of a body part through space and time.

Adding the dimension of time increases the complexity of the data, and its potential expression. Rather than points in space describing the position of a body at a single point in time, several frames start to show the dynamics of movement. How we render lines between this data influences how we may express or hide certain qualities of movement.

On this page, data points show the position of the feet, hips and shoulders of one body. Connect the dots to render movement as the body moves through space.

is it clear what the bodies do, and how? Effort, time, space and weight?

is there a correspondence between the drawing action and the movement it describes?

does the tool that you use have an influence on the dynamic qualities that it visualises / expresses?

how do different visual characteristics inform about different ways of moving?

Merging Bodies

More bodies and several frames increase expressivity: we may be able to start seeing how one body moves differently in relation to the other body, and we might choose to enhance this difference through the way in which we render lines between data points. For example, the female body and the male body in the image below may be expressed in different ways to emphasise their qualities of movement.

In this process, dimensionality emerges: we may start to see how one body moves in relation to the other. What we may see from one perspective, will be different from another. Connecting multiple expressions of moving bodies renders a form, where two bodies merge into one new body. Still, the way in which the qualities of movement are rendered, may tell who they belong to or how this body moves.

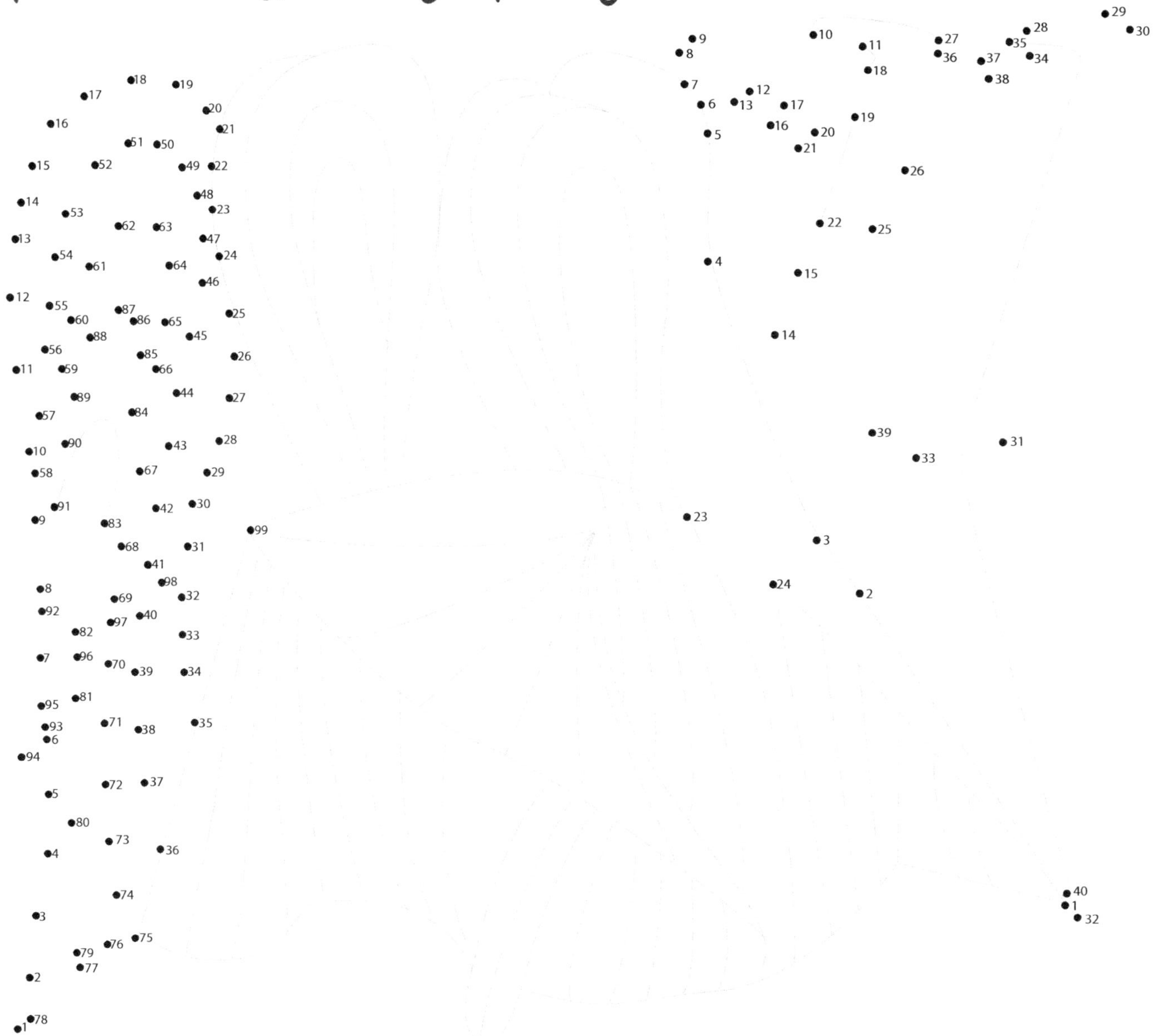

can you describe the directions of the forces that emerge in this process?

is there a relationship between your effort and the effort that the movement demanded?

Generating Form

The presence of a space around a form, is yet another way to express movement and what qualities are perceivable. The figures on this space show a digitally produced rendering of the tango dance explored in the previous pages, where the movements of two bodies are visualised in a single solid form.

Expressions in Form

Resolution, texture and perspective are other ways in which we may highlight qualities of movement. In this example, different colours are used to emphasise the intersecting movement of two different bodies, one silver, one gold.

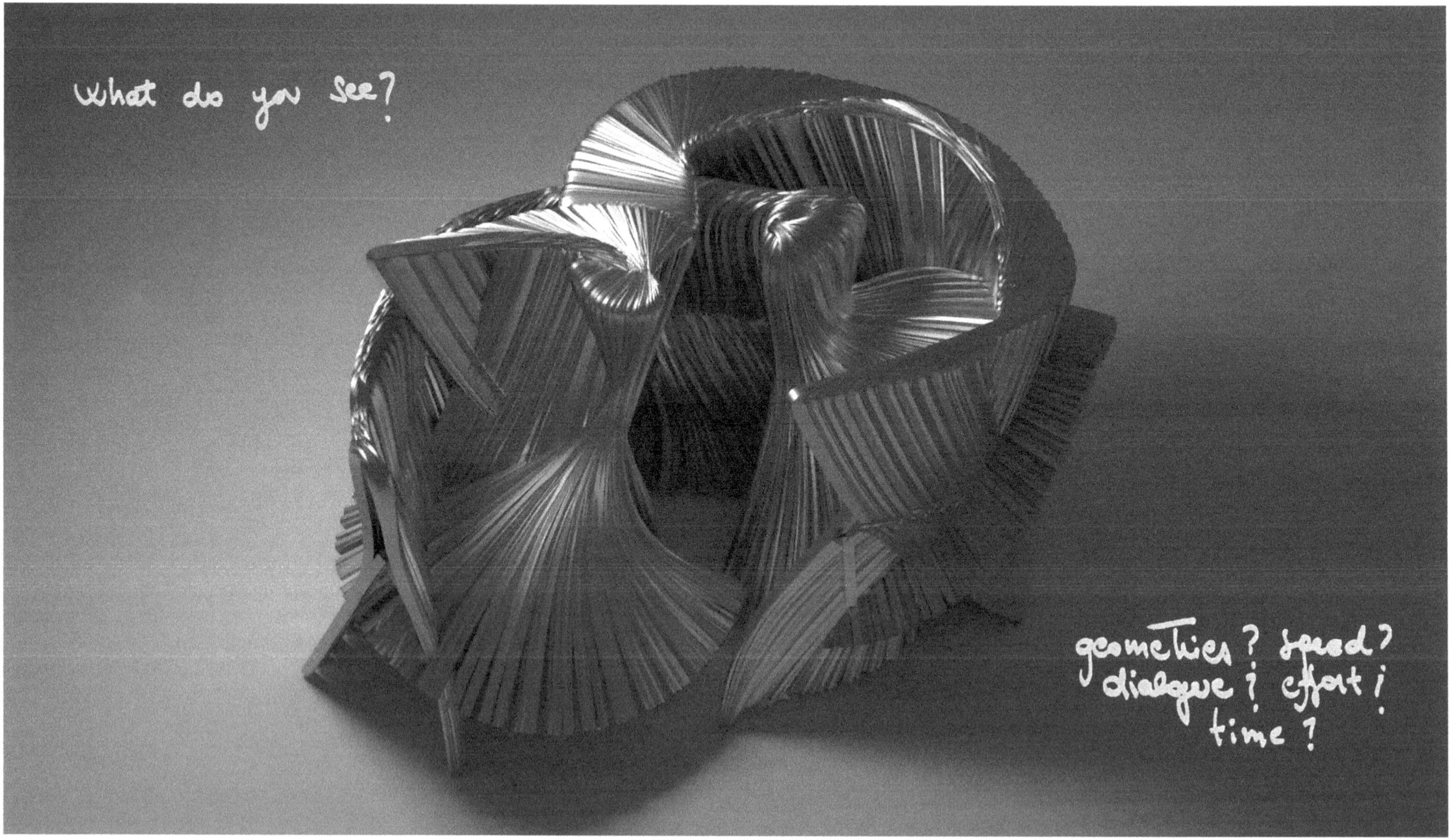

Conclusion

In this pictorial, we return to the core activity of the *MoCap Tango* project. We focus on the design process in which data captured from dancing bodies is visualised with the aim of understanding qualities of movement and eventually, transposing such qualities into other domains of design. Such transposition is not addressed in this pictorial, but in other work [10].

We use a series of tasks for the reader, based on the principle "connect the dots", to convey part of this designerly analysis. The dots in these tasks represent and abstraction of the raw coordinate data that is collected through digital capturing. Through these tasks, we actively involve the reader in moving between levels of abstractions and expressions of movement, with the scope of producing a deeper understanding on the data. We claim that such movement between levels of abstraction and expression constitutes a designerly way of analysing data. By designerly way we mean rendering them in meaningful ways that preserve dynamic and emotional qualities .The different tasks elicit a series of questions, which provoke reflections on the various expessivities that the tasks have generated.

In this endeavour, this pictorial become itself a research vehicle, where we explore how the generative activity of design, where tacit knowledge and intuitive understanding form an important part of every process, may be conveyed in a way that is experienceable, in addition to described.

Future Research

In future research work, we aim to further explore how formal communication formats may used creatively in order to create space for parts of the design (research) process to be conveyed to the reader in a way that requires active engagement. Part of this work will revolve around investigating how the tasks in this pictorial have been interpreted and executed. We therefore kindly ask interested readers to share their expressions on Instagram or Twitter, marked with *#mocaptangodots*.

Acknowledgements

We would like to thank the team that has contributed with their valuable skills, expertise and knowledge to various branches of the *MoCap Tango* project: Murat Erdemsel, Sigrid van Tilbeurgh, Olov Långström, Nicole Sampanidou, Willem Zwagers, Ronald Helgers, Daphne Muller, Stoffel Kuenen and Nigel Papworth. Special thanks to Marlies Peeters for her valuable contribution to the development of the concept of this pictorial.

References

1. Paul Dourish. 2001. Where the Action is: The Foundations of Embodied Interaction. Cambridge: MIT Press.
2. Thomas Dykes, Jayne Wallace, Mark Blythe, and James Thomas. 2016. Paper Street View: A Guided Tour of Design and Making Using Comics. In Proceedings of the 2016 ACM Conference on Designing Interactive Systems (DIS '16). ACM, New York, NY, USA, 334-346. DOI: https://doi.org/10.1145/2901790.2901904
3. Nadine Jarvis, David Cameron, and Andy Boucher. 2012. Attention to detail: annotations of a design process. In Proceedings of the 7th Nordic Conference on Human-Computer Interaction: Making Sense Through Design (NordiCHI '12). ACM, New York, NY, USA, 11-20. DOI: https://doi.org/10.1145/2399016.2399019
4. Elvin Karana, Elisa Giaccardi, Niels Stamhuis, and Jasper Goossensen. 2016. The Tuning of Materials: A Designer's Journey. In Proceedings of the 2016 ACM Conference on Designing Interactive Systems (DIS '16). ACM, New York, NY, USA, 619-631. DOI: https://doi.org/10.1145/2901790.2901909
5. Caroline Hummels, Kees C. Overbeeke, and Sietske Klooster. 2007. Move to get moved: a search for methods, tools and knowledge to design for expressive and rich movement-based interaction. Personal Ubiquitous Comput. 11, 8 (December 2007), 677-690. DOI=http://dx.doi.org/10.1007/s00779-006-0135-y
6. Ilpo Koskinen, John Zimmerman,, Thomas Binder, Johan Redström, and Stephan Wensveen. Design Research Through Practice: From the Lab, Field, and

Showroom. Amsterdam: Elsevier; 2011. 224 p.
7. Lian Loke and Toni Robertson. 2011. The lived body in design: mapping the terrain. In Proceedings of the 23rd Australian Computer-Human Interaction Conference (OzCHI '11). ACM, New York, NY, USA, 181-184. DOI=http://dx.doi.org/10.1145/2071536.2071565
8. Lian Loke, Tony Roberston. 2010. Studies of Dancers: Moving from Experience to Interaction Design. International Journal of Design. Aug 31;4(2):39–54.
9. Sarah Fdili Alaoui, Thecla Schiphorst, Shannon Cuykendall, Kristin Carlson, Karen Studd, and Karen Bradley. 2015. Strategies for Embodied Design: The Value and Challenges of Observing Movement. In Proceedings of the 2015 ACM SIGCHI Conference on Creativity and Cognition (C&C '15). ACM, New York, NY, USA, 121-130. DOI: https://doi.org/10.1145/2757226.2757238
10. Jeroen Peeters, Stoffel Kuenen, and Ambra Trotto 2017. Unveiling the Expressivity of Complexity: Drifting in Design Research. In Proceedings of the 2017 Design and Semantics of Form and Movement Conference (DeSForM '17). , InTech, DOI: 10.5772/intechopen.71123.
11. Jeroen Peeters, Ambra Trotto, and Stoffel Kuenen. 2016. MoCap Tango: Traces of Complexity. In Proceedings of the TEI '16: Tenth International Conference on Tangible, Embedded, and Embodied Interaction (TEI '16). ACM, New York, NY, USA, 545-550. DOI: https://doi.org/10.1145/2839462.2856544
12. Jeroen Peeters, Ambra Trotto. 2015. Reflections on Designing for Aesthetic Engagement. In: Proceedings of the 2nd Biennial Research Through Design Conference, 25-27 March 2015, Cambridge, UK, Article 12. DOI: 10.6084/m9.figshare.1327999.
13. Philip Ross, Stephan Wensveen. 2010). Designing aesthetics of behavior in interaction: Using aesthetic experience as a mechanism for design. International Journal of Design, 4(2), 3-13.

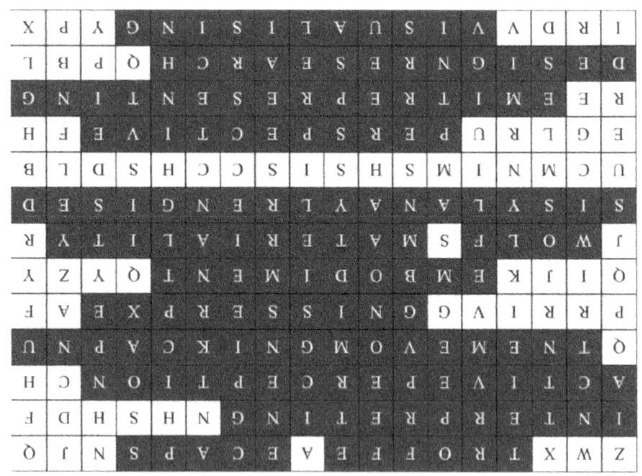

Aeroquake: Drone Augmented Dance

Heesoon Kim
Stanford University
Stanford, CA USA
heesoon0823@gmail.com

James A. Landay
Stanford University
Stanford, CA USA
landay@cs.stanford.edu

ABSTRACT
As drone-based entertainment becomes more popular, researchers have explored different forms of expression and systems to support drone performances. However, most of these systems are pre-programmed and do not interact with the body movement of dancers in real-time. In response, some have presented drone performances using bulky camera systems to track the performer's body movement. We introduce Aeroquake, an augmented dance system that uses simple wearable microphones to enhance a dancer's body movement with sound and control the movement of drones in real-time. Dancers experience a simulation of "quaking" the space around them: upon stomping, the movement is translated into sound and vertical motion across multiple drones. Aeroquake allows dancers to improvise choreography and explore their creativity in the space in which they choose to dance. We worked with a dancer to validate our system by performing before a live audience.

Author Keywords
Drone, UAV, Human-drone Interaction, Augmented Dance Design, Interactive Dance

ACM Classification Keywords
H.5.m [Information Interfaces and Presentation]: Miscellaneous; J.5 [Arts and Humanities]: Performing arts.

INTRODUCTION
The ability to control and fly several objects in 3D space gives the potential to transform live performances. As such, performances using multiple autonomous drones have started to appear in popular culture (e.g., at Disney [1]). Yet, this is still a developing area. There are few examples of *interactive* performances between dancers and autonomous drones, and these have used bulky, multi-camera systems to track the motion of the performers and control the drones. At the same time, there are many examples of interactive dance and performance that leverage simpler sound, visual, and sensing technologies without drones.

DIS '18, June 9–13, 2018, Hong Kong

ACM ISBN 978-1-4503-5198-0/18/06...$15.00
DOI: https://doi.org/10.1145/3196709.3196798

How can multiple autonomous drones help performers to augment their expression in a live performance? In this paper, we introduce Aeroquake, a novel drone-augmented dance system that uses a simple microphone sensor, and the enhanced expression it provides. In our system, we chose to realize this expression through sound and drone-movement. To contribute to future research in designing interactive live performance using autonomous drones, we describe our design process, the system implementation, joint choreography with a dancer, and our validation through a dance performance with Aeroquake before a live audience.

RELATED WORK
We begin by describing the prior work that uses drones in entertainment systems and interactive dance performances. We also review how other technologies have been used to augment dance and describe principles that have been previously developed for augmented dance design.

Drone Entertainment Shows
Recently, drone entertainment shows and the systems that support them have advanced considerably [2]. For example, a swarm of 13 drones was used to light an indoor concert [3]. The drones were both pre-programmed and manually flown by operators, requiring a team of specialists. Entertainment drones have also been used outdoors [1,4,5]; a swarm of more than 100 drones was used for a sky light show at Disney World. These large swarms use pre-programmed systems that limit the drones' motion to predefined trajectories.

There have also been examples in which dancers or actors perform with drones. For example, Cirque du Soleil collaborated with Verity Studios to include drones in a Broadway show [6], and a drone-based dance act performed on "Britain's Got Talent" [7]. In these cases, the performance is with a small swarm of drones. The drones do *not* react to the body movements of the dancers or actors in real-time, limiting the performers to moving their body along with the pre-programmed movement of the drones. For these performances, choreographing and programming both the dance and the drone movements is a long, intensive process.

Interactive Drone Performances
In response to some of the issues with manually controlled or pre-programmed drone entertainment, some researchers have presented swarm drone performances where the drones interact with the body movement of actors in real-time. MagicLab and Rhizomatiks Research created a performance using 24 autonomous drones that fly around the performers like a flock of trained birds in response to the movement of the performer [8]. Similarly, Elevenplay performed live with

24 drones on the TV show "America's Got Talent" [9]. In both performances, the drones interact with the performers' body movements in real-time. These shows rely on large and bulky multi-camera systems to allow the systems to track the performers' body movements and automatically fly the drones to move in concert. Such systems limit the possible types of performance spaces and are time consuming to setup.

Augmented Dance

Researchers have also used similar tracking systems (or more limited systems such as the Microsoft Kinect) to explore various types of augmented dance using other technologies [10,11,12]. Many of these systems attempt to enhance a dancer's choreography by displaying or modifying sound and/or projected visualizations that accompany the dance. Again, such systems often limit the type of space or the size of space in which the performer can dance.

In contrast to camera-based systems, others have explored using wearable devices containing accelerometers or gyro sensors to track the dancer's motion [13,14]. For example, Sony demonstrated the Motion Sonic Project, which uses a microphone-based wearable sensor containing a three-microphone array, accelerometer, and gyro sensor to augment the dancer's movements with sound in real-time [15]. This system allowed dancers to create various kinds of sound synchronized with their choreography. Motion Sonic uses the microphones to collect the sound of the wind produced when the dancer moves their body, amplifies the sound, and adds to or changes the sound effects in real-time using the output of the accelerometer and gyro. These wearable devices do not limit the performance environments in the way the multi-camera systems do in other prior work.

Aeroquake was inspired by these prior wearable sensor systems. It uses a simple wearable microphone worn on the ankle both to enhance a dancer's body movement with sound and to control the movement of autonomous drones in real-time. We used the same experimental wearable device that Sony used in the Motion Sonic Project.

Augmented Dance Design Principles

In designing Aeroquake we used Gonzalez and colleague's 5 design principles for technology-augmented dance [16]:

1. Connected Kinetics

Audience members should be able to tell that dancers' movements control, manipulate, or influence the kinetics of the visualizations.

2. Augmented Expression

The technology should enrich the mediums of expression available to the choreographer and dancers or provide entirely new mediums of expression.

3. Aesthetic Harmony

A relationship should be established between the dancers and visualizations such that they complement each other to create an integrated aesthetic.

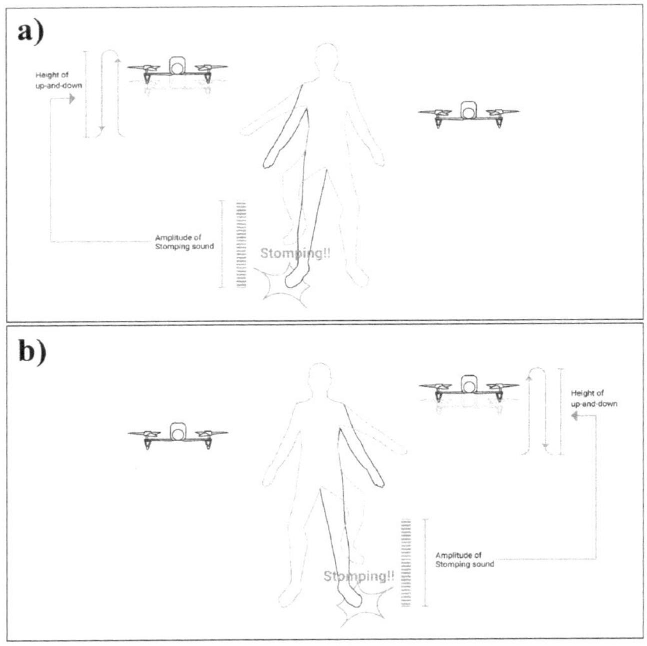

Figure 1. Quaking. a) Quake right drone with right foot stomping. b) Quake left drone with left foot stomping.

4. Interactive Build

The variability and intensity of the visualizations and interaction should progress throughout the dance to match the build of the choreography.

5. Integrated Process

The technologist should be integrated into the choreographic design process to better inform the development of the technology, visualizations, and choreography to support their subsequent union.

We used these principles to help design our system and, more importantly, the resulting augmented dance performance in concert with a hip-hop dancer.

AEROQUAKE INTERACTION

Aeroquake is a novel augmented dance system that enhances a dancer's body movement with both sound and the movement of a swarm of drones in real time. In particular, Aeroquake allows the dancer to create sound to go along with their improvised foot stomping choreography and transform it into visualized movement across multiple drones. This is accomplished by sensing the stomping motions through ankle-worn microphones. Aeroquake gives dancers a new form of augmented dance expression that simulates the "quaking" of the space around them. It was inspired by the movements of Japanese movie monsters with huge bodies like Godzilla. We explored two types of augmented dance expression, Quaking and Waving.

Quaking

Quaking is a drone-augmented expression to simulate quaking the space through the dancer's stomping. In response to the dancer's foot stomping, one of two drones floating on either side of the dancer flies up-and-down to go along with the sound wave produced by the stomping.

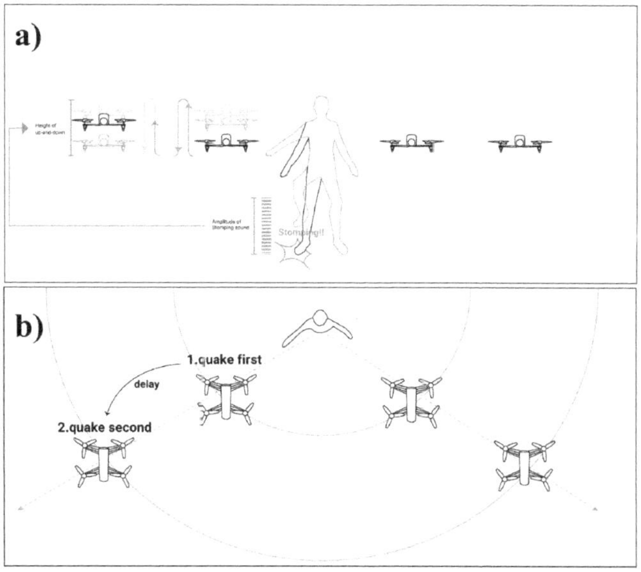

Figure 2. Waving. a) Waving propagates out through multiple drones in the direction of the stomping foot. b) Waving uses a delay to emphasize the outward movement of the shaking.

Depending on whether the right or left foot was used, a drone floating on the same side of the dancer flies up-and-down, where the height of the movement is proportional to the amplitude of the stomping sound wave (see Figure 1). This allows dancers to express the direction and strength of quaking the space through their stomping choreography. As the drone flies up-and-down, the system creates a loud quaking sound to go along with the dancer's own stomping.

Waving

Waving is a drone-augmented expression that allows the dancer to quake through a wider space. Using four drones, two on each side of the dancer, allows the dancer to produce a quaking animation that starts in the drones near the dancer and propagates with a delay to the outer drones (see Figure 2). Waving allows dancers to express the quaking sound and movement over a larger space and a longer time period.

AEROQUAKE IMPLEMENTATION

Here we give an overview of the Aeroquake system, describe how sound is sensed and processed, explain how sound effects are created, and detail the drone control.

System Overview

The Aeroquake system consists of wearable microphones, multiple drones, a laptop PC, and an audio interface with a low latency audio Bluetooth receiver and speaker. The microphones worn on the dancer's ankles capture the sound produced by the feet. Each captured sound is sent to the laptop through the audio interface with less than 40ms latency. The laptop control application analyzes the sound, outputs new quaking sounds, and controls the drones.

Sound-Based Motion Sensing

The microphone captures the sound produced by the dancer's stomping motions and sends it continuously along with its foot ID (right or left) to the control application, which only processes sound with a frequency lower than 10 Hz. We consider higher frequency sounds to be noise since we wish to sense ground motion like a geophone [17] does, and these typically sense frequencies under 10Hz.

Motion Sound Effects

The next step in the process is to amplify and modify the stomping sounds. The sound waves are first amplified by the laptop PC control application, which then adds a quaking effect. To create this sound, we add a bass boost effect to enhance the original low frequency wave and then a modulation effect to produce vibrato and echo. In particular, we delay the incoming sound signal by a few milliseconds and use a Low Frequency Oscillator to modulate the delayed signal. This process allows the dancer to create a sound that resembles the quaking of the ground.

Drone Animation Control

The control application sends commands to the drones based on the foot IDs and the amplitude of the sound detected by the corresponding microphone on the dancer's foot. First, the foot IDs enable the control application to determine which drones to send the control message to. In addition, the height of the up-and-down movement sent in the control message is proportional to the peak level of the frequency of the sound wave. That is, the height of the up-and-down movement of the drone, $H_{drone\ height}$, is calculated by multiplying the peak level of the frequency of the quaking sound signal, $F_{peak\ level}$, and the amplitude coefficient, $a_{coefficient}$.

DESIGNING A DRONE AUGMENTED PERFORMANCE

We collaborated with a hip-hop dancer to design a Drone Augmented Dance using the five design principles for augmented dance by Gonzalez and colleagues [16]. In this section, we describe how we used these principles.

Interaction Design for Drone Augmented Dance

In the early phases of our design process, we explored our interaction design concepts for drone augmented dance by considering the principles of *Connected Kinetics* and *Augmented Expression*. Connected Kinetics is expressed by 1) having the drones move up and down in time with the dancer's stomping and changing the height of the motion based on the strength of the stomping, and 2) controlling drones on the right or left based on which foot is stomping.

The Augmented Expressions for Aeroquake are Quaking and Waving. We developed and refined these two expressions through several prototyping exercises with the dancer. We experimented with using one drone, two drones, and four drones. In this *Integrated Process*, we first had an operator manually control the drones from the laptop. They reacted to what they saw the dancer doing as quickly as they could.

One Drone

At the start of our design process with the dancer, we tried using a single drone near the dancer and had it move up-and-down a constant height in reaction to her improvised stomping choreography. We found it was insufficient to move the drone a constant height, regardless the strength of

Figure 3. Performance design for Aesthetic Harmony. a) Shaking the body while waving all the drones. b) Moving right arm up-and-down while quaking the right drone. c) Moving left arm up-and-down while quaking the left drone.

each stomp. Thus, we explored changing the height depending on the magnitude of the stomping. This seemed to better implement Connected Kinetics. Unfortunately, this did not give the feeling that the dancer was quaking the space *around* her. A single drone appeared insufficient to meet the Augmented Expression principle for quaking the space.

Two Drones
We next explored using a drone on each side of the dancer and reran the single drone experiment. We could now feel the dancer quake the space around her. But, we also found that moving both drones along with any stomping motion regardless of right or left foot resulted in a weak implementation of the Connected Kinetics principle. Next, we tested moving only the drone corresponding to the foot that the dancer had stomped. This allowed the dancer to better make the Augmented Expression of quaking the space in the specific direction of their foot movement.

Four Drones
Finally, we tested four drones to enhance the Augmented Expression of quaking an even wider space. We flew two drones on each side of the dancer. First, we tested moving each of the two drones on the right or left around the dancer up-and-down at the same time to go along with the right or left stomping as we did in the two-drone experiments. This resulted in a sense of the dancer quaking a wider space, but the dancer could not feel the perspective of the wider space. In response, we added a delay in the motion as it went out from the dancer to the outer drone. This gave the dancer a better sense of quaking the wider space. We called this Augmented Expression "waving" the wider space.

Performance Design for Drone Augmented Dance
In the final part of our design process, we again used an *Integrated Process* together with the hip-hop dancer to design a dance performance with *Aesthetic Harmony*. Aesthetic Harmony is created through the synchrony of the up-and-down movement of the drones with the dancer's other movements. For example, the dancer shook her entire body to accompany a waving movement of the drones caused by her stomping both feet (see Figure 3a). Similarly, when quaking the right drone with a right foot stomp, she moved her right hand to match the motion (see Figure 3b) and then did the same on her left side (see Figure 3c).

During this process, we started to use the automated Aeroquake prototype that we described earlier. We practiced in a dance studio with large mirrors so that the dancer could explore the Aesthetic Harmony between her improvised choreography and the drone movement. She gradually started to iteratively explore how to increase the amplitude of the drone movement to accompany her own stomping and create an *Interactive Build* as the music progressed. We had finally created a performance such that the dancer's choreography and the movement of the drones complemented each other with an integrated aesthetic.

PERFORMANCE AND VALIDATION
The hip-hop dancer whom we had collaborated with during our design process gave a short performance using the Aeroquake system to a live audience of ten people. For this performance, we used four drones. After this experience, the dancer reported that "I had never before experienced a dance where I could extend my movement outside of my body, and I really appreciated this opportunity to create new visuals and expand my conceptions of dance."

We also surveyed the individuals in the audience. We asked questions that probed whether the performance satisfied the first three design principles for technology-augmented dance. For example, to probe for Connected Kinetics we asked, "Were you aware that the dancer's movement affected the motion of the drones?" All five respondents answered "Yes." To test for Augmented Expression, we asked, "Please indicate how engaging you find multimedia enhanced dances (1-not at all engaging to 10-extremely engaging)." The average was 7. To test for Aesthetic Harmony, we asked, "How often did Aeroquake hold your attention?" 80% answered most of the time to the entire time. From these results, the reports of the dancer, and our own reflection on the design process, we believe Aeroquake satisfied the design principles for technology-augmented dance.

CONCLUSIONS
We introduced Aeroquake, a novel drone augmented dance system that enhances a dancer's body movement using sound and the movement of multiple drones. Aeroquake gives the dancer the augmented expressions of Quaking and Waving. Quaking is an expression that shakes the space near the dancer along with her stomping choreography. Waving is an expression that appears to quake a wider space by propagating the quaking farther from the dancer. By collaborating with a hip-hop dancer, we designed the basic interaction concepts and choreographed a performance using the key design principles for technology-augmented dance. The dancer successfully performed with Aeroquake before a live audience, helping to validate that our design satisfied these principles.

REFERENCES

1. Brian Barret. 2016. Disney's Latest Attraction? 300 Drones Flying in Formation. Retrieved September 16, 2017 from https://www.wired.com/2016/11/disneys-latest-attraction-300-drones-flying-formation/
2. Waibel, M., Keays, B. and Augugliaro, F. 2017. Drone shows: creative potential and best practices. Retrieved March 5, 2017 from https://veritystudios.com/whitepaper/
3. CAST Software Blog. 2016. BlackTrax flies high for Muse on its Drones worldwide arena concerts. Retrieved March 28, 2018 from http://cast-soft.com/blog/2016/03/blacktrax-flies-high-muse-drones-worldwide-arena-concerts/
4. Ken Kaplan. 2016. 500 Drones Light Night Sky to Set Record. Retrieved July 5, 2017 from https://iq.intel.com/500-drones-light-show-sets-record/
5. Donaupark. 2016. DRONE 100 - Spaxels über Linz. Retrieved July 5, 2017 from https://www.aec.at/radicalatoms/de/drone100/
6. Gordon Cox. 2016. Drones Make Theater, Not War in Broadway 'Paramour'. Retrieved July 5, 2017 from http://variety.com/2016/legit/news/paramour-drones-cirque-du-soleil-broadway-1201782129/
7. Britain's Got Talent. 2016. Flying Bebop and their drones are out of this world | Semi-Final 3. Retrieved December 9, 2016 from https://www.youtube.com/watch?v=cwNwdN2tpqY&list=RDcwNwdN2tpqY&t=1
8. MagicLab and Rhizomatiks Research. 2016. 24 Drone Flight. Retrieved November 4, 2016 from https://research.rhizomatiks.com/en/works/marco_tempest_magic.html
9. Elevenplay and Rhizomatiks Research. 2016. America's Got Talent. Retrieved November 4, 2016 from https://research.rhizomatiks.com/works/agt_elevenplay.html
10. Baptista, Filipe, Pedro Faria Lopes, and Pedro Santana. 2016. MotionDesigner: Augmented artistic performances with kinect-based human body motion tracking. *Computação Gráfica e Interação (EPCGI)*, 1-7. DOI: 10.1109/EPCGI.2016.7851195
11. Miao Song, Serguei A. Mokhov, Sudhir P. Mudur, and Peter Grogono. 2015. Rapid interactive real-time application prototyping for media arts and stage performance. In *Proceeding of SIGGRAPH Asia 2015* Courses (SA '15). ACM, New York, NY, USA, Article 14, 11 pages. DOI: https://doi.org/10.1145/2818143.2818148
12. Danilo Gasques Rodrigues, Emily Grenader, Fernando da Silva Nos, Marcel de Sena Dall'Agnol, Troels E. Hansen, and Nadir Weibel. 2013. MotionDraw: a tool for enhancing art and performance using kinect. In *Proceeding of CHI '13 Extended Abstracts on Human Factors in Computing Systems* (CHI EA '13). ACM, New York, NY, USA, 1197-1202. DOI: https://doi.org/10.1145/2468356.2468570
13. Hyun Yi Jung, Dohee Kim, and Hyunggi Kim. 2015. Study on Interactive Dance Performance based on Wearable Sensor Technology. *Advanced Science and Technology Letters* Vol. 96 (IRTT 2015), 14-18. DOI: http://dx.doi.org/10.14257/astl.2015.96.04
14. Yu-I Ha and Yi-Kyung Kim. 2014. The Design Process of Wearable Computers for Extending the Performer's Expression. In Proceeding of *HCI International 2014 - Posters' Extended Abstracts*. HCI 2014. Communications in Computer and Information Science, vol 434. Springer, Cham. 421-426. DOI: https://doi.org/10.1007/978-3-319-07857-1_74
15. Nathan Ingraham. 2017. Sony's Motion Sonic wristband makes sound with a wave of your arm, Retrieved March 15, 2017 from https://www.engadget.com/2017/03/14/sony-motion-sonic-wristband-makes-sound-with-a-wave-of-your-ar/
16. Berto Gonzalez, Erin Carroll, and Celine Latulipe. 2012. Dance-inspired technology, technology-inspired dance. In *Proceedings of the 7th Nordic Conference on Human-Computer Interaction: Making Sense Through Design* (NordiCHI '12). ACM, New York, NY, USA, 398-407. DOI: https://doi.org/10.1145/2399016.2399078
17. Zou, Zhihui, Hua-wei Zhou, Fan Jiang, and Hui Liu. 2010. Assessing the reliability of low frequencies in geophone records. In *Proceeding of SEG Technical Program Expanded Abstracts 2010*, 121-126. DOI: https://doi.org/10.1190/1.3513064

Author Index